"I feel that it is workable, it is flexible and it is strong enough to hold the country together both in peace-time and in war-time. Indeed, if I may say so, if things go wrong under the new Constitution, the reason will not be that we had a bad constitution. What we will have to say is that Man was vile."

B.R. AMBEDKAR
Chairman, Drafting Committee of the Constituent Assembly

To live by the Rule of the Constitution ought not to be regarded as slavery, but rather as salvation

ARISTOTLE

CONSTITUTIONAL GOVERNMENT IN INDIA

Prof. (Dr.) M.V. PYLEE

Emeritus Professor
and
Former Vice Chancellor
University of Cochin
National Research Professor
(Padma Bhushan Awardee)

Eighth Revised & Enlarged Edition

S. CHAND & COMPANY PVT. LTD.

(AN ISO 9001: 2008 COMPANY)

RAM NAGAR, NEW DELHI-110055

S.CHAND
PUBLISHING
empowering minds

S. CHAND & COMPANY PVT. LTD.

(An ISO 9001 : 2008 Company)

Head Office: 7361, RAM NAGAR, NEW DELHI - 110 055
Phone: 23672080-81-82, 9899107446, 9911310888 Fax: 91-11-23677446
www.schandpublishing.com; e-mail: helpdesk@schandpublishing.com

Branches

Ahmedabad	:	Ph: 27541965, 27542369, ahmedabad@schandpublishing.com
Bengaluru	:	Ph: 22268048, 22354008, bangalore@schandpublishing.com
Bhopal	:	Ph: 4274723, 4209587, bhopal@schandpublishing.com
Chandigarh	:	Ph: 2725443, 2725446, chandigarh@schandpublishing.com
Chennai	:	Ph. 28410027, 28410058, chennai@schandpublishing.com
Coimbatore	:	Ph: 2323620, 4217136, coimbatore@schandpublishing.com (Marketing Office)
Cuttack	:	Ph: 2332580; 2332581, cuttack@schandpublishing.com
Dehradun	:	Ph: 2711101, 2710861, dehradun@schandpublishing.com
Guwahati	:	Ph: 2738811, 2735640, guwahati@schandpublishing.com
Hyderabad	:	Ph: 27550194, 27550195, hyderabad@schandpublishing.com
Jaipur	:	Ph: 2219175, 2219176, jaipur@schandpublishing.com
Jalandhar	:	Ph: 2401630, 5000630, jalandhar@schandpublishing.com
Kochi	:	Ph: 2378740, 2378207-08, cochin@schandpublishing.com
Kolkata	:	Ph: 22367459, 22373914, kolkata@schandpublishing.com
Lucknow	:	Ph: 4026791, 4065646 lucknow@schandpublishing.com
Mumbai	:	Ph: 22690881, 22610885, mumbai@schandpublishing.com
Nagpur	:	Ph: 6451311, 2720523, 2777666, nagpur@schandpublishing.com
Patna	:	Ph: 2300489, 2302100, patna@schandpublishing.com
Pune	:	Ph: 64017298, pune@schandpublishing.com
Raipur	:	Ph: 2443142, raipur@schandpublishing.com (Marketing Office)
Ranchi	:	Ph: 2361178, ranchi@schandpublishing.com
Siliguri	:	Ph: 2520750, siliguri@schandpublishing.com (Marketing Office)
Visakhapatnam	:	Ph: 2782609 visakhapatnam@schandpublishing.com (Marketing Office)

First Edition 1960
Subsequent Editions 1984, 2003, 2006, 2007
Eighth Edition (Revised and Enlarged) 2012
Reprint 2016

ISBN : 978-81-219-2203-6 **Code :** 1017A 130

PRINTED IN INDIA

By Vikas Publishing House Pvt. Ltd., Plot 20/4, Site-IV, Industrial Area Sahibabad, Ghaziabad-201010 and Published byS.Chand & Company Pvt. Ltd., 7361, Ram Nagar, New Delhi -110 055.

To
MY PARENTS

Extracts from Reviews on the Earlier Editions

This clearly written and comprehensive book is the best that so far has been published on the structure and working of the Indian Constitution......

The author's conclusion, which few who have followed his admirable exposition will desire to controvert, is that in spite of difficulty which he sets out so frankly, India can feel satisfied with the progress so far made towards the goal - even if the goal is far away - of the complete and unqualified triumph of the rule of law under the constitution.

Literary Supplement of the Times
London

DR. M.V. PYLEE .... presents a well balanced exhaustive reference work on constitutional government in India which emphasises the historical background to constitutionalism in India as well as an analysis of the longest constitutional document itself.

Journal of Asian Studies
U.S.A.

Since it first appeared in 1960 Professor Pylee's book has become established as an authoritative work in its field. Its handling of the complicated issues relating to constitutional government in India is at once scholarly, exhaustive and lucid.

—British Book News
London

Dr. Pylee's Constitutional Government in India is an authoritative work on the subject and gives a clear exposition not only of the constitution itself, but also the machinery by which it works.

—The Sunday Statesman
Calcutta

This account of the creation and working of the Indian Constitution is a book of great interest and it is hoped that many English people will read it...

Dr. Pylee's notable work should be included in every library with any claim to importance.

—Law Journal
London

Many books have appeared in recent years on the subject of the Constitution of India. All the same, this book by Dr. Pylee fulfils a real need.

—The Hindu
Madras

Indeed, this work will have reasons to claim very good credit. It may even claim the best political commentary on the Constitution of India and its working........

Finally, a good work of praise to the author and publishers for the excellent bibliography and the immaculate production.

—Hindustan Standard
Calcutta

This volume of Constitutional Goverment in India aims not only at describing and analysing the formal articles of the Indian Constitution, but also to explain how the Constitution has been actually working.

—Hindustan Times
New Delhi

The learned author attempts to relate every Article and Chapter of the Constitution to its political background. The fact that the Constitution is a living document and vital element in India's political destiny is clearly brought out by the author. In his study the author has tried to be objective and seeks to focus the attention of those interested in the subject on the way the different aspects of the Constitution have been in operation on their proved merits and demerits......

With numerous references to major legal points decided by the courts in the course of the working of the Constitution, extracts from debates in the Constituent Assembly and exhaustive notes, the book will be found of absorbing interest to the constitutional lawyers, administrators, students and those doing research work in the field. The publishers also must be congratulated for bringing out such a nice edition.

—All India Reporter

This book deals exhaustively with the Constitution of India. Into its more than seven hundred pages the author has put in a vast amount of scholarship and intellectual labour.

—The New Administrator
Madras

This is certainly a well documented book........ It is bound to be of help both to the informed citizen and the enquiring student........... The author's style is simple and lucid, without ceasing to be scholarly. It is a notable contribution to the literature on the subject.

—The Sunday Tribune
Chandigarh

PREFACE TO THE EIGHTH REVISED EDITION

I am happy that the Seventh Edition has been sold out nearly a year ago.

The distinguishing feature of this Edition is that it contains details about the fifteenth Lok Sabha Elections that took place during 2009. It was a massive, gigantic exercise the world has never seen before. India can feel proud that such an exercise was held peacefully and in an orderly manner. The results of that election reaffirmed India's determination to uphold stability and orderly progress. The Government headed by Dr. Manmohan Singh continues to hold office for a second term.

I want to express my deep sense of gratitude to all those readers who encouraged me by sending to me their comments, criticisms and also appreciation.

I want also to thank the publishers, S. Chand and Company, to produce the book in a most attractive manner.

KOCHI **Emeritus Professor Dr. M.V. Pylee**
May 2011

PREFACE TO THE FIRST EDITION

The first major achievement of independent India was the framing of a new constitution based on the ideals of justice, liberty, equality and fraternity. But the Constitution has been criticised for being unusually long and complex. In one or two respects there is some justification in this criticism. But by and large, the alleged over-elaboration and complexity are more apparent than real.

No other constitution-making body had ever faced a task so difficult as the Constituent Assembly of India. Any constitution that is designed to provide for the government machinery of a vast country like India with 360 million people was bound to be complicated. But with India it was not merely a matter of number or size. There was a perplexing diversity — of language, race, religion and culture.

Prior to 1947, there were two Indias politically, British India and Indian India. The former was under the direct rule of Britain for two centuries. The latter was a political medley, composed of hundreds of heterogeneous Princely States, some big but most of them small, some modern but most of them feudal, some liberal but most of them autocratic, and all equally under the paramountcy of the British Crown.

Economically, although improverished in general as a result of colonial exploitation, India nevertheless provided a paradox — certain areas were comparatively advanced and prosperous while others were unbelievably backward; certain classes fabulously rich, others living in abject poverty. Socially, the evils of a degenerated caste-system, the curse of untouchability and the canker of communalism based upon religious differences were destroying the very vitals of the once-dynamic Indian society.

Despite all the artificial barriers, political, economic and social, there had still been a cultural unity pervading the entire country. But that too was fast disappearing under the influence of fissiparous forces. On top of all, there came the partition of the country into India and Pakistan, and all pangs of that painful process.

It was difficult to find a more baffling political entity with such complex social and economic problems, than the India of 1947. To evolve out of the weltering chaos a compact, well-knit nation was the task that confronted the constitution-makers.

The Constitution of India attempts to tackle this by laying down the fundamental law of the new nation. It is not merely a document dealing with the governmental machinery for running the administration of the country, but in fact, an embodiment of the ideals and aspirations of the people of India. .At the same time, it is also the product of the pattern of social forces that prevailed in India in the wake of her winning political independence.

Naturally, such a document is bound to be long, complicated and, at least in parts, beyond the comprehension of the layman. But such complexity was not the result of deliberate intent, nor the product of loose thinking and poor drafting. Every part of it has a history behind it; every part of it has a definite purpose to serve; every part of it is the result of a sustained effort by best intellects in India that got together in the Constituent Assembly. It has, nevertheless some imperfections, like all things human.

Almost every modern constitution is a complicated document. This is mainly because of the complications involved in the mechanism of modern government, which is no longer the simple thing that government was in the past. It is no longer the embodiment of the traditional concept of 'a hindrance to hindrances to the good life'. Today it has to play a positive role. It has to lead and guide human beings in many of their activities.

The layman is comparatively ignorant of the working of the complicated mechanism of modern government just as he is incapable of understanding the complicated mechanism of a technological device. It is a field for the expert and even experts do not know all about it. Yet the ordinary man is capable of judging whether that mechanism works well or ill on the basis of the benefits that he enjoys through it.

It is not the simplicity or the complexity of the Constitution that matters. What matters is how it works; whether or not its objectives are being realized in practice. The text may be long or short, simple or obscure. But if it works well and produces good results, it is a good constitution. This is the test that we should apply to the Constitution of India.

A decade is too short a period for this purpose. Yet, during the last ten years, the Constitution has more or less been meeting the requirements of the country that has embarked upon a programme of revolutionary but peaceful change. How it has actually been working in the circumstances is a matter that calls for careful study. This book attempts to do that in a detailed manner. It strives to be an objective study that seeks to focus the attention of those interested in the subject on the way the different aspects of the Constitution have been in operation, on their proved merits and drawbacks. The impact of a reasonably successful system of constitutional government in India will not be confined to the four hundred million people of India; it will affect the destiny of many nations of Asia and Africa who have recently achieved or are in the process of achieving their political independence.

Since the text went to the printers, two significant constitutional developments have taken place, both of which call for constitutional amendments. The first of these relates to the special safeguards provided to the Scheduled Castes, Scheduled Tribes and Anglo-Indians under the Constitution. The second envisages the division of the present bilingual Bombay State into two unilingual states, Bombay and Gujarat.

As originally conceived, the special constitutional provisions intended to protect the political, educational and service interests of the Scheduled Castes, Scheduled Tribes and Anglo-Indians were to last only for a period of ten years from the commencement of the Constitution. The ten-year period, however, does not seem to have produced the expected results. The dominant opinion in the country seems to be that these special provisions should continue for another period of ten years. Accordingly, Parliament has recently passed a Bill amending the Constitution (Eighth Amendment) and extending the continuance of the special safeguards until 26 January 1970.

A major reorganisation of the State-system had taken place in 1956 following the publication of the Report of the States Reorganization Commission. The pattern that emerged as a result was largely one of unilingual States. The one notable exception was the bilingual State of Bombay. The Marathi-speaking and Gujarati-speaking peoples who mainly composed the population of the State, however, were not satisfied by bilingual arrangement. A powerful and persistent campaign for the division of the State into two unilingual States has gone on for three years; and the demand is now being accepted. The break-up of Bombay may be reckoned to be another triumph of 'people's will' in the evolution of constitutional government in India.

At the present juncture of India's development, the most powerful unifying ideal seems to be the linguistic principle. It is difficult to forecast to what extent it will affect the unity of the nation in the long run. Despite the almost fanatic linguistic fervour, deep-seated sentiments of national unity are visible in many forms in all parts of the country today. But as the present national leadership gradually disappears and the consciousness of the common struggle for Independence fades, it is difficult to foresee whether the same sentiments of national unity will prevail.

I wish to express my deep gratitude to all those who have encouraged me in writing this book, particularly a number of my colleagues. Of the many to whom I am deeply obliged, I wish to mention specially my friend Prof. V.V. John, for carefully reading through the text and making many valuable suggestions.

Delhi
June 1960 **Dr. M.V. PYLEE**

OTHER BOOKS OF THE AUTHOR

India's Constitution at Work

India's Constitution

The Federal Court of India

Constitutional History of India

Industrial Policy

A Tribute to India

International Joint Business Ventures (CO-AUTHOR)

Worker Participation in Management : Myth and Reality

Russia of my Experience

A Study of Coir Industry in India

An Introduction to Managerial Economics (CO-AUTHOR)

Professional Management in India (EDITOR)

Essentials of Materials Management (EDITOR)

Crisis, Conscience and the Constitution

An Introduction to the Constitution of India

Emerging Trends of Indian Polity

Our Constitution, Government and Politics

Constitutions of the World

Select Constitutions of the World

Constitutional Amendments in India

Looking Back-Reflections and Reminiscences

The author has written fourteen other books which are in Malayalam language.

CONTENTS

PART I

INTRODUCTORY

1

THE LONGEST CONSTITUTIONAL DOCUMENT

The Dawn of a New Era

THE TWENTY-SIXTH January 1950 marked a great event in the long and chequered history of India. For, on that day, was brought into force the present Constitution of India, which announced to the world the birth of a new republic. It was in fact the re-birth of an ancient country, after centuries of dire vicissitudes.

The struggle for national independence was over by 15 August 1947. On that day the two-hundred-year-old British rule in India was brought the to an end by the transfer of political authority to Indian hands. However, the attainment of independence was not an end in itself. It was only the beginning of a new struggle, the struggle to live as an independent nation and, at the same time, to establish a democracy based upon the ideals of justice, liberty, equality and fraternity. The need of a new constitution forming the basic law of the land for the realization of these ideals was paramount. Therefore, one of the first tasks undertaken by independent India was the framing of a new constitution. The present Constitution of India is its result. It represents the political, economic and social ideals and aspirations of the vast majority of the Indian people of the present generation.

A constitution is a set of laws and rules setting up the machinery of the government of a State and which defines and determines the relations between the different institutions and areas of government, the executive, the legislature and the judiciary, the central, the regional and the local governments. The first well-known instance of a written constitution was that of the United States of America which set up an original pattern, and which for its 'brevity, restraint and simplicity' is universally hailed as a remarkable document. The makers of the Indian Constitution drew much from the American Constitution though not its brevity, and added to that the experience of later constitutions in different parts of the world, especially much from the British-made Government of India Act of 1935. Thus, the Constitution of India is the result of considerable imitation and adaptation rather than of originality.

Napoleon once told Talleyrand, his leading political adviser, that a 'constitution ought to be short and clear'. But the latter countered, 'No, Sire, it ought to be long and obscure!' Of the two qualities prescribed by the ingenious Frenchman, there can be no doubt that the Indian Constitution possesses the first; it is debatable whether we have achieved the second quality. The Constitution in XXII parts'[1] with its 395 Articles,[2] many of which

1. The Forty-second Amendment added two new parts, Part IV-A and Part XIV-A.
2. The total number of Articles also has gone up as a result of numerous amendments of the constitution.

contain a number of exceptions, limitations and qualifications, and 9 Schedules and 82 Amendments (so far), runs into some 300 pages making it the longest in the history of constitutions.[1]

The Elephantine Size of the Constitution

What made the Constitution so 'bulky' is perhaps the first question which anyone who glances over it might ask. To begin with, therefore, we may deal with the question.[2] The size of the Constitution is the result of many contributory factors. The most important of these are as follows :

1. India has a federal constitution. Normally, a federal constitution, because of the detailed provisions that it embodies with respect to the division of powers between the federation and the States, is longer than the constitution of a unitary State. But the Constitution of India is not merely that of a federation. Unlike most federal constitutions it prescribes not only a constitution for the Union but also for the States, Part VI of the Constitution which contains eighty-six articles (Art. 152 to 237) forms a standard constitution for the States of the Indian Union which neither a State Legislature nor the Parliament of India alone can amend. Part VIII consisting of three articles (Art. 239 to 241) deals with the Union Territories, territories that fall directly under the jurisdiction of the Union Government and which are administered under its direct supervision. Part X consisting of Article 244 and 244A deals with the Scheduled and Tribal Areas. These are areas scattered in different parts of the country and inhabited by aboriginal tribes, whose economy and social organization are in varying stages of development. Since they need special treatment, the Constitution has devoted Part X to this purpose. The provisions of the Fifth and Sixth Schedules also apply to the administration and control of the Scheduled Areas and Scheduled Tribes. While the Fifth Schedule, with four sections, deals with the administration and control of the scheduled areas and tribes in general, the Sixth Schedule, with twenty-one Parts applies to the administration of the tribal areas in the States of Assam, Meghalaya and Mizoram.

2. The Constitution seeks to regulate the relations between the Union and the States in a detailed and thorough manner. Experience of the working of the older federations shows that one of the most prolific sources of conflict leading to unending litigation has been the result of a lack of clear-cut and well-defined division of powers between the Union and the States. By providing for a detailed demarcation of the respective jurisdictions of the Union and the States, the Constitution has made an earnest attempt to bring down the chances of conflict between them to the minimum. Part XI, entitled 'Relations between the Union and the States' consists of two chapters, 'Legislative Relations' and 'Administrative Relations' and runs into twenty-one articles (Art. 245 to 263). Besides, it also incorporates the Seventh Schedule consisting of three legislative lists, the Union List, the State List and

---

1. There was as time when the Ugoslavians claimed that theirs was the longest constitution in the world with as many as 406 articles. That claim is no more valid as the Republic of Ugoslavia got disintegrated as a result of the Civil war in 1993.
2. Speaking about the size of the Constitution, H.V. Kamath said in the Constituent Assembly that we were proud of the fact that our Constitution was the bulkiest in the whole world' 'The emblem and the crest that we have selected for our assembly is an elephant. It is perhaps in consonance with that our Constitution too is the bulkiest that the world has produced'. C.A.D. VII, p. 1042. The same member said on another occasion: 'I am sure, the House does not agree that we should make the Constitution an elephantine one' C.A.D. VIII, p. 127.

the Concurrent List. Part XII consisting of thirty-nine articles (Art. 264 to 300) deals, in elaborate terms, with the financial relations between the Union and the States as well as the financial dealings of the Union and the States with third parties. Part XIII with seven articles (Art 301 to 307) deals with inter-state trade and commerce.

3. Part III of the Constitution embodies the Fundamental Rights and consists of twenty-seven articles (Art. 12 to 35). Most of the modern constitutions have a chapter on fundamental rights. But seldom has any constitution attempted to set out these rights in such detail. Because of the peculiar conditions and circumstances prevailing in India, the framers of the constitution were compelled not only to incorporate rights which are unknown to other constitutions[1] but also details which may be considered unnecessary elsewhere. The Constituent Assembly thought fit to include also a chapter on 'Directive Principles of State Policy' occupying seventeen articles (Art. 36 to 51). Part IV contains these directives which, although, according to the Constitution, not 'enforceable by any court of law', are nevertheless fundamental in the governance of the country.

4. There are problems peculiar to India which, in the opinion of the Constituent Assembly, required special treatment in the Constitution itself. These include the 'Services under the Union and the States', Part XIV with sixteen articles (Art. 308 to 323); special provisions relating to classes such as the Scheduled Castes, Scheduled Tribes and Anglo Indians, Part XVI with thirteen articles (Art. 330 to 342); official languages, dealt with under Part XVII with nine articles (Art. 343 to 351) and the Eighth Schedule'[2] and the Emergency Provisions under Part XVIII occupying nine articles (Art. 352 to 360). The Constitution has also a chapter each, on 'Elections', Part XV, consisting of six articles (Art. 324 to 329); on 'Miscellaneous Provisions', Part XIX, with eight articles (Art 361 to 367); and 'Temporary and Transitional Provisions', Part XXI, covering nineteen articles (Art. 369 to 392). Almost three fourths of the Constitution is covered by the items mentioned above, and that explains the size of the Constitution.

5. The justification for the inclusion of provisions for what would otherwise be regulated by ordinary legislation is to be found in the constitutional history of India under the British rule. The Constitution derives directly from the Government of India Act, 1935, many of its provisions almost verbatim. That Act was the largest ever passed by the British Parliament and its main purpose was to transfer power, subject to numerous so-called safeguards, from British officials to Indian politicians. It had to create a new federal legislature and, at the same time, reform the Governments of the former British Indian Provinces and establish new relations with the former Indian Princely States. As Sir Ivor Jennings said, 'The Government of India had been an autocracy whose powers were at first limited in the interests of British politicians and subsequently in the interests of Indian politicians'. The problem in 1935 was re-distribution of the powers of the British Government in India to reconcile the Indian demand for full self-government and the British determination to keep India under their control. Hence, the Constitution Act of 1935 was full of compromises designed to meet this double objective resulting in a extremely elaborate and complex document. Although the Government of India Act of 1935 was not fully put into operation, an important part of it was implemented in 1937 and, in any case, Indians had become familiar with its provisions ever

1. For instance, the abolition of 'Untouchability' and making its practice in any form an offence punishable under law.
2. The Schedule lists eighteen languages recognised as the national languages of India.

since. The same Act was suitably modified to become the Constitution of the Dominion of India between 15 August 1947 and 26 January 1950, the date of commencement of the present Constitution. It was only natural, therefore, that the fathers of the Constitution should borrow many provisions of the Act of 1935 and make them part of the new constitution they were framing. Making a specific reference to this aspect of the Constitution, Ambedkar, the Chairman of the Drafting Committee, said in the Constituent Assembly:

> As to the accusation that the Draft Constitution has reproduced a good part of the provisions of the Government of India Act, 1935 I make no apologies. There is nothing to be ashamed of in borrowing. It involves no plagiarism. Nobody holds any patent rights in the fundamental ideas of a Constitution. What I am sorry about is that the provisions taken from the Government of India Act, 1935, relate mostly to the details of administration. I agree that administrative details should have no place in the Constitution. I wish very much that the Drafting Committee could see its way to avoid their inclusion in the Constitution. But this is to be said on the necessity which justifies their inclusion. Grote, the historian of Greece, has said that:
>
> The diffusion of constitutional morality, not merely among the majority of any community but throughout the whole, is the indispensable condition of government at once free and peaceable; since even any powerful and obstinate minority may render the working of a free institution impracticable, without being strong enough to conquer ascendancy of themselves.'
>
> By constitutional morality Grote meant a paramount reverence for the forms of the Constitution, enforcing obedience to authority acting under and within these forms yet combined with the habit of open speech, of action subject only to definite legal control and unrestrained censure of those very authorities as to all their public acts combined too with a perfect confidence in the bosom of every citizen, amidst the bitterness of party contest, that the forms of the Constitution will not be less sacred in the eyes of his opponents than in his own.
>
> While everybody recognizes the necessity of the diffusion of constitutional morality for the peaceful working of a democratic constitution, there are two things inter-connected with it which are not, unfortunately, generally recognized, One is that the form of administration has a close connection with the form of the Constitution. The form of the administration must be appropriate to and in the same sense as the form of the Constitution. The other is that it is perfectly possible to pervert the Constitution, without changing its form by merely changing the form of the administration and to make it inconsistent and opposed to the spirit of the Constitution. It follows that it is only where people are saturated with constitutional morality such as the one described by Grote the historian that one can take the risk of omitting from the Constitution details of administration and leaving it for the Legislature to prescribe them. The question is, can we presume such a diffusion of constitutional morality? Constitutional morality is not a natural sentiment. It has to be cultivated. We must realize that our people have yet to learn it. Democracy in India is only a top-dressing on an Indian soil which is essentially undemocratic.[1]

6. Another consideration that influenced the founding fathers of the Constitution was the existence of certain factors which were peculiar to India. Most of the members of the Constituent Assembly, particularly the leading lights had the unpleasant experience of having undergone varying terms of imprisonment while non-violently fighting against the British rule. Very often, it was an arbitrary Government decision that sent them to jail. This convinced them of the necessity to limit, rigidly by law, the powers of government. Consequently, they made a special effort to go into as much details as possible in every part of the Constitution.

7. India is a land of immense diversity. From a religious point of view, Hindusim and Islam are the leading faiths. But there are considerable numbers of adherents of other religions like Christianity, Sikhism, Buddhism, Jainism, Zoroastrianism and Judaism. Among the Hindus, who are traditionally divided into different castes, were a large number of the so-called 'Untouchables'. There are also the tribal people who occupy certain isolated

---

1. CAD VII. p.38

pockets in different parts of the country, almost cut off from the rest of the people. From a racial point of view there are at least three major groups, the Indo-Aryans, the Dravidians and the Mongolo-Aryans. There are not less than a dozen well-developed major languages spoken in different parts of the country. Some of these have a literature as old as 3,000 years. From a cultural point of view also, great differences can be noticed between different areas within the Indian sub-continent. The Constitution-makers were called upon to draw up a document which adequately protected the interests of these various minorities and yet safeguarded the essential unity of the nation. This again tended to enlarge the size of the Constitution.

8. One can easily notice the spirit of not only political democracy but also economic democracy that breathes through many parts of the Constitution, particularly in Part IV which deals with the Directive Principles of State Policy. This is the result of an ardent desire of the framers to effect a rapid modernization of economic and social institutions. It was impossible to think of a constitution of 1950 creating the framework of a *laissez-faire* State rather than a Welfare State. The American Constitution, which was framed in the 'horse and buggy' days of the eighteenth century, could rightly ignore such a consideration. But India, after two centuries of foreign rule and economic exploitation, and with a huge population, could not leave this matter to either legislative discretion or judicial interpretation.

9. The exercise of both judicial and administrative functions by the same officer was one of the controversies of British India. The Collector, the head of a district, was more often than not, a local dictator. This was due to the combination of executive and judicial functions in his office. Agitation for the separation of these functions has a century-old history in India. Hence, it was no surprise that the Constitution-makers should have dealt with this problem in detail. As a result, the doctrine of the separation of powers has received a new interpretation in India. Such separation calls for not merely the independence of the superior courts but also a differentiation of local functions. Judicial administration, even at the lower levels, has become a subject of constitutional importance. The articles of the Constitution dealing with the judiciary are based on the theory that the subject is of such great importance that it should be dealt with in detail by constitutional law and not by ordinary law.

10. All these special problems and circumstances have made their conspicuous contribution to making the Constitution a bulky and even complex document. The predominance of the lawyer-element in the making of the Constitution may have been an additional factor, although the same circumstance did not have a similar effect on the American Constitution which is a marvel of brevity and simplicity. This difference was probably due to the different background against which that Constitution was drawn up. The American Constitution was the product of a revolution. Its framers started on a clean slate. On the contrary, the Indian Constitution-makers were not framing a constitution anew after a 'bloody' revolution. Political power was transferred in a peaceful manner in India. Hence, the framers did not and could not altogether ignore, in the new framework, the administrative structure which was in existence and had been working for a long time.

The Alleged Paradise of the Lawyers

One of the most frequently heard complaints against Constitution, both in the Constituent Assembly during the discussion of the Draft Constitution and outside it, was that it was 'a lwayer's paradise'. Making a general comment on the Constitution, a member said that :

The Draft tends to make people more litigious, more inclined to go to law courts, less truthful and less likely to follow the methods of truth and non-violence. If I may say so, the Draft is really a lawyer's paradise. It opens up vast avenues of litigation and will give our able and ingenious lawyers plenty of work to do.[1]

Another member said :

I should, however, like to say that the draft of the articles that have been brought before the House by Dr. Ambedkar seems to my mind to be far too ponderous like the ponderous tomes of a law manual. A document dealing with a Constitution hardly uses to much of padding and so much of verbiage. (The member compared the Constitution of India with that of West Germany and said that the latter was only a little pamphlet of 52 pages containing 146 articles).... All this verbiage reflects the mind of lawyers who have spent most of their lives in arguing and bandying words with each other in courts and does not reflect the spirit of a people, the fighting spirit of a people who have been through the fire and steel of the freedom struggle and who have solemnly assembled to infuse our Constitution with life and light. Unfortunately, the Drafting Committee has been weighted with men who have led a sheltered existence, who have been hardly touched by the effulgent light of a deathless ideal, and who have spent most of their lives in the service of the Government. Perhaps it is difficult for them to compose a document which should be, to my mind, not a law manual but a socio-political document, a vibrating, pulsating and life-giving document. But to our misfortune, that was not to be, and we have been burdened with so much of words, words and words which could have been very easily eliminated.[2]

It is true that the Constitution is a complex document. The complexity, as we have noted above, is mainly due to the difficult problems which the framers confronted at the time of its making and their attempt to embody solutions for them in the Constitution itself. It is also because of the elaborate and detailed language in which the provisions of the Constitution are couched. Further, the phraseology adopted is that which is familiar only in courts of law. A striking feature of the Constitution in this context is the numerous exceptions, qualifications and explanations that one finds along with almost every provision. Whatever might be the reasons for their inclusion, their presence makes the understanding of the Constitution extremely difficult for the ordinary reader. Only an experienced lawyer, well versed in constitutional law, can understand the implications of the legal language in which most of these provisions are couched. This would seem to justify the description of the Constitution as a lawyer's paradise.

On a closer examination, however, it will be seen that such a description is the result of misunderstanding and a misplaced apprehension. The fact that the Constitution is a complex document need not necessarily mean that it should become a prolific source of litigation. Neither the length nor complexity of a legal document has in itself a direct relation to litigation. An apparently simple and easily understood provision might provide a fertile field for unending litigation. A classic example is the 'Commerce Clause' of the American Constitution which provides that 'the Congress shall have power to regulate commerce with foreign Nations, and among the several States, and with the Indian Tribes'.[3] It is almost impossible to think of simpler terms to describe the idea embodied in this clause. Apparently, no legal assistance is required for anyone to understand its meaning. And yet, the Commerce Clause has been a veritable source of unending litigation throughout the history of the American Republic. The number of cases in which the Supreme Court has been called upon to interpret the scope of this apparently simple provision is legion. This is true of several other apparently simple and easily understood provisions of the American Constitution. The 'General Welfare' clause is another example.

1. Himmat Singh. K. Maheswari, C.A.D. VII, p. 293
2. Panjab Rao Deshmukh, C.A.D. IX, 613.
3. Art. I, Sec. 8.

We may take yet another example, this time from another constitution, the Constitution of Australia, which also attempted to formulate in simple terms the provision dealing with inter-state trade and commerce.[1] It is well known that the provision has been perpetual source of litigation. Both the Australian High Court and the Judicial Committee of the Privy Council were compelled to read into the provision various exceptions and qualifications from time to time to reconcile the interests of local autonomy with the principle of freedom of inter-state trade and commerce. Commenting about the provision an Australian writer observes:

> The paragraph is in the laymen's language. It reads more like a slogan than as part of a legal document ..... The history of the section is a conspicuous example of the pit-falls likely to be encountered by a rigid Constitution in a changing world. No section in the Constitution has given rise to so much litigation or difference of judicial opinion.[2]

As has already been pointed out, the American Constitution, compared to its Indian counterpart, is a marvel of brevity and simplicity. But this has not in any way cut down litigation. On an average the Supreme Court of the United States in called upon to decide thirteen hundred cases a year.[3] In contrast, the Supreme Court of India with its wider jurisdiction has yet to reach half as much of constitutional cases a year in its career to far. The number of cases that comes before the Supreme Court compares favourably with that which comes before other federal Supreme Courts such as the Canadian Supreme Court and the Australian High Court.

The elaborate nature of the Indian Constitution, instead of enhancing the scope of litigation, has in fact helped to reduce it to a minimum. The best example of this is provided by those chapters of the Constitution which deal with the relations between the Union and the States. Under any federal system, one of the biggest sources of litigation is provided by the part of the constitution which deals with the division of powers between the Union and the States. This has been the case in the United States, in Canada and Australia. But in India, during a period of over five decades of the working of the Constitution, there has been a proportionately small number of cases in the field. The credit for this comparatively smaller amount of litigation should go largely to the detailed character of the provisions of the Constitution.

If there is any part of the Constitution which can be called a lawyer's paradise on the basis of the extent of litigation that it has caused so far, it is the chapter which embodies the Fundamental Rights. Even a causal glance over the pages of the *Supreme Court Reports* will show that there have been more cases in this area than in any other. Critics of the Constitution were severe on these provisions at the time of their adoption and predicted that they would beat all records as a source of litigation. One must admit that this prediction has largely come true. Normally, fundamental rights, by their very nature, provide a continuously rich source of litigation. The conflict between man and the State is a perennial problem. As such, any constitution that guarantees fundamental rights and makes the

---

1. Section 92: 'On the imposition of uniform duties of customs, trade, commerce and intercourse, among the States, whetehr by means of internal carriage or ocean navigation, shall be absolutely free'.
2. Nichols, *The Australian Constitution* (1948), p. 129.
3. Taking a ten-year period of 1944-53, the maximum number of 1,510 cases were filed in 1946 while the minimum was, 1,181 in 1950. See William O. Douglas, *We the Judges, p.* 64. The number has been steadily on the increase. For example, from 1953 when it was 1463 it rose to 5311 in 1981. See 1983 U.S. News and World Report, Inc.

judiciary its protector makes also an invitation to litigation. The Bill of Rights under the American Constitution is the best example. The fact that the American Bill of Rights is couched in the simplest language imaginable did not in any way reduce litigation. On the contrary, the American Supreme Court, again and again, in thousands of cases, was called upon to adjudicate the competing claims of individual freedom and social control. It is not a fact that in India, the litigation arising out of the provisions of the chapter on fundamental rights has been due to the detailed nature of the provisions or because of the numerous exceptions and qualifications. Such litigation is an inevitable expression of the democratic vigilance in regard to the freedom of the individual. It is a sign of health, and not the result of any defects in the law.

Constitutional litigation is generally a product of verbal defects such as ambiguity, vagueness of the expressions used and the lack of precision and certainty. Viewed from this point, one could find several provisions in the Constitution of India, as originally passed, which were far from satisfactory. This is one of the reasons for the comparatively large number of amendments, forty-six of them in the relatively short period of the first thirty years. Article 31 which dealt with the right to property which caused, perhaps, the largest amount of litigation on any single article, provides one of the best illustrations of such provisions. As an extreme example of compromise, in its original form, the right to property and the power of the State to acquire private property compulsorily, was expressed in vague language. When the Supreme Court interpreted its meaning and held that 'compensation meant full compensation in all cases of compulsory acquisition and equivalent to the market value of the property at the time of acquisition,' the spokesmen of the Government protested that such was not what had been intended when the Article was adopted by the Constituent Assembly. The provision was then amended. But no one could legitimately blame the Supreme Court for its interpretation of the article as it originally stood.

In an unusually long constitutional document like the Constitution of India, which attempts to provide almost a panacea for the many political, social and economic ills which the country had been suffering from at the time of its Independence, it is not impossible to find provisions that may be vague or ambiguous. But to denigrate the Constitution as a lawyer's paradise on account of its detailed provisions or of its complex nature is not justified. On the contrary, the Constitution has so far not yielded overabundant opportunities for unending legal wrangles, and it is improbable that it will ever do so in future. It was certainly no conspiracy of the lawyer-Constitution-makers that made the Constitution complex. The problems which India faced in the wake of freedom were multifarious and complex. No Constituent Assembly charged with the task of framing a democratic document ever faced such diverse and difficult problems. Simplicity in itself is not a virtue. Adequacy is a more essential quality in a legal document. And the virtue of the Constitution is finally to be judged from the results it produces.

***

2

SOME FURTHER POINTS OF CRITICISM

APART FROM the large size and the complexity which made the critics of the Constitution assail it as a lawyer's paradise, there were also other serious criticisms which deserve at least a brief analysis.

1. One of the most important of these criticisms has been that no part of the Constitution represents the ancient polity of India, its genius and the spirit of its hallowed and glorious traditions. Many members in the Constituent Assembly drew the attention of the House and the country to this omission. Some of them also pointed out that the Constitution did not embody the principles for which 'Gandhism' stood or the ideology of the Indian National Congress. A prominent member even went to the point of attributing this 'lapse' to Ambedkar's non-participation in the Gandhian movement and the antagonism towards Gandhian ideas:[1] The Constitution, according to some of them, ought to have been drafted on the ancient Hindu model of a State and that, instead of incorporating western theories, it should have been 'raised and built upon village panchayats and district panchayats'. A few extremists even advocated the abolition of the Central and the Provincial Governments. They just wanted an India full of village governments.

Answering these criticisms, Ambedkar said in the Constituent Assembly:[2]

> The love of the intellectual Indian for the village community is of course infinite if not pathetic (laughter). It is largely due to the fulsome praise bestowed upon it by Metcalfe who described them as little republics having nearly everything that they want within themselves, and almost independent of any foreign relations. The existence of these village communities each one forming a separate little State in itself has, according to Metcalfe, contributed more than any other cause to the preservation of the people of India, through all the revolutions and changes which they have suffered, and is in a high degree conducive to their happiness and to the enjoyment of a great portion of the freedom and independence. No doubt the village communities do not care to consider what little part they have played in the affairs and the density of the country ; and why? Their part in the density of the country has been well described by Metcalfe himself who says:
>
> Dynasty after dynasty tumbles down. Revolution succeeds to revolution. Hindoo, Pathan, Mogul, Maharatha, Sikh, English are all masters in turn but the village communities remain the same. In times of trouble they arm and fortify themselves. A hostile army passes through the country. The village communities collect their little cattle within their walls, and let the enemy pass unprovoked'.
>
> Such is the part the village communities have played in the history of their country. Knowing this, what pride can one feel in them? That they have survived through all vicissitudes may be a fact. But mere survival has no value. The question is on what plane they have survived. Surely on a low, on a selfish level. I hold that these village republics have been the ruination of India. I am therefore surprised

1. T Prakasam, C.A.D. VII, p. 387.
2. C.A.D. VII, p, 38.

that those who condemn provincialism and communalism should come forward as champions of the village. What is the village but a sink of localism, a den of ignorance, narrow-midedness and communalism? I am glad that the Draft Constitution has discarded the village and adopted the individual as its unit.

Ambedkar's criticism has been largely justified in the light of the performance of village panchayats wherever they have been established in the country ever since Independence. There can be no doubt that the stability and security of Indian democracy depend largely on the successful functioning of the village panchayats which have to become its real back-bone. But the fact is that the village panchayats, today, are nowhere near that position. And it is doubtful whether they would in the near future develop themselves to assume such a role. At present, speaking comparatively, the best organized and the best-run political institution in the country except in one or two States, is the Central Government. As we go down the line from the Centre to the States, the districts, the sub-divisions, the taluqas and to the villages, the quality of the administration and its standards mark a steady deterioration. Nothing but all-round education and the cultivation of civic virtues and responsibilities at the village level can build, over a period of years, a sound foundation for a democratic system to flourish in the country. If the Constitution had attempted to establish straightaway 'village republics' in mid-twentieth century on the plea that such institutions flourished in the country in the remote past, ignoring the conditions of the modern technological age, there would have been nothing but chaos and anarchy, and the unity that was established as a result of so much sacrifice would have been lost in no time once again, perhaps for ever.

After nearly half a century after the inauguration of the Constitution, the Seventy-third Amendment of the Constitution in 1973 has provided for the establishment of the Panchayati Raj system to usher in a new era of decentralisation to ensure the villages of India to become the primary units of self Government. The process which began in 1965 was to establish itself and it is hoped that eventually the Gandhian dream of Gram Swaraj would become a reality.

2. Critics of the federal provisions can be divided into two categories. According to most of them, the Centre has been made too strong. But some of them wanted it to be made stronger. The Constitution, according to the Drafting Committee, has struck a balance. Ambedkar said:

However much you may deny powers to the Centre, it is difficult to prevent the Centre from becoming strong. Conditions in the modern world are such that centralisation of powers is inevitable. One has only to consider the growth of the Federal Government in the U.S.A. which notwithstanding the very limited powers given to it by the Constitution, has outgrown its former self and has overshadowed and eclipsed the State Governments. This is due to modern conditions. The same conditions are sure to operate on the Government of India and nothing that one can do will help to prevent it form being strong. On the other hand, we must resist the tendency to make it stronger. It cannot chew more than it can digest. Its strength must be commensurate with its weight. It would be a folly to make it so strong that it may fall by its own weight.[1]

The experience of over five decades shows that the federal system as envisaged under the Constitution, on the whole, has worked reasonably well. The apprehensions of the critics that the Union being too strong would either devour the States or reduce them to the status of administrative units of the Union or that of municipalities within a State, have not materialized. On the other hand, the States have been holding their own and maintaining

1. C.A.D. VII, p. 42.

their individuality within the framework of the Constitution. No doubt, centralized planning and an integrated programme of economic development for the entire country through successive Five Year Plans have brought about unrivalled supremacy of the Union in the economic and financial sphere. But this is not the product of any specific provision in the Constitution. By and large, the States have voluntarily acceded to this situation in a crucial period of development and there is nothing that prevents them later from going back to a position of greater autonomy in the economic sphere.

A wholesome feature in the working of the federal system under the Indian Constitution is that litigation in the field of Centre-State relationship has been conspicuous by its negligible size rather than its enormity which is one of the common defects of the older federations. Although there had been several amendments to the Constitution within the first few years after its inauguration, none of these seriously affected the field of Centre-State relationship except for minor changes. The fear that the existence of a long Concurrent List, instead of reducing litigation, might lead to an increase of it,[1] has been falsified. In fact, the success of the federal system is largely the result, while distributing and allocating legislative powers, of taking into account the political and economic conditions obtaining in the country, rather than of relying on *a priori* theories of federalism.

3. Perhaps, the most criticized part of the Constitution is that which deals with the Fundamental Rights. It has been alleged that every fundamental right embodied in the Constitution is riddled with so many exceptions and qualifications that these have eaten up the rights altogether. Further, it is pointed out that the life and liberty of the subject has been placed at the mercy of the executive government and there is hardly any protection against tyrannical laws.[2]

Answering these criticisms Ambedkar said in the Constituent Assembly:

> In the opinion of the critics, fundamental rights are not fundamental unless they are also absolute rights. The critics rely on the Constitution of the United States and the Bill of Rights embodied in the first ten Amendments to that Constitution in support of their contention. It is said that the fundamental rights in the American Bill of rights are real because they are not subjected to limitations or exceptions.
>
> I am sorry to say that the whole of the criticism about fundamental rights is based upon a misconception. In the first place, the criticism in so far as it seeks to distinguish fundamental rights from non-fundamental rights is not sound. It is incorrect to say that fundamental rights are absolute while non-fundamental rights are created by agreement between parties while fundamental rights are the gift of the law. Because fundamental rights are the gift of the State it does not follow that the State cannot qualify them.
>
> In the second place, it is wrong to say that fundamental rights in America are absolute. The difference between the position under the American Constitution and the Draft Constitution is one of form and not of substance. That the fundamental rights in America are not absolute rights is beyond dispute. In support of every exception to the Fundamental Rights set out in the Draft Constitution one can refer to at least one judgement of the United States Supreme Court. It would be sufficient to quote one such judgement of the Supreme Court in justification of the limitation on the right of free speech contained in Article 13 of the Draft Constitution. In Gitlow *vs.* New York,[3] in which the issue was the constitutionality of a New York 'criminal anarchy' law which purported to punish utterances calculated to bring about violent change, the Supreme Court said:
>
> 'It is a fundamental principle, long established, that the freedom of speech and of the press, which is secured by the Constitution, does not confer an absolute right to speak or publish, without responsibility, whatever one may choose, or an unrestricted and unbridled licence that gives immunity for every

1. K.C. Wheare, *Modern Constitutions*, p. 53.
2. P.R. Das, Presidential Address, The Indian Civil Liberties Conference, 1949.
3. 268 U.S. 652, 1925

possible use of language and prevents the punishment of those who abuse this freedom. It is therefore wrong to say that the fundamental rights in America are absolute while those in the Draft Constitution are not[1].

The difficulty in formulating any set of fundamental rights is now widely recognized by writers on constitutional government. As Wheare points out:

> The declaration of rights provides a great problem for the makers of Constitution. If they are not inserted, some influential body of opinion may be alienated and the Constitution may fail to be accepted. But if they are to be inserted, it is extremely difficult to define the nature and extent of those rights in such a way that something significant and realistic is achiéved. If a Government is to be effective, few rights of its citizens can be stated in absolute form.......... There must be, it would seem, some restrictions on these rights. Most constitutions which contain a declaration of rights do recognise that some qualifications must be attached to their exercise...... No realistic attempt to define the rights of citizens indeed fail to include qualification.[2]

4. The criticism that the protection against tyrannical laws and the arbitrary conduct of the executive against the life and liberty of the subject is too slender, has a good deal of force in it. For, under Article 21, life and liberty can be taken away so long as it is done in accordance with the procedure established by law. Similarly, private property can be compulsorily acquired by the State for a public purpose and the Legislature may at its will fix the quantum of compensation[3]. In both these cases, the ultimate power is vested in the Legislature to fix the limits and the citizen has hardly any (except rarely from the judiciary) remedy against an oppressive legislative majority, a serious drawback from the point of view of fundamental rights. The existence of a provision which permits 'preventive detention' for the purposes of the State leaves in the hands of the executive an extraordinary power to curb individual freedom. And this power was used more often than not all these years by the governments in India both at the Centre and in the States. These are serious limitations on the scope of fundamental rights and, as such, they form a weighty criticism of an important part of the Constitution.

Some of the most important amendments of the Constitution have been designed to bring about profound changes in the scope of the rights. Among them are the First, the Fourth and the Twenty-fifth Amendments, the former dealing with the freedom of speech and the latter (both,) with the right to property. The main justification for these amendments is the increasing need, in the light of the socio-economic development of the country, for greater social control of the freedom of the individual in order to facilitate the planned growth and ćhange of the society as a whole.

5. The inclusion of a set of non-justiciable rights — the Directive Principles of State Policy — in the Constitution has been criticized as the inclusion of a set of pious declarations which have no binding force. According to Ambedkar, this Criticism is superfluous:

> The Constitution itself says so in so many words. If it is said that the Directive Principles have no legal force behind them, I am prepared to admit it. But I am not prepared to admit that they have no sort of binding force at all. Nor am I prepared to concede that they are useless because they have no binding force in law.[4]

Apart from the fact that the Directive Principles form a code of conduct both for legislators

1. C.A.D. VII, p. 40
2. Op. cit. pp. 55.7
3. Right to Property is no more a Fundamental Right. It was abolished by the Forty fourth Amendment, 1979.
4. C.A.D. VII, p. 41

and administrators and set before the country a socio-economic objective that is to be realized as early as possible, they help the people to assess in the light of a clearly laid-down standard, the achievements of each government in office at the time of every general election. Further, the separation of non-justiciable rights from justiciable ones has a special advantage. It avoids the necessity of bringing under the same category, rights of varying value. In fact, this plan may be claimed to be preferable to that adopted in the Declaration of Rights contained in the Preamble of the Fourth Republic of France in regard to the legal value of which widely differing views have been expressed. It is maintained by some that it represents no more than a collection of pious hopes, whereas the view is held by others that the principles enunciated therein are intended to be legally binding on all future legislators, though the French Constitution makes no provision for conformity. The Preamble was the result of a compromise between the individualist and the socialist schools of thought and in which liberal and collectivist doctrines are mingled together.[1]

In contrast, the Directive Principles in the Indian Constitution have not created any such conflicting legal views. The Governments in India — Central as well as State—have been trying their utmost for the translation of these principles into reality. The value attached to them has been so much that when there was a conflict between a directive principle and a fundamental right and the Supreme Court declared the latter to prevail over the former, the Constitution itself was amended to modify the fundamental right. Thus, the criticism that the Directive Principles are only pious wishes has been already falsified. In fact, they are the real guiding stars of State activity in India. Being non-justiciable, the Supreme Court said that it cannot enforce these principles. But even the Court has recognized the value of these principles and has been giving them due recognition in its decisions so long as they do not come in direct conflict with any fundamental rights. Of late the Supreme Court has been taking a more active stand regarding Directive Principles and this is reflected in some of its decisions. Today, the Directive Principles are a really important part of India's constitutional system.[2]

6. The Constitution has been criticized by some for the special safeguards that it provides for minorities and certain classes who are socially and educationally backward. Commending the wisdom underlying these provisions, Ambedkar said:

> Speaking for myself, I have no doubt that the Constituent Assembly has done wisely in providing such safeguards for minorities as it has done. In this country both the minorities and the majorities have followed a wrong path. It is wrong for the majority to deny the existence of minorities. It is equally wrong for the minorities to perpetuate themselves. A solution must be found which will serve a double purpose. It must recognise the existence of the minorities to start with. It must also be such that it will enable majorities and minorities to merge some day into one. The solution proposed by the Constituent Assembly is to be welcomed because it is a solution which serves this two-fold purpose. To diehards who have developed a kind of fanaticism against minority protection I would like to say two things. One is that minorities are an explosive force which, if it erupts, can blow up the whole fabric of the State. The history of Europe bears ample and appalling testimony to this fact. The other is that the minorities in India have agreed to place their existence in the hands of the majority. In the history of negotiations for preventing the partition of Ireland, Redmond said to Carson, 'Ask for any safeguard you like for the Protestant minority but let us have a United Ireland'. Carson's reply was, 'Damn your safeguards, we don't want to be ruled by you'. No minority in India has taken this stand. They have loyally accepted the rule of the majority which is basically a communal majority and not a political majority. It is for the majority to realize its duty not to discriminate against minorities. Whether the minorities will continue

1. Taylor, *Constitution and Political Parties inthe Fourth Republic of France.*
2. This aspect is discussed at length later in the chapter on Directive Principles (see Chatper 23).

or will vanish must depend upon this habit of the majority. The moment the majority loses the habit of discriminating against minority, the minorities can have no ground to exist. They will vanish.[1]

The safeguards provided in this context can be divided into two categories; First, those that are guaranteed for a specified period, namely, ten years from the commencement of the Constitution; secondly, those which form part of the Fundamental Rights. A ten-year period was considered sufficient by the Constituent Assembly to remove some of the glaring political and educational disabilities of certain backward classes and put them on a level of equality with the rest of the people.[2] As for the Fundamental Rights, they are conceived in a spirit of generosity on the part of the majority and accommodation and understanding on the part of the minorities. As such, they ought to provide a lasting solution for this highly complicated problem. They, as Ambedkar confidently hoped, should, in the course of time, remove all the artificial barriers which separate minorities from majorities and create a composite society in the country.

The Draft Constitution was discussed in most of the Provincial Assemblies even before it was considered in detail by the Constituent Assembly. A remarkable trend of these discussions was the general consensus of opinion on the soundness of its fundamentals, and the firm hope that the Constitution would prove a working document for a new India that was taking shape. The only serious criticism voiced was about the Centre-State financial provisions which, it was feared placed the States at the mercy of the Centre in the financial field. It is significant to note that no section of the people, however advanced or backward their views were, denounced the Constitution in *toto*. In fact, two political parties, the Socialist Party of India and the Hindu Mahasabha, had prepared their own constitutions[3] for free India. And the most striking feature of these constitutional drafts was that both of them were in agreement with the main features of the Constitution as adopted by the Constituent Assembly.

No constitution is perfect and the Constitution of India is no exception to this universal rule. There can however be no doubt that it is a workable document. It is a blend of idealism and realism. In hammering it out, the framers traversed all the processes of 'democratic manufactory' and ranged through the whole gamut of democratic factors. There have been careful thought, close analysis, argument and counter argument. There was even fierce controversy, so fierce that, as Frank Anthony a leading member of the Assembly, observed, it was apprehended at times that the members might reach the stage of what the Romans called *argumentum and baculum,* i.e. settling it by actual physical force. But in the final analysis, a real sense of accommodation prevailed and a real sense of forbearance.[4] As a result, the Constitution emerged as foundation for all the people of India to work in co-operation and collaboration in a mighty endeavour to build a new, free India. As Ambedkar said:

> I feel that it is workable, it is flexible and it is strong enough to hold the country together both in peace-time and in war-time. Indeed, if I may say so, if things go wrong under the new Constitution, the reason will not be that we had a bad Constitution. What we will have to say is that Man was vile.[5]

***

1. C.A.D. VII; p. 39.
2. Some of these have been extended beyond the ten-year period, *e.g.*, the reservation of seats in Parliament and State Legislatures for the Scheduled Castes and Scheduled Tribes. The seventy-ninth Amendment Act of 1999 extends the period of reservation to the year 2009.
3. *Draft Constitution of the Indian Republic and the Constitution of the Hindustan Republic.*
4. C.A.D.X, p. 38.
5. C.A.D. VII, P. 44.

3

BASIC PRINCIPLES

IF THE division of power is the basis of civilized government, a constitution is the best device by which such division could be facilitated. Constitutionalism is an achievement of the modern world. But it is a comparatively recent achievement. As such, it has not become fully stabilized. Meanwhile, every constitution aims at building up a governmental structure based on certain basic principles. And these principles are more or less well-established. Although some of these principles are common to most constitutions, there are others which vary from constitution to constitution. Such variations are the product of the varying conditions and circumstances that determine the principles of the constitution. The Constitution of India is no exception to this rule and it has its own basic principles. We shall therefore begin by a study of the basic principles of the Constitution, which form the foundations of democratic government in India.

A careful study of the Constitution will show that there are at least seven basic principles which are embodied in it and which form the foundations of democracy in India. These are :

1. popular sovereignty;
2. socialism;
3. secularism;
4. fundamental rights;
5. directive principles of State policy;
6. judicial independence;
7. federalism; and
8. cabinet government.

We may examine briefly the scope of each of these principles.

Popular Sovereignty

The Constitution proclaims the sovereignty of the people in its opening words. The Preamble begins with the words, 'We the people of India, having solemnly resolved to constitute India into a sovereign democratic republic'. The idea is reaffirmed in several places in the Constitution, particularly in the chapter dealing with 'Elections'. Article 326 declares that 'the elections to the House of the People and to the Legislative Assembly of every States shall be on the basis of adult suffrage'. As a result, the governments at the Centre and in the States derive their authority from the people who choose their representatives for Parliament and the State Legislatures at regular intervals. Further, those who wield the executive power of the government are responsible to the legislature and through them to the people. Thus, in the affairs of the State, it is the will of the people that prevails ultimately and not the will of a few selfish individuals. This is the principle of popular sovereignty.

There have been kings, revolutions, constitutions and vast bureaucracies since time immemorial. But the idea of adult suffrage and the common man as elector are of very recent origin. To Aristotle the ideal form of democracy meant that the vital decisions affecting the community were made by the assembly of the whole citizenry in the market-place. Today, it means that every adult citizen-men and women alike-goes to the polling booth and casts his vote in favour of those who, in his opinion, are the best persons to represent him in the management of the affairs of his government. Elections are not the only possible method for securing representatives. But they are considered the most democratic method. They are democratic because every adult citizen gets a chance at regular intervals to participate in the selection of those who will rule over him. 'The real backbone of the elective system is the cautious, steadfast, men and women of common-sense who can see the forest rather than the trees'[1]

It is impossible to over-emphasize the importance of free popular elections to ensure a democratic government based upon the consent of the governed. At pointed out by a distinguished contemporary political scientist:[2]

> The decisive safeguard against the abuse of political power is the institution of periodic popular elections. The very fact that political power is subject to recall and can be taken for granted only for limited periods of time limits the duration of political power with mechanical sharpness. But it also limits the freedom with which political power can be used as long as it lasts. For since the holders of political powers have a natural tendency to keep themselves in power by getting themselves re-elected, they must use their political freedom with a view to winning the ever impending elections. Thus the preferences of the electorate, real or fancied, are an everpresent limitation on the freedom of the holders of political power to use that power as they would like to. The absolute ruler is free to govern as he sees fit, subject only to the limits of physical nature. The freedom of constitutional government is hemmed in not only by institutional devices and, as it is democratic, by the mechanical limits of popular elections, but also by the political dynamics of the democratic process. It is this contrast between the complete freedom of the absolute ruler to exercise the authority of government at his discretion and the limits within which constitutional government must operate, which Theodore Roosevelt had in mind when the expressed the wish to be for twenty-four hours President, Congress, and Supreme Court at the same time.
>
> The democratic processes, in order to be able to delimit the freedom of the rulers to govern, must themselves be free to bring the will of the majority to bear upon the personnel and policies of the government. The freedom of the governed to control and replace the rulers and the limitations upon the rulers' freedom to govern are the two sides of the same coin, the latter being a function of the former. Without that freedom of the governed, democracy loses its substance; for it no longer provides the people with the freedom of choosing rulers and, through them, policies. A democracy which loses that freedom can only survive as the occasional plebiscitarian approval of the personnel and the policies of the government. This is the totalitarian type of democracy.

In spite of the ignorance and illiteracy of large sections of the India people, the Constituent Assembly adopted the principle of adult franchise with an abundant faith in the common man and the ultimate success of democratic rule. The Assembly was of the opinion that democratic government on the basis of adult suffrage would bring along enlightenment and promote the well-being, the standard of life, the comfort and decent living of the common man. The principle was adopted in no light-hearted mood but with

1. Karl Friedrich, *Constitutional Government and Democracy, 1950,* p *275.*
2. Hans J. Moregenthau, 'Dilemmas of Freedom', *The American Review,* vol. II, no. 4, pp. 38-9.

the full realization of its implications. If democracy is to be broad-based, and the Government is to have the ultimate sanction of the people as a whole, in a country where the large mass of people are illiterate, and the people owning property are so few, the introduction of any property or educational qualifications for the exercise of franchise would be a negation of the principles of democracy.[1]

The principle of popular sovereignty has not been a mere ideal embodied in the Constitution but has been a living reality during a period of over five decades during which the Constitution has been in operation. The thourteen general elections the country has had so far (1951-52, 1957, 1962, 1967, 1971, 1977, 1980, 1984, 1989, 1991, 1996, 1998, 1999, 2004 and 2009) have demonstrated that the illiterate and presumably ignorant masses of India are not altogether incapable of independently exercising the right of franchise. In fact, this precious right in their hands, which ensures the democratic ideal of 'one man, one vote, one value', irrespective of his wealth, education, social status and 'importance', had, in fact, enhanced their self-respect as citizens of a democratic India. It has instilled in them the belief that they are no mere 'hewers of wood and drawers of water', but are important enough as members of a vast new human society engaged in the great co-operative enterprise of building up a new nation. The awareness that the strength of the State is the aggregate strength of its individual citizens is fast dawning upon them. They are also fast realizing that suffrage is the link that binds, in a bond of mutual interest and responsibility, the fortunes of the citizen to the fortunes of the State. It is this realization and its increasing impact in successive elections in the future that will prove the strongest and the most enduring base on which the superstructure of democratic government in India is to flourish.

Free elections are, perhaps the greatest forum of mass education. The dangers inherent in adult suffrage among largely illiterate people can be mitigated only by the blessings of universal education. In a country like India, nearly fifty per cent of whose population is illiterate, the attainment of universal education is a goal still a long way off. But this need not necessarily mean that until a certain minimum standard of universal education is realized, the Indian masses are incapable of properly exercising their right of franchise. Illiteracy is not quite the same thing as ignorance. A free election which ensures the free exchange of ideas and free canvassing by contending parties who stand for differing programmes of social organization for the realization of the common welfare, offers the best medium for the political education of the illiterate masses. It is this that the Constitution guarantees.

The Constitution-makers were not satisfied by merely providing for adult suffrage. They wanted to ensure free elections by creating an independent constitutional authority to be in charge of everything connected with elections. Free election is a reality in India. It ensures for the electors both the freedom of choice and secrecy of the ballot. The thirteen general elections have demonstrated that the ordinary man, in spite of his so-called illiteracy, has been able to exercise his robust commonsense in electing candidate of his choice. Neither money nor social status nor official position has been powerful enough to make him a convenient tool in the hands of self-seeking politicians. This perhaps is the surest and the most welcome guarantee that popular sovereignty will remain a living reality in India despite the fact that most of its people are steeped in ignorance, poverty and social backwardness and selfish politicians have been trying to use money power and muscle power to vitiate the process of free elections.

---

1. Alladi Krishnaswami Aiyar, C.A.D. X, p. 834.

Socialism

Increasing intervention as well as participation by the State in the economic field has been a distinguishing feature of the twentieth century. There is hardly any country today in which the State is not actively engaged in a variety of economic activities. In varying degrees, governments everywhere are involved in economic, industrial and commercial management. This is broadly described as the influence of socialist ideas on State activity.

Even before the adoption of the new Constitution, the Government of Independent India had made clear its policy to enter the economic field in a very active manner. The Industrial Policy Resolution of 1948 gives ample evidence of this. It envisaged a greater role for the State in the economic development of the country. Certain Industries such as atomic energy, manufacturing of arms and ammunition and Railways were declared to be the sole monopoly of the State. The right of the State to nationalise any major industry and bringing it within the public sector was also clearly stated. Nevertheless the Constitution did not explicitly state anywhere that it stood for the establishment of a socilist State.

The Directive Principles of State Policy, however, unmistakably set out the socialist objective of the Constitution, although one might point out that they do not go far enough to establish a full-fledged socialist order. But then it is also clear that our Constitution with its emphasis on a set of guaranteed fundamental rights did not envisage a collectivist socialist State like those existed in Eastern Europe during 1945 and 1990. On the contrary, it aims at establishing a democratic socialist State which, while moving progressively towards the socialist ideal, wants at the same time to protect and preserve basic human rights.

Nevertheless successive amendments to the Constitution clearly show that the direction was more towards the realisation of socialist than the democratic ideal. The Constitution was amended several times with a view to realising the objective. Among those amendments, special mention may be made of the First, Fourth, Seventeenth, Twenty-fifth. Twenty-ninth, Thirty-fourth and Forty-second Amendments. Almost everyone of these gives precedence to the Directive Principles over Fundamental Rights in the implementation of certain legislative enactments. The Forty-second Amendment (1976) went a step further and amended the Preamble of the Constitution to include specifically the term "socialist" which was absent in the original form in which it was enacted.

Nearly for a period of thirty years since the inauguration of the Constitution the socialist ideal seems to have influenced the policy makers of the country both in the legislative and the executive spheres. This was evident in the policies of the Central and State Governments in setting up hundreds of large public sector enterprises and investing, most of the country's resources in those enterprises. Unfortunately, these enterprises did not produce the resources they were expected to generate. While India was largely a failure in its effort to bring about a socialist pattern of society, its Asian neighbours such as Sri Lanka, Malaysia, Thailand, Taiwan, Hong Kong, South Korea and Japan made spectacular progress without adopting a socialist approach. Hence there was a gradual shift in the policies beginning from the mid eighties culminating in the new economic policy inaugurated in the year 1991. That policy still continues and is likely to continue in the days to come. Policy makers do not any more swear by the socialist ideal of the past. They seem to be convinced of the importance of private initiative and liberalism in the onward march of the country.

Secularism

The Constitution aims to establish a secular State. The concept of secular State envisaged by the Constitution is that the State will not make any discrimination whatsoever on the ground of religion, caste or community against any person professing any particular form of religious faith. No particular religion will be identified as State religion nor will it receive any State patronage or preferential status. The State will not establish any state religion; nor will the State accord any preferential treatment to any citizen or discriminate against him simply on the ground that he professes a particular form of religion. The fact that a person professes a particular religion will not be taken into consideration in his relationship with the State or its agencies.

Although the term *secular* was not included anywhere in the Constitution as it was originally passed in 1949, the fathers of the Constitution were clear in their mind as to what they meant by secularism. Ambedkar, Chairman of the Drafting Committee, while participating in the debate in Parliament on the Hindu Code Bill in 1951, explained the secular concept as follows:

"It (secular state) does not mean that we shall not take into consideration the religious sentiment of the people. All that a secular state means is that this parliament shall not be competent to impose any particular religion upon the rest of the people. This is the only limitation that the Constitution recognises."[1] In the Constituent Assembly itself several members had expressed similar ideas in more elaborate terms.[2]

The Forty-second Amendment of the Constitution (1976) sought to make the position explicitly clear by introducing the term *secular* as part of the Preamble of the Constitution. As a result the Preamble now reads : "We the people of India, having solemnly resolved to constitute India into a Sovereign, Socialist, Secular, Democratic Republic ...."

The concept of secularism as interpreted in the West — and we have undoubtedly borrowed the concept from the West — owes its origin to the beginning of Christianity. And Christianity is characterised by its recognition and teaching of basic duality, spiritual and temporal, each with its appropriate set of loyalties. This is reflected in the famous biblical precept: Render unto Caesar the things that are Caesar's and unto God the things that are God's. But this was not easy in practice. Hence there was frequent conflict between the loyalties of the Christians to the State (to the king) and to their Church. The Edict of Milan of Roman Emperor Constantine made the practice somewhat better in terms of the following proclamation: "Liberty of worship shall not be denied to any, but that the mind and the will of every individual shall be free to manage divine affairs according to his own choice."

The concept of secularism as evolved over the centuries in the West, however, took an anti-religious character. This is why perhaps the Encyplopaedia Britannica defines secular as non-spiritual, having no concern with religious or spiritual matters. The term is used in the wider sense of "anything which is distinct, opposed to, or not connected with religion or ecclesiastical things, temporal as opposed to spiritual or ecclesiastical. The Encyclopaedia of Religion and Ethics describes secularism as a movement intentionally ethical, negatively religious, with political and philosophical antecedents. The relation of secularism to religion

1. Parliamentary Debates 1951 Vol. III Part II p. 2466.
2. See. C.A.D. Vol. VI, P. 825 TO 831.

is defined as mutually exclusive rather than hostile. The secular movement away from religion need not imply total abandonment of it. It is perfectly possible to advocate both secularism and religion. Secularism is not opposed to religion as such; it is opposed rather to the use of religious institutions and religious motivations in the legal, political and educative processes. So long as religion does keep to its own sphere, secularism is religiously neutral, it neither endorses nor disapproves of religiousness.

The concept of secularism as embodied in the Constitution of India cannot be viewed in the sense in which it is viewed in the West as described above but in the context of the following provisions of the Constitution. The Constitution guarantees freedom of conscience, freedom to profess, practise and propagate religion and also freedom to establish religious institutions and manage or administer their affairs. It prohibits discrimination on grounds of religion and guarantees legal and social equality to all by providing for equality before the law and equal protection of laws, prohibiting discrimination with regard to places of public importance and providing for equal opportunity in matters of public employment. The constitution also guarantees religious minorities the right to establish and administer educational institutions of their choice and to conserve their script, language and culture.

These provisions would naturally indicate that our Constitution endeavours to build up in India the philosophy of secularism on freedom, equality and tolerance in the field of religion. And viewed in this context it is clear that the Constitution of India does not build a wall of separation between the state and religion. The essence of secularism is that the State is non-partisan in its relations to citizens, no matter to whatever religion they belong.

Thus the distinguishing features of a secular democracy as contemplated by the Constitution of India are: (1) that the State will not identify itself with or be controlled by any religion; (2) that while the State guarantees to every one the right to profess whatever religion one chooses to follow (which includes also the right to be an agnostic or an atheist), it will not accord any preferential treatment to any of them; (3) that no discrimination will be shown by the State against any person on account of his religion and faith; and (4) that the right of every citizen, subject to any general condition, to enter any office under the State will be equal to that of his fellow citizens. Political equality which entitles any Indian citizen to seek the highest office under the State as opposed to what obtains in a theocratic State is the heart and soul of secularism as envisaged by the Constitution.

Fundamental Rights

Discussing the implications of democracy in his *Liberty in the Modern State*, Professor Laski says that, first, it involves a frame of government in which men are given the chance of making the government under which they live, at stated intervals. We have seen above how this principle is safeguarded under the Constitution. Secondly, he says, it involves the securing to the citizens certain fundamental human rights and the maintenance of those rights by the separation of the judicial from the executive powers. Thirdly, it involves the bringing into existence of a Bill of Rights for safeguarding the fundamental human rights, such as freedom of speech, protection from arbitrary arrest and the like. According to Laski, the supremacy of the 'rule of law' is essential for the working of a democracy. Only where the rule of law prevails, true democracy can function and the success or failure of a democracy depends largely on the extent to which civil liberties are enjoyed by the citizens in general.

Liberty, however, is not an easy word to define. On 18 April 1864, soon after the American civil war on the question of slavery, President Abraham Lincoln said:

> The world has never had a good definition of the word liberty, and the Amerincan people, just now, are much in want of one. We all declare for liberty; but in using the same word we do not all mean the same *thing*. With some the word liberty may mean for each man to do as he pleases with himself, and product of his labour; while with others the same word may mean for some men to do as they please with other men, and the product of other men's labour. Here are two, not only different, but incompatible things called by two different and incompatible names — liberty and tyranny.

Genuine democracy must forever guard against the temptation to transform itself into a system under which the ruling majority claims infallibility for itself. While democracy requires that the will of the people limit the freedom of the government, it also requires that the freedom of the popular will be limited. A popular will, not so limited, becomes the tyranny of the majority which destroys the freedom of political competition and thus uses the powers of the government to entrench itself permanently in the seat of power and to prevent a new majority from forming. Further, it will tend to think and act as if it will provide the ultimate standard of thought and action and there is no higher law to limit its freedom. As Laski has put it, 'If in any State there is a body of men who possess unlimited political power, those over whom they rule can never be free'. The emergence of such a state of affairs will synchronize with the disappearance of certain vital characteristics of democracy, the spirit of questioning and individual initiative. Their place will be taken up by unquestioned submissiveness and conformity, the most distinguishing characteristics of a totalitarian system. This is perhaps the most serious danger inherent in the dynamics of modern democracy which is to be strongly guarded against.

There are two possible alternative safeguards which a constitution can provide to remedy the situation. First, it can guarantee certain basic rights to the individual citizen against all encroachment by the State. Secondly, it may so divide the powers of the State and entrust them to separate agencies that no body of men possesses unlimited power. The Constitution of India has chosen the first alternative and tries to achieve the objective by embodying in it a set of fundamental rights and guaranteeing them through an independent judiciary. These rights impose limitations both on legislative and executive powers. One the one hand, the Legislature is prohibited from passing certain laws which would curtail individual's freedom. On the other, the Executive is compelled to adhere to certain formalities and procedures when it deals with the citizens. Thus, in an attempt to secure fundamental freedoms, the Constitution delimits the respective spheres of activity of the State and the individual and erects a wall, as it were, between the government and the people.

The Constitution affirms the basic principle that every individual is entitled to enjoy certain rights as a human being and the enjoyment of such rights does not depend upon the will of any majority or minority. No majority has the right to abrogate such rights. In fact, the legitimacy of the majority to rule is derived from the existence of these rights. These rights include all the basic liberties such as freedom of speech, movement and association, equality before law and equal protection of laws, freedom of religious belief, and cultural and educational freedoms. The Constitution has classified these rights into seven categories and one of them is the right to constitutional remedies which entitles every aggrieved person to approach either a High Court or the Supreme Court of India to restore to him any fundamental right that may have been violated.

It is, thus, a basic affirmation of the Constitution that the political system that it establishes should provide conditions favourable for the maximum development of the individual's personality. The framers of the Constitution were conscious of the of the fact that in the absence of the enjoyment of the above-mentioned rights, such development of the personality was impossible and democracy would sound an empty word. Having spent most of their lives under a foreign rule and having fought relentlessly for the enjoyment of these rights by themselves, it was only natural that they should have wanted to embody them in the Constitution they framed for the establishment of a democratic political order. They hoped to build this political order upon the firm foundation of the freedom of political competition. The prime importance of these rights is that while the will of the majority decides how these freedoms are to be implemented, the existence of the freedoms themselves is not subject to that will. On the contrary, these freedoms set the conditions under which the will of the majority is to be formed and exercised. They establish the framework of 'democratic legitimacy' for the rule of the majority.

It must be stressed, however, that the fundamental freedoms guaranteed to the individual under the Constitution are not absolute. Individual rights, however basic they are, cannot override national security and general welfare. For, in the absence of national security and general welfare, individual rights themselves are not secure. Freedom of speech does not mean freedom to abuse another; freedom of movement does not mean freedom of physical attack on others. The Constitution has made express provisions dealing with such limitations of fundamental rights so that those who seek to enjoy the rights may also realize the obligations attending them.

Directive Principles of State Policy

The wall of separation which the Fundamental Rights erect between the government and the people is indeed one of the greatest and surest safeguards of the life, liberty and property of the individual. But conditions of absolute and unhindered growth of private power, like absolute government power, are capable of destroying individual freedom. Concentration of private power, mainly in the form of economic controls, in the hands of a few individuals is equally destructive of the dynamic qualities of a democratic society as a dictatorial government could be. In a highly capitalist society, a few giants in the industrial and financial world, who concentrate in themselves the bulk of economic power, can easily subject the rest of the community to the travails of a new feudalistic order. After having provided against the emergence of a totalitarian system through the constitutional guarantees of fundamental rights, the framers turned their attention to deal with the possible future menace of a private capitalist concentration of economic power and to ensure the establishment and sustenance of a socialistic society which provided for the diffusion of economic power among the different sections of the people. The methods they sought to provide for the purpose are embodied in the chapter on Directive Principles of State Policy, which embodies another basic principle of the Constitution.

Writing about post-war constitutions which are estimated to number over fifty, a thoughtful critic has observed:

> Liberty, the constitutions could and did promise, but not bread and the modicum of economic security the little man yearns for. To him it is the plain and unadorned truth that the political decisions which are vital for the well-being of all, no longer occur within the frame of the constitution. The

social forces move and battle extra-constitutionally because the constitutions did not even attempt the required solutions.[1]

Critics of the Constitution of India cannot accuse the framers of any lack of awareness of this problem or of not attempting to provide solutions for it. They were one with *The Federalist* who wrote over two hundred years ago about the same problem thus:

> It is of great importance in a republic, not only to guard the society against the oppression of its rulers but to guard one part of the society against the injustice of the other part. Different interests necessarily exist in different classes of citizens. If a majority be united by a common interest, the rights of the minority will be insecure. There are but two methods of providing against this evil: the one by creating a will in the community independent of the majority, that is, of the society itself; the other by comprehending in the society so many separate descriptions of citizens, as will render an unjust combination of a majority of the whole very improbable, if not impracticable.[2]

While many of the older constitutions including that of the United States adopted the second method, namely the separation of powers for avoiding the evil and largely failed in the attempt, the Constitution of India adopts a different method, following the example of the Constitution of the Irish Republic. According to this method, the State and every one of its agencies are commanded to follow certain fundamental principles while they frame their policies regarding the various fields of State activity. These principles, on the one hand, are assurances to the people as to what they can expect from the State and, on the other, are directives to the Government, Central, State, and local to establish and maintain a new 'social order in which justice, social, economic and political, shall inform all the institutions of national life'. The State shall in particular direct its policy towards securing:

(a) That the citizens, men and women equally, have the right to an adequate means of livelihood;

(b) That the ownership and control of the material resources of the community are so distributed as best to subserve the common good;

(c) That the operation of the economic system does not result in the concentration of wealth and the means of production to the common detriment;

(d) That there is equal pay for equal work for both men and women;

(e) That the health and strength of workers, men and women, and the tender age of children are not abused and that citizens are not forced by economic necessity to enter advocations unsuited to their age or strength;

(f) That childhood and youth are protected against exploitation and against moral and material abandonment.

These and other principles that follow them unmistakably set out the socialist objective of the Constitution, although one might complain that they do not go far enough to establish a full fledged socialist order. But then, it is also clear that our Constitution with its emphasis on a set of guaranteed Fundamental Rights does not envisage a collectivist Socialist State. On the contrary it aims at establishing a democratic socialist state which while moving progressively towards the socialist ideal wants at the same time to protect and preserve

1. Loewenstein, 'Reflections on the Value of Constitutions in our Revolutionary Age' in *Constitutions and Constitutional Trends Since World War II*, 1951, p. 191.
2. *The Federalist*, no. 51.

basic human rights. Nevertheless successive amendments to the Constitution clearly show that the direction is more toward the realisation of the socialist than the democratic ideal. The Constitution was amended several times with a view to realising this objective. Among those Amendments special mention may be made of the First, Fourth, Seventeenth, Twenty-fifty, Twenty-ninth, Thirty-fourth and Forty-second amendments. Almost every one of these gave priority to Directive principles over Fundamental Rights in the implementation of certain legislative enactments. The Forty-second Amendment went a step further and amended the Preamble to include specifically the term "socialist" which was absent in the original form in which it was enacted.

The right to work and the right to education are as essential to a free citizen as the right to life and liberty. No person can develop his personality 'sanely, soundly and completely' and maintain his self-respect, without the opportunity of employing himself in worthwhile work in terms of appreciation by the community, expressed in regular remuneration. As one of the most important freedoms of the modern age, the right to work has yet to receive the recognition that it deserves. The right to education also is an equally important right. The difficulty with respect to these and such other rights has been, however, the State's inability to guarantee them on account of its inadequate resources. A constitution can easily provide guarantees for freedoms such as those of speech, movement, religion etc.. For, these are only negative obligations on the State or prohibitions on State action. But such rights as the right to work, education, etc. involve positive action, making available to the citizens physical satisfaction in certain basic requirements of theirs. This is why the Constitution makes these rights non-justiciable — not enforceable through a court of law — while the Fundamental Rights are made justiciable. Nevertheless, they are of fundamental importance in the governance of the State and, therefore, are not mere pious declarations.

Speaking about the value of their inclusion in the Constitution, Ambedkar said in the Constituent Assembly:

> The Draft Constitution as framed only provides a machinery for the government of the country. It is not a contrivance to install any particular party in power, as has been done in some countries. Who should be in power is left to be determined by the people, as it must be, if the system is to satisfy the tests of democracy. But whoever captures power will not be free to do what he likes with it. In the exercise of it, he will have to respect these instruments of instructions which are called Directive Principles. He cannot ignore them. He may not have to answer for their breach in a Court of Law. But he will certainly have to answer for them before the electorate at election time. What great value these directive principles posses will be realized better when the forces of the right contrive to capture power.[1]

No one will seriously contend today that the Directive Principles are mere pious declarations. They have now become the real yardstick to measure the social and economic progress of the Indian people. The success or failure of a government either of the Centre or of the States is premised on the extent to which they have translated the Directive Principles into reality. No political party which contests for power dare condemn these principles as pious platitudes. On the contrary, every one of them is pledging itself to make them real to the people at the earliest possible time. Prime Minister Nehru once declared in Parliament that the Directive Principles are more important than even the Fundamental Rights and if there arise a conflict between the two, the former should prevail

1. C.A.D. VII, p. 41.

over the latter. In conformity with this declaration, the Constitution was amended several times during the period that it has been in operation.[1]

Judicial Independence

'Justice is the end of government', said *The Federalist*. 'It ever has been and ever will be pursued until it be obtained, or until liberty is lost in the pursuit'. No wonder, therefore, if justice has been often characterized as the primary, or even the only *ideal* purpose of government.

The judicial function is indeed a delicate and difficult one. It involves the process of deciding what is just in a controversy between two or more contending parties. If the parties have no confidence in the impartiality of the judiciary, justice becomes an empty word. Man's long struggle has been to live under a government of laws, not of men. Equal justice under law has for long been his cherished ideal, a system under which the same law is applicable to all alike. Man has in all ages been striving to escape the regime that dispenses justice according to the political or religious ideology of the litigant or the whim or caprice of those who run the government. As a consequence of this struggle, he established a principle of abiding value, that no judiciary can be impartial unless it is independent. In fact, the judicial process ceases to be judicial the moment those who seek to judge cease to be independent of every form of external influence. Hence the importance of judicial independence.

As Lord Hewart has pointed out, the independence of the judiciary is essential because many of the significant victories for freedom and justice have been won in the law courts and the liberties of the citizen are closely bound up with the complete independence of the Judges.[2] Obviously, the men who are to administer justice in the Courts, the methods by which they are to be chosen, the way in which they are to perform their function, the terms upon which they shall hold power, these and their related problems become inseparably bound up with the ideal of judicial independence. Judicial independence acts as a safeguard, not merely against the manipulations of the law for political purposes at the behest of the government in power, but also against the corruption of judicial organs of the State by bribery and intimidation by powerful outside interests which threaten the impartial administration of justice from time to time.[3] As Graham Wallas pointed out, "We make a judge independent not to spare him personal humiliation, but in order that certain motives shall not and certain other motives shall, direct his official conduct.[4]

The framers of the Constitution were aware that democratic freedoms were meaningless in the absence of an independent machinery to safeguard them. No subordinate or agent of the Government could be trusted to be just and impartial in judging the merits of a conflict in which the Government itself was a party. Similarly, a judiciary subordinate either to the Centre or the States could not be trusted as an impartial arbiter of conflicts and controversies between the Centre and the States. These were the compelling reasons for the creation of an independent judiciary as an integral part of the Constitution and for the adoption of judicial independence as a basic principle of the Constitution.

In its bid to establish complete independence of the judiciary, the Constitution has first erected a barrier that separates the executive from the judiciary. After effecting such separation, it has created conditions that are conducive to making the judiciary independent.

---

1. The First and Fourth Amendments. Also 73rd and 74th Amendments.
2. Lord Hewart, *The New Despotism*, p. 102.
3. W.A. Robson, *Justice and Administrative Law*, p. 45.
4. Graham Wallas, *Our Social Heritage*, p. 188.

Thus, rigid qualifications are laid down for the appointment of judges and provision has been made for compulsory consultation of the Chief Justice of India in the appointment of every Judge of the Supreme Court and the High Courts. The Judges are appointed almost for life[1] and their conditions of service cannot be altered to their disadvantage, once they are appointed. They are given relatively high salaries and their conduct is made a subject beyond the scope of discussion in the Legislature. They can be removed from office only for proved misbehaviour. For this purpose, both the Houses of Parliament will have to pass resolutions against a Judge supported by a two-third majority of the total membership of the House.

The judiciary in India, even under the British rule, was noted for its integrity and independence. Under the Constitution, its position has been made doubly secure so that it can become in reality the most impartial arbiter of the conflicts and controversies which fall within its jurisdiction. Anyone can approach even the highest court in the land, the Supreme Court of India, to secure the restoration of a fundamental right whenever it is violated. Even a casual analysis of the hundreds of decisions which the Supreme Court and the High Courts have given so far will easily prove that the judiciary in India is working in a spirit of impartiality and in an atmosphere of independence.

Federalism

Federalism is one of the most important aspects of modern constitutionalism. It is true that there exists a certain vagueness and even confusion about its meaning. But this is the result of a formalistic and juristic approach to the concept of federalism. From a practical point of view, its fundamentals as a constitutional form are not in doubt. It is established all over the world, perhaps, as the only form of political organization suited to communities with a diversified pattern of objectives, interests and traditions, who seek to join together in the pursuit of common objectives and interests and the cultivation of common traditions. The basic objective of federalism is unity in diversity, devolution in authority and decentralisation in administration. Its fundamental characteristic is the division of powers between two sets of governments — a Central Government and Local or State Governments — each independent of the other in its own sphere of activity. The unity which federalism achieves is not unity through compulsion but unity through willing consent and voluntary co-operation. Under it, the different units which agree to join together and establish a new central Government, enjoy the same status and the same privileges and have the same obligations.

Whenever and wherever the necessity arose for setting problems of a multi-lingual and multi-racial character and welding together diverse communities living over a vast area into a single, compact governmental system, federalism alone offered a possible solution. This is why the framers of the Constitution turned to federalism as a solution of a number of problems they confronted in their attempt to frame a constitution for a new, united India. Particularly, they wanted to preserve both the 'infinite variety and the innate unity' that animated the length and breadth of India. The situation in India had been described in the following words written many years ago by Jawaharlal Nehru:

> I think, the glory of India has been the way in which it has managed to keep two things going at the same time: that is, its infinite variety and at the same time its unity in that variety. Both have to be kept, because if we have only variety, then that means separation and going to pieces. If we seek to impose some kind of regimented unity, that makes a living organism rather lifeless.

The choice of federalism as a constitutional form and as the basis of a national

1. Retiring age for Supreme Court and High Court judges is sixty-five and sixty-two years respectively.

government in India was not a sudden development upon the transfer of power on 15 August 1947. It was there for many years and, in a limited form it was already in operation in British India. For the solution of the constitutional problem of a multi-racial, multi-lingual and multi-communal country like India with a vast area and a huge population, federalism was only a natural choice. Nevertheless, the framers were cautious to ensure that the unity they sought to establish through federalism was of an abiding nature, and in case of a future conflict between that unity and the diversity preserved under the Constitution, the former should prevail over the latter. In other words, it was their intention to create an indestructible Union.

Fully conscious of the many disruptive tendencies prevailing in the country, the framers provided for special powers to the Central Government to act during emergencies in the interest of preservation of national unity. The operation of these emergency provisions will automatically convert the federal system into one of a unitary character. As soon as the emergency is over, the federal system would be re-established. This is a special feature of the federalism established under the Constitution. But this does not in any way affect the form of the Constitution which, during all normal times, is federal. Thus, federalism forms one of the foundations of constitutional government in India.

During the past five decades and more since the inauguration of the Constitution, a system of federal government that is suited to the peculiar needs of a vast and complex country like India has been in operation. We will have occasion to see later in the course of this study the details of the working of that system. Suffice it here to say that the Union Government and the twenty-eight State Governments in India today are dividing the totality of governmental power between them and are functioning as governments responsible for their respective spheres of activity and to that extent independent of one another. The States are not administrative units of the Union nor are the State Governments subordinate agencies of the Union Government. Here is the essence of federalism in action, making it a basic principle of the Constitution.

Cabinet Government

The most distinctive characteristic of a cabinet system of government is the complete and continuous responsibility of the Executive to the Legislature. The Cabinet is composed of the Prime Minister, who is the chief of the executive, and his ministerial colleagues who share the responsibility with him for the formulation and execution of the policies of the government. In contrast to a system of checks and balances as obtains under the presidential system of the United States, the cabinet system embodies the principle of concentrated authority under strict control. The Cabinet is the central shaft to which all the other agencies of government are geared. Individual members of the Cabinet are the heads of the different departments of the administration[1]. Collectively, the Cabinet shapes the programme of legislation which is submitted to Parliament and from it emanate the broad and general policies. Parliament also checks and controls the performance of the administration. Thus, the cabinet system facilitates, on the one hand, the intimate co-operation between the exclusive and the legislature and, on the other, ensures the responsibility of the executive to the legislature, the representative of the people.

Under the Cabinet System, the Head of the State occupies a position of great dignity, but practically all authority, nominally vested in him, is exercised by the Cabinet or the Ministry which assumes full responsibility for acts performed in his name. The unity and collective responsibility of the Cabinet are achieved through the Prime Minister, who is the keystone of the Cabinet arch. His colleagues in the Cabinet are appointed on his

1. Quoted in Wade and Phillips, *Constitutional Law,* Second Edition, 1955 p. 23.

recommendation and they always go out of office along with him. He is thus central both to the formation and the dissolution of the Cabinet.

The real merit of a cabinet system is that the Executive being responsible to the Legislature it is always being watched. The moment it proves unequal to the task, or it goes off the track or flouts the will of the Legislature, it can be removed from the office by a successful vote of no-confidence. Under the modern party system, if the party in office has a stable majority in the Legislature, the Cabinet may wield overwhelming power so long as the members of the party are solidly behind it. Under such conditions, as Herman Finer put it, the Cabinet although a creature of Parliament becomes a creature which leads its creator. But under different conditions, Parliament will assert itself and no Cabinet will be able to dominate. If instability of cabinet does not become chronic as was the case under the Fourth Republic of France, a parliamentary executive is preferable to a presidential executive whose main merit is the stability of the executive for a fixed period.

Comparing the merits of the parliamentary and the presidential systems, Lord Balfour made the following significant observations:

> Under the Presidential system the effective head of the national administration is elected for a fixed term. He is practically irremovable. Even if he is proved to be inefficient, even if he becomes unpopular, even if his policy is unacceptable to his countrymen he and his methods must be endured until the moment comes for a new election.
>
> He is aided by ministers, who however able and distinguished, have no independent political status, have probably had no congressional training and are by law precluded from obtaining it during their term of office.
>
> Under the Cabinet system everything is different. The head of the administration commonly called the Prime Minister is elected for the place on the ground that he is the statesman best qualified to secure a majority in the House of Commons. He retains it only so far as that support is forthcoming; he is the head of his party. He must be a member of one or the other of the two Houses of Parliament; and he must be competent to lead the House to which he belongs. While the Cabinet ministers of a President are merely his officials, the Prime Minister is *Primus inter pares* in a Cabinet of which (according to peace-time practice) every member must, like himself, have had some parliamentary experience and gained some parliamentary reputation. The President's powers are defined by the Constitution, and for their exercise with the law he is responsible to no man. The Prime Minister and his Cabinet, on the other hand, are restrained by no written constitution, but they are forced by critics and rivals whose position though entirely unofficial is as constitutional as their own; they are subject to perpetual stream of unfriendly questions, to which they must make public response, and they may at any moment be dismissed from power by a hostile vote.

The Constitution of India has adopted as a basic principle the British Cabinet System almost in its entirety. The only feature of the Indian Constitution which deserves special mention in this context is the position of the Prime Minister. The Constitution expressly gives him a distinctly superior position by making him the head of the Council of Ministers. In Britain, although in practice the Prime Minister holds a superior position, he is, at least in theory, described as first among equals. In India, the cabinet system of government under the Constitution is established not only at the Central level, but also in the States. In every state there is a Council of Ministers headed by a Chief Minister, just like the Prime Minister who heads the Central Cabinet.

Special Features

Apart from the basic principles which form the foundations of the Constitution, one notices certain special features which deserve mention. Of these, the most important are the innovations which the Constitution introduces in the federal system that it seeks to establish.

1. Almost every federal system is cast in a tight mould of federalism. No matter what the circumstances, it cannot change its form and shape. It can never be unitary. But the Constitution of India can be both federal and unitary according to requirements and the circumstances. It is framed to work as a federal system during normal times. But in times of war, insurrection or the breakdown of constitutional machinery in the States, it is designed to work as though it was a unitary system. With the proclamation of an emergency by the President, the federal system could automatically be transformed into a unitary State. The Union Government can exercise, if it so chooses, (i) the power to legislate upon any subject even though it may be in the State Legislative List, (ii) the power to give directions to the States as to how they should exercise their executive authority in matters which are within their charge, (iii) the power to vest authority for any purpose in any officer, and (iv) the power to suspend the financial provisions of the Constitution. Such a power of converting itself into a unitary State no other federation possesses.

The two most common drawbacks from which a federal system is alleged to suffer are rigidity and legalism. A federal constitution cannot but be a written constitution and a written constitution must necessarily be a rigid constitution. Similarly, the division of powers between the Centre and the States has two necessary consequences: first, that any invasion by the Centre in the field assigned to the States and *vice versa* becomes a breach of the Constitution, and secondly, such breach is a justiciable matter to be determined by the judiciary only. Hence the criticism that 'federalism is legalism'. The Constitution of India has attempted to reduce the disadvantage arising out of the rigidity and legalism inherent in the federal system by adopting the following provisions:

(a) Following the Australian federal model which too has tried to assuage the rigours of rigidity and legalism, the Constitution of India has adopted a long list of subjects for concurrent powers of legislation. Further, the subjects included in the Union List cover a larger area than has ever been covered by any other federal system. A large area of concurrent powers with federal supremacy over it, is bound to produce a reasonably large measure of flexibility in the operation of the federal system.[1]

(b) Parliament is given power to legislate in normal times even on those subjects included in the State List under certain circumstances. According to this, Parliament can legislate on a State subject if it becomes a matter of national concern, provided a resolution is passed by a two-third majority of the Council of States in favour of such action.

(c) Under an emergency, Parliament is empowered to legislate on all items included in the State List.

(d) Parliament can exercise the power of legislation with respect to any subject included in the State List if two or more States make a request for such legislation. In this case, Parliamentary legislation is applicable to only those States which make the request.

(e) The rigidity of the Constitution is mitigated also by the provisions relating to the amendment of the Constitution. For the purpose of amendment, the Constitution may be divided into two parts. Provisions under one part can be amended by Parliament alone, by a majority of at least two-thirds of those who sit and vote and an absolute majority of the total membership. For amending the provisions of the second part, in addition to the majorities prescribed above, at

1. Ambedkar, C.A.D.VII, p. 36.

least half of the States should also agree to such amendment. In either case, the amending process is far simpler than that in other federations. These provisions, as a whole, make the Indian federation a flexible system.

2. Although the Constitution has adopted the principle of federalism, it has at the same time rejected the principle of dual citizenship which is a feature of many federal constitutions. Instead, it has embodied in clear terms the principle of single citizenship for the whole of India. It is a great step forward in the creation of an integrated Indian society. As a result, the citizens of India are clothed with common civil and political rights all over India. Not only is there no restriction for any Indian citizen to move about and settle in any part of the country but he also acquires all the political rights incidental to his residence in a particular place. He is entitled to participate as a voter or as a candidate in the elections to local bodies, the State Legislature or Parliament by satisfying a residence qualification covering a short period.

3. Another special feature of the Constitution is the single system of judiciary that it establishes. Usually, a federal system being a dual polity has a dual system of judiciary. If there are ten States in the Union it is not surprising to find eleven sets of courts, one for each of the States and another for the Union, and also eleven sets of legal systems. The United States provides the best example. The result has been an enormous amount of conflict of laws, jurisdiction and litigation. In contrast, under the Constitution of India, there is uniformity in fundamental laws civil and criminal. All these laws are applied by all the courts in India which are organized in a hierarchical manner. The Supreme Court of India stands at the apex of this hierarchical system of judiciary, bringing about unity in the legal and judicial systems of the country through its power of interpretation of all laws, and of superintendence of the lower courts.

4. The provisions dealing with the All India Services are, again, a special feature of the Constitution. Usually, under a federal system, there are separate services for the Union and the States. Because of the complete separation of the State and the federal civil services, one often notices the glaring differences between the standards of administration at the Centre and the States. The Constitution provides a remedy for this by permitting the creation of all India Services without depriving the States, at the same time, of their right to form their own civil services. The All India Services are recruited on an All-India basis with common qualifications, with uniform scales of pay and only the members of these services may be appointed to certain important posts in the States as well as the Union.

5. There is the office of the Comptroller and Auditor-General. The provisions dealing with the Comptroller and Auditor-General are designed to create an independent audit authority under the Constitution itself. His position is made more or less similar to that of a Supreme Court Judge as far as his independence is concerned. By providing for the audit of the entire financial transactions of the Government — Central as well as State — the Constitution has recognized the importance of an independent external check upon the authority of the government in its financial policies, dealings and procedures.

6. Finally, the Election Commission of India is again a constitutionally created authority with considerable powers to conduct elections to the Parliament and the State Legislatures from time to time. The Commission is also entrusted with the power to hold elections to the offices of the President and the Vice President of India.

***

PART II

THE GROWTH OF CONSTITUTIONALISM IN INDIA

4

HISTORICAL BACKGROUND

The East India Company

THE ORIGINS of the Constitution of the Indian Republic, to a great extent, are rooted in the history of India under the British rule. That history began with the incorporation in England of the East India Company in 1600, although the British had not become a ruling power of India until the second half of the 18th century. The essentially commercial character of the company in the beginning gradually underwent a complete change in the course of a century and a half. The downfall of the Mughal Empire — which was the main unifying force in the country — by the end of the 18th century, the consequent disintegration of a centralised administration, and the rise of innumerable local rulers who rivalled among themselves, provided the Company with an opportunity to enter the field of Indian politics. The victory of the Company's forces in the battle of Plassey in 1757 against Suraj-ud-Doula, the Nawab of Bengal, had laid the foundation of the British Empire in India.

As the Company began to transform itself from a commercial concern into a territorial power, there was a corresponding change in the attitude of the British Parliament toward it. Through a series of enactments the Parliament increased its control over the affairs of the Company in India. The Regulating Act, 1773, Pitt's India Act, 1784, and a series of Charter Acts that followed them are important in this connection. The net result of these enactments was the emergence of a highly centralised British administration in India.

The Revolution of 1857

The revolution of 1857 which had been characterised by the British as the "Sepoy Mutiny" was, on the one hand, an abortive attempt to oust the foreign ruler, and, on the other, a valiant protest against the autocratic and irresponsible character of the government that prevailed in India. It also exposed the utter incapacity of the company to handle the government of a vast territory, in spite of a certain amount of control by the British Parliament. There was an uproar in England against the continuance of the Company's rule in India any further. As a result in 1858, the Government of British India was transferred from the Company to the British Crown. This, indeed, was a land-mark in the political evolution of India.

Queen Victoria's proclamation of 1858 which brought the East India Company's century-old rule to an end said among other things:

1. Now, therefore, we .... have taken upon ourselves the said Government.

2. We appoint him, Viscount Canning, to be our First Viceroy and Governor-General in and over our said territories, and to administer the government thereof in our name and

generally to act in our name and on our behalf, subject to such orders and regulations as he shall, from time to time, receive through one of our Principal Secretaries of State.

3. We hereby announce to the native princes of India that all treaties and engagement made with them by or under the authority of the East India Company are by us accepted and will be scrupulously maintained, and we look for the like observance on their part.

4. We desire no extension of our present territorial possessions; and while we will permit no aggression upon our dominions or our rights to be attempted with impunity, we shall sanction no encroachment of those of others.

5. We shall respect the rights, dignity and honour of native princes as our own; and we desire that they, as well as our subjects, should enjoy that prosperity and that social advancement which can only be secured by internal peace and good government.

6. We hold ourselves bound to the natives of our Indian territories by the same obligations of duty which bind us to all our other subjects and those obligations, by the blessing of almighty God, we shall faithfully and conscientiously fill.

7. We disclaim alike the right and the desire to impose our convictions (religious) on any of our subjects. We declare it to be our royal will and pleasure that none be in anywise favoured, none molested or disquieted by reason of their religious faith or observances, but that all shall alike enjoy the equal and impartial protection of the law; and we do strictly charge and enjoin all those who may be in authority under us that they abstain from all interference with the religious belief or worship of any of our subjects on pain of our highest displeasure.

8. And it is our further will that, so far as may be, our subjects, of whatever race or creed, be freely and impartially admitted to office in our service, the duties of which they may be qualified by their education, ability and integrity duly to discharge.

9. We know and respect the feelings of attachment with which the natives of India regard the lands inherited by them from their ancestors and we desire to protect them in all rights connected therewith, subject to the equitable demands of the State; and we will that generally, in framing and administering the law, due regard be paid to the ancient rights and customs of India.

10. When, by the blessing of Providence, internal tranquility shall be restored, it is our earnest desire to stimulate the peaceful industry of India, to promote works of public utility and improvement, and to administer the Government for the benefit of all our subjects resident therein. In their prosperity will be our strength, in their contentment our security and in their gratitude our best reward.

The Emergence of Bureaucratic Government

When the Crown assumed direct responsibility for the Government of India in 1858, all powers — legislative, administrative and financial — came to be centralised in the Secretary of State for India and his Council on behalf of the Crown. As a necessary consequence, in India, also, power came to reside in the hands of the Governor-General in Council and it was exercised through a vast network of officials spread over the whole country. The resulting form of administration has been called "Bureaucratic Government".

In this form, the administration was carried on by a hierarchy or gradation of officers, the lower officers being the agents of and, therefore, entirely responsible to those superior to them. At the top of this bureaucratic hierarchy stood the Secretary of State for India and his Council responsible to the British Parliament for the administration of India. Below him was the Viceroy and Governor-General of India who was at the head of the Indian administration and the "Man on the spot". Then came a number of Governors, Lieutenant-Governors and Chief Commissioners who were at the head of various classes of Provinces into which the country was divided and who were the agents of and, therefore, responsible to the Governor-General in Council. Finally, within the Provinces a more or less uniform system of administration came to be established, the unit of which was the District. The chief executive officer of the District was the Collector-Magistrate or the Deputy Commissioner. Thus, the whole system from top to bottom was well-knit and, therefore, highly centralised and behaved like an unbreakable steel-frame with all the characteristics of a full-fledged autocracy.

Movement toward Decentralisation

The defects of this highly centralised system of administration had become obvious even before the process of centralisation itself was complete. The realisation of this provided an impetus to give a start to an opposite process — a process of decentralisation as between the Central and the Provincial Governments. The rapid growth of communications, the introduction and spread of English education, the assimilation, of western ideas of Parliamentary Government by Indians and the consequent modernisation of their outlook, all these must have been contributory forces for the introduction of this new process of decentralisation and the gradual change in the tone and character of the British Indian Government. If one word could summarise the most striking characteristic of the British administration in India prior to 1858, that was "centralisation". Similarly, if one word could sum up the post-1858 administration of the British in India, it was "decentralisation" which gradually led the way for the introduction of a federal system of Government as embodied, first, in the Constitution Act of 1935, and then in the Constitution of the Indian Republic in 1950.

The Stages of Decentralisation

The process began with the passing of the Indian Councils Act in 1861 which, for the first time, introduced the principle of consultation in the Indian political scene by the British rulers. However indirect and unsatisfactory the nature of that consultation might have been, it sought, for the first time, the co-operation of the Indian people in the administration of the country. It was a movement in the right direction.

The Minto-Morley Reforms of 1909 tried to mitigate the evils of bureaucracy in two ways: first, by further decentralising the existing authority through encouragement of local self-government and giving wider powers of the Legislative Councils and increasing Indian representation in them. The Act of 1909 was essentially of an evolutionary character extending the application of the principle already enunciated. It was only a mild response to the moderate character of the political demands made during the pre-1909 period by Indian nationalism. However, when put to the test, it created only disillusionment. The extent of decentralisation embodied in the Act was not sufficient enough to modify the character of British Indian bureaucracy to the extent demanded by public opinion. The agitation for greater share in the administration continued unabated.

A series of developments, both in India and abroad soon after created a favourable situation to the Indian cause. Of these, the outbreak of the First World War was the most important. Britain was anxious to enlist Indian support in the war effort. Consequently, the British Government announced its new policy toward India. That policy envisaged the increasing association of Indians in every branch of the administration with a view to the gradual development of self-governing institutions. Closely following upon the announcement, Montagu, the then Secretary of State, visited India and in consultation with Lord Chelmsford, the Governor-General, drew up a report on Indian Constitutional Reforms, popularly known as the Mont-Ford Report. On the basis of the Report, a new Act was passed by the British Parliament — the Act of 1919.

The Government of India Act of 1919 and Dyarchy

The Act was based on the principles set forth in the above Report. It had two important features. First, it envisaged the maximum amount of decentralisation through the division of authority between the Central and the Provincial Governments in the various fields of administration and, secondly, the introduction of "Dyarchy" in the Provinces, a division of the executive power between the Indian representatives and the British advisers of the Governor.

The principles of division of authority between the Centre and the provinces was that subjects of all-India importance were to be allotted to the Central Government and matters which were of predominantly local interest to the Provincial Governments. It must be noted, however, that the division was not as rigid as it is in a federation. This is clear from the fact that the Central Legislature was competent to legislate on Provincial subjects. In other words, there was still no federal principle in operations and the government of India still remained essentially unitary in form and substance. Nevertheless, the powers that were given to the Provinces in matters of legislation, finance and administration were substantial.

In spite of all the decentralisation and some democratisation brought about by the Act of 1919, the results, as evidenced through its working, did not enthuse the people. Instead, there was widespread dissatisfaction and all-round disappointment. The chief reason for this was the failure of dyarchy as a constitutional experiment. The most important feature of the Act of 1919 was the introduction of dyarchy in the Provinces. When put to the test of practice, it was found that there was no substantial transfer of power to the representatives of the people. The entire scheme of the Act was bound to fail in the absence of co-operation from the "Swarajists" who formed the majority group in most of the Provincial Legislatures. But even those optimists like the "Liberals" who gave a fair trial to the Act, found it wanting in the essentials of a responsible government and were, therefore, terribly disappointed.

Demand for Complete Transfer of Power

The result was the emergence of a new spirit, zeal and unity of the educated classes under the leadership of the Indian National Congress. The non-violent non co-operation movement started by Gandhiji gathered momentum and assumed the shape of a full-fledged agitation for complete transfer of power to Indian hands. Every one felt the need of a new, constitution which would suit the needs and conditions of India. The only difference of opinion was as to the nature of the new Constitution, whether it should be federal or unitary in structure.

The Simon Commission, which was appointed by the British Government in 1927 to report on constitutional reforms in India, had recommended against an all-India federation. The Nehru Committee, an Indian parallel to the Simon Commission, and appointed by the Indian National Congress, on the other hand, had recommended the formation of such a federation. Powerful spokesmen of the Indian Princes, too, had expressed themselves in favour of an all-India federation. The British Government, who were undecided for a time, discarded the Report of the Simon Commission and expressed themselves also in favour of establishing a federation for India as a solution to the constitutional problem. To facilitate the formation of the federation by drawing up a constitution, a series of conferences were held in London known as the Round Table Conferences.

The Indian National Congress, on account of serious differences with the British Government with regard to the nature of self-government that was to be established in India under the proposed constitution, withdrew itself from these deliberations. But the British Government was bent upon imposing a new constitution on India. With this object in view, they introduced a new Bill in the Parliament which, after prolonged discussions and deliberations, was finally passed in 1935 and become the Goverment of India Act, 1935.

The Constitution Act of 1935

There were two very important provisions in the Government of India Act, 1935, which deserve special mention. They were (1) the introduction of a federal polity in India, and (2) the establishment of Provincial autonomy in the British Indian Provinces. Both these were radical changes. In place of the old unitary form of government the new federal form was to bring in both the British Indian Provinces and the Indian States into one organic union embracing the entire country. Both the Provinces and the States were to function as constituent units of the federation, the former self-governing and the latter self-acting.

The all-India federation that was contemplated by the Act did not, however, materialise during the period of its operation. All that was effected by the Act only a semi-federation of the British Indian Provinces. Still the change was of great significance. In the words of the first Chief Justice of India, Sir Maurice Gwyer, "there came into being in place of the pre-existing Provinces which were under the tutelage of the Central Government, eleven autonomous States, pulsating with a vigorous life of their own and dividing with the Government of India the legislative and executive powers of government, that is to say, a federation of the eleven British Indian Provinces associated together in an organic union".

Provincial Autonomy

April 1937 marked a historic event when constitutional progress in India recorded the beginning of a new chapter. General elections under the Constitution Act were already over in all the eleven Provinces and responsible governments were installed in every one of them by that date. The Congress Party which secured overwhelming majority in seven Provinces was entrusted with the administration in those Provinces and in the remaining ones coalition governments controlled the administration.

Despite all the misgivings expressed about the new set-up, it must be admitted that the Ministries in the Provinces functioned with remarkable success. There was a spirit of accommodation both on the part of the British Government in the Provinces who were at the head of the administration and the Indian leaders who accepted office and wanted to give a trial to the new experiment in constitutionalism. The result was a smooth and efficient functioning of governments in the Provinces according to the well-known principles of parliamentary democracy. However, this was destined to be a shortlived experiment as events with far-reaching consequences were developing in the horizon of international politics with their inevitable impact on India.

The Impact of the Second World War

The outbreak of the Second World War in September 1939, created a first class constitutional crisis in India threatening the very foundation of the existing responsible government in the Provinces. The crisis was precipitated by the short-sighted policy of the British authorities who were then at the helm of affairs in the country. The Governor-General, Lord Linlithgow, made an automatic declaration of war on Germany following a similar one in the British Parliament by the Prime Minister of Great Britain. The high-handed behaviour on the part of the Governor-General gave an unexpectedly rude shock to the popular Ministries in the British Indian Provinces. It was not the declaration of war as such that shocked them, but the manner in which it was done. The British bureaucracy never thought that it was necessary for them even to consult the popular political forces in India before committing the country to world war. The importance of this action can be fully realised if we consider the cases of British Dominions like Canada, Australia and South Africa which, instead of making automatic declaration of war, submitted the matter to their respective Parliaments for decision. It was only at the will of their Parliaments that they could commit themselves to the war.

The Governor-General's autocratic action led the Indian leaders to the inevitable conclusion that Britain still considered India only as one of her colonies. It was their duty to fight that disgraceful position and establish the complete independence of the country. In a statement issued by the Working Committee of the Indian National Congress on 14 September 1939, it said among other things: "If Great Britain fights for maintenance and extension of democracy, then she must necessarily end imperialism in her possessions and establish full democracy in India and the Indian People must have the right of self-determination by framing their own constitution through a Constituent Assembly. A free democratic India will gladly associate herself with other free nations for mutual defence against aggression. Therefore it was only a natural consequence of their renewed determination to fight for their independence that they tendered the resignation of their offices in the Provincial administration. But the Governor-General and his henchmen in India wanted to impose their dictatorial will on the people of India even against their will. An emergency was declared all over India and the administration of the whole country was concentrated into the hands of the Governor-General through the Governors and the Indian Civil Service. A series of new emergency Ordinances were passed to meet any opposition from the popular forces in the country. Most of the national leaders has been arrested and sent to jail. Provincial autonomy, which was the foundation of the limited federal system that existed under the Constitution Act was no more a living constitutional feature but only a dream of the past. Indian administration, once again, was pressured into the all-India steel-frame of the old centralised bureaucracy.

The Cripps Mission

The first two years of the war were the most disastrous for Great Britain during the whole of her history as a world power. Not only that Britain was fighting for her life at home against German air attacks but she was also losing her colonies in the East to Japan which was almost at the door-step of the Indian Empire. These set-backs compelled her to revise the British policy towards India. With this end in view, Sir Stafford Cripps was sent to India on a special mission for finding a "just and final solution" of the constitutional crisis.

The Cripps Mission envisaged complete transfer of power to Indians after the war, and partial transfer during the war. In return for this, Britain wanted the Indian leaders to support and work wholeheartedly for the prosecution of the war. The Indian National Congress declining the 'Cripps Offer' declared that the essential condition was the freedom of India without the realisation of which the hearts of millions of Indians could not be illumined nor could they be moved into action. This the British Government was not prepared for and, therefore, the Cripps Mission failed.

The Quit India Resolution

"...........The Committee is of opinion that immediate ending of British rule in India is an urgent necessity, both for the sake of India and for the success of the cause of the United Nations. The continuation of that rule is degrading and enfeebling India and making her progressively less capable of defending herself and of contributing to the cause of world freedom.............

"The freedom of India must be the symbol of and the prelude to the freedom of all other Asian nations under foreign domination. Burma, Malaya, Indo-China, the Dutch Indies, Iran and Iraq must also attain their complete freedom.

"The Committee is of opinion that the future peace, security and orderly progress of the world demanded a world-federation of free nations and on no other basis can the problems of the modern world be solved.........An independent India would gladly join such a federation and co-operate on an equal basis with other countries in the solution of international problems."

The British Government in reply at once arrested all the Congress leaders and banned all Congress organisations throughout India. The arrest of the leaders of the nation provoked a widespread revolution in India, known as the August Revolution. Thousands became prey to the onslaughts of the British Police forces in India and the war-efforts of the Government were seriously hampered by the apathy of the public. However, the August Revolution was suppressed with an iron hand.

The Simla Conference

Victory for the Allies came in Europe in May, 1945. Three years had passed since the Cripps Mission. All this time the national leaders were in jail. In June 1945, the Governor-General announced the release of the Congress leaders as a preparatory measure for negotiations with them. A conference was called, soon after, at Simla where all the leading political parties took part. But it could not arrive at any agreed solution. Immediately after this, Lord Wavell, the then Governor-General, visited England where there had taken place tremendous political changes due to the defeat of the Conservative Party in the general elections and the formation of the Labour Government. On his return to India in September

1945, Lord Wavell announced the determination of the British Government to go ahead with the hope of bringing India to self-government speedily.

Parliamentary Delegation

In February, 1946, the British Prime Minister, Clement Attlee announced in the House of Commons that a Parliamentary Delegation would visit India with a view to meeting the national leaders and discuss the various problems connected with self-government in India. The Delegation, consisting of members of Parliament belonging to all important parties, visited India soon after and spent over four weeks in the country. This paved the way of further progress in Indo-British understanding regarding India's constitutional problem. By this time, the Labour Government was convinced of the imperative necessity to grant India complete self-government.

All this time, the Viceroy was in constant touch with the British Cabinet with a view to finalize the next plan of action. The Labour Government thought that the situation in India demanded an altogether different approach than what had been hitherto going on. The Viceroy too, agreed with the new approach. Accordingly, it was announced on 19, February 1946 in the House of Lords by Lord Pethik-Lawrence, the Secretary of State for India, that a Cabinet Mission consisting of himself, Sir Stafford Cripps (President of the Board of Trade) and A.V. Alexander (First Lord of the Admiralty) would soon visit India to seek, in association with the Viceroy, a settlement of the constitutional issue.

The Cabinet Mission Scheme

The three Cabinet Ministers arrived in New Delhi on 24 March, 1946. Immediately after their arrival they held negotiations with the Viceroy and various party leaders. These negotiations lasted over seven weeks and the leaders met included Gandhi, Azad, Nehru, Patel, Jinnah, Shyama Prasad Mukherjee, Ambedkar, Jagjivan Ram, Tara Singh, Tej Bahadur Sapru and M.R. Jayakar. The Cabinet Mission had done their best to bring the Congress and the League together for a settlement. But like all the previous attempts by others, theirs too failed. Yet, the Mission decided to put forward what they considered to be the best possible proposals. These were included in a statement which they issued on 16 May 1946 and became known as the Cabinet Mission Plan.

The Plan can be divided into three parts. First, the examination of the proposals for the partition of the country and the creation of a new independent State called Pakistan; secondly, a scheme for the setting up of an Interim Government; thirdly, a plan for a long-term settlement.

Examining the case for establishing a new sovereign State of Pakistan consisting of the six Provinces (Assam, Bengal, the Punjab, Sind, NW.F.P and Baluchistan) claimed by the League, the Mission said that they were unable to agree with the proposal. This was because it would not solve the problem of communal minorities as the Provinces included also areas which were predominantly non-Muslim. They further examined an alternate proposal according to which the proposed Pakistan State should consist of only the Muslim majority areas of these Provinces. The Muslim League itself was against such proposal because it would be quite impracticable. The Cabinet Mission were convinced that a solution involving the partition of the Punjab and Bengal would be contrary to the wishes and interests of a very large proportion of the inhabitants of these Provinces. Moreover, a division of the Punjab would necessarily involve the division of the Sikh community. Further, there were also weighty administrative, economic and military considerations against the creation of a sovereign State of Pakistan. Therefore, the Cabinet Mission rejected the plea for the partition of the country and the creation of a separate State of Pakistan.

The Mission recommended the following plan for a long-term settlement:

1. There should be a Union of India, embracing both British India and the States which should deal with the following subjects: defence, foreign affairs and communications.
2. The Union should have an executive and a legislature constituted of British Indian and States' representatives. Any question raising a major communal issue in the Legislature should require for its decision a majority of the representatives present and voting of each of the two major communities as well as a majority of all the members present and voting.
3. All subjects other than the Union subjects and all residuary powers should vest in the Provinces.
4. The States would retain all subjects and powers other than those ceded to the Union.
5. Provinces should be free to form groups with executives and legislatures and each group could determine the provincial subjects to be taken in common.
6. The constitution of the Union and of the groups should contain a provision whereby the Province could by a majority vote of the Legislative Assembly call for a reconsideration of the terms of the constitution after an initial period of ten years and at ten-yearly intervals thereafter.
7. The constitution-making body should be constituted immediately through indirect election. (Direct election based on adult franchise would lead to long delay). For this purpose, each Province was to be allotted a number of seats proportional to its population, roughly to the ratio of one to a million. The total number of seats thus arrived at for each Province was to be divided among the main communities in proportion to their population and that the representatives allotted to each community were to be elected by the members of the same community in the Legislative Assembly. (The communities recognized for this purpose were General, Muslim and Sikhs).
8. The representatives so elected would meet together in New Delhi as one body, together with the representatives of the Indian states to constitute a constitution-making body.
9. The Constituent Assembly would separate into three sections:

   Section A. Madras, Bombay, U.P., C.P., Bihar and Orissa.

   Section B. Punjab, N.W.F.P and Sind.

   Section C. Bengal and Assam.
10. Each section would decide its own provincial constitutions and also whether any constitution for the group as a whole to be set up and if so the extent of its powers.
11. After the group constitutions are settled, the groups would assemble together to settle the Union Constitution.

12. The Union Constituent Assembly would negotiate a treaty with the United Kingdom to provide for certain matters arising out of the transfer of power.

The short-term plan of the Mission envisaged the immediate setting up of an Interim Government having the support of all the major political parties in order to carry on the administration while the constitution-making was in progress. In the Interim Government all the portfolios would be held by Indians. The British Government would give its fullest measure of co-operation in the accomplishment of the tasks confronted by the Interim Government.

The Mission concluded its long statement in the following words:

> We hope that the new independent India may choose to be a member of the British Commonwealth. We hope in any event that you will remain in close and friendly association with our people. But these are matters for your own free choice. Whatever the choice may be, we look forward with you to your ever-increasing prosperity among the great nations of the world, and to a future even more glorious than your past.

The proposals of the Cabinet Mission soon became the object of close examination by the different political parties. The reactions were on the whole favourable. Nevertheless, there were a number of details which were subjected to criticism by each party on the basis of its own stand. The main objection of the Congress was against those provisions relating to the grouping of Provinces. Jinnah was unhappy over the rejection of the League's claim for the setting up of a separate, sovereign Pakistan. The Sikhs were considerably disturbed by the proposals which, they felt, would leave them without sufficient safeguards against a Muslim majority in Group B Provinces.

On 6 June 1946 the Council of the Muslim League passed a resolution accepting the Cabinet Mission's proposals with a number of reservations The Congress Working Committee met on 25 June and expressed its disapproval of the system of grouping of Provinces. The Committee decided, however, to join the proposed Constituent Assembly with a view to framing the constitution of a free, united and democratic India. With respect to the formation of an Interim Government, the Committee said that it would co-operate only if its national, non-communal character was recognized in the selection of members to the Executive Council.

When the Cabinet Mission left India on 29 June leaving the Indian political scene still in an atmosphere of uncertainty, it was difficult for any one to characterize the Mission a success. Yet there were some positive achievements. First, the problem of the future of India had been brought down from the clouds of nebulous theories to the plane of hard realities. Secondly, there had been the welcome realization that the Labour Party in England meant to keep their pledge to withdraw from India as soon as possible. Finally, both the Congress and the Muslim League had indeed accepted the long-term plan although each party had its own reservations and interpretations of almost all the controversial issues.[1]

Meeting at Bombay on 6 June 1946, the All India Congress Committee ratified the resolution of the Working Committee on the Cabinet Mission Plan. But in his presidential address to the Committee Jawaharlal Nehru, who was then just elected as the Congress president for the fourth time, declared that as far as he could see it was not a question of the Congress accepting any plan, long or short. It was merely a question of their agreeing to enter the Constituent Assembly, and nothing more than that. 'We are not bound by a single

1. V.P. Menon, on cit., p. 279.

thing', he declared, 'except that we have decided for the moment to go into the Constituent Assembly'. Nehru elaborated this later in a press conference and asserted that there would be no grouping of Provinces as envisaged in the Statement of the Cabinet Mission.

These and other utterances of responsible Congressmen were taken up by Jinnah who characterized them as a complete repudiation of the basic form upon which the long-term scheme rested. He demanded clarification on this matter from the British Government. In a debate that took place soon in the British Parliament, both the Secretary of State and Sir Stafford Cripps explained the position and tried to show that Jinnah's fears were not justified. Jinnah, however, was not satisfied. At a meeting of the League Council on 27 July in Bombay, the League went back on its earlier stand and rejected the Cabinet Mission Plan in its entirety. It went one step further to reiterate its earlier stand for a sovereign Pakistan and also decided to draw up a plan of 'direct action'. Accordingly, the League declared 16 August 1946 as 'Direct Action Day'.

Elections to the proposed Constituent Assembly were completed by now in all the Provinces. Both the Congress and the League had won almost all the seats in their respective spheres.[1] In the meantime, the Viceroy had been negotiating with party leaders with a view to forming an Interim Government. The basis of his negotiations was a Council of 14 members, with 6 Congress nominees (including a scheduled caste representative), 5 Muslim League nominees and three representatives of the minorities to be nominated by the Viceroy. Jinnah did not agree with this plan mainly on the same ground which he raised at the Simla Conference. Thereupon, the Viceroy asked Congress to form the Interim Government to which it responded enthusiastically.

Accordingly, on the second day of September 1946, for the first time in the two-centuries-old history of British rule in India, a fully popular Governor-General's Council consisting of national leaders like Jawaharlal Nehru, Vallabhbhai Patel, Rajendra Prasad and Rajagopalachari took over the reins of Indian administration. Nehru was its first Vice-President.

The Muslim League's observance of 16 August as Direct Action Day was an invitation to violence. The result was an unprecedented holocaust in Calcutta and other cities of India where thousands of people were butchered in communal riots. These unfortunate happenings shook the confidence of Lord Wavell who thought that the only solution to get over the difficult situation was to persuade the Muslim League to enter the Interim Government. This he managed after protracted negotiations with Jinnah lasting over six weeks, and the Muslim League's five representatives joined the Government on 26 October 1946.

The Interim Government, however, did not function successfully. This was mainly because of the intransigent attitude of the Muslim League which did not want the Interim Government to function as a harmonious team as it feared that it might consolidate the position of the Congress. In fact, the Muslim League's anxiety to enter the Interim Government was motivated more by considerations of thwarting Congress doing well in Government than by its sharing political power. Hence, it became evident soon that the League contingent in the Government was using its position in Government for the realization of the League's ambition of establishing a sovereign Pakistan. Lord Wavell tried his best to persuade Jinnah to rescind the League's Bombay resolution by which it rejected the Cabinet

1. The Congress won all the general seats except nine while the League won 73 out of a total of 78 allotted to Muslims.

Mission Plan. He made it clear that the League's entry into the Interim Government was conditional on its acceptance of the Cabinet Mission's Statement of 16 May. But Jinnah adopted an evasive attitude. Further, the League representatives in the Interim Government refused to accept Nehru's leadership as Vice-President of the Council, and flouted the principles of collective responsibility. When the Constituent Assembly met for the first time on 9 December 1946, the League representatives boycotted it. There were also during this difficult period communal disturbances in different parts of the country to make the situation worse for bringing about any settlement.

In a last bid to break the deadlock, the British Government invited the leaders of the two parties to meet with them in London. Nehru represented the Congress, Baldev Singh the Sikhs, and Jinnah and Liaquat Ali Khan the League. The discussions at London, however, failed to find a solution. Soon after the return of the leaders to India, both the All India Congress Committee and the Muslim League Council reiterated their respective stands. The League's failure to enter the Constituent Assembly and its continued demand for Pakistan made the Congress and the minority representatives in the Executive Council to demand the resignation of the League members from the Council. An extremely difficult situation arose when none could forecast the grave repercussions of the withdrawal of the League members from the Council or, in the alternative, that of the Congress members. Unfortunately, Lord Wavell wavered and could not find a satisfactory course of action. He was not happy to dismiss the League members nor could persuade Jinnah to co-operate with the Congress in the Government and the Constituent Assembly in order to create an atmosphere of goodwill and trust which might lead to mutual understanding.

On 20 February 1947, Prime Minister Attlee made a statement in the House of Commons announcing the British Government's definite intention of taking necessary steps to effect the peaceful transfer of power into responsible Indian hands by a date not later than June 1948. If no agreement was reached by then between the leading political parties in India, the British Government would have to consider to whom it should transfer the powers of the Central Government, whether as a whole to some form of Central Government for British India, or in some areas to the existing Provincial Governments, or in some other way as may seem most reasonable and in the best interests of the Indian people. Simultaneously, he also announced that Lord Wavell would be succeeded by Lord Mountbatten who would be entrusted with the task of transferring to Indian hands responsibility for the Government of British India in a manner that would best ensure the future happiness and prosperity of India.

When Lord Mountbatten arrived in Delhi on 22 May 1947, the general situation in the country was so bleak that it appeared as though it was heading for immediate and inescapable disaster. The Muslim League was preaching direct action and conducting civil disobedience against some of the Congress ministries in the Provinces. Hindu-Muslim differences were at their worst. Even the Services who were traditionally loyal to the Government and impartial in their approach were divided in their loyalty and had begun taking sides in the political controversy.

The Mountbatten Plan

Immediately after his arrival at Delhi, Mountbatten plunged straight and deep into the constitutional problem. It was his objective to find an agreed solution on the basis of the

Cabinet Mission Plan. He set about this task in the most zealous and expeditious manner. But the initial round of talks that he had with the party leaders, particularly Jinnah and his colleagues, convinced him that it was impossible to find an agreed solution for a united India. Hence, he directed his energies towards the acceptance of an alternative plan based upon the statement of Prime Minister Attlee in the House of Commons on 20 February. According to this, if the representatives of the predominantly Hindu and Muslim areas of Bengal and the Punjab voted for partition, these Provinces were to be partitioned; the predominantly Muslim district of Assam, namely Sylhet, should have the option to join the Muslim Province. The plan envisaged the holding of a referendum to ascertain the wishes of the people of the North West Frontier Province. Thus the responsibility for the partition of the country was to be placed on the shoulders of the Indian people themselves who were affected by the measure.

The Mountbatten Plan became ultimately the basis for the partition of the country which was accepted, although with great unwillingness, by the parties. The inevitability of partition was recognized and acknowledged by the Congress leaders by early 1947. In a public speech on 20 April 1947 Nehru said, 'The Muslim League can have Pakistan, if they wish to have it, but on the condition that they do not take away other parts of India which do not wish to join Pakistan'. Rajendra Prasad, President of the Constituent Assembly, declared in the Assembly on 28 April:

> While we have accepted the Cabinet Mission's Statement of May 16, 1946, which contemplated a Union of the different Provinces and States within the country, it may be that the Union may not comprise all Provinces. If that unfortunately comes to pass, we shall have to be content with a constitution for a part of it. In that case, we can and should insist that one principle will apply to all parts of the country and no constitution will be forced upon any unwilling part of it. This may mean not only the division of India, but a division of some Provinces. For this we must be prepared and the Assembly may have to draw up a constitution based on such a division.

The communal situation in the Punjab, N.W.F.P. and Sind had by now reached alarming proportions. Organized disturbances resulting in the death of thousands of people and destruction of property worth millions became the order of the day. The Viceroy found that the only way in which these unhappy occurrences could be stopped was to speed up the implementation of his plan. With this object in view, he initiated another round of talks with the Indian leaders and also got in touch with the British Government. The result was the acceptance of the plan for the partition of the country into India and Pakistan which were to be given immediately the status of a Dominion in the British Commonwealth of Nations and to advance the date of transfer of power to 15 August 1947. The Plan was announced officially on 3 June 1947 by Prime Minister Attlee in the British Parliament, later to be known as 'the June 3rd Plan', and on the basis of which the necessary legislation was soon introduced in Parliament.

The Indian Independence Act, 1947

The Indian Independence Bill which was designed to transfer power to the people of India was introduced in the House of Commons on 4 July and was piloted through Parliament in a record time and received the Royal Assent on 18 July. The main provisions of the Indian Independence Act, 1947, are as follows:

1. As from 15 August 1947, two independent Dominions shall be set up in India, to be known respectively as India and Pakistan.

2. The territories of India shall include all the British Indian Provinces except those that comprise Pakistan.

3. The territories of Pakistan shall include the areas covered by the Provinces of East Bengal, West Punjab, Sind, Baluchistan and the North West Frontier Province. (The Province of East Bengal includes also the district of Sylhet of Assam Province.)

4. The Indian States are free to accede to either of the two new Dominions.

5. For each of the new Dominions, there shall be a Governor-General who shall be appointed by His Majesty and shall represent His Majesty for the purposes of the Government of the Dominion.

6. The Legislature of each of the new Dominions shall have full power to make laws for the Dominion, including laws having extra-territorial operation. No such law shall be void on the ground that it is repugnant to the laws of England or any provision of any existing or future Act of Parliament of the United Kingdom nor an Order-in-Council shall extend to the new Dominions.

7. As from the 15th Day of August 1947, the Government of the United Kingdom have no responsibility as respects the government of any of the territories which, immediately before that day, were included in British India.

8. The suzerainty of His Majesty over the Indian States lapses, and with it, all treaties and agreements in force at the date of the passing of this Act, between His Majesty and the rulers of Indian States.

9. The Constituent Assembly of each Dominion shall exercise all powers exercised by the Legislature of the Dominion.

10. The Governor-General shall by order make such provision as appears to him to be necessary or expedient for bringing the provisions of this Act into effective operation and all matters incidental to it.

It was indeed a formidable task to carry out the partition of a vast country of four hundred million people and effect the transfer of power to two independent governments in a period of about ten weeks The task was, however, achieved with commendable success. Mountbatten flew to Karachi on 13 August to inaugurate the Dominion of Pakistan. He flew back to Delhi on 14 August. On the night of that day, the Constituent Assembly met and in a memorable speech, Jawaharlal Nehru called upon the members and through them the entire people of India to take a pledge of dedication to the service of India. He said:

Long years ago we made a tryst with destiny, and now the time comes when we shall redeem our pledge, not wholly or in full measure, but very substantially. At the stroke of the midnight hour, when the world sleeps India will awake to life and freedom. A moment comes, which comes but rarely in history, when we step out from the old to the new, when an age ends, and when the soul of a nation, long suppressed, finds utterance. It is fitting that at this solemn moment we take the pledge of dedication to the service of India and her people and to the still larger cause of humanity.

It was a fitting tribute to the signal service of Lord Mountbatten that the Constituent Assembly unanimously endorsed the proposal of the Congress leadership that he should become the first Governor-General of Independent India. Lord Mountbatten responded by saying: 'I am proud of the honour and I will do my best to carry out your advice in a constitutional manner'. On 15 August he was sworn in as Governor-General in a colourful ceremony and thus began the life of a new nation ending the 182 years old British rule in India and the mightiest of empires history has ever known.

***

5

THE CONSTITUENT ASSEMBLY

THE CONSTITUENT ASSEMBLY met, for the first time, on 9 December 1946. It was a historic occasion. Following the example of such occasions elsewhere, the oldest member of the Assembly, Sachidananda Sinha, presided over the first meeting[1]. Three messages of goodwill were received by the Constituent Assembly at the inaugural session, one each from the U.S.A., the Republic of China and the Government of Australia and the Chairman read them out to the Assembly as the first item of the day. Later, Rajendra Prasad, one of the outstanding leaders of the Indian National Congress, was unanimously elected President of the Assembly.

A question that faced the Assembly at the very outset was whether or not it was sovereign body. From a strictly legal and constitutional point of view, it seems that the assembly was not a sovereign body[2]. For, it was the British Government that brought it into being and it could abolish it. From a political point of view, however, this was extremely unlikely when once the Assembly had actually come into being. According to the rules drafted by the Expert Committee, the Assembly had the right to frame its own rules and the leaders of the Congress Party asserted that the Assembly was a sovereign body the moment it started functioning. This position was contested by M.R. Jayakar on the floor of the Assembly in the opening session. According to him, the Assembly was not sovereign; it was subject to the limitations imposed by the Statement of the Cabinet Mission. Those limitations could be removed only by agreement with the Muslim League and the Indian States. Jayakar not only opposed the Objectives Resolution moved by Jawaharlal Nehru but even characterized it as 'wrong, illegal, premature, disastrous and dangerous.'

Jayakar's arguments were countered by N. Gopalaswami Ayyangar and Alladi Krishnaswami Aiyar. The former thought that the Constituent Assembly had in full the residuary power for accomplishing the tasks which it had undertaken. 'Whatever is not said but necessary for the accomplishment of our task, is within our powers to regulate'. Alladi thought that the Cabinet Mission Statement basically established the sovereign character of the Constituent Assembly. The Assembly proceeded on the basis of this assumption and adopted the draft rules framed by the Procedure Committee. There were two significant rules among these which proclaimed the sovereign character of the Assembly. First, the President was named the guardian of the privileges of the Assembly, its spokesman and representative and its highest executive authority. Secondly, the

1. Acharya J.B. Kripalani proposed Sinha's name for election as temporary Chairman.
2. Winston Churchill had doubted the validity of the Constituent Assembly itself in a parliamentary debate. The Muslim League also was opposed to it.

Assembly could not be dissolved except by its own resolution passed at least by two-thirds of all the members of the Assembly.

It may be interesting to record here the method adopted by the Constituent Assembly to conduct its work. First it laid down its 'terms of reference' as it were, in the form of an Objectives Resolution which was moved by Nehru in an inspiring speech and which later constituted the Preamble of the Constitution. It then proceeded to appoint a number of committees to deal with the different aspects of the Constitutional problem. Several of these had as their chairman either Jawaharlal Nehru or Vallabhbhai Patel, to whom therefore should go the credit for laying down the fundamentals of the Constitution. On the basis of the reports of these committees, a draft constitution was prepared by B.N. Rao, the Constitutional Adviser, who brought to bear on this task both his knowledge of the conditions of this country and the constitutions of other countries. The Assembly then appointed a Drafting Committee, with B.R. Ambedkar as its Chairman, which worked on the original draft and produced the Draft Constitution. This Draft was considered by the Assembly at great length, particularly at the second reading stage.

The Constituent Assembly took almost three years (two years, eleven months and seventeen days, to be precise) to complete its historic task of drafting the Constitution for Independent India. During the period, it held eleven sessions, covering a total of 165 days. Of these, 114 days were spent on the consideration of the Draft Constitution. The Constitutional Adviser's text on which the Drafting Committee worked consisted of 243 Articles and 13 Schedules. The Draft Constitution prepared by the Committee consisted of 315 Articles and 7 Schedules. At the end of the consideration stage, the number of Articles grew to 386. In its final form, the Constitution had 395 Articles and 8 Schedules.

As to the composition of the Assembly, members were chosen by indirect election by the members of the Provincial Legislative Assemblies according to the Scheme recommended by the Cabinet (British) Mission. The arrangement was (1) 292 members were elected through the Provincial Legislative Assemblies, (2) 93 members represented the Indian Princely States and (3) 4 members represented the Chief Commissioners' Provinces. Thus the total membership of the Assembly was to be 389. However, as a result of the partition of the country and the creation of Pakistan under the Mountbatten Plan of June 3, 1947, a separate Constituent Assembly was set up for Pakistan and representatives of some Provinces ceased to be members of the Assembly. As a result, the membership of the Assembly was reduced to 299.

The work on the Constitution was conducted in a democratic manner. To the Draft Constitution, not less than 7,635 amendments were tabled by the members. Of these, 2,473 were actually moved, discussed and disposed of. This alone should show the manner in which the Assembly conducted its business. To anyone who goes through the proceedings of the Assembly, it will be abundantly clear that it was indeed a great democratic exercise. Discussion was encouraged to the maximum. There was great tolerance of criticism and no impatience with long drawn-out debates, no attempt to hustle through, no endeavour at imposition. It was a full-fledged democratic procedure of which India can be proud.

Against this background it may be seen that the time taken by the Assembly was not too long. In fact, it compares well with similar and comparable work elsewhere. For example, the American Constitutional Convention took four months; that of Australia nine years and Canada two years and five months. In these cases, the constitutions adopted were much smaller in size than the Constitution of India. Moreover, they had not faced the problem of amendments. They were passed as moved. Further, the Constituent Assembly of India was a much larger body. The size of the Assembly and the prolonged discussions were partly responsible for the three years that it took to complete its task. The Assembly cost the people of India Rs. 6.4 million.

Important Committees of the Constituent Assembly and its Chairmen

	Committee		Chairman
1.	Drafting Committee	:	B.R. Ambedkar
2.	Union Powers Committee	:	Jawaharlal Nehru
3.	Union Constitution Committee	:	Jawaharlal Nehru
4.	Committee on the Rules of Procedure	:	Rajendra Prasad
5.	Steering Committee	:	Rajendra Prasad
6.	Finance & Staff Committee	:	Rajendra Prasad
7.	Credentials Committee	:	Alladi Krishnaswami Aiyar
8.	House Committee	:	B. Pattabhi Sitaramayya
9.	Order of Business Committee	:	K.M. Munshi
10.	Ad hoc Committee on National Flag	:	Rajendra Prasad
11.	Committee on the Function of the Constituent Assembly	:	J.V. Mavalankar
12.	States Committee	:	Jawaharlal Nehru
13.	Advisory Committee on Fundamental Rights, Minorities & Tribal & Excluded Areas	:	Vallabhbhai Patel
14.	Minorities Sub-committee	:	H.C. Mukherjee
15.	Fundamental Rights Sub-committee	:	J.B. Kripalani
16.	North East Frontier Tribal Areas & Assam Excluded & Partially Excluded Areas Sub-committee	:	Gopinath Bardoloi
17.	Excluded & Partially Excluded Areas (other than those in Assam) Sub-committee	:	A.V. Thakkar

A discussion on the work of the Constituent Assembly is not complete without a brief mention of the role played by those who contributed most to the making of the Constitution. In this respect, the Drafting Committee members come first. It is difficult to exactly assess the contribution of each member of the committee. Theirs was primarily a teamwork. Yet, some of them deserve special recognition for the outstanding service that they rendered in the framing of the Constitution.

B.R. AMBEDKAR

Ambedkar went into the Constituent Assembly as a 'protestant'. Acknowledged as almost the undisputed leader of the Scheduled Castes by the British, he was a relentless opponent and uncompromising critic of the Indian National Congress in its policies towards his community. Naturally, the Congress was not interested in sponsoring his election to the Assembly however eminent and talented a person he was. Ambedkar, however, got elected to the Constitution-making body through the strength of his supporters in the Bengal Assembly. In the opening session of the Assembly he was one of the very few who opposed the Objectives Resolution moved by Nehru. But subsequent developments culminating in the partition of the country made him realize that political realism demanded a moderate attitude on his part towards those who had in their hands effective political power. The Congress leaders responded to this gesture so generously that they elected him the Chairman of the Drafting Committee. They could not have made a decision which was or could be more right. For, Ambedkar not only fully justified his selection but added lustre to the work he undertook.

Ambedkar brought to bear upon his task a vast array of qualities, erudition, scholarship, imagination, logic, eloquence and experience. He had a rare mastery over even the most complicated problems and situations and an ability to put across his ideas in the most lucid and forceful manner. With a rich treasure of knowledge of constitutional principles and practices in most of the leading countries, and his thorough and intimate understanding of the working of the Government of India of 1935, Ambedkar was able to meet any critic in the Assembly and expound the principles underlying the Constitution in an admirable manner. Whenever he spoke in the House, usually to reply to the criticisms advanced against provisions of the Draft Constitution, there emerged a clear and lucid exposition of the provisions of the Constitution. As he sat down, the mist of doubts vanished, as also the clouds of confusion and vagueness. In the Constituent Assembly none else was so forceful and persuasive in argument, clear and lucid in expression, quick and arresting in debate. And yet, he had always the generosity to concede the credit to a critic who made a valid point and to frankly acknowledge it. Ambedkar's contribution to the Constitution is undoubtedly of the highest order. Indeed, he was a modern Manu and deserves to be called the father or the chief architect of the Constitution of India.

ALLADI KRISHNASWAMI AIYAR

Alladi was undoubtedly the leading constitutional lawyer in the Assembly. His knowledge of constitutional law was encyclopaedic and it proved to be of great assistance in the drawing up of many important parts of the Constitution. Those parts of the Constitution which deal with the Fundamental Rights, the Supreme Court and High Courts bear particularly the stamp of Alladi's scholarship and legal acumen.

N. GOPALASWAMI AYYANGAR

With all the experience of a seasoned administrator at his disposal, Gopalaswami Ayyangar rendered sterling service to the work of the Assembly by assisting in the drawing up of many provisions which dealt with administrative matters. It was he who piloted the discussions dealing with the language question, one of the knottiest problems that faced the Assembly.

K.M. MUNSHI

Munshi was one of the very firsts to associate himself with the work of the Assembly. He had an important role in preparing the draft of the Objectives Resolution and the Rules of Procedure regulating the business of the Assembly. With his wide knowledge, sharp intellect and ready resourcefulness to bring about compromises, Munshi did commendable work to give the final shape to many of the important aspects of the Constitution.

T.T. KRISHNAMACHARI

Krishnamachari had the distinction of being the only non-lawyer member of the Drafting Committee. Yet, the manner in which he dealt with the different aspects of the Constitution on the floor of the Assembly speaks highly of his mastery over legal and constitutional problems. He rendered immense assistance to Ambedkar with his ready repartee, sharp intellect and thorough grasp of various complicated constitutional problems. Krishnamachari's contribution is particularly noteworthy in respect of those provisions of the Constitution which deal with the federal system, finance and inter-state commerce.

There were two other members of the Drafting Committee, namely, Mohamed Saadulla and Madhava Rao, both distinguished in their own way as political leaders. But their work as members of the Committee was comparatively less significant. Among the other members of the Assembly, the following persons stand out for their outstanding work.

RAJENDRA PRASAD

The unanimous election of Rajendra Prasad as President of the Constituent Assembly itself was a proof of the great esteem and respect that he enjoyed among the members. Like George Washington, who with general acclamation presided over the American Constitutional Convention, Rajendra Prasad conducted the proceedings of the Assembly in his inimitable manner, with dignity, gravity and impartiality. He maintained meticulous order in the House. He was quite firm without being harsh or rude. The President was an embodiment of courtesy and politeness. He was liberal yet firm in his decisions, sympathetic yet practical in his approach and tolerant yet unbending in his attitude. He gave adequate opportunity to those who differed from the decision of the Drafting Committee to express their opinions. He was particularly considerate to members who represented the minority communities and interests. Often he displayed his great mastery over procedure and his command over the law and the ability to interpret it. His decisions as President were always justified and hailed by all sections in the Assembly. No one disobeyed the President or challenged his decisions, or showed any resentment at his rulings. Occasionally, he brought to the Assembly's proceedings a sense of humour, rare and dignified.

President Prasad was not merely a presiding officer. He was, at times, a brilliant participant in the discussions. With the vast and rich experience that he had as a lawyer, a public leader and a man of erudition, he raised vital and pertinent questions which could sometimes make even the encyclopaedic Ambedkar look puzzled and tongue-tied for a moment. He did not hesitate even to cross-examine the Chairman of the Drafting Committee with the view to fully clarifying difficult and complicated provisions. It was such searching analysis by the President that brought forth the best in Ambedkar, illuminating the entire situation. President Prasad was indeed an inspiring example of a presiding officer who made a great contribution to the successful completion of the work of the Constituent Assembly. Like George Washington in America, he was not only elected the First President of the new republic whose Constitution was framed and adopted under his able guidance but was also re-elected for a second term.

JAWAHARLAL NEHRU

As Prime Minister and leader of the Congress Party, Nehru's influence in solving almost every difficult problem that confronted the Assembly was far-reaching. He moved the Objective Resolution which really laid the foundations of the Constitution. Everytime the Assembly faced an almost insoluble problem, he came on the scene and gave a lead that was at once inspiring and decisive. Nehru was the Chairman of the Union Constitution Committee of the Constituent Assembly. He moved the compromise resolution dealing with the right to property under Article 31 of the Constitution which, after a marathon debate, was finally adopted by the Assembly. He was a source of strength and help to the Drafting Committee not only through his remarkable leadership in every difficult situation that confronted the Assembly in its work, but also through his abilities as a writer and a draftsman to touch up particular articles before they were presented for the consideration of the Assembly.

VALLABHBHAI PATEL

The influence which Patel wielded in the councils of the Constituent Assembly was only next to that of Nehru. He was the Chairman of most of the important committees appointed by the Assembly such as the Fundamental Rights and Minorities Committee and the States Committee. Whenever the Sardar spoke in the Constituent Assembly, he spoke with rare authority and tremendous power. He had an unique ability to silence his opponents with usual tact and an iron will. He produced on the floor of the Assembly many unanimous decisions on problems which had baffled the country for many decades. He solved, for example, not only the problem of minorities but also that of the States — two of the most difficult problems that plagued the Indian body politic throughout the first half of this country — within a short period of two years with the skill of a magician.

B.N. RAU

As Constitutional Adviser to the Constituent Assembly, Rau was a perennial source of assistance to its deliberations. It was he who paved the way of the Assembly's task by producing the first draft of the Constitution for the consideration of the Drafting Committee. Besides, he greatly lightened the task of the Members of the Assembly with several brochures, papers and notes based on a careful study of different aspects of the constitutions and of the constitutional precedents of several countries. If Ambedkar was the skilful architect of the Constitution through all its different stages, Rau was the person who visualised the plan and laid its foundation. His superb draftsmanship as well as his clear, illuminating and precise style were of great assistance to the Assembly[1].

There were a number of others who played their part in making the work of the Assembly smooth, vigorous and successfully democratic. The services of the Vice-President

1. See in this connection Rajendra Prasad in Foreword to B.N. Rao, *India's Constitution in the Making* (1960).

of the Assembly, H.C. Mukherjee, who presided over it on a number of occasions in the absence of President Prasad, deserves special mention. But it was those who worked as the 'self-appointed' members in opposition who contributed most to the vigour and liveliness with which the Assembly conducted its work, and weighing the merit of each and every article, both in its form and substance, in the balance. Among them were the indefatigable H.V. Kamath, who had the credit of moving the largest number of amendments, the inimitable Naziruddin Ahmed, who was ever vigilant even over every punctuation mark in the Constitution, the indomitable Shibban Lal Saksena, who had always something original to suggest, the erudite K.T. Shah who fought a lone battle for the adoption of a presidential form of government, the moderate H.N. Kunzru, the methodical Thakur Das Bhargava, Frank Anthony, the Anglo-Indian leader, Jaipal Singh, the Jharkhand leader and a number of others. The lighter side of the discussions was almost invariably provided by the Assembly's humorist-trio, Brajeswar Prasad, Mahabir Tyagi and Rohini Kumar Chaudhary. Among the women members, Mrs. Durgabai deserves special mention.

A special virtue of the Constituent Assembly was its cosmopolitan character. Although the Congress Party could nominate its own partymen for every available seat in the Assembly and win almost every one of them they did not adopt such a narrow-minded course of action. On the contrary, they were keen on bringing into the Constituent Assembly men of ability, integrity and erudition whatever their political background. Thus, there were a large number of non-partymen in the Assembly. A notable example of such members was Jerome D'Souza, a Jesuit Priest from Madras. Such members not only brought to the floor of the Assembly a freshness in outlook and an individuality in approach but also made its composition broad-based and its complexion cosmopolitan.

The Constitution was formally adopted on 26 November 1949 and the members appended their signatures to it on 24 January 1950. In all 284 members actually signed the document.

***

PART III

PREAMBLE, TERRITORY AND CITIZENSHIP

6

THE PREAMBLE

EVERY CONSTITUTION has a Preamble with which it begins and which embodies its objectives or basic purposes. A notable exception to this almost universal rule was the Government of India Act of 1935, the only one of its kind ever passed by the British Parliament. What made the tradition-bound framers of that constitutional enactment discard the age-old practice, no one knows precisely. Perhaps, they themselves were not quite certain about the objectives of the new constitution they were framing, or it may be that they desisted from stating their objectives clearly lest they should incur displeasure or antagonize public opinion, both Indian and British. In contrast, the framers of the Constitution of the Republic of India were in a most happy position. Here was an opportunity for them to give expression to the dreams of a new order they had been dreaming of for years. Naturally, they were eager to draw up a Preamble which embodied the fundamental principles of that new order.

From a strictly legal point of view, the importance of a Preamble is limited. It cannot qualify the provisions of the enactment so long as its text is clear and unambiguous. In the words of the United States Supreme Court:

> Although the preamble indicates the general purposes for which the people ordained and established the Constitution, it has never been regarded as the source of any substantive power conferred on the Government of the United States or any of its Documents. Such powers embrace only those expressly granted in the body of the Constitution, and such as may be implied from those powers[1].

But if the statute is ambiguous, the Preamble can be referred to in order to explain and elucidate it as 'it is a key to open the minds of the makers of the Act, and the mischiefs they intended to redress'.[2]

The Supreme Court of India is substantially in agreement with this position. In the words of Justice Patanjali Sastri, 'The Court could only search for the objective intent of the Legislature primarily in the words used in the enactment, aided by such historical material as reports of statutory committees, preambles etc.'[3] While Justice Sastri was prepared to give only secondary importance to the Preamble in the interpretation of the provisions of the Constitution, Justice Mahajan seems to go a step further when he said, 'The interpretation that I am inclined to place on clause (5) of Article 22 is justified by the solemn words of the declaration contained in the Preamble to the Constitution. It is this declaration that makes our Constitution sublime....'[4] The Court was, however, against the importation of the idea of

---

1. Jacobson *vs*. Massachussets, 1905 19/U.S. 11.
2. Sussex Peerage case, 1844, II CL & F. 85, 143.
3. A.K. Gopalan *vs* State of Madras, 1950 S.C.J., p. 236.
4. Ibid, p. 249.

'the spirit of the Constitution' in the interpretation of its provisions on the strength of the declaration of its objectives embodied in the Preamble, such as the establishment of justice, liberty, equality, fraternity, etc.[1]

The Preamble of the Constitution of India as it was originally enacted reads as follows:

WE, THE PEOPLE OF INDIA,

having solemnly resolved to constitute India into a

SOVEREIGN, DEMOCRATIC REPUBLIC[2]

and to secure to all its citizens:

JUSTICE, social, economic and political;

LIBERTY of thought, expression, belief, faith and worship;

EQUALITY of status and of opportunity; and to promote among them all

FRATERNITY assuring the dignity of the individual and the unity of the nation;

IN OUR CONSTITUENT ASSEMBLY this twenty-sixth day of November 1949

do HEREBY ADOPT, ENACT, AND GIVE TO OURSELVES THIS CONSTITUTION.

The sentiments expressed in the Preamble were those described by Jawaharlal Nehru in the Objectives Resolution which he moved in the Constituent Assembly in its first session and which the Assembly adopted unanimously.[3] But Nehru's resolution itself had

---

1. It was Ambedkar who, appearing before the Supreme Court in 1952, advanced the plea to adopt such an interpretation. See State of Bihar *vs.* Kameshwar Singh, 1952, S.C.J., p. 361. See also Mahajan J., in A.K. Gopalan's case, 1950 S.C.J., p. 246; also Syed Mohammed and Company *vs.* State of Andhra, A.I.R. 1952 S.C. 314; State of Punjab *vs.* Ajaib Singh, 1953, S.C.R. 254; Chiranjit Lal Chowdhuri *vs.* The Union of India, 1950, S.C.R. 869 and Dwarakadas Srinivas *vs.* Sholapur Spinning and Weaving Co. A.I.R. 1954, S.C. 119. Also see Wanchoo J. in Golaknath case, A.I.R. 1967, S.C. 1943.
2. The Forty-second Amendment added "Socialist, Secular" after sovereign, making it read as Sovereign, Socialist, Secular, Democratic Republic. It also added 'integrity' after 'unity'.
3. The text of the Resolution is as follows:

This Constituent Assembly declares its firm and solemn resolve to proclaim India as an Independent Sovereign Republic and to draw up for her future governance a Constitution.
WHEREIN the territories that now comprise British India, the territories that now form the Indian States, and such other parts of India as are outside British India and the States as well as such other territories as are wiling to be constituted into the independent Sovereign India shall be a Union of them all; and
WHEREIN the said territories, whether with their present boundaries or with such others as may be determined by the Constituent Assembly and thereafter according to the law of the Constitution, shall possess and retain the status of autonomous powers and functions of government and administration, save and except such powers and functions as are vested in or assigned to the Union, or as are inherent or implied in the Union or resulting therefrom; and
WHEREIN all powers and authority of the Sovereign Independent India, its constituent parts and organs of Government; are derived from the people; and
WHEREIN shall be guaranteed and secured to all the people fo INDIA.
Justice, social, economic and political;
Equality of status, of opportunity, and before the law;
Freedom of thought, expression, belief, faith, worship, vocation, association and action, subject to law and public morality; and
WHEREIN adequate safeguards shall be provided for minorities, backward classes; and tribal areas, and depressed and other backward classes; and
WHEREIN shall be maintained the integrity of the territory of the Republic and its sovereign rights on land, sea and air according to justice and the law of civilised nations;
And
this ancient land attain its rightful and honoured place in the world and make its full and willing contribution to the promotion of world peace and the welfare of mankind.

taken shape out of what had been already said many times by Mahatma Gandhi. In 1931 when Gandhi was standing on the deck of a ship taking him to London, as the spokesman and representative of nationalist India to the Second Round Table Conference, he was asked by a newspaper correspondent as to what constitution he would bring back if he could help it. Gandhi's reply is worth reproducing here:

> I shall strive for a Constitution, which will release India from all thraldom and patronage, and give her, if need be, the right to sin. I shall work for an India, in which the poorest shall feel that it is their country in whose making they have an effective voice; an India in which there shall be no high class and low class of people; an India in which all communities shall live in perfect harmony. There can be no room in such an India for the curse of untouchability or the curse of intoxicating drinks and drugs. Women shall enjoy the same rights as men. Since we shall be at peace with all the rest of the world, neither exploiting nor being exploited, we should have the smallest army imaginable. All interests not in conflict with the interests of the dumb millions will be scrupulously respected, whether foreign or indigenous. Personally, I hate distinction between foreign and indigenous. This is the India of my dreams.

It is not an exaggeration to say that not only in the Preamble but in several other parts of the Constitution, there is a perceptible vibration of the Gandhian concept of independent India.

Reading through the Preamble, one can see the purposes that it serves, namely, the declaration of (*i*) the source of the Constitution, (*ii*) a statement of its objectives and (*iii*) the date of its adoption.

The opening words of the Preamble emphasize the ultimate authority of the People from whose will the Constitution emerges. Most of the modern constitutions emphasize the same principle.[1] Since the Constituent Assembly 'enacted and adopted' the constitution in the name of the people of India, the question has been asked whether the Assembly was really representative of the people of India. 'Does the Constitution reflect the will of the people of India?' This question was raised both within and outside the Assembly. Notice of a motion to this effect was given by a member of the Assembly who asked the House to adjourn the discussion on the Draft Constitution altogether and called for a new House on the basis of adult franchise to be elected, claiming that such a House alone should deal with the framing of the Constitution.[2] The motion was, however, rejected by the Assembly as there was no one to support it.

The circumstances under which the Constituent Assembly came into being will show that it was impracticable to constitute such a body in 1946 with adult suffrage as its basis. No part of the country had the experience of adult suffrage. To prepare an electoral roll on that basis would have certainly taken a number of years. It was rightly thought unwise to postpone the task of constitution making until such an election was held. At the same time, the necessity for having a new Constitution made by Indians to suit the conditions and circumstances in the country was keenly felt. This was the main justification for accepting the Cabinet Mission Plan for constituting the Assembly through indirect election.

If the time factor was the main consideration in 1946, one might ask the question : 'What prevented the Constitution being referred to the people through a referendum in 1950 for their approval?' Such a procedure would have established the popular character of

1. The Constitution of U.S.A., Eire and Burma.
2. Maulana Hazrat Mohani, C.A.D. VII, pp. 17, 44 and 211.

the Constitution despite the fact that the Assembly was not elected on a popular basis. Here again, the answer is simple. To conduct a nation-wide referendum involving some 180 million voters was indeed a task which involved elaborate preparation and enormous expense. But the effect of such a referendum was soon provided by the First General Elections of 1951-52 conducted under the new Constitution on the basis of adult suffrage. In that election some of the leading opposition parties had declared that if they were returned to power, they would scrap the present Constitution and write an altogether new one. But the results of the election proved beyond any doubt that the Constituent Assembly, although elected indirectly, was a fully representative body and the Constitution was an instrument of the popular will. For, not only were those parties who opposed the Constitution severely defeated at the polls, but almost every member of the Constituent Assembly who stood for election was returned to the new Parliament of India or a State Legislature with convincing majorities. The talk of scrapping the Constitution has not been heard since then, and today, every all India political party in the country is wedded to the principle of supporting and upholding the Constitution and to working within its four corners if elected to power. No one will seriously challenge today what Ambedkar said on the floor of the Constituent Assembly in 1949.

> I say that this Preamble embodies what is the desire of every member of the House, that this Constitution should have its root, its authority, its sovereignty from the people. That it has.[1]

An amendment moved in the Assembly by H.V. Kamath sought the Preamble to begin with the words, 'In the name of God'.[2] The debate that ensured highlighted the sympathies of many members in favour of the amendment. However, those who opposed it pointed out that it was inappropriate for a Constitution which professed to establish a secular democracy (which will include believers in god as well as non-believers) to begin with such an invocation to God. The amendment was put to vote and declared lost with forty-one in favour and sixty-eight against.

The Preamble proclaims the solemn resolution of the people of India 'to constitute India into a sovereign, democratic republic'. India had already ceased to be a dependency of the British Empire by the passing of the Indian Independence Act, 1947. From 15 August 1947 to 26 January 1950, her political status was that of a Dominion in the British Commonwealth of Nations. But with the inauguration of the present Constitution, India became a 'Sovereign Republic' like the United States of America or the Swiss Republic. However, India is still a member of the Commonwealth of nations. This peculiar position is the result of an agreement reached at the Prime Ministers' Conference in London in April 1949. There, India made a declaration to the effect that notwithstanding her becoming a sovereign independent Republic, she would continue 'her full membership of the Commonwealth of nations and her acceptance of the King (of England) as the symbol of the free association of Commonwealth.' But it is to be noted in this connection that this declaration was extra-legal. There is no mention of it in the Constitution of India. It is a voluntary declaration which indicates a free association with no legal obligation. Its acceptance of the King of England as a symbolic head of the Commonwealth does not create any allegiance of the citizens of India to the King of England. Hence this voluntary association of India with

---

1. CAD X. p. 456.
2. Ibid. p. 439.

the Commonwealth does not affect her sovereignty in any manner, and it would be open to India to cut off that association as easily as it had been declared.[1]

The term 'democratic' is comprehensive in nature. In a narrow political sense it refers only to the form of Government, a representative and responsible system under which those who administer the affairs of the State are chosen by the electorate and accountable to them. But in its broadest sense, it embraces, in addition to political democracy, social and economic democracy as well. It is in this sense that the term 'democratic' is used in the Preamble.

The term 'republic' implies an elected head of the State. A democratic State may have an elected or a hereditary head. Britain is perhaps the best example of the latter type. There, the monarch, a hereditary ruler, is no hindrance to democratic government as the real power of the State is in the hands of the representatives of the electorate. Under a republican form, on the contrary, the head of the State, single or collective, is always elected for a prescribed period. For example, in the United States the head of the State and Chief Executive — the President — is elected for a fixed period of four years. In Switzerland, on the other hand, a collegium of seven members is elected for a period of seven years to constitute the Executive. By deciding to become a republic, India has chosen the system of electing one of its citizens as its President — the head of the Statc — at regular intervals.

The Preamble proceeds further to define the objectives of the Indian republic. These objectives are four in number: Justice, Liberty, Equality and Fraternity. Justice implies a 'harmonious reconcilement of individual conduct with the general welfare of society'. The essence of justice is the attainment of the common good. It embraces, as the Preamble proclaims, the entire social, economic and political spheres of human activity.

The term 'liberty' is used in the Preamble not merely in a negative but also in a positive sense. It signifies not only the absence of any arbitrary restraint on the freedom of individual action but also the creation of conditions which provide the essential ingredients necessary for the fullest development of the personality of the individual. Since society is constituted of individuals, social progress depends on the progress of the individual. Hence it is in the interest of society to ensure the maximum liberty of thought and action of the individual commensurate with social conditions and circumstances.

Liberty and equality are complementary. Equality does not mean that all human beings are equal mentally and physically. It signifies equality of status, the status of free individuals, and equality of opportunity. As the French revolutionaries proclaimed: 'Men are born and remain free and equal in rights. Social distinctions are based only upon public utility'. Equality of opportunity implies the availability of opportunity to every one to develop his or her potential capacities. The declaration of the Rights of Man and Citizen said:

Law is the expression of the public will. It must be same for all, whether it protects or

---

1. Lord Jowitt, the Lord Chancellor, referring to a broadcast on India and the Commonwealth given by B.N. Rau from lake Success during February 1949 had commented in the course of a letter: "It is true that it is the essence of our Commonwealth that all of its members are equal in status. It is, of course, a club from which any member can resign, if he is so minded...." B.N. Rau Ibid. chap. 23 entitled *India and the Commonwealth*.

   On 7 May 1949, the Constituent Assembly adopted a Resolution moved by Prime Minister Nehru ratifying the official statement issued at the conclusion fo the Conference of the Commonwealth Prime Ministers in London on 27 April 1949.

punishes... All citizens, being equal in its eyes, are equally eligible for all public dignities, places and employments according to their capacities and without distinction of their virtues and talents.

The concept of equality that is envisaged in the Preamble, as it embraces both of status and of opportunity, is of the widest in scope.

Finally, the Preamble emphasizes the objective of fraternity in order to ensure both the dignity of the individual and the unity of the nation. The necessity of the spirit of brotherhood among the citizens was first emphasized by the French Revolution which adopted it along with liberty and equality as the foundations of the new order that it aimed to establish. Ever since the French declaration it has become a slogan of universal application. In its Declaration of Human Rights, the United Nations proclaims:

> All human beings are born free and equal in dignity and rights. They are endowed with reason and conscience and should act towards one another in a spirit of brotherhood.

It is this spirit of brotherhood that is emphasized by the use of the term 'fraternity' in the Preamble. In a country like India with many disruptive social forces, communal and caste, sectional and denominational, local and regional, linguistic and cultural, the unity of the nation can be preserved only through a spirit of brotherhood that pervades the entire country, among all its citizens irrespective of their differences. Through the establishment of a new nation based upon justice, liberty and equality, all must feel that they are the children of the same soil, of the same motherland and members of the same fraternity.

The Preamble of the Constitution of India after the Forty-second Amendment of the Constitution in 1976 reads as follows:

"WE, THE PEOPLE OF INDIA having solemnly resolved to constitute India into a SOVEREIGN, SOCIALIST, SECULAR, DEMOCRATIC REPUBLIC and to secure to all its citizens;

JUSTICE, social, economic and political;

LIBERTY of thought, expression, belief, faith and worship;

EQUALITY of status and of opportunity; and to promote among them all;

FRATERNITY assuring the dignity of the individual and the unity and integrity of the nation;

IN OUR CONSTITUENT ASSEMBLY this twenty-sixth day of November 1949 do HEREBY ADOPT, ENACT, AND GIVE TO OURSELVES THIS CONSTITUTION".

The Preamble of the Constitution of India is one of the best of its kind ever drafted. A glance over the preambles of constitutions all the world over will show that both in ideas and ideals and in expression, ours is unrivalled. It embodies the spirit of the Constitution, the determination of the Indian people to unite themselves in a common adventure of building up a new socialist, secular'[1] democratic nation which will ensure the triumph of justice, liberty, equality and fraternity. Commending the beautiful form in which the Preamble is couched, one of the members in the Constituent Assembly rose to poetic heights when he said: 'The Preamble is the most precious part of the Constitution. It is the soul of the Constitution. It is a key to the Constitution.... It is a jewel set in the Constitution. It is a superb prose-poem, nay, it is perfection in itself.[2]

***

1. See Excel Wear *vs.* Union of India (1978) 4 Sec. 224 to understand the effect of introducing the term 'socialist; in the Preamble.
2. Pandit Thakur Das Bhargava, C.A.D.X., p. 682.

7

THE UNION AND ITS TERRITORY

THE FIRST article of the Constitution declares that India is a Union of States. The text of the article, 'India, that is Bharat, shall be a Union of States', was adopted after heated and prolonged discussion in the Constituent Assembly. The controversy mainly centred on the terms 'India' and 'Union of States'. Those who wanted to adopt India as the nation's name pointed out that it was the name by which the country was known all over the world throughout history and it was a great advantage to preserve it as the official name for the future. Those who opposed this view contended that the real and original name of what is known as 'India' was 'Bharat' and, therefore, that alone should be the name to find its place in the Constitution. A compromise was finally arrived at, as a result of which the present text, 'India, that is Bharat', was adopted.[1]

Explaining the significance of the term 'Union of States', Ambedkar said that it implied two things: first, the Indian Federation was not the result of an agreement among the units. Secondly, the component units had no freedom to secede from the Union.[2] Those who opposed the term Union contended that it did not sufficiently emphasize the federal nature of the Constitution. They wanted the adoption of the term 'Federation of States'.

An important feature of the States in the Indian Union, which may be mentioned in this context, is that none of them was a sovereign entity at the time of the formation of the Constitution. The British Indian Provinces, under the Constitution Act of 1935, were at best only autonomous units. The Indian States, until 15 August 1947, were under the paramountcy of the British Crown not only in the field of external affairs but even in respect of internal administration. Perhaps, in a technical sense, they all became sovereign on 15 August 1947, as a result of the Indian Independence Act and the consequent lapse of British paramountcy. But whatever the content of the sovereignty of the Rulers, it was surrendered by them to the Goverment of India during the 1947-50 period on a negotiated basis.

Thus, none of the constituent units of India was sovereign in the sense the thirteen American Colonies after the Declaration of Independence or the Swiss Cantons were before they decided to enter into federal compacts by pooling their sovereignty. Nor was the Constituent Assembly a representative of the units. It derives its power from the sovereign people and, therefore, was entirely unfettered by any previous commitment in evolving a constitutional pattern suitable to the genius and requirements of the Indian people as a

1. C.A.D. VII, pp. 399-404 and IX, pp. 1674-83.
2. The adoption of the term 'Union' was inspired by the example of the Canadian Constitution which, though federal in form, preferred the term Union to Federation.

whole. Thus, the significance of the provision, 'India is a Union of States', is that although it establishes a federal polity, the units have no right to secede from the Union as the federal system is the result of an expression of the will of the people through the Constituent Assembly. Therefore, unlike the United States of America, the Indian Union is not an 'indestructible Union composed of the indestructible States' in that the Union alone is indestructible but the individual States are not.[1]

Under Article 2, the Parliament of India is empowered to admit into the Union, or establish, new States on terms and conditions it thinks fit. Thus, it may form a new State by separation of territory from any State or by uniting two or more States or parts of States or by uniting any territory to a part of any State. In the process, it can increase or decrease the area of any State, or alter the boundaries, or change the name of any State (Art. 3). Although the power of Parliament in this respect is exclusive, the Constitution provides for a procedure which enables the legislatures of the States concerned to express their opinion in the matter. According to this, every Bill contemplating any of the above changes can be introduced in Parliament only on the recommendation of the President and after prior reference by the President to the Legislature of the State concerned for its opinion. The procedure thus helps Parliament to have in view the sentiments of the people of the State concerned before taking a final decision.[2] Any such change made by Parliament and the consequent alterations effected in the Constitution will not amount to an amendment of the Constitution (Art. 4).

Is Parliament competent, under Article 3, to make a law with a view to transferring a part of the territory of the Indian Union to another country? This question came up for detailed examination by the Supreme Court on a reference made to it by the President in 1962. The reference was necessitated by the controversy that arose from a decision of the Government to transfer part of a territory known as Berubari Union (West Bengal) to Pakistan in exchange of Pakistani territory in pursuance of the agreement between the Governments of India and Pakistan in 1958. The Court held that Parliament was not competent to make a law under Article 3 for the implementation of the agreement. The implementation could only be effected by an amendment of the Constitution under Article 368. Subsequently the Constitution (Ninth Amendment) Act, 1960, was passed to give effect to the transfer of the territory concerned.[3] However, in a later case[4] the Court held the view that a mere adjustment of boundaries between India and a foreign state can be effected by an executive act. No legislation is needed for the purpose. The Court laid down this principle in Kutch Award Tribunal case.

At present, the Union of India according to the Constitution is composed of twenty-eight States which are the units of the federal Union and nine territories which are under the direct administration of the Central Government. As such, the political map of India today presents a comparatively simple picture in contrast to what it was in 1947 when India became independent and in 1950 when the present Constitution was inaugurated. But this was mainly the result of the successful execution of a gigantic task of integration and reorganization during the first ten years of independent India. The process was indeed a difficult and even painful one and it cannot yet be said with certainty that the pattern

1. *Report on the Reorganisation of States*, p. 9.
2. Babulal Parate *vs*. The State of Bombay, (1960) S.C.J. 107.
3. Indo-Pakistan Agreement Relating to Berubari Union and Exchange of Enclaves, in re (1960) S.C.J. 933.
4. Maganbhai *vs*. Union of India, A.I.R. 1969 S.C. 583.

which emerged and which exists at present is the final one. An attempt is made here to give a short account of the story of this integration and reorganization.

The Story of Reorganization of States

During the early phase of the rise of the British power in India, the accretion of territories, as we have seen earlier, was gradual and, therefore, the need for the rationalization of administrative units was not seriously felt. British rule in India started with small settlements in the coastal regions established at different times during the seventeenth century. From the middle of the eighteenth century they provided the basis from which British authority expanded inwards by the acquisition of further territories which were attached to one of the three presidencies of Bengal, Madras and Bombay. As more territories were acquired, new provinces were created. Thus, by the end of the nineteenth century, besides the three Presidencies headed by Governors, there were about a dozen Provinces some of which were headed by Lieutenant-Governors and the rest by Chief Commissioners on the basis of their area, population, strategic importance or administrative convenience. The point that needs emphasis here, however, is that the formation of these Provinces did not follow a rational pattern. Naturally, it was a haphazard growth and needed large scale re-adjustments. This was why the Indian Statutory Commission, 1930, observed:

> Although we are well aware of the difficulties encountered in all attempts to alter boundaries, and of the administrative and financial complications that arise, we are making a definite recommendation for reviewing and, if possible, resettling the provincial boundaries of India at as early a date as possible.[1]

Although no major reorganization of Provinces was attempted to implement this recommendation, by 1936 two new Provinces were created, namely, Orissa and Sind. In 1947 when the British left India, the provincial organization remained in the same form in which it was operating under the Constitution Act of 1935 except for the changes that resulted from the partition of the country.

We have already discussed the consequences of the lapse of British paramountcy over the Indian States in August 1947. But even while the Indian Independence Bill was on the Parliamentary anvil, negotiations were started with a number of Indian Rulers with a view to bringing their States into the Indian Union through accession and their example compelled others soon to follow suit. The policy of accession ensured the fundamental unity of the country. India had become one federation, with the Provinces and the States as its integral parts. Further, the Standstill Agreements between the States and the Goverment of India provides the basis for retaining intact the many agreements and administrative arrangements which had been built up over a century for safeguarding all-India interests and which, with the termination of paramountcy, had threatened to disappear and in the process throw the whole country into a state of chaos and confusion.[2]

In his address to the Constituent Assembly on 15 August 1947, Lord Mountbatten referred to the success of the accession policy and paid a tribute to Sardar patel as a far-sighted statesman who played the most important role in bringing about such a satisfactory situation. He said:

---

1. *Report of the Indian Statutory Commission*, vol. II, para 25. The Commission is popularly known as Simon Commission.
2. For a detailed discussion on this question, see V.P. menon, *The Story of the Integration of the Indian States*, Chapter II.

It is a great triumph for the realism and sense of responsibility of the rulers and the Governments of the States as well as the Government of India that it was possible to produce an instrument of accession which was equally acceptable to both sides: and one, moreover, so simple and so straightforward that within less than three weeks practically all the States concerned had signed the Instrument of Accession and the Standstill Agreement. There is thus established a unified political structure.

The period immediately following the transfer of power to India saw a revolutionary change come over the Indian States with dramatic speed. Once the States had acceded to India it was impossible for them to resist such a change, however much they had disliked it. Two strikingly novel devices were made use of to bring about this change, 'integration' and 'merger'. Integration represented the joining of two or more contiguous States in order to form a new viable unit of the Union. By merger was meant the outright disappearance of a State unit by its incorporation into a Province within which it was situated. As a result of this process of integration and merger, the number of State units in the Indian Union was brought down to a very small one from a number which stood around six hundred. Of these, 216 States having a population of a little over 19 million were merged in the Provinces; 61 States having a population of about 7 million were constituted into new centrally administered units; and 275 States with a population of about 35 million were integrated to create five new viable administrative units. Only three of the former States survived this process of integration and merger, namely, Hyderabad, Mysore, and Jammu Kashmir.

Side by side, with the development of integration, there was also the extension of the Authority of the Central Government. Further, under the initiative of the Centre, federal financial integration with the States was also realized. The movement for democratization of the administrative setup in the States had already made considerable progress and in many States or States-unions, fullfledged responsible government had already taken over the reins of administration. Thus, the Provinces and the States became equal partners in the Union. This equality embraced four major areas:[1]

1. The Central Government's performing the same functions and exercising the same powers in the States as in the Provinces.
2. The Central Government's functioning through its own executive organizations in the States as in the Provinces.
3. Uniformity and equality on the basis of contributions to Central resources from the Provinces and the States.
4. Equality of treatment as between Provinces and States in the matter of common services rendered by the Central Government and the sharing of divisible federal taxes, grants-in-aid, subsidies and all other forms of financial and technical assistance.

The States in 1947 were in varying stages of development. In most cases, the advance had to be made from the starting-point of pure autocracy. Having regard to the magnitude of the task which confronted the governments of the States-unions in the transitional period, and to the fact that either the Services inherited by them or the political organizations as they existed there, were in a position to assume, unaided, full responsibilities of the administration, the Central Government made a provision in some of the covenants that

1. See *White Paper on States*, July 1948 and *Report on States Ministry*, March 1949. Also C.A.D.X, PP. 161-96.

till the new Constitution came into operation in these unions the *Rajapramukhs* and the Council of Ministers should in the exercise of their functions be under the general control of the Government of India and comply with the instructions issued by that Government from time to time. This policy of the transitional period was subsequently made applicable to all States and it continued even after the inauguration of the Constitution in 1950 and ended only with the implementation of the provisions of the States Reorganization Act of 1956, and was fully justified by the unsatisfactory manner in which democratic institutions functioned in most of them during the period.

While factors such as linguistic and ethnic homogeneity or historical tradition were taken into consideration to the extent practicable in the process of integration and merger, the compulsion of the dynamic urges of the time necessitated prompt decisions. A number of settlements, therefore, made in respect of these States had to be in the nature of transitional expedients. Hence, it was inevitable that some of the features of the old order had to be incorporated in the Constitution. The result of all these had been the emergence of a peculiar state-system established under the Constitution as it was originally passed in 1949. Under this system, the constituent units of the Union had no uniform status. Instead, they were recognized under three separate categories. Part A, part B and Part C States.

There were ten Part A States which were, generally speaking, the Provinces that constituted the bulk of former British India which formed part of the Indian Union. Some of these had become larger in size, as a result of the merger of some former Indian States in their territory, while others had become smaller owing to the partition of the country. All the Part A States were fullfledged members of the Union and their status was based on the concept of federalism.

There were eight Part B States. These were mostly the products of integration. They too enjoyed a status similar to that of Part A States as members of the federal union. Yet, they were a step below the Part A states in political progress and, as such, were not entitled to enjoy the fullest measure of autonomy as defined by the Constitution. This was embodied in Article 371 of the Constitution,[1] according to which the Government of every Part B State was to be under the general control of and comply with, such particular directions of the Central Goverment. Another distinguishing feature of the Part B States was that they were headed by *Rajapramukhs*[2] and not Governors as in the case of Part A States.

The Part C States, although they were called as such, were not really States in the federal union; for, they were territories directly administered by the Centre on a unitary

Table 1
States under Parts A, B, C and D

	Name of the State	*Area (sq. miles)*	*Population*
PART A	Andhra	63,608	20,801,192
	Assam	85,012	9,043,707

1. This provision of the original Constitution has disappeared as a result of the Seventh Amendment of the Constitution, 1956.
2. *Rajapramukhs* were those former Rulers of Indian States who were recognized as Heads of Part B States.

	Bihar	70,330	40,225,947
	Bombay	111,434	35,956,150
	Madhya Pradesh	130,272	21,247,533
	Madras	60,263	35,736,489
	Orissa	60,136	14,645,946
	Punjab	37,378	12,641,205
	Uttar Pradesh	113,409	63,215,742
	West Bengal	30,775	24,810,308
PART B	Hyderabad	82,168	18,655,108
	Jammu & Kashmir	92,780	4,410,000
	Madhya Bharat	46,478	7,594,254
	Mysore	29,489	9,074,972
	PEPSU*	10,078	3,493,685
	Rajasthan	130,207	15,290,797
	Saurashtra	21,451	4,137,359
	Travancore-Cochin	9,144	9,280,425
PART C	Ajmer	2,417	693,372
	Bilaspur	453	126,099
	Bhopal	8,878	836,474
	Coorg	1,586	229,405
	Delhi	578	1,744,072
	Himachal Pradesh	10,451	983,367
	Kutch	16,742	567,606
	Manipur	8,628	577,635
	Tripura	4,032	639,029
	Vindhya Pradesh	23,603	3,574,690
PART D	The Andaman and Nicobar Islands	3,215	30,791

*Patiala and East Punjab States Union.

Note: The table shows the position at the time of the inauguration of the Constitution, 1950, with the modification that resulted from the coming into being of the State of Andhra in 1953 which was a part of Madras until then.

basis. They were in all ten in number. Some of these were the former Chief Commissioner's Provinces under the British. Although some of them had been allowed from 1952 to have Legislative Assemblies of their own and ministers responsibie to them, the powers of these Assemblies were subject to the direct control of Parliament and the Union Executive was responsible to Parliament for their administration.

Apart from these three categories of States in the Union, there were also territories under Part D which formed part of the country. The only territories under Part D were the islands of the Bay of Bengal — Andaman and Nicobar Islands — which were under the direct and full control of the Central Government. The names of the different States under Part, A, B and C and the territories under Part D, as well as the area and population of each in 1950, at the time of the inauguration of the Constitution, are given in (See Table 1.)

The constitutional provisions establishing the three-tier state-system were the product of expediency. No one was happy with the desperate status of the constituent units of the Union. Naturally, there was a widespread desire to end this unnatural arrangement at the earliest opportunity. Evidence of this could be seen even in the change-over unless there were compelling circumstances to prolong the existing arrangement. But the situation underwent an unexpected change in 1952 when the Central Government took a sudden decision to create a separate State of Andhra out of certain parts of the former undivided Part A State of Madras, on account of the compelling demands of the Telugu-speaking people of Madras State. The State of Andhra came into existence on 1 October 1953. The inauguration of the new State was not, however, an isolated incident. Formation of new States on a linguistic basis and the consequent reorganisation of the entire state-system became almost a militant demand all over the country. Political leadership found it no longer possible to stem the tide of this surging demand. The result was the appointment of the States Reorganization Commission in December 1953 to go into the entire question of reorganization 'objectively and dispassionately' and make its recommendations with a view to settling this tangled problem.

The Commission was headed by a former Justice of the Supreme Court of India, Fazl Ali, and had, in addition, two distinguished public men, H.N. Kunzru and K.M. Panikkar, as members. The task before the Commission was set out in the following terms:

> The Commission will investigate the conditions of the problem, the historical background, the existing situation and the bearing of all important and relevant factors thereon. They will be free to consider any proposal relating to such reorganization. The Government expect the Commission to make recommendations with regard to the broad principles which should govern the solution of this problem.[1]

The Commission took over a year and a half for their work and submitted their report on 30 September 1955.

Although the reorganization of States which ushered in the present pattern was mainly the result of the Commission's Report, mention must be made, in this connection, of the various studies and attempts made in the past regarding this question, both under the auspices of the State and other agencies.

During the British period, territorial changes were governed mainly by imperial interests. The Montagu-Chelmsford Report, 1918, examined a serious suggestion for the formation, within the existing Provinces, of sub-Provinces on a linguistic and racial basis. Although the idea was rejected as impracticable, they commended the objective of smaller and more homogeneous units. Twelve years later, the Indian Statutory Commission, after examining the question in detail, could give only partial support to the principle of linguistic and racial redistribution of Provinces. The Joint Committee on Indian Constitutional Reforms, 1933-34, however, in recommending the formation of a new Sind Province gave greater measure of support to the principle.

The Indian National Congress lent indirect support to the linguistic principles as early as in 1905 when it backed the demand for ending the partition of Bengal. The Congress gave its direct and pronounced support to the idea by forming Congress Provinces all over

1. Resolution of the Government of India in the Ministry of Home Affairs, no. 53 of 29 December 1953, para 7.

India for the All Parties Conference of 1928 which lent its powerful support to the linguistic principle. Thereafter, it became almost an annual affair of the All India Congress meetings to reaffirm the principle.[1]

There was, however, a slight change in the Congress attitude by the time the Constituent Assembly seriously started its work. Speaking in the Assembly (Legislative) in 1947, soon after the Partition, Prime Minister Nehru, while conceding the linguistic principle, remarked that 'first things must come first and the first thing is the security and stability of India'. Nevertheless, on the recommendation of the Drafting Committee, the Dar Commission was appointed to enquire into and report on the desirability or otherwise of the linguistic redistribution of some of the Provinces. The Dar Commission not only expressed itself strongly against any reorganization at the time but also held that the formation of Provinces on a linguistic basis was inadvisable. Its emphasis was primarily on administrative convenience. Among many other factors which should be given due weight, the Commission mentioned history, geography, economy and culture.[2] The Dar Commission Report was soon followed by the report of a committee composed of Jawaharlal Nehru, Vallabhbhai Patel and Pattabhi Sitaramayya appointed by the Jaipur Session of the Congress in 1948. The Report sounded a note of warning against the linguistic principle, the first of its kind from an official Congress body. It emphasized that the primary consideration must be security, unity and the economic prosperity of India and every separatist and disruptive tendency should rigorously be discouraged. The Committee admitted, however, that if public sentiment was insistent and overwhelming, the practicability of satisfying public demand with its implications and consequences must be examined. The J.V.P. Committee Report was adopted by the Congress Working Committee in 1949. Since then, the Congress has been broadly adhering to the views expressed in the report.[3]

The linguistic redistribution of States also figured prominently in the resolutions and election manifestoes of other Indian political parties. The Socialist Party declared that it was in favour of the redistribution of States on a linguistic basis consistent with geographic contiguity and economic viability. The Communist Party stood for national States on a linguistic basis enjoying wide powers including the right of self-determination. The Hindu Mahasabha believed in the policy of the formation of Provinces on a linguistic basis but was of the opinion that due regard should be given to the problem of defence and to other factors like area and economic stability.

With so many studies, reports, resolutions and opinions at its disposal, the S.R.C. had a comparatively easy task although the problem was in itself overwhelmingly complex. After considering fully all the aspects of the problem, the Commission arrived at four major principles which were to be given the highest importance in any scheme of reorganization of States. These are:

(a) Preservation and strengthening of the unity and security of India;

(b) Linguistic and cultural homogeneity;

(c) Financial, economic and administrative considerations; and

1. See, *e.g.*, the resolutions of the Calcutta Session, 1937, the Wardha Resolution of July 1938 and the Election Manifesto of 1945-46.
2. *Report of the Linguistic Provinces Commission*, para 131.
3. See, *e.g.*, the Election Manifesto of the Congress in 1951 and the resolutions passed by it since 1949.

(d) Successful working of the national development plans.

In addition to these major principles, the Commission thought that there were others which ought to be given due weight although they came only next to these in importance. Among these were a common historical tradition which fosters a sense of kinship and oneness, geographical contiguity, administrative considerations and the wishes of the people to the extent that they were objectively ascertainable and which did not come into conflict with larger national interests. Despite the enunciation and enumeration of these principles, the Commission recognized that the problems of reorganization varied from region to region.

> It has to be kept in mind that the interplay for centuries of historical, linguistic, geographical, economic and other factors has produced peculiar patterns in different regions. Each case, therefore, has its own background. Besides, the problems of reorganization are so complex that it would be unrealistic to determine any case by a single test alone. All the committees and commissions which have previously gone into the matter such as the Dar Commission and the J.V.P. Committee have rightly expressed themselves against a monistic approach to the problem. We have, accordingly, examined each case on its own merits and its own context and arrived at conclusions after taking into consideration the totality of circumstances and on an overall assessment of the solutions proposed.[1]

In making their recommendations, the Commission dealt with not only territorial readjustments but also other matters such as financial implications, administrative changes, integration of services, *etc*. Taking these as a whole, the following recommendations deserve special mention:

1. Abolition of the classification of States into three categories, Parts A, B and C, which was essentially a temporary expedient and the constitution of States enjoying a uniform status.
2. Abolition of the special agreements entered into with the Union in consequence of the financial integration of Part B States. Also, abolition of the general control vested in the Government of India by Article 371 as well as the abolition of the institution of *Rajapramukhs*.
3. Since there was no adequate recompense for all the financial, administrative and constitutional difficulties which the Part C States presented, they, with the exception of three (Delhi, the federal capital, Manipur and the Andaman and Nicobar Islands, to be centrally administered), should be merged with the adjoining States.
4. On the basis of these changes, there should be 16 States and 3 centrally administered territories as shown in Table 2.

In addition to these major recommendations, the Commission had also recommended a number of consequential measures to be adopted in order to see that the reorganization did not create unduly severe hardships for those who were adversely affected by these changes. Among these were a number of recommendations dealing with safeguards for linguistic minorities, integration of services, division of assets and liabilities, legislation regarding river valleys and water disputes, regional grievances, special development boards, the constitution of a body to look into the economic grievances of areas and industrial location plans.

---

1. *S.R.C. Report*, para 235.

The publication of the S.R.C. Report precipitated disturbances in many parts of the country. Where wholesale changes in the existing system were recommended, it was only natural that many interests should be adversely affected. Further, where sentiments could be aroused and tempers frayed on account of these, the results could never be happy. And where people imagined that political pressure and agitation could possibly dictate the course of action on the part of those who were in power anything could happen. This was what happened after the publication of the Report. No one could claim that the recommendations of the Commission were flawless. For one thing, despite all the major principles to which the commission gave due weight in the scheme of reorganization, the pattern that emerged from their recommendations consisted of practically unilingual States only. But that was perhaps inevitable in the context of prevailing conditions and circumstances in the country.

Table 2
States and Territories

States	*Area (in sq. miles approximately)*	*Population (in millions, approximately)*
Madras	50,170	30.0
Kerala	14,980	13.6
Karnataka	72,730	19.0
Hyderabad	45,300	11.3
Andhra	64,950	20.9
Bombay	151,360	40.2
Vidarbha	36,880	7.6
Madhya Pradesh	171,200	26.1
Rajasthan	132,300	16.0
Punjab	58,140	17.2
Uttar Pradesh	113,410	63.2
Bihar	66,520	38.5
West Bengal	34,590	26.5
Assam	89,040	9.7
Orissa	60,140	14.6
Jammu and Kashmir	92,780	4.4
	Territories	
Delhi	578	1.7
Manipur	8,628	0.6
The Andaman and Nicobar Islands	3,215	0.03

Note: The table represents the recommendations of the States Reorganization Commission, 1956, with regard to reorganization.

The Goverment failed to handle with efficiency and expedition the situation that developed. There were indications of vacillation and uncertainty as to what should be done. There was failure to give a lead to the country on this vexed question. The Report was finally placed before Parliament which discussed it at length. Even during these debates there was failure to give the necessary lead. After prolonged discussion in Parliament and the State Legislatures, and after protracted negotiations between the Union Cabinet and the interested parties, the Government announced its decision which was embodied in a Bill called the States Reorganization Bill. The Constitution also needed amendment at many places as a result of the proposed reorganization. Both the amendment of the Constitution[1] and the Reorganization Bill were passed in 1956 and were implemented on 1 November 1956.

The provisions of both the Amendment and the Act were based upon the recommendations of the S.R.C. except in a few instances. The most important of these were the decisions with respect to the formation of the Bombay State and the immediate creation of a united Telugu-speaking State of Andhra Pradesh. The number of the centrally administered areas also was increased from the recommended three to six. The following table will show the reorganized States as they emerged from the States Reorganization Act, 1956 (See Table 3).

As may be seen from the table, the Union of India consisted of fourteen States and six centrally administered territories.

That position, however, did not last long. The pattern underwent a further change in 1960 on account of intense and persistent popular demand. Bombay was divided on linguistic basis to form two new States, a Marathi-speaking State of Maharashtra and a Gujarati-speaking State of Gujarat.

In 1961 yet another new State was created when, under the Nagaland (Territorial Provisions) Regulations promulgated by the President, the areas comprised of Naga Hills and Tuensang Area assumed the name of Nagaland and was given the status of the sixteenth state of the Indian Union.

Table 3
Rorganised States

Name of State	*Area in Sq. miles*	*Population*	*Capital*	*Principal language*
1. Andhra Pradesh	105,963	31,260,333	Hyderabad	Telugu
2. Assam	50,043	9,043,707	Shillong	Assamese
3. Bihar	67,164	38,784,172	Patna	Hindi
4. Bombay	190,919	48,265,221	Bombay	Marathi and Gujarati
5. Jammu and Kashmir	85,861	4,021,615	Srinagar	Kashmiri and Urdu
6. Kerala	15,035	13,549,118	Trivandrum	Malayalam
7. Madhya Pradesh	171,201	26,071,637	Bhopal	Hindi

1. The Seventh Amendment of the Constitution (1956).

8. Madras	50,110	29,974,936	Madras	Tamil
9. Mysore	74,326	19,401,193	Bangalore	Kannada
10. Orissa	60,136	14,645,946	Bhuvaneswar	Oriya
11. Punjab	47,456	16,134,890	Chandigarh	Punjabi and Hindi
12. Rajasthan	132,077	15,970,774	Jaipur	Rajasthani and Hindi
13. Uttar Pradesh	113,409	63,215,742	Lucknow	Hindi
14. West Bengal	34,945	26,310,992	Calcutta	Bengali
Centrally Administered Territories				
1. Delhi	578	1,744,072	Delhi (union Capital)	Hindi, Urdu, Punjabi
2. Himachal Pradesh	10,904	1,109,466	Simla	Hindi and Pahari
3. Manipur	8,628	577,635	Imphal	Manipuri
4. Tripura	4,032	639,029	Agartala	Bengali and Tripuri
5. Andaman and Nicobar Islands	3,215	30,971	Port Blair	Bengali
6. Laccadive, Minicoy and Amindivi Islands	10	21,035	Kozhikode	Malayalam

Note: The table shows the position immediately after the reorganization of States, 1956.

During the next ten years five more new States were created. The first of these was Haryana by reorganizing Pubjab to form two States, Punjab and Haryana, in 1966. In 1970 Himachal Pradesh which had been a Union Territory until then, was made a fullfledged State. Manipur and Tripura, both Union Territories, were given the status of States in 1971. In the same year yet another State was created to make the total twenty-one. The new State was Meghalaya which comprised the territories specified in the North-Eastern Areas (Reorganization) Act, 1971. These territories were part of the State of Assam until then.

In 1975 Sikkim acceded to India and was given the status of a state, thus raising the total number of States to twenty-two.

The number of Union Territories also has registered an increase since 1956. In August 1961 Dadra and Nagar Haveli were integrated with the Union of India at the request of the Varishta Panchayat and the people of Free Dadra and Nagar Haveli. Similarly, Goa, Daman and Diu were also united with India in December 1961 and thus the remnants of Portuguese colonialism, which was the last to disappear, were brought to an end. Pondicherry, a former French colony, became a Union Territory in 1962 along with other French establishments in India. In 1966 as a part of the reorganization of Punjab which resulted in the emergence of Haryana, Chandigarh was made a Union Territory. Two more Union Territories were created a few years later (1971). They are Mizoram and Arunachal Pradesh both in the north-eastern part of the country. Both of them became fullfledged States soon. Goa was the last to join the rest thus making the total twenty-five.

In the year 2000 three more new States were created namely, Jharkhand, Uttaranchal and Chhatisgarh making the total twenty-eight. Eighteen districts of South Bihar were brought together to form the new State of Jharkhand. Thirteen districts of Uttar Pradesh in the north western part of the State formed the new State of Uttaranchal and sixteen districts of Madhya Pradesh in the south-east part of the State were put together to form the new State of Chhatisgarh.

Before the reorganisation of States in 1956, Madhya Pradesh was the largest among the States with an area of 130, 272 square miles, as large in size as two-thirds of France. But as a result of reorganization, Bombay became first with an area of 190,668 square miles, almost as large as France. But with the division of Bombay into Maharashtra and Gujarat, Madhya Pradesh once again became the largest State in India. The creation of Chhatisgarh as a separate State, however, reduced the size of Madhya Pradesh considerably and made it smaller in size than Rajasthan. Hence Rajasthan has become the largest State in India. Sikkism remains the smallest state.

From population point of view Uttar Pradesh comes first with more than 130 million people which is more than the population of Federal Republic of Germany and France put together. Sikkim has the smallest population, approximately a little more than 400,000. But if density of population is taken into consideration, West Bengal comes first with about 775 people per square kilometre, perhaps the most densely populated State in the world.

Table 4
States of India (2000)

Sl. No.	*Name of State*	*Area sq. km.*	*Population (1991)*	*Capital*	*Principal language*
1.	Andhra Pradesh	2,75,068	66,304,854	Hyderabad	Telugu
2.	Arunachal Pradesh	83,743	858,392	Itanagar	Bengali, English
3.	Assam	78,400	22,294,562	Guwahati	Assamese
4.	Bihar	94,163	64,686,853	Patna	Hindi
5.	Chhatisgarh	1,35,100	17,610,000	Raipur	Hindi
6.	Gujarat	1,96,024	41,174,060	Gandhinagar	Gujarati
7.	Goa	3,814	1,168,622	Panaji	Konkani
8.	Haryana	44,212	16,317,715	Chandigarh	Hindi
9.	Himachal Pradesh	55,673	5,111,079	Simla	Hindi
10.	Jammu & Kashmir	2,22,236	7,718,700	Srinagar	Kashmiri, Urdu
11.	Jharkand	79,714	21,840,000	Ranchi	Hindi
12.	Karnataka	1,91,791	44,817,398	Bangalore	Kannada
13.	Kerala	38,863	29,011,237	Thiruvana-nthapuram	Malayalam
14.	Madhya Pradesh	3,08,346	48,525,862	Bhopal	Hindi
15.	Mizoram	21,081	686,217	Aizwal	Mizo, English

16. Maharashtra	3,07,690	78,706,719	Mumbai	Marathi
17. Manipur	22,327	1,826,714	Imphal	Manipuri
18. Meghalaya	22,429	1,760,626	Shillong	English
19. Nagaland	16,579	1,215,573	Kohima	English
20. Orissa	1,55,707	31,512,070	Bhubaneswar	Oriya
21. Punjab	50,362	20,190,795	Chandigarh	Punjabi
22. Rajasthan	3,42,239	43,880,640	Jaipur	Hindi
23. Sikkim	7,096	403,612	Gangtok	Hindi, Nepali
24. Tamil Nadu	1,30,058	55,638,318	Chennai	Tamil
25. Tripura	10,486	2,744,827	Agarthala	Bengali
26. Uttaranchal	55,845	7,040,000	Dehradun	Hindi
27. Uttar Pradesh	2,38,566	131,720,417	Lucknow	Hindi
28. West Bengal	88,752	67,982,732	Kolkata	Bengali

UNION TERRITORIES

1. Andaman & Nicobar Islands	8,249	277,989	Port Blair	Bengali
2. Chandigarh	114	140,725	Chandigarh	Hindi & Punjabi
3. Dadra-Nagar Haveli	491	138,542	N. Haveli	Gujarati
4. Delhi	1,483	9,370,475	New Delhi	Hindi
5. Lakshadweep	32	51,681	Kavarati	Malayalam
6. Pondicherry	492	789,426	Pondicherry	Tamil
7. Daman & Diu		101,439	Daman	Guajarati

A comparison between a country like India and a continent like Europe makes an interesting study from many points of view, such as area, population, language and races. India is two-thirds of the whole of Europe in size. But population of India is more than double that of Europe. From a linguistic point of view, while Europe has a score of main languages, India too has a linguistic diversity which is not less pronounced. From a racial point of view, the people of India present a greater diversity than what the whole of Europe presents. But while India is today a single political entity with a population of over a thousand million, Eurpoe has over a score of sovereign States. How difficult a problem would it be if an attempt is made to weld together Europe minus Russia into a single political entity? The efforts to form a Western European Federation are yet to find fruition. It is well to remember these facts while dealing with the problems of India, a sub-continent which presents both immensity in size and perplexing diversity.

***

8

CITIZENSHIP

THE CONSTITUENT Assembly took more than two years to arrive at a final decision with respect to the provisions dealing with citizenship. This was mainly due to some special problems created by the partition of India as well as the presence of a large number of Indians abroad. Between 1947 and 1949, millions of people had crossed and re-crossed the frontiers that separate India from Pakistan, in order to make final choice of their nationality. On the one hand, Hindus and Sikhs, who were born and domiciled in that part of India which became Pakistan and who migrated to India, had to be given the citizenship of new India; on the other, Muslims who left India to become citizens of Pakistan had to be excluded. There was also the case of persons of Indian origin living abroad, in many countries and for many years, and who might now prefer to reside in India permanently as she had become a free nation. Several drafts were prepared and set aside by the Drafting Committee in its effort to cover all the cases which it was thought necessary and desirable to cover. Even so, the final draft that it placed before the Assembly had to face a veritable barrage of amendments, as many as 140, thereby indicating how difficult it was to reach a solution of this complicated problem.[1] The provisions as finally passed are covered by Articles 5 to 11 and are embodied in Part II of the Constitution.

Article 5 refers to citizenship not in any general sense but to citizenship on the date of the commencement of the Constitution. It is not the object of this article to lay down a permanent law of citizenship for the country. That business is left to the Parliament of India. Accordingly, at the commencement of the Constitution, every person who had his domicile in the territory of India and (*a*) who was born in India, or (*b*) either of whose parents was born in India, or (*c*) who had been ordinarily resident in India for not less than five years immediately preceding the commencement of the Constitution, was to be considered a citizen of India. Persons of Indian orgin who had been residing outside India at the commencement of the Constitution were given the free choice of becoming Indian citizens under the above provisions if they so desired. The only condition that they had to fulfil in this connection was to get themselves registered as Indian citizens by the diplomatic or consular representative of India in the country where they were residing (Art. 8).

Articles 6 and 7 deal with two categories of persons, namely, those who were residents in India but had migrated to Pakistan and those who were residents of Pakistan but had migrated to India. Those who migrated from Pakistan to India were divided into two categories, (*a*) those who came before 19 July 1948, and (*b*) those who came after that date. According to Article 6, those who came before 19 July would automatically become citizens on the

1. C.A.D. IX, pp. 343-448.

commencement of the Constitution, provided they had been registered in the form and manner prescribed for this purpose by the Government of India[1]. These two articles thus provided for all cases of mass migration from Pakistan to India without making any distinction between one community and another, although the partition of the country itself was based upon such a distinction.

Article 7 provided for those who had migrated to Pakistan[2] but who had returned to India from Pakistan with the intention of permanently residing in India. Such a provision had to be made because the Government of India, in dealing with persons who left India for Pakistan and who subsequently returned from Pakistan to India, allowed them to come and settle permanently under what is called a 'permit system'. This permit system was introduced from 19 July 1948. Under this system, every person who desired to return to India and permanently reside in India was required to get a separate permit. Thus, Article 7 of the Constitution clearly overrides Article 5. It is peremptory in its scope and makes no exemption for even such a case as the wife of a citizen of India migrating to Pakistan leaving her husband in India and later returning to India claiming Indian citizenship.[3]

It is clear from the nature of these provisions that their object was not to place before the Constituent Assembly anything like a code of nationality laws. In fact, there is hardly any constitution in which attempt has been made to embody a detailed nationality law. But since India's constitution is of a republican character and provision is made throughout the Constitution for election to various offices under the State by and from among the citizens, it was thought essential to have some provisions which precisely determined who was an Indian citizen at the commencement of the Constitution. Otherwise, there could have arisen difficulties in connection with the holding of particular offices and even with the starting of representative institutions in the country under the republican Constitution. This is why the Parliament of India has been given plenary power to deal with the question of nationality and enact any law in this connection that it deems suited to the conditions of the country. Such parliamentary power embraces not only the question of acquisition of citizenship but also its termination as well as any other matter relating to citizenship (Art. 11). Also, under Article 9 of the Constitution, any person who voluntarily acquires the citizenship of any foreign state, even if qualified for Indian citizenship under any provision of the Constitution, may not be a citizen of India.[4]

The Citizenship Act, 1955

A comprehensive law dealing with citizenship was passed by Parliament in 1955 in accordance with the powers vested in it by Article 11 of the Constitution. The provisions of the Act may be broadly divided into three parts, acquisition of citizenship, termination of citizenship and supplemental provisions. The Act provides five modes of acquiring the citizenship of India. These are:

1. *By Birth*. Every person born in India, on or after 26 January 1950, shall be a citizen of India by birth. There are two exceptions, however, to this rule, namely, children born to

---

1. Shanno Devi *vs.* Mangal Sain, 1961 S.C.J. 201.
2. The State of Andhra Pradesh *vs.* Abdul Khader, (1962) I S.C.J. 100. See also the State of Assam *vs.* Jilkader (1974) 1 S.C.J. 201 and State of Gujarat *vs.* Yakub Ibrahim A.I.R. (1974) Sec. 645.
3. The State of Bihar *vs.* Kumar Rani Sayedda Khatoon, 1955, S.C.J. 311.
4. For a discussion on problems relating to citizenship in India, see S.P. Sathe, *Citizenship in India—Some Problems regarding the determination of* (1962) I S.C.J. p. 67.

foreign diplomatic personnel in India and those of enemy aliens whose birth occurs in a place then under occupation by the enemy.

2. *By Descent.* A person born outside India on or after 26 January 1950 shall be a citizen of India by descent if his father is a citizen of India at the time of his birth. Children of those who are citizens of India by descent, as also children of non-citizens who are in service under a government of India, may also take advantage of this provision and become Indian citizens by descent, if they so desire, through registration.

3. *By Registration.* Any person who is not already an Indian citizen by virtue of the provisions of the Constitution or those of this Act can acquire citizenship by registration if that person belongs to any one of the following five categories:

(a) Persons of Indian origin who are ordinarily resident in India and who have been so resident for at least six months immediately before making an application for registration;

(b) Persons of Indian origin who are ordinarily resident in any country or place outside undivided India;

(c) Women who are, or have been, married to citizens of India;

(d) Minor children of persons who are citizens of India; and

(e) Persons of full age and capacity who are citizens of the Commonwealth countries or the Republic of Ireland.

4. *By Naturalization.* Any person who does not come under any of the categories mentioned above can acquire Indian citizenship by naturalization if his application for it has been acceded to by the Government of India and a certificate is granted to him to that effect. An applicant for a naturalization certificate has to satisfy the following conditions:

(a) He is not a citizen of a country which prohibits Indians becoming citizens of that country by naturalization;

(b) He has renounced the citizenship of the country to which he belonged;

(c) He has either resided in India or has been in the service of a government in India, normally, for one year immediately prior to the date of application;

(d) During the seven years preceding the above-mentioned one year, he has resided in India or been in the service of a government in India for periods amounting in the aggregate to not less than four years;

(e) He is of good character;

(f) He has an adequate knowledge of a language specified in the Constitution;

(g) If granted a certificate, he intends to reside in India or enter into, or continue in, service under a Government in India.

The Act provides, however, for a conspicuous exemption under which any or all of the above conditions may be waived in favour of a person who has rendered distinguished service to the cause of science, philosophy, art, literature, world peace or human progress generally. Every person to whom a certificate of naturalization is granted has to take an oath of allegiance solemnly affirming that he will bear true faith and allegiance to the Constitution of India as by law established, and that he will faithfully observe the law of India and fulfil his duties as a citizen of India.

5. *By Incorporation of Territory.* If any territory becomes part of India, the Government of India, by order, may specify the persons who shall be citizens of India by reason of their connection with that territory.

Losing of Citizenship

The Act envisages three situations under which a citizen of India may lose his Indian nationality. These are:

1. *By Renunciation.* If any citizen of India who is also a national of another country renounces his Indian citizenship through a declaration in the prescribed manner, he ceases to be an Indian citizen on registration of such declaration. When a male person ceases to be a citizen of India, every minor child of his also ceases to be a citizen of India. However, such a child may within one year after attaining full age, become an Indian citizen by making a declaration of his intention to resume Indian citizenship.

2. *By Termination.* Any person who acquired Indian citizenship by naturalization, registration or otherwise, if he or she voluntarily acquired the citizenship of another country at any time between 26 January 1950, the date of commencement of the Constitution, and 30 December 1955, the date of commencement of this Act, shall have ceased to be a citizen of India from the date of such acquisition.

3. *By Deprivation.* The Central Government is empowered to deprive a citizen of his citizenship by issuing an order under Section 10 of the Act. But this power of the Government may not be used in case of every citizen, as it applies only to those who acquired Indian citizenship by naturalization or by virtue only of Clause (*c*) of Article 5 of the Constitution[1] or by registration.[2] The possible ground of such deprivation are: the obtaining of a citizenship certificate by means of fraud, false representation, concealment of any material fact; disloyalty or disaffection towards the Constitution shown by act or speech; assisting an enemy with whom India is at war; sentence to imprisonment in any country for a term of not less than two years within the first five years after the acquisition of Indian citizenship and continuous residence outside India for a period of seven years without expressing in a prescribed manner his intention to retain his Indian citizenship. The Act also provides for reasonable safeguards in order to see that a proper procedure is followed in every case of deprivation of citizenship.

Can a Company be a Citizen of India?

This question was considered by the Supreme Court in the State Trading Corporation of India *vs.* Commercial Tax Officer.[3] When the company was sought to be taxed in respect of sales effected by it, the company contended that its transactions related to inter-state sales which are exempted from tax by Article 286(1)(*a*). The tax sought to be imposed had, therefore, constituted an infringement of their fundamental rights under Article 19(1)(*g*). Since Article 19 could be invoked only by citizens the question arose whether a company could be a citizen of India. The case was heard by a Special Bench of 9 judges which held by a majority of 7 to 2 that a company is not a citizen of India and cannot, therefore, claim such

1. Any person who has been ordinarily resident in the territory of India for not less than five years immediately preceding the commencement of the Constitution.
2. Section 10(1) of the Act.
3. A.I.R. 1963 S.C. 1811.

of the fundamental rights as have been conferred on citizens. Part II of the Constitution dealing with citizenship is concerned only with natural persons. The Citizenship Act, 1955, expressly excludes, a Company from the scope of the Act. In Tata Engineering and Locomotive Co. *vs.* State of Bihar[1] an interesting argument was advanced before the Supreme Court. It was contended that if all shareholders of the Company are citizens, the veil of the corporate or legal personality of the company might be lifted and thus the fundamental rights of the citizens — members of the company — might be protected. Rejecting this argument the Supreme Court held that if this plea was accepted, it would mean that what a company could not get directly could be achieved by it indirectly by relying upon the doctrine of lifting the veil.[2]

Commonwealth Citizenship

India's Commonwealth tie is reflected in the Citizenship Act by providing for the status of a Commonwealth citizen. According to this, every person who is a citizen of a Commonwealth country, by virtue of that citizenship, has been given the status of a Commonwealth citizen in India. Further, the Central Government is empowered to make provisions on a basis of reciprocity for the conferment of any of the rights of a citizen of India on the citizens of Commonwealth countries. During the discussion on the Citizenship Bill in Parliament, it was stressed on behalf of the Government that the privileges extended to Commonwealth citizens would be available only to the citizens of those Commonwealth countries which extended to Indians, the same privileges. A striking suggestion made in the course of the debate was that there could be a common citizenship for the countries subscribing to the doctrine of *Pancha Shila*[3] While the idealism behind the suggestion was fully recognized by all, it was felt that it could not be entertained as a serious practical proposition for immediate realization.

The Citizenship Act, on the whole, is one of the most liberal enactments of its kind anywhere. Not only does it provide for the acquisition of Indian citizenship in a comparatively simple and easy manner, but it even recognizes dual nationality under certain circumstances. The attacks on the provisions dealing with Commonwealth citizenship and the criticism that Indian citizenship has been made very cheap do not stand serious examination in the light of India's relationship with the Commonwealth, and the modern conditions and circumstances which facilitate social mobility on an international basis.[4] Of a different sort was the criticism, made both in Parliament and outside, on the provisions dealing with the deprivation of citizenship. Under the Act, a committee of three appointed by the Goverment will sit in judgment over such cases. Critics of the measure were of the opinion that every case of deprivation of citizenship ought to have been made justiciable.

Single Citizenship

The most important aspect of the constitutional provisions dealing with citizenship is that it has established a uniform or single system of citizenship law for the whole country.

1. (1964) I S.C.J. 666.
2. See also Barium Chemicals Ltd. *vs.* Company Law Board, A.I.R. 1967 S.C. 29.
3. The five principles of co-existence. With the Chinese aggression of India's territory in 1962, *Pancha Shila*, whatever might be its inherent worth, has lost its original appeal.
4. The Commonwealth citizenship has lost its original importance as Indian citizens do not get any free entry in most of the Commonwealth countries.

A citizen of India is accepted legally as citizen in almost every part of the territory of India with almost all the benefits and privileges that attend such a status. This is in striking contrast to the system of double citizenship that prevails in some federal states.[1] Before the inauguration of the Constitution, there were two broad divisions among Indian citizens. British Indian subjects and State subjects. Since there were over 500 Indian States, the State subjects themselves were further subdivided into as many groups of citizens as there were States. Thus, the term Indian citizenship had little precise legal significance except that the Indian people as a whole came under the overall jurisdiction of the British Government that ruled India. The abolition of such distinctions makes the essential unity of the nation a reality. A single citizenship for the entire country removes much of the artificial State barriers that prevailed in pre-Independence days and facilitates the freedom of trade, commerce and intercourse throughout the territory of India.

There is, however, one barrier that still hinders the full realization of the ideal of a single citizenship established under the Constitution. This is the existence of what are known as 'domiciliary rules' in the different States in India. The term 'domicile' is difficult to define.[2] According to the rules prevailing today in the different States in India, domicile requirements vary from three to fifteen years' continuous residence within the State in addition to other conditions. Thus, the status of domicile is given only to a permanent resident of the State. On the basis of such a distinction, there exist practices in different States which amount to gross discrimination as between citizen and citizen. They also engender provincialism and parochialism which tend to disrupt the unity of the nation. Domiciliary rules which govern eligibility to public services in most of the States illustrate this point. Such rules are applied in some States not only to determine eligibility for appointment to public services but also to regulate the awards of contracts and rights in respect of fisheries, ferries, toll-bridges, forests and excise shops. The conditions to be satisfied for acquiring a domicile in some of the States are of such an extremely rigorous nature that it is almost impossible for any person to satisfy them.

It is unnecessary to emphasize that such stipulations are not only inconsistent with the Fundamental Rights of equality before law, equal protection of laws, equality of opportunity in matters of public employment and freedom to practise any profession or carry on any occupation, trade or business, but strike at the very root of the conception of an Indian citizenship.[3] Until and unless the artificial restrictions arising out of the still existing domiciliary laws are removed and the citizens of India can feel confident that their rights as citizens are respected and accepted in practice wherever they go within the territory of India, the intention with which the Constituent Assembly passed part II of the Constitution, and Parliament enacted the citizenship law, will remain only half-fulfilled. The remedy is the passing of appropriate parliamentary legislation as contemplated under Article 35 of the Constitution and the strict enforcement thereof. Parliament has already attended to this in so far as it concerns opportunities of public employment. The judiciary has, in one of the States, already declared the domiciliary rule unconstitutional.

---

1. For example, in the United States of America, a citizen of the United States is also a citizen of one of the States.
2. According to an English Judge, "that place is properly the domicile of a person in which his habitation is fixed without any present intention of removing therefrom.' See in this connection Central Bank of India Ltd. *vs.* Ram Narain, 1955, S.C., p. 4.
3. The States Reorganization Commission had discussed this question at considerable length. (See Part VI of the Report).

A Full Bench of the Bombay High Court in a case,[1] has declared the unconstitutionality of such laws. According to the unanimous decision of the Court, any issue of a certificate of local 'domicile' hereafter by the Presidency Magistrates' Establishment (Bombay) will be illegal. The learned judges declared:

> It is a total misapprehension of the position in law in our country to talk of a person being domiciled in a Province or in a State. A person can only be domiciled in India as a whole. That is the only country that can be considered in the context of the expression 'Domicile' and the only system of law by which a person is governed in India is the system of law which prevails in any Province or State. Therefore, in India a person has one citizenship of India. He has one domicile, the domicile in India and one legal system, the system that prevails in the whole country. The expression 'domicile' used in any State or Provincial law is, therefore, a misnomer and it does not carry with it the implications that expression has when used in the context of International law. It has no more importance or significance than the expression 'permanently resident'.

The question of domicile had not come before the Supreme Court until 1984 when the Court held that to have domicile, there shall be intention on the part of the person who seeks it. The concept of domicile is used in relation to the Union and not with reference to the States.[2] The Court warned against the use of the word in a loose sense as it is dangerous to the unity and integrity of the nation. It requires the State governments to do away with the wrong expression and also they should desist from incorporating domicile as a condition precedent for admission to institutions.[3]

***

1. The State *vs* N.M. Dayme, 1958 A.I.R., Bom. 68.
2. Louis De Racdt *vs.* Union of India, AIR 1991 SC 1886.
3. Pradeep Jain *vs.* Union of India, AIR 1984 SC 1420.

PART IV

FUNDAMENTAL RIGHTS AND DIRECTIVE PRINCIPLES

9

FUNDAMENTAL RIGHTS : GENERAL NATURE

THE CONFLICT between man and the State is as old as human history. Despite centuries-old attempts at a proper adjustment between the competing claims of the State and the individual, the solution seems to be still far off. This is primarily because of the dynamic nature of human society where old values, ideas and forces constantly yield place to new ones. It is obvious that if individuals are allowed to have unqualified freedom of speech and action, the result would be chaos, ruin and anarchy. On the other hand, if the State personifies absolute power to delimit personal liberty, the result would be tyranny. Hence, the eternal problem that faced statesmen and constitutionalists was how to make a fitting adjustment between individual independence and social control[1], the need for protecting personal liberty against governmental power and that of limiting personal liberty by governmental power.

This problem assumes extreme difficulty only under a democratic system of government. For, the success or failure of a democracy depends largely on the extent to which civil liberties are enjoyed by the citizens in general. A democracy aims at the maximum development of the individual's personality; and the personality of the individual is inseparably bound with his liberty. Only a free society can ensure the all-round progress of its members which ultimately helps the advancement of human welfare. Therefore, every democracy pays special attention to securing this bare objective to the maximum extent without, at the same time, endangering the security of the State itself. A common device that is adopted by most of them for this purpose is to incorporate a list of fundamental rights in their constitutions and guarantee them against violation by executive and legislative authorities.

The British Position

Almost every modern constitution has followed this pattern. The only exception to this almost universal rule is the case of British Parliament as a constitution-making body. This is why the written constitutions of British Dominions like Canada and Australia embody no fundamental rights. British politicians and constitutionalists are generally of the view that written rights are not of much practical value. Abstract declarations, according to them, are useless unless there exists the will and means to make them effective[2]. The real

1. John Stuart Mill, *On Liberty*, p. 6.
2. When Gladstone introduced the Irish Home Rule Bill of 1893 a clause, which sought to guarantee life, liberty, property and due process of law, was assailed as vague, 'full of ambiguity abounding in pitfalls and provocative of every kind of frivolous litigation'. The clause was subsequently abandoned.

guaranty of liberty lies in an effective public opinion and the existence of a government that is amenable to such public opinion.

Fundamentally, this is a sound position. It is true that in Great Britain today there is perhaps more individual freedom than in most of the countries of the world. Yet, the British attitude towards written rights is not unimpeachable. For, one might ask the simple question: How long has it taken Britain to reach the present position ? And at what price ? One can easily point out at least two revolutions in the process, one 'bloody' and the other 'bloodless'. For establishing the liberties which the present generation of Englishmen enjoy, thousands of their ancestors paid a heavy price with their life, liberty and property. Further, no one can ignore the stupendous importance of documents like the Magna Charta, the Bill of Rights, the Petition of Rights, *etc.* in establishing the basic rights which a citizen ought to enjoy both as a human being and as a member of a given political society, and safeguarding them against all encroachments by the executive authority of the State. The most striking feature of the fight of the British people for civil liberties was that it was always directed against the arbitrary power of the Executive but seldom against the Legislature. This was because the despotic power of the King stood in the way of Parliament, the representative of the people. Hence, the British were always anxious to cut down the power of the executive and correspondingly increase that of the legislature. This is why the great charters like the Magna Charta speak only of limiting the powers of the King. The British never accepted the idea that a legislature could also become a tyrannous body and that hence the individual's liberties are to be safeguarded against legislative majorities too. The doctrine of parliamentary sovereignty is the product of such an attitude.

The American Position

In contrast, the framers of the American Constitution, although most of them were educated in the British tradition, were unwilling to accept the British position. They did not believe in the sovereignty of the Legislature however popular that body might be. True, the original constitution had not included in it a Bill of rights. But within two years of the inauguration of the Constitution, a series of amendments were enacted in order to constitute such a Bill of Rights. But within two years of the inauguration of the Constitution, a series of amendments were enacted in order to constitute such a Bill of Rights. The task of enforcing and protecting these rights was entrusted to the judiciary, particularly to the Supreme Court of the United States. The American concept, as one can see from the nature of these rights as well as the manner in which they are safeguarded, is that fundamental rights are not matters to be drawn into the vortex of political controversy or to be placed at the mercy of legislative majorities. They are to be definitely recognized in the constitution and protected against any violation either by the authority of the Executive or by the Legislature through an independent and impartial judiciary. This idea is clear from what Thomas Jefferson, the author of the American Declaration of Independence, wrote in a letter to one of his friends in the early days of the American Republic:

> The executive in our government is not the sole, it is scarcely the principal, subject of my jealousy. The tyranny of the legislature is the most formidable dread at the present and will be for long years. That of the executive will come; but it will be at a remote period.

Naturally, Jefferson was the most ardent protagonist of the 'inclusion of a Bill of Rights in the Constitution to guard against legislative tyranny'.

Why Guaranteed Rights ?

What is the purpose of guaranteed fundamental rights ? Their very purpose is to withdraw certain subjects from the changing pattern of political controversy, to place them beyond the reach of a majority in legislatures and officials in the government and to establish them as legal principles to be applied by the Courts. For, if the danger of personal rule by despotic rulers has more or less disappeared as a result of representative institutions coming into their own, that from legislative interference has correspondingly increased because of the high-handed manner in which majorities might manage affairs in legislatures. A dominant group of legislators could pass any discriminatory or unjust legislation and prejudice the interests of considerable sections of the people. This meant in reality the substitution of one kind of tyranny by another, the replacement of the personal rule of the monarch by the tyranny of a legislative majority. One's right to life, liberty and property, to free speech and free expression, freedom of worship and assembly, and other fundamental rights are not subjects to be submitted to vote. They do not depend on the outcome of elections.

When legislatures were prohibited from encroaching upon certain rights through constitutional safeguards, the protection of these rights was achieved against the arbitrary conduct of both the Executive and the Legislature. When an independent judiciary was made the guardian of these rights by the constitution itself, the process of the protection of fundamental rights was complete and the enjoyment of these rights by all irrespective of wealth or social status, race or religious belief, was fully ensured. Herein lies the importance of fundamental rights. The United States has led many countries in this respect. Today, the idea of a list of written rights as an integral part of a new constitution has been generally accepted. Even the British did not seriously contest the wisdom of this arrangement and were prepared to concede its value at least to a limited extent.

The Indian Demand for Fundamental Rights

The idea of incorporating a list of fundamental rights in a new constitution of India had excited the imagination of almost all political thinkers and constitutionalists in India from the time the idea of the transfer of power from Britain to Indian hands had taken shape. The American Bill of Rights had tremendous impact on Indian thinking on this subject. The Indian National Congress, the Liberals, moderates of all shades and the religious minorities like the Muslims, the Christians and the Sikhs, considered it not only desirable but essential, both for the protection of the rights of minorities and for infusing confidence in the majority community. The Nehru Committee endorsed it. The Muslim League lent its full support to it. The Simon Commission, however, ridiculed the idea and rejected it. But in spite of the Commission's adverse report, the matter came up for discussion during the Round Table Conferences held in London to consider constitutional reforms for India.

During the Second Round Table Conference, 1931, Ramsay MacDonald, the then Labour Prime Minister of Britain, announced that he was in favour of incorporating a list of fundamental rights in the proposed federal constitution of India for safeguarding the interests of minorities. But a little later, when Conservative leaders joined the Conference as spokesmen of the National Government of Britain, the official stand underwent a change. Lord Reading was the first to ridicule the idea. He was followed by Sir John Simon who had headed the Indian Statutory Commission in 1927. Sir John gave three major arguments in support of his contention. First, the British Constitution does not recognize any fundamental rights. The concept of the British Constitution implied the sovereignty of Parliament. All rights in Britain originate, therefore, from Parliament. Secondly, the necessity of fundamental rights arises only where autocracy rules. But where there is a parliamentary system of government, there is no necessity for fundamental rights and guarantees. Thirdly, there can only be two possibilities with regard to fundamental rights; either they are justiciable or non-justiciable. Take the first right: 'All men are equal before law'. On what ground can this form the matter of adjudication in a court of Law ? It is so general and has no specific application that it cannot by itself form the subject matter of any litigation. Therefore, in describing these laws as fundamental you are really misleading the citizens and giving them a false sense of security.

Unfortunately for India, the Indian representatives at the Conference failed to drive home the necessity of including such rights in the Constitution of India. They could not convince the authorities at Westminster that the Constitution which was envisaged for India had fundamental differences from the British Constitution. After all, the British Constitution was largely an unwritten one, the product of centuries of evolutionary process. Moreover, Britain had never faced the astonishing diversity of interests which, in India, are based on religious, linguistic and cultural differences. It is surprising that the British spokesmen never fully recognized these facts.[1] Those who think like Sir John forget that fundamental rights taken at their lowest value could at least be said to establish a social philosophy, to lay down a set of rules of conduct as much for legislatures and governments as for individuals. They form a code of social philosophy regulating the conduct of every one. On the one hand, they remind legislatures and executives, whenever they begin to trample over these rights, that they are treading on a prohibited area. On the other, they provide an opportunity for citizens to create public opinion against such measures. Above all, in a country of such bewildering diversity as India, incorporation of fundamental rights in the constitution would infuse confidence in various religious, linguistic and cultural minorities. But the British constitutionalists have often displayed a tendency to insist that what is good for Britain ought to be good for others also. Hence, the Constitution Act of 1935 was passed without any Bill of Rights incorporated in it.

The absence of guaranteed fundamental rights showed how free the Government of India was to do whatever it liked however illegal it was. During the war years, civil liberties lost all their meaning in India and the courts including the Federal Court of India found it impossible to safeguard them. A series of ordinances by the Governor-General replaced legislative enactments in this field. Special Courts were set up to try persons for all types of political activities. Such courts ignored even the provisions of the Code of Criminal Procedure. Their decisions were placed beyond any review by High Courts. When the Federal Court declared the ordinance which established these Courts invalid, thereby rendering the imprisonment of some 8,000 persons illegal, the Governor-General promulgated another ordinance in identical terms the very next day![2] Hundreds of cases were brought before the various High Courts but the Courts could not help, for there was no constitutional guarantee under which they could act. A decade of the working of the Constitution Act of 1935 amply demonstrated the imperative necessity of incorporating a list of fundamental rights in the constitution of independent India.

---

1. See for example, the views of Ivor Jennings who in 1951 more or less repeated the views expressed earlier by Simon in his *Some Characteristics of the Indian Constitution,* Chapter 11.
2. For a detailed account of this, See Pylee, M.V., The Federal Court of India, 1967, Chapt. XI.

Another argument of the British also deserves mention in this context. It was a standing contention of the British that Indians did not deserve independence because they were so divided by religion, caste, race, language and culture that normal democratic government could never work in this country. The only way in which Indian participation in government could be facilitated was by giving separate representation to all these interests. Hence, the communal electorates. The Indian national movement never accepted this thesis but branded it as a cover to the imperial design to 'divide and rule'. According to the national movement, the answer to the communal, religious or caste problem was a guaranteed Bill of Rights. Communalism is irrelevant to politics where irrespective of religious differences citizens can join together for the management of the affairs of State. In fact, communalism is a cultural problem and it will solve itself if the individual is guaranteed his freedoms. Hence, what is required is a constitutional guarantee of fundamental liberties and not separate electorates. By 1946, even the British accepted the soundness of this stand. As a result, the Cabinet Mission agreed upon the necessity of the incorporation of a separate chapter of fundamental rights in the future constitution of India.

Attitude of the Constituent Assembly

When the Constituent Assembly met for the first time in 1946, no member opposed the idea of a chapter of fundamental rights as an integral part of the Constitution. In fact, it was unreservedly supported by all sections of opinion in the Assembly. Over the Special committee appointed for the purpose, Sardar Patel Presided and it included prominent members of the various minority communities. The committee made a detailed study of the whole problem and recommended a number of measures. On the basis of this report, the Drafting Committee of the Constituent Assembly prepared the provisions on Fundamental Rights as embodied in the Draft Constitution.

Even a rapid glance over the two chapters of the Constitution—Fundamental Rights and Directive Principles—will satisfy any impassioned observer that the one desire that was dominant in the framers of the Constitution was for the rapid modernization of the country's political, social and economic institutions. That desire has found its expression in the chapter on Fundamental Rights along with that on Directive Principles. In this regard, they were primarily guided by the ideals of the American and Frech Revolutions. Intellectually, the leaders of contemporary India are the children of the West, that region of the world where modernism had its birth and growth. Hence, it was no wonder that in the constitution they framed, an important place was given to these rights with a view to modernizing their political, social and economic institutions.

The real problems that faced the framers of the Indian Constitution in this connection, however, related to the selection of rights which were to be regarded as fundamental and the creation of institutions to safeguard them.[1] The framers of the American and the French constitutions who were the first to solve these problems were naturally guided in their task by their own historic experience and the philosophical doctrines that arose out of it. In their view, rights are ultimately the remedies for wrongs done to their subjects by the despotic rulers of the age and there were, therefore, as many rights as there were wrongs to be remedied. The vocal sections of eighteenth century Europe and America were the rising middle classes who were eager to apply the results of the ever-expanding experimental

1. See in this connection B.N. Rau, op. cit. p. 245.

sciences to trade, business and industry and maximize their profits. Among the wrongs which they suffered at the hands of their despotic rulers were arbitrary taxation, arbitrary imprisonment, arbitrary control over freedom of speech and expression, religious persecution and other restrictions on personal freedom. These stood in the way of the spread of the ideas of the new science. There was also arbitrariness in the making and administering of law. Society too was hierarchically organized with different levels of nobility and aristocracy enjoining special status and privileges. The enterprising middle class was denied equality of opportunity in securing a fair share in administration, especially in the higher ranks of the public services both civil and military. These were the wrongs to be remedied and the remedies found for each one of them were elevated to the rank of fundamental rights. Right to property, to which a central place was given, was for instance a remedy for arbitrary exploitation; freedom of person was the remedy for religious persecution. Thus, in selecting the rights which they came to regard as fundamental, they were guided by the nature of the disabilities from which they suffered at the hands of their rulers.

The rights which were thus selected fell broadly into two categories—public and private—but both had the same purpose in view, namely, to put an end to arbitrary rule. Among the public or political rights were the right of men to choose their rulers, the right to hold them responsible for their conduct, the right to a share in law-making and the right to bear arms. Among the private rights were the right to personal freedom, the right to freedom of religious belief, the right to freedom of thought and expression, the right to equality and to the possession and use of property. Political thinkers of the age gave a philosophical explanation for these rights being regarded as fundamental. Assuming that happiness is the goal of human life, they pointed out, that man had, independently of his government, a right to the enjoyment of all those conditions which are essential for the pursuit of happiness. To such conditions, the term 'Rights' was applied and this meaning of Rights has, on the whole, come to stay although political thinkers of more recent times refer to the goal of human life as the development of personality. From their point of view, rights are those conditions which a person should possess if he is to develop his personality and become the best that he is capable of becoming. The two views do not however make much of a difference so far as the enunciation of fundamental rights is concerned. By about the beginning of the nineteenth century, philosophers as well as statesmen were able to evolve a formula of fundamental rights and those who framed new constitutions in the subsequent period had not much difficulty in selecting the rights to be safeguarded as fundamental for incorporation in the constitution.

The fathers of the Indian Constitution were, therefore, in a happy position to examine the experience of a variety of constitutions from different parts of the world. Of these, the Bill of Rights of the American Constitution, French Declaration of the rights of Man and the Irish Constitution of 1935—all of the era preceding the Second World War—were the most important which influenced them. Among the post-war constitutions, those of Japan (which was American-inspired) and Burma[1] (which had many problems similar to those of India) were the two which attracted them most. There was also the influence of the Universal Human Rights Charter which was almost at its final stage of adoption by the United Nations. It must be emphasized, however, that the Indian constitution-makers were

1. Now renamed as Myanmar.

not content with merely borrowing from experience abroad. They were profoundly influenced in the selection of these rights by at least three other factors peculiar to the situation in India. First, there were the special disabilities from which they suffered during the British rule, the disabilities which were similar to those to which the peoples of the West were subject in the days of depotism, but with the added circumstance of alien domination. The second was the institution of caste which was the dominant feature of the Indian social system as a consequence of which a large section of the people came to be treated as 'untouchables'. The third was the existence of a number of religious, linguistic and racial minorities in the country whose cultural rights had to be safeguarded. Some of the rights included in the Constitution, therefore, owe their origin to one or other of these three factors.

The real problem that confronted the framers, however, was how to limit their selection of rights to certain categories only. What rights were fundamental and what were not, and why ? If the right to life, liberty and property were fundamental, what about right to employment and education ? Has not the traditional concept of fundamental rights in its individualistic setting undergone a change in the modern era of Welfare State ? The framers had no doubt about the answers to these questions. They were quite conscious of the change in the character of the modern State. They knew that the age of the American Bill of Rights which believed in the 'perfectibility of man and the malignancy of government' had gone for ever. And yet, it was a task of utmost difficulty. This was because the State in India was not yet in a position to guarantee the right to employment or education. It was a matter of physical impossibility, not the lack of will. Hence, they divided these rights into two categories, justiciable and non-justiciable. Justiciable rights are those which can be enforced by a court of law. Part III of the Constitution which is entitled 'Fundamental Rights' contains justiciable rights like the right to life, liberty and property. Part IV, 'The Directive Principles of State Policy', contains non-justiciable rights such as right to employment and education. The citizen has no judicial remedy if he is denied the enjoyment of these rights.

Special Features

Of the many constitutions that incorporate a declaration of human rights, the Constitution of India has the most elaborate and complex one. There are in all 24 articles which deal with these rights. They are divided into eight sections, the first of which contains certain general provisions applicable to all the rights enumerated, and each of the remaining seven sections deal with a different category of rights. These are: Right to Equality; Right to Freedom; Right against Exploitation; Right to Freedom of Religion; Cultural and Educational Rights and Right to Constitutional Remedies.

The Fundamental Rights under the Constitution of India place limitations not only on the Union Government, but also on the States and on every authority that has got either the power to make laws or the power to have discretion vested in it. Thus, they are binding not only on the Central and State Governments but also on such bodies as District Boards, Municipalities, Taluk Boards, Village Panchayats, *etc.*[1] The fundamental nature of these rights lies in the emphasis which they place on the basic unity of India in spite of the fact that it is divided into so many different units and provides for many separate authorities.

1. C.A.D. VII, p. 610.

With respect to these rights, the citizen is entitled to have the same treatment at the hands of all these authorities. In contrast to such a position, it is interesting to note that the Bill of Rights under the American Constitution was intended to place limitations on the national Government alone. Ever after the passing of the Fourteenth Amendment, the question whether the Bill of Rights as a whole or in part is binding on the States is still debated in the United States.

The Rights embodied in Part III of the Constitution are not couched in absolute terms.[1] The Constitution itself enumerates in each case the exceptions, limitations and qualifications. It is true that rights are not absolute even if they are expressed in absolute terms. Yet, there is a special significance that deserves attention here. Where the Constitution speaks of no limitations, it becomes the duty of courts to prescribe them while interpreting the Constitution. But this is a long and tedious process as has happened in the United States. The Framers of the Indian Constitution were not in favour of such a process but permitted the State directly to impose limitations upon the fundamental rights.[2]

The Constitution draws a distinction between citizens and aliens in the matter of enjoyment of these rights. While such rights as equality before law, religious freedom, *etc.* are applicable to citizens and aliens alike, rights such as freedom of speech, assembly, and cultural and educational rights are available only to citizens. This distinction can easily be noticed by the use of the two terms 'citizens' and 'persons' at the appropriate places where the scope of each right is expressed. Even in the absence of such a classification all these rights would not have been available to every person, citizen or alien. But, there again, the matter would have been left undecided until the Supreme Court came on the scene and determined the category of persons to whom each of these rights is to be made applicable.

One important feature of the Fundamental Rights is the absence of a provision corresponding to the Ninth Amendment of the United States Constitution. According to this provision, the American people are not denied the enjoyment of other fundamental rights because of the fact that the Constitution enumerates certain rights as such. Under the Indian Constitution, the position is different. No individual can claim a fundamental right against the State outside the chapter on Fundamental Rights. This precludes the chance of the Indian Courts from enquiring about any fundamental right that is not enumerated in the Constitution. This, again, is a restriction on the scope of judicial review in India as against that in the United States where, under the guise of a theory of natural rights, the judges may enlarge the scope of interpretation to whatever extent they may choose.

Indian fundamental rights in their application embrace not only the State and its agencies but in certain cases also private individuals and organizations. Thus, the practice of 'untouchability' in any form by any individual is an offence punishable under law. Similarly, certain forms of discrimination indulged by individuals are punishable under law. In all such cases, the law that will govern them will have to be passed exclusively by the Parliament of India.

The Indian Constitution is not satisfied by a mere enumeration of a series of fundamental rights but has also made the right to constitutional remedies itself a fundamental right. It is difficult to exaggerate the importance of this provision. Declaration of rights in general terms without prescribing definite remedies to enforce them in case of infringement

1. Ram Singh *vs.* The State of Delhi, 1951 S.C.R. 451.
2. C.A.D. VII, p 41.

may even fail to make these rights real. A fundamental right becomes real only when the Constitution provides a remedy for the violation of it. This has been ensured by making the right to constitutional remedies a fundamental right under which the Supreme Court and High Courts are empowered to issue appropriate writs or orders as the occasion demands for the restoration of the enjoyment of a right that is violated.

Although the framers of the Constitution were eager to guarantee the maximum number of rights as fundamental and make them available uninterrupted by any authority, they were also conscious of the times of the emergency which might demand the suspension of some of these rights. Accordingly, the Constitution provides for the suspension of various rights guaranteed under the 'Right to Freedom' such as freedom of speech, movement, association, *etc.* under an emergency declared by the President of India. Further, the Constitution empowers the President to suspend, under an emergency, the right to move any court of law for the enforcement of any of the Fundamental Rights.

There is yet another special feature that deserves mention here. That relates to the power that is vested in Parliament to amend the provisions dealing with the Fundamental Rights. India's is a federal constitution. Under a federal system, the usual feature is that a constitutional amendment can be brought about only by concurrent action on the part of both the Union and the States. This is true of India also so far as it relates to certain parts of the Constitution, especially those which deal with the federal system. But Fundamental Rights chapter is an exception to this. Parliament can amend this part of the Constitution with an affirmative two-thirds majority of those who sit and vote. Such two-thirds majority should in no case be less than an absolute majority of the total membership of Parliament.

This position which appeared to have been accepted by all concerned until 1967 underwent a dramatic change as a result of the decision of the Supreme Court in the now famous Golak Nath case.[1] By a majority of six to five the Court held that Parliament has no power to take away or abridge any of the fundamental rights guaranteed by the Constitution through constitutional amendments. The decision of the Court let loose a great debate all over the country focusing attention on both the competence of Parliament to amend Fundamental Rights and the Supreme Court's power to take away through constitutional interpretation a right which Parliament was exercising for seventeen years. In 1971, soon after the fifth General Elections, Parliament acted decisively by passing the Twenty-fourth Amendment of the Constitution reaffirming its right to amend the Constitution in accordance with the procedure laid down in Article 368 of the Constitution. But the decision of the Supreme Court in Kesavananda Bharati[2] has conclusively re-established the authority of the Court to review any Parliamentary enactment including amendment of the Constitution under the Doctrine of Basic Structure.

We may now consider in detail the various provisions relating to Fundamental rights.

General Provisions

Article 12 defines the term 'State' as it applies to the provisions of this chapter.

---

1. (1967) 2 S.C.R. 762; A.I.R. 1967 S.C. 1643. See also the following decisions of the Court regarding its views on the general nature of Fundamental Rights:
   L.N. Mishra Institute *vs*. State of Bihar, A.I.R. 1988 S.C. 1136 and Kishore Darius *vs*. Union of India, A.I.R. 1990 S.C. 605.
2. Kesavananda Bharati *vs*. State of Kerala, A.I.R. 1973 SC 1461.

According to it, State includes the Government (Executive) and Parliament and the Government and the Legislature of each of the States and all local and other authorities within the territory of India or under the control of the Government of India. The definition is made so comprehensive that it includes every governmental authority, legislative or executive, Central, State or Local and the rights are guaranteed against violation by any one of these authorities. Local authority will include bodies such as District Boards, Janpad Sabhas, Taluk Boards, Village Panchayats and Municipalities—in fact, every authority that has been created by law and has got the power to make laws, rules, regulations or by-laws.[1] The inclusion of the term 'under the control of the Government of India' in this Article was thought necessary because apart from territories which form part of India, there may be other territories which may not form part of India but may nonetheless be under the control of the Government of India such as a territory under trusteeship from the United Nations. There ought to be no discrimination so far as the citizens of India and the residents of such territories are concerned in regard to Fundamental Rights.[2] Objection was raised in the Constituent Assembly for the loose manner in which the term 'State' was used in the Constitution to signify different meanings at different places and thereby creating confusion.[3] The Drafting Committee, however, did not accept this criticism, but pointed out that there was no confusion as to the meaning of the term in the context in which it occurred.

Article 13 has two important aspects. On the one hand, it invalidates all laws which were in force at the commencement of the Constitution in so far as they were consistent with Fundamental Rights and to the extent of their inconsistency with those rights. On the other, it imposes a prohibition upon the State not to make any law which takes away or abridges the rights conferred by this chapter. In case any law is made in contravention of this provision, such law would be invalid to the extent of its inconsistency with any of the rights guaranteed. It should be emphasized, however, that the Article does not declare any law void independently of the existence of the rights guaranteed by this chapter. It is only in relation to the various freedoms embodied in the chapter that the provisions of Article 13(1) come into play.[4]

The importance of this provision is that it makes express provision for judicial review of legislative enactments as to their conformity with the Constitution. This is in contrast with the provision for judicial review in the United States—the land of such reviews' birth and growth—where the Supreme Court assumed extensive power of reviewing legislative acts under cover of the widely interpreted 'due process' clause in the Fifth and Fourteenth Amendments.[5] In the opinion of Chief Justice Kania in Gopalan *vs.* the State of Madras, the inclusion of Article 13(1) and (2) in the Constitution appears to be a matter of abundant caution. Even in their absence, if any of the Fundamental Rights was infringed by any

1. C.A.D. VII, p. 610. See Electricity Board *vs*. Mohanlal, A.I.R. 1967 S.C. 1857 and Ajit Singh *vs*. State of Punjab, A.I.R. 1967 S.C. 856. Statutory corporations carrying on business of public importance such as the Life Insurance Corporation or Industrial Finance Corporation are authorities within the meaning of Art. 12. See Sukhdev Singh *vs*. Bhagat Ram (1975) I SCC. 421. See also M.C. Mehta *vs*. Union of India, AIR 1987 S.C. 1086, Ajay Hasia *vs*. Sehravardi, A.I.R. 1981 SC 487 and Unnikrishnan *vs*. State of A.P. A.I.R. 1993 S.C. 2178.
2. Ibid. p. 606
3. Ibid. P. 404.
4. Nabhirajaiah *vs*. State of Mysore 1952, S.C.R. 744.
5. State of Madras *vs*. V.G. Appa Rao, 1952. S.C.R. 597.

legislative enactment, the Court has always the power to declare the enactment, to the extent it transgresses the limits, invalid. The existence of Article 13, therefore, is not material for the decision of the question of what fundamental right is given and to what extent it is permitted to be abridged by the Constitution intself.[1] The Supreme Court ruled, however, that the Article can have no retrospective effect but is wholly prospective in its operation. Thus, the Court could give no protection to a person who had offended the law before the commencement of the Constitution and was as a consequence sentenced to imprisonment, even though that law became invalid after the commencement of the Constitution.[2] Putting such a time-bar for the enjoyment of a fundamental right seems to be really hard on citizens who should be in a position to claim these rights without time limits.

To determine the characteristics of a 'State' the Supreme Court has laid down the following principles as important in the case of Ajay Hasia *vs.* Sehravardi.[3]

1. If the entire share capital is held by the government;
2. Where the financial assistance of the State is great;
3. If the corporation enjoys a monopoly status conferred by the State;
4. Existence of deep and pervasive State control;
5. If the functions of State government are closely related to that of government and
6. If a department of Government is transferred to the corporation.

In addition to Articles 12 and 13, Articles 33, 34 and 35 in the chapter on Fundamental Rights also contain certain general provisions. Article 33 gives the power to Parliament to suitably modify the Fundamental Rights so as to apply them to the Armed Forces with a view to ensuring the proper discharge of their duties and the maintenance of discipline among them. Article 34 deals with the restriction of Fundamental Rights while martial law is in force in any area. If the right to life and personal liberty cannot be violated except according to procedure established by law, the application of martial law might become impossible in the country and it would be impossible for the State to restore order quickly in an area which has become rebellious, riotous or in any other way violently disorderly. Therefore, it was thought necessary to make a special provision to permit any act proclaimed by the Commander-in-Chief of the area where martial law prevails as an offence to be reckoned under the established law. Similarly, the procedure prescribed by him shall be procedure deemed to have been established by law.[4] Further, Parliament is empowered to indemnify any person in respect of any act done by him in connection with the restoration and maintenance of order in any area where martial law was in force. Thus, Article 34 makes the operation of martial law and the consequent restoration of peace possible.

Article 35 deals with legislation intended to give effect to some of the provisions dealing with Fundamental Rights. Under this, Parliament has been given exclusive power to make laws with respect to the following matters: right to constitutional remedies;

---

1. 1950, S.C.R. 88.
2. Keshavan Madhav Menon *vs.* State of Bombay, 1955, 1955, S.C.R. 228. See also Behram Khurshed Pesikaka *vs.* State of Bombay, 1955, S.C.R. 613 for the Court's interpretation of the term 'void' in Article 13. Also see A.S. Krishna *vs.* State of Madras, 1957, S.C.J. 216.
3. C.A.D. X, p. 577. See also the State of Pubjab *vs.* Khan Chand (1974) 1 Scc. 549 and N.P. Natwani *vs.* The Commissioner of Police (1976) 78 Bom. L.R.I.
4. AIR 1981 S.C. 487.

prescribing residence qualifications required for public employment; Armed Forces; and martial law. Parliament is given exclusive power also for prescribing punishment for those acts which are declared to be offences under the chapter on Fundamental Rights. The Constitution in express terms prohibits the States from passing any law with respect to these items. The purpose of these provisions is clearly to establish uniform standards for the whole country as these are subjects which if handled by the States would create different standards which would be detrimental to the ideals of single citizenship and national unity which the Constitution aims to establish.

***

10

THE RIGHT TO EQUALITY

(Articles 14, 15, 16, 17 and 18)

ARTICLE 14 declares that 'the State shall not deny to any person equality before the law or equal protection of the laws within the territory of India'. The phrase 'Equality before the law' occurs in almost all written constitutions that guarantee fundamental rights. The American Constitution uses the expression, 'equal protection of laws'. The Constitution of India adopts both the expressions in the same Article which deals with the right to equality. Both the expressions may appear to signify the same thing but in fact, they mean different things. Equality before the law is an expression of English Common Law[1] while 'equal protection of laws' owes its origin to the American Constitution.[2] Both the phrases aim to establish what is called the 'equality of status and of opportunity' as embodied in the Preamble of the Constitution.

While equality before the law is a somewhat negative concept implying the absence of any special privilege in favour of any individual and the equal subjection of all classes to the ordinary law, equal protection of laws is a more positive concept implying equality of treatment under equal circumstances. Thus, Article 14 stands for the establishment of a situation under which there is complete absence of any arbitrary discrimination by the laws themselves or in their administration. The significance of the equal protection clause is explained in the following words by a judge of the Supreme Court of the United States:

> The clause undoubtedly intended, not only that there should be no arbitrary deprivation of life or liberty or arbitrary spoilation of property, but that equal protection and security should be given to all under like circumstances in the enjoyment of their personal and civil rights, that all persons should be equally entitled to pursue their happiness and acquire and enjoy property; that they should have like access to the courts of the country for the protection of their person and property, the prevention and redress of wrongs, and the enforcement of contracts; that no impediments should be interposed to these pursuits by others under like circumstances; that no greater burdens should be laid upon one than are laid upon others in the same calling and condition; and that in the administration of criminal justice no different or higher punishment should be imposed upon one than such as is prescribed to all for like offences.

Interpreting the scope of equal protection of laws, the Supreme Court of India held in

---

1. A.V. Dicey, *Law of the Constitution,* chapter on the Rule of Law.
2. Fourteenth Amendment, See for similar provisions Article 40 (1) of the Irish Constitution and Article 18 of the Universal Human Rights Charter.

Chiranjit Lal Choudhury *vs.* The Union of India[1] that: (*a*) Equal protection means equal protection under equal circumstances; (*b*) The State can make reasonable classifications for purposes of legislation; (*c*) Presumption of reasonableness is in favour of the legislation; and (*d*) The burden of proof is on those who challenge the legislation. Explaining the scope of reasonable classification, the Court held that 'even one corporation or a group of persons can be taken to be a class by itself for the purpose of legislation, provided there is sufficient basis or reason for it. The onus of proving that there were also other companies similarly situated and this company alone has been discriminated against, was on the petitioner'.

The following two interpretations by two of the High Courts in India deserve attention in this connection:

> The guarantee of the equal protection of the laws means the protection of equal laws. It forbids class legislation but does not prohibit classification which rests upon reasonable grounds of distinction. It merely requires that all persons subjected to such legislation shall be treated alike under like circumstances and conditions both in the privileges conferred and in the liabilities imposed. Mathematical nicety and perfect equality are not required, and one who assails classification must carry the burden of showing that it does not rest upon any reasonable basis.[2]

> The guarantee of equality before the law or equal protection of the law means substantial equality of treatment under the laws. Equal treatment does not necessarily mean identical treatment. In fact, identical treatment in unequal circumstances amounts to inequality. In other words, in different circumstances the variation in legal procedure is not only permissible but necessary. Equal protection of laws does not mean identical laws. Sometimes, it is necessary to abridge the ordinary procedure in the interest of justice itself. Of course, in abridgement of legal procedure which curtails the essential safeguards can be permitted. A detailed procedure in normal times and in ordinary cases may become harmful in abnormal times or in extraordinary and special cases.[3]

---

1. 1950, S.C.R. 869. Hundreds of cases have been decided by the Courts in India interpreting this article since January 26, 1950. Of these, the following deserve special mention: State of West Bengal *vs.* Anwar Ali Sarkar 1952, S.C.R. 284; Satish Chandra Anand *vs.* The Union of India 1953, S.C.R. 655; Syed Mohammed and Co. *vs.* The Union of Andhra, A.I.R. 1954, S.C. 314; Yusuf Abdul Aziz *vs.* The State of Bombay, A.I.R. 1954, S.C. 321; Shri Kishen Singh *vs.* The State of Rajasthan 1955, 2 S.C.R. 531; Budhan Choudhry *vs.* The State of Bihar 1955, 1 S.C.R. 1045; Bidi Supply Co. *vs.* The Union of India, A.I.R. 1956, S.C. 479, Babulal mehta *vs.* Collector of Customs, Calcutta, 1957, S.C.J. 828; M.H. Rao *vs.* State of Andhra Pradesh 1958, S.C.J. 129; Baldeo Singh *vs.* State of Bihar, 1957 S.C.J. 535; Attar Singh *vs.* The State of U.P. 1959 S.C..J. 474; K. Haldar *vs.* State of West Bengal 1960, S.C.J. 629; M.T. Moopil Nair *vs.* State of Kerala (1961) II S.C.J. 269; J.D. Rama Rao *vs.* State of Andhra Pradesh (1961) I S.C.J. 310; Instalment Supply (Private) Ltd. *vs.* The Union of India (1961) II S.C.J. 625; The Collector of Sea Customs *vs.* N.S. Chetty (1962) I S.C.J. 68; Mohanlal Jain *vs.* Ex-Ruler of Jaipur (1962) I S.C.J. 104; K. Kunhikoman *vs.* State of Kerala (1962) I S.C.J. 510; The State of Jammu and Kashmir *vs.* Ghulam Rasool (1962) I S.C.J. 552; B. Agarwalla *vs.* The State of Bihar (1962) II S.C.J. 27; Southern Roadways (P) Ltd. *vs.* The Union of India (1962) II S.C.J. 310; Sant Ram, *In re* (1961) I S.C.J. 98; and J.K. Vellukunnel *vs.* The Reserve Bank of India (1963) I S.C.J. 210.

   For the interpretation of the scope of 'equal protection of laws', see particularly The State of Jammu and Kashmir Vs. Ghulam Rasool, Ibid; Jyoti Prasad *vs.* The Administrator for the Union Territory of Delhi (1962) II S.C.J. 58 and J.P. Sharma *vs.* The State of U.P. (1963) I S.C.J. 115.

   See also State of Nagaland *vs.* Ratan Singh, A.I.R. 1967 S.C. 158; State of Gujarat *vs.* Shri Ambika Mills Ltd. (1974) 2 S.C.J. 211; Shastri *vs.* Union of India I.LR. (1971) I Delhi 131 and Erusian Equipment and Chemicals Ltd., A.I.R. 1975 S.C. 266. Also See Benerjee *vs.* Anita Pan A.I.R. 1975 S.C. 1146.

2. Sir Kameswar Singh *vs.* State of Bihar, A.I.R. 1951, Patna 91.

   See also Maneka Gandhi *vs.* Union of India, 1978, I S.C.C. 248.

3. Abdul Rahim *vs.* Joseph A. Pinto, petition nos. 14-20 of 1950, Hyderabad.

In its struggle for social and political freedom mankind has striven continuously towards the ideal of equality for all. The urge for equality and liberty has been the motive force of many revolutions. The Charter of the United Nations records the determination of the member nations to reaffirm their faith in the equal rights of men and women. Indeed, real and effective democracy cannot be achieved unless equality in all spheres is realized in a full measure. However, complete equality among men and women in all spheres of life is a distant ideal to be realized only by the march of humanity along the long and arduous path of economic, social and political progress. The constitution and laws of a country can at best assure to its citizens only a limited measure of equality. The framers of the Indian Constitution were fully conscious of this. This is why while they gave political and legal equality the status of a fundamental right, economic and social equality was largely left within the scope of Directive Principles of State policy.

The Right to Equality affords protection not only against discriminatory laws passed by legislatures but also prevents arbitrary discretion being vested in the executive. In the modern State, the executive is armed with vast powers, in the matter of enforcing by-laws, rules and regulations as well as in the performance of a number of the other functions. The equality clause prevents such power being exercised in a discriminatory manner. For example, the issue of licences regulating various trades and business activities cannot be left to the unqualified discretion of the licensing authority. The law regulating such activities should lay down the principles under which the licensing authority has to act in the grant of these licences. Among the cases on this point a leading one is Satwant Singh *vs.* A.P.O., New Delhi[1] where the executive claimed a right to refuse a passport at its discretion and the Court held that such discretion would be inconsistent with Article 14.

> An executive arbitrariness can prevent one from doing so (going abroad) and permit another to travel merely for pleasure. While in the case of enacted law one knows where he stands, in the case of unchannelled arbitrary discretion, discrimination is writ large on the face of it. Such a discretion patently violates the doctrine of equality, for the difference in the treatment of persons rests solely on the arbitrary selection of the executive.

Article 14 prevents discrimination only by the State and not by individuals. For instance, if a private employer like the owner of a private business concern discriminates in choosing his employees or treats his employees unequally, the person discriminated against will have no judicial remedy. One might ask here, why should the Constitution not extend the scope of this right to private individuals also. There is good reason for not doing so. For, such extension to individual action may result in serious interference with the liberty of the individual and, in the process, fundamental rights themselves may become meaningless. After all, real democracy can be achieved only by a proper balance between the freedom of the individual and the restrictions imposed on it in the interests of the community. Yet, even individual action in certain spheres has been restricted by the Constitution, for example, the abolition of untouchability and its practice in any form by any one being made an offence. Altogether, Article 14 lays down an important fundamental right which has to be closely and vigilantly guarded. And in interpreting it, it is to be presumed that the courts will not adopt a doctrinaire approach which might choke legislation beneficial to the community at large.[2]

---

1. A.I.R. 1967 S.C. 1836.
2. Among the cases reported on fundamental rights the largest number relates to the interpretation of Article 14. In 1968 for example, out of 43 cases reported, Article 14 was involved in not less than 34 cases.

There is just another important point that deserves consideration here. The right to equality and equal protection of laws loses its reality if all the citizens do not have equal facilities of access to the courts for the protection of their fundamental rights. The fact that these rights are guaranteed in the Constitution does not make them real unless legal assistance is available for all on reasonable terms. There cannot be any real equality in the right to 'sue and be sued' in the same manner as others unless the poorer sections of the community have equal access to courts as the richer sections. It is the realization of this feeling that led to the passing, in England, of the Legal Aid and Advice Act, 1949. There is no such provision under the existing Indian Law. It would seem necessary for the Parliament of India and the State Legislatures, therefore, to pass suitable legislation in order to translate the ideal of equal protection of laws into the realm of reality for the millions of impecunious Indian citizens.[1]

Prohibition of Discrimination on Certain Grounds (Art. 15)

Not content with a mere general declaration of the right to equality, and fully conscious of the types of discrimination prevalent in the country, the framers went a step further in Article 15, which is more illustrative in character than introducing anything substantially new. Yet, there is one striking feature in it which brings within its scope, although in a limited way, the actions of private individuals. According to the article:

> The State shall not discriminate against any citizen on grounds only of religion, race, caste, sex place of birth or any of them. Further, on the basis of any of these grounds a citizen cannot be denied access to shops, public restaurants or the use of wells, tanks, bathing ghats, roads and places of public resort maintained wholly or partly out of State funds or dedicated to the use of the general public.

According to Ambedkar, the term shop is used here in its generic sense. It is a place where the owner is prepared to offer his service to anybody who is prepared to go there seeking his service. Further, it is used in the sense of entry for services if the terms of service are agreed to, and not in the sense of mere right of entry.[2] As such, a shop includes such places as laundry, shaving saloon, the offices of a lawyer and the clinic of a doctor. Similarly, places of public resort will include a burial ground, subject to the fact that such a burial ground is maintained wholly or partly out of state funds.[3] The public character of a place is determined on the basis of whether or not it is maintained wholly or partly out of state funds. It has nothing to do with definition given in the Indian Penal Code.[4]

Interpreting the scope of the Article, the Supreme Court held that 'it is plain that the fundamental right conferred by Article 15(1) is conferred on a citizen as an individual and is a guarantee against his being subjected to discrimination in the matter of rights, privileges and immunities pertaining to him as a citizen generally'.[5] In another decision the Court rejected the plea that residence in the State was equivalent to place of birth and held that these are two distinct conceptions with different connotations both in law and in fact, and when Article 15(1) prohibits discrimination based on the place of birth, it cannot be read as

1. Considerable groundwork has already been done by 1980 in the establishment of a system of legal aid to the needy.
2. C.A.D. VII, p. 661.
3. and
4. Ibid, p. 662.
5. Nain Sukh Das *vs.* The State of U.P. 1953, S.C.R. 1184.

prohibiting discrimination based on residence.[1] Residence as a qualification for certain purposes such as employment may not be classed with discrimination based on caste and place of birth. The significance of the article is that it is a guarantee against every form of discrimination by the State on the basis of religion,[2] race, caste[3] or sex. It also strikes at the root of provincialism by prohibiting discrimination based upon one's place of birth. It also goes well with the ideal of single citizenship which the Constitution establishes for the entire country. By including within its scope certain discriminatory actions of private individuals, the Article anticipates Article 17 which abolishes untouchability and facilitates the removal of discriminatory practices indulged in by the higher castes against the lower castes and helps in a substantial measure the progress of social equality.

Article 15 has, however, two notable exceptions in its application. The first of these permits the State to make special provision for the benefit of women and children. The second allows the State to make any special provision for the advancement of any socially and educationally backward classes of citizens or for the Scheduled Casts and the Scheduled Tribes. The special treatment meted out to women and children is in the larger and the long-range interest of the community itself. It also recognizes the social customs and background of the country as a whole. The second exception was not in the original constitution but was later on added to it as a result of the First Amendment of the Constitution in 1951. The amendment was necessitated by a decision[4] of the Supreme Court by which it invalidated what is known as the Communal G.O. of the Madras Government reserving seats for various communities in certain educational institutions under the State. The Government of Madras argued that it was the duty of the State to protect the interests of socially and educationally backward communities as provided for in the Directive Principles. If they were not given a favoured treatment in such matters as admission to technical institutions, *etc.* and were placed on par with members of other communities who were more advanced and if merit alone were made the governing principle for admissions, then, they would remain always backward as they would not be able to successfully compete with others. Hence, the Constitutional amendment providing for such reservations.[5]

What is to noted here is that Article 15(3) and (4) are enabling provisions. They permit discrimination popularly known as compensatory discrimination. For more details on 15(4) see Balaji *vs.* State of Mysore, A.I.R. 1963 S.C. 649, State of U.P. *vs.* Pradeep Tandon, A.I.R. 1975 SC 563 and Jayasree *vs.* State of Kerala, AIR 1976 S.C. 2381. In Chandrasekhar Paswan *vs.* State of Bihar A.I.R. 1976 S.C. 959 it was held that a single post could not be reserved. Factors to determine the backward classes of citizens are largely economic and caste criteria (Vasant Kumar *vs.* State of Karnataka A.I.R. 1985 S.C. 1495) But in Indra Sawhoney *vs.* Union of India 1992 Sup. (3) S.C.C. 217 it was held that economic criterion need not be considered for determining the backwardness of a class, for what is aimed at is not poverty alleviation.

---

1. D.P. Joshi *vs.* State of Madhya Bharat 1955, I S.C.R. 1215.
2. and
3. The State of Rajasthan *vs.* Thakur Pratap Singh (1961) I S.C.J. 143.
4. Srinivasan *vs.* State of Madras 1951, S.C.R. 226.
5. It is interesting to recall in this connection that Ambedkar was against any special protection for Scheduled Castes and Tribes under Article 15, as he feared that instead of removing the disabilities of these people, it might perpetuate their social aloofness. See C.A.D. VII, p. 661.
   For the views of the Supreme Court in this connection See A.I.R. 1864 S.C. 1923. Also Jayasree *vs.* The State of Karala A.I.R. 1976 S.C. 2381 and Subhash Chandra *vs.* State of U.P. A.I.R. 1975 S.C. 563.

Equality of Opportunity in Matters of Public Employment (Art. 16)

Article 16 guarantees equality of opportunity in matters of public employment. In the first part of the article, the general rule is laid down that there shall be equal opportunity for all citizens, wherever they are living, in matters of employment under the State; thereby the universality of Indian citizenship is postulated. In the next section, the general principle is explained in detail. According to this, the State is prohibited from showing any discrimination against any citizen on the grounds of religion, caste, race, sex, descent,[1] place of birth or residence. The next clauses are in the nature of exceptions. According to the first, residence qualifications may be made necessary in the case of appointments under the State for particular positions. But instead of leaving it to individual States to make any rules they like in this regard, the power is vested in Parliament to prescribe the requirement as to residence within the State. This is intended to make the qualifying test uniform throughout India. The second exception is in favour of reservation of positions in public employment for any backward class of citizens. This is meant to help those who have had very little share so far in public employment. The determination of a backward community is a matter that is left to each State Government.[2] The third exception seeks to take out of the scope of the general principle the management of the affairs of any religious or denominational institution under any special law providing for the same.

Although Article 16 guarantees equality of opportunity in matters of public employment for all citizens and is expected to provide a bulwark against considerations of caste, community and religion, the result so far has been far from satisfactory. This has been fully brought out in judicial decisions as well as reports and findings. The States Reorganisation Commission observes:

> Recruitment to the services is a prolific source of discontent among linguistic minorities. The main complaint is that a number of States confine entry to their services to permanent residents of the States, 'permanent residents' being defined in varying ways. These domicile tests, it is contended, have been so devised as to exclude the minority groups from the services.
>
> The residence required under these rules varies from three years in certain cases to fifteen years. These rules are, strictly speaking, in contravention of Article 16(1) of the Constitution. They have apparently been allowed to continue in terms of Article 35(*b*) pending a general review of the position.[3]

In Venkataramana's case,[4] the Supreme court declared invalid the Communal G.O. of the Madras Government reserving posts in the public services for various communities on the principle of communal representation. According to the Court, the ineligibility of the petitioner for appointment to the Madras Provincial Service created by the Communal G.O. was not sanctioned in spite of the exception that permitted the State to provide for reservation of appointments in favour of backward class citizens and, therefore, it was an infringement of the fundamental right guaranteed to him as an individual citizen under Article 16(1). The Communal G.O. was repugnant to the provisions of the article and, as such, void and illegal. In K.C. Nayar *vs*. The Chairman, Central Tractor Organisation,[5] the Court held that the

1. G.D. Rama Rao *vs*. The State of Andhra Pradesh (1961) I S.C.J. 310.
2. C.A.D. VII, p. 701.
3. S.R.C. Report, paras 786 and 787.
4. Venkataramana *vs*. State of Madras, A.I.R. 1951, S.C. 229 See also Mervyn Coutinho *vs*. Collector of Customs, A.I.R. 1967 S.C. 52.
5. (1962) I S.C.J. 715.

fundamental right guaranteed by the Constitution is not only to make an application for a post under the Government but the further right to be considered on merits for such post. The Court held in another case,[1] however, that the State if justified in laying down requisite qualifications for a particular service. It is open to the appointing authority to lay down such pre-requisite conditions of appointment as would be conducive to the maintenance of proper standards amongst government servants and such conditions will not infringe the rights guaranteed under Article 16. In yet another case, the Court held that a contract with the government for the supply of goods is not a contract of employment in the sense in which the word is used in the article. The article "both in terms and in the collocation of the words, indicates that it is confined to 'employment' by the State, and has reference to employment in service rather than as contractors".

Hardly any other constitution has gone into such details in regard to the question of equality in public services. Yet, the operation of these provisions has not been in accordance with their spirit, and has been a source of discontent among large sections of people. Provincialism, communalism, and 'casteism' have been making serious inroads into the arena of the public services. The real problem that confronts the State today is how, on the one hand, it can ensure the building up and maintenance of a public service which is not torn by dissensions and asundered by divisions based on caste and group, community and region, and which evinces social cohesion and civic solidarity, and has its foundation in merit, while, on the other hand it also provides an opportunity for those who have been the victims of a petrified social system to come forward and become equal partners of their more fortunate brethren sharing the responsibilities of office in a common national endeavour. It is indeed a difficult problem and it still awaits a satisfactory solution.

In this context the Supreme court has stressed the need for balancing the competing interests of the entire community in having equal opportunities and the interest of the community in promoting the advancement of the backward classes. However, protective discrimination in favour of backward classes should not be stretched so far as to completely eliminate the value of equal protection of law. Defining the constitutional policy that motivates protective discrimination the Court held in Triloki Nath *vs*. State of Jammu and Kashmir:[2] "In a country where there are different strata of society ranging from highly sophisticated to lowly backward the concept of equality will drive the latter to the wall. Their condition would become worse than what it is. So in order to give a real opportunity to them to compete with the better placed people clause (3) and (4) are introduced in the article (16)'. However, protective discrimination should not result in the perpetuation of the caste-wise division of the society. The Court has, therefore, disapproved the caste-wise definition of backwardness.

Equality of opportunity in matters of public employment as a right is applicable not only to new appointments but also to promotions for those in service. But the Supreme Court held that equality in matters of promotion must mean equality as between members of the same class of employees and not between members of separate independent classes.[3]

1. Banarsidas *vs*. State of Uttar Pradesh. See also 1953, S.C.R. 655 and 1952, S.C.R. 435. The Court's views on this problem were further amplified in a case involving the milki rules of Andhra Pradesh. Narasimha Rao *vs*. State of A.P. A.I.R. 1970 S.C. 432.
2. A.I.R. 1967 S.C. 1889; see also Rajendra *vs*. State of Madras, A.I.R. 1968 S.C. 1012 State of Andhra Pradesh *vs*. P. Sagar A.I.R. 1968 S.C. 1379 and Ranjendran *vs*. Union of India, A.I.R. 1968 S.C. 507.
3. Station Masters' and Assistant Station Master's Association *vs*. General Manager, Central Railway (1960) S.C.J. 344.

In another case,[1] examining the scope and effect of the reservation of posts in public service for candidates belonging to the Scheduled Castes and Tribes, the Court held that the reservation is also applicable to promotion of such candidates to selection posts.

Serious efforts have been made in recent times to make progress towards a solution by which the backward sections of the people are rehabilitated as quickly as possible. A concrete step in this direction was the appointment of a Backward Classes Commission in 1953 to determine the criteria to be adopted in considering any section of the people as socially and educationally backward classes, and to investigate the conditions of such classes and the difficulties under which they labour. The Commission submitted a voluminous report but found it difficult to answer the first question in a clear and satisfactory manner. A plethora of claims was pressed before the Commission for the acceptance of various groups as distinct and separate categories of backward classes. The Commission accepted most of them with the result that there were as many as 2,399 communities in their list. Of these, 913 alone account for an estimated population of 115 million; Scheduled Castes and Tribes will make up another 70 million. Women as a class have also been regarded by them as backward, though they have not listed them as backward classes since they do not form a separate community. In this way, the bulk of the country's millions could be counted as coming within the category of backward, thus making the report not a very useful document for the purpose of making special provisions for those who are really backward in the context of the country's present development. In one sense, however, these figures serve a very useful purpose. They show the general backwardness, social, educational and economic, of the country as a whole and also of the fact that the difficulties and handicaps from which the backward classes suffer differ only in intensity and not in kind from the general problem which applies to the country in its entirety. Nevertheless, the recommendations of the Commission have served a valuable purpose by focusing the attention of both the Central and State Governments on the specific disabilities of various sections of the community so that the governments may formulate appropriate programmes of development.

Abolition of domicile tests for eligibility to state services is sought in a new Act that has been passed by Parliament seven years after the inauguration of the Constitution. The measure, the Public Employment (Requirement as to Residence) Act, 1957, seeks to repeal all existing domiciliary laws in the country which prescribe a period of residence within a particular State or Union Territory for any public employment there. This is one of the safeguards for linguistic minorities suggested by the States Reorganisation Commission in regard to employment in public services. The Central Government as a result is empowered to draft service rules with due regard to the requirements of different areas. The implementation of this Act,[2] which aims at the control of this field by the Central Government, will indeed go a long way in translating into reality the fundamental right of equality in public employment.

By the end of 1962 the framing of rules in conformity with the provisions of the Act was completed in all the States. This means that domicile test has been, at last, done away with in the matter of recruitment to public services. Most of the States have also framed the rules to the effect that language is not a bar to recruitment. The test of proficiency is held only after the selection and not at the stage of selection. The medium of examinations

1. The General Manager, Southern Railway *vs.* Rangachari (1961) II S.C.J. 424.
2. The Public Employment (Requirement as to Residence) Act, 1957.

conducted by the State Public Service Commissions still continues to be English and an option is given to the regional language where candidates prefer to use that language as medium. A somewhat dependable administrative machinery also appears to have been evolved by holding an annual Chief Ministers' Conference when problems of this nature are discussed and decisions are made. The Ministry of Home Affairs of the Central Government plays a key-role at these Conferences.

At a time when emotional integration is of paramount importance to the future of the Nation, the removal of unfair restrictions like the domicile test and the language qualification was an obvious desideratum. While the removal of domicile test will make the concept of single citizenship real, that of language qualification will do justice to linguistic minorities. It is impossible to exaggerate the effectiveness of such practical measures to promote national unity. The Union Government should, however, exercise vigilance to ensure that the States act not only in letter but also in the spirit of these provisions and the old restrictive provisions are not reintroduced by the backdoor under some other guise.

The Central Government has been taking several measures to translate the ideal embodied in Article 16 into practice. It convenes, on a regular basis, a conference of State Ministers of Backward Classes with a view to assessing the measures already taken and suggesting necessary modifications to existing practices in order to produce better results. It also advises the State Governments from time to time on specific actions, such as the deletion of references to caste from official records and application forms for admission to educational institutions and issuing warnings against the practice of untouchability to all Government servants, etc. The States are also advised to adopt economic criteria for the determination of the backwardness of a particular class. But the Governments in the States which are really concerned with the implementation of these proposals have yet to change their attitudes. Most of them are still so much influenced by caste and communal considerations that it seems unrealistic to expect much from them in the near future. Rapid industrialization and the availability of plenty of new jobs along with a simultaneous expansion of educational opportunities for the backward sections of the community as well as a change in the outlook and attitude of those classes and groups which hold a traditional monopoly in public services will gradually facilitate the realization of the ultimate goal of equal opportunity in public services.[1]

In Indra Sawhoney's case[2] which arose out of the implementation of the Mandal Commission Report, the Supreme Court extensively dealt with the question whether Article 16(4) was an exhaustive provision with reference to backward class citizens, whether class can be identified with caste, the viability of means test, the categorisation of backward classes into backward and non-backward classes, extent of reservation etc.

The Court categorically held that the principles of reservation are applicable only to initial appointments and not to promotions. But the state can extend concessions to reserved categories. Article 16(4) is not an exception to proviso to Article 16(1) but it is an empahtic statement of Article 16. The court further held that caste can be and often is a social class in India. If it is a socially backward one, then it benefits from 16(4). But there are differences between caste and class. The Court said that "caste is a socially and occupationally homogenous class". Therefore, caste can be the basis of identification of backward classes at least in the beginning.

1. See in this connection Thomas *vs*. The State of Kerala 1974 A.I.R. 601.
2. 1992 Sup. (3) S.C.C. 217.

The Abolition of Untouchability (Art. 17)

Article 17 abolishes 'untouchability', and its practice in any form is made an offence punishable under the law. No article in the Constitution was adopted with such unanimity and so great an acclamation and enthusiasm as this article. It was the only one which had the special distinction of having been adopted with cries of *'Mahatma Gandhi ki Jai'*. Some critics of the Constitution ask the question: 'What is the right that is created by this article?' It is true that it does not create any special privileges for any one. Yet, it is a great fundamental right, a charter of deliverance to one-sixth of the Indian population from perpetual subjugation and despair, from perpetual humiliation and disgrace.[1] We have already seen, while discussing the nature of fundamental right, that a right is a remedy against a disability. The abolition of untouchability becomes a right in that sense. The custom of untouchability had not only thrown millions of the Indian population into abysmal gloom and despair, shame and disgrace, but it had also eaten into the very vitals of the nation. There could be no better sign of the determination to eradicate the evil than incorporating this article into the chapter on Fundamental Rights in the Constitution.[2]

It may not be inappropriate in this context to recall what Ghandhi feelingly said on one occasion on the subject. He said:

> I do not want to be re-born, but if I am re-born, I wish that I would be re-born as a Harijan, as an untouchable, so that I may lead a continuous struggle against the oppression and indignities that have been heaped upon these classes of people.

Again, it may not be inappropriate to recall here that it was an irony of fate that a man who was driven from one school to another, who was forced to take his lessons outside the classroom and who was thrown out of hotels in the dead of night, all because he was an untouchable, was entrusted with the task of framing the Constitution which embodies this article and which dealt the death blow to this pernicious social perversion.

With the epic fast of Mahatma Gandhi in 1932 in protest against the 'communal award' by which the Scheduled Castes were to be given a separate electorate, a vigorous movement against untouchability was launched on a national basis. Solemn pledges were taken by many members of the Indian National Congress and others that untouchability would no longer find any asylum in the country. The movement brought forth some good results. Many temples were thrown open, and the rigours of untouchability had become a thing of the past at least in the urban centres of the country. But the evil of untouchability still lingered in many forms and in many parts of the country. No wonder Ambedkar had said that though born a Hindu, "I shall never die as one". The only way, he thought, he could escape the curse of caste was by conversion to an egalitarian religion. With vast number of his followers he embraced Buddhism, a religion of egalitarianism. Since then many of his followers embraced Buddhism or other egalitarian religions to escape the wrath of caste. Speaking on the Untouchability Offences Bill, which was passed into an Act in 1955, the Home Minister of India said:

> This cancer of untouchability has entered into the very vitals of our society. It is not only a blot on the Hindu religion, but it has created intolerance, sectionalism and fissiparous tendencies. Many of the evils that we find in our society today are traceable to this heinous monstrosity. It was

1. C.A.D. VII, p. 665.
2. See Ambedkar, B.R., *States and Minorities* 1947, for a detailed discussion of the subject.

really strange that Hindus with their sublime philosophy and their merciful kind-heartedness even towards insects should have been party to such an intolerable dwarfing of manhood. Yet, untouchability has been there for centuries and we have now to atone for it..... The idea of untouchability is entirely repugnant to the structure, spirit and provisions of the Constitution.

The Untouchability Offences Act came into force in June 1955. In one sense it may be said to be an extension of Article 15 of the Constituion.[1] The Act intends to make the enforcement of any disability against the Scheduled Castes illegal. It provides that when the victim is a member of a Scheduled Caste, the commission of a forbidden act should be presumed to have been done on the ground of untouchability. It has laid down that whatever is open to the general public or to Hindu generally should be equally open to members of the Scheduled Castes also. Thus, for example, no shop may refuse to sell and no person may refuse to render any service to any person on the ground of untouchability. Every person is entitled to such services on the terms on which they may be obtained in the ordinary course of business by any other person. Any refusal on that ground entails cancellation of any licence required in respect of such profession. Any act which interferes in any manner with the exercise of such rights by any person is an offence punishable with imprisonment for six months or a fine up to Rs. 500 or both. A subsequent offence is punishable with both imprisonment and fine. All offences under the Act are cognizable and may be compounded with leave of the Court.[2]

In 1976 the name of the untouchability (Offences) Act has been changed as Protection of Civil Rights Act.

Even before the passing of this Act, there has been attempts on the part of State legislatures to remove some of the social disabilities by legislation. There were over twenty such enactments in operation at the time when the Untouchability Offences Act was passed. The Bengal Hindu Social Disabilities Removal Act of 1948 was one such enactment. The Act was challenged as *ultra vires* of the Constitution in the Calcutta High Court in Banamali Das *vs*. Pakhu Bhandari.[3] The facts of the case are interesting. A Banamali Das lodged a complaint against a Pakhu Bhandari and others alleging that the accused had refused to cut the complainant's hair and also to render similar services to others who belonged to the same caste as the complainant, his caste being that of cobbler. As a result, proceedings were initiated against the accused under the abovementioned Act. The defendants contended that the Act was invalid as it unreasonably restricted the exercise of their profession, the calling of a barber. They also attacked the validity of the Act as discriminatory in its tendency.

The Court, in a unanimous decision, rejected these contentions. It said that there was nothing in the Act which cut down the right to carry on the profession of a barber.

All it does is to prohibit him from discriminating between one Hindu and another in carrying out his duties as a barber. The Act compels him to serve all and really enlarges the scope of his services rather than restrict the same.... The citizens of India should not be subdivided, but should form a united body and that is an end that is rightly sought for by our law-making bodies. The makers

1. See *Social Legislation, Its Role in Social Welfare* 1956, p. 220.
2. An amendment to the Act of 1955 introduced in Parliament in 1972 envisaged a jail term to be made mandatory for those convicted of untouchability offences. The new law prescribes a minimum punishment of one month's imprisonment and fifty rupees as fine. A new definition would make it an offence to justify the practice of untouchability on historical, philosophical or religious grounds.
3. A.I.R. 1951, Calcutta 167.

of the Constitution have recognised it and have abolished untouchability and have also provided that there should be no discrimination only on the ground of caste or religion..... The Act does not discriminate, but penalises and abolishes tendencies in Hindu society to discrimination.... [It] does not deny any person equality before law. It tends to make all persons equal in society and before the law and it cannot possibly be argued that this Act denies any person equal protection of laws.

In a similar case,[1] the U.P. Removal of Social Disabilities Act, 1947, was challenged in a joint appeal by five barbers and two *dhobies* (washermen) before the Allahabad High Court. Here also the decision of the Court, which was unanimous upheld the Act. The Court held that the applicants had no right to refuse to render their service because the persons demanding it belonged to a Scheduled Caste.

The Court also held that non permission to certain communities to enter temples would violate Article 17.[2]

In spite of the constitutional provisions, the operation of the Untouchability Offences Act and judicial pronouncements, India cannot yet claim to have rooted out the evil of untouchability completely. In the fight against social evils, legislation is only one of many weapons. To adopt an article in the Constitution against untouchability and make it a fundamental right or pass an Act of Parliament making its practice an offence and then expect overnight to have a society devoid of this centuries-old evil would be too optimistic. There is no room for complacency in spite of the existence of these enactments. Legislation is a poor remedy for prejudices. The battle against every form of untouchability and social discrimination has to be carried to the hearts and minds of prejudiced people through mass contact, the mustering of public opinion and social action. Simultaneously, there must be a vigilant watch over offenders with a view to punishing every aggressive manifestation of caste discrimination.

A relevant report[3] of the Commissioner for Scheduled Castes and Tribes reveals that untouchability is gradually disappearing as a result of the efforts made by official and non-official agencies. But it is doubtful whether the evil will be completely rooted out before the specific period of safeguards provided in the Constitution comes to an end in 2010. Maharashtra was the only State, according to the Commissioner, which has set up a specific machinery to assess the prevalence of untouchability and formulate measures to get rid of it before the period of constitutional safeguard was over. If every State sets up a Committee of experts from each of the fields of anthropology, psychology, sociology, economics, political science and history besides representatives of the administration and a few social workers of experience and repute to investigate into the problem of untouchability in all its aspects and follows up the recommendations of such a committee and evaluates the progress made every year, the results are bound to be more substantial. An enhancement of the powers of the Commissioner which includes his direct contacts with various State authorities to ensure that the directives issued by the Union Government with regard to the safeguards and the implementation of the welfare schemes are duly and promptly carried out also is necessary to ensure better rate of progress.

---

1. State *vs*. Banwari, A.I.R. 1951, Allahabad, 615.
2. See Venkiteramana *vs*. State of Maysore AIR 1958 S.C. 255.
3. Tenth Report of the Commissioner for Scheduled Castes and Scheduled Tribes, 1962. The Subsequent reports of the Commissioner, however, do not portray such an encouraging picture.

The Abolition of Titles (Art. 18)

In the creation of a society which seeks to establish political, social and economic equality and thereby aspires to become truly democratic, there is no room for some individuals to hold titles thus creating artificial distinctions among members of the same society. Recognition of titles and the consequent creation of a hierarchy of aristocracy had been denounced as an anti-democratic practice as early as the eighteenth century by both the American[1] and the French Revolutions. A democracy should not create titles and titular glories. In India, the practice of the British Government conferring a number of titles every year mostly on their political supporters and government officers had already created a peculiar class of nobility among the people. It was difficult, on principle, for Independent India to recognize and accept these titles apart from considerations of the merit of those who held them. Article 18, therefore, abolishes all titles and the State is prohibited from conferring titles on any person. The only exception made to the strict rule of non-recognition of titles is that provided in favour of academic or military distinctions.[2]

Ambedkar explained in the Constituent Assembly that Article 18 did not create a justiciable right.

> The non-acceptance of titles is a condition of continued citizenship, it is not a right, it is a duty imposed upon the individual that if he continues to be the citizen of this country, then he must abide by certain conditions. One of the conditions is that he must not accept a title, if he did, it would be open for Parliament to decide by law what should be done to persons who violate the provisions of this article. One of the penalties may be that he may lose the right of citizenships.[3]

Thus, under Article 18, not only is the State in India prevented from conferring titles on any person, but Indian citizens are forbidden to accept any title from a foreign State without the consent of the President of India. The prohibition applies not only to the acceptance of titles but also to that of any present, emolument or office of any kind from any foreign State by any person holding an office of profit or trust under the State.

The battle against the titles conferred by the British monarch started with the passing of the United States Constitution in 1787 which prohibited all titles of nobility in the United States. Another British dependency, Ireland, on establishing its independence followed suit and its constitution too prohibits the conferring of titles by the State.[4] India and Burma were the next to follow the example, the former despite the fact that she decided to continue to be a member of the Commonwealth of Nations whose head was the British monarch.

Apart from its inherent undemocratic character, conferment of titles by the State has in it another serious objectionable aspect. The State's action in this regard is in reality the result of decisions made by the government of the day. Since the Government of the day is a party government, its decisions on matters like this are likely to reflect political considerations. In other words, it is not always merit or objective considerations but partisanship and personal factors that dominate such divisions. However honest or objective

---

1. Section 9, Sub-section 8 of the First Article of the United States Constitution reads: 'No title of nobility shall be granted by the United States and no person holding any office of profit or trust under them shall, without the consent of the Congress, accept any present, emolument, office or title of any kind whatever from any king, prince or foreign State.'
2. Art. 18(1) reads: 'No title, not being a military or academic distinction, shall be conferred by the State.'
3. C.A.D. VII, p. 709.
4. Art. 40(2). See also similar provisions in the Constitution of Japan, Art. 19.

a government may be in this matter today, it is no guarantee for similar conduct on the part of future governments. This is the fundamental objection to all cases of nominations, however desirable and advantageous they may otherwise be. The lofty ideal with which such a process marks its beginning may soon degenerate into favouritism and corruption. As an illustration, one may point out the classic case of the Canadian Senate where members for existing vacancies are nominated for life by the government of the day. Originally, it was not meant to be a device for indulging in patronage but for getting elder statesmen for the Legislature as such men might not like to contest elections. Yet, in course of time, the Canadian Senate earned the notorious name of 'the bribery fund' of the party in power.

Viewed against this background, there could be objections to the President of India conferring awards and distinctions such as *Bharat Ratna, Padma Vibhushan, etc.* on Indian citizens.[1] True, the Government does not consider them as titles or anything equivalent to titles. They are only tokens of public recognition of the meritorious service rendered by individual citizens to the country or community. Yet, the way in which they are conferred and the categories into which they are divided, all smack of the evil that it purported to be abolished by Article 18 of the Constitution. Even the Warrant of Precedence of the Government of India recognizes the superior status of persons on whom such honours have been conferred.[2] Apart from the fundamental objections already pointed out the practice in fact amounts to an attempt to make an evaluation of the comparative merits of the services of different individuals, which often becomes an impossibility. To adjudge comparatively, in terms of actual merit, the services of two persons working in two fields of activity altogether different from each other may be impracticable. How then may one of them receive an honour that is rated superior to the other as for instance a *Padma Vibhushan* instead of a *Padma Shri* ? This naturally creates heartburning in those who receive the lower honours and even engenders a spirit of unhealthy and unfair comparison. If the person concerned happens to be a government servant, he dares not, even if he does not feel happy with the particular honour that is being conferred upon him, refuse it. Legally these honours may not be recognized by the Government as titles. Yet in effect they almost amount to the same and are open to the objections which are advanced against the conferment of titles.

The urge to recognize meritorious services and to give picturesque or effective verbal expression to such recognition has ever been a human habit. Whether governments officially recognized them or not, the people at large were keen to express their esteem and devotion in this form. The classic example of it in India was the title of *Mahatma* (great soul) which

---

1. At present there are four such awards and distinctions. There are : (i) *Bharat Ratna*: (Jewel of India) the highest of its kind. The award is made for outstanding work for the advancement of art, literature and science and in recognition of public service of the highest order. (ii) *Padma Vibhushan*: The award is made for exceptional and distinguished service in any field, including service rendered by government servants (iii) *Padma Bhushan:* This award stands next in order and is made for distinguished service of a high order in any field, including service rendered by government servants (iv) *Padma Shri:* the last in order of merit, is awarded for distinguished service in any field, including service rendered by government servants. For a short period, 1977-79, when the Janata Government was in power, these awards were discontinued. They were, however, revived in 1980.
2. For instance, holders of Bharat Ratna decorations are given the ninth place in the National Warrant of Precedence. See *India* 1974.

   Also see "It is no Honour to figure in a Crowd", Times or India, Feb., 20, 1999 and Malhotra, Awards Losing their Shine, The Hindu, Feb. 3, 1999.

came to be universally accepted, and became an inseparable part of the name of Gandhi. It was not the result of conferment or recognition by any State. It was the result of a national urge on the part of the people who wanted to recognize, in an appropriate manner, the services of a great hero. There was nothing undemocratic in it. But when the State enters the field, the results are not so happy. This is the rationale behind the abolition of titles as well as a prohibition on the State to confer titles. The high-minded purpose of Article 18 will become a reality only when its provisions are respected not only in form but also in the spirit.

For the first time when the Republic Day awards by the President of India was instituted over decades ago, the reactions of the public varied from downright hostility to plain indifference. There was certainly no popular enthusiasm over what in fact was a major national innovation since Independence. Critics objected to the revival of titles in a new form because they feared that this was an uningenuous attempt to reverse the process of creating a classless society. Indifference was the result of a feeling that the new awards were inadequate in comparison with those which existed during the British regime. But the passage of time appears to have brought about a definite change in the attitude of the public. This is evident from the eagerness with which the Honours List is awaited on the Republic Day and the subsequent esteem shown to the recipients. It is also a fact, that, by and large, the awards were made to individuals who had rendered meritorious work. But there have been instances where individuals have refused to accept them or where the recipients were later found to be lacking in the qualities for which they were presumed to have been honoured. This should provide a warning for the future. The practice can certainly degenerate into a system of political or narrow group interest being rewarded by those in office for the time being. The existing procedure by which candidates are chosen is also one which is capable of being abused at the whims and fancies of a privileged few[1]. Therefore, if the Honours List has to become one of really honoured ones, the selection procedure has to be made most acceptable.

The urge to revolt against all forms of inequalities is natural to man. Stable democratic conditions to which equality is well adjusted are the gateways to social, political and economic justice to which the Constitution is dedicated. If any democratic system of government is to produce wholesome lasting results, it is necessary that the desire for establishing equality must characterize and influence its operations. Only a society which succeeds in establishing equality among its members will be able to produce satisfactory democratic values. Any democratic polity which does not include an investigation of the values of equality would belie its name.

***

1. An independent member of Parliament and a veteran freedom fighter, J.B. Kripalani, moved in the Lok Sabha a Bill (1972) to abolsih State decorations like the Republic Day awards describing them as unconstitutional, anti-democratic and anit-socialistic. He said that the State awards violated the fundamental right to equality, demoralised the people and degraded the giver as well as the reciever.

11

THE RIGHT TO FREEDOM : I

(Art. 19)

PERSONAL LIBERTY is the most fundamental of fundamental rights. Articles 19 to 22 deal with the different aspects of this basic right. Taken together, these four articles form a charter of personal liberties, which provides the backbone of the chapter on Fundamental Rights. Of these, Article 19 is the most important and it may rightly be called the key-article embodying the 'Basic Freedoms' under the Constitution, guaranteed to all citizens These are the rights :

1. to freedom of speech and expression;
2. to assemble peaceably and without arms;
3. to form associations or unions;
4. to move freely throughout the territory of India;
5. to reside and settle in any part of the territory of India; and
6. to practise any profession, or to carry on any occupation, trade or business.

It is impossible to exaggerate the importance of these freedoms in any democratic society. Indeed, the very test of a democratic society is the extent to which these freedoms are enjoyed by the citizens in general. These freedoms, as a whole, constitute the extent of liberty of the individual, and liberty is one of the most essential ingredients of human happiness and progress. The most important among the inalienable rights of man, according to the Declaration of American Independence, are 'Life, Liberty and the Pursuit of Happiness'. The preamble of almost every constitution declares the same in one form or another as its objective. The Preamble of the Constitution of the United States, for instance, declares that one of its objects is 'to secure the blessings of liberty to ourselves and to our posterity'. The Preamble of the Indian Constitution too proclaims that one of its objectives is to secure Liberty—liberty of thought, expression, belief, faith and worship.

The inclusion of the right to freedom of speech as an integral part of a written constitution was first attempted in the American Constitution. The political theory behind the guarantee of this right was most eloquently expounded by Thomas Jefferson in 1779 in the following words:

> That the opinions of men are not the object of civil government, nor under its jurisdiction; that to suffer the civil magistrate to intrude his powers into the field of opinion and to restrain the profession or propagation of principles on supposition of their tendency is a dangerous fallacy, which at once destroys all religious liberty, because he being of course the judge of that tendency

will make his opinions the rule of judgement, and approve or condemn the sentiments of others only as they shall square with or suffer from his own; that it is time enough for the rightful purposes of civil government for its officers to interfere when principles break out into overt acts against peace and good order; and finally, that truth is great and will prevail if left to herself; that she is the proper and sufficient antagonist to error, and has nothing to fear from the conflict unless, by human interposition, disarmed of her natural weapons, free argument and debate; errors ceasing to be dangerous when it is permitted freely to contradict them.

This Jeffersonian theory found powerful support, although much later, in the philosophy of John Stuart Mill who wrote:

If all mankind minus one, were of one opinion, and only one person were of the contrary opinion, mankind would be no more justified in silencing that one person, than he, if he had the power, would be justified in silencing mankind.

Freedom of speech, however, is not absolute. One's freedom to express oneself does not permit the liberty to abuse or slander the good name of others. But so far as questions of public import are concerned, there should be scope for full and free debate. There must even be scope for advocacy. Ideas are, of course, dangerous—perhaps the most dangerous forces in the world. Advocacy of an idea may be an incitement too powerful for any resistance. Every speech is indeed an incitement—sometimes an incitement to action, sometimes to mediation. Civilized man has known as much from the beginning.[1] But dangerous as advocacy and the excitement of ideas are, there is even greater danger in suppression. A government that enters upon a programme of suppression may have its own views of the public good in mind. But what is good for the government may be anathema to the people. Henry VIII banned the reading of the Bible in churches, for he thought that the ideas of liberty contained therein might make the common people restless. The Tibetan monasteries feared for long mass education more than Chinese invasion. These were after all manifestations of absolute autocracy. But where the doctrine of 'consent of the governed' is to be real, the people ought to have full opportunity to learn. For, freedom to learn is, indeed, the most important product of freedom of speech.

Nevertheless, even the freedom of political expression has to have certain limits. It is restricted in the interests of society itself, its preservation, its orderliness and its progress. But where shall we draw the line ? It is here that we run into serious difficulties. The extent of freedom of expression enjoyed by citizens under different political systems, even if basically they are democratic in nature, is bound to vary in degree on account of the differing political and socio-economic developments they have achieved. It seems that a doctrinaire approach here is as dangerous to the stability of the political system itself as an attempt to suppress free speech and expression altogether.

Social discipline and anarchy are not mutually complimentary or supplementary. When individuals and groups in their overt actions begin to practise the ideologies of revolutions and anarchy, they sow the seeds of their own destruction. While social discipline alone can make men safe in their moorings, social indiscipline opens so wide a door to tendencies which lower the standards of morality all-round. Lawlessness in private conduct soon ends in public disaster. A tendency that is seen in many newly independent societies is a lack of balance in the exercise of individual liberty and social control. It is a difficult adjustment to be brought about by the written laws of a Constitution. We may examine what guidance India's Constitution has to offer in this connection.

1. William O. Douglas, *We the Judges*, p. 300.

The articles dealing with the Right to Freedom are the product of a compromise of the two extremes. Having achieved political freedom only recently, the urge to exercise unfettered right to freedom was very much there. At the same time, there was also the realization that the State that had been brought into existence was an infant State and if the newly-won freedom was to be guaranteed by a stable political order, it depended on the continued existence of that infant State which had yet to pass through many troubles. Therefore, the State should be preserved even if that entailed the abridgement to some extent of the rights guaranteed. The Drafting Committee, therefore, chose the golden mean of providing a proper enumeration of those rights that are considered essential for the individual and, at the same time, putting such checks on them as will ensure the security of the State. They thought that the working of these rights depended on the genius of the Indian people, on how they developed their ideas of liberty which at the time of the drafting of the Constitution were in a rather undeveloped state.[1]

There was, however, vehement criticism in the Constituent Assembly against the restrictions on the enjoyment of these freedoms. One member observed:

> In fact, the freedoms guaranteed by this article (19) become so elusive that one would find it necessary to have a microscope to discover where these freedoms are whenever it suits the State or the authorities to deny them.[2]

On personal liberty he said :

> The constitution was drafted at a time when people were going through extraordinary stress and strain. The tragic happenings of some twelve or fourteen months ago (the partition, mass killings and mass migrations) were no doubt responsible for influencing those who drafted the Constitution that in the then prevailing 'goonda raj'[3] it was necessary to restrict somehow the freedom of the individual.[4]

Another member said :

> If we leave these rights to this very body (legislature), which in a democracy is nothing beyond a political party, to finally judge when these rights so sacred on paper and glorified as fundamental rights are to be extinguished, we are certainly making these freedoms illusory.[5]

As it stands, now, there are eight restrictions on the freedom of speech and expression. These are: the sovereignty and integrity of India, the security of the State; friendly relations with foreign States; public order, decency or morality; contempt of court; defamation; and incitement to an offence. As it was passed originally by the Constituent Assembly, the restrictions were fewer and confined only to 'libel' slander, defamation; contempt of court; any matter which offends against decency or morality, or which undermines the security of, or tends to overthrow, the State'. These were modified into their present form as a result of the First Amendment of the Constitution, 1951, necessitated by the decision of the Supreme Court in Romesh Thapar *vs.* the State of Madras, and also the sixteenth Amendment of 1963. The Court held in Thapar's case that unless a law restricting freedom of speech and expression were directed solely against the undermining of the security of

1. C.A.D. VII, p. 771.
2. K.T. Shah, Ibid, pp, 714 and 726.
3. The rule of the thugs.
4. K.T. Shah, Ibid.
5. Sardar Hukum Singh, p. 734. Hukum singh was the Deputy Speaker of the Lok Sabha between 1957 and 1962 and its Speaker since September 1962, indeed in a privileged position to safeguard these rights.

the State or its overthrow, the law could not be held a reasonable restriction though it sought to impose a restraint for the maintenance of public order.[1] Speaking for the Court, Justice Patanjali Sastri said:

> There can be no doubt that freedom of speech and expression includes freedom of propagation of ideas, and that the freedom is ensured by the freedom of circulation. Liberty of circulation is as essential to that freedom as the liberty of publication. Indeed, without circulation the publication would be of little value... Similarly, the Constitution in formulating the varying criteria for permissible legislation imposing restrictions on the fundamental rights enumerated in Article 19(1), has placed in a distinct category those offences against public order which aim at undermining the security of State or overthrowing it and made their prevention the sole justification for legislative abridgement of freedom of speech and expression, that is to say, nothing less than endangering the foundations of the State or threatening its overthrow could justify curtailment of the rights to freedom of speech and expression, while the right of peaceable assembly and the right to association may be restricted under clauses 3 and 4 of Article 19 in the interest of public order, which in those clauses includes the security of the State..... The Constitution thus requires a line to be drawn in the field of public order or tranquility, marking off, more of less roughly, the boundary between those serious and aggravated forms of public disorder which are calculated to endanger the security of the State, and the relatively minor breaches of the peace of a purely local significance treating for this purpose differences in degree as if they were differences in kind.... Deletion of the word sedition from the draft (Constitution) therefore, shows that criticism of the government existing disaffection or bad feelings towards it is not to be regarded as a justifying ground for restricting the freedom of expression and of the press, unless it is such as to undermine the security or tend to overthrow the State. It is also significant that the corresponding Irish formula of undermining the public order or the security of the State,[2] did not find favour with the framers of the Indian Constitution. Thus, very narrow and stringent limits have been set to permissible legislative abridgement of the right of free speech and expression and this was doubtless due to the realisation that freedom of speech and of the press lay at the foundation of all democratic organisation, or without free political discussion no public education, so essential for the proper functioning of the processes of popular government, is possible. A freedom of such amplitude might involve risks of abuse.
>
> We are, therefore, of opinion that unless a law restricting freedom of speech and expression is directed solely against the undermining of the security of the State or the overthrow of it, such law cannot fall within the reservation under clause (2) of Article 19, although the restrictions which it seeks to impose may have been conceived generally in the interests of securing public order. It follows that section 9(1-A) which authorises imposition of restrictions for the wider purpose of securing public safety or the maintenance of public order falls outside the scope of authorised restrictions under clause (2) and is, therefore, void and unconstitutional[3].

On the basis of this interpretation of the Supreme Court, some of the High Courts gave decisions to the effect that even incitement to individual murder or promoting disaffection among classes could not be restricted under the permissive limits set in Article 19(2). This was indeed a drawback which required rectification. The First Amendment of the Constitution made the necessary provision to obviate this difficulty by including 'public order' along with other grounds for restricting the freedom of speech and expression. Thus, the scope of restriction under the present provision is broader than what it was under the original provision. Yet, in every case the judiciary gets a chance to test the validity of

---

1. The impugned legislation in this case was the Madras Maintenance of Public Order Act, 1947, particularly its section 9(1—A).
2. Article 40 of the Constitution of Ireland 1937.
3. See in this connection, Tara Singh *vs.* State, 1951, A.I.R, Punjab 29; Srinivas *vs.* State of Madras 1951, A.I.R. Madras 70 and *In re* Bharati Press A.I.R. 1951, Patna 12.

the executive action or legislative enactment against its reasonableness. In fact, the word 'reasonable' is the life and soul of the entire article. Interpreting the meaning of this word the Supreme Court said :

> The phrase 'reasonable restriction' connotes that the limitation imposed upon a person in enjoyment of a right should not be arbitrary or of an excessive nature beyond what is required in the interest of the public. Legislation which arbitrarily or excessively invades the right cannot be said to contain the quality of reasonableness, and unless it strikes a proper balance between the freedom guaranteed and the social control permitted under Article 19 it must be held to be wanting in reasonableness.[1]

While there can be a definite or positive standard of reasonableness, the reasonableness of the legislation, it need hardly be pointed out, must be germane to the nature and objects of the legislation concerned.[2] Despite the First Amendment which enlarged the scope of the restrictions, the courts, during the course of over three decades, have given a number of pronouncements showing that they are on the side of tolerance for speech and expression.

A few representative selections may not be out of place in this context. In Brij Bhushan *vs*. The State of Delhi[3] the Supreme Court held:

> There can be little doubt that the imposition of pre-consorship on a journal is a restriction on the liberty of the press which is an essential part of the right of freedom of speech and expression declared by Article 19(1)(*a*)

However, the Court held in the State of Bihar *vs*. Shailabala Devi,[4] that:

> Speeches and expressions on the part of an individual which incite to or encourage the commission of violent crimes, such as murder, cannot but be matters which would undermine the security of the State and come within the ambit of a law sanctioned by Article 19(2).

But the Court said that the document in question in this particular case did not fall within the statutory prohibitions as it merely consisted of empty slogans'. Justice Mahajan wrote:

> Writing of this character at the present moment and in the present background of our country neither excite nor have the tendency to excite any person from among the class which is likely to read a pamphlet of this nature..... The writing has to be considered as a whole and in a fair and free and liberal spirit.

The test to determine the validity of an impugned Act curtailing freedom of speech and expression is to see the effect of that on the abridgement of the Fundamental Right.[5] In Indian Express *vs*. Union of India[6] imposition of customs duty on newsprint only because it was said to be minimal was held to be violative of freedom of the press under the Article. The Court held that the levying newsprint on insufficient and unconvincing grounds was violative of Article 19(1)(*a*).

In Ramji Lal Modi *vs*. State of U.P.,[7] the validity of Section 295-A of the Indian

1. Dwarka Prasad *vs*. State of U.P., A.I.R. 1954, S.C. 224.
2. Chintaman Rao *vs*. The State of Madhya Pradesh 1950, S.C.R. 759. See also Cooverjee Bharucha *vs*. Excise Commissioner 1954, S.C.R. 873; Saghir Ahmed *vs*. The State of Uttar Pradesh 1955, S.C.R. 707, p. 726; R.L. Modi *vs*. The State of Uttar Pradesh 1957, S.C.J. 522 and Virendra *vs*. The State of Punjab 1958, S.C.J. 88.
3. 1950, S.C.R. 605.
4. 1952, S.C.R. 654. See also Ram Singh *vs*. State of Delhi 1951, S.C.R. 451.
5. Express Newspapers Ltd. Union of India AIR 1958 SC 5789.
6. AIR 1986 SC 515.
7. 1957, S.C.J. 522. See also Virendra *vs*. State of Punjab 1958, S.C.J. 88 and Hamdard Dawakhana *vs*. Union of India, 1960 S.C.R. 611.

Penal Code was challenged on the ground that it interfered with the petitioner's right to freedom of speech and expression guaranteed to him as a citizen of India by Article 19(1)(*a*) of the Constitution. In an unanimous decision, the Court rejected this plea and held that the impugned section of the Penal Code was within the protection of Clause (2) of Article 19 as being a law imposing reasonable restrictions on the exercise of the right to freedom of speech and expression.

> Section 295-A of the Penal Code does not penalise any and every act of insult or attempt to insult the religion or religious beliefs of a class of citizens, which are perpetrated with the deliberate and malicious intention of outraging the religious feelings of that class. Insults to religion offered unwittingly or carelessly or without any deliberate or malicious intention of outraging the religious feelings of that class do not come within the section. It only punishes the aggravated form of insult to religion when it is perpetrated with the deliberate and malicious intention of outraging the religious feelings of that class. The calculated tendency of this aggravated form of insult is clearly to disrupt the public order and the section (295-A) which penalises such activities, is well within the protection of clause (2) of Article 19...

The Court also pointed out that the scope of the expression 'in the interest of public order' is much wider than 'for maintenance of public order'. If therefore, certain activities have a tendency to cause public disorder, a law penalising such activities as an offence cannot but be held to be a law imposing 'reasonable restriction' 'in the interests of public order although in some cases those activities may not actually lead to a breach of public order.[1]

In K.N. Singh *vs.* State of Bihar the Court held:

> Freedom has to be guarded against becoming a license for vilification and condemnation of the Government established by law, in words which incite violence or have the tendency to create public disorder. A citizen has a right to say or write whatever he likes about the Government... so long as he does not incite people to violence...

On this basis the anti-sedition section of the Indian Penal Code was upheld by the Court with the condition that it applied only 'when the words... have the pernicious tendency or intention of creating public disorder or disturbances of law and order. In this decision the Supreme Court was one with its predecessor, the Federal Court, which had expressed similar views in 1942.

As a general rule, the Court is prepared to concede that the Executive has the authority to impose restrictive measures as an incidence of its police power. But the Court has, at the same time, insisted that there should be more than "remote or fanciful connections between the impugned act and the public order." The interest of public order does not ignore the necessity for an intimate connection between the act and the public order sought to be maintained by the act. Further, restriction made "in the interest of public order" must have reasonable relation to the object to be achieved, namely, public order. "A reasonable restriction should be one which has a proximate connection or nexus with public order, but not one far-fetched, hypothetical or problematical or too remote in the chain of its relation with the public order."

The net result of the various decisions of the Supreme Court in this sphere seems to leave the balance of advantage in the hands of the Executive although the Court has the

---

1. For a detailed discussion on the scope of 'public order' by the Supreme Court, see K.N. Singh *vs.* The State of Bihar (1963) I S.C.J. 18; Supt., Central Prison *vs.* R.M. Lohia, 1960 S.C.J. 567; B. Parate *vs.* The State of Maharashtra (1961) I S.C.J. 554. Also see D.C. Srivastava, *Concept of Public Order in India,* 1960 S.C.J. 241.

final say in every case where the action of the police is challenged.[1]

The Sixteenth Amendment of the Constitution (1962) has brought about a further modification in the scope of Article 19(2) and added an additional restriction to the freedom of speech and expression: "in the interest of sovereignty and integrity of India". The object of this Amendment is to make potentially illegal any political agitation for dismembering the Indian Union or for ceding any portion of Indian territory to a foreign State. The Supreme court has yet to interpret the scope of the new limitation. It would be interesting to wait for the Court's reaction in a situation where local politicians indulge in agitations of a political nature, such as linguistic demands or greater regional or local autonomy, and the State taking action against them under the provisions of the Sixteenth Amendment.

Freedom of the Press

There had been much criticism, both within the Constituent Assembly and outside, of the omission of a specific reference to Freedom of the Press and the failure to guarantee it along with the freedom of speech.[2] The omission was considered a serious lapse on the part of the Drafting Committee by the protagonists of a 'Free Press' as a separate right. No doubt the freedom of the Press was one of the most precious rights for the recognition of which bitter constitutional battles had been fought in the eighteenth and nineteenth centuries in Europe and America. The First Amendment of the American Constitution, and most of the European constitutions, embody the freedom of the Press as a separate right. Nevertheless, the Drafting Committee did not think it necessary to incorporate a separate right of this nature in the chapter on Fundamental Rights.

Speaking on behalf of the Committee, Ambedkar said that the Press was merely another way of denoting an individual or a citizen.

> The Press has no special rights which are not to be given or which are not to be exercised by the citizen in his individual capacity. The editor of a press or the manager of the press are all citizens and, therefore, when they choose to write in newspapers, they are merely exercising their right of expression and in my judgment, therefore, no special mention is necessary of the freedom of the Press at all.[3]

The word 'expression' that is used in Article 19(1) (*a*) in addition to 'speech' is comprehensive enough to cover the Press. In fact, the lack of a specific mention of the Press in the Constitution created no difficulty when the Supreme Court was called upon to protect the freedom of the Press in Romesh Thapar's case.[4] Further, modern science and technology have invented and are still inventing and bringing into use many forms of expression through which communication of ideas is facilitated. The radio, the cinema, the telephone, television and internet are a few important examples of these new forms. Some of these may become in the course of time even more powerful and important media of expression than the Press itself. So, there seems to be no justification to single out any of them or mentioning all of the existing dominant forms in the Constitution, as such detailed mention would not serve any purpose which is not served by the word 'expression'.

---

1. See in ths connection Anantha Prabhu *vs*. The District Collector, Ernakulam, 1974 KLT 291 and Maneka Gandhi *vs*. Union of India (1978) I Scc. 248.
2. C.A.D. VII, 382, 712, 714. Also see vol IX, pp, 841–53 and 1182–3.
3. C.A.D. VII, pp. 779-80.
4. Also see Shanker *vs*. State, 41 A.I.R. 562 and *In re* Venugopal, 41 A.I.R. 901; Express Newspapers *vs*. The Union of India 1958, S.C.J. 1113.

Hence, the criticism of the Constitution for not including the 'Freedom of the Press as a separate right can hardly be justified.

Yet, the scope of the freedom of the press figured prominently when the Supreme Court examined the ambit of certain provisions included in the Newspaper (Price and Page) Act, 1956 in the case of Sakal Papers (P) Ltd. *vs.* The Union of India.[1] The main question that called for a decision was whether the State could restrict the freedom of a newspaper to publish any number of pages or to circulate it to any number of persons as an integral part of the freedom of speech and expression. The Court held that a restraint placed on either of them was a direct infringement of the right to freedom of speech and expression. "The Newspaper Act was intended to affect circulation and thus directly affect the freedom of speech. The Act seeks to achieve its object of enabling what are termed the smaller newspapers to secure larger circulation by provisions which without disguise are aimed at restricting the circulation of what are termed the larger papers with better financial strength. The impugned law far from being one, which merely interferes with the right of freedom of speech incidentally, does so directly though it seeks to achieve the end by purporting to regulate the business aspect of a newspaper. Such a course is not permissible and the Courts must be ever vigilant in guarding perhaps the most precious of all the freedoms guaranteed by our Constitution. The freedom of speech and expression is of paramount importance under a democratic constitution which envisages changes in the composition of legislatures and governments and must be preserved...

"The object of giving some kind of protection to small or newly started newspapers may be desirable but for attaining that object the State cannot make inroads on the right of other newspapers which Article 19(1) (*a*) guarantees to them. The only restrictions which may be imposed on the rights of an individual under Article 19(1) (*a*) are those which clause (2) of Article 19 permits and no other.

"Accordingly, section 3(1) of the Newspaper (Price and Page) Act 1956 which is its pivotal provision is unconstitutional and, therefore, the Daily Newspaper (Price and Page) Order, 1960 made thereunder is also unconstitutional. If section 3(1) is struck down as bad, nothing remains in the Act itself."

In Virendra *vs.* State of Punjab[2] the action of the State authorities in prohibiting the entry or publication of materials they believed would stir up Hindu-Sikh conflict during a tense communal situation was challenged as unreasonable restriction on the freedom of expression. The Court upheld the arguments of the State on the basis that the State authorities alone were the best judges of the threat to law and order under specific circumstances. It also agreed that under such circumstances the State had the right to exercise pre-censorship and to restrict the dissemination of press materials from outside the State for temporary periods during an emergency. The Court, however, insisted that the restrictions placed on the press must specify the material not to be printed, the reasons, and the duration for which the restrictions would be in force. There must also be provision for representation to the Government against any restrictive order in this context.

In Express Newspapers (Private) Ltd. *vs.* The Union of India[3] an attempt was made by some newspapers to seek refuge from labour laws under Article 19(1) (*a*). The Court,

1. (1962) II S.C.J. 400.
2. A.I.R. 1958 S.C. 986. See also Naresh *vs.* State of Maharashtra, A.I.R. 1967 S.C. I.
3. 1959 S.C.R. 12.

rejecting the plea of the newspapers, held the view that although the press could not be singled out for discriminatory legislation, freedom of the press did not include immunity from ordinary taxation or general labour laws, particularly so far as they applied to working conditions. The Court also held that the content of commercial advertisements is not covered by Article 19(1) (*a*) since the object of such advertisements is not the propagation of social, political or economic ideas or the furtherance of literature or human thought but commercialization of a product.[1] The decision also upheld the Government's right to regulate advertisements for drugs and "magical remedies". The decision is not clear, however, as to what would be the attitude of the Court towards paid advertisements which may deal with ideas or ideologies and which also the State may seek to regulate. Since such advertisements are deliberately meant to propagate political or other ideas, they should normally be considered to fall within the protection of free speech and expression. Paid political advertisements in the press, however, are yet to become an important medium of communication in India. On the whole, the judiciary has been a true guardian, to the extent possible under conditions existing in India, to uphold the freedom of the press both from pre-censorship and other interference under ordinary conditions by the State and its agencies.

The Right of Assembly [Art. 19(1) (*b*) and 19(3)]

One of the basic protections of free speech is the right of free assembly. In fact, freedom of assembly and freedom of speech go hand in hand. The framers of the Constitution knew that the right to assemble in peace for public debate and discussion, for political activities and such other purposes was essential to make the freedom of speech and expression real. Hence the constitutional guarantee to assemble peaceably and without arms. Some members of the Constituent Assembly thought that the right to bear arms also should have been made available. Some of them pointed out that the Karachi session of the Congress in 1930 had in its Resolution on Fundamental Rights included the right to keep and bear arms.[2] Gandhi had included it as one of his 'Eight Points' which he wanted to be accepted by Lord Irwin, the Governor-General, in 1930. The question of this right dates back to the year 1858 when, after the Mutiny, the British Government disarmed the nation. The achievement of Independence ought to have, according to some members, reestablished the right in unmistakable terms. Answering the critics, Ambedkar pointed out that the circumstances under which the Congress Party had passed resolutions on the right to bear arms did not exist any longer.

> My submission is that so far as bearing of arms is concerned, what we ought to insist upon is not be the *right* of an individual to bear arms but his duty to bear arms.[3]

The right to assembly can be restricted only in the interest of public order and the restrictions ought to be reasonable. Interpreting the scope of this provision, the Patna High Court, in the case of Indradeo Singh *vs.* the State[4], in which the Bihar Maintenance of Public Order Ordinance of 1949 was challenged as invalid, held that what the Court had to decide was whether or not the restrictions were reasonable.

---

1. Hamdard Dawakhana *vs.* Union of India, Ibid.
   See also Reliance Petrochemical Ltd. *vs.* Proprietors of Express Newspapers, Bombay AIR 1989 SC 140.
2. C.A.D. VII, pp. 719 and 764.
3. Ibid. p. 780
4. 1951, A.I.R. Patna 242. See also in this connection the views of the Supreme Court in Babulal Parate *vs.* The State of Maharashtra 1961 I.S.C.J. 554.

The question is whether the relevant section of the Ordinance relating to the banning of public procession *etc.* was an unreasonable restriction in the exercise of the right conferred by the above clause [Art. 19(3)] of the Constitution. In my opinion, it is sufficient to state that the restriction imposed by the Act so far as it related to public processions *etc.* was not unreasonable; and, therefore, it cannot be held that the sentence passed against the petitioners fell along with the relevant section of the Order. The restriction actually imposed cannot be said to be unreasonable judged by any standard.

The Right to Form Associations or Unions [Art. 19(1) (*c*) and 19(4)]

The right guaranteed to form associations or unions is more or less a charter for all working people in this country. Trade union activity was not only discouraged by most of the western countries until comparatively recenly, but in many countries it was even looked upon as an anti-social and anti-state activity. Workers had to undergo great suffering before they could obtain even the elementary rights that vitally affected their existence as a separate group or class in society. It was only in the twentieth century, particularly after the end of the First World War, that any significant measures were undertaken to ensure the legitimate rights of workers through labour and industrial legislation. To make these rights fundamental and embody them as such in a constitution was indeed a much bolder step forward. Fully recognizing the trend of the times, the Constitution of India has made the worker's right to form Unions a fundamental one.

The right to form associations or unions can be restricted only in the interests of public order or morality. There can be no association or union for an illegal or conspirational purpose. Nor can there be an association to further immorality. Interpreting the scope of the right the Supreme Court held in the case of the State of Madras *vs.* V.G. Rao:[1]

> The right to form associations or unions has such wide and varied scope for its exercise and its curtailment is fraught with such potential reactions in the religious, political and economic fields, that the vesting of authority in the executive government to impose restrictions on such rights, without allowing the grounds of such imposition, both in thier factual and legal aspects, to be duly tested in a judicial enquiry, is a strong element which, in our opinion, must be taken into account in judging the reasonableness of the restrictions imposed on the exercise of the fundamental right under Article 19(1) (*c*) .... The formula of subjective satisfaction of the government or its officers, with an Advisory Board thrown in to review the materials on which the government seeks to override a basic freedom guaranteed to the citizen, may be viewed as reasonable only in very exceptional circumstances, and within the narrowest limits and cannot receive judicial approval as a general patten of reasonable restrictions on fundamental rights.[2]

The right to form associations or unions, however, is not available to every citizen in the same measure. A member of the public services, although he is a citizen, cannot claim the right to the extent that a private citizen can. Being a government servant, he is bound by his service rules and he cannot challenge his service rules on the ground that they stand in his way of fully enjoying the right to form associations. This has been made clear by the Supreme court in P. Balakotiah *vs.* The Union of India.[3] In this case, the appellants contended that the orders terminating their services under the Security Rules (of the Railway Services)

---

1. See also Raja Kulkarni *vs.* State of Bombay A.I.R. 1954, S.C. 73 and Ramakrisnayya *vs.* President, District Board, A.I.R. 1952, Madras 253.
2. See also Raja Kulkarni *vs.* State of Bombay A.I.R. 1954, S.C. 73 and Ramakrishnayya *vs.* President, District Board, A.I.R. 1952, Madras 253.
3. 1858, S.C.J. 451.

amounted to a denial to them of the freedom to form associations. Speaking for an unanimous Court, Justice Venkatarama Aiyar said:

> ...(we) do not see how any right of the appellants under Article 19(1) (*c*) has been infringed. The orders do not prevent them from continuing to be Communists or trade unionists. Their right in that behalf remains after the impugned orders precisely what they were before. The real complaint of the appellants is that their services have been terminated; but that involves, apart from Article 311, no infringement of any of their constitutional rights. The appellants have no doubt a fundamental right to form associations under Article 19(1) (*c*), and when the services are terminated by the State, they cannot complain of the infirngement of any of their Constitutional rights, when no question of violation of Article 311 arises.[1]

But in another case,[2] the Court declared Rule 4-B of Central Government Service invalid as it contravened Article 19(1) (*c*) of the Constitution which guaranteed the right to form associations. The Rule prohibits a Government servant from joining or continuing to be a member of any association of Government servants which has not been recognized or whose recognition has been withdrawn by the Government. The Court also held that Rule 4-A which prohibited any form of demonstration was equally violative of the Government servant's fundamental rights.

The Right to Free Movement, to Residence and to Property [Art. 19(1) (*d*), (*e*), (*f*) and 19(5)]

The right to freely move throughout the territory of India, to reside and settle in any part of it and to acquire, hold and dispose of property are guaranteed under sub-clauses (*d*), (*e*) and (*f*) respectively of Clause (1) of Article 19. The importance of the freedom of movement cannot be exaggerated. In fact, the enjoyment of the freedoms guaranteed under the other rights depends largely on the freedom of movement unhampered and uncircumscribed. The State's power to place reasonable restrictions on these freedoms is limited to two: the interests of the general public and the protection of the interests of any Scheduled Tribe. For instance, it is in the interests of the general public to restrict the free movement of a person suffering from a contagious disease. Similarly, the Scheduled Tribes form separate communities by themselves, backward and unsophisticated, with separate cultural and property interests. Although, complete segregation of the tribal people in the name of their separate culture and general backwardness is wrong and against the ultimate aim of complete national integration, certain safeguards as are envisaged here seem to be justified. Otherwise, the tribal people may become easy victims of exploitation at the hands of their more 'civilized', shrewd and designing brethren. Hence there are various provisions disabling them from alienating thier own properties except under special conditions. In their own interest and for their benefit, laws may be made restricting the ordinary rights of citizens to go and settle in particular areas inhabited by the tribal people or acquire property in them. The reference to the interests of the Scheduled Tribes makes it clear that the free movement spoken of in the clause relates not to general rights of locomotion but to the particular right of shifting or moving from one part of the Indian territory to another, without any sort of discriminatory barriers.[3]

---

1. Article 311 deals with certain protections provided for the members of the Public Services.
2. Accountant-General *vs.* E.X. Joseph
   See also Police Nongazetted Kamachari Singh *vs.* Union of India A.I.R. 1987 S.C. 379.
3. Gopalan *vs.* The State of Madras, 1950, S.C.R. 269.

Almost from the very start of the Constitution, the Courts were called upon to interpret the scope of these freedoms. In Ismail *vs.* the State of Orissa[1] the Orissa Maintenance of Public Order Act, 1950 was challenged as invalid under the Freedom of Movement clause of the Constitution. The Act had provided for internment of persons up to a maximum of one year without trial. Further, there was no provision either for consulting an Advisory Council or for even giving the internee an opportunity of making representations to the government. In an unanimous decision, the Orissa High Court declared the disputed provisions of the Act invalid. Considering the reasonableness of restrictions contemplated by the Constitution, the Court held:

> ...(The) Court has to consider whether the fundamental principles of natural justice which require that no party ought to be condemned, or to have a decision given against him, unless he has been given reasonable opportunity of putting forward his case before an impartial tribunal, have been contravened. Judged by the standard the provisions of section 2(1) (*b*) and section 3 of the Act cannot be held to authorise the imposition or reasonable restrictions on the fundamental rights guaranteed to a citizen under Article 19(1) (*d*) of the Constitution.

In Ismail Khan *vs.* the State,[2] the Assam High Court held:

> The validity of the legislation permitting restrictions on the right to move freely throughout the territory of India is justiciable. It is open to the courts to consider the reasonableness of the restrictions. It is also open to the Court to examine the procedure to be followed before any restrictions on the right to move freely throughout the territory of India can be imposed.

The question of the freedom of movement and its relation to preventive detention for which provision has been made in the Constitution under Article 22 came up for exhaustive discussion in Gopalan *vs.* The State of Madras,[3] one of the most important cases ever decided by the Supreme Court of India. The petitioner, who was held in detention under the preventive Detention Act, 1950, challenged its validity, among other, on the ground that he had a right to move freely throughout the territory of India guaranteed by the Constitution. It was contended that the right to move freely was the very essence of personal liberty and in as much as the detention authoritized by the Act was not a reasonable restriction which Parliament could validly impose on such right, the Act was void. Dealing with the right to move freely the Court held:

> Article 19(1)(*d*) protects a specific aspect of the right of free locomotion, namely the right to move freely throughout the territory of India which is regarded as a special privilege or right of an Indian citizen and is protected as such. The protection of Article 19 is co-terminous with the legal capacity of a citizen to exercise the rights protected thereby, for sub-clauses (*a*) to (*e*) and (*g*) of Article 19(1) postulate the freedom of the person which alone can ensure the capacity to exercise the right protected by these sub-clauses. A citizen who loses the freedom of his person by being lawfully detained whether as a result of a conviction for an offence or as a result of preventive detention loses his capacity to exercise those rights and, therefore, has none of the rights which sub-clauses (*a*) to (*e*) and (*g*) may protect.[4]

In Khare *vs.* The State of Delhi, the President of the All India Hindu Mahasabha, who had served with an order of externment directing him not to remain in the Delhi

---

1. A.I.R. 1951, Orissa 86.
2. A.I.R. 1951, Assam 106.
3. A.I.R. 1950, S.C. 27.
4. 1950, S.C.R. 579. See also Gurbachan Singh *vs.* State of Bombay 1952, S.C.R. 737. See also Rahimtoola *vs.* The State of Bombay 1960, S.C.J. 50 and State of M.P. *vs.* Baldeo Prasad 1960, S.C.J. (Notes) 33.

District for a period of three months, challenged the validity of the order under the freedom of movement clause. The Court held that there was nothing unreasonable in the order as the ground under which the order was served could not be described as vague, insufficient and incomplete.

> In is expressly stated that the activities of the petitioner, who is the President of the Hindu Mahasabha, since the disturbances between two communities in East and West Bengal, have particularly been of a communal nature which excited hatred between the communities. It is further stated that having regard to the recent disturbances in Delhi, the population of which is composed of both these communities, the excitement of such hatred is likely to be dangerous to the peace and maintenance of law and order. Far from being vague, I think that these grounds are specific and if honestly believed can support the order.

In Malik Singh's Case[1], it was held that in making surveillance over notorious characters, their privacy should not be encroached upon.

The right to acquire, hold and dispose of property is no more a Fundamental right. It was a part of the Constitution as originally passed but was abolished by the Forty-fourth Amendment (1978). There are however some important Supreme Court decisions which deserve a brief mention.

The scope of the right to acquire, hold and dispose of property was considered at length by the Supreme Court in Chiranjital Choudhri *vs.* The Union of India[2] which challenged the validity of the Sholapur Shinning and Weaving Company (Emergency Provisions) Act of 1950 under which the above company was taken over by the Government to avoid its closing down owing to mismanagement and to protect the interests of workers as well as to maintain the supply of the goods produced by the company for the use of the general public. The petitioner contended that his right as a shareholder to hold, acquire or dispose of property in his shares of the company was restricted by the above Act which was an unreasonable restriction on his fundamental right. The Court held that there was no such restriction. He still held the shares and he could dispose of them if he so desired. But even if for the sake of argument it was held that the disabilities imposed amounted to restrictions on his proprietary right, they might very well be supported as reasonable restraints imposed in the interests of the general public, *viz.* to secure the supply of a commodity and prevent serious unemployment amongst a section of the people and were, therefore, protected completely by Clause (5) of Article 19.[3]

Dealing with the scope of Article 19(1) (*f*) in its application to certain religious and charitable institutions, Alladi Krishnaswami Aiyar observed:

> In terms, Article 19(1) (*f*) applies to citizens as such, as the expression 'citizen' under the Constitution can apply only to natural persons. *vide,* Article 5 of the Constitution, Neither a juristic person like an idol enshrined in a temple, nor a juristic personality as an institution like a *Mutt,* is or can be a citizen within the meaning of the article.

The actual words employed in clause (*f*) of Article 19(1), *viz.* 'to acquire, hold and dispose of property' read in the context of other sub-clauses in Article (19)1, make it quite clear that a juristic person like an idol or a religious institution like a *Mutt* could not have

1. A.I.R. 1981 SC 760.
2. 1951, S.C.R. 29.
3. In this connection, see also Narinder Kumar *vs.* Union of India 1960, S.C.J. 3; Krishna Sugar Mills *vs.* Union of India 1960, S.C.J. 1119; The Collector of Customs *vs.* N.S. Chetty (1962) I.S.C.J. 68; Steelworth Ltd. *vs.* The State of Assam (1962) II S.C.J. 301 and Bishan Das *vs.* The State of Punjab (1963) I S.C.J. 405

been intended to be covered by Article 19(1) (*f*).[1]

In another decision the Court held that a company could not claim the fundamental rights guaranteed to the citizens under the Constitution. Natural persons alone could be citizens. As such, a company registered under the Indian Companies Act, which was only a juristic and not a natural person, could not claim fundamental rights guaranteed to citizens under Article 19 of the Constitution. The decision was given on a petition filed under Article 32 of the Constitution by the State Trading Corporation of India (a public sector undertaking) challenging the levy of sales-tax by the Andhra Pradesh and Bihar Governments on the ground that it was a citizen and its fundamental rights under Article 19 had been violated. The Court held that it was a mistake to confuse nationality with citizenship. While it was correct that the S.T.C. having been incorporated in India under the Companies Act was a national of India, it would be wholly erroneous to think that it also became on such incorporation a citizen of India. Neither the provisions of Part III of the Constitution (fundamental rights) nor of the Citizenship Act, the Court held, either conferred the right of citizenship on or recognized as citizens, any person other than a natural persons.[2]

The Freedom of Profession, Occupation, Trade or Business [Art. 19(1) (*g*) and 19(6)]

Article 19(1) (*g*) guarantees the freedom to practise any profession, or to carry on any occupation, trade or business. A doubt was expressed in the Constituent Assembly whether these were fundamental rights at all.[3] Perhaps the only other constitutions which have given them the status of fundamental rights are those of Ireland and Switzerland. It seems that the framers of the Indian Constitution had been influenced by the complex social system that prevailed in India in seeking to guarantee rights such as these. It has been a bane of India's social life that professions were inherited rather than acquired. A society dominated by caste, and professions based upon caste or religion have little to offer for the building up of a community enlivened by social mobility and dynamism. Such a society is often intolerant to persons who change the traditional profession of their ancestors and is eager to maintain a petrified social order. A constitutional guarantee of the right to take up the profession, calling, trade or business of one's choice is indeed a significant aid to the building up of a dynamic and democratic society. The framers of the Constitution have done well to incorporate these rights in the chapter on Fundamental Rights and have thereby helped the evolution of a truly democratic society. The State's power to restrict the enjoyment of these freedoms is limited to the making of any law imposing reasonable restrictions in the interests of the general public in so far as it relates to: (*i*) the prescribing of professional or technical qualification necessary for practising any profession or carrying on any occupation, trade or business or (*ii*) the carrying on by the State or by a corporation owned or controlled by the State, of any trade, business, industry or service.[4]

---

1. Srinivas Sastri Lecutre (1952) published under the title 'The Constitution and Fundamental Rights' 1955, pp. 41-3. See in this connection the decision of the Supreme Court in the Commissioner, Hindu Religious Endowments, Madras *vs*. L.T. Swamiar 1954. S.C.J. 335.
2. State Trading Corporation of India *vs*. Commercial Tax Officer A.I.R. 1963 S.C. 1811. Also see Pathumma *vs*. State of Keral A.I.R. 1978 S.C. 771.
3. C.A.D. VII, 755.
4. This Clause (b) was added to the original Constitution by the First Amendment of 1951 in order to remove all possiblae doubts that might arise as a result of the State's economic, industrial and commercial activities, which might otherwise be interpreted as possible infrigements of this right.

In Rashid Ahmed *vs.* The Municipal Board, Kairana,[1] the Supreme Court had occasion to discuss in detail the scope of the rights guaranteed under the clause regarding the freedom of profession. Rashid Ahmed was carrying on wholesale business in fruits and vegetables in one of the bazaars of Kairana, a town in Uttar Pradesh, In April 1949, a set of new by-laws framed by the Kairana municipality came into force. Anticipating the coming into force of the by-laws, the Board had auctioned the contract for wholesale trade in vegetables on the basis of a monopoly right. The contract was given to one Habib Ahmed. Subsequently the Board notified a specified place as the market for wholesale business in vegetables. Thereupon the petitioner applied for a licence to carry on his business at his shop. The Board rejected the application and the decision was communicated to the petitioner, It said:

> According to resolution number 188 dated 22 December 1949, the application of Mr. Rashid Ahmed is rejected and he be informed accordingly.

The resolution contained no reason for the rejection of the application. Soon after, notice was served on the petitioner by the Board asking him to stop selling vegetables at once as it would be a breach of the by-laws of the Board. In short, the petitioner could not do any wholesale business in vegetables at the appointed market or at his own shop where he had been doing business at least for two years prior to the coming into effect of the by-laws. His business had been wholly stopped and the was being prosecuted for alleged breach of the by-laws. By-law 2 ran thus:

> No person shall establish any new market or place for wholesale transaction without obtaining the previous permission of the Board and no person shall sell or expose for sale any vegetable, fruit *etc.* at any place other than the fixed by the Board for the purpose.

Speaking on behalf of a unanimous Court, Justice S.R. Das observed:

> The Constitution by Article 19(1) (*g*) guarantees to the Indian citizen the right to carry on trade or business subject to such reasonable restrictions as are mentioned in clause 6 of that Article. The position, however, under by-law 2 is that while it provided that no person shall establish a market for wholesale transaction in vegetables except with the permission of the Board, there is no by-law authorizing the respondent to issue the licence. The net result is that the prohibition of this by-law, in the absence of any provision for issuing licences, becomes absolute. Further, the Board has granted a monopoly to Habib Ahmed and has put it out of its power to grant a licence to the petitioner to carry on wholesale business in vegetable either at the fixed market or at any other place within the municipal limits of Kairana. This certainly is much more than reasonable restrictions on the petitioner as are contemplated by Clause (6) of Article 19 of the Constitution...
>
> We are satisfied that in this case the petitioner's fundamental rights have been infringed and he is entitled to have his grievances redressed. The proper order in such circumstances would be to direct the respondent Board not to prohibit the petitioner from carrying on the trade of wholesale dealer and commission agent of vegetables and fruits within the limits of the Municipal Board of Kairana, except in accordance with the byelaws as and when framed in future according to law and further to direct the respondent municipal Board to withdraw the pending prosecution of the petitioner and we order accordingly.

In Motilal *vs.* Uttar Pradesh,[2] Chief Justice Malik of the Allahabad High Court held that 'reasonable restriction also meant total stoppage'. The word in Article (19)(6) was not 'regulation' but 'reasonable restrictions'. If by reason of the nature of the trade which

---

1. 1950, S.C.R. 566.
2. A.I.R. 1951, Allahabad, 257. See also Excel Weat *vs.* Union of India (1978) 4 Scc. 224.

might be against public morality, or for any other reason, it was deemed necessary in the general interest to stop totally any trade or business, there was no reason why it could not be included in the word restriction.

In Chandrasekhara *vs.* the Income-tax Commissioner,[1] the Madras High Court held that the criteria by which certain categories of persons were disqualified from appearing on behalf of assessees in income-tax cases were a reasonable restriction on the exercise of the right conferred by Article 91(1) (*g*). Similarly, in S.P. Mukherjee *vs.* Chatterji[2] the Calcutta High Court in an unanimous decision held that to keep a watch over the activities of a particular 'bath and massage clinic' by the posting of plainclothes policemen by the State near the premises to see whether unlawful acts were being committed in the said premises would not amount to a violation of the right guaranteed by the freedom of profession clause.

In Chintaman Rao *vs.* the State of Madhya Pradesh[3] the Supreme Court held invalid the Central Provinces and Berar Regulation of Manufacture of Bidis (Agricultural purposes) Act, 1948, because it totally prohibited the manufacture of bidis during the agricultural season in certain parts of the State. The Court said that such a prohibition, on the face of it, was of an arbitrary nature and, therefore, could not be said to be a reasonable restriction on the exercise of the right to carry on a profession, trade or business. But in another decision the Court held that the requirement of a permit as required by the law cannot be regarded as an unreasonable restriction on the citizen's right under the freedom of profession clause.[4] In Kapur *vs.* the State of Punjab[5] the Court upheld the nationalization of textbooks by the Government of Punjab. 'The action of the Government may be good or bad. It may be criticised and condemned in the Houses of Legislature or outside but this does not amount to an infraction of the fundamental right guaranteed by Article 19(1) (*g*)'.

In Sodan Singh *vs.* New Delhi Municipal Committee[6] the matter that came up for consideration was the right of pavement occupiers. The Court held that they had a right to carry on trade subject to reasonable restrictions under Article 19(6). In Goodwill Paints and Chemicals Industry *vs.* Union of India[7] it was held that a trade or business involving inherent danger to public health and safety could be restricted by Parliament.

As a whole, the tendency of the judiciary with regard to the freedom of profession has been not to block in any way the increasing state activity that is bound to take place in a Welfare State but, at the same time, to give the individual maximum protection from high-handed executive actions or discriminatory legislative enactments. Whenever the

---

1. A.I.R. 1951, Madras 897. See also Sakhwat Ali *vs.* State of Orrisa 1955. I S.C.R. 1004; Babul Chandra *vs.* Chief Justice and Judges A.I.R. 1954, S.C. 529.
2. D.L.R. Calcutta, 28.
3. 1950, S.C.R. 759.
4. Harishnakar Bagla *vs.* Madhya Pradesh State A.I.R. 1954, S.C. 465. See also Seshadri *vs.* District Magistrate, Tanjore A.I.R. 1954, S.C. 747.
5. 1955, 2 S.C.R. 225. See also Ram Chandra Palai *vs.* State of Orrisa A.I.R. 1956, S.C. 298; Bijay Cotton Mills Ltd. *vs.* State of Ajmer 1955, 1 S.C.R. 752; T.B. Ibrahim *vs.* Regional Transport Authority, Tanjore 1953, S.C.R. 290; Harman Singh *vs.* R.T.A. Culcutta Region A.I.R. 1954, S.C. 190; Hamdard Dawakhana *vs.* Union of India, 1960 S.C.J. 611; The Union of India *vs.* Bhanamal Gulzarimal, Ltd. 1960 S.C.J. 584 and Mohan Lal *vs.* The State of Punjab 1960 S.C.J. (Notes) p. 40.
6. A.I.R. 1989 S.C. 1988
7. 1992 Supp. (1) SCC 16.

action of the State was in the interest of the general public, even if it involved the restriction of the individual's freedom of action in the economic sphere, the Courts did not seem hesitant to support it.[1] This was the main reason that impelled them to uphold many legislative enactments of nationalization of public utilities such as road transport, electricity, *etc.* even before the First Amendment had made a special provision in support of such State actions and the consequent expansion of the economic and commercial activities of the State.

***

1. R.M.D. Chamarbaugwalla *vs*. Union of India 1957, S.C.J. 493; Lilavati Bai *vs*. The State of Bombay 1957, S.C.J. 557; Bhatnagar *vs*. The Union of India 1957, S.C.J. 546 and Diwan Sugar and General Mills *vs*. The Union of India 1959, S.C.J. 663. Also see H.C.Narayanappa *vs*. The State of Mysore (1961) I S.C.J. 7; G. Nageswara Rao *vs*. Andhra Pradesh State Raod Transport Corporation 1959, S.C.J. 967; Fedco (P.) Ltd. *vs*. S.N. Bilgrami, 1960 S.C.J. 235; R.D.J. Parkash *vs*. Union of India (1962) II 445 and A.H. Quraish *vs*. The State of Bihar (1962) II S.C.J. 523. See also the following: Nataraja Mudaliar *vs*. State Transport Authority (1978) 4 S.C.C. 290. Union of India *vs*. Indo-Afgan Agencies Ltd. 91968) 2 S.C.C. 365 and Madan Mohan Pathak *vs*. Union of India, A.I.R. 1978 S.C. 803.

12

THE RIGHT TO FREEDOM : II

(Arts. 20,21 and 22)

Protection in respect of Conviction for Offences

ARTICLE 20 affords protection against arbitrary and excessive punishment to any person who commits an offence. There are four such guaranteed protections: (*i*) A person can be convicted of an offence only if he has violated a law in force at the time when he is alleged to have committed the offence. (*ii*) No person can be subjected to a greater penalty than what might have been given to him under the law that was prevalent when he committed the offence. (*iii*) No person can be prosecuted and punished for the same offence more than once. (*iv*) No person accused of an offence can be compelled to be a witness against himself. The Draft Constitution did not contain the term 'prosecuted' in the clause prohibiting double punishment. It was pointed out in the Constituent Assembly that such a word was necessary because punishment here meant only that which was given by a Court of law. Departmental punishment would not be taken as 'punishment' in the sense in which the word is used in the Constitution. Nor would any punishment given in Court of law preclude departmental action leading to punishment for the same offence committed by the same official. This means that disciplinary action may be taken by the Government against an official despite the sentence of a Court of law[1] and such action will not infringe the right guaranteed under this article.

Taken together, these provisions guard against retrospective application of a punitive law and double punishment for the same offence.[2] These are indeed guarantees of great importance which establish 'the primacy of law over the passions of man'. In Kedar Nath *vs.* the State of West Bengal,[3] the Supreme Court held that for an offence committed in 1947, the penal provisions of an amended Act dealing with the same offence passed in 1949 were not applicable.

What is prohibited in article 20 is the conviction of a person or his subjection to a penalty under *ex-post facto* laws. The prohibition under the article is not confined to the passing or the validity of the law, but extends to the conviction or the sentence and is based on its character as an *ex-post facto* law. The fullest effect, therefore, should be given to the words used in the article. Nor

---

1. C.A.D. VII, p. 795.
2. For a detailed discussion on the scope of Article 20, see Virendra Kumar Sirkar, "The Scope of Judicial Review with regard to Right to Life and Personal Liberty in India." (1961) I S.C.J. 47.
3. 1953, A.I.R. S.C. 404.

does such a construction result in giving retrospective operation to the fundamental right thereby recognised. This article must accordingly be taken to prohibit all convictions or subjections to penalty after the constitution in respect of *ex-post facto* law whether the same was a post-Constitution law or a pre-Constitution law.[1]

In Hathisingh Manufacturing Co. *vs*. The Union of India,[2] the Court reiterating its earlier decisions held that the protection of Article 20(1) avails only against punishment for an act which is treated as an offence, which when done was no offence.

Interpreting Caluse (2) of Article 20, the Court held:

In order that the protection of Article 20(2) be invoked by a citizen there must have been a prosecution and punishment in respect of the same offence before a Court of law or a tribunal required by law to decide the matters in controversy judicially on evidence on oath which it must be authorised by law to administer and not before a tribunal which entertains a departmental or administrative enquiry even though set up by statute but not required to proceed on legal evidence on oath.[3]

In Rattanlal *vs*. The State of Punjab[4] it was held that the doctrine of Ex-post Facto law was not applicable to a provision which confers some benefit to the accused. In this case though the accused was convicted, the Supreme Court held that he could get the benefit of the Probation of Offender's Act 1958 although it was a legislation subsequent to the offence.

Section 304-B of the IPC was enacted in 1986 so as to punish offences relating to dowry death. It therefore creates a substantive offence. Taking these facts into account the Supreme Court in Soni Devaraj Bhai *vs*. State of Gujarat[5] held that it was not applicable retrospectively since it would be hit by Article 20 (1).

The words 'prosecuted and punished' are to be taken not distributively so as to mean prosecuted or punished. Both the factors must co-exist in order that the operation of the clause may be attracted.[6] If there is no punishment for an offence as a result of the prosecution, Clause (2) of Article 20 has no application. An appeal against an acquittal wherever such is provided by the procedure is in substance a continuation of the prosecution.[7] Further, where there are two alternative charges in the same trial, the fact that the accused is acquitted of one of them will not prevent the conviction on the other.[8]

The Supreme Court also held that Article 20(3) does not apply at all to a case where the confession is made with any inducement, threat or promise.[9] In M.P. Sharma *vs*. Satish

1. Rao Shiv Bahadur Singh *vs*. The State of Vindhya Pradesh 1953, S.C.R. 1100.
2. (1961) I S.C.J. 22. See also K.S. Singh *vs*. The State of Punjab 1960, S.C.J. 863.
3. Maqbool Hussain *vs*. The State of Bombay 1953, S.C.R. 730.
4. A.I.R. 1965 S.C. 444.
5. A.I.R. 1991 S.C. 2173.
   Please see also State of Bihar *vs*. Murad Ali Khan (1988) 4 S.C.C. 655 and Union of India *vs*. K.V. Janaki Raman A.I.R. 1991 S.C. 2010.
6. Venkataraman *vs*. The Union of India 1954, A.I.R. S.C. 375. See also Ebrahim Vazir *vs*. The State of Bombay 1954, A.I.R. S.C. 229; Thomas Dana *vs*. The Superintendent 1958, S.C.J. 301.
7. Kalavati *vs*. The State of Himachal Pradesh 1953, S.C.R. 546.
8. The State of M.P. *vs*. Veereshwar Rao Agnihotri 1957, S.C.J. 519. See also Tripati *vs*. The State of Bhopal 1957, S.C.J. 405; Thoma Dana *vs*. The State of Punjab 1959, S.C.J. 669 and The State of Bombay *vs*. S.L. Apte (1961) I S.C.J. 685.
9. Kalavati *vs*. The State of Himachal Pradesh, 1953, S.C.R. 546. See also in this connection T.G. Gaokar *vs*. R.N. Shukla, 1968, A.I.R. S.C. 1050 and Yusuf Alli *vs*.State of Maharashtra, 1968, A.I.R. S.C. 147.

Chandra,[1] it was contended on behalf of the petitioner that the provision under section 96(1) of the Criminal Procedure Code which authoritized search and seizure violated the right guaranteed by Article 20(3). The Court rejected this contention and held that a power of search and seizure is in any system of jurisprudence an overriding power of the State for the protection of social security and that power is necessarily regulated by law. When the Constitution-makers have thought fit not to subject such regulation to Constitutional limitations by recognition of a fundamental right to privacy, analogous to the American Fourth Amendment, there is no justification to import it into a totally different fundamental right by some process of strained construction. Nor is it legitimate to assume that the constitutional protection under Article 20(3) would be defeated by the statutory provisions for searches.[2]

In Delhi Judicial Association *vs.* State of Gujarat[3], it was held by the Court that there must be the following ingredients to invoke Article 20(3); (*a*) One should be accused of an offence, (*b*) Element of compulsion to be a witness should be there, (*c*) That too should be against himself. But the Court was wise enough not to stultify the scientific development in the legal field. In Gautam Kundu's case[4] the Court held that the blood group testing to determine the parentage of a child was not hit by the Article. In Kripal Singh *vs.* Collector[5] it was held that serving out the sentence would not wipe out civil liability to pay the penal amount.

Protection of Life and Personal Liberty (Art. 21)

Article 21 is one of the hottest in the Constitution over which there took place one of the longest and most thorough-going discussions in the Constituent Assembly. It enacts that 'No person shall be deprived of his life or personal liberty except according to procedure established by law'. The article as it stands now is a revised version of what originally was in the Draft Constitution, according to which 'no person was to be deprived of his life or liberty *without due process of law*'. The Drafting Committee gave two reasons for this change. First, the word 'liberty' should be qualified by the word 'personal' in order to avoid the possibility of too wide an interpretation which might include even the freedoms already dealt with under Article 19. Secondly, the expression 'procedure established by law' is more definite and such a provision finds place in the same context in the Japanese Constitution of 1946.[6]

---

1. 1954, A.I.R. 300. The State of Bombay *vs.* K.K. Oghad (1963) I S.C.J. 195 the Supreme Court examined the scope of Art. 20(3) in great detail. See also Mohamed Dastigar *vs.* The State of Madras 1960, S.C.J. 726 and Raja Narayanlal Bansilal *vs.* M.P. Mistry (1961) I S.C.J. 353.
2. An attempt was made in the Constituent Assembly to include the right of 'protection against search and seizure' through an amendment to the present Article 20. The move was, however, defeated. See State of U.P. *vs.* Boota Singh, A.I.R. 1978 S.C. 1770.
3. A.I.R. 1991, S.C. 2176.
4. A.I.R. 1993, S.C. 2295.
5. 1992 Supp. (3) S.C.C. 183.
6. C.A.D. VIII, p. 844. Article 31 of the Japanese Constitution reads as follows: 'No person shall be deprived of his life or liberty nor shall any other criminal penalty be imposed, except according to procedure established by law. Article 40 of the Constitution of Ireland reads: 'No person shall be deprived of personal liberty save in accordance with law'.

It was this rather radical modification made by the Drafting Committee that touched off a great debate in the Assembly centering on the relative virtues and vices that might flow from the adoption of either 'procedure established by law' or 'due process of law'. The debate, in which almost every prominent lawyer in the Assembly participated, indeed touched great heights. The mastery with which each side drove home its points, again and again, emphasizing the relative advantages of adopting its own point of view and the disadvantages involved in the adoption of the opposite view made the situation fluid and even confused. The Drafting Committee itself, in spite of its recommendation for the revised version, was divided and two of its prominent members, Alladi and Munshi, were in opposite camps as if they were their self-appointed leaders. Strangely enough, Chairman Ambedkar, after weighing the pros and cons of the issues in a magnificent speech, was inclined to leave the matter as an open question to be decided by a free vote in the House.

Pandit Thankur Das Bhargava who opened the vigorous attack against the revised version and who advocated the retention of the 'due process' clause said:

> We want two bulwarks for our liberties. One is the legislature and the other is the judiciary. But even if the legislature is carried away by party spirit and is sometimes panicky, the judiciary will save us from the tyranny of the legislature and the executive. Hence 'due process of law' should be retained. I want the judiciary to be exalted to its right position of palladium of justice and the people to be secure in their rights and liberties under its protecting wings.[1]

Leading some eight other speakers who voiced similar views, K.M. Munshi said:

> This clause would only have meaning if the Courts could examine that not merely the conviction has been according to law or according to proper procedure but the procedure as well as the substance of the case. We want to set up a democracy and the essence of democracy is that a balance must be struck between individual liberty on the one hand and social control on the other. We must not forget that the majority is more anxious to establish social control than to serve individual liberty. Some scheme, therefore, must be devised to adjust the needs of individual liberty and the demands of social control.[2]

The arguments in favour of 'due process' were countered by Alladi by pointing out the vagaries of judicial pronouncements in the United States where the 'due process' had its origin and growth as a constitutional guarantee.[3] He said:

> In the development of the doctrine of due process the United States Supreme Court has not adopted a consistent view at all and the decisions are conflicting..... One decision is very often reversed by another decision.... It all depended upon the particular judges that presided on the occasion...[4]

According to Justice Douglas of the U.S. Supreme Court:

> Due process as used in the Fourteenth Amendment was wholly undefined. It would have such a meaning as judges from time to time might give it. That had the advantage of great flexibility. By it also had inherent dangers. For, Due Process like Natural Law, could come to reflect the individual idiosyncracies of the judge, his predilection, his favoured economic creed or philosophical theory. The absence of guides or standards might allow judicial whim or caprice to play havoc with legislative programme.[5]

---

1. C.A.D. VII, p. 848.
2. Ibid., pp. 851-3.
3. Both the Fifth and Fourteenth Amendments of the American Constitution embody the 'due process' clause.
4. C.A.D. VII, pp. 853-4.
5. Douglas, J. *We the Judges*, p. 264.

Speaking on the attitude of the Court toward social legislation Douglas said:

> It seemed for a while that the Due Process Clause had given the Supreme Court powers comparable to a super-legislature. For the Court had so construed Due Process in a substantive sense as to curtail drastically the power of the States to legislate.[1]

Reviewing the discussion as a whole, Ambedkar summarized the arguments on both sides skilfully in the following words:

> ...We are, therefore, placed in between two difficult positions. One is to give the judiciary the authority to sit in judgment over the will of the legislature and to question the law made by the legislature on the ground that it is not a good law, in consonance with fundamental principles. Is that a desirable principle ? The second position is that the legislature ought to be trusted not to make bad laws. It is very difficult to come to any definite conclusion. There are dangers on both sides. For myself, I cannot altogether omit the possibility of a legislature packed by party men making laws which may abrogate or violate what we regard as certain fundamental principles affecting the life and liberty of the individual. At the same time, I do not see how five or six gentlemen sitting in the federal or Supreme Court examining laws made by the legislature, and by the dint of their own individual conscience or their bias or prejudices, be trusted to determine which law is good and which law is bad. It is rather a case where a man has to sail between Charybdis and Scilla and I, therefore, would not say anything. I would leave it to the House to determine in any way it likes.[2]

Ultimately, the Assembly decided in favour of the revised version. It seems that the Japanese example had a decisive role in arriving at the decision. The fact that the Japanese Constitution of 1946 which was drafted under American guidance and inspiration had preferred 'procedure established by law' to 'due process of law' was a factor which went against the latter phrase. The Constituent Assembly finally veered round to 'procedure established by law' owing to two reasons. First, they wanted to avoid the uncertainty, vagueness and changeability that have grown around the doctrine of due process. Secondly, they were prepared rather to trust the legislature not to make bad laws than to trust the judiciary not to become a super-legislature.

The key word in Article 21 is 'law'. What does law enacted by a competent legislative body or fundamental or natural law mean ? This was the question that confronted the Supreme Court soon after the inauguration of the Constitution. The question was discussed at length is Gopalan's case[3] reference to which has already been made. It was contended on behalf of the petitioner that the Indian Constitution gives the same protection to every person in India, as in the United States, except that in the United States 'due process of law' has been construed by its Supreme Court to cover both substantive and procedural law, while in India only the protection of procedural law is guaranteed. It was contended that the omission of the word 'due' made a difference to the interpretation of the words in Article 21. The word 'established' was not equivalent to 'prescribed'. It had a wider meaning. The word 'law' did not mean enacted law because that will be no legislative protection at all. If so construed, any Act passed by Parliament or a State Legislature, which was otherwise within its legislative power, can destroy or abridge this right. On the same line of reasoning, it was argued that if that was the intention there was no necessity to put this as a fundamental right at all. As to the meaning of the word 'law' it was argued that it meant principles of natural justice.

---

1. Douglas, J. Ibid.
2. C.A.D. VII, p. 1000.
3. 1950, S.C. J. P. 175.

The Court, however, did not accept this line of argument. Chief Justice Kania said that there was no ambiguity in the meaning of the article.

> Normally read, and without thinking of other Constitutions, the expression 'procedure established by law' must mean procedure prescribed by the law of the State.... To read the word 'law' as meaning rules of natural justice will land one in difficulties because the rules of natural justice as regards procedure are nowhere defined and in my opinion, the Constitution cannot be read as laying down a vague standard. This is particularly so when in omitting to adopt 'due process of law' it was considered that the expression 'procedure established by law' made the standard specific.[1]

This opinion of the Chief Justice was supported by four other judges of the Court. Justice Patanjali Sastri said:

> ....I am unable to agree that the term 'law' in Article 21 means the immutable and universal principles of natural justice. 'Procedure established by law' must be taken to refer to a procedure which has a statutory origin, for no procedure is known or can be said to have been established by such vague and uncertain concepts as the immutable and universal principles of natural justice. In my opinion, 'law in Article 21 means 'positive or State-made law'.

The importance of the right embodied in Article 21, even if it does not place limitations on legislative power, is indicated by Justice Mukherjea in the same case in the following words:

> The fundamental rights not merely imposed limitations upon the Legislature, but they serve as checks on exercise of executive powers as well, and in the matter of depriving a man of his personal liberty, checks or the high-handedness of the executive in the shape of preventing them from taking any step, which is not in accordance with law, could certainly rank as fundamental rights. In the Constitutions of various other countries, the provisions relating to protection of personal liberty are couched very much in the same language as in Article 21. It is all a question of policy as to whether the Legislature or the judiciary would have the final say in such matters and the Constitution-makers of India deliberately decided to place these powers in the hands of the Legislature. Article 31 of the Japanese Constitution, upon which Article 21 of our Constitution is modelled, proceeds upon the same principle.

In spite of Justice Mukherjea's pious hope the response of the Supreme Court to the numerous petitions complaining violations of Article 21 cannot be said to be consistent. The Court seems to have found it difficult to enunciate any objective test in interpreting this Article. The Court has assumed an activist tendency with its historic decision in Maneka Gandhi *vs*. the Union of India (A.I.R.) 1978 S.C. 498). During the eighties and nineties through its many decisions the court appears to have incorporated the concepts of natural justice, human rights, public health, public interest, social justice, legal aid, environmental protection, rights of prisoners and the like within the ambit of Article 21. As a result, the meaning of the words in the Article has changed substantially. A few examples are in order.

In Francis Coralie *vs*. Administrator, Union Territory of Delhi (A.I.R. 1981, S.C. 746) the concept of life has got a more meaningful definition. It said, ".....right to life includes the right to live with human dignity and ... the bare necessities of life such as adequate nutrition, clothing and shelter..... facilities for reading, writing and expressing oneself in diverse forms". (See also Vikram Das Singh *vs*. State of Bihar A.I.R. 1988 S.C. 1782) Rejecting the stand in A.K. Gopalan's case as to the concept of life, Maneka Gandhi's case inducted the concept

1. 1950, S.C.J., pp. 184-6. For a more recent discussion on the subject by the Court, see Sant Ram *In re* (1961) I S.C.J. 98 and Ram Chandra Prasad *vs*. The State of Bihar (1962) II S.C.J. 13.

of natural law into it. Krishna Iyer J. said that "law in Article 21 is a reasonable law, not any enacted piece". (See also Sunil Batra *vs*. Delhi Administration (1978 4 S.C.C. 499). Similarly on Olga Tellis *vs*. Bombay Municipal Corporation (A.I.R. 1986, S.C. 180) which is popularly called the pavement dwellers' case, the Court held that the procedure established by law must be just, fair and reasonable. Such a stand is different from that in Gopalan's case.

Delay in effecting death sentence would violate Article 21 as there could be procedural unfairness. This was made clear in Triveni Bai *vs*. State of Gujarat (A.I.R. 1989, S.C. 1335) in which the delay in execution of death sentence was challenged. In Sunil Batra *vs*. Delhi Administration (Supra) solitary confinement of an awardee of capital punishment was held violative of Article 21. (See also Hussainara Khatun *vs*. Home Secretary, Bihar (1981, S.C.C. 115), Vatheeswaran *vs*. State of Tamil Nadu A.I.R. (1983, S.C. 361) arose out of the death sentence awarded to a murderer. It was held that a delay of two years in the execution of death sentence would help quashing it.

In M.H. Hosket *vs*. State of Maharashtra (A.I.R. 1978 S.C. 1548) the right to free legal aid was held to be implied in Article 21 (See also Kendra Phadia *vs*. State of Bihar A.I.R. 1981, SC 939) The Court further said that it includes speedy investigation and trial also. (See Raghu Bir Singh *vs*. State of Bihar A.I.R. 1987, S.C. 149).

Unnecessary handcuffing of under-trial prisoners was held to be violative of Article 21. (See Sunil Gupta *vs*. State of Madhya Pradesh (1990, S.C.C. 119).

In the 1980's Article 21 was interpreted to include right to healthy environment, (See M.C. Mehta *vs*. Union of India A.I.R. 1988, S.C. 1037) popularly known as Ganga Pollution (Tanneries) case. This was a Public Interest Litigation (PIL) to issue a writ of Mandamus to restrain the respondents from letting out harmful effluence into the river Ganga. The Court said that "life, health and ecology have greater importance to the people than unemployment, loss of revenue etc. due to the closure of the tanneries. (See also Subhash Kumar *vs*. State of Bihar A.I.R. (1991, S.C. 420) in which for the first time 'life' under Article 21 was made to include the right to pollution-free water, air and environment.

In J.P. Unnikrishnan *vs*. State of Andhra Pradesh (A.I.R. 1993, S.C. 2173) the Court held that the "right to life" includes right to free primary education. (See also Mohini Jain *vs*. State of Karnataka A.I.R. 1992, S.C. 1858). The observation of the Court on this case covers wide spectrum of rights within the amplitude of the right to personal liberty.

21A. Right to education-

The State shall provide free and compulsory education to all children of the age of six to fourteen years in such manner as the State may, by law. determine.

Until 2002 the right to education was only a Directive Principle of State Policy. However, this amendment makes it a Fundamental Right. The corresponding provision in Part IV, Directive Principles of State policy, namely article 45 also been amended. These Amendments have been made under the constitution eighty-sixth Amendment Act, 2002.

Protection against Arrest and Detention (Art. 22)

Article 22 guarantees three rights. First, it guarantees the right of every person who is arrested to be informed of the cause of his arrest; secondly, his right to consult, and to be defended by a lawyer of his choice. Thirdly, every person arrested and detained in custody shall be produced before the nearest Magistrate within a period of twenty-four hours and shall be kept in continued custody only with his authority. All these rights are without any qualifications and are, therefore, in absolute terms. It is interesting to note in this connection that Article 22 was not in the Draft Constitution at all. It was added to the Constitution almost towards the end of the deliberations of the Constituent Assembly. Ambedkar explained the circumstances under which the article was added in the following words:

...A large part of the House including myself were greatly dissatisfied with the wording of Article 15 (present 21)... There is no part of the Constitution which has been so violently criticised by the public outside as Article 15 because all that it does is this: it only prevents the Executive from making an arrest. All that is necessary is to have a law and the law need not be subject to any conditions or limitations. It was felt that while this matter was being included in the chapter dealing with fundamental rights, we were giving a *carte blanche* to Parliament to make and provide for the arrest of any person under any circumstances as Parliament may think fit. By Article 15A (present 22) were making a compensation, if I may say so, for what was done then in passing Article 15... We are providing substance of 'due process' by the introduction of Article 15A (present Art. 22).

It merely lifts from the Criminal Procedure Code two of the most fundamental principles which every civilised country follows as principles of international justice. By making these parts of the Constitution, we are making a fundamental change because we put a limitation on the authority of both Parliament and State Legislatures not to abrogate these two provisions because now they are part and parcel of the Constitution itself....the provisions contained in this are sufficient against illegal or arbitrary arrests.[1]

There are, however, two exceptions to the universal application of the rights guaranteed under the first two clauses of Article 22. These relate to:

(a) any person who is for the time being an enemy alien; or

(b) any person who is arrested or detained under any law providing for preventive detention.

The first exception was accepted by the Constituent Assembly without any opposition as it embodied a sound principle. For instance, if India were at war with another country, considerations of national security may demand the arrest and detention of a person who is the citizen of the enemy country. He may not be given the rights guaranteed under Article 22(1) and (2). But no such easy justification is available for the second exception which provides for preventive detention even during normal times. Discussion on this clause in the Constituent Assembly was stormy and acrimonious.

The reasons for the introduction of such a clause were explained by Ambedkar thus:

It has to be recognised that in the present circumstances of the country, it may be necessary for the Executive to detain a person who is tampering either with public order or with the Defence Services of the country. In such case, I do not think that the exigency of the liberty of the individual shall be placed above the interest of the state.[2]

Ambedkar's explanation, however, failed to satisfy a considerable section of the Assembly who criticized the provision in strong terms. For example, H.V. Kamath, quoting the Bible 'where there is no vision the people perish', said that it seemed to him that they were making a short-term constitution. For, those who might get into office first might make use of it to suppress others and their liberties constitutionally.[3] In a remarkable speech Bakshi Tek Chand assailed the provision in the severest terms which included the following question:

I will ask Dr. Ambedkar and Mr. Munshi and Sir Alladi and others if there is any written constitution in the world in which there is provision for detention of persons without trial in this manner in normal times ?[4]

---

1. C.A.D. IX, p. 1496.
2. Ibid.
3. Ibid., p. 1501.
4. Ibid., p. 1529.

Replying to the debate, Ambedkar laid emphasis on the special safeguards embodied in the Constitution even when a person is arrested and detained under a preventive detention law. He said:

> If all of us follow purely constitutional methods to achieve our objective, I think the situation would have been different and probably the necessity of having preventive detention might not be there at all. But I think in making a law we ought to take into consideration the worst and not the best..... There may be many parties and persons who may not be patient enough to follow constitutional methods but are impatient in reaching their objective and if for that purpose (they) resort to unconstitutional methods, then there may be a large number of people who may have to be detained by the Executive. In such a situation, would it be possible for the Executive to prepare the cases and do all that is necessary to satisfy the elaborate legal procedure prescribed ? Is it practicable ? [1]

Ambedkar, however, pointed out the safeguards provided in the Constitution to mitigate the rigours of an apparently absolute power of preventive detention permitted under Article 22(3). Firstly, every case of preventive detention must be authorised by law. It cannot be at the will of the Executive. Secondly, no law of preventive detention shall normally authorize the detention of a person for a longer period than three months. Thirdly, every case of preventive detention for a period longer than three months must be placed before an Advisory Board composed of persons qualified for appointment as judges of a High Court. Such cases must be placed before the Board within the three months' period. The continued detention after three months should be only on the basis of a favourable opinion by the Board. The only exception to this provision is when Parliament prescribes by law the circumstances under which a person may be kept in detention beyond three months even without the opinion of the Advisory Board. Fourthly, no person who is detained under any preventive detention law can be detained indefinitely. There shall always be a maximum period of detention which Parliament is required to prescribe by law. Fifthly, in cases which are required to be placed before the Advisory Board, the procedure to be followed by the Board shall be laid down by Parliament. Sixthly, when a person is detained under a law of preventive detention, the detaining authority shall communicate to him the grounds on which the order has been made. It should also afford him the earliest opportunity of making a representation against the order.

The greatest safeguard, according to Ambedkar, is that preventive detention takes place only under the law. It cannot be at the will of the Executive. It is also necessary to make a distinction between different categories of cases. There may be cases of detention where the circumstances are so serious and the consequences so dangerous that it would not even be desirable to permit the members of the Board to know the facts regarding the detention of any particular individual. The disclosure of such facts may be too dangerous to the security of the State or its very existence. But even here there are two mitigating circumstances. First, such cases will be defined by Parliament. They are not to be arbitrarily decided by the Executive. Secondly, in every case there shall be a maximum period of detention prescribed by law.[2]

It has already been pointed out that the Draft Constitution did not contemplate preventive detention; the idea came up only at a very late stage of constitution-making. What then were the motives that impelled the framers to incorporate such a drastic and

1. Ibid., p. 1556.
2. C.A.D. X., p. 575.

undemocratic provision in the Constitution ? What happened during the 1946-49 period to justify the inclusion of such a provision ?

In many ways both the Executive and the Judiciary were put to a severe strain during the first years of independence. This was due to the impact of two contradictory forces on the political life of India. The ideal of a democracy with maximum scope for civil liberties was in the air. The judiciary was eager to ensure for the individual the maximum of these liberties both in spirit and in reality. At the same time, the Executive being charged with the very survival of the newly-won freedom and independence was anxious to nip in the bud every threat to national security from within. The division of the country into India and Pakistan and the consequent influx of millions of refugees—who were dissatisfied and disappointed with their lot—the war in Kashmir, the food scarcity and near-famine conditions in many parts of the country, the exploitation of such a bleak situation by political opportunists and adventurers, profiteers and foreign agents—who constituted threat to political security and economic stability of the country—all these contributed to a situation unprecedented in the annals of any democracy. It was the realization of these difficulties and the determination to deal with them in an effective manner so that civil liberties could flourish in an orderly society, devoid of subversion, sabotage and anti-social activities, that the Constitution-makers, as a precautionary measure, added a 'preventive detention clause' to the original draft of the Constitution along with those very freedoms which form the foundations of a democratic order.

There is no authoritative definition of the term 'preventive detention' in Indian law. The expression has its origin in the language used by judges in England while explaining the nature of detention under the Defence of the Realm Act, 1914, passed on the outbreak of the First World War. The same language was repeated in connection with the Emergency Regulations made during the Second World War. The word 'preventive' is used in contradistinction to the word 'punitive'. In Rex *vs*. Halliday,[1] Lord Finaly said that

> ... it is not a punitive but a precautionary measure. The object is not to punish a man for having done something but to intercept him before he does it and to prevent him from doing it. No offence is proved, nor any charge formulated; and the justification of such detention is suspicion or reasonable probability and not criminal conviction which can only be warranted by legal evidence.

Detention in such a form is unknown in the United States except what took place in the case of the Japanese domiciled in the country during the last War. It was resorted to in England only during war-time but no democratic country in the world has made this an integral part of its constitution as has been done in India. Justice Mukherjea of the Supreme Court of India observed:

> This is undoubtedly unfortunate but it is not our business to speculate on questions of policy or to attempt to explore the reasons which led the representatives of our people to make such a drastic provision in the Constitution itself which cannot but be regarded as a most unwholesome encroachment upon the liberties of the people.[2]

The First Preventive Detention Act was passed by Parliament in 1950. The validity of the Act was soon challenged before the Supreme Court in Gopalan *vs*. the State of Madras.[3]

1. 1917, A.C. 260.
2. 1950, A.I.R. S.C. 92.
3. Ibid.

The case was heard by six judges of the Court and each of the judges wrote a separate opinion. Each examined in general the scope of fundamental rights under the Constitution besides analysing in detail the content of personal liberty. By a 4:2 majority, the Court upheld the Act except Section 14 of the Act which was unanimously declared invalid. The invalidity of this section, however, did not affect the rest of the Act as it could be severed from the remaining provisions. Section 14 according to Justice Mahajan was

> ...in the nature of an iron curtain around the acts of the authority making the order of preventive detention. The Constitution has guaranteed to the detained person the right to be told the grounds of his detention. He has been given a right to make a representation; yet section 14 prohibits the disclosure of the grounds furnished to him or the contents of the representation made by him in a Court of law and makes a breach of this injunction punishable with imprisonment.... It is a guaranteed right of the person detained to have the very grounds which are the basis of the order of detention. This Court would be entitled to examine the matter and so see whether the grounds furnished are the grounds on the basis of which he has been detained or they contained some other vague or irrelevant material.... It [section 14] virtually amounts to a suspension of a guaranteed right provided by the Constitution in as much as it indirectly by a stringent provision makes administration of the law by this Court impossible and at the same time it deprives a detained person from obtaining justice from this Court.[1]

Although the Court has upheld the validity of the Act in terms of the powers of Parliament to pass such a legislation, the judges were agreed on denouncing the idea of preventive detention during normal times. Justice Mahajan said:

> Preventive detention laws are repugnant to democratic constitutions and they cannot be found to exist in any of the democratic countries of the world... Curiously enough, this subject has found a place in the Constitution in the Chapter in Fundamental Rights.[2]

Chief Justice Kania observed:

> It may be noticed that neither the American nor the Japanese Constitution contains provisions permitting preventive detention, much less laying down limitations on such right of detention in normal times... Preventive detention in normal times, *i.e.*, without the existence of an emergency like war, is recognised as a normal topic of legislation (under our Constitution).[3]

According to Justice Mukherjea:

> ...no country in the world that I am aware of has made this (preventive detention) an integral part of their Constitution as has been done in India. This is undoubtedly unfortunate...which cannot but be regarded as a most unwholesome encroachment upon the liberties of the people.[4]

In Ram Krishna Bardwaj *vs.* the State of Delhi,[5] Chief Justice Patanjali Sastri said:

---

1. 1950, S.C.J., pp. 259-60.
2. 1950, S.C.J. p. 247.
3. 1950. S.C.J. p. 189. 3 Ibid., p. 263.
4. 1953, S.C.R. 708.
5. 1954, A.I.R. S.C. 179. See also Naranjan Singh *vs.* State of Punjab 1952, S.C.R. 395; Parulekar *vs.* District Magistrate, Thana 1952, S.C.R. 683; Tarapada De. R. *vs.* State of West Bengal 1951, S.C.R. 212; Ram Singh *vs.* State of Delhi 1951, S.C.R. 451; State of Bombay *vs.* Atma Ram Shridhar Vaidya 1951, S.C.R. 167; S. Krishnan *vs.* The State of Madras 1951, S.C.R. 621; N.C. Ganguli *vs.* The State of West Bengal, 1960, S.C.J. 303, Jagan Nath Sathu *vs.* The Union of India, 1960 S.C.J. 975 and Nirmal Kumar Khandelwal *vs.* Union of India (1978) 2 S.C.C. 508.

Preventive detention is a serious invasion of personal liberty and such meagre safeguards as the Constitution has provided against the improper exercise of the power must be jealously watched and enforced by the Court.

In Shibban Lal *vs.* the State of U.P.[1] the Court held that the sufficiency of the particulars conveyed to the detenu in accordance with the provision embodied in article 22(5) is a justiciable issue, the test being whether they were sufficient to enable the detenu to make an effective representation.[2]

The Court had also questioned the detention orders if the detaining authority acted *mala fide* or if the grounds were irrelevant. It has thus made extensive use of the procedural safeguards provided for in the Constitution and has exercised substantial influence in the liberalization of the law of preventive detention in favour of the detenus. Indeed, the Court has invariably taken a very strict view of preventive detentions and has interpreted the provisions of the law in such a way as to restrict the powers of preventive detention as far as possible.

In Motilal *vs.* State of Bihar[3] the Court held that the grounds communicated to the detenu were vague and incomplete. Speaking on behalf of the Court, Justice Hegde observed: "Preventive detention is a serious invasion of personal liberty and such safeguards as the Constitution has provided against the improper exercise of the power must be jealously watched and enforced by the Court".[3]

Whenever the Court got an opportunity to examine a case where the detention was made otherwise than under the Preventive Detention Act, the Court was quick and decisive to come to the aid of the aggrieved citizen by upholding his right under Article 22. In Keshavram *vs.* Nafisul Hassan[4] the Court set free with dramatic speed the editor of *Blitz,* a Bombay journal, who was arrested and kept under custody at Lucknow under the orders of the Speaker of the Uttar Pradesh Legislative Assembly for alleged contempt of the Assembly. Before the detained editor could be produced before the Assembly, a writ petition was moved on his behalf in the Supreme Court on the ground that he was not produced before a Magistrate within twenty-four hours after his arrest as required by Article 22(2) of the Constitution. Thereupon the Court ordered his immediate release as his detention violated the right guaranteed under Article 22(2).

For a period of two decades—from 1950 to 1970—a parliamentary enactment on preventive detention had continued to exist in the country. The Preventive Detention Act of 1950 was amended seven times, each time for a period of three years, thus extending it up to December 31, 1969. It was not further extended and hence there has been since then no preventive detention law for the country as a whole. Some of the States, however, passed laws on preventive detention in 1970. In 1971 Parliament passed a modified version of the old Preventive Detention Act under the title Maintenance of Internal Security Act.

Every time in the past when the Government moved to extend the Act, it provoked a heated debate in Parliament. This was particularly so in 1957 and 1960. Opposing the extension of the life of the Act, some members of the Opposition made the serious allegation that the Act had been used primarily to suppress political opposition. This allegation was refuted by the Government spokesmen by pointing out that out of a total of 106 detained on

1. For a discussion on 'preventive detention', see R.N. Mathur, "Right to Life and Personal Liberty", (1963) I S.C.J. 4.
2. 1968, A.I.R. S.C. 1509.
3. 1954, A.I.R. S.C. 636.

September 30, 1960, there were only eight who could be categorized as members of opposition parties. But they denied that the detention was for political reasons. The Government spokesman went further and asserted that for a large country like India where many fissiparous tendencies against national integrity still existed and subversive elements operated, the number of persons detained under the Act (about 500 between 1959 and 1960) in the interest of the security of the nation was not too much of a price. According to the Home Minister, as against nearly 11,000 persons who were in detention in 1950, there were only about a 100 at the time of extending the Act in 1960. In September 1957 the total was 205, December 1959, 96; January 1960, 98; and September 1960, 106. He added that there was a time when the number of detenus under the Act for the whole of India fell to as low a figure as a dozen.

The Opposition, however, was not impressed by these figures. Nor were they convinced of the need of extending the Act. They were almost unanimous in condemning it as a black Act and characterizing it as repugnant to all that was decent and precious in the political life of the country. One Member said that the right of individuals is not measured in quantitative terms. To say that only 500 were detained showed a 'blunting of sensitivity'. Even one person's liberty is precious and in guarding and protecting it the conscience of the whole nation had to be aroused. It was also pointed out that the circumstances which prevailed in 1950 when the Act was first passed had completely changed and that there was no justification for such a measure in 1960. Of course, the cry of State in danger has been used in all ages in all countries by those who wanted to perpetuate themselves in power; but often, this cry has little relation to reality. Those who make laws should remember that a law misused is worse than no law at all. Some of the leaders of the Opposition made a joint appeal to the Prime Minister to refer the matter to the Law Commission so that the Commission could examine the provisions of the Act, "particularly the procedures which give authority to the executive to act in an arbitrary manner so as to undermine civil liberties of the citizens. We continue to be not convinced of the need of such wide powers which are repugnant to the spirit of the Constitution and the rule of law we cherish. If the Act has to be extended, it should be extended only till the new Parliament is elected (1962) and the new House should be given an opportunity at the earliest to review the law *de novo.*"

The Government did not, however, agree to refer the Act to the Law Commission as it was a matter for the Executive to decide and no points of constitutional nature were involved which required a verdict of the Commission. The spokesmen of the Government emphasized that the retention of the Act in the Statute Book had by itself a restraining influence on anti-social and subversive elements. They also pointed out that the powers under the Act were used only sparingly as was shown by the figures of detention during the first decade since the Act was first passed. No one could seriously contest the fact that there existed in the country forces of separatism, parochialism, linguism and antinationalism. Some of these forces were in conspiracy with foreign powers who had evil designs on the country's integrity. Where large groups of citizens indulge in hostile activities or are suspected of espionage, where members actively participate in the process of law-making within the Legislatures but undermine the very same laws through coercive methods, such as, civil disobedience and fasting, where democratic freedoms are abused by organized sections to destroy the very same freedoms of others, the State should have effective powers, it was forcefully argued on behalf of the Government, for the protection of the civil liberties of the millions and the security of the State.[1]

The Forty-fourth Amendment of the Constitution (1978) while retaining the provision for preventive detention, made the conditions of preventive detention more rigorous in the interest of the individual. The amendment provision, for instance, reduced the initial period of detention from three months to two months. Further, the conditions under which the period can be extended have been made more difficult.

In a landmark decision—Additional Secretary to Government of India *vs*. Alka Subhash 1992 Supp. (1) S.C.C. 496, the Supreme Court held that the rights of a detenu are not confined to the Article 22 (5) but also extends to Articles 14, 19 and 21.

Apart from the Preventive Detention Act of 1950 which was the forerunner of all the preventive detention laws in the country, from time to time, similar laws were passed and implemented. Among them are COFFEPOSA (1974) Prevention of Blackmarketing and maintenance of Supplies of Essential Commodities Act, (1980), Prevention of Illicit traffic in Narcotic Drugs and Psychotropic Substances Act (1988) and Terrorists and Disruptive Activities (Prevention) Act (TADA) (1985). Prevention of Terrorism Bill 2000 is now on the anvil to replace the existing TADA.

Looking back on the life of Republican India, one may feel reasonably satisfied with the extent of personal liberty the Indian people at large have been enjoying. Democratic freedom in India is still too young and tender a plant to be capable of defending itself easily against overt or covert onslaughts that may be directed against it by elements which have no regard either for democratic liberties or orderly progress. Vigilance is still required to protect the country's hard-won freedom and national unity from forces of subversion and violent revolution. Until and unless every party or group accepts constitutional means to achieve its objectives and practises them, special provisions such as the preventive detention law may still be needed in India. But, whatever be the justification, so long as any provision similar to preventive detention remains on the statute book, there will also remain an unseemly blot on the fair face of democracy in India.

***

1. In April 1973, by a unanimous decision in Sambhu Nath Sarkar *vs*. State of West Bengal the Supreme Court struck down Sec. 17(A) of the Maintenance of Internal Security Act as being inconsistent with Clause 7 (A) of Article 22 of the Constitution. Section 17(1) had provided that during the period of operation of the emergency issued on December 3, 1971 "any person including a foreinger in respect of whom an order of detention has been made under this Act, may be detained without obtaining the opinion of the Advisory Board for a period longer than three months, but not exceeding two years, from the date of his detention." In this case Sarkar was kept in detention for 21 months without consulting an Advisory Board under order of the District Magistrate of Hooghly.

13

THE RIGHT AGAINST EXPLOITATION

(Arts. 23 and 24)

ARTICLES 23 and 24 deal with the right against exploitation. Article 23 which prohibits traffic in human beings and *begar*[1] and similar forms of forced labour are comparable to the Thirteenth Amendment of the American Constitution abolishing slavery or involuntary servitude. At the time of the adoption of the Constitution there was hardly anything like slavery or the widespread practice of forced labour in any part of India. The national freedom movement, since the twenties of last century, had been a rallying force against such practices. However, there were many areas of the country where the 'untouchables' were being exploited in several ways by the higher castes and richer classes. For example, in parts of Rajasthan in western India, which was in pre-independence days a cluster of Princely States, there existed a practice under which labourers who worked for a particular landlord could not leave him to seek employment elsewhere without his permission. Very often this restriction was so absolute that he was just a slave in reality. The local laws had supported such practices. Speaking about the evils of *begar*, a member of the Constituent Assembly from Rajasthan said:

> This article is a complement to the charter of freedom (Art. 19). This frees the poor, downtrodden and dumb people of the Indian States from the curse of *begar*. This begar has been a blot on humanity and has been a denial of all that has been good and noble in human civilisation. Through the centuries, this curse has remained as a dead weight on the shoulders of the common man, like the practice of slavery.[2]

Evils like the *Devadasi* system under which women were dedicated in the name of religion, to Hindu deities, idols, objects of worship, temples and other religious institutions, and under which they, instead of living a life of dedication, self-renunciation and piety, were the life-long victims of lust and immorality, had been prevalent in certain parts of southern and western India. Vestiges of such evil customs and practices were still there in many parts of the country. The Constitution-makers were eager to proclaim a war against them through the Constitution as these practices could have no place in the new political and social concept that was emerging with the advent of independence. The ideal of 'one man, one vote, one value', equality before law and equal protection of laws, freedom of profession and the right to move freely throughout the country—all these would have no

1. The term *begar* has been defined as labour or service without any remuneration. See PUDR *vs.* Union of India A.I.R. 1982, S.C. 1473, popularly known as Asjad Case.
2. Raj Bahadur, C.A.D. VII, p. 809.

meaning if 'one man' was subjugated by 'another man' and one's life was at the mercy of another.

As a result of Article 23 as many as twelve Central and State Laws that sanctioned forced labour under certain circumstances became void and as many as some 26 million people, mostly hillmen, got relief from forced labour.

Although any form of forced labour is an offence punishable under law just as untouchability is an offence, this consitutional guarantee is only against private individuals and organizations. An important exception is made in favour of the State which may impose compulsory service for public purposes.[1] Compulsory military service or compulsory work for nation-building programmes may provide examples of such service. The State may, for instance, pass a law by which it may compel every University graduate to spend six months in villages, immediately after leaving the University, on literacy work or other social service among the village people. Such a law, however, may not make any discrimination on grounds of religion, caste or class, or any of them. A member moved an amendment to this provision in the Constituent Assembly urging payment for such compulsory service. The chairman of the Drafting Committee did not agree to the proposal. He said:

> The fundamental proposition enunciated in sub-clause (2) is this: that whenever compulsory labour or compulsory service is demanded, it shall be demanded from all and if the State demands service from all and does not pay any, I do not think the State is committing any very great inequity...[2]

The Indian Penal Code and the Criminal Procedure Code have separate provisions prohibting traffic in human beings. According to the Penal Code, selling, letting for hire or otherwise disposing of, or buying, hiring or otherwise obtaining possession of any girl under 18 years of age for the purpose of prostitution or for any unlawful or immoral purpose is an offence. Importing into India girls under 21 years of age for immoral purposes is also an offence. In 1958, by a Central enactment organized prostituion as a profession has been abolished all over the country and the running of brothels has been made an offence.[3] In most of the States, there have already been enactments supressing immoral traffic. By 1953 there were no less than seventeen such enactments.[4] Some of the more important among these which deserve special mention are: The Madhya Pradesh Supression of Immoral Traffic Act, 1953; The Travancore-Cochin Supression of Immoral Traffic Act, 1952; and the Madras Devadasi (Prevention of Dedication) Act, 1947. The Madras Act makes any person participating in the cremeony of 'dedication' including the woman dedicated, liable to imprisonment for six months or a fine of Rs. 500, or both.

Prohibition of Child Labour

According to Article 24, no child below the age of fourteen years shall be employed to work in any factory or mine or engaged in any other hazardous employment. This article is intimately related to a directive principle of State policy which calls upon the

1. Article 23(2).
2. C.A.D. VIII, p. 812.
3. The Suppression of Traffic in Women and Girls Act, 1958, came into effect from 1 May 1958. The Act was challenged as unconstitutional on the ground that it was inconsistent with the provisions of fundamental right to carry on any trade, *etc.* but it was of no avail. See Sharma *vs.* State of Uttar Pradesh 1959, A.I.R. All. 57.
4. *Social Legislation: Its Role in Social Welfare* (Issued on behalf of the Planning Commission, Government of India), 1956, p. 261.

State to enforce universal compulsory and free primary education to all children in the country up to the age of fourteen years. This comes of the realization that children should prepare during this period for the tasks of the future as useful and responsible citizens. Employment of children is an uncivilized and even inhuman practice. It is an exploitation which stunts their growth, corrupts their morals and often drives them to delinquency. Naturally, it must be prohibited and incentives to divert them from employment should be provided.

Yet, only recently have attempts to prohibit the exploitation of child labour become successful even in the most advanced countries of the West. In the United States, for instance, since the Bill of Rights provided no remedy, the Congress had to resort to devious methods such as prohibition of inter-State commerce in the products of child labour (using its powers under the 'Commerce clause') and the Child Labour Tax Law, 1919. But the United States Supreme Court, by a narrow majority struck down both laws as unconstitutional on the ground that they transcended the authority of the Congress over commerce and interfered with the authority of the States. One of the most famous dissents of Justice Holmes was delivered in this connection.[1] He said:

> The notion that prohibition is any less prohibition when applied to things now thought evil I do not understand. But if there is any matter upon which civilised countries have agreed,—far more unanimously then they have with regard to intoxicants and some other matters over which this country is now emotionally aroused,—it is the evil of premature and excessive child labour. I should have thought that if we were to introduce our own moral conceptions where, in my opinion, they do not belong, this was pre-eminently a case for upholding the exercise of all its powers by the United States. But I had thought that the propriety of the exercise of a power admitted to exist in some cases was for the consideration of Congress alone, and that this Court always had disavowed the right to intrude its judgment upon questions of policy or morals. It is not for this Court to pronouce when prohibition is necessary to regulation if it ever may be necessary—to say that it is permissible as against strong drink, but not as against the product of ruined lives.[2]

It took some fifteen years more for the Court to reverse itself and uphold Congressional legislation designed to eradicate the evil of child labour and which was passed under the New Deal regime of President Roosevelt.[3]

The framers of the Indian Constitution were aware of this American experience under a federal system and were resolved to avoid its repetition in this country. It must, however, be pointed out that there were already some laws in the country at the time of the passing of the Constitution under which child labour was prohibited. The Indian Factories Act, 1948, for instance, made it an offence to employ any person, who had not completed his fourteen years, in a factory. After the inauguration of the Constitution, several such laws have been passed extending the scope of the constitutional prohibition under Article 24 to more defined areas of employment activity. The Plantation Labour Act of 1951 prohibits the employment of child workers in plantations. Similarly, according to the Mines Act of 1952, no child under fifteen years of age may be employed in any mine.

In spite of the existence of several laws which seek to provide protection of the right against exploitation, there still remain in many parts of the country many forms of exploitation that come within the scope of this right. The efforts so far made by the State in

---

1. Hammar *vs*. Dagenhart 1918, 247 U.S. 251 and Bailey *vs*. Drexel Furniture Co. 1922. 258 U.S. 20.
2. Hammer *vs*. Dagenhart, Ibid.
3. N.L.R.B. *vs*. Jones and Laughlin Steel Corporation 1937, 301 U.S. I.

this direction are marked by timidity rather than determination. There is an undercurrent of indifference even in the law-enforcing officials with respect to these rights. Many of them think, for instance, that attempts to close down brothels altogether are foredoomed to failure. Society must awaken to the full realization that *begar* and immoral traffic are the products of poverty and neglect. A Committee appointed some years ago by the Central Social Welfare Board to go into all aspects of immoral traffic reported that the question of women and girls generally is so closely linked up with prostitution that it is not possible to suggest measures to wipe out the one without taking into consideration the other. The question cannot be considered except in the context of national progress, full employment, economic advancement, social justice and the general raising of the standard of living of all sections of the people. Nevertheless, the adoption of preventive measures would reduce the incidence of these evil practices. For this, it is necessary for the State to pursue a more vigorous policy. In the words of the abovementioned Committee : Nothing but firm meausres carefully formulated and vigorously implemented can produce the result even if it takes time.

***

14

THE RIGHT TO FREEDOM OF RELIGION

(Arts. 25 to 28)

IT IS a paradox that while almost every religion stands for and preaches the universal brotherhood of man, religion has been a constant source of conflict in human history. India has been most unfortunate in this respect, particularly during the last thousand years of her history. The British did not desist from exploiting this situation for their own advantage so as to continue their rule in India as long as they could. We saw in the earlier part of this discussion how religion shattered the unity of the nation and how the country was partitioned on a religious basis. Yet the problem of religious minorities in independent India was not solved and it remained as difficult as ever. Despite the creation of Pakistan, there were more than forty million Muslims in India scattered all over the country. There were, in addition, some ten million Christians. Five million Sikhs and considerable numbers of Parsees, Jains, Buddhists and Jews. Those who professed the Hindu religion formed an overwhelming majority, some 85 per cent of the total population. If they chose to act together as a religious group in representative institutions, they could pass any law they liked and have absolute control over the governmental machinery and all its activities. The slightest tendency towards such an attitude would have undermined the confidence of the religious minorities, and democracy in India might have become a label without meaning, a form without substance.

The idea of guaranteed fundamental rights itself was a device directed towards the avoidance of such a contingency. The right to freedom of speech and expression and the right to form associations and unions are also rights which guarantee religious speech and expression and the right to form religious associations and unions. But the Constituent Assembly was not satisfied with such provisions alone in its bid to infuse complete confidence in the religious minorities. It went a step further and adopted a separate group of articles dealing solely with the right to freedom of religion.[1] The freedoms provided in Articles 25, 26, 27 and 28 are conceived in most generous terms to the complete satisfaction of religious minorities. They were in fact the result of an agreement with the minorities, almost unanimously arrived at in the Minorities Committee constituted by the Constituent Assembly. Such unanimity created an atmosphere of harmony and confidence in the majority community.[2] Further, these provisions embodied in detail one of the objectives of

1. For the meaning of religion and religious denominations, See S.P. Mittal *vs.* Union of India, AIR 1983 S.C.I.
2. C.A.D. VII, p. 837.

the Constitution as declared in the Preamble; 'to secure to all its citizens. ... liberty of faith, belief and worship'.[1]

Religious Freedom and the Secular State

It was argued on the floor of the Assembly that the religious freedom guaranteed under the Constitution was antithetical to the concept of a secular State which the Constitution aimed to establish.[2] This proposition was successfully challenged by several prominent members including those of the Drafting Committee. Some of the observations made in this context deserve reproduction in original. According to Lakshmi Kant Maitra the above-mentioned conception of a secular State was wholly wrong. He said:

> By secular State, as I understand it, is meant that the State is not going to make any discrimination whatsoever on the ground of religion or community against any person professing any particular form of religious faith. This means in essence that no particular religion in the State will receive any State patronage whatsoever. The State is not going to establish, patronise or endow any particular religion to the exclusion of or in preference to others and that no citizen in the State will have any preferential treatment or will be discriminated against simply on the ground that he professed a particular form of religion. In other words, in the affairs of the State, the professing of any particular religion will not be taken into consideration at all. This I consider is the essence of a secular State.[3]

H.V. Kamath said:

> When I say that a State should not identify itself with any particular religion, I do not mean to say that a State should be anti-religious or irreligious. We have certainly declared India to be a secular State. But to my mind, a secular State is neither a God-less State nor an irreligious nor an anti-religious State[4].

Participating in the debate on the Hindu Code Bill in Parliament in 1951, Ambedkar explained the concept of secularism as follows:

> It [secular State] does not mean that we shall not take into consideration the religious sentiments of the people. All that a secular State means is that this Parliament shall not be contempetent to impose any particular religion upon the rest of the people. That is the only limitation that the Constitution recognises.[5]

The significance of secularism as it relates to the State in India has been dealt with at length by India's first Vice-President, Radhakrishnan,[6] in the following words:

> When India is said to be a secular State, it does not mean that we reject the reality of an unseen spirit or the relevance of religion to life or that we exalt irreligion. It does not mean that secularism itself becomes a positive religion or that the State assumes divine prerogatives. Though faith in the Supreme is the basic principle of the Indian tradition, the Indian State will not identify itself with or be controlled by any particular religion. We hold that no one religion should be given preferential status, or unique distinction, that no one religion should be accorded special privileges in national life or international relations for that would be a violation of the basic principles of

1. While the Constitutional provisions are hailed as most generous, the procedural safeguards seen to be far from that; *e.g.* see D.C. Srivastava, "Procedural Impediments on Religious Freedom" (1961) I.S.C.J. 41.
2. Ibid., p. 822.
3. Ibid. VII, p. 831.
4. Ibid., p. 825. Speaking about the term secular. Jawaharlal Nehru once said: "the word secular perhaps is not a happy one. And yet for want of a better word we have used it."
5. *Parliamentary Debates* 1951, vol III, part II, 2466.
6. Dr. Radhakrishnan was elected President of India in 1962.

democracy and contrary to the best interests of religion and government. This view of religious impartiality of comprehension and forbearance has a prophetic role to play within the national and international life. No group of citizens shall arrogate to itself rights and privileges which it denies to others. No person should suffer any form of disability or discrimination because of his religion but all alike should be free to share to the fullest degree in the common life. This is the basic principle involved in the separation of Church and State. The religious impartiality of the Indian State is not to be confused with secularism or atheism. Secularism as here defined is in accordance with the ancient religious tradition of India. It tries to build up a fellowship of believers, not by subordinating individual qualities to the group-mind but by bringing them into harmony with each other.[1]

Thus the distinguishing features of a secular democracy as contemplated by the Constitution of India are : (*i*) that the State will not identify itself with or be controlled by any religion; (*ii*) that while the State guarantees to every one the right to profess whatever religion one chooses to follow (which includes also the right to be an agnostic or an atheist), it will not accord any preferential treatment to any of them; (*iii*) that no discrimination will be shown by the State against any person on account of his religion or faith, and (*iv*) that the right of every citizen, subject to any general condition, to enter any office under the State will be equal to that of his fellow-citizens. Political equality which entitles any Indian citizen to seek the highest office under the State is the heart and soul of secularism as envisaged by the Constitution. It secures the conditions of creating a fraternity of the Indian people which assures both the dignity of the individual and the unity of the nation.[2]

Freedom of Conscience, etc.

Article 25 (1) enacts that all persons are equally entitled to freedom of conscience and the right freely to profess, practise and propagate religion.[3] The wording of the article has been largely based upon the judicial interpretation of freedom of religion in the United States. Interpreting the scope of religious freedom as guaranteed under the First Amendment, the American Supreme Court held:

> Freedom of religious belief and to act in the exercise of such belief cannot override the interests of peace, order or morals of the society and to that extent the freedom of religion is subject to the control of the State[4].

This is in conformity with the modern idea that anything may not, in the name of religion, have the unrestricted right to practise or propagate itself.

The problem of interpreting the right to freely practise and propagate religion, however, has never been an easy task for the Courts[5]. This is evident from the contradictory decisions of the United States Supreme Court on such an apparently simple matter as to whether an Ordinance enjoining every citizen to salute the National Flag interferes with religious freedom. As Justice Felix Frankfurter pointed out in one of these decisions,

1. *Recovery of Faith,* N.Y. Harper Bros., 1955, p. 202.
2. See in this connection Sharma G.S. (Ed), *Secularism: Its Implications for Law and Life in India* (1966); also Setalvad, M.C. *Secularism* (Patel Memorial Lectures, 1967). See also Suresh Chandra *vs*. The Union of India, A.I.R. 1975 Del. 168.
3. The wearing and carrying of *Kirpans* shall be deemed to be included in the profession of the Sikh religion.
4. Davies *vs*. Beason 133, U.S. 333.
5. cf. Minersville School Dist. *vs*. Gobitis 1940, 310, U.S. 586 and West Virginia State Boarding of Education *vs*. barnette 1943, 319, U.S. 624.

of course patriotism cannot be enforced by the flag salute. But neither can the liberal spirit be enforced by judicial invalidation of illiberal legislation..... Reliance for the most precious interests of civilisation, therefore, must be found outside of their vindication in courts of law. Only a persistent positive translation of the faith of a free society into the convictions and habits and actions of a community is the ultimate reliance against unabated temptations to fetter the human spirit.[1]

Yet in its zeal to uphold the right of religious enthusiasts, the Court has on occasions gone to the limit of approving actions such as ringing door bells and disturbing householders, accosting passers-by and insulting them in their religious beliefs, soliciting funds even in an intimidating manner and 'peddling doctrinal wares in the street.'[2] These decisions of the Court show how essential it is for the text of the Constitution to give a positive lead to the Courts by specifically laying down as clearly as possible the permissive limits to which legislation regulating the practice and propagation of religion can go. The idea of laying down such restrictions finds wide acceptance today.[3]

The framers of the Indian Constitution accepted this idea and made it a part of Article 25(a) by placing three restrictions to the freedom of religion, namely, public order, morality and health. The full implications of these qualifications have not yet been discovered. Naturally, they will have to grow with the growing social and moral conscience of the people as well as authoritative judicial pronouncements. The State is also permitted to regulate economic, financial, political or other secular activities which may be associated with religious practice.[4] Further, it may also provide for social welfare and reform or the throwing open of Hindu religious institutions of a public character to all classes and sections of Hindus.[5]

In S.P. Mittal *vs*. The Union of India the petitioners challenged the validity of the Auroville (Emergency Provision) Act of 1980, which provided for the taking over the management of Auroville founded by Aurobindo for a limited time. It was held by the Supreme Court that the Aurobindo Society or the Auroville Township does not constitute a religious denomination and teachings of Aurobindo does not represent religion (See also in this connection Acharya Jagadeswaranand *vs*. Commissioner of Police, AIR 1984 SC 51 for the definition of the concepts.)

In Bijo Emmanuel *vs*. State of Kerala (AIR 1987 SC 748) the Court laid down the tests to determine the ambit of freedom of conscience under Article 25(1). In this case the Court held that standing respectfully without singing the National Anthem due to religious prescriptions can be permitted under Article 25(1). It reversed the decision of Kerala High Court in Bijo Emmanuel *vs*. State of Kerala 1986 KLT 227.

The word 'propagate' does not find a place in any other constitution where it deals with religious freedom. A few members of the Constituent Assembly were vehemently opposed to the inclusion of this term as they thought that it may be perilous to guarantee it and might freely be used for the purpose of wholesale conversion.[6] But the overwhelming majority of members did not agree to this view. As one member pointed out:

---

1. 319, U.S. 624.
2. See in this connection E.S. Corwin, *The Constitution and What It Means Today*, 10th edition, p. 200.
3. See the decision of the Australian High Court which deals with the subject rather exhaustively in Adelaide Company of Jehovah's Witness *vs*. The Commonwealth, 67 C.L.R. 116.
4. Article 25(2)(a).
5. Article 25(2)(b)
6. C.A.D. VII, pp, 882-4.

After all, propagation is merely freedom of expression. I would like to point out that the word 'convert'; is not there...... Those who drafted this Constitution have taken care to see that no unlimited right of conversion has been given. People have freedom of conscience, and if any man is converted voluntarily owing to freedom of conscience, then well and good. No restrictions can be placed against. it.[1]

Speaking on behalf of the Drafting Committee, K.M. Munshi said:

.....Moreover, I was a party from the very beginning to the compromise with the minorities....and I know that it was on this word the Indian Christian community laid the greatest emphasis, not because they wanted to convert people aggressively, but because the word 'propagate' was a fundamental part of their tenet. Even if the word were not there, I am sure, under the freedom of speech which the Constitution guarantees, it will be open to any religious community to persuade other people to join their faith. So long as religion is religion, conversion by free exercise of the conscience has to be recognised.[2]

Advocating the inclusion of the word 'propagate', another member observed:

It is generally understood that the word propagate is intended only for the Christian community. But I think it is absolutely necessary, in the present context of circumstances, that we must educate our people on religious tenets and doctrines. So far as my experience goes, the Christian community has not transgressed their limits of legitimate propagation of religious view, and on the whole, they have done well indeed. It is for other communities to emulate them and propagate other religions as well.... The different communities may well.... propagate their religion and what it stands for. It is not to be understood that when one propagates his religion he should cry down other religions. It is not the spirit of any religion to cry down another religion. Therefore, this is absolutely necessary and essential.[3]

According to Alladi Krishnaswami Aiyar:

.......it was probably unnecessary to have included the expression 'propagate' in view of that fact that freedom of expression is already guaranteed under article 19, but the expression was inserted by way of abundant caution to satisfy certain missionary interests who were zealous about it.[4]

The Supreme Court had occasion to interpret the right of religious freedom under Article 25 in the case of Commissioner of Hindu Religious Endowment *vs*. L.T. Swamiar.[5] The Court held that article 25 guarantees to every person subject to public order, health and morality, a freedom not only to entertain such religious belief as may be approved of by his judgment and conscience, but also to exhibit his belief in such outward acts as he thinks proper and to propagate or disseminate his ideas for the edification of others. The expression 'practice of religion' denotes that the Constitution not only protects the freedom of religious opinion but also acts done in pursuance of a religion.

Article 26 is, in fact, a corollary to Article 25 and guarantees the freedom to manage religious affairs. According to this, every religious denomination is given the right: (*i*) to establish and maintain institutions for religious and charitable purposes; (*ii*) to manage its own affairs in matters of religion' (*iii*) to own and acquire movable and immovable property'; and (*iv*) to administer such property in accordance with law. Article 27 provides an additional protection to religious activity by exempting funds appropriated towards the

---

1. K. Santhanam, C.A.D. VII, p. 835.
2. Ibid,. p. 837.
3. L. Krishnaswami Bharati, C.A.D. VII, p. 833.
4. K. Santhanam C.A.D. VIII.
5. 1954, A.I.R. S.C. 282. See also the sirur Mutt case 1954, S.C. J. 335.

promotion or maintenance of any particular religion from the payment of taxes.[1]

Some of these provisions have already come up before the Supreme Court for interpretation. In the Madras case cited above, the Court held that the freedom of religion is not confined to religious beliefs only but it extends to religious practices as well. Under Article 26(*b*), therefore, a religious denomination or organization enjoys complete autonomy in the matter of deciding as to what rites and ceremonies are essential according to the tenets of the religion they hold and no outside authority has any jurisdiction to interfere with their decision in such matters.[2] However, the right of a religious denomination to manage its own affairs in matters of religion is subject to, and can be controlled by, a law protected by Article 25(2) (*b*) throwing open a Hindu public temple to all classes and sections of Hindus.[3] Under Article 26 (*d*) it is the fundamental right of a religious denomination or its representative to administer its properties in accordance with law, and the law therefore must leave the right of administration to the denomination itself subject to certain restrictions.[4] In Sri Jagannath *vs*. the State of Orrisa,[5] the Orrisa Hindu Religious Endowments Act of 1939 was challenged as invalid on the ground that it authorized the State to collect certain contributions which was an infringement of Article 27. The Court did not agree with this contention and held that

> What is forbidden by article 27 is the specific appropriation of the proceeds of any tax on payment of expenses for the promotion or maintenance of any particular religious denomination. The object of the contribution is not the fostering or preservation of the Hindu Religion or of any denomination within it; the purpose is to see that religious trusts and institutions wherever they exist are properly administered. Therefore, article 27 does not apply.

The provision that empowers the State to override religious injunctions prohibiting certain classes from entering temples or other religious institutions is, again, a unique one. The obvious object is to remove a potent cause of disunion and inequality among the various castes of the Hindus. It is indeed a corollary to the abolition of untouchability. However, the opening of temples to all Hindus by the State is confined to only public institutions, that is, those which have been intended for the Hindu public either by grant or user. It means that the scope of this provision will not extend to private institutions established by individual or family endowments.

A provision that is similar to the above is that which deals with social reform. A secular State which protects all religions equally is by no means bound to protect every kind of human activity under the guise of religion. There are religions which bring under their own cloak every human activity and it would be absurd to suggest that a secular state should protect them all. Here again, Indian conditions have had their particular impact in

1. Tracing the genesis of this article, Alladi points out that it was intended as a possible protection against the predominant Hindu or Muslim Provinces as the case may be (under the Cabinet Mission Plan) levying taxes for the maintenance of the religion professed by the majority in a particular State Op. cit., p. 48. See also Bashir Ahmad *vs*. State of West Bengal, A.I.R. 1976. Cal. 142 and State of Rajasthan *vs*. Sajjan Lal, A.I.R. 1975 S.C. 706.
2. Sarup Singh *vs*. Stae of Punjab, 1959 S.C.J. 715. See also Durga Committee *vs*. Syed Hussain, 1961 A.I.R. S.C. 1402 T.S.G. Maharaj *vs*. State of Rajasthan, (1964) II S.C.J. 715 and N.H. Quereshi *vs*. State of Bihar (Popularly known as Cow Slaughter Case), 1958 S.C.J. 975.
3. Sri Venkataramana Devaru *vs*. The State of Mysore 1958, S.C.J. 382.
4. Ibid., 1954. A.I.R. S.C. 282.
5. 1954, A.I.R. S.C. 400.

the minds of the fathers of the Constitution. Mention has already been made of the degradation of certain social institutions like caste. The importance of this provision is that it does not allow social inequalities to be perpetuated under the cloak of religion. Where there is conflict between religious practice and social reform, religion must yield.[1] The conception of religion in India, as Ambedkar explained in the Constituent Assembly, is so vast that it covers every aspect of life from birth to death.[2] If the State were to accept this conception of religion, the country would come to a standstill in regard to reforms. It may be expected that no sensible State, in the name of social reform, would interfere with the essence of any religion. The legislation for social reform would touch only questionable practices and dogmas and the like, which would stand in the way of social progress of the country.

Religious Instruction in Schools

Article 28 prohibits religious instruction in any educational institution wholly maintained out of State funds whether such instruction is given by the State or by any other body. But this prohibition will not apply to any educational institution which is established under any endowment or trust which requires that religious instruction should be imparted in such institution, even if it happens to be administered by the State. After having thus settled the question of religious instruction in State schools, the Constitution deals with this matter in State-aided or State recognized schools.[3] No person attending such institutions can be compelled to take part in any religious instruction without the consent of the person concerned or, if the person is a minor, without the consent of his guardian. This again is a provision which seeks to accommodate the interests of religious minorities. Although educational institutions run by them may receive State aid, this does not prohibit their imparting religious instruction to those who are willing to attend[4]. Thus, while secular character of the State is demonstrated by all State educational institutions, private or denominational institutions, even when they receive State aid, are given freedom to maintain their religious character.

The subject of religious instruction in schools raised some controversy in the Constituent Assembly. While some members thought that religious instruction should not be allowed in any educational institution, others thought that there should be provision for it in every school including State schools. 'There was no reason to prohibit religious instruction in State Schools', said one member. 'What was needed as the consent of the parties or their parent.' Another member[5] wanted the State to endeavour to develop religious tolerance and morality among its citizens by providing suitable courses on various religions in the schools. Winding up the discussion, Ambedkar pointed out the reasons that impelled the Drafting Committee to adopt the existing provisions. First, the multiplicity of religions and their sub-divisions makes it impossible for the State to treat the children of all these communities on a footing of equality and to provide religious instruction even if the principle were accepted. Secondly, the religions as they prevail in this country are not merely non-

---

1. See in this connection B.N. Chobe, "Religious Freedom and Religious Trusts Bill," (1961) I S.C.J. 9.
2. C.A.D. VII, p. 781.
3. Article 28(3).
4. Mohamed Ismael Sahib, CAD VII p. 866.
5. Shibban Lal Saksena Ibid., p. 867.

social but were even anti-social, one religion claiming that its teachings constitute the only right path for salvation, that all other religions are wrong.

> In view of this, it seems to me that we should be considerably disturbing the peaceful atmosphere of an institution if these controversies were brought into juxtaposition in the school itself. Therefore, in laying down that in State institutions there should be no religious instruction, we have in my judgment travelled the path of complete safety.[1]

The second clause, in Ambedkar's opinion, tries to regularize the claim of a community which has started educational institutions for the advancement of its own children either in education or in cultural matters, to be permitted to give religious instruction in such institutions, notwithstanding the fact that they receive certain aid from the State. But such institutions shall not give religious instruction to the children of other communities without the consent of their parents. A double purpose has been thus achieved and those who want religious instruction to be given are free to establish their own institutions, claim aid from the State and give religious instruction, but shall not be in a position to force such religious instruction on other communities. Hence, it is not proper to say that religious instruction is barred by this provision.[2]

---

1. Ibid., p. 883.
2. The plea for giving religious instruction in all educational institutions with a view to building up a high sense of morality and character among the young men and women who attend these institutions has been passionately advocated by several eminent men in India. C. Rajagopalachari was a champion among them. See *e.g.*, his Annual Convocation Address to the graduates of Agra University in 1956.

15

CULTURAL AND EDUCATIONAL RIGHTS

(Arts. 29 and 30)

UNDER ARTICLES 29 and 30, certain cultural and educational rights are guaranteed. Section (1) of Article 29 guarantees the right of any section of the citizens residing in any part of the country having a distinct language, script or culture of its own to conserve them. Section (2) prohibits any discrimination baed only on religion, race, caste, language or any of them in the matter of admission to State or State-aided educational institutions. Section (1) of Article 30 provides that 'all minorities, whether based on religion or language, shall have the right to establish and administer educational institutions of their chocie'. According to Section (2), the State shall not, in granting aid to educational institutions, discriminate against any educational institution on the ground that it is under the management of a minority, whether based on religion or language.

These propvisions are unique in their thoroughness. There is nothing comparable to these rights in the Bill of Rights of the U.S. Constitution. Two constitutions which do have provisions which resemble certain parts of these two articles are the Burmese and the Irish Republic's. According to Article 22 of the Burmese Constitution, 'no minority, religious, racial or linguistic, shall be discriminated against in regard to admission to State educational institutions'. Article 42 of the Irish Constitution has two significant provisions:

> 1. The State shall not oblige parents in violation of their conscience and lawful preference to send their children to schools established by the State or to any particular type of school designated by the State.
>
> 2. Legislation providing State aid for schools shall not discriminate between schools under the management of the different religious denominations.

It is worth remembering in this context that Ireland has a religious-denominational problem. Although the population belongs almost entirely to the Christian religion, it is divided between two principal denominations, namely the Catholic and the Protestant. The Irish Protestants are a small minority. Burma has religious, racial and linguistic minorities. A third country which has a similar problem and which too thought in terms of making an express provision in this regard is West Germany. According to Article 113 of the West German Constitution:

> Sections of the population of the Reich speaking another language may not be restricted whether by way of legislation or administration in their free racial development. This applies specially to the use of their mother tongue in education as well as the question of internal administration and the administration of justice.

None of these constitutions, however, goes as far as the Constitution of India. This will be clear when provisions under Articles 29 and 30 are considered along with other provisions in the chapter on Fundamental Rights and elsewhere in the constitution safeguarding the rights of religious, linguistic and racial minorities. It is the sole purpose of these provisions to reassure the minorities that certain special interests of theirs which they chreish as fundamental to their life are safe under the Constitution. These are in conformity with the right to religious freedom and an extension to certain specific aspects of that right, like the freedom to maintain separate educational institutions, etc. already referred to. One speical feature of these provisions, however, is that the term 'minority' has been given a wide connotation. Here a minority is recognized as such on the basis not only of religion but also on language, script or culture. The importance of the provision will be evident in view of the existence of not less than a dozen well-developed languages within the territory of India.

As in the case of other Fundamental Rights, the Constituent Assembly witnessed a long debate on these provisions as well. Leading the critics who advocated even more liberal provisions, Z.H. Lari thought that the provisions under Article 29 on language or script and culture were not sufficient to protect the linguistic and cultural interests of the minorities. He wanted the original provision in the recommendations of the Fundamental and Minority Rights Committee to remain.[2] That provision stood as follows:

> Minorities in every unit shall be protected in respect of their language, script and culture, and no laws and regulations may be enacted that may operate oppressively or prejudicially in this respect.[3]

Further, Lari made a specific suggestion that the right to be educated through the mother tongue during the primary stage of education should be safeguarded.[4]

Giving the reasons for changing the original draft, Ambedkar first explained the difference in the meaning of the word minority used in the usual, technical sense of a religious minority, and the use of the word to denote cultural or linguistic units. He then said:

> In order to meet the situation of migration from one Province to another, we felt it was desirable that such a provision should be incorporated in the Constitution. Further, it does not impose any obligation or burden upon the State. The government shall not be required by law to finance any project of giving education to such minorities in their own language. The only limitation is that if the minority wants to preserve its language etc., the State shall not by law impose upon it any other culture which may be either local or otherwise.
>
> Although the word 'minority' has been omitted, we have very greatly improved upon the protection that was given in the original article. As a result, we have converted it into a fundamental right so that if a State made any law which was inconsistent with the provisions of this article, then that much of the law will be invalid.[5]

Ambedkar also explained the difficulties involved in incorporating a provision guaranteeing primary education through the medium of mother tongue. The main difficulties, he said, were practical:

---

1. The Eighth Schedule of the Constitution recognizes eighteen languages of India.
2. C.A.D. VII, p. 893.
3. P. 30 of the *Report*.
4. Pandit H.N. Kunzru supported Lari's plea in this regard. C.A.D. VII, p. 919.
5. C.A.D. VII, p. 922.

Who will decide whether or not the minorities are in substantial numbers to justify such facilities? Neither the executive nor the judiciary can be entrusted with this task. The former is not reliable. It is not advisable to entrust the latter with such a task; perhaps, it is not competent to do it.[1]

While Lari and others thought that the constitutional provisions did not go far enough, others denounced them as too great a concession to fissiparous tendencies. Leading such critics, Damodar Swarup Seth said that he feared that 'educational institutions based on religion or community will block the national unity and secularism, and promote communalism and a narrow antinational outlook with disastrous results'. He was, however, in favour of guaranteeing the right of linguistic minorities in this respect up to and including secondary education.[2]

Despite these extreme views, the bulk of the members in the Assembly, including members belonging to linguistic and religious minorities, hailed these provisions as generous and satisfactory. Jaipal Singh, the Jharkhand leader from Chotanagpur, said:

> This article [29] seems to open a new era for Indians.... I hope that the Provincial Govenrments will act according to the spirit of this article long before the Constitution actually comes into existence, so that the bitterness that there is in the Provinces on account of this linguistic warfare may gradually disappear, and all linguistic minorities may feel that their languages will not be victimised, that they may develop their languages as they like and that their language has a rightful palce in the country.[3]

Speaking on the merits of Article 29, K. Santhanam said:

> This article solves one of the most difficult problems which free India will have to face. The problems of religious minorities and of Scheduled Castes are legacies of the past and I expect that in the near future they will simply lapse owing to the lapse of time and owing to circumstances. But the question of linguistic minorities will be a problem for many decades to come and I am afraid, it is going to cause the country a great deal of trouble.[4]

The debate in the Constituent Assembly gives one the impression that in the framing of these articles, particularly Article 29, the framers were more concerned with the question of linguistic and cultural minorities rather than that of religious minorities. The problem of religious minorities was already dealt with in detail under the provisons on the right to freedom of religion. The difficulty of finding a solution to the problem of linguistic or cultural minorities arose from the fact that they formed islands of their own within the territory of each state. On the one hand, they wanted to conserve their own language and culture and impart education to their children through the medium of the mother tongue. On the other, it was the general interest that such a right should not interfere with the historical process of assimilation of these minorities with the rest of the people in these areas. Otherwise, they would remain perpetually a sort of aliens in the areas they lived, hampering the building up of an integrated society. Hence, any provision which sought to protect the mother tongue of every child automatically, irrespective of the area in which it lived, although seemingly an attractive idea from the point of view of the linguistic or cultural minorities, was harmful from a national point of view. But the process of integration could not be sudden. It could not be a forced one either. Article 29 takes care of these

1. Ibid.
2. Bombay Education Society *vs.* The State of Bombay, 56, Bom. L.R. 655.
3. State of Madras *vs.* Champakam Dorairajan and State of Madras *vs.* C.R. Srinivasan, 1951, S.C.J. 313.
4. C.A.D. VII, p. 899.

competing considerations and strikes a balance which makes it highly realistic from both points of view. Nevertheless, it must be pointed out that Article 29 alone does not provide a solution to this problem. The picture becomes complete only when Articles 15, 16 (non-discrimination) and 46 (the State's special responsibility to backward classes) are read along with Article 29.

Interpreting the scope of Article 29, the Bombay High Court held that it embodied two important principles:[1]

> One is the right of the citizen to select any educational institution maintained by the State and receiving aid out of State funds. The State cannot tell a citizen, 'you shall go to this school which I maintain and not to the other.' Here we find reproduced the right of the parent to control the education of the child.

The scope of Article 29(2) came up for detailed interpretation before the Supreme Court in two cases,[2] both of which were appeals against decisions of the Madras High Court, relating to admission in educatinal institutions maintained by the State. The facts were as follows. The State of Madras maintained four medical colleges and four engineering colleges, with 330 and 395 seats respecively. These seats, for many years before the commencement of the Constitution, had been apportioned among candidates on the basis of what used to be called the Communal G.O. According to this, for every fourteen seats to be filled by the selection committee, candidates used to be selected on the folowing basis: Non-Brahmin Hindus 6; Backward Hindus 2; Brahmins 2; Harijans 2; Anglo-Indians and Indian Christian 1; and Muslims 1. The same system continued even after the inauguration of the Constitution.

In June 1950, Dorairajan and Srinivasan, two candidates seeking admission to a medical college and an engineering college respectively, made applications to the Madras High Court praying for the issue of writs of mandamus or any other appropriate order restraining the State Government from enforcing the Communal G.O. as it violated their fundamental rights under Articles 15(1) and 29(2).

The Madras High Court declared the Communal G.O. invalid by a unanimous decision. The state of Madras preferred to appeal to the Supreme Court and the Supreme Court upheld the decision of the High Court. Speaking for a unanimous Court, Justice S.R. Das after enumerating the two clauses of Article 29 said:

> It will be noted that while clause (1) protects the language, script or culture of a section of the citizens, clause (2) guarantees the fundamental right of an individual citizen. The right to get admission into any educaitonal institution of the kind mentioned in clause (2) is a right which an individual citizen has as a citizen and not as a member of any community or class of citizens. This right is not to be denied to the citizen on ground only of religion, race, caste, language or any of them. If a citizen who seeks admission into any such educational institution has not the requisite academic qualifications and is denied admission on that ground, he certainly cannot be heard to complain of an infraction of his fundamental right under this Article. But, on the other hand, if he has the academic qualifications but is refused admission only on ground of religion, race, caste, language or any of them, then there is a clear breach of his fundamental right.

On behalf of the State, it was contended that Article 46 charged the State with promoting, with special care, the educational and economic interests of the weaker sections of the people, and, in particular, of the Scheduled Castes and the Scheduled Tribes, and

1. Bombay Education Society *vs*. The State of Bombay, 56 Bom. L.R. 655.
2. C.A.D. VII, p. 908.

with protecting them from social injustice and all forms of exploitation. Although this being a directive principle was a non-justiciable right, it was nevertheless obligatory on the part of the State to enforce it in practice. The Court rejected this argument and declared:

> The directive principles of State policy, which by article 37 are expressly made unenforceable by a Court cannot override the provisions found in Part III which, notwithstanding other provisions, are expressly made enforceable by appropriate writs, orders or directions under Article 32. The Chapter of Fundamental Rights is sacrosanct and not liable to be abridged by any Legislative or Executive act or order, except to the extent provided in the appropriate Article in Part III. The directive principles of State policy have to conform to and run as subsidiary to the Chapter of Fundamental Rights. In our opinion, that is the correct way in which the provisions found in Parts III and IV have to be understood. However, so long as there is no infringement of any Fundamental Rights, to the extent conferred by the provisions in Part III, there can be no objection to the State acting in accordance with the directive principles set out in Part IV, but subject again to Legislative and Executive powers and limitations conferred on the State under different provisions of the Constitution.
>
> The classification in the Communal G.O. proceeds on the basis of religion, race and caste. In our view, the classification made in the Communal G.O. is opposed to the Constitution and constitutes a clear violation of the fundamental rights guaranteed to the citizen under Article 29(2)[1]

Article 30 is a charter of educational rights. It guarantees in absolute terms the right of linguistic and religious minorities to establish and administer educaitonal institutions of their choice and, at the same time, claim grants-in-aid without any discrimintion based upon religion or language. The fact that the Constitution does not impose any express restriction in the scope of the enjoyment of this right, unlike most of the rights included in the chapter on Fundamental Rights, shows that the framers intended to make its scope unfettered. This does not, however, mean that the State cannot impose reasonable restrictions of a regulatory character for maintaining standards of education. This point has been made abundantly clear in judicial pronouncements. In the Bombay Education Society case,[2] Chief Justice Chagla, speaking for a unanimous Court, said:

> It is not as if the State is helpless before minorities who may set up any kind of educational institutions. The important corrective that the State has and possesses is that unless the educational institution conforms to and complies with the proper rules laid down by the State, the State may deny to the educational institution any aid from its funds, except where the State is bound to grant aid to any particular minority[3] under the Constitution. But the right of the State is not to dictate to the minority what the nature of its educational institution should be; its right is not to recognise a particular educational institution.

The Supreme Court has upheld this view of the Bombay High Court and said that "the power of the State to make reasonable regulations for all schools ... or to prescribe a curriculum for institutions which it supports" cannot be questioned. The 'choice' of the minorities to establish and administer educational institutions is not unfettered and the State can make reasonable regulations[4] in the interest of efficiency of instruction, discipline,

---

1. The effect of this decision has been affected to some extent by the First Amendment of the Constitution (Article 15) which permits the State to make such reservatins in the interests of socially and educationally backward classes of people.
2. Bombay Education Society *vs.* State of Bombay, 56, Bombay L.R. 643.
3. The only such minority which is entitled to such grant is the Anglo-Indian community. (See Art. 337 of the Constitution).
4. State of Bombay *vs.* Bombay Education Society, A.I.R. 1954, S.C. 561. See in this connection the opinion of the Supreme Court of the United States in Pierce *vs.* Society of Sisters, 268, U.S. 510.

health, sanitation, morality, public order and tne like. In the Gujarat University Case, A.I.R. 1963, S.C. 540, the Court refused to express any opinion on the alleged infringement of fundamental rights of the petitioner under Article 29(1) as the decision in the case was given in the light of the extent of the power of the State Legislature to legislate on the medium of instruciton in universities.

The scope of Article 30 was interpreted at length by the Supreme Court in a reference made to it by the President. The subject of the reference was the constitutional validity of certain provisions of the Kerala Education Bill, 1957, which was submitted to the Presidnet for his assent.[1] The Bill had been the cause of agitation by certain religious minorities in the State of Kerala ever since its introduction in the State Assembly in 1957, and those who opposed it contended that it violated the fundamental rights guaranteed under the Constitution, especially those under Article 30. In a six to one decision, the Court held that Clause 3(5) of the Bill was invalid.[2] The clause read as follows:

> After the commencement of this Act, the establishment of a new school or the opening of a new class in any private school shall be subject to the provisions of this Act and the rules made thereunder and any school or higher class established or opened otherwise than in accordance with such provisions shall not be entitled to be recognised by the government.

Speaking for the majority on the content of Article 30(1) Chief Justice Das said:

> The first point to note is that the Article gives certain rights not only to religious minorities but also to linguistic minorities. In the next place, the right conferred on such minorities is to establish educational institutions of their choice. It does not say that minorities based on religion should establish educational institutions for teaching religion only, or that linguistic minorities should have the right to establish educational institutions for teaching their language only. What the Article says and means is that the religious and the linguistic minorities should have the right to establish educational institutions of their choice. There is no limitation placed on the subjects to be taught in such educational institutions. All such minorities will ordinarily desire that their children should be brought up properly and efficiently and be eligible for higher university education and go out in the world fully equipped with such intellectual attainments as will make them fit for entering the public service. Educational institutions of their choice will necessarily include institutions imparting general secular education also.

Thus the Chief Justice said that the article gave all minorities whether based on religion or language two rights, namely the right to establish and the right to administer educational institutions of their choice. The key to the understanding to the true meaning and implication of the article under consideration were the words 'of their choice'.

The educational institutions established or administered by the minorities in exercise of the rights conferred by Article 30(1), the Chief Justice said, might be classified into three categories: (*i*) those which did not seek either aid or recognition from the State; (*ii*) those which wanted aid and (*iii*) those which wanted only recognition but not aid. In regard to educational institutions in the first category, he held that by Clause 38 of the Bill, they were, *prima facie*, outside the purview of the Bill. As regards the second category, the Chief Justice said that they had to subdivide it into two classes, namely, (*a*) those which were by the Constitution itself expressly made eligible for receiving grants, and (*b*) those

1. The Bill was submitted to the President for his assent because of certain of its provisions which empowered the State Government to acquire compulsorily private property. Under Article 31 of the Constitution, Presidential assent is essential for the validty of such laws.
2. Kerala Education Bill (1957), *In the matter of*, 1959, S.C.J. 321.

which were not entitled to such grant, but nevertheless sought aid.

The Chief Justice observed that the Anglo-Indian educational institutions established prior to 1948 used to receive grants from the Governments of those days. Article 337 of the Constitution preserved this bounty for a period of ten years. The Anglo-Indian educatinal institutions in Kerala had, before the passing of the Bill, been receiving grants from the Madras State and also the Travancore-Cochin State. After the formation of Kerala, too the bounty continued. In the circumstances, the amount received by the Anglo-Indian institutions as grant under Article 337 should be construed as aid within the meaning of the Bill and educational institutions in receipt of such grant payable under Article 337 should accordingly be regarded as aided schools.

Referring to the argument that no conditions could be imposed in regard to the administration of institutions run by the minorities, the Chief Justice said that the right to administer could not obviously include the right to maladminister. It stood to reason that the constitutional right to administer an educational institution of their choice did not necessarily militate against the claim of the State to insist that in order to grant aid the State might prescribe reasonable regulations to ensure the excellence of the institutions to be aided.

In regard to educational institutions of minorities which sought only recognition, but not aid from the State, the Chief Justice said that without recognition the educational institutions established or to be established by the minority communities could not fulfil the real object of their choice. The right to establish educational institutions of their choice should, therefore, mean the right to establish real institutions which would effectively serve the needs of their community and the scholars who attended such institutions. To deny recognition to educational institutions except on terms tantamount to the surrender of their constitutional right to administer educational institutions of their choice was in truth and effect to deprive them of their right under Article 30(1). The Chief Justice said:

> We the people of India have given unto ourselves the Constitution which is not for any particular community or section but for all. Its provisions are intended to protect all, minority as well as majority communities. There can be no manner of doubt that our Constitution has guaranteed certain cherished rights of the minorities concerning their language, culture and religion. These concessions must have been made to them for good and valid reasons.
>
> So long as the Constitution stands as it is and is not altered, it is, we conceive, the duty of this Court to uphold the fundamental rights and thereby honour the scared obligations to the minority communities who are of our own. Throughout the ages endless inundations of men of diverse creeds, cultures and races — Aryans and non-Aryans, Dravidians and Chinese, Scythians, Huns, Pathans and Mughals — have come to this ancient land from distant regions and climes. India has wlecomed them all. They have met and gathered, given and taken and got mingled, merged and lost in one body. India's tradition has thus been epitomised in the noble lines: 'None shall be turned away from the shores of this vast sea of humanity that is India' (Tagore). Indeed India has sent out to the world her message of goodwill enshrined and proclaimed in our national anthem. It is thus that the genius of India has been able to find unity in diversity by assimilating the best of all creeds and cultures.

If one considers the Kerala Education Bill case from the point of view of the uncompromising "wall of separation between State and Church" doctrine envisaged under the U.S. Constitution by Thomas Jefferson, the Supreme Court's advisory opinion may sound the deathknell of the secular state in India. But taking into acount the extremely complicated religious minority situation in the country, it appears that the Court had no choice but to save Article 30(1) and the rights of minorities from meaninglessness. The other alternative for the Court would have been to subscribe to the Kerala Education Bill in toto. This would have meant upholding a rigid form of secularism and in the circumstances a hostile attitude in effect towards certain religious minorities, a solution which would have far-reaching political implications and which might have gone against the professed constitutional protections the religious minorities are supposed to enjoy. It seems that the Court is of the view that it is possible to reconcile the secular outlook with religious freedom of minorities and in the process a fair degree of discrimination in favour of religious minorities is justified. In this respect, it acted on the same principle which it has applied to backward classes, the principle of protective discrimination. But while the *ratio legis* behind this principle is to help backward classes in spite of religious tradition, the *ratio decidendi* behind protective discrimination in favour of religious minorities is to secure to the Christians, Muslims and such other minorities a fair deal in the name of religion and to secure customary religious tolerance which India has displayed throughout the ages.[1]

The educational rights of religious minorities under Article 30(1) came up again in a big way before the Supreme Court, nearly a decade later, in the now famous Aligarh Muslim University case.[2] In this case the petitioners challenged the constitutionality of the Aligarh Muslim University (Amendment) Act of 1951 and the (Amendment) Act of 1965 on the ground that these Acts violated the provisions of Article 30(1).

The main contention of the petitioners was that the Aligarh Muslim University was established by the Muslim minority in India and, therefore, the Muslims alone had the right to administer it and as the above two Acts took away or abridged any part of that right, they violated Article 30(1) of the Constitution. This contention was challenged by the Union of India on the grounds that:

(1) The Aligarh University was established in 1920 by the Central Act of 1920 and not by the Muslim minority as contended by the petitioners and, therefore, the Muslim minority cannot claim any fundamental right to administer the Aligarh University under Article 30(1).

(2) The Aligarh University was established as a result of the Act of 1920 and hence Parliament had the right to amend that Statute in the interest of education and the amendments made by the two Acts in question were valid because there was no question of their taking away any fundamental right of the Muslim community.

(3) The fact that under the Act of 1920 the Court of the Aligarh University was to be composed entirely of Muslim did not give any right to the Muslim community as such to administer the University, which had been administered by the authorities established by the Act of 1920.

The Supreme Court examined in great detail the contentions of both parties and in the process traced the history of the University right from the inception of the Aligarh College in the eighteen seventies, the establishment of the University in 1920 and the constitution of the different University authorities set up under the Act of 1920. In the course of its analysis the Court came to the following conclusions:

1. See in this connection Alexandrowiecz, C.H., 'Secular State in India and the United States', *Journal of the Indian Law Institute,* Vol. 2 (1960), p. 273.
2. Azeez Basha *vs.* Union of India, S.C.J. (1968) II, 299.

(1) The University is open to all persons of either sex and of whatever race, creed or class. (2) The final control of the University was vested with the Lord Rector who was the Governor-General of India. There was no condition that the Lord Rector and the members of the Visiting Board must belong to the Muslim community. Various other provisions of the Act implied the ultimate control of the Governor-General. (3) The provision that the Court of the University shall consist only of Muslims does not necessarily mean that the administration of the University was vested or was intended to be vested in the Muslim minority. (4) With the inauguration of the Constitution in 1950 an amendment of the Act of 1920 became necessary to take away the power of the University Court to make statutes providing for religious instruction. Otherwise the University would have lost the financial grant given to it by the Government of India in view of Article 28(3) of the Constitution dealing with religious instruction. The amendments made provision for non-Muslims to become members of the University Court. These amendments of 1951 were not challenged until 1965 when further amendments reduced the supremacy of the Court of the University, reduced its powers and increased those of the Excutive Council of the University.

The Court did not accept either of the contentions of the petitioners that the University was established by the Muslim minority and that the right to administer it vested in that minority. The University was established by the Act of 1920 and hence the Muslim minority could not claim any right to administer it. The Court thus rejected the claim of the petitioners that the amending Act of 1965 was unconstitutional.

The Aligarh Muslim University Act was further amended in 1972 to ensure that the University would henceforth be administered on the lines of proposals set out in the Gajendragadkar Committee report.[1] The new legislation while preserving the unitary and residential character of the University strengthened the academic community within the University and introduced much-needed and long-delayed structural and procedural reforms providing for the smooth functioning and academic autonomy of this national institution. With some 90 per cent of the total annual budget of the University (1971-72) provided by the Government of India through the University Grants Commission, the Union Government had to ensure that the University functioned in a manner that satisfied the requirements of public accountability. The Government took the firm stand, quite rightly, that "no Government under India's Constitution can pronounce an educational institution which is largely maintained by funds provided by it to be a minority institution."

In Proost *vs.* State of Bihar,[2] the petitioners (the management of a private college) challenged the validty of Section 48-A of the Bihar State Universities Act of 1960 as amended by the Act of 1961 on the strength of Articles 29 and 30 of the Constitution. Section 48-A of the impugned Act had imposed several restrictions on the management in the appointment of teachers and taking disciplinary action against them by centralizing most of the powers in this connection in the University Service Commission which was established by the Act. While the petition was pending before the Supreme Court, Section 48-B was inserted in the impugned Act by a Governor's Ordinance (1968). Section 48-B read as follows:

---

1. The Government of India had appointed a former Chief Justice of the Supreme Court, Gajendragadkar, in 1969 to study and report to the Government on the modifications necessary to the existing legislation in order to make the University function as a national institution for higher education, specializing in the study of Islamic religion and philosophy.
2. S.C.J. (1969) II, 700.

Notwithstanding anything contained in sub-sections 6, 7, 8, 9, 10 and 11 of Section 48-A. The Governing body of an affiliated college established by a minority based on religion or language, which the minority has the right to administer, shall be entitled to make appointments, dismissals, removals, termination of service or reduction in rank of teahcers or take other disciplinary measures subject only to approval of the Commission and the Syndicate of the University.

The contention of the petitioners was that their college St. Xavier's College, Ranci, was one established by a minority based on religion or language and therefore be exempted from the operation of Section 48-A and be protected under the new Section 48-B. The State of Bihar contended that the Jesuits being a minority based on religion had a right to establish and administer educaitonal protection under Article 29(1) was only a right to conserve a distinct language, script or culture of its own and hence the college did not qualify for the protection of Article 30(1) because it was not founded to conserve them.

The Supreme Court did not accept this contention and held:

"The width of Article 30(1) cannot be cut down by introducing in it considerations on which Article 29(1) is based. The latter article is a general protection which is given to minorities to conserve their language, script or culture. The former is a special right to minorities to establish educational institutions of their choice. This choice is not limited to institutions seeking to conserve language, script or culture and (this) choice is not taken away if the minority community having established an educational institution of its choice also admits members of other communities. That is a circumstance irrelevant for the application of Article 30(1) since no such limitation is expressed and none can be implied. The two articles create two separate rights although it is possible that they meet in a given case."

The Court further held that the St. Xavier's College was founded by the Catholic minority community based on religion and as such could be protected under Article 30 of the Constitution, and be exempted under Section 48-B of the Bihar Act.

"In our judgment, the language of Article 30(1) is wide and must receive full meaning. We are dealing with protection in minorities and attempts to whittle down the protection cannot be allowed. We need not enlarge the protection but we may not reduce a protection naturally following from the words. Here the protection clearly flows from the words and there is nothing on the basis of which aid can be sought from Article 29(1)."

The Court reiterated the same interpretation in two other cases which came up, again, from Bihar a year later. These were: The Rt. Rev. Bishop S.K. Patro and others *vs.* The State of Bihar and S.V. Qadir *vs.* The State of Bihar,[1] the former an appeal against a decision of the High Court of Patna and the latter a writ petition. Amplifying its earlier interpretation of Article 30(1) the Court held that the minority competent to claim the protectin must be a minority of persons residing in India and they must form a well defined religious or linguistic minority. It does not confer upon foreigners not resident in India the right to set up educational institutions of their choice.

The most comprehensive decision of the Supreme Court so far as on Minority Rights has been that in the Ahmedabad St. Xavier's College Society *vs.* State of Gujarat.[2] Interpreting the combined effect of Article 29(1) and 31(1) Chief Justice Ray speaking on

1. S.C.J. (1970) I, 370.
2. (1974) 1 S.C.J. 381.

behalf of himself and five of his colleagues said: "It will be wrong to read Article 30(1) as restricting the right of minorities to establish and administer educational institutions of their choice only to cases where such institutions are concerned with language, script or culture of the minorities. If the scope of Article 30(1) is to conserve language, script or culture of minorities, it will render Article 30 redundant. If rights under Article 29(1) are the same, then the consequence will be that any section of citizens, not necessarily linguistic or religious minorities, will have the right to establish and administer educational institutions of their choice. The scope of Article 30 rests on linguistic or religious minorities and no other section of citizens of India has such a right. Article 30(1) covers institutions imparting general secular eduation.

In St. Stephen's College *vs.* Delhi University (1992) SCC 558 the Court again studied the implications of Articles 29 and 30 in depth. This case arose when the petitioner, a minority institution, made their own procedure for admission although affiliated to the University which was challenged before and stayed by the Delhi High Court. It was held that though Article 29(2) was there to prevent discrimiantion on certain grounds, still it was not to nullify the effect of Article 30. After studying the relationship between the articles conferring minority rights the Court held that through rights conferred on the minorities are unrestricted, they are not absolute rights. It was in this decision that the Court fixed the maximum number of seats for the minority as 50 per cent of the total number of seats in the institution.

In Christian Medical College Employees Union *vs.* CMC Vellore Association (AIR 1988 SC 57) it was held that regulations for labour welfare were not violative of Article 30(1). Similarly, in All Bihar Christian Schools Association *vs.* State of Bihar (1988 SC 305) it was held that statutory measures regulating standard of excellence of minority educational institutions do not offend the Articles. (For the implications of the provisions relating to Cultural and Educational Rights further, see the following cases also:

Theclamma *vs.* Union of India AIR 1987 SC 1210; Frank Anthony Public School Employees Association *vs.* Union of India, AIR 1987 SC 311 and Mar Athenasius College *vs.* State of Kerala (1993) 4 SCC 347.

Though there is no fundamental right of a minority institution to affiliation to a university, any law which provides for affiliation on terms which will involve abridgement of the right of linguistic and religious minorities to administer and establish educational institutions of their choice will offend Article 30(1)."

Although the Judges spoke in different expressions, it was clear that they were all agreed that minority institutions had no right to lower the standard of education, misuse state subsidy or maladminister them. They also made it clear that the State could regulate the minority rights to safeguard standards of education, improve excellence of the minority institutions and ensure their proper administration. However, autonomy in administration precluded the State from interfering with the constitution of the governing body of the minority educational institution. The right to administer could validly be regulated by measures which aimed at improving the administration of the institution through the existing management and not by displacing it.

Judicial interpretations of Article 29 and 30 so far lead us to the following conclusions:

Firstly Articles 29 and 30 create two separate rights although it is possible that they may meet in a given case. Secondly, whether a particular community is a minority or not is to be judged on the basis of the entire population of the area to which the particular legislation applies. Thirdly, a minority can effectively conserve its script, language and culture by and through educational institutions and therefore the right to establish and maintain educational institutions of its choice is a necessary concomitant to the right to conserve its distinctive culture, language and sript. Fourthly, the language of Article 29(2) is wide and unqualified and covers all citizens whether they belong to the majority or minority groups. The Article confers a special right on citizens for admission into educational institutions maintained or aided by the State. Citizens belonging to the majority community cannot be discriminated against in case of institutions which receive State aid. Fifthly, the right of getting admission into an educational institution is a right which an individual citizen has as a citizen and not as a member of a community or class of citizens. Hence this right cannot be denied to citizens on grounds only of religion, race, caste, language or any of them. Sixthly, in case of minority based on religion and language, the right to impart instruction in their own institutions to the children of their community in their own language must be protected. In such a case, the power of the State to determine the medium of instruction must yield to the fundamental right of the minority to the extent it is necessary to give effect to that right and cannot be permitted to run counter to it. Seventhly, the words 'establish and administer' in Article 30(1) must be read conjunctively and if done so, the minority is entitled to the right to administer an educational institution provided the said institution has been established by the minority and not otherwise. Finally, the protection implied in Articles 29 and 30 applies not only to educational institutions established after the commecement of the Constitution but also to those established before it.

The rights of the minorities, however, cannot be absolute. They must be subject to restrictions in the interest of education as well as in pursuance of socio-economic objectives embodied in the Directive Principls of State Policy. The purpose of the provisions guaranteeing rights to the minorities was not to create vested interests in separateness of the minorities. The Constitution gave these cultural and educational rights with a view to enabling the religious and linguistic minorities to maintain their individuality as well as distinct identity of their language and culture. But the preservation of such distinctiveness should not result in the minorities remaining isolated from the mainstream of national life. As the nation makes progress, the barriers that divide the citizens into majority and minority compartments should gradually disappear and a rigid, tradition-bound society in India should become transformed into a composite, dynamic and progressive society cherishing common national ideals and aspirations. Educational and cultural institutions should become the agents of such change rather than perpetuating narrow barriers between citizen and citizen.

Taking the rights guaranteed under religious, educational and cultural fields as a whole, it will be noted that these are couched in the most comprehensive language and a very large measure of freedom is guaranteed to the minorities, religious and linguistic. The special significance of these provisions is that while the impact of other rights in Part III of the Constitution is on the people of India as a whole, irrespective of religion, race, caste or language, that of these rights is only on the minorities. The democratic basis of the Constitution would have been questioned if the minorities were not given adequate protection to preserve their religious beliefs and institutions of education and culture. The Constitution might then have been branded as an instrument for the furtherance of the majority community and the language of the majority. Naturally, there would have resulted much resentment against such a position among the minorities all over the country, as religious minorities lived in all States of India and linguistic monorities totalled not less than 200 million at the time of Indepenence. Moreover, such a position would have discredited the foundation of the national movement against foreign rule in which almost every religious and linguistic minority in India was represented and solemn promises had been made by representatives of the majority community to safeguard the legitimate interests of the minorities against all forms of tyranny in a free India.

***

16

THE RIGHT TO PROPERTY

(Arts. 31, 31A, 31B and 31C)

As a result of the adoption of the Forty-fourth Amendment of the Constitution (1978), Article 31 entitled *the Right to Property* was omitted from the chapter of Fundamental Rights. At the same time Arts. 31A, 31B and 31C which are related to the Right to Property still continue to find a place in the Constitution. In order to understand their relevance and significance, it is necessary to recount the circumstances which led to the adoption of the original provisions by the Constituent Assembly and how they had undergone changes through a succession of Amendments to the Constitution beginning with the First Amendment in 1951.

In a country so vast as India with a population of over 1,000 million and with one of the lowest standards of living in the world, the gravity of the economic problems needs no emphasis. During the last two hundred years India remained a reservoir of plentiful raw materials for industrial Britain and a vast market for her finished products. Basic industries which transform the economy of a country from foreign dependence to self-reliance had not even been given a start in India all these years. As a result, when political freedom was won, India was economically on the verge of collapse. The partition of the country and the loss of vast areas of food-producing lands to Pakistan aggravated the situation.

With a view to simplifying the collection of land revenue, the British had, in the early days of their rule, assigned large plots of land to individuals, themselves mostly land-owners. These 'Zamindars' in their turn parcelled out the land and gave small plots to tenants who cultivated it and paid annual rents to the Zamindars. Some of these tenants were the original small owners, and others new persons. In the course of generations, the relationship between the Zamindar and the tenant got reduced to rent-paying and rent-receiving. As a result, there arose a double evil in the country. On the one hand, the tenant, feeling that the land was not his, never effected any permanent improvements on the land but was interested only in his immediate gain. This contributed in a large measure to the qualitative deterioration of the land and the consequent diminishing returns. On the other hand, a new class of people emerged in India, a class that lived almost entirely on the fruits of the labour of others. Thus, both on the economic and social levels there was degeneration and the consequent lack of vitality among large sections of Indian society. It was widely recognized that the only solution to this problem was suitable land reforms.

But the importance of land reform was not merely economic. It was also political. The successful solution of the land problem would lead to the emergence of a contended landed gentry and would be a solid foundation for a stable political order. The importance of this factor will be fully realized when we take into consideration the facts that 80 per cent of India's population is wedded to agriculture. If the 500 million and more people who depend upon land for their sustenance are satisfied, Indian democracy will soon find its roots on firm ground.

But the settlement of the land problem in itself would not be enough for the economic well-being and advancement of the nation. In the present age, no nation can advance without industrial and technological progress. In the case of India there was need for not only vast but also quick progress in this field in order to make up for her extreme backwardness. It was realized that to achieve rapid results in industrialization, the State had to play a positive role. Naturally, this was bound to affect the right to ownership of property by the individual citizen. These considerations figured prominently in the background when the Constituent Assembly deliberated on the provisions of the Constitution relating to property rights.

One of the articles that experienced the greatest difficulty in getting into shape in the Constituent Assembly was that which dealt with the right to property under Article 31. We have already seen the scope of the right to acquire, hold and dispose of property under Article 19. We have also seen under the same article the right to practise any profession or to carry on any occupation, trade or business. The Assembly thought fit to have in addition an altogether separate section to deal with property rights, because it realized that in the absence of such a section it would be impossible to solve the conflicts involved in the right of the individual to own property and the duty of the State to enter the economic field with a view to bringing about badly-needed reforms. In fact, Articles 31 and 31A attempted to reconcile the competing claims of the right of the individual to property and the duty of the State to acquire private property for public purpose or general welfare.

It was a difficult problem. Neither in the Congress Party in the Assembly, nor in the Indian Cabinet was there any unanimity on the approach to the problem. Opinion was sharply divided into at least three major groups, an extreme left which favoured nationalization even without compensation, an extreme right which favoured nationalization with full compensation at the market value of the property acquired and a middle group which presented a more moderate yet progressive attitude. These conflicting attitudes to this complex problem were reflected in the debates of the Assembly.

An unusual and interesting feature about Article 31 was that it was Prime Minister Nehru who moved its amended version in the Constituent Assembly. In a long speech,[1] he made the following main points: (*i*) There will be no expropriation so fair as this Constitution is concerned. (*ii*) If the State takes over property, 'fair and equitable' compensation will have to be given. But we must remember that equity does not apply only to the individual but also to the community. No individual can override ultimately the rights of the community at large. No community shall injure and invade the right of the individual unless it is for the most urgent and important reasons. (*iii*) Criticisms of this article as vague or lacking in clarity is inevitable to some extent when 'you try to bring together a large number of ideas and approaches and factors and put them in one or a number of phrases.' (*iv*) This draft article is the result of a greant deal of consultation, of an attempt to bring together and

1. C.A.D IX, pp. 1191-6.

compromise various approaches to this question. (*v*) On a proper construction of this clause, normally speaking, the judiciary should not and does not come in. Parliament either fixes the compensation itself or the principles governing that compensation and they should not be challenged except for one reason, where it is thought that there has been a fraud on the Constitution. (*vi*) The power of the President is only to check and to see that no wrong has been done in a hurry by the Legislature, and to suggest changes if necessary. (*vii*) The House has to keep in mind the transitional and the revolutionary aspects of the problem 'because when you think of the land question in India today you are thinking of something which is dynamic, moving, changing, and revolutionary. We have to view this question in this context.' (*viii*) We have taken a pledge to abolish the Zamindari system and we must honour our pledge.

The Prime Minister's speech was followed by a long drawn out debate, a real battle of wits, in which more than a score of members participated. Each gave vent to his own feeling and apprehensions rather than provide an assessment of the merits of the proposition. One member asserted that socialization would be impossible.[1] Another said that he was against the judiciary coming into the field: "It will be a lawyer's paradise if this is passed in this form."[2] Yet another said that Parliament alone should be the ultimate authority to determine compensation.[3] A fourth differed from the Prime Minister on whether there should be no expropriation without compensation.[4] In the words of still another: 'The draft article is one of the most wonderful examples of chaos and confusion of ideas. The industrialists are not satisfied with it; the landed magnates are not; nor the teeming millions.'[5] A member from Mysore[6] wanted compensation to be fixed at 5 per cent of the market value of the property acquired. As against these, there were those who wanted fair and adequate compensation and wanted the judiciary to determine ultimately the question of compensation.[7] A large number of amendments were formally moved but, in the end, the article as moved by the Prime Minister was passed except for a minor verbal change.[8]

Article 31 as originally passed reads as follows:

31.(1) No person shall be deprived of his property save by authority of law.

(2) No property, movable or immovable, including any interest in, or in any company, owning, any commercial or industrial undertaking, shall be taken possession of or acquired for public purposes under any law authorising the taking of such possession or such acquisition, unless the law provides for compensation for the property taken possession of or acquired and either fixes the amount of the compensation, or specifies the principles on which, and the manner in which, the compensation is to be determined and given.

(3) No such law as is referred to in clause (2) made by the Legislature of a State shall have effect unless such law, having been reserved for the consideration of the President, has received his assent.

(4) If any Bill pending at the commencement of this Constitution in the Legislature of a State has, after it has been passed by such Legislature, been reserved for the consideration of

1. Damodar Swarup Seth, C.A.D. IX, p. 1199.
2. Shibban Lal Saksena, Ibid, p. 1201.
3. H.V. Kamath, C.A.D. IX, p. 1201.
4. K.T. Shah, Ibid, p. 1215. See also Mahavir Tyagi, VII, p. 361.
5. Jaduhans Sahay, C.A.D. IX, p. 1221.
6. S. Dasappa, Ibid, p. 1224.
7. Thakur Das Bhargava and Nazirunddin Ahmed, Ibid, p. 1226 and p. 1233.
8. K.M. Munshi, Ibid, p. 1265.

the President and has received his assent, then, notwithstanding anything in this Constitution, the law so assented to shall not be called in question in any court on the ground that it contravenes the provisions of clause (2).

(5) Nothing in clause (2) shall affect—

(a) the provision of any existing law other than a law to which the provisions of clause (6) apply, or

(b) the provisions of any law which the State may hereafter make

(i) for the purpose of imposing or levying any tax or penalty, or

(ii) for the promotion of public health or the prevention of danger to life or property, or

(iii) in pursuance of any agreement entered into between the Government of the Dominion of India or the Government of India and the Government or any other country, or otherwise, with respect to property declared by law to be evacuee property.

(6) Any law of the State enacted not more than eighteen months before the commencement of this Constitution may within three months from such commencement be submitted to the President for his certification, and thereunpon if the President by public notification so certifies, it shall not be called in question in any court on the ground that it contravenes the provisions of clause (2) of this article or has contravened the provisions of sub-section (2) of Section 299 of the Government of India Act, 1935.[1]

While the Constitution thus afforded protection to private property in general, it declared under Clauses (4) and (6) that the validity of certain specific laws affecting property rights shall not be challenged in any court on the ground that they violated the safeguards detailed above. These were laws which abolished the Zamindari system or absentee landlordism in different states. The object of this special provision was to remove any uncertainty and make safe the main agrarian reforms which sought to do away with this evil system and thwart the attempts of the landlords to fight these laws through the courts of law. The Constitution also provided under clause (5) that the compensation clause would not apply in the following cases: (*i*) laws providing for the imposition or levying of any tax or penalty; (*ii*) laws made for the promotion of public health or the prevention of danger to life or property; and (*iii*) laws relating to evacuee property.

The special protection given to the various Zamindari abolition laws, however, did not prove to be of much avail. Soon after the inauguration of the Constitution the Zamindars tested the validity of these laws against some of the fundamental rights. The first round of the battle was fought in the High Courts of Patna, Allahabad, and Nagpur. In the Patna High Court they succeeded in getting the Bihar Land Reforms Act, 1950, declared invalid.[2] The decision of the High Court was unanimous. It was based on the equality provision (Art. 14) of the Constitution and not under the property right clause 31. The Allahabad High Court, however, found the Uttar Pradesh Zamindari Abolition and Land Reforms Act, 1950, valid in all respects.[3] The decision of the Nagpur High Court also went in favour of the State law.[4] But the Zamindars were not disheartened. They carried the battle to the Supreme Court in appeal.

1. Sub-section (2) of Section 299 of the Government of India Act of 1935 provided for the payment of compensation for property compulsorily acquired by the State.
2. Kameswar Singh *vs.* State of Bihar, A.I.R. 1951, Patna 91.
3. Suryapal Singh *vs.* U.P. Government, A.I.R. 1951, Allahabad 675.
4. The Madhya Pradesh Abolition of Proprietary Rights (Estates, Mahals, Alienated Lands) Act, 1950. A Full Bench of the High Court upheld the validity of the Act on 9 April 1951.

The First Amendment

When it was found that the legal battle was going to consume an unduly long time with consequent frustration for the general mass of people and the loss of confidence in the governments, new ways and measures were sought to combat the deteriorating situation. Accordingly, it was decided to amend the Constitution whereby judicial roadblocks could be removed and immediate implementation of the land reform legislation could be made possible. The First Amendment of the Constitution was accordingly passed in 1951 adding two new Articles 31A and 31B, with a view to fully safeguarding the various land reform laws against possible attack arising from any fundamental right in the Constitution. Further, a new schedule containing all such State laws — the Ninth Schedule — was added to the Constitution to make the scope of the new amendment abundantly clear. The amendment read as follows:

31A. (1) Notwithstanding anything in the foregoing provisions of this Part, no law providing for the acquisition by the State of any estate or of any rights therein or for the extinguishment or modification of any such rights shall be deemed to be void on the ground that it is inconsistent with, or takes away or abridges any of the rights conferred by any provisions of this Part.

Provided that where such law is a law made by the legislature of a State, the provisions of this article shall not apply thereto unless such law, having been reserved for the consideration of the President, has received his assent.

(2) In this article

(a) The expression 'estate' shall, in relation to any local area, have the same meaning as that expression or its local equivalent has in that existing law relating to land tenures in force in that area, and shall also include any *Jagir, Inam or muafi* or other similar grant;

(b) the expression 'rights' in relation to an estate, shall include any rights vesting in proprietor, sub-proprietor, under-proprietor, tenure-holder or other intermediary and any rights or privileges in respect of land revenue.

31B. Without prejudice to the generality of the provisions contained in Article 31A, none of the Acts and Regulations specified in the Ninth Schedule nor any of the provision thereof shall be deemed to be void, or ever to have become void, on the ground that such Act, Regulation or provision is inconsistent with, or takes away or abridges any of the rights conferred by any provisions of this Part, and notwithstanding any judgement, decree or order of any court or tribunal to the contrary, each of the said Acts and Regulations shall, subject to the power of any competent Legislature to repeal or amend it, continue in force.

The appeals to the Supreme Court were still pending when the first amendment was passed. Anticipating the strong position of the State under the new amendment, the Zamindars carried their battle even against the constitutional amendment on the plea that Parliament as it was then constituted was not competent to pass the amendment. Since the decision of the Court on this question was to affect the fate of the appeal cases, the Court, instead of proceeding with the appeals, first considered the validity of the Amendment itself. The main attack on the Amendment was that it was passed by a Parliament which had only one House[1] whereas the amendment procedure prescribed in the Constitution spoke of two Houses of Parliament. The intention of the framers of the Constitution, therefore, was to undertake any amendment of the Constitution only after the new Parliament consisting

1. Until the reconstitution of Parliament after the first General Elections in 1951-52, the old Constituent Assembly in a reconstituted form continued as the Provisional Parliament of India. It was this body that passed the amendment.

of both Houses had been constituted as the result of a general election. The Court rejected this plea and gave a unanimous verdict in favour of the competence of the provisional Parliament to amend the Constitution.[1]

By 1952, the Court also finally disposed of the appeals which at last put the stamp of final authority on those hotly contested legislative measures.[2] There were, however, interpretations of the Court which did not quite accord with some of the observations of the Prime Minister which he had made while moving the property right clause in the Constituent Assembly. These related mainly to the terms 'public purpose' and 'compensation'. According to the Court:

> The existence of a 'public purpose' is undoubtedly an implied condition of the exercise of compulsory powers of acquisition by the State, but the language of article 31(2) does not expressly make it a condition precedent to acquisition. It assumes that compulsory acquisition can be for a public purpose only which is thus inherent in such acquisition. Hence, article 31(4) does not bar the jurisdiction of the Court from enquiring whether the law relating to compulsory acquisition of property is valid,.... to see whether the acquisition has been made for a public purpose. It is unnecessary to state in express terms in the statute itself the precise purpose for which property is being taken, provided from the whole tenor and intendment of the Act it could be gathered that the property was being acquired either for purposes of the State or for the purposes of the public and that the intention was to benefit the community at large. The Legislature is the best judge of what is good for the community, by whose suffrage it comes into existence and it is not possible to say that there was no public purpose behind the acquisition.... The phrase 'public purpose; has to be construed according to the spirit of the times in which the particular legislation is enacted....

In a later decision[3] the Court held that the phrase 'public purpose' has been used in a generic sense and will include any purpose in which even a fraction of the community may be interested or may be benefited.

What Justice S.R. Das observed in Subodha Gopal's case[4] appears to be the right approach to the problem of public purpose. He said:

> With the onward march of civilisation our notions as to the scope of the general interest of the community are fast changing and widening with the result that our old and narrower notion as to the sanctity of the private interest of the individual can no longer stem the forward flowing tide of time and must necessarily give way to the broader notions of the general interest of the community. The emphasis is unmistakably shifting from the individual to the community.

Prima facie the State would be the judge to decide whether a purpose is a public one or not. But it is not the sole and final judge. The courts have the jurisdiction and it is their duty to determine whether a particular purpose is a public purpose or not.[5] In determining what is a public purpose, the directive principles of state policy may be taken into consideration. If no public purpose is established in a particular case, the court will be justified in declaring the concerned law unconstitutional. It is not obligatory on the State to state in express terms in the statute itself the precise purpose for which property is being

1. Shankari Prasad Singh *vs.* Union of India, 1951, S.C.R. 89.
2. The State of Bihar *vs.* Kameswar Singh, 1952, S.C.J. 354.
3. B.B. Thakur *vs.* The State of Bombay, 1960, S.C.J. (Note) 22. But the Court is of the view that the term 'public purpose' has to be given a restricted meaning when applied to acquisition of private property for a company. A declaration of 'public purpose; by Government will not be conclusive to determine the public purpose character of the acquisition, *vide* R.L. Arora *vs.* The State of U.P. (1963) I.S.C.J. 33.
4. A.I.R. 1954 S.C. 92.
5. Raja Suryapal Singh's case, 1952 S.C.R. 1056.

acquired. The intention may be gathered from the act. Here the Court seems to be quite close to the *intention* of the constitution-makers.

But the position was quite different in the case of term 'compensation'. Although the Constitution does not say 'just' or 'full' or 'adequate' compensation, the Court said that compensation here meant just compensation determined on the basis of the market value of the property acquired.[1] They went one step further and said that in addition to 100 per cent market value to be paid in every case of acquisition, a solatium of 15 per cent more is to be given to compensate the compulsory nature of the acquisition which was already in vogue in India under the Land Acquisition Act of 1894. According to the Allahabad High Court:

> Compensation in Article 31(2) means the equivalent in value of property taken or acquired, subject only to this qualification that such equivalent need not be paid in money. Any provision for giving by way of compensation less than the equivalent will not amount to compensation in law and will constitute a contravention of that clause.[2]

The Calcutta High Court also expressed the same view:

> Article 31, Clause 2 requires a just amount to be given for any property acquired and if the amount a law gives is not just or reasonable, then it cannot be regarded as compensation within the clause.[3]

Other High Courts also gave interpretations to the same effect.

The Supreme Court affirmed this interpretation of the High Courts in its decision on the Zamindari abolition cases. In Mrs. Bela Banerjee *vs.* State of West Bengal[4] the Court went a step further and said:

> While it is true that the legislature is given the discretionary power of laying down the principles which should govern the determination of the amount to be given to the owner for the property appropriated, such principles must ensure that what is determined as payable must be compensation, that is, just equivalent of what the owner has been deprived of.

In Dwarkadas Shrinivas *vs.* Sholapur Spinning and Weaving Company[5] the Court examined the correlation of Article 31(1) and 31(2) and said:

> From the language employed in the different sub-clauses of Article 31, it is difficult to escape the conclusion that the words 'acquisition' and 'taking possession' used in Article 31(2) have the same meaning as the word 'deprivation' in Article 31(1).

It further said that the protection in Article 31 is against loss of property to the owner and there is no protection given to the State by the article. The decision of the Court in this case made invalid a Central enactment by which the above-mentioned Company was taken over by the Government. According to the Court, the statute had overstepped the limits of legitimate social control legislation and had infringed the fundamental right of the Company guaranteed to it under Article 31(2) and was, therefore, unconstitutional.

---

1. Reading Article 31(2) one is tempted to suggest that the omission of the adjective 'just' or 'adequate' or 'full' before the word 'compensation' was deliberate. For comparison, see corresponding provisions in the Fifth Amendment of the U.S. Constitution, and Article 23 of the Burmese Constitution, all of which use one or the other of these adjectives with the word 'compensation'.
2. Raja Suryapal Singh *vs.* U.P. Government.
3. West Bengal Settlement Kunungo Co-operative Society Ltd. *vs.* Mrs. Bela banerjee, A.I.R. 1951, Calcutta 32.
4. A.I.R. 1954, S.C. 170.
5. A.I.R. 1954, S.C. 624. See also Thakur Amar Singhji *vs.* State of Rajasthan 1955, 2 S.C.R. 303, Shanti Sarup *vs.* Union of India A.I.R. 1955, S.C. 624, Hanumantappa *vs.* Union of India 1955, 1 S.C.R. 769; Gohil *vs.* State of Bombay 1955, 1, S.C.R. 691; Lilavati Bai *vs.* The State of Bombay, 1957, S.C.J. 557; and Amar Singh *vs.* Custodian, Evacuee Property, Punjab 1957, S.C.J. 574.

These judicial pronouncements had far-reaching consequences. They showed that legislation on social and economic welfare, which necessitated the acquisition of various forms of private property, was virtually impossible because of the prohibitive cost involved in the payment of compensation. Further, such enormous public cost would have made meaningless certain reforms which were intended to be a part of the social engineering with a view to bringing about a social order in which economic and social justice was to be ensured. The compelling motive underlying these measures was to narrow down the gap that existed between the affluent and the downtrodden, the rich and the poor of Indian society. Zamindari abolition was only the first stage in a planned programme of legislation for social and economic welfare. Other equally important legislative measures were planed to follow suit. Some of the most important of these were: (*i*) the fixing of limits to the extent of agricultural land that may be owned or occupied by any person, the disposal of any land held in excess of the prescribed minimum and the further modification of the rights of land owners and tenants in agricultural holdings; (*ii*) the proper planning of urban and rural areas, the beneficial utilisation of vacant and waste lands and clearance of slum areas. (*iii*) the taking over of the control of the mineral and soil resources of the country in the interests of national economy; (*iv*) the taking over of the management by the State, for temporary periods, of commercial and industrial undertakings in the public interest or to secure better management; (*v*) reforms in company law administration including the elimination of the managing agency system; and (*vi*) nationalization of public utility undertakings. But so long as the compensation clause of the Constitution remained in the manner in which it was interpreted by the Supreme Court, it was pointed out by spokesmen of the Government, no progress could be made along these lines. Thus, according to them, the compensation clause and the power of the Courts to enforce it stood in the way of planning and the implementation of a programme of planned development.[1] The Government wanted to remove this hindrance and have a free hand in the evolution of a new society. The only way to accomplish this was by further amending the Constitution. The result was the Fourth Amendment of 1955.

The Fourth Amendment

The chief provision of the Amendment is that compensation under Article 31 is no more a justiciable matter under the Constitution. The Amendment does not say that no compensation will be paid in future for property compulsorily acquired, nor is it its intention to abolish compensation altogether. All that it says is that although compensation should be paid in all cases of acquisition, it is the sole business of the Legislature to determine the amount of compensation or the principles or the manner in which it will be paid and no Court of Law will sit over it in Judgment. Thus, the question of compensation is withdrawn from the field of judicial determination and placed exclusively at the will of the legislature[2]. The following is the text of the Amendment:

---

1 cf. the speech of the Prime Minister in the Lok Sabha on 20 December 1954 moving the Bill to amend the Constitution.

2. Lilavarti Bai *vs.* The State of Bombay 1957 S.C.J. 557 and Prem Nath Kaul *vs.* The State of Jamkmu and Kashmir 1959 S.C.J. 797. See also the Okhla Electric Supply Company *vs.* The State of Punjab, 1960 S.C.J. 502; Moopil Nair *vs.* State of Kerala (1961) II S.C.J. 269; B.B. Thakur *vs.* The State of Bombay (1961) II S.C.J. 392 and K. Kunhikoman *vs.* State of Kerala (1962) I S.C.J. 510.

31(2) No property shall be compulsorily acquired or requisitioned save for a public purpose and save by authority of a law which provides for compensation for the property so acquired or requisitioned and either fixes the amount of the compensation or specifies the principles on which, and the manner in which, the compensation is to be determined and given; and no such law shall be called in question in any court on the ground that the compensation provided by that law is not adequate.

(2A) Where a law does not provide for the transfer of the ownership or right to possession of any property to the State or to a corporation owned or controlled by the state, it shall not be deemed to provide for the compulsory acquisition or requisitioning of property, notwithstanding that it deprives any person of his property.

31 A.(1) Notwithstanding anything contained in Article 13, no law providing for

(a) the acquisition by the State of any estate or of any rights therein or the extinguishment or modification of any such rights, or

(b) the taking of the management of any property by the State for a limited period either in the public interest or in order to secure the proper management of the property, or

(c) the amalgamation of two or more corporations either in the public interest or in order to secure the proper management of any of the corporations, or

(d) the extinguishment or modification of any rights of managing agents, secretaries and treasurers, managing directors, directors or managers of corporations, or of any voting rights of shareholders thereof, or

(e) the extinguishment or modification of any rights accruing by virtue of any agreement, lease or licence for the purpose of searching for, or mining, any mineral or mineral oil, or the premature termination or cancellation of any such agreement, lease or licence.

shall be deemed to be void on the ground that it is inconsistent with, or takes away or abridges any of the rights conferred by Article 14, Article 19 or Article 31.

Provided that where such law is a law made by the Legislature of a State, the provisions of this article shall not apply thereto unless such law, having been reserved for the consideration of the President, has received his assent.

Whatever might be the compelling reasons for the adoption of such measure, the Fourth Amendment, according to its critics, has brought about a major departure from the original intentions of the framers of the Constitution. They argued that if the right to property is not justiciable, it is no longer a fundamental right. For as we have seen earlier, the distinguishing feature of a fundamental right is that it is guaranteed against not only Executive 'despotism' but also the 'tyranny' of legislative majorities. That feature has now little application to the right to property embodied in the chapter on Fundamental Rights in the Constitution. In other words, parliamentary supremacy is the rule so far as this right is concerned. Parliamentary supremacy today means, in fact, the will of the party in power. Since the Government or the Cabinet is composed of the leaders of the ruling party, parliamentary supremacy ultimately amounts in practice to the will of the Executive. Thus, the right to property under the Constitution is not even a right that depends on the will of the Legislature but is in reality only a right at the mercy of the Executive. A right that depends on the mercy of the Executive can never be a fundamental right. Thus, in the opinion of those critics, who assailed the Fourth Amendment both on the floor of Parliament and outside, 'the sanctity of property is lost; unjust compensation is legalised and the totalitarian trends are encouraged under cover of the doctrine of Parliamentary supremacy.'

In view of such a situation, it was asked in Parliament: "Why not altogether take away the right to property from the Constitution?" In reply, the Home Minister pointed out that the judiciary could still come into the picture. If any law providing for compensation was a 'fraud on the Constitution', the judiciary could intervene and still declare it invalid. But more important than this perhaps was his assurance as to how the measure would work. According to him, the basic principles of justice, equity and good conscience would guide both the Centre and the States in this respect. Moreover, the States will to some extent be further circumscribed by the need to receive Presidential assent, which in effect means Central approval for their proposed actions under the amended property right clause. Thus, there was reasonable possibility for a uniform national policy to emerge ensuring justice, equity and fair play in the enjoyment of the right to property by all.

This was clearly demonstrated in all cases of nationalization that soon followed the Fourth Amendment. Among these, the nationalization of the Imperial Bank of India, the private airlines, and the life insurance business was undertaken by the Government of India and that of the Kolar Gold Mines by the Government of Mysore. In all these cases the compensation paid by the Government was hailed as not only just and equitable but even generous.

The Supreme Court, however, showed a marked tendency to interpret Article 31-A rather narrowly. The best example of this perhaps is its decision in Kochunni *vs.* State of Madras.[1] In that decision the Court held:

> Under Article 31(1) a person cannot be deprived of his property save by authority of law. The law must be a valid law. Under Article 13(2) a law depriving a person of his property cannot take away or abridge the rights conferred by Part III of the Constitution. Hence a law depriving a citizen of his property will be invalid if it infringes Article 19(1)(f) unless it imposes reasonable restrictions on the citizen's fundamental right.

We have seen earlier that Article 31-A was intended to facilitate the passing of legislation embodying economic reforms which were immune from challenge in courts on the ground of its alleged inconsistency with Articles 14, 19 and 31. But decisions like those in Kochunni case made it clear that the Supreme Court might not uphold every piece of legislation which claimed itself to bring about economic reform. Hence the Government decided to further amend Article 31-A with a view to protecting a large number of land reform enactments passed by different States. The Seventeenth Amendment of the Constitution, 1964, was the result.

The Seventeenth Amendment

The Amendment introduced the following new provisions:

1. In Article 31-A of the Constitution

(i) in clause (1), after the existing proviso, the following proviso shall be inserted, namely:

> Provided further that where any law makes any provision for the acquisition by the State of any estate and where any land comprised therein is held by a person under his personal cultivation, it shall not be lawful for the State to acquire any portion of such land as is within the ceiling limit applicable to him under any law for the time being in force or any building or structure standing thereon or appertenant thereto, unless the law relating to the acquisition of such land, building or structure, provides for payment of compensation at a rate which shall not be less than the market value thereof.

(ii) In Clause (2), for sub-clause (a), the following sub-clause shall be substituted and shall be deemed always to have been substituted, namely:

1. (1961) II S.C.J. 444.

(a) the expression "estate" shall, in relation to any local area, have the same meaning as that expression or its local equivalent has in the existing law relating to land tenures in force in that area and shall also include—

(i) any *jagir, inam* or *muafti* or other similar grant and in the States of Madras and Kerala, an *janam* right;

(ii) any land held under ryotwari settlement;

(iii) any land held or let for purposes of agriculture or for purposes thereto, including wasteland, forestland, land for pasture or sites of buildings and other structures occupied by cultivators of land, agricultural labourers and village artisans.

The Ninth Schedule of the Constitution has been amended to add 44 new land reform enactments to the original list of 20. Thus, the Nith Schedule consisted of a total of 64 such enactments in 1964. By making them part of the Constitution they have been taken out of the reach of judicial review so far as their validity with respect to any provision embodied in Part III of the Constitution is concerned.[1] But that was not the end of the story.

The validity of the Seventeenth Amendment was challenged in Sajjan Singh *vs.* The State of Punjab[2] but the Supreme Court held that the Amendment was constitutionally valid. The spirit of this decision was practically nullified by the later decision of the Court in the Golak Nath case.[3] Although the amendment was saved by a new doctrine called 'prospective over ruling the Court held that Parliament had no power to amend the Fundamental Rights under the Constitution and it will not tolerate any amendments in the future.

Indeed the Seventeenth Amendment has had a salutary effect on the Supreme Court in so far as its attitude towards questions of compensation related to land reform and other economic reforms legislation. This was evident in a number of its decisions during the post-1964 period. For example, in Udai Ram *vs.* Union of India,[4] Justice Mitter speaking on behalf of the majority of the Court observed:

> Schemes of the magnitude of the plan for the development of Delhi or for the establishment of an iron an steel plant did not have to be considered in pre-Constitution days. The Land Acquisition Act of 1894 contained sufficient measures to allow acquisition of small parcels of property for the different schemes of the extent and magnitude which had to be considered in the past. Even then law regard to compensation did not remain static from the days of the Act of 1870 to 1923.

While the attitude of the Court toward land reform legislation has been liberal on the whole, especially since the Seventeenth Amendment, no such attitude has been evident in its decision dealing with other cases involving questions of compensation. In fact, the Court has been assuming the role of a champion who stood almost fanatically to ensure the right to get full compensation every time private property was acquired or requisitioned by the State for a public purpose. The net result of the many decisions of the Court on this subject has been utter confusion and complete uncertainty regarding the meaning of the

1. Subsequent amendments (Twenty-ninth, 1972, Thirty-fourth, 1974, Thirty-ninth, 1975, and Fortieth, 1976) raised the total number of such enactments included in the Ninth Schedule to 188.
2. A.I.R. 1965 S.C. 845.
3. A.I.R. 1967 S.C. 1643. See detailed discussion of this deision in Chapters 22 and 50.
4. A.I.R. 1968 S.C. 1138. See also State of U.P. *vs.* Anand Brahma, A.I.R. 1967 S.C. 661; Inder Singh *vs.* State of Punjab, A.I.R. 1967 S.C. 1776; P.S. Chalil *vs.* State of Punjab, A.I.R. 1967 S.C. 930.

Constitution. Further, it defeated the clearly expressed intention of the Constitution that a law of acquisition would not be challenged in courts on the ground that the compensation it provided was inadequate.

In Vajravelu *vs.* Sp. Deputy Collector,[1] Justice Subba Rao speaking for the Court observed that it would strike down a law as a fraud on the Constitution if the principles for determining compensation were irrelevant to the value of the property at or about the time of acquisition or if the law provided for illusory compensation. The decision of the Court in this case almost resurrected that in the Bela Banerji case which was supposed to have been buried deep by the Fourth Amendment of 1955. In the Union of India *vs.* Metal Corporation,[2] two years later, the Court reiterating the above stand struck down the Metal Corporation of India (Acquisition of Undertaking) Act, 1965, on the ground that the principles for the payment of compensation provided thereunder were irrelevant to the value of the property acquired and hence in effect the impugned legislation did not provide for the payment of compensation. It must be pointed out, however, that the Act had laid down principles for compensation with regard to the acquisition of the property of the said company in accordance with the provisions of the Fourth Amendment of the Constitution; and hence these principles could hardly be called irrelevant. This decision of the Court ignored the distinction between the determination whether the compensation was illusory and the determination whether the compensation was inadequate. This was indeed an over-exercise of judicial power. Undoubtedly the Court was changing its own value judgment on the adequacy of compensation which as a consequence of the Fourth Amendment it was not competent to do.

In State of Gujarat *vs.* Shantilal Mangaldas[3] the Court laid down as follows:

> .... But compensation fixed or determined cannot be permitted to be challenged on the somewhat indefinite plea that it is not just or a fair equivalent. Principles may be challenged on the ground that they are irrelevant to the determination of compensation, but not on the plea that what is awarded as a result of the application of these principles is not just or fair compensation. A challenge to a statute that the principles specified by it do not awared a just equivalent will be a clear violation of the constitutional declaration that inadequacy of compensation provided is not judiciable.

In the Bank Nationalization case,[4] however, the Court held:

> Article 19(1) (f) enunciates the right to acquire, hold and dispose of property. Clause (5) of Article 19 authorises imposition of restriction upon this right. Article 31 assumes the right to property and grants protection against the exercise of the authority of the State. Clause (5) of Article 19 and clauses (1) and (2) of Article 31 prescribe restrictions upon State action subject to which the right to property may be exercised. Article 19(5) is a broad generalisation dealing with the nature of limitations which may be placed by law on the right to property. The guarantees under Article 31(1) and (2) arise out of the limitations imposed upon the authority of the State by law to take over the individual's property. The true character of the limitations under the two provisions is not different. Clause (5) of Article 19 and clauses (1) and (2) of Article 31 are parts of a single pattern. 19(1) (f) enunciates the basic right to property of the citizens and Article 19(5) and clauses (1) and (2) of Article 31 deal with limitations which may be placed by law subject to which the right may be exercised.

---

1. A.I.R. 1965 S.C. 1017.
2. A.I.R. 1967 S.C. 637. It is interesting to note that it was Chief Justice (as he then was) Subba Rao who delivered the judgement in this case.
3. A.I.R. 1969 S.C. 634.
4. A.I.R. 1970 S.C. 564.

Having explained this position the Court further laid down:

We are therefore unable to hold that the challenge to the validity of the provision for acquisition is liable to be tested only on the ground of non-compliance with Article 31(2). Article 31(2) requires that property must be acquired for a public purpose and that it must be acquired under a law with characteristics set out in that Article. Formal compliance with Article 31(2) is not sufficient to negative the protection of the guarantee of the right to property. Acquisition must be under the authority of the law and the expression 'law' means a law which is within the competence of the Legislature, and does not impair the guarantee of the rights in Part III. We are unable therefore to agree that Articles 19(1) and 31(2) are mutually exclusive.

The effect of this judgment was that a law under Article 31(2) will have to stand the test of Article 19(5) and also other relevant Articles under Part III of the Constitution. This meant that the authority of the State to acquire or requisition property became subject to many more restrictions.

Such successive overrulings by the Court had brought about complete uncertainty in the law and defeated the clearly expressed intention that a law of acquisition would not be challenged in courts on the ground that the compensation it provided was inadequate. The only way to remedy this unsatisfactory situation was by further amending the Constitution. But since the Golak Nath decision still held the ground and prohibited Parliament from amending the Fundamental Rights, the first step required was to restore to Parliament its power to modify any part of the Constitution including the chapter on Fundamental Rights. The Twenty-fourth Amendment (1971) restored Parliament's amending power. Soon after, the Twenty-fifth Amendment was passed suitably amending the provisions dealing with property rights to remove all uncertainties created by conflicting judicial pronouncements.

Twenty-fifth Amendment

The following is the text of the Amendment:

1. This Act may be called the Constitution (Twenty-fifth Amendment) Act, 1971.

2. In Article 31 of the Constitution; (A) for clause (2), the following clause shall be substituted, namely:

(2) No property shall be compulsorily acquired or requisitioned save for a public purpose and save by authority of a law which provides for acquisition or requisitioning of the property for an amount which may be fixed by such law or which may be determined in accordance with such principles and given in such manner as may be specified in such law: and no such law shall be called in question in any court on the ground that amount so fixed or determined is not adequate or that the whole or any part of such amount is to be given otherwise than in cash.

Provided that in making any law providing for the compulsory acquisition of any property of an educational institution established and administered by a minority, referred to in clause (1) of Article 30, the State shall ensure that the amount fixed by or determined under such law for the acquisition of such property is such as would not restrict or abrogate the right guaranteed under that clause.

(B) After clause (2A), the following clause shall be inserted, namely:

(2B) Nothing in sub-section (f) of clause (1) of Article 19 shall affect any such law as is referred to in clause (2).

3. After Article 31B of the Constitution, the following Article shall be inserted, namely:

31C. Notwithstanding anything contained in Article 13, no law giving effect to the policy of the State towards securing the principles specified in clause (B) or clause (C) of Article 39 shall be deemed to be void on the ground that it is inconsistent with or takes or abridges any of the rights conferred by Article 14, Article 19 or Article 31, and no law containing a declaration that it is for giving effect to such policy shall be called in question in any court on the ground that it does not give effect to such policy.

Provided that where such law is made by the legislature of a State, the provisions of this Article shall not apply thereto unless such law, having been reserved for the consideration of the President, has received his assent.

The Twenty-fifth Amendment has tremendous political, economic and constitutional significance. Parliament has, through this Amendment reasserted its position as the most important agency for bringing about radical socio-economic changes. The effect of the decision of the Supreme Court in the Bank Nationalization Case has been nullified. The Courts can no more sit in judgement on the adequacy of the *amount*[1] payable by the State when it takes over private property for a public purpose. The possibility for the application of the concept of 'market value' in such cases has been altogether removed except in cases of the compulsory acquisition of any property of an educational institution established and administered by a minority referred to in Article 30(1). The Amendment has thus established the principle that in a matter of public importance, the fundamental rights of the individual with regard to property rights will give place to the Directive Principles of State Policy. Article 31(C) gives the necessary protection for the implementation of the principle. Henceforth individual rights of property will yield second place to the supervening rights of society. After two decades of uncertainty and utter confusion, right to property under the constitution appeared to have become a settled issue.

In Kesavananda Bharati *vs.* State of Kerala, [2]however, the Supreme Court held that the last part of Article 31C, namely, "and no law containing a declaration that it is for giving effect to such policy shall be called in question in any court on the ground that it does not give effect to such policy was invalid as it imposed a blanket prohibition on the Court to examine the validity of such laws."

Forty-Second Amendment

The Forty-second Amendment of the Constitution (1976) not only sought to nullify the effect of this decision but went ahead and took a major step by further enlarging the scope of the Article to cover "all or any of the Principles laid down in Part IV" of the Constitution. A new Article was also added — 31D — providing for the saving of existing laws or making of new laws by Parliament to prevent or prohibit the formation of anti-national associations or their activities. This Article however was deleted by the Forty-third Amendment of 1978.

The enlarged scope of Article 31C under the Forty-second Amendment was challenged in the Minerva Mills case (1980) and the Court held that these changes damaged the basic feature of the Constitution and violated the Court's judgment in the Kesavananda Bharati case. While striking down Article 31C as amended, the Court dealt with the relative roles of Directive Principles and Fundamental Rights in the constitutional scheme and held that "to destroy the guarantees given by Part III in order purportedly to achieve the goals of Part IV

1. The Amendment does not use the term 'compensation' anywhere in the text. Instead the new term used is 'amount', a term which has not acquired any special legal connotation as in the case of compensation.
2. (1973) 4 S.C.C. 225.

is plainly to subvert the constitution by destroying its basic structure." The decision in effect was a reiteration of the Court's position in 1973 as expounded through the Kesavananda case.[1]

Of all the rights included in the chapter on Fundamental Rights and indeed of all provisions in the Constitution, the right to property has been the one which was subjected to the largest number of Amendments so far. It shows on the one hand the complex nature of the right itself and on the other the difficulty of the State to find a satisfactory balance between the individual's right to property and its social control under laws made by the State.

Forty-Fourth Amendment

This was evident in a dramatic manner when Parliament again sought to amend the right to property when it took up for consideration the Forty-fourth Amendment of the Constitution in 1978. There was, however, a striking contrast this time to the approaches of the past. According to the Forty-Fourth Amendment the Right to Property will no longer be a Fundamental Right. Hence from Article 19, sub-clause (i) (f) namely, *the right to acquire, hold and dispose of property* has been taken away. The sub heading "Right to property" occurring after Article 30 has been omitted. Article 31 which deals with Property has been altogether omitted. Consequential changes have been made in Article 31A and 31C. However, the right of persons holding land for personal cultivation and within the ceiling limit to receive compensation at the market value will not be affected. Similarly a new clause after clause (1) of Article 30 has been inserted to protect the right of minorities to establish and administer educational institutions in all cases of compulsory acquisition of property.

Looking back at the many constitutional amendments and the bitter costly legal battles on the right to property as a Fundamental Right, the latest amendment appears like an anti-climax. What its effect will be the future alone can unfold.

The Forty-fourth Amendment Act of 1979 took away from the chapter on Fundamental Rights the Right to Property. That means Article 31 which dealt with the Right to Property — the right to acquire, hold and dispose of property as a Fundamental Right, has been altogether omitted.

---

1. In Wamah Rao *vs.* Union of India AIR SC 271 it was held that amendments made in the Ninth Schedule before the Kesavananda Bharati decision are valid while the later ones would have to satisfy the 'test that they did not damage the basic structure of the Constitution.'

17

THE RIGHT TO CONSTITUTIONAL REMEDIES

(Art. 32)

A DECLARATION of fundamental rights is meaningless unless there is an effective machinery for the enforcement of the rights. In England, even though there is no formal declaration of rights as fundamental, individual rights are safeguarded by means of the 'prerogative writs'. Professor Dicey calls them the bulwark of English liberty. The fathers of the U.S. Constitution assumed that these Common Law Writs would be available in the United States as they had already been used to them during the colonial regime. Therefore, they made no specific provision in the Constitution for the issue of these writs. However, they made a special constitutional limitation of the suspension of the writ of *habeas corpus*.[1] In addition, federal laws have been enacted in the U.S. laying down the conditions and the procedure for the issue of these writs.

The framers of the Indian Constitution were in favour of adopting special provisions guaranteeing the right to constitutional remedies. This, again, is in tune with the nature in general of the various provisions embodied in the chapter on Fundamental Rights. Defending these special provisions, Ambedkar said:

> I prefer the British method of dealing with rights. The British method is a peculiar method. British jurisprudence insists that there can be no right unless the Constitution provides a remedy that makes the right real. If there is no remedy, there is no right at all, and I am, therefore, not prepared to burden the Constitution with a number of pious declarations which may sound as glittering generalities but for which the Constitution makes no provision by way of a remedy. It is much better to be limited in the scope of our rights and to make them real by enumerating remedies than to have a lot of pious wishes embodied in the Constitution.[2]

Article 32 has four sections. The first section is general in scope and says that 'the right to move the Supreme Court by appropriate proceedings for the enforcement of the rights conferred by this Part is guaranteed.' The second section deals, in more specific terms, with the power of the Supreme Court to issue writs including writs in the nature of *habeas corpus, mandamus,* prohibition, *quo warranto* and *certiorari* for the enforcement of any of the rights.[3] The third section empowers Parliament to confer the power of issuing

---

1. Article I Section 9(2).
2. C.A.D. VII, p. 953.
3. See in this connection Khajoor Singh *vs.* Union of India 1961, II S.C.J. 235 and the State of Jammu & Kashmir *vs.* Ghulam Rasool 1962, I S.C.J. 552.

writs or orders on any other court without prejudice to the power of the Supreme Court in this respect.[1] So far, Parliament has not passed any law conferring the power of issuing writs on any courts. The last section deals with the conditions under which this right can be suspended.

The first three sections of the Article, taken together, make fundamental rights under the Constitution real and, as such, they form the crowning part of the entire chapter. Adverting to the special importance of this Article, Ambedkar declared in the Assembly:

> If I was asked to name the particular article in this Constitution as the most important without which this Constitution would be a nullity, I could not refer to any other article except this one. It is the very soul of the Constitution and the very heart of it and I am glad that the House has realised its importance. Hereafter, it would not be possible for any legislature to take away the writs which are mentioned in this article. It is not that the Supreme Court is left to be invested with the power to issue these writs by a law to be made by the legislature as its sweet will. The Constitution has invested the Supreme Court with these rights and these writs could not be taken away unless and until the Constitution itself is amended by means left open to the legislatures. This in my judgement is one of the greatest safeguards that can be provided for the safety and security of the individual.[2]

This opinion of the Chairman of the Drafting Committee has been reaffirmed by the Court itself on several occasions. In Romesh Thapar *vs.* The State of Madras[3] the Court held:

> Article 32 provides a guaranteed remedy for the enforcement of the rights conferred by Part III (of the Constitution) and this remedial right is itself made a fundamental right by being included in Part III. The Court is thus constituted the protector and guarantor of fundamental rights and it cannot, consistently with the responsibility so laid upon it, refuse to entertain applications seeking protection against infringement of such rights.

However, the Court will not entertain any application under Article 32 unless the matter falls within the scope of any of the fundamental rights guaranteed in Part III of the Constitution.[4]

As the guardian of fundamental rights the Supreme Court has two types of jurisdiction, original and appellate. Under its original jurisdiction, any person who complains that his fundamental right has been violated within the territory of India may move the Supreme Court seeking an appropriate remedy. The fact that he may have a remedy in any of the High Courts does not preclude him from going directly to the Supreme Court.[5] However,

1. Under Article 226(1), the Constitution confers similar power on the High Courts within their own jurisdiction.
2. C.A.D. VII, p. 953.
3. 1950, S.C.R. 869.
4. The Court expressed this opinion first in A.K. Gopalan's case and subsequently in a number of other cases and refused to hear many of them on account of this reason, e.g. see Ram Chandra Palai *vs.* State of Orissa A.I.R. 1956, S.C. 298; Gangasahai *vs.* Union of India, A.I.R. 1956, S.C. 175; Nain Sukh Das *vs.* The State of U.P. 1953 S.C.R. 1184, and Cooverjee *vs.* Excise Commissioner, Ajmer, A.I.R. 1954, S.C. 220.
   See also Fertilizer Corporation *vs.* Union of India, A.I.R. 1981, S.C. 344 and Bandhu Mukti Morcha *vs.* Union of India, A.I.R. 1984, S.C. 802.
5. In Romesh Thapar's case the Advocate-General of Madras argued that as a matter of orderly procedure, the aggrieved person must first go to the High Court of appropriate jurisdiction. But the Supreme Court did not accept this contention. See also D.S. Rathi *vs.* The State of Punjab, 1958, S.C.J. 425 and Vinod Kumar *vs.* The State of Himachal Pradesh 1959, S.C.J. 275.

it is not the Court's policy to encourage the practice of direct approach except for good reasons[1] as otherwise the Court's load of work would be unnecessarily enhanced. The scope of Article 32 has been explained at length by the Court in Chiranjit Lal Choudhary *vs.* the Union of India.[2] There are four points that stand out prominently in that decision with respect to Article 32: (i) The sole object of Article 32 is the enforcement of the Fundamental Rights guaranteed under the Constitution. (ii) What is aimed at is the enforcement of Fundamental Rights, no matter whether the necessity arises out of an action of the Executive or of the Legislature. (iii) Any person who complains of an infraction of any of the Fundamental Rights guaranteed under the Constitution is at liberty to move the Supreme Court. (iv) Article 32 gives the Court very wide discretion in the matter of framing a writ to suit the exigencies of particular case and the application of a petitioner cannot be thrown out simply on the ground that the proper writ or direction has not been prayed for. Ever since the inauguration of the Constitution in 1950 there have been numerous occasions when the Court exercised its power of issuing orders, directions or writs as the protector of Fundamental Rights guaranteed under the Constitution.

At the time when the article was under consideration of the Constituent Assembly and even after the adoption and implementation of the Constitution, there was apprehension in enlightened quarters of the wisdom of investing an original jurisdiction in the Supreme Court in regard to the infringement of the fundamental rights in a big country like India. There was also the feeling that the Supreme Court might be flooded with work, and with its present strength it might not be able to cope with all the spheres of work arising under different heads. But the experience so far of the Court's work has not only belied these fears but also demonstrated the beneficent nature of the provision.

> It has solved expeditiously many a difficult and knotty problem which might have otherwise taken several years if the aggrieved citizen had to go from Court to Court for the redress of his grievances. The jurisdiction vested in the Supreme Court does not interfere with the rights of the High Court in the first instance, if the aggrieved party invokes the jurisdiction of the High Court and avails himself of the remedy before the High Court.[3]

We have already seen under Article 32(4) that the right to constitutional remedies may be suspended under certain circumstances. These circumstances are dealt with in detail in the chapter on Emergency Provisions of the Constitution. Chiefly, these emergencies are three: external aggression, internal disturbance and breakdown of constitutional machinery in States. Under such conditions the President of India is empowered to proclaim an emergency/ During the period of emergency he *may* by order declare that the right to move any Court for the enforcement of any fundamental right shall remain suspended up to a maximum period of the existence of the emergency (Art. 359). Every such order should be placed before each House of Parliament as soon as possible.[4]

The provision for the suspension of the right to constitutional remedies was severely criticized by some members in the Constituent Assembly. But Ambedkar had convincing arguments for the inclusion of such an apparently undemocratic provision. He said:

---

1. M.K. Gopalan *vs.* State of M.P. A.I.R. 1974, S.C. 362.
2. 1950, S.C.R. 869.
3. Alladi Krishnaswami Aiyar, op. cit., p. 53.
4. Although an emergency was proclaimed by the Defence of India Ordinance in 1962 as a result of the Chinese aggression, the right to constitutional remedies was not suspended. This was true in the case of proclamation of emergency on later occasions also.

There can be no doubt that while there are certain fundamental rights which the State must guarantee to the individual in the order that the individual may have some security and freedom to develop his own personality, it is equally clear that in certain cases, where, for instance, the State's very life is in jeopardy, those rights must be subject to a certain amount of limitation. In times of emergency, the individual himself will be found to have lost his very existence. Consequently, the superior right of the State to protect itself in times of emergency, so that it may survive that emergency and live to discharge its functions in order that the individual under the aegis of the State may develop, must be guaranteed as safely as the right of the individual. I know of no Constitution which gave fundamental rights but which gives them in such a manner as to deprive the State in times of emergency to protect itself by curtailing the rights of the individual.[1]

The Supreme Court began to widen the scope of Article 32 when it began to entertain Public Interest Litigation (PIL). On such occasions rules of Locus Standi have been liberalised. (See for example, S.P. Gupta *vs.* Union of India 1981 Supp. S.C.C. 81. For more details see Janata Dal *vs.* Chowdhary (1992) 4 S.C.C. 305 and Sheela Barse *vs.* Union of India, A.I.R. 1988 S.C. 2211).

Provision for the Issue of Writs

In view of a general provision under which power was conferred upon the Supreme Court to issue appropriate orders, directions or writs in order to safeguard fundamental rights, the propriety of certain writs being particularly mentioned was questioned in the Constituent Assembly. The necessity for mentioning and making reference to these particular writs, according to Ambedkar, was obvious. He said:

These writs have been in existence in Great Britain for a number of years. Their nature and the remedies that they provided are known to every lawyer and consequently we thought that as it is impossible even for a man who has the most fertile imagination to invent something new, it was hardly possible to improve upon the writs which have been in existence for probably thousands of years and which have given complete satisfaction to every Englishman with regard to the protection of his freedom. We, therefore, thought that a situation such as the one which existed in English jurisprudence which contained these writs and which, if I may say so, have been found to be knave-proof and fool-proof ought to be mentioned by their name in the Constitution without prejudice to the right of the Supreme Court to do justice in some other way if it was felt it was desirable to do so.

The importance of these writs which have been given by this article lies in the fact that they are prerogative writs; they can be sought for by an aggrieved party without bringing any proceedings or suit. Ordinarily, you must first file a suit before you can get any kind of an order from the Court, whether the order is in the nature of *mandamus*, prohibition or *certiorari* or anything of the kind. But, here, so far as this article is concerned, without filing any proceedings you can straightway go to the Court and apply for the writ. The object of the writ is really to grant what I may call interim relief. For instance, if a man is arrested, without filing a suit or a proceeding against the officer who arrests him, he can file a petition to the Court for setting him at liberty. It is not necessary for him to first file a suit or a proceeding against the officer. In a proceeding of this kind where the application is for a prerogative writ, all that the Court can do is to ascertain whether the arrest is in accordance with law. The Court at that stage will not enter into the question whether the law under which a person is arrested is a good law or a bad law, whether it conflicts with any of the provisions of the Constitution.... When a person is actually arrested and his trial has commenced, it is in the course of these proceedings that the

1. C.A.D. VII, p. 950.

Court would be entitled to go into the facts and to come to a decision whether a particular law under which a person is arrested is a good law or a bad law. Then the Court will go into the question whether it conflicts with the provisions of the Constitution.[1]

A Note on Writs

Habeas Corpus

'Habeas corpus' is a Latin term which literally means 'you may have the body'. Under the law of England, as a result of long usage, the term came to signify a prerogative writ, a remedy with which a person unlawfully detained sought to be set at liberty. It is mentioned as early as the fourteenth century in England and was formalized in the Habeas Corpus Act of 1679. The privilege of the use of this writ was regarded as a foundation of human freedom and the British citizen insisted upon this privilege wherever he went whether for business or for colonization. This is how it found a place in the Constitution of the United States when the British colonies in America won their independence and established a new State under that Constitution.

In India, under the Constitution, the power to issue a writ of habeas corpus is vested only in the Supreme Court and the High Courts. The writ is a direction of the Court to a person who is detaining another, commanding him to bring the body of the person in his custody at a specified time to a specified place for a specified purpose. In the famous words of Blackstone:

> The great and efficacious writ, in all manner of illegal confinement, is that of *habeas corpus ad subjiciendum*, directed to a person detaining another, and commanding him to produce the body of the prisoner, with the day and cause of his caption and detention, to do, submit and receive whatsoever the judge or court awarding such writ, shall consider it in that behalf.[2]

According to Broom:

> This great constitutional remedy rests upon the common law declared by Magna Carta and the statutes, which affirm it, rests, likewise, on specific enactments ensuring its efficiency, extending its applicability, and rendering more firm and durable the liberties of the people.... and the right to claim it cannot be suspended, even for one hour, by any means short of an Act of Parliament.[3]

A writ or habeas corpus has only one purpose: to set at liberty a person who is confined without legal justification; to secure release from confinement of a person unlawfully detained. The writ does not punish the wrong-doer. If the detention is proved unlawful, the person who secures liberty through the writ may proceed against the wrong-doer in any appropriate manner. The writ is issued not only against authorities of the State but also to private individuals or organizations if necessary.

The writ is obtained by any person on behalf of the detailed person if the prisoner himself is unable, for any reason, to move for it. Normally, there is no difficulty for a detained person to make an application for the writ and all facilities are provided for doing so. In fact, most of the habeas corpus petitions which are filed before the High Courts and the Supreme Court are made by the detained persons themselves. But the privilege extended to any person to file a petition on behalf of a detained person is an added safeguard.

---

1. C.A.D. VII, pp. 951-2.
2. *Commentaries*, p. 131.
3. See Rex *vs.* Halliday 1917, A.C. 260, p. 296.

However, this privilege cannot be abused. In Vidya Verma *vs.* Shiv Narain,[1] the Supreme Court held:

Where an advocate presents a petition under Article 32 for a writ of habeas corpus on behalf of a lady and appeals as her next friend but the petition does not disclose that he made any attempt to consult the person who he said was the husband of the lady nor does it show that he made any attempt to contact either the lady or even her uncle, and he had three hearings in the Court despite the warning he was given about costs, and when the permission is refused and the petition dismissed, the advocate should be made to pay the costs personally.

Under the Constitution, the writ of habeas corpus is sought to safeguard the fundamental rights guaranteed under Articles 19 (right to freedom), 21 (protection of life and personal liberty) and 22 (protection against arrest and detention). The law that the has been most assailed by those who sought the writ is the Preventive Detention Act and its later version the Maintenance of Internal Security Act which has been in existence ever since the inauguration of the Constitution. The principles underlying the many decisions which the Supreme Court has given in connection with preventive detention have been brought together by the Court in its decision in the following case.[2]

Where power is vested in a statutory authority to deprive the liberty of a subject on its subjective satisfaction with reference to specified matters, if that satisfaction is stated to be based on a number of grounds or for a variety of reasons, all taken together, and if some out of them are found to be non-existent or irrelevant, the very exercise of that power is bad. That is so because the matter being one for subjective satisfaction, it must be properly based on all the reasons on which it purports to be based. If some out of them are found to be non-existent or irrelevant, the Court cannot predicate what the subjective satisfaction of the said authority would have been on the exclusion of those grounds or reasons. To uphold the validity of such an order in spite of the invalidity of some of the reasons or ground would be to substitute the objective standards of the Court for the subjective satisfaction of the statutory authority. In applying these principles, however, the Court must be satisfied that the vague or irrelevant grounds are such, if excluded, might reasonably have affected the subjective satisfaction of the appropriate authority. It is not merely because some ground or reason of a comparatively unessential nature is defective that such an order based on subjective satisfaction can be held to be invalid. The Court while anxious to safeguard the personal liberty of the individual will not lightly interfere with such orders.

In Sabastian Horgray *vs.* Union of India AIR 1984 SC 571 the Supreme Court held that it would be reluctant to issue an exparte writ of habeas corpus if the fact of detention may be controverted or it may become necessary to investigate facts.

Mandamus

The Latin word 'mandamus' means 'we order'. The writ of mandamus is an order of the High Court or the Supreme Court commanding a person or a body to do that which it is his, or its duty to do. Usually, it is an order directing the performance of ministerial acts. A ministerial act is one which a person or a body is obliged by law to perform under given circumstances. For instance, a licensing officer is obliged to issue a licence to an applicant if the latter fulfils all the conditions laid down for the issue of such licence. Similarly, an

1. A.I.R. 1956, S.C. 108.
2. Dwaraka Das Bhatia *vs.* The State of Jammu and Kashmir, 1957, S.C.J. See also ADM Jabalpore *vs.* Shukla, A.I.R. 1776.

appointing authority should issue a letter of appointment to a candidate if all the formalities of selection over and if the candidate is declared fit for the appointment. But despite the fulfilment of such conditions, if the officer or the authority concerned refuses or fails to issue the licence or the appointment letter, the aggrieved person has a right to seek the remedy through a writ of mandamus.

There are three essential conditions for the issue of a writ of mandamus. Firstly, the applicant must show that he has a real and special interest in the subject matter and a specific legal right to enforce. Secondly, he must show that there resides in him a legal right to the performance sought, and finally, that there is no other equally effective, convenient and beneficial remedy.[1]

If in the performance of official duty, a public body or officer fails to observe the principles of natural justice, a writ of mandamus may be sought against him or that body. Thus, the Calcutta High Court held in Dasgupta *vs.* Bijoy Ranjan Rakshit[2] that the State Medical Faculty or the governing body in performing its duty of deciding whether the candidates have been guilty of unfair means and what punishment should be inflicted, must not only act in good faith but also fairly and reasonably and without violation of notice to the candidates of the charges against them. There having been no opportunity whatsoever of showing that the allegation was not true, or that even if true, the punishment should be different from what the governing body proposed and there being no individual consideration of the different candidates, a writ of mandamus may issue to ensure that it performs its duties properly.

In the State of Bombay *vs.* the United Motors (India) Ltd.[3] the Supreme Court held that the principle that a court will not issue a prerogative writ when an adequate alternative remedy was available could not apply where a party came to the Court with an allegation that his fundamental right had been infringed and sought relief under Article 226. The Court will also consider whether the alternative remedy is of 'an onerous and burdensome character'.

Where an officer is empowered to use his discretion in the exercise of his duty to do either one way or another, and if he has honestly and reasonably exercised his discretion in one way, he cannot be compelled through a mandamus writ to exercise it in the alternative way. But if he refuses to act either way, then he can be compelled through the issue of the writ to act their one way or the other. Further, the writ is not a substitute for appeal or what has been called in U.S. a writ of error. In reversing a decision of the Orissa High Court in which the Court had declared invalid a decision of the Syndicate of Utkal University declaring an examination cancelled on account of leakage of a question paper, the Supreme Court held:

> The substance is more important than the form and if there is substantial compliance with the spirit and substance of the law, an unessential defect in form cannot defeat what is otherwise a proper and valid resolution....

---

1. Shankeramma *vs.* Government of Hyderabad, A.I.R. 1953, Hyd. 79; Ajit Kumar *vs.* Collector A.I.R. 1953, Cal. 653. Also see Y.M. Sheriff *vs.* Mysore State Transport Authority, 1960 S.C.J. 402; T.G. Gaokar *vs.* R.N. Shukla, A.I.R. 1968 S.C. 1050.
2. 56 C.W.N. 861.
3. 1953, S.C.R. 572. See also Mehta *vs.* Madhya Pradesh 1964, S.C.J. 445.

The question was one of urgency and the Vice-Chancellor and the members of the Syndicate were well within their rights in exercising their discretion in the way they did. It may be that the matter could have been handled in some other way, as, for example, in the manner the learned judges indicate, but it is not the function of courts of law to substitute their wisdom and discretion for that of the person to whose judgement the matter in question is entrusted by law. The University authorities acted honestly as reasonable and responsible men confronted with an urgent situation are entitled to act... This was decidedly not the sort of case in which mandamus ought to issue.[1]

In Barium Chemicals Ltd. *vs.* Company Law Board[2] the Supreme Court held that Courts might intervene in the exercise of administrative discretion if it has been exercised on grounds extraneous to the legislation even if there be no malafide or oblique motive.

Normally, a writ of mandamus does not issue and an order in the nature of mandamus is not made against a private individual. However, the Supreme Court held that:

....such an order may be made against a person directing him to do some particular thing specified in the order, which appertains to his office and is in the nature of a public duty.... Where a person has apparently entered into *bona fide* possession of a property without knowledge that any person has been illegally evicted therefrom, a mandamus will not lie against the person in possession to restore possession to the person claiming to have been illegally evicted therefrom.[3]

In England, the operation of mandamus was at one time confined to a limited class of cases affecting the administration of public affairs, and in particular it was invoked to compel inferior courts to proceed in matters within their jurisdiction or public officers to perform their duties. But many Acts of Parliament which confer powers and obligations upon public utility undertakings of all descriptions normally require the execution of certain works for the benefit of private persons, e.g. landowners who may have been dispossessed of their property or some of its amenities by the undertaking. An Act may impose the duty of erecting a bridge over a new railway, or of constructing a road in place of one which has been closed. The execution of works of this description is enforceable by mandamus at the instance of the persons aggrieved.[4] The position in India is also the same.[5]

Prohibitiion

A Writ of prohibition is issued primarily to prevent an inferior court from exceeding its jurisdiction, or acting contrary to the rules of natural justice, for example, to restrain a judge from hearing a case in which he is personally interested. The term 'inferior courts' contemplates special tribunals, commissions, magistrates and officers who exercise judicial powers affecting the property or rights of the citizen and act in a summary way or in a new course different form the common law.[6] It is well established that the writ lies only against a body exercising public functions of a judicial or quasi-judicial character and cannot in the nature of things be utilized to restrain legislative powers.[7]

---

1. Vice-Chancellor, Utkal University *vs.* Ghosh 1954, S.C.J. 252.
2. A.I.R. 1967 S.C. 295. See also Lakhanpal *vs.* Union of India, A.I.R. 1967 S.C. 1507. See also R.P. Singh *vs.* State of Bihar (1978) I S.C.C. 37.
3. Sohan Lal *vs.* The Union of India 1957, S.C.J. 489.
4. Wade and Phillips, *Constitutional Law* (Fifth edition), pp. 318-19.
5. State of Bombay *vs.* The United Motors (India) Ltd. 1953, S.C.J. 373; Mohamed Yasin *vs.* the Town Area Committee 1952, S.C.J. 162.
6. *Bunill's Law Dictionary.*
7. Shankeramma *vs.* The Government of Hyderabad, A.I.R. 1953, Hyd. 79.

The writ of prohibition is the counterpart of the writ of certiorari which too is issued against the action of an inferior court. The difference between the two was explained by Justice Venkatarama Aiyar of the Supreme Court in the following terms:

Whenever an inferior court takes up for hearing a matter over which it has no jurisdiction, the person against whom the proceedings are taken can move the superior court for a writ of prohibition and on that an order will issue forbidding the inferior court from continuing the proceedings. On the other hand, if the court hears the cause or matter and gives a decision, the party aggrieved would have to move the superior court for a writ of certiorari and on that an order will be made quashing the decision on the ground of want of jurisdiction.[1]

According to Halsbury's *Laws of England*:

Prohibition lies not only for excess of or absence of jurisdiction, but also for the contravention of some statute or the principles of the common law; it does not, however, lie to correct the course, practice or procedure of an inferior tribunal, or a wrong decision on the merits of procedings.[2]

There must remain something to which prohibition can apply, some act which the authority, if not prohibited, may do in excess of jurisdiction. Hence, an application for prohibition is never too late, so long as there is something left for it to operate upon.

The writ will not be readily issued if there is a right of appeal from the inferior court which has not been used. However, tribunals exercising judicial and quasi-judicial functions are only too anxious in modern democracy to be covetous of jurisdiction and it is up to the superior courts to curb the tendency. As aptly observed by an English Judge:

My view of the power of Prohibition at the present day is that courts should not be chary of exercising it and that whenever the legislature entrusts to any body of persons the power of imposing an obligation on individuals, the courts ought to exercise as widely as they can the power of controlling those bodies, if they admittedly attempt to exercise powers beyond those given to them by Act of Parliament.[3]

With regard to the grounds for issuance of the writ of prohibition, the Supreme Court held that it is established law that they are identical to those on which the writ of certiorari is issued, the only difference being in the stages of their issuance.[4] The conditions for granting the writ were stated afresh by the Court in Govinda Menon *vs.* Union of India[5] and reiterated the view that through this writ the superior court supervises whether the inferior tribunals act within their jurisdiction and in conformity with the principles of natural justice. In another case[6] the Court held that the issuance of a writ being discretionary it is subject to only self-imposed limitations of the Court concerned. On this ground the Supreme Court refused to interfere with the discretion of the High Court.

Certiorari

Certiorari is an ancient prerogative writ which orders the removal of a suit from an inferior court to a superior court. It may be used before a trial to prevent an excess or abuse

---

1. Harivishnu *vs.* Ahmed Ishaque A.I.R. 1956, S.C.J. 33.
2. Second Edition, IX, p. 820.
3. Esher, L.J. in Queen *vs.* Local Board, 1883, (10) Q.B.D. 309.
4. H.V. Kamath *vs.* Ahmed Ishaque, A.I.R. 1955, S.C. 233.
5. A.I.R. 1967, S.C. 1274.
6. Income-tax Officer *vs.* Short Bros. Ltd., A.I.R. 1967, S.C. 81.

of jurisdiction and to remove the case for trial to a higher court. It is invoked also after trial to quash an order which has been made without jurisdiction or in defiance of the rules of natural justice.[1]

Speaking on the scope of the writ, the Supreme Court, in the State of Bombay *vs.* Advani,[2] held:

(i) When any body of persons having legal authority to determine questions affecting the rights of subjects and having the duty to act judicially, act in excess of their legal authority, a writ of certiorari lies. It does not lie to remove or cancel executive or administrative acts. (ii) For this purpose, the term judicial does not necessarily mean acts of a judge or legal tribunal sitting for the determination of matters of law, but for the purpose of this question a judicial act seems to be an act done by competent authority, upon considerations of facts and circumstances, and imposing liability or affecting the rights of others.[3]

In Prem Singh *vs.* Deputy Custodian-General,[4] the Court held:

A writ of certiorari may be issued to correct an error of law apparent on the fact of the record. It is difficult to lay down any general test as to when an error ceases to be a mere error and becomes an error apparent on the face of the record. What is an error apparent on the face of the record cannot be defined precisely or exhaustively, there being an element of indefiniteness inherent in its very nature and it must be left to be determined judicially on the facts of each case.

In Sangram Singh *vs.* Election Tribunal, Kota,[5] the Court held:

The jurisdiction which Article 226 and 136 confer entitle the High Court and this Court to examine the decisions of all tribunals to see whether they have acted illegally. That jurisdiction purports to confer power on a tribunal to act illegally by enacting a statute that its illegal acts shall become legal the moment the tribunal chooses to say they are legal. The legality of an act or conclusion is something that exists outside and apart from the decision of an inferior tribunal. It is a part of the law of the land which cannot be finally determined or altered by any tribunal of limited jurisdiction. The High Courts and the Supreme Court alone can determine what the law of the land is vis-a-vis all other courts and tribunals and that alone can pronounce with authority and finality on what is legal and what is not. All that an inferior tribunal can do is to reach a tentative conclusion which is subject to review under Articles 226 and 136.

Often a writ of certiorari is sought along with prohibition, so that not merely may an invalid act be reviewed by a superior court (certiorari), but its operation may also be restrained (prohibition). While prohibition and certiorari are so intimately related to each other, prohibition is the converse of mandamus. The former is invoked to prevent a Court or other authority from doing something which it has not the power to do, while the latter is called in aid to require it to do something which it is bound to do.

Quo Warranto

The writ of quo warranto is a common law process of great antiquity. According to this, the High Courts or the Supreme Court may grant an injunction to restrain a person from acting in an office to which he is not entitled and may also declare the office to be vacant. What the Court has to consider in an application for writ of quo warranto is whether there has been usurpation of an office of a public nature and an office substantive in

1. For a discussion on the subject see S.N. Shukla, "The Grounds for Certiorari", 1960, S.C.J. 247.
2. 1950, S.C.R. 621.
3. See also Mineral Development Ltd. *vs.* The State of Bihar, 1960, S.C.J. 643.
4. 1958 S.C.J. 29.
5. 1955, S.C.J. 431. See also Election Commission *vs.* Venkata Rai 1953, S.C.J. 293 and Basappa *vs.* Nagappa 1954, S.C.J. 695.

character, i.e., an office independent in title. It is a remedy given by law at the discretion of the Court and is not issued as a matter of course.[1]

There seems to be divergence of opinion as to who can claim the issue of a writ of quo warranto. One view is that unless there is an infraction of a personal right, a person has no right to maintain an application for the issue of a writ of quo warranto under Articles 226 or 32 of the Constitution of India.[2] The other view is that a member of the public may challenge a public act of the State in a writ of quo warranto 'provided he does so *bona fide* and is not a man of straw set up by others as a mere pawn in the game and provided it is in the interests of the public that the legal position should be judicially decided once for all'.[3] The latter view has the merit of safeguarding the interests of the public by recognizing, as the Court of King's Bench in England did,[4] that in proceedings of the issue of a writ of quo warranto, the relator need not necessarily have a direct and personal interest except what he may have in common with the public.

An application for the issue of a writ of quo warranto is maintainable only in respect of offices of a public nature which are the creation of statute and not against private institutions.[5] In the case of domestic tribunals, the order of the tribunal will not be disturbed unless it is attacked on the ground of *bona fides* or *vires*[6] . Thus, it has been held that a member of a Legislative Assembly has every right to know by what authority the Speaker of the body functions as such, if he *bona fide* thinks that the Speaker holds his officer without authority and the application for a writ of quo warranto is maintainable.[7]

In the State of Orissa *vs.* Binapani Dei[8] the Supreme Court refused to accept the contention of the Orissa Government that the Court has no right to intervene in a matter concerning an order which was administrative in nature. It held that even an administrative order which involved civil consequences should be made consistently with the rules of natural justice. "If there is power to decide and determine to the prejudice of a person, duty to act judicially is implicit in the exercise of such power."

The meaning of "wrong occupation of public office" was considered in the State of Assam *vs.* Ranga Muhammad.[9] In two writ petitions one Ranga Muhammad contended that in view of the ruling in Chandra Mohan *vs.* the State of U.P.[10] the 'transfer' and 'posting' of two District judges by the State Government being unconstitutional, they were illegal occupiers of the said public offices. While the Supreme Court agreed that the transfer of a District Judge falls within the exclusive jurisdiction of the High Court and in the 'posting' of such judges the High Court must be consulted and their advice cannot be easily bypassed as the High Court is best suited to judge these matters, yet in the opinion of the Court the petition for quo warranto was not entertainable as the irregularity was not of such a nature as could justify the issuance of a writ. It was further pointed out that for such a writ there must be "wrong occupation" of the public office as opposed to mere irregularity.

---

1. Govinda Panicker *vs.* Balakrishna Marar A.I.R. 1955, Travancore-Cochin 42.
2. Grama *vs.* Agarwal A.I.R. 1953, Nagpur 81.
3. Chakkari Chettiar *in re* A.I.R. 1953, Madras 96. Also see P. Lakhanpal *vs.* The President of India (1962) I S.C.J. 670.
4. Rex *vs.* Speyer 1915, 1 K.B. 595.
5. Amarenda Chandra *vs.* Basu, 56, C.W.N. 449.
6. Surendra Mohan *vs.* Gopal Chandra A.I.R. 1952, Orissa 359.
7. Nesamony *vs.* Verghese 5 D.L.R. (T.C.) 402.
8. A.I.R. 1967 S.C. 1269. See also Gopal Krishna *vs.* State of M.P., A.I.R. 1967 S.C. 240. On the question whether and when the same function of the executive which first starts as purely administrative one and then converts into a quasi-judicial function, see Lakhanpal *vs.* Union of India, A.I.R. 1967, S.C. 1507.
9. A.I.R. 1967 S.C. 903. Also see Statesman (P) Ltd. *vs.* H.R. Deb, A.I.R. 1968 S.C. 1495.
10. A.I.R. 1966 S.C. 1967.

18

AN ASSESSMENT

THE CHAPTER on Fundamental Rights in the Constitution has been the subject of criticism both in India and outside ever since its adoption. Broadly classified, the critics are of three types. Firstly, there are those who think that the Constitution does not embody fundamental rights in reality but only an apology for them. According to them, many fundamental rights such as the right to work, education, etc. which ought to have found a place in the chapter have been ignored.[1] Secondly, there are those who think that the spirit that pervades the whole chapter and much of its substance are taken away by the extraordinary provisions such as preventive detention, suspension of the right of constitutional remedies, etc. These critics allege that what has been given by one hand has been taken away by the other.[2] Thirdly, there are those who argue that even those rights that are attempted to be safeguarded are hedged in with so many exceptions, explanations and qualifications that it is difficult to understand what exactly is available to the individual by way of fundamental rights. One of these critics sarcastically suggested that the chapter on Fundamental Rights should be renamed as 'Limitations on Fundamental Rights, or, Fundamental Rights and Limitations Thereon.'[3]

It is true that the right to work, the right to rest and leisure, material security, etc. are not included in the chapter on Fundamental Rights. Even the right to education does not find a place there. The reason why they have not been included is not far to seek. Every one of the rights in this chapter is a justiciable right. For every violation of these rights, there is a judicial remedy, which makes the right a practical proposition. On the other hand, take, for example, the right to education: 'Every child under the age of fourteen shall have the right to free education.' It is a positive right. To translate it into reality, the State should have provided immediately thousands of schools all over the country. Was it possible under the conditions prevailing in India at the time of the adoption of the Constitution to have this right realized in practice? Needless to say, it was possible. It is a right which can reach the realm of physical possibility only in the course of decades. This is why the right to education has been included in the chapter on Directive Principles of State Policy and a time of ten years was fixed.[4]

The fundamental difference between Fundamental Rights and Directive Principles is that the former are justiciable rights — rights that can be enforced by a court of law — while the latter are non-justiciable rights. The fact that certain rights have been made non-

1. C.A.D. X, p. 618.
2. Ibid, VII, p. 305, pp. 370-74 and X, p. 732.
3. Jaspat Roy Kapoor C.A.D. IX, p. 1541.
4. It is now fully recognized that even by 2000 this goal will not be realized.

justiciable does not make them useless or meaningless as has been alleged by some critics.[1] The distinction can be understood only in the light of the evaluation of the theory and practice relating to fundamental rights in the nineteenth and twentieth centuries. Consequent upon the Industrial Revolution in Europe, the labouring classes became politically conscious and realized that the conditions which they required for the development of their personality, whose fulfilment they demanded, were different from those which the middle classes of the seventeenth and eighteenth centuries required and demanded. What the working classes wanted was better conditions of work in the factories: better housing, better sanitation, medical relief and social security. They wanted education for their children. They stood for more equitable distribution of wealth and higher and heavier taxation of the wealthy. The right to freedom of expression and religion, etc. demanded by the middle classes called for negative action by the State. These rights could become real when restrictions on the press or dictating religion to its subjects. But the conditions of good life demanded by the labourers called for positive action by the State, such as factory legislation, compulsory and free education, old age pensions, unemployment relief and so on. This is the difference between the rights demanded during the nineteenth and the twentieth centuries. Those who question the utility of non-justiciable rights do not appreciate this distinction. The right to employment or education are not rights which can be safeguarded by courts of law. When courts start safeguarding such rights they will cease to be courts. These are rights which ought to come within the scope of legislative policy. They are not appropriate for judicial action. The remedy for them lies in the legislature which is elected on the basis of adult franchise. In a democracy based on adult suffrage, legislatures are bound to take action and see that such rights remain not mere platitudes on paper but as effective as justiciable rights.

The provisions dealing with preventive detention and the suspension of constitutional remedies are indeed difficult to defend. Nevertheless, there are considerations which can be urged in their favour. It has already been pointed out that restrictions on individual freedom are necessary in the interests of society. The framers of the Constitution were not unaware of the dangers to the existence and safety of the Republic they were establishing.[2] They were giving it shape at a time when the country was passing through extraordinary stress and strain There were groups and parties in India who made no secret of their opposition to the new democratic order that was emerging in the country. The assassination of Gandhi was itself the most eloquent indication of this. Where organized groups swear by force and violence to achieve their objectives which strike at the very roots of democratic institutions, no constitution can be accused of whittling down fundamental rights if a freely elected Parliament is given power to enact a law of preventive detention. In the opinion of a British writer on Fundamental Rights in India, preventive detention is an administrative necessity in India, and likely to cause less human misery than might result from likely alternative measures to deal with persons who cannot be successfully prosecuted for their activities, though they are a menace to public security and order. The danger and consequences of public disturbances in India are too grave to justify any Indian government in giving the tub-thumping demagogue, and the conspiratorial member of a political cell the freedom he enjoys in Britain.[3]

1. *e.g.* Ivor Jennings, *Some Characteristics of the Indian Constitution,* Chapter II.
2. C.A.D. X, p. 837.
3. Alan Gledhill, *Fundamental Rights in India*, p. 126. Although the Preventive Detention Act ceased to exist by 1973, its place was taken more or less in the same form by a new Act under the title Maintenance of Internal Security Act, passed in 1973 and renewed periodically in later years.

It goes to the credit of democratic India that, in spite of the extremely trying circumstances under which it has been functioning over the past three decades and more, the number of persons taken into custody under the preventive detention laws has been comparatively small in relation to the gigantic proportions of the country, both in area and population and in the magnitude of the problems confronting it. The only exception to this was a short period of internal emergency during 1975-77 which was revoked in early 1977. This, of course, should not be taken as a strong defence of an unwholesome provision like preventive detention. Yet it might help place the problem in proper perspective.

The operation of several other Fundamental Rights, however, was seriously affected by the Proclamation of Emergency by the President in 1962 and later in 1965, 1971 and 1975. The Proclamation was followed by the Defence of India Act, investing the Government with vast powers over the liberty of the citizen. In fact, Article 358 of the Constitution provides for the automatic suspension of the seven freedoms such as the right to freedom of speech, assembly, association, movement, etc. embodied in Article 19 of the Constitution as a result of the proclamation. Article 359 enables the President by order to suspend the right to constitutional remedies provided under Article 32.[1] Since there is no provision for the automatic suspension of any other fundamental right, orders were issued soon after the Proclamation suspending the enforcement of Article 14 (equality before the law), Article 21 (right to life and personal liberty), and Article 22 (protection against unlawful arrest and detention) in so far only as they might affect the constitutionality of the Defence of India Act, the Rules made under it and also any order made in pursuance of them.

In addition to the already existent powers under the Preventive Detention Act, the Defence of India Act had provided for the detention of any person "whom an authority suspects on grounds appearing to that authority to be reasonable, of being of hostile origin, of having acted, acting, being about to act or being likely to act in a manner prejudicial to the defence of India and civil defence, the security of the State, the public safety or interest, the maintenance of public order, India's relations with foreign States, the maintenance of peaceful conditions in any part of India or the efficient conduct of military operations." The Government may also impose restrictions, short of detention, regulating the conduct in any such manner as may be specified in the order. Restrictions may also be imposed in respect of enjoyment of association or communication with other persons or against propagation of opinion.

Suffice it to say that these are by any standard extraordinary powers to be exercised by the Executive under a democratic system of government. This is particularly so when there is no provision for an independent review of orders made under the Act. Under the cloak of emergency these powers could be abused by an unscrupulous and power-seeking party in office to destroy forever the cherished ideals of the Constitution. If the emergency is unnecessarily prolonged or the power under it are misused for political purposes, it will sound the deathknell of the democratic character of the Constitution. It is true, as Lord Justice Scrutton once observed that a war could not be conducted on the principles of Magna Charta or those of the Sermon on the Mount. Fundamental Rights are bound to be curtailed during a period of grave national emergency in the interests of the security of the State. But the term 'security of the State' has to be properly interpreted and it should not be

1. Articles 20 and 21 are exempted from the purview of Article 359.

equated with the 'security of the Government' of the day. The extent of regulation of individual liberty even during a war emergency should conform to the spirit of Lord Atkin's celebrated dictum: "Amid the clash of arms, the laws are not silent. They may be changed but they speak the same language in war as in peace."

The Supreme Court of India has been very vigilant to safeguard the fundamental rights of citizens even during times of national emergency. This is clear from some of the decisions of the Court interpreting the orders issued by the President under Article 359. In M.S. Tarasikka *vs.* State of Punjab,[1] the Court upheld the validity of an order under Article 359 but gave relief to the petitioner against *mala fide* and illegal actions of the Executive. In Ghulam Sarwar *vs.* Union of India[2] the Court held that the order of the President under Article 359 was subject to the restrictive provisions of Part III of the Constitution. Under Article 359 the President has to make an order declaring that the right to move a court in respect of a fundamental right is suspended. Under this he can make only an order which is valid. An order making an unjustified discrimination in suspending the right to move a Court will be void at its inception. So viewed, the order must satisfy Article 14.

The Court held at the same time that the differential treatment given to foreigner under the order was justified in view of the danger of internal sabotage and espionage. There was also danger from the activities of some nationals and hence they had to be treated differently under the Defence of India Rules.[3]

In Mohammed Yaqub *vs.* State of Jammu and Kashmir,[4] however, the Court chose to retrace its steps from the position it took in Ghulam Sarwar case and held that Article 359 gave the President absolute power to suspend the enforcement of fundamental rights during an emergency. Hence the Court would give maximum consideration to the judgment of the Executive as the stake involved was the security of the nation. Even so, the Court might interfere in extreme cases of executive excesses if the evidence justified such interference. Through strict construction of the Defence of India Rules the Court tried to provide this and thus gave maximum protection to individual liberty. In Lakhanpal *vs.* the Union of India[5] the Court held that although the decision to detain a person under the D.I.R. is purely to be based on the subjective satisfaction of the Government, the continuance of such detention beyond the period of six months must be based on objective standards. In State of M.P. *vs.* Bharat Singh,[6] the Court held that the suspension of fundamental rights envisaged under Article 358 was prospective. It did not operate to validate a law which was invalid when enacted due to its inconsistency with the fundamental rights guaranteed by Article 19. If the Act was enacted before 1962 it was void at its inception and subsequent proclamation of emergency did not revive it. These decisions clearly show how anxious the Court was to safeguard fundamental rights, especially personal freedom, even during a period of national emergency. The decision of the Court in ADM Jabalpore *vs.* Shukla,[7]

1. A.I.R. 1964 S.C. 381.
2. A.I.R. 1967, S.C. 1335.
3. For detailed discussion see Koppell, G.O., "The Emergency, the Courts and Indian Democracy", 8 J.I.L. I, 1966, 287.
4. A.I.R. 1968, S.C. 765.
5. A.I.R. 1967, S.C. 1507
6. A.I.R. 1967, S.C. 1170.
7. A.I.R. 1976, S.C. 1207.

however, has been severely criticized bringing into sharp focus the need to amend the emergency provisions of the Constitution. The Forty-fourth Amendment has been able to achieve it up to a point.

The third line of criticism that the fundamental rights are couched in difficult language, that they are beyond the comprehension of an ordinary reader of the Constitution, that the rights are hedged in with numerous exception and qualifications, is justified. It is a feature that runs through the entire Constitution which made a critic remark that it was not a Constitution but a constitutional treatise. Compared with the Indian Fundamental Rights, the U.S. Bill of Rights is a marvel of clarity and conciseness. The fathers of the U.S. Constitution reduced their ideas of fundamental liberties to a few simple propositions and made them part of their Constitution. The rest of the job was left trustfully to the judges. The Constituent Assembly, on the contrary, instead of leaving it to the courts to read into the law the necessary exceptions and limitations, sought to express them in a compendious form in the Constitution itself. It is also well to remember in this connection that the difficulty of understanding the different constitutional provisions is not actually a problem of language alone. It also arises out of the unfamiliarity of a new constitutional system that requires close study and deep understanding which alone can make it a part of the common national heritage.

A close study of the provisions of the chapter on Fundamental Rights will show that it is not the product of a consistent philosophy. Such a philosophy was perhaps possible a century ago and in countries characterized by a homogeneity of language, religion and culture. But India presented something totally different, complex, heterogenous and diversified. Naturally, the Constitution was bound to reflect it; and the chapter on Fundamental Rights is its most powerful mirror. There is some justification in the following words of a critic of this chapter:

> A thread of nineteenth century liberalism runs through it; there are consequences of the political problems of Britain in it; there are relics of the bitter experience in opposition to British rule; and there is evidence of a desire to reform some of the social institutions which time and circumstances have developed in India. The result is a series of complex formulae, in twenty-four articles, some of them lengthy, which must become the basis of a vast and complicated case law.[1]

It is generally true that, in the ultimate analysis, fundamental rights are not protected by courts of law but by public opinion. But the effectiveness of public opinion as the guardian of fundamental rights depends upon how well organized and effective is public opinion in a country. India is vast in size and has a huge population. It is also a poor and backward country. Education and civic consciousness are yet to reach a commendable level in India. How difficult it is to organize effective public opinion in a country like India needs no special mention . In the absence of really effective public opinion, it would have been suicidal to leave the protection of fundamental liberties to the discretion of executive authorities or the caprices of legislative majorities. Even in England it took centuries for public opinion to assert itself as a champion of human rights. It is this that adds to the importance of incorporating the Right to Constitutional Remedies as an integral part of the chapter on Fundamental Rights. Nevertheless, there is the utmost need for the building up of a vigorous, effective public opinion in India as an important additional

1. Ivor Jennings, *op. cit.*

safeguard to fundamental rights. Eternal vigilance is the price of liberty.[1]

There is another aspect of this problem which deserves consideration. While great emphasis is often placed on one's rights, there is no corresponding stress on one's duties. For, rights and duties are the two sides of the same coin. Those who passionately claim their rights should at the same time have also the duty to respect and uphold the rights of others. There is a good deal of strength in the saying that if duties are fulfilled, the rights will take care of themselves. It has been rightly said that one's right to swing one's arms stops where the other man's nose begins. For, he has a right to keep his nose where it should be. If our recent history has been marked by fierce interregional, intercommunal and intercaste conflicts, it is not because the Constitution has not put adequate emphasis — nor too much of it — on fundamental rights, but because powerful parochial and narrow-minded groups have tended to treat these rights with contempt. On the one hand, linguistic and communal majorities have failed to win the confidence of the minorities. On the other, some of the minorities have tended to take too narrow and selfish a view of their own interests. Such an attitude is not conducive to the creation of an atmosphere which permits the proper enjoyment of the fundamental rights by the community as a whole. Further, it also makes the task of enforcing the rights extremely difficult. Hence, if public opinion has to be vigilant and expose every encroachment of the individual's liberty by the State, it has to be equally vigilant to denounce the actions of individuals and groups who subvert the rights of others. Thus, an atmosphere of understanding and tolerance should prevail all over the country as a precondition to the flourishing of these fundamental rights.

By no means was it an easy problem for the Constituent Assembly to draw up a simple list of fundamental rights. What has been finally adopted is the product of a difficult compromise. It is still too early to pronounce a judgement on the wisdom of the Assembly. One thing, however, is already clear. The Supreme Court of India has been deciding more cases dealing with Fundamental Rights[2] than those connected with the rest of the Constitution. The Court's decisions as the guardian of these rights have had, indeed, a salutary influence both on the Executive and the Legislature against whom those rights have been primarily guaranteed. The Court has been generally prompt and forthright in curbing legislative exuberance by declaring those enactments of Parliament and the State Legislatures invalid whenever it found them transgressing the defined limits within which they are permitted to impose reasonable limitations on the freedom of the individual. Similarly, it has successfully prevented on many occasions the excess and abuse of administrative power and the illegal and high-handed actions of the Executive. Further, every time the fundamental right of the individual has been upheld against the Executive and the Legislature, it has had wholesome and far-reaching repercussions. But while the Court has been thus rendering a remarkable service in safeguarding the Fundamental Rights embodied in the Constitution, it was unfortunate that it became the subject of an acute, nation-wide controversy through its decision in the Golak Nath case. In this case the Court was not only sharply divided — six against five — but it negatived its own consistent stand in a number of cases over a period of seventeen years. But even more important was the stand of the majority that the Fundamental Rights are outside the amendatory process

1 For a critical review of the operation of fundamental rights, see B.K. Sharma, "A Pragmatic Evaluation of Fundamental Rights", 1960 S.C.J. 18.

2. See R.V.R. Chandrasekhara Rao, "Fundamental Rights and the Problem of Judicial Review," 1961, II S.C.J. 71.

prescribed by the Constitution if the amendment seeks to abridge or take away any of these rights. Chief Justice Subba Rao who was the chief spokesman of the majority went to the extent of characterizing the fundamental rights as transcendental in nature, a claim which hardly any founding father of the Constitution would have made and in favour of which one finds little evidence in the entire debates in the Constituent Assembly. Moreover, it is hardly appealing to reason that certain constitutional provisions enacted at a particular time, however valid and important they might be at that time, will continue to be so for all time to come in a fast-moving and changing world.

Every constitution has, as an integral part of it, definite provisions dealing with the manner in which it can be amended. So has the Constitution of India. Part XX of the Constitution titled "Amendment of the Constitution" does not indicate any limitation, express or implied. If the Fundamental Rights were to be excluded it could have been titled "Amendment of the Constitution except Part III".

If the intention of the Constituent Assembly was to make these rights transcendental, the members of the Assembly would have expressed it either on the floor of the Assembly or later. But the members of the Constituent Assembly were members of the first Parliament and it was that Parliament which passed the First Amendment, modifying the scope of some of the Fundamental Rights. But nobody at any stage raised an argument of this type. Again, the Fourth Amendment which was necessitated by the interpretations of the Supreme Court was passed in 1954 when most of the founding fathers, including Ambedkar, were alive. Since he was then a leading member of the opposition, Ambedkar would not have kept quiet if Parliament was incompetent to amend the Fundamental Rights. In fact, Ambedkar's speech in the Constituent Assembly while moving the provisions dealing with the amending process bears ample testimony to his own acceptance of the possible need for amending the Fundamental Rights and Parliament's power to do so.

A close study of the decisions of the Supreme Court in four important cases — the Subodh Gopal case, the Kochunni case, the Golak Nath case and the Bank Nationalization case, each one dealing with property rights — will show how a narrow majority of judges of the Court has been displaying undue solicitude to property and too much of a conservative attitude in dealing with problems affecting property. It is gratifying to note, at the same time, the liberal outlook and attitude of the judges who held a different view. A typical example is the following observation of Justice S.R. Das who in the Subodh Gopal case said:

> It is futile to cling to our notions of absolute sanctity of individual liberty or private property and to wishfully think that our Constitution-makers have enshrined in our Constitution the notions of individual liberty and private property that prevailed in the sixteenth century when Hugo Grotius flourished, or in the eighteenth century when Blackstone wrote his Commentaries or when the Federal Constitution of America was framed. We must reconcile ourselves to the plain truth that emphasis has now unmistakably shifted from the individual to the community. We cannot overlook that the avowed purpose of our Constitution is to set up a welfare State by subordinating the social interest in individual liberty or property to the larger social interest in the rights of the community.

When the country has been passing through a momentous period of socio-economic change and planned development, it is only natural that conflicting viewpoints with regard to the competing claims of the individual and social control come to the forefront and judges like others get involved in these controversies. The twenty-fourth and twenty-fifth amendments of the Constitution and the marathon arguments and counterarguments adduced before the Supreme Court regarding the constitutional validity of these amendments, again, showed how deep and sharp are the differences that still exist among the custodians of the highest tribunal in the land. Indeed, Fundamental Rights are bound to produce the same conflicting situation in the years to come since the conflict between man and State is bound to continue and different individuals are apt to view them differently from time to time.

Despite the fact that some of the Rights have been substantially modified in scope as a result of constitutional amendments, the chapter on Fundamental Rights taken as a whole remains a formidable bulwark of individual liberty, a code of public conduct and a strong and sustaining basis of Indian democracy.

Nevertheless, a word of caution seems to be appropriate here. The fact that a remedy is available from the Supreme Court for the violation of every fundamental right does not mean in fact that it is available to all. This is because of the heavy cost involved in the process of moving the Court. Effective enforcement of these rights from the point of view of the ordinary Indian citizen is possible only when justice becomes less expensive, less complex and more speedy.

***

19

THE DIRECTIVE PRINCIPLES

PART IV of the Constitution dealing with the Directive Principles of State Policy provides one of the most novel and striking features of modern constitutional government. It seems that the framers of the Constitution were in this respect influenced most by the Constitution of the Irish Republic which embodies a chapter on 'Directive Principles of Social Policy'. The Irish themselves had, however, taken the idea from the Constitution of Republican Spain which was the first ever to incorporate such principles as part of a Constitution. But the idea of such principles can be traced back to the Declaration of the Rights of Man and Citizen proclaimed by revolutionary France and the Declaration of Independence by the American Colonies. The influence of these declarations was so profound on millions of people in Europe and America that they inspired organized efforts, on the one hand, to overthrow all forms of political tyranny, and, on the other, to compel the State to take positive measures for the removal of many antisocial practices which had been considered as normal in those days.

In more recent times, thinkers on political and social reforms who did not agree with the Marxian approach for the eradication of the ills and evils of modern society advocated such principles to be made the guiding force of State activity. The ideas of Jeremy Bentham, the political and social strand of the Liberal and Radical parties of Western Europe, the major principles of Fabian Socialism and, to some extent, those of Guild Socialism, are all taken to much of what is embodied in this Part of the Constitution. Ivor Jennings claims that the ghosts of Sidney and Beatrice Webb stalk through the pages of the entire text and this part of the Constitution expresses Fabian Socialism without the word 'socialism', 'for only the nationalisaiton of the means of production, distribution and exchange is missing'.[1] But this would be to give an exaggerated importance to the Fabian influence, for one finds other documents and proclamations of more recent date that could have influenced the framers even more. Mention has already been made of the Irish Constitution. The Sapru Committee had recommended a division of fundamental rights into two classes—judiciable and nonjudiciable.[2] The Constitution Act of India, 1935, itself provided for 'Instruments of Instructions' which were a fruitful idea. Ambedkar said:[3]

> The Directive Principles are like the Instruments which were issued to the Governor-General and the Governors of Colonies, and to those of India by the British Government under the 1935 Government of India Act. What is called 'Directive Principles' is merely another name

---

1. Jennings, *op. cit.*
2. Costitutional Proposals of the Sapru Committee (1946).
3. C.A.D. VII, p. 41.

for the Instrument of Instructions. The only difference is that they are instructions to the legislature and executive. Whoever captures power will not be free to do what he likes with it. In the exercise of it he will have to respect these instruments of instructions which are called Directive Principles. He cannot ignore them.

But there were other influences too. The Charter of the United Nations as well as the Universal Human Rights Chapter influenced the Constitution-makers. The discussions on the Charter of Human Rights were in progress during the same period as the Constituent Assembly was deliberating upon the Constitution.

It would however be wrong to suppose that the various principles embodied in this chapter are mere foreign borrowings or adaptations of principles of recent Western political or social philosophy. In fact, a number of these principles are entirely Indian, particularly those which formed an integral part of the very foundations of the national movement. Provisions dealing with village panchayats, cottage industries, prohibition, protection against cow-slaughter, Scheduled Castes, Scheduled Tribes and other socially and educationally backward classes, are all formally and essentially Indian and some of these were the cherished ideals for the recognition of which Gandhi had striven throughout his life.

As the title itself indicates, the principles embodied in this chapter are directives to the various governments and government agencies[1] (including even village panchayats) to be followed as fundamental in the governance of the country. It shall be the duty of the State to apply these principles in making laws.[2] Thus, they place an ideal before the legislators of India while they frame new legislation for the country's administration. They lay down a code of conduct for the administrators of India while they discharge their responsibilities as agents of the sovereign power of the nation. In short, the Directive Principles enshrine the fundamentals for the realization of which the State of India stands. They guide the path which will lead the people of India to achieve the noble ideals which the Preamble of the Constitution proclaims: Justice, social, economic and political; Liberty; Equality; Fraternity. It is this realization that impelled a member in the Constituent Assembly to demand the placing of this chapter immediately after the Preamble in order to give it 'greater sanctity' than others.[3] There was also a suggestion to change the title of the chapter to 'Fundamental Principles of State.'[4]

The Advisory Committee on Fundamental Rights had made a definite recommendation to the Constituent Assembly for the inclusion of such a chapter. The committee reported:

> We have come to the conclusion that in addition to these fundamental rights, the Constitution should include certain directives of State Policy which, though not cognisable in any court of law, should be regarded as fundamental in the governance of the country.[5]

Speaking about the purpose of this chapter, Ambedkar said:

> In enacting this Part of the Constitution, the Assembly is giving certain directions to the future legislature and the future executive to show in what manner they are to exercise the legislative and the executive power they will have. Surely it is not the intention to introduce in this part these principles as mere pious declarations. It is the intention of this Assembly that in

1. Ibid, pp. 477-8.
2. Article 37.
3. C.A.D. VII, p. 382.
4. Ibid., p. 473.
5. Para 2 of the Reprot.

future both the legislature and the executive should not merely pay lip-service to these principles but that they should be made the basis of all legislative and executive action that they may be taking hereafter in the matter of the governance of the country.[1]

There are nineteen articles of the Constitution that deal with the Directive Principles. These cover a wide range of State activity embracing economic, social, legal, educational, administrative, cultural and international problems. The most important of these are the following:

1. To secure and protect a social order which stands for the welfare of the people. (Art. 38).
2. In particular, the State shall direct its policy towards securing:

(a) adequate means of livelihood to all citizens;
(b) a proper distribution of the material resources of the community for the common good;
(c) the prevention of concentration of wealth to the common detriment;
(d) equal pay for equal work for both men and women;
(e) the protection of the strength and health of the workers and avoiding circumstances which force citizens to enter avocations unsuited to their age or strength; and
(f) the protection of childhood and youth against exploitation or moral and material abandonment. (Art. 39).

3. To provide free legal aid to ensure that opportunities for securing justice are not denied to any citizen by reason of economic or other disabilities (Art. 39A).

4. To organize village panchayats as units of self-government. (Art. 40).

5. To secure the right to work, education and public assistance in cases of undeserved want, such as unemployment, old age, sickness, etc. (Art. 41).

6. To secure just and humane conditions of work and maternity relief. (Art. 42).

7. To secure work, a living wage, a decent standard of life, leisure and social and cultural opportunities for people, and in particular to promote cottage industries. (Art. 43).

8. To secure the participation of workers in the management of undertakings engaged in any industry. (Art. 43A).

9. To secure a uniform civil code applicable to the entire country. (Art. 44).

10. To provide, within ten years from the commencement of the Constitution, free and compulsory education to all children up to the age of fourteen years. (Art. 45).

The Constitution Eighty-sixth Amendemnt Act of 2002 has amended this provision as follows :

45. Provision for early childhood care and education to children below the age of six years : The State shall endeavour to provide early childhood care and education for all children until they complete the age of six years.

Amendment of Article 51A :-

In Article 51A of the Constitution, after clause (j) the following clause shall be added, namely :

(k) Who is a parent or guardian to provide opportunities for education to his child or as the case may be, ward between the age of six and fourteen years.

11. To promote with special care the educational and economic interests of the weaker sections of the people, especially the Scheduled Castes and Tribes. (Art. 46).

12. To secure the improvement of public health and the prohibition of intoxicating drinks and drugs. (Art. 47).

13. To organize agriculture and animal husbandry on scientific lines and preserve and improve the breeds and prohibit the slaughter of cows, calves and other milch and draught cattle. (Art. 48).

---

1. C.A.D. VII, p. 476.

14. To protect and improve the environment and to safeguard the forests and wild life of the country. (Art. 48A).

15. To protect all monuments of historic interest and national importance. (Art. 49).

16. To bring about the separation of the judiciary from the executive. (Art. 50).

17. To endeavour to secure:

(a) the promotion of international peace and security;

(b) the maintenance of just and honourable relations between nations;

(c) foster respect for international law and treaty obligations in the dealings of organised people with one another; and

(d) the settlement of international disputes by arbitration. (Art. 51).

Taken together, these principles lay down the foundations on which a new democratic India will be built up. They represent the minimum of the ambitions and aspirations cherished by the people of India, set as a goal to be realized in a reasonable period of time. Indeed, when the State of India translates these principles into reality, she can justly claim to be a Welfare State.

Principles in Practice

How far the State has moved, so far, towards the realization of these principles is a question that deserves an answer in this context. It may be stated in general that the achievements of the first thirty-five years have not made the country a welfare state. Nevertheless, no impassioned observer can miss the direction towards which it is moving, if not fast, at least at a reasonable pace.

The efforts of the State to translate the Directive Principles into reality are concentrated primarily in the national Five Year Plans, the first of which was initiated soon after the inauguration of the Constitution. The central objective of public policy and national endeavour as evinced through these plans has been the promotion of rapid and balanced economic development which will raise living standards and open out to the people new opportunities for a richer and more varied life. Such development is intended to expand the community's productive power and provide the environment in which there is scope for the expression and application of diverse faculties and urges. It follows, therefore, that the pattern of development must be related to the basic objectives which the Constitution has kept in view. These objectives are defined and explained from time to time in order that they may guide the State in planning as well as ensure their conformity with the Directive Principles. The basic objectives have been summed up in the phase 'socialistic pattern of society'. What it stands for is explained by the Second Five Year Plan in the following terms:

> Essentially this means that the basic criterion for determining the lines of advance must not be private profit but social gain, and that the pattern of development and the structure of socio-economic relations should be so planned that they result not only in *appreciable increases in national income and employment, but also in greater equality in incomes and wealth.*[1] Major decisions regarding production, consumption and investment — in fact, all significant socio-economic relationships — must be made by agencies informed by social purpose. The benefits

1. Emphasis ours.

of economic development must accrue more and more to the relatively less privileged classes of society, and there should be a progressive reduction of the concentration of incomes, wealth and economic power. The problem is to create a milieu in which the small man who has so far had little opportunity of perceiving and participating in the immense possibilities of growth through organised effort is enabled to put in his best in the increase of a higher standard of life for himself and increased prosperity for the country. In the process, he rises in economic and social status.... For creating the appropriate conditions, the State has to take on heavy responsibilities as the principal agency speaking for an acting on behalf of the community as a whole....[1]

Economic policy and institutional changes have to be planned in a manner that would secure economic advance along democratic and egalitarian lines. Democracy, it has been said, is a way of life rather than a particular set of institutional arrangements. The same could be said of the socialistic pattern.[2]

The Third Five Year Plan spells out even more explicitly the meaning and implications of the Indian concept of socialist pattern. In the first chapter of this document[3] titled "Objectives of Planned Development", it is stated:

Progress towards socialism lies along a number of directions, each enhancing the value of others. Above all, a socialist economy must be efficient, progressive in its approach to science and technology, and capable of growing steadily to a level at which the well being of the mass of the population can be secured.... In the second place a socialist economy should ensure equality of opportunity to every citizen.... In the third place, through the public policies it pursues, a socialist economy must not only reduce economic and social disparities which already exist, but must also ensure that rapid expansion of the economy is achieved without concentration of economic power and growth of monopoly. Finally, a society developing on the basis of democracy and socialism is bound to place the greatest stress on social values and incentives and developing a sense of common interest and obligations among all sections of the society.[4]

These statements of objectives make it clear that the Directive Principles are not allowed to remain in the Constitution as platitudes, but are systematically put into application with a view to transforming Indian society and bringing about a social order in conformity with these principles.[5] It is difficult to bring within the scope of this discussion a detailed survey of the concrete measure the State has taken so far and the results achieved therefrom. Yet, one may broadly indicate the trends which would help the better appreciation of the situation. For example, there has been a substantial increase in the vesting of both ownership and control of material resources of the community in the State during the first three decades. The great multipurpose river valley projects such as Bhakra-Nangal, Damodar Valley and Hirakud, iron and steel producing centres such as Bhilai, Rourkela, Durgapur and Bokaro, shipbuilding centres like Vizag, Cochin and other concerns such as the Sindri Fertilizers, Hindustan Machine Tools, Chittaranjan Locomotives, Hindustan Aircraft etc. which contribute substantially to the basic economic development of the country, are owned and managed by the State. The choice, in fact, is being forced on the State almost continuously and as a result new economic functions are being undertaken by the State machinery.

1. *Second Five Year Plan*, p. 22. 2. Ibid., p. 24.

3. This chapter is reported to have been written by Prime Minister Nehru himself.

4. *Third Five Year Plan* (1961), pp. 9-10.

5. The Forty-second Amendment of the Constitution added the term 'socialism' to the Preamble of the Constitution making socialism one of the basic objectives of the Constitution.

It is true that the State has not yet moved very far on the road of achieving objectives such as full employment, public assistance during old age, sickness, etc. Nevertheless, most of them have found a place in the development plans. Great emphasis was laid on the creation of employment opportunities. Steps are being taken to bring into being a scheme of unemployment insurance. A limited scheme of workmen's insurance against sickness, accident and disease is already in operation. Minimum wages are fixed in a number of spheres of employment. Equal wages for equal work are being paid to both men and women in almost every area of activity. The community development programme which has been in operation in many parts of the country aimed at the transformation of the rural economy, particularly the reorganization of agriculture and animal husbandry on scientific lines. Besides, most of the States have passed laws designed to prohibit the slaughter of cows, calves and other milch and draught cattle.[1] Mention has already been made of a number of laws which have been passed with a view to protecting children and youth against exploitation.[2] The Central Council of Health established in 1952 deals with matters connected with health, hygiene, nutrition, etc. on a national basis. Great emphasis has been placed on Panchayati Raj institutions all over the country with the passing of the Seventy-third Amendment of the Constitution in 1993 and decentralisation in administration has been steadily in progress.

The passing of a uniform civil code is not an easy measure in India where adherents of every religion have their own personal laws. The Hindu Code that is being passed in instalments (*e.g.*, the Hindu Marriage Act, 1955, and the Hindu Succession Act, 1956) is a right move towards the ultimate realization of a uniform civil code for the entire country. In the field of free and compulsory primary education for children, great strides have already been made. But it is not widely realized that the ten years' limit that was set in the Constitution to make such education available to every child in the country was impossible to adhere to. It seems that India will require another decade or two to make this principle a practical proposition.[3] A number of measures have already been taken to promote the educational and economic interests of the weaker sections of the people, especially the Scheduled Castes and Tribes. With a view to specially benefitting the backward class of citizens economically, efforts are being made for the setting up of more cottage and small-scale industries and also to give liberal financial aid for such activities undertaken by them. A vigorous policy of prohibition was inaugurated with the adoption of the Constitution, and at least a few States in India have achieved the goal of complete prohibition of intoxicating liquors throughout their territory. Unfortunately, in later years, prohibition seems to have got a setback almost throughout the country. The principle of the complete separation of the judiciary from the executive is yet to be fully realized. But every State has adopted a definite programme in this respect and, according to this, every year a certain number of districts are being brought under the scheme.[4] Finally, it is perhaps unnecessary to detail the efforts made by India towards the promotion of international understanding, peace and security. Suffice it to say that her contribution in this field is widely and generously acknowledged by almost all nations of the world.

---

1. See in this connection Quareshi *vs.* State of Bihar 1958, S.C.J. 983.
2. *e.g.* see The Women's and Children's Institution (Licensing) Act of 1958.
3. The present expectation is that by 2000 universal free primary education will become a near reality throughout the country. See Shame of Illiteracy by K.B. Sahay in Hindustan Times, 24 October, 1997.
4. So far the States of Andhra Pradesh, Maharashtra, Kerala, Assam, Gujarat, Himachal Pradesh, Delhi, Karnataka, Madhya Pradesh, Orissa, Rajasthan, Tamil Nadu, Uttar Pradesh, West Bengal and Punjab have completed the process.

Non-Justiciable Character

According to Article 37, Directive Principles, though they are fundamental in the governance of the country and it shall be the duty of the State to apply these principles in making laws, are expressly made non-justiciable. It means that the Courts in India including the Supreme Court have no power to enforce them. This is in contrast with the position of Fundamental Rights which are justiciable and, therefore, enforceable by the courts of law. Thus, while there is a judicial remedy for every violation of a fundamental right, there is none for the enforcement of Directive Principles. Would this mean that these are a set of platitudes designed by clever politicians to hoodwink the credulous Indian masses? Is there no remedy at all if the government that is in power ignores and even flagrantly violates these principles which are of a fundamental character in the governance of the country? The answer is 'no' to the first and 'yes' to the second. No doubt, there is no direct judicial remedy, but other remedies there are and they are reasonably effective.

The Twenty-fifth Amendment of the Constitution (1971) has given precedence to the principles embodied in Article 39(b) and (c) over fundamental rights embodied in Articles 14, 19 and 31. This is indeed a revolutionary measure. The Supreme Court also played its role in this connection by declaring that primary education is a Fundamental Right (Unnikrishnan *vs.* State of Andhra Pradesh, 1993 SCC 645).

It must be remembered in this connection that the Constitution establishes a democratic form of government, a representative government. It is also a responsible government, one that is continuously and always responsible for all its actions to the representatives of the people and through them to the people in general. Those who are in power are there because the people of India, who have been guaranteed universal adult suffrage, have given them that power. They are not the masters of the people but their 'servants'. They are voted into power to translate into practice the provisions of the Constitution which the people have given unto themselves. If they fail in this solemn duty, then they have no right to continue in office and they can be and should be removed from office when the stocktaking of their work is done at the end of every five years at the time of the general elections in the country. Since the Constitution ensures, free choice by the people from amongst competing candidates with differing policies and programmes, the electorate can choose those who, in their opinion, are likely to transform these principles into reality. These directives, thus seen, constitute a kind of basic standard of national conscience and those who violate its dictates do so at the risk of being ousted from the positions of responsibility to which they have been chosen. The agents of the State at a given time may not be answerable to a court of law for their breach of these principles, but they cannot escape facing a higher and more powerful court which will at regular intervals do the reckoning. When a member in the Constituent Assembly moved an amendment which sought to make the Directive Principles justiciable, another pointed out:

> There is no use being carried away by sentiments. We must be practical. We cannot go on introducing various provisions here which any government, if it is not indifferent to public opinion, can ignore. It is not a Court that can enforce these provisions or rights. It is the public opinion and the strength of public opinion that is behind a demand that can enforce these provisions. Once in four (or five) years elections will take place and then it is open to the electorate not to send the very persons who are indifferent to public opinion. That is the real sanction and not the sanction of any court of law.[1]

1. C.A.D. VII, p. 475.

There are, however, two important questions that are intimately related to the non-justiciable character of these principles and have created some confusion in the minds of those interested in India's constitutional law. Of these, the first deals with the attitude of the President or the Governor towards a Bill containing provisions that contravene any of these principles. One view is that since the President, or the Governor, as the case may be, has taken oath to defend and uphold the Constitution, he should refuse to give his assent to a Bill which violated a Directive Principle.[1] Ambedkar opposed this view, characterized it as a 'dangerous doctrine' and contended that 'the Constitution does not warrant it'.[2] The apprehension that these principles might lead to a conflict between the President and the Prime Minister or between the Governors and the State Cabinets was expressed in the Constituent Assembly itself. 'What happens if the Prime Minister of India ignores these instructions?'[3] There has so far been no occasion for such a conflict. Yet the problem has to be faced if and when it arises. The main factor that should be remembered in this context is the system of government which the Constitution establishes — a parliamentary system under which the executive is responsible to the legislature. So long as the executive has the confidence of the legislature, a constitutional head of the State will find it difficult to go against the will of the legislature.

It is also relevant to remember in this context that the President is not directly elected by the people and hence can claim no direct mandate. If at any time Parliament or a State Legislature decides to pass a law which contravenes a Directive Principle, there must be weighty reasons for it. And if it is the considered opinion of the legislature to pass such a law and if the voting on it reflects a substantial majority in its favour, the President will have little justification to withhold his assent to the Bill. Perhaps, the President could send the Bill back to Parliament for reconsideration in the light of his objections to it . And if Parliament passes it a second time, the President will have no justification to withhold his assent. After all, Parliament alone is competent to change even the Directive Principles by a constitutional amendment. Moreover, however fundamental these principles might be today, they can have no claim to permanent sanctity. They cannot be considered as embodying eternal verities. As society changes in character, its needs also undergo corresponding changes. What is considered as fundamental today may become inessential and unimportant a hundred years hence or earlier. Under a democratic system, all these questions are to be determined first by the representatives of the people and finally by the people themselves. Hence, it would seem wise for the President not to use his veto power over a Bill that is passed by the legislature merely on the ground that in his view it violates a directive principle.

Fundamental Rights *vs.* Directive Principles[4]

The second question is this: Where there is a conflict between a Fundamental Right and a Directive principle, which should prevail? This question was answered by the Supreme Court , for the first time, in Champakam Dorairajan's case.[5] Speaking for a unanimous Court, Justice S.R. Das said:

1. V.G. Ramachandran, S.C.J. 1955, p. 37.
2. Foreword to Basu's *A Commentary on the Constitution of India*, p. vii.
3. *A Commentary on the Constitution of India*, pp. 263-4.
4. For a general discussion discussion on the subject see Chandra Appa Rao, "Fundamental Rights vis-a-vis Directive Principles in the Constitution." (1961) II S.C.J. 11.
5. 1952, S.C.J. 354.

The Directive Principles of State Policy which by Article 37 are expressly made unenforceable by a court cannot override the provisions found in Part III which, notwithstanding other provisions, are expressly made enforceable by writs, orders or directions under Article 32. The chapter on Fundamental Rights is sacrosanct and not liable to be abridged by any legislative or executive act or order except to the extent provided in the particular Article in Part III. The Directive Principles of State Policy have to conform to and run subsidiary to the chapter on Fundamental Rights. In our opinion, that is the correct way in which the provisions found in Part III and Part IV have to be understood.

It was mainly this decision of the Court that led to a constitutional amendment to Article 15 in 1951, under which the State was permitted to make special provisions to protect the interest of socially and educationally backward classes. A year later, when the Court dealt with the Zamindari abolition cases, its attitude was considerably modified. In the State of Bihar *vs.* Kameswar Singh,[1] the Court used the Directive Principles for its guidance in determining a crucial question on which the validity of the Bihar Act hinged. The question was whether there was any 'public purpose' to justify the legislation which acquired compulsorily vast lands of private owners. Answering the question, Justice Mahajan said, after quoting Article 37:

Now it is obvious that the concentration of big blocks of land in the hands of a few individuals is contrary to the principles on which the Constitution of India is based. The purpose of the acquisition contemplated by the Act, therefore, is to do away with the concentration of big blocks of land and means of production in the hands of a few individuals and to distribute the ownership and control of the material resources which come in the hands of the State, so as to subserve the common good as best as possible.

Here the judge was absolutely guided by the Directive Principles. Justice S.R. Das substantially reproduced the same language in the same case. After quoting Articles 38 and 39 of the chapter on Directive Principles, he said:

In the light of this new outlook, what I ask is the purpose of the State in adopting measures for the acquisition of Zamindaries and the interests of intermediaries. Surely, it is to subserve the common good by bringing the land which feeds and sustains the community and also produces wealth by its forest, mineral and other resources, under State ownership or control. This State ownership or control over land is a necessary preliminary step towards the implementation of Directive Principles of State Policy and it cannot but be a public purpose.

This question came up again a few years later in the course of arguments in the President's reference to the Supreme Court of the Kerala Education Bill. The Court had no hesitation to uphold its earlier stand in the Zamindari abolition cases, namely, that the Directive Principles cannot be altogether ignored by it in spite of their non-justiciable character.[2] However, the Court is certain that the Directive Principles cannot override the categorical restriction imposed on the legislative power of the State through the Fundamental Rights. "A harmonious interpretation has to be placed upon the Constitution and so interpreted that it means the State should certainly implement the directive principles but it must do so in such a way that its laws do not take away or abridge the fundamental rights, for otherwise the protecting provisions of Chapter III will be a mere rope of sand."[3]

---

1. *Op. cit.*
2. See in this connection Chandra Appa Rao, "Judicial Analysis of the Directive Principles of State Policy", (1961) I S.C.J. 83.
3. Quareshi *vs.* The State of Bihar (1958) S.C.J., p. 983. The Supreme Court will have to modify its stand substantially in view of the Twenty-fifth Amendment of the Constitution (1971).

Speaking on the motion by which he introduced the Fourth Amendment to the Constitution in Parliament, Prime Minister Nehru observed that where there was a conflict between a Fundamental Right and a Directive Principle, the latter should prevail. This opinion may appear to be in direct conflict with the view of the Supreme Court. But on closer examination it will be seen that the conflict is apparent rather than real. For, as far as the Supreme Court is concerned, where there is a clear conflict between the two, it should uphold the Fundamental Right being justiciable, against the Directive Principle, which is a non-justiciable right. But this solution is only a judicial solution of the matter. The courts cannot go further than that, but Parliament can. The final solution is arrived at only when the social conflict arising out of the competing claims of a justiciable and a non-justiciable right are resolved. The guiding principle here is the superiority of the social interest over that of the individual. To facilitate the putting into effect of this principle, the Constitution may have to be amended and the Directive Principle allowed to prevail. The Constitution was amended seven times (the First, Second, Fourth, Seventeenth, Twenty-fifth, Forty-second and Forty-fourth Amendments) with this object in view. It should, however, be added that whenever the Court is called upon to resolve a conflict between a Fundamental Right and a Directive Principle, it is the duty of the Court to resolve the conflict with an eye on the fundamental spirit of the Constitution and with a view to harmonizing differences to the extent that is possible and feasible.

The significance of Directive Principles in relation to that of Fundamental Rights can be determined only by making a reference to the object of the Constitution-makers in making these principles an integral part of the Constitution. According to Supreme Court justices Hegde and Mukherjea: "The Fundamental Rights and the Directive Principles constitute the 'Conscience' of our Constitution. The purpose of the Fundamental Rights is to create an egalitarian society, to free all citizens from coercion or restriction by society and to make liberty available for all. The purpose of the Directive Principles is to fix certain social and economic goals for immediate attainment by bringing about a non-violent social revolution. Through such a social revolution, the Constitution seeks to fulfil the basic needs of the common man and to change the structure of our society. It aims at making the Indian masses free in the positive sense. Without faithfully implementing the Directive Principles, it is not possible to achieve the welfare state contemplated by the Constitution."[1]

In the words of Justice Chandrachud (as he then was), "Our Constitution aims at bringing about a synthesis between Fundamental Rights and the Directive Principles of State Policy, by giving to the former a pride of place and to the latter a place of permanence. Together, not individually, they form the core of the Constitution. Together, not individually, they constitute its true conscience."[2] As has already been pointed out, they represent the basic principles which aim at the creation of a Welfare State.[3] Taken together, these principles form a charter of economic and social democracy in India. On the one hand, they are assurances to the people as to what they may expect, while on the other, they are directives to the governments, Central and State, as to what policies they ought to pursue. It is unfair to the people as well as what policies they ought to pursue. It is unfair to the people as well as inconsistent with the spirit of the Constitution to allow those principles

1. (1973) 4 SCC 225. 2. (1973) 4 SCC 225.

3. See Justice K.K. Mathew, the Welfare State, Rule of Law and Natural Justice.

to remain pious wishes. Every effort should be made by the representatives of the people and the agents of the government to translate them into reality. Nothing should be allowed to stand in their way, even the fundamental rights guaranteed to the individual. After all, the progress and welfare of society as a whole should not be hampered by the rights of the individual. This is why every fundamental right is subject to reasonable restrictions in the interests of the general public, whether such restrictions are on account of public order, morality, decency, health or anything else. It is in this sense that the Fundamental Rights are to subserve the Directive Principles. Indeed, there can be no real conflict between the two. They are intimately related to and inseparably bound up with each other.

The Value of These Principles

A constitution framed in the middle of the twentieth century could hardly do without a chapter on directive principles of the type the Indian Constitution has. The establishment of political democracy is a fundamental aim of the Constitution. But that in itself is not enough. The sustaining forces of that political democracy have to be carefully built up. The most effective force which will sustain a political democracy is the simultaneous existence of an economic democracy. Where there is no economic democracy, political democracy is bound to degenerate soon into a dictatorship. If the fundamental rights guarantee a political democracy in India, the Directive Principles ensure the eventual emergence of an economic democracy to sustain the former. Thus, the Directive Principles of State Policy become the greatest guarantee for a genuine democracy in India. In the light of these considerations, it would betray a lack of discernment to consider these directives as a mere political manifesto without any legal sanction,[1] or to characterize them as vague and indefinite serving no useful purpose[2] or to dismiss them as a mere moral homily. The last five decades and more demonstrate that such criticism has neither substance nor relevance today. If K.T. Shah were alive now, he should certainly have revised the opinion that he expressed in the Constituent Assembly that these principles "are like a cheque on a bank payable when able, only when the resources of the bank permit."[3]

Another apparently weighty criticism of the Directive Principles is implied in the question whether it is worth-while to insert in a constitution of today a collection of political principles taken from the experience of the nineteenth century England or Western Europe, and to deem them to be suitable for India in the middle of the twentieth century.[4] The question whether they would be suitable for the twenty-first century when the Constitution is hoped to be still in operation is difficult to answer. It is probable that they may become outmoded by then. Who can predict the precise nature of the potentialities of an atomic or a hydrogen age? It may revolutionize the whole economic system of the present day and convert India into a land of plenty where all human wants in the material field are fully and instantaneously satisfied. In such a state of affairs, the Directive Principles will indeed look not only outmoded but even reactionary. But as far as the twentieth century was concerned, India had yet to reach in many spheres of economic activity a standard

---

1. K.C. Wheare, "India's New Constitution", 54, C.W.N.
2. M. Ramaswamy, Can Bar Rev. 14.
3. C.A.D. VII, p. 479.
4. Ivor Jennings, *op. cit.*

comparable to that which existed even in the nineteenth century in Western Europe. Thus, even assuming that the Directive Principles reflect the nineteenth century political ideas of the West, their value in twentieth century India was not lost. Besides, it is not quite correct to characterize these principles as borrowings from aborad. As has been pointed out elsewhere, there are many provision in this chapter which prove the originality of the Constitution-makers and reflect the genius of the Indian people.

If and when the Directive Principles become outmoded, they can be suitably amended or altogether abolished. The process of amending these provisions is simple. But by the time such amendments take place, India will have benefited immensely by the Directive Principles, and an economic democracy will have sent its roots deep into the Indian soil and the present form in which these principles are embodied will have realized its goal. Moreover, these principles would have become part and parcel of the Indian heritage. Thus, one can see the immense educative value of these principles. They will instil in the minds and thoughts of the coming generations of Indian youth the fundamental values of a stable political order and a dynamic economic system. A constitution is primarily concerned with the present. The future will take care of itself if the present is built on solid foundations. It is quite unnecessary, therefore, to think of the distant future with reference to certain provisions of a constitutional document.

The real importance of the Directive Principles is that they contain the positive obligations of the State towards its citizens. No one can say that these obligations are of an insignificant type, or that even if they are fulfilled, the pattern of society in India will still remain more or less the same. In fact they are revolutionary in character and yet to be achieved in a constitutional manner. Herein lies the real value of embodying these principles as an integral part of the Constitution. Through the Directive Principles of State Policy, the Constitution of India will steer clear of the two extremes, a proletarian dictatorship which destroys the liberty of the individual and a capitalist oligarchy which hampers the economic security of the masses.

***

20

FUNDAMENTAL DUTIES

The Forty-second Amendment of the Constitution added a new Part to the Constitution—Part IV-A-incorporating ten Fundamental Duties of the citizen under Article 51-A. "What is the use of mere enumeration of such duties in the Constitution in the absence of suitable provisions to enforce them?" Critics may ask such a question and it is not easy to give a very satisfactory answer. However, the intention is quite clear and that is to place before the country a code of conduct which the citizens are expected to follow in their actions and conduct. The Fundamental Duties are as follows:

It shall be the duty of every citizen of India

(a) to abide by the Constitution and respect its ideals and institutions, the National Flag and the National Anthem;

(b) to cherish and follow the noble ideals which inspired our national struggle for freedom;

(c) to uphold and protect the sovereignty, unity and integrity of India;

(d) to defend the country and render national service when called upon to do so;

(e) to promote harmony and the spirit of common brotherhood amongst all the people of India transcending religious, linguistic and regional or sectional diversities; to renounce practices derogatory to the dignity of women;

(f) to value and preserve the rich heritage of our composite culture;

(g) to protect and improve the natural environment including forests, lakes, rivers and wild life, and to have compassion for living creatures;

(h) to develop the scientific temper, humanism and the spirit of inquiry and reform;

(i) to safeguard public property and to abjure violence;

(j) to strive towards excellence in all spheres of individual and collective activity, so that the nation constantly rises to higher levels of endeavour and achievement.

Although these Duties were on the statute book, no concrete steps had been taken by the Governments both at the Centre and in the States for years. Like several Directive Principles of State Policy, these Duties also remained in the Constitution as a set of platitudes.

Perhaps that is the reason why in May 1998 the Supreme Court issued a notice to the Government of India to enquire about the Government's plan to operationalise the suggestion to teach Fundamental Duties to the citizens of the country. The Court's notice was based on a letter which it received from Justice Ranganath Misra (former Chief Justice of the Supreme Court) stating that "all of us are experiencing to our horror degrading human behaviour in society every day. The deterioration is gradually becoming sharper and unless this fall is immediately arrested and a remedial measure found out and enforced, the situation would not improve... Fundamental Duties have remained in the Constitution Book and have not come out to reach even the class of people who handle the Constitution".

It has been further stated that "the Constitution within a quarter of a century, brought about a right-oriented society. The Indian approach of ensuring rights through performance of one's duties was totally abandoned. Article 51-A in its ten clauses covers several aspects, the lack of which has been responsible for today's evils. If society becomes duty based, every one in India should turn attention on performance of duties and through such performance ensure and be entitled to the rights of a citizen".

As a nation-building measure, teaching Fundamental Duties in every educational institution and as a measure of in-service training everywhere is necessary as these cannot be inculcated in our citizens unless these are brought into their minds and living process through teaching and education. It is the obligation of the State to educate the citizens in the matter of Fundamental Duties so that a right balance between rights and duties may emerge.

In response to the Supreme Court's notice, the Government of India set-up a Committee to examine all aspects of operationalisation of Fundamental Duties for an effective inculcation of the same by the citizens.

The terms of reference of the Committee were as follows:

(i) To develop a package for teaching Fundamental Duties at primary, secondary, senior secondary and university levels.

(ii) To decide the activities as part of curriculum and co-curricular activities.

(iii) To review the existing programme already being implemented by the NCERT* under the National Curricular Framework and need for identifying additional inputs into it.

(iv) To develop programme packages for pre-service/in-service training of teachers at various levels.

(vi) To develop a separate package for the training of citizens through non-formal education/adult education programme/media (print, electronic, etc.)

In its Interim Report submitted in 1999, the Committee has emphasised the following:

Standards in Public Life: It is the duty of every citizen to obey the constitutional mandate. Every holder of a public office has to superadd to his duties, as a citizen, the additional duties imposed by virtue of the office she/he holds. Sensitivity of all enforcement agencies is essential for realising the promise held out in the Constitution. It is important to draw our attention to "The Seven Principles of Public Life" contained in the First Report of the United Kingdom's Committee on Standards in Public Life — Vol-I by Lord Nolan, Chairman, which are reproduced below:

*National Council for Educational Research and Training.

Selflessness: Holders of public office should take decisions solely in terms of the public interest. They should not do so in order to gain financial or other material benefits for themselves, their family or their friends.

Integrity: Holders of public office should not place themselves under any financial or other obligation to outside individuals or organisations that might influence them in the performance of their official duties.

Objectivity: In carrying out public business, including making public appointments, awarding contracts, or recommending individuals for rewards and benefits, holders of public office should make choices on merit.

Accountability: Holders of public office are accountable for their decisions and actions to the public and must submit themselves to whatever scrutiny is appropriate to their office.

Openness: Holders of public office should be as open as possible about all the decisions and actions they take. They should give reasons for their decisions and restrict information only when the wider public interest clearly demands.

Honesty: Holders of public office have a duty to declare any private interests relating to their public duties and to take steps to resolve any conflicts arising in a way that protects the public interest.

Leadership: Holders of public office should promote and support these principles by leadership and example.

National Policy on Education 1986/1992: A significant exhortation in the National Policy on Education (1986) with modifications undertaken in 1992 incorporates the basic spirit of Article 51-A and reads thus: "The National System of Education will be based on a national curricular framework which contains a common core along with other components that are flexible. The common core will include the history of India's freedom movement, the constitutional obligations and other contents essential to nurture national identity. These elements will cut across subject areas and will be designed to promote values such as India's common cultural heritage, egalitarianism, democracy and secularism, equality of the sexes, protection of the environment, removal of social barriers, observance of the small family norm and inculcation of the scientific temper. All educational programmes will be carried on in strict conformity with secular value".

Against the conceptual backdrop of such deliberations, the Committee applied its mind to a multiplicity of issues concerning Fundamental Duties. It took stock of some of the judicial decisions relevant to enforcement of Fundamental Duties, studied schemes or programmes related to National Integration and Communal Harmony, Culture and Values and Environment as already in operation. It undertook analysis of school curriculum, programmes of Non-formal and Adult Education as well as teacher education curriculum from the standpoint of Fundamental Duties and also attempted ascertaining the status of Fundamental Duties in higher and professional education.

The Committee noted that a number of judicial decisions are available towards enforcement of several provisions of Article 51-A. What is needed is their operationalisation in compliance of the provisions of the various Acts. Also the educational system has to create proper and graded curricular inputs from early years of education to the higher and professional levels of education.

There is no finality in these efforts but a continuance of endeavour in achieving the objectives related to the values underlying the constitutional provisions. They require a constant reminder to the citizen to continue to strive towards display of better and better citizenship behaviour so necessary for a patriotic fervour. These aspects are to be nurtured through educational programmes, through informal, non-formal, formal and media interventions.

Although the Fundamental Duties like the Directive Principles of State Policy cannot be enforced by the judiciary, the Court can certainly take them into consideration while interpreting a law which is amenable to more than one interpretation. For example, Article 51-A (g) regarding protection of environment has come up before the High Courts and the Supreme Court again and again, and the Courts have been responding positively in the interest of environmental protection.

In the ultimate analysis, however, the only way to bring adherence to Fundamental Duties is through a vigorous public opinion all over the country. Our educational institutions and voluntary agencies can do much in highlighting the values of these Duties and giving a lead in upholding the need to adhere to them for the orderly progress of our society. There has been too much emphasis on Fundamental Rights hitherto. Hereafter, we should have equal emphasis on Fundamental Duties also.

***

PART V

THE GOVERNMENT OF THE UNION

21

THE UNION EXECUTIVE

THE CONSTITUTION of India has adopted the British model of the Cabinet system of responsible government. On the question of the form of government, opinion in the Constituent Assembly was at first divided. There were those who advocated the adoption of the presidential system of government prevalent in the United States of America.[1] They had two major arguments in support of their view. Firstly, the presidential form of government enables the executive head (the President) to be elected directly by the people. A presidential system could ensure stability as the head of the Executive is elected for a fixed period.[2] However, those who advocated the presidential system formed only a small minority in the Assembly. At least one member pleaded for the Swiss form of Collegiate Executive which combined the merits of both presidential and parliamentary systems by providing stability and responsibility at the same time.[3] As against these, the overwhelming majority was decisively in favour of the cabinet system of government.

The decision to adopt the cabinet system was the result of a long discussion in the Assembly in one of its earlier sessions. It had in its support the favourable recommendation of the Constitution Committee (for the Union Government) presided over by Nehru. The two issues which were raised during the discussion were: (i) What would make for the strongest Executive consistently with a democratic constitutional structure? (ii) What was the form of Executive which was suited to the conditions of this country? Giving his views in answer to these questions, K.M. Munshi said:

> The strongest government and the most elastic executive have been found to be in England and that is because the executive powers vest in the Cabinet supported by a majority in the Lower House which has financial powers under the Constitution. As a result, it is the rule of the majority in the legislature, for it supports its leaders in the Cabinet, which advises the head of the State, namely, the King. The King is thus placed above party. He is made really the symbol of the impartial dignity of the Constitution. The Government in England is found strong and elastic under all circumstances....
>
> We must not forget a very important fact that, during the last hundred years, Indian public life has largely drawn upon the traditions of British constitutional law. Most of us have looked up to the British model as the best. For the last thirty or forty years some kind of responsibility has been introduced in the governance of this country. Our constitutional traditions have become parliamentary

1. K.T. Shah was the most ardent champion of this group. C.A.D. VII, pp. 975-80.
2. Ibid., p. 284.
3. Ibid., p. 296.

and we have now all our Province functioning more or less on the British model. Today, the Dominion Government of India is functioning as a full-fledged parliamentary government. After this experience, why should we go back upon the tradition that has been built for over a hundred years and try a novel experiment?....[1]

These considerations were reinforced by two additional arguments of special significance from Alladi Krishnaswami Aiyar.[2] The first of these related to the form of government in the States. A presidential system at the Centre postulated a similar system in the States as well. This meant that

The Rulers of the States would again be invested with real executive power and the legislature be confined purely to their legislative functions. It will be against the marked tendency of the times. It will create insuperable difficulties in the Indian States.

Secondly:

There are obvious difficulties in the way of working the Presidential system. Unless there is some kind of close union between the Legislature and the Executive, it is sure to result in a spoils system.... Parliament may take one line of action and the Executive may take another line of actin. An infant democracy cannot afford, under modern conditions, to take the risk of a perpetual cleavage, feud or conflict or threatened conflict between the Legislature and the Executive. The object of the present constitutional structure is to prevent a conflict between the Executive and the Legislature and to promote harmony between the different parts of the governmental system.... After weighing the pros and cons of the Parliamentary Executive as they obtain in Great Britain, in the Dominions and in some of the Continental Constitutions, and the Presidential type of government as it obtains in the United States of America, the Indian Constitution has adopted the institution of Parliamentary Executive.

Prime Minister Nehru also spoke in the Assembly on this subject and said that after giving 'anxious thought to this matter' they had come to the conclusion that emphasis should be given to the 'ministerial character of the government and power resided in the Ministry and in the Legislature and not in the President as such.

Office of the President

Since India is a Republic, the Constitution provides for a President of India and the executive power of the Union Government, including the supreme command of the defence forces, is vested in him. The Constitution prescribed only simple qualifications for a presidential candidate. He should be a citizen of India who has completed the age of 35 years and is qualified to be elected as a member of the House of the people. No person who holds any office of profit under the Government of India or any State Government or local authority is eligible for election as President. But there are certain positions in the Government which are excluded from the scope of this provision. These are the offices of the President, Vice President, Governors and Ministers of the Central and State Governments. The President not be a member of Parliament or a State Legislature. Any member of a legislature who is elected as President shall cease to be such a member on the date he assumes the office of President. Further, the President is prohibited from holding any other office of profit. He is entitled to have his official residence free of rent. He is also entitled to such salaries, allowances and privileges as may be determined by Parliament. At present, his salary is fixed at Rs. 50,000 a month. His salaries and allowances cannot be diminished during his term of office. He is also entitled for an annual pension of Rs. 3 lakhs on the expiry of his term or on resignation.

1.C.A.D. VII, p. 984. 2. Ibid., pp. 985-6.

Election

The President is elected for a period of five years by an electoral college which is composed of (i) the elected members of Parliament and (ii) the elected members of the State Legislative Assemblies. With a view to ensuring uniformity in representation of the different States at the presidential election and party between the States as a whole and the Union, the Constitution has prescribed an ingenius method. Normally, it should have been possible to achieve this uniformity by the simple device of assigning each member of the electoral college one vote. Such uniformity would however have been invidious because in different States different ratios prevailed between the population and the number of legislators. For example, in one State it may be one representative for every 50,000 of the population while in another the proportion may be one to 75,000 or more. The most populous State of Union, Uttar Pradesh, has only 425 members in the Legislative Assembly for a population of over 140 million, while Assam has 126 members for a population of about 25 million. That being so, the problem was to ensure that the votes cast will have a value in proportion to the population that the votes represented.

According to the special method devised to ensure this, each elected member of the State Assemblies has a certain number of votes on the basis of the relation between the total number of the elected members of the State Assembly and the total population of the State. The number is worked out in the following manner: Divide the total population of the State, first by the total number of elected members in the Assembly. Divide the quotient obtained by the above division by 1,000. Fractions of half or more should be counted as one and added to the quotient which will be the number of votes each member of the Assembly will have in the presidential election.

The following illustration will help to make the process clear. We may worked out the actual number of votes a member of the Uttar Pradesh Legislative Assembly had in the presidential election in 1962.

Total population of Uttar Pradesh (1951 census): 63,215,742

Total number of elected members in the Legislative Assembly: 430

The number of votes of each number: $\frac{63{,}215{,}742}{430 \times 1000} = 147\frac{13}{1000} = 147$

The figures for the remaining States in the same election were as follows: Andhra Pradesh, 104; Assam, 94; Bihar and Bombay, 122 each; Kerala, 108; Madhya Pradesh, 91; Madras, 146; Mysore, 93; Orissa and Punjab, 105 each; Rajasthan, 91; West Bengal, 104; Jammu and Kashmir, 59.

The corresponding figures for the Presidential election of 1969 were as follows: Andhra Pradesh, 125; Assam, 94; Bihar, 146; Gujarat, 123; Haryana, 94; Jammu and Kashmir, 51; Maharashtra, 146; Nagaland, 7; Orissa, 125; Punjab, 107; Tamil Nadu, 144; Rajasthan, 100; Uttar Pradesh, 174; West Bengal, 125; Kerala, 127; Mysore and Madhya Pradesh, 109 each.

By the time presidential election of 1982 took place, the figures had undergone further changes and also in a substantial measure as can be seen from the following:

Andhra Pradesh: 148, Assam: 116, Bihar: 174, Gujarat: 147, Haryana: 112, Himachal Pradesh: 51, Jammu and Kashmir: 83, Karnataka: 131, Kerala: 152, Madhya Pradesh: 130, Maharashtra: 175, Manipur: 18, Meghalaya: 17, Nagaland: 9, Orissa: 149, Punjab: 116, Rajasthan: 129, Sikkim: 7, Tamil Nadu: 176, Tripura: 26, Uttar Pradesh: 208 and West Bengal : 151.

In the Presidential election of 1992 the number of votes of each elector was as follows:

State	No. of Assembly Seats (Elective)		Value of Votes: Of a Member of Legislative Assembly		Value of Votes: Total Votes for the State
Andhra Pradesh	294	×	148	=	43,512
Arunachal Pradesh	60	×	8	=	480
Assam	126	×	116	=	14,616
Bihar	324	×	174	=	56,276
Goa	40	×	20	=	800
Gujarat	182	×	147	=	26,754
Haryana	90	×	112	=	10,080
Himachal Pradesh	68	×	51	=	3,468
Jammu & Kashmir	87	×	72	=	6,264
Karnataka	224	×	131	=	29,344
Kerala	140	×	151	=	21,280
Madhya Pradesh	320	×	130	=	41,600
Maharashtra	288	×	175	=	50,400
Manipur	60	×	18	=	1,080
Meghalaya	60	×	17	=	1,020
Mizoram	40	×	8	=	320
Nagaland	60	×	9	=	540
Orissa	147	×	117	=	21,903
Punjab	117	×	116	=	13,572
Rajasthan	200	×	129	=	25,800
Sikkim	32	×	7	=	224
Tamil Nadu	234	×	176	=	41,184
Tripura	60	×	26	=	1,560
Uttar Pradesh	425	×	208	=	88,400
West Bengal	294	×	151	=	44,394
Total	3,972		Total value		5,44,971

(A) Vote value per MP = 544,971divided by (543[1] + 233[2] = 776) = 702.7282 or 702 (rounded)

1. Total number of elected members of Lok Sabha.

2. Total number of elected members of Rajya Sabha.

(B) Total vote value for MPs = 702 × 776 = 544,752
Grand total = 544,971 + 544,752 = 10,89,723

The number of votes each elected member of Parliament is entitled to in the Presidential election is arrived at by dividing the total number of votes given to all the elected members of the State Assemblies by the total number of elected members of the State Assemblies by the total number of elected members of both houses of Parliament.[1] The election is held in accordance with the system of proportional representation by means of the single transferable vote. The voting at the election is by secret ballot. On the whole, this is a unique system of presidential election and one is tempted to ask what prompted the constitution-makers to adopt such a system.

First, in view of the adoption of a cabinet system of government under which the President was to function as constitutional head of the State, direct election by the entire electorate as in the case of the President of the United States was considered neither necessary nor advisable.[2] Yet, it was thought desirable to have the President elected by as popular a body as possible. Both these purposes have been realized under the present system. The election becomes indirect and also simple when the electorate consists of only the elected members of the State Legislative Assemblies and Parliament. The elected members of the State Assemblies are themselves elected on adult suffrage. The House of the People of Parliament is also elected on the same basis. The Council of States is elected by the State Assemblies which are also elected on adult suffrage. The electoral college is thus not only broad based but also is substantially large in size.[3]

The significance of an electoral college composed of not only the members of both Houses of Parliament but also those of various State Assemblies needs emphasis. In an election where the head of the nation is chosen, if the members of Parliament alone participate it is possible that a party that has a clear majority in Parliament can easily see its candidate elected. But when the members of the State Assemblies also participate in the election, the picture is likely to undergo a substantial change. For, it is quite possible that the Party which has won a majority in Parliament may be a minority in many State Assemblies or even in most of them. Under such conditions, a Party supported by a majority of members in Parliament will not by itself be able to elect its candidate to the office of President.

---

1. In the 1962 elections this number was 495. In 1969 it was 576. In 1982 it was 702 In 1992 it was 776.
2. C.A.D. VII, p. 998.
3. In the 1952 election there were 3, 559 members in the electoral college and a total of 616,913 votes were cast. In the 1957 election the total number of valid votes polled was 463, 196; of these, Rajendra Prasad secured 459,698, Nagendra Narayan Das, 2,000 and Chowdhry Hari Ram, 1,418.
In 1962 the electoral college had a strength of 3,920. Of these, 3,094 participated in the election. The total number of valid votes was 562,945. Of these, S. Radhakrishnan secured 553,067, Chowdhry Hari Ram, 6,341 and Yamuna Prasad Trisulia, 3,537 votes. In 1967 Zakir Husain secured 471,244 votes as against 363,971 secured by his rival, K. Subha Rao. Zakir Husain died in office in 1969. Subsequetnly, there was election in the same year which was fought by fifteen candidates, of whom the most prominent were V.V. Giri, Sanjiva Reddy and C.D. Deshmukh. In the count of the first preference votes Giri obtained 401,515 votes, Reddy 313,545 and Deshmukh 112,769. As no one got the requisite quota of 50 per cent plus one of the votes polled, second preference votes were counted. As a result, Giri secured 420,077 as against Reddy's 405,427. Hence Giri was elected as the fourth President of India.

The use of the term 'proportional representation' was objected to in the Assembly because only one person was to be elected as President.[1] Critics asked; 'What significance has it in the absence of a multi-member constituency?' It is significant because, first it ensures an absolute majority of the total number of votes polled for a candidate to be elected,[2] instead of a simple majority or a plurality of votes as in the elections to Parliament and the State Legislative Assemblies. Since the President is the head of the State and represents the nation which includes all parties and groups, and since he should stand above party considerations, it is desirable that he is elected with as large majority as possible. But under the simple majority system there is no guarantee for this. The present system ensures his election with at least an absolute majority. Secondly, it often helps the smaller parties in Parliament or regional parties who are strong only in some State Assemblies to have some voice in the election of the President. If no party can claim an absolute majority of the total votes of the electoral college, a candidate, to win the election, has to seek the support of two or more parties. This gives an opportunity to smaller parties to influence the election. In the words of Ambedkar:

> ....Obviously no member of the House would like the President to be elected by a bare majority or by a system of election in which the minorities has no part to play. That being so, the election of the President by a bare majority has to be eliminated and we have to provide a system whereby the minorities will have some voice in the election of the President. The only method, therefore, that remained was to have a system of election in which the minorities will have some hand and some play and that is undoubtedly the system of proportional representation.[3]

Although, on paper, the presidential election is a complicated process, in practice, it is a comparatively simple process.[4] Moreover, this method of electing the President seems to be much more in consonance with the federal principle than that which obtains in the United States, where the President is supposed to be elected by the electors but, in reality, directly by the people. The election of the American President raises the greatest political battle in the world for the election of any head of the State. But, in India, such a contest will pass off without a ripple of popular excitement. No doubt, it is a matter of all-India significance. And yet, since those who directly participate in it number just a few thousands (about 5000) it passes off in a quiet, business-like manner.[5]

Although the President is only a constitutional head of the State who has little effective power at his disposal, the office of the President carries with it great dignity and prestige. These are reflect in certain legal privileges which the President enjoys. Thus, he is not

---

1. C.A.D. VII, pp. 1003, 1005 and 1006.
2. According to the Election Rules (1952) the method prescribed is commonly known as the alternative vote in a single-member constituency. The quota is determined by dividing the total number of valid votes by one plus one and adding one to the quotient so obtained. If the first counting does not give any candidate the quota of votes, the candidate who got the least number of votes is eliminated and his votes transferred to the remaining candidates on the basis of the preferences shwon. The process is repeated until one candidate reaches the requisite number fixed by the quota.
3. C.A.D. VII, p. 1017.
4. In 1952 Parliament passed for the first time an Act providing details regarding election to the offices of President and Vice-President of India. The Act was amended in 1962 and again in 1969.
5. The only occasion when the election of the President became exciting was in 1969 when at the first counting no condidate could secure an absolute majority.

answerable to any court of law for the exercise and performance of the powers and functions of his office. No criminal proceedings can be instituted against him nor can he be arrested or imprisoned during the tenure of his office. No civil proceedings even can be instituted against him without, at least, two months' written notice regarding the relief claimed.

Before entering upon his office, the President has to make and subscribe in the presence of the Chief Justice of India an oath or affirmation in the following form:

I, A.B., $\frac{\text{Do swear in the name of God}}{\text{Solemnly affirm}}$ that I will faithfully execute the office of President (or discharge the functions of the President) of India and will, to the best of my ability, preserve, protect and defend the Constitution and the law and that I will devote myself to the service and well being of the people of India.

This oath or affirmation is important because it is on the basis of the pledge that he has taken that, if an occasion arises, impeachment proceedings are taken against him.

Normally, the President's office becomes vacant in three ways: death, resignation or removal by impeachment. The Constitution lays down a detailed procedure for the impeachment of the President, which is almost identical to that in the United States except for one major difference. In India the charge may be preferred by either House of Parliament while in the United States the House of Representatives alone has the power to try the impeachment. The President can be impeached only for the violation of the Constitution, a form which is comprehensive enough to cover crimes such as treason, bribery and other crimes.[1] Before the charge is preferred by either House of Parliament, the proposal should be embodied in a resolution moved after a notice of at least fourteen days. The notive must be signed by at least one-fourth of the total number of members of the House. The charge shall be preferred only if such a resolution is passed by a two-third majority of the total membership of the House. Once the charge has been so preferred in one House, the other House will investigate the charge or appoint a special body for such investigation. If the result of such investigation is that the charge against the President has been sustained and to this effect a resolution is passed by the House with a two-third majority of its total membership, the President cease to hold the office of the President of India from the date of passing such resolution. The provisions dealing with impeachment have, thus, four important aspects:

(a) The motion of impeachment may be initiated in either House of Parliament;

(b) Such motion must have the support of two-thirds of the total membership of the House;

(c) The House which has passed the motion for investigation shall not be entitled to investigate the charge;

(d) If the investigating House finds the President guilty, it must do so by a two-third majority of its total membership.

The justification for a special majority is the gravity of the action. An impeachment is not like a no-confidence resolution which invovles no disgrace or imputation of moral turpitude but only the disapproval of the Government's policy. If the President is convicted on a motion of impeachment, it will practically amount to the ruination of his public career.

1. C.A.D. VII, p. 1081.

Hence it is desirable that such an important consequence should not be permitted to follow from the decision of a bare majority but at least a two-third majority.

When a vacancy arises in the office of the President owing to any one of the above causes, it will be filled by the Vice-President until a new President is elected. But the new President should be elected before six month elapse after the vacancy has occurred. When a new President is elected in this manner he will hold office for the full term of five years. When Zakir Husain died in office in 1969 the then Vice-President V.V. Giri took over as acting President. He, however, resigned soon in order to contest the election to the Office of President. In the meanwhile, Parliament passed the President (Discharge of Functions) Act of 1969 providing for discharge of functions of the Office of President in the event of occurrence of vacancies in the Office of both the President and Vice-President. It provided that in such a contingency, the Chief Justice of India or in his absence of senior-most judge of the Supreme Court of India available shall discharge the functions of the President until a new President enters upon his office. Accordingly, in Giri's resignation, Chief Justice Hidayatulla was sworn in for discharging the functions of the President. The results of the election were declared on August 20 and the new President entered upon his office on August 24, 1969. There is no constitutional bar against the President's re-election. Every doubt and dispute arising out of the President election shall be finally decided by the Supreme Court of India. The Court held in this connection that it would entertain any doubt or dispute in a presidential election only after the completion of the entire process called the election and not at any earlier stage.[1]

The election of Giri as President in 1969 was challenged as invalid on the ground that undue influence was exercised on the minds of voters on behalf of him. A Special Bench of five judges of the Supreme Court was constituted for the purpose and for the first time in such a case evidence was recorded in proceedings before the Court. The Supreme Court upheld the election.

Until 1972, any two electors could nominate a presidential candidate as proposer and seconder. Misusing this simple provision of the law, several aspirants to the presidential office managed to enter the contest in a light-hearted manner although they knew that they had no chance whatsoever to get elected. To discourage this unhealthy tendency the law was amended and, as a result, henceforth any candidate seeking election to the office of President would be required to have the backing of at least 40 electors of whom at least two should be members of Parliament and at least 24 belonging to State Assemblies. The new law has removed the earlier provision relating to the offence of bribery or undue influence for chanllenging an election to the presidential office.

It also provides that there should be a minimum of 40 electors joined together as petitioners for challenging an election to the office of President of whom at least 12 should be members of Parliament and at least 24 members of State Assemblies. Another change is that the fact of wrong acceptance of the nomination of any candidate other than the successful candidate who had withdrawn, cannot constitute a ground for setting aside the election. The new law also provides for a deposit of Rs. 2,500 for a candidate

1. Dr. N.B. Khare *vs*. The Election Commission of India, 1957, S.C.J. 663. Also see Dr. N.B. Khare *vs*. The Election Commission of India (1958), S.C.J. 278 and N.P. Ponnuswami *vs*. Returning Officer, Namakkal, 1952, S.C.R. 218.

seeking election which is liable to be forfeited if the candidate fails to secure at least one-sixth of the number of votes necessary to secure the return of a candidate.

Powers of the President

Under Article 53 of the Constitution the executive power of the Union is vested in the President who is empowered to exercise it either directly or through officers subordinate to him. Some members of the Constituent Assembly thought that it was unnecessary to specify the exercise of presidential power through officers subordinate to him. But on behalf of the Drafting Committee it was pointed out that by putting in the word 'officers' all the theory of delegation which loomed large in the U.S. Constitution would be put at rest in its application to the Indian Constitution in this context.[1] The list of powers which the Constitution confers upon the President is long and impressive. These may be broadly classified under three categories: Executive powers, Legislative powers and Emergency powers.

Executive Powers

The Constitution lays down the general principle that the executive power of the Union is coextensive with its legislative power. Interpreting the scope of this power the Supreme Court held that it embraced not only matters upon which Parliament has already passed legislation but also those on which it is competent to pass legislation.[2] Since the President is the head of the Union Executive naturally his executive power embraces the entire field of activities of the Union. It has already been pointed out that he is the Commander-in-Chief of the Defence Forces. By making the President the Commander-in-Chief, the Constitution ensures the subordination of the entire Armed Forces to the civil authority at all times. In addition, the President has vast powers of appointment. He appoints the Prime Minister and other members of the Council of Ministers and makes rules for the transaction of the business of the Government of India and for the allocation, among the Ministers, of that business. He appoints the Attorney-General, the Chief Justice and Justices of the Supreme Court and those of the High Courts, the members of the Union Public Service Commission and the Election Commission, the Comptroller and Auditor-General of India, Ambassadors and other diplomatic representatives of India abroad, the Governors and the Chief Commissioner of Union Territories. In fact, every appointment in the Union Government is made in the name of the President or under his authority. But in most of the above cases the appointments are made by the President 'by warrant under his hand and seal'.

Under Article 72 the President is given the power to grant pardons.[3] According to this, in all Court Martial cases as well as cases involving the breach of a Union law where a punishment or sentence is inflicted on any person, the President may grant pardon or any other appropriate mercy such as reprieve, respite, remission, or suspension, or commutation of the sentence. A member proposed in the Constitution Assembly that the President should be given exclusive power of pardon in all cases involving the death sentence.[4] The proposal

1. C.A.D. X, p. 358.
2. 1955, 2 S.C.R. 225.
3. Pardoning power is sometimes characterized as a judicial power of the President. This is wrong because granting of pardon is a prerogative of the Executive and, as such, an executive power.
4. C.A.D. VII, p.1118.

was, however, negatived by the Assembly on Ambedkar's opposition, to it. He said that the power of commuting death sentence was vested in both the President and the Governors. Since the offence was committed in a particular locality, the Home Minister of the State Government would be in a better position to advise the Governor having regard to the intimate knowledge of the circumstances of the case and the situation prevailing in that area. There was, however, a safeguard over the decision of the Governor if he rejected the mercy petition. The person concerned might approach the President and move him for a reprieve.[1]

The power of pardon is a constitutional responsibility of the President, according to the Supreme Court. (Kehar Singh *vs.* Union of India A.I.R. 1989 S.C. 653). This was a case arising out of the murder of former Prime Minister Indira Gandhi. The power of pardoning under Article 72 rests on the advice of the Central Government. The convict seeking relief under Article 72 has no right to personal oral hearing. Though the Court can go into the nature and extent of the power under Article 72. The exercise of the power on merits is not open to a judicial review. (Kehar Singh *vs.* Union of India-Supra).

Legislative Powers

In the legislative field too the President has important powers. In fact the President forms an integral part of the legislative process in that, without his assent, no Central Bill can become law. He summons the Houses of Parliament, prorogues the Houses and may dissolve the House of the People. He may address either House of Parliament or both Houses assembled together or seen messages to them. He nominates twelve members to the Council of States and may nominate two members of the Anglo-Indian community to the House of the People. Every Bill passed by Parliament must be presented to the President for his assent. He may, except in the case of a Money Bill, withhold his assent or return it to Parliament for reconsideration. He causes to be laid before Parliament the annual budget showing the estimated receipts and expenditure of the Union for each year. No demand for a financial grant can be made in Parliament except on his recommendation.

Perhaps, the most important legislative power of the President is his power to promulgate ordinances under Article 123. It is a power somewhat analogous to what the British Emergency Powers Act, 1920, confers upon the King to issue a proclamation when Parliament is not in session. According to Article to Article 123 the President is empowered to promulgate ordinances, except when both Houses of Parliament are in session, if he is satisfied that circumstances exist compelling him to take immediate action. A Presidential ordinance has the same force and effect as an Act of Parliament within six weeks from the reassembly of Parliament. Failure to comply with this condition, or Parliamentary disapproval within the six weeks' period, will make the ordinance invalid. The President may also withdraw the ordinance at any time he likes. Thus, the ordinance will remain in force as long as Parliament does not meet. Since the Constitution insists that not more than six months will pass between two sessions of Parliament, there is the possibility of a maximum life of six months for the ordinance before Parliament reassembles. And, even when Parliament meets, the ordinance will not expire immediately but will remain in force for six weeks from its reassembly unless it is disapproved earlier by both Houses. Thus, an ordinance may last for a maximum possible period of seven and a half months.

---

1. ibid., pp. 1119-20.

In the Constitution Assembly, several members deplored the possibility of such a long period of life for a Presidential Ordinance which in reality was an exercise of legislative power by the Executive under exceptional circumstances.[1] Some members were against even the principle of promulgating ordinances.[2] But Ambedkar justified the provisions with the following arguments:

> It is not difficult to imagine cases where the powers conferred by the ordinary law existing at any particular movement may be difficult to deal with a situation which may suddenly and immediately arise. The executive must have the power to deal with the situation. This is possible only if the President has the power to issue an Ordinance as the Executive cannot deal with the situation by resorting to the ordinary process of law because the legislature is not in session. Therefore, fundamentally there can be no objection to the provision.

With regard to the period, he thought that it was not in the interests of the Executive to resort to any dilatory process with a view to keeping the Ordinance in operation for an unduly long period. More than anything else, it is necessary for the Government of the day to maintain the confidence of Parliament in it.[3]

Emergency Powers

The President is empowered to declare three different types of emergency. He may declare an emergency either in any part or the whole of India, if he is satisfied that there is a threat of war or external aggression or internal disturbance. Further, he is empowered to declare an emergency in case of a breakdown of the Constitutional machinery in any State of the Union. He may also declare, in case of a financial breakdown, a financial emergency. (As there is a separate chapter dealing with these powers and their implications, it is not proposed to deal with these powers and their implications, in detail here).

The President, a Constitutional Head of the State

Taken as a whole, and on their face value, the presidential powers are indeed formidable. There is hardly any other constitution which gives such a long and detailed list of powers to its Chief Executive. The question, however, is how far all or any of these powers will be really exercised by him. On the answer to this question will depend the real position of the President in the governmental system established by the Constitution rather than what may appear from a literal reading of the constitutional provision. It is here that we have to turn to the nature as well the working of the Government of India. It has already been pointed out that the form of government which the Constitution aims to establish is modelled on the British parliamentary or cabinet system and not the presidential type of the United States. Under the British system, the monarch (the King or the Queen) is only a ceremonial head of the State. He does not possess the tremendous powers technically ascribed to him. They belong to a convenient myth or 'working hypothesis' called the Crown. Almost all the powers which theoretically belong to the Crown are in reality exercised by the Cabinet. The position under the Indian Constitution too is the same, that the President of India is only the Constitutional Head of the State who is a necessary adjunct of cabinet government, his position and powers being more or less the same as those of the British monarch.

1. C.A.D. VIII, p. 206.
2. Ibid., pp. 207-13.
3. Ibid., p. 213.

This question was discussed at length in the Constituent Assembly at different times and every time the point that was most stressed was the constitutional character of the head of the State. A few of the more important statements which were made during these discussions may be noted. Introducing the Draft Constitution, Ambedkar said:

In the Draft Constitution there is placed at the head of the Indian Union of functionary who is called the President of the Union. The title of this functionary reminds one of the President of the United States. But beyond identity of names there is nothing in common between the form of Government prevalent in America and the form of government proposed under the Draft Constitution. The two are fundamentally different. Under the Presidential system of America, the President is the Chief head of the Executive. The administration is vested in him. Under the Draft Constitution the President occupies the same position as the King under the English Constitution. He is the head of the State but not of the Executive. He represents the nation but does not rule the nation. He is the symbol of the nation. His place in the administration is that of a ceremonial device on a seal by which the nation's decisions are made known.[1]

During the general discussion on the Constitution, at the concluding stage. T.T. Krishnamachari said:

It has been mentioned that one of the chief defects of this Constitution is that we have not anywhere mentioned that the President is a constitutional head and the future of the President's powers is, therefore, doubtful....... This is a matter which has been examined by the Drafting Committee to some extent. The position of the President in a responsible government is not the same as the position of the President under representative Government like America and that is a mistake that a number of people in the House have been making, when they said that the President will be an autocrat, and no one appears to realise that the President has to act on the advice of the Prime Minister........ So far as the relationship of the President with the Cabinet is concerned, I must say that we have, so to say, completely copied the system of responsible government that is functioning in Britain today; we have made no aviation from it and the deviations that we have made are only such as are necessary because our Constitution is federal in structure.[2]

Participating in the same discussion, President Prasad said:

We have had to reconcile the position of an elected President with an elected legislature, and in doing so, we have adopted more or less, the position of the British monarch for the President........ His position is that of a constitutional President. Then we come to the Ministers. They are, of course, responsible to the Legislature and tender advice to the President who is bound to act according to that advice. Although there are no specific provisions, so far as I know, in the Constitution itself making it binding on the President to accept the advice of his Ministers, it is hoped that the convention under which in England the King acts always on the advice of his Ministers will be established in this country also and the President, not so much on account of the written word in the Constitution, but as a result of this very healthy convention, will become a constitutional President in all matters.[3]

With this background in view one may examine the constitutional provisions that deal with the relationship of the President with the Council of Ministers in order to see how far are these claims justified. Articles 74, 75 and 78 are important in this connection. They provide that:

1. There shall be a Council of Ministers with the Prime Minister at the head to aid and advise the President who shall, in the exercise of his functions, act in accordance with such advice.

1. C.A.D. VII, p. 32.
2. C.A.D. VII, p. 988.
3. C.A.D. X, p. 956.

Provided that the President may require the Council of Ministers to reconsider such advice, either generally or otherwise, and the President shall act in accordance with the advice tendered after such reconsideration. (Article 74 in its original form was first amended by adding the last part in 1976 through the Forty-second Amendment. The Proviso was added by the Forty-Fourth Amendment of 1978.)

2. No court of law has power to enquire as to whether any advice was given the Ministers and, if so, what it was.

3. The Prime Minister shall be appointed by the President and, on the advice of the Prime Minister, the President will appoint other Ministers.

4. The Ministers shall hold office during the pleasure of the President.

5. The Council of Ministers shall be collectively responsible to the House of the People.

6, It shall be the duty of the Prime Minister:

(a) to communicate to the President all decisions of the Council of Ministers;

(b) to furnish such information relating to the administration of the Union and proposals for legislation as the President calls for, and

(c) to submit for the consideration of the Council, if the President so desires, any matter on which a decision has been taken by a Minister but which has not been considered by the Council.

These provisions, taken as a whole, fairly establish the claim of Ambedkar and his colleagues that the authors of the Constitution wanted to adopt the British pattern of cabinet government. At the same time, it is also clear that they did not want to use expressions which would take away the flexibility that is the heart and soul of the British system. The difficulty of the Drafting Committee was to state precisely in a written constitution certain well-established constitutional conventions that regulate the relationship between the King and the Cabinet in Britain. This is why, while certain provisions convey their meaning in unmistakable terms, there are others that are not equally clear. Thus, it is quite clear that, for the exercise of his functions, there must be a Council of Ministers with the Prime Minister at the head to aid and advise the President. But does this mean that the President is always bound by the advice of the Council? Ambadkar answered it in the positive. "The President of the Indian Union will be generally bound by the advice of his Ministers. He can do nothing contrary to their advice, nor can he do anything without their advice"[1]

According to those who supported Ambedkar, "It is the Prime Minister's business, with the support of the Ministers, to rule the country and the President may be permitted now and then to aid and advise the Council of Ministers. Therefore, we should look at the substance and not at the mere phraseology which is the result of conventions.[2] Further, the expression 'said and advise' is only a constitutional euphemism.[3] It has been used, in pursuance of past practice, both for the maintenance of the outward dignity of the office of the President and for avoiding some practical difficulties of a constitutional character. Every one in the Constituent Assembly was, however, not satisfied with the language of

1. C.A.D. VIII, p. 32.
2. K. Santhanam, Ibid, VII, p. 1155.
3. Alladi Krishnaswami Aiyar, Ibid, X, p. 270.

the provision and least of all President Rajendra Prasad. The following exchange between the President and Ambedkar is illuminating:[1]

Mr. President: There is another amendment which has been moved by Sardar Hukum Singh in which he says that the President may promulgate ordinances after consultation with his Council of Ministers.

The Honourable Dr. B.R. Ambedkar: I am very grateful to you for reminding me about this. The point is that amendment is unnecessary because the President could not act and will not act except on the advice of the Ministers.

Mr. President: Where is the provisions in the Draft Constitution which binds the President to act in accordance with the advice of the Ministers?

Dr. Ambedkar: I am sure that there is a provision and the provisions is that there shall be a Council of Ministers to aid and advise the President in the exercise of his functions.

Mr. President: Since we are having this written Constitution, we must have that clearly put somewhere.

Dr. Ambedkar: Though I cannot point it out just now, I am sure there is a provision. I think there is a provision that the President will be bound to accept the advice of the Ministers. In fact, he cannot act without the advice of his Ministers.

Some Honourable Members: Article 61(1).

Mr. President: It only lays down the duty of the Ministers, but it does not lay down the duty of the President to act in accordance with advice given by the Ministers. It does not lay down that the President is bound to accept the advice. Is there any other provision in the Constitution? We will not be able even to impeach him, because he will not be acting in violation of the Constitution, if there is no provision.

Dr. Ambedkar: May I draw your attention to Article 61, which deals with the exercise of the President's functions. He cannot exercise any of his functions, unless he has got the advice, 'in the exercise of his functions'. It is not merely 'to aid and advise'. 'In the exercise of his functions', those are the most important words.

Mr. President: I have my doubts if this word could bind the President. It only lays down that there shall be a Council of Ministers with the Prime Minister at the head to aid and advise the President in the exercise of his functions. It does not say that the President will be bound to accept that advice.

Dr. Ambedkar: If he does not accept the advice of the existing Ministry, he shall have to find some other body of Ministers to advise him. He will never be able to act independently of the Ministers.

Mr. President: Is there any real difficulty in providing somewhere that the President will be bound by the advice of the Ministers?

Dr. Ambedkar: We are doing that. If I may say so, there is a provision in the Instrument of Instructions.

Mr. President: I have considered that also.

Dr. Ambedkar: Paragraph 3 reads: in all matters within the scope of the executive power of the Union, the President, shall in the exercise of the powers conferred upon him, be guided by the advice of his Ministers. We propose to make some amendment to that.

1. Ibid, VIII, pp. 215-6.

Mr. President: You want to change that. As it is, it lays down that the President will be guided by the Ministers in the exercise of the executive powers of the Union and not in its legislative power.

Dr. Ambedkar: Article 61 follows almost literally various other constitutions and the Presidents have always understood that language means that they must accept the advice. If there is any difficulty, it will certainly be remedied by suitable amendment.

In accordance with this statement of the Chairman of the Drafting Committee the Draft Constitution had incorporated in it a schedule of instructions to the President and one of whose clauses had provided that, in the exercise of his functions under the Constitution, he must be generally guided by these instructions. These instructions had provided *inter alia* that he must act on ministerial advice. Ultimately, however, the instructions as well as the clause were omitted as unnecessary. When a number of members objected to this and questioned the wisdom of our depending on the conventions of the British Constitution, Ambedkar said that even without them the President was bound to act on the advice of the Council of Ministers. If the President did not act so, Ambedkar had not the slightest doubt that it would amount to a violation of the Constitution for which the President could be impeached. On this assurance, the Assembly agreed to omit the schedule and the clause[1] and the article was left as it originally was without making a specific provision by which the President was bound by the advice of the Ministry. What, then, is the present position? Is the President bound by the advice of the Council of Ministers? The answer is: *yes normally*.

In a parliamentary system of government, the Executive is responsible to the Legislative. As such the Council of Ministers hold their offices not as a grace of the President (or literally during his pleasure) but because of the confidence of Parliament which they enjoy. They go out of office not because the President has lost confidence in them but because they have lost the confidence of Parliament to which they are jointly and directly responsible. There can be no conflict between the will of Parliament, the representative of the electorate, and that of the President. If at all there arises such a conflict, the will of Parliament ought to prevail. That is why the Constitution vests in Parliament the power to impeach the President. Therefore so long as the Council of Ministers has the confidence of Parliament, the President is literally bound by their advice and, in reality, it is the President who is cast in the role of an adviser.

This view about the position of the President vis-a-vis the Council of Ministers was shared also by the Supreme Court which expressed its opinion in the following language:

> In India, as in England, the executive has to act subject to the control of the legislature; but in what way is this control exercised by the legislature? Under Article 53(1) of our Constitution, the executive power of the Union is vested in the President but under Article 75 there is to be a Council of Ministers with the Prime Minister at the head to aid and advise the President in the exercise of his functions. The President *has thus been made a formal or Constitutional head of the executive and the real executive powers are vested in the Ministers or the Cabinet*.....[2] In the Indian Constitution, therefore, we have the same system of Parliamentary executive as in England, and the Council of ministers consisting, as it does of the members of the legislature is, like the British Cabinet, 'a hyphen which joins, a buckle which fastens the legislative part of the State to the executive part.' The Cabinet enjoying, as it does, a majority in the legislature concentrates in itself the virtual

1. C.A.D.X, pp. 268-71.
2. Emphasis ours.

control of both legislative and executive functions; and as the Ministers constituting the Cabinet are presumably agreed on fundamental and act on the principle of collective responsibility, the most important questions of policy are all formulated by them.[1]

The working of the Constitution so far shows that the President is, in reality, only the Constitutional Head of the State. On the eve of the 1951-52 General Elections in India, President Rajendra Prasad sent a message to Parliament explaining his views on the Hindu Code Bill which was then under consideration. In that message he said that personally he was opposed to the passing of the Bill but, if adopted by Parliament, he would give his assent to it, however reluctant he might be. During the first two decades the country has had five General Elections each followed by a reconstitution of the Council of Ministers. During this period there were also major political changes and far-reaching economic development programmes. The State Reorganization Act, 1956, has brought about a complete redrawing of the political map of India. There were over two dozen constitutional amendments some of which were of a far-reaching character. *In all these cases, the decisions were of the Ministry (the Cabinet) and there was never a question of the 'President exercising executive powers and the Ministers only advising him'.*

At least on two occasions during his second term, President Prasad sought the advice of the Attorney-General regarding the President's position in his capacity as Visitor of Central Universities and that as the Supreme Commander of the Armed Forces. What the President wanted to know as whether he was bound by the advice of the Council of Ministers while discharging his functions in either of these capacities. The Attorney-General advised the President that he was so bound in either capacity[2] and hence the President acted as advised by the Ministry.

Fortunately for India, there was during this period a stable government, one that always enjoyed the confidence of Parliament. In fact, the characteristic feature of this period was the massive majority of the Congress party in Parliament and the comparative insignificance of the opposition. The Congress party, on its own strength, could pass any legislative measure including constitutional amendments which required a special majority. So overwhelming was the position of the party that it appeared as if India had a one-party government which was likely to assume the character of one-party dictatorship.[3] With so formidable a position enjoyed by the Congress party and so dominant a position held by its unchallenged leader, there was little room for the President to play any role of political significance.

The situation has undergone a gradual but unmistakable change ever since 1962, beginning with the Chinese aggression against the country late that year. One of the most significant developments in that context was the reconstitution of the Nehru Cabinet after obliging the then Defence Minister, a close associate of Nehru, to tender his resignation. No authoritative information is available to the public at large on the inside story of the Defence Minister's resignation. Informed reports in newspapers of those days, however, indicate that the President played a significant role in the political developments of that period.

---

1. (1955) 2 S.C.R. 225; S.C.J. 304.
2. *The Times of India*, Delhi Edn., 30 November 1961.
3. Prime Minister Nehru was at one time reported to have been unhappy with this situation and was even interested to help the development of a strong opposition. !

The death of Nehru in 1964 and Lal Bahadur Shastri's assumption of the Prime Minister's office soon afterwards brought about a substantially different situation. The new Prime Minister had yet to establish his mastery over the party, Parliament and the country. But before this could be achieved, Shastri left the scene. Indira Gandhi succeeded him, after a fight within the party against Morarji Desai who had been an aspirant to the office even earlier. The fight for leadership and the lack of unity within the party thereafter weakened the position of the Prime Minister considerably. This was reflected in the general elections of 1967 and, for the first time since 1947, the Congress party lost control of the Governments of a majority of States. In Parliament, although the party still commanded a majority, it was a somewhat precarious one.

It was this situation that compelled the Congress party to seek the support of some of the opposition parties as well as independent legislators in 1967 in favour of its nominee, Dr. Zakir Husain, for President. Dr. Zakir Husain's sudden death in office, Vice-President Giri's temporary assumption of the office of President, his later election as President defeating the official Congress condidate and the consequent split in the Congress party are events full of political and constitutional significance. What is relevant, however, to our discussion here is the impact of all these new developments on the office of the President. The unmistakable impression that one gets is that had that situation continued, the President, unlike his predecessors, would have been called upon to play a decisive role in the affairs of the nation, a role very different from that of a constitutional head of the State. The crucial fact that he has to reckon with is that although for the time being the government enjoys the confidence of parliament, the party which supports it has either no majority of its own in the Lok Sabha or its majority is too slender.[1]

Let us consider some of the possibilities that are inherent in such a situation. Suppose the Council of Ministers loses the confidence of Parliament or is torn by internal dissensions and factions impairing that confidence. The President's relations with the Council at once become difficult and delicate. The President will have to assess carefully the position of the Council in relation to Parliament and the Prime Minister in relation to the Council. If the Council loses Parliament's confidence, the normal course open to the Council is to resign. Instead, if the Council advises the President to dissolve the Lok Sabha, should the President accept the advice and act accordingly? Is he bound by it? Should he not explore the possibilities of another Government? If the defeated Council of Ministers advises the President to dissolve the Lok Sabha and at the same time a clear majority of members of the House in writing plead with him to constitute a new Council, what should he do?[2]

Similarly, in case of acute differences within the Council of Ministers, should the President dismiss individual Ministers on the advice of the Prime Minister? Or, if a majority of the Council headed by one of the Ministers is opposed to the Prime Minister, should the President call for the resignation of the Council with a view to reconstituting it with a new Prime Minister? One might say that the answers to these questions are to be provided by the party in power and the Parliament. But a particular action on the part of the President at a crucial moment may swing the pendulum to either side and hence he can, if he cares to

1. The General Elections of 1971 returned the Congress party with a massive majority to the Lok Sabha and, as a consequence, the political uncertainty of the earlier period disappeared almost overnight.
2. It is important to remember in this context that the President may have been elected with the support of a large section of the opposition in Parliament as in the case of Giri's.

do so, decisively influence the situation. If the President happens to be a man of political ambition, he could with impunity take advantage of a crucial situation and indulge in the game of political patronage in the formation and dissolution of Ministries.

India has a federal system of government under which the totality of governmental power is divided between the Union Government and the States. The Union and States have their own separate governments and these governments, as has already been demonstrated by the general elections of 1967 and some of the later general elections may belong to different political parties. In such circumstances, the party in power at the Centre could misuse or abuse its position either to assist its own supporters or to spite the party or parties in power in the States. For example, a legislative enactment affecting property right passed by a State Legislature requires Presidential assent. The Central Cabinet could advise the President not to give his assent to the new measure. Is the President bound by that advice even when he is convinced that the Ministry's advice was politically motivated?

Similarly, if a particular decision of the Council of Ministers is likely to undermine the Constitution or go against any of its provisions or, in the President's considered view, against the interest and welfare of the people of India as a whole, should he accept that decison?[1] if he does so, is he not violating the pledge that he has taken at the time when he entered upon his office?

The President has a special role as an integral part of the Parliament of India. Without his assent no Bill can become law. He is empowered, under Article 111 of the Constitution, to send back to Parliament any Bill (except a money bill) if he is of the view that it should be reconsidered. Here again, it is unlikely that he will act on ministerial advice. To take yet another example relating to Parliament, a situation may arise in which the Prime Minister and the Speaker do not see eye to eye. Will the President, in such circumstances blindly accept the Prime Minister's advice or decide the issue on its merits? Similarly, how should he act when advised to issue ordiances or to prorogue the Houses, merely on the advice of the Ministry?

Is the President justified in accepting every advice of the Ministry in making the highest appointments which are specified under the Constitution to be made by warrant under his hand and seal? If he is convinced that an appointment is politically motivated, the person appointed unfit or ill qualified for the job or corrupt, is he obliged to act according to the Ministry's advice? The answer is "no".

Since the Constitution specifically makes the President the Supreme Commander of the Armed Forces, has he not a special duty to keep the armed forces immune from political partisanship? If the Union Government of the day, motivated by partisan politics, makes use of the armed forces to destroy self-government in any State or effect undeserving and unjust promotions within the armed forces, is the President bound to support them because the Ministry has advised him to do so? We can multiply such instances. The crucial point is: Is the President always bound by the advice of the Council of Ministers? The answer is quite obvious; not always and in all circumstances.

If the President does not act in accordance with the advice of the Ministry what is the remedy? Impeachment. But no impeachment can succeed unless those who move for

1. President Sanjiva Reddy refused to accept some of the recommendations of the Charan Singh Government in 1979.

impeachment can get the support of a two-thirds majority in each House of Parliament. Where such a two-thirds majority is not commanded by the ruling party or the combination of parties, the President is his own master and may act as he likes in conformity with the terms of his oath of office.

Thus, it seems possible to fix two limits, an inner one within which the President is always acting on the advice of the Council of Ministers and an outer one beyond which he finds it impossible to form an alternative Ministry to carry on the administration. If he refuses to accept the advice of the Council, he even faces impeachment. In between these two limits there is an area, however narrow it is, where he is his own master and is neither bound by the advice of the Council nor runs the risk of a successful impeachment against him. Within this area he may act in his own discretion and may ignore or disregard the advice of the Ministry and act in a manner which according to him is in conformity with the oath that he has taken before entering upon his office, 'to faithfully execute the office of the President and to preserve, protect and defend the Constitution and the law and devote myself to the service and well-being of the people of India'. Such discretion would have been taken away if the framers had made the provision which would bind the President to act under *all* circumstances in accordance with the advice of the Ministry.

It is possible that the framers had been influenced by another consideration. What judicial remedy is there if the President does not act in accordance with the Ministry's advice, assuming that the Constitution expressly provided for his accepting their advice? There is none in view of Article 74(2) which states that the question whether any, and if so what, advice was tendered by Ministers to the President shall not be inquired into any Court. Hence it does not appear to be sound to give more importance to what is legally permissible than what is politically wise in view of the fact that the remedy is political. The Ministry may precipitate a political crisis in which the President cannot find an alternate Ministry that enjoys Parliament's confidence, or Parliament may start proceedings for his impeachment. Both these alternatives are available even in the absence of a specific provision which expressly ties down the President to the Ministry's advice. The present wording provides the necessary elasticity that suits any political situation and avoids all rigidity. The President, after taking stock of the situation, may use his discretion and act constitutionally in the interest of the country.

What is the scope of presidential discretion? According to Ambedkar, The President has no discretionary *functions* at all. All that he will have are certain *prerogatives* but not functions. He said:

> Under a parliamentary system of government, there are only two prerogatives which the King or the Head of the State may exercise. One is the appointment of the Prime Minister and the other is the dissolution of Parliament. With regard to the Prime Minister, it is not possible to avoid vesting the discretion in the President. The only other way..... is to require that it is the House which shall in the first instance choose its leader and then, on the choice being made of a motion or resolution, the President should proceed to appoint the Prime Minister. But it seems that this is quire unnecessary.[1]

In either case, the purpose is to test the confidence of Parliament in the new Prime Minister. That confidence is reflected, before assuming the office, through a resolution as pointed out above or after assuming the office through a no-confidence motion. Ambedkar stated:

1. C.A.D. VII, p. 1158.

One way is as good as the other and it is, therefore, felt desirable to leave this matter to the discretion of the President.

With regard to the dissolution of the House, there again, there is not any definite opinion so far as the British constitutional lawyers are concerned. There is a view held that the President or King must accept the advice of the Prime Minister for a dissolution if he finds that the House has become recalcitrant or that the House does not represent the wishes of the people. There is also the other view that notwithstanding the advice of the Prime Minister and his Cabinet, the President if he thinks that the House has ceased to represent the wishes of the people can *suo moto* and of his own accord dissolve the House..... These are purely prerogatives and they do not come within the administration of the country.[1]

Nevertheless, these are discretionary powers which can vitally affect the proper functioning of parliamentary democracy in this country. This was clearly and even dramatically demonstrated in 1979 when President Sanjiva Reddy invited Charan Singh to form a new Government to replace the Janata Government headed by Morarji Desai and later dissolving the Lok Sabha when Charan Singh failed to secure a vote of confidence of the House. President Reddy's action in appointing Charan Singh as Prime Minister and later his dissolution of the Lok Sabha were both severely criticized resulting in a wide-spread controversy. That was the first time when a President in office became subject of such severe criticism, a direct result of the use of his discretionary power.[2] In 1989 President Venkitaraman's action in inviting Rajiv Gandhi to explore the possibility of forming a stable government was criticized because the Congress Party had failed to get a majority of seats in the General Elections. Rajiv Gandhi however declined the offer and hence the President invited V.P. Singh to form the government after ensuring that he had majority support. But the government formed by V.P. Singh was shortlived as the Janata Dal Party got split and the Prime Minister failed to win the Confidence vote in the Lok Sabha. The group that broke off from the Janata Dal Party was led by Chandra Sekhar who claimed to form the new government with the support of the Congress Party. At that point the President insisted that Rajiv Gandhi as leader of the Congress Party should give in writing that his Party would support Chandra Sekhar to form the new government which he did. However, the Chandra Sekhar government did not last long. In the ensuing General Elections in 1991, again, no party had a majority of seats in the Lok Sabha. The Congress Party had the largest number which was only 239. Yet the President invited the leader of the Congress Party, P.V. Narasimha Rao to form the government and he was sworn in as Prime Minister. The President was criticised for this action on the ground that he was violating the convention he himself had established. Narasimha Rao however was able to win the vote of confidence in support of his government.

In the General Elections of 1996 no Party was able to secure majority in the Lok Sabha. The BJP was the leading Party although far short of majority. Yet, President Shankar Dayal Sharma not only invited Atal Behari Vajpayee, the leader of the BJP, but had sworn him as Prime Minister. But Vajpayee failing to get adequate support to win confidence vote in the Lok Sabha had to resign. Was the Presidential action in swearing Vajpayee as Prime Minister without ensuring the possibility of a stable government right?[3] Later, when

1. Ibid., p. 1159.
2. See Pylee, M.V., Crisis, Conscience and the Constitution, Asia Publishing House, Bombay (1981), Chapter 1.
3. See in this connection Pylee M.V., *Where the President has gone wrong ?* Hindustan Times, 29-5-1996.

Deva Gowda and I.K. Gujral were successively appointed Prime Ministers, the President took care that both of them had majority support in the Lok Sabha.

In 1998 also the General Elections did not give majority in the Lok Sabha to any Party. As leader of the leading Party, Atal Behari Vajpayee was called upon by President K.R. Narayanan to explore the possibility of forming a stable government. The President ensured that Vajpayee had a clear majority supported by documentary evidence before he was sworn as Prime Minister. He applied the same test in 1999 also. In all these cases the Presidents have been using their discretion by using the authority vested in them by the Constitution. The manner in which conventions will develop regulating the use of these discretionary powers by the President will determine, in the long run, the success or failure of the working of a cabinet system of government in India. The President will have to be very cautious and judicious in exercising his discretion for rejecting the advice of the Ministry. Before taking his final decision, he should exercise all his influence and persuade the Ministry to accept his point of view. The President's personality and the esteem and prestige that he enjoys in the country will weigh very much on such occasions. In the actual working of the Constitution, personal factors will have great scope and, in course of time, suitable conventions will have been established to smooth the sharp edges of the Constitution. But conventions can be built up only by precedents drawn from constitutional practice; their growth is, however, often a slow and even painful one.

Apart from the two discretionary powers discussed above and which depend upon conventions yet to develop in India for determining the manner in which they will be exercised, there are a few others, though comparatively less important, for which provision is made under the Constitution. These are:

1. The President's power to call for information relating to the administration of the affairs of the Union and proposals for legislation; and

2. His power to ask the Prime Minister to submit to the consideration of the Council any matter on which a decision has been taken by a Minister but which has not been considered by the Council.[1]

Under the first of these provisions, the President needs no advice of the Ministry to ask the Prime Minister for information about the Council's decisions. It is his prerogative to be informed, again a well-established convention of the English Constitution. Under the second provision, the President can ensure collective action within the cabinet in those matters which, in his discretion, he thinks as deserving of such action but has not had it.

When Rajiv Gandhi failed to report to the President about the policies of the Government for a prolonged period, president Zial Singh not only reminded him of his obligation but even threatened to take punitive action against the Prime Minister if the infirmity was not corrected. Rajiv Gandhi made amends immediately.

When President Rajendra Prasad expressed his views on the Hindu Code bill to Jawaharlal Nehru or President Zial Singh returned the Postal Bill passed by Parliament they were giving notice to the government of the day that they were not bound by the advice of the Cabinet. In 1997 President K.R. Narayanan sent back to the Government for reconsideration the Cabinet decision to dismiss the Kalyan Singh Government of Uttar Pradesh. On reconsideration the Cabinet decided to abide by the President's advice. Again

1. Article 78.

President Narayanan sent back to the Vajpayee Government the Cabinet's decision to dismiss the Rabri Devi Government of Bihar in 1999 for reconsideration. In all these cases the Presidents have shown that they are not a rubber stamp and no government should take the President for granted. During the time of caretaker governments the President's position becomes active. President Venkitaraman was called by some critics as an activist President.

He justified the position by saying that when there is no government and the country is placed into a position in which immediately a government cannot be formed, then the responsibility for the President arises to see that the administration is being carried on according to norms and to see that democratically elected government comes into power. He did not mind being called an activist President. In his view during the period of a caretaker government the President's role undergoes a change and he becomes active to ensure that the constitutional provisions are upheld and adhered. President Sanjiva Reddy has acted in the same manner when Charan Singh was caretaker Prime Minister.

In 1991 during the period when Chandra Sekhar was caretaker Prime Minister, some of his Cabinet colleagues questioned the concept of caretaker government saying that the Constitution does not speak of a caretaker government. But President Venkitaraman did not yield. He was against the Ministry taking any policy decisions.[1] President Narayanan also has shown that he was not a rubber stamp although politicians in power resented it.

As President Venkitaraman said in his Farewell Address in 1992, the President of India as the Head of the State is like an 'emergency light' which lights up when power fails. "Unfortunately power in Delhi fails too often and too frequently and for too long a time. And therefore, it looks as if the President is active". Under such circumstances the President has to apply his mind and act according to his understanding of the situation.

3. Article 103 requires that if any question arises whether any member of Parliament has become subject to any of the disqualifications mentioned in Article 102, the President must obtain the opinion of the Election Commission and decide the question accordingly and that decision is final. There is hardly any room for ministeral advice here.

4. Article 111 authorizes the President to declare that either he assents to a Bill passed by the Houses of Parliament or he withholds assent therefrom and return it to Parliament for reconsideration. It is very unlikely, although altogether not inconceivable, that Ministers responsible to Parliament would advise the President to withhold assent from a Bill passed by both Houses.

Those who place too much of reliance on British constitutional conventions to guide the President in all his actions will do well to give due importance to certain features of the Constitution of India which provide for a position of the Head of the State different from that of Britain. These are:

1. India has a written Constitution.

2. India has an elected President who is eligible for re-election as against a hereditary monarch in Britain. He is, therefore, answerable to his constituents for his acts which implies that he should have freedom to act as he thinks right.

3. India has a federal constitution which divides the powers of the Government

1. See in this connection " Government in Name only, M.V. PYLEE on Caretaker Administrations, Hindustan Times, New Delhi, February 3, 1998.

between a Central Government and the State Governments. The President cannot be either a partisan or a silent partner if the Central Cabinet through its 'dictatorial' actions try to subvert the federal structure of the Constitution.

4. The Constitution has a list of guaranteed fundamental rights. It is through the enforcement of these rights that the Constitution seeks to inspire confidence in the cultural, linguistic and religious minorities. The President cannot be a party to the activities of a ministry which seeks to undermine these rights through a tyrannical legislative majority which the ministry may command at a time.

5. Similarly, the Constitution has a chapter on 'Directive Principles of State Policy'. These are expressly stated to be fundamental in the governance of the country and 'it shall be the duty of the State to apply these principles in making laws". If a Bill is passed which, in the opinion of the President, violates one of these Principles, is he bound to act according to ministerial advice and give assent to it? If he does so, he may be accused of having violated the Constitution which he is bound, under oath, to uphold and defend.

6. The Constitution provides for three different types of emergencies. One of these authorizes the President to dismiss a State Ministry on account of the failure of the Constitutional machinery in the State. If ministerial advice to dismiss a State Ministry is based on narrow political and party considerations (the parties in power at the Centre and the State being rivals), is the President bound to act on that advice?

All these will show that there are clear constitutional provisions which make a distinction between the President as a mere titular head of the Union and an arbiter or umpire between competing claims and contesting parties. Therefore, it does not seem to be correct to equate his powers to those of the British monarch and repeat Walter Bagehot's famous words that he has only the right "to be consulted to encourage and warn".[1] On the contrary, the President can function under the Constitution as an effective, influential and sobering force without being dominant or dictatorial. This is why the President of India need not be a mere figurehead as the French President happened to be under the Fourth Republic At the same time, it is difficult to agree with the observation that under the present provisions, "he is an ambiguous figure, three quarters a British monarch and one quarter an American President.[2]

1. Such thoughts must have been uppermost in President Prasad's mind when in November 1960, on the occasion of laying the foundation-stone of the Indian Law Institute in New Delhi, he suggested to the Institute a study of the powers and functions of the President under the Constitution. The occasion, the man, the office he held, and his experience in that office and the part he played in drafting the Constitution were all more than adeauate assurance that he would not have lightly raised an issue of such vital import on the working of the Constitution. The President's statement unleashed the floodgates of a great controversy that raged among constitutional lawyers all over the country. As is often usual in such a controversy, there was more of thunder but less of light although much was written to prove that the President was a mere figurehead or a power to reckon with. To remove all doubts, a member of Parliament, Bhupesh Gupta, proposed two amendments to the Constitution to make ministerial advice binding on the President. The Member could not, however, eanlist adequate support to his move and hence the proposal was lost (*The Times of India,* Delhi End., II March 1961).
2. P.B. Chakravarti, *Link,* 29 January 1961, p. 59. See also the opinions of several other constitutionalists in the same issue on the powers of the President.

The office of the President is indeed one of great dignity as well as authority. The framers of the Constitution had a very difficult task in designing it. For, unlike the British monarch's it was to be an elective office. But like that of the British monarch his was to be of great dignity. Further, they had to keep in view the special features of the Constitution in contrast to that of Britain, its written character, the federal system, the guaranteed rights of the citizen and the Directive Principles of State policy. There is enough of evidence in the Constitution to show that they did not want to make the position of the President so rigid as to rule out the possibility of flexibility under differing conditions and circumstances in the country.

This discussion may be concluded by detailing the circumstances under which the President will have occasion to make use of his discretionary powers in a decisive manner. Firstly, when no party in Parliament (the House of the People, to be more precise) has a clear majority, the President's choice of a particular person as Prime Minister may decisively swing the pendulum one way or the other. If, unfortunately India follows the French pattern of political uncertainty of the past, which was the result of a multitude of small parties and none capable of forming a stable Ministry, an ambitious President will be able to dictate terms to any Prime Minister or a prospective Prime Minister. Secondly, when the majority party which holds the reins of power is torn asunder by internal disputes and dissensions, the President's inclination to support or denounce a particular leader is bound to have far reaching consequence. When discipline in the ruling party degenerates, when groups and factions undermine party cohesion, when adventurous and unscrupulous group-bosses try to capture office through questionable means and, finally, when corrupt practices tarnish the reputation and goodwill of the ruling party, there will be an opportunity for the President to play a decisive role in the machinery of the government. In the ultimate analysis, it is the political climate that will dictate the use of his power.

***

22

THE COUNCIL OF MINISTERS AND THE PRIME MINISTER

WE HAVE already seen the relationship of the President with the Council of Ministers. In that connection we saw the special status the Constitution confers on the Prime Minister as the head of the Council of Ministers. Justifying the provision, Ambedkar sad that "there can be hardly any objection to giving statutory recognition to the position of the Prime Minister which is established for long by convention in England".

The special position of superiority given to the Prime Minister is essential in the interest of the principle of collective responsibility to the House of the People as laid down under article 75(3). The essence of collective responsibility is that all members of the Council of Ministers will speak in public with a united voice. This does not necessarily mean that all of them see eye to eye with one another on every problem the Ministry faces. The different points of view are expressed freely in the meetings of the Council so as to arrive at the best decision in the circumstances.[1] Once such a decision is taken, every Minister is expected to stand by the decision without any reservation. Thus, responsibility for governmental action becomes collective on the part of the Ministry which will 'sink or sail as a whole'.

Nevertheless, if a Minister violates the principle by openly criticizing the decision of the Ministry, he cannot be prosecuted in a court of law for a breach of the principle of collective responsibility. Obviously, there is no legal sanction for collective responsibility. What is expected of a Minister as normal practice is that he should tender has resignation if he finds himself so sharply in conflict with his colleagues that it is no longer honestly possible for him to defend the Government's policies. But if he fails to do so, the Prime Minister can enforce collective responsibility through either of two ways. He may advise the President to dismiss the Minister, since the President has appointed the Minister on the advice of the Prime Minister. If the Prime Minister is not inclined to adopt this course, he may tender the resignation of the entire Ministry and form a new Ministry excluding the undesirable Minister. Thus, the realization of the principle of collective responsibility is made possible by placing the Ministers under the Prime Minister in the matter of appointment as well as dismissal.

Collective responsibility under the leadership of the Prime Minister ensures against the possibilities of intrigues among the members of the Ministry. If there was no Prime

1. In the words of Gladstone: "Differences of views stated, and if need be argued, and then advisedly surrendered with a view to common conclusion, are not dissension."

Minister, it would then be possible for the President to control and influence individual Ministers and thereby cause disruption among them. This happened in Britain, before the principle of collective responsibility was fully established, when the King used to disrupt the Cabinet. But once the position of the Prime Minister as *primus inter pares* (first among equals) was established, collective responsibility became a reality. Today, through the office of the Prime Minister, collective responsibility has become an abiding principle of cabinet government. Thus, he is the keystone of the Cabinet arch and this is what the Constitution achieves by making the Prime Ministers the head of the Council of Ministers.

According to Article 75(2), "the Ministers shall hold office during the pleasure of the President". Explaining the significance of this provision, Ambedkar said that a Minister would be liable to removal on two grounds.

> One ground on which he would be liable to dismissal would be that he has lost the confidence of the House. Secondly, that his administration is not pure, because the word here used is 'pleasure'. It would be perfectly open under that particular clause for the President to call for the removal of a particular Minister on the ground that he is guilty of corruption or bribery or maladministration, although that particular Minister probably is a person who enjoyed the confidence of the House. The two conditions that govern the tenure of a Minister of Office are purity of administration and confidence of the House. These are provided for in the Article.[1]

A striking feature of the cabinet system of government is that Ministers who hold the top positions in the Executive are, at the same time, members of Parliament also. But a rigid adherence to this rule might deprive the Executive of the services of men of ability who may not for the time being, be members of the Legislature. To avoid this difficulty, the Constitution provides a maximum period of six months for a Minister to become a member of the Legislature if he is already not such a member. There was opposition to this provision in the Constituent Assembly. "If nominated members of the legislature have no right even to participate in the election of the President, how could they (or non-members) become Ministers?" asked one member.[2] Ambedkar replied:

> It is perfectly possible to imagine that a person who is otherwise competent to hold the post of a Minister has been defeated in a constituency for some reason.... But it is not a reason why such a member so competent as that should be not permitted to be appointed a member of the Cabinet on the assumption that he may be able to get himself elected from some other constituency. After all, the privilege that is extended is only six months. Secondly, a nominated member being made a Minister does not violate the principle of collective responsibility, nor does it violate the principle of confidence, because if he is a member of the Cabinet, if he is prepared to accept the policy of the Cabinet, stands part of the Cabinet, and resigns with the Cabinet when he ceases to have the confidence of the House, his membership of the Cabinet does not in any way cause any inconvenience or breach of the fundamental principles on which parliamentary government is based.[3]

Nevertheless, the tendency so far in India has been against the appointment to the Ministry of nominated members and those who have been defeated in the election.[4]

---

1. C.A.D. VII, P. 1158
2. Shibban Lal Saksena, Ibid., p. 1174
3. C.A.D. VII, p. 1186.
4. Two notable exceptions to this tendency, which is fast becoming a convention, took place in 1952 after the first General Election in the states, when Morarji Desai who was defeated in the election to the Assembly was sent to the Council and appointed Chief Minister of Bombay, and when C. Rajagopalachari was nominated by the Governor to the Legislative Council and then appointed Chief Minister of Madras. In 1964 Indira Gandhi was appointed a minister of the Union Cabinet although she was not a member of either Houses of Parliament. Manmohan Singh in 1991 was another exception.

The Constitution also provides for the salaries and allowances of Ministers. But the details of these, such as the amount, etc. may by law be determined by Parliament from time to time. When compared with the salaries and allowances of the members of the Viceroy's Executive Council during the British regime, the salaries and allowances of the members of the present Government cannot be said to be high. Yet they are high enough in a comparatively poor country like India.[1] There were anxious voices raised in the Constituent Assembly emphasizing the need for purity in administration. It was suggested that every Minister at the time of joining office should declare all his assets, interests in property, etc. so that purity in service could be maintained. This suggestion was supported by many member who sought to incorporate it in a specific provision of the Constitution. This was, however, not accepted by the Drafting Committee. Yet, Ambedkar was personally in favour of some such provision. He thought that there ought to be at least some sanction in law for maintaining purity in administration. Firstly, every Minister should declare his assets and liabilities at the time he assumes office. He should also make such a declaration of his assets on the day that he quits office. If there is an abnormal increase in his assets there must ba provision to charge him for explaining how he managed to amass such large wealth. Secondly, if the explanation is not satisfactory, such abnormal increase should be declared an offence followed by a penalty or fine. He confessed that these were, however, very inadequate remedies. The machinery is inadequate and the remedy may be worse than the disease. "We have a better sanction and that is public opinion as mobilized and focused in the legislature." When one member asked, "Is it not a more impossible task?" the learned Doctor snapped back: "Democracy has to perform many more impossible tasks. If you want democracy you must face them."[2]

We have already seen the position of importance which the Constitution confers upon the Prime Minister. Though the President makes the appointment normally, it is only a constitutional formality as the person appointed has the political and parliamentary support to claim such an appointment. Similarly, though the President appoints other Ministers, they are so appointed only on the advice of the Prime Minister and, in reality, they are the nominees of the Prime Minister. The Ministry's decisions and actions are transmitted to the President only through the Prime Minister. Again, the Ministry is jointly responsible to the House of the People whose leader is the Prime Minister. Thus, the Prime Minister is a connecting link between the Ministry and the President on the one hand and also between the Ministry and Parliament on the other. This special position that he enjoys both in the Government and in Parliament makes his office the most important under the Constitution of India.

The long list of powers that are vested in the President are powers exercised in reality by the Prime Minister. As the leader of the party that commands the majority in Parliament and thus in fact as the leader of Parliament itself, and, in addition, as the head of the Council of Ministers, he really leads the Council of Ministers, Parliament an the nation. This is what makes him the most powerful functionary under the governmental system established by the Constitution. During any period of emergency, his power will

---

1. In the context of the general level of salaries in the country, they are by no means low, With free residence, travel, medical and other facilities besides a handsome monthly salary the Ministers of the Central Government are expected to maintain a decent standard of living and conforms which will keep them away from corrupt practices.
2. C.A.D. VII, 1189.

increase as the administration of the area affected by the emergency comes directly under the Union Government. Naturally, the personality of the Prime Minister will have an influence either in enhancing the actual powers of the President or limiting them to his constitutional functions.

The great concentration of power in the hands of the Prime Minister was an object of severe criticism in the Constituent Assembly. 'This Constitution concentrates so much power and influence in the hands of the Prime Minister, in regard to the appointment of judges, ambassadors or governors to such an extent', said K.T. Shan, 'that there is every danger to apprehend that the Prime Minister may become a dictator if he chooses to do so. I think there are cases which ought to be removed from his political influence.....'[1] Although such strong words were not used by him. Ambedkar also drew a picture of the Prime Minister almost in similar terms on one occasion when he was comparing the offices of the Prime Minister and the President.[2] On another occasion he said, 'If any functionary under our Constitution is to be compared with the United States President, he is the Prime Minister and not the President of the Union.'[3] Other members also expressed opinions reflecting the same apprehension which Shah had expressed. But the Constitution does not provide any special remedy except the accountability of the Ministry to Parliament.

India is gradually developing a well-defined party system which is an indispensable aid, to the evolution of a successful parliamentary government. The national election in the United States once every four years is meant primarily to select the President who would become the head of the nation and the Chief Executive for four years . In India, the general election once every five years becomes a great battle which determines the party that will rule the country for the next five years. But, to a large extent, it will also decide the person who will become the Prime Minister of India. For the party which secures a majority in Parliament is sure to have its leader appointed Prime Minister by the President. In fact, the President himself is often the nominee of the party and the leader of the party is sure to have a substantial influence in the selection of the presidential candidate.[4]

The Council of Ministers and the Cabinet

There is some confusion as a result of the indiscriminate use of the terms 'Cabinet' and 'Council of Ministers' in connection with the activities of the government. Often they are used as interchangeable terms. But, in fact, they are not. The Council of Ministers, or

1. C.A.D. VIII, p. 234.
2. C.A.D. VIII, p. 1036.
3. C.A.D. VII, p. 998.
4. In 1950 Prime Minister Nehru was in favour of electing C. Rajagopalachari, the last Governor-General of India, as the first President. Because of the strong opposition within the Congress party to C. Rajagopalacharis's election, Nehru yielded to party pressure and supported Rajendra Prasad who was unanimously elected President. In 1957, Nehru was reported to have favoured Vice President Radhakrishnan as President but Rajendra Prasad was unwilling to leave the scene and a large section of the party was supporting his re-election for another term. Again, Nehru yielded and Prasad was elected. In 1969 Sanjiva Reddy was the party nominee against the wishes of Prime Minister Indira Gandhi. In the closely contested election that followed, V.V. Giri, who was supported by the Prime Minister, won the contest, although by a narrow margin. Fakruddin Ali Ahemad and Gyani Zail Singh were both Indira Gandhi's choices. The Prime Minister was able to do so both because of her unrivalled position in the Congress Party and also because the Congress Party had massive majority in Parliament and majority support in most of the State Legislatures. Sanjiva Reddy's election as President in 1977 was unanimous.

the Ministry as it is usually called, consists of all the different categories of Ministers of the Government of India. Ar present, there are three such categories, namely, Cabinet Ministers, Ministers of State and Deputy Ministers. Of these, the Cabinet Ministers by themselves form a separate body called the Cabinet, which, in fact, is the nucleus of the Council of Ministers. There is not a word mentioned about the Cabinet in the Constitution which, as we have already seen, speaks only of the Council of Ministers. Yet, today, the functions of the Cabinet for all practical purposes are identified with those assigned to the Council under the Constitution.

The Cabinet provides the best example of conventions so far established under the Constitution. No doubt, the organization and working of the British Cabinet have provided the example. Yet, the Indian Cabinet is not a carbon copy of the British original, for, it has developed its own special features. At the time when power was transferred to Indians in 1947, there was no such institution as Cabinet in India. What existed then as a comparable body at the highest level in the Government was the Governor-General's Executive Council. But with the establishment of responsible government on 15 August 1947, the Executive Council was transformed into a Ministry responsible to Parliament. The two significant results of this transformation were the recognition of the principle of collective responsibility and the acceptance of the Prime Minister as the leader and head of the Ministry. The term 'Cabinet' was used thereafter as an alternative to 'Ministry' so much so that for some time these two terms were in use synonymously. All members of the Ministry or the Cabinet except the Prime Minister had the same status. But the situation soon underwent a change on account of the appointment of junior Ministers to the Council of Ministers.

During the transition period (till the inauguration of the Constitution in 1950), it was not possible to go into the various aspects of this and other developments, in administration. Nevertheless, the Cabinet was seized of the problem even before 1950 and entrusted the task of studying the problem and making suitable recommendations to one of its senior members, Gopalaswami Ayyanagar. It was the Ayyanagar Report of November 1949 which formed the basis of a comprehensive reorganization of the machinery of the Government at its highest level. The most significant part of this scheme or reorganization was the categorization of Ministers and defining the functions and responsibilities of each category and thus bringing about a rational system in place of the haphazard and even chaotic growth that had already taken place.

According to the scheme, a three-tier ministerial hierarchy was established with the Cabinet Ministers at the top, Ministers of State in the middle and Deputy Ministers at the lowest rung of the ladder.[1] A clear distinction was draw between Ministers who were members of the Cabinet and others. The Cabinet was composed of the seniormost Ministers

---

1. The total strength of the Council in 1964 under Prime Minister Nehru was 50 of which 13 were Cabinet Ministers, 15 Ministers of State and 22 Deputy Ministers. When Lal Bahadur Shastri succeeded him as Prime Minister in June 1964 the composition of the Council was somewhat altered with 16 Cabinet Ministers, 15 Ministers of State and 20 Deputy Ministers.

   In 1973, with Indira Gandhi as Prime Minister, there were 60 ministers in the Council of which 17 were Cabinet Ministers, 21 Ministers of State and 22 Deputy Ministers. Prime Minister Desai's Council (1977-79) had a maximum of 44 Ministers of which 20 were Cabinet Ministers and the rest Ministers of State. The Council of Ministers in 1981 with Indira Gandhi as Prime Minister consisted of 18 Cabinet Ministers, 21 Ministers of State and 10 Deputy Minister, 49 in all. Prime Minister Vajpayee's Council of Ministers, the latest of 2000, has been the largest with 74 Ministers in all, with 30 Cabinet Ministers and 44 Ministers of State of which 7 were with independent charge.

who were not mere departmental chiefs but whose responsibilities transcended departmental boundaries into the entire field of the administration. It was, naturally, a smaller body and the most powerful body in the Government. Thus, the growth of the Cabinet as a separate body from the Council of Ministers was only a natural product of the application of the administrative theory of organization. Soon, the Cabinet became not only a distinct entity, different from the Council of Ministers, but also an institution with its own detailed organization. In the process, it has also taken over functions assigned by the Constitution to the Council. For instance, the Council had the constitutional responsibility of advising the President. But this function is exercised exclusively by the Cabinet at present.

Members of the Cabinet are the principal Ministers who are chosen generally for their established reputation and ability in the political and administrative fields. Looking from another angle, one might say that the Cabinet is composed of Ministers who hold charge of the most important portfolios such as Finance, External Affairs, Defence, Communications, Home Affairs, Industry, Railways, etc. In the selection of Cabinet Ministers, the most important factor is the choice of the Prime Minister although he himself is bound to be influenced by political and party considerations. It is also necessary to keep the Cabinet a reasonably small body in order to make it 'a widely thinking, planning and deliberating body'. The size of the Indian Cabinet has remained around 13 to 20.

As the topmost body in the Government, the Cabinet has four major functions:

(a) To approve all proposals for legislation embodying the policies of the Government;
(b) To make all major appointments;
(c) To settle all inter-departmental disputes; and
(d) To co-ordinate the various activities of the Government and watch the progress in the execution of its policies.

Thus, the Cabinet is the formulator of national policies, the highest appointing authority, the arbiter of inter-departmental disputes and the supreme organ of coordination in the Government.

As a decision-making body, the Cabinet meets regularly (once a week is the present practice) and takes decisions on various items falling in one or other of the spheres of governmental activity which are presented for its consideration by individual Ministries and departments. Every matter that is submitted to the Cabinet for its decision is accompanied by an explanatory memorandum. If the matter concerns more than one department, all departments concerned supply such explanatory memoranda. These are circulated among the members of the Cabinet sufficiently in advance so that the members can attend Cabinet meetings well prepared after studying the issues involved in each question. As each item on the agenda is taken up, discussion takes place followed by decisions which also are recorded and transmitted. In its work the Cabinet is assisted by the Cabinet Secretariat which is headed by one of the seniormost members of the Civil Service designated as Cabinet Secretary.

In view of the tremendous growth in the volume and complexity of government business and also in view of the fact that Cabinet is the supreme organ of coordination, it had been found necessary to effect a division of labour among the members of the Cabinet as well as effective delegation within the Cabinet. This has been achieved through the constitution of Cabinet Committees. These committees are of two types, standing committees which are of a permanent nature and *ad hoc* committees. There are four standing committees of the Cabinet: Defence Committee, Economic Committee, Administrative Organization Committee and Parliamentary and Legal Affairs Committee. *Ad hoc* committees are constituted from time to time as and when new problems of great importance arise, requiring special study by a group within the Cabinet before final decision is taken by the Cabinet as a whole. Within the respective fields of activities of these committees, there is also provision for the setting up of sub-committees as and when necessary. These committees have functioned as effective agencies through which the functions of the Cabinet are discharged efficiently, expeditiously and with a considerable degree of expertise.

Ministers of State come next to Cabinet Ministers in the ministerial hierarchy. There are Ministers of State who hold independent charge of individual Ministries and perform the same functions and exercise the same powers as a Cabinet Minister. The only difference between such a Minister of State and a Cabinet Minister is that he is not a member of the Cabinet, and attends Cabinet meetings only when specially invited to do so in connection with the subject for which he is responsible. There are, however, some Ministers of State who do not hold independent charge but work directly under Cabinet Ministers. Thus, the existing position with respect to Ministers of State is not uniform. Selection to this category of Ministers seems to be made with the expectation that they would, in due course, rise to Cabinet rank after gaining experience.

Deputy Ministers are junior Ministers who do not have specific administrative responsibility for the conduct of business of any department but are practically understudies for eventual appointment as Ministers of State Normally, their duties include: (i) answering of questions in Parliament on behalf of the Ministers concerned and helping to pilot Bills; (ii) explaining policies and programmes to the general public and maintaining liaison with members of Parliament, political parties and the press; and (iii) undertaking special study or investigation of particular problems which may be entrusted to them by the Ministers concerned. The Deputy Minister in India, thus, holds a position equivalent to that of Parliamentary Secretaries in Britain. There are Parliamentary Secretaries in India also. But they are not members of the Council of Ministers and have no administrative responsibility whatever. Their function is confined to assisting Ministers in the discharge of their parliamentary functions such as answering questions in Parliament on behalf of the Ministers concerned.[1]

The Cabinet and Parliament

The most distinguishing feature of a parliamentary system of government is the unqualified and continuous responsibility of the Cabinet to Parliament for all its actions. Besides collective responsibility, there is also the individual responsibility of Ministers to Parliament for their actions arising out of their own administrative charges. Under the Constitution, ministerial responsibility is confined to the House of the People, (Lok Sabha) the Lower House of Parliament. This is in recognition of the popular character of that House which is a directly elected body, whereas the Council of States (Rajya Sabha) (the Upper House of Parliament) is indirectly elected.

1. There were 12 Parliamentary Secretaries on 1 April 1949. Their number in 1964, however, was only six. In 1973 there were no Parliamentary Secretaries. They ceased to exist thereafter.

Two special features of parliament government in India deserve mention in this connection. A person who is not a member of either House of Parliament can be a Minister. Secondly, a Minister, whether he is a member of Parliament or not, has the right to attend both House and participate in the discussions. The only restriction placed upon him is that he cannot vote. Similarly, a Minister who is a member of either House has the right to appear in the other House and participate in its proceedings, except for voting. So far, the Prime Minister has always been a member of the House of the People.[1] But one or other of his senior colleagues in the Cabinet has always been a member of the Council of States so that he could be its leader.

There are several methods by which Parliament ensures ministerial responsibility. Questions in Parliament, budget discussions, adjournment motions, discussions on reports by departments are some of the common and regular devices by which accountability is ensured. But the most important device at the disposal of Parliament is a no confidence motion with which Parliament's confidence in the Ministry can be tested. A successful no confidence motion will result in the defeat and overthrow of the Ministry. Thus, under the parliamentary system of government, the Cabinet is the creature of Parliament. But the working of the parliamentary system will show that although the Cabinet is the creature of Parliament, it is a creature that leads its creator.

The strength of the Indian Cabinet in the past had been the result of the support that it received from the party to which it belongs and the overwhelming strength of the party in Parliament. With a stable parliamentary support, the Cabinet, in reality, becomes the leader of Parliament. The initiative for all the policies and programmes of the Government are in the hands of the Cabinet. Nevertheless it must be pointed out that the Indian Cabinet has been treating Parliament with greater consideration and respect than is usual elsewhere under conditions of overwhelming parliamentary majorities. This has been mainly due to two reasons. First, on questions of great importance which vitally affect the nation as a whole, the Cabinet itself has given over the initiative to Parliament. The best example of this is provided by the initiative taken by Parliament in settling the question of the reorganized State of Bombay at the time of the adoption of the States Reorganization Act of 1956. Second, members of Parliament have often evinced a willingness to forget party affiliations when questions of purity in administration are brought before it. On such occasions, the Indian Parliament has shown that it is the mirror and custodian of public opinion in the country and a true representative of the electorate and is second only to the electorate itself. The manner in which Parliament dealt with the allegations brought before it against a state enterprise like the Life Insurance Corporation in 1957 is an example in point. Another good example is the Bofors case. A Parliamentary committee was constituted to probe into the alligation of corruption in the gun-deal in spite of the massive majority of the Rajiv Gandhi Governments.

The short period of internal emergency under Indira Gandhi during 1975-77 was the only exception.

Parliamentary pressure has also brought about perceptible changes in recent years in the policies of the Government towards industry, labour, taxation, defence, etc.

---

1. But this convention has been broken twice in the States when in 1952 the Chief Ministers of Bombay and Madras were members of the Upper House. The former as Chief Minister was such a member only for a short while, as he got elected to the Assembly some months later.

One must also point out in this connection the willingness and even the openmindedness displayed by the Indian Cabinet in dealing with such matters. The Government, with its steamroller majority and ability to crack the party whip against every recalcitrant member showing any sign of defiance, could have imposed its will on Parliament and carried on in a dictatorial manner. But experience so far shows that cabinet dictatorship is still foreign to India although the conditions and circumstances during the first two decades have been abundantly in its favour. Adherence to the fundamental principles of parliamentary government has been almost a passion with the Indian Cabinet which has been eager to build up conventions of an abiding nature to make its working smooth and successful. The flowering of parliamentary government may yet be a long way off in India. But its roots are growing fast in the Indian soil and there is reason to believe that, in future, it will flourish and become a part of the best of parliamentary heritage.

***

23

THE VICE PRESIDENT AND THE ATTORNEY-GENERAL

THE CONSTITUTION provides for a Vice President whose role in the Government is comparatively insignificant. Going through the provisions dealing with his office, one can easily see a striking similarity between the role of the Vice President of India and that of his counterpart in the United States. The U.S. Vice President is sometimes called "His Superfluous Highness' to characterize his comparative insignificance in the administration. But there is a provision in the U.S. Constitution which makes the Vice President potentially important. According to this, if the President dies in office, the Vice President takes over the President's office and continues in that capacity for the full length of the unexpired term. But under the Indian Constitution, if the President dies or resigns or is otherwise incapacitated and as a result, the presidential office becomes vacant, the Vice President will act as President only for a maximum period of six months. This difference seems to be the product of two reasons. First, the President of India is not elected in a general election involving the whole nation as is the case with the U.S. President. Second, since the Constitution insists that not more than six months should elapse between two sessions of Parliament and those of the State Legislatures, even if the Legislatures are under dissolution at the time when a vacancy occurs in the office of the President, election of the new President can be held within a maximum period of six months as the new Legislatures would have come into being during that period. As such, the maximum possible delay in the election of a new President will be only six months. Hence the provision for the Vice President to act as President up to a maximum period of six months.

The main function of the Vice President like that of his U.S. counterpart is to preside over the Upper House of Parliament, the Council of States. He is its *ex-officio* Chairman.

The Vice President is elected by the members of both Houses of Parliament at a joint meeting. The election will be conducted in accordance with the system of proportional representation by means of a single transferable vote. The voting will be by secret ballot. Explaining the reason for the adoption of a different system from that by which the President is elected, Ambedkar said:

> The difference is based upon the functions which the two dignitaries are supposed to discharge. The President is the Head of the State and his powers extend both to the administration by the Centre as well as of the States..... But when we come to the Vice-President, his normal functions are merely to preside over the Council of States. It is only on a rare occasion, and that too for a temporary

period, that he may be called upon to assume the duties of the President. That is the justification for a distinction in the methods of election of these two dignitaries.[1]

The salary of the Vice President as notified in 2000 is Rs. 40,000 p.m. The Vice President will take over the office of the President, normally, under four situations: death of the President, resignation of the President; removal of the President from his office through impeachment or otherwise; and finally, when the President is unable to discharge his functions owing to absence, illness or any other cause. The last of these clearly provides for any temporary period of incapacity which makes the President incapable of discharging his responsibilities.[2] This is a good provision, the absence of which in the U.S. Constitution created serious constitutional difficulties some years ago when President Eisenhower was ill.[3]

During the period when the Vice President is acting for the President he will have all the powers and immunities of the President. He is also entitled for such salary and allowances and privileges as may be determined by Parliament by law for the purpose. At present, according to the Second Schedule to the Constitution, the Vice President is entitled to the same emoluments, allowances and privileges as the President while he discharges the functions of or is acting as the President.

Any Indian citizen who has completed thirty-five years of age and who is qualified for election as a member of the Council of States is eligible for election as Vice President. But no person who holds an office of profit under the Government of India or any State or local or other authority in India is eligible for the purpose. The Vice President cannot be a member of either House of Parliament or a member of any State legislature. He can be removed from office by a majority of all the then members[4] of the Council and agreed to by the House of the People. But this procedure does not seem to be sufficient if, at the time such removal is sought, the Vice President is acting for the President. If he is to be removed from office while he acts in the latter capacity, the provisions ought to be exactly the same as are applicable to the impeachment of the President. All disputes in connection with the elections of the President and Vice President will be settled by the Supreme Court of India.

Although the Constitution does not confer upon the Vice President the great authority that it vests in the President as the Head of the State, the office of the Vice President has nevertheless been one of great dignity and prestige.[5] The personality of its incumbents who have all been eminent men has been one of the major reasons. The dignity and prestige that are established today may be expected to remain with the office of the Vice President in the years to come.

---

1. C.A.D. VII, p. 1100.
2. This provision has been taken advantage of in 1961 and 1964 when President Rajendra Prasad and President Radhakrishnan respectively were ill. Again in 1978 and 1982 when President Sanjiva Reddy and Presidednt Zail Singh respectively were away abroad to undergo treatment.
3. The same difficulty occurred during the second term of Wilson's Presidency between the years 1919 and 1920.
4. The word 'then' qualifying 'members' means the total number of members on the roll of the Council at the time of voting.
5. According to the present Warrant of Precedence, the Vice President comes as number two, next to the President. Originally, his place was number three, as the second place was taken by the Prime Minister. At present, the Prime Minister figures as number three in the order of precedence.

The Attorney-General

In order to advise the Union Government in legal matters as well as to perform such other duties of a legal character as may be assigned by the President, the Constitution has provided for the office of the Attorney-General for India. The attorney-General must have the qualifications of a judge of the Supreme Court of India. He is appointed by the President and shall hold office during the pleasure of the President. The President may determine the remuneration to be paid to the Attorney-General.

The Attorney-General is a member of the Cabinet in Britain. But in India, there is a Minister of Law in the Cabinet to deal with legal affairs at government level. The Attorney-General, however, has the privilege of addressing both Houses of Parliament just as a Minister has, irrespective of his membership of the House. He also enjoys the same privileges and immunities as the members of Parliament. The Constitution expressly guarantees his right of audience in all courts in India in the performance of his duties.

In 1962 the Government made a proposal to merge the office of the Attorney-General with that of the Minister of Law. The proposal envisaged even an amendment of the Constitution if it was found necessary for the purpose. But it soon raised a controversy all over the country as to the constitutionality and the propriety of the step. The main arguments advanced by the Government in support of the proposal were (1) that the Attorney-General had no responsibility to the Government; (2) that the Government normally sought the advice of the Law Minister; (3) that the question of an independent adviser was necessitated by economy and the emergency.[1] It was also pointed out that under the British Parliamentary model of Government which India had adopted the Attorney-General was normally a member of the Cabinet.

These arguments were ably countered by the opponents of the proposal, particularly a large majority of the lawyers in the country.[2] Their main arguments were: (1) It is wrong to compare the British practice with the position of the Attorney-General under the Constitution. This is because of the existence of Parliamentary supremacy in England. Indian Parliament, on the contrary, is limited in its powers. The most significant part of the work of the Attorney-General is to advise on the competence of Parliament to pass laws without infringing the guaranteed fundamental rights and without transgressing the legislative field demarcated for the States under the federal system. Such advice can be given in an independent and forthright manner if only the Attorney-General is independent of the Central Cabinet and not responsible for the policies formulated by it. (2) The Law Minister being a Member of the Cabinet cannot be expected to give such independent advice. He is a party to the policy and hence his judgment is likely to be coloured by the political overtones of the question. (3) The framers of the Constitution envisaged a separate office for the Attorney-General, independent of and separate from that of the Law Minister. (4) If the Attorney-General is not an independent adviser, the President would be denied of independent advice as and when he needs it. (5) Considerations of economy and emergency cannot ignore the fundamental principles of the Constitution and the intentions of the framers.

The opposition to the proposal was so strong that the Government was compelled to abandon the ill-advised move within a few months.

***

1. The country was at war with China in 1962 and consequently an emergency was declared.
2. Cf Ashok H. Desail, "Law Minister as Attorney-General", *The Economic and Politicial Weekly,* Annual Number 1963, pp. 129-32 and V. Venkatarama Ayyar, "Attorney-General and Law Minister", *The Hindu,* 22 January 1963.

24

THE UNION LEGISLATURE : THE PARLIAMENT OF INDIA

THE GENERAL objective of every scheme of representation is efficacy in securing responsibility in government. In a general sense, modern government can be interpreted as an effort to produce the responsible conduct of public affairs with a view to realizing mutually acceptable interests. Such interests are generally characterized as 'public interests' which become the basis for evaluating the actions of public authorities. But who is competent to judge the soundness or otherwise of governmental action in relation to public interest? The most common and popular answer is: the public. The public, however, in a modern State means millions and millions of people. They cannot gather together at one place in the manner in which the ancient Athenians used to assemble in their market place and transact public business. Hence, new devices were called for, which would facilitate on the one hand the participation of the public and, on the other, the evaluation of governmental action in the light of public interest. The most widely accepted device for securing this double purpose is the creation of representative institutions. The emergence of legislatures, parliaments, congresses and such other bodies as representative institutions is the result of the application of this device. By representing the public, they reflect the conflicting interests that exists among the public. But the common good demands that these conflicting interests should compromise. And compromise is brought about by argument and discussion. Through such argument and discussion interests become articulated and get rationalized. Thus, Parliaments serve the tow-fold purpose of public interests and popular representation. In spite of their defects and drawbacks, legislatures justify themselves by fulfilling these two cardinal functions.

The working of modern representative institutions has a comparatively short history in India although the history of ancient India bears testimony to the widespread prevalence of different types of representative institutions. The village panchayats and janpad sabhas are two examples from among many such institutions which served the people at the basic levels of civic life. These institutions, however, disappeared in course of time as a result of invasions and the establishment of dictatorial or monarchical regimes. The first attempt to introduce modern representative institutions in India under the British, as we have seen earlier, was made after the transfer of power from the Company to the Crown. The Indian Councils Act of 1861 is sometimes called as 'the Prime Charter of the Indian Legislature'. But the so-called legislatures in India during the nineteenth century were at best a miniature version of a real legislative body. The representation of the public in these bodies was even less than nominal. But substantial progress was made in the twentieth century. The Government of India Acts of 1909, 1919 and 1935 set up legislative bodies both at the Centre and in the Provinces, each successive Act setting up such institutions on the basis of a more broad-based representative character. Side by side with these, there were also developments in some of the Indian States[1] which favoured the creation of legislative bodies. But the Indian national movement which gathered momentum in the thirties of this century was not satisfied with the existing basis of representation nor with the sort of responsible government that prevailed in India. With the passage of the Indian Independence Act of 1947 and the establishment of a full-fledged Indian Government, the principle of legislative supremacy was established for the first time in India. This was the position when the Constituent Assembly took up the question of establishing a new Parliament under the Constitution of independent India.

Under the Constitution, the Legislature of the Union is called Parliament. The Indian Parliament is constituted on the basis of the principle of bi-cameralism, that is, the Legislature having two Houses or Chambers. As the Constitution established a federal system of government, there was almost unanimity among the framers for achieving a balance between the direct representation of people and the representation of units as such by setting up two Houses, one representing the people as a whole and the other the federated units. The two Houses of Parliament are the House of the People (the Lok Sabha) and the Council of States (the Rajya Sabha). The name of the Houses fairly reflect the character of the composition. The House of the People is composed of directly elected representatives on the basis of adult franchise and territorial constituencies. The Council of States is composed mainly of representatives of the States elected by the State Assemblies.

As has been pointed out earlier, the President is an integral part of Parliament. Under Article 79, Parliament shall consist of the President and the two Houses. Making the President a part of Parliament is in conformity with the principles and traditions of parliamentary government. In England, Parliament is constituted of the King, the House of Lords and the House of Commons. In contrast, the President of the United States is not a part of the U.S. Congress. Whereas the presidential system of government emphasizes the separation of the executive and legislative powers, the parliamentary system lays stress on the intimate relationship and the interdependence of the Executive and the Legislature. Members of the Government are at the same time members of the Legislature. His participation in the legislative process is ensured by making him a part of Parliament. The fact that he is the chief executive authority and that the executive power is coextensive with the legislative power also makes it necessary that he should become an integral part of the Legislature.[2]

The House of the People (The Lok Sabha)

The House of the People is commonly known as the Lok Sabha and its members are elected directly by the people. Unlike many other constitutions, the maximum number of members to be elected to the Lok Sabha was originally fixed at 500. But the Seventh Amendment of the Constitution, following the reorganization of States in 1956, raised the limit to 520 (Art. 81). The Thirty-first Amendment, 1973, further raised the limit to 545. Of these, 20 seats are reserved for members from the Union territories who may be elected

1. The most notable examples are Mysore, Travancore-Cochin and Baroda.
2. C.A.D. VII, p. 1198.

directly or otherwise as Parliament by law may provide. The remaining 525 members are to be chosen by direct election from territorial constituencies in the States. For this purpose, a certain number of seats is allotted to each State on the basis of its population in proportion to the total population of all the States. For the purpose of election, each State is divided into territorial constituencies which are more or less of the same size in regard to population.

The fixation of a maximum number of seats for a House elected by popular vote does not seem to be a sound principle. The provision was criticized in the Constituent Assembly. K.T. Shah said:

> It is not in accord with the correct principle of popular representation that it must be the final authority in the governance of the country calling itself a democracy. Under such a principle, the constitution should not fix permanently the maximum number of representatives for the popular chamber. Where the population is making a steady increase, if a permanent maximum is fixed the representative character of each representative would become lesser and lesser, as he would be representing a larger and larger number.[1]

Apart from this, for a population of over 1000 million people 545 representatives seem to be too small a number. For example, in Britain, for a population of 55 million the House of Commons has a membership of 640; in France for 50 million the National Assembly under the Fourth Republic had 595 and under the Fifth Republic 540 members; the House of Representatives in the United States has 435 members for a population of some 260 million and the Lower House of the Supreme Soviet of the U.S.S.R. had over 700 members for a population of some 270 million. The fixation of a maximum was proved inexpedient within six years after the inauguration of the Constitution and the Seventh Amendment raised the upper limit of elected members from 500 to 520. In 1973 the upper limit was further raised to 545. The only argument in favour of fixing a maximum of 500 at the time of the adoption of the Constitution was that more than 500 would constitute too large a body which would hamper the efficiency of the work of the House.[2] But in the light of the examples cited above, this apprehension would seem to be baseless.

The present strength of the House is 545. These include the two Anglo-Indian representatives who have been nominated to the House by the President. This is in accordance with a special provision of the Constitution under which the President will nominate not more than two members of the Anglo-Indian community to the Lok Sabha if no member of that community is elected to that House.[3] On the basis of the 1951 census, India had a population of 360 million. But in 1961 it was about 440 million and in 1971 about 560 million. By 1981 it was over 683 million. By 2000 it has gone above 1000 million.

With 543 elected members in the House, one member at present represents about two million of the population, a very low rate of representation indeed. The representation from the various States may be seen in the following table:

---

1. C.A.D. VII, p. 236.
2. C.A.D., p. 1260.
3. Vide Article 331.

Name of the State	Number of Members
1. Andhra Pradesh	42
2. Arunachal Pradesh	1
3. Assam	14
4. Bihar	40
5. Chhatisgarh	11
6. Goa	2
7. Gujarat	26
8. Haryana	10
9. Himachanl Pradesh	4
10. Jammu & Kashmir	6
11. Jharkhand	14
12. Karnataka	28
13. Kerala	20
14. Madhya Pradesh	29
15. Maharashtra	48
16. Manipur	2
17. Meghalaya	2
18. Mizoram	1
19. Nagaland	1
20. Orissa	21
21. Punjab	13
22. Rajasthan	25
23. Sikkim	1
24. Tamil Nadu	39
25. Tripura	2
26. Uttaranchal	5
27. Uttar Pradesh	80
28. West Bengal	42
Union Territories	
1. Andaman and Nicobar Islands	1
2. Chandigarh	1
3. Dadra and Nagar Haveli	1
4. Delhi	7
5. Lakshadweep	1
6. Pondicherry	1
7. Daman and Diu	1
Special Representation	
Anglo-Indians	2

The election to the House is conducted on the basis of adult franchise, every man or woman who has completed the age of eighteen years being eligible to vote. The Constitution provides for secret ballot. According to the present system, a candidate who secures the highest number of votes is declared elected. Some members had advocated the system of proportional representation for the election of members to the Lok Sabha. This was opposed by Ambedkar for two reasons:

> Proportional Representation presupposes literacy on a large scale.....I think having regard to the extent of literacy in this country, such a presupposition would be utterly extravagant....Further, proportional representation is not suited to the form of government which this Constitution lays down..... Where there is a parliamentary system of government you must necessarily have a party which is in majority and which is prepared to support the government. A disadvantage of the system of proportional representation is the fragmentation of the legislature into a number of small groups. If Parliament is divided into so many small groups, every time anything happened which displeased certain groups in Parliament, they would on that occasion withdraw their support from the Government with the result that the Government would fall to pieces. Now, I have not the least doubt in my mind that whatever else the future government provides for, whether it relieves the people from the wants from which they are suffering now or not our future government must do one thing, namely, it must maintain a stable government and maintain law and order.[1]

The normal life of the House of the People is five years from the date of its first meeting, but it may be dissolved earlier by the President of India.[2] The President is also empowered to extend the life of the House for one year at a time during a national emergency. But in any case, the life of the House cannot be extended beyond six months after the promulgation of the emergency has ceased to operate. The House shall meet at least twice a year and the interval between two consecutive sessions shall be less than six months. The time and the place of meeting will be decided by the President who will summon the House to meet. He has also the power to prorogue the House.

Qualifications for Election to Parliament

There is hardly any qualification that the Constitution prescribes for a member of Parliament except that he should be an Indian citizen and has completed the age of twenty-five years if he seeks election to the House and thirty years if he seeks election to the Council. A striking feature of the electoral law is that a candidate for election to the House of the People may stand from any parliamentary constituency from any of the States in India. Such a provision, which is almost unknown in other federal States, is an incidence of the principle of single citizenship which emphasizes the unity of the nation. In the United States, for instance, a contesting candidate for a seat in the House of Representatives must be, when elected, "An inhabitant of that State in which he shall be chosen." A person who seeks election to the Council of States, however, should be an elector in any of the parliamentary constituencies of the State from which he is standing for election. This emphasizes the principle that the Council of States is the representatives of the States.

---

1. C.A.D. VII, p. 1262.
2. Such a dissolution took place for the first time in 1971, at the end of four years. Again the House was dissolved in 1979 before it could complete half of its full term of 5 years. Again, it was dissolved in 1991, 1998 and 1999 each time before it completed five years.

The question of fixing some special qualifications for parliamentary candidates as well as those for State legislatures had been raised in the Constituent Assembly. K.T. Shah was the Champion of this cause and advocated at least certain minimum literacy qualifications for every candidate.[1]

We have an appalling volume of ignorance in this country—utter illiteracy. And the danger of illiteracy becoming predominant or rather the danger of illiterate candidates coming into the legislature appears to me to be so great that In think that we would do well to lay down a positive requirement or qualification for candidates seeking election to the legislature, to be literates at least.

According to R.R. Diwakar, qualifications should have been prescribed for candidates in order to ensure a minimum standard. "We want a legislator who is not merely a representative but also a representative who can legislate and who has a certain perspective".[2] But the most powerful argument came from President Prasad in his Concluding address to the Assembly:

I would have liked to have some qualifications laid down for members of the legislatures. It is anomalous that we should insist upon high qualifications for those who administer or help in administering the law but none for those who make it except that they are elected. A law-giver requires intellectual equipment but even more than that the capacity to take a balanced view of things, to act independently and above all to be true to those fundamental things of life, to have character. It is not possible to devise any yardstick for measuring the moral qualities of a man and so long as that is not possible, our Constitution will remain defective.[3]

Ambedkar was of opinion that this was a question that should be left to the legislature to decide.[4]

The Constitution has, however, laid down certain disqualifications for membership. These are as follows:

1. No person can be a member of both Houses of Parliament or a member both of Parliament and of a State Legislature. There is no bar to a candidate contesting at a same time as many seats as he likes or to as many legislatures as he likes. But if he is elected to more than one seat, he should vacate all except one according to his choice. If the same person is elected to both a parliamentary seat and a seat in a State Legislature and if he does not resign his seat in the State Legislature before a specified period, his seat in Parliament will become vacant.
2. A person will be disqualified if he absents himself for a period of sixty days from the meetings of the House without the permission of the House.
3. He will be disqualified if he holds an office of profit under any Government in India.[5]

---

1. C.A.D. VIII, p. 552, also see Ibid., p. 135.
2. C.A.D. VII, p. 291.
3. Ibid., X, p. 993.
4. Ibid., VIII, p. 553.
5. Ministers are exempted from this provision. Parliament has defined the term 'Office of Profit' in order to specify its limits in respect of many offices of a semi or quasi governmental character. See *Report of the Committee on Offices of Profit,* Lok Sabha Secretariat, 1955. There is a Joint Committee of Parliament to look into this matter.

4. He will be disqualified if he is of unsound mind.
5. He will be disqualified if he is an undischarged insolvent.
6. He will be disqualified if he voluntarily acquires the citizenship of another State or is under any acknowledgment of allegiance to a foreign State.[1]

In pursuance of the powers granted under Article 327 to regulate matters of election, Parliament passed the Representation of the People Act in 1951 which too lays down certain conditions for disqualification. These are:

1. A member of Parliament should not have been found guilty by a Court or an Election Tribunal of Certain election offences or corrupt practices in election.
2. He should not have been convicted by a Court in India of any offence and sentenced to imprisonment for a period of not less than two years.
3. He should not have failed to lodge an account of his election expenses within the time and in the manner prescribed.
4. He should not have been dismissed for corruption or disloyalty from Government service.
5. He should not be a director or managing agent or hold an office of profit under any corporation in which the Government has any financial interest.
6. He should not have any interest in government contract, execution of government work or service.

These disqualifications should not exist on the date of nomination of a candidate for election and on the date when the results are declared.[3]

Officers of Parliament: The Speaker

The House of the People is presided over by the Speaker who is elected by the House from among its own members. The office of the Speaker has been held in great esteem throughout the history of over three hundred years of parliamentary government in Britain. This is because of the manner in which he has discharged his responsibilities as presiding officer, and the detachment and objectivity which he brought to bear upon all his decisions. That the frames of India's Constitution were quite conscious of this role of impartiality of the Speaker is evident from the provisions in the Constitution dealing with the office of the Speaker. For instance, Article 94(c) provides for the removal of the Speaker by a resolution of the House passed by a majority of all the then members of the House. Removal of officers from their positions in this manner, namely, by such special resolutions and by such special majorities, is restricted to only a few offices such as those of the President, the Vice President, the Presiding Officers of both Houses of Parliament, Judges of the Supreme Court, etc. as these officers are expected to discharge their responsibilities without political and party considerations.

---

1. H.V. Kamath wanted a provision in the Constituion authorizing the recall of legislators. The move was, however, rejected by the Assembly. C.A.D. VII, p. 134.
2. These are applicable to memebrs of State legislatures also. See, also the Prevention of Disqualification Act, 1958, in this connection.
3. Section 7, Representation of the People Act, 1951. See also the Amending Act of 1955.

The importance of the office of the Speaker can be seen also from the functions that he performs and the powers that he exercises. He presides over the meetings of the House. He adjourns the House or suspends its meeting if there is no quorum. While questions are decided in the House, he is not entitled to vote in the first instance (which emphasizes his impartiality) but he shall exercise a casting vote in case of a tie. Any member of the House who resigns his office should address his letter of resignation to the Speaker. The decision of the Speaker as to whether or not a Bill is a Money Bill shall be final. The Speaker will have to endorse or certify it before such a Bill is transmitted to the Council of States or presented to the President for his assent. He will be consulted along with the Chairman of the Council of States by the President while making rules of procedure with respect to joint sittings of the two Houses. In such sittings it is the Speaker's right to preside. In conformity with the Speaker's power to conduct the business of the House, he is empowered to allow any member to speak in his mother tongue if he cannot adequately express himself either in Hindi or English. With respect to the discharge of his powers and functions, the Speaker is not answerable to anyone except the House. No court of law can go into the merits of a ruling given by the Speaker.

In addition to these constitutional provisions, the Rules of procedure of the House confer upon the Speaker a variety of powers in the detailed conduct of the business of the House. Under these, his decision to admit notices of questions, motions, resolutions, bills, amendments, etc. is final. There are certain guiding principles which the Rules of Procedure lay down for determining the admissibility of notices of motions, etc. The interpretation of these rules as well as their application to specific situations and circumstances is the prerogative of the Speaker. He is the sole authority for giving priority or urgency to a matter so that it may be placed before the House in the national interest. He is not expected to give reasons for his decisions which cannot be challenged by any member. His powers to maintain discipline in the House and to conduct its proceedings in accordance with the rules are formidable. Similarly his powers in connection with the constitution as well as the working of parliamentary committees also are enormous. The Speaker is thus the guardian and custodian of the rights and privileges of the members, both in their individual capacity and on the group or party basis. The Speaker, in short, is the representative of the House itself in its powers, proceedings and dignity.

A special feature of the Speaker's office is that even when the House is dissolved, the Speaker does not vacate his office. He will continue in office until a new Speaker is elected when the new House meets. Parliament is empowered to fix the salary and allowances of the Speaker and these are charged on the Consolidated Fund of India.

The esteem with which the office of the Speaker is looked upon is reflected in the following observation of Prime Minister Nehru at the time of the unveiling of the portrait of the late V.J. Patel (the first Indian who presided over the Central Legislative Assembly) on 8 March 1948 in the Constituent Assembly of India. He said:

> Now Sir, on behalf of the Government, may I say that we would like the distinguished occupant of the Chair now and always to guard the freedom and liberties of the House from every possible danger, even from the danger of executive intrusion. There is always a danger.....from a majority that it may choose to ride rough-shod over the opinions of a minority, and it is there that the Speaker comes in to protect each single member or each single group from any such unjust activity by a dominant group or a dominant Government..... The Speaker represents the House. He represents the dignity of the House, the freedom of the House and because the House represents the nation, in a

particular way, the Speaker becomes the symbol of the nation's freedom and liberty. Therefore, it is right that that should be an honoured position and should be occupied always by men of outstanding ability and impartiality.

Within the relatively short period of over five decades during which the Speaker's office has been in existence, conventions of an abiding nature have already been established and the Speaker has, indeed, become a true symbol of the dignity and independence of the House as well as the guardian of the rights and privileges of its members. There was, however, one occasion during this period when a motion of no confidence was moved against the Speaker supported by a combined opposition alleging that "he has ceased to maintain an impartial attitude necessary to command the confidence of all the sections of the House".[1] The motion was defeated after a detailed discussion in which a large number of members including Prime Minister Nehru participated. But it had its lessons. The entire discussion highlighted the importance of the Speaker's office, its dignity and authority, and the necessity for the maintenance of absolute impartiality by the Speaker in the discharge of his official functions and in the exercise of his powers. The then Deputy Speaker who presided over the memorable occasion affirmed: "I agree that even if one honourable member is not treated impartially, he may have a grievance and many honourable members may support him". In fact, the Speaker has a special obligation to protect the rights of the minorities—groups or parties—in the House. General recognition of these principles and scrupulous adherence to them by the Speaker alone will not produce the desired results. There is a corresponding obligation on the part of those who are in power as well as those in opposition to respect the Speaker, to adbide by his rullings unreservedly and desist from any attempt to censure him at the slightest provocation. It is only such a spirit of give and take that can build up the enduring foundations of an effective parliamentary forum.

The Deputy Speaker

The Deputy Speaker who presides over the House in the absence of the Speaker is elected in the same manner in which the Speaker is elected by the House. He can be removed from office also in the same manner. When he sits in the seat of the Speaker, he has all the powers of the Speaker and can perform all his functions. One of his special privileges is that when he is appointed as a member of a parliamentary committee, he automatically becomes its Chairman. By virtue of the office that he holds, he has a right to be present at any meeting of any committee if he so chooses and can preside over its deliberations. His rullings are generally final, in any case, so far as they are related to the matters under discussion, but the Speaker may give guidance in the interest of uniformity in practice. Whenever the Deputy Speaker is in doubt, he reserves the matter for the ruling of the Speaker.

The Deputy Speaker, however, is otherwise like any ordinary member when the Speaker presides over the House. He may speak like any other member, maintain his party affiliation and vote on propositions before the House as any ordinary member. It seems desirable, however, that he keeps himself aloof from controversies and narrow partisan activities. This will enable him to cultivate the virtue of impartiality and exercise it whenever he presides over the House. Moreover, this will make it easy for the House to elect him

1. The motion was moved on 18 December 1954 and the Speaker concerned was G.V. Mavlankar, the first to occupy the office under the present Constitution.

unanimously as its Speaker if and when the Speaker's office becomes vacant. The Deputy Speaker is entitled to a regular salary.

Panel of Chairmen

To facilitate the work of the House in the absence of the Speaker and the Deputy Speaker, there is provision for one of the members of the House out of a panel of six Chairmen whom the Speaker nominates from time to time, to preside over its deliberations. When the Chairman sits in the Speaker's chair, he has all the powers of the Speaker just as the Deputy Speaker has when he acts for the Speaker. The Chairman, however, is just an ordinary member as soon as he vacates the Speaker's chair. A healthy convention has been built up by which the Speaker nominates members on the Panel of Chairmen irrespective of their party affiliations. As a result, some of the members of the panel come from the ranks of the opposition parties.

Secretary

The Constitution authorizes each House of Parliament to have its own secretarial staff and also gives them the power to regulate by law the conditions of service of those appointed to the secretarial staff. Such a provision was not in the original draft of the Constitution. The decision to incorporate it in the Constitution was taken by the Drafting Committee as a result of the recommendation of the Speakers' conference of 1949. The principle behind the provision is that a secretariat responsible to the Speaker and independent of the Executive is essential to maintain the independence of the House, the efficient transaction of its business and the dignity of the Speaker. The Lok Sabha Secretariat is now headed by a Secretary General who is a permanent officer. He discharges on behalf of the Speaker the various administrative and executive functions connected with the work of the House. In many ways, he is like an adviser to the House, its committees, the Speaker, the Deputy Speaker, and individual members. His role in the work of the House is that of a permanent civil service officer in the Secretariat of the Government of India. In discharging his functions, he is not concerned with the party affiliations of the members or the political cross-currents within the House.

Chairman

While the presiding officers of the House of the People are called the Speaker and the Deputy Speaker, the officers in the Council of States are called the Chairman and the Deputy Chairman respectively. It has already been mentioned that the Vice President of India is the *ex-officio* Chairman of the Council of States. We have also seen in that connection the method of his election, the manner in which he may be removed from office and his functions and powers. As the presiding officer of the Rajya Sabha his functions and powers are the same as those of the Speaker. He is however not a member of the House. We have seen now the Vice President will act for the President under certain contingencies. During such periods, he will not perform the duties of the office of the Chairman of the Council nor will he draw the salary or allowances payable to the Chairman.

Deputy Chairman

In the absence of the Chairman, the Council is presided over by the Deputy Chairman.

He is a member of the House and is elected by the members of the House. When he ceases to be a member of the Council, he automatically vacates the office of the Deputy Chairman. He can resign his office by writing to the Chairman. He may be removed from his office by a resolution passed by a majority of all the then members of the Council. The Deputy Chairman is empowered to discharge all the functions and to perform all the duties of the office of the Chairman whenever the Chairman's office is vacant or when the Vice President is acting for the President. As a presiding officer of the Council he is also given a regular salary and other allowances such as Parliament by law has fixed. The Council of States also has a panel of members called Vice Chairman nominated by the Chairman for the purpose of presiding over the House in the absence of both the Chairman and the Deputy Chairman. The Secretariat of the Rajay Sabha is headed by a Secretary who discharges the same functions as the Secretary General of the Lok Sabha.

The Council of States (The Rajya Sabha)

The Council of States is the Upper House of Parliament and is sometimes called the 'House of Elders'. In spite of the academic and theoretical denunciations of second chambers, the Constituent Assembly was practically unanimous[1] about the usefulness and necessity of the Council of States as an integral part of the general scheme of the Union Government. There was however divergence of opinion with respect to its composition, maximum membership and functions.[2] One member wanted the numerical strength of the House to be fixed at 150. Several suggestions were made in connection with the composition of the House. Some wanted equality of status among the States in the matter of representation while others denounced it as undermocratic and outmoded. Some were bitterly opposed to nomination of members while others wanted functional representation. While indirect election was opposed by some, election by the method of proportional representation was welcomed by others. One member suggested that an advisory body of professional and special interests should be set up to advise Parliament. Despite the large number of amendments based upon these and other ideas, the provisions embodied in the Draft Constitution were passed without any substantial modification except in regard to the method of the election of members.[3]

The maximum membership of the Council of States is limited to 250, just half of the maximum membership originally fixed for the House of the People. Its composition is unique. There is an attempt to combine different principles of representation in the composition of the same legislative body. The American principle of equality of States in representation, which has been followed by several federal constitutions was rejected as undermocratic. At the same time, the election of the majority of its members by the State Assemblies is intended to give recognition to the federal principle. The provision of nomination seeks to bring into the Council persons of special talents and accomplishments who may not otherwise become members.

The present strength of the Council is 244. Of these, 232 are elected by the various State Legislative Assemblies, thus making the council predominantly and indirectly elected

1. There was only one member to move an amendment which sought to remove the Council altogether. C.A.D. VII, p. 1195.
2. Ibid. p. 1202.
3. Ibid., pp. 1200-31.

body. For the purpose of this election, a certain number of seats is allotted to each State in the Council. The main basis of such allotment is the strength of the population in each State. But this is not the sole consideration. The smaller States have been accorded some weightage in representation. Thus, for example, Uttar Pradesh, with a population of over 110 million, has been given only 34 seats while 7 seats have been allotted to Assam with a population of a little over 19 million. While Kerala with a population of 25 million has 9 seats, only 22 seats have been allotted to Bihar with a population of some 70 million. To take a more glaring example, Delhi with a population of little over six million has 3 seats while West Bengal has only 16 seats despite her population of over 54 million. (These population figures are based on 1981 census).

Member of each State Legislative Assembly form the electorate for the purpose of electing the requisite number of members allotted to each State, thus ensuring the principle of the State representation in the Upper Chamber of Parliament. This arrangement seems to have two advantages over the senatorial elections in the United States and Australia. First, the election is much simpler. Second, the voters are the State's representatives.[1] The election of members to the Council from the State Assemblies is conducted in accordance with the system of proportional representation by means of single transferable vote and voting is by secret ballot. The Draft Constitution had not provided for the elections to the Council by the system of proportional representation. But a passionate plea for it by H.N. Kunzru who argued that proportional representation alone would ensure the representation of different views in the Upper House had the desired effect.[2]

Another principle that is given recognition in the composition of the Council of States is representation of talent, experience and service. Here the example of the Seanad Eireann of the Irish Republic seems to have influenced the constitution-makers of India.[3] However, the number of members nominated by the Present of India to the Council is very small in comparison with the number of elected members. The number of nominated members is constitutionally limited to twelve. Such members should be persons having special knowledge or practical experience in respect of matters like literature, science, art or social service. The following table shows the State-wise representation in the Council of States:

Name of the State	*Number of Members*
1. Andhra Pradesh	18
2. Arunachal Pradesh	1
3. Assam	7
4. Bihar	17
5. Chhatisgarh	5
6. Goa	1
7. Gujarat	11

1. In the United States, on the contrary, both the Senators and the Representatives are elected by the people directly, the only difference being the relative size of the constituencies. Until 1913, the Senators were elected by the members of the State Legislatures. The constituency of a Senator embraces the whole State; but that of a Representatives is only one District.
2. C.A.D. VII, p. 1124.

8. Haryana	5
9. Himachal Pradesh	3
10. Jammu and Kashmir	4
11. Jharkhand	6
12. Karnataka	12
13. Kerala	9
14. Madhya Pradesh	11
15. Maharashtra	19
16. Manipur	1
17. Meghalaya	1
18. Mizoram	1
19. Nagaland	1
20. Orissa	10
21. Punjab	7
22. Rajasthan	10
23. Sikkim	1
24. Tamil Nadu	18
25. Tripura	1
26. Uttaranchal	3
27. Uttar Pradesh	31
28. West Bengal	16
Union Territories	
1. Delhi	3
2. Pondicherry	1
Nominated	12
Total	224

The Council of States is a permanent body like the U.S. Senate. Like the U.S. Senators the members of the Rajya Sabha are elected for six years. At the end of every second year, one-third of the members are re-elected. This provision enables the Council to retain its political complexion in a more stable manner than the House of the People which after every election is a completely new House.

The House *vs.* the Council

Although the participation and collaboration of both Houses are essential for all legislative activities and without such collaboration practically nothing can be done in the legislative field, the Constitution has recognized the overriding powers of the House of the People over the Council in certain respects. The first and perhaps the most important of these is the relationship between Parliament and the Council of Ministers. The Upper House has hardly any control over the Ministers who are jointly and individually responsible for their actions to the House of the People. Not that the Ministers, if they so choose, can ignore the Council of States. The Council has every right to be fully informed of all matters connected with the Government's activities which are raised on its floor. But it has no right to pass a censure motion against the Government of the day. The confidence of

Parliament means the confidence of the House of the People, and the responsibility of the Executive means responsibility to the House of the People. This principle can be justified only on the basis of the popular character of the House. In a parliamentary democracy, the government of the day must be accountable to the people. Within the mechanism of the government such accountability is made possible through the peoples' representatives, and the House of the People alone is composed of the directly elected representatives of the people. It was England which first established this principle by ensuring cabinet responsibility to the House of Commons and, today, it has become an accepted principle in every parliamentary democracy including India.

Secondly, the power of the Council with regard to Money Bills is almost negligible. Every Money Bill should be introduced in the House of the People. The fundamental principle of every taxation measure is that taxes should be collected only with the consent of the people. In a democracy, the people's consent is essential both for the raising of public revenues and their spending. Here again, the people's consent can be expressed only by a House which is elected directly by the people. Under the procedure established by the Constitution, however, the Council is not altogether prevented from scrutinizing Money Bills. But its power is only of an advisory character. Every Money Bill passed by the House will go to the Council for its consideration and within fourteen days after the receipt of the Bill the Council must take whatever action it deems fit. It may pass it in which case the Bill goes to the President for his assent. If the Bill is amended or rejected by the Council it goes back to the House where it is reconsidered and voted by a simple majority and sent to the President. Thus, in financial matters, the Council has only an advisory role and the House has the final say.

In all other matters of legislation, including constitutional amendments, the extent of the Council's power is the same as that of the House. A Bill can be initiated either in the House or in the Council. The Council may amend or reject a Bill that is passed by the House. If the House does not agree with the action of the Council, the contested measure is placed before a joint sitting of both Houses and passed by a simple majority. As the total membership of the Council is less than even half the total strength of the House of the People, the latter will naturally win in a conflict of this nature.[1] A Bill passed in a joint sitting is sent straight to the President for his assent. Thus, unlike the Senate in the U.S. the Council of States has comparatively less power. The U.S.. Senate with its special powers in connection with appointments and treaty-making, in addition to its normal powers of legislation, is immensely more powerful than the House of Representatives of the U.S. Congress, and is easily the most powerful second chamber in the world. In contrast, the Canadian Senate, which was modelled after the House of Lords, stands at the other extreme.

The relative status of the two Houses of Parliament has been a subject of discussion at least once so far in the life of Parliament. It was raised in the Rajya Sabha by one of its Members[2] who referred to the exception taken by a Member of the Lok Sabha to the

1. So far there has been only one occasion (1961) when the two Houses sat in joint session. It was to resolve their differences with respect to certain provisions of the Dowry Prohibition Bill of 1960. The joint sitting lasted for two days during which the differences between the two Houses were resolved and the Bill was passed.
2. Bhupesh Gupta was the Member who raised the subject in the Rajya Sabha and his reference was to the point made by H.V. Kamath in the Lok Sabha. (See the Hindu, 5 March 1963).

discussion of the Railway and General Budgets by the Rajya Sabha first. The Vice President who was in the Chair at the time said that "under the Constitution there was no question of any superiority of one House over the other. It was incontrovertible".

Of all the second chambers in the Commonwealth of Nations, the Australian Senate seems to be the most powerful. It shares power with the House of Representatives on the basis of equality. Even in the case of Money Bill, it has the power to reject. By the exercise of this power it may even force a dissolution of both chambers. Nevertheless, in practice, the Australian Senate has not established any position as a rival, much less any position of superiority, to the House of Representatives.

In India, the Council of States in relation to the House of the People is nowhere as powerful as the U.S. Senate, nor is it on a par with the Australian counterpart; but it is much more powerful than the Canadian Senate. It is true that the Constitution clearly recognizes the supremacy of the House of the People over the Council in certain matters, but not in all. The co-equal power of the Council on constitutional amendment is of great significance. It means that the Constitution cannot be amended unless the Council of States as the representative of the States also agrees to such a change. This provision alone will show the important role the framers of the Constitution have assigned to the Council. In addition, in all matters of legislation except finance it shares equal powers with the House.

Besides, there are two other provisions which confer upon the Council, as the sole representative of the States, powers in its own right and to the exclusion of the House. These are of considerable importance from a constitutional point of view. Under Article 249, the Council with the support of two-thirds of its members sitting and voting, is empowered to declare that, in the national interest, Parliament should make laws with respect to a matter that is included in the State Legislative List. On the passing of such a resolution, it becomes lawful for Parliament of make laws with respect to that matter for the whole or any part of India for a period of one year. There are two reasons why such a power is vested in the Council. First, since the Council and not the House of the People is representative of the States, it is but proper that any temporary transfer of an item included in the State List to the jurisdiction of the Union should be done only with the authority of the Council even if such transfer is in the national interest. Second, since the Council is a permanent body, immediate action can be taken in this respect if a situation calling for such action arises after the House has been dissolved prior to an election. A suitable Bill may be introduced in the Council and thus, a major part of the step to meet the new situation can be completed before a dissolved House of the People reassembles after elections.

The second exclusive power of the Council is connected with the setting up of all India Services.[1] The special characteristic of an all India Service is that it is common to the Union and the States. As such, the setting up of such a service affects the powers of the Sates. Therefore, here again, the Council is given the power to decide by a resolution supported by a two-thirds majority the question of setting up an all India Service. Hence, any laws connected with such a service can be initiated only if the Council passes such a resolution. Thus, in both these cases, the House of the People comes into the picture only after the Council has acted.

These provisions make the Council an important part of the governmental machinery and not an ornamental superstructure or an inessential adjunct. It was not designed to play

1. Article 312.

the humble role of an unimportant adviser, nor of an occasional check on hasty legislation. Its comparatively smaller and therefore more compact size, its permanent character which ensures a certain degree of stability and continuity in thought and action, its having a large number of 'elder statesmen' among its members, and its broad-based representative character—all these, in course of time, should help establish it not only as a respectable but also beneficial and influential body though not equal in power with the House of the People.

Conduct of Business

Each House has a Roll of Members which is to be signed by very member before taking his seat. Every member should also make and subscribe to an oath or affirmation while he formally assumes seat. With the Speaker or any other presiding officer in the Chair and in the presence of at least one-tenth of its total membership which is the quorum , the House can begin its business. If at any time during a meeting of the House there is no quorum, the presiding officer will either adjourn or suspend the work of the House. Normally, all questions are decided by a majority of the votes of members present and voting. The presiding officer may vote only when the House is equally divided.

Question Hour

The first hour of each sitting is devoted to parliamentary questions and interpellations. Normally, this is the time when the House is most lively. The main purpose of questions is to seek information and draw attention to grievances of public importance. There are elaborate Rules of Procedure to determine the admissibility of questions. The Speakers's decision in this respect is final. Usually every question is sent days in advance of the session so that all relevant information is collected in the department concerned and transmitted to the House. There is, however, a provision for asking short notice questions under certain conditions.

Every main question and its answer are followed by supplementary questions. These highlight the different aspects of the problem raised by the questions. It is an occasion which calls for quickness, alertness, ingenuity and comprehension on the part of both the members and the Ministers. The question time is apply regarded as searchlight turned on the activities of the Government. It often provides a means for Ministers to look into questions of public importance which they might otherwise not have come across; it also enables the public to have a peep into many an act of commission and omission of the Government. In fact, question time is a real testing-time for the Government.[1]

After the question hour the House takes up, item by item, the business that is allotted for the day. The business takes different forms and for each of these, a separate procedure is prescribed. The more important of these which deserve special mention are adjournment motions, resolutions, no confidence motions, other motions for discussion, legislative business and financial business. There are also other types of business such as statements on policy made by Ministers from time to time and laying of papers and documents on the Table of the House. In the latter case, the Minister concerned will rise in his seat and make a formal statement drawing the attention of the House to the document that is placed on the Table.

1. See, for a detailed disucssion, *Question Hour in Parliament,* Lok Sabha Secretariat, 957.

Adjournment Motions

Adjournment motions are an unusual feature. A motion for adjournment is meant to draw the attention of the House to a matter of public importance which has arisen suddenly and which deserves immediate attention. It should deal with a specific matter of recent occurrence and of urgent public importance. Such a motion is intended to direct the attention of the House to a particular action or inaction of the Government. It also compels the Government to act in a manner that is appropriate to the situation on penalty or otherwise losing the confidence of the House. Thus, an adjournment motion is the nearest to a censure motion against the Government. The practice that has developed during the last few years indicates that only very rarely an adjournment motion is allowed to be moved. The Speaker announces in the House that he has received notion of such a motion and calls upon the Minister concerned and enquires whether he has anything to say on the matter. The Minister may make a statement on the spot or request time to collect relevant information regarding the matter. Once the position is fully clarified, there is usually no need to pursue the matter and the motion is either withdrawn or ruled out. But in case the Speaker allows the motion to be moved, a discussion take place before it is finally disposed of.

Resolutions

A resolution is a device by which the House is made to declare an opinion on a particular matter. A resolution should equal with only one issue and should be worded clearly and precisely. It should not contain arguments, imputations or defamatory statements nor refer to the conduct and character of persons except in their official or public capacity. Further, it should not relate to a matter which is under the consideration of a court of law. The Speaker's decision to disallow a resolution, either as a whole or a part of it, is final. When once a resolution is moved in the House, amendments can be moved subjective to the conditions mentioned above.

No Confidence Motion

No confidence or censure motions are a rare feature. A censure motion is an expression of want of confidence in the Ministry. Permission to move such a motion will be given only if at least fifty members in the House rise in support of it. If leave is granted to move the motion, a date is fixed for discussion and the Speaker may allot one or more days for the purpose. Resort to a no confidence motion is not usually made unless the Opposition has a reasonable chance of defeating the Ministry. But sometimes it is also made use of as a political weapon to discredit a Ministry or highlight its various failures in the public eye with a view to bringing down its prestige[1] and image.

Motion for Discussion

Under the Rules of procedure, a member can, with the consent of the Speaker, move a motion for the discussion of a matter of general public interest. If admitted, the Speaker will allot a day or more for its discussion, depending upon the availability of time during a particular session. Sometimes, the Government itself may bring forward such motions in view of the importance of the matter involved. This provision is, in a way, one that enables

1. In the history of Parliament a no confidence motion was moved against the Ministry for the first time in 1963. But thereafter it became almost a regular feature.

members as well as the Government to bring to the floor of the House any matter of public importance which is not covered by legislative proposals and other parliamentary business.

Closure Motion

There is also provision to cut short the discussion on any matter by moving what is known as a 'closure motion'. Any member can move such a motion and if the House adopts it, discussion is stopped forthwith and the matter before the House is voted upon. Sometimes when the time set for a particular measure is already over despite the fact that the discussion on all its parts has not been completed, a vote is taken on the motion before the House. Then the rest of the measure is put to vote without discussion. This procedure is described as the 'guillotine'.

There are at present 389 rules which regulate the procedure in the House covering every aspect of its activities. These are supplemented by 'Directions by the Speaker'. There are 123 directions by the Speaker which are codified for the use of members and others concerned. Such directions are added from time to time. Taken together, these form the foundations of parliamentary procedure in India, which facilitate the orderly transaction of business in Parliament. But the picture is not complete with these alone. One must add to it the numerous rulings of the presiding officers, precedents and conventions, all of which, in a substantial measure, serve the successful working of the Houses of Parliament.[1]

***

1. See Rules or procedure and Conduct of Business in Lok Sabha, Eighth Edition 1995, Lok Sabha Secretariat.

25

LEGISLATIVE PROCEDURE

THE PRIMARY function of Parliament is law making. Historically it was the function of making laws that made the legislature a distinctly separate department of government. In spite of all the additional functions that a legislature takes up as a result of the complexities of modern government, law making still remains its most important activity. A parliament without legislative work ceases to be a parliament in the real sense, whatever else it might be.

A law maker has to look to the future, while being rooted in the experience of the past. He has to take into consideration the conditions and circumstances of the society to which the laws would be applicable. Modern society is so complex that laws which govern it have necessarily to be complex. Naturally, law making too has become a complex process. This will be illustrated by the process prescribed under the Constitution of India.

The first stage of legislation is the introduction of a Bill embodying the provisions of the proposed law, accompanied by the 'Statement of Objects and Reasons'. If a private member desires to introduce a Bill, he must give notice of his intention to the Speaker. Every Bill that is introduced in the House has to be published in the Gazette. There is provision, however, for the publication of any Bill with the consent of the Speaker even before its formal introduction. Usually, at the time of the introduction of a Bill there is no debate. The person who is given leave to introduce the Bill, if he so chooses, may make a short statement indicating broadly its aims and objects. But if the introduction of the Bill is opposed, then the Speaker may allow one of the opposing members to give his reason too, after which he will put the question to vote. If the House is in favour of the introduction of the Bill, then it goes to the next stage. The introduction of the Bill is also called the first reading of the Bill.

There are four alternative courses of action open at the second stage. The Bill may be taken into consideration; it may be referred to a Select Committee of the House; it may be referred to a Joint Committee of both Houses; or it may be circulated for the purpose of eliciting public opinion. In the case of every proposed legislative measure which is likely to arouse public controversy and agitate public opinion, resort to the last step is invariably made. But there are many Bills which are of minor importance or pertain to routine matters, and others of an urgent nature, which may not therefore permit any long delay. In their cases one or the other of the first three alternatives is adopted.

The Select Committee or Joint Committee is expected to give its report within a specified date. The members of the Select Committee are selected generally on the basis of their ability or expert knowledge on the subject. The usual practice is that the mover of the Bill will himself propose the names of members of the committee and the House adopts them. Members of the Opposition are well represented on the committee. In the case of a Joint Committee, the concurrence of the other House is taken. Of the total number of members on the Joint Committee two-thirds belong to the Lok Sabha and one-third to the Rajya Sabha. The committee may give a unanimous report or a majority report. In the latter case, members in a minority have the right to give minutes of dissent. Submission of the report of the Committee may be taken as the beginning of the third stage. It is during this stage that members can add their amendments to the different provisions of the Bill.

After the committee's report has been considered and the motion that the Bill as reported by the committee be taken into consideration is adopted, the fourth stage begins when a detailed clause to clause discussion of the Bill begins. Each clause is taken up by the House and amendments are moved, discussed and disposed of. The amendments that are moved in the House are those which have already been checked by the Secretariat with a view to seeing that they are within the scope of the Bill and relevant to the subject matter and satisfy all the conditions laid down in regard to their admissibility. This is the stage when the Bill undergoes substantial changes, should they be found necessary. It is also the most time-consuming stage. Once the clause by clause consideration is over and every clause is voted, the second reading of the Bill is over.

The next stage is the third reading stage when the member in charge who has piloted it moves that 'the Bill be passed'. Such a motion may be moved either immediately after the second reading or on a subsequent date. Unless there is any great urgency, the third reading takes place after sufficient time is given to members to study the Bill in the amended form in which it was passed at the second reading. At the third reading, normally, only verbal or purely formal amendments are moved and discussion is limited and progress is quick. When once all the amendments are disposed of the Bill is sent to the other House for its action.

A fourth stage starts with the consideration of the Bill by the other House where it goes through the same procedure and the different stages. The House has three alternatives before it. It might finally pass the Bill as sent by the originating House. It might amend or altogether reject the Bill. In the last two cases, the Bill may be returned to the originating House. Or it may not return it at all within six months after the receipt of the Bill, which will mean the same as rejection.

At the fifth stage, the returned Bill is considered by the House in the light of the amendments made by the other House. If the amendments are accepted, it sends a message to the other House to that effect. If they are not accepted then the bill is returned to the other House with a message to that effect. If in this process of sending the Bill up and down, the Houses do not come to an agreement, the only solution is a joint sitting of the two Houses called for the purpose by the President. The disputed provision is then finally adopted or rejected by a simple majority vote of those who are present and voting.[1]

1. For a more detailed discussion on the subjuect, see S.P. Sen-Verm. 'The Birth of a Statute", (1961) II S.C.J. 23.

A Bill that is finally passed by both Houses goes, with the signature of the Speaker, to the President for his assent. This is normally the last stage. If the President gives his assent, the Bill becomes an Act and is placed on the Statute Book. But even at this last stage, the Bill can be stopped from becoming an Act. The President, as we have already seen, is empowered, if he so chooses, to refuse assent to a Bill that is placed before him. He may send the Bill back to Parliament for reconsideration This will reopen almost the whole process and if the Bill is passed by both Houses again with or without amendments, it will be sent to the President for a second time. At this stage, the President shall not withhold his assent. Thus, it can be seen how long, detailed and time-consuming is the process of modern legislation and how difficult it is if a Bill has to be passed within a short time. The magnitude of the work will be fully understood only if one takes into consideration the number of bills which Parliament is called upon to pass every year. This also highlights the importance of drafting, a highly skilled technical job which would facilitate the smooth passage of the Bill without unnecessary discussions on matters of minor importance such as language sequence of sentences, arrangement of matter, numbering of clauses, punctuation, etc. If a Bill is properly drafted, its passage becomes easy and smooth to a great extent. Successful and expeditious law making also involves the skilful handling of the provisions of a Bill on the floor of the House by those who are in charge of piloting it and the maximum measure of support they can enlist from members in general and particularly from those in opposition.

Financial Procedure

It is the unquestioned right of Parliament under any responsible system of Government not only to ensure that public funds are raised only with its consent but also to exercise complete control over the way in which the nation's revenues are spent by the Government. The framers of the Constitution had kept in view these considerations while laying down the principles which would guide the operation of public finance and the procedure that would regulate the financial transactions of the Government. The basic principles underlying the financial provisions of the Constitution are as follows:

1. There shall be no taxation without a law authorizing it. If any levy is to be made upon the people, the sanction must be that of law.[1]
2. There shall be no expenditure without the authority of Parliament. Such authority should be embodied in an Act of Parliament and not merely expressed by a resolution.[2]
3. As an essential safeguard for the sound administration of the nation's finances, Parliament should have unrestricted power to superintend, scrutinize, regulate and determine financial administration.[3]
4. The executive should alone have the initiative in making proposals for taxation and expenditure and no such proposals can be initiated by a private member.[4]
5. The House of the People should have supremacy over the Council of States in all financial matters.

---

1. C.A.D. VII, p. 723.
2. Ibid., p. 730.
3. Ibid, p. 735.
4. Ibid., p. 776.

6. All revenues received by the Union Government should form the Consolidated Fund of India from which alone the Government shall withdraw money for its expenditure and repayment of debts.[1]
7. To meet unforeseen requirements exceeding the authorized expenditure, a reserve fund called the Contingency Fund of India should be placed at the disposal of the Government facilitating advances subject to subsequent regularization[2].
8. The President shall not withhold his assent from a Money Bill passed by Parliament. In the matter of finance, Parliament is supreme.[3]

On the basis of these principles the Constitution proceeds to lay down a detailed financial procedure. In laying down such a detailed procedure the framers were influenced by a set of established principles. These are:

1. Procedure should not obscure fundamental issues;
2. Procedures should ensure that no bad or irresponsible decisions are taken by the Executive;
3. Procedures should make it possible or consider the budget as a whole and as an integral part of national accounting rather than as a series of unrelated parts;
4. Procedures should ensure a complete and coordinated circuit between expenditure and resources;
5. Procedures should leave ample scope for long-term economic planning and development, treating annual allocations and sanctions as effective and strong links of such planning and development.

With these principles in view one may examine the mechanics of the financial procedure. Under Article 112, every year "the President shall cause to be laid before both the Houses of Parliament" the annual financial statement, popularly known as the budget. The person through whom the President acts in this respect is the Finance Minister who is the custodian of the nation's finances. The budget will show the estimated receipts and expenditure for that financial year. According to custom, it is presented on the last day of February in order that Parliament will have sufficient time to discuss the proposals in general and authorize appropriation before the beginning of the new financial year on the first day of April. There will be no discussion of the budget on the day on which it is presented to Parliament; this is to give members time to study the proposals before the discussion of the budget begins.

The expenditure embodied on the budget is divided into two separate parts: the expenditure charged upon the Consolidated Fund of India which are no-votable, and the sums required to meet other expenditure from the Consolidated Fund which are votable. The following items belong to the charged expenditure: (i) the salary and allowances of the President; (ii) the salaries and allowances of the Presiding Officers of the Houses of Parliament; (iii) debt charges of the Government of India; (iv) the salaries and allowances of the judges of the Supreme Court, the Comptroller and Auditor-General and pension

1. Ibid., IX p. 201.
2. Ibid., X, p. 201.
3. Ibid., VIII, p. 726.

payable to retired judges of the Federal Court; (v) sums required to satisfy any Court decree or award and any other expenditure declared by the Constitution or by Parliament to be so charged. Although Parliament does not vote on these items as these payments are guaranteed under the Constitution,[1] there is no bar to a discussion on any of them by either of the two Houses. With respect to the second part of expenditure, estimates are to be submitted in the form of demands for grants to the House of the People. The House has the power to assent, reduce, or reject these demands. Every demand for a grant should be made only with the recommendation of the President.

The term Consolidated Fund of India was a new one coined by the Drafting Committee in place of the old Public Account of the government of India to mean the consolidated fund into which moneys received on account of the revenues of the Government are paid and credited, and from which alone all disbursements by the Government are made. "A Consolidated Fund is necessary to prevent the proceeds of taxes being frittered away by laws made by Parliament in individual purposes without regard to the general necessity of the people at all".[2]

Although the Consolidation prohibits the appropriation of funds from the Consolidated Fund without specific demands for grants, it provides, under Article 116, for a grant in advance pending completion of the regular procedure so that the Government may be able to carry on until grants are finally voted after detailed discussion. Such grants are made usually to cover the expenditure for a period of three to four months and only a discussion of a general character takes place before they are voted. Voting on these demands are called Votes on Account. In addition, the Constitution also provides, under the same article, for Votes of Credit and Exceptional Grants. A vote of credit is a grant obtained for meeting an unexpected demand upon the resources of India when, on account of the magnitude or indefinite character of the service, the demand cannot be stated with detail ordinarily given in the budget. An exceptional grant is one which forms no part of the current service of any financial year. Although the Constitution has made provision for these special cases, there has been no occasion so far to make use of them.

We have already seen that a Money Bill has to be introduced in the House of the People. The Constitution has defined a Money Bill under Article 110. A Money Bill, according to this article, deals in general with all proposals of taxation and expenditure, borrowing policy of the Government and measures declaring any expenditure as charged, etc. A Money Bill can be introduced only with the recommendation of the President. We have also seen that the power of the Council of States with the respect to a Money Bill is only advisory and if the Bill is not returned to the House within a period of fourteen days, the Bill will be taken as passed at the end of that period in the form in which it was sent to the Council.

Under the rules of procedure, ordinarily a separate demand has to be made in respect of the grant proposed for each Ministry and each demand should contain not only a statement of the total grant proposed, but also a detailed estimate under each grant divided into

1. If Parliament is to have the power of voting on these items, these officers would not be able to function independently, as one of the most important elements of independence is a guaranteed minimum salary during the peirod when one holds the position.
2. Ambedkar, C.A.D. VIII, p. 723.

items. The discussion on the budget can be divided into two parts: a general discussion, and a detailed discussion which takes place when every time a separate demand is placed before the House. During the general discussion, the accent is on general problems connected with the nations's finances and the principles involved in the budget proposals. At the end of the discussion the Finance Minister has a right to reply.

It is during the second stage that members get the opportunity to move cut motions to reduce the amount of a demand. Every cut motion to a demand for grants represents disapproval of some aspect or other of the governmental policy or administration involved in the demand. The procedure recognizes three different types of cut motions. If the cut motion aims to reduce the demand by one rupee only, the motion will be known as Disapproval of Policy Cut. The motion in this case represents disapproval of the policy underlying the demand. If the reduction demanded is either in the form of a lump sum or omission or reduction of an item in the demand, the motion which embodies such cut is known as Economy Cut. There the object of the motion is economy in Government spending. If the motion seeks to reduce the demand by a cut of Rs. 100 it aims to ventilate a specific grievance which is within the sphere of the responsibility of the Government and such a motion is known as a Token Cut. The admissibility of these cut motions is regulated by rules which lay down conditions. The cut motions provide the maximum opportunity for members to examine every part of the budget and subject it to detailed criticism and offer suggestions for improvement.

Voting on demands by itself does not complete the formalities connected with the provision of funds to the Government. There should be legal sanction for the appropriation of sums from the Consolidated Fund. To facilitate this the procedure provides for two different pieces of financial legislation. One is the Appropriation Act and the other is the Finance Act. The former fixes the amount which can be drawn out of the Consolidated Fund for meeting the expenditure against each grant. The Constitution does not permit any withdrawal in excess of the amount provided in the Act. The Finance Act deals with the legislation which authorizes the raising of funds through taxation as embodied in the financial proposals of the year.

Mention has been made earlier of the constitutional prohibition against funds being withdrawn from the Consolidated Fund except under appropriations made by law. But it has been found, from time to time, that the expenditure voted by Parliament for a Department is not enough because of unforeseen or unexpected reasons. If the expenditure is incurred without parliamentary authorization, it would be illegal. But if the Executive awaits parliamentary sanction before incurring the expenditure, the Department concerned will be put to great inconvence. Besides the expenditure may be urgently required and the inability of the Government to make provision for it may be detrimental to the public interest. To provide for such contingencies, Parliament is authorized under Article 267, to establish a "Contingency Fund of India into which shall be paid, from time to time, such sums as may be determined by law." This Fund is placed at the disposal of the President to enable advances to be made by him for the purpose of meeting unforeseen expenditure pending its authorization in accordance with the established financial procedure. The idea of the Contingency Fund, as most of the other ideas in the financial filed, is taken from England. The Contingency Fund stands at Rs. 150 million now.

Once advances have been made available from the Contingency Fund for meeting the unforeseen and urgent financial needs of the Department in excess of the authorized amount, such advances have to be regularized. As we have seen, the Executive cannot spend funds without the specific authority of Parliament. The situation is met through the device of a supplementary budget. A supplementary budget is one which includes all those sums which the department has drawn in excess of the annual grant. It is presented during the course of the financial year. The procedure for getting supplementary grants is similar to that prescribed for the annual budget. When the supplementary demands are passed, advances taken from the Contingency Fund are returned to it in order to restore the Fund to its original amount.

A discussion of the financial procedure is not complete without going into the respective roles of three committees of Parliament whose activities have an important bearing on the financial affairs of the Government. These are the Estimates Committee, the Public Accounts Committee and the Committee of Public Undertakings. The work of these committees is dealt with along with that of other parliamentary committees in a separate section. Mention must also be made of the role of the Comptroller and Auditor-General of India which is also dealt with separately. Taking into consideration the impact of all these controlling agencies on the financial policies, programmes and activities of the Government, one major conclusion emerges that the fundamental principles which have been embodied in the financial provisions of the Constitution are substantially realized in practice. The fact that the government of the day enjoys the support of a party with even an overwhelming majority in Parliament has not made the parliamentary control of public finances any the less real.

***

26

PRIVILEGES AND COMMITTEES

THE PROVISIONS of the Constitution dealing with parliamentary privileges and immunities bear a special mark of indebtedness to the centuries-old conventions established and maintained in this regard by the mother of parliaments, the British Parliament. In fact, this is the only section where a direct reference to the House of Commons was made in the Constitution. Article 105 deals with the powers, privileges and immunities of the Houses of Parliament, their members and committees. It guarantees to every member freedom of speech in Parliament and grants immunity from proceedings in any court of Law in respect of anything said or any vote given by him in Parliament or in any of its committees. A similar immunity is granted in respect of any public, under the authority of either House of Parliament, of reports, papers, votes or proceedings:

In other respects, the powers, privileges and immunities of each House of Parliament and of the members and the Committees of each House, shall be such as may from time to time be defined by Parliament by law, and, until so defined, shall be those of that House and its members and committees immediately before coming into force of the Forty-fourth Amendment of the constitution (1978).

As originally provided under Article 105 section (3) the powers, privileges and immunities, except for those defined by Parliament by law, were to be those of the House of Commons of the Parliament of the United Kingdom and of its members and Committees at the commencement of the Constitution, that is 1950.

This provision provoked a heated debate in the Constituent Assembly during which several members assailed the direct reference to the House of Commons in the text of the Constitution. H.V. Kamath said:

I venture to state this is the first instance of its kind where reference is made in the constitution of a free country to certain provisions obtaining in the constitution of another State. Is it necessary or desirable when we are drafting our own Constitution that we should lay down explicitly in an article that the provisions as regards this matter will be like those of the House of Commons in England ?[1]

K.T. Shah, supporting Kamath, said:

A sovereign legislature is the sole judge of the privileges of its members as well as of the body collectively. Hence any breach thereof should be dealt with by the House concerned.[2]

Speaking on behalf of the Drafting Committee, Alladi Krishnaswami Aiyar countered these arguments and said:

---

1. C.A.D. VIII, p. 144.
2. C.A.D., p. 145.

I may share the sentiment but it is also necessary to appreciate it from a practical point of view. It is common knowledge that the widest privileges are exercised by members of Parliament in England. The present legislatures in India, according to judicial verdict, have no right to punish for contempt. The British Parliament has such powers. The Dominion Parliaments too have such powers. Should we not have that power ?..... If you have the time and leisure to formulate all the privileges in a compendious form, it will be well and good. The Committee appointed by the Speaker has found it extremely difficult. Under these circumstances, I submit, there is absolutely no *infra dig*. We are having our Constitution in English. Why object only to a reference to the privileges in England ?

The other point is that there is nothing to prevent Parliament from setting up the proper machinery for formulating privileges. The Article leaves wide scope for it..... It does not in any way fetter your discretion. You may enlarge the privileges, you may curtail the privileges, you may have different kinds of privileges.... This is only a temporary measure..... Under these circumstances, far from this article being framed in a spirit of servility or slavery or subjection to Britain, it is framed in a spirit of self-assertion and an assertion that our country and our Parliament are as great as the Parliament of Great Britain.[1]

The reference to the House of Commons, in fact, was a saving provision because when India inaugurated a new Constitution, she was, at least from the point of view of the working of parliamentary institutions, embarking on a somewhat uncharted sea. It was wise to adopt, until such time as her own constitutional practices crystallized into a sufficiently authoritative body of precedents on the basis of which the law of privileges and immunities could be formulated, the conventions evolved by a body like the British Parliament which has had a long tradition behind it and the procedures of which were well known in India. So far, Parliament has not been able to do much by way of formulating the powers, privileges and immunities of its members, committees and the Houses.

What has been done so far is included in the Rules of Procedure. This deals mainly with two questions: questions of privileges, and arrest or detention of members. A question of privilege can be raised by any member provided it satisfies the conditions laid down for its admissibility. The matter is then referred to the Committee of Privileges if the House agrees to that and appropriate action is taken by the House on the basis of the recommendations of the committee.

When a member is arrested or detained on a criminal charge or sentenced to imprisonment by a Court, the authority concerned should immediatley inform the Speaker or the Chairman, as the case may be, indicating the reasons for the arrest, detention or imprisonment. Similarly, when member is released from detention, such fact also should be communicated to the Speaker. The Speaker will infor the House of the contents of such communications as early as possible. No member can be arrested within the premises of Parliament without the permission of the Speaker. Similarly, no legal process, civil or criminal, can be served on members within the precincts of the Houses without obtaining the Speaker's or the Chairman's permission.[2]

---

1. Ibid., p. 148. The Government of India Act of 1935 has an identical provision. Section 49 of the Australian Constitution also contains a direct reference to the Parliament of the United Kingdom. Ambedkar too supported the provisions with a long speech. Ibid., p. 582.
2. Has a member of Parliament the right to stay within Parliament House after the day's business ? The Speaker of the Lok Sabha answered the question in the negative while giving a ruling on a question of privilege raised in the House by one of its members. The Speaker said that it was his right and privielege to decide how long a member could be allowed to stay within Parliament House after the day's business. See the Statesman (Delhi Edition), 19 March 1964.

The Lok Sabha made history on 29 August 1961 by reprimanding a journalist at the Bar of the House for publishing words calculated to bring a Member of the House into odium, contempt and ridicule, Administering the reprimand the Speaker said. "This offence of yours was further aggravated by the type of explanation you chose to submit to the Committee of Privileges. In the name of the House, I accordingly reprimand you for committing a gross breach of privilege and contempt of the House." The journalist concerned, the Editor of *Blitz,* a Bombay weekly, had earlier moved the Supreme Court in a desperate bid to challenge the warrant issued against him summoning him before the Bar of the House on the ground that it was in violation of a fundamental right guaranteed to him by the Constitution. The Supreme Court, however, rejected the petition and reaffirmed its decision in an earlier case[1] of a similar nature when it held that the right to freedom of speech was subject to the right or privilege of the Legislature to prohibit the publication of even a true and faithful report of the proceedings that took place in the House. According to the Court, the real remedy lies only with the Legislature itself by passing a comprehensive law defining and codifying its privileges. Then the citizen will known how far do these parliamentary privileges restrict his fundamental right to freedom of speech and expression.

It is true that, under a system of parliamentary government, the privileges of the legislature, its members and committees are an essential guarantee of its efficient working. The concept of parliamentary privileges, however, rests mainly on parliamentary privileges in England. There, these have been evolved for the purpose of maintaining the independence and dignity of the House and its members. In the words of Erskine May,[2] "the distinctive mark of a privilege is its ancillary character. They are enjoyed by individual members because the House cannot perform its functions without unimpeded use of the service of its members, and by each House for the protection of its members and the vindication of its own authority and dignity." By the very origin and nature of these privileges, they do not accrue by reason of any exalted position of the House of its members, but because they are absolutely necessary for the proper and effective discharge of the functions of a legislative body. But the manner in which issues on privilege are raised again and again on the floor of the Houses of Parliament and the State Legislatures gives one the impression that the parliamentarians in India are too sensitive to criticism from outside. This is not a trend meriting encouragement from any quarter. After all parliaments and their members and committees are neither infallible nor embodiments of all wisdom. Being the representatives of the people they must always be prepared to face public criticism and should never consider themselves to be above such criticism.

The Indian Parliament, it should be pointed out, is very different in at least one important respect from the British Parliament. While the latter has sovereign powers at least in theory, the Indian Parliament has only limited powers. Parliamentary supremacy is inconsistent with the written Constitution of India which has imposed prohibitions on Parliament to pass certain kinds of legislation.[3] Such a Parliament cannot pretend, under the cover of Article 105(3), to have unlimited powers and privileges.

1. M.S. M. Sharma *vs*. Sri Krishna Sinha. 1959 S.C.J. 925.
2. Erskine May is the author of the famous book May's Parliamentary Procedure.
3. These prohibitions are the result of the existence of constitutionally guaranteed Fundamental Rights as well as the division of powers betweenm the Union of India and the constitutent States.

As an aftermath of the *Blitz* case, the Indian Federation of Working Journalists organized late on 1961 a two-day seminar in New Delhi to discuss the subject of "Privileges of Parliament and the Press."[1] The discussions at the seminar highlighted the extremely unsatisfactory position resulting from the recent decisions of the Courts on parliamentary privileges, the undue sensitivity of legislatures to criticism and the lack of a codified system of law on the subject. One of the journalists pointed out that there had been considerable curtailment of freedom of the press in reporting the proceedings in Parliament since Independence. He asserted that the extent of freedom enjoyed by the Press in reporting the proceedings of the Central Assembly under British rule was much greater than what it had today in reporting the Indian Parliament. For example, today, a question cannot be published until it was admitted and circulated and an adjournment motion cannot be reported until it is read out by the Speaker in the House. So-called breaches of privileges were raised on inconsequential matters. Members even complained of discrimination "if they were given only two lines in the press as against five to someone else". He criticised the government for not carrying out for fourteen years its solemn undertaking to define the privileges of Parliament. "It was the freedom of the press to determine what is publishable, to introduce slant and to question political motives." Another speaker complained that the theory privileges as practised in India was completely out of tune with the concept of parliamentary democracy. "Had Senator McCarthy been a member of India's Parliament," he added, "any criticism on his activities would have been taken up as a breach of privileges." He pleaded for the acceptance of the principle that any verdict by Parliament of a breach of privilege should be justiciable.

Thus the consensus among those who spoke for the Press was in favour of clearly defining privileges and codifying the complex field of privileges.[2] But others opposed this position, among whom were the Law Minister of the Government of India and the Deputy Speaker of the Lok Sabha who is also the Chairman of the Privileges Committee. The Law Minister said that a few recent cases had highlighted the privileges issue but the problem was not as serious as was often thought. Parliament had tried to keep the area of immunity as wide as possible and also sought to be "quite insensitive". But he frankly conceded that Parliament must restrain itself in the exercise of its "unbounded" privileges and added that "there should be no privilege of Parliament in supersession of the fundamental rights guaranteed in the Constitution." The Deputy Speaker held that Parliament should retain powers for its proper functioning and not transfer them to the judiciary. It would be below the dignity of Parliament, if every time there was a question of breach of privileges, a member of Parliament had to go to the judiciary. He was in favour of maintaining the "supreme authority" of Parliament. Once the privileges were codified, he added, it would be subject to the scrutiny of the judiciary. Further it was not easy to define the privileges because there were practical difficulties. Freedom of Parliament was very important and should be safeguarded. "If Parliament itself is not free, nothing will be free. There will be no freedom of the individual or of the Press". A Member of Parliament who followed him went to the extent of saying that any step, which might have the effect of subjecting Parliament to the jurisdiction of the courts would be the greatest national calamity, and

1. *the Times of India*, 4 and 5 November 1961.

2. The press in India appeared generally to be of the same view; see for example *The Times of India*, 13 November 1961 and *The Indian Express* 22 July 1961.

asked: "What will be the position of Parliament represented by the Speaker, when standing as suppliant before a Court ?"

As against these two opposed views, the Secretary to the Legislative Department of the Ministry of Law took a middle course and suggested the appointment of an influential Commission consisting of eminent judges, jurists and legislators, to examine the jurisdiction of courts and Parliament in cases affecting parliamentary privileges and recommend measures to define the thin line between the competence of courts and the exclusive jurisdiction of the Houses of Parliament in this matter. He also suggested that section 2 of Article 19 of the Constitution relating to contempt of court be amended so as to include a reference to concept of Parliament and State Legislatures. This, if done, would be in accord with the decision of the Supreme Court and in keeping with the spirit of the Constitution and at the same time would not unduly restrict the freedom of the Press.

The cases relating to parliamentary privileges and the nation-wide discussion that they provoked seem to have already produced some beneficial results. It was announced by the Deputy Speaker at the Seminar that the suggestion for the appointment of a committee to define Parliament's privileges was under active consideration. However, no such committee was appointed.

But even if parliamentary privileges are codified, controversies arising out of questions of privilege are bound to continue. Perhaps with the creation of a codified law of privileges there is even the possibility of the large volume of litigation in the field. It is idle to imagine that a detailed law on the subject will by itself minimize conflicts. For conflicts arise as a result of differing views and conduct on the part of members within and others outside Parliament. While the need for such a law seems to be compelling, it is also important to build up healthy conventions which will regulate the conduct of all concerned in the entire field. After all, the role of conventions in smoothening the working of parliamentary institutions of England is universally acknowledged. Such conventions should be deliberately established in India and followed with determination. In a free society freedom of speech and expression has to be responsible while Parliaments have to be responsive to the ideas and urges of the mass of the people. When India's parliamentary institutions as well as their critics are habitually inspired by these basic principles of a democracy, the problems arising from parliamentary privileges will become much easier to solve.[1]

Under Article 106, members are entitled to receive such salaries and allowances as may from time to time be determined by law made by Parliament.

It is not easy to quantify what a member of Parliament earns in that capacity.

He draws a regular monthly salary of Rs. 4000/- In addition he draws a per diem allowance of Rs. 400/-, office expense of Rs. 2500/- per month, secretarial allowance of Rs. 6000/- and Mandalam allowance of Rs. 8000/-. He is entitled to 32 free air tickets per annum from his place of residence to Delhi and back. For journeys undertaken by road he may claim road mileage at the rate of Rs. 6 per km. He can get a car loan advance of Rs. 100,000. Free electricity up to 15000 units, free water supply up to 2000 kl. and 100,000 free telephone calls a year. He is entitled for a monthly pension of Rs. 2500/- Family pension provided is Rs. 1000/- per month. AC first class (free) railway travel anywhere in

1. For a more detailed discussion see Pylee, M.V., "Free Speech and Parliamentary Privileges in India", *Pacific Affairs*, Vo. XXXV, No. 1, Spring 1962.

India for both husband and wife is also permitted. Every member is provided subsidised accommodation, house or flat, in Delhi.

Taking all these together, it is estimated that the total recurring expenditure per year per member would be around Rs. 15.05 lakhs and a non recurring expenditure of Rs. 5.65 lakhs. MPs enjoy a special discretionary quota for granting out of turn gas connection, 160 a year. Similarly, they get a quota of 50 phone connections a year. They also get a Local Area Development Fund of Rupees one crore. This may go up to 2 crores. By an Act passed by Parliament in 2001, the salary of MPs has been trebled. All allowances have also been substantially enhanced.

Parliamentary Committees

Under a parliamentary system of government, Committees of Parliament are a necessary adjunct of the work of Parliament. They make parliamentary work smooth, efficient and expeditious. They provide a certain expertise to the deliberations of Parliament. They also help to realize better and more constructive co-operation from the Opposition for various measures initiated by the Government. It must be mentioned, however, that committees of legislature under a parliamentary system stand on a different plane from those under a presidential system where there is separation of powers between the Executive and the Legislature. They are essentially subordinate bodies of the Legislature created only for the purpose of rendering assistance to the Legislature primarily in its work as a legislative body. In contrast, the Congressional Committees in the United States not only function as subordinate bodies of the Congress to assist it in its legislative work but also have assumed the role of investigating bodies looking into the activities of the Executive. There is less scope for a Parliamentary Committee in India to assume such a role.

Members of the committees are appointed or elected by the House or nominated by the Speaker. Before a member's name is proposed to a committee, his willingness to serve on the committee is ascertained. The inclusion of a member in a committee may be objected to on the ground that he has a personal, pecuniary or direct interest of such an intimate character that may affect prejudicially the deliberations of the committee. Whenever such object is raised, the Speaker will investigate the grounds of objection and will give his verdict in the matter which shall be final. The Chairman of a committee is appointed by the Speaker from among its members. But if the Deputy Speaker happens to be a member, he shall be appointed Chairman. One-third of the total membership constitutes the quorum and questions are decided by a majority of votes with provision for a casting vote by the Chairman in case of a tie. A Committee of Parliament has the power to appoint sub-committees. The sittings of the committee are normally held within the precincts of Parliament House and deliberations are held in private. It has the power to take evidence from witnesses called for the purpose. It has also the power to send for persons, papers and records. The report of a parliamentary committee is presented to the appropriate House by its Chairman. Members have generally the right to submit minutes of dissent if they do not agree with the report of the majority. The Speaker has the power to give directions to the committee for the purpose of regulating its procedure and the organization of its work.

According to the *Rules of Procedure and Conduct of Business in the Lok Sabha,* there are twelve Committees of Parliament. The following is a brief survey of the work of these committees which should give one a general perspective of the work of Parliament itself.

1. The Business Advisory Committee

This committee is constituted at the commencement of the House with a view mainly to regulating the time-table of the work of the House. It has fifteen members. The Speaker may assign to the committee any other function. The members of the committee are nominated by the Speaker who himself will be its Chairman. In the work of this committee, the Leader of the House (the leader of the Party in power) as well as the leaders of various parties and groups actively, participate in order to run the business of the House smoothly, efficiently and with the co-operation and support of all sections of the House.

2. The Committee on Private Members' Bills and Resolutions

This again is a committee of fifteen whose members are nominated by the Speaker and whose tenure is for a period of one year. The main function of the committee is to examine all private members' bills, to categorize them as important and less important or urgent and less urgent, to scrutinize whether or not any provision of such bills seeks to initiate legislation outside the legislative competence of the House, to recommend the time that should be allotted for discussion, *etc.*

3. Select Committees on Bills

The occasion for the appointment of a Select Committee on any Bill arises as and when a motion that the Bill be referred to a Select Committee is made. Member of a Select Committee are appointed by the House. There is no rigidity about the number of members, which may vary from committee to committee on the basis of the type and magnitude of the proposed legislation. A Select Committee may hear expert evidence and representatives of special interests affected by the measure before them. Any member of the Select Committee may record a minute of dissent on any matter connected with the Bill. But such dissent should be "couched in temperate and decorous language and shall not refer to any discussion in the Select Committee nor cast any aspersion on the Committee."

4. The Committee on Petitions

This committee is nominated by the Speaker at the commencement of the House and will have a strength of fifteen members. A feature of this committee, as in the case of certain other committees also, is that no Minister can be a member on it. The function of the committee is to examine every petition referred to it and report to the House after taking such evidence as it deems fit and to suggest remedial measures to the House.

5. The Estimates Committee

The financial business of Parliament, as we have already seen, is so complex that, constituted as it is, Parliament is unable to devote to it the time and energy required for discharging satisfactorily its responsibilities of financial control. Hence three committees have been set up to enable Parliament to discharge its functions in this connection more efficiently. *viz.* the Estimates Committee, the Public Accounts Committee and the Committee on Public Undertakings.

The Estimates Committee is charged with the detailed examination of the budget estimates and, therefore, is in a powerful position to influence the activities of the Government not only in the financial field but also in other fields. There are four specified functions allotted to the committee:

(*a*) To report what economies, improvements in organization efficiency or administrative reform, consistent with the policy underlying the estimates, may be effected;

(*b*) To suggest alterantive policies in order to bring about efficiency and economy in administration;

(*c*) To examine whether the money is well laid out within the limits of the policy implied in the estimates; and

(*d*) To suggest the form in which the estimates shall be presented to Parliament.

It is clear from these functions that the committee is empowered not only to examine such of the annual estimates of the Government as it considers fit and suggest economies consistent with the policy underlying these estimates, but also to suggest alterantive policies in order to bring about efficiency and economy in administration. The very nature of these functions show how difficult is the role that the committee has to play and how much expert knowledge it needs to discharge its responsibilities satisfactorily. The committee was constituted for the first time in 1952 replacing the then Standing Finance Committee of Parliament. The Estimates Committee has so far produced several hundred reports dealing with different departments and agencies of the Government. For its more efficient work the committee divides itself into groups or sub-committees and to each of these groups is allotted certain departments for examination and report. Since the financial procedure permits the vote-on-account system, the reports of the committee become a valuable aid to the House at the time when demands are finally voted.

The committee has thirty members who are elected in accordance with the system of proportional representation from among the members of the Lok Sabha for a period of one year.[1] One special feature of the work of the committee is that its work is not over with the final passage of the budget even though it is mainly concerned with estimates. It goes on working all the year round, selecting any department or agency of the Government according to its own choice for the purpose of its scrutiny. Of all the committees of Parliament, the Estimates Committee has a leading role to play in ensuring the accountability of government activities. But one serious handicap resulting from the present set-up of the committee deserves mention here. From the nature of its functions, it has to perform the duties of an expert body. But its members are not experts. There is not even a good chance of its members becoming experts as a result of continuous work with the committee over a number of years. Because every year the membership is decided by the election and there is no guarantee that one who was a member in the previous year will be re-elected. Further, the committee has not the assistance of an expert like the Comptroller and Auditor-General who advises the Public Accounts Committee. These are serious limitations which need to be suitably remedied in order to make the committee a more authoritative and really effective instrument of parliamentary control.

---

1. Some years ago the committee critisized, in one of its reports, the present set-up of the Planning Commission and suggested certain modifications. The Cabinet took objection to this and characterized it as interference with policy for which the committee had no business. Whatever might be the practical difficulties involved, one thing is certain. The functions of the committee at present permit it to suggest alternative policies in the interest of efficiency and economy in administration. See Estimates Committee, *Twenty-first Report,* 1958.

6. The Public Accounts Committee

The Public Accounts Committee is the twin-sister of the Estimates Committee. If the latter is concerned with the examination of estimates, the former is concerned with the manner and results of spending public funds. The Public Accounts Committee is not new to India. As early as 1923, a Public Accounts Committee was set up by the Central Legislative Assembly. Consequently, the committee today has behind it a set of well-established traditions.

The committee consists of twenty-two members of whom seven are from the Rajya Sabha.[1] The Members are elected by the system of proportional representation. No Minister a can be a member of the committee. The term of office of the members shall not exceed one year.

The function of the Committee is the examination of accounts of the Government in all its financial transactions. In this respect it is its duty to scrutinize the appropriation accounts and the report of the Comptroller and Auditor-General of India. The committee should satisfy itself (*i*) that the moneys shown in the accounts as having been disbursed were legally available for, and applicable, to the service or purpose to which they have been applied or charged; (*ii*) that the expenditure conforms to the authority which governs it; and (*iii*) that every re-appropriation has been made in accordance with the provisions made in this behalf under rules framed by competent authority. It is also the duty of the committee to examine the statements of accounts showing the income and expenditure of state corporations, and manufacturing schemes, autonomous and semi-autonomous bodies, together with their balance sheets and profit and loss accounts. If any money has been spent on any service during a financial year in excess of the amount granted by the House for that purpose, the Committee shall examine with reference to the facts of each case the circumstances leading to such an excess and make such recommendation as it deems fit.

Unlike the Estimates Committee, the Public Accounts Committee has at its disposal the expert advice of the Comptroller and Auditor-General based upon a thorough study and detailed examination of the Government's accounts. Thus, the intricacies of the process of modern accounting need not baffle or hinder the committee in its work. Further, the committee examines departmental witnesses who are summoned to appear before it and to answer the criticism of the comptroller and Auditor-General in the working of their departments. The committee also appoints sub-committees for efficient discharge of its responsibilities.

There is no doubt that the Public Accounts Committee is really an expert body. Perhaps it is the only expert body of Parliament composed of its own members, as a result of its intimate association with the Comptroller and Auditor-General. Its proceedings are conducted in a judicial and non-party manner. It can aptly be termed "a Committee of judges putting aside for the time being all party considerations". Its decisions and recommendations have an effect on the future expenditure of the government and lead towards improvement in the financial machinery.

1. Originally, there was no provision for members of the Rajya Sabha to associate themselves with the committee. It was only after much debate that the Lok Sabha agreed to add seven members from the Rajya Sabha also to the Committee.

Nevertheless, its action is only of a deterrent nature. It is sometimes said that the committee's function is like flogging a dead horse. It comes across and unearths the irregularities of the Government's financial transactions some years after they have occurred. And by the time they are pointed out, many changes might have occurred in the administrative machinery, thus making it very difficult if not impossible to take effective measures against those responsible. Unless the committee's reports can direct attention on the activities of the immediate past, the value and effectiveness of these reports are bound of suffer.

Despite these drawbacks, the Public Accounts Committee is indeed a powerful instrument of parliamentary control of public finances. Its power mainly lies in its ability to create public opinion by giving due publicity to any matter that comes before it. The fear of the committee and the very searching examination that takes place before it helps greatly to keep members of the public services on the path of rectitude and carefulness.

7. The Committee on Public Undertakings

The Lok Sabha adopted a motion in November 1963 to set up a Committee on Public Undertakings consisting of ten members of the Lok Sabha and five of the Rajya Sabha. The Committee will examine (*a*) the reports and the accounts of the public undertakings; (*b*) the reports, if any, of the Comptroller and Auditor-General on the public undertakings and (*c*) in the context of the autonomy and efficiency of the public undertakings whether their affairs are being managed in accordance with sound business principles and prudent commercial practices. It will also examine such functions at present vested in the Public Accounts Committee and the Estimates Committee in relation to public undertakings as may be allotted to that Committee by the Speaker from time to time. Matters of major Government policy as distinct from business or commercial functions, matters of day to day administration, and matters for the consideration of which machinery is established by any special statute, will not the examined by the Committee.

One-fifth of the Committee shall retire every year by rotation and members to retire by rotation every year shall be those who have been longest on office since their last election. The undertakings over which the Committee will have jurisdiction are: the Damodar Valley Corporation, Industrial Finance Corporation, Indian Airlines, Air-India, Oil and Natural Gas Commission and all government companies.

8. The Committee on Privileges

The Speaker nominates this committee of fifteen members at the commencement of the House. It is concerned with the examination of questions of privilege and the determination of any breach of privilege in the cases referred to it.

9. The Committee on Subordinate Legislation

The main function of this committee is to scrutinize and report to the House whether the powers to make regulations, rules, sub-rules, bye-laws, *etc.* conferred by the Constitution or delegated by Parliament are being properly exercised within the limits of such delegation. It will have a maximum membership of fifteen, who will hold office for a year. The members are nominated by the Speaker. Membership of this committee is not open to Ministers.

10. The Committee on Government Assurances

It is the function of this committee to scrutinize the various assurances promises and undertakings given by Ministers, from time to time on the floor of the House and to report on the extent to which such assurances have been implemented, and, where implemented, whether such implementation has taken place within the time necessary for the purpose. This committee too has a membership of fifteen, who are nominated for one year by the Speaker. Ministers are not eligible to be members of this committee.

11. The Committee on Absence of Members from the Sittings of the House

This is also a fifteen-member committee whose members are nominated by the speaker for a year. The committee considers all applications from members for leave of absence from the sittings of the House and will examine every case where a member has been absent for a period of sixty days or more, without permission, from the sittings of the House and will report whether the absence should be condoned or the seat of the member be declared vacant.

12. The Rules Committee

The main function of the Rules Committee is to consider matters of procedure and conduct of business in the House and to recommend any amendments or additions to these rules that may be deemed necessary. The committee is nominated by the Speaker, has fifteen members, and the Speaker himself is its *ex-officio* Chairman.

13. Committee on Papers Laid on the Table

This is a Committee of fifteen members. The members are nominated by the Speaker for a term of one year. The function of the Committee is to examine all the papers laid on the Table of the House by the Ministers and to report to the House whether there has been compliance of the provisions of the Constitution, Act, Rule or Regulation under which the paper has been laid. The Committee will also look into any delay in laying the Paper and if there has then any delay whether a statement explaining the reasons for such delay has been laid and whether these reasons are satisfactory.

14. Committee on the Welfare of Scheduled Castes and Scheduled Tribes.

This is a thirty member Committee of which twenty members are from the Lok Sabha who are elected on the principle of proportional representation and the remaining ten nominated by the Rajya Sabha. The term of the Committee is one year. The main function of the Committee is to consider the reports of the Commission for Scheduled Castes and Tribes under Article 338(2) of the Constitution and to report as to the measures that should be taken by the Union Government in respect of matters with regard to the Union Territories. Also to examine the measures taken by the Union Government to secure due representation for the Scheduled Castes and Tribes in services and posts under the Centre having regard to the provisions of Article 335 of the Constitution.

15. Departmentally-related Standing Committees

These are called Standing Committees. There is a Standing Committee for each Ministry or Department of the Union Government in each House of Parliament. The

Committees also make reports on Bills moved in the House. The Reports of the Committee are based on unanimous recommendations. However, there is provision for giving notes of dissent. The notes of dissent are presented to the House along with the Report. The Standing Committees shall not work in any other place except the precincts of the Parliament House unless other wise specifically permitted by the Speaker or the Chairman of the Rajaya Sabha. The Standing Committee may avail of expert opinion or public opinion. A Standing Committee shall not generally consider the matters which are considered by the other Parliamentary Committees.

16. Committee on Empowerment of Women

This Committee which has been the latest to be constituted (1997) consists of 30 members, 20 of them from the Lok Sabha nominated by the Speaker and the remaining ten from the Rajya Sabha nominated by the Chairman of that House. The term of office of the Committee is one year. Ministers shall not be nominated as Members of the Committee.

The functions of the Committee are as follows. To consider the reports by the National Commission for women and reports on the measures that should be taken by the Union Government for improving the status of women in respect of matters within the purview of the Union Government.

These committees were created with a view to developing specialisation and expertise in members in those activities of the state in which they are interested and to give members opportunity to look closely at the activities of the different Ministries.

It is unnecessary to stress the importance of these committees in the work of Parliament. In order to become a more efficient instrument of public action, Parliament may, in fact, have to establish more of these committees. From a comparative point of view, the number of parliamentary committees in India is small. Almost every other country with a parliamentary system of government has more of these committees. To quote one example, France under the Fourth Republic had no less than nineteen of them. In the context of the objective of a socialist pattern of society and the enormous increase of State activity which is its direct result, parliamentary work will continue to increase in the years to come. To cope with this increased load, one possible measure is an increase in the number of these committees and the division of work of some of them. More parliamentary committees will also bring about greater decentralization of parliamentary power. At present, some of the committees are big power-centres. Membership of such committees, in course of time, will become seats of patronage and there will be contests for capturing those seats. An increase in the number of committees is also necessary for increasing the efficiency in the working of these committees. Moreover, an increase in the number of these committees will give better opportunity to a larger number of members to participate in parliamentary work more actively and thus make them really useful representatives of the electorate.

Subordinate Legislation

We have already seen that the most important function of Parliament is legislation. The scope of legislation in a modern state has enormously increased as a result of the unprecedented increase in state activity. A modern government provides a variety of services to advance the social welfare of the people and directly or indirectly controls the economic resources of the State. As a result, public administration pervades every walk and aspect of a citizen's life. Naturally, therefore, the scope of legislation has become unbelievably wide and varied, and the number of laws is incomparably large.

That being so, it is possible for any body of legislators to deliberate upon, discuss and approve every little rule or regulation, which may be essential for the purpose of administering the various laws, schemes, *etc.* which the Government may sponsor. There is also the limitation of time on account of the various duties and obligations that Parliament has to perform; it has to keep a general supervision and watch over the Executive; it has to exercise control over finance; it has to lay down general policies for the guidance of the Executive, and attend to many other matters. Parliament can, therefore, lay down, even the matter of legislation, only the broad aspects of a measure and leave the details to be worked out by the Executive to give effect in the desired manner to the wishes as expressed by the Legislature in an enactment.

Such a development has necessitated the delegation of the parliamentary power of legislation to the Executive within the scope and limits that legislation may impose. Experience has shown that the work of the Government has to be carried on more by the rules made by the Executive then by the few principles which are laid down for the government by Parliament.[1] The rule-making powers thus vested in the Executive by legislation has given rise to a kind of 'new despotism' as experienced parliamentarians in the United Kingdom have put it. It is for the purpose of keeping this new despotism under control within due limits and on proper lines that Parliament has established as special Committee on Subordinate Legislation in order that it may function effectively through it. The committee, in fact, is the custodian of the duties of Parliament to watch as to how the power given the Parliament is being exercised in action and to keep the administration within the bounds intended by parliament.

The committee came into being in 1953. Within a year it submitted its first report which contained the important recommendation that bills containing proposals for delegation of legislative powers should invariably be accompanied by the memorandum containing the details and the scope of such proposals. The committee also made certain recommendations for the purpose of bringing about uniformity in the practice of delegating legislative powers.

In September 1954, the committee presented its second report to the Lok Sabha. The committee examined many bills and statutory orders and pointed out where legislation had gone beyond the limits of the rule-making authority. Subsequent reports also have made several valuable recommendations.

The Speaker has appointed a member of the Opposition as the Chairman of the committee. This is a healthy innovation, and perhaps as a result the committee has functioned entirely free from the control of any of the Ministers. The members of the committee act in a business-like manner and are absolutely free from any party whip; they never approach any problem actuated by the party spirit. In fact, it has functioned very satisfactorily as a business committee charged with the responsible duty of checking and eliminating the chance of the possible transgression of authority prescribed by Parliament. Matters are decided by the general consensus of opinion of the members present and the Chairman is

1. See P.L. Shrivastava. "Sub-Delegation of Legislation Power", (1962) II S.C.J. 15.

spared the necessity of taking any votes. The committee is particularly interested in insisting on the compliance with the rule that all subordinate legislation must be placed on the table of the House and every dereliction is promptly censured.

The reports of the committee show that it has received the co-operation of the different Ministries and the officers, whenever it had occasion to seek information from them or to send for them or to interrogate them as to the propriety of the subordinate legislation they had promulgated. Whenever the committee pointed out to a Ministry or the rule-making authority that the rules have gone beyond the limits prescribed or that they were not in conformity with the spirit of the Statute, the department or the official concerned have accepted the committee's viewpoint and have attempted to rectify the matter. In particular, the committee has been careful scrutinizing the measures so as to ensure that the jurisdiction of the courts of law should not be ousted. The danger of executive despotism becomes serious if judicial review is sought to be altogether ousted by the rule-making authority.

It is now fully recognized that the delegation of power is both a necessity and a risk. The real function of the committee is to minimize the inherent risk in the improper exercise of rule-making powers. It is often very difficult to find the dividing line between policy and detail. The Rules of Procedure of Parliament have, however, some salutary provisions on the subject. Members need not take them as the final word. The committee, so far, has not functioned as an Opposition to the Executive, but as a responsible body appointed by Parliament in order to subject to detailed scrutiny the voluminous output of subordinate legislation in an independent and non-partisan manner to eliminate, as far as possible, the abuse of authority or any encroachment on Paliament's powers under the Constitution.

***

27

AN ASSESSMENT OF PARLIAMENT'S WORK

ALTHOUGH a full-fledged system of parliamentary government was in operation ever since India's political independence in August 1947, the establishment of a Parliament as envisaged under the Constitution was possible only by 1952 with the conclusion of the first general elections. The most significant feature of the results of these elections was the overwhelming majority with which the Congress Party was voted to both Houses of Parliament. The Opposition was not only too small in size but also suffered from the further weakness of being divided into too many groups of widely differing political platforms. As a result, no party in the opposition was entitled to be recognized as an official opposition party for which status the minimum requirement is one-tenth of the total membership of the House.

With a steamroller majority at its behest, the ruling Congress Party could get through Parliament any measure it proposed. The party was so strong that it could pass even a constitutional amendment depending only on its own strength. Naturally there was a widespread felling that Parliament would become a convenient "rubber stamp" in the hands of the Executive which was dominated by the Congress Party leadership. As the Leader of the House, Prime Minister Nehru was anxious to dispel this impression and this was perhaps what prompted him to declare on the floor of the House while speaking on the First Amendment of the Constitution (1951) that "after all, the responsibility for the Government of India, for the advancement of India, lies on this and future Parliaments of India and if this Parliament or future Parliaments of India do not come up to our expectations, then it will bode India no good." The functioning of Parliament since 1952 shows that this expectation was substantially fulfilled and parliamentary authority has come to be accepted not only in theory but fully in practice. But it must be pointed out that this acceptance was a gradual process and it had its own limitations.

In a nation of India's size and complexity, issues of virtual national importance are so difficult of solution that as long as a democratic system prevails, decisions affecting them are not easy to be made by an Executive, however great and powerful are the men who constitute it. This is really the rationale behind the gradual but steady growth of parliamentary power in India within a decade. When the nation faced some of the most difficult problems in history which sought solutions of general national acceptability, Parliament alone was found to be the final arbiter. In the process, Parliament asserted itself in every matter of national importance.

The first and perhaps the most decisive occasion arose in 1955-56 when the problem of reorganizing the States was taken up in the light of the report of the States Reorganization Commission. The great debate that took place in Parliament on the Commission's Report clearly showed that it was no rubber stamp of either the Executive or the party in power. In fact, the final decision to create a bilingual Bombay State, an altogether new proposal, was a product of spontaneous parliamentary initiative. There were also other important decisions which emanated in the light of the discussions in Parliament. No close student of India's democracy could miss the frequency with which the Executive of the day was vacillating between constantly varying positions and the eagerness with which it solicited parliamentary approval for a particular line of action it sought to adopt.

Another sphere where the Executive has been seeking the approval of Parliament is the manner in which planned development of the nation is brought about. Planning is indeed a prerogative of the Executive. Yet, apart from the fact that the Five Year Plans had been subjected to comprehensive and critical appraisal in Parliament, every formulation of economic policy by the government and every modification of that policy was being scrutinized by Parliament. In fact, the manner in which Parliament went about examining the different aspects of the successive Five Year Plans, particularly through its Committees, shows that there was closer and more detailed scrutiny of the later plans than the earlier ones giving us a glimpse of the increasing parliamentary hold on this most important sector of national endeavour.

Every occasion when the President declared a constitutional emergency in any of the States was one which gave Parliament an opportunity to show its real position and authority. Even when the proclamation was made under non-controversial conditions, parliamentary vigilance was a powerful force to compel the Executive to uphold the rule of law and to act with restraint and caution. There have been occasions when Parliament had compelled the Executive to adopt procedures acceptable to it rather than what the latter thought to be adequate in its opinion. Some of the measures taken with respect to matters affecting Kerala (1959) and Orissa (1960) during the pendancy of constitutional emergency in these States are examples.

The decision of the Executive to cede certain parts of the Berubari Union of West Bengal to Pakistan as a part of an agreement between the Prime Ministers of India and Pakistan and the subsequent intervention of Parliament to disapprove the manner of cession is an example of the way in which India's Parliament has asserted itself. The Government was compelled to seek the advice of the Supreme Court in the matter, according to the advice of the Court a constitutional amendment was required to give effect to the agreement. The government was originally of the view that it could implement the agreement even without Parliament coming into the picture and even if necessary, nothing more than an ordinary legislative enactment was required.

There have been occasions when revelations in Parliament have ultimately forced ministers to resign, officials to be dismissed and investigations into the working of organizations ordered.[1] Parliament has also inflicted punishments on individuals for contempt of that august body.[2] While these are all important stages which gradually built

1. The resignations of T.T. Krishnamachari (1958) and Keshav Deo Malaviya (1963) are only two of the most important examples.
2. e.g. The Blitz editor's case (1961).

up Parliament as the sheet-anchor of the Republic's democratic structure, it was the national emergency of 1962 which accorded the greatest recognition to Parliament as the sovereign institution of the nation's political power. The discussion on the Presidential proclamation of emergency prior to its approval by Parliament marked the triumph of Parliament as the most decisive factor of our constitutional government. Never before has Parliament asserted itself in the manner in which it asserted on that occasion. And never before had the Executive with an overwhelming majority in Parliament behind it sought parliamentary approval on a variety of its actions on that occasion in the manner in which it did. On the face of it, it was an astounding performance on the part of a body which a decade earlier appeared to be the mouthpiece of an unrivalled Executive and an all powerful party.

Confidence in the valuable role which Parliament could play in the nation's affairs has also been growing steadily and uniformly. Every one of the existing parties has accepted the parliamentary system without reservations. Even the Communist Party, which at one time thought of Parliament as merely another arena of struggle in the process of the dictatorship of the proletariat, has radically changed its attitude by proclaiming its confidence in the parliamentary method to bring about peaceful transition to socialism. In fact, there exists no organized section of public opinion in the country, except perhaps a few individuals and small groups here and there who contemptuously discard the parliamentary role as insignificant.

The attitude of the ruling party too has been conducive to strengthen the usefulness of Parliament. The Congress Party could, if it wanted to do so nullify the effectiveness of Parliament by taking legislative decisions during party meetings and subsequently getting them formally adopted by Parliament in a mechanical fashion. Not only that the party did not adopt this technique but went to the extent of treating the fragmented and heterogeneous opposition with respect and consideration. It is indeed significant that the party has not used its overwhelming majority to ride roughshod over the Opposition. On the contrary, it has permitted the Opposition to take almost as much time for discussions as itself thereby upholding in practice its faith in the need and effectiveness of opposition for the successful functioning of a parliamentary system. There have been even occasions when members of the ruling party playing the role of the opposition and enhancing the value of parliamentary discussions.

The annual working days of Parliament, the volume of its work, the variety of subjects that it has been handling, the diverse methods it has been employing to control the Executive and the different procedures it has adopted to ensure accountability of the Executive, all this will show that Parliament has its grip over the pulse of the nation. On an average, both Houses of Parliament have been holding at least three sessions a year. The Lok Sabha sits for about 160 days a year while the corresponding figure for the Rajya Sabha is 120 days. In order to get an idea of the volume and variety of the work of Parliament during a year, we may consider a particular year. For example in 1962 as many as 93 official Bill were considered by the Houses and 71 of these were enacted. There were 59 new Bills introduced by private members in the same year. The Government accepted some of these for circulation in order to elicit public opinion and others for study and report by a Joint Committee of both Houses. Several non-legislative matters also came up for detailed discussion in the Houses. Among these were the situation created by the Chinese aggression, the Colombo Proposals, the second and third reports of the Commissioner for Linguistic

Minorities and the Krishnamachari[1] Report on Indian and State Administrative Services and the Problems of District Administration. During the year, 1,333 assurances given by Ministers were recorded in the proceedings of both Houses. Of these, as many as 874 assurances were implemented, a handsome record indeed. Under the auspices of the Department of Parliamentary Affairs, as many as 114 meetings of the Consultative Committees attached to the various Ministries and Departments were held during the year. The Department also arranged a large number of visits of groups of Members of Parliament to various development projects all over the country. To these must be added the thousands of regular and short notice questions asked and answered on the floor of either House, the large number of Resolutions discussed, Adjournment Motions moved and statements made by government spokesmen on matters of public importance. Mention must also be made of the work done by the various Parliamentary Committees and the reports produced by them, especially those of the Estimates Committee, the Public Accounts Committee and the Committee on Subordinate Legislation.

All these, as a whole, are heartening signs of the manner in which parliamentary institutions and practices are steadily gaining ground in the country. This, however, is only one side of the picture. We must also consider the opposite side in order to have a proper perspective of the situation as is obtained today.

The quality of work of any Parliament depends on the quality of its members, particularly the ordinary member. In this respect, India's Parliament has yet to go a long way. As in the case of almost any Parliament of a democracy, there is no special qualification prescribed in India for a member to be elected. But in the context of the country's educational backwardness this has serious consequences. A large proportion of the members elected to Parliament are incapable of discharging the responsibilities of a parliamentarian on account of their lack of ability to participate intelligently in the proceedings. As a result the successful conduct of parliamentary work depends almost entirely on a small group of able and educated men, who are willing to work. Unfortunately, the number of such members who can be identified as expert and effective parliamentarians is decreasing alarmingly; losses are scarcely filled by competent young members. Fewer men and women of high academic distinction are entering Parliament in successive elections. The situation cannot easily be remedied as it will take many years to make India educationally advanced. The only short-term remedy lies in the hands of the political parties. Since an overwhelming number of members are elected as party nominees, if parties decide to select properly qualified candidates only, the quality of the ordinary member would go up automatically and Parliament would have better qualified members. In this respect, the leading political parties have the greatest responsibility as their members form an overwhelming majority in Parliament.

Although the dignity and decorum with which the Houses of Parliament have been conducting their business has been satisfactory in the early years there was still much room for improvement. Discipline is a prime prerequisite of Parliament's smooth and efficient functioning. Since Parliament functions through its presiding officers—the Speaker or the Chairman—it is of paramount importance that every member should abide by the presiding officer's rulings. But there have been several occasions when members have

1. V.T. Krishnamachari who was associated with the Planning Commission for many years either as its Member or Deputy Chairman.

behaved in an unruly fashion, ignored or defied the Speaker's rulings and acted in an undignified manner. There have also been occasions when the Speaker was compelled to "name" members, order them out of the House, suspend them from participating in the proceedings of the House and at least on one occasion called the sergeant on duty to forcefully remove defiant members from the House.[1]

The all-round and fullest realization that when members uphold the authority of the presiding officer they are only upholding the authority and dignity of the House is yet to get firm roots in the parliamentary practice.

Indiscriminate and improper use of raising points of order is a tendency which has been gaining steady ground in Parliament. Points are often raised by members which are no points of order at all but are intended merely either to seek information from the Government or for placing before the House the member's own views or his observations or comments on what a Minister or another member has said on the floor of the House. Sometimes points of order are raised during the course of a speech by a member deliberately to interrupt or confuse him. Resort to points of order is also made sometimes when a business has first been finished and before the next item has been taken up. Sometimes they are not even related to the business before the House at all.

Another tendency which has been on the increase is the manner in which some members indulge in interrupting another member's speech. This assumes unusual proportions when some Ministers are addressing the House. These interruptions sometimes take the shape of a running commentary on the speech by those who interrupt. The present practice in the House is that a member may interrupt another if the member in possession of the House is willing to give way. But no member has a right to force another nor can the Speaker force the member on his feet to give way. Even if the member who interrupts intends to correct an erroneous observation on the part of the member who has the floor, the purpose is seldom served on account of the general confusion that ensues such interruptions.

Some members while speaking in the House raise their hands in wild gesticulations or point their fingers at others or speak at the top of their voice. They seem to forget that the place of their address is the floor of India's Parliament and not the crowded and confused mass gatherings at open-air political meetings. Very often such gestures and behaviour give rise to counter-gestures and shouting from other members and this gives the appearance of utter disorder and affects the dignity of the proceedings and the decorum in the House.

Motions seeking the adjournment of the House to discuss a matter of urgent public importance is a device which the opposition has been employing to arrest the attention of the House and the Government. But if this device is used indiscriminately its value gets easily nullified. In a period of three years—1957-60—there were over 350 adjournment motions for which notices were given by members but only three of them were allowed to be discussed. This addiction to adjournment motions appear to be the lingering influence of an old habit. Under the Government of India Act of 1919, adjournment motions were invariably allowed in the Central Legislative Assembly because they did not amount to a censure of the Government. They also then provided an avenue for members to raise a

1. There have also been occasions, although very few, when the Speaker had to warn individual members who challenged others for a fight or who were on the verge of violence to settle a point with one or more of their fellow parliamentarians.

discussion or ventilate a grievance. Members seem to forget that they function today in an entirely different House which is the repository of the national will and which affords them many other means to raise discussions on every matter of public importance.

There have been occasions when members, especially a few from the Opposition, took unfair advantage of their Parliamentary privilege to level charges or make insinuations against officials and private individuals during debates. They conveniently forget that the individuals whom they attack in this manner cannot make use of the same forum in replying or rebuffing such accusations. This has also occurred in debates or questions concerning the service personnel including promotions. A strong sense of responsibility must accompany privileges if democratic practices are to prevail in Parliament.

A matter which often created confusion in the House, generated unnecessary heat and aroused passions, is the language problem. The normal practice at present is that members should speak in English or Hindi. But if a member cannot express himself in either of these, he may speak through his mother tongue with the permission of the Speaker. But this privilege is seldom made use of and whenever a member spoke in a language other than either English or Hindi, it is understood by such a small number of members that its practical utility becomes almost nil. As a result, there are many members who have never spoken in the House. Even when members speak either in English or Hindi a good proportion or members cannot follow what is said. Unless there is an arrangement by which simultaneous translation of speeches can be made, the effectiveness of the House will remain at a low level so far as members conveying their views to their colleagues is concerned.

The quorum required to transact business in the House is one tenth of its total strength. This means that the Lok Sabha should have at least fifty-five members present in the House to conduct its business. One would think that this is an abnormally small number in a House of over 540 members. Yet, there have been many occasions when the members present number less than what was required to constitute a quorum. At least on one occasion there were only ten members in the House. Such poor attendance has often compelled the House to be adjourned and to upset its time-schedules seriously affecting its programme of work. If the nation's Parliament cannot set an example in matters like this how can one expect the other, less important, institutions and functionaries display a high sense of responsibility in the conduct of their affairs ?

The tendency for legislators to speak irrelevantly or indulge in pointless perorations is not confined to India's Parliament. This is one of the drawbacks of legislatures all over the world. But any one who makes a casual glance over the voluminous parliamentary reports will realize the need for improving this aspect of Parliament's work. It is often the result of poor organization of parliamentary business as well as the lack of proper division of work among members. When every organization in Government is striving to improve its efficiency in every way, particularly, through the application of the principles of scientific management, Parliament alone cannot lag behind in this important aspect of its work.

The efficient transaction of the business of Parliament, to some measure at least, depends on the presiding officers also. In this respect, the Speaker's role is of utmost importance. A Speaker has to discipline himself rigidly particularly in two respects: to avoid being dubbed as a partisan; and to avoid entering the arena of controversial subjects. The first will ensure the members' confidence in him and the second the dignity of his office. In this context, the record of the Speakers, although on the whole satisfactory, is not as good as it should be. There was at least one occasion when a no confidence motion was moved against the Speaker alleging partisanship in his actions, even though the motion was defeated by a overwhelming majority. In another case, the Speaker got involved in a controversy by publicly criticizing family planning, a policy adopted by Government and approved by Parliament. A healthy convention demands that such views should not be made in public by the Speaker.

On a number of occasions senior Ministers have expressed their inability to share information with members on important matters such as aspects of national defence, defence production, financial estimates of certain public sector enterprises, terms of certain foreign collaboration agreements, *etc.* The general plea that is almost invariably put forward is that it is not in public interest or in the interest of national security. But every time such a reply is given, Parliament appears to lose all its majesty and paramount authority. Further, such answers restrict the limits within which the House can debate usefully problems of that nature without in any way impinging on genuine security interests. Sometimes, they provide a convenient cover for inefficient or even questionable practices within Ministries and Departments of the government.

There can be no doubt that a reconciliation of the interests of the House with those of national security in such circumstances is not easy. Yet it is necessary for Parliament to find suitable remedies. One way may be to covert the House into a Committee of the whole House while such discussions take place so that the Ministers can speak more freely and frankly. The real difficulty, however, seems to be the absence of a sufficiently large and effective Opposition. So long as the Opposition is small, the Government is likely to feel reluctant to share confidential information with members since an irresponsible Opposition may not feel obliged in keeping such information confidential. This situation no more exists as the Opposition since 1991 has been of large enough in size.

A peculiarly intriguing situation emerges occasionally when a Minister makes a statement in Parliament about a matter in which he is involved or in connection with which his integrity is questioned. But the statement becomes meaningful to the House only if all facts are made known to the House. On the contrary, in the absence of such facts, such statements create confusion as well as suspicion on the minds of the members and the general public regarding the bonafides of the Minister concerned. Giving full information to Parliament in order to make its proceedings more meaningful becomes important on such occasions.

There have also been occasions, although rare, when Ministers have either refused or showed reluctance to give details regarding certain transactions of the government with parties from abroad or concerns dealing with defence equipment. Sometimes the plea was that Parliament could not be given the details without the consent of the other party. On one such occasion, the Speaker intervened and gave the ruling that even if the other party did not agree, the information sought by the House should be given by the Government. He ruled that nothing should be spent from the Consolidated Fund of India without the permission of the House. "If someone in the House had sought details such as deployment of forces, the government had a right to withhold them in public interest." "But", he warned, "if any conern would agree to a transaction only on the ground that the details thereof should not be divulged to Parliament, it is better that such a transaction is not entered into".

Few Deputy Ministers and even Ministers of State have been able to make a mark in Parliament during the fairly long period of Parliament's existence. This is not a welcome feature of Parliament's work. After all at least theoretically, these are the functionaries groomed for development and eventually to take over from the senior Ministers. It seems that working under the shadow of their senior colleagues, they usually remain unnoticed and unimpressive. Even when they get an independent portfolio, it is often of relatively unimportant nature. There have, of course, been exceptions to this but, speaking generally, the Parliament of India has not afforded much opportunity to build up future senior ministers. In the same manner, the gap between the experienced front blenchers whether of the ruling party or the parties of the opposition and the backbenchers has always been too wide making an imbalance in the intellectual equipment of the House.

India has always been famous for her tolerant attitude towards differing ideas, views and opinions. This great national quality is often reflected during discussions in the Houses of Parliament. Yet there have been occasions when members, grouped on linguistic or regional considerations, betrayed their narrow loyalties and extreme intolerance. Discussions on the official language have almost invariably created an atmosphere of hostility between rival sections who advocated divergent policies. This attitude of intolerance has, of late, been showing an increasing rather than decreasing tendency.

The Year 2000 marks the completion of the first fifty years of the functioning of the Indian Parliament. As a representative body representing India's millions, how effective, how efficient and successful it has been during this period is a big question which cannot be easily answered. No doubt, as has been pointed out earlier in this chapter, Parliament had played a great role in settling many vexed complex problems which confronted the nation during the early years of its Independence. Gradually, however, Parliament appeared to lose its majesty and became a handmade in the hands of clever, unscrupulous and power hungry politicians. Although Nehru gave great importance for the Parliament's role in the country's administration, Indira Gandhi had little respect for Parliament and she seldom attended its sessions and gave it the necessary leadership that is expected of the Prime Minister. During the period of internal emergency Parliament was reduced to the position of a rubber stamp. The Janata Government which followed hers was so short-lived that it could not mend the situation. Neither during the second term of Indira Gandhi nor during Rajiv Gandhi's rule that followed it did re-establish Parliament as a truly representative body. The brute majority of the Congress Party under Rajiv Gandhi made Parliament subservient to the whims and fancies of the party leadership.

The last decade of the twentieth century saw the emergence of a large number of small parties in Parliament, with the national parties losing their decisive voice in parliament. This has led to two serious consequences. First the instability of governments; second, frequent general elections. In ten years India has had eight governments and five general elections, a sort of a record indeed. This had brought down the prestige of Parliament and quality of parliamentary government. With the multiplicity of parties each of whom working at cross purposes, parliament became a hot bed of intrigue, fight and disorder rather than an orderly business-like body dealing with the many complex problems facing the country. But that is not all.

In recent years India's Parliament has become an utterly indisciplined and unruly body. Indeed, those interested citizens who have been watching the Lok Sabha (also Rajya

Sabha) proceedings on television, when important debates were telecast live would be left wondering whether it is the highest representative body of India or a boisterons mob embroiled in a street battle. The Speaker, or the Chairman repeatedly reminding the agitated members that "the nation is watching them" and exhorting them of the need to maintain discipline and decorum but finding that his appeals are of no avail, ordering the TV cameras be switched off and finally adjourning the House for the day. Such happenings have not been rare in India's Houses of Parliament but have become a common place.

According to the Rules of Procedure of Parliament, "whenever the Speaker rises he shall be heard in silence and any member who is then speaking or offering to speak shall immediately resume his seat". Rule 361(i). This rule is followed often in its breach rather than its adherence. Instances of members violating rules and established conventions of good behaviour at the slightest provocation from any quarter of the House have become the order of the day. And political parties, small or large and cutting across the ideological divide, have been indulging in such unwholesome behaviour pattern with impunity. Shouting slogans in the House is forbidden. But who cares. Not only ordinary members but even party leaders indulge in this despicable behaviour. They choose the Well of the House for slogan shouting so that the high pitch sound so generated reverberates the entire hall making it impossible for others to remain in the Hall. The tragedy is that it is often a small group, less than ten per cent in a House of 545, which makes the orderly functioning of the House impossible and the presiding officer has no other alternative except to adjourn the House. Thus entire day's parliamentary work is lost.

This kind of utter degeneration in the functioning of Parliament started as a regular feature during the Tenth Lok Sabha and continues unabated since then. In fact, pendemonium leading to adjournments has become an established practice in the proceedings of the Parliament of India. It is such reprehensible happenings which might have impelled a junior judge of a Delhi Court to characterise the Parliament as a fish market while addressing a former Minister who appeared before him on charges of corruption. Although the Delhi High Court later expunged those remarks from the records, the fact remains that the concerned judge had the courage to make such a statement in an open court. Session after session of Parliament has been wasted without transacting any business making parliamentary responsibility a mockery. In this nefarious game the culprits are not only the small parties which are often irresponsible but even the leading parties of the country the Congress (I) and the BJP. Indeed, it looks as if the political parties irrespective of their ideological diversity, seem to have arrived at a consensus not to condemn the disruption of Parliament, And the effect of this is not far to seek.

One has only to go through the proceedings of the Houses of Parliament to realise that issues of importance, whether they are serious charges of corruption against Ministers or the commission and omission of acts of the Government, or any other important matter affecting the country's interests, they have hardly been addressed in any sense of seriousness since 1999. In fact, many members who are interested in serious parliamentary work and who would like to maintain orderly behaviour are frustrated and hence they keep off from attending the sessions. Even if a member takes the trouble to study thoroughly a problem, in the prevailing atmosphere in the House, he will not get the opportunity to present it and create the desired impact.

There was a time when Parliament witnessed a sense of accountability from the members of the Treasury Benches but that too has disappeared in the nineties and Ministers can get away whatever be the quality of their performance. With the kind of coalition governments that have become the order of the day, as many as twenty or more of them getting together to form a government, the principle of parliamentary responsibility of the Executive also has largely disappeared from the Indian parliamentary scene.

The average cost of running the Parliament is estimated to be Rs. 2570 a minute. This is based on calculations of cost in the year 1992. It should be substantially more in 2000. Let some one work out the cost of wasted hours in Parliament only to get an idea of the stupendous cost involved just to maintain a non functioning Parliament.

The view has been expressed by some critics that parliamentary democracy does not suit a country like India on account of the peculiar conditions like illiteracy, poverty and the caste system. They do not however say what needs to be done to make it serve better the interests of the country. Everyone knows how demagogues and unscrupulous power seekers can exploit the ignorance of an electorate unable to assess the performance, not to speak of the promises, of a multiplicity of parties. But no one has an answer to the question how the system of popular direct elections based on adult suffrage can be done away with without making room for a despotic on a totalitarian system of government.

Sometimes one hears of vague proposals that the parties should resolve their differences and evolve a common programme. But this is to beg the question. For, it is because they cannot agree on a common programme that they have organized themselves into different parties. The fact is that in a country of India's size and perplexing problems, it is impossible to expect a common programme. The best that can be expected is a certain measure of unity among the political parties with regard to the basic objectives such as welfare measures and development programmes. Such unity is already in existence. But there are many other issues as well as different policies for implementation on which widely differing views exist and so long as such differences continue to exist, different political parties will also exist.

What is needed is not the abolition of parties nor their merger into one entity, but the adherence to the rules of the game by all the parties. This will mean that every party will endeavour to instil in its members a sense of discipline and dedication for national welfare through constitutional means. Only when every party stands by the ideal of constitutional morality can the country expect to derive the best results of a party system of government. A determined and sustained programme of education in the fundamentals and foundations of State policy among the rank and file of the parties as well as a leadership that adheres to a minimum code of behaviour in the spirit of the Constitution can ensure better and more enduring results.

Parliament and the Party System

The essence of parliamentary democracy is party government. And a party government cannot succeed without an organized party system. To maintain the democratic character of a party government, there should be continuous and responsible criticism both within the Legislature and elsewhere. In the absence of such criticism, the government would soon become an autocracy and, later, a tyranny. But criticism cannot be effective if it is only sporadic; it becomes even useless when it is only casual. To make it sustained and effective, it should be organized. Hence the necessity for deliberately organized political parties whose business it is to oppose the government, to expose its defects and depose it when the time is ripe.

Effective and sustained criticism by organized political parties in opposition not only prevents a party government from becoming autocratic; it also helps to make the Government a more efficient instrument of democracy. Every government, however democratic and welfare-minded it may be, is apt to make mistakes. Often they are not aware of them. Sometimes they hide them and on occasion they even try to justify them. An organized opposition, functioning effectively within the Legislature, can make use of the various parliamentary methods in order to compel the government to admit its mistakes and adopt appropriate measures to remedy them. Responsible opponents, who believe in principles and dare to criticize, contribute more to the success of a party government than indulgent party men who have an 'endearing tendency' to blind the government with their 'songs of praise'.

While the government of the day should be open to constant criticism and should be challenged almost every day, it should not be overthrown every day. That would be disastrous. While the government should be sensible enough to be influenced by justifiable criticism, it should be strong enough to resist criticism who, units view, is not justified, and to remain in office. A government formed on the basis of a popular election and backed by members of a victorious party has a mandate from the people to be in charge of the nation's affairs for at least a few years. Then alone it can give political peace, continuity of policy and stability in administration. Instability in government will lead to frequent elections, political turmoil, administrative choas, widespread insurrections and even civil war. Not party government can effectively function so long as its life hangs constantly in the balance.

The stability of parliamentary government is a product of the party system. The members of the party in power are organized into a cohesive and united force, disciplined and imbued with common ideals and pursuing common objectives and policies. So also are those in the opposition, although on certain matters affecting the nation as a whole such as national security, the Government and the Opposition stand on the same plane. If the voters come to dislike the policies of the party in power, they can exert pressure through the Opposition and will eventually get an opportunity to change the government at the next election. The party system provides for a ready Opposition to take over the responsibility of Government whenever the occasion arises. If such an alternative is not possible or available, either an autocracy or chaos will be the result.

The success of parliamentary democracy depends not only on the party system but also on the acceptance of certain common objectives and principles by all parties. The most important of these seems to be the unqualified acceptance of the parliamentary principle by all. They must also believe in the principle of constitutionalism, that every change of government must be brought about in a peaceful, constitutional manner as opposed to one of conspiracy and violence.

Political parties not only organize the people in the peaceful process of political action but also create and sustain public opinion. They give an opportunity to the average citizen to express his opinions and canvass support for them on a wider plane. They bring to his knowledge a mass of information on public affairs. Even if they occasionally falsify the perspective of the issues that arise, they are a sure guarantee that ultimately the correct perspective would emerge. In short, they create an atmosphere conducive to the exchange in ideas and constitute an insurance against bigotry and fanaticism. Thus, the political education they provide and the opportunity that they create for the ordinary man to come forward in the field of public affairs will ensure a healthy and dynamic democracy.

Finally, the party system enables the poor and the uneducated in society to fight the rch and the socially advanced on an equal footing for positions in the nation's parliament. Each party has its funds and these can be made available to meet the election expenses of those deserving but poor candidates. The fact that such candidates can get elected to Parliament will go a long way to instil a spirit of devotion to the idea of party government among the common people, thereby supplying a broadbased foundation for the parliamentary principle. Thus, the party system lies at the very hart of parliamentary democracy. Without it party government has no basis and it will soon degenerate into the dictatorship of a dominant group.

These underlying principles of a party system are inherent in the working of the parliamentary democracy that is established under the Constitution of India. It is true that the Constitution does not give expression to them except in an oblique manner. The only provision which has anything directly to do with this is Article 75(3) which ensures the collective responsibility of the Council of Ministers to the House of the People. But the spirit that underlies the fundamentals of the Constitution envisages a party system which implies all the above principles. To a great extent, even legal sanction has been given to them by the Election Commission of India, officially recognizing political parties in India on an all India or regional basis for the purposes of conducting elections.

The Evil of Defection

Defection of legislators was practically unknown in India until 1967. The fourth general elections in 1967 was a watershed in the electoral politics of the country. For, it was during that year that the Indian National Congress lost its majority in parliament and several state legislatures. While the Congress Party lost majority its position was not wrested by any other single party. As a result, a new system of Government came into being almost all over the country. Samyukt Vidhayak Dal (SVD) or United Front Governments, that was the first large scale experiment in coalition politics in India. Though it failed to work effectively, it left its seeds of revival in one form or another since then. Instability of governments, particularly in the States, almost became chronic. The main cause for instability was the frequent defections of members inspired by the lure of ministerial office. Defections brought down even single party governments. Haryana provided the classic example of a single member defecting and changing parties twice on the same day. This was characterised by the then Home Minister Y.B. Chavan as the "spectacle of *Aya Ram* and *Gaya Ram*".

Defections had been made possible and profitable by the change in the size of the Council of Ministers. Since there was no constitutional bar on the size of the Cabinet, more and more ministers could be added as and when the situation demanded. Defections, split of parties and uneasy combination of groups and parties and unstable coaliation governments became a common feature of parliamentary system of government in India. Such a situation was perhaps not anticipated by the Constituent Assembly. Not that apprehensions were not expressed in the Assembly. When some members moved amendments to limit the size of the Council of Ministers to fifteen members the Chairman of the Drafting Committee, B.R. Ambedkar, opposed them and hence they were rejected. His argument was that the Prime Minister should not be bound constitutionally to appoint a fixed number of Ministers.

It may be relevant to point out here that the Constitution of Ireland stipulates a minimum of seven and a maximum of fifteen ministers. In Japan the Constitution empowers the parliament to fix the strength of the ministers by law. Even in Britain where conventions take precedence, there is a law which restricts the number of Ministers. The Government of India Act of 1935 had set a ceiling of ten Ministers. It is unfortunate that the Constituent Assembly did not follow these examples.

The question of defection had been a subject of heated discussion repeatedly in Parliament since 1967 and as a result an Ethics Committee was constituted under the Chairmanship of Y.B. Chavan, the then Home Minister. Following up the Committee's report, a Bill was introduced in Parliament in 1971 to deal with the problem. The Bill, however, lapsed soon after as a result of the dissolution of the Lok Sabha.

No further effort was made until 1985 when the Rajiv Gandhi Government brought about the fifty second Constitutional Amendment in 1985 with a view to banning defections. It added the Tenth Schedule to the Constitution which may be called the Anti-defection law. But one single provision in the law has virtually defeated the very purpose of the law, namely that if one-third of the members of a party decides to break away it will not be deemed to be defection. This one provision has played havoc to parliamentary government in India. The number of splits since 1990 has been legion particularly in view of the fact that the number of smaller parties has been going up election after election. The smaller the party the splitting process becomes easier as a small number could make up the one-third required.

Another major defect of the law has been the provision for vesting in the Speaker the final authority to determine whether or not there has been defection. Partisan Speakers played havoc with the law by recognising or not any break-away group according to his discretion and political alignment. Innumerable cases relating to the issue of disqualification on the ground of defection have come up creating utter confusion and chaos. It is well known that many of the defections are engineered by vested interests and corruption of various forms plays an important role in them. The lure of ministerial positions has been used to break parties, manipulate majorities, destabilise and topple governments. Decisions of Speakers have been challenged in Courts. Although judicial review has been prohibited by the Amendment on the Speaker's decisions, Courts have ruled that judicial review is part of the basic structure of the Constitution and cannot be ruled out.

It has become a practice that members involved in defection are generally given almost automatically a berth in the Cabinet. As a result, Cabinets have become "Jumbo Cabinets", making infra structure facilities in State secretariates difficult to be provided for ministers. Also not enough of portfolios to be distributed among ministers. Uttar Pradesh under Chief Minister Kalyan Singh (1998) had ninety ministers. The number of MLAs supporting the government was just a bare majority in the Assembly. That means over 40 per cent of members were ministers: The position was not different in Bihar under Laloo Prasad Yadav or Rabri Devi. In a small State like Arunachal Pradesh the Ministry at one time consisted of over 50 percent of the total membership of the Assembly. Most of the smaller States in the north-east were no exception.

At the time the matter was under discussion in Parliament in the late sixties, the dominant view was that the maximum strength of the Cabinet should be limited to 10-11 per cent of the total membership of the legislature. However no law could be passed embrodying this view except the National Capital Territory Act which has limited the number of ministers to seven. The only State which follows now the norm of 10 percent is Kerala which has only 14 ministers in an Assembly of 140 members (1996-2001)[1]. Unless drastic measures are taken to curb defections parliamentary democracy in India is doomed to become corrupt, inefficient and undemocratic.

A Code of Conduct for Members of Parliament

In 1997 the Rajya Sabha set up an Ethics Committee with a view to overseeing the moral and ethical conduct of its members and to examine cases referred to it with reference to their ethical and other misconduct. In its first report the Committee has proposed a Code of Conduct for members consisting of twenty broad principles and guidelines which the members should abide in their dealings. The Code requires the members to always see that their private financial interests and those of their immediate family members did not conflict with the public interest. The code has suggested that members should never expect or accept any fee, remuneration or any benefit for a vote given or not given by them on the floor of the House for introducing a Bill, for moving a resolution or desisting from moving a resolution, putting a question or for participating in the deliberations of the House or a Parliamentary Committee.

The Code has suggested that the members should not accept a gift which may interfere with honest discharge of their official duties. They should desist from giving certificates to individuals and institutions of which they have no personal knowledge and are not based on facts. Members should not misuse the facilities and amenities made available to them.

The Committee has desired that it should be made compulsory for the members to declare their assets and liabilities and those of their immediate family members including spouse, dependent daughters and sons before the Committee. The Committee proposes to place those statements' on the Table of the House.

The Committee plans to consider in its subsequent reports the procedures for making a complaint to the Committee or taking up a matter *suo moto* by it, the mechanism for investigation of a complaint and the question of providing penalties for violation of the Code. It will recommend specific measures to the House for taking a view in each case referred to it on the basis of public perception of credentials.

Taking note of the emerging trend of cross voting in the elections for the Rajya Sabha and the Legislative Councils in States, the Committee suggests that instead of secret ballot the question of holding elections by open ballot may be examined. The Committee is of the view that the question of corporate funding of political parties and its ramifications needs to be further examined. It felt that donations received by political parties, the source of which lies in a foreign country should be totally banned.

It is heartening to note that the Rajya Sabha has taken the initiative to establish a Code of Conduct for its members. We may expect the Lok Sabha and the State legislatures too emulate this example and set up appropriate committees to deal with this matter.

***

1. The UDF Ministry of 2001 however, consisted of 20 Ministers.

28

THE UNION JUDICIARY : THE SUPREME COURT

THE ESSENCE of a federal constitution is the division of governmental power between a central government and state governments and this division is expressed in written words. Since language is apt to be ambiguous, and its meaning may not be taken as the same by all at all times, it is certain that in any federation there will be disputes between the centre and the units about the terms of the division of powers and the respective areas of their authority. All such disputes are to be settled with reference to the constitution which is the supreme law and which embodies the manner in which powers are divided between the centre and the units. Justice demands, at the same time, that such conflicts should be settled by an independent and impartial arbiter. A supreme court under federal constitution is such an arbiter and is, therefore, an essential part of a federal system. It is at once the highest interpreter of the constitution and a tribunal for the final determination of disputes between the Union and its constituent units. This is one of the most important functions of the Supreme Court of India under the federal system established by the Constitution.

The Supreme Court of India, however, is more than a federal supreme court. For, as we have already seen, under Article 32 the Court is made the protector of all the Fundamental Rights embodied in the Constitution and it has to guard these rights jealously against every infringement at the hands of either the Union Government or the state governments. By declaring the significance and operation of these rights from time to time, it protects the citizens from unconstitutional laws passed by the legislatures and arbitrary acts done by the administrative authorities.

The Supreme Court is also an all India supreme appellate court having both criminal and civil jurisdictions. The Constitution invests the Court with extensive powers of reviewing the decisions of the courts below it in criminal and civil cases. In the process, it gets an opportunity to construe not only the Constitution and the laws enacted by Parliament but also the laws passed by the various State Legislatures. Thus, in resolving finally a controversy between two private parties over a certain property, the Court may take into consideration even a local custom and determine the respective rights of the parties in its light.[1] With the exercise of the civil and criminal appellate jurisdictions, the Court has assumed the role which the Privy Council had been performing for about a century in the Indian judicial sphere.

1. Singh *vs*. Singh 1954, S.C.J. 562. Also see Inder Singh *vs*. Gurdial Singh (1962) II S.C.J. 459.

Further, the Supreme Court of India plays a unique role by giving its advice, from time to time, to the President of India on questions of law or fact which are of such a nature and of such public importance that the President refers them to the Court for its consideration and opinion. It is doubtful whether there is any other court of law to which has been assigned so much power under any constitution. The highly important position that the Court holds under the Constitution was described by a leading member of the Drafting Committee. Alladi Krishnaswami Aiyar, in the following terms:

> ...... The future evolution of the Indian Constitution will thus depend to a large extent upon the work of the Supreme Court and the direction given to it by that Court. From time to time, in the interpretation of the Constitution, the Supreme Court will be confronted with apparently contradictory forces at work in the society for the time being. While its functions may be one of interpreting the Constitution... it cannot in the discharge of its duties afford to ignore the social, economic and political tendencies of the times which furnish the necessary background. It has to keep the poise between the seemingly contradictory forces. In the process of the interpretation of the Constitution, on certain occasions, it may appear to strengthen the Union at the expense of the units and at another it may appear to champion the cause of provincial autonomy and regionalism. On one occasion it may appear to favour individual liberty as against social or state control and at another time it may appear to favour social or state control. It is the great tribunal which has to draw the line between individual liberty and social control.[1]

A Single Judicial System

Unlike many countries with federal constitutions, India has a single judicial system. This, however, is not an altogether novel feature that has been established by the present Constitution. It was there, in a limited sense, under the Constitution Act of 1935 with the Federal Court as the highest Court within India in all constitutional matters. But the Federal Court was not the ultimate judicial authority, as appeals could go to the Judicial Committee of the Privy Council in London even from the Federal Court.

The absence of a unifying organ embracing all the different areas in the judicial system was keenly felt for many years in the country. The movement for the establishment of such a body was brought to the forefront during the discussions of the Round Table Conferences. Both in the executive and in the legislative fields there were such unifying organs, the Central Executive and the Central Legislature. The Privy Council was too remote to become a similarly unifying judicial organ. Hence, the Federal Court playing that role, though in a limited manner, was a welcome development. Today there are no such limiting factors in the Supreme Court filling the role.

The Supreme Court stands at the apex of India's judicial hierarchy with effective power to supervise and control the working of the entire system and to ensure the realization of the high judicial standards that it might set as an integral part of the democratic system of government sought to be established by the Constitution. Explaining the nature of this system, Ambedkar said in the Constituent Assembly:

> The Indian federation, though a dual polity, has no dual judiciary at all. The High Courts and the Supreme Court form one single integrated judiciary having jurisdiction and providing remedies in all cases under the Constitutional law, the Civil law or the Criminal law. This is done to eliminate all diversities in a remedial procedure. Canada is the only country which furnishes a close parallel. The Australian system is only an approximation.[2]

1. C.A.D. VIII, pp. 223-4.
2. C.A.D. VII, p. 36.

The single hierarchical system of judiciary has brought about not only jurisdictional unity, but also the establishment of a single judicial cadre, as it were, for the whole country. Although there is nothing that prevents a direct appointment to the Supreme Court from the Bar, there has been none so far, and all the appointments to the Supreme Court were made from the High Courts. Similarly, a good many appointments to the High Courts are made from among the judges of the lower courts, particularly the District and Sessions judges. Further, there is also a provision for the transfer of judges from one High Court to another in any part of the country. The Indian judiciary, thus, with the Supreme Court at its apex, is a fully integrated system in every sense of the term. The writ of the Supreme court runs not only all over the country, Central, State and local areas, but also within all fields of law, constitutional, civil and criminal.

The Supreme Court was formally inaugurated on 28 January 1950.

An Independent Court (Art. 124)

The Supreme Court at present consists of the Chief Justice and twenty-five other judges. In 1950, when the Court was inaugurated with the new Constitution, it had only eight judges. But a parliamentary enactment in 1957 increased the number to a total of eleven. At present twenty-six judges including the Chief Justice comprise the Court.

The Constitution envisages an independent Court. Every member in the Constituent Assembly had been eager to see that the Court was made as independent as it possibly could be. There was detailed discussion on this very important matter. As a member emphasized:

> This is the institution which will preserve those fundamental rights and secure to every citizen the rights that have been given to him under the Constitution. Hence, it must naturally be above all interference by the Executive. The Supreme Court is the watch-dog of democracy.[1]

The independence of the judges is ensured by eight main provisions.

1. Appointment

Every judge of the Supreme court is appointed by the President of India after consultation with such of the judges of the Supreme Court and the High Courts of the States as the President may deem necessary for the purpose. But in the appointment of a judge other than the Chief Justice, consultation of the Chief Justice of India by the President is obligatory.

As would be clear from our earlier discussions, the President here means "the President aided and advised by the Council of Ministers". Will not such a body bring in politics in the appointment of judges ? This was the question which the framers were called upon to answer, and if the answer to it was 'Yes', they were to provide the necessary safeguards. It was pointed out that in England appointments to the judiciary were made by the Crown. There is no limit whatever placed on this power which in effect is wielded by the Executive of the day. In the United States, on the contrary, appointments to the Supreme Court are made only with the concurrence of the Senate. Ambedkar said:

> It seems to me, that in the circumstances in which we live today, where the sense of responsibility has not grown to the same extent to which we find it in the United Kingdom, it would be dangerous to leave the appointments to be made by the President without any kind of reservation

1. C.A.D. VIII, p. 257.

or limitation. Similarly, it seems to me that to make every appointment which the Executive wishes to make subject to the concurrence of the Legislature is also not a very suitable provision. Apart from its being cumbrous, it also involves the possibility of the appointment being influenced by political pressure and political considerations. The draft article, therefore, steers a middle course. It does not make the President the supreme and the absolute authority in the matter of making appointments. It does not also import the influence of the Legislature. The provision in the article is that there should be consultation of persons who are *ex-hypothesi* well qualified to give proper advice in matters of this sort.[1]

Barring the emergency period of 1975-77 the constitutional provisions regarding the appointment of judges worked quite satisfactorily during the first three decades. Some of the appointments made during the period of emergency were severaly criticised as partisan and politically motivated. Appointment of Justice Ray as Chief Justice over the heads of three other senior judges created almost a crisis in the functioning of the Supreme Court but that was a short-lived aberration. Nevertheless, after a short period of the Janata Government, with Indira Gandhi again in power, the situation had undergone a sea change. An infamous circular of 1980 providing for the transfer of a number of judges from one State to another created an atmosphere of anxiety and mistrust in the Executive. This was reflected in the decision of the Supreme Court in S.P. Gupta *vs*. Union of India (AIR 1982 SC 149) where the Court had pointed out the deviations and the distortions that had crept into the system. Nevertheless, the Court stood by the constitutional provisions and affirmed the existing method of appointment. There was, however, one significant aspect of that decision and that was the removal of the decisive voice which the Chief Justice of India enjoyed until then in the appointment of judges. The result was the absolute use of political power by the Executive and merit becoming a casualty in judicial appointments. The role of the Chief Justice of India became nominal and minimal. The resultant dissatisfaction led to the decision in the Advocates on Record Association case (AIR 1994 SC 268). The majority of judges in this case caused the pendulam to swing to the opposite side and the power of appointment was concentrated in the judiciary itself by making the Chief justice and two senior-most judges together practically taking the decisions and making the Executive to have little say in the matter. In that decision the meaning of the word 'consultation' was made to become 'concurrence'. This was indeed a great setback to the role of the Executive in the appointment of judges. Naturally it became a serious matter of contention at the highest levels in Government. It was contended that the selection process for appointment of judges was questionable as the consultation process for it was not followed resulting in deadlock over the issue. Matters came to a head when some senior advocates of the Supreme Court submitted a memorandum to the President of India urging him to supercede the senior-most judge of the Supreme Court M.M. Punchhi in the impending appointment of the next Chief Justice, and those advocates were removed from the Bar Association membership by an overwhelming majority of the Supreme Court Bar Association. The upshot of this rather sordid controversy was the recommendation of the Bajpai Government to the President of India to make a reference to the Supreme Court seeking the Court's opinion in the disputed matter. Accordingly, the President referred to the Court on 27-07-1998 nine questions dealing with all aspects of the problem seeking its opinion.

A special nine-judge Bench of the Court in its unanimous opinion on the Presidential

1. C.A.D. VIII, p. 258. It was revealed in the Assembly that the question as to how politics could be kept out of the appointment of judges was referred to the Federal Court and the High Courts by the Assembly. The advice suggested the following procedure for the appointment of judges to the High Courts: The Chief Justice should send his recommendation in that behalf directly to the President. After consultation with the Governor, the President should make the appointment with the cocurrence of the Chief Justice of India. Ibid. VIII, p. 232.

reference held that the Chief Justice of India must make a recommendation to appoint a judge of the Supreme Court and to transfer a Chief Justice or a puisne judge of a High Court in consultation with the four senior-most puisne judges of the Supreme Court. The expression 'consultation with the Chief Justice of India' in Articles 217(1) and 222(1) of the Constitution requires consultation with a plurality of judges in the formation of the opinion of the Chief Justice. It is to be noted in this context that the process of appointment of judges is an integrated participatory consultative process for selecting the best and most suitable persons available and all the constitutional functionaries must perform this duty collectively to reach an agreed decision subserving the constitutional purpose.

To deal with the appointment and all related matters a National Judicial Commission was proposed from time to time by the Law Ministry and several other authorities.

However, so far the proposed National Judicial Commission has not yet been constituted. That means, today for all practical purposes, the Chief Justice of India and four senior most judges of the Supreme Court of India decide every matter connected with the appointment of both Supreme Court and High Courts in India. They also decide the question of transfer of judges from one High Court to another. They also deal with any other matter connected with the functioning of the High Courts including the discipline of the High Court judges.

2. Qualifications

The elimination of politics in the appointment of judges is further achieved by prescribing high minimum qualifications in the Constitution itself. This is also intended to enhance the competence of those appointed as the judges of the highest court in the land. The qualifications are: the person concerned must be a citizen of India and (a) has been a judge of a High Court at least for five years; or (b) has been for at least ten years an advocate of a High Court; or (c) is in the opinion of the President a distinguished jurist. The inclusion of the last provision which would enable the President to appoint a distinguished jurist on the Supreme Court, even if he did not qualify by a specified number of years of practice at the Bar, was intended to open a wider field of choice. Under this provision, for instance, a distinguished jurist who holds a Chair in a university will be qualified for appointment to the Supreme Court.[1]

3. Tenure

Although the Constitution does not provide for life tenure, the existing provision in effect amounts to nearly the same, as judges once appointed, hold office until they complete the age of sixty-five years. A retiring age of sixty-five is, by Indian standards, very high, considering the average expectation of life in India and the average fitness of persons for work in old age. The age of superannuation for central civil services is fixed at sixty and retirement age for university teachers also is normally sixty. Physical and mental incapacity overtake most people (particularly in India) after the age of sixty-five. Answering those who criticized the fixation of age for retirement. Ambedkar said:

> If you fix any age-limit, what you are practically doing is to drive out a man who, notwithstanding the age that we have prescribed, is hale and hearty, sound in mind and sound in body, and capable for a certain number of years of rendering perfectly good service to the State. I entirely agree that sixty-five cannot always be regarded as the zero-hour in a man's intellectual ability. Hence, the special provision in the Constitution (Art. 128) for appointing a retired judge.[2]

---

1. For appointment on the International Court of Justice, the only qualification prescribed is that the person concerned should be a distinguished jurist.
2. Under Art. 128 the Chief Justice of India may, at any time, with the previous consent of the President, request any retired judge of the Supreme Court to sit and act as a judge of the Supreme Court.

Therefore, there is less possibility of losing the talent of individual people who have already served on the Supreme Court.[1]

4. Prohibition of Practice after Retirement

A retired judge of the Supreme Court is prohibited from practising law before any court or authority within the territory of India. But there is no constitutional prohibition against a retired judge being appointed for a specialized form of work by the Government. It was pointed out in the Assembly that a retired judge should never be appointed for any office of profit under the Government[2] and that they should be placed on the same footing, in this respect, with retired members of the Public Service Commissions. Ambedkar, however, drew a distinction between the two categories of work and pointed out that the work of the Public Service Commission was one which was intimately connected with that of the Executive:

> It is quite possible that a Minister in charge of a portfolio may influence a member of the Public Service Commission by promising something else after retirement if he were to recommend a certain candidate in whom the Minister was interested. Between the Commission and the Government, the relation was a very close and integral one.[3]

There was no such intimate relation between the Executive and the judiciary. In fact, there is complete separation between the functions of the two. Consequently, the chances of the Government influencing the conduct of a member of the judiciary are remote. Besides, there are many cases where the employment of judicial talent in a specialized form is necessary for certain purposes, such as conducting enquires, special investigations, *etc.*[4] Ambedkar further said that he was personally against a sitting judge of the Supreme Court being assigned to any non-judicial work *e.g.*, a diplomatic assignment, and then his returning to the judiciary. It was highly objectionable. But if a retired judge or a judge who does not revert to the judicial assignment were to be appointed to such a position, it would not undermine the independence of the judiciary.

5. Removal

A judge of the Supreme Court can be removed from his position only on the ground of proved misbehaviour or incapacity. Parliament is empowered to regulate the procedure for the investigation and proof of such misbehaviour or incapacity. But whatever be the procedure, each House in order to remove the judge, will have to pass a resolution supported by two-thirds of the members present and voting and a majority of the total membership of the House. Such a resolution will be addressed to the President who will then pass the order of removal of the judge.[5]

1. C.A.D. VIII, p. 257.
2. Ibid. p. 239.
3. C.A.D. VIII, p. 260.
4. It may be pointed out, however, that the employment of retired judges should be strictly restricted to specialized forms of work where judicial talent is of special significance. Such purely political appointments as governorships do not seem to be a legitimate use of high judicial talent.
5. So far there was only one occasion when there was an allegation against a judge of the Supreme Court that he was incapacitated and a demand was made for his removal. But the judge concerned soon after resigned, thus preventing the necessity of the matter being pursued further.

The process of impeachment, however, does not appear to be effective to remove a delinquent judge. This was demonstrated in the Ramaswami case the only one of its kind in the last fifty years. Justice V. Ramaswami was the Chief Justice of the Punjab and Haryana High Court against whom were several charges of misconduct. On a resolution adopted by Parliament to initiate the process of impeaching him, the Cheif Justice of India constituted a High Power Tribunal in accordance with the provisions of the Judges Inquiry Act of 1968 to enquire into the charges. The Tribunal came to the unanimous conclusion that Ramaswami was guilty and recommended further action. However, when the matter came up for consideration in Parliament, it did not get the required support of members and therefore it was rejected. It was alleged that the voting was on political lines which showed the weakness of the constitutional provision. This episode has led to a demand that an alternative mechanism must be devised and incorporated in the Constitution to check deviant behaviour on the part of members of higher judiciary.

6. Remuneration

A very important element that determines the independence of any functionary is the remuneration that he receives as well as its dependence or otherwise on the will of somebody else. With respect to the judges of the Supreme Court, the Constitution has taken good care of this. Unlike many other constitutions which leave the fixation of salary to the Legislature, it has prescribed that a salary of Rs. 4,000 per month should be paid to every judge except the Chief Justice who should receive a salary of Rs. 5,000 per month. In addition, each judge is also entitled to a free house and certain other allowances and privileges. Neither the salary, allowances and privileges nor his rights in respect of leave of absence or pension (to which he is entitled after retirement) can be varied to his disadvantage after his appointment. There is, however, one exception to this almost absolute rule. The salaries of the judges may be reduced by a law of Parliament during a grave financial emergency declared by the President.

By an amendment of the law relating to the salaries and allowances of Judges in 2000, the salary of the Chief Justice of the Supreme Court has been raised to Rs. 33,000 per month and that of other judges to Rs. 30,000. There has been corresponding revision in their pensionary and other benefits.

These salaries and allowances compare favourably with those else where, as for instance, the salaries of the judges in Britain, Canada or Australia. As we have already seen, the salaries of the Supreme Court judges are charged on the Consolidated Fund of India. This means that these are not subject to the vote of the House of the People. They are a primary charge on the public exchequer.

It is not desirable for retired judges to accept the position of Governor of a state or membership of legislatures. Independence and accountability, excellence and creativity are the finest facets of judicial performance. However, as the International Commission of Jurists has observed, "Independence of Judges and lawyers is not an end in itself; it is a means placed at the service of the community. The judiciary must not stake its claim in the name of the privileges of its members or the pleasure of an Olympian affirmation of its own power. Its independence and dignity must be defended in the common interest of our people, and in particular in the name of the most humble elements of society, of those who most intensely rely upon a free, efficient, altruistic, honest and wise system of justice."[1]

7. Establishment

The framers were not content with salary alone. They went a step further and authorized the Supreme Court to have its own establishment and to have complete control over it. In the absence of such a provision they thought that the Court's independence may become illusory. If the establishment looks for preferment or for promotion to other quarters, it is likely to sap the independence of the judiciary.[2] Hence all appointments of officers and servants of the Supreme Court are to be made by the Chief Justice or any other judge or officer whom he may direct for the purpose. The conditions of service of such officers and servants also are determined by the Court. Further, all administrative expenses, salaries, *etc.*, connected with these officials and servants as well as the other maintenance charges of the Court's establishment as a whole are charged on the Consolidated Fund of India.

8. Immunities

Finally, the independence of the Court is further safeguarded by making all the actions and decisions of the judges in their official capacity immune from criticism. This does not mean that no one may subject a decision of the Court or an opinion of a judge to a critical academic analysis. All that is prohibited is the imputation of movities on the part of the judges in arriving at decisions and taking action. Even Parliament may not discuss the conduct of a judge except when a resolution for his removal is before it. In order to maintain the dignity of the Court and to protect it from malicious and tendentious criticism, it has the power of initiating contempt of court proceedings against any alleged offender and take appropriate action.

The Court had occasion to discuss this question when an editorial comment on one of its decisions in a leading newspaper was made the subject of contempt proceedings against the authorities of the journal concerned.[3] The Court held:

> No objection could have been taken to the article, had it merely preached to the Court of law the sermon of divine detachment. But when it proceeded to attribute improper motives to the judges it not only transgressed the limits of fair and *bona fide* criticism but had a clear tendency to affect the dignity and prestige of this Court. The article in question was thus a gross contempt of court. It is obvious that if an impression is created in the minds of the public that the judges in the highest court in the land act on extraneous considerations in deciding cases, the confidence of the whole community in the administration of justice is bound to be undermined and no greater mischief than that can possibly be imagined. It was for this reason that the rule was issued against the respondents.

The Court has resorted to contempt proceedings not only to safeguard its dignity, honour and prestige, but also to stop any act that might prejudicially affect its arriving at an impartial and independent decision In Dixit *vs*. State of U.P.,[4] the Court said:

> ... that the object of writing this paragraph and particularly of publishing it at the time it was actually done was quite clearly to affect the minds of the judges and to deflect them from the strict

1. The International Commission of Jurists, Global Advocates of Human Rights, (University of Pennsylvania Press, p. 225).
2. C.A.D. VIII, p. 391.
3. In the matter of the Editor, Printer and Publisher, *The Times of India,* 1953, S.C.R. 215.
4. A.I.R. 1954, S.C. 743.

performance of their duties. The offending passage and the time and the place of its publication certainly tended to hinder or obstruct the due administration of justice and was a contempt of Court.

As Ambedkar said in the Assembly, it was the intention of the framers to create a judiciary and to give it ample independence so that it could act without fear or favour of the Executive or anybody else. There was no intention, however, to create an *imperium in imperio*[1] which would have created unwanted rivalries between the judiciary and the Executive resulting in unexpected conflicts. The work of the Court so far has vindicated to a substantial measure the expectations of the framers of the law.

The Law Commission of India, presided over by the Attorney General M.C. Setalvad however, had expressed anxiety in one of its reports,[2] regarding certain disquieting trends that adversely affect the judiciary as a whole including the Supreme Court. According to the Commission, political, communal and regional considerations as well as the Executive's influence have been responsible for some appointments of the Supreme Court, with adverse effect on the quality and efficiency of administration of justice. The Commission recommended that efforts should be made to recruit the judges of the Supreme Court directly from among distinguished members of the Bar, with a tenure of at least ten years. The practice of appointing the seniormost puisne judge of the Court as the Chief Justice of India is not desirable because the duties of the latter require not only a person of ability and experience but also a competent administrator capable of handling complex matters. Merit should be the sole criterion in appointing judges, and for the purpose of recruitment, the entire country should be treated as one unit. An *ad hoc* body presided over by the Chief Justice of India should be created to draw up a panel of persons suitable for such appointment. The meagre pensions which at present judges get do not induce members of the Bar to accept judgeship in the Supreme Court. These are indeed observations which merit the most serious consideration in order to make the Supreme Court discharge its onerous responsibilities most satisfactorily.

The present practice, however, is to appoint the senior-most judge as the Chief Justice of the Court.

Jurisdiction

A survey of the leading constitutions would show that the Supreme Court of India has wider jurisdiction than any other superior court in any part of the world.[3] But this was not the position in the Draft Constitution which had envisaged only a narrower jurisdiction for the Supreme Court than it has today. Some of the prominent lawyer-members[4] of the Constituent Assembly took the lead in enlarging the jurisdiction of the Supreme Court.

The jurisdiction of the Court can be divided into three categories, original, appellate and advisory.

Original Jurisdiction (Art. 131)

The Supreme Court has original and exclusive jurisdiction in any dispute (a) between

1. C.A.D. VIII, p. 399.
2. *Fourteenth Report,* 1959. Among the members of the Commission were several judges of the Supreme Court and High Courts. The Commission was reconstituted in 1971 with a more limited membership.
3. Alladi Krishnawami Aiyar, C.A.D. VIII, p. 596.
4. Among these, Pandit Thakur Dass Bhargava, Frank Anthony, and P.K. Sen deserve special mention.

the Government of India and one or more States; or (b) between the Government of India and any State or States on one side and one or more other States on the other; or (c) between two or more States. It is also provided that the dispute should involve a question, whether of law or of fact, on which depends the existence or the extent of a legal right which the Court is called upon to determine. The main difference of this provision from similar provisions in other federal constitutions like those of the United States and Australia is that in India the Supreme Court will have no original jurisdiction to decide dispute between residents of different States or those between a State and the resident of another State. Such disputes will come up to the Supreme Court only under its appellate jurisdiction. But there is one field where the Constitution permits an aggrieved person to approach the Court directly. That comes under Article 32 of the Constitution which permits the Court to entertain a writ petition from a party which complains of the violation of a Fundamental Right. But this original jurisdiction of the Court is not exclusive. The aggrieved party might as well approach the High Court for the issue of a writ or an order.

There has been only one important instance when the Supreme Court was called upon to decide a case in exercise of its original jurisdiction, that of State of West Bengal *vs*. Union of India.[1] In this case the Court held that the States under the Constitution are not sovereign and that the Union has authority to acquire compulsorily land belonging to State governments. In the same decision, the Court has also pointed out the types of dispute which are to be excluded from the original jurisdiction of the Court.

Appellate Jurisdiction (Art. 132 to 136)

The appellate jurisdiction of the Court can be divided into four main parts, constitutional, civil, criminal and special.

Article 132(1) provides that "An appeal shall lie to the Supreme Court from any judgment, decree or final order of a High Court in the territory of India, whether in a civil, criminal or other proceeding, if the High Court certifies that the case involves a substantial question of law as to the interpretation of the Constitution." Even if the High Court refuses to give such a certificate the Supreme Court can grant special leave to appeal if the Court is satisfied that the case involves a substantial question of law as to the interpretation of the Constitution. When once such a certificate is given or such leave is granted, any party to the case may raise before the Supreme Court any matter which in its opinion has been wrongly decided by the High Court in that particular case. Thus, in every matter which involves an interpretation of the Constitution, whether it arises under civil, criminal or any other proceeding, the Supreme Court has been made the final authority to expound the meaning and intent of the Constitution. This is what makes the Court the ultimate interpreter and guardian of the Constitution.[2]

The Supreme Court's appellate jurisdiction in civil cases is of a restricted character. According to this, a party to a civil suit is permitted to appeal to the Supreme Court if the High Court certifies that the value of the subject matter of the dispute is not less than

---

1. A.I.R. 1963 S.C. 1241.
2. Nar Singh *vs*. State of U.P. A.I.R. 1954, S.C. 457. See also Saifuddin Saheb *vs*. State of Bombay, 1958, S.C.J. Sadhu Singh *vs*. State of PEPSU A.I.R. 1954, S.C. 271; The State of Jammu and Kashmir *vs*. Thakur Ganga Singh, 1960 S.C.J. 231 and Harbans Singh *vs*. The State of Punjab (1962) II S.C.J. 662.

Rs. 20,000[1] or that the case is fit for appeal to the Supreme Court. Further, when once the Court is seized of the appeal, it is open to any party to challenge a decision of the High Court in that case an invalid so far as it dealt with the interpretation of the Constitution. The appellate jurisdiction of the Court in civil cases can be enlarged if Parliament passes a law to the effect.

The Draft Constitution had no provision for the criminal appellate jurisdiction of the Supreme Court. As has been pointed out above, many members referred to it as a serious defect of the Constitution and demanded the inclusion of certain provisions to ensure and maintain a high degree of criminal justice through the Court's appellate powers. "We ought to provide in a handsome manner in the Constitution itself," said P.K. Sen, "for a right of appeal to the Supreme Court in all cases of the death sentence."[2] This was opposed by K.M. Munshi on the basis of cost as well as the physical impossibility of the Supreme Court dealing with so many cases. "It is only in cases of miscarriage of justice on matters relating to the nature of evidence or procedure that the Privy Council gives special leave."[3] He advocated, therefore, the same principle to guide the criminal appellate jurisdiction[4] of the Supreme Court. The present provisions substantially conform to this proposal and was hailed as "a well-balanced one".

There are three circumstances under which criminal appeals to the Supreme Court will be permitted. They are, if a High Court (i) has on appeal reversed an order of acquittal of an accused person and sentenced him to death; or (ii) has withdrawn for trial before itself any case from any court subordinate to its authority and has in such trial convicted the accused person and sentenced him to death; or (iii) certifies that the case is a fit one for appeal to the Supreme Court. Parliament is empowered, in this connection also, to enlarge the Court's jurisdiction. These provisions, according to Ambedkar, "ought to be made, having regard to the enlightened conscience of the modern world and of the Indian people."[5] When President Prasad asked the question why it was that no provision was made to cover cases where death sentence was passed as a result of enhancement of sentence on appeal, the Chairman of the Drafting Committee replied:

> The amendment recognizes conviction or acquittal as the basis for a right of appeal to the Supreme Court. It does not recognize the nature of sentence or the type of punishment as the basis. Further, in the case of enhancement of sentence, the punishment is not for the first time. The accused already stands convicted.[6]

The criminal appellate jurisdiction of the Court has been a prolific source of appeals. In the course of deciding these cases, the Court has had many occasions to interpret the scope of the Constitutional provisions dealing with this jurisdiction. Some of the principles established as a result deserve to be mentioned here.

---

1. The minimum amount has now become Rs. 200,000 as a result of an amending law passed by Parliament in 1970.
2. C.A.D. VIII, p. 604.
3. Ibid. p. 607.
4. On the same question Bakshi Tek Chand said: "It is undesirable to convert the Supreme Court into a Court of Criminal Appeal for all types of cases.... Life and liberty are certainly more important than property, but an unrestricted right of appeal either in civil or criminal matters will do incalculable harm to society. After all, there must be some limit to appeals and further appeals". Ibid., p. 850.
5. C.A.D. VIII, pp. 853-7.
6. Ibid.

1. The grant of a certificate under Article 134(1)(c) is not a matter of course; the power has to be exercised after considering what difficult questions of law or principle were involved in the case, which would require the further consideration of the Supreme Court. The word 'certifies' in sub-article (1) (c) is a strong word which requires the High Court to look closely into the case to see if any special considerations arise. If a case does not involve any question of law, then, however difficult the question of fact may be that would not justify the grant of a certificate, because if the High Court has any doubt about the facts of a criminal case, the benefit of that doubt must to go the accused.[1]

2. The Court will not entertain a criminal appeal except in special and exceptional cases where it is manifest that by a disregard of the forms of legal process or by a violation of the principles of natural justice grave injustices has been done.[2]

3. The Court would not be justified in disturbing a decision of the Courts below on special leave merely on the ground that perhaps a different inference could also have been drawn from the facts found in the case.[3]

4. When the Court of first instance and the Court of appeal arrive at concurrent findings of fact after believing the evidence of a witness, the Supreme Court as the final Court will not disturb such findings, except in most exceptional cases where grave and substantial injustice has resulted.[4]

5. The exercise of the extraordinary jurisdiction vested in the Supreme Court by Article 136 is not justifiable in criminal cases unless exceptional or special circumstances are shown to exist or that substantial and grave injustice has been done. The exercise of jurisdiction would not be justified for merely correcting errors of fact or law; but an occasion for interference may arise where a High Court acts perversely or otherwise improperly, or has been deceived by fraud.[5]

These principles establish that the Supreme Court does not adopt too narrow an approach in hearing criminal appeals, although the Court is anxious to avoid any undue expansion of this jurisdiction through its interpretations of Article 134, lest it should be confronted with an impossible number of cases. In one case, the Court pointed out:

> We have examined the evidence at length in this case, not because it is not decisive to depart from our usual practice of declining to reassess the evidence in an appeal here but because there has been in this case a departure from the rule that when an accused person puts forward a reasonable defence which is likely to be true, and in addition, is supported by two prosecution witnesses, then the burden on the other side becomes all the heavier.[6]

Going through the hundreds of cases which the Court has decided under its criminal appellate jurisdiction, one is left with the impression that the framers have done a wise

1. Sunder Singh *vs*. State of U.P. A.I.R. 1956, S.C. 411. See also Kalawati *vs*. Himachal Pradesh, 1953, S.C.R. 546 in which the Court ruled that it cannot be converted into an ordinary court of criminal appeal for any reason.
2. Mohinder Singh *vs*. The State, A.I.R., 1953, S.C. 415.
3. Vijendrajit *vs*. State of Bombay, A.I.R. 1953, S.C. 247.
4. Hanumant *vs*. State of M.P. 1952, S.C.R. 1091. See also A.I.R. 1954, S.C. 271 in which the Court held that it will not by special leave convert itself into a Court to review evidence for a third time.
5. State of M.P. *vs*. Ramakrishna, A.I.R., 1954, S.C. 20.
6. Hate Singh *vs*. State of M.B., A.I.R. 1953, S.C. 468.

thing in incorporating these provisions in the Constitution.[1] It stands as a living testimony to the increasing recognition that is accorded to the sanctity of human life in recent times in contrast to the incredible frequency with which capital punishment was awarded for the most petty and trifling offenders in the past.

One might wonder whey the Constitution makes separate sets of provisions dealing with questions of constitutional law and those which do not raise such questions. The reason why this separation is made between the two sets of appeals is to be made clear. Under Article 132, whenever an appeal comes before the Supreme Court and if it involves questions of constitutional law, the minimum number of judges who would sit to hear such a case shall be five, while in other cases of appeal, the matter is left to the Supreme Court to determine the number of judges. According to the practice established by the Court, in constitutional matters often more than five judges sit to hear the case. But in civil and criminal appeals the Bench will consist of three judges only. With twenty-six judges on the Court, there could be one Constitutional Bench and seven Benches for Civil or criminal appeal cases at the same time.

Special Appeals

From a jurisdictional point of view Article 136 is of utmost importance. It enacts:

> Notwithstanding anything in this Chapter, the Supreme Court may, in its discretion, grant special leave to appeal from any judgment, decree, determination, sentence or order in any cause or matter passed or made by any Court or tribunal in the territory of India.

The only exception to this all-embracing power of judicial superintendence is the decisions of any Courts constituted under any law relating to the Armed Forces. Explaining the comprehensive nature of the Article and the plenitude of jurisdiction that it confers on the Supreme Court, Alladi Krishnaswami Aiyar said:

> The jurisdiction of the Supreme Court extends over every order in every cause or matter passed by any Court, or tribunal in the territory of India. Secondly, the Supreme Court is free to develop its own rules and conventions in the exercise of its jurisdiction. For example, there is nothing to prevent the Court from interfering even in a criminal case where there is miscarriage of justice, where a Court has misdirected itself or where there is a serious error of law..... The Supreme Court is able to develop its own jurisprudence according to its own light, suited to the conditions of the country in such a way that it could do complete justice in every kind of case or matter.[2]

Although the Court's intervention under this jurisdiction is often sought, it has been reluctant to make too frequent use of it. The Court held:

> On a careful examination of article 136 along with the preceding article, it seems clear that the wide discretionary power with which the Supreme Court is invested under it is to be exercised spartingly and in exceptional cases only, and as far as possible a more or less uniform standard should be adopted in granting special leave in the wide range of matters which can come up before it under this article.[3]

In another case[4] the Court held:

---

1. Rajendra Saran Agarwal, "Appeal to Supreme Court in Criminal Cases," 1960 S.C.J. 197.
2. C.A.D. VIII, p. 638.
3. Pritam Singh *vs.* The State 1950, S.C.r. 453.
4. Dhakeswari Cotton Mills *vs.* Commissioner of Income-tax, West Bengal, A.I.R. 1955, S.C. 154. See also Balwan Singh *vs.* Lakshmi Narain, 1960 S.C.J. 717.

It is not possible to define with any precision to limitations on the exercise of discretionary jurisdiction vested in the Supreme Court by the Constitutional provision made under article 136. The limitations, whatever they be, are implicit in the nature and character of the power itself. It being an exceptional and overriding power, naturally it has to be exercised sparingly, and with caution and only in special and extraordinary situations. Beyond that, it is not possible to fetter the exercise of this power by any set formula or rule. All that can be said is that the Constitution having trusted the wisdom and good sense of the judges of the Supreme Court in this matter, that itself is a sufficient safeguard and guarantee that the power will only be used to advance the principles which govern the exercise of overriding constitutional powers.

It is open to the Supreme Court at the time of hearing an appeal by special leave to consider whether the leave was properly granted and whether the appellant is to be heard on the merits. Further, save in exceptional and special circumstances the Court would not exercise its power under Article 136 in such a way as to bypass the High Court and ignore the latter's decision which has become final and binding on the parties thereto by entertaining an appeal directly from the orders of a tribunal.[1] The Court has also made it a more or less settled policy not to entertain direct appeal for special leave without exhausting all other remedies.[2]

In Raj Krishna *vs.* Vinod[3] the Court showed its disapproval of any attempt on the part of the Legislature to whittle down its power under Article 136. In that case, the Legislature had made the orders of an Election Tribunal final and conclusive and the Tribunal had ruled that the successful candidate was illegally elected because of certain alleged corrupt practices. The Court disagreed with the Tribunal on its construction of the election law and set aside its order. The Court further held that its power under Article 136 includes the power to review orders of an Election Tribunal and this power "cannot be taken away or whittled down by the Legislature", and that so long as it remains, the discretion of the Court to allow an appeal and to pass on the merits of the issue presented is "unfettered". In another election case[4] the Court held:

The jurisdiction with which the Election Tribunal is endowed is undoubtedly a special jurisdiction, but once it is held it is a judicial tribunal empowered and obliged to deal judicially with disputes arisng out of or in connection with elections, the overrding power of this Court to grant special leave, in proper cases, would certainly be attracted and this power cannot be excluded by parliamentary legislation.

Apart from Election Tribunals, the special appellate power has become a handy weapon in the hands of the Court to review the decisions of labour and industrial Tribunals. In the Calcutta Tramways Company's case[5] the Court said that

.....wide and undefinable with exactitude as the powers of the Supreme Court are it is now well settled that generally the necesary pre-requisites for the Court's interference to set right decisions arrived at by Tribunal on questions of fact are final. These can be classified under the following categories, namely, (i) where the Tribunal acts in excess of the jurisdiction conferred upon it under the statute or regulations; (ii) where there is an apparent error on the face of the decision and (iii)

1. C.P. Chokhani *vs.* The State of Bihar (1962) I S.C.J. 138.
2. Ram Saran Das *vs.* The Commercial Tax Officer (1962) II S.C.J. 210.
3. A.I.R. 1954, S.C. 202.
4. Durga Shankar *vs.* Raghuraj Singh A.I.R. 1954, S.C. 520. See also Singh *vs.* E.T. Kota 1955, 2 S.C.R. 1 and Nagappa *vs.* Basappa A.I.R. 1955, S.C. 756.
5. 1957, S.C.J. 23.

where the Tribunal has erroneously applied well accepted principles of jurisdiction. It is only where errors of this nature exist that iterference is called for.

In Bharat Bank *vs*. Employees of Bharat Bank,[1] the Court held that the functions and duties of the Industrial Tribunal are very much like those of a body discharging judicial functions, although it is not a Court which has all the necessary attributes of a court of justice. In Muir Mills *vs*. Suti Mills Mazdoor Union,[2] the Court reiterated the same view and held that it has exceptional and overrriding powers to intervene where it reaches the conclusion that a person has been dealt with arbitrarily or that a Court or Tribunal within the territory of India has not given a fair deal to a litigant.

The Court, however held that "it is not the practice of the Supreme Court in special leave cases and in exercise of its overriding powers to interfere with a matter which vests in the discretion of the High Court except in very exceptional cases'.[3] Similarly, the Court held on another occasion that it would normally be slow to interfere, in appeal, with an order passed by virtue of such wide powers as are vested in the Custodian-General under the Administration of the Evacuee Property Act of 1950.[4] Nevertheless, the reach of Article 136 is indeed formidable. It has become a convenient instrument at the disposal of the Court to check arbitrary acts and unjust decisions of the ever-increasing number of administrative tribunals whch the Union and the States are setting up almost daily in the process of seeking the objectives of a socialistic pattern of society.[5]

For the scope of discretionary power of the Supreme Court under Article 136, see also the following cases: I.J. Divakar *vs*. Government of A.P. (AIR 1982 SC 1555) Union Carbide Corporation *vs*. Union of India (1991) 4 SCC 584, Chandra Bensi Singh *vs*. State of Bihar (AIR 1984 SC 1767), S.G. Chemicals and Dyes Trade Employees Union *vs*. S.G. Chemicals and Dyes Trading Ltd. (1986) 2 SCC 624, Bihar Legal Support Society *vs*. Chief Justice of India (AIR 1987 SC 38), Indira Kaur *vs*. Sheo Lal Kapoor (AIR 1988 SC 1074), Mithilesh Kumari *vs*. Prem Bihari Khare (AIR 1989 SC 1247) and Junior Telecom Officers' Forum *vs*. Union of India (AIR 1993 SC 787).

Review

As a measure of abundant caution the framers have invested the Court with the power of reviewing its own decisions and orders. It has been said that while a lower Court is concerned with facts and a High Court with error (of judgment of the lower court), a Supreme Court is concerned with wisdom. But even a Supreme Court may go wrong and there must be a provision by which such wrongs can be rectified. This has been ensured under Article 137 which empowers the Court to review its own judgments or orders. So far, there have been only very few occasions for the Court to exercise its powers under this provision.[6]

1. 1950, S.C.R. 459.
2. 1955, 1 S.C.R. 991. See also Buckingham and Carnatic Co. *vs*. Workers of Backingham and Canatic Co. 1953, S.C.R. 219.
3. Shareef *vs*, Nagpur High Court 1955, I.S.C.R. 757. See also Nageshwara Rao *vs*. Madras High Court 1955, I.S.C.R. 1055.
4. Sohan Lal *vs*. Custodian of Evacuee Property A.I.R. 1956, S.C. 77.
5. Ambika Ram *vs*. The Commissioner of Income-tax, 1960, S.C.J. 292 and Kanhaiyalal Lohia *vs*. The Commissioner of Income-tax West Bengal (1962) I S.C.J. 127.
6. Cf. B.C. Trivedi *vs*. M.N. Nagrashna (1961) II S.C.J. 84.

Enlargement of Jurisdiction

Parliament is empowered to enlarge the jurisdiction of the Supreme Court with respect to any matter included in the Union List of legislative powers.[1] The Government of India and the Government of any State may enter into an agreement under which any matter may be placed under the jurisdiction of the Supreme Court provided Parliament passess a law for the purpose. Further, Parliament may by law confer on the Supreme Court power to issue directions, orders or writs for purposes even other than the enforcement of fundamental rights already provided for under Article 32 of the Constitution. Parliament may also confer upon the Supremee Court such supplemental powers not inconsistent with any of the provisions of tghe Constitution as to enable the Court to exercise its jurisdiction more effectively.

The Court as an Adviser (Art. 143)

The role of the judiciary as adviser to the executive or legislative department of the government was unknown to India until the inauguration of the Government of India Act of 1935. The enunciation of this principle as embodied in Section 213 of the Act shows an attempt to follow the old English practice of the Executive consulting the judiciary. With the establishment of the Federal Court of India in 1937 and the number of important advisory opinions rendered by the Court since then, judicial circles in India were by and large convinced of the usefulness of conferring a jurisdiction of this nature on the highest Court of the land. There was, therefore, hardly any criticism in the Constituent Assembly on Article 143 of the Constitution which provides for the advisory role of the Supreme Court.

Advisory function of a court of law, however, has always been a controversial question. Under the U.S. Constitution, there is not only no provision for the Supreme Court to render such advice, but the Court has always resisted any attempt by the Executive to make the Court accede to its request for advice. During his presidency, Washington asked for such advice, but the Court refused to oblige. Most American jurists are of the view that advisory opinions are legislative in nature and the doctrine of separation of powers prohibits such opinions. According to them, the Court in such cases is not assisting in the legislative function but are telling the legislature in advance how it would exercise its judicial function. According to Justice Felix Frankfurter of the United States Supreme Court:

> ....to submit legislative proposals to judicial judgement, instead of the deliberate decision of the legislature, is to submit legislative doubts instead of legislative convictions.... Advisory opinions are bound to move in an unreal atmoshpere.[2]

The Australian High Court also has refused to give advisory opinions on the ground that the essential function of the judiciary is the decision of actual disputed matters between parties and not the consideration of abstract legal questions.

---

1. The Forty Second Amendment of the Constitution, 1976 had effected certain amendments to the Jurisdiction and powers of the Supreme Court. The Forty-fourth amendment however abolished those provisions and restored the original provisions of the Constitution.

   See also Re. Cauvery Water Disputes Tribunal (IMR 1992) SC 522 and S. Nagaraj *vs.* State of Karnataka (1993) Supp. (4) SCC 595.

2. *Harvard Law Review,* Vo. XXXVII, p. 1002.

The position of Canada, however, is different. The Canadian Supreme Court Act in 1906 empowers the Governor-General-in-Council to refer important questions of law touching certain matters to the Supreme Court for hearing and consideration. The exercise of advisory jurisdiction by the Privy Council in Britain is a well-known fact. In the international sphere too, the role of the judiciary as an adviser has been accepted by embodying the principle in the Charter of the Permanent Court of International Justice and the World Court unde the United Nations Charter. More recently many constitutions, formed after the end of the Second World War, have adopted provisions embodying the consultative role of their highest courts. Burma is a notable example nearer home. Article 143(1) enacts:

> If at any time it appears to the President that a question of law or fact has arisen or it likely to arise, which is of such a nature and of such public importance that it is expedient to obtain the opinion of the Supreme Court upon it, he may refer the question to that Court for consideration and the Court may, after such hearing as it thinks fit, report to the President its opinion thereon.

The President can, thus, refer to the Court either a question of law or a question of fact provided that it is of public importance. There is no constitutional compulsion for the Court to give its advice. Further, it is up to the Court to decide as to what type of hearing it will adopt for the purpose. In this respect, the Court has adopted the same procedure as in the case of a regular dispute that comes before it. The hearing is in the open Court; interested parties are heard in the usual manner, and the opinion of the court is announced in the open Court. Judges are allowed to divide themselves and give their opinions jointly or severally, concurring or dissenting.

Under Section (2) of Article 143, the President is empowered to refer to the Supreme Court for its opinion disputes arising out of any treaty, agreement, *etc.*, which had been entered into or executed before the commencement of the Constitution. In such cases, it is obligatory for the Court, under the Constitution, to give its opinion to the President. The treaties, agreements *etc.*, referred to here, are those which the Government of India has entered into with the former Princely States and their Rulers between 1947 and 1950 during which period the territorial integration of the Indian Union was accomplished.

There have been only a limited number of occasions so far when the President referred questions to the Supreme Court for its opinion. The first of these, which was in 1951, dealt with the scope of delegation of legislative power in India.[1] The Court was asked to determine the validity or otherwise of certain provisions of three enactments, the Delhi Laws Act, 1912, the Ajmere-Merwara (Extension of Laws) Act, 1947 and the Part C States (Laws) Act, 1950. The Court was unable to give a unanimous opinion in answer to the specific questions referred to it. Yet the different opinions expressed by the judges who heard the case are hailed as 'momentous' on the subject of delegation of legislative power.[2]

The second refernece,[3] by the peculiar nature of its subject matter, is almost unprecedented in the annals of advisory jurisdiction. It dealt with a Bill passed by the Legislature of the State of Kerala in 1957, which sought to reorganize the educational system at the primary and secondary stages in that State. As the Bill contained certain provisions which authorized the State Government to take over schools managed by private

1. 1951, S.C.J. 527.
2. See for an illuminating discussion on the subject, Alexandrowiz, *Constitutional Development in India*, 1957, Chapter 6.
3. In the matter of the Kerala Education Bill 1957, 1959, S.C.L. 321.

agencies and, as such, came within the scope of the property right provisions of the Constitution, presidential assent became necessary for its validty. Since there were serious and acrimonious controversies within the State about the validity of several provisions of the Bill in the light to some of the fundamental rights under the Constitution, and representations were made to the President not to give his assent to such an 'unconstitutional piece of legislation', the President decided to send the Bill for the opinion of the Court. Here again, the opinion of the Court has become one of the most important ever given by the Court, interpreting the scope of the constitutional guarantees ensuring the cultural and educational rights of linguistic or religious minorities.

The third occcasion which necessitated the President to make a reference to the Court for its opinion was also under unusual circumstances. The Prime Ministers of India and Pakistan, acting on behalf of their respective Governments, had entered into an agreement in 1958 called the Indo-Pakistan Agreement of Exchange of Berubari Union and Cooch-Behar Enclaves by which certain territories of India were to be ceded to Pakistan. Subsequently, there was doubt regarding the competence of Parliament to implement the agreement by an ordinary legislative enactment under Article 3 since the subject matter of the legislation related to cession of national territory to a foreign State. One view was that the implementation of the Agreement necessitated a Constitutional amendment under Article 368. The Court held that the power to cede national territory cannot be read in Article 3(c) of the Constitution by implication, and so, if a part of the Union territory is to be ceded to a foreign State, no law relating to Article 3 would be competent in respect of such cession. If that be the true position, cession of a part of the Union territories would inevitably have to be implemented by legislation relating to Article 368 of the Constitution.[1] This opinion of the Court was directly against the views of the Government of India which thought that Parliament was competent to implement the Agreement by an ordinary enactment.

The fourth occasion necessitating reference by the President arose in connection with the validity of a proposed amendment to the Sea Customs Act of 1878 by Parliament.[2] Some of the State Governments expressed the view that the amendments as proposed in the Bill might not be valid constitutionally in view, of the provisions of Article 289 read with the deinitions of 'taxation' and 'tax' in clause 28 of Article 366 of the Constitution. The Government of India, on the other hand, was of the view that Parliament was competent to enact the proposed amendment. The Supreme Court, after considering the issues in all aspects, expressed the view that the proposed amendments were not inconsistent with the provisions of Article 289 of the Constitution.

The fifth occasion necessitating Presidential reference arose out of, perhaps, the most unprecedented circumstances related to a grave jurisdictional conflict between the Legislature of Uttar Pradesh and the High Court of the State.[3] The facts of this case are given in detail elsewhere and, therefore, it is not proposed to recount them here (refer to Chapter 36 under sub-heading Legislative Privileges). this reference, the President included five separate issues for the Supreme Court's consideration. Of these, the most important was whether in entertaining a petition on an issue involving a legislature's contempt or breach of privilege, a High Court judge himself commits contempt of the legislature and

1. Indo-Pakistan Agreement, *In re,* 1960, S.C.J. 933.
2. A.I.R. 1963, S.C. 1760.
3. A.I.R. 1965, S.C. 745.

whether the legislature is competent to take action against such a judge. The other four issues related to the specific case of the Uttar Pradesh Legislative Assembly from the statge the High Court entertained the petition of a Socialist woker who was punished by the Assembly for contempt of the Assembly's direction for the production of the two judges (who heard the petition) before it "in custody". The answer of the Court on all the issus amounted to the upholding of the action taken by the judges of the High Court and against the Uttar Pradesh Legislative Assembly.

In 1978 the President sought the Court's advice on the constitutional validity of setting up special courts to try emergency offences and the Court gave its verdict in the affirmative.

In 1991 the President sought the advice of the Supreme Court on the Cauvery Water dispute. The Court in its unanimous opinion pointed out that though the waters of an inter-state river pass through the territories of the riparian States, such waters cannot be said to be located in any one State. The Court also drew attention to the acknowledged principle of distribution and allocation of waters between the riparian States on the basis of the equitable share of each State. The equitable share of a State in the given case will, however, depend on the facts of the particular case.

The latest and perhaps the most momentous of these Presidential references has been the one in which the President sought the opinion of the Court in 1998 on the question of the consultative process involved in the appointment and transfers of judges and related issues. The nine-judge Bench which gave its verdict on these questions spelt out the details regarding the consultative process.

The first three opinions of the Court however are enough to prove the beneficent results of its advisory jurisdiction. The experience of Britain and Canada, and recently of Burma and India, does not justify the abhorrence displayed towards advisory opinions by the American and Australian Courts. So long as the independence and integrity of the judiciary can be maintained intact, and at the same time it can materially contribute to the lessening of the evil of enormous litigation, advisory opinions are eminently worthwhile. There was a time when courts occupied the position of "only the namesis of wrongdoers'. But that position has undergone a change and, in addition to this role, they have assumed a new role by becoming the guardians and advisers of those who respect law. A judge in the modern age, like a physician who is not only concerned with curative but also preventive medicine, ought to be interested not only in settling conflicts but also in preventing their occurrence. Advisory opinions are a help to preventing litigation or reducing it to a considerable extent. That alone should justify the role of the Supreme Court as an adviser to the Executive.

A Court of Record (Art. 129)

Article 129 makes the Supreme Court a court of record. The significance of a court of record is twofold: first, the records of such a Court are admitted to be of evidentiary value and are not questioned when they are produced before any Court. Second, once a Court is made a Court of Record by statute, its power to punish for contempt necessarily follows from that position. In spite of this, the Constitution has specifically provided for the power of the Supreme Court to punish for contempt of itself. Explaining the reason for this, Ambedkar said that in England, "the power to punish for contempt was derived largely from the Common Law; in this country we felt it better to state the whole position in the statute itself"[1].

In 1972, E.M.S. Nambudiripad, then Chief Minister of Kerala, was held guilty of contempt for stating that judges are prey to the biases of their class and are weighted against the exploited and working classes. Similarly in 1978 the Court initiated contempt proceedings for an article criticizing the judgment in the ADM Jabalpur case during the Emergency holding that all Fundamental Rights including the right to life stood suspended and the Courts could not be approached even for the protection of individual's life. More recently, the Chief Secretary of the Karnataka Government, a senior IAS officer, was sentenced to three months imprisonment for not implementing an order of the Supreme Court intended to render justice to the people.

The definition of criminal contempt is wide enough to cover gross interference with the administration of justice. In Waryam Singh *vs.* Sadhu Singh (A.I.R. 1972, S.C. 905) the court held three police officers guilty of contempt for arresting and threatening ordinary citizens with the object of stifling prosecution in a criminal complaint against the police.

The Constitution also prescribes the seat of the Court which is Delhi or any other place which the Chief Justice of India may, from time to time, appoint with the approval of the President.

All judgements of the Supreme Court will be delivered in the open Court. The judgement or opinion, as the case may be, of the Court will be in accordance with the majority of the judges present at the hearing of the case. A judge not concurring with the majority view is entitled to deliver a dissenting judgment or opinion.

Court Rules (Art. 145)

The Supreme Court is authorized, with approval of the President and subject to any law made by Parliament, to make rules for regulating the practice and procedure of the Court.[2] These include the rules as to:

1. the persons practising before the Court;
2. the procedure for hearing appeals;
3. the proceedings in the Court for the enforcement of any of the Fundamental Rights;
4. the entertainment of appeals under Article 134(1)(c) [if the High Court certifies that the case is a fit one for appeal to the Supreme Court];
5. the conditions subject to which any judgment or order of the Court is to be reviewed;
6. the costs of, and incidental to, any proceedings in the Court, and the fees to be charged in respect of proceedings therein;
7. granting of bail;
8. stay of proceedings;

---

1. C.A.D. VIII, p. 382.
2. The rules which regulate the practice and procedure of the Court as amended in the present form and which came into force with effect from 15 April 1959 may be seen as Supplement appended to the Journal Section of 1959 S.C.J.

9. providing for the summary determination of any appeals;
10. the procedure for enquiries for the removal of members of the Public Service Commission.

The scope and extent of the rule-making power of the Supreme Court under Article 145 came in for detailed examination by the Court in a decision of 1960. The main question that called for a determination by the Court in this case[1] was whether it had the jurisdiction under Article 145 to prepare and publish lists of touts, (a tout is a person who habitually procures business for an Advocate in consideration of remuneration) and by general or special order exclude them from the precincts of the Court. In the course of its judgement, the Court held:

> The Supreme Court has the inherent jurisdiction to regulate the proceedings relating to the conduct of persons appearing before it, in and out of the Court, in so far as such conduct has a bearing on their professional relations and ethics apart from the Constitutional provisions of Article 145. Apart from inherent jurisdiction, the Constitution itself has authorized the Court to make rules for regulating generally the practice and procedure of the Court. The expression practice and procedure of the Court in Article 145 must be considered in its fullest amplitude and must include regulating the conduct of all persons appearing before the Court in relation to the business of the Court. Thus the conduct of Advocates and their assistants in relation to the business of the Court must form the subject matter of regulation by the rules of the Court.
>
> All persons who frequent the precincts of the Court shall be dealt with under the same rules and all persons included in the list of touts will be liable to be dealt with in the same way, irrespective of any other considerations.

The Court's Judicial Supremacy

We have already seen how the Supreme Court is the ultimate interpreter of the Constitution and, as such, its guardian. The authority of the Court is further enhanced by the provision that "the law declared by the Supreme Court shall be binding on all Courts within the territory of India" (Art. 141). Further, in the exercise of its jurisdiction, the Court is authorized to pass appropriate decrees or orders in the interests of complete justice in any case before it. Such decrees and orders are enforceable throughout the territory of India in such manner as may be prescribed by the law of Parliament. The Supreme Court has also the power to secure the attendance before it of any person within the territory of India or to order the discovery and production of any documents, or the investigation or punishment of any contempt of itself (Art. 142).

An enumeration of the various powers of the Supreme Court will show how impressive and formidable they are. To recount the most important of them, the Court is the ultimate interpreter of the Constitution. As the final interpretational authority of the Constitution, its power embraces not only the interpretation of the Constitution but also that of the laws of the Union, the States and local authorities. Under its original jurisdiction, it settles all disputes between the States and the Union or those between the States themselves. Its appellate jurisdiction embraces not only constitutional but also civil and criminal matters. And through the exercise of its power to grant special leave to appeal, it is competent to review any decision by any Court or tribunal in the country. The law declared by the Supreme Court is binding on every Court in India. Further, it has the

1. Sant Ram, *In re*, (1961) I S.C.J. 98. See Also Rahimtola *vs.* The State of Bombay (1960) S.C.J. 50.

power of superintendence and control over every High Court in India. Its orders are enforceable throughout the country and it can order any one to appear before it or call for any document. Its decisions can invalidate the laws made by even the highest legislative authority in the land — the Parliament of India. Above all, the Court is the protector of the Fundamental Rights guaranteed under the Constitution. In the exercise of its power it can issue writs or orders to any administrative authority in any part of India with a view to preventing the infringement of any fundamental right guaranteed under the Constitution. The combination of such wide and varied powers in the Supreme Court makes it indeed not only the supreme authority in the judicial field but also the guardian of the Constitution and the laws of the land.

The Court and Stare Decisis

By virtue of its supremacy in the judicial field, the law declared by the Supreme Court is binding on every Court in India. But to what extent does it bind the Supreme Court itself? This is a difficult question to answer. If the Supreme Court resolutely follows the principle of *state decisis,* the principle of strict adherence of prior decisions, it will fetter its vision, curb its initiative and destroy its dynamism. For, a constitution is not dead wood. It has to become a living and dynamic thing because it gives shape to the Government of a living and growing people. But a constitution, when written, does not breathe. It gets life and begins to grow only when human elements gather and work it. As time passes by, it is suitably moulded and controlled and kept current with the times by those who are entrusted with the task of working it. In this process of growth, the contribution of a Supreme court is indeed very great, perhaps the greatest. But how is this possible if the Court unflinchingly adheres to its past decision, meant to suit the conditions and circumstances of a past age? Naturally the Court cannot be a slave to *stare decisis*.

On the contrary, imagine a Supreme Court which frequently and constantly reverses its own past decisions. Not only would it thereby make it impossible for others to follow its lead with reasonable certainty, but it will also ruin the fabric with which the entire constitutional structure is built up. There will no more be reasonably ascertainable constitutional principles governing the working of the Government but, instead, only the pet theories and wild fancies of different sets of judges who sit on the supreme bench from time to time. This will not advance the course of constitutionalism but will create only uncertainty and confusion. Hence it is essential that a Supreme Court imposes on itself a self discipline which binds it, as far as practicable, to its earlier decisions. As the Supreme Court of the United States pointed out in a famous decision:

> We recognize that *stare decisis* embodies an important social policy. It represents an element of continuity in law, and is rooted in the psychological need to satisfy reasonable expectations. But *stare decisis* is a principle of policy and not a mechanical formula of adherence to the latest decision, however recent and questionable, when such adherence involves collision with a prior doctrine more embracing in its scope, intrinsically sounder and verified by experience.[1]

In another case, the same Court observed:

> In reaching this conclusion, we are not unmindful of the desirability of continuity of decision in constitutional questions. However, when convinced of former error, this Court has never felt constrained to follow precedent. In constitutional questions, where correction depends on amendment

1. Helvering *vs.* Hallock, 309, U.S. 106.

and not upon legislative action, this Court throughout its history has freely exercised its power to re-examine the basis of its constitutional decisions. This has long been accepted practice, and this practice has continued to this day.[1]

Throughout the U.S. history the Supreme Court has not hesitated to overrule constitutional decisions that did not seem to fit the requirements of the new age. A classic example is provided by the desegregation decision of the Court which sought to bring together the Negro and the White children in the same school. The decision has completely reversed the earlier stand of the Court which had favoured "equal facilities but in separate schools". However, the overruling of a decision in constitutional law is, at times, not the true measure of the change. "Commonly the change extends over a long period; the erosion of a precedent is gradual. The overruling does not effect an abrupt change in the law; it rather recognizes a *fait accompli*"[2]

The tendency in India too has been the same. In Charanjit Lal Chowdhury *vs.* Union of India,[3] the Supreme Court upheld the special law under which the Government had taken over the Sholapur Spinning and Weaving Company and declared that there had been no violation of the right to equality and equal protection under Article 14 of the Constitution. But four years later, the Court gave a decision which practically wiped out the substance of the above decision. In Shrinivas *vs.* Sholapur Spinning and Weaving Company,[4] the Court answered the question 'whether it was bound by its own decision' in the negative. In that case, the subject mater for decision centered on the Government taking over the same Company and the law by which it was taken over, but the challenge came from a different Fundamental Right — the constitutional guarantee against compulsory acquisition of private property without compensation. The Court held, after explaining its earlier decision in Charanjit Lal Chowdhury's case, that the Government could not hold the Company under its control and management indefinitely without paying the compensation guaranteed under Article 31. Thus, the second decision practically cancelled out the first, and the principle that the Supreme Court is not bound by its own decisions and may even reverse a previous decision, especially on constitutional questions, was openly acknowledged by the Court. However, the Court pointed out at the same time that it would surely be slow to do so unless such previous decision appeared to be obviously erroneous.[5]

The second time the Supreme Court reversed its own earlier decision was when it gave its verdict in the Bengal Immunity Company Ltd. *vs.* the State of Bihar.[6] The Court reiterated its earlier stand and said:

> There is nothing in the Indian Constitution which prevents the Supreme Court from departing from a previous decision of it, if it is convinced of its error and its baneful effect on the general interests of the public.[7]

To quote Justice Douglas again, in support of this view of the Supreme Court:

---

1. 321, U.S. 665.
2. William O. Douglas, *We the Judges*, 1956, p. 432.
3. 1950, S.C.J. 29.
4. 1954, S.C..J. 175.
5. A.I.R. 1954, S.C. 119.
6. 1955, S.C. 611.
7. The decision overruled was a majority decision in the State of Bombay *vs.* The United Motors (India) Ltd., 1953, S.C.R. 1069 and it related to the question of inter-state sales tax. Undoubtedly, the most important decision of the Court in this context was that in Golaknath Case, A.I.R. 1967, S.C. 1643. See also A.I.R. 1967, S.C. 997.

So far as constitutional law is concerned, *stare decisis* must give way before the dynamic component of history. Then the cycle starts again. Today's new decision becomes a coveted anchorage for new vested interests. The former proponents of change acquire an acute conservatism in their new *status quo*. It then takes an oncoming group from a new generation to catch the broader vision which may require the undoing of the work of their predecessors.

That is the way it must be if the Constitution is to remain a living vital force in the affairs of each generation.[1]

In England, the House of Lords, until some years ago, was bound by its earlier decisions on question of law. In 1966, however, the Lord Chancellor ruled that the House of Lords, while treating their former decisions as normally binding, will depart from a previous decision when it might appear right to do so. The Judicial Committee of the Privy Council is free to overrule its earlier decisions. The Australian High Court is neither legally nor technically bound by its past decisions.

Prospective Overruling

The Supreme Court made history in 1967 by propounding a new doctrine by its decision in the Golaknath case,[2] the doctrine of prospective overruling. Normally the decision of a Court acts retrospectively. But there may be circumstances which might lead the Court to the conclusion that to give retrospective effect to the decision would introduce chaos and unsettled conditions in the country. The Court has to find a way out to meet such a situation. In the words of Chief Justice Subba Rao, who wrote the majority opinion in the Golaknath case, "we must evolve some doctrine which has roots in reason and precedents so that past may be preserved and future protected." He referred to George F. Canfield who said that a Court should recognize a duty to announce a new and better rule for future transactions whenever the Court has reached the conviction that the old rule (as established by the precedents) is unsound even though feeling compelled by *stare decisis* to apply the old and condemned rule to the instant case and transactions which have already taken place.

Five of the eleven judges who heard the Golaknath case accepted the doctrine of prospective overruling and laid down that their decision that Parliament has no power to abridge Fundamental Rights would not affect the validity of constitutional amendments which have already been incorporated in the Constitution (First, Fourth and the Seventeenth Amendments). Hence the Golaknath decision has only prospective operation. After having thus laid down the doctrine of prospective overruling, the five judges considered the possible objections to the doctrine and laid down the following guidelines for the operation of the doctrine:

1. The doctrine of prospective overruling can be invoked only in matters arising under the Constitution.
2. It can be applied by the highest Court of the country only. That means the Supreme Court alone can declare the manner of application of the doctrine.
3. The scope of the retroactive operation of the law declared by the Supreme Court superceding its earlier decisions is left to its discretion to be moulded in accordance with the justice of the cause or matter before it.

---

1. A.I.R. 1967, S.C. 1643.
2. Ibid, p. 433.

The doctrine of prospective overruling, by its very nature, seems to be more of an expediency than a sound principle. It has the potentiality of being used as a convenient device to confront progressive legislation and hinder much-needed social change. It is doubtful whether it will have lasting effect on the judicial scene of India.

The Supreme Court and Judicial Review

Over a century and a half ago, the Supreme Court of the United States made a famous pronouncement of far-reaching importance. It was in the course of its judgment in the famous case of Marbury *vs.* Madison.[1] The judge who spoke for the unanimous Court was the great John Marshall, Chief Justice of the United States. Marshall said:

> ...certainly all those who have framed written constitutions contemplate them as forming the fundamental and paramount law of the nation, and, consequently, the theory of every such Government must be that an act of the Legislature, repugnant to the constitution, is void.

On the strength of this theory, the Court declared a Congressional enactment invalid and thereby firmly established the doctrine of judicial review. The essence of judicial review is the competence of a court of law to declare the constitutionality or otherwise of a legislative enactment. The division of powers between the Union and the States and the express constitutional prohibitions on legislative authority are the two main sources for the exercise of the judicial veto on legislation.

The Constitution of India, in this respect, is more akin to the U.S. Constitution than the British or any other Constitution of the English-speaking peoples.[2] In Britain, the doctrine of parliamentary supremacy still holds good. No court of law there can declare a Parliamentary enactment invalid. On the contrary, every court is constrained to enforce every provision of a law of Parliament. Under the Constitution of India Parliament is not supreme.[3] Its powers are limited in two ways. First there is the division of powers between the Union and the States. Parliament is competent to pass laws only with respect to those subjects which are guaranteed to the citizen against every form of legislative encroachment. Being the guardian of the Fundamental Rights and the arbiter of constitutional conflicts between the Union and the States with respect to the division of powers between them, the Supreme Court stands in a unique position wherefrom it is competent to exercise the power of reviewing legislative enactments both of Parliament and the State Legislatures. This is what makes the Court a powerful instrument of judicial review under the Constitution.

The position was made abundantly clear by Justice B.K. Mukherjea (as he then was) in the following words:

> The Constitution of India is a written Constitution and though it has adopted many of the principles of the English Parliamentary system, it has not accepted the English doctrine of the absolute supremacy of Parliament in matters of legislation. In this respect, it has followed the American Constitution and other systems modelled on it. Notwithstanding the representative character of their political institutions, the Americans regard the limitations imposed by their Constitution upon the action of the Government, both legislative and executive, as essential to the preservation of public and private rights. They serve as a check upon what has been described as the despotism of the majority...

---

1. 1, Cranch, 137.
2. See in this connection Patanjali Sastri J. 1950, S.C.J. 237.
3. See Mukherjea J., 1950, S.C.J. 262.

In India it is the Constitution that is supreme and Parliament as well as State legislatures must not only act within the limits of their respective legislative spheres as demarcated in the three lists occurring in the Seventh Schedule to the Constitution, but Part III of the Constitution guarantees to the citizen certain fundamental rights which the legislative authority can no account transgress. A statute or law to be valid, must in all cases be in conformity with the Constitutional requirements and it is for the judiciary to decide whether any enactment is unconstitutional or not.[1]

The power of the Court to declare legislative enactments invalid is expressly enacted in the Constitution under Article 13 which declares that every law in force or every future law inconsistent with or in derogation of the Fundamental Rights shall be void, and under Article 32 which vests in the Supreme Court the power to enforce these Rights. Articles 131 to 136 which deal with the jurisdiction of the Court also expressly vest in the Supreme Court the same power of reviewing legislative enactments of the Union and the States. Article 246 which deals with the nature of the division of legislative power between the Union and the States is also equally relevant in this context. But even in the absence of some of these express provisions, the Court would have had the power of review. Speaking about the significance of Article 13, Chief Justice Kania said:

> The inclusion of Article 13(1) and (2) in the Constitution appears to be a matter of abundant caution. Even in their absence, if any of the Fundamental Rights was infringed by any legislative enactment, the Court has always the power to declare the enactment, to the extent if transgresses the limits, invalid. The existence of Article 13(1) and (2) in the Constitution therefore is not material for the decision of the question what fundamental rights is given and to what extent it is permitted to be abridged by the Constitution itself.[2]

The Court's power of reviewing legislative enactments has not been a subject of controversy in India. It is an accepted and established fact. Chief Justice Mukherjea writing on the subject reiterated in Deo *vs.* the State of Orissa[3] what he had said in 1950:

> If the Constitution of a State distributes the legislative powers among different bodies, which have to act within their respective spheres marked out by specific legislative entries, or if there are limitations on the legislative authority in the shape of fundamental rights, questions do arise as to whether the Legislature in a particular case has or has not... transgressed the limits of its constitutional powers. Such transgression may be patent, manifest or direct, but it may also be disguised, covert and indirect... In other words, it is the substance of the Act that is material and not merely the form or outward appearance... The Legislature cannot violate the constitutional prohibitions by employing an indirect method.

The fact that judicial review under the Constitution is not a controversial matter in India does not in itself settle the question as to what its scope or extent is in this country. Since the example of judicial review is provided by the practice obtaining in the United States, it has been argued by some that the scope of judicial review in India is as wide as in the U.S.[4] The Supreme Court, however, does not seem to accept this view. Proof of this may be seen in a number of observations made by the judges from time to time in different cases. Speaking of the position of the judiciary in India under the present Constitution,[5] Justice S.R. Das (as he then was) said:

---

1. Ibid.
2. A.K. Gopalan *vs.* The State of Madras, 1950, S.C.J. 179.
3. 1954, S.C.J. 597.
4. See the arguments of the counsel on behalf of the petitioner in Gopalan's case already referred to. Ambedkar argued along the same lines and urged the Court to go into "the spirit of the Constitution" while arguing on behalf of the Zamindars in the Zamindari Abolition cases referred to earlier.
5. 1950, S.C.J. 284-5.

It is necessary to bear in mind the scope and ambit of the powers of the Court under the Constitution. The powers of the courts are not the same under all constitutions. In England Parliament is supreme and there is no limitation upon its legislative powers. Therefore, a law duly made by Parliament cannot be challenged in any Court. The English Courts have to interpret and apply the law; they have no authority to declare such a law illegal or unconstitutional. But the Constitution of the United States is supreme above all the three limbs of government and, therefore, the law made by the Congress, in order to be valid, must be in conformity with the provisions of the Constitution. If it is not, the Supreme Court will intervene and declare that law to be unconstitutional and void. As will be seen more fully hereafter, the Supreme Court of the United States, under the leadership of Chief Justice Marshall assumed the power to declare any law unconstitutional on the ground of its not being in "due process of law" an expression to be found in the Fifth Amendment (1791) of the United States Constitution and the Fourteenth Amendment (1868) which related to the States' Constitution. It is thus that the Supreme Court established its own supremacy over the Executive and the Congress. In India the position of the Judiciary is somewhere between the Courts in England and the United States. While in the main leaving our Parliament and the State Legislatures supreme in their respective legislative fields, our Constitution has, by some of the Articles, put upon the Legislature certain specified limitations some of which will have to be discussed hereafter. The point to be noted, however, is that in so far as there is any limitation on the legislative power, the Court must, on a complaint being made to it, scrutinize and ascertain whether such limitation has been transgressed and if there has been any transgression the Court will courageously declare the law unconstitutional, for the Court is bound by its oath to uphold the Constitution. But outside the limitations imposed on the legislative powers, our Parliament and the State Legislatures are supreme in their respective legislative fields and the Court has no authority to question the wisdom or policy of the law duly made by the appropriate Legislature. Our Constitution, unlike the English Constitution, recognizes the Courts supremacy over the legislative authority, but such supremacy is a very limited one, for it is confined to the field where the legislative power is circumscribed by limitations put upon it by the Constitution itself. Within this restricted field the Court may, on a scrutiny of the law made by the Legislature, declare it void if it is found to have transgressed the constitutional limitations. But our Constitution, unlike the American Constitution, does not recognize the absolute supremacy of the Court over the legislative authority in all respects, for outside the restricted field of constitutional limitations our Parliament and the State Legislatures are supreme in their respective legislative fields and in their wider field there is no scope for the Courts in India to play the role of the Supreme Court of the United States. It is well for us to constantly remember this basic limitations on our own powers.

The same question was dealt with by Justice Mahajan (as he then was) in the following terms:[1]

There can be no doubt that the legislative will expressed herein would be enforceable unless the Legislature has failed to keep within its constitutional limits. It is quite obvious that the Court cannot declare a statute unconstitutional and void simply on the ground of unjust and oppressive provisions or because it is supposed to violate natural, social or political rights of citizens unless it can be shown that such injustice is prohibited or such rights are guaranteed or protected by the Constitution. It may also be observed that an Act cannot be declared void because in the opinion of the Court it is opposed to the spirit supposed to pervade the constitution but not so expressed in words. It is difficult on any general principles to limit the omnipotence of the sovereign legislative power by judicial interposition except in so far as the express words of the written constitution give that authority. Article 13(2) of our Constitution gives such an authority and to the extent stated therein. It says that the State shall not make any law which takes away or abridges the rights conferred by this Part and any law made in contravention of this clause shall to the extent of the contravention be void.

1. 1950, S.C.J. 246.

The above two opinions are supported by Chief Justice Kania who said:[1]

> There is considerable authority for the statement that the Courts are not at liberty to declare an Act void because in their opinion it is opposed to a spirit supposed to pervade the Constitution but not expressed in words. Where the fundamental law has not limited, either in terms or by necessary implication, the general powers conferred upon the Legislature we cannot declare a limitation under the notion of having discovered something in the spirit of the Constitution which is not even mentioned in the instrument. It is difficult on any general principles to limit the omnipotence of the sovereign legislative power by judicial interposition, except so far as the express words of a written Constitution give that authority. It is also stated, if the words be positive and without ambiguity, there is no authority for a Court to vacate or repeal a statute on that ground alone. But it is only in express constitutional provisions limiting legislative power and controlling the temporary will of a majority by a permanent and paramount law settled by the deliberate wisdom of the nation that one can find a safe and solid ground for the authority of Courts of Justice to declare void any legislative enactment. Any assumption of authority beyond this would be to place in the hands of the judiciary powers too great and too indefinite either for its own security or the protection of private rights.

Pronouncements of this type could be multiplied from several other opinions given by the judges of the Supreme Court from time to time. The obvious conclusion that is to be drawn from these statements is as follows. The scope of judicial review in India is not as wide as it is in the United States. This is because the Supreme Court has consistently refused to declare legislative enactments invalid on the ground that they violate the natural, social or political rights of citizens, unless it could be shown that such injustice was expressly prohibited by the Constitution.

The scope of judicial review is limited in India in contrast to that in the United States owing also to the fact that the Constitution of India goes into great detail in dividing the legislative power between the Union and the States, in the creation of a long Concurrent List covering vast areas involving possible conflicts between the Union and the States, and in making the Union supreme in that field. Although there were apprehensions that such detailed provisions would increase the scope of litigation, they have not been borne out by facts. So far, the number of cases in this field has been small and comparatively insignificant in contrast to any other federal system. It was the general structure of the United States Constitution as opposed to the detailed structure of the Constitution of India that provided a greater scope of judicial review in the United States. The general structure of the U.S. Constitution is described by Professor Munro in the following words:[2]

> The architects of 1787 built only the basement. Their descendants have kept adding walls and windows, wings and gables, pillars, and porches to make a rambling structure, which is not yet finished. Or, to change the metaphor, it has a fabric which, to use the words of James Russel Lowell, is still being 'woven on the roaring loom of time. That is what the framers of the original Constitution intended it to be. Never was it in their mind to work out a final scheme for the government of the country and stereotype it for all time. They sought merely to provide a starting point.

The same aspect is emphasized in Professor Willis's book, *Constitutional Law* and Cooley's *Constitutional Limitations*. In contrast to the U.S. Constitution, the Indian Constitution is a very detailed one. The Constitution itself sets forth in minute detail the legislative powers of Parliament and the State Legislatures. The same feature is noticeable in the provisions concerning the judiciary, finance, trade, commerce and services. The

1. 1950, S.C.J. 191.
2. *Government of the United States*, Fifth edition, p. 53.

Constitution is thus quite detailed, and the whole of it has the same sanctity as the provisions of Part III or Article 246 dealing with the legislative powers of the Union.

The detailed manner in which the framers have drawn up the Fundamental Rights has also contributed to the restricted scope of judicial review in India. The U.S. Bill of Rights has couched every human right included in it in absolute terms. But human rights by their very nature are not absolute. They are subject to social control. But who will determine the nature and extent of that social control? The U.S. Constitution vested this power in the Supreme Court. Naturally, the Supreme Court from time to time, while interpreting the scope of these rights as opposed to social control, had to propound new doctrines and theories. The doctrines of 'police power', 'general welfare', *etc.* are the products of the Court's interpretation. In the process, the U.S. Supreme Court has assumed the role of a Super Legislature, a position which is inconsistent with the democratic concept. At times, the Court became a major obstacle to social reform and the judges interpreted the Constitution in the light of their own political or social philosophy. This brought the Court into direct conflict with both the Legislature and the Executive and the Court became a subject of acute and acrimonious controversy.

The framers of the Indian Constitution did not want repetition of the U.S. experiences in India and, therefore, embodied in the Constitution itself the limitations and qualifications of each fundamental right to restrict the scope of the Supreme Court's power of review.

Nevertheless, the scope of judicial review in India is sufficient to make the Supreme Court a powerful agency to control the activities of both the Legislature and the Executive. While the Constitution expressly provided for the power of regulation of fundamental rights by the Legislature, it also insists that such regulations must be "reasonable". The Supreme Court is the ultimate authority to decide what is reasonable. Here is, then, a sizable measure of power for the Court to determine the reasonableness or otherwise of a piece of legislation in the light of the Constitutional provisions. As Justice Mukerjea said:

> Where there is limitation on the legislative power, the Court must on a complaint being made to it, scrutinize and ascertain whether such limitation has been transgressed and if there has been any transgression the Court will courageously declare the law unconstitutional, for the Court is bound by its oath to uphold the Constitution.[1]

This the Court did in one of the very first major cases that came up before it in which the Preventive Detention Act (1950) was challenged as invalid. The Court by a unanimous decision declared Section 14 of the Act invalid and thus manifested its competence to declare void any parliamentary enactment repugnant to the provisions of the Constitution. Since then, the Court has had many occasions to declare Central or State legislations invalid either wholly or partly.[2]

The Court's power of review also embraces the activities of administrative agencies. We have already seen this while discussing the power of the Court to grant special leave under Article 136. We have also seen the ruling of the Court that this power cannot be taken away or whittled down by the Legislature.[3] Therefore, the scope of judicial review

1. 1950, S.C.J. 260.
2. During the first decade of the Constitution the Supreme Court declared invalid only one of a total of 694 Acts passed by Parliament (Act XXVIII of 1950). During the same period the Court declared six State laws invalid. During the second decade, however, the number in both categories was much larger.
3. 1955, S.C.J. 723.

of administrative action, although it is still in an evolutionary stage, appears to be vast in the context of the unprecedented increase of such activities resulting from the manifold forms in which state activity is expanding.

As far as judicial review is concerned, India stands between the two extremes of parliamentary supremacy in Britain and judicial supremacy in the United States. As Justice S.R. Das said:

> Subject to the ...limitations I have mentioned which are certainly justiciable, our Constitution has accepted the supremacy of the Legislative authority and, that being so, we must be prepared to face occasional vagaries of that body and to put up with enactments of the nature of the atrocious English statute to which learned counsel for the petitioner has repeatedly referred, namely that the Bishop of Rochester's cook be boiled to death. If Parliament may take away life by providing for hanging by the neck, logically there can be no objection if it provides a sentence of death by shooting by a firing squad or by guillotine or in the electric chair or even by boiling in oil. A procedure laid down by the Legislature may offend against the Court's sense of justice and fair play and a sentence provided by the Legislature may outrage the Court's notions of penology, but that is a wholly irrelevant consideration. The Court may construe and interpret the Constitution and ascertain its true meaning but once that is done the Court cannot question its wisdom or policy. The Constitution is supreme. The Court must take the Constitution as it finds it even if it does not accord with its preconceived notions of what an ideal constitution should be. Our protection against legislative tyranny, if any, lies in the ultimate analysis in a free and intelligent public opinion which must eventually assert itself.

On 17 September 1949, Ambedkar moved a Bill in the Constituent Assembly to abolish once for all appeals from India to the Privy Council. The Bill was adopted unanimously. Speaking on the occasion K.M. Munshi paid a handsome tribute to the Privy Council and expressed the hope that

> ...the Supreme Court of India will carry forward the traditions of the Privy Council, traditions which involve that judicial detachment, that unflinching integrity, that subordinating of every thing to the rule of law, and the conscientious regard for the rights and for justice not only between subjects and subjects but also between the State and the subjects.[1]

Alladi Krishnaswami Aiyar, while joining his colleague in that tribute, sounded a note of caution and warning. He said:[2]

> There is, however, one point which I would like to emphasise, *viz.*, the Supreme Court should not blindly follow the precedents of the Judicial Committee. It is hoped that the Court will evolve a jurisprudence suited to the genius of the people and the conditions of our country. The Supreme Court will occupy a position of unique importance and the verdict of history would largely depend upon the independence, the ability and the learning which they would bring to bear upon their task.

There could be no difference of opinion that what the Court needs is a combination of the qualities and approach mentioned in the speeches quoted above. Practically the same sentiments were echoed by Chief Justice Kania, the first Chief Justice of India under the new Constitution, on 25 January 1950, when he addressed the inaugural session of the Court. Among other things the Chief Justice said:

---

1. C.A.D. IX, p. 1614.
2. Ibid., p. 1615. For the opinion of the Court regarding the scope of interpretation of the Constitution, see also the Jiyajeerao Cotton Mills Ltd. *vs.* The State of Madhya Pradesh (1962) II S.C.J. 145 and The State of Bihar *vs.* Motilal Jute Mills (1960) S.C.J. 255.

The duty of interpreting the Constitution falls on the Supreme Court. The Supreme Court will declare and interpret the law of the land and with the high traditions of the judiciary in this country, we are convinced that the work will be done in no spirit of formal or barren legalism... The Supreme Court, however, under the colour of interpretation cannot alter or amend the law. But within the limits prescribed we are quite sure that the Supreme Court will be able to make a substantial contribution toward the formation of India into a great country retaining its own civilization, traditions and customs. With the establishment of the Supreme Court of India we shall develop our own jurisprudence based on our historical background and we trust that will be an important and useful contribution to the creation of international law.

The role of the highest court of law in a free, democratic society functioning under a written constitution is difficult and delicate. The best illustration of this is perhaps the Supreme Court of the United States which has a history of two centuries behind it. During this long period, the Court had to face severe criticism on several occasions; it was branded as a citadel of conservatism and reaction, a roadblock to social change and progress. Whenever the Court was moving against the current of public opinion and interpreted law in isolation, it was in difficulties, a role which no Supreme Court can dare to play long. As Justice Holmes said in one of his famous observations: "The life of law has not been logic; it has been experience. The felt necessities of time, the prevalent moral and political theories, intuitions of public policy, avowed or unconscious, even the prejudices which the judges share with their fellowmen, have had a good deal more to do than the syllogism in determining the rules by which men should be governed. The law embodies the story of nation's development through many centuries, and it cannot be dealt with as if it contained only the axioms and corollaries of a book of mathematics."[1]

Focussing the attention on the attitude the Supreme Court ought to have, Justice William O. Douglas said: "The problems before the Supreme Court require at times the economist's understanding, the poet's insight, the executive's experience, the politician's scientific understanding and the historian's perspectives."[2]

It is difficult to decide the manner in which the Supreme Court of India had fulfilled its onerous role as the final interpreter of the Constitution. Perhaps, even a half century is not long enough to give an answer to the question. We may, however, attempt to note the trends which have become unmistakably clear. In this context we may also note the special advantages the Court has as a judicial body. Being a court of law, it is far removed from the political arena than the legislative and administrative agencies. It keeps itself aloof and detached from the community, not subject to political stress and storms of the other branches of the Government. The judges have security of tenure and other protections against the political forces of the day. Naturally they can function in an atmosphere of freedom and independence.

Such an atmosphere has, on the whole, helped the Court to maintain its integrity and impartiality but it has also made several of the judges to exhibit too much of their individuality. This was evident in some of the early judgments of the Court when almost every judge who sat on the Bench wrote a separate opinion.[3] This created three serious problems. First, the logic and reasoning of each judge in arriving at the conclusion, even when the conclusion was the same, were often different and sometimes contradictory.

1. *Common Law*, p. 1.
2. Cornell Law quarterly, val. 45, 1960, p.3.
3. See, for example, the judgment in A.K. Gopalan *vs.* The State of Madras.

Second, it was difficult to say what the views of the Court as a whole were, although the views of individual judges could be listed. Third, when the majority is very narrow, as in the Golaknath case (six against five), and several individual opinions are given, it is difficult to believe that the Supreme Court, as a whole, as the final interpreter of the Constitution, has a point of view. Further, it is even more difficult to believe that through such a process a fundamental change in the meaning of the Constitution could be brought about. As Nath Pai (who introduced a Bill to amend the Constitution to restore to Parliament the power of amending Fundamental Rights which it had lost as a result of the Golaknath decision) observed[1] rather caustically:

> ...(T)hat till the 27th of February 1967 — that means till the judgment by six judges against the five in Golaknath case was delivered — the Constitution of India gave the Parliament the power to amend the fundamental rights. This power was confirmed by the Supreme Court in its earlier decisions, but on the 27 of February, there was a basic change in the Constitution. Who made this change? That is the question. Till the 27th of February, Parliament had certain powers. On the 27th it ceased to have the power. That means there was a change in the Constitution. That means there was an amendment of the Constitution. Who carried out this amendment?... Six judges of the Supreme Court of India. Is it the function of judges to go on amending the Constitution?

A multiplicity of dissenting and concurring opinions of judges who sit on the Bench will take away an essential quality of the law, *viz. certainty*. It is essential that law should be certain, if not ideal. The Supreme Court of the United States has shown better appreciation of this problem and has followed the practice of delivering majority and minority judgments and not individual judgments by different judges.

In the early decisions the Supreme Court several judges showed a certain lack of confidence and even immaturity regarding constitutional theory. This was evident from the numerous quotations they freely made use of from the decisions of other Supreme Courts, especially that of the Supreme Court of the United States, as well as foreign (mainly U.S.) writers on the constitution and constitutional law of the United States. This is to some extent understandable in view of the fact that our lawyers of the pre-Independence era had little to do with constitutional law as a subject of study when they were students of law and even in the case of those who did study the subject had the opportunity of studying only the British constitutional law. This was indeed a serious handicap in dealing with the complex problems arising out of a written constitution which was of federal type and with an elaborate list of fundamental rights. By the time the Court was in the second decade of its existence, this handicap was to a large extent overcome and our judges showed better familiarity with the different aspects of the subject.

During the first decade, the Court was very reluctant to declare any parliamentary enactment invalid. In fact, whenever it did so, it did with great caution and hesitation. That position had undergone considerable change during the second decade, especially during its second half. The Golaknath decision marks the height of that tendency. That decision in effect told Parliament that it was only a mere "creature" of the Constitution and as such it could not amend Fundamental Rights which are of a "transcendental character". That decision also made the Supreme Court the centre of an unhappy controversy and a challenger of Parliament's legitimate powers embodied in the Constitution. The controversy has not enhanced the reputation of the Court.

1. *Parliament and Constitutional Amendment*, Inst. of Const. and Parliamentary Studies, 1970, p. 145.

But during the same period, one can point out with considerable satisfaction that the Court has been a real custodian of personal liberty and the guaranteed rights of linguistic, religious and cultural minorities. There had been numerous occasions when aggrieved individuals went directly to the Supreme Court seeking a remedy and the Court generously gave them a hearing and provided a remedy wherever it was warranted. In fact, the Court proved itself a zealous guardian of personal liberty irrespective of the political ideologies and antecedents of the individuals involved. The A.K. Gopalan case is perhaps a classic example in point.

While the Court has thus been a champion of personal liberty, its performance in the field of socio-economic legislation has not been very happy. While interpreting Article 21 (personal liberty) it relied on the proceedings of the Constituent Assembly but the same approach was not adopted while interpreting Article 31 (right to property). If the Court's attitude towards personal liberty was that of a "progressive liberal" its attitude towards the right to property was that of a "diehard conservative". Decisions of the Court in the Golaknath case and the Bank Nationalization case demonstrated that a majority of Supreme Court judges were deeply wedded to the traditional concept of property right and were not much concerned by considerations of a welfare State. As a result, the Court became a target of severe criticism both in Parliament and outside. The Twenty-fifth and the Twenty-sixth Amendments of the Constitution were the direct results of such decisions of the Court. The decision of the Court that a popularly elected Parliament was not competent under any conditions to amend the Fundamental Rights even though the Constitution has a specific provision to that effect and that these rights as framed by the fathers of the Constitution in 1949 were transcendental in nature sound like views voiced by persons who are not bothered by economics or sociology in an economically poor and sociologically backward country like India.

During the seventies and the early eighties the Court has been going through a difficult period of trial to maintain its exalted position as the guardian of the Constitution. Several decisions of the Court became subjects of acute national controversy and the judges appeared to belong to different and even hostile ideological and political camps. The decision in the Kesavananda case is a classic example. Although the opinions of the different judges who heard the case ran into hundreds of printed pages, there was no clear indication of the verdict of the Court. Similarly the Court's majority decision in the now famous Judges' Transfer case (1981) has also been disappointing in many respects. The separate judgments added together ran to as many as 1484 pages, perhaps a record in the annals of judicial pronouncements anywhere ! Such decisions have not enhanced the reputation of the Court.

The Kesavananda Bharati decision is indeed a watershed in the annals of judicial performance. It is the most important so far from the point of view of its far-reaching effect. By that decision the Court struck down a constitutional amendment on the ground that it violated the basic structure or framework of the Constitution. The concept of basic structure is a creative and innovative interpretation of the Constitution. The Court has, however, not spelt out as to what it meant by basic structure of the Constitution or a list of its basic features but has reserved its right to declare these as and when the situation arises. For instance it has held that secularism is a basic feature of the Constitution. Similarly it has declared that Fundamental Rights, Judicial Review and Parliamentary system of Government are all basic features of the Constitution.

There have also been occasions when individual judges of the Court were guilty of impropriety. In 1967, the then Chief Justice of the Supreme Court, Subba Rao, resigned his position to accept the invitation of the Opposition to become its candidate to contest the Presidential election. In 1983, a sitting judge of the Court, Baharul Islam, resigned from the Court to contest Parliamentary elections in Assam as a candidate of the ruling Party. Such conducts on the part of the judges of the highest Court in the country casts suspicion on their impartiality and independence and is violative of the principle that once appointed, their biases should be constitutional and judicial, not political or ideological. It was the intention of the framers of the Constitution that the judges of the Supreme Court should be free from temptation or fear even after they retire from the Court.

Man's long struggle has been to live under a government of laws, not of men. His search has been for equal justice under law, for a system of law applicable to all alike. He has ever sought to escape from a regime that dispenses justice according to the political or religious ideology of the litigant or the whim or caprice of government officials. A judiciary dedicated to a government of laws creates confidence in the body politic and a sense of responsibility both in lawmakers and in those who administer the law. To become the real guardian of the Constitution, the Supreme Court should symbolize that idea.

Judicial Activism

Judicial activism has not been a spontaneous development. It is the consequence of a situation which necessitated it. In 1985, the then Chief Justice of India, Justice P.N. Bhagavati converted a letter written to him on a post card by an aggrieved person into a public interest litigation. That was the beginning of judicial activism. By the middle of the nineties the Court's role in this field became well understood and widely appreciated. The Court's role in sensitising the Central Intelligence Agencies to discharge their constitutional obligations in the hawala cases in which top leaders both in the Government and in the Opposition were involved, its various judgments ranging from the need to have a uniform civil code, pollution control, preservation of historical monuments, cleaning and keeping the metropolises more hygienic, directing the eviction of unauthorised occupation of government buildings, in camera trial of rape victims and the award of compensation to them, punishing senior civil servants for contempt, prohibiting children employed in hazardous industries, directing the closure of all acqua farms in coastal areas and a host of such other decisions have attracted both praise and criticism.

Following the example set by the Supreme Court, the High Courts also followed suit. For example, the Delhi High Court directed the Delhi Government and Archeological Survey of India to prepare a scheme for the restoration of the 'haveli' (house) in which the legendary Urdu poet, Mirza Galib, lived in the nineteenth century. The Kerala High Court declared "*Bandh*" organised by political parties which brought public life to a standstill illegal and unconstitutional. The same Court ordered to stop smoking in public places. Even a subordinate Court took courage to criticise the Executive and the Legislature. An additional sessions Judge of Delhi even went to the extent of calling the Parliament of India a fish market and members of Parliament irresponsible, unruly and indisciplined crowd. Although the Delhi High Court later expunged the remarks of the judge, the incident showed the prevailing mood of the judiciary. A decade ago such observations and decisions were unimaginable in the country. They have become almost commonplace today.

In a democracy, functioning on the basis of a written constitution, the function of an independent judiciary is to act as an umpire, to ensure that state agencies operated within limits and the citizen's rights are protected. Under a federal constitutional system where power is distributed between the Union and the States, the federal Supreme Court is an arbiter between the Union and the States regarding their respective legislative authority. Indeed, the role of the Court is limited to this function and any exercise of power beyond this limit is looked upon with suspicion by the executive and the legislature.

In the historic judgement of the Supreme Court of India in the Judges' Transfer case, the seven-judge Constitution Bench held that any member of the public even if not directly involved, but having "sufficient interest" can approach the High Court under Article 226 of the Constitution, or in case of breach of Fundamental Rights, the Supreme Court for redressal of the grievances of the persons who are not able to move the Court because of "poverty, helplessness or disability or socially or economically disadvantaged position". After this judgment it has become open to public-minded individual citizens or social organisations to seek judicial relief in the interest of the general public.

Delivering the N.D. Krishna Rao Memorial Lecture in Bangalore (See the Hindu Sept. 3, 1997) Justice A.S. Anand of the Supreme Court (as he then was) exhorted courts not to shy away from discharging their constitutional obligations to protect and enforce human rights and while acting within the bounds of law must always rise to the occasion as guardians of the Constitution, notwithstanding the criticism of judicial activism. To the extent judicial activism is making the legislative and executive branches function properly in accordance with law, the court's functioning is unexceptionable, but we must remember, he said, that the sole check on judicial power is the use of proper judicial restraint by the judges in the discharge of their functions. The Courts in exercise of their power of judicial review must base their decisions on recognised doctrines or principles of law; for "judicial activism and judicial restraint are two sides of the same coin".

Inaugurating the SAARC Law Conference in New Delhi on 29.10.1998, Chief Justice Anand reiterated his above mentioned view that "Criticism notwithstanding, our experience is that the activist role of the judiciary, used with proper self-restraint is desirable for the general good of the people for whom the courts of law ultimately exist."

The trend of judicial scrutiny of governmental action and the readiness even of the executive to seek judicial determination of debatable or controversial issues have resulted in enhancing the significance of the role of judiciary in India. Judiciary has intervened in certain areas because of the people's perception that judicial intervention is perhaps the only feasible correctional remedy available. There is therefore no need to treat this exercise as an attempt by the judiciary to either clutch at jurisdiction or to usurp the function of any other organ of the State. What might appear to be non-traditional at the time of performance of such a task by the judiciary, when considered in proper perspective, might turn out to be really the process of development of law to respond to the needs of the society. In human affairs there is a constant recurring cycle of change and experiment. A society changes as the norms acceptable to the society undergo a change. Judges are alive to this reality and discharge their constitutional obligation to develop and expound the law on these lines acting within the bounds and limits set out for them by the Constitution. Judicial creativity is often called as judicial activism. But it was needed as a means of evolving new juristic principles for the development and growth of law. The courts do not interfere in matters which do not have judicially manageable standards or matters which concern policy such as fiscal policy.

Inaugurating the Golden Jubilee celebrations of the Rajasthan High Court in Jodhpur on August 30, 1999, Chief Justice Anand reiterated his views on judicial activism and called for proper balance between judicial activism and judicial restraint. He emphasised that impartiality and independence of the judiciary depended on the high standards of conduct followed by judges. "The judiciary cannot afford to adopt an uncritical attitude towards itself. Judges must, make themselves accountable and ensure that their actions were transparent and within the parameters of the Constitution."

While there has been considerable appreciation and even approbation on the part of different sections of the public regarding the new innovative role of the judiciary, criticism was not lacking and there were apprehensions from many influential quarters, particularly the executive wing of the government. While inaugurating the All India Lawyers' Convention in New Delhi (1997) Prime Minister I.K. Gujral (as he then was) lamenting on the 'misuse' of public interest litigation commented that "the PIL was on distorted path." Although the Gujral Government had abandoned the controversial move of its predecessor government to introduce a legislation restricting the frequent resort to PIL, the attempt by the judiciary to raise the issue of accountability of civil servants and cleanse public life of venality has raised a storm in the political arena. All of a sudden, complaints of 'co-option by courts' and charges that the judiciary is exceeding its boundaries and thus entering into the policy domain of the executive are levelled by politicians and bureaucrats frequently.

Has the Judiciary overstepped its limits and thus altered the balance of power between the three organs of the State? Is PIL a mere radical gimmick of judicial activism which is destroying political reputations and careers while bringing in accolades from the people on the pavements? The answer is not far to seek. The achievements of PIL are already documented in published reports of hundreds of cases both of the Supreme Court and the High Courts. An academic work of considerable scholarship has thrown adequate light on the subject. This work which is the first of its kind has systematically documented almost all the reported and unreported cases on PIL since 1977.[1]

Public Interest Litigation which may be more appropriately called as social action litigation is the most important innovation in Indian jurisprudence. It arose like the phoenix from the ashes of the Emergency. It emerged in response to a need to make judicial process more accessible to the disadvantaged sections of society and to ensure adequate judicial protection of their human rights. Although PIL was primarily a creation of judges, it also arose due to a "happy conspiracy between the Bench and the Bar". While the traditional paradigm of the judicial process primarily designed for private law adjudication emphasised dispute resolution, public law litigation is essentially concerned with conflict resolution. Thus courts began playing a political role in securing human right entitlements guaranteed by the Constitution.

By liberally reinterpreting Article 32 and 226 of the Constitution, PIL expanded the scope of fundamental rights. The courts not merely jettisoned the narrow concept of *locus standi* prevalent until then, but also brought many issues such as inhuman prison conditions, exploitation of quarry workers, problems of bonded labrourers and landless tribals, reduction of vehicular emissions, closing of polluting industries etc., to the attention of the Court. As

1. Sangeeta Ahuja, People, Law and Justice (two volumes) Published by Orient Longmans (1997).

Justice Krishna Iyer[1] has argued, it has democratised the judiciary by not only fighting the violations of the law but directly provided rights to the people.

Although PIL comes within the writ jurisdiction of the Supreme Court and the High Courts, they have also originated in trial courts. The first case in environmental law, Ratalam Municipality *vs.* Vardhichand can be traced to a trial court. So also was the prosecution of former Chief Minister of Maharashtra, A.R. Antulay, which was under the Prevention of Corruption Act. Both these cases involved questions of abuse of public power. Neither of them was a mere dispute between contesting private parties, nor could they be described as class action suits since the petitioners were not seeking any benefit to themselves.

The revolutionary upsurge that was witnessed in the field of PIL during a period of two decades seems to have lost its momentum by the end of the century due to various reasons. First, there was an overenthusiasm on the part of lawyers, particularly the younger ones, who promoted too many of these cases. The over enthusiastic members of the public also joined hands. The result was the opening of the flood gates, as it were, and the courts were finding it a little too much to handle. Between 1984 and 1994, for instance, there were over 1,50,000 letter petitions addressed to the Supreme Court alone. And the Court was able to handle only around 500. Despite the fact that action was initiated in most of these cases convictions were few. This has created a sort of public cynicism and PIL is gradually losing its initial impact. There is a general feeling that courts are not going far enough to monitor the work of the investigating agencies in handling PIL. At the same time there have been powerful voices both from the Executive and the Legislature criticising the new trend as an usurpation of power by the judiciary.

At a conference of the Presiding Officers of Legislatures (1996) in New Delhi, the Speaker of the Lok Sabha cautioned the judiciary and appealed for restraint. There were others, Speakers of Legislative Assemblies from several States who strongly voiced their apprehension that the courts were overstepping the boundaries of their jurisdiction. Inaugurating the Conference on Legal Aid in Ahmedabad (1998) Union Home Minister, L.K. Advani, said that the system of dispensation of justice has become problem-ridden and insensitive to the needs of the common man because a larger malaise on the past couple of decades particularly because of the decay and atrophy that had afflicted the basic institutions of democracy. He maintained that the values and standards governing public life have shown an alarming decline with corruption, criminalisation and arbitrariness becoming the norms in more and more spheres of national life and the judicial system which till recently remained immune to the decline and command respect from the common masses had also fallen prey. The result is that the legal system instead of being a part of the solution has ironically become a part of the problem.

Nevertheless it is obvious that unless the Executive and the Legislature begin to respond to the needs of the citizens and discharge their responsibilities, public interest litigation and judicial activism are bound to remain centre stage as long as courts continue to respond the way they do now. As justice Pandiyan, a former judge of the Supreme Court has said on judicial creativity[2]: "In a country like ours more than eighty percent of people are economically backward and they are subjected to discrimination as a rule. In such an explosive situation causing adverse effect on society, when the executive and

1. Former judge of the Supreme Court of India
2. L.K. Jha Memorial Lecture, Bharatiya Vidya Bhavan (1996).

legislature are apathetic and fail to discharge their constitutional duties and deliver the goods, the apex court which is the custodian of the citizen's rights and liberties and which in that capacity acts as sentinel on the *qui vive* has no other choice but to step in and direct these constitutional functioneres to discharge their obligations. When the bureaucracy shows a callous indifference and insensitivity to its mandatory duties which affect the basic rights of the people and when the law enforcing agencies exhibit their brutality in the process of implementation of law, should the court remain a passive observer of the scenario? Will judges of the highest court be justified sitting in an ivory tower like an Olympian closing their eyes to the stress and storm that affect society and remain into cocoons or in isolated and protected cells without giving appropriate mandates and thereby protecting the Fundamental Rights and liberties of the citizens of the country, asks Justice Pandian.

Speaking on the subject of Social Legitimacy and Institutional Viability, former Chief Justice of the Supreme Court, Justice A.M. Ahmadi said: "To successfully refute the charge of undemocratic conduct and uphold the legitimacy of judicial review, the judiciary must strive to maintain the respect it commands amongst the masses for its independence and integrity. Judicial activism within limits is bound to have a salutary effect on all authorities under the Constitution to do what is expected of them.

Two centuries ago, John Marshall, the Chief Justice of the United States Supreme Court said thus on the role of the Court : "We must never forget that it is the Constitution that we are expounding intended to endure for ages to come". And that made the Supreme Court of the United States Supreme in due course of time. Our Supreme Court also might aspire to have the same position in the fullness of time. Nevertheless, neither the judiciary nor the supporters of its new role of judicial activism should forget that courts are no substitute to the Executive or Legislature. All the three must play their roles in a manner that will appropriately bring into effect the provisions of the Constitution.

Accountability Of Judiciary

Of all the institutions established by the Constitution the higher judiciary seems to have acquitted itself in the last fifty years as the best in a relative sense. The most respected public institution in India is the Supreme Court, respected by the elite and the illiterate alike. If the Court has come increasingly effective in its role as the final arbiter of justice, it is because of the confidence the common man has placed in it. The Court has no army at its command. It does not hold any purse strings. Its strength lies largely in the command it has over the hearts and minds of the public and the manner in which it can influence and mould public opinion. As the distinguished French author Alexis de Toqueville describes the power wielded by judges is the power of public opinion.

The citizen's disillusionment with almost all our public institutions and functionaries has reached nearly its melting point. In that context, his last hope is the Supreme Court. Hence it is important that the Court maintains its effectiveness undiminished and reputation unsullied. The challenges before the Court today are many and multifarious. Perhaps no other apex court in the world has faced such grave challenges before. The great number of cases coming before it and their variety, constitutional, civil, criminal, advisory, special and extraordinary, is itself frightening indeed. The list of subjects is unending. The question is whether there is any subject under the sun which it is not called upon to deal with. A dispute may begin at the village level and ultimately it may end up in the Supreme Court.

Our legal system, adopted largely from the British counterpart is based on written laws and rules. This means normally the result of a dispute should be predictable. A reasonable degree of predictability alone can earn the enduring respect of the common man for the rule of law. "Who will watch the watchman"? is a big and difficult question to answer. The least incorrect answer may be "self restraint". Any effort to reduce the degree of judicial uncertainty and unpredictability will certainly be a step forward in making the rule of law real and meaningful. An increase in the degree of predictability of judgement can liberate the judicial system from the growing number of frivolous and chance-taking litigations that are choking it.

While there has been alround appreciation and even approbation of the splendid work of the Supreme Court, it has not been altogether free from blemish and criticism. Some of the decisions of the Court were subjected to criticism both by lawyers and politicians. For instance, the Court's decision in the hawala case was attacked as an extreme case of judicial usurpation of the functions of the Executive and Parliament. Giving detailed directions on appointment, tenure and termination of posts such as the Director of CBI, the Central Vigilance Commissioner and constitution of committees have been cited as transgression of the Constitutional scheme of division of powers by the Court. It has been pointed out that the Court adheres to virtually no rules to control the size and quality of its docket. The procedure for admitting cases depends, it has been alleged, on judicial idiosyncracy. Thus the writ jurisdiction has become a forum of appeal. The very special powers of the Supreme Court to accept appeals — special leave petitions — have virtually dwarfed the rest of its jurisdiction. The Doctrine of Judicial Restraint seems to have altogether disappeared. Principles of institutional comity between the organs of government have fallen down as lawyers have pressed the judges to claim jurisdiction in more and more areas of governance. One of the key concepts of the Constitution stipulates that governmental and legislative actions should be measured by the test of reasonableness. Yet, the Court has not laid down any authoritative guidance on what reasonableness means other than the altogether undependable formula that it depends on the facts and circumstances of the case. Similarly, the Court, it is said, in its eagerness to do justice in every matter it considers important, justice is distributed on an adhoc basis that often defies logic and gives rise to suspicion on grounds of inconsistency. In short, the allegation is that the Court is exercising power without accountability and there are no safeguards in the Constitution to make it accountable for its exercise of power. No doubt, the Judiciary has to act as watch dog of public life, as it has to uphold probity in public life, but this can hardly be accomplished if the members of the judiciary themselves do not behave like Caesar's wife.

It is in this context that the demand for judicial reforms assumes special significance. There has been growing discontentment among litigants across the country over the tardy pace and circuitous route to justice. According to one estimate, at the end of 1999 there were over three crores of cases pending in different courts in the country. Inordinate delay is a characteristic feature of the Indian judicial system. Justice delayed is justice denied. Almost every conference of judges or lawyers emphasises this aspect. It has been reported that there are cases which are yet to be settled even after fifty years. Generations have changed in the meantime.

An Attorney-General of India observed that the increase of pending cases, multitudes of ill-conceived and ill-drafted laws, frequent adjournment of cases and judicial authoritarianism are the causes impeding the entire judicial process. He has suggested a national judicial commission empowered to act against errant judges. He was also of the view that provision should be made for ad hoc appointment of retired judges at all levels of the judiciary to clear up the backlog of pending cases. Mere increase in the number of judges alone would not improve judicial performance, rather it is important to make the right choices for appointment.

Widespread discussions have been going on in the country for quite some time, both in the government circles and outside, that a National Judicial Commission should be set up for the appointment of judges. To facilitate the constitution of such a Commission, the Constitution has to be amended (Articles 124, 126, 217, 220 and 221(1). The basic question, however, is whether such measures would be able to reduce litigation, clear the enormous backlog and help litigants in getting justice.

Indian legal system has several inadequacies. So also the legal education and training of legal professionals. But precious little has been done so far to remove these inadequacies. It is an appropriate time to take necessary measures not only to clear the backlog of pending cases but also to bring about transparency in the appointment of judges and making the judicial system accountable.

The concept of accountability involves not only the method of appointment but also the method of removal for deviant behaviour. In this context the only method available now is impeachment. But impeachment has lost much of its sanction and sanctity due to the political approach adopted by the ruling Congress party in the Ramaswamy Case which showed how ineffective the method of impeachment could be. In a Paper under the title "Who Judges the Judges? A well known Australian judge, Justice Gordon J. Samuel says (1986) that : "Judges ought to be answerable for the way in which they perform their duties is an undeniable proposition which all the judges of the Supreme Court then available explicitly acknowledged in their public statement of 1986. No institutional power in society should be uncontrolled and judges are no exception."

Judiciary cannot be an imperium in imperio. That is why its accountability is important. The performance and discipline of judges and the audit and enquiry in this behalf cannot be ruled out altogether but may be responsibly regulated and reasonably restrained by carefully drawn up procedures. No democratic institution including the judiciary can be above the rule of accountability in the absence of which there is the possible danger of developing absolutism. The people of India look upon the Supreme Court as an instrument of social justice and a guarantor of the great ideals enshrined in the Preamble of our Constitution, "Justice, social economic and political, liberty, equality before law and equal protection of laws." Misbehaviour by a judge, whether it takes place on the Bench or off the Bench undermines public confidence in the administration of justice and also damages public respect for law and judges. A single dishonest judge not only dishonours himself and disgraces his office but jeopardises the integrity of the entire judicial system.

As the Supreme Court has said in one of its decisions (J.T. 1991 3SC 198) "A Judicial scandal has always been regarded as far more deplorable than a scandal involving either the executive or a member of the legislature. The slightest hint of irregularity or impropriety in the court is a cause for great anxiety and alarm. A legislator or administrator may be found guilty of corruption without apparently endangering the foundation of the State.

But a judge must keep himself absolutely above suspicion to preserve the impartiality and independence of the judiciary and to have public confidence thereof".

If any noble profession has to command the confidence of the community it can only do so by high standards maintained by its members. It is essential therefore that a Code of Conduct is drawn up and compliance with it monitored if the high esteem of the judiciary is to be protected and maintained. In this connection it is heartening to note that the Supreme Court of India has taken the initiative to adopt a 'statement of values of judicial life.'

***

PART VI

THE MACHINERY OF GOVERNMENT IN THE STATES

29

THE STATE EXECUTIVE : THE GOVERNOR

THE MACHINERY of government in the States is organized on the same pattern as that of the Union Government. Hence, in the light of our discussion on the machinery of the Union Government, the task of analyzing the organization and working of the State Government becomes comparatively easy. As in the Union, the government in the States is also organized on the parliamentary model. The Head of the State is called the Governor, who is the constitutional head of the State as the President is for the whole of India. The Chief of the State Government is called the Chief Minister who is the counterpart of the Prime Minister of India in the State. There is a Council of Ministers for each of the States as in the Union. The organization of the State Legislature is also more or less on the model of the Indian Parliament. In the judicial field, the High Courts, for all practical purposes, occupy the same position within the States as the Supreme Court does for the whole of India. Thus, the State Government is a true replica of the Union Government within the jurisdiction of each State; this helps the States to draw examples and inspiration from the working of the Union Government in almost every field of activity.

The executive power of the State is vested in a Governor who is appointed by the President and who holds office during the pleasure of the President. The vesting of the entire executive power of the State in the Governor shows that—he occupies the same constitutional position within the State as the President does with respect to the Government of India. Normally, the Governor holds office for a period of five years from the date on which he enters upon his office.

The qualifications for appointment as a Governor are simple and few. He should be a citizen of India and must have completed the age of thirty-five years. The Governor cannot be a member of either House of Parliament or of a State Legislature. Nor can he hold any other office of profit. He is entitled to a free official residence, a regular monthly salary and other allowances. At present, his salary is Rs. 36,000 per month. His salary and allowances cannot be reduced during his term of office. They are charged on the Consolidated Fund of the State and, as such, are non-votable. One striking provision which has found a place in the Constitution as a result of the Seventh Amendment is that one and the same person may be appointed Governor of more than one State.[1] Before entering upon his office, the Governor has to make and subscribe, in the presence of the Chief Justice of the High Court of the State, an oath or affirmation to preserve, protect and defend the Constitution.

1. This provision, however, has so far been taken advantage of only in the case of the north-eastern States of Assam, Meghalaya, Manipur, Tripura and Nagaland with the same person as Governor for each of them.

There has been severe criticism of the appointment of Governors, the persons appointed and the manner in which the appointments are made. Since the Constitution has not prescribed any specific qualifications for the governor, anybody could be a Governor and the Union Executive has been misusing the power to appoint anyone it liked. In the early years most of the persons selected were persons of distinction who had established their reputation as administrators or leaders of the freedom movement, That practice gradually disappeared and politics became the main consideration for the appointment of Governors, Politicians who were defeated at the polls or retired politicians who were on the look out for a senecure position or those who were rivals to local leaders or trouble makers, retired bureaucrats who are favourites of the central leadership, even retired judges, all these figured in the list of Governors. Many of them have been quite old, in their seventies, so much so that some of them died in office. As the governors held the office during the pleasure of the President, change of government at the Centre resulted in the summary termination of those who were persona non grata to the government. While some of the Governors were given a term of five years, others were given extension or a second term of five years. Earlier there was only one Governor for all the small States of the North East but now, everyone of them has a separate governor. Thus the Governor's office has been subjected to political abuse of the worst order bringing down its prestige and dignity. The Sarkaria Commission which enquired into the problem of Centre-State relations has very critical observations on the manner in which some Governors have functioned. The Commission has offered many valuable suggestions to make the office of the Governor non-controversial.

Why an Appointed Governor ?

In August 1947, when the question of the Head of the State was discussed at a joint meeting of the Union Constitution Committee and the Provincial Constitution Committee, there were two diametrically opposed views, one urging the adoption of the U.S. model and the other the British. As has been pointed out earlier, the latter view prevailed. Yet, it was decided then that the Governor should be elected. It seems that this decision was in conformity with the idea of giving each State the maximum autonomy as units of a federation. In this matter, the position of the State Governor in the United States must have been the greatest influence upon the framers. In May 1949, however, the original decision was reversed and the provision for an appointed Governor was adopted. The reasons for this *volte face* deserve analysis, as they vitally concern the overall pattern of the governmental system established under the Constitution.

Speaking in the Assembly, Prime Minister Nehru said that it was the two years' experience (1947-49) of running the administration that made the framers to reverse the original proposal. One of the most serious problems that confronted the Central Government during this period was the separatist tendencies which assumed many forms and made many claims threatening the very foundations of the Indian Union. Many members in the Constituent Assembly gave evidence of this tendency by advocating the creation of a federal system in which the Centre was to have the minimum powers and the States the maximum autonomy. The problem of the integration of Princely States was still in progress and the progress was indeed painful and hard. The impact of these was so severe on the thinking of those who held the reins of power at the Centre that they abandoned many of their old ideas, like maximum autonomy for States, linguistic redistribution of Indian territory, etc. At the same time, began devising means with which they could hold intact the unity of the nation and the stability of the democratic order they were building up. In the words of Prime Minister Nehru:

> In providing for a stable democratic machine, it is very important for us not to take any step which might tend towards loosening the fabric of India or loosening the governmental machinery and thus producing conflicts. We have passed through very grave times and we have survived them with a measure of success. We have still to pass through difficult times and I think we should always view things from this context of preserving unity, the stability and security of India and not produce too many factors in our constitutional machinery which will tend to disrupt that unity by frequent recourse to vast elections which disturb people's minds and, at the same time, divert a great deal of our resources towards electoral machines rather than towards the reconstruction of the country.[1]

The four alternative methods of selecting the Governor which the Assembly discussed before finally adopting appointment by the President were: (i) election by adult suffrage; (ii) election by the members of the Lower House or both Houses of the State Legislature either by the system of proportional representation or otherwise; (iii) selection by the President out of a panel submitted by the Lower House of the Legislature and (iv) appointment by President. The arguments for the rejection of the first three alternatives are worth recounting.

1. In a parliamentary system of government a popularly elected Governor does not fit in at all. When the Governor is elected directly by the people on the basis of adult franchise, he becomes a direct representative of the people and may very well try to exercise his powers not as a constitutional head of the State, but as its real head. Such a position is very likely to create a rivalry between the Governor and the Council of Ministers whose members also are directly elected by the people. In the event of any conflict between the two, the Governor, with the prestige of a general election by adult franchise behind him, might seek, in a given contingency, to override the powers of the Chief Minister as the power of dismissal is vested in him. This is totally against the basic principle of parliamentary government under which the real power of the State is vested in a Ministry which is responsible to the Legislature. Since the federal states in the U.S. have a presidential system of government just as in the case of the federal government in the country they do not face a problem of rivalry between the Governor and his Cabinet.[2]

Intervening in the debate, Ambedkar put forward the case against direct election of the Governor in the following terms:

> The Governor has no functions which he is required to exercise either in his discretion or his individual judgement. According to the principles of the Constitution, he is required to follow the advice of his Ministry in all matters... If the Governor has no power of interference in the internal administration of a Ministry which has a majority (in the Legislature), then it seems to me that the question whether he is elected or appointed is a wholly immaterial one.[3]

2. Apart from the possibility of a clash between the Governor and the Council of Ministers, the direct election of the Governor creates a serious problem of leadership at the time of a general election. During election, a political party will have to rally round a

---

1. C.A.D. VIII, p. 455. 2. C.A.D., VIII, p. 430.
3. Ibid, p. 469.

leader. Who will be the leader, the candidate for the office of the Governor or the Chief Minister ? Since the effective power of the State Government is in the hands of the Chief Minister and his colleagues in the Ministry, the top leaders of the Party are likely to contest the election with a view to securing these positions. This will inevitably lead to the selection of a second-rank leader to contest the election for the office of Governor. "Why waste money and energy in a huge election for a second-rate man in the Party at the head of the Government ?", asked K.M. Munshi. "It would mean also that the Governor will be subsidiary in importance to the Chief Minister as he would be his nominee. If this is going to be the case, why this farce of an election ?"[1]

3. If, instead of the Governor being elected directly by the people, he were elected by the State Legislature, there does not seem to be so much chance of a rivalry between him and the Ministry as in the former case. For, the Ministry is responsible to the same Legislature which elects the Governor. But the defect of such an arrangement seems to be the danger of the Governor becoming a pawn in the hands of a political party or parties that secure his election. Since he would not be elected to the office on a permanent basis, the temptation to play into the hands of the majority Party on crucial occasions in order to show his gratitude for getting elected or to ensure his re-election is irresistible.

4. The third method proposed for the selection of the Governor, namely, appointment by the President out of a panel of names submitted to him by the Legislature of the State, was also rejected as unsound. In the selection of names on the panel, there is bound to be factions and groups coming into play. Each group would like to see a member of it to be placed on the panel. This group affinity reflected in the selection of group men on the panel and the ultimate selection of one man from the panel might undermine party cohesion. Further, if the President chooses one down in the line from the panel, those who nominated the first name are bound to nurse a grouse against such a man. This may even lead to bad relations between the Governor and the State Cabinet.[2]

5. A Governor, directly or indirectly elected, is unlikely to fit into a federal system of Government which aims to create a very powerful Centre. For, the Governor, in either case, is a representative of the State who receives his authority from the will of the people of the State. In the event of a conflict between the State and the Union, which involves the security of the nation, there is no guarantee that the Governor would act in the interests of the nation and as an instrument of the Union Government. On the other hand, the Governor may create difficulties in the path of the Union's authority and may even conspire with the State Cabinet to defy the Union and undermine the foundations of national unity. This is not in harmony with the idea of emergency powers embodied in the Constitution under which, in certain circumstances, the federal system ceases to function and the Union takes over the powers vested in the State Government.

6. The original idea of the framers was not to have as powerful a Union as was eventually established under the Constitution. The maximum possible autonomy for the States was the ideal they had originally set before the country. But as Nehru pointed out in the Assembly, the experience of running the administration during the 1947-49 period compelled them to revise their ideas and it was decided that what India needed was a strong Union and comparatively weak Sates. Among the causes that contributed to this

1. Ibid, p. 452.
2. C.A.D.VIII., p. 428.

major change in the basic structure of the Constitution were the partition of the country and the various problems created by the partition, the food crisis, the urge for integrated economic and social planning for the entire country, the upsurge of provincialism and communalism and the fear of the possible instability of State Ministries. It was thought that both for the preservation of the newly-won independence and the planned development of the country, central direction was essential. From this point of view, an elected Governor was not desirable. He should be one who could be commanded by the President in times of emergency to translate the will of the Union into action within the State.

7. It was thought that in the wake of newly established self-government, the emergence of rival groups and factions was inevitable within the State Legislature and the State as a whole. The majority Party itself might split into two or more factions resulting in rivalry between two or more aspirants for Chief Ministership. Under such conditions, a Governor from within the State directly or indirectly elected was likely to become an interested party rather than an impartial and independent mediator between rival factions. If the Governor is the President's nominee, there is little possibility of such a danger.

8. So long as State politics is stable, so long as the Ministry has the solid backing from the Legislature, a Governor appointed by the President is bound to function as the constitutional head of the State like the President himself. The change in his role is envisaged only under exceptional circumstances. Under such circumstances, the Governor has to exercise his discretion. He has to report to the President and act under his instructions. An appointed Governor will, thus, eminently suit all the requirements of the responsibilities envisaged of the office of Governor. The present provision was thus the product of mature thought and abundant caution, and the Constitution-makers have been justified in their decision by events in some of the States during the last few years. The Canadian Constitution which has a strong Centre seems to have particularly influenced the Drafting Committee in this connection. In that country, the Governors of the Provinces are appointed by the Governor-General and they hold office during the pleasure of the Governor-General. Alladi Krishnaswamy Aiyar said:

> On the whole, in the interests of harmony, in the interests of good working, in the interests of sounder relations between the Provincial Cabinet and the Governor, it will be much better if we accept the Canadian model.[1]

Thus, the Constitution vests complete power in the President for the selection and appointment of the Governor. This means in effect that he is a nominee of the Central Government. But a healthy convention has grown up during the last many years which makes the Governor not merely a nominee of the Central Government but also one who is agreeable to the State concerned. Such a result is obtained by the Central Government consulting the State Cabinet prior to the appointment of a new Governor. No person who is *persona non grata* to the State Government will be imposed upon it by the Centre. This enables the selection of an agreed candidate who is capable of discharging his responsibilities as the head of the State and "a sagacious counsellor and adviser to the Ministry, one who can throw oil on the troubled waters" of the State politics.[2] Thus, the

1. C.A.D. VIII, p.432.
2. There has been criticism that this healthy convention which was built up over many years has been violated in recent years because the Union Government and a particular State Government belonged to different political parties.

present method of selection has removed the evils which would have otherwise resulted from any of the alternative methods of election originally contemplated by the Constituent Assembly.

Another convention has also been fairly well established and this too has contributed to making the position of the Governor one above party and group politics within the State. According to this, the person selected as the Governor of a State is normally an outsider, a resident of another State, one who has had no political entanglements within the State. This has, on the whole, proved to be of great advantage. Not only does this keep the Governor out of the local politics, but it also enables him to look at the problems of the State and the problems of Union-State relationship with detachment and objectivity. There have been only two exceptions so far to the rule of 'non-resident' Governors.[1] These appointments, however, do not seem to have produced any undesirable results. Nevertheless, it is likely that this convention would become an integral part of the Constitutional practice.

Powers and Functions of the Governor

The executive power of the State is vested in the Governor who is empowered to exercise it either directly or through officers subordinate to him, and the executive power of the State extends to all matters on which the State Legislature has the power to make laws. In the discharge of his responsibilities as the Head of the State, the Governor exercises functions similar to those of the President as the Head of the Union. He appoints the Chief Minister and other members of the Council of Ministers who hold office during his pleasure. He allocates the business of the Government among the Ministers and makes rules for the more convenient transaction of such business. All executive actions of the Government are taken in his name. He appoints the Advocate-General and other officers of the State. In the States of Bihar, Madhya Pradesh and Orissa, it is the special responsibility of the Governor to see that a Minister is placed in charge of tribal welfare. In Assam, the Governor is given certain special powers with respect to the administration of the tribal areas as provided in the Sixth Schedule of the Constitution.[2] In Nagaland, Manipur and Sikkim also the Governor is vested with special responsibilities.

Like the President's power of pardon, the Governor too is empowered to grant pardons. This may apply to all persons convicted of any offence against any law relating to a matter to which the executive power of the State extends.[3]

In the legislative field, the Governor has considerable powers. He is an integral part of the State Legislature. He convenes the State Legislature, addresses it in person or sends messages to it, and can prorogue or dissolve it. During every financial year, he causes the Budget to be laid before the House. Demands for grants in the Legislature can be made

1. The first exception was in the case of the late Governor of West Bengal, H.P. Mukerjee, who was himself not a politician but an eminent educationist. The second was in the case of the former Princely ruler of the State of Mysore who was appointed Governor in 1957 after the reorganization of States brought about by the Seventh Amendment of the Constitution (1956).
2. The special provision for a Minister of Tribal Affairs was the result of the recommendation of Sub-Committee on Tribal People appointed by the Minorities Committee of the Constituent Assembly. The Committee recommended that there should be a statutory provision for such appointment. C.A.D. VII, p. 521.
3. For the scope of the Governor's pardoning power, see K.M. Nanavati *vs*. The State of Bombay (1961) II S.C.J. 100.

only on his recommendation. Every Bill that is passed by the State Legislature has to be presented to the Governor for his assent. The Governor has three alternatives before him with respect to such a Bill. He may give his assent to it, in which case it becomes law. Or, he may return it to the Legislature with a message suggesting alterations or modifications. The Governor has, however, no power to return a Money Bill. Or again, he may reserve the Bill for the assent of the President if, in his opinion, it contains provisions which might endanger the position envisaged for the High Court under the Constitution.

The Governor has also the special legislative power of promulgating Ordinances during the recess of the State Legislature, if he is satisfied that there exist circumstances which make it necessary for him to take immediate action. But with respect to three matters, the Governor is prohibited from promulgating Ordinances without prior instructions from the President. These are: (i) the provisions which, if embodied in a Bill, would require the previous sanction of the President for introduction in the State Legislature; or (ii) if the Governor would have deemed it necessary to reserve a Bill containing the same provisions for the consideration of the President; or (iii) if an Act of the State Legislature containing the same provisions would be invalid without the assent of the President.

Every Ordinance promulgated by the Governor has the same force and effect as an Act of the State Legislature. But every Ordinance should be laid before the State Legislature when it reassembles and if the Ordinance is not passed by the Legislature, it becomes invalid. The Governor is empowered to withdraw the Ordinance any time he likes. The Ordinance will be invalid if it has provisions which would not be valid if enacted in an Act of the State Legislature to which the Governor gives his assent.

During a period of emergency, the Governor comes into his own as the real head of the executive in the State. With the proclamation of an emergency by the President, the entire State administration comes directly under the control of the Union. Being the 'man on the spot' and the 'agent' of the President in the State, the Governor during the period of emergency takes over the reins of administration directly into his own hands and runs the State with the aid of the civil service.

***

30

THE GOVERNOR AND THE COUNCIL OF MINISTERS

IN THE exercise of all his functions, except when he is expressly required to act in his discretion the Governor is aided and advised by a Council of Ministers headed by a Chief Minister. But if there is a conflict of opinion between the Governor and the Ministry as to whether or not a particular matter falls within the scope of the Governor's discretionary power, the decision of the Governor in his discretion shall be final. Further, the validity of anything done by the Governor cannot be called in question on the ground that he ought or ought not to have acted in his discretion. Although the Governor has to act on the advice of the Ministers, the question whether any, and if so what, advice was tendered by the Ministers to the Governor cannot be enquired into in any court of law.

The Governor appoints the Chief Minister and on the latter's advice appoints the other Ministers. The Ministers hold office during the pleasure of the Governor. Before the inauguration of the Constitution, the terms 'Prime Minister' and 'Premier' were indiscriminately in use to refer to the head of the Council of Ministers both at the Centre and the Provinces. This created a certain amount of confusion in constitutional parlance, which has been removed now by the introduction of the term 'Chief Minister'. The Ministers are collectively responsible to the Legislative Assembly of the State. The Governor administers the oath of office to each Minister before he enters upon his office. The Governor can appoint as Minister a person who is not a member of the State Legislature at the time of the appointment. But such a Minister should become a member of the Legislature within six months after entering upon his office.

We have already noticed that all executive action of the State Government is taken in the name of the Governor. In this connection the Governor is authorized to make rules for the more convenient transaction of the business of the State Government. He is also empowered to allocate among the Ministers the business of the Government except where he is expected to act in his discretion. It is the duty of the Chief Minister as the head of the Council of Ministers to communicate to the Governor all decisions of the Council relating to the administration of the affairs of the State and proposals for legislation. He has also to furnish any information which the Governor calls for and which is connected with any administrative or legislative matter of the State. Again, it is the duty of the Chief Minister to place before the Council, if the Governor so requires, any matter on which a decision has been taken by a Minister but which has not been considered by the Council.

These provisions of the Constitution vest in the Governor a fairly long list of powers which, if taken on their face value, will add up to formidable proportions. Yet, as we have already seen from statements made in the Constituent Assembly, the Governor is only the constitutional head of the State. This means that although he is the Chief Executive, in the exercise of his functions, the real power is in the hands of the Council of Ministers. This was pointed out again and again by authoritative spokesmen in the Constituent Assembly. Speaking about the nature of the Governor's functions, Ambedkar said that the Governor would have *"no functions* which he is required [to perform] either in his discretion or in his individual judgement. According to the principles of the Constitution, he is required to follow the advice of the Ministry in all matters".[1]

Interpreting the scope of the provision that "the Ministers shall hold office during the pleasure of the Governor", Ambedkar said:

> I have no doubt that it is the intention of this Constitution that the Ministry shall hold office during such time as it holds the confidence of the majority. It is on this principle that the Constitution will work. The reason why we have not so expressly stated it is because it has not been stated in that fashion or in those terms in any of the Constitutions which lays down a Parliamentary system of Government. 'During pleasure' is always understood to mean that the 'pleasure' shall not continue notwithstanding the fact that the Ministry has lost the confidence of the majority, it is presumed that the Governor will exercise his 'pleasure' in dismissing the Ministry and, therefore, it is unnecessary to differ from what I may say the stereotyped phraseology which is used in all responsible governments.[2]

The Constituent Assembly witnessed one of the longest debates in discussing the position and functions of the Governor under the Constitution. A dominant note that ran through the entire discussion was the almost fanatical opposition which practically every member displayed against the vesting of any discretionary power in the Governor. It seems that most of them, while speaking on the subject, had before them the image of the erstwhile British Governor under the Government of India Act of 1935, a repository of extraordinary powers and a symbol of imperialist power, acting in his discretion and individual responsibility. Many of them, when they found that the same language as was used in the Act of 1935 dealing with a number of important powers of the Governor was repeated verbatim in the new Constitution, naturally grew suspicious of the role of the 'new' Governor. This was what made Ambedkar and others to reiterate and even overemphasize the constitutional nature of the Governor's office and the 'passive' role he was expected to play in the scheme of the State Government. To quote Ambedkar again, while pleading for the rejection of the elective principle for the selection of the Governor, he had declared that the Governor's powers "will be so limited, so nominal, his position so ornamental" that it was a waste to spend public resources on a popular election for Governorship.

The Governor under the present Constitution cannot be compared with the Governor under the Act of 1935. The latter was a really powerful functionary, who was the real master of the situation under almost all conditions. But it was fundamentally owing to the nature of the Government that then existed. It was not a fully responsible Government, and it was a government which was a *de facto* and *de jure* agent of an alien power. It is difficult, however, to think of a Governor, under a fully responsible system of government established on the broadest possible popular basis, to behave in a manner that smacks of

1. C.A.D.VIII, p. 467.
2. C.A.D. VIII, p. 520.

authoritarianism. When a Cabinet composed of popular Ministers, collectively responsible to the Legislature, is to aid and advise the Governor in the discharge of his functions, occasions are almost nonexistent for him to overrule them or act in a manner contrary to their advice. But does this mean that he is a mere figurehead, "a rubber-stamp of his Cabinet or a post-office between his Cabinet and the President or between his Cabinet and the official gazette ?" A careful reading of the constitutional provisions and an appreciation of them in the perspective of the totality of the constitutional scheme will show that the Governor is neither a figurehead nor a rubber-stamp but a functionary designed to play a vital rôle in the administration of the affairs of the State. This was clearly demonstrated during the period 1967-72 when political instability undermined the smooth functioning of several State Governments and compelled the Governors to intervene and advise the President to proclaim a constitutional emergency. Quite often, such action provoked controversy and the parties adversely affected even went to the extent of assailing the Governor personally and accusing him as a partisan of the ruling party at the Centre. A typical example of such accusation runs as follows:

> The State Governors were designed by our Constitution-makers to be liaison officers between the Central and the State Governments. For the rest, they were expected to be the constitutional heads of the State Governments. But, as they have been allowed to function, they have arrogated to themselves more powers than any other functionary in our democracy.
>
> They wield more power in their States than does the Prime Minister at the Centre or the President of India. They can put in office as Chief Ministers those who do not command a majority in the State Assemblies. They can appoint as Chief Ministers those who are not members of the Assemblies or Councils, but whom they nominate as members of the latter body on some pretext or other. They thus violate the spirit of the Constitution since nominated members lack a representative character.
>
> They can dismiss Chief Ministers, who have not lost their majorities in their respective assemblies. They can dissolve assemblies at the bidding of Chief Ministers who have lost the majority support in their legislatures. They can, of course, adjourn and prorogue the House just to oblige Chief Ministers, who no more command majorities. They can dissolve the legislatures and advise tne President to impose his rule, which in effect means their own rule. They can also keep Assemblies in animated suspension.
>
> The President of India cannot do all these things: nor can the Prime Minister. While the President of India can be impeached by Parliament for violating the Constitution or for misbehaviour or incapacity, the Governors cannot be removed or so impeached by the State Legislatures or Parliament. The Governors' decisions cannot be questioned in a court of law. If a politician, who loves power more than an exalted position, were given a choice between becoming the President of India and a Governor of a State, he would prefer the latter office.[1]

To what extent is this strong criticism justified, coming as it does from a veteran political leader ? From the point of view of the vital role played by the Governor, we may briefly examine those of his functions which give him the opportunity to act at his discretion. Those functions are as follows:

1. The selection of a Chief Minister prior to the formation of a Council of Ministers;
2. Dismissal of a Ministry;
3. Dissolution of the Legislative Assembly;

1. J.B. Kripalani, *The Indian Express*, 3 April 1973.

4. Asking information from the Chief Minister relating to legislative and administrative matters;
5. Asking the Chief Minister to submit for the consideration of the Council of Ministers any matter on which a decision has been taken by a Minister but which has not been considered by the Council;
6. Refusing to give assent to a Bill passed by the Legislature and returning it for reconsideration.
7. Reserving a Bill passed by the State Legislature for the assent of the President;
8. Seeking instructions from the President before promulgating an Ordinance dealing with certain matters;
9. Advising the President for the proclamation of an emergency; and
10. In the case of the Governor of Assam, certain administrative matters connected with the tribal areas and settling disputes between the Government of Assam and the District Council (of an autonomous district) with respect to mining royalties.

Each of these functions deserves detailed consideration.

If, at the end of every General Election, every State in India finds one Party with a stable majority in the Legislative Assembly, the Governor will have no opportunity to exercise his discretion in the selection of a Chief Minister with a view to forming a Council of Ministers.[1] But all States may not be blessed with such a happy situation. At the end of the first General Elections in 1952, there were at least two States, Madras and Travancore-Cochin, where no party had emerged with a clear majority. At the end of the second General Elections in 1957, Kerala repeated the Travancore-Cochin situation of 1952. The situation in 1967 at the end of the fourth General Elections was substantially different from that in the past. There were several States with no clear majority for any political party in the State legislature. Under such a situation, it is natural that the parties and groups in the Assembly will try to get together with a view to producing a majority and claiming the right to form a new Government. Often, such claims are made on the basis of alliances which have no cohesive force behind them except the eagerness to somehow get into office. Naturally, under situation of this type, the Governor will have an important role to play both in taking stock of the situation and reporting to the President, and in selecting a leader who might reasonably be expected to form a stable Ministry.[2]

---

1. It is an established practice now in India that soon after the election every Legislature Party meets and elects its leader. This enables the Governor to send for the acknowledged leader of the Party. The Governor has no discretion in the matter.
2. Orissa has provided two occasions in the course of fourteen months for the Governor to use his discretion in the selection of a Chief Minister; firstly, immediately after the second General Elections in 1957 and secondly in 1958 when the Mahtab Ministry submitted its resignation. In the latter case, despite the claim of the Opposition leader that he had a majority in the Assembly, the Governor, on investigation, did not find it justified and, therefore, did not call upon him to form a new Ministry. Here is a clear case of the Governor acting in his discretion.

   In 1965 the Governor of Kerala (V.V.Giri) recommended to the President the dissolution of the Assembly even before it met after Elections as there was no Party or combination of parties to form a government.

2. It is possible that a Ministry has lost the confidence of the Legislature as a result of a split in the Party in power and one of the groups crossing the floor to join the ranks of the opposition. But the Ministry may like to continue in office, and it may advise the Governor to prorogue the Assembly with a view to avoiding a censure motion which is likely to be passed. Or, in the alternative, the Council may ask the Governor to dissolve the Assembly. In the meantime, a majority of members in the Assembly may submit a petition to the Governor to the effect that the Ministry does not enjoy the confidence of the Legislature any longer and that it should be dismissed. What should the Governor do under such conditions ? Here is a clear case where he is called upon to use his discretion with a view to solving the political crisis in the State. He may adopt any of the alternatives including the dismissal of the Ministry. Although the Governor will not normally dismiss a Ministry so long as it enjoys the confidence of a majority in the Assembly, yet the Governor's use of his discretion to dismiss a Ministry which still enjoys the support of a majority (after consultation with the President) will be justified if he is convinced that there have been clear cases of corruption to which the Ministry is a party and, in the interests of purity in administration, the Ministry should be dismissed from office. The same opinion was expressed by Ambedkar, although in a different context. He was speaking of the powers of the President to dismiss a Minister. He said:

> It would be perfectly open under that particular clause [the Ministers shall hold office during the pleasure of the President] to call for the removal of a particular Minister on the ground that he is guilty of corruption, bribery or maladministration although that particular Minister probably is a person who enjoyed the confidence of the House. The two conditions that govern the tenure of a Minister in office are purity of administration and confidence of the House.[1]

The discretionary power of the Governor to dismiss a Ministry also seems to exist if the Governor has reasons to believe that the Ministry is engaged in activities which are likely to endanger national security or solidarity. If a Party has come into office with avowed professions of allegiance to the Constitution and after joining office makes use of the privileged position of power to undermine the unity of the nation and establish an independent State or enter into secret negotiations with a foreign power with a view to breaking away from the federal union, the Governor may justifiably dismiss such a Ministry even if it enjoys a majority in the Legislature.[2] Although, these are not normal circumstances, yet in a country where democratic institutions are in a stage of evolution, and regional, linguistic and other disintegrating loyalties are still reigning supreme in several parts of the country, the probability of such contingencies is not remote. And the Governor is the only person on the spot who can take stock of the situation and initiate appropriate action including the dismissal of the Ministry.[2]

3. It is not a normal practice to dissolve a Legislature before it has completed its prescribed period of life. Yet, dissolution at an earlier date with a view to appealing to the electorate and seeking to solve a situation of political instability is an accepted principle of the parliamentary system of government. The power of dissolution is vested in the Governor. Is he bound to accept the advice of the Ministry in this respect ? The British practice more

1. C.A.D. VII, PP. 1185-86 2. 2.
2. The dismissal of Sheikh Abdullah Ministry of Jammu and Kashmir in 1953 is a good example in point. Majority in the Legislature is a rather vague term. For it can be as overwhelming a majority as 70 per cent or more and as slender as a majority dependent on a single vote.

or less has established the convention that a defeated Ministry has a choice between meeting the electorate to seek a fresh mandate in support of its policies and resignation. But in Britain such elections have been rare. If the British convention had been made applicable to France under the Fourth Republic, the French people would have been perpetually preparing for general elections. This is why the Constitution of the Fourth Republic made a specific provision in this connection, 'and took away from a defeated Ministry the right to enforce a dissolution of the National Assembly. In India, there is no specific provision in the Constitution to govern a situation of this nature. Here again, the matter comes within the discretion of the Governor. In 1954, a defeated Ministry in the State of Travancore-Cochin (which now forms part of the present Kerala State) advised the Rajpramukh (Head of the State) to dissolve the Legislative Assembly. The advice was accepted and the Assembly was dissolved. But in 1955 in the same State, the advice of another defeated Ministry to dissolve the Assembly was rejected. If these instances can be relied upon, they prove only this: the Ministry's advice in this respect does not bind the Governor. In his discretion, he may accept or reject such advice.

At the Governor's Conference held in 1970 and presided over by the President a five-member Committee of the Governors was set up to frame guidelines for the Governors. The Committee presented its report to the President in 1971. Among the recommendations it made the following observations on these questions.

The Committee considered and held that a Governor had the right to dismiss a Ministry if the Chief Minister shirked his primary responsibilities of facing the Assembly within the shortest possible time to test the confidence of the legislature in him. The report said that the test of confidence in the Ministry should normally be left to a vote in the Assembly. The Chief Minister's refusal to test his strength on the floor of the Assembly could be interpreted *as prima facie* proof that he no longer enjoyed the confidence of the legislature. If formation of an alternate Ministry was not possible, the Governor would be left with no alternative but to make a report to the President under Article 356 and to recommend at the same time the dissolution of the Assembly.

The Committee also expressed itself against making a person, who was not a member of the legislature or a nominated member, as Chief Minister.

On coalition ministries, the Committee felt that a Chief Minister derived his pre-eminence solely from the agreement among the partners. A Chief Minister was the keystone of the arch of the Cabinet but this could apply only when he headed a team which collectively had majority support in the legislature. Thus, the Chief Minister in a coalition "could not claim the right of advising the Governor in the matter of appointment or dismissal of a Minister in such a manner as to break the arch and yet claim the right to continue as Chief Minister".

If some Ministers in a coalition belonging to a particular party or group themselves resigned due to disagreement with the Chief Minister, the Committee felt that the Chief Minister might not necessarily resign. If, however, his majority in the Assembly was threatened by the resignations, it would be expected of him to demonstrate his continuing strength in the Assembly by advising the Governor that the Assembly be summoned within the shortest possible time and its verdict be obtained in his favour.

On relationship between the Governor and the Chief Minister, the report said that the Constitution, properly observed by both the Governor and the political parties, made sufficient provisions for dealing with all situations and for ensuring stable government in the State. The Committee also suggested the setting up of a special cell in the President's Secretariat to put the Governors in possession of authentic information regarding political and constitutional developments in the states from time to time. All the facts ascertained in a particular case and communicated confidentially to all the Governors with the President's permission would assist them in knowing how and why a particular Governor took a certain action and the circumstances that led to it.

On the position of the Governor, the Committee pressed the view that he, as head of the State, was in no sense agent of the President and his functions were laid down in the Constitution. The findings of the Committee throw considerable light on the difficult role of the Governor and hence their recommendations are bound to assist both the Governor and the Ministry in developing healthy traditions and practices for the smooth functioning of the State Governments.

4. It needs no argument to show that the power of the Governor to ask for information from the Chief Minister relating to legislative and administrative matters is a power that he exercises in his discretion. It is a duty cast on the Chief Minister by the Constitution to supply the Governor with such information that he calls for. The fact that the Governor has the power to call for such information does not mean that he can, on the basis of such information, overrule the Ministry on any particular matter. On the contrary, even when the Governor is personally opposed to a particular decision of the Ministry, he is generally bound to accept it. But since the Ministry is to hold office during his pleasure, he has to see whether and when he should exercise his pleasure against the Ministry. Moreover, it is his duty, as Ambedkar pointed out, 'to advise the Ministry, to warn the Ministry, to suggest to the Ministry an alternative and to ask for a reconsideration."[1]

> The Governor is the representative not of a party; he is the representative of the people as a whole of the State. It is in the name of the people that he carries on the administration. He must see that the administration is carried on at a level which is regarded as good, efficient and honest administration. How can the Governor discharge these duties, if he has not before him certain information ? It is to enable the Governor to discharge his functions in respect of a good and pure administration that we propose to give the Governor the power to call for any information.[2]

5. Under Article 167(c) the Governor is empowered to ask the Chief Minister to submit for the consideration of the Council of Ministers any matter on which a decision has been taken by a Minister but which has not been considered by the Council. This power is intimately related to his power of asking for information. For, while going through the decisions of the Government both by the Cabinet and individual Ministers, the Governor may come across a particular decision made by a Minister which, in his opinion, requires reconsideration by the Cabinet as a whole. As K.M. Munshi pointed out, the Governor may say:

> 'Here is a particular order. I feel that it is a matter of great importance. I want that by virtue of collective responsibility, all the Ministers must meet together and consider it'. ...If they accept it, he is bound to accept their advice. He has no right to overrule them. It is merely a matter of caution

1. Ambedkar drew a distinction between the functions of the Governor and his duties. He thought that in the exercise of the former he has no discretion while in the discharge of the latter he has.
2. C.A.D.VIII, p. 545.

that a decision, which, in the opinion of the constitutional head, is such as requires the *imprimatur of the* whole Cabinet and not of a single Minister, should so receive it. Therefore, it is a safeguard which preserves the collective responsibility....[1]

This power of the Governor does not in any way amount to an interference in the administration of the affairs of the Government. It places the Governor in a position to enable him to perform the duties "which every Governor ought to discharge."[2]

6. Under Article 200, power is vested in the Governor to return a Bill passed by the State Legislature and presented for his assent with a message requesting the Legislature to reconsider the Bill, either as a whole or any part of it, and suggesting recommendations for amendments. The Governor, however, cannot return a Money Bill. Although this power of the Governor can be made use of by the Ministry as a safeguard against hasty legislation,[3] it appears to be of little significance if its use is restricted to this purpose only. In fact, under a parliamentary system, almost all legislation is a product of the Government's initiative. If a Private Member's Bill finds an occasional place in the huge volume of Government business in the Legislature, even that cannot be passed without the support of the Government which commands a clear majority. In other words, almost every Bill that is presented to the Governor for his assent is the result of policy decisions taken at Cabinet level and of detailed consideration in the Legislature.

It is unlikely that such legislative enactment would be sent back for reconsideration either as a whole or in part at the instance of the Cabinet. This should lead us to the conclusion that the Governor, in his discretion, may return a Bill for reconsideration and suggest suitable amendments although the occasions for the exercise of such a power seem to be rare.

7. There is another provision under Article 200 which empowers the Governor to reserve a Bill for the consideration of the President if in the opinion of the Governor the provisions of the Bill will "so derogate from the powers of the High Court as to endanger the position which the Court is by this Constitution designed to fill". Although the Constitution has special provisions safeguarding the independence of the High Court and its powers and jurisdiction are defined therein, it operates within the boundaries of the State and as an integral part of the overall machinery of the State Government (consisting of the Executive, the Legislature and the Judiciary). Hence the State Legislature is competent to legislate on a number of matters which will directly or indirectly affect the working of the High Court. This provision, therefore, safeguards the position of the High Court against any measure that may affect its independence.

8. The power of promulgating Ordinances is a power which the Governor exercises with the aid and advice of the Ministry. But there are three circumstances under which the

---

1. Ibid., p. 541.
2. Ambedkar, Ibid., p. 546.
3. Both Ambedkar and Krishnamachari stressed in the Constituent Assembly that this was only a saving clause. Ambedkar pointed out that the Governor has no discretionary power here and this is why the words "in his discretion' used in the original draft of the Constitution were removed. (C.A.D. IX, pp. 41 and 61). But the existence of the words 'in his discretion' is not necessary for the Governor to use his discretion. Moreover, if these words had remained, the Governor would have become more than a constitutional head and even as a normal practice he would have the power of veto over legislation.

Governor cannot promulgate Ordinances without prior instructions from the President. The second of these states:

> The Governor shall not, without instructions from the President, promulgate any such Ordinance if he would have deemed it necessary to reserve a Bill containing the same provisions for the consideration of the President.

The power of the Governor to reserve a proposal of the State Cabinet to issue an Ordinance, for instructions from the President, should naturally be one that he exercises in his discretion.

9. There can hardly be any doubt as to the decisive role which the Governor is called upon to play prior to the promulgation of an emergency by the President as a consequence of a breakdown of the Constitutional machinery. The assessment of the situation that necessitates presidential intervention is primarily the task of the Governor.[1] In that context he is the President's adviser on the spot. Although the Governor will have the benefit of the advice of the Ministry in this respect, he is not bound by it. It is possible that the Government of the day may be against presidential intervention whereas the Governor himself is in favour of it. In such circumstances, if the Governor is to recommend to the President his intervention, he can do so only if he acts in his discretion.

It is true that the breakdown of the constitutional machinery is not a normal feature. But the record of even the first decade shows that it is not an altogether rare feature either. There were six different States,[2] where, during such a short period, the constitutional machinery broke down and, the Centre had to take action under the emergency provisions. The record of the second, third and fourth, decades shows many more such occasions. These instances show that parliamentary government in several States of the Union has yet to reach a degree of stability that makes the possibility of presidential intervention remote. So long as such a situation continues to exist, the Governors will be called upon to exercise real as against nominal power, which latter is the normal course.

10. Finally, the Governor of Assam has two special powers, the exercise of which in his discretion is expressly provided in the Constitution. Both of them are embodied in the Sixth Schedule of the Constitution. The first of these deals with disputes between the Government of Assam and an autonomous Tribal District Council with respect to the sharing of royalties that accrue from the lease of mining rights within the autonomous district.[3] The second relates to the manner in which the Governor may apply certain special administrative provisions in the Constitution with respect to tribal areas in Assam vis-a-vis a particular tribal area.[4]

It is well to remember Article 163(2) while dealing with the discretionary powers of the Governor. The section reads:

---

1. This was clearly demonstrated in July 1959 when the President proclaimed an emergency as a result of which the Kerala State Ministry was dismissed from office, the State Legislative Assembly dissolved and the administration of the State taken over by the Centre. When the Proclamation was subsequently placed before Parliament for its approval, it was pointed out by the Union Home Minister that the decision was taken on the basis of the report by the Governor. A summary of the Governor's report itself was also placed before Parliament.
2. The States concerned are: Punjab, PEPSU, Andhra, Travancore-Cochin. Kerala and Orissa.
3. Section 9 (2).
4. Section 18(3).

> If any question arises whether any matter is or is not a matter as respects which the Governor is by or under this Constitution required to act in his discretion, the decision of the Governor in his discretion shall be final, and the validity of anything done by the Governor shall not be called in question on the ground that he ought or ought not to have acted in his discretion.

Since nowhere in the Constitution (except where it deals with the Governor of Assam) there is express mention of the discretionary powers of the Governor, whatever powers the Governor has to exercise in his discretion are inherent in a particular situation. Being above party politics and as the Head of the State, he is expected to look at problems of the State with a detached view and if a particular situation demands the exercise of certain powers of his in his discretion no one can prevent him from doing so. It is to facilitate this and also to protect the Governor from being made a subject of unseemly controversies that the provision dealing with the discretionary powers of the Governor is couched in such general terms. If the Governor has no discretionary powers under the Constitution, this provision has no meaning and is superfluous. If his discretionary powers could be precisely pinned down to a few situations in the working of the State Government, the Constitution could have made specific provisions for them and avoided a general statement. Further, one should also recognize the significance of the place where this clause is inserted in the Constitution. It comes immediately after defining the relationship between the Governor and the Council of Ministers. The corresponding provision which deals with the relationship between the President and the Council of Ministers (of the Union) is not followed by such a provision dealing with the President's discretionary powers (Art. 74).

The inescapable inferences in the circumstances are:

(a) that the framers of the Constitution contemplated the exercise of discretionary powers by the Governor;

(b) that such exercise is not confined to one or a few occasions which can be precisely defined and embodied in the Constitution;

(c) that it is a power which is of a general nature and its use by the Governor will depend upon the circumstances that obtain in the State in a particular context or situation: and

(d) that the use of discretionary power by the Governor should be guided by conventions that grow up from time to time in the working of the Constitution.

The intentions of the framers become even clearer from a decision of the Constituent Assembly which has a direct bearing on this question. The Drafting Committee had originally provided for a Schedule embodying the 'Instrument of Instructions' to the President and the Governors to govern the relationship between the President or the Governor and the Ministers. But towards the end of the deliberations of the Assembly, the idea of incorporating the Instrument of Instructions was abandoned. Moving an amendment to this effect, T.T. Krishnamachari said:

> The Fourth Schedule was necessary because certain provisions were put in the Constitution in order to describe the relations of the President and the Governors vis-a-vis the Ministers. It has now been felt that the matter should be left entirely to convention rather than to be put into the body of the Constitution as a Schedule in the shape of an Instrument of Instructions, and there is a fairly large volume of opinion which favours that idea....[It] is felt to be entirely unnecessary and superfluous to give such directions in the Constitution, which really should arise out of conventions that grow

up from time to time and the President and the Governors in their respective spheres will be guided by these conventions.[1]

Supporting this view, Ambedkar said:

> The Instrument of Instructions had significance so long as ultimately every Viceroy or Governor was responsible to the Secretary of State who could remove them. So far as our Constitution is concerned, there is no functionary created by it who can see that this instrument of Instructions is carried out faithfully by the Governor.[2] It is, therefore, felt that no such directions should be given.[3]

It should be pointed out that the Governor's discretion under Article 163(2), although it appears to be absolute, cannot in reality be absolute. For, absolute discretion is an element of autocracy. The Governor can under no circumstances be an autocrat, so long as he functions within the framework of a democratic Constitution. What, then, is the check on his discretionary power? Neither the Ministry nor the State Legislature can control the Governor in this respect; but the President can. This means that the Governor is not a free agent in the exercise of his discretion. If he misused it either as a result of personal ambitions or as a partisan in the currents and cross-currents of State politics, the President can always check him; if necessary he may even dismiss him. Thus, in the final analysis, the Governor is not a free agent, either during normal times or abnormal times. For, in the discharge of his functions normally he is aided and advised by the Council of Ministers. So long as the Council has the confidence of the State Legislature, the Governor will not be able to substitute his discretion for the advice of the Council. If he attempts to do that, it will lead to political complications which will ultimately lead to his dismissal. On the contrary, under abnormal conditions such as an emergency caused by war, internal rebellion or a breakdown of the Constitutional machinery, he will be acting as an agent of the President and not as the absolute master of the situation. No doubt, during such times his powers are more real than during normal times when his powers are practically nominal.

The dismissal of the Rama Rao Ministry of Andhra Pradesh by Governor Ram Lal was a unique case when a Ministry with clear majority in the Legislative Assembly was dismissed by a Governor. Ram Lal soon after lost his job as a result of relentless opposition against him in the State and Ram Rao was soon after reinstated as Chief Minister. In the Bommai case, the Supreme Court for the first time declared the Governor's action in dismissing a Ministry invalid as the Ministry had not lost the confidence of the Legislature. By the same reason the Court had declared that the dismissal of the Ministry in Meghalaya in 1991 was also invalid. The matter has been dealt with at length by the Sarkaria Commission which made detailed recommendations as to how the Governor should act in such cases of constitutional break down.

All things taken together, the emphasis on the Governor's office seems to be on his role as an adviser.[4] On the one hand, he is a non-partisan adviser to the Ministry. By virtue of his position as the Head of the State, he has a right to be consulted, the right to encourage and the right to warn. He is a detached spectator, from a position of vantage and authority,

1. C.A.D., X.P.114.
2. This opinion does not appear to be correct. For, the President is competent to see that the Instrument of Instructions to the Governors is carried out just as the Secretary of State under the Act of 1935.
3. C.A.D.X, p. 115.
4. See in this connection the views of R.R. Diwakar, "The Governor and the State Administration" in G.S. Halappa (ed.). *Studies in State Administration,* pp. 76 & 83. Shri Diwakar was Governor for five years.

of what is going on in the State. Placed in that position, he maintains the dignity, the stability and the collective responsibility of the State Government. On the other, he is the agent of the President, his adviser on the affairs of the State and the representative of the Union in the State. He is the link that fastens the Federal-State chain, the channel which regulates the Union-State relationship. Thus, he is an essential part of the Constitutional machinery, fulfilling an essential purpose and rendering an essential service. In the words of one who was privileged to know the position from inside.

> A Governor can do a great deal of good if he is a good Governor and he can do a great deal of mischief, if he is a bad Governor, in spite of the very little power given to him under the Constitution we are framing.[1]

When some members of the Opposition attacked the Governor's office as superfluous in the Madras Legislative Assembly (1952), Rajaji who was then Chief Minister of the state said that the Governor was like a fire-fighting vehicle. So long as there was no fire, fire engines would be idle, but they would be pressed into service if there was a fire. If the fire service system were to be done away with any major fire could prove disastrous. When a political crisis arises it is the Governor who often has to resolve the crisis.

Although the Governor is appointed by the President (Central Government) he is not a servant of the Centre. He is an independent constitutional authority as the Head of the State and discharging functions assigned to him under the Constitution. Writing about his experience as Governor of Maharashtra, C. Subramaniam observed that the Governor can discharge many useful functions; first in the field of administration; second, in the field of education as Chancellor of the Universities; third, in the field of social service as the patron of voluntary organisations; and finally, in the field of fine arts, A governor should never be a partisan politician. Active politicians whenever appointed governors have almost invariably proved misfits to hold the exalted office.

A study team constituted by the Administrative Reforms Commission, explaining the nature of the Governor's role, observed that the office of the Governor is not meant to be an ornamental sinecure. It pointed out that his character, calibre and experience must be of an order that enables him to discharge with skill and detachment his dual responsibility towards the Union and the State of which he is constitutional head, This duality is perhaps its most important and certainly its most unusual feature. It is vitally important therefore that what the Governor is required to do should be clearly understood by him, by the State government and by the Centre. And it is equally important that the Governor should discharge his functions judiciously, impartially and efficiently."

The Sarkaria Commission has observed that "discarded and disgruntled politicians from the party in power in the Union, who cannot be accommodated elsewhere, get appointed (as Governors). Such persons, while in office, tend to function as agents of the Union Government rather than as impartial constitutional functionaries. The number of Governors who have displayed the qualities of ability, integrity and impartiality and statesmanship has been on the declining side,"

Taking into consideration what happened during the past fifty years we are led to the conclusion that the Governor's office requires better definition in the Constitution.

---

1. B.G. Kher (Chief Minister of Bombay as he then was), C.A.D. VIII, p. 434.

The Advocate-General for the State

Like the Attorney-General who is the legal adviser to the Union Government, the Constitution provides for a legal adviser to the State Government known as the Advocate-General for the State. He is appointed by the Governor and holds office during his pleasure. To be appointed as Advocate-General, a person should have the same qualifications as would make him eligible for appointment as a judge of the High Court. The Advocate-General will receive such remuneration as the Governor may determine.

It is the duty of the Advocate-General to give advice to the State Government on legal matters referred to him as well as to perform certain other duties of a legal character which are assigned to him from time to time. In the discharge of these duties he is entitled to appear before any court of law within the State or the State Legislature as and when required.

***

31

THE STATE LEGISLATURE

THE CONSTITUTION provides for a Legislature for every State in the Union. But it does not adhere to the principle of bicameralism in the case of every State Legislature. There are six States, namely Bihar, Maharashtra, Jammu and Kashmir, Karnataka, Uttar Pradesh and Madhya Pradesh, each of which has two Houses in the Legislature, while the remaining States have unicameral Legislatures. Where there are two Houses of the Legislature, one is known as the Legislative Assembly and the other, the Legislative Council. Where there is only one House, it is known as the Legislative Assembly. The Governor of the State is an integral part of the Legislature.

The State Legislative Assembly is a replica of the House of the People while the Legislative Council has a resemblance to the Council of States. An interesting feature of the debates in the Constituent Assembly about the Legislative Councils was that the Assembly as a whole did not want to take a decision on the question of establishing Legislative Councils in the States. The matter was left to be decided by the members from each State. This accounts for the anomaly of certain States having two Houses while others are provided with only one House. This was really the result of the choice made by members representing each State. Although the Constitution provides for bicameral Legislatures for certain States and unicameral ones for others, the question of the organization of State Legislatures in a single House or two Houses is still left an open one. Article 169 provides a special procedure for the creation and abolition of Legislative Councils in the future. According to this, Parliament is empowered to create a Legislative Council in a State having no such Council or abolish the Council where it exists, provided the Legislative Assembly of the State passes a resolution to that effect supported by not less than a majority of the total membership of the House and a majority of not less than two-thirds of those who sit and vote.[1] Any law passed by Parliament in this regard should contain the necessary amendments to the provisions of the Constitution which are affected by such law. But these amendments will not be considered as regular amendments to the Constitution for which a special procedure is prescribed.

Composition of the Legislative Assembly

The Assembly is composed of members chosen by direct election. The only exception

1. Taking advantage of this provision, Madhya Pradesh and Mysore established new Legislative Councils for them (Seventh Amendment of the Constitution, 1958), while West Bengal and Punjab abolished their existing Councils by the West Bengal Legislative Council (Abolition) Act, 1969, and the Punjab Legislative Council (Abolition) Act, 1969, respectively. The Legislative council of Andhra Pradesh was abolished in 1985 that of Tamil Nadu was abolished in 1986.

to this rule is the representation of the Anglo-Indian community. If no member of that community secures election to the Assembly, the Governor is empowered to nominate one or more members on behalf of it as members of the Assembly.[1] The Constitution has fixed a maximum number of 500 members for any State Assembly and a minimum of 60 members.[2] For purposes of election, the State is divided into as many territorial constituencies as there are seats in the Assembly. As far as possible, the ratio between the population of each constituency and the number of seats allotted to it will be the same throughout the State. At the end of each decennial census, the constituencies will be recast to make the necessary adjustments to meet the variations in population. At present, the number of voters in each constituency is around 100,000. The number of members in each State Legislative Assembly may be seen from the table on page 379.

Composition of the Legislative Council

Several members in the Constituent Assembly were opposed to the idea of constituting an Upper House for the States. They thought that an additional House to the Legislative Assembly in the States was superfluous. Some of them even doubted the financial ability of several States to maintain this "costly ornamental luxury"[3]. These criticisms were mainly responsible for the Assembly allowing the members from different States to decide the question themselves, and leaving the future of the Councils in a fluid state in the Constitution itself. In these circumstances, the Drafting Committee found it difficult at first to present to the Assembly a definite plan for the composition of the Council. In fact, when the Assembly took up the Constitutional provisions in this regard for detailed consideration, the matter was quite open, with scores of amendments proposed by members and the Drafting Committee without any readymade pattern. Some of the members found fault with the Committee for their lack of interest and indecision in this matter. When Ambedkar said that "since the Drafting Committee had not finally decided upon this question, they wanted to leave it to Parliament", some members took objection to this attitude of the Committee. President Prasad, intervening in the debate, said:

> I confess to a sense of disappointment at the Drafting Committee not being able to find a solution for this question. (Hear, hear.) It is an important matter in the Constitution that the composition of the Chambers of the Legislature should be laid down definitely.... I do not blame the Drafting Committee for it, As Dr. Ambedkar had pointed out, there has been such a jumble of amendments suggested, so many viewpoints put forward, that they found it impossible to reconcile all these and they take the line of least resistance by putting it off till the Legislative Assembly meets and decides the question. If it is at all possible, I would at this late stage suggest that the question might be referred back to the Drafting Committee....

Ambedkar said sportingly, "We can have another go at it".[4]

Accordingly, the Committee later presented a new article dealing with the composition of the Council which, as Ambedkar acknowledged, was mainly based upon an amendment in this regard moved earlier in the House by Shibban Lal Saksena.[5] After a long debate, the

1. Article 333.
2. The only exception to this is the Sikkim Legislative Assembly which has only 30 members now. Article 371F adopted by the Thirty-sixth Amendment of the Constitution makes special provisions with respect to the State of Sikkim and this is one of those special provisions.
3. C.A.D. IX, pp. 1-37.
4. C.A.D. IX. p. 37.
5. Ibid., p. 473.

Table 1

Name of State	*Number of Members*	*Nominated*
Andhra Pradesh	294	1
Assam	126	–
Bihar	324	1
Chatisgarh	90	–
Gujarat	182	–
Haryana	90	–
Himachal Pradesh	68	–
Jammu and Kashmir	76	–
Jharkhand	81	–
Karnataka	224	1
Kerala	140	1
Madhya Pradesh	320	1
Maharashtra	288	1
Manipur	60	–
Meghalaya	60	–
Nagaland	60	–
Orissa	147	–
Punjab	117	–
Rajasthan	200	–
Sikkim	30	–
Tamil Nadu	234	1
Tripura	60	–
Uttaranchal	70	–
Uttar Pradesh	425	–
West Bengal	294	4

article was finally adopted with some minor modifications and became Article 171 of the Constitution. The main provisions of the article are as follows:

1. The total number of members in the .Legislative Council should not exceed one-third of the total number of members in the Legislative Assembly.[1] But in any case, it should not be less than forty.
2. There are five different categories of representation to the Council. These are:
   (a) One-third of the total membership to be elected by electorates consisting of members of self-governing local bodies like Municipalities, District Boards, etc., in the State.
   (b) One-third to be elected by the members of the Legislative Assembly of the State.
   (c) One-twelfth to be elected by electorates consisting of university graduates (of at least three years' standing) or others recognized as possessing equivalent qualification and who are residing in the State.

1. As originally passed, the proportion fixed was one-fourth. But the Seventh Amendment (1956) altered it to one-third.

(d) One-twelfth to be elected by electorates consisting of secondary school teachers or those in higher educational institutions, with at least three years' experience in teaching.

(e) The remainder to be nominated by the Governor on the basis of their special knowledge or practical experience in literature, science, art, the co-operative movement or social service.

3. The election of the first four categories is to be held in accordance with the system of proportional representation by means of the single transferable vote.
4. Voting shall be by secret ballot.
5. Parliament is empowered to make any change with regard to the nature of representation detailed above.

These provisions, it must be said, are not the result of mature consideration on the question. As it stands at present, there is a combination of direct election, indirect election and nomination which makes the Council a hotch - potch of representation. The right of franchise given to teachers and members of local government bodies indicate that the emphasis is primarily on functional representation. But, from that point of view, the representation is too narrow. There are many professions and interests in addition to these whose representation in the Council is desirable and likely to prove of great benefit. Too much weight has been given to the members of the Assembly by providing for one-third of the Council membership to be elected by them. The percentage of seats reserved for nomination, on the other hand, seems to be too small. Men of merit from the fields of art, science, literature and social service should have formed a large number among the members of the Council in order to make it a body of meritorious elders who can effectively help in the work of legislation, supervise or watch over the administration.

Table 2 shows the membership of the Legislative Councils in different States with a detailed statement of the constituencies from which they are elected.

Table 2

LEGISLATIVE COUNCILS

Name of the State	Total number of members	Elected by the Legislative Assembly	Elected by Local Authorities			
Bihar	72	25	23	6	6	12
Jammu and Kashmir	36	21	7	Nil	2	6
Karnataka	63	21	21	6	6	9
Madhya Pradesh	90	31	31	8	8	12
Maharashtra	78	30	22	7	7	12
Uttar Pradesh	72	24	24	6	6	12

The normal life of the Assembly is five years: but it may be dissolved earlier by the Governor. In case of an emergency, its life may be extended by a law of Parliament, one year at a time, but in any case not beyond six months after the Proclamation of Emergency has ceased to operate. The Council, on the other hand, is a permanent body which renews one-third of its membership after every two years. In this respect, it follows the pattern of the Council of States.

There is hardly any special qualification fixed for election to the State Legislature except one of age. As in the case of a member of the House of the People, a member of the Assembly should have completed the minimum age of twenty-five years at the time of election. In the case, of a member of the Council the minimum age prescribed is thirty years.

The Assembly has two elected officers, the Speaker and the Deputy Speaker, to conduct its business. The position of these two officers in the conduct of the business of the House, and their powers and functions in the Assembly, are respectively same as those of the Speaker and the Deputy Speaker of the House of the People. They may be removed from office by a resolution of the House supported by a majority of all the existing members of the House. The Council has a Chairman, and a Deputy Chairman, both elected by the Council, and they have the same powers and functions as their counterparts in the Assembly. They also can be removed from office by a resolution of the Council supported by a majority of the existing members in the Council at the time of passing such resolution. The Constitution provides for each House of the State Legislature a separate secretarial staff whose members are independent of the Executive in matters of recruitment and conditions of service.

Conduct of Business

There is hardly anything special to be pointed out in this context which is different from that of the two Houses of Parliament. Most of the articles in this part of the Constitution are a reproduction, almost verbatim, of those which deal with corresponding provisions regarding the two Houses of Parliament. Ambedkar acknowledged this in the Constituent Assembly and pointed out that that was one of the reasons why there were very few amendments to the various articles in that part of the Constitution. In view of the detailed discussion on parliamentary procedure given in an earlier chapter, it is not necessary to go into any detail regarding the procedure in the State Legislatures. A brief resume of it is given below.

The State Legislature must meet at least twice a year and the interval between any two sessions should not be more than six months. Usually, a new session begins with an opening address by the Governor which outlines the policy of the State Government. The address is then subjected to a debate and finally voted upon in the form of a resolution expressing thanks to the Governor. It is during this debate that the opposition parties get the best opportunity to criticize in general the policies and programmes of the Government.

Any Bill, except a Money Bill, may be introduced in either House of the Legislature. The Bill is finally passed with its third reading. Then it goes to the Governor for his assent. But the Governor may send it back for reconsideration. When it is passed again by the Legislature, the Governor cannot withhold his assent. But he may reserve certain Bills for the consideration of the President,[1] who may ask the Governor to place it before the .Legislature for reconsideration.. When it is passed again, with or without amendment, it goes to the President for his consideration. The President is not bound to give his assent

1. Any Bill which in the opinion of the Governor, if it becomes law, so derogate from the powers of the High Court as to endanger the position which that Court is by this Constitution designed to fill.

even though the Bill has been reconsidered and passed for a second time by the State Legislature.

What is the effect of the dissolution of the Assembly on pending Bills? According to Article 196, Bills that are pending in the Assembly or Bills which have been passed by the Assembly but are pending in the Council alone will lapse as a result of dissolution. Bills which have been duly passed by the Assembly (where there is only one House) and by the Assembly and the Council (where there are two Houses) and are awaiting the assent of the Governor or the President shall not lapse as a consequence of the Assembly's dissolution. Further, a Bill which has been returned either by the Governor or the President for reconsideration can be considered and passed by the newly constituted Assembly although the Bill was originally passed by the dissolved House. These points have been settled by the Supreme Court in one of its decisions[1] in 1961 when the Court was asked to declare invalid the Kerala Agrarian Relations Act of 1961 on the ground that the Bill was pending before the President for assent when the Assembly was dissolved in 1959 following the Proclamation of emergency in the State by the President.

Assembly vs. Council

A significant point of difference between the relationship of the two Houses of Parliament and that of the two Houses of the State Legislature (wherever two Houses exist) is the comparatively less important role which the Legislative Council plays in contrast to that of the Council of States. As we have already seen, the Council of States has, except in the field of Money Bills, co-equal powers with the House in all legislative matters. When there is an irreconcilable conflict between the two, the deadlock is resolved in a joint sitting of the two Houses. In the State Legislature, on the contrary, the Council is designed to play a definitely inferior role. Its functions are of an advisory nature only. Ambedkar pointed out in the Assembly that the provisions adopted by the Constitution to resolve conflicts between the two Houses of the State Legislature were based on the provisions of the (British) Parliament Act of 1911.[2]

According to this, a Bill can have only two journeys from the Assembly to the Council. When a Bill goes to the Council for the first time from the Assembly, the Council has four courses of action: (i) it may reject the Bill; (ii) it may amend the Bill; (iii) it may take no action on it (but when three months have elapsed since its receipt by the Council and the Council does not inform the Assembly the action it has taken on the Bill, it is deemed to have been rejected by the Council); and (iv) it may pass the Bill as sent by the Assembly. In the first three cases the Assembly takes up the consideration of the Bill for a second time. It may or may not accept the amendments made by the Council and passes the Bill. It now goes for the second time to the Council which can adopt any of the above alternative courses of action except that it can delay the Bill only for a month instead of three months as in the first instance. The Assembly acts again according to the same procedure as before, if the Council does not again agree with it. Thus, only twice will the Bills travel from the Assembly to the Council and the latter has only the power of a suspensory veto, the first time for a period of three months and the second time for a month. These provisions clearly establish the absolute superiority of the Assembly over the Council. In respect of Money Bills, the powers of the State Assembly are the same as those of 'the House of the

1. P. Nambudiri vs. The State of Kerala, (1962) I S.C.J. 477.
2. C.A.D.IX,p.41.

People, which we have already dealt with. There is also a special procedure prescribed for financial matters on the same pattern as obtaining in Parliament.

Legislative Privileges

The powers, privileges and immunities of the State Legislature and their members are the same as those of Parliament and its members. Members are entitled to receive such salaries and allowances as are determined by the Legislature. At present, there is no uniformity with regard to these among the various States. While some of them give regular monthly salaries and certain allowances to their legislators, others give either a fixed sum of money for the year or only certain allowances.

The question of the privileges and immunities of the legislature and its members figured prominently in several cases where attempts were made to persuade the High Courts and the Supreme Court to interfere with the working of the State Legislative Assemblies. Of these, Misra vs. Nand Kishore[1] was a case which came up before the Orissa High Court in which the petitioner challenged the action of the Speaker who disallowed certain questions which he asked on the floor of the Orissa Assembly. The High Court declined to interfere as this was a matter which fell within the exclusive rights of the Legislature to regulate. In the second case. Singh vs. Govind,[2] the Allahabad High Court was asked to determine the legality or otherwise of certain disciplinary action taken against the petitioner as a member of the Uttar Pradesh Assembly. Here again, the Court refused to interfere. Speaking on behalf of the Court. Justice Sapru said:

> Obviously, this Court is not in any sense whatever, a Court of appeal or revision against the Legislature or against the rulings of the Speaker, who, as the holder of an office of the highest distinction, has the sole responsibility cast upon him of maintaining the prestige and dignity of the House.

He added that under Article 194, the Legislature has the right (i) to be the exclusive judge of the legality of its own proceedings, (ii) to punish its members for their conduct in the House, and (iii) to settle its own proceedings.

The matter came before the Supreme Court for the first time in the case of *The Searchlight* and the Court gave its verdict in favour of the Legislature.[3] The case arose out of the publication by *The Searchlight* of certain references in the Legislative Assembly of the Slate of Bihar relating to the conduct of the Chief Minister of the State and an ex-Minister. The newspaper reported that a member of the Assembly made a bitter attack on the Chief Minister and his ex-colleague with respect to their activities regarding selection of Ministers and the glaring instances of encouragement of corruption by the Government. Soon after, the Secretary of the Bihar Legislature issued a notice to the Editor of *The Searchlight* for the breach of privilege of the House inasmuch as he was alleged to have published a perverted and unfaithful report of the proceedings. The notice asked the Editor to appear before the Privileges Committee which had found a *prima facie* case against him and show cause why action should not be taken against him. The Editor challenged the validity of the notice by a petition filed in the Supreme Court under Article 32 of the Constitution.

The Court said that it was called upon to answer two questions: (i) whether the House of the Legislature could prohibit the publication of publicly seen and heard

---

1. 40 A.I.R.III. 2. 41 A.J..R 319.
3. M.S.M. Sharma *vs.* Sri Krishna Sinha. 1959, S.C.J. 925. See also 1960 S.CJ. Notes 21.

proceedings; and (ii) whether the privileges of the House under Article 194(3) prevailed over the Fundamental Rights of the citizen under Article 19(1) (a). A four to one majority of the Court answered both questions in the affirmative. Speaking on behalf of the majority. Chief Justice S.R. Das held that in the absence of a law made by the Legislature, the Legislature shall have all the privileges, powers and immunities enjoyed by the House of Commons in England at the commencement of the Constitution of India and the citizen could not insist on the faithful publication of the proceedings of the Legislature if the Legislature chose not to permit him to do so. The fundamental right of freedom of speech guaranteed to a citizen under Article 19(1) (a) could not override the privileges of the Legislature. It must not be overlooked that they (the privileges) were conferred by constitutional laws and not ordinary laws made by Parliament and, therefore, they are as supreme as the Chapter on Fundamental Rights.

In his dissent. Justice Subba Rao said that the reasoning adopted in the majority judgment would unduly restrict and circumscribe the wide scope and content of one of the cherished fundamental rights, namely, the freedom of speech in its application to the Press. The learned judge asked: "Why should Article 194 be preferred to Article 19(1) (a) and not vice versa ?" According to him, if there is a conflict between a legislative privilege and a fundamental right, the former should yield to the latter to the extent that is necessary to uphold the fundamental right. The Legislature has only the privilege of preventing, *mala fide* publication of the proceedings. Article 19(2) gives ample scope for such reasonable restrictions to be imposed by a duly enacted law. The privilege of the Legislature can be adequately protected by applying the test of reasonable restrictions envisaged under Article 19(2). Hence it is unnecessary to accord a preferred position to the privilege of the Legislature over the fundamental right of the citizen expressly guaranteed by the Constitution.

In spite of the Supreme Court's verdict in *The Searchlight* case holding the supremacy of legislative privilege over the right to freedom of expression, it must be emphasized that the interests of parliamentary democracy demand the need to ensure the freedom of the press in an adequate measure. The press should not get the impression that the House was trying to "terrorize" it into refraining from fair comment. As there is no possibility for appeal against any decision taken by the House, fairness demands of Members to act with great responsibility and utmost impartiality in deciding what they should object to and what action they should take. Unfortunately, there exists a tendency among legislators in India to invoke privilege too frequently. This seems to be the product either of insufficient appreciation of the rights of others to criticize what they do on the floor of the House or of an exaggerated feeling of importance of their parliamentary role. The best example of this is provided by the episode of a conflict between the Legislative Assembly and the High Court of Madras which took place during 1960, an incident unparalleled, perhaps, in the annals of parliamentary privileges.

The Government of Madras had appointed one Mr. Alagirisami as Government Pleader after his retirement from judicial service in the State. The appointment was challenged through a writ petition in the High Court by an Advocate of the Court. The Court however dismissed the petition, saying that from a strict "legal point of view" the Government could make the appointment and the Court could not interfere.[1] But one of

1. Judiciary vs. Speaker, *The Current*, 21 September 1960.

the judges who heard the petition made stringent remarks by way of *obiter dicta* imputing motives to the Minister in charge of law who also happened to be the Leader of the House in the Assembly. A member of the government party (the Congress Party), during the next session of the Assembly, moved a privilege motion in the House alleging that the Court had in some of its observations in the decision of the above case "usurped the powers and privileges of the legislature." He said that the matter was a fit case to be referred to the Committee on Privileges, as, in the Court's order, "strong observations have been made affecting the conduct, character, prestige and privilege of a member and Leader of this House and powers which essentially belong to the Legislature have been assumed by the High Court, thereby affecting the powers and privileges of this House". The Speaker announced that views of the leaders of parties in the House would be elicited on the privilege motion two days later when the motion would be considered by the House.

The day after the motion was moved in the Assembly, the same Advocate who had moved the High Court earlier filed a petition before the Court praying that action might be taken against the member who moved the privilege motion for contempt of court. He pointed out that no member of the legislature had any right to discuss the conduct of any High Court judge and anything in regard to pronouncements made by him in the discharge of his official duties (Article 211).[1] This provision was embodied in the Constitution to ensure that judges could administer justice without fear or favour. The privilege motion, he alleged, had cast aspersions on a judge of the High Court. The two judges who heard the petition admitted it and ordered issue of notice to the member. The Court also issued a notice to the Speaker of the Assembly to show cause why a writ of mandamus directing the Speaker to forbear from allowing consideration or discussion of a certain privilege motion tabled in the Assembly should not be issued against him. On the following day the Speaker made a rather dramatic announcement of the notice in the Assembly and added that he did not propose to subject himself to the authority of any court in the exercise of his powers (in accordance with Article 212 of the Constitution).[2] The Court regretted the uncooperative attitude of the Speaker in helping it to clear up the conflict between Article 211 and 212 but proceeded to examine the issue of privilege involved in the case. The Chief Justice, who went into this aspect in considerable detail, pointed out that the criticism levelled against the Minister in the court order was in relation to a member of the Executive Government and not to a member of the Legislature. The functions of the Legislature and the Executive were different. The Executive was not protected by privileges in the actions and, therefore, he could not understand whether there was *prima facie* any privilege involved in the orders of the Court. As regards the stand of the Speaker that the Court could not issue notice to him relating to his duties in the Assembly, the Chief Justice observed that notice could be issued to anybody in the land excepting foreign dignitaries. It was a different question whether the Court had any jurisdiction to pass an order of injunction.

This unfortunate episode of a constitutional clash between the High Court and the Speaker, arising out of an undue emphasis on legislative privilege, came to a happy end,

1. Article 211: "No discussion shall take place in the Legislature of a State with respect to the conduct of any Judge of the Supreme Court or of a High Court in the discharge of his duties."
2. Article 212: "(I) The validity of any proceedings in the Legislature of a State shall not be called in question on the ground of any alleged irregularity of procedure; (2) No Officer or member of the Legislature of a State in whom powers are vested by or under this Constitution for regulating procedure or the conduct of business, or for maintaining order, in the Legislature, shall be subject to the jurisdiction of any court in respect to the exercise by him of these powers".

however, by the adjournment of the House *sine die* without discussing the privilege motion and by the subsequent decision of the Speaker not to proceed with the matter.[1]

The clash between the Madras Assembly and the High Court over legislative privileges versus contempt of court becomes a minor scuffle when compared to the unprecedented Jurisdictional fight, four years later, between the Uttar Pradesh Assembly and the Allahabad High Court. The circumstances which led to this unusual incident were as follows. The U.P. Legislative Assembly passed a resolution on 14 March 1964, recommending that a Socialist worker, Keshav Singh, be sentenced to simple imprisonment for seven days for committing contempt of the House by defying its order. Subsequently, the High Court, acting on a writ petition, released Keshav Singh on bail pending the final disposal of the petition. The Assembly discussed the action of the Court and decided by an overwhelming majority that it amounted to a contempt of the House. It adopted a motion that the two judges who heard the writ petition as well as Keshav Singh and his counsel should be produced before the bar of the House for the breach of privilege. The High Court reacted to this move of the Assembly swiftly and firmly. A full bench of the Court consisting of twenty-eight judges passed an interim order on the following day, staying the implementation of the Assembly's controversial resolution which had already provoked an unprecedented constitutional crisis. Further, the Court reserved orders on three petitions intended to institute contempt of court proceedings against the Assembly, the Speaker, the Marshall (who was asked to serve the warrant on the judges) and the mover and the supporter of the resolution in the Assembly.

By now, the U.P. happenings were attracting nationwide attention and attempts were made to discuss the matter in the Lok Sabha. A few days later, having failed to find a satisfactory solution to the constitutional impasse, the ruling Congress Party steamrolled a resolution through the State Assembly virtually rescinding its earlier resolution and requesting Presidential intervention under Article 143 of the Constitution in order to settle its conflict with the High Court. Thus the matter reached the President who, under Article 143, referred it to the Supreme Court for its advice.[2] The Court held that the High Court was competent to entertain the petition filed by Keshav Singh challenging the legality of the sentence of imprisonment imposed on him by the Assembly. It also held that the Assembly was not competent to direct the production of the two judges of the High Court who ordered the release of Keshav Singh.

The extent to which claims to parliamentary privileges can go was further shown in a decision of the Supreme Court in January 1961. In this—a defamation case—a member of the West Bengal State Assembly contended that there was an absolute privilege in favour of a member and that he, therefore, could not be prosecuted for having published subsequently questions which had been disallowed by the Speaker. In January 1954, he had given notice of his intention to ask certain questions in the Assembly. The questions were disallowed. He then published them in a local journal. The person whose conduct had formed the subject matter of the questions filed a complaint against the Assembly member, and also the editor and publisher of the journal, alleging that the published matter contained scandalous imputations against him and was intended to tarnish his reputation. In a unanimous verdict the Supreme Court held that there was no absolute privilege attaching

1. See in this connection D. Gopalakrishna Sastri, "Conflict in Privileges of Courts and Legislative Bodies", (1961) I S.C.J. 21.
2. A.I.R. 1965 S.C. 745.

to the publication of extracts from proceedings and that, if the extracts contained defamatory matter, the member concerned 'should face the consequences as in any ordinary case of defamation.[1]

What happened in the Tamil Nadu Legislative Assembly, on 22 March 1999 was another instance of unruly behaviour of legislators which has become almost the rule across the country during the past one decade. In the instant incident, a member of the Assembly, Thamaraikani, assaulted the Minister of Agriculture, Veerpandi Arumugam, and seriously injured him. It was part of ugly scenes of violence witnessed in the Assembly in which DMK and AIADMK members freely exchanged blows. The Speaker of the Assembly later got the offending MLA arrested from a private hospital and suspended him from the Assembly for the rest of the session and sentenced him for 15 days imprisonment. On the following day, a habeas corpus writ petition was moved on his behalf before the Madras High Court and a Division Bench of the court ordered his release. In the meantime the Assembly by a resolution sentenced the offending MLA for 15 days' imprisonment. In accordance with this resolution the MLA was rearrested and sent to jail. On the next day a fresh petition was filed before the Court challenging the resolution of the Assembly and praying for his release. The Court also admitted a contempt petition submitted by the MLA's counsel. Naturally, the matter developed into a major row between the High Court and the Assembly. However, better counsels prevailed as the Chief Minister and the Speaker adopting a conciliatory attitude with a view to avoiding a confrontation with the High Court. Thamaraikani was released but his suspension from the rest of the session from the Assembly was not annuled, Once again, the exaggerated claims of the Assembly regarding its "sovereignty and constitutional immunity from judicial intervention" was proved to be a false claim. Neither the Speaker nor the Legislature has authority to sit as a criminal court of law.

***

1. Dr. J.C. Ghosh vs. H.S. Mukherjee, (1962) I.S.C.J. 411.

32

JUDICIARY IN THE STATES

EVERY STATE has a High Court operating within its territorial jurisdiction except some of the small States and every High Court is a Court of Record,[1] which has all the powers of such a Court including the power to punish for contempt of itself. Neither the Supreme Court nor the Legislature can deprive a High Court of its power of punishing a contempt of itself.[2]

Most of the High Courts in India have a long and rich history behind them. They were established during the British period by Royal Charters and were virtually the highest courts in the country within their own territories. The only tribunal to which appeals could be taken from the High Courts was the Judicial Committee of the Privy Council. With the establishment of the Federal Court of India under the Constitution Act of 1935, appeals on constitutional matters from the High Courts went first to the Federal Court and then to the Privy Council. But the Federal Court had no appellate jurisdiction in criminal or civil matters, and, therefore, appeals in these matters went straight to the Privy Council. This position continued, even after the transfer of power, up to 1949 when the Privy Council appeals were abolished.

We have already seen the position of the Supreme Court with the inauguration of the new Constitution in 1950, and how it affected the position of the High Courts by bringing them directly under the Supreme Court as parts of a single, integrated, and hierarchical, all India judicial system. The Constitution does not, however, vest in the Supreme Court any direct administrative control over the High Courts which would substantially affect their functioning as independent judicial institutions.

The position of the High Courts under a federal Constitution like that of India is substantially different from that of the State Courts under most other federations, notably that of the United States of America. There, the State Courts are constituted under the State Constitutions and, as such, do not in any way link themselves up with the federal judicial system. The method of appointment and conditions of service of the judges of the State Courts as well as their respective jurisdictions vary from State to State. In India, on the contrary, there is uniformity in all these matters and the Constitution lays down detailed provisions dealing with them. Neither the State Executive nor the State Legislature has any power to control the High Court, or to alter the constitution or organization of the

1. The significance of a Court of Record has already been dealt with in connection with the powers of the Supreme Court.
2. Sukhdev Singh vs. Teja Singh A.I.R. 1954, S.C. 186. See also H.P. Singh vs. Thakur Prasad Tewari A.I.R. 1953, S.C. 436.

High Court.[1] Whatever that is permissible, short of a constitutional amendment, is vested in Parliament. These provisions have great importance in determining the independence of the High Courts.

Unlike the Supreme Court, there is no fixed minimum number of judges for the High Court. The President, from time to time, will fix the number of judges in each High Court and it varies from Court to Court. For example, the Andhra Pradesh High Court has at present only twenty-six judges whereas the Allahabad High Court has as many as sixty judges.

Every judge of the High Court is appointed by the President of India after consultation with the Chief Justice of India, the Governor of the State and, in the case of the appointment of a judge other than the Chief Justice, the Chief Justice of the High Court concerned. If he is appointed on a permanent basis, he will hold office until he completes the age of sixty-two years.

Appointment of Judges

Differing legal perceptions on the scope and content of the consultation process between the Executive and the Chief Justice of the Supreme Court led to the President referring the matter to the Supreme Court for its opinion in 1998, The Court held that the expression "Consultation with the Chief Justice of India" in Articles 217(1) and 222(1) of the Constitution requires consultation with a plurality of judges in the formation of the opinion of the Chief Justice, Plurality here means two senior-most judges of the Supreme Court. In the case of transfer of High Court judges, the Court held that the recommendation should be made by the Chief Justice in consultation with four seniormost judges of the Supreme Court.

The minimum qualifications prescribed for appointment are Indian citizenship and at least ten years' experience either as an advocate of a High Court in India or as a judicial officer in the territory of India.' In computing the ten-year period for the purpose of appointment, experience as an advocate can be combined with that of a judicial officer. A judge of the High Court can be removed from office only for proved misbehaviour or incapacity and only in the same manner in which a judge of the Supreme Court is removed.

The Chief Justice and the other judges of the High Court are paid monthly salaries of Rs. 30,000 and 26,000 respectively. In addition, they are also entitled to certain allowances and a pension on retirement. The salary and allowances of a judge of the High Court cannot be varied to his disadvantage after his appointment. Further, these sums are charged on the Consolidated Fund of the State and, as such, are excluded from being voted on in the State Legislature. The Constitution imposes on judges of High Courts certain restrictions with respect to legal practice after retirement. According to this, they cannot practise before any Court except the Supreme Court and High Courts other than those in which they were judges.[2] These provisions which are almost identical with those dealing with the judges of the Supreme Court are intended to safeguard the independence of the High Courts.

There are, however, certain special provisions which make the organization and

1. "The only matter that is left to the State Legislatures is to fix the jurisdiction of the High Court in a pecuniary way or with regard to the subject matter. The rest of the High Court is placed within the jurisdiction of the Centre". Ambedkar, C.A.D. IX, p. 781.
2. According to the original Constitution, there was a total prohibition on practising after retirement. The present provision is the result of the Seventh Amendment of the Constitution, 1956.

functioning of the High Court different from those of the Supreme Court. Of these, the power of the President to transfer a judge from one High Court to another seems to be the most important one. Every such transfer is to be made only after consultation with the Chief Justice of India. This provision may not seem to be quite in harmony with the concept of judicial independence. Yet, it has some justification. The services of a competent judge may be required in any part of the country as a matter of national interest, and this provision enables the President to choose such a judge from any of the High Courts in the country. This will also facilitate the better selection of judges and to keep the question above State or regional barriers. Secondly, unlike the provisions in regard to the Supreme Court, there is a provision for the appointment of additional and acting judges to the High Court. Additional judges are appointed for a period not exceeding two years to meet any temporary increase in the work of the Court or to dispose of arrears of accumulated work. An acting judge is appointed in the place of a permanent judge of the Court when the latter is away on leave or on some other duty.[1]

Both in the Constituent Assembly and outside, during the time of the framing of the Constitution and after, the provisions dealing with the conditions of service of judges of the High Court were subjected to three major criticisms. The most important of these related to the fixation of sixty years as the retiring age as was then provided. It was pointed out that when the age of retirement of the judges of the Supreme Court was fixed at sixty-five years, there was little justification for fixing that of the High Court judges at sixty. There is hardly any reason to suppose that the judges of the Supreme Court will do better after sixty than the judges of the High Court. There is no fundamental difference between the types of work of the Supreme Court and the High Court, nor in the conditions under which the judges work. It may be that a brilliant or sound judge of the High Court who is physically fit has the opportunity to be appointed to the Supreme Court and thereby continue in service until he completes sixty-five years of age. But vacancies on the Supreme Bench are not of frequent occurrence. In comparison with the number of judges who retire every year from the High Courts, possible vacancies in the Supreme Court during the same period are negligible. Fixation of sixty as the retiring age may also prevent the top men in the Bar who have crossed the age of fifty years from accepting appointments as judges of High Courts. These criticisms went home substantially as a result of which the Sixteenth Amendment of the Constitution provided the retiring age to be raised to sixty-two years.

The second criticism was against the restriction on legal practice after retirement. The original provision had imposed a total prohibition on practice. In support of this, it was pointed out that if a judge was allowed to practise after retirement, "during the last years of his tenure there might be a temptation to so behave as to attract practice after retirement".[2] But this argument has no relevance with respect to practise in other High Courts or the Supreme Court. If a person is appointed as a judge of the High Court at the age of say, fifty-five years, the pension that he earns at the time of retirement is a very small amount. Since he is prohibited from practising after retirement and the pension that

1. For example, a judge of the High Court may be away as the Chairman or member of an investigating Committee or a Commission of Enquiry. The Chief Justice of the High Court acts as the Governor of the State, in case of a sudden vacancy in the Governor's office due to death or resignation, until a new Governor is appointed. During such periods the necessity for temporary appointments will arise as one of the permanent judges will be appointed as the Acting Chief Justice.
2. C.A.D. IX, p. 670.

he earns on retirement is very small, he has little inducement to accept an appointment as a judge. Such a situation is a serious hindrance to the recruitment of able and experienced persons as judges of the High Courts. These were the main reasons which compelled the constitutional amendment which permitted retired judges of High Courts to practise before the Supreme Court or other High Courts than the one in which they were judges.

The third criticism was directed against the inadequacy of the salaries of High Court judges. All of them except the Chief Justices, get only Rs. 3,500 per month. This, it was pointed out, was much smaller than the average monthly income of a top-ranking advocate of a High Court. As such, the top men in the legal profession would not be attracted by positions on the Bench, and the choice may have to be from the ranks of mediocrity. There is an element of truth in this criticism, but it fails to keep in view an overall perspective of the conditions in the country. It is true that at present, there are a few hundred lawyers in the country whose average monthly income exceeds the salary of a judge of the High Court. But the legal and judicial talent in the country is not confined to this small number. Moreover, there is no guarantee that a brilliant lawyer will make himself a good or sound judge. Salaries of every category of public officials have to be related to the general economic standards in the country. They should also be comparable to other categories of salaries within the State. One must also take into consideration the dignity, the honour and the prestige of a particular office. Taking all these into consideration, there is hardly any reason to fear that able and talented people will not be available as judges of the High Courts at the prevailing rate of salary and allowances. As K.M. Munshi said in the Constituent Assembly:

> ...ultimately the success of the Court depends upon whether the distinction and prestige of a High Court judge is such as to attract talented people.... If we invest the High Courts with the prestige they enjoy in England. I am sure talent will be drawn to this office whether the pension is meagre or adequate.[1]

The Law Commission has highlighted these and other criticisms with a view to bringing about necessary reforms which will further raise the standard of efficiency of the High Courts as key agencies of the country's administration of justice.[2] The Commission recommended that Article 217 of the Constitution should be amended to provide that a judge of a High Court should be appointed only on the recommendation of the Chief Justice of the High Court and with the concurrence of the Chief Justice of India. Merit should be the only criterion in appointing judges and every effort should be made to eschew political, communal and regional considerations and the influence of the Executive. The practice of appointing the seniormost puisne judge of the court as the Chief Justice is not desirable as the duties of the latter require not only a person of ability and experience but also a competent administrator capable of handling complex matters. An *ad hoc* body presided by the Chief Justice of India should be created to draw up a panel of persons suitable for appointment and the entire country should be treated as one unit for the purpose. The present rules of pension of the judges of the High Court should be revised and the benefits substantially enhanced in order to attract top men from the Bar to accept judgeships. The Commission pointed out that retired Judges resumed practice at the Bar or sought employment due to the inadequacy of the pensions they got at present. Among the other recommendations of the Commission are the raising of the permanent strength of the High

---

1. C.A.D. IX p. 670
2. *Fourteenth Report*, 1959.

Courts in view of the recent increase in their work, increasing the number of working days in a year and the working hours of a day to at least 200 and five respectively and the creation of a Central Ministry of Justice to promote effective coordination between the judicial systems obtaining in the various States and ensure that the High Courts possess adequate and competent personnel.[1]

Jurisdiction

The Constitution does not attempt detailed definitions and classification of the different types of jurisdiction of the High Courts as it has done in the case of the Supreme Court. This is mainly because most of the High Courts at the time of the framing of the Constitution had been functioning with well-defined jurisdictions, whereas the Supreme Court was a newly-created institution necessitating a clear definition of its powers and functions. Moreover, the High Courts were expected to maintain the same position that they originally had as the highest courts in the States even after the inauguration of the Constitution.[2] It was provided, therefore, that the High Courts would retain their existing jurisdiction subject to the provisions of the Constitution and any future law that was to be made by the appropriate Legislature. Further, in future, there would be no restriction as in the past to the exercise of original jurisdiction by the High Courts in matters concerning "revenue or its collection". The High Courts have also been given full powers to make rules to regulate the business before them and such other incidental power as is required in relation to the administration of justice which falls within their jurisdiction.

That the coming into being of the Constitution has not affected the jurisdiction and powers of the High Courts as they existed before 1950 was affirmed by the Supreme Court in one of its decisions in 1953.[3] It was argued before the Court that simultaneously with the repeal of Section 108 of the Government of India Act, 1915, and enactment of its provisions in Section 223 of the Government of India Act 1935, and later on in Article 225 of the Constitution of India, there had not been any corresponding amendment of Clause 15 of the Letters Patent and as such the High Court had no power to make rules regarding the manner in which it could conduct its business. Speaking for a unanimous Court, Justice Mahajan said:

> This objection, in our opinion, is not well-founded as it overlooks the fact that the power that was conferred on the High Court by Section 108 still subsists, and it has not been affected in any manner whatever either by the Government of India Act, 1935, or by the new Constitution. On the other hand, it has been kept alive and re-affirmed with great vigour by .the statutes. The High Courts still enjoy the same unfettered power as they enjoyed under Section 108 of the Act of 1915, of making rules and providing whether an appeal has to be heard by one judge or more judges or by Division Courts consisting of two or more judges of the High Court. It is immaterial by what label or nomenclature that power is described in the different statutes or in the Letters Patent. The power is there and continues to be there and to be exercised in the same manner as it could be exercised when it was originally conferred.

Apart from the normal original and appellate jurisdiction, the Constitution also vests four additional powers in the High Courts. These are: (i) the power to issue writs or orders for the enforcement of the Fundamental Rights or for any other purpose; (ii) the power of

1. *Fourteenth Report*, 1959.
2. C.A.D. IX, p. 671.
3. National Sewing Thread Co. Ltd. *vs.* James Chadwick and Bros., Ltd. 1953, S.C.R. 1028.

superintendence over all Courts in the State: (iii) the power to transfer cases to itself from subordinate Courts concerning the interpretation of the Constitution; and, (iv) the power to appoint officers and servants of the High Court.

Under Article 226, the High Courts have been made the protectors of the Fundamental Rights guaranteed under the Constitution within their respective territorial jurisdictions. We have already seen that under Article 32, the Supreme Court is the ultimate protector of these fundamental rights. But if the protection of fundamental rights was entrusted to the Supreme Court alone, many an aggrieved citizen would have found it impossible to approach the Court for the enforcement of a right of his which has been violated. By giving this power to the High Courts also, these rights have been made more real for the ordinary citizen. In the exercise of this power, the Court may issue the same type of writs, orders or directions which the Supreme Court is empowered to issue under Article 32.

Speaking on the scope of this power of the High Courts, the Supreme Court said:

> The jurisdiction under Article 226 is exercised by the High Court in order to protect and safeguard the rights of the citizens and whenever the High Court finds that any person within its territories is guilty of doing an act which is not authorised by law or is violative of the fundamental rights of the citizens, it exercises that jurisdiction in order to vindicate his rights and redress his grievances and the only conditions of its exercise of that jurisdiction are: (1) the power is to be exercised throughout the territories in relation to which it exercises jurisdiction, that is to say, the writs issued by the Court do not run beyond the territories subject to its jurisdiction: (2) the person or authority to whom the High Court is empowered to issue such writs must be within those territories which clearly implies that they must be amenable to its jurisdiction either by residence or location within territories.[1]

In another case, the Court said:

> Such writs as are referred to in Article 226 are obviously intended to enable the High Court to issue them in grave cases where the subordinate tribunals or bodies or officers act wholly without jurisdiction, or in excess of it, or in violation of the principles of natural justice, or refuse to exercise a jurisdiction vested in them or there is an error apparent on the face of the record, and such act, omission, error or excess has resulted in manifest injustice.[2]

On another occasion[3] the Court held that the remedy provided for in Article 226 is a discretionary remedy and the High Court has always the discretion to refuse to grant any writ if it is satisfied that the aggrieved party can have adequate or suitable relief elsewhere. The Court further said that "the High Courts do not, and should not act as Courts of Appeal under Article 226".[4]

Under Article 227, every High Court has the power of superintendence over all Courts and tribunals except those dealing with the Armed Forces functioning within its territorial jurisdiction. In the exercise of this power the High Court is authorized (i) to call for returns from such courts; (ii) to make and issue general rules and prescribe forms for regulating the practice and proceedings of such Courts; and (iii) to prescribe forms in

1. A.T.K. Kasuliar *vs.* M.V. Potti, A.I.R. 1956, S.C. 256.
2. Veerappa Pillai *vs.* Raman and Raman Ltd. 1952, S.C.R. 583; see also The Bhopal Sugar Industries *vs.* The Income-tax Officer 1961, I S.C.J. 191; S. Jhunjhunwala *vs.* The State of Bombay (1961) II S.C.J. 553 and Burmah Construction Company *vs.* The State of Orissa 1962, II S.C.J. 148.
3. K.S. Rashid *vs.* T.I.I. Commission, A.I.R. 1954, S.C. 207.
4. Sangram Singh vs. Election Tribunal, Kota, 1955, II S.C.R. 1. See also Election Commission *vs.* Venkata Rao 1953, S.C.R. 210.

which books, entries and accounts shall be kept by the officers of any such Courts. Interpreting the scope of this power, the Supreme Court said that all types of tribunals including the Administrative Tribunals operating within a State are subject to the superintendence of the High Court and further, that the "superintendence is both judicial and administrative". While under Article 226 the High Court can only annul the decision of the Tribunals, it can under Article 227 do that and also issue further directions in the matter.[1]

Article 228 vests in the High Courts the power to transfer constitutional cases from lower Courts. According to this, if the Court is satisfied that a case pending in one of its subordinate Courts involves a substantial question of law as to the interpretation of the Constitution, the determination of which is necessary for the disposal of the case, it shall then withdraw the case and may either dispose of the case itself or determine the constitutional question and then send the case back to the Court wherefrom it was withdrawn. By vesting this power in the High Court, the framers of the Constitution have safeguarded against the possible multiplicity of constitutional interpretations at the level of subordinate Courts.[2] As it is, in addition to the Supreme Court every High Court is authorized to interpret the Constitution which means that there are at least eighteen Courts undertaking this interpretation work. Conflicts in interpretation are not unusual or unnatural under such conditions. The Supreme Court does not get an opportunity in every case to resolve such conflicts as there is no provision for automatic revision by the Court. If the lower courts also were invested with the power of, interpreting the Constitution, it would have created an extremely confusing situation. That possibility has been completely eliminated by the provisions under Article 228.

If the High Courts are to function independently they should also have at their disposal adequate staff and the power of controlling the members of that staff. These are ensured under Article 229. According to this, the Chief Justice of the High Court is empowered to appoint officers and servants of the Court. The Governor may in this respect require the Court to consult the Public Service Commission of the State. The Chief Justice is also authorized to regulate the conditions of service of the staff subject to any law made by the State Legislature in this respect. The rules relating to salaries, allowances, leave or pensions require the approval of the Governor. The power of the Chief Justice to appoint any member of the Staff of the High Court also includes his power to dismiss any such member from the service of the Court. Giving this interpretation to Article 229, the Supreme Court said that there could be no argument or doubt about it as "a power of appointment includes the power to suspend or dismiss".[3] The Constitution also provides for charging all the administrative expenses of the High Court on the Consolidated Fund of the State.

We have already noted that, subject to the provisions of the Constitution, the State Legislature is empowered to modify the jurisdiction of the High Court. Thus, for instance, the Legislature may enlarge or restrict the scope of the Court's jurisdiction in civil matters by prescribing a pecuniary limit, as Ambedkar pointed out in the Constituent Assembly. But Parliament alone is empowered to enlarge or restrict the territorial jurisdiction of a particular High Court by extending or excluding such jurisdiction from any Union Territory.

1. Hari Vishnu Kamath vs. Syed Ahmed Ishaque, 1955,1 S.C.R. 1104. See also Waryam Singh *vs*. Amar Nath A.I.R. 1954, S.C. 215. Also see S.L. Hegde *vs*. M.B. Tirumale 1960, S.C.J. 1065.
2. Raja Ganga Partap Singh *vs*. Allahabad Bank Ltd., 1958, S.C.J. 431.
3. Pradyat Kumar *vs*. Chief Justice of the Calcutta High Court, A.I.R. 1956, S.C. 285.

The Legislature of a Union Territory, if it has one, has no power to deal with the jurisdiction of the Court in any manner. Parliament is also empowered to establish common High Courts for two or more States and a Union Territory. Although not much use has been made of this provision except in the case of Assam and other north-eastern States, it is possible for better organization of the judicial system at the level of the High Courts with this provision as and when appropriate conditions present themselves in future.

The following table shows the various High Courts in India, the places where they are located and the number of judges in each High Court.

Table 1. High Courts

Name of the State	*Seat of the High Court*	*Number o/ Judges*
Andhra Pradesh	Hyderabad	26
Assam and other North Eastern States	Guwahati	9
Bihar	Patna	35
Gujarat	Ahmedabad	20
Himachal Pradesh	Simla	5
Jammu & Kashmir	Srinagar	7
Karnataka	Bangalore	24
Kerala	Cochin	25
Madhya Pradesh	Bhopal	29
Maharashtra	Bombay	43
Orissa	Bhubaneswar	10
Punjab & Haryana	Chandigarh	23
Rajasthan	Jaipur	18
Sikkim	Gangtok	2
Tamil Nadu	Madras	25
Uttar Pradesh	Allahabad	60
West Bengal	Calcutta	39
Delhi	Delhi	27

A Constitution, being the basic law, does not usually go into such details as the provisions dealing with the organization and working of subordinate courts. Such subjects are left to be dealt with by the Legislature. The Constitution of India departs from this practice by incorporating detailed provisions concerning even the subordinate judiciary. This is mainly due to certain peculiar conditions which existed in India at the time of the making of the Constitution.

During the British rule, executive and judicial functions were combined in the same officer at the lower levels of the administration in order to suit the convenience of a foreign government. Each Province was divided into a number of districts which were the pivotal units of administration. Each of these districts was headed by an officer called the Collector-Magistrate who combined in his office both executive and judicial functions. The combination of both executive and judicial powers in his office made this officer, more often than not, behave as a dictator. The evils of this system were so far-reaching that it became an instrument of terror during the national movement. There was almost universal condemnation of the system and the demand for the complete separation of the judiciary from the executive was persistent and vociferous. This accounts for the constitution-makers dealing with this problem in detail. As we have seen earlier, one of the Directive Principles is the separation of the judiciary from the executive. They were not satisfied with this alone. They wanted also to see that the judiciary at the lower levels was made completely independent of the executive; they sought to establish a judicial system under which, from the highest court in the land to the lowest, every layer and each unit in every layer functioned in a spirit of judicial independence. The special significance of the powers of superintendence which the High Court exercises over the subordinate judiciary is to be assessed in this context.

The constitutional provisions dealing with the Subordinate Courts, therefore, are intended to secure a two-fold objective. First, to provide for the appointment of District and Subordinate Judges and their qualifications and second, to place the whole of the civil judiciary under the control of the High Court.[1] The importance of these provisions can hardly be exaggerated in the context of the Indian situation. It is the subordinate judiciary that comes into most intimate contact with the ordinary people in the judicial field. Therefore, it is particularly necessary that its independence is placed beyond question in order to infuse public confidence in it.

The Constitution draws a distinction between two categories of Subordinate Courts, namely, the District Courts and others. Judges of the District Courts are appointed by the Governor in consultation with the High Court. Further, a person to be eligible for appointment as a District Judge should be either an advocate or a pleader of seven years' standing,[2] or an officer in the service of the Union or of the State. In the case of every advocate or pleader, the appointment should be on a recommendation by the High Court.

Appointment of persons other than District Judges to the judicial service of a State is made by the Governor in accordance with rules made by him in that behalf after consultation with the High Court and the State Public Service Commission. The practice that exists in most States at present is that the Public Service Commission conducts competitive examinations for the selection of candidates for appointment to the State judicial service. The Commission lays down certain minimum educational and professional qualifications for candidates who intend to compete in these examinations. At least three years' experience as an advocate or a pleader is one of the principal qualifications. The selected candidates are given special training for a certain period before regular appointment to the service, and thereafter they come under the superintendence of the High Court in the discharge of their responsibilities.

In order to bring about better quality and efficiency in the administration of Justice at lower levels, the Law Commission has made a number of suggestions.[3] The Commission recommends that there should be one State judicial service divided into two classes: Class I consisting of district judges or other equivalent posts and Class II comprising two grades of officers, namely, munsifs and subordinate judges. In States where the judiciary has been separated from the executive, the civil and criminal judiciary should be unified and

---

1. Ambedkar, C.A.D. IX, p, 1571.
2. See in this connection Rameshwar Dayal *vs*. The State of Punjab 1961, II S.C.J. 285.
3. *Fourteenth Report,* 1959.

formed into an integrated cadre. Recruitment to the State Judicial Service, Class II, should be made on the result of a competitive examination conducted by the Public Service Commission, with the upper age limit at thirty years and a minimum of three years' practice at the Bar as one of the qualifications. In order to attract to the judiciary capable young graduates, an all-India Judicial Service should be created which should man 40 per cent of the posts in the State Judicial Service, Class I. Officers for this service should be selected by means of an all-India competitive examination and their emoluments should be the same as those of the I.A.S. officers. The remaining sixty per cent of the posts should be filled in by promotion from the State Judicial Service, Class II, and by direct recruitment from the Bar with a minimum requirement of seven years' practice and an upper age limit of forty years. The pay scales of judicial officers should be the same in all States as they do exactly the same work and have precisely the same qualifications. The age of retirement of officers of the subordinate judiciary should be raised to 58 years and they should not be re-employed under government after retirement. Promotions should not be on the basis of mere seniority but on grounds of merit and ability alone.[1]

Article 235 specifies the nature and extent of the High Courts control over the subordinate judiciary. According to that Article, the High Court exercises control over the District Courts and the courts subordinate to them in matters such as posting, promotions, and the granting of leave to all persons belonging to the State Judicial Service. The Governor is empowered to extend the scope of these provisions in order to include different classes of magistrates in the State who do not belong to the regular judicial service.

Except for minor local variations, the structure and functions of the subordinate courts are uniform throughout the country. Each State, for the purpose of judicial administration, is divided into a number of districts, each under the jurisdiction of a District Judge. Under him is a hierarchy of judicial officers exercising varying types of jurisdiction. As a result of the progressive implementation of the principle of the separation of the judiciary from the executive, a subordinate judiciary in most parts of the country is already functioning separately. The Constitutional safeguards are bound to provide for its firm establishment as a truly independent institution as the framers intended it to be.

***

1. Most of these recommendations have already been implemented.

33

UNION TERRITORIES

WHILE DISCUSSING the reorganization of States which took place in 1956, we had occasion to deal with the Part C States and the territories under Part D established under the original Constitution. There were in all ten Part C States. The territories under Part D were Andaman and Nicobar islands. What should be the status of these States and territories under the reorganized set-up was a question which the States Reorganization Commission was called upon to deal with. There were three alternative courses of action possible. First, to recommend the continuance of the Part C States and make them equal in status to the Part A States; second, to allow the *status quo* to continue; and, third, to abolish them as separate entities and merge them with the neighbouring States. The Commission gave adequate consideration to the pros and cons of each of these alternatives. They said:

> Separated from each other by long distances they have greater economic, linguistic and cultural affinities with the neighbouring States than with each other. Politically, economically and educationally, they are in varying phases of development. Even in the constitutional field, they do not follow a uniform pattern in that some of them have legislatures and ministries and others only advisory councils. Two are administered through Lieutenant Governors and the remaining through Chief Commissioners.[1]

Summing up their discussion on these States, the Commission said:

> The position is that there is a general consensus of opinion that the existing set-up of the Part C States is unsatisfactory. The solution suggested by the official representatives of the Part C States, namely, a constitutional status which is identical with that of Part A States will only remove the Constitutional anomalies. These small units will still continue to be economically unbalanced, financially weak, and administratively and politically unstable.
>
> The democratic experiment in these States, wherever it has been tried, has proved to be more costly than was expected or intended and this extra cost has not been justified by increased administrative efficiency or rapid economic and social progress. Quite obviously, these States cannot subsist as separate administrative units without excessive dependence on the Centre, which will lead to all the undesirable consequences of divorcing the responsibility for expenditure from that for finding the resources.
>
> Taking all these factors into consideration, we have come to the conclusion that there is no adequate recompense for all the financial, administrative and constitutional difficulties which the present structure of these States present and that, with the exception of two, to be centrally administered, the merger of the existing Part C States with the adjoining States is the only solution of their problems.[2]

1. *S.R.C. Report*, p. 70.
2. *S.R.C. Report*, pp. 74-5.

The reorganization plan of the Commission envisaged only two categories of units in the Indian Union: (i) 'States[1] forming primary constituent units of the Indian Union having a Constitutional relationship with the Centre on a federal basis. These units were to cover virtually the entire country, (ii) 'Territories' which for vital strategic or other considerations cannot be joined to any of the States and are therefore, centrally administered. This plan was accepted and given effect to in the Seventh Amendment of the Constitution and the States Reorganization Act, 1956. To these were added later the former French and Portuguese colonies which became parts of the Union in the course of the next five years. This is the story of the origin of the Union territories.

But some of the former Union Territories were later given the status of States and were thus elevated to the position of fullfledged members of the Union. This was mainly due to the local public demand which was eventually acknowledged and given effect by the Union Government through appropriate legislation. The former Union Territories which were thus elevated to statehood are Himachal Pradesh, Tripura and Manipur, all of which got the new status in 1971. Arunachal Pradesh and Mizoram became fullfledged States in 1987.

There are in all seven Union Territories.[2] These are :

1. Delhi
2. Andaman and Nicobar Islands
3. The Lakshadweep, Minicoy and Amindivi Islands
5. Dadra and Nagar Haveli
6. Pondicherry
6. Chandigarh
7. Daman and Diu

Of these, Delhi[3] is the federal capital. As such, it could not be made part of a fullfledged constituent unit of the Indian Union. Even under a unitary system of Government, the normal practice is to place national capitals under a special dispensation. London and Paris are perhaps the best examples where there is a greater degree of Central control over the city administration than over other municipalities. Under a federal system there is an additional consideration. Any constitutional division of powers, if it is applicable to a unit functioning in the seat of the national government, is bound to give rise to embarrassing situations. This is why most federal capitals are under the Central Government. Washington D.C., the capital of the United States, and Canberra, the federal capital of the Australian Commonwealth, are two good examples. This does not however stand in the way of giving the federal capital territory a measure of self government. This is the rationale behind Delhi, the federal capital territory of India, which has a legislature and a cabinet responsible to the Legislative Assembly.

Andaman and Nicobar Islands in the Bay of Bengal and the Lakshadweep, Minicoy and Amindivi Islands in the Arabian Sea are groups of islands which form two separate Union Territories. Daman and Diu as well as Dadra and Nagar Haveli are former Portuguese colonies. Similarly, Pondicherry is a former French colony, They have distinct cultures of

---

1. For details regarding these Territories, see the First Schedule of the Constitution of India.
2. Delhi's present official name is National Capital Territory.

their own and as such claimed special status for themselves instead of merging in the neighbouring states. In 1966 when Punjab was reorganized to form two separate States of Punjab and Haryana, Chandigarh, the capital of undivided Punjab, was made a Union Territory where the new States could locate their capitals.

The Constitutional provisions dealing with these Union Territories attempt to set out the basic pattern of administration for them. Its main features are as follows:

(a) The Union territories are to be administered by the President through an administrator to be appointed by him with a suitable designation. Parliament, however, is empowered to make any other provision by law for the administration of any of these territories.

(b)The President may, if he so chooses, appoint the Governor of a State as the administrator of an adjoining Union Territory. In the exercise of his functions as administrator of the Union Territory, the Governor will act independently of his Council of Ministers.

(c) The President may make regulations for the peace, progress and good government of the Union Territories of the Andaman and Nicobar Islands, and the Lakshadweep, Minicoy and Amindivi Islands. Any such regulation made by the President may repeal or amend any existing Act dealing with the administration of these islands and will have the same effect as a Parliamentary enactment.

(d) Parliament is empowered to constitute a High Court for any Union Territory or to declare any existing court there to be a High Court. Such a High Court will have the same functions and powers as any other High Court in India except for such modifications or exceptions as Parliament may provide by law. Until such a High Court is established, those High Courts under whose jurisdiction these territories had remained will continue to exercise such jurisdiction in relation to those territories. Parliament has the power to make any change with respect to this jurisdiction.

Of all the Union Territories, Delhi alone has a separate High Court of its own.

By the Fourteenth Amendment of the Constitution in 1962, Parliament is empowered to create local legislatures or Council of Ministers in the Union Territories. Accordingly legislatures and Council of Ministers have been created in the Union Territories of Pondichery and Delhi.

***

PART VII

THE FEDERAL SYSTEM

34

THE SCHEME OF DIVISION OF POWERS

MOVING THE consideration of the Draft Constitution in the Constituent Assembly, Ambedkar said that the form of the Constitution was federal. "It establishes a dual polity with the Union at the Centre and the States at the periphery, each endowed with sovereign powers to be exercised in the field assigned to them respectively by the Constitution. The Union is not a League of States, united in a loose relationship, nor are the States the agencies of the Union, deriving powers from it. Both the Union and the States are created by the Constitution; both derive their respective authority from the Constitution. The one is not subordinate to the other in its own field; the authority of one is coordinate with that of the other."[1]

Dealing with the criticism of overcentralization in the Constitution, Ambedkar said:

A serious complaint is made on the ground that there is too much centralization and that the States have been reduced to municipalities. It is clear that this view is not only an exaggeration but is also founded on a misunderstanding of what exactly the Constitution contrives to do.

As to the relations between the Centre and States it is necessary to bear in mind the fundamental principle on which it rests. The basic principle of Federalism is that the legislative and executive authority is partitioned between the Centre and the States not by any law to be made by the Centre but by the Constitution itself. This is what the Constitution does. The States are in no way dependent upon the Centre for their legislative or executive authority. The States and the Centre are co-equal in this matter.

It is difficult to see how such a Constitution can be called centralism. It may be that the Constitution assigns to the Centre a larger field for the operation of its legislative and executive authority than is to be found in any other federal constitution. It may be that the residuary powers are given to the Centre and not to the States. But these features do not form the essence of federalism.

The chief mark of federalism lies in the partition of the legislative and executive authority between the Centre and Units by the constitution. This is the principle embodied in our Constitution. There can be no mistake about it. It is therefore wrong to say that the States have been placed under the Centre. The Centre cannot by its own will alter the boundary of this partition. Nor can the judiciary. For as has been well said: 'Courts may modify, they cannot replace. They can revise earlier interpretations as new arguments, new points of view are presented, they can shift the dividing line in marginal cases, but there are barriers they cannot pass, definite assignments of power they cannot re-allocate. They can give a broadening construction of existing powers, but they cannot assign to one authority the powers explicitly granted to another.'[2]

Ambedkar was supported in these views by his colleagues on the Drafting Committee and by others whose opinions carried weight and authority in the deliberations of the

1. C.A.D.VII, p. 33.
2. C.A.D. VII, p. 33.

Assembly. Yet, the controversy continued. A large number of members still thought that the Centre was invested with excessive power and, in the process, the federal principle which was to form the very foundation of the State-system under the Constitution was "brutally butchered". Some of them thought that it was a betrayal on the part of the leaders to go back on the solemn pledges they had made again and again before the achievement of Independence. Representatives of the former Princely States deprecated almost unanimously the manner in which the original idea of establishing fully autonomous units had yielded place to one of an 'overcentralized' Union with weak units.

The controversy did not end even with the adoption of the Constitution. From the floor of the Assembly it spread to a wider arena, among political scientists and constitutional lawyers both within and outside the country. According to some, the Constitution is 'quasi-federal'; it establishes a unitary State with subsidiary federal features rather than a federal State with subsidiary unitary features.[1] Others are of opinion that the unitary features are so strong that the federal framework of the Constitution is nothing but a facade without the substance of federalism in it. To them it is only a pseudo-federation. But there are others who think that the Constitution embodies the federal principle in such substantial measure that it is truly a federal Constitution.[2]

These conflicting opinions arise from the conflicting ideas on federalism that prevail among constitutional theorists. Hence, the question whether the Constitution is federal or not cannot be satisfactorily answered without going into the meaning of federalism and the essential elements that constitute a federal state.

What is federalism ? Is it such a rigid concept that it can be applied to governmental organizations like a mathematical equation ? Such an approach appears to be highly impracticable. Generally speaking, federal schemes seek to combine a measure of unity with a measure of diversity. Usually, the diversity follows a territorial pattern based upon language, culture, race or geography, and unity in the pursuit of common objectives and interests and the cultivation of common traditions; Often, the federal principle is characterized by a tendency to substitute coordinating for subordinating relationships or, at least, to restrict the latter as much as possible; to replace compulsion from above with reciprocity, understanding and adjustment; to supplant commands by persuasion, and force by law. The basic aspect of federalism is pluralistic; its fundamental tendency is harmony and its regulative principle is solidarity.

Until the year 1787 when the United States Constitution was framed, the word federal signified little more than a League of States resting upon the good sense of the parties, formed for a specific purpose and dictated by expediency. It was an improvization for facing some imminent danger that threatened their individual existence. A war or a common enemy was enough to rally a number of small States together into a Union to ward off the danger. But the moment the threatened danger vanished, the Union too dissolved and the old order again set in. No new government was created as a common factor for all the members of the Union with specific powers.

The earliest examples of such loosely-knit leagues of States are found in the history of ancient Greece. They were neither rigid nor permanent. The cities of ancient Greece

1. Wheare, K.C., *Federal Government,* Third edition, p. 28.
2. K. Santhanam, *Union Slate Relations in India*, p. 8.

occasionally joined together in temporary alliance in the face of a common enemy and those Unions had varying degrees of cohesion.[1] The causes that led to the formation of such Leagues in ancient times continued throughout the Middle Ages, resulting in the formation of medieval unions like the Swiss and the German confederations. Although these confederations were somewhat improved forms of the Leagues, they did not establish any federal state in the sense in which we understand the term today.

The emergence of the United States of America in 1787 as a federal state effected a complete change in the conception of federation. It substituted not only a federation for confederation, but an efficient federation for an inefficient federation. The United States established a government based upon a novel principle, the principle of division of powers between the national and state governments, each independent within its sphere. Thus, the word 'federal', which signified little more than a league of States resting upon the good faith of parties up to 1787, came to possess a new meaning, the meaning which we understand today.[2]

If the popular usage of the time had been followed, the United States should have used some word other than 'federal' to describe its constitution. Nevertheless, it was called federal and the government which it established upon this new principle was also called federal. As this government developed, the new principle became firmly established and with the end of the Civil War in 1865, it became an accepted doctrine of the Constitution. Since the U.S. is nowadays regarded as the typical federal government, it is appropriate to confine the use of the term federal to the principle embodied in the Government of the United States under the Constitution of 1787. For, to a large extent, the federal principle has come to mean what it does today because the United States has come to be what it is.

Not that the federal pattern established by the United States is so inflexible that it does not admit of any variations. In fact, the federal system established by its closest neighbour, Canada, has many material points of difference. The first European country which substantially followed the American federal model was Switzerland. Yet, the Swiss did not fully adhere to the federal principles of the United States. The closest follower of the U.S. in this respect was perhaps the Commonwealth of Australia; but even that country did not ignore the distinctive features of the federal governments in Canada and Switzerland.[3]

During the last sixty years, the federal principle has been made use of in almost every part of the world with innumerable variations in form.[4] Today, federalism is no more a constitutional experiment; it has fully established its lasting influence as a distinct form of government. Its remarkable achievements as a unifying force, under widely differing conditions, make political thinkers and Constitution-makers look upon it as a possible device for the solution of many complicated political problems. Such has been the success of the federal principle in solving multi-national and multi-lingual problems that the peace-makers of Versailles turned to it for resolving world conflicts and ensuring lasting peace. The League of Nations could not achieve any success because it could not apply the federal

---

1. Freeman, *History of Federal Government*, Vol. I, p. 127.
2. Morison, *History of the U.S.A.*, Vol. I, p. 87.
3. For example, compare the Senate of the United States with that of the Australian Commonwealth and see the striking contrast in the powers of the two.
4. For a detailed and theoretical discussion of different types of federations, see Wheare, K.C., *Federal Government*, third edition, Chapters I and 2.

principle successfully. When the Second World War ended, a war-torn humanity again turned to federalism. The United Nations, with an embryonic World Parliament in its General Assembly, has not been able to employ the federal principle in any spectacularly different manner from that of the League. And yet, it is a better mechanism of federalism than the one made use of by the League of Nations.

What is significant is not the achievement but the movement in itself. Federalism is like any other idea in government, and the correct approach to it should be empirical; the search for its beneficial results is more important than any insistence on rigidity in its form. Hence, theoretical definitions[1] of federalism which ignore the historical evolution of federalism and its potentialities as a dynamic idea for future experimentation are of little value.

True, the federal principle is no more the vague idea that it was two centuries ago. Federal compacts are easily distinguishable from confederations or leagues. Similarly, the differences between a federal and a unitary State are also ascertainable with reasonable accuracy. Yet, to adhere to rigid definitions and to characterize federalism as an inflexible pattern is to miss its purpose. In its application to concrete political problems, federalism becomes a relative and dynamic principle. It may vary its form to suit particular situations. One may distinguish between a centrifugal and a centripetal federalism. The federalist tendencies of Continental Europe in the nineteenth and twentieth centuries were mainly centrifugal—a reaction against the unitarism which was built up in France during the monarchy and put into practice by the Jacobins and Napoleon.

With the rapid spread of nationalist ideas during the last half century, the principle of federalism acquired a new and even peculiar significance. Linguistic, racial and cultural differences replaced, to a great extent, differences in religion and custom as factors endangering civic equality. Federalism could be applied within a State, where such differences existed, so as to organize regional groups on a new basis by which regional autonomy could be achieved without sacrificing national unity. This new basis limited on every side the action of a Central government and split up the strength of the State among coordinate and independent authorities. Dicey was one of the first writers on constitutional government to recognize not only the distinguishing features of federalism but even to acknowledge its obvious advantages over a highly centralized unitary system as obtained in Great Britain.[2] Gradually, the federal principle became the unifying force of multilingual and multi-national States. Centrifugal and centripetal forces found an ideal compromise in the larger interest of vast areas and large populations,

Thus, federalism in the modern age is a principle of reconciliation between two divergent tendencies, the widening range of common interests and the need for local autonomy. This is why Lord Acton said:

> Of all checks on democracy, federalism has been the most efficacious and the most congenial. The federal system limits and restrains the sovereign power by dividing it, and by assigning to the government only certain defined rights.[3]

The reconciliation that is established in a State between the individual self-sufficiency

---

1. As for example, see the definition of Wheare, *op. cil.*, p. 4. See also the definition of Sir Robert Garren quoted in Report of the Royal Commission on the Australian Constitution at p. 230.
2. See A.V. Dicey, Law of the Constitution, Chapter III.
3. Acton, Essays on Freedom and Power, p. 163.

of the citizen and his allegiance to the State is, in a measure, federal in essence.[1] Modern forms of federations arose either out of the imperfections or limitations of the large, unitary democracy or the defence and economic necessities of the small individual State. What is needed is neither complete independence nor total dependence but an interdependence that creates harmony, orderly progress and prosperity. It looks almost contradictory in appearance but it is the essence of federalism; and only federalism can provide such an effect. Unity while allowing for diversity and oneness while providing for division are the outstanding characteristics of modern federalism. It finds an institutional means whereby the solution of conflicts between social interests could be provided for. The means remain the same in different parts of the world, however much they vary in detail to suit environment and circumstances.

When federalism is viewed in a broad sense as discussed in the foregoing analysis, there is hardly any possibility for a controversy on the federal character of the Constitution. This will become clear as we progress with the analysis of the federal provisions of the Constitution.

Legislative Relations Between the Union and the States

A common feature of many federal constitutions which follow the U.S. federal model is to enumerate a list of legislative powers and assign them to the Union and leave the residue to the States. The Canadian Constitution, on the other hand, follows a different System according to which there are two lists of legislative powers, one for the Centre and the other for the Provinces and the residue is vested in the Centre. The Constitution of India follows a system similar to the Canadian, but with more elaborate lists which include an additional one called the Concurrent List. In drawing up an elaborate Concurrent List, the framers followed the Australian pattern of federal division of powers. Under the Australian Constitution, concurrent subjects are 39.[2] Under the Draft Constitution they were 37. (In the final form of the Constitution the number increased to 47). The scheme is almost the same as in the Government of India Act of 1935.[3]

In place of the existing system, Alladi Krishnaswami Aiyar had proposed a simpler and more logical scheme of division of powers between the Union and the States. According to this, there would be only two Lists, an exclusive State List and a Concurrent List with federal supremacy. The rest of the powers would be vested exclusively in the Union. Further, there was to be a provision for the supremacy of Union law over State law if there was a conflict between the two even with respect to items included in the State list. Alladi contended that such a scheme of division was more logical in the context of and in keeping with the change in the pattern of federalism. Federalism, according to him, had already become a Centre-dominated system. The residuary power being with the Centre, three lists were unnecessary. The simpler scheme he suggested would eliminate almost completely the possibility for litigation under the current pattern of division of powers.[4]

1. According to Harold Laski. "....since society is essentially federal in nature, the body which seeks to impose the necessary unity must be so built that the diversities have a place therein." See *A Grammar of Politics*, Chapter VII.
2. Ambedkar, C.A.D. VII, p. 37.
3. The main difference between the two is that under the Act of 1935, the residuary powers were vested in the Governor-General.
4. C.A.D.VII!, p.795.

In spite of the advantages claimed for it, Alladi's scheme was not accepted by his colleagues on the Drafting Committee. They did not contest the obvious advantages of the Alladi scheme. In fact, most of them conceded and even openly acknowledged them. But they argued that it did not aim at any change in the substance of the existing scheme but only in its form. There was a distinct advantage in the existing system, namely, that it was familiar to all in the country. Since 1937, under the Government of India Act of 1935 the Centre and the Provinces had been operating on the basis of such a scheme. The Federal Court and the High Courts had given a number of decisions interpreting the scope of different legislative items under the scheme. Hence, there was no necessity to introduce a new system unless there were compelling reasons for it.

The scheme established by the Constitution, as pointed out earlier, consists of three Lists, the Union List, the State List and the Concurrent List.[1] The Union List which consists of ninety-seven items is the longest of the three.[2] It includes items such as defence, armed forces, arms and ammunition, atomic energy, foreign affairs, diplomatic representation, United Nations, treaties, war and peace, citizenship, extradition, railways, shipping and navigation, airways, posts and telegraphs, telephones, wireless and broadcasting, currency, coinage and legal tender, foreign loans, the Reserve Bank of India, foreign trade, interstate trade and commerce incorporation and its regulations, banking, bills of exchange, insurance, stock exchange, patents, establishment of standards in weights and measures, control of industries, regulation and development of mines, minerals and oil resources, maintenance of national museums, libraries and such other institutions, historical monuments, the Survey of India, Census, Union Public Services, elections, parliamentary privileges, audit of Government Accounts, constitution and organization of the Supreme Court, High Courts and the Union Public Service Commission, income-tax, customs duties and export duties, duties of excise, corporation tax, taxes on capital value of assets, estate duty, terminal taxes, taxes on the sale or purchase of newspapers, *etc., which are of common interest to the Union and with respect to which uniformity of legislation throughout the Union is essential.* As such, Parliament has exclusive power of legislation with regard to the items mentioned in this List.

The State List consists of sixty-six items.[3] *The selection of these items made on the basis of local interest and it envisages the possibility of diversity of treatment with respect to different items in the different States of the Union.* The scope of the application of the federal principle in India is to be determined by the scope of State legislation arising out of items included in this List. Some of the more important of these items are as follows: public order; police; administration of justice; prisons and reformatories; local government; public health and sanitation; prohibition; burials and burial grounds; education; libraries and museums controlled by the State; intra-state communications; agriculture; animal husbandry; water supplies and irrigation; land rights; forests; fisheries; trade and commerce within the State; gas and gas-works; markets and fairs; moneylending; theatres; betting and gambling; local elections; legislative privileges; salaries and allowances of all State officials; State public services and the State Public Service Commission: treasure trove;

1. The three Lists are embodied in the Seventh Schedule of the Constitution.
2. As originally provided there were only ninety-seven items in the List. The Sixth Amendment of the Constitution added one more item to the List. The Forty-second Amendment added one and deleted another.
3. As originally provided there were only sixty-six items. The Seventh Amendment and the Forty-second Amendment removed five items from the original List thereby reducing it to sixty-one.

land revenue; taxes on agricultural income; taxes on lands and buildings; estate duty and succession duty on agricultural land; duties of excise on alcoholic liquors, opium, *etc.* produced within the State; taxes on the entry of goods into a local area; taxes on electricity (its sale and consumption); taxes on the sale and purchase of goods other than papers; taxes on advertisements except those in newspapers: taxes on goods and passengers carried by road or inland waterways; taxes on vehicles; taxes on animals and boats; tolls; taxes on professions, trades and callings; capitation taxes; taxes on luxuries; *etc.* The State Legislature has the exclusive power of legislation with regard to every one of the items included in the State List.

The Concurrent List consists of fifty-two items.[1] *These are items with respect to which uniformity of legislation throughout the Union is desirable but not essential.* As such, they are placed under the jurisdiction of both ' the Union and the States. The List includes items such as detention for reasons connected with the security of the State; marriage and divorce; education, transfer of property other than agricultural land, contracts; bankruptcy and insolvency; trust and trustees; civil procedure; contempt of court; vagrancy; lunacy and mental deficiency; adulteration of food stuffs; drugs and poisons; economic and social planning; commercial and industrial monopolies; trade unions, social security; labour welfare; legal, medical and other professions; vital statistics; trade and commerce in a number of items; price control; factories; electricity; newspapers, books and printing presses; stamp duties, etc. The Parliament of India and the State Legislatures have concurrent power of legislation over the items included in this List. So long as Parliament does not pass a law on any of these items, the States may pass any law they like on these items. But once Parliament does enact a law on such items, parliamentary law shall prevail over any State law in this regard. There is, however, one exception to this general rule. According to this, a later law of the State Legislature on any item in the Concurrent List shall prevail over an earlier law of Parliament on the same subject, if the State law was reserved for the consideration of the President and received his assent. This is a novel and original feature which enables a State to pass a more advanced piece of legislation than an existing parliamentary law, or to provide through a new law with the consent of the Union for any special conditions and circumstances which prevail in a State.

The idea of a Concurrent List was borrowed from the Government of India Act of 1935. The coordinating and unifying power which is given to Parliament over the subjects included in the Concurrent List is specially valuable to a country of India's size and complexity. The Joint Parliamentary Committee of 1934 expected :

> .....to secure uniformity in the main principles of law throughout the country, in others to guide and encourage provincial effort, and in others again to provide remedies for mischiefs arising in the provincial sphere but extending or liable to extend beyond the boundaries of a single Province. Instances of the first are provided by the subject matter of the great Indian Codes, second by such matters as labour legislation, and of the third by legislation for the prevention and control of epidemic disease. It would in our view be disastrous if the uniformity of law which the Indian Codes provide were destroyed or whittled away by the uncoordinated action of Provincial Legislatures.[2]

In framing the three elaborate legislative lists and demarcating the respective areas of competence for the Union and the States, it is clear that the fathers of the Constitution

1. As originally provided the Concurrent List consisted of only 47 items. By successive Amendments (Third and Forty-second), five more items were added.
2. *Report of Joint Committee on Indian Constitutional Reform*, 1934, Vol. I, p. 31.

had in mind three main considerations: first, to ensure the autonomy of the States as well as their initiative; second, to vest the necessary power in Parliament to intervene as and when required in the interest of the maintenance of national unity; and, third, to secure flexibility in working and promoting joint consultation and action between the Union and States in essential fields of activity.

In view of the detailed and comprehensive enumeration of subjects in the three lists, the scope for residuary legislative power under the Constitution of India is indeed very limited. Yet the possibility of the "residue of legislative power unallocated" cannot altogether be ruled out and hence Article 248 confides such exclusive power to the Union parliament. In this respect India follows the well-known example of the Canadian Constitution (Section 91). Speaking about the rationale of 'residuary powers', the Joint Committee on Indian Constitutional Reform observed:

> It would ...... be beyond the skill of any draftsman to guarantee that no potential subject of legislation, unknown and unsuspected at the present time, may not hereafter arise; and therefore, however carefully the lists are drawn, a residue of subjects must remain, however small it may be....[1]

This power includes the power of making laws imposing any taxes not mentioned in either of the State or Concurrent Lists. Parliament is also empowered to establish additional Courts for the better administration of laws made by it on any matter included in the Union List. Besides, Parliament has the exclusive power of legislation to give effect to any treaty, agreement or convention with any other country or international body.

Although the States have the exclusive power of legislation over every item in the State List, there are two exceptions to this general rule.

1. *Under Article 249*

If the Council of States declares by a resolution supported by two-thirds of the members present and voting that it is necessary or expedient in the national interest that Parliament should make laws with respect to any matter enumerated in the State List, then Parliament is competent to make laws on that matter for the whole or any part of India. Such a resolution remains valid for a year. If, however, the situation under which the resolution was passed continues to exist even at the end of the one year period, another resolution to the same effect may be passed. In the absence of such a resolution, the Parliamentary law passed in this connection will automatically cease to be in force within six months after the end of the year.[2]

Although the power vested in Parliament under this article is an exceptional one and only for a limited period and that too in the national interest, it was vehemently opposed by some members in the Constituent Assembly[3] on the ground that "it enables the Centre to go beyond the scope of the division of powers. It has great potentiality for mischief, to interfere with the autonomy of the States". It was further pointed out that Article 252 which empowers Parliament to take the initiative at the instance of two or more States would be enough to cover such contingencies. T.T. Krishnamachari countered these arguments by saying that Article 252 was

1. *Report of Joint Committee on Indian Constitutional Reform,* 1934, Vol. 1, p. 32.
2. The significance of the power to pass this resolution being vested in the Council of States has been discussed earlier.
3. C.A.D.VIII, p. 800.

.....premised on voluntary cooperation of two or more States—a process not easily given shape at any rate at the instance of the Centre—and as such, there can be no guarantee that speedy action when required can be taken. The legislation for one year at a time also is important. For, it gives the States an opportunity to review the legislation, its scope and its operation and if thought in that light unnecessary, they can instruct their representatives in the Council not to extend its life. Hence, the time limit is a real safeguard against unnecessary extension of the Central power.[1]

A year is a short period. The Centre will not easily succumb to the temptation of augmenting its power for just a year, considering the effort that is required for accomplishing it. Again, to pass such a resolution a simple majority of the Council is not enough. These measures are adequate safeguards against any attempt on the part of the Centre to extend its power without grave justification.

2. *Under Article 250*

Parliament is empowered to make laws on any item included in the State List for the whole or any part of India while a Proclamation of Emergency is in operation. The maximum period for which such a law can be in force is the period for which the Emergency lasts and six months beyond that period.

In addition to the two occasions when the Union, on its own initiative, extends its legislative power to embrace that of the States, there could be a third occasion when action on the part of two or more States will enable Parliament to make laws on any item included in the State List. Article 252 deals with this contingency. According to this article, if the Legislatures of two or more States pass resolutions to the effect that it is desirable to have a parliamentary law regulating any of the matters included in the State List, it is lawful then for Parliament to make laws regulating that matter. Such laws can be extended to any other State as and when the Legislature of the State passes a resolution to that effect. If any such law is to be amended or repealed, it can be done by Parliament alone but the initiative rests with the States. The merit of this provision is that parliamentary action is the result of the initiative taken by the States in a matter in which they have a common interest but are unable to act individually because the suggested legislation goes beyond their respective territorial jurisdictions. Further, the States will retain the same initiative to amend or repeal such Parliamentary law when it no longer serves the purpose for which it was originally passed or its need has ceased to exist.

A comparison with other federal constitutions will show, first of all, that none of them has attempted such a detailed division of legislative powers between the Union and the States. In the Indian Constitution, the subjects have been formulated precisely so as to lead to a minimum of controversy and litigation. If the framers, for the sake of brevity, had dealt with this subject in such general terms as in the United States Constitution, it would have led to an enormous amount of litigation. The litigation that centers on the Commerce Clause of the U.S. Constitution is sufficient to indicate the vast scope of judicial interpretation and the dependence on such interpretation whenever the Centre or the States wish to take any particular action that they consider as falling within their respective fields.

The provision for a Concurrent List consisting of a fairly large number of items has two advantages. First, it affords an opportunity to States which are forward-looking to go ahead and pass appropriate legislation on any item included in the List. This is likely to be emulated by other States in course of time in which case the matter becomes one of national

1. C.A.D. VIII., p. 802.

importance and Parliament can step in and pass a uniform law in the field. Second, in spite of the fact that there exists a Central law on a subject included in the List, special provisions can be made because of special circumstances prevailing in a State. The Concurrent List thus is like a twilight zone as it were, for both the Union and the States are competent to legislate in this field without coming into conflict. The possibility of mutual encroachment between the Union and the States is reduced to a minimum by including in the Concurrent List all those matters over which conflicts of jurisdiction are most likely to arise. While the State List is based upon local interests and the Union List on national interests, the Concurrent List includes matters which have varying degrees of local and national interests. If these matters had figured in either the State List or the Union List, conflicts would have arisen. As it is, the Concurrent List is like a shock-absorber which enables both the Union and the States to go beyond their own exclusive legislative spheres, as necessity arises, to meet exigencies without transgressing the boundaries of each other. This has already been demonstrated during the five decades of the working of the Constitution.

The experience of the United States, Canada and Australia was taken note of in adopting the type of division of powers attempted in the Indian Constitution. Among federations, the largest amount of litigation centering on the division of legislative power between the federation and the units arose in the United States. One of the reasons for this was the enumeration of the federal powers alone in the Constitution.[1] In addition to this, The Tenth Amendment specifically vests in the States or the people the powers not delegated to the Union or prohibited to the States. Interpreting the scope of the residuary powers of the States, the United States Supreme Court said that they include "the right to pass laws, to give effect to law through executive action, to administer justice through the Courts and to employ all necessary agencies for the legitimate purposes of State governments."[2]

In theory, it would appear that the federal powers in the United States are severely restricted to the limited number enumerated in the Constitution. But this is not so in actual practice. Ever since the inauguration of the Constitution, the federal power has been gradually on the increase, although it has had occasional rebuffs. In fact, during the twentieth century and particularly during the last five decades, the federal power in the United States has extended itself like the tentacles of an octopus, embracing almost every field of State activity. This growth largely induced by national emergencies, was facilitated by the constitutional interpretations of the Supreme Court. The Court devised a number of doctrines in this connection. The most prominent of these are the doctrines of (i) implied powers, (ii) immunity of instrumentalities, and (iii) implied prohibition. Chief Justice Marshall initiated the process with his celebrated decision in McCulloch vs. Maryland,[3] the spirit of which reverberated through more than a century culminating in some of the New Deal decisions,[4] recognizing Congressional power to enact social security measures under the power to tax and to provide for the general welfare. In the case of the United States *vs.* S.F. Underwriters' Association[5] the Court reversed its seventy-five year old precedent of excluding insurance from federal control, another instance of the recognition of national requirements. The alleged ground was again the Commerce Clause, which was construed as a positive power. The Court said:

1. Article 1, Section 8.
2. President, Directors and Co. of Veazie Bank *vs*. Feremiah Fenno. 8 Wall. 533; 19 Law ed. 482.
3. 4 Law, ed. 579.
4. For example, Steward Machine Co. *vs*. Davis, 301 U.S. 548.
5. 322, U.S., 533.

It is the power to legislate concerning transactions which reaching across Slate boundaries affect the people of more Sates than one..... This federal power to determine the rules of intercourse across State lines was essential to weld a loose confederacy into a single indivisible Nation.

The march of events from 1787 to 1954 has reversed the old rule of the American federal system that "government by the Centre was the exception and government by the States was the rule."

The Supreme Court of the United States through its decisions has ingeniously removed the multitude of restrictions upon national power. Today the national authority has become a question of governmental policy and has substantially ceased to be one of constitutional law. But the process has been slow and at times painful, leaving behind an enormous amount of litigation.

Under the Canadian Constitution there was no need to adopt the doctrine of implied powers to further the national interest. There, the constitution had itself provided for it by adopting two lists, a federal legislative list and a State List and vesting the residuary powers in the Union. When the Australians adopted their federal constitution, they adopted a new device to avoid the federal-state conflicts regarding division of powers. They made a list of concurrent powers—subjects over which both the States and the federation have authority to legislate. India synthesized the principles of both Canada and Australia and adopted three long lists, Union, State and Concurrent, with a special provision that residuary powers would rest with the Union. Thus, the need of applying the doctrine of implied powers has been completely eliminated. This is the most meritorious aspect of the division of powers under Indian federalism. The question came up for discussion in the Supreme Court soon after the inauguration of the Constitution. In R.K. Ramnath *vs.* Kamptee Municipality.[1] petitioner Ramnath challenged the validity of a municipal tax in the form of octroi duty on tobacco as such duty conflicted with the Central Excises and Salt Duty Act of 1944 by which the Central Government levied a duty on tobacco. He contended that the octroi duty which was levied on his tobacco by the Municipality was already covered by the Central excise duty which he had paid. In other words, his tobacco was not subject to both the Central excise duty and the municipal octroi duty. The tobacco was being taken to the municipal limits for the manufacture of *bidis* which were not sold within the municipal limits but outside.

In a unanimous decision of the Court, Chief Justice Kania rejected this contention.

....It is natural enough, when considering the ambit of an express power in relation to an unspecified residuary power, to give a broad interpretation to the former at the expense of the latter. The case however is different where, as in the Constitution Act, there are two complementary powers each expressed in precise and definite terms. There can be no reason in such a case for giving a broad interpretation to one power rather than to the other; and there is certainly no reason for extending the meaning of the expression duties of excise at the expense of the provincial power to levy taxes on the sale of goods.

This decision clearly illustrates the refusal of the Supreme Court of India to apply the doctrine of implied powers to give strength to the federal power at the expense of the State power.

Speaking on the nature of the division of powers in Australia, Justice Stark said in South Australia *vs.* the Commonwealth:

The Government of Australia is a dual system based on the separation of organs and powers.

1. A.I.R., 1950, S.C.ll.

The maintenance of the States and their powers is as much the object of the Constitution as the maintenance of the Commonwealth and its powers. Therefore, it is beyond the power of either to abolish or destroy the other.[1]

The Australian Constitution gives the Commonwealth Parliament directly the power of incidental legislation under Section 51. Despite the wide power given to the States in Australia, the original rigidity of the federal power has been relaxed by judicial interpretation, always resulting in the all-round recognition of federal powers.[2] In the Uniform Tax case,[3] it was held that though the Commonwealth cannot directly prohibit the States from exercising their constitutional functions, it can indirectly exclude the States from a field of taxation under the grants power. This was a result of war emergency conditions. The defence of the country was the responsibility of the Centre and in order that its finances be strong, federal control of taxation was necessary.

The makers of the Indian Constitution were eager to avoid the long, winding way along which federal power had advanced slowly and painfully in the older federations. If India, struggling for political unity and economic stability, were to depend on judicial intervention for the enhancement of national powers, no one could say how successful she would have been in realizing these objectives. In all probability, she might have failed in both. The Constitution had to provide for any contingency that might arise in future. In short, the special virtue of the division of powers under the federal system established by the Constitution is its unique combination of rigidity and flexibility, which provides for adaptability to suit the needs of the political and economic situation in the country.

The entire scheme of the distribution of legislative powers undoubtedly displays a strong tendency towards a high degree of centralization. This has been praised by some as the product of realism and a genuine understanding of the general tendency towards centralization in all federations whatever be the nature of the division of powers in them as shown by the original, written provisions. At the same time, others have denounced it as a deviation from a strictly federal pattern and an attempt to embody unitarism in a federal form. Here we may recall our earlier discussion on the meaning of federalism and point out that there is no strictly rigid federal system set as a pattern for all to copy, nor any sanctity attached to any particular form of federation. Federal government is not always and everywhere good government. It is not an end in itself, but a means for ensuring good government. Nevertheless, there are critics who point out that in a vast country like India, the danger of excessive centralization which may lead to "apoplexy at the Centre and anaemia at the circumference" cannot altogether be ruled out in practice.

The Union Government, by virtue of its position, is called upon to coordinate the activities of the various State Governments in the interests of uniformity without which there is the risk of fissiparous tendencies growing unchecked.

This has been stated in unmistakable terms by the Union Powers Committee of the Constituent Assembly in the following manner:

> Now that partition [between India and Pakistan] is a settled fact, we are unanimously of the view that it would be injurious to the interests of the country to provide for a weak Central authority which would be incapable of ensuring peace, of coordinating vital matters of common concern and

1. 65, C.L.R. 373.
2. Australian Railway Union *vs.* Victoria Railway Commissioners, 44, C.L.R. 319.
3. South Australia vs. Commonwealth 65, C.L.R. 373.

of speaking effectively for the whole country in the international sphere. At the same time, we are quite clear in our minds that there are many matters in which authority must be solely with the Units and that to frame a Constitution on the basis of a unitary State would be a retrograde step, both politically and administratively. We have accordingly come to the conclusion—a conclusion which was also reached by the Union Constitution Committee—that the soundest framework for our Constitution is a Federation, with a strong Centre.[1]

Moreover, the trend towards centralization is not peculiar to India. War, economic depression, the growth of social services, the mechanical revolution in transport and industry, planning, the receipt by the States of financial assistance from the Union and judicial interpretation, all these have promoted the increase of federal power in the United States, Canada, Australia and Switzerland.[2] As pointed out by an Indian critic of the Constitution:

> What, notwithstanding the fiercely avowed intentions and policies of the founders of the American Constitution, has taken place in the United States, and what local and provincial antagonisms have been unable to prevent in Canada and Australia, has now been statutorily formulated in India.[3]

Nevertheless, a careful reading of the sixty-six items over which the States have exclusive jurisdiction along with the powder they enjoy in the Concurrent field should make it clear that the States are not reduced to a position of insignificance in the scheme of division of powers. On the contrary, they have at their disposal substantial powers covering a large area which enable them, if they so choose, to function as effective agencies of the sovereign power which they share with the Union. Take, for instance, items like public health, agriculture and fisheries which are placed within the jurisdiction of the States. Considering the importance of these items from a national point of view, one could even doubt the wisdom of leaving them in the State List. As a keen observer of the working of the administrative system has pointed out:

> Epidemics respect no State boundaries, and for other reasons look national health is increasingly a national problem. Neither agriculture nor fisheries has greater local significance than national if as much. In a nation dedicated to the Welfare State ideal, the food supply and the welfare of farm families are inescapably national responsibilities. Almost all economic activities are carried on in localities but this fact does not make their significance local. The Constitutional effort to specify scopes of national and state powers so precisely would appear to raise the most serious barriers before national needs to develop and execute national programmes in the interest of national economy and the national public.[4]

The crucial question, however, is whether all these matters can be satisfactorily dealt with in time by a central government whose decision-making centres are often far-removed and distant. India is not a small country. It has a population of over 1000 million. Some of its States are much larger than most countries of the world. The degree of development varies from State to State and region to region. In this context, the question is often asked whether the Union Government, during the last three decades and more, has acquired powers which it cannot usefully discharge or powers which ought to belong to the States.

---

1. C.A.D. VIII. p. 60.
2. See *e.g.*, Leonard D. White, *The States and the Nation,* 1953; Dawson, R.N., *The Government of Canada,* 1960; Miller, J.D.B., *Australian Government and Politics,* 1959, and Rappard, W.E,, *The Government of Switzerland,* 1936.
3. Ramaswami Iyer, C.P., *U.P.Sc.,* Vol. XI (1950).
4. Paul H. Appleby. *Public Administration in India: Report of a Survey,* p. 17.

If the answer to this question is in the positive, then it is time to consider how some of these powers can be transferred to the States so that the distortions that have crept into the Constitutional system can be remedied and a better balanced federal system could be established.

According to the Administrative Reforms Commission, with the undertaking of economic and social planning, a subject included in the Concurrent List, the Centre has taken an active role in the formulation and the over-seeing of the execution of plan programmes in fields which also include subjects which fall in the State List. The role of the Central agencies which had, prior to the advent of planning, been to function as observers, coordinators and advisers, has expanded greatly and tended to overstep its legitimate jurisdiction. The Commission's report was submitted in 1969. Much has happened since then to further augment the powers of the Centre instead of any attempt to reverse the trend. Hence the time is ripe to give serious consideration for a review of Union-State relations. In this connection the appointment of the Sarkaria Commission[1] by the Union Government in 1983 to make a comprehensive review of the relationship between the Union and the States was a step in the right direction. Although the Commission has made many recommendations of far-reaching significance hardly anyone of them has been implemented so far (2000).

***

1. Justice R. S. Sarkaria was appointed Chairman of the Commission.

35

ADMINISTRATIVE RELATIONS BETWEEN THE UNION AND THE STATES

ONE OF the most difficult problems under a federal system is the adjustment of administrative relations between the Union and the States. In the absence of clear provisions in the Constitution, considerable difficulty is often experienced by the Union and the States in the discharge of their responsibilities. The framers of the Indian Constitution therefore decided to include detailed provisions so as to avoid clashes between the Union and the States in the administrative field. Here again, the pattern that is adopted is based mainly on that which was established under the Government of India Act of 1935.

According to Article 256, the executive power of every State is to be exercised in such a way as to ensure compliance with the laws made by Parliament. Further, the Union Executive is empowered to give such directions to a State as may appear to the Government of India to be necessary for the purpose. The idea of the Union giving directions to the States is foreign to most federations. It is looked upon with suspicion and distrust in the United States. In Australia too, the position is more or less the same. Section 61 of the Australian Constitution provides that "the Executive power of the Commonwealth extends to the execution and maintenance of the Constitution and the laws of the Commonwealth". Yet, in the process of execution, the Commonwealth Government has had to face interferences from the States. The High Court of Australia had to intervene by declaring such interferences invalid.

Explaining the object of Article 256, Ambedkar said that it envisaged two propositions:

> The first proposition is that generally the authority to execute laws which relate to what is called the Concurrent field, whether the law is passed by the Central Legislature or it is passed by the State Legislature, shall ordinarily apply to the State. The second proposition it lays down is that if in any particular case Parliament thinks that in passing a law which relates to the Concurrent field, the execution ought to be retained by the Central Government, Parliament shall have the power to do so.[1]

Ambedkar also said that if the Centre did not have such power, it would become impossible to secure the proper execution of the laws which Parliament was obliged to enact. Take, for instance, laws such as the untouchability abolition law, factory legislation, and child marriage abolition law.

Is it desirable that these legislations of the Central Government be mere paper legislations

1. C.A.D.VII, p. 1136.

with no effect given to them ? Is it logical, is it fair, that the Centre on which responsibility has been cast by the Constitution in the matter of untouchability should merely pass a law and sit with folded hands waiting and watching as to what the State Governments are doing in the matter of executing all these particular laws? Should it allow the States the liberty to do what they liked with the legislation made by Parliament with such intensity of feeling and such keen desire of putting it into effect ? Should not the Centre which enacts a law of this character have the authority to execute it ? How can effect be given to them unless the Centre has got the same authority to make good the administration of the laws which it makes ? I think it is a crying situation which ought to be rectified, which the provision seeks to do.[1]

Not satisfied with the general power of the Union to give directions to the States, the Constitution goes a step further and calls upon every State (under Article 257) not to impede or prejudice the executive power of the Union in the State. If any Union agency finds it difficult to function within a State, the Union Executive is empowered to issue appropriate directions to the State Government to remove all obstacles. The Union's power of giving directions in this regard includes certain specific matters such as (i) the construction and maintenance of means of communication which are of national or military importance, and (ii) the protection of railways within the State. This power of giving directions does not in any way affect the power of Parliament to declare highways or waterways or the power of the Union to construct and maintain means of communication as part of its functions with respect to naval, military or air force works.

The Draft Constitution had not provided for the Union giving directions to the States with respect to the protection of railways. Introducing this provision in the form of an amendment. Ambedkar said:

All police, first of all, are in the List II (State List). Consequently, the protection of railway property also is within the field of State Governments. It was felt that in particular cases, the Centre might desire that the property of the Railway should be protected by taking special measures by the Slate and for the purpose the Centre now seeks to be endowed with power to give directions in that behalf.[2]

It is possible that by-reason of the special directions given by the Centre some extra cost above normal may be incurred by the States in the performance of the service. The Constitution provides for compensating the States for the extra expenditure they incur on account of undertaking such tasks. Under this provision, the Union is obliged to come to an agreement with the States about the amount that is to be paid. If, however, the parties fail to reach an agreement, the matter will be referred to an arbitrator appointed by the Chief Justice of India. Such an arbitrator will decide the extra costs incurred which the Union should make good to the State concerned.

The Constitution also empowers the Union Executive, with the consent of the Government of a State, to entrust to that Government or its officers functions which fall within the scope of the Union's executive functions. Parliament is also empowered, in a similar manner, to confer powers or impose duties on State officers through any of its laws which has application in a State. The Union Government will pay to the State the cost involved in the discharge of such functions by the State or its officers. Here again, if any dispute arises, it will be settled by an arbitrator appointed by the Chief Justice of India.

Under Article 260 the Government of India may undertake any executive, legislative

1. C.A.D.VII, p. 1139.
2. C.A.D.DC, p.1185.

or judicial functions in a foreign territory on the basis of an agreement with the Government of that territory. The provisions of such agreements are governed by laws relating to the exercise of foreign jurisdiction and, as such, they will not come within the scope of the provisions dealing with the normal administrative relationship between the Union and the States. The necessity of this provision was obvious in the context of territories belonging to foreign powers within the geographical boundaries of the Indian Union at the time the Constitution came into effect. With the incorporation of territories such as Pondicherry in the Union, this provision has little significance today.

Another provision that facilitates the smooth transaction of administrative business is embodied in Article 261. According to this, full faith and credit shall be given to public acts, records and judicial proceedings of the Union and the States in all parts of the Indian territory. The manner in which these acts and records will be proved and their effect determined will be provided by Parliamentary enactments. Provision is also made for the execution of final judgments or orders delivered or passed by civil courts in any part of India.

The Constitution has an important provision embodied in Article 262 dealing with the waters of inter-State rivers and river valleys. Aware of the unending inter-State disputes over this subject in other federations, particularly the United States, the Constitution-makers decided that the power to deal with this subject should be vested exclusively in Parliament. Thus, Parliament may by law provide for the adjudication of any dispute or complaint with respect to the use, distribution or control of the waters of any inter- State river or river valley. Parliament may also provide that neither the Supreme Court nor any other Court shall exercise any jurisdiction in respect of any such dispute or complaint. The importance of this provision is evident in the context of the many inter-State multi-purpose river valley projects like the Damodar Valley Corporation, which are being undertaken in different parts of the country.

The Draft constitution had not envisaged a provision of this nature. It was incorporated later on through an amendment. Moving the amendment in the Assembly, Ambedkar said:

> In view of the fact that we are now creating various corporations and these corporations will be endowed with the power of taking possession of property and other things, very many disputes may arise and consequently it would be necessary to appoint a permanent body to deal with these questions. Hence it has been felt that the original draft was too hidebound and too stereotyped to allow any elastic action that may be necessary to be taken for meeting these problems. Hence, the new article leaves it to Parliament to make laws for the settlement of these disputes.[1]

In pursuance of its constitutional authority under Article 262, Parliament passed the Inter-State Water Disputes Act, 1956, which has empowered the Union Government to set up a tribunal for the adjudication of water disputes at the request of any party to such disputes. The decision of the tribunal is final and binding upon all parties to the dispute. In spite of the constitutional provision and the existence of the Inter-State Water Disputes Act, however, some of the long-standing and acrimonious disputes that have been existing for several years between some of the States regarding the use of inter-State rivers and river waters have remained unsolved. The Kaveri water dispute between the States of Karnataka and Tamil Nadu is perhaps the best example in this connection.

Finally, to facilitate the smooth working of the administrative machinery of the

---

1. C.A.D. IX. p. 1187.

country as a whole as well as to ensure better coordination of policy and action between the Union and the States or between the States themselves, the Constitution empowers the President under Article 263 to appoint an Inter-State Council whenever the necessity is felt. The Council is charged with the following three specific duties:

(a) To enquire into and advise upon disputes which may have arisen between States;

(b) To investigate and discuss subjects in which the States or the Union and the States have a common interest; and

(c) To make recommendations upon these subjects and, in particular, recommendations for the better coordination of the policy and action with respect to these subjects.

The President is empowered not only to establish such a Council but also to determine its organization and procedure and to define the nature of its duties. The President may set up more than one Inter-State Council to deal with the subjects mentioned in the Article. The Union . Government does not seem to have taken much advantage of this Article. The only body that comes within the scope of this Article which has been set up by the President is the Central Council of Local Self-Government composed of all State ministers in charge of local self-government.

An analysis of the legislative and administrative relations between the Union and the States shows that the federal system established under the Constitution, like other similar systems, aims to achieve the fundamental objective of unity in diversity. A federation, being a dual polity based on the division of authority in all the principal departments of the government, is bound to produce diversities in laws, administration and judicial protection. Up to a certain point, the diversity is to be welcomed as an attempt to accommodate the powers of government to local needs and circumstances. But when it goes beyond a point, it is capable of creating chaos and has indeed produced chaos in many federal States. The framers of the Indian Constitution were aware of the inherent dangers of a federal system which, as Dicey pointed out, provides for the predominance of legalism and produces a weak government. It is possible that Lord de Villier's observation at the time of the consideration of a new constitution for South Africa was ringing in their ears; Lord de Villier said that in the light of the experience of the U.S., Canada and Australia, South Africa ought to avoid federalism if it was at all possible to do so. South Africa establishes perhaps the most highly decentralized governmental system short of being a federation. Conditions in India at the time of the transfer of power and immediately afterwards were such that those in authority feared that a federal set-up without special safeguards to preserve unity would dissipate the century-old effort at national unity.[1]

At the same time, it would have been politically unwise and impossible in practice to abandon altogether the idea of establishing a federal system. Moreover, when vast areas are brought under a single national government, perhaps no constitutional form except federalism can weld them together as willing partners of an integrated system. The urge

1. There were a few members in the Constituent Assembly who consistently opposed any kind of federal set-up and advocated a full-fledged centralized government for the whole country. Some of them were of the view that India could be most efficiently governed under a unitary system with the whole country divided into some 250 to 300 Districts, each placed under the charge of a District Officer who is directly responsible to the Government of India at Delhi.

for conserving power to rule over oneself and to be independent is as old as humanity. Dependence on others in any form is to be compensated by considerations of relative advantage. As independence without security would be shortlived, the predominant consideration in devising a federal Union was the urge for the preservation of independence. But for this paramount consideration and the existence of a vague, underlying cultural unity, India presents a picture of perplexing diversity. It has an area almost as large as Europe minus Russia and a much larger population than that of the whole of Europe. The number of well-developed languages in India is more than that in the whole of Western and Central Europe and the racial and cultural differences more pronounced than in continental Europe. In these circumstances it was not easy to ensure the framing of a federal constitution that could satisfy at once the urge for independence and the paramount need for security. The framers of the Constitution, in their attempt to satisfy these objectives, designed a federal system embodying several special features not generally found in other federations. It is also quite possible that their intimate knowledge of the working of the paramountcy powers, which the British Government had over the Indian States during the pre-Independence days, made them realize that a system similar to that within the federal framework was what India needed in the circumstances.

We have dealt with most of the special features of the federal system in different places. It may be appropriate here to collect them together so .as to obtain a clear perspective of these distinctive features which place the Indian federation in a class by itself.

1. The division of powers between the Union and the States is the most elaborate ever attempted by a federal constitution. Although the idea of a Concurrent List of powers is not new, no other constitution has enumerated the items in such detail and included in it a variety of subjects with a view to eliminating as far as possible, litigation between the Union and the States, and also the diversity of laws, courts and procedures. The residuary powers are vested in the Union.

2. Usually, under a federal system, the States have their own constitutions separate from that of the Union. This is the case in the United States. The Indian Constitution, on the contrary, embodies not only the Constitution of the Union but also those of the States. Further, the States of the Indian Union have a uniform constitution. The amending process, both for the Constitution of the Union and the Stales, is the same.

3. Under the Indian federation, the territorial jurisdiction of each of the States can be changed. States themselves abolished and new States created, without resorting to the procedure prescribed for amending the Constitution (art- 3). That is, the territorial, pattern of the federal system as it exists today can be reorganized with suitable adjustments without resorting to the comparatively difficult process of a constitutional amendment or any other special procedure.

4. Dual citizenship is a usual feature that goes with the dual form of government established under a federation. As a result, each member-state has the right to grant its citizens or residents certain rights which it may deny, or grant on more difficult terms, to non-residents. This was a striking feature of the U.S. federation in its early days. As time passed by, the rigours of dual citizenship have grown less. Still the idea continues' to be associated with the federal system of government. In India, however, it has no place. The Constitution has established a single citizenship. All Indians, no matter where they reside, are equal in the eyes of the law.

5. Dual polity involves in certain federations a double system of judiciary. For example, in the United States, the States have their own judicial system unrelated to and uncoordinated with the federal judiciary. Australia too follows more or less the same pattern. But in India, the Supreme Court and the High Courts form a single integrated judicial system. They have jurisdiction over cases arising under the same laws. constitutional, civil and criminal. The civil and the criminal laws are codified and are applicable to the entire country. To ensure their uniformity, they are placed in the Concurrent List.

6. A unique feature of the Indian federal system is its ability to adapt itself to changing circumstances. This is in contrast with the general characteristic of rigidity associated with federal constitutions. Normally, the Indian Constitution is meant to be federal. But under an emergency it can assume a unitary character. The process of change-over does not involve any complicated constitutional process.

7. The Constitution vests certain extraordinary powers in the Union Government even during normal times. Thus, a resolution supported by a two-thirds majority in the Council of States can temporarily transfer any item from the State List to the Union List, enabling Parliament to pass laws on such items in the national interest. It also provides for Parliament to pass laws on items on the State List if two or more States ask for it.

8. The Heads of the States—the Governors—are appointed by the President. They hold office during his pleasure.

9. The Constitution has certain special provisions to ensure the uniformity of the administrative system and to maintain minimum common administrative standards without impairing the federal principle. These include the creation of all India Services such as the Indian Administrative and Police Services and placing the members of these Services in key administrative positions in the States.

10. Appointments to the High Courts are made by the President, and the judges of the High Court can be transferred by the President from one High Court to another.

11. The Comptroller and Auditor-General of India has an organization managed by the officers of the Indian Aduti and Accounts Services—a Central Service, who are concerned not only with the accounts and auditing of the Union Government but also those of the States.

12. The Election Commission, a body appointed by the President, is in charge of conducting elections not only to Parliament and to other elective office of the Union, but also those to the State Legislatures.

13. Although every Bill passed by the State Legislatures normally becomes law with the assent of the Governor, certain Bills have to be reserved for the assent of the President. Only with the assent of the President can such Bills become law.

14. The provision for giving grants-in-aid and loans from the Union to the States and the consequent power which the Union has to influence the State is again a special feature of the Constitution.

15. The Constitution vests powers in the Union and its agencies to resolve conflicts that arise between the Union and the States. The Finance Commission, the Inter-State Council *etc.* are examples of such agencies.

16. Finally, constitutional amendment too is a comparatively simple process in India.

This, again emphasizes the flexibility of the federal constitution. Ultimately, the test of a constitution is in its working. If it is found to be defective in any respect in its actual working, it should be amended. For this, the amending process should be reasonably simple and easy.

The list is indeed formidable. Almost every one of these emphasizes the supremacy of the Union and its compulsive power to discipline the States. Where the Union has such predominant powers, can the system be called federal? Once again, it may seem that there is some validity in the viewpoints of some of the critics of the Constitution referred to earlier. But if we take into account the manner in which the States in India have been functioning during the last three decades and more, and the substantial autonomy they have been enjoying in ordering their affairs within the sphere of power allocated to them, the conclusion will be different. Even when the Centre took over, under the emergency provisions, the administration of some of the States for the States for short periods, it was done only for reestablishing responsible government in those States where, owing to political instability, such government had become impossible.[1] The only occasion when the Union availed itself of Article 249 and passed a law on a subject included in the State List was in 1951 when there was acute food scarcity and such a law became essential in the economic interests of the nation. But the operation of the law lasted only for a short period of two years and the States got back their powers in this regard when the scarcity conditions disappeared.

An objective study of the Constitution at work cannot miss a basic fact of constitutional government in India, namely, the existence and functioning of fullfledged parliamentary and cabinet government in the States of the India Union. As Alexandrowicz points out:[2]

> A local executive fully responsible to a local Legislature ensures a good deal of local internal sovereignty and sovereignty means a statehood, limited as it may be by the distribution of powers. Local States pursue local policies, sometimes in accordance with policy of the Centre, sometimes not. This distinguishes them precisely from the position which prevails in administrative federations in which local units must toe the line and always follow the policy of the Centre. India is undoubtedly a federation in which the attributes of statehood are shared between the Centre and local States. Instead of defining her by the vague term of 'quasi-federation', it seems more accurate to exclude her from the category of administrative federations and to consider her a federation with vertically divided sovereignty. Moreover, the position of local States is also strengthened by two significant developments, one connected with the formation of position or coalition governments in a number of local States, the other with the reorganization of the Union on linguistic lines.

About the operation of the federal system from an administrative point of view and the trend it indicates for the future, here are a few significant observations which Paul Appleby made after his study of India's administrative system:

> It is not too unfair, I think, to say that except for the character of its leadership, the new national government of India is given less basic resource in power than any other large and important nation, while at the same time having rather more sense of need and determination to establish programmes dealing with matters important to the national interest. The administrative trend is evidently to go still further, to give over to the States some financial resources now in the province of the Centre, to minimize in practice some of the marginal or interpretative zones of power, and to retreat before an opposition State minister's charge of 'interference' with the States.

1. This question is dealt with in detail in the chapter on the Emergency Powers.
2. *Constitutional Developments in India,* pp. 168-9.

No other large and important national government, I believe, is so dependent as India on theoretically subordinate but actually rather distinct units responsible to a different political control, for so much of the administration of what are recognized as national programmes of great importance to the nation.

The power that is exercised organically in New Delhi is the uncertain and discontinuous power of prestige. It is influence rather than power. Its method is making plans, issuing pronouncements, holding conferences. In reference to two different programme fields I have been authoritatively informed at both the Centre and in the States that the Centre's administrative function is performed by annual or semi-annual conferences. Any real power in most of the development field is the personal power of particular leaders and the informal, extra-constitutional, extra administrative power of a dominant party, coherent and strongly led by the some leaders. Dependence for achievement, therefore, is in some crucial ways, apart from the formal organs of governance, in forces which in the future may take quite different forms.[1]

Appleby has been largely proved correct. Appleby's criticisms focusing attention on the weakness of the Central power may be countered by pointing out the different instruments of control with which the Centre may bring the States to its way of thinking. The role of the Planning Commission, an extra-constitutional body created by the Centre and the manner in which it acts as a 'Super Cabinet' for the whole of India, directing and regulating the entire socio-economic activity on a national basis, may be cited as an illustration.

But what is often forgotten in this context is that the Planning Commission has neither constitutional nor statutory authority. The entire scheme of planning that has been taking place in a highly centralized manner as a governmental activity is, more or less, on an informal basis. It is perfectly right for a State, if it so chooses, to argue that it is not bound by the decisions of the Commission and the Central Government is powerless to discipline the State through constitutional means. The reasons why no State has so far not taken such an attitude are not far to seek. First, during most of the period since India's Independence, one Party has ruled the country except in the case of a few States for brief periods.* When the ruling Congress Party had taken a decision to introduce centralized planning for the whole country in 1950, the decision was binding on every Government in the country, Central and State. It was a decision based upon willing consent on the part of all those who had been chosen by the people to rule the country.

Secondly, the financing of the Plan has been an equally important factor. The Central Government undertook the major burden of financing the Plan and a State could refuse to fall in line only at the risk of foregoing the massive financial assistance offered by the Union. Thus, both on political and financial grounds it was only natural for the States to come in. Once they came into the system and started the gigantic task of building up the backward economy, it was almost impossible to get out of it even if a different Party had captured power in a State and wanted to do so.

Further, the entire planning has been going on an Executive level with only formal Parliamentary approval. No rigid boundaries have been demarcated between the Union and the States regarding the amounts to be allotted or the measures to be taken. As such, the whole process could be readjusted from time to time. So long as the Union and the States were agreeable to execute the Plan, there were no legal difficulties in its formulation

1. Appleby *op. cit.*, pp. 17-22.

*The only exceptions are West-Bengal and Tripura.

and implementation.[1] In fact, the Planning Commission assumed from the very beginning that the federal nature of the Constitution would not give them any trouble. The First Plan stated:

"Under the Constitution, India is organized as a federation in which the Central Government and the governments of the States have their assigned spheres of action. There are certain concurrent subjects in which the Centre as well as the States have to work in unison."[2]

But the Commission's work was not all dictation from above. In order to get the willing cooperation of the States, the Commission evolved a suitable machinery. The most significant part of its is the National Development Council composed of all the Ministers of the Central Cabinet, members of the Planning Commission and the Chief Ministers of the States. The decisions of the Planning Commission are ratified by the National Development Council presided over by the Prime Minister. By convention it has been established that the decisions of the Council are binding on all the State Governments and the Government of India. Thus the position of the National Development Council is somewhat like that of a super cabinet for the entire Indian Federation, at least in the field of its economic activities.

Attempts are also made by the Planning Commission and the Central Government to be in constant touch with the States and consult them in all matters affecting the programme of planned development. Innumerable conferences are being regularly held where the State representatives, Ministers or Heads of Departments, have an important role to play. Decisions taken in these conferences are naturally joint decisions. It is these decisions which become parts of the programme under the successive Five Year Plans and which are implemented by the States. If planning, thus, has superseded in practice the federal theory that is embodied in the Constitution, the supersession has not been brought by legal or constitutional means but by agreement and consent. From the operative point of view inter-governmental cooperation and not competition, is the underlying spirit of India's federal system. Economic development through the successive Five Year Plans is brought about through Union-State partnership based on mutual understanding and cooperation. Hence it seems appropriate to call the federal system that exists in the country today by the name Cooperative Federalism. In such a conception of federal relationship, the States and the national government are regarded as mutually complementary parts of a single system of government whose powers are intended to realize the common objectives set for the nation as a whole.

If planning has substantially affected the working of the federal system in the economic sphere, its influence in the political sphere has not been so conspicuous. In fact, from this point of view, despite the predominance of a single political Party in the governmental sphere, federalism has been a powerful decentralizing force. The formation of linguistic States was the most important single factor which contributed to this development. Linguism is a fact that is to be reckoned with for the figure as it is unlikely to change its character as a result of planning. In addition, if at any time in the future, a considerable number of State Governments should belong to parties different from that

---

1. K. Santhanam, *o cit.,* pp 44-48.
2. *First Five Year Plan Report,* Chap. 1.

which controls the Central Government or if the Centre finds it necessary to curtail drastically its financial assistance to the States, it is reasonable to forecast that an opposite trend, which will rehabilitate the autonomy of the States to the fullest extent provided by the Constitution, is bound to develop. This trend is unmistakable in recent years.

Whatever the possibilities of the future may be, the basic fact remains today that India is not ruled by one Government from New Delhi with subordinate agencies at the various State headquarters, but simultaneously by one National Government and twenty-eight State Governments, sharing between them the totality of governmental powers under the Constitution. Such sharing of sovereign powers by different governments under the same constitution is possible only under a federal system and that is what makes India a federal union and its constitution a federal constitution.

***

36

FINANCIAL RELATIONS

NO OTHER federal constitution makes such elaborate provisions as the Constitution of India with respect to the relationship between the Union and the States in the financial field. In fact, by providing for the establishment of a Finance Commission for the purpose of allocating and adjusting the receipts from certain sources, the Constitution has made an original contribution in this extremely complicated aspect of federal relationship. The significance of this provision becomes evident when one takes into account the unending conflicts between the federation and the units in the financial field that characterize the working of the older federations. Often the federation and the units have tried to raise revenue by taxing the same sources such as earned income. While in theory it may look alright, in practice it created great inconvenience. The federation thought that the States stood in its way of enhanced taxation while the States looked upon the federation as a hindrance to their financial soundness. At the same time, the people thought that they were subjected to double or excessive taxation. There was a constant challenge by the States to the authority of the federation to impose a particular tax. At the same time, the federation too resorted to the same process against the States. Individual citizens too challenged the authority of either the federation or the States so as to suit their interests. The result was an enormous amount of litigation. The Courts tried to solve the problem by propounding new doctrines of interpretation. The doctrine of Immunity of Instrumentalities as propounded by the Supreme Court of the United States is an example in point.

The Government of India Act of 1935 had attempted a solution of the problem by a better device. To avoid all confusion, it tried to allocate every possible source of taxation either to the Centre or the Provinces. In some cases, the Centre was allowed to levy and collect the tax but distribute the proceeds to the Provinces. But the real drawback of the Act of 1935 was the extremely limited revenue resources of the Provinces. The makers of the present Constitution, while following the same system as obtained under the 1935 Act, wanted to avoid the repetition of its defect. As a result, the Constitution lays down a broad scheme for the distribution of revenue resources between the Union and the States. But it left the task of detailed allocation to the Finance Commission to be set up by the President within two years after the inauguration of the Constitution.

The basic principles that guide the allocation of resources between the federation and the units are efficiency, adequacy and suitability. It is indeed difficult to achieve all three ends at the same time. Constitutional, natural and economic considerations often stand in the way. Even if a certain system might suggest itself as the most acceptable, it would not satisfy the claims and counter-claims of the various States. Hence, the

Constitution has attempted a compromise. According to this, the subject is divided into two parts, namely (i) the allocation of revenues between the Union and the States, and (ii) the distribution of grants-in-aid. The following list will show the sources of revenue for the Union and the States.

I. Union Sources

1. Corporation tax
2. Currency, coinage and legal tender; foreign exchange
3. Duties of customs including export duties
4. Duties of excise on tobacco and certain goods manufactured or produced in India
5. Estate duty in respect of property other than agricultural land
6. Fees in respect of any of the matters in the Union List, but not including any fees taken in any Court
7. Foreign loans
8. Lotteries organized by the Government of India or the Government of a State
9. Post Office Savings Bark
10. Posts and Telegraphs: Telephones, wireless, broadcasting and other like forms of communication
11. Property of the Union
12. Public Debt of the Union
13. Railways
14. Rates of stamp duty in respect of Bills of Exchange, Cheques, Promissory Notes, *etc.*
15. Reserve Bank of India
16. Taxes on income other than agricultural income
17. Taxes on the capital value of the assets, exclusive of agricultural land, of individuals and companies
18. Taxes other than stamp duties on transactions in stock exchanges and future markets
19. Taxes on the sale or purchase of newspapers and on advertisements published therein
20. Terminal taxes on goods or passengers, carried by railways, sea or air.

II. State Sources

1. Capitation taxes
2. Duties in respect of succession to agricultural land
3. Duties of excise on certain goods produced or manufactured in the State, such as alcoholic liquids, opium *etc.*
4. Estate duty in respect of agricultural land
5. Fees in respect of any of the matters in the State List, but not including fees taken in any court
6. Land Revenue
7. Rates of stamp duty in respect of documents other than those specified in the Union List
8. Taxes on agricultural income
9. Taxes on land and buildings

10. Taxes on mineral rights, subject to limitations imposed by Parliament relating to mineral development
11. Taxes on the consumption or sale of electricity
12. Taxes on the entry of goods into a local area for consumption or sale therein
13. Taxes on the sale and purchase of goods other than newspapers
14. Taxes on advertisements other than those published in the newspapers
15. Taxes on goods and passengers carried by road or on inland waterways
16. Taxes on vehicles
17. Taxes on animals and boats
18. Taxes on professions, trades, callings and employments
19. Taxes on luxuries, including taxes on entertainments, amusements, betting and gambling
20. Tolls.

III. Taxes Levied and Collected by the Union but Assigned to the States (Art. 269)

1. Duties in respect of succession to property other than agricultural land.
2. Estate duty in respect of property other than agricultural land.
3. Taxes on railway fares and freights.
4. Taxes other than stamp duties on transactions in stock exchanges and futures markets.
5. Taxes on the sale or purchase of newspapers and on advertisements published therein.
6. Terminal taxes on goods or passengers carried by railways, sea or air.
7. Taxes on the sale or purchase of goods other than newspapers where such sale or purchase takes place in the course of inter-State trade or commerce.

IV. Duties Levied by the Union but Collected and Appropriated by the States (Art. 268)

Stamp duties and duties of excise on medicinal and toilet preparations (those mentioned in the Union List) shall be levied by the Government of India but shall be collected (i) in the case where such duties are leviable within any Union territory, by the Government of India, and (ii) in other cases, by the States within which such duties are leviable.

V. Taxes which are Levied and Collected by the Union but which may be Distributed between the Union and the States (Arts. 270 and 272)

1. Taxes on income other than agricultural income.
2. Union duties of excise other than such duties of excise on medicinal and toilet preparations as are mentioned in the Union List and collected by the Government of India.

'Taxes on income' does not include corporation tax. The distribution of income-tax proceeds between the Union and the States is made on the basis of the recommendations of the Finance Commission.

In spite of Articles 269 and 270 which provide for the collection of taxes by the Union either to be assigned to the States or to be shared between the Union and the States, Parliament is, under Article 271, authorized to impose a surcharge for the purposes of the

Union on all items of tax included in Articles 269 and 270. The entire proceeds of such a surcharge will form part of the Consolidated Fund of India.

Taxes on Professions, Trades, etc. (Art. 276)

Although the imposition and collection of income-tax are within the jurisdiction of the Union, the States are permitted to impose a tax on professions, trades, callings or employments. Such a tax will not be invalid on the ground that it relates to a tax on income. Taxes on professions, *etc.* are generally made use of for the benefit of local self-governing institutions such as municipalities, local boards, etc. If such a tax were not allowed, an important source of income of these bodies would come to an end, adversely affecting their already depleted sources of income. There is, however, an upper limit of Rs. 2500 per annum prescribed for this tax.

These elaborate provisions regarding the allocation of tax items between the Union and the States have several advantages. Firstly, overlapping jurisdictions and double taxation of income are avoided. Secondly, excluding corporation tax from the divisible pool has avoided the distribution of income-tax on the basis of origin. Thirdly, centralization of customs duties and excises has achieved operational efficiency and has ensured a common market throughout the country. Finally, uniformity in excises in company and personal taxation will facilitate economic growth. Although centralization of major taxes has given the Union a predominant position in the country's financial field as a whole, if used properly, it can assist the evolution of a fiscal policy for balanced economic growth and stability.

Grants-in-Aid (Art. 275)

Federalism is not only a unifying but also a levelling-up force. Among the constituent States of the Union are some which are developed and others underdeveloped and backward. One of the results expected of a federal Union is the opportunity that it should provide for the socially and economically backward units to better their lot. A common method adopted for this purpose is the system of the Union giving grants to the needy States. Article 275 provides for this by empowering Parliament to pay, out of the Consolidated Fund of India, certain sums every year as grants-in-aid of the revenues of such States to the extent that such assistance is adjudged necessary. The grants so fixed are based upon the recommendations of the Finance Commission. It is not necessary that every State should get grants-in-aid every year. If in the opinion of the Finance Commission a particular State does not need such assistance. Parliament may leave it out while allocating such grants. The Constitution, however, makes it obligatory for the Union Government to pay such grants-in-aid to cover the schemes of development undertaken by a State with the approval of the Union for the purpose of promoting the welfare of the Scheduled Tribes in that State or raising the level of administration of the Scheduled areas.

Giving grants by the Union to the States is not a routine ritual. Nor is it necessary or desirable that every State receives such grants. The principles which govern such grants especially in the context of the national plans are as follows: 1. Planning priorities are observed. 2. These priorities are adapted to the needs of individual States. 3. The Slates are given the maximum incentive to develop and augment their own resources. 4. All resources, whatever their origin, are employed with the maximum economy and efficiency. 5. The States are encouraged to contribute creatively to the planning process.

Bills Affecting Taxation in which the States are Interested (Art. 274)

In the case of all Bills relating to taxation in which the States are interested, the Constitution requires the prior recommendation of the President. Thus, when a Bill which affects the meaning and scope of the term 'agricultural income' as applied to Indian income-tax is to be introduced in the House of the People, the President's recommendation is necessary. The purpose of such recommendation by the President is to safeguard the interests of the States by making it obligatory for the Union Government to consult them through the President.

The Finance Commission (Arts. 280 and 281)

As has been pointed out earlier, the constitutional requirements of setting up a Finance Commission is an original idea. According to this, the President should, within two years from the inauguration of the Constitution and thereafter on the expiry of every fifth year or at such earlier intervals as he thinks necessary constitute a Finance Commission. The Commission will consist of a Chairman and four other members who are all to be appointed by the President. As the Commission has to be constituted at regular intervals, a certain measure of continuity in the work of these Commissions is ensured. And each Commission profits by the work of its predecessors.

Parliament is empowered to determine by law the qualifications of the members of the Commission and the manner of their selection. The powers of the Commission in the performance of their functions are also to be laid down by parliamentary enactment. In pursuance of these provisions, a Finance Commission Act was passed in 1951. The Act was amended in 1955.[1] Some of the provisions of the Act are worthy of note in view of the important position which the Commission occupies in the financial scheme of the federal system.

1. The Chairman shall be selected from among persons who have had experience of public affairs and the four other members shall be selected from among persons who:

   (a) are, or have been, or are qualified to be appointed as High Court Judges; or
   (b) have special knowledge of the finances and accounts of the Government; or
   (c) have had wide experience in financial matters and in administration; or
   (d) have special knowledge of economics.

2. Before appointing a person the President shall satisfy himself that the person will have no such financial or other interests as is likely to affect prejudicially his functions as a member of the Commission.

3. The Commission shall determine its procedure and, in the performance of its functions, shall have all the powers of a civil court.

4. The Commission shall have the power to require any person to furnish information which may be useful for its work.

The Constitutional provisions dealing with the work of the Commission are interspersed in many articles covering the financial relations between the Union and the States. For Convenience of reference, these are collected together and enumerated below.

According to Article 280, the Finance Commission has to make recommendations

1. See Appendix II of the *Report of the Finance Commission*, 1957.

to the President on two specific matters and on any other matter referred to the Commission by the President in the interests of sound finance.

The two specific matters are:

(i) the distribution between the Union and the States of the net proceeds of taxes which are to be, or may be, divided between them and the allocation between the States of the respective shares of such proceeds; and

(ii) the principles which should govern the grants-in-aid of the revenues of the States out of the Consolidated Fund of India.

The Constitution makes it mandatory under Article 270 to divide taxes on income other than agricultural income between the Union and the States, For this purpose, taxes on income exclude corporation tax and any surcharge which may be levied for Union purposes. To the extent that the proceeds of taxes on income represent proceeds attributable to Union territories or to taxes payable in respect of Union emoluments, they are retained by the Union. The Constitution also contains in Article 272 an enabling provision under which, if Parliament so prescribes by law, Union duties of excise other than duties of excise on medicinal and toilet preparations may be divided.

In the case of income-tax, the Commission is charged with the duty of making the following recommendations:

(*i*) The percentage of the net proceeds of taxes on income excluding the taxes payable in respect of Union emoluments, which shall be deemed to represent proceeds attributable to Union territories;

(*ii*) The percentage of the net proceeds in any financial year of tax on income other than agricultural income, except in so far as those proceeds represent proceeds attributable to Union territories or to taxes payable in respect of Union emoluments, which shall not form part of the Consolidated Fund of India but shall be assigned to the States within which that tax is leviable in that year and the manner in which, and the time from which, such percentage shall be distributed among the states.

The President, after considering the recommendations of the Finance Commission, prescribes by order the percentages and the manner of distribution. Parliament is not directly concerned with the assignment and distribution of income tax.

The position is different in respect of the distribution under Article 272 of Union duties of excise. This article does not refer to the Finance Commission. The Commission's jurisdiction to deal with this distribution is derived from the provisions of Article 280(3)(a). It is also open to the President to make a specific reference of this matter to the Commission. There is no obligation on the part of the Union to share the excise duties with the States. When it decides to do so, this has to be done by a law of Parliament, which has to prescribe which of the excise duties should be paid out of the Consolidated Fund of India to the States. The principles of distribution among the States have also to be prescribed by law. In the case of excise duties, the Finance Commission's recommendation will assist the Union Government in placing appropriate legislation before Parliament.

Article 280, as originally enacted, required the Commission to make recommendations on another matter, namely, the continuance or modification of the terms of any agreements entered into under Articles 278 and 306 with States in Part B of the First Schedule. The Constitution (Seventh Amendment) Act, 1956, abolished Part B States and deleted these two articles as well as the sub-clause of Article 280 dealing with such agreements.

The Commission has also to make recommendations to the President in regard to the sums which may be prescribed by him under Article 273 as grants-in-aid of the revenues of the States of Assam, Bihar, Orissa and West Bengal in lieu of the assignment of any share of the net proceeds in each year of export duty on jute and jute products. These sums are payable so long as any export duty on jute products continues to be levied by the Government of India or until the expiration of ten years from the commencement of the Constitution, whichever is earlier.

Article 275 deals with the grants-in-aid of the revenues of the States. These grants-in-aid are to be provided by law of Parliament; but Clause (2) of this article states that until provision is made by law, the President may exercise this power by order. His power is, however, conditioned by the proviso "that after a Finance Commission has been constituted no order shall be made under this clause by the President except after considering the recommendations of the Finance Commission". No reference to the Commission is necessary, if the grants-in-aid are provided by law of Parliament or if the President considers that no State is in need of assistance. The President did, however, refer the matter to all Finance Commissions for their recommendations.

Under Article 280(3) (b) the Finance Commission has the duty of making recommendations as "to the principles which should govern the grants-in-aid of the revenues of the States out of the Consolidated Fund of India."

Under Article 280(3) (c) the President may refer to the Commission any matter which he considers to be in the interests of sound finance, Under this provision, they were asked to make recommendations as to the principles which should govern the distribution, among the States, of the net proceeds in any financial year of :

(*a*) the estate duty in respect of property other than agricultural land:

(*b*) the tax on railway fares; and

(*c*) the additional duties of excise on mill-made textiles, sugar and tobacco (including manufactured tobacco), to be levied in replacement of the sales taxes on those articles.

In the case of the last item, the Commission had been asked to recommend the amounts which should be assured to each State as the income, now derived by it from the levy of the sales taxes on these commodities.

The Commission had further been asked, under the same provision, to recommend modifications, if any, in the rates of interest and the terms of repayment of the loans made to the various States by the Government of India between 15 August 1947 and 31 March 1956.

The recommendations regarding the three additional items of taxation mentioned above have to be implemented by law of Parliament, while those relating to loans may be given effect to by executive order.

The estate duty and the tax on railway fares are taxes included in Article 269 of the Constitution. Clause (2) of that article states that

...the net proceeds in any financial year of any such duty or tax, except in so far as those proceeds represent proceeds attributable of Union territories, shall not form part of the Consolidated Fund of India, but shall be assigned to the States within which that duty or tax is leviable in that year, and shall be distributed among those States in accordance with such principles of distribution as may be formulated by Parliament by law.

Except in relation to the Union territories and to the extent of a central surcharge, if any, the Union Government has no share in these taxes and is entrusted merely with their levy, collection and distribution. It is obvious that these taxes have been placed under the Union Government to ensure uniformity of taxation and convenience of collection. As regards distribution, though Parliament is free to formulate any principles of distribution in respect of these taxes, the Commission considered that, to the extent to which they can be reasonably ascertained or estimated, each State should receive from these taxes as nearly as may be the amounts which it would have raised if it had the power to levy and collect them.

The recommendations of the Commission thus fell under the following categories for the purpose of implementation:

(*i*) those that have to be implemented only by Presidential order, namely, those relating to the distribution of income tax and grants-in-aid in lieu of assignment of any share of the net proceeds of export duty on jute and jute products;

(*ii*) those that may be implemented by law of Parliament and till the enactment of such law, by Presidential order, namely, those relating to the grants-in-aid under the substantive portion of Article 275;

(*iii*) those that have to be implemented by law of Parliament alone, namely, those relating to the distribution of excise duties, estate duty, tax on railway fares and additional duties of excise; and

(*iv*) lastly, those that may be implemented by executive order, namely, those relating to the modification of rates of interest and the terms of repayment of loans.

The importance of the Finance Commission as a constitutional instrument capable of settling many complicated financial problems that affect the relationship of the Union and the States may be seen from the recommendations of various Commissions. For the purpose of illustration we may note a few of the more important recommendations of the Seventh Commission.[1]

The Seventh Finance Commission was constituted in June 1977. The Commission's recommendations cover a period of five years commencing from 1 April 1979. Besides, recommending devolution of taxes and duties and grant-in-aid to the States, (in need of assistance) the Commission, was asked to make an assessment of the non-plan capital gap of the States and suggest appropriate measures to deal with it. The Commission was also asked to review the policy and arrangements in regard to financing of relief expenditure by the States affected by natural calamities,

The Commission submitted its report in October 1978. All the recommendations of the Commission except those relating to grants-in-aid to compensate the loss in excise revenue consequent on the introduction of prohibition and conversion of outstanding small

1. *See Report of the Seventh Finance Commission,* 1978. Altogether there had been eleven Finance commissions by the year 2000.

savings loans into "loans in perpetuity", have been accepted by the Government. The Commission had raised the share of the States in income-tax pool from 80 to 85 per cent and doubled the share of the States in basic excise duties other than the duty on electricity. In the case of excise duty on electricity, the net proceeds were to be passed on to the States from where they were collected. The Commission had recommended grants totalling Rs. 1,173 crores during the period 1979-84 to eight States which were likely to have gap in their revenue account as per the Commission's assessment. In addition, the Commission had also recommended Rs. 437 crores to 17 out of 22 States for upgradation of standards in certain sectors of administration like police, justice, revenue, district and tribal administration, *etc.*

To enable the States to meet their non-plan capital gap, the Commission had recommended a scheme for relief in the repayment of outstanding central loans to the Union government. It envisages write off of central loans to the extent of Rs. 943 crores. The consolidation of outstanding central loans as on 31 March 1979 was expected to give a debt relief of Rs. 2,156 crores to the States during the period 1979-84.

For financing relief expenditure, the Commission had made large annual provisions in its re-assessment of the forecast on receipts and expenditure of the States. For drought relief expenditure in excess of the amount allowed by the Commission, the States are expected to make a contribution from their plan expenditure not exceeding 5 per cent. The requirement of States for drought relief expenditure over and above the annual amount permitted by the Commission and contribution of the States, is to be met by the Central Government by way of assistance, half as grant and half as loans. In case of natural calamities like floods, cyclones and others, the central government's relief assistance is to be made available as non-plan grant to the extent of 75 per cent of the total expenditure in excess of the annual amount provided in the Commission's assessment. The transfers under the Commission's award as per its estimates during the period 1979-84 would be of the order of Rs. 23.063 crores.[1]

The Report of the Eleventh Finance Commission was placed before Parliament in its winter session in 2000. The Report of the Commission was criticised by some of the States, particularly the southern States, as discriminatory. They voiced their concern for poor allocation of incentive funds for them. Though the Eleventh Finance Commission provides for the States a share of 29.50 per cent of the "net proceeds of all Union taxes and duties" the above mentioned States found a sizeable drop in the individual share of transfer from the Centre against what the Tenth Finance Commission had recommended.

The Report of the Commission recommending the setting up of a two-part Incentive Fund to address the concerns of all States, has clearly stated that fiscal reforms at the State's level were the need of the current economic situation. Even as States would not like their financial position to deteriorate, the burden on the Centre's finances should also be modest, the report stated. Within this broad framework, Part A of the Incentive Fund would comprise 15 per cent of the grants recommended to cover the revenue account deficits of State Governments. The release from this withheld portion would be tied to the performance of the States in implementing a monitorable programme of fiscal reforms.

Part B of the Fund to be created by an equal contribution by the Central Government,

---

1. One crore is equivalent to 10 million.

envisages an incentive component to be provided to all States. The initial eligibility for each State has been arrived at based on their population in 1971. The crux of the issue was that the additional incentive worked out "in addressing concerns of better performing States was too small as even earlier levels of vertical transfer from the Centre had not been maintained by the Eleventh Finance Commission. On the whole, the Report of the Eleventh Finance Commission's recommendations regarding transfer of funds to the relatively better developed States had been disappointing to them. This goes against the very spirit of cooperative federalism which is supposed to animate the working of the financial relations between the Centre and the States.

The chief merit of the work of the Commission lies in its impartial and objective outlook as a steadying force in the finances of the federal system and its ability to take the question of distribution of finances out of the vortex of federal-state political pressures and controversies. In fact, the Commission acts as a buffer between the Union and the States, checking the clamorous, finance-hungry States bent upon applying political pressure on the Union, and, at the same time, making the latter give as much as possible to the needy States. It will be almost impossible for the Union to go against the recommendations of the Commission.

Many members in the Constituent Assembly were opposed to the procedure prescribed in the Constitution by which the Finance Commission's report, along with the Executive's action on it as shown in the explanatory memorandum, is placed before Parliament. They thought that this was an infringement of the sovereign right of Parliament to have the last word over all financial matters. It would not be right to confront Parliament with a *fait accompli*. Therefore, it was urged that Parliament must discuss the Report first and in the light of that should come the action of the Government.[1] The Drafting Committee, however, did not agree. Ambedkar said that the matter would come before Parliament for its sanction when a Money Bill was introduced in the House of the People to sanction the levy of the taxes and duties and the manner in which they were to be allocated.[2]

The Principle of Immunity of Instrumentalities

The principle of reciprocal immunity of instrumentalities springs from the very basis of a federal system. It recognizes the right of both the Union and State Governments to exist and effectively function as governments. This will not be possible, if either the federal or the State authority taxes the property or the personnel of the other in an indiscriminate manner. In the United States the principle developed through judicial interpretation just as did several other principles of the U.S. Constitution and, in course of time, it became a doctrine of that Constitution. When the Australians adopted a federal constitution they followed the U.S. example and made an express provision in their Constitution embodying this principle.[3] But the principle of reciprocal immunity created many complications as the character and functions of the State changed. So long as the activities of the State were confined to the traditional functions of a government such as law and order, administration of justice, defence, etc. there was no difficulty. But when once the State accepted the goal of socialism, and commercial, industrial and trade activities were undertaken, adherence to the principle of reciprocal immunity became difficult. As a result, the doctrine of

1. C.A.D. IX, p. 321.
2. Ibid., 328.
3. Section 114 of the Australian Constitution.

immunity of instrumentalities came to be practically abandoned in both the United States and Australia.

The framers of the Constitution of India were aware of this problem. As a result, they did not agree with a powerful section of the Constituent Assembly, especially those who hailed from some of the former Indian States[1] who suggested adoption of the principle of full reciprocal immunity from taxation for both the Union and the States. At the same time, the principle has been embodied in the Constitution in a modified form with adequate safeguards against its abuse by the States as they expand their activities. Justifying these provisions Alladi Kishnaswami Aiyar said:

> We have to look at the problem in the larger perspective of Indian industry and Indian advancement.... Our objective may be towards socialisation of key industries but if that objective is to fructify and to yield excellent results, it has to be necessarily a little slow.... Parliament should have the power to consider each case and impose taxes. Therefore, having regard: (a) to the plenary power of Parliament to exempt any particular industries and particular businesses from the operation of the tax provision, (b) having regard to the fact that it is not obligatory on Parliament to levy any tax, (c) that the very conception of the industry may change with the further evolution of the States and the changing times, and (d) to the inter-connection between one State and another, it will be very difficult to differentiate between particular States, between States which have been working certain industries and other States. To lay down a general principle of exemption would lead to wild-goose schemes being started by various States. They may not take into account the general interests of trade and industry in the whole country.[2]

Under Article 285, the property of the Union is exempt from all taxes imposed by a State or any local authority unless Parliament provides otherwise. This provision was opposed by some members on the ground that the States were entitled to tax the Union property and this would not be possible if they gave protection to such property. They argued that the general principle applicable to private property and that belonging to State Governments should be followed in regard to taxation of Union property as well.[3] Ambedkar, opposing this view, pointed out:

It is impossible theoretically to conceive of any property of a person who is not represented or whose interests are not represented in a particular organisation to allow that organisation a right *ad infinitum* to levy any tax upon the property of such persons. Secondly, the taxing authority of a local body is derived from a law made by the legislature of the State. Consequently, not knowing what is the nature of the tax and the extent of the tax, it is impossible to expect of the Central Government to surrender or submit itself to the authority of the local body.[4]

But Parliament may voluntarily agree to submit Union property to local taxation after examining the taxation proposals.[5] Thus, there is flexibility in the operation of the provision.

There are two more constitutional prohibitions upon the States in the matter of imposing .taxes on Union activities. These relate to the consumption of electricity and

---

1. C.A.D. IX. 1161-7.
2. C.A.D. IX, p. 1167.
3. Ibid., pp. 1148 and 1152.
4. Ibid., p. 1157.
5. *e.g.* The Railways Local Authorities Taxation Act, 1941, by which Parliament allows local bodies to tax railway property.

water by the Union or its agencies. Under Article 287, no State law can impose, unless Parliament provides otherwise, a tax on the consumption, or sale of electricity which is (a) consumed by the Government of India or sold to the Government of India for consumption; or (b) consumed in the construction, maintenance or operation of any railway by the Government of India or a railway company operating that railway, or sold for such consumption. Similarly, under Article 288, no State law in force at the time of the inauguration of the Constitution was competent to impose a tax (unless the President by order provided otherwise) in respect of any water or electricity stored, generated, consumed, distributed or sold by any authority established by Parliament for regulating or developing any inter-State river or river-valleys. The object of this provision is obvious in the light of the plan for establishing inter-State multi-purpose river-valley projects. Here again, there is a saving clause. The opportunity for the States to tax such activities is not altogether ruled out for the future since, under Article 288(2), a State may impose such tax with the prior consent of the Union. For this purpose, every such law to have effect should be reserved for the assent of the President and should receive his assent.

The principle of reciprocal immunity is partially recognized under the Constitution through the provision under Article 289. According to this, the property and income of a State are exempt from Union taxation. But this general prohibition does not stand in the way of Parliament's power to impose any tax in respect of a trade or business of any kind carried on by, or on behalf of, the Government of a State. However, Parliament may declare any trade or business as incidental to the ordinary functions of a State Government in which case those activities will be exempt from central taxation.

Since several members from the former Indian States expressed their anxiety that the Union's power of taxing industrial or commercial activities might prejudicially affect the financial stability of the States, the then Finance Minister of the Government of India, John Mathai, gave an assurance on behalf of the Government to the members in the Constituent Assembly that "if this provision should have the slightest effect in checking industrialisation in any of the States concerned, then we would be the last to make use of this provision." He said that if members assumed that there was an inevitable conflict between the financial objectives of the Centre and the States, nothing could be farther from the truth.

> As things are shaping today, and as we realise more and more the need for a united structure in the country, both politically and economically, the identity of interests between the Centre and the States is bound to be extremely close. If by the operation of a provision of this kind it is found that the finances of a State are rendered difficult, then it will be a problem that will cause anxiety not merely to the State, but to the Centre also. Hence necessary adjustments will be made. It is not our intention to levy any tax on industries run by the States whose object is to produce services of a public utility character.... If it happens that the revenue resources of a State are seriously crippled by taxation under this provision, then, assuming that the development projects are projects of national importance, it automatically follows that there is a corresponding obligation which will fall upon the Centre to make up so far as its resources permit such shortfall as might occur in the financial resources of the States.[1]

Analysing the provisions dealing with reciprocal immunity in the light of this and other official statements as detailed above, we are led to the conclusion that the framers were not taking a doctrinaire view but were influenced by realistic considerations. If the

1. C.A.D. IX, p. 1169.

Constitution had provided for complete mutual exemption of taxation, it would have given rise to the same problems which the United States and Australia faced and which compelled them to modify the original rigid nature of the doctrine of reciprocal immunity. The merit of the Indian Constitution in this regard is that it accepts the doctrine to the extent that it is practicable while expressly providing for Parliament to take stock of any special situation and accord any special treatment as the situation demands.

Miscellaneous Financial Provisions

1. The Union and the States are empowered to make grants for any public purpose even though that purpose may not fall within their respective legislative powers (Art. 282). This is virtually a saving clause which will enable the Union or a State to meet an unforeseen contingency.

2. The power to make laws regulating the payment of moneys into, withdrawals from, and custody of the Consolidated Fund of India, is vested in Parliament. A similar power is vested in the State Legislatures with respect to the Consolidated Funds of the States (Art. 283).

3. All moneys received by any officer employed in connection with the affairs of the Union, other than revenues or public moneys raised or received by the Government of India, are to be paid into the public account of India. Moneys received or deposited with any court also will be paid into the same account. Similarly, such moneys received by State officers will be paid in the public account of the State (Art. 284)

4. Article 290 provides for adjustments between the Union and one or more States, of expenses incurred on behalf of any Court or Commission which rendered service to both, or on account of the pension payable to a person who was in the service of the Crown in India before the commencement of the Constitution or had been in the service of the Union or of a State after the inauguration of the Constitution. If the Union and the State concerned do not come to an agreement in such a matter, it will be determined by an arbitrator appointed by the Chief Justice of India.

5. *Borrowing*. The Union Executive is empowered under Article 292 to borrow from anywhere it likes upon the security of the Consolidated Fund of India. However, Parliament may fix from time to time the limits within which such borrowings could be made as well as the giving of guarantees within such limits. Under Article 293, the State Executive also is empowered to borrow on the security of the Consolidated Fund of the State, but the area from which it can borrow is limited to the territory of India. The State Legislature has the power to fix limits as well as regulate the giving of guarantees within such limits.

The Government of India may, subject to any conditions which Parliament may lay down in this regard, make loans to any State within the limits fixed by Parliament or give guarantees in respect of loans raised by any State. So long as such loans or parts thereof are still outstanding, the State concerned may not raise another loan without the consent of the Government of India. When such consent is sought, the Government of India may grant it subject to such conditions as it may think fit to impose. The provision for the Union making loans to the States has been fully made use of by the States. The nature and extent of it may be seen from the following statement of the second Finance Commission:

> In recent years there has been a phenomenal growth in the number and amount of the loans given by the Government of India to the States. On 15th August 1947, the total debt of the Provincial

Governments to the Centre was only Rs. 43.97 crores. Between that date and 31st March 1951, the number of loans had risen by about 220 and the outstanding amount had gone up to Rs. 195.41 crores. During the period of the first Five Year Plan, namely, from 1st April 1951 to 31st March 1956, the number of outstanding loans rose by about 2570, the total outstanding debt on the latter date being approximately Rs. 900 crores. These loans have been made for a variety of purposes, but largely to implement the Plan. The amounts of individual loans have ranged from small sums to crores of rupees. The rates of interest have varied from 1 to 5 per cent, some of the loans being free of interest. Except where a concessional rate has been given, the rates have generally been determined with reference to the redemption yield of Central loans with a remaining maturity approximating to the period for which the loans are given. A number of loans are due to be repaid in equated annual instalments, including both principal and interest. Others are repayable in periods ranging from 1 to 40 years.[1]

The Commission has made a number of significant observations on the manner in which the financial relations between the Union and the States are affected as a result of these loans. The following observations deserve special mention in this context:

> The large number of loans given and the wide variation in the rates of interest and the terms of repayment have introduced unavoidable complication in the financial relations between the Union and the States. It will simplify matters and save a great deal of labour and accounting, if these loans are consolidated and the rates of interest and the terms of repayment rationalized.
>
> We have already indicated our objection to the grant of an indirect subsidy by way of concessional interest. At the same time, we think that the Union should not deal with the States as if it were a commercial banker. The Union and the States are partners in the big enterprise of national development, and while there is no reason why the Union should lend to the States at less than the true cost of its borrowing, there is no justification either for charging more than the true cost. In calculating such cost, all factors which affect the cost of borrowing should be taken into consideration.[2]

6. Property, Contracts, *etc*. Articles 294 and 295 provide for the succession to property, assets, rights, liabilities and obligations resulting from the coming into being of the Republic of India on 26 January 1950. Since the transfer of power in India was a peaceful process, there was hardly any complication arising out of these matters. The two significant factors to be taken into account were the partition of the country between India and Pakistan and the accession of the princely states to the Indian Union. Provision has been made for both under the two Articles mentioned above. According to them

> ...subject to the adjustments under the partition of the country and the conditions under which the former Indian States acceded to the Union, the new Governments of India and the States succeeded to all property and assets, as well as all rights, liabilities and obligations which the Governments of the Dominion of India, the Provinces and the acceded Indian States had prior to the coming into operation of the Constitution.[3]

7. Territorial Waters. The provision on territorial waters was introduced in the Constitution at a very late stage. Explaining the reason for its inclusion, Ambedkar said that it was meant to remove any possibility of a future claim by any one of the maritime States which acceded to the Indian Union that the territorial waters of these States were free from the jurisdiction of the Central Government although the States themselves had acceded to the Union. "The Constitution hence expressly states that if any maritime State

1. *Report of the Finance Commission*, 1957, p. 52.
2. Ibid., p. 53.
3. See the interpretation of the Supreme Court of Art. 294(b) in Maharaj Umeg Singh vs. State of Bombay, 1955, 2 S.C.R. 164.

joined the Union, the territorial waters of such State will go to the Central Government. That kind of question shall never be subject to any kind of dispute or adjudication."[1]

According to Article 297, "all lands, minerals and other things of value underlying the ocean within the territorial waters of India shall vest in the Union and be held for the purposes of the Union."

The question of the jurisdiction over territorial waters has been a prolific source of litigation in some of the older federations, notably the United States where the controversy mostly centered on the exploitation of mineral and oil resources in territorial waters. The matter was taken to the Supreme Court of the United States on several occasions and every time the Court gave a verdict in favour of the Federal Government. The Court held that the United States had paramount rights in the lands in question, since the ocean is of vital importance to the national interest. both commercially and for the purposes of national defence, and those interests are primarily the responsibility of the nation as a whole, rather than of a particular State.[2] But the effect of these decisions of the Court was partly nullified by an Act of the U.S. Congress of 1953 which ceded the oil rights in these submerged lands to the States from whose shores they extend.

8. *Power to Carry on Trade, etc.* Article 298 embodies a rather unusual provision which empowers the executives of the Union and of each State to carry on any trade or business and to acquire, hold and dispose of any property and to enter into contracts for any purpose to the extent permitted by the respective legislative powers of Parliament and the State Legislatures. There was no such provision in the Constitution as originally passed in 1949. It was added in 1956 by the Seventh Amendment of the Constitution. The addition of the Article was necessitated by the controversy between the citizen and the State on the scope of the Fundamental Rights guaranteeing the right to carry on any trade or profession. It was contended on behalf of the citizen that the State was not justified in depriving him of his right to carry on any trade or business through its policy of nationalization or socialization of a particular activity. On the other hand, it was argued on behalf of the State that it was justified in undertaking such activities in the public interest in conformity with the objectives embodied in the Directive Principles of State Policy. A large number of cases had come up before the High Courts and the Supreme Court in this connection. Some of these cases have been referred to earlier. The provisions of Article 298 seek to remove all doubts in the matter and establish the validity of the activities of the State in the economic and commercial spheres.

9. *Contracts.* Every contract that is entered into by the Government of India with any party has to be expressly made by the President. Similarly, in the case of every contract by a State, it has to be expressly made by the Governor. But all such contracts may be executed on behalf of the President or the Governor by any authorized person in a manner that is prescribed for the purpose (Art. 299). The fact that every contract is entered into by the President or the Governor does not mean that either of them has any personal liability in the matter. Similarly, an officer who has been authorized to enter into such contract also has no personal liability.

Interpreting the scope of this article, the Supreme Court held:

---

1. C.A.D.VIII, p. 891.
2. United States *vs.* California, 332, U.S. 19.

We do not think [that] the provisions were inserted for the sake of mere form. We feel that they are there to safeguard Government against unauthorised contracts. If in fact a contract is unauthorised or in excess of authority, it is right that the Government should be safeguarded. On the other hand, an officer entering into a contract on behalf of Government can always safeguard himself by having recourse to the proper form. In between is a large class of contracts, probably by far the greatest in numbers, which though authorised, are for one reason or other, not in proper form. It is only right that an innocent contracting party should not suffer because of this and if there is no other defect or objection. We have no doubt that Government will always accept the responsibility. If not, its interests are safeguarded as we think the Constitution intended that they should be.[1]

10. *Suits and Proceedings*. The Government of India is authorized under Article 300 to sue or be sued by the name of the Union of India. Similarly, the Government of a State may sue or be sued by the name of the State. For instance, if a dispute arises between the Government of India and the Government of Punjab and the matter is taken to the Supreme Court by the Government of India, the case will be known as the Union of India *vs*. the State of Punjab.

To examine the financial relations between the Union and the States is indeed to traverse difficult terrain. The provisions are detailed, often expressed in difficult and clumsy legal terminology. Moreover, almost every general proposition is qualified or modified by exceptions or limitations. Nevertheless, these detailed provisions have the merit of eliminating the possibility of much litigation which has been the bane of the older federations. Critics of the bulkiness of the Constitution should take special note of this. It is a striking feature in the working of the Constitution that the volume of litigation in this field so far has been negligible.

Thus, the financial provisions of the Constitution have on the whole avoided the pitfalls of several other federal constitutions. This has been achieved by sharply demarcating the tax jurisdictions of each authority —Union and State—in order that conflicts in the concurrent zone of tax jurisdiction may not arise. The Constitution has not followed the simple dichotomy of direct and indirect tax commonly followed in some federations. Both direct and indirect taxes have been allocated to the Union and the States. The rationale of the division is the fundamental principles of federal finance, namely, efficiency and suitability. The principle of adequacy has been met by the provisions dealing with federal grants-in-aid. The framework of the entire financial fabric is based upon the assumption of Union-State coordination, so that the fiscal relations between the Union and the States may be harmonious.

Viewing the Union-State relationship in the financial field as a whole, one finds that it is in harmony with the general nature of the Indian federalism, namely, the tendency for centralization. The Union Government is financially stabler and stronger than the State Government. This was necessary to facilitate the planned development of the country as a whole and to check parochial and even separatist tendencies in the economic activities within individual States. As it is, the States are, in view of their limited resources, bound to look up to the Union for financial aid for most if not all of their developmental projects. Naturally, they will have to follow the lead of the Union and at times, even submit to its dictation. This has its merits as well as defects.

But in the present context, marked as it is by low growth rates of Gross Domestic Product, absence of significant amelioration in the conditions of the mass of the people below the poverty line, widening regional disparities within the country and the ever increasing inflationary potential, there is need for a review of the existing Union-State financial relations in the spirit of cooperative federalism that the country endeavours to

1. Chaturbhuj Vithaldas *vs*. Moreswar Parashram, A.I.R. 1954, S.C. 236.

develop. If this is accepted by the Union Government, and this is bound to happen, the existing financial relations between the Union and the States are bound to change in future as the pattern of Indian economy undergoes change. Adjustments will have to be made in the light of such change. Legislative enactments on taxation cannot be made for all time to come. The relation of the State Governments to the Union Government is a dynamic relation; and its problems cannot be solved once for all any more than the problems of life itself.

Towards A more Federal India

Federalism in India from the very beginning of the Constitution was highly centralized. We have seen earlier the reasons for such a development. But over-centralisation is not a virtue. On the contrary, it is in itself a cause of discord and dissatisfaction, particularly in a country of India's size and linguistic and cultural diversity. The Constitution should make express provision for the reflection of such geographic, linguistic and cultural diversity. It is generally accepted by all that the Centre is overloaded with powers and functions. Decentralisation is therefore the foremost agenda to make Indian federalism more efficient and healthy. In fact, a single constitution for a country of many and varied subnationalities is an anachronistic centralism. Already there is evidence of it in the Constitution with Jammu & Kashmir having a special position.

The starting point for fresh thinking in regard to devolution has to be the recognition of sub-nationalism as a growing reality. The federal centre has to be viewed as the focal point at which the various sub-national identities converge rather than as a source from which power is imposed upon them. Devolutionary measures as a consequence should be worked out in a spirit of partnership between the federal and sub-national levels rather than unilaterally by a dominant Centre.

This problem has been highlighted in a Memorandum by the West Bengal government some years ago by pointing out that the unity of the country has been subjected to considerable strain by concentration of all powers and responsibilities in the Centre. The consequence, according to the Memorandum, was a deviation from democratic norms, aggravation of tension and distrust and denial of the rights of various economic and social and cultural groups. The excessive outlay on Defence, the Police and the Intelligence network was a negative feature of this development. Since the autonomy of the States was deliberately sought to be suppressed, economic growth was stultified. To reverse this trend, it seems necessary to amend the Constitution to enshrine in full the majesty of the federal principle.

The federal system is a living organism which can survive and flourish only if the constituent units function in an atmosphere of true autonomy and freedom. A more federal India must, therefore, strive to be attractive enough for all its units to want to stay as its integral parts, willingly and with a sense of belonging. Its rich civilisational heritage must remain eclectic and indeed become more so rather than be distorted by those who want to make it narrowly exclusive. The benefits of its common market in goods, services and employment must be seen to flow equitably to all, whether rich or poor, whether of the so-called mainstream or of the periphery. The advantages of belonging to a common polity and having a common citizenship must become evident to all. Simultaneously it is necessary to initiate measures which will facilitate the devolution of more powers to the States. It is not impossible to progress towards a more federal India with attributes that include rather than exclude. In this context the Commission that was set up in 2000 to review the working of the Constitution with a view to bringing about necessary changes deserves widespread attention.

***

37

INTER-STATE TRADE AND COMMERCE

FROM THE very beginning of its deliberations, the Constituent Assembly was keen to ensure the freedom of inter-state trade and commerce throughout the Union. In fact, one of the primary purposes of a federal Union itself is the establishment of the freedom of commerce. According to some writers, it is the Commerce Clause of the U.S. Constitution which made the United States one united nation. For, under the Commerce Clause, the national government of the United States assumed enormous powers of regulating a wide variety of activities of the citizens and of the constituent States. Today, its powers embrace not only the direct control over inter-state commerce but indirectly also intra-state commerce. In one of its famous decisions, the Supreme Court of the United States said that the U.S. Congress has a right to regulate that which regulated inter-state commerce.[1] But the process has involved an unending legal conflict which is still raging between the Union and the States even after two centuries of the working of the Constitution. In Australia too, the situation is not happy owing to the omnibus character of the right to inter-state trade and commerce that is embodied in the Constitution. Section 92 of the Constitution is the relevant provision there and according to Australian critics it stands as a bar to any progressive legislation which the Commonwealth Government would want to introduce. For example, when the Australian Government wanted to nationalize banking, Section 92 was held as a bar to such action on the part of the Government.

The framers of the Indian Constitution had the benefit of these experiences at the time of drafting the provisions dealing with inter-state trade and commerce as embodied in the Constitution. That is why Articles 301 to 307 form a well thought out scheme and, in the opinion of one of the members of the Drafting Committee, "are about as nearly perfect as human ingenuity could possibly make them."[2] The objective behind the principle of freedom of inter-state commerce is that within the country, trade and commerce should develop to the largest possible extent: it should not be hindered by artificial barriers and restrictions imposed by the various States of the federation. The Drafting Committee had given the utmost consideration to this objective while framing the provisions dealing with inter-state trade and commerce.

Originally, the Draft Constitution had no chapter dealing with inter-state trade and commerce. The articles dealing with freedom of trade and commerce were scattered in different parts of the Draft Constitution. One article, found its place even in the chapter on Fundamental Rights which said that "trade and commerce, subject to any law made by

1. The Minnesota Rate cases, 230, U.S. 352.
2. T.T. Krishnamachari, C.A.D. VIII, p. 1138.

Parliament, shall be free throughout the territory of India."[1] As a result, members had considerable difficulty in understanding the implications of these provisions as a whole.

In order, therefore, to give the House a complete picture of all the provisions relating to freedom of trade and commerce, the Drafting Committee felt that it was much better to assemble all these different articles scattered in the different parts of the Draft Constitution into one single part and to set them out *seriatim*, so that at one glance it would be possible to know what are the provisions with regard to the freedom of trade and commerce throughout India.[2]

The scheme as finally embodied in the Constitution has taken into account the larger interests of India as a whole as well as the interests of particular States and the wide geography of this country in which the interests of one region differ from those of another.

In a federation, one has to take into account the large interests of the country and permit freedom of trade and commerce as far as possible. Secondly, you cannot ignore altogether regional interests. Thirdly, there must be power of intervention of the Centre in any case of crisis to deal with peculiar problems that might arise in any part of India. The scheme has taken into consideration all these three factors.[3]

Speaking on the general nature of the provisions, Ambedkar said:

I should also like to say that according to the provisions contained in this part, it is not the intention to make trade and commerce absolutely free, that is to say, deprive both Parliament and States of any power to depart from the fundamental provision that trade and commerce shall be free. The freedom of trade and commerce is subject to certain limitations which may be imposed by Parliament or by the Legislatures of the various States, subject to the fact that the limitations contained in the power of Parliament is confined to cases arising from scarcity of goods in one part of the territory of India, and in the case of the States it must be justified on the ground of public interest.[4]

Article 301 is general in scope and enacts that "subject to the other provisions of this Part, trade, commerce and intercourse throughout the territory of India shall be free."[5] Explaining the scope of the freedom embodied in this provision, the Supreme Court held that "the freedom of inter-state and intra-state trade or business embodied in Article 301 is not a fundamental right conferred by Part III of the Constitution and, therefore, cannot be enforced by a petition under Article 32."[6] In other words, freedom of trade and commerce is not a matter of civil liberty. Yet it is not a declaration of a mere platitude or the expression of a pious hope of a declaratory character; it is also not a mere statement of a directive principle of State policy; it embodies and enshrines a principle of paramount importance that the economic unity of the country will provide the main sustaining force for the stability and progress of the political and cultural unity of the country.[7]

After having stated the general nature of the freedom of trade and commerce, the Constitution details the limitations to this freedom. There are five such limitations.

1. Parliament may impose restrictions in any part of the territory of India in the public interest (Art. 302). The purpose of this provision is to allow the Government of

---

1. Art. 16 of the Draft Constitution.
2. Ambedkar. Ibid., p. 1124.
3. Alladi Krishnaswami Aiyar, C.A.D. VIII, p. 1141.
4. Ibid., p. 1124.
5. See in this connection, T.K. Tope, "Freedom of Trade and Commerce under the Indian Constitution" (1962) I S.C.J. 29.
6. Ram Chandra Palai vs. State of Orissa, A.I.R. 1956, S.C. 298. See also the Bangalore Woollen, Cotton and Silk Mills Co. Ltd. vs. The Corporation of Bangalore, (1962) I S.C.J 214.
7. Attibari Tea Co. Ltd. vs. The State of Assam, A.I.R. 1961, S.C. 232.

India to restrict the movement of goods so as to ensure a well-balanced economy and the proper organization and ordering of supplies of goods and services. Famine may be raging in one part of the country while there is plenty in another part, as has been the experience of the country in regard to food during the last several years. If Parliament has no effective powers to check such abnormal situations, freedom of trade and commerce, instead of being a blessing, will become a menace to the freedom of life itself.

2. Although Parliament is empowered to restrict the free movement of articles of trade and commerce, the laws passed by Parliament in this context ought to be normally non-discriminatory in character. In other words, it should not prefer one State to another. But when any part of the country is suffering from scarcity of goods. Parliament may, to meet such a situation, pass even a discriminatory law (Art. 303).

3. A State Legislature may impose on goods imported from other States any tax if similar goods produced in that State also are taxed in a like manner. A State Legislature is also authorized to impose reasonable restrictions on the freedom of trade and commerce with or within that State as may be required in the public interest (Art. 304). Here is a certain amount of discretion given to the States to regulate inter-state trade and commerce under exceptional conditions. But this is subject to central control. According to this, any Bill which seeks to introduce such restrictions can be introduced in the State Legislature only with the previous sanction of the President. The purpose of the provision is obvious. If, on account of parochial patriotism or provincialism and in disregard of the larger interests of India as a whole, a Bill or an amending Bill to an existing law is being introduced in a State Legislature, it will be open to the President to withhold the sanction. The President will have opportunity to see that the legislation is in the public interest and the restriction imposed is reasonable.

The Supreme Court had occasion to consider all these aspects when it was called upon to declare invalid the Assam Taxation (on Goods Carried by Roads or Inland Waterways) Act of 1954, as the Act was alleged to have put a direct restriction on the freedom of inter-state trade and commerce. The Court held that the Act, while it had made a direct restriction on trade, had not received the assent of the President as required by Article 304(b) and, therefore, was invalid.[1]

4. Under Article 305, tax laws existing at the time of the inauguration of the Constitution were safeguarded even if they violated the freedom of inter-state trade and commerce and power of Parliament to regulate it.[2] At the same time, the President was empowered to make any changes to those laws as thought fit. This article in its present form was added by the Fourth Amendment of the Constitution. 1955, which saves also all laws providing for State monopolies which were passed before the coming into effect of the Fourth Amendment.[3] The fact that every restriction should be reasonable in relation to its objective leaves the Supreme Court with adequate power to examine and adjudicate upon the reasonableness of such restrictions and declare invalid those that are unreasonable in its view.

5. Finally, under Article 307, Parliament is empowered to appoint such authority as

1. A.I.R. 1961, S.C. 232.
2. See in this connection V.G. Ramachandran, "Is Taxation Law Subject to Exercise of Fundamental Rights ?" (1961) I S.C.J. 3i.
3. Ram Chandra Palai vs. State of Orissa, op. cit.

it considers appropriate for carrying out the purposes of Articles 301 to 304 and to confer on that authority such powers and duties as it thinks necessary. Speaking on this provision. Ambedkar said:

> [It] is merely an article which would enable Parliament to establish an authority such as the Inter- State Commission as it exists in the U.S.A. Without specifically mentioning any such authority it is thought desirable to leave Parliament freedom to establish any kind of authority that it may think fit.

Australia too has such an Inter-State Commission which renders valuable service in the field of inter-state trade and commerce.

Taxes on Inter-State Sales and Purchases (Art. 286)

The constitutional provisions dealing with taxes on purchase and sale of goods were not in the original draft of the Constitution. They were introduced by Ambedkar in the form of amendments almost towards the end of the deliberations of the Constituent Assembly. Speaking on the necessity of these provisions, he said that although

> ....the financial system which has been laid down in the scheme of the Draft Constitution is better than any other financial system that I know of, I think it must be said that it suffers from one defect. That defect is that the Provinces [States] are very largely dependent for their resources upon the grants made to them by the Centre.... I think, therefore, that while a large number of resources on which the Provinces depend have been concentrated in the Centre, from the point of view of constitutional government it is desirable at least to leave one important source of revenue with the Provinces.[1]

While it was felt that an important source of income should be left to the States by allowing them to tax the purchase or sale of goods, it was also keenly felt that the use of such tax power by the States should not be allowed to affect prejudicially the freedom of inter-state trade and commerce. Hence Article 286(1) provided that no State could impose a tax on the sale or purchase of goods if such sale or purchase took place (a) outside the State;[2] or (b) in the course of the import of the goods into, or export of the goods out of, the territory of India. There was, however, an Explanation to sub-clause (a) above which provided that "a sale or purchase shall be deemed to have taken place in the State in which the goods have actually been delivered as a direct result of such sale or purchase for the purpose of consumption in that State, notwithstanding the fact that under the general law relating to sale of goods the property in the goods has by reason of such sale or purchase passed in another State". Section (2) of Article 286 provided that "except as permitted by Parliament, no State shall impose a tax on the sale or purchase takes place in the course of inter-state trade or commerce."[3] Finally, under section (3) of the same article, a Slate Legislature was prohibited from imposing a tax on the sale or purchase of any goods declared by Parliament as essential to the life of the community, unless assent to such law was given by the President.[4]

The operation of sales tax laws made by the States under these provisions, however, soon created practical difficulties; and controversies which resulted from them reached

---

1. C.A.D.IX.339.
2. Copper Corporation Ltd. vs. The State of Bihar (1961) I S.C.J. I S.C.J. 457. Also see The State of Kerala *vs.* Coal Company Ltd. (1961) II S.C.J. 20 and Burmah Shell Ltd. *vs.* The Commercial Tax Officer (1962) II S.C.J. 251.
3. E. Narasimhan *vs.* The State of Orissa (1962) I S.C.J. 54.
4. Stockholders' Association Ltd. *vs.* The State of M.P- (1963) I S.C.J. 383.

the Supreme Court in appeals from the High Courts. In the first of the two Travancore-Cochin cases,[1] the Court considered the scope of Article 286(1) (b) and held:

A sale by export involves a series of integrated activities commencing from the agreement of sale with a foreign buyer and ending with the delivery of the goods to a common carrier for transport out of the country by land or sea. Such a sale cannot be dissociated from the export without which it cannot be effectuated.

In the second case,[2] however, the Court held:

The last purchase of goods made by the exporter for the purpose of exporting them to implement orders already received from a foreign buyer or expected to be received subsequently in the course of business, and the first sale by the importer to fulfil orders pursuant to which the goods were imported or orders expected to be received after the import, are not within the prohibition of Article 286(1) (b). What is exempted is the sale or purchase taking place in the course of import into or export out of the territory of India. The word 'course' etymologically denotes movement from one point to another, and the expression 'in the course of' not only implies a period of time during which the movement is in progress but postulates also a connected relation.

The scope of Article 286(1) (a) was first interpreted by the Supreme Court in the case of the State of Bombay vs. the United Motors (India) Ltd.[3] A majority of the Court then held that:

Article 286(1) (a), read with the Explanation thereto and construed in the light of Articles 301 and 304, prohibited the taxation of sales or purchases involving inter-State elements by all States except the States in which the goods were actually delivered for the purpose of consumption therein and that clause (2) of Article 286 did not affect the power of the State in which delivery of the goods was so made to tax the sales or purchases of the kind mentioned in the Explanation, the effect of which was to convert such inter-State transactions into intra-State transactions and to take them out of the operation of clause (2) of that Article.

The Court was called, upon two years later, in the case of Bengal Immunity Company vs. the State of Bihar, to reverse this decision and give its verdict against any State Sale's Tax law that hindered the flow of inter-state trade and commerce.[4] It was not easy for the Court to reverse its own decision, particularly one of recent date. Yet, it decided in favour of it. Speaking for the majority,[5] the then Acting Chief Justice S.R. Das said:

The majority decision does not merely determine the rights of the two contending parties to the Bombay appeal. Its effect is far-reaching as it affects the rights of all consuming public. It authorises the imposition and levying of a tax by the State on an interpretation of a constitutional provision which appears to us to be unsupportable. To follow that interpretation will result in perpetuating what, with humility we say, an error and in perpetuating a tax burden imposed on the people which, according to our considered opinion, is manifestly and wholly unauthorised. It is not an ordinary pronouncement declaring the rights of two private individuals *inter se*. It involves an adjudication on the taxing power of the States as against the consuming public generally. If the decision is erroneous, as indeed we conceive it to be, we owe it to that public to protect them against the illegal tax burdons which the States are seeking to impose on the strength of that erroneous recent decision.

The difference between the majority and minority opinions centered on the scope of Article 286(1) (a) read with the Explanation following it and Article 286(2). The respective

1. 1952, S.C.R. 1112.
2. 1954, S.C.R. 53..
3. 1953. 2 S.C.R. 603.
4. 1955, 2 S.C.R. 603.
5. Of the seven judges who heard the appeal, four were in favour of reversal while the remaining three were opposed to it.

positions of the majority and minority Judges were summarized by Justice Sinha (who voiced the minority view) as follows:

Coming to the merits of the case in hand, we are all agreed that' the Explanation to Article 286(1) (a) of the Constitution has created a legal fiction as a result of which a transaction of sale or a purchase partaking of an inter- State character has been treated as a domestic transaction. The fiction has localized sales or purchases contemplated by the Explanation, by converting such transactions as would otherwise have been inter-State .sales or purchases into sales or purchases inside one State in a sense in which it is placed in a class distinct and separate from what is referred to as sales or purchases "outside the State" in the main body of Article 286(l)(a) which prohibits imposition of tax by any State. There is a general agreement amongst us, 1 take it, that the main purpose of creating the fiction is to prevent multiple taxation at the same transaction, but, it may be added, not altogether to stop the taxation of such transactions. We are also agreed that full effect must be given to the legal fiction on the supposition that the putative state of affairs is the real one- While thus agreeing on the general principle bearing on the question of the purpose and scope of a legal fiction, we are again divided on the question of how far the legal fiction should be carried in its actual application. For the reasons given by my brother Judge Venkatrama Ayyar, I agree with him that the fiction created by the Explanation brings such a sale within the taxing power of the State within which such a sale is said to have taken place. Such a result is brought about not by holding that the Explanation has conferred positively the power on the relevant State to impose sales-tax, but by holding that such an inside sale is beyond the scope of the prohibition contained in the main body of Article 286(1) (a) which interdicts the imposition of a tax on a sale "outside the State". The Explanation has got to be read as an integral part of Article 286(1) (a), and thus read, it means negatively that a sale or purchase outside a State cannot be taxed; and by necessary implication, that a sale or purchase outside a State cannot be taxed; and by necessary implication, that a sale or purchase inside a State may be taxed by that State as falling outside the mischief of the prohibition directed against the imposition of a tax on a sale or purchase of goods outside a State; in other words, as soon as a sale or purchase of goods is declared to be outside the pale of the prohibition contained in Article 286 (1) (a), the State's power of imposing a tax contained in Article 246 read with item 54 of List II of the Seventh Schedule comes into operation. I do not find myself in agreement with the view propounded by my brother Judge S-R. Das chiefly because that view goes beyond the purpose of the creation of the fiction which admittedly was to prevent multiple taxation. The view as propounded by him besides preventing multiple taxation, goes to the length of prohibiting any imposition of sales-tax by any State. Such, in my opinion, was not the intention of Constitution. Whereas the imposition of multiple sales-tax on transactions of sale or purchase may be an obstacle to the free flow of inland trade and commerce, the imposition of sales-tax by a single State in which the sale or purchase may be an obstacle to the free flow of inland trade and commerce, the imposition of sales-tax by a single State in which the sale is deemed to have taken place by virtue of the Explanation cannot be predicted as having such an effect. The view propounded by my learned brother Judge Venkatrama Ayyar is thus not inconsistent with the avowed purpose of the Constitution, as expressed in Article 301, which provided that trade, commerce and intercourse shall be free throughout the territory of India. In my opinion, the view propounded by my learned brother Judge S.R. Das about the actual application of the legal fiction stops short of giving full effect to that fiction. Allied with this question is the controversy as to whether clause (2) of Article 286 is subject to Article 286 (1) (a) read with the Explanation or vice versa.

The Court's divided decision as well as its reversal of its own earlier decision put the whole question of taxes on inter-state sales by the States in a new perspective. The decision, as it stood, prohibited the States from imposing sales tax on any inter-state transaction until Parliament by law provided otherwise. The upshot of the divergent opinions of the judges was the Sixth Amendment of the Constitution. The Amendment retained Clause (1) of Article 286 in the original, form, but, for the rest, the following provisions were substituted:

286(2). Parliament may by law formulate principles for determining when a sale or purchase of goods takes place in any of the ways mentioned in clause (1).

286(3). Any law of a State shall, in so far as it imposes, or authorises the imposition of, a tax on the sale or purchase of goods declared by Parliament by law to be of special importance in inter-State trade or commerce, be subject to such restrictions and conditions in regard to the system of levy, rates and other incidents of the tax as Parliament may by law specify.

In accordance with these provisions, Parliament passed the Central Sales Tax Act, 1956, embodying the above mentioned principles. The principles and their objects are outlined in the Prefatory Note of the Act itself which reads as follows:

In the interest of the national economy of India certain amendments were undertaken in the Constitution by the Constitution (Sixth Amendment) Act, 1956, whereby:

(a) taxes on sales or purchases of goods in the course of inter-State trade or commerce were brought expressly within the purview of the legislative jurisdiction of Parliament;

(b) restrictions could be imposed on the powers of State legislatures with respect to the levy of taxes on the sales or purchases of goods within the State where the goods are of special importance in inter-State trade or commerce.

The amendments, at the same time, authorized Parliament to formulate principles for determining when a sale or purchase takes place in the course of inter-state trade or commerce or in the course of export or import in or outside a State in order that the legislative spheres of Parliament and the State legislatures become clearly demarcated. In the case of goods of special importance in inter-state trade or commerce, a law of Parliament is to lay down the restrictions and conditions subject to which any State law may regulate the tax on sales or purchases of such goods in the State. As specifically pointed out in the Prefatory Note:

This Bill seeks to provide for the legislation authorised by the Constitution as amended above with a view to enabling the State Governments to raise additional revenues by levying tax on inter-State transactions which are at present immune from tax under their respective sales-tax law. After taking into account the recommendations of the Taxation Enquiry Commission and in consultation with the States, the Government of India are of the view that the following principles should govern the scheme of the detailed legislation on the subject:

(*i*) The Central Government should authorise the State Government to impose on behalf of the 'Central Government a tax on the sale or purchase of goods in the course of inter-state trade or commerce. The Central legislation should also delegate to the States the Central Government's power to levy and collect the tax and for this purpose prescribe the same system of registration, assessment, etc. as prevails in the States concerned under their own sales-tax system.

(*ii*) An important aspect of the Central legislation will be concerned with the definition of the locale of sales for the purpose of defining in detail the relative jurisdiction, firstly of the Union and the States and, secondly, of the States *inter se*. It is therefore necessary that the law should define clearly, with specific reference to sales-tax, the circumstances in which a sale or purchase becomes taxable by a particular State and no other. It should also define for the purpose of the Constitutional restrictions on the States' power to impose a tax under item 54 of the State List, when a sale or purchase of goods may be said to take place:

(*a*) in the course of export out of India,

(*b*) in the course of import into India, and

(*c*) in the course of inter-State trade of commerce.

(*iii*) The Central legislation should provide for the declaration of certain commodities which are in the nature of raw materials and of special importance in inter-state trade or commerce and lay down the restrictions, and conditions as to the rate, system of levy and other incidents of tax subject to which the States may impose tax on the sale or purchase thereof.

The matter does not seem to have reached a finality as a result of this legislation. In fact, it has been only the beginning. The Union Government has been attempting to increase the list of items on which State sales tax is exempted. The States have been resisting this attempt as they fear that the only significant source of increasing revenue for them will eventually dry up. The Union Government has been assuring the States that adequate compensation will be paid to them for the items which are taken out of the purview of the sales tax law. The States, however, are generally unwilling to accept this position and hence an unending controversy has been the result. From time to time efforts have been made under the leadership of the Union to find an amicable solution to this problem. In the year 2000 an attempt was made to bring down extreme differences between different States regarding the rates of sales tax on certain items but several States have expressed their reservation in accepting and implementing the Central proposals. It is unlikely that this problem will get solved amicably to the satisfaction of all concerned.

***

38

EMERGENCY PROVISIONS

NO CHAPTER of the Constitution has been the subject of more acrimonious attack by its critics than that dealing with the Emergency Provisions. The Constituent Assembly witnessed one of the most agitated scenes during the discussion on these provisions. Many prominent members of the Assembly opposed the inclusion of these provisions in the Constitution as they thought that they were inconsistent with the democratic provisions embodied elsewhere. The majority of the members however favoured the inclusion of these provisions, although somewhat reluctantly, as a precautionary measure against possible disruptive forces destroying the newly established Union.

The Constitution provides for three different categories of emergency and in each case the President is empowered to declare the Emergency.

War Emergency (Art. 352)

If the President is satisfied that a grave emergency exists whereby the security of India or any part of its territory is threatened by war, external aggression or armed rebellion, he may proclaim a state of emergency. The Proclamation may be revoked subsequently; if not, it should be laid before Parliament. If Parliament does not approve of it within two months, it will become ineffective.

It may be that at the time of the Proclamation, the House of the People has been dissolved or its dissolution takes place within two months after the Proclamation. In either case, it shall be laid before the Council of States. If the Council passes it, it must still be approved by the House within thirty days after the meeting of the new House of the People. If, on the other hand, the Council itself has not approved the Proclamation, it will cease to be valid.

The power of the President to declare an Emergency may be made use of even before the actual occurrence of the aggression or disturbance, if the President is satisfied that there is imminent danger.

A Proclamation so approved shall operate in the first instance for a period of six months but may be extended for a further period of six months if approved by Parliament.

Effect of the Proclamation (Arts. 353 and 354)

As soon as the Emergency is proclaimed, the federal provisions of the Constitution may cease to function in the area affected by the Proclamation. As a result, there is a two-fold expansion of the authority of the Union. Firstly, the executive power of the Union will extend to the giving of any directions to any State Executive in the emergency area. Secondly, Parliament's law-making power will extend to the subjects enumerated in the State List. Further, the President is empowered to restrict or prohibit by order the distribution of revenues that are normally to be assigned entirely to the States under the financial provisions of the Constitution. However, all such orders have to be placed before each House of Parliament for its approval. The combined effect of the operation of these provisions is the emergence of a fullfledged unitary government.

The first Proclamation of Emergency under Article 353 by the President of India after the inauguration of the Constitution was in 1962 as a result of the Chinese attack on India's territories during November that year. The President also promulgated an Ordinance incorporating the provisions of the Defence of India Act of 1939 to enable the Government of India to meet the situation created by the national emergency. Both Houses of Parliament were summoned to meet soon after the Proclamation. Parliament, after approving the Proclamation, passed the Defence of India Act and rules were framed under the Act for the implementation of its provisions. The Proclamation lasted only for a short time and was withdrawn during January 1963. The second and the third Proclamations of Emergency under Article 352 were made in 1965 and 1971 respectively. On both occasions it was Pakistani aggression that compelled on President to proclaim the Emergency. The Proclamation was followed, each time, by the same steps which were taken at the time of the Proclamation of Emergency in 1962. The fourth Proclamation of Emergency under Article 352 was made in June 1975. The Proclamation declared that "a grave emergency exists whereby the security of India is threatened by internal disturbances". The Proclamation was placed before both Houses of Parliament a month later and was approved by both Houses in July 1975.

Under Article 355 of the Constitution the Union has the obligation to protect every State against external aggression and internal disturbance and to ensure that the government of every State is carried on in accordance with the provisions of the Constitution.

Constitutional Emergency in the States (Art. 356)

If the President is satisfied on receipt of a report from the Governor or otherwise that a situation has arisen in which the government of a State cannot be carried on in accordance with the provisions of the Constitution, he is empowered to proclaim an Emergency. As a result, (i) he may assume to himself all or any of the functions of the State or he may vest all or any of those functions in the Governor or any other executive authority; (ii) he may declare that the powers of the State Legislature shall be exercisable by Parliament; and (iii) he may make any other incidental or consequential provisions necessary to give effect to the objects of the Proclamation. The President, however, cannot assume to himself any of the powers vested in a High Court.

The Proclamation will have to be approved by the Houses of Parliament in the same manner in which a war emergency Proclamation has to be approved. But even if Parliament has approved the Proclamation, it will normally cease to operate six months after the Proclamation. The Proclamation can be extended if necessary so as to allow the period of Emergency to continue for a maximum of one year.

If the Emergency Proclamation authorizes Parliament to exercise the powers of the State Legislature, it is open to Parliament to adopt one or the other of two courses. It may pass all legislative enactments for the State including financial legislation. But if Parliament does not find it convenient to do all this additional work, it may confer on the President the power of the State Legislature to make laws, or authorize the President to delegate this power to any suitable authority. Parliament is also empowered to authorize the President to sanction expenditure from the Consolidated Fund of the State, if the House of the People is not in session, pending approval of such expenditure by Parliament. It is also provided that any law made by any of the authorities mentioned above will cease to have validity at the end of a year after the Proclamation has ceased to operate.

Suspension of Fundamental Rights (Arts. 358 and 359)

During the period of Emergency as declared under either of the two categories discussed above, the State is empowered to suspend the Fundamental Rights guaranteed under Article 19 of the Constitution. The term 'State' is used here in the same sense in which it has been used in the chapter on Fundamental Rights. It means that the power to suspend the operation of these Fundamental Rights is vested not only in Parliament but also in the Union Executive and even in a subordinate authority. Further, the Constitution empowers the President to suspend the right to move any court of law for the enforcement of any of the Fundamental Rights except those under Articles 20 and 21. It means that virtually the whole chapter on Fundamental Rights except articles 20 and 21 can be suspended during the operation of the Emergency. However, such orders are to be placed before Parliament as soon as possible for its approval.

Financial Emergency (Art. 360)

If the President is satisfied that a situation has arisen whereby the financial stability or credit of India or any part of it is threatened, he may declare a Financial Emergency. The Proclamation in this case also should be approved by Parliament as in the other two cases of emergency.

During the Financial Emergency, "the executive authority of the Union shall extend to the giving of directions to any State to observe such canons of financial propriety as may be specified in the direction" or any other directions which the President may deem necessary for the purpose. Such directions may include those requiring the reduction of salaries and allowances of government servants and even those of the judges of the Supreme Court and the High Courts.

Criticism in the Constituent Assembly

Critics in the Constituent Assembly characterized these provisions as too sweeping and autocratic. K.T. Shah observed:

> Coming to this grand finale and the crowning glory of this chapter of reaction and retrogression I find one cannot but notice two distinct currents of thought underlying and influencing throughout the provisions of this chapter. (1) To arm the Centre with special power against the units and (2) to arm the government against the people.... Looking at all the provisions of this chapter particularly and scrutinising the powers that have been given in almost every article, it seems to me, the name only of liberty or democracy will remain under the Constitution.[1]

H.V. Kamath, who was another severe critic, said:

---

1. C.A.D. VIII, p. 196.

I fear that by this single chapter we are seeking to lay the foundation of a totalitarian State, a police State, a State completely opposed to all the ideals and principles that we have held aloft during the last few decades, a State where the rights and liberties of millions of innocent men and women will be in continuous jeopardy, a State where if there be peace, it will be the peace of the grave and the void of the desert, 1 only pray God that He may grant us wisdom, wisdom to avert any such catastrophe, grant us fortitude and courage.[1]

According to B. Das, these provisions would make the President "a new Frankenstein, something like the South American Presidents who could usurp all powers, including financial, and starve the Provinces". There were others who pointed out that the whole chapter reminded them of Article 48 of the Constitution of the Weimar Republic (1919) of Germany providing for emergency powers, under whose shadow Hitler rode to the seat of supreme power. According to H.N. Kunzru, the emergency financial provisions were a serious threat to the financial autonomy of the States.

While the whole chapter on emergency provisions was the subject of severe attack, two articles in the chapter were its special target. These were Articles 358 and 359 which dealt with the suspension of the freedoms guaranteed under Article 19 and the suspension of the provisions for the enforcement of Fundamental Rights through the courts including the Supreme Court. Dealing with these provisions, Kamath said:

The Constitution has been founded.... on what I would call 'the Grand Affirmation of the Fundamental Rights'. We have tried to build on that the edifice of democracy, but I find surmounting that edifice is the arch of the 'Great Negation'.... and Article 359 to my mind is the key-stone of this arch of autocratic reaction..... As an autocratic negation of liberty, this article takes the palm over all other constitutions in the world. The combined effect of Articles 358 and 359 is that during the emergency all the freedoms guaranteed under Article 19 will be automatically suspended throughout the Union and further the citizen is denied the right of access to courts of law for making complaints about the violation of not only the rights of individual freedom but all other fundamental rights during the period of emergency. A general authorisation of this kind for restricting individual freedom has no parallel anywhere else.[2]

Suspension of the fundamental rights to move the courts was severely criticized by several other speakers also. K.T. Shah drew the particular attention of the House to the precious nature of this right when he said:

Here is one right more precious than perhaps any other because it makes other rights workable, real, concrete and actually experienceable, so that if anybody feels aggrieved because of any of the Fundamental Rights mentioned in Part III being denied, such a person shall be in a position to move the Court which may give him appropriate relief or remedy.[3]

On the same article, Shibban Lal Saksena said:

When we were in jails in 1942, even though it was during the war, the foreign government did not think it fit to deprive us of the right of *habeas corpus*. So if the power is given to the President to abrogate this right, it will be a slur on our Constitution and it should not be allowed to be included in it.

He also pointed out that neither in the Canadian nor in the Australian Constitution was there such a provision.[4]

---

1. Ibid., p. 539.
2. C.A.D. IX, pp. 533-8.
3. Ibid., p. 539.
4. Ibid., p. 541.

All these criticisms were serious and they reflected the fears of many members of the Constituent Assembly as well as large sections of the public. Nevertheless, looking back, one feels that much of it was the result of imaginary fears, an extreme sense of idealism, lack of appreciation of the general nature of the Constitution and the working of federal constitutions in general. The fierce attacks made against these provisions and the fears expressed about them in the Assembly and outside during the time of the framing of the Constitution seem to have lost their sharpness in the light of the experience gained so far. An analysis of these criticisms becomes easier now since the working of the Constitution until now has demonstrated certain reasonably clear trends. For such an analysis, it is proposed to classify these criticisms under the following heads:

1. The federal character of the Constitution will be destroyed and the Union will become all-powerful.
2. The powers of the State—both the Union and the Units—will entirely be concentrated in the hands of the Union Executive.
3. The President will become a dictator.
4. The financial autonomy of the States will be nullified.
5. Fundamental rights will become meaningless and, as a result, the democratic foundations of the Constitution will be destroyed.

These may be examined one by one. It is true that the federal character of the Government can be transformed into a unitary one as a result of the Proclamation of Emergency. But this is more or less true of almost any federation during a period of grave national emergency. The safety and security of the nation is the responsibility of the Union. The claim for the maintenance of the federal character has not the same importance as the requirements of national security. In case of a conflict between the two, the latter should prevail. But such a situation is an exceptional one. Hence the provisions to meet any emergency are the result of abundant caution. As Ambedkar told the critics:

> ....these overriding powers are not the normal feature of the Constitution. Their use and operation are expressly confined to emergencies only. The second consideration is: Could we avoid giving overriding power to the Centre when an emergency has arisen ? Those who do not admit the justification for such overriding powers to the Centre even in an emergency, do not seem to have a clear idea of the problem which lies at the root of the matter.
>
> The solution of this problem depends upon one's answer to this question which is the crux of the problem. There can be no doubt that in the opinion of the vast majority of the people, the residual loyalty of the citizen in any emergency must lie to the Centre and not to the constituent States. For it is only the Centre which can work for a common purpose and for the general interests of the country as a whole. Herein lies the justification for giving to the Centre certain overriding powers to be used in an emergency. And after all what is the obligation imposed upon the constituent States by these emergency powers ? No more than this, that in an emergency, they should take into consideration alongside their own local interests, the opinion and interests of the nation as a whole.[1]

Members of the Assembly were conscious of the many disruptive forces which were operating in different parts of the country even while constitution-making was in progress. As one member[2] pointed out:

> This is the most important provision in the Constitution.... I submit that we must take not a

1. C.A.D.VII,p.42.
2. Naziruddin Ahmed, C.A.D. IX, p. 116.

theoretical view of the affair, but rather a practical view. I submit that there are real dangers threatening the internal peace of the country, apart from the fear of external aggression.... There are many dangers lurking in the way of the establishment and maintenance of democracy in this country. There are forces of disintegration and disorder already visible everywhere.

The specific circumstances under which the Centre may be called upon to take over the administration of a State were detailed by another member[1] in the following terms:

There may be a physical breakdown of the government in the State owing to widespread internal disturbances or external aggression and for some reason or other, law and order cannot be maintained. Naturally, without the Centre's intervention there will be nothing but chaos. Then there may be political breakdown. This is a point which requires careful analysis. A political breakdown can happen when no Ministry can be formed or the Ministries that can be formed are so unstable that the government actually breaks down. Normally, according to the Constitution, when there is great instability in government, the proper procedure will be to dissolve the lower House and reconstitute it. If after a dissolution also, the same factions are reproduced in the local legislature and they make a Ministry impossible, it will then be inevitable for the Centre to step in.... Then there is a third contingency of economic breakdown. Suppose, for instance, in a State the Ministry is alright, but it wants to make itself popular by reducing or cancelling all taxes and running its administration on a bankrupt basis..... Here again, the Centre will have to be very careful. But ultimately it will have to step in.

The necessity for a strong Union to meet any eventuality was widely accepted during the period when the Constitution was being framed. The war in Kashmir, the recalcitrant attitude of some Princely States against joining the Union, armed insurrection in the Telengana region of the Hyderabad State, the circumstances that called for the 'police action' in Hyderabad and a number of other forces—all these were shaking the very foundations of the newly founded Union. Commenting on the federal system envisaged under the Constitution, The Times (London) observed:

The Union must have a strong centre both to protect against disruptive influences and to deal with a number of federating units which differ widely in efficiency, ranging from the long-established regimes of the former British Indian Provinces to the new and untried administrations now controlling territories carved from former Indian States.

It is difficult to question the force of this argument. For the first time in centuries, India has established a single administration embracing the entire country. The Union was a precious achievement; it could not be allowed to be destroyed under the impact of disruptive forces generated by linguism, regionalism or provincialism from within or aggressive forces from without. The States are incapable of successfully facing an external threat and are not always trustworthy in meeting an internal crisis. Diversity of authority in an emergency will spell disaster.

A difficult case may arise when some States are governed by political parties which are different from the political party which is governing at the Centre and the majority of the other States. In such circumstances there is the possibility, through political prejudice, of the Centre taking intolerant action against a State. The framers were aware of such possibilities. Replying to the general debate Ambedkar said:

I do not altogether deny that there is a possibility of these articles being abused or employed for political purposes. But that objection applies to every part of the Constitution which gives power to the Centre to override the Provinces......(The) proper thing we ought to expect is that such articles will never be called into operation and that they would remain a dead letter.[2]

---

1. K. Santhanam, ibid-, p. 153 2. C.A.D.IX,P.177.

In the words of T.T. Krishnamachari, "these emergency provisions have got to be tolerated as a necessary evil and without these provisions it is well nigh possible that all our efforts to frame a Constitution may ultimately be jeopardised."[1]

The very first decade of the working of the Constitution did vindicate the wisdom of these provisions. During this period there was neither a war emergency nor a financial emergency; but there had been six occasions when the President had to proclaim an emergency as a result of the breakdown of constitutional machinery in some of the States. As we have seen earlier, it was in the twelfth year of the Union that a War Emergency was proclaimed following the Chinese aggression on the Indian territory.

The first Proclamation under Article 356 was made in 1951 when in Punjab the Bhargava Ministry resigned and an alternative Ministry could not be formed. The proclamation of emergency was made on the basis of a report of the then Governor of Punjab, to whom was later delegated by the President the executive power to carry on the State's administration during the period of emergency. At the same time, the legislative power of the State was given over to Parliament. The emergency, however, was only for a short period and parliamentary government was reestablised immediately after the termination of the emergency. Not only did the Centre show eagerness to keep the State under its direct control longer than was absolutely necessary, but it also helped the local political conditions to stabilize in order that a Ministry could soon be formed.

The second occassion for the proclamation of emergency arose in 1952 when after the first general elections the formation of a stable Ministry was found impossible in the PEPSU State.[2] There was first a Congress Ministry which soon lost its majority in the Legislature. A coalition Ministry which followed it was incapable of functioning smoothly on account of dissensions within the coalition. As a result of the proclamation of emergency, the State Legislature was dissolved. The Union appointed one of its senior civil service officers as Adviser to the *Rajpramukh* to carry on the administration during the emergency. Within six months new elections were held and a Congress Ministry came back to power with a stable majority.

The third occasion arose in 1954 in the newly created Andhra State under rather unusual circumstances. The ruling Prakasam Ministry was supported by the Congress Party and a number of Independents. But the Government had only a slender majority in the State Legislature. The defection of some of its supporters in a crucial vote of no-confidence, arising out of the implementation of the recommendations of a Committee which reported on the working of prohibition in the State, brought about its downfall. The opposition members who joined hands to defeat the Ministry belonged to three parties besides Independents and dissident Congress members. Naturally, it was not easy for such disparate elements to join together for the formation of a new Ministry. Moreover, the members of the then State Assembly were elected in the first general elections to the Legislature of the former composite State of Madras from which Andhra was created in 1953. In the circumstances, public opinion within the State itself was in favour of a new election. But the defeated Prakasam Ministry was unwilling to carry on even as a caretaker government during the period required for holding the new election. The Governor's

1. Ibid., IX, p. 125.
2. Patiala and East Punjab States Union, a Part B State, which with the 'States' reorganization in 1956 became part of the State of Punjab.

report had made these points clear and in the light of them the President proclaimed the emergency and took over the administration. The President's rule however, came to an end with the formation of a stable Government after the election in 1954.

The fourth occasion which necessitated the proclamation of emergency arose in 1956 when the then Congress Ministry of the former State of Travancore-Cochin[1] resigned as a result of its loss of majority in the Legislature. Since no other party was capable of forming an alternate Ministry, taking over of the administration by the Union became inevitable. As in the case of PEPSU an Adviser was appointed to assist the *Rajpramukh* to whom was delegated the executive power of the State. The emergency lasted for about a year during which the new State of Kerala was formed and the Second General Elections held. Although the election did not produce a stable majority for any party in the State Legislature, a coalition of the Communist members and some Independents made the restoration of parliamentary government possible in the State in 1957 immediately after the results of the election were declared.

The fifth occasion necessitating the proclamation of emergency by the President arose under unusual circumstances once again in the State of Kerala. These circumstances developed after the assumption of power in that State in April 1957 by the Communist Party of India. A popular agitation in the State supported by all the Opposition Parties began gathering momentum from the beginning of 1959. Soon it assumed formidable proportions and under its auspices a State-wide civil disobedience movement was launched against the Ministry, demanding its immediate resignation from office. In a House of 127 the Ministry had the support of a majority of two votes. Although there was no vote of no-confidence against the Ministry in the State Legislature, the magnitude and intensity of the popular agitation led by the combined Opposition became such that the Governor of the State reported to the President in July 1959 that, considering the present situation, he had come to the conclusion "that the administration of the State (could) not be carried on in accordance with the Constitution any longer." On the basis of this report, the President issued a Proclamation of Emergency on 31 July 1959 under Article 356 of the Constitution.

The Report[2] of the Governor, a voluminous document, detailed the circumstances which led to the emergence of this unprecedented situation. It said that the charges against the Communist Ministry in respect of the release of prisoners who were Communists or party-sympathisers, widespread insecurity of person and property, attempts at the indoctrination of students, demoralization of the services, especially the police, by the interference of Party men, the use of cooperative societies for the consolidation of the Party, discrimination in administration, deterioration in the financial position of the State, etc. were substantially true. It was the combined effect of these acts of commission and omission that made non-Communists in the State to combine against the Ministry and organize a mass upsurge for its removal from office.

The crux of the legal and constitutional question is whether the Kerala Government has lost the support of the overwhelming majority of the people and whether the allegations made of mal-administration and subversion of democracy are substantially true. I have already expressed my view on both these points. The allegations made against Government are substantially true

---

1. As a result of the reorganization of the States in 1956, Travancore-Cochin became part of the present State of Kerala.
2. A fifteen-page summary of the Report was placed before Parliament on 17 August 1959 at the time when the Lok Sabha debated the proclamation before its approval by the House.

and I am convinced also that the Government has lost the support of the majority of the people. The figures given by me above will bear out this fact. While the securing of a majority of seats in the legislature, however meagre, is very relevant at the time of forming a government, it cannot be pleaded as conferring a continuing right to claim the confidence of the majority. There is no doubt that there has been a tremendous shift in the minds and in the feelings of the people. I do not think that this public opinion can be ignored without serious consequences for the future. The only solution which is available to us therefore, is the exercise of power under Article 356 of the Constitution.

Moving the resolution in the House of the People approving the President's proclamation, the Home Minister G.B. Pant, made abundantly clear the attitude and policy of the Central Government in a matter like this. He said:

So far as this resolution is concerned, it gives me no pleasure to move it. I really regret that an occasion should have arisen which left us no alternative but to advise the President to issue the proclamation. There are, I know, differences of opinion over this matter, but I would respectfully submit that the Central Government has no desire, and has never been anxious to interfere with or even intervene in, the affairs of the States. In fact, with every passing year, the co-operation between the States and the Centre is growing.

After detailing the various steps the Union Government has taken to accommodate the Kerala Government, the Home Minister continued:

Even the step [the issue of the proclamation] has been taken, I can say, because the circumstances left us no alternative. The tension that was there at fever heat and the hatred and animosity that had grown in the course of the two and a half years had come to divide the entire community into Communists and fellow-travellers or their sympathisers and non-Communists, and had affected every nook and comer of that State and had made it very difficult for the administration to be conducted according to the Constitution.... In the circumstances, the Central Government thought that when other alternatives that were suggested to the Kerala Government had not been accepted,[1] the only way out was the issuing of the Proclamation.

After referring to the long struggle for achieving Independence and to the drawing up of a new constitution as one of the first tasks undertaken by independent India, the Minister said:

Today the basis of all our activity is our Constitution. That Constitution was framed with due care and some of us had the good fortune of taking part in the framing of that Constitution. Perhaps some of us also tried to enlarge and amplify the scope of provincial autonomy. So the Constitution has our unreserved allegiance. It was denounced by the Communist Party once in., I think, very deprecatory terms. But I was glad to see a turn in their attitude towards the Constitution and also to the parliamentary system as such. Of course, I do not know whether we all have exactly the same conception about democracy a word which is used and bandied about very often. But I am not sure whether we all use it in the same sense. So far as we are concerned we are wedded to democracy.

When an Opposition Member interrupted the Home Minister by saying that all weddings are not faithful, the latter retorted:

We shall be faithful to democracy, to its ideals, to its fundamentals and to its objectives in an unreserved and unqualified way..... We have no reservations and we do not interpret democracy as people's democracy, as is done in certain countries, but as a democracy, in which every citizen in the country is a participant and has a right to see that the welfare of the Slate and its progress and advancement requires a spirit of accommodation. We have, in administering the affairs of the State,

1. One of these alternatives was the holding of mid-term elections to the State Legislature with a view to testing the popular confidence or otherwise of the Ministry.

so far as it lies with us, tried to adhere to these principles. There have been many agitations, sometimes they have been accompanied by even violence and some very serious consequences have followed in certain places, but we have tried to stick faithfully to what we believe to be the right course and fair means. And I venture to submit that but for the compelling circumstances, we would not have in any way intervened in the affairs of Kerala.

In spite of the elaborate explanations of the Home Minister and the overwhelming majority of Parliament in support of the Government's action, there existed serious doubts among constitutional experts and lovers of constitutional government in the country about the wisdom of proclaiming emergency in a State where the party in power had a majority in the Legislature.[1] They thought that it would become a bad precedent. Once a party is elected to power, the rules of the game of parliamentary government demand that it should continue in office so long as it enjoyed the confidence of the Legislature. The means by which the opposition can remove the Ministry from office should be strictly constitutional and not based on civil disobedience. For, there is little justification to resort to civil disobedience to remove from the seat of power a government established by law. The motives behind the proclamation would also become politically suspect when the dismissed Ministry belonged to a Party which was in opposition in Parliament. One might earnestly hope that the Kerala instance would provide valuable lessons for the future and the proclamation of an emergency under similar conditions would not be repeated.

There was, however, one subsequent development which gave the Union Government considerable satisfaction in justification of its action. That was the severe defeat which the Communist Party suffered in the mid-term elections in Kerala in 1960 following the proclamation of emergency. Soon after the elections, a new Ministry was formed with the support of an overwhelming majority of members in the State Legislature and the emergency was brought to an end.

The sixth occasion when the President proclaimed an emergency in a State was in 1961 when the constitutional machinery in Orissa broke down as a result of the break-up of the Coalition Ministry which functioned in that State since the second General Elections of 1957 and no alternative Ministry commanding the confidence of the Legislature could be formed. Within a few months after the proclamation of the emergency, statewide elections were held as a result of which the Congress Party secured a clear majority in the Legislature which enabled the Party to form a new Ministry facilitating the revocation of the emergency,

The constitutional machinery broke down again in Kerala, for a third time, necessitating the seventh proclamation of emergency by the President in 1964 as a result of a successful no confidence motion against the Ministry. Since the opposition parties could not unite to form a new government the President had to proclaim an emergency which lasted until 1967.

The eighth occasion necessitating the Proclamation arose in Goa, Daman and Diu in 1966 to facilitate the conduct of a referendum under the direct supervision of the Central authority to determine whether or not Goa, Daman and Diu should merge in Maharashtra.

Between 1967 and 2000 there were in all sixty-six Proclamations of Emergency in the States. Most of these were due to political instability following the General Elections. There were several States with no single party emerging victorious at the end of the elections in 1967. This resulted in the formation of United Front Ministries in those States. Most of

1. C. K. Santhanam, "President's Rule in Kerala" in Democratic Planning, Problems and Pitfalls, 1961, p. 181.

these United Fronts were opportunist alliances with the sole purpose of enjoying power. Such alliances, by their very nature, could not last long. Legislators who did not get ministerial or comparable positions changed party allegiance at will and the degrading spectacle of members crossing and re-crossing the floor of the House became too frequent a feature in several State Legislatures. For example, in Haryana at one time 22 out of 30 members of the Vishal Haryana Party were made Ministers in order to prevent floor-crossing. And yet, in the State Assembly two members crossed the floor back and forth four times, two thrice and six twice within a short period. Defection among legislators had become an accepted common characteristic during the 1967-71 period of constitutional government in India. No wonder that the President had to intervene with a Proclamation of Emergency as that was the only remedy to meet with a hopelessly unstable political situation in several States. In fact, the Proclamation was a blessing in disguise both for the State and the politicians who indulged too much in the game of floor-crossing. There were very few States in the whole country which had not been affected by it.

At the same time, it must be pointed out that the ruling Party at the Centre has exploited this provision on many occasions to gain political advantage and install its own State Government or a Government in which it has a leading role. Such abuse of Article 356 became possible largely because of the vagueness of the Article itself. Article 356 can be invoked if there exists a situation "in which the Government of the State cannot be carried on in accordance with the provisions of this Constitution". What are the ingredients of such a situation ? Unless these are specifically detailed, the vagueness will continue and it is bound to be exploited to suit the political expediency of the Party in power at the Centre.

It is possible to indicate the following situations which justify the invocation of Article 356 :[1]

1. The existence of a political deadlock where a ministry having resigned, the Governor finds it impossible to form an alternative government.

2. Where a ministry, although properly constituted, acts contrary to the provisions of the Constitution or seeks to use its powers for purposes not authorised by the Constitution and the Governor's attempts to call the ministry to order have failed.

3. Where the ministry fails to carry out the directives issued to it validly by the Centre in the exercise of its powers under the Constitution.

4. Where no Party has a clear majority and the government somehow or other formed, has been defeated in the Assembly, and would prefer to have fresh elections.

5. Where the Assembly, for whatever reason, stands dissolved around February or March, without leaving a constitutional alternative for the budget to be passed.

6. Where the Chief Minister advises the Governor to dissolve the Assembly but does not tender his own resignation although the defeat of his ministry is imminent, or tenders it only after the dissolution of the Assembly.

7. Where there is a complete breakdown of law and order in a State, when the State Government itself is unable to maintain the safety and security of the people and property in the State.

---

1. Both the Congress Party and the Janata party at the Centre are guilty of such abuse.

Thus, it is clear that although the Constitution requires some provision to deal with a situation of constitutional failure in the States, Article 356 as it now exists requires suitable amendment to minimise its abuse which has been very much in evidence, especially since 1967. It may be pointed out, however, that Central intervention had, on many occasions, brought about the emergence of stable ministries at the termination of emergency. The provision has proved not only a protective device for responsible government in politically unstable States but also a blessing to political parties which are unwilling to shoulder responsibility for a time on account of group rivalries or any other unfavourable circumstances.

During a period of emergency it is natural that the Executive becomes unusually powerful. This is a tendency of governments all over the world, federal or unitary. The powers of the U.S. President, the Chief Executive of a supposedly weak federation, during the two world wars were enormous. This is in spite of the fact that there exists in the United States in practice the principle of separation of governmental powers. In contrast, there is a parliamentary system in India where, although the Executive is directly responsible to the Legislature, the Executive, by virtue of its leadership over the party in power in the Legislature, leads the Legislature. Nevertheless, the experience of parliamentary democracies indicate that a parliament is vigilant and, through the members of the Opposition particularly, it manages to compel the Executive to account for all its actions. Thus Parliament has the power to check the Executive whenever the latter goes beyond reasonable limits. Emergency provisions do not in any way cut Parliament out of the picture. As T.T. Krishnamachari pointed out:

> After all, we are not suspending by means of these provisions sittings of Parliament. We are not suspending Parliament's power..... and Parliament has always the right to call the Executive to order; and if they find that the Executive had exceeded their powers in regard to the operation of any of the provisions enacted under the emergency laws, they can always pull them up; they can dismiss the Ministry and replace them so that it would appear on examination that we have taken very great care to see that Parliament's powers shall be kept intact and Parliament shall be summoned with the least possible delay.[1]

Explaining the provision for delegating legislative powers, Alladi Krishnaswami Aiyar said:

> The primary responsibility with regard to legislative matters is vested in Parliament. But at the same time, having regard to the multifarious work in which Parliament is engaged and the exigencies of Indian conditions, it will be impossible for Parliament to carry on the daily work of legislation though the ultimate responsibility will be that of Parliament, Hence the provision for delegation.

It may be contended that the House of the People may be dissolved and thus made incapable of discussing the emergency measures. But such action can at the most put off the discussion to a maximum of six to eight months. Even if the House is dissolved, the Proclamation of Emergency will have to be laid before the Council of States—the representatives of the States—within two months and if the Council does not approve of it, the Proclamation becomes invalid. This indeed is an effective check on any Executive bent upon creating an imaginary emergency.

How effectively Parliament would and could function during a period of national emergency was a subject of speculation until 1962, when the President proclaimed emergency under Article 352. But the manner in which Parliament has dealt with the

1. C.A.D.IX, p.124.

Emergency and functioned during the Emergency shows that instead of the Executive arrogating to itself the powers of Parliament in the name of emergency, Parliament has subjected the Executive to greater control and scrutiny in all its actions vitally, affecting the nation. In fact, the debates in Parliament demonstrated the eagerness with which the Executive sought the approval of Parliament not only with regard to the actions already taken by the Government but also those proposed for the future.

Many critics have drawn attention to the position of the President during an emergency. They think that the President can become a dictator, if he so wishes, during the emergency. But this is not quite so. We have already seen the real scope of the President's powers. The chances of his becoming a Caesar or a Tsar are practically nil. There is hardly an occasion when the President can rule the country without the assistance of a Council of Ministers. To think of the President and the Ministers combining in a conspiracy to flout the Constitution by maintaining a perpetual emergency and dissolving the House of the People every time it comes into being is a fear arising more out of a basic mistrust in the strength of democracy and its institutions that an understanding of the working of democratic governments. No constitution can avoid such a situation if those who are charged upon to work it deliberately try to wreck it. It cannot be helped under any system of Government, whatever might be the constitutional provisions.

Even if the President is bent upon acting autocratically, with or without the Ministry, by declaring emergencies, it is impossible for him to carry on the administration without the approval of Parliament. For, there is no provision in the Constitution authorizing the President to appropriate funds without Parliamentary sanction. Hence, at the most, the President may carry on his 'autocratic rule' only until the end of the current financial year; to run the administration any further he would need the support of Parliament.

It is not correct to compare the emergency provisions with either Section 102 or Section 93 of the Government of India Act, 1935. The President, acting under a democratic Constitution, cannot be compared with the Governor-General acting under the British rule. The President acts on the advice of a Ministry which is responsible to a national Parliament. In Parliament there are members representing the States whose Governments may be affected by the Proclamation of Emergency. The temporary suspension of the autonomy of the States does not proceed from, or end in, autocracy.

The fact that the President is a constitutional head was again and again emphasized by members of the Drafting Committee during the course of the discussion on emergency provisions. 'The whole scheme of the Constitution", declared Krishnamachari, "has been envisaged on the basis that the President is a constitutional head even though we have not put it in so many words within the Constitution...."[1] Emphasizing the same point, Alladi said:

> The President means *the Central Cabinet responsible to Parliament*[2] in which are representatives from various units which form the component parts of the Federal government. Therefore, the provincial machinery having failed, the Central Cabinet assumes the responsibility instead of the Provincial Cabinet.[3]

The provisions dealing with financial emergency were introduced at a time when the economic situation in India, soon after the coming of Independence, had become

1. C.A.D. IX, p. 150. 2. Emphasis ours. 3. C.A.D.IX.P. 124.

suddenly serious. Explaining the reasons for their incorporation in the Constitution, Ambedkar said:

This article more or less follows the pattern of what is called the National Recovery Act of the United States passed in 1930 or thereabouts,, which gave the President power to make similar provisions in order to remove the difficulties, both economical and financial, that had overtaken the American people, as a result of the great depression. The reason for its inclusion in our Constitution is that in the U.SA., such legislation was challenged and declared unconstitutional by the Supreme Court with the result that after such declaration by the Court, the President could hardly do anything which he wanted to do under the provisions of the National Recovery Act. A similar fate perhaps might overwhelm our President if he were to grapple with a similar financial and economic emergency. In order to prevent such difficulty, we thought it was much better to make an express provision in the Constitution itself and that is the reason why this article has been brought forth.[1]

The provisions for financial emergency, again, show how the framers of the Constitution have drawn upon the experience of the working of federalism elsewhere- There has however been no occasion so far to make use of these provisions.

Finally, one may consider the provision for the suspension of fundamental rights. Apparently this is by far the most unwholesome provision in the Constitution. In the United States this power is vested in the Congress. According to Ambedkar "the American President has an *ad interim* power to suspend fundamental rights." But in any case, there the Supreme Court can set aside both the Presidential and the Congressional action if it feels that it is unjustified under the circumstances. In Britain, the British Emergency Powers Act, 1920, provides that the Proclamation should be laid before Parliament within five days of its issue and would cease to operate after seven days if Parliament does not approve of it.

The conflicting claims which figured prominently in the Constituent Assembly in this connection were those of the State and those of the citizen; and those of security against those of liberty. Excessive emphasis on security may result in autocracy whereas too great a claim for liberty might result in licence. It seems that the framers were fully aware of this. Yet, in the interests of the Union they were prepared to place greater emphasis on security than on liberty. As Alladi Krishnaswami Aiyar said:

I will remind the House in this connection that 'a war cannot be fought on principles of the Magna Carta'. Freedom of speech, right of Assembly and other rights have to be secured in times of peace, but if only the Slate exists and if the security of the State is guaranteed. Otherwise, all these rights cannot exist. We are envisaging a situation threatened by war, in a country with multitudinous people with possible divided loyalties, though technically they may be citizens of India.... Freedom of speech may be used for the purpose of endangering the State and resulting in crippling all the resources of the country. If only we realise that the country must exist, if liberty and other things are to be guaranteed, there can be no possible objection to this article.....It will be the life of this Constitution, it will save democracy from danger and annihilation,[2]

The provision for the suspension of constitutional rights does not mean that with every proclamation of emergency, there will be an automatic suspension of fundamental rights. It may be quite possible to keep the enforcement of the fundamental rights intact and there need not be a universal suspension throughout the country merely by reason of the Proclamation. Further, the order of suspension should be placed before Parliament and it will be free to take whatever action it deems fit,

Despite these safeguards, Ambedkar was not very happy over these drastic provisions. This can be seen from what he said while replying to the final debate on the emergency provision. He said:

1. C.A.D.X,p.361.
2. C.A.D. IX, p.545.

The article deals with fundamental matters relating to the rights of people, and it is therefore proper that we should approach a subject of this sort with caution—but I am also prepared to say—with some emotion. We have passed certain fundamental rights already and when we are trying to reduce them or to suspend them we should be very careful as to the ways and means we adopt in curtailing or suspending them.

Therefore, my friends who have spoken against the article will, I hope, understand that I am in no sense an opponent of what they have said. In fact, I respect their sentiments very much. All the same, I remain quite unconvinced. I may also say .that I am no less fond of fundamental rights than they are.

The working of the Constitution so far shows that the suspension of fundamental rights took place only rarely. That happened as a result of the proclamation of national emergency only. The proclamation did not, however, affect all the fundamental rights embodied in the Constitution. Those affected were Articles 14,19 and 22. The implications of such suspension have been dealt with earlier in this work.

Suspension of fundamental rights, however, even during a period of national emergency is an utterly undemocratic practice whatever may be the case in its favour. Its immediate result is that a sanctuary of human rights which has been a prohibited area for the Executive is thrown open for its unrestricted action. In the process, individual liberty is bound to suffer. For, where the Executive is at liberty to act with impunity, abuse of power becomes its natural concomitant. Hence, there is great need for Parliament to be extra vigilant and create, if necessary, a suitable machinery which could review every case of curtailment of the individual's freedom. If emergency is used as a cover for political gain or vindictiveness by the Party in power, it will amount to a fraud on the Constitution.

In contrast to the demands of national emergency declared under Article 352, fundamental rights were never suspended during any of the emergencies proclaimed in the States. That remains a good precedent. Even during a national emergency, suspension of fundamental right should be restricted to the absolute minimum. There have been no instances so far of the Union Executive ignoring Parliament in the name of emergency except perhaps during the comparatively short period of Internal Emergency (1975-77). The apprehension that the President may act as a dictator is not one of the acute discomforts of our political thinking. On the other hand, the emergency provisions have been on the whole, justified when viewed from the experience of the past.

The only exceptions have been the occasions when constitutional emergency was declared in States when governments with majority support in the legislative assembly was in office. There have been quite a few occasions of that type. The action of the Janata Government of Morarji Desai soon after it came to power in 1977 in dismissing the Congress Governments in several States was condemned by not only opposition parties but also by large sections of the public as politically motivated. In 1980 when Indira Gandhi came back to power, she paid back in the same coin by dismissing the Janata Governments which were then in power in the States. Such actions were undoubtedly not in the spirit of the Constitution.

The landmark verdict of the Supreme Court in the Bommai case seems to have made the Union government to realise that judicial intervention might declare invalid a declaration of emergency if imposed without adequate justification. The Court also held that the State Assembly should not be dissolved until the Presidential proclamation was approved by Parliament. That means if Parliament does not ratify the proclamation the Assembly will continue to function. That indeed has been a healthy development.

***

39

THE ZONAL COUNCILS AND INTER STATE COUNCIL

THE ZONAL Councils have come into existence following the reorganization of States in India. The idea of Zonal Councils is not a product of post-Independence thinking. It figured even earlier as a device to give economic complexion to certain political plans such as those formulated for the purpose of having an attenuated centre with interposed sub-federations.[1] Nor is the idea something peculiar to India. In the United States, for example, beginning with the inter-state parole and probation compact of 1934, collective State action has been a regular feature to promote inter-state cooperation of such fields as the abatement of water pollution, conservation of oil and gas, development of inter-state parks and the conservation and development of Atlantic marine fisheries. Australia is yet another country which has undertaken such an effort to evolve a common approach to problems of inter-state character.

The Indian scheme for the Zonal Councils owes its origin to Prime Minister Jawaharlal Nehru's suggestion in the Lok Sabha in December 1955, that the reorganized States might be grouped into four or five zones, each with an Advisory Council with a view to developing the habit of cooperative working. He said:

> ....Finally, the more I have thought about it, the more I have been attracted to something which I used to reject seriously... That is, the division of India into four, five or six major groups regardless of language, but always, I will repeat, giving the greatest importance to the languages in those areas. [2]

The Home Minister G.B. Pant's statement in the same context came as an explanation to the Prime Minister's proposal.

> While the States have to be carved in accordance with their natural affinities, the supreme objective of strengthening the unity, the cohesion of the nation and the country, has to be given the first and foremost consideration.... So far as the economic and developmental requirements of the country are concerned, these linguistic affinities do not mark the bounds of the various territories. Rivers do not determine their course in accordance with the language of the people who make them their homes. The mines that lie deep down in the bosom of the earth do not follow any regional pattern, much less any linguistic pattern. So, for the purpose of economic development at least, if not for anything else, it would be desirable to have councils of this type.[3]

Thus, the idea of Zonal Councils took a concrete shape from the just and wholesome

1. For example, Coupland's Plan of 1944.
2. Lok Sabha Debates, 1955, States Reorganization, p. 881.
3. *Lok Sabha Debates*, 1955, States Reorganization, p. 1407.

revulsion against the ugly passions displayed by the reactions of linguistic communities during the discussions on the proposals of the States Reorganization Commission. The idea as expressed by the Prime Minister and explained by the Home Minister on the floor of Parliament in December 1955 soon matured and found expression in the Resolution of the Government of India published on 16 January 1956 containing the decisions on most of the proposals of the Commission. Among other things it stated:

> The Government of India propose to establish Zonal Councils which may deal with matters of common concern to the States in different zones, including economic planning and questions arising out of reorganization.

The country has thus been divided into five zones taking into account several factors such as the natural divisions of the country, requirements of economic development, cultural and linguistic affinity, river systems, means of communication and requirements of security and law and order. The five zones are:

(*i*) The Northern Zone: This is comprised of the States of Haryana, Punjab, Rajasthan, Jammu and Kashmir and Himachal Pradesh and the union territories of Delhi and Chandigarh. This Zone was inaugurated on 23 April 1957 with headquarters at New Delhi.

(*ii*) The Southern Zone: The States included in this Zone are Andhra Pradesh, Tamil Nadu, Kerala and Karnataka. The Union Territory of Pondicherry was added to it later. It was inaugurated on 11 July 1957 with Madras as headquarters.

(*iii*) The Central Zone: This has only two States, namely, Uttar Pradesh and Madhya Pradesh. It was inaugurated on 1 May 1957 with Allahabad as headquarters.

(*iv*) The Eastern Zone: This contains the States of Bihar, West Bengal, Orissa, Assam, Manipur, Tripura, Meghalaya, Nagaland, Mizoram and Arunachal Pradesh with Calcutta as headquarters. It was inaugurated on 30 April 1957.

(*v*) The Western Zone: Maharashtra, Gujarat and Goa at present constitute this Zone.

This main objectives of these Zonal Councils are:

(*a*) to achieve an emotional integration of the country;

(*b*) to help in arresting the growth of acute State consciousness, regionalism, linguism and particularist trends;

(*c*) to help in removing the aftereffects of separation in some cases so that the processes of reorganization, integration and economic advancement may coalesce and synchronize;

(*d*) to enable the Centre and the States which are dealing increasingly with matters economic and social, to cooperate and exchange ideas and experience in order that uriform policies for the common good of the community are evolved and the ideal of a socialistic society is achieved;

(*e*) to cooperate with each other in the successful and speedy execution of major development projects; and

(*f*) to secure some kind of political equilibrium between different regions of the country.

In short:

> ...what we have in view now is an inter-state forum without impinging on the legislative and executive authority either of the Centre or of the States, the idea to provide in each Zone a common meeting-ground where the States could be associated with each other to promote and facilitate co-operative effort towards the economic and social development of each Zone and towards the unity and welfare of the nation as a whole.[1]

Each Zonal Council is composed of a Union Minister nominated by the President,[2] the Chief Minister of each of the States of the Zone and two Ministers in addition from each of the States nominated by the Head of the State concerned. The Union Minister is to preside over the meetings of the Council, Each Council will have a secretariat of its own with a Secretary, a Joint Secretary and such other officers as the Chairman may appoint. The Chief Secretaries of the States of the Council will act as Secretary to the Council by rotation. Besides the Chief Secretaries, the Development Commissioners from all the member States and a representative of the Planning Commission also attend the proceedings of the Council as advisers. The advisers have the right to take part in the discussions of the Council.

A Zonal Council will meet at such time as the Chairman may fix, normally after three months, by rotation in the States included in that zone. Decisions may be taken at such meetings by majority of votes of the members present. However, in practice, the decisions are taken only by common consent. The proceedings of every meeting of a Zonal Council are forwarded to the Central Government and the State Governments concerned. A joint meeting of two or more Zonal Councils may decide issues of common interest to States of more than one zone. The Central Government reserves the power to make rules for regulating the procedure at such joint council meetings. The Councils have also the power to appoint committees of their own members and advisers.

The Zonal Councils are deliberative and advisory bodies. According to the Government of India, their creation will not, therefore, in any way detract from the context of the legislative or executive authority of the States. This official clarification should dispel notions that these Councils will amount to the creation of a sub-federal structure under the Constitution. In other words, what is aimed at is the best possible utilization of the human and material resources of the zone while retaining for each constituent State liberty of action within its own legislative and executive spheres. Though advisory in character, the Council with the Chief Minister and two other Ministers from each State on it is bound to make its deliberations well- informed and the advice authoritative. While the Council no doubt serves as a forum for each State to put forward its particular point of view, it enables the State to see the other points of view represented at the Council and to consider its own problems in the larger perspective of zonal needs and resources.

Each Council may discuss any matter in which some or all the States represented in the Council, or the Union and one or more of the States represented in that Council, have a common interest. In particular, a Zonal Council may discuss and make recommendations with regard to:

(*a*) any matter of common interest in the field of economic and social planning;

---

1. The Home Minister's speech at the Inaugural Meeting of the Northern Zonal Council on 23 April 1957.
2. At present the Union Home Minister is the Chairman of all the Zonal Councils.

(*b*) any matter concerning border disputes, linguistic minorities, or inter-state transport; and

(*c*) any matter connected with, or arising out of, the reorganization of the States.

However, the ability and utility of the Councils to resolve such problems as border disputes and linguistic minorities seem to be doubtful. So far, the Councils have little to their credit in these fields of conflict. If problems like border disputes are settled, they are due to the good offices of the Centre rather than the resolutions of the Zonal Councils.

In contrast, the Councils can and are playing an important role in the field of economic and social planning and collaboration. In matters such as rationalization of inter-state road transport regulations, coordination of irrigation plans, pooling of facilities for technical and other types of higher education, assessing manpower requirements, uniformity of sales tax, restrictions of inter-state trade, enforcement of prohibition and similar matters on which there is hardly any room for serious dispute and much scope for cooperation, the Zonal Councils are in an advantageous position to settle matters more quickly and easily than all India bodies and conferences. Further, the Councils can act as checkposts to ensure that in the Five Year Plan proposals regional considerations are not left out of account.

The idea of the Zonal Council, despite its lofty aims, has had no unanimous support in the country. Even in the official sphere there was opposition to the zonal scheme from its very inception. The Chief Minister of Uttar Pradesh[1] turned out to be the most powerful opponent of the scheme. In a statement made on 21 April 1957 he said: "We should have either a unitary government or the present system under which the States are sovereign in the sphere of their listed powers." Any departure from the present system, he said, could either be towards a unitary form of government or towards more delegation of powers to the States. But Zones did not seem to fall in either of these categories. While conceding the need for resolving inter-state problems without the States working at cross purposes, he claimed that the creation of ad hoc committees of the Chief Ministers or the Ministers of the States concerned for specific problems would be preferable to permanent zones. In the sphere of development too, a permanent Zonal Council with a permanent secretariat would be no better than a fifth wheel. While the Chief Minister and the members of the Council would be responsible to their respective legislatures, committed to specified policies subject to intra-party control, the Council as a whole would be a relatively free body, responsible to none but its collective consciousness.

The period during which the Zonal Councils has operated is long enough to consider their usefulness as effective for inter-state cooperation and coordination. The record, so far, shows two clear trends. Firstly, the ability of the Zonal Councils to settle political questions seems to be remote. Secondly, in the economic and social sphere they are capable of producing some good results. In the administrative sphere too they have been able to forge some common policies and actions. Among the achievements of the Zonal Councils are the following:

1. Effective measures for inter-state cooperation in the field of training of technical personnel in the zones and making available such personnel for those States which have them in short supply;[2] 2. Coordinated development of electrical power

1. Sampurnanand was the then Chief Minister.
2. One of the salutary decisions taken in this context by the Northern Zonal Council is the removal of domiciliary restrictions for admissions to technical institutions.

resources; 3, Solving some of the problems confronting inter-state transport; 4. Promoting better maintenance and coordination of control, and construction of bridges on inter-state roads; 5. Review of agricultural production and development programmes in the Zones; and 6. Constituting common police reserve forces in the Zones.

The reorganization of States led to the break-up of composite States and created a new state system based predominantly on the principle of unilingual States. But the Zonal Councils have sprung up to bring them together again on a regional basis as equal and independent partners in a common venture. The meetings of these Councils remind the people of India that the demarcation of State boundaries for administrative purposes cannot and does not mean the abandonment of the tradition of the people of a region working together on a regular basis for the solution of their common problems.

If the reorganization of States had set in motion forces of linguistic separatism, the Zonal Councils have proved to be an attempt to reverse the trend by promoting habits of cooperation among neighbouring States for the solution of common problems.[1] Unilingual States have the merit that they can transact their business easily through the medium of a single language. But carried to extremes, linguism is bound to engender feelings of separatism and linguistic fanaticism to the detriment of the unity of the nation. By providing a regular forum for discussing matters of common interest, these Councils have become clearing houses of ideas and not a mere device for registering agreements. So long as they enable members to understand one another's difficulties and needs, and help in building up an atmosphere of fellowship, they will perform a useful and vital function in the evolution of a novel feature in the governmental system in India. In this respect, the conventions which these Councils have developed in the initial stages will have abiding influence on their evolution and growth. Unfortunately, after the initial enthusiasm with which the zonal councils started functioning was not sustained in the later years. The meetings of the Councils have not been regular and their effectiveness as councils of regional cooperation and collaboration in economic and developmental areas has been minimal.

Inter State Council

The Inter State Council is a step ahead of the Zonal councils and is a highly representative body embracing the entire country. It was conceived as a political consensus-building forum on major issues.

The Council is headed by the Prime Minister and consists of six Cabinet Ministers and all Chief Ministers of States and heads of Union Territories. Although its role is advisory in character, its recommendations are bound to be taken almost binding because of its composition making it almost a national cabinet.

Its inauguration on 10 October 1990 by the former Prime Minister V.P. Singh was a euphoric occasion and it was expected to play a major role as national consensus builder. It was expected to meet at least thrice a year. However, the Council was a non-starter in taking up Centre-State and inter-state relations although many controversial issues have been bedeviling the country, particularly during the nineties as a result of political control swiftly changing with each major political party being in control in one State or another.

1. For a detailed study of the working of a Zonal Council, see S. Maheswari, "Zonal Council: A Study of the Northern Zonal Council" in A. Awasthi and S.N. Varma (eds.), *Aspects of Administration*, 1963.

The Council was charged with the duty of (a) enquiring into or advising upon disputes which may have arisen between States; (b) investigating and discussing subjects in which some or all States or the Union and one or more States have a common interest or (c) making recommendations upon any such subject and, in particular recommendations or the better coordination of policy and action with respect to that subject.

It took four years for the Council to meet again and that was to consider the recommendations of its own sub-committee headed by the then Home Minister S.B. Chavan. The Committee was entrusted with the task of examining the recommendations of the Sarkaria Commission. All controversies that have arisen in the intervening period had been ignored. Subjects such as consignment tax, the unending controversy over Article 356 empowering the centre to propose president's rule in States, powers and composition of the Election Commission of India and the environmental Ministry's notification imposing a ban on mining etc., were never taken up by the Council for consideration.

Altogether there had been only 5 meetings of the Council until 2000. Successive Prime Minister's did not show much interest in making use of the Council to tackle the most vexing problems confronted by the country. At its fifth meeting in January 1999 the Council endeavoured to find a consensus on Article 356, but failed to find a common ground. While states like Tamil Nadu, Punjab and West Bengal stood for the abolition of the Article altogether, there were others who advocated radical modification. Several States demanded a redefinition of the basis of or division of financial resources between the Union and States and bring about a more rational and equitable redistribution of the country's financial resources. The meeting was successful in bringing about an agreement on the modalities of securing the President's assent for the State Bills relating to the Concurrent List of the Seventh Schedule. It also accepted the recommendations of the Sarkaria Commission. The Council reconstituted its Standing committee with the Home Minister as Chairman and 5 Central Ministers and 7 Chief Ministers as members.

***

PART VIII

MISCELLANEOUS PROVISIONS

40

THE COMPTROLLER AND AUDITOR GENERAL OF INDIA

THE PROVISION for independent audit is an essential ingredient of parliamentary democracy. The fundamental basis of a parliamentary system of government is the responsibility of the Executive to the Legislature for all its actions. The Legislature will be able to enforce this executive responsibility only if it is competent to scrutinize the activities of the Executive and exercise on each of them its judgement in an appropriate manner. There are certain activities of the Executive which can easily be scrutinized by any one, while others are difficult for a group of laymen to scrutinize. Checking of accounts and assessing the soundness or otherwise of the financial transactions of the Executive is a technical job which falls in the latter category and Parliament, composed as it is by laymen in general, is not a competent, suitable instrument for making such scrutiny. Yet, it is a function of Parliament to scrutinize the financial dealings of the government and to ensure that the taxpayer's money is properly spent. Parliament needs the assistance of an expert for this purpose and it is in this context that the office of the Comptroller and Auditor-General who, through his expert advice, enables Parliament to discharge this function efficiently. By performing such an important function the Comptroller and Auditor-General makes himself as indispensable instrument in the proper working of a parliamentary government. It is this important role that makes his office "one of the four pillars of our democratic Constitution, the other three being the Legislature, the Executive and the Judiciary."

There is nothing strikingly original in the provisions of the Constitution dealing with the office of the Comptroller and Auditor-General. Such an office (the Auditor-General of India) had already been in existence as an integral part of India's constitutional machinery since 1919. The idea of the office itself comes from England where it has a history of over a century. Until the year 1866 when Gladstone got the new Audit Exchequer Act passed, the conception of parliamentary financial control did not actually extend over the manner in which money voted by Parliament was spent. This was considered to be the sphere of the Treasury which had uncontrolled and unquestioned powers in the matter. The Treasury had its own audit agency whose examination of the accounts gave it the necessary material for exercising administrative control over the departments. Evidently, the audit in those days acted more as a help to the administration than as control by Parliament. Then came the Act of 1866 where it was specifically laid down that the report of the Comptroller and Auditor-General should be laid before the House of Commons. This was further clarified in 1921 when an amendment to the Act of 1866 stated that the Appropriation Accounts of various Ministries "shall be examined by the Comptroller and Auditor-General on behalf of the House of Commons".

The Auditor-General received statutory recognition for the first time under the Government of India Act 1919. Such recognition, however, did not mean complete independence from the Executive. The Auditor-General was to conduct an audit "subject to any general or special orders of the Secretary of State-in-Council and his reports on the Government Accounts were to be sent to that authority through the Governor-General". The Government of India Act of 1935 substantially increased the independence of the Auditor-General by abolishing the control of the Secretary of State and the Auditor-General was required to submit his annual audit reports to the respective legislatures through the Government of India and those of the Provinces. Thus, at the time of the transfer of power, the Auditor-General was already functioning as a substantially independent authority entrusted with powers of scrutinizing the financial activities of the Government.

The framers of the Constitution, realizing the importance of an independent agency for audit under parliamentary democracy, made the Comptroller and Auditor-General fully independent so that he could discharge his functions efficiently and fearlessly. Speaking in the Constituent Assembly on the position of the Comptroller and Auditor-General under the Constitution, Pattabhi Sitaramayya said:

> We have done a great thing in respect of the position that we have assigned to the Comptroller and Auditor-General. No matter how perfect your Constitution may be, no matter how numerous may be the checks and balances and safeguards for the right conduct of the business of the future, it is money that counts and we have to deal with huge sums and if all this money is not spent alright, and if the people deliver cheap gibes at men like me who count money... then there is no government at all worth mentioning; it is anarchy; it is chaos; it is loot; it is dacoity. And who is to control this? The Comptroller and Auditor-General must be supreme and independent as the judges of the Supreme Court, perhaps even more so. He is not merely an Auditor-General, but he represents a judicial authority, with a judicial frame of mind and his acts must be acts of justice between what he considers to be right and what is actually done by the Executive. At times, he is called upon to criticise the Executive and to expose it even to contempt. He should not, therefore, come under the ire of the Government or any party or of the Finance Department.... Till 1921 in this country we never thought of the independence of the Auditor-General. Later on, we built up step by step and stage by stage so that today we have installed him as a supreme master who has his own judgment to look to and who has no fears or favours to be guided by from outside. The Comptroller and Auditor-General should be the supreme arbitrator of India's finances and then alone our *swaraj* will be a proper *swaraj*[1].

Independence of the Comptroller and Auditor-General

Let us examine how and to what extent is the office of the Comptroller and Auditor-General made independent under the Constitution. Under Article 148, the Comptroller and Auditor-General of India is to be appointed by the President by warrant under his hand and seal, just as a judge of the Supreme Court is appointed. He can be removed from office only in like manner and on the like grounds as a judge of the Supreme Court. Every person appointed to be the Comptroller and Auditor-General, before he enters upon his office, has to make and subscribe before the President an oath or affirmation in a form prescribed for the purpose. His salary and other conditions of service may be determined by Parliament. But once appointed, neither his salary nor his rights in respect of leave of

1. C.A.D. X, p. 943.

absence, pension or age of retirement[1] can be varied to his disadvantage. At present, the Comptroller and Auditor-General receives a salary of Rs. 30,000 per month, the same salary as that of a judge of the Supreme Court. After retirement or resignation from office, he is not eligible for any office under the Government of India or any State Government. The administrative expenses of the office of the Comptroller and Auditor-General, including the salaries of the office staff, are charged upon the Consolidated Fund of India. It is also provided that the conditions of service of persons serving in the Indian Audit and Accounts Department and the administrative powers of the Comptroller and Auditor-General will be prescribed by rules made by the President after consultation with the Comptroller and Auditor-General. Such rules, however, are subject to the provisions of the Constitution as well as any law made by Parliament on this behalf.

A comparison of these provisions with the corresponding provisions dealing with the judges of the Supreme Court will show that they are substantially the same in scope, and that the office of the Comptroller and Auditor-General, as far as its independence is concerned has been modelled on the Supreme Court. As such, the Comptroller and auditor-General can function, in the discharge of his responsibilities, as an authority established under the Constitution, whose independence is safeguarded by the express provisions of the Constitution. Nevertheless, there is one matter in which the Comptroller and Auditor-General does not enjoy the powers that the Supreme Court has. This is with respect to the powers of the Comptroller and Auditor-General in the matter of the appointment of staff. Ambedkar confessed in the Constituent Assembly that he was not happy over the matter. If he had his choice, he said, he would have made the office of the Comptroller and Auditor-General even more independent than the Supreme Court. The following are his words:

> I am not very happy over these provisions. Personally, speaking for myself, I am of opinion that this dignitary or officer is probably the most important officer under the Constitution of India. He is the one man who is going to see that the expenses voted by Parliament are not exceeded or varied from what has been laid down by Parliament in what is called the Appropriation Act. If this functionary has to carry out the duties — and his duties I submit are far more important than the duties even of the judiciary — he should have been certainly as independent as the judiciary. But comparing the articles above relating to the Auditor-General, I cannot help saying that we have not given him the same independence that we have given to the judiciary, although I personally feel that we ought to have given him far greater independence than the judiciary itself.[2]

About the absence of the power to appoint staff, Ambedkar said:

> The absence of such a power means that the staff of the Auditor-General shall be appointed by the Executive. Being appointed by the Executive, the staff shall be subjected to the Executive for disciplinary action. I have not the slightest doubt in my mind that if an officer does not possess the power of disciplinary control over his immediate subordinate, his administration is going to be thoroughly demoralised. From that point of view, I should have thought that it would have been proper in the interests of the people that such a power should have been given to the Auditor-General. But sentiment seems to be opposed to investing the Auditor-General with such a power. For the moment, I feel that noting more can be done than remain content with the sentiment such as it is today[3].

---

1. The maximum age limit for the Comptroller and Auditor-General is fixed at sixty-five years by an Act of Parliament (1972) dealing with the conditions of service, duties and powers of the Comptroller and Auditor General of India.
2. C.A.D. VIII, p. 407.
3. Ibid., p. 408. This aspect of Ambedkar's criticism seems to have been proved invalid in the light of the existing practice under which the Comptroller and Auditor-General exercises full control over the officials of his department.

After emphasizing the qualifications of a good Auditor-General, K.T. Shah wanted the Constitution to lay down specific minimum qualifications as it had done in the case of judges. He said that the Comptroller and Auditor-General ought to be a qualified Account Officer (Registered Accountant) with at least ten years' practical experience. Dealing with this suggestion, T.T. Krishnamachari said that the idea was original and was in conformity with ideas prevalent in the commercial world.

> But this is not in tune with the existing practice here or elsewhere. Actually the man who is the Accountant-General is not an accountant *per se*. He has a number of other duties to perform and in so functioning he has got to have a knowledge of the entire administration. He must be a good administrator, who must have experience in the intricacies of financial problems. He must have not merely an arithmetic or accounting knowledge, but a comprehensive knowledge of the entire administration. From this point of view, Shah's view is extremely narrow[1].

Duties and Powers of the Comptroller and Auditor-General

Article 149 and 150 deal with the powers and duties of Comptroller and Auditor-General. According to Article 149, Parliament is empowered to prescribe the powers and duties of the Comptroller and Auditor-General in relation to the accounts of the Union and the States and any other authority or body established either by the Union or the States. It is also provided that until Parliament prescribes such powers and duties, he will perform such duties and exercise such powers as those exercised by the Auditor-General of India immediately before the commencement of the Constitution. Parliament passed an Act in 1972 dealing with these matters. It upholds the independence of the Comptroller and Auditor-General of India and enables him to work effectively and efficiently. According to Article 150, the Comptroller and Auditor-General has the power to prescribe the form and manner in which the accounts of the Union and the States shall be kept, subject to the approval of the President.

The system that is followed in India with regard to the manner in which accounts are kept is analogous to that in Britain. There are, however, two differences. The Comptroller and Auditor-General of India is responsible for both the accounts and audit while in Britain, the work of accounting is done by the Accounting Officer appointed in every department for this purpose. The other difference is that unlike the Comptroller and Auditor-General of India, his counterpart in England, besides functioning as an auditor, also controls the receipt and issue of public money and it is his duty to see that nothing is paid out of the account at the Bank of England without legal authority. This system of control over the issue of public money not only prevents withdrawal for an unauthorized purpose but also prevents expenditure in excess of the grants made by Parliament. In contrast, the Comptroller and Auditor-General in India comes in to the picture only at the audit stage when the expenditure has already taken place. After the commencement of the Constitution, there has been a desire to introduce the British practice in India in order to exercise better control over the withdrawals from the Consolidated Fund. But no action has yet been taken in this regard. India's first Comptroller and Auditor-General, Narahari Rao, had the following to say on this question before the Public Accounts Committee in December 1952.

1. Ibid., p. 410.

If a satisfactory system of Exchequer control is to be introduced in India, I consider that we will have to resort, as the first step, to the system of having separate Accounts Officers for each of the ministries and major spending departments as in the United Kingdom with whom all payments will be centralised in respect of such ministry or department. A corollary to this will be that the State Governments will have to take over the maintenance of the Accounts which under the Transitional Provisions of the Constitution is, at present, the responsibility of the Comptroller and Auditor-General. The present position of making the same agency responsible for the maintenance of accounts and also the audit of the accounts is defective... The separation of audit from accounts and the organisation of the necessary accounting machinery under the administrative departments with a view to removing these serious defects and the enforcement of effective exchequer control are essential and overdue, and I, as Comptroller and Auditor-General, attach the greatest importance to these reforms, being carried out after the minimum interval required to carry out the necessary organisational changes.

India's second Comptroller and Auditor-General, Ashok Kumar Chanda, summed up the situation when he said in one of his speeches in 1955:

Our Constitution re-designated the office I hold as the Comptroller and Auditor-General, as it was recognised that the functioning of a Comptroller-General was indispensable in the enforcement of Parliamentary control. This designation of Comptroller-General has, under the present state of affairs, become an honorific prefix without any function. If I am to ensure on behalf of Parliament that Governmental expenditure is kept within the funds appropriated—department and vote-wise—the departmentalisation of accounts is inescapable.[1]

The department of the Comptroller and Auditor-General is expected to discharge three main functions:

(a) to audit the Government's expenditure;

(b) to see that the financial rules and orders which have a bearing on governmental expenditure are obeyed; and

(c) to satisfy itself that those who sanction expenditure have the power to do so.

In the words of A.K. Chanda :

The Comptroller and Auditor-General examines the accounts to satisfy himself that the parliamentary grants have been applied to the purposes for which they were intended...and that they have been spent according to law, rules and regulations. He certifies that the accounts are correct, subject to whatever reservation he chooses to make and make his report to Parliament. He reports on any waste and inefficiency. He comments also on important occurrences which are topical matters of accounting or financial principles which are in dispute, transactions where heavy losses have occurred or might occur, expenditure on new services and departure from settled precedents and procedure.

It is the Comptroller and Auditor-General of India who, after examining the accounts in the manner mentioned above, draws the attention of the Public Accounts Committee of Parliament to cases of apparent waste and extravagance although it is not one which forms part of his statutory obligations. Wherever a parliamentary system of government prevails, this is considered to be the most important function of the Office of the Comptroller and Auditor General.

1. Inaugural Address at the Annual Meeting of the Class II Officers Association of the Internal Audit and Accounts Department, 15 January 1955, p. 12.

The Comptroller and Auditor-General and the Public Accounts Committee

As has been pointed out in an earlier chapter, it is the duty of the Public Accounts Committee to examine the appropriation accounts and the reports the Comptroller and Auditor-General on them and such other accounts laid before Parliament as the Committee may think fit. The purpose of such examination is to ensure the accountability of the Executive to Parliament with respect to all its activities in the financial field. In carrying out its investigations, the Committee receives the expert advice of the Comptroller and Auditor-General who takes it through the intricacies of government accounts. The Committee examines departmental witnesses who are summoned to appear before it and to answer the criticism which the Comptroller and Auditor-General has brought against the working of their departments in his annual reports. It is widely accepted that the success or failure of the work of the Public Accounts Committee depends mainly on the quality of the reports of the Comptroller and Auditor-General. His reports will not only ensure that the appropriations made by Parliament are not exceeded without supplementary grants but also that the expenditure conforms to the rules. In addition, he must also satisfy himself on behalf of Parliament about the wisdom, faithfulness and economy of the spending programme of the Government.

Under Article 151, the reports of the Comptroller and Auditor-General relating to the accounts of the Union are submitted to the President. Those relating to the accounts of the States are submitted to the Governors. These reports are laid before Parliament and the State Legislatures repspectively.

There has been some controversy, arising out of certain new governmental functions and the role of the Comptroller and Auditor-General in that connection. In its endeavour to achieve rapid industrialization in the country the Government has set up a large number of statutory corporations and government companies. From a strictly juridical point of view, these are autonomous bodies. It means that they are not to be included as part of the ordinary or traditional operations of the Government. This, however, does not take away their accountability to Parliament. But being autonomous, the details or the manner in which the funds allocated by the Government are being spent on these concerns annually are not fully explained in the audit of these concerns. Unless the Statute or the Articles of Association specifically nominates the Comptroller and Auditor-General as auditor of these concerns, he has no right to examine their accounts as he has in the case of ordinary departments of the Government. The result is that although public funds are spent on a large scale on certain activities undertaken by the Government, the Comptroller and Auditor-General, "the supreme arbiter of the nation's public finances", is not permitted to examine them and report on them to Parliament.

The problem of accountability arising out of the setting up of government corporations and companies was commented upon as early as 1952 by Narahari Rao as follows:

> I refer to the formation of private companies under the Indian Companies Act for the management of government industrial undertakings from the Consolidated Fund. This private limited companies are, in my opinion, a fraud on the Companies Act and also on the Constitution, because money cannot be taken away from the Consolidated Fund for the establishment and transformation of certain concerns into private companies in the name of the President and Secretary to Government.... To convert a government concern into a private company solely by

executive action is unconstitutional. While recognising that the management of industrial and business concerns differs from the normal day-to-day duties of administration and that special organisation and delegation of authority more in accordance with speedier business practices may be necessary, the Government should have the backing of suitable Parliamentary enactment for the setting up of Corporations.

There is another important point involved in this procedure of creating a private company under the Companies Act. Private Companies are to be audited by auditors nominated by the Board of Directors. The Comptroller and Auditor-General will not therefore, have any automatic right to audit such a company... It is true that the company may request him to be the auditor, if necessary by incorporating suitable provisions in its Articles of Association, but this would be neither proper nor binding, as the Comptroller and Auditor-General's duties and functions are prescribed by Parliament and cannot be regulated by the Articles of Association of a company. Further-more, even if he undertakes audit on a consent basis on payment of fees, he only submit his audit reports to the company and not to Parliament through the President. Parliament cannot watch through the Public Accounts Committee the regularity of the operations and the financial results of such company.[1]

On the other hand, it is pointed out by those who are opposed to the Comptroller and Auditor-General being brought into the picture that his role in this context is a hindrance to the efficient conduct of public enterprises in India. For instance, when the question of the auditing of the Life Insurance Corporation came up for discussion in Parliament, the then finance Minister of the Government of India, Chintaman D. Deshmukh, opposed the idea of entrusting the task to the Comptroller and Auditor-General on the ground that his audit was conventional and mechanical and, therefore, unsuitable to the requirements of the proposed enterprise.

Others have criticised his role in more severe terms and accused him of being the primary cause of a "widespread and paralysing unwillingness to decide and act" on the part of those who are in charge of these concerns.

Auditors do not know and cannot be expected to know very much about good administration; their prestige is highest with others who do not know much about administration.... Auditing is a necessary but highly pedestrian function with a narrow perspective and very limited usefulness... Many of the Comptroller's reports are mere substitutions of hindsight for the kind of judgment possible and necessary and proper at the time of action.[2]

Such criticisms have helped the Executive to keep the Comptroller and Auditor-General out of the sphere of public enterprises. But Parliament urged by its Public Accounts Committee, always showed its interest in bringing him into the sphere of the working of all State enterprises. As a result of such interest and systematic effort, there has been an extension of the jurisdiction of the Comptroller and Auditor-General. The Companies Act of 1956 was suitably amended to give him the right (a) to direct the manner and to give instructions about the way the accounts shall be audited; (b) to conduct a supplementary or test audit; (c) to comment upon or supplement the audit report which was to be submitted to him by the auditors; and (d) to advise in the matter of appointment of auditors. The practice that exists at present in public enterprises other than Government companies also conforms, more or less, to this pattern except in the case of two statutory corporations, the State Bank of India and the Life Insurance Corporation.[3]

---

1. Statement made before the Union Public Service Accounts Committee, December,1952.
2. Appleby, A *Re-examination of India's Administrative Sytem, pages 28 and 42.*
3. When Lok Sabha was considering a bill dealing with the conditions of service, duties and powers of the C.A.G. in 1971, some members made an attempt to enlarge the scope of the existing powers of the C.A.G. in this context. But the Finance Minister who piloted the bill did not agree to do so.

If the function of the Comptroller and Auditor-General with respect to the working of the public enterprises is to become more effective, the attitude and approach of his department to the problems of these enterprises should undergo a radical change. It is necessary that the Auditor should lay greater emphasis on the assessment of results rather than on the meticulous implementation of rules and procedures. As regards the failures or mistakes, the effort should be to suggest ways and means which will lead to the avoidance of abuse or irregularity in the future. Further, audit report should be oriented in a positive way so as to lead to purposive action.[1]

If the object of auditing is to be a broad one, namely, the examination of of the efficiency of a concern as a whole, the Comptroller and Auditor-General does not seem to be able to serve this purpose. For, after all, the task is performed not by the Auditor-General himself but by the staff of his Department. Unless the members of the Staff have special training in assessing the efficiency of public enterprises, they cannot render really useful service by prying into ;the operations of these concerns. In the process of ensuring financial accountability through the Comptroller, the Government cannot afford to allow the initiative and enterprise of those who run these concerns destroyed as a consequence of indiscriminate criticism. The problem of the accountability of these concerns should be solved through other bodies which are more competent for the purpose. The role of the Estimates Committee is worth mentioning in this context. Parliament has always the plenary power to set up appropriate machinery for the purpose. It is under such powers that Parliament set up the Committee on Public Undertakings.

But this need not detract from the importance of the Comptroller and Auditor-General. Even in the narrow field within which he operates, his service is of inestimable value to safeguard the interests of the taxpayer. Audit is the watchdog of the finances of the nation and the Comptroller and Auditor-General is the supreme overseer of the Government's financial activities on behalf of Parliament. In a country like India where public expenditure is increasing at a fast pace year after year, there is scope both for widening and intensifying the role of the Comptroller and Auditor-General for the better realization of the democratic ideals embodied in the Constitution.

***

1. See in this connection, Laxmi Narain, "The Comptroller and Auditor-General and Public Enterprises in India," *The Ind. Journal of Pub. Admn.*, Vol. IX, No. 1. pp. 72-87.

41

THE PUBLIC SERVICE COMMISSIONS

AT THE TIME of the framing of the new Constitution, India had had some experience of Public Service Commissions functioning as integral part of the old Constitution. The Government of India Act of 1935 had provided for the establishment of Public Service Commission both at the Centre and in the Provinces.[1] When the present Constitution was being framed the Federal Public Service Commission was already functioning. The experience of the working of the Commission was of value to the framers of the Constitution in dealing with this part. Except for a few changes, they have in fact closely followed the provisions of the Government of India Act of 1935.

Why Public Service Commissions?

Experience in most democratic countries has shown that under the old system of private and political patronage the government used to be deprived of the services of the most able men. This was because their place was taken by those whose main qualification was the possession of influence. Civil servants actually in office were discouraged from giving of their best to their work, because advancement depended not on their ability and zeal, but on the extent of political and private favouritism. The civil service was unable to provide continuity of administrative experience for the benefit of successive governments, because the senior posts changed hands when governments changed. The number of civil servants was often unnecessarily enlarged in order to provide posts for the dependents of those who held the reins of political power. By drawing on the widest possible field for recruitment, the public service gets more able people than when it relied on a system of personal contacts. Moreover, it was able to divide the talent more evenly amongst all the government departments.

In a country like India the necessity and importance of Public Service Commissions should be evident. The population of over 1,000 million is multi-lingual and multi-racial. One must also take note of the existence of a number of religious minorities and socially and educationally backward classes and communities. If political consideration and favouritism dominate the recruitment to the public services under these conditions, the injury to the nation will be incalculable. It will certainly affect the efficiency and integrity of the public services. What the Royal Commission on the Indian Civil Service wrote in 1924 is true even today:[1]

---

1. It is interesting to note that the introduction of responsible governments was the starting point for the institution of Public Service Commissions in India. The idea behind them was the protection of Public Services from the political influence of the popular ministers who assumed office for the first time under the Government of India Act of 1919. See the *First Despatch on the Indian Constitutional Reforms,* 5 March 1999, para 55. Also see *Report of the Royal Commission on Superior Services in India*, 1924.

Wherever democratic institutions exist, experience has shown that to secure an efficient Civil Service it is essential to protect it, so far as possible, from political and personal influences and to give it that position of stability and security which is vital to its successful working as the impartial and efficient instrument by which Governments, of whatever complexion, may give effect to their policies. In countries where this principle has been neglected, and where the 'spoils system' has taken its place, an inefficient and disorganised civil service has been the inevitable result and corruption has been rampant.

The function, therefore, of a Public Service Commission is two fold: first, it must, to adapt a famous phrase in American history, 'keep the rascals out'; secondly, it must try to put the best men in. It is difficult to overemphasize the importance of this function.

That the Constituent Assembly was fully aware of this vital role of the Public Service Commission was made clear by the members who participated in the discussion on the subject. For the purpose of illustration, we may note some of their observations. Jaspat Roy Kapoor said:

Entrusted with the task of selecting candidates to fill various posts under the Union and State Governments the formation of both the Central and State Public Service Commissions becomes of very great importance. On its proper formation and on the proper selection of the members of such Commissions depend the proper selection of persons who will be called upon to discharge the responsible and onerous duties of the Government in the various Departments[1].

H.N. Kunzru was of the opinion that the efficiency of the administration of the State will depend upon the manner in which recruitment was made. "It is, therefore, of the utmost importance that the body making the recruitment should possess within limits as much independence as possible."[2] The importance of Public Service Commission was emphasized by H.V. Kamath in a long speech. Among other things, he said:

It is imperative that whichever government comes into power the permanent services should carry out the policy laid down by the Government for the time being in office. In countries where the principle has been neglected and where, instead, the spoils system has taken its place, an inefficient and disorganised civil service has been the inevitable result, and corruption has become rampant with all its attendant consequences. It is, therefore, of the utmost importance that the Public Service Commissions that we contemplate under these articles should be completely independent of the Government of the day whether at the Centre or in the States. Otherwise, I am afraid the civil services will apprehend that amenability to Ministerial pressure and a correct attitude towards questions in which a little coterie or group for the time being in power is interested, will secure them promotions, rather than merit or efficiency...

Most of the democratic countries in the world have set up Public Service Commissions to free the matter of appointments from patronage, and in order to protect Ministers against group interest at the expense of the national. And to protect the Ministers against such charge, it is necessary that the Public Service Commissions must be kept completely independent of the Executive...[3]

Constitution of the Union Public Service Commission

Article 315 makes it obligatory for the Union to constitute a Public Service Commission. It is presided over by a Chairman who is designated as the Chairman, Union Public Service Commission. The Chairman and the members of the Commission are

1. C.A.D. IX, p. 576. See also p. 555.
2. Ibid, p. 583.
3. C.A.D. IX, p. 585. See also p. 605.

appointed by the President. They hold office for a period of six years from the date they join duty or until they attain the age of sixty-five years; whichever is earlier. It is provided that at least one half of the members of the Commission should be persons with a minimum of ten years' experience in Government Service. This is intended to ensure always the presence of men of experience in civil service on the Commission so that it may function as an expert body. The number of members on the Commission is determined by the President by regulations. At present there are eleven members on the Commission including the Chairman.

A member of the Commission is ineligible for the same appointment for a second term. His further employment elsewhere also is severely restricted. The Chairman of the Union Public Service Commission is ineligible for further employment either under the Government of India or under the Government of a State. A member other than the Chairman is eligible to become either the Chairman of the U.P.S.C. or the Chairman of a State Public Service Commission. But for these two offices, he is ineligible for appointment to any post under the Union Government or any State Government in India.

The President is empowered to determine by regulations the salary and other conditions of service of the members of the Commission. He may also make regulations with respect to the strength of the staff of the Commission and their conditions of service. It is provided that the conditions of service of a member of the Commission cannot be varied to his disadvantage after his appointment. The Chairman and members of the Commission are paid Rs. 30,000 and Rs. 26,000 per month respectively as salary. These amounts compare favourably with the salaries of comparable positions at the highest level in the Government. The entire expenses of the Commission, including the salaries and allowances of its members, are charged to the Consolidated Fund of India.

A member of the Union Public Service Commission can be removed from office only by an order of the President on the ground of misbehaviour. The Constitution prescribes a procedure to prove such misbehaviour. According to this, the matter will be referred to the Supreme Court by the President and the Court will conduct an enquiry in accordance with the procedure prescribed under Article 145 of the Constitution and will submit a report to the President. Pending the enquiry by the Supreme Court, the President may suspend the member concerned. The President is empowered to remove by order a member also on the following grounds:

1. if he is adjudged an insolvent; or
2. if he engages during his term of office in any paid employment outside the duties of his office; or
3. if he is, in the opinion of the President, unfit to continue in office by reason of infirmity of mind or body; or
4. if he becomes in any way concerned in any contract or agreement made by or on behalf of the Government of India or a State Government or in any way participates in its profit or benefits except as an ordinary member of an incorporated company.

All the provisions are intended to make the Commission an independent and impartial body to discharge its responsibilities in an efficient manner.

Constitution of State Public Service Commissions

Under Article 315, each constituent State of the Union should also have a Public Service Commission. There is however provision for setting up Joint Public Service Commissions each serving more than one State.[1] But such Commissions may be set up only by the law of Parliament on a request for them by the States concerned. The Constitution also permits the Union Public Service Commission to render its services to a State for all or any of the needs of the State with the approval of the President.

The members of a State Public Service Commission are appointed by the Governor, and those of a Joint Commission by the President. As in the case of the Union Commission, the appointment is for a maximum period of six years. But if a member attains the age of sixty-two years while in service, irrespective of his having completed six years, he must retire from service. The members of State and Joint Public Service Commissions are not eligible for any appointment under the Union or the States except that a Chairman may become the Chairman or a member of the Union Public Service Commission or the Chairman of any other State or Joint Public Service Commission and a member may, in addition to the abovementioned offices, become the Chairman of the Commission of which he is a member. The conditions of service of the members of the State Public Service Commissions are more or less the same as those of the Union Commission. The only significant point of difference is in salary which varies from State to State. The conditions of service of a member of a State Public Service Commission may not be varied to his disadvantage after his appointment. The number of members on the State Commissions also varies from State to State. The basis and the procedure for the removal of the members of the State or Joint Commissions are the same as for the members of the Union Public Service Commission.

Functions of the Commission

Under Article 320, the Commissions have the following functions:

1. To conduct examinations for appointments to the services of the Union or the States;
2. To assist the States in framing and operating schemes of joint recruitment if two or more States request the Union Commission in this behalf;
3. To advise the Union or State Governments
   (*a*) on all matters relating to methods of recruitment to civil services and for civil posts;
   (*b*) on the principles to be followed in making appointment to civil services and civil posts and promotions, transfers, etc. from one service to another;
   (*c*) on all disciplinary matters affecting Government servants of the Union or the States;
   (*d*) on claims for costs of legal proceedings instituted against a Union official or a State official;
   (*e*) on claims for the award of pension in respect of injuries sustained by a Union official or a State official on duty; and
   (*f*) any other matter specifically referred to it by the President or the Governor.

1. So far no Joint Public Service Commission has been set up.

The Union or State Governments are empowered to frame rules from time to time regulating the scope of these advisory functions of the Commissions. Those which regulate the scope of the Union Public Service Commission's functions in this sphere are known as the U.P.S.C. (Exemption and Consultation) Regulations. The Government's power to amend these rules can substantially modify the Commission's powers. For example, an amendment of 1961 provided that "it shall not be necessary for the President to consult the Commission in any case where he proposes to make an order of dismissal, removal or reduction in rank after being satisfied that such action is necessary in the interest of the security of the State." Similar drastic amendments were made in 1962 affecting a variety of advisory functions of the Commission following the Proclamation of Emergency by the President.[1]

Under Article 321, the functions of the Union Commission or a State Commission may be extended by an Act made by Parliament or the Legislature of the State concerned. Such an Act may also bring within the scope of the functions of the Commission matters connected with the services of public institutions such as local bodies or public corporations under the Union or State Governments. This is important in view of the fact that as the activities of both the Union and the State Governments increase, more and more of public corporations and such other institutions are bound to be established involving the employment of an ever increasing number of officials.

Report of the Commissions

The Union Public Service Commission has to submit to the President an annual report on the work done by the Commission. The report accompanied by a memorandum explaining the action taken by the Government on the recommendations of the Commission is to be placed before both Houses of Parliament. Similarly, a State Commission has to submit to the Governor an annual report which, with the memorandum explaining the action taken by the State Government on the Commissioner's recommendations, is placed before the State Legislature. The memorandum should explain the reasons for the non-acceptance of the recommendations of the Commission by the Government if there are any such cases.

It must be observed here that the Public Service Commissions envisaged under the Constitution including the U.P.S.C. are only advisory bodies. It might be asked why the recommendations of such an important body as the Public Service Commission are not obligatory on the Government. The framers of the Constitution, in this respect, have followed the practice that obtained under the Constitution Act of 1935. Experience has shown that the recommendations of the Commission have more influence if they are advisory than mandatory in character. The danger is that if the Commission is given mandatory powers there is a possibility of conflict between the Commission and the Government and there may arise situations when they behave as rival governments in the same territory, each trying to establish its will over the other. The real safeguard against the rejection of any recommendations of the Commission lies in the parliamentary control that is provided for by the Constitution. The Government has to justify its action before the Legislature which has the power of repudiating the Government's action.

The Public Service Commissions in India are in a much stronger position from a constitutional point of view than statutory bodies or Commissions set up in Britain or the

1. Union Public Service Commission (Exemption from Consultation) Second Amendment Regulations, 1962.

United States. This is because these Commissions are set up by the same sovereign authority which sets up the Executive, the Legislature and the Judiciary. All of them are created by the Constitution itself. But in Britain, the United States and elsewhere, Public Service Commissions are the creations of the Legislature and, as such, the British Parliament and the United States Congress have the power to modify them as they like. In other words, they are subordinate bodies. In India, the Public Service Commissions are in no way subordinate to the Legislature or the Executive. Thus, while a Public Service Commission would not ordinarily like to withhold information on any particular subject, its constitutional right to withhold any such information should be recognized.

Obviously, the Constitution-makers wanted to provide all reasonable safeguards to make the Public Service Commissions in India immune from undue influence and to enable them to carry out their duties with impartiality, integrity and independence.

Magnitude of the Commission's Work

A glance over the annual reports of the Public Service Commissions — Union as well as the State Commissions — will show the variety and volume of their work. Conducting competitive examinations for recruiting personnel to the various services is one of the most arduous tasks undertaken by these Commissions. In one of its reports the Union Public Service Commission gives the following details with regard to some of its functions:

During the period 1998-99

(a) UPSC made 10877 recommendations regarding suitability of candidates/ officials for recruitment, confirmation, promotion, etc.

(b) UPSC tendered advice in 331 disciplinary cases.

(c) UPSC tendered advice on 267 cases relating to Recruitment Rules, Service matters, etc. All these had been substantially more than the previous years. It is significant to note that Government did not accept 12 recommendations of the UPSC of which one relates to recruitment by interview, two relate to promotion within Central Services and four disciplinary cases involving nine charged officers.

During the 1998-99 period UPSC conducted 13 examinations; received 8,53,995 applications; interviewed 4,500 candidates based on the results of 7 examinations and recommended 5,042 candidates for various posts.

UPSC also received 70,355 applications for recruitment by interview to various posts, interviewed 5,610 candidates and recommended 1,191 candidates for appointment.

Also UPSC tendered advice in 629 references received from various Ministries/ Departments of the Union Government regarding Recruitment Rules and Service Rules. It also considered the service records of 25,296 officers; held 704 Selection Committee/ Department Promotion Committee Meetings and recommended—

211 officials for induction into All India Services, 2,871 officials for promotions in Central Services, 295 officials for appointment on transfer or deputation/transfer and 1,110 officials for confirmation.

The Commission made recommendations to 82% and 77% of the posts reserved for SC, ST and OBC candidates through recruitment by interview respectively.

The Commission disposed of 579 disciplinary cases out of which in respect of 302 cases effective advice was tendered; in 20 cases earlier advice was reiterated; in one case de novo proceedings were recommended; in 8 cases miscellaneous advice was tendered. 239 cases were returned to the Government for completion of documents and compliance to prescribed procedures and 6 cases were returned as the reference did not lie with UPSC.

The Commission penalised 17 candidates who resorted to malpractices during examinations. Altogether, this is a very impressive record.

The Commission in its reports has acknowledged that apart from a few isolated instances, the Ministries and Departments generally observed the provisions of the Constitution. It means that on the whole the recommendations of the Commission are accepted and acted upon by the Government. In fact, most of the reports show that there was not even one case where the Union Government had not accepted the recommendations of the Commission. No greater test is required to prove the effectiveness of the Commission as an independent body under the Constitution even though its recommendations are only of an advisory nature.

While the Union Public Service Commission's performance, on the whole, has been of very high order, the same cannot be said of that of the State Public Service Commissions. In recent years, in several States, the members of the Commission have not been appointed with sole reference to their merit but other considerations such as caste, community, religion or even political affiliation. This has resulted in the alarming deterioration of the quality of performance of these Commissions. If suitable measures are not taken in time to remedy this situation and tone up their functioning, this would ultimately be reflected in the quality of performance of the public services as a whole.

***

42

PUBLIC SERVICES

THE STANDARD and efficiency of administration in any country depend ultimately on the calibre, training and integrity of the members of the Public Services. When the aim of a constitution is the establishment of a Welfare State, it is evident that the functions of such a State will embrace a wide range of activities. The successful operation of these activities depends upon the availability of men of vision, ability, honesty and loyalty to man and administrative apparatus of the State. The concern of the framers of the Constitution to ensure this is clear from the provisions dealing with the constitution and functions of the Public Service Commissions. We have also seen the constitutional guarantee of equality of opportunity in matters of public employment. Not content with these, they went further and made certain special provisions dealing with the Public Services in India in order to make them feel contended and secure in their positions.

As was pointed out by a member in the Constituent Assembly:

> Without an efficient civil service, it will be impossible for the government to carry on and the continuity of policy to be kept. The importance of governmental administration has been in fact that there is continuity and unless there is continuity there is chaos. In the contentment of the civil services lies the safety of the country.[1]

Another member put it more forcefully in the following terms:

> With the independence of our country, the responsibilities of the services have become onerous. They may make or mar the efficiency of the machinery of administration, a machinery so vital for the peace and progress of the country. A country without an efficient civil service cannot make progress in spite of the earnestness of the people at the helm of affairs in the country. Wherever democratic institutions exist, experience has shown that it is essential to protect the public service as far as possible from political or personal influence and to give it that position of stability and security which is vital in its successful working as an impartial and efficient instrument by which government, of whatever political complexion, may give effect to their policies.[2]

One of the major problems of a democratic government is the proper adjustment between the 'political wing' and 'civil service wing' of the administrative machinery. The former are the representatives of the people, and, as such, enter and leave office according to the will of the people. The latter, on the other hand, are permanently in office and are often called upon to serve different masters at different times: to translate into action different policies at the behest of different masters. This they can do only if they maintain an attitude of political detachment and eschew all partisan approach. At the same time, they should be loyal to the government of the day.

---

1. P. Subbaroyan, C.A.D. IX, p. 962.
2. H.V. Kamath, Ibid, p. 585.

As pointed out by A.D. Gorwala:

> Bad government and good administration, for example, are at best a temporary combination. The interplay between the two being continuous and unremitting, the quality of the administration is bound to be affected by that of the Government. Government for its part derives the main features of its strength or weakness from the character of the people, their leaders and the nature of the prevailing political set-up. Since administration has to be considered not merely as a machine but as the vital instrument through which a democracy carries out its policies, its organic connection for good or ill with the body politic in general and with the Ministry, Parties and Legislature in particular cannot be ignored.

To what extent has this ideal been translated into practice in India can be assessed only in the light of the constitutional provisions dealing with the services and their operation.

Article 309 empowers Parliament and the State Legislatures to regulate the recruitment and the conditions of service of the Public Services of the Union and the States respectively. Article 310 ensures that all persons who are members of the Defence Services or of the Civil Services of the Union or of All India Services hold office during the pleasure of the President. Similarly, members of the State Services hold office during the pleasure of the Governor. Since the President or the Governor is only the constitutional head of the State, the powers of the President or the Governor here are those which are exercised by the Union Cabinet or the State Cabinet. Hence, the Cabinet wields the real power of controlling all categories of services. This is in harmony with the democratic and responsible character of the Government which ensures the responsibility of the Executive to the Legislature.[1]

To hold office during the pleasure of the President or Governor does not, however, mean that a member of the public services can be dismissed arbitrarily by the President or the Governor. There are certain constitutional safeguards against such an action. These are embodied in Article 311 in the following manner:

1. No member of a civil service of the Union or an All India Service or a State Service can be dismissed or removed by an authority subordinate to that by which he was appointed.
2. No such member shall be dismissed or removed or reduced in rank until he has been given a reasonable opportunity of showing cause against the action proposed to be taken in regard to him.

The purport of this article, as Ambedkar made it clear in the Constituent Assembly, is to lay down a general proposition that in every case of action which affects a member of the Civil Service adversely, notice shall be given. "I should have thought that that was probably the best provision that we have for the safety and security of the civil service, because it contains a fundamental limitation upon the authority to dismiss."[2] There can hardly be any doubt that one of the most important aspects of the public services is 'permanence in office'. This is so closely associated with the 'security of service' that it is difficult to think of the one without at once associating it with the other. Continuity of personnel is of great importance. Constant change in the services is costly in terms of money and more costly in effectiveness. Civil servants must be given such security of

1. For a detailed discussion on the subject, see Om Prakash Motiwal, "Doctrine of Pleasure and the Services in the Indian Constitution," *The Ind. Jour. of Pub. Admn.,* Vol. IX, No. 1, pp. 64-73. See also A.I.R. 1971, S.C. 1997.
2. C.A.D. IX, p. 1112.

tenure as will give them confidence to deal forthrightly with their 'masters'. This is to a large extent obtained by the constitutional guarantees mentioned above.

Under the Government of India Act of 1935, the control of the Civil Services was vested in the Secretary of State, beyond the control of the Indian Legislatures. But under the Constitution, Parliament and the State Legislatures have become the controlling authorities. Elaborate procedures have been devised to protect the security of tenure of the civil servant. These involve enquiries and investigations by officers of high standing appointed specially for the purpose. The report of the findings of such enquiries are made available to the Public Service Commissions and adverse action is taken against a civil servant only with the concurrence of the Commission.

There are, however, a few exceptions where the civil servant is not given all these facilities to defend himself. These are:

(i) Where a person is dismissed or reduced in rank on the ground of conduct which has lead to his conviction on a criminal charge.

(ii) Where it is impracticable to give the civil servant an opportunity to defend himself. (But the authority taking action against him shall record the reasons for such action).

(iii) Where in the interest of the security of the State, it is not expedient to give such an opportunity to the civil servant.

Ambedkar explained the scope of these restrictive provisions in the following terms:

> The question has been raised that any person who has been convitced in any criminal case need not be given notice. There, again, I must submit that there has been a mistake, because the regulations made by a State may well provide that although a person is convicted of a criminal offence, if that offence does not involve moral turpitude, he need not be dismissed from State service. It is perfectly open to Parliament to so legislate. It is not every criminal charge, for instance, under the motoring law or under some trivial law made by Parliament or by a State making a certain act an offence, that would necessarily be not a ground for dismissal. It may, *e.g.*, exclude political offences... That liberty of Parliament is not touched or restricted by sub-clause (a).
>
> With regard to sub-clause (b), this has been bodily taken from Section 240 of the Government of India Act... Even the British people, who were very keen on giving protection to the civil services, thought it necessary to introduce a proviso like sub-clause (b). With regard to (c) the President may say that in certain cases a notice shall not be served. I think that is a very salutary provision and notwithstanding the obvious criticism that may be made that it opens a wide door to the President to abrogate the provisions contained in sub-clause (2), I am inclined to think that in the better interests of the State, it ought to be retained.[1]
>
> Coming to clause (3) this has been deliberately introduced. Suppose this clause was not there, what would be the position? Any person, who has not been given notice under sub-clause (a) or (b) or (c), would be entitled to go to a Court of law and say that he has been dismissed without giving an opportunity to show cause. Now, Courts have taken two different views with regard to the word 'satisfaction': it is a subjective state of mind of the officer himself or an objective state, that is to say, depending upon circumstances. It has been felt in a matter of this sort, it is better to oust the jurisdiction of the Court and to make the decision of the officer final. That is the reason why clause (3) had to be introduced that no court shall be able to call in

1. Those who bitterly opposed this provision included H.V. Kamath, Shibban Lal Saksena, etc. See C.A.D. IX, pp. 1108-12.

question if the officer feels that it is impracticable to give reasonable notice or the President thinks that under certain circumstances notice need not be given.

...Under the provisions relating to Public Service Commissions, there is a provision that every civil servant who is aggrieved by any action taken by an officer relating to the conditions of service will have a right of appeal to the Public Service Commission. Therefore, even in cases where the Government has not given the officer an opportunity to show cause, even such an officer will have the right to go to the Public Service Commission and to file an appeal that he has been wrongfully dismissed contrary to the provisions contained in the rules made relating to his service...[1]

Ever since the inauguration of the Constitution, the High Courts and the Supreme Court were, in a series of cases, called upon to adjudge the validity or otherwise of dismissals or removals of public servants from service by the Union or the States in the light of the protections provided by the Constitution. In Shyamlal *vs.* State of U.P.[2] the Supreme Court held that "a compulsory retirement does not amount to dismissal or removal and, therefore, does not attract the provisions of the Article 311." Similarly, termination of contractual service by notice under one of the provisions of the contract also does not amount to dismissal or removal contemplated under Article 311.[3] In Mahesh Prasad *vs.* State of U.P.[4], the Court held that Article 311(1) does not mean that the removal from service must be by the very same authority who made the appointment or by his direct superior. It is enough if the removing authority is of the same rank or grade. Giving reasonable opportunity of showing cause against the action proposed to be taken in regard to a civil servant does not imply giving more than one such opportunity. Further, if the civil servant concerned does not make use of such opportunity given to him, he does so at his own risk.[5]

The question as to whether non-compliance with the provisions of Article 320, under which the Government is expected to consult the Public Service Commission in every case of disciplinary action, will affect an action properly taken against a civil servant under Article 311 came up for consideration before the Supreme Court in State of U.P. *vs.* M.L. Srivastava[6]. The Court held that "Article 320 cannot be held to be mandatory and is not in the nature of a rider to Article 311 is not controlled by Article 320 for the following reasons :

(i) The proviso to Article 320 would not be there if the intention of the makers of the Constitution was that it should be mandatory

(ii) It does not extend to making the advice of the Commission binding on the Government.

(iii) Chapter II, Part XIV containing Article 320 and other articles deal with the constitution of the Public Service Commission, the conditions of service of its members and also their duties and functions and the relation between the Government and the Commission and between the Commission and a public servant; it does not confer any

---

1. C.A.D. IX, p. 1112.
2. A.I.R. 1954, S.C. 369. See also State of Bombay *vs.* S.N. Doshi, 1954, S.C.J. 161, Dalip Singh *vs.* The State of Punjab (1961) II S.C.J. 58, Union of India *vs.* J.N. Sinha, A.I.R. 1971, S.C. 40. The State of Assam *vs.* D.P. Deka, A.I.R. 1971, S.C. 173 and B. Jena *vs.* State of Orissa, A.I.R. 1971, S.C. 1516.
3. Satish Chandra Anand *vs.* Union of India, 1953 S.C.R. 655. See also H.P. Singh *vs.* State of U.P. 1958, S.C.J. 148.
4. 1951, I.S.C.R. 965.
5. Joseph John *vs.* State of Travancore-Cochin, 1955, S.C.R. 1011.
6. 1958, S.C.J. 150.

rights or privileges on an individual public servant, nor any constitutional guarantee of the nature contained in Chapter I of Part XIV, particularly Article 311.

(iv) Further, the Constitution does not provide that in the event of non-compliance with the requirements of Article 320(3) (c), the proceedings ending with the Government order are invalid."

In this case, as the provisions of Article 311 had been fully complied with, the public servant had no remedy against any irregularity that the State Government may have committed and irregular compliance with the provisions of Article 320(3) (c) did not afford a cause of action to the public servant.

In another case,[1] the Court held that the power of the President to impose any punishment for any misdemeanour found proved against a delinquent public servant is unrestricted. The Constitution merely guarantees the protection of a reasonable opportunity of showing cause against the action proposed. It does not guarantee that the punishment shall not be more sever than a prescribed punishment.

In 1958, the Supreme Court had occasion to make an exhaustive analysis of the scope and ambit of the constitutional safeguards embodied in Article 311 in the light of all judicial decisions pronounced until then in the case of Purushotam Lal Dhingra *vs.* Union of India[2]. The facts of this case, briefly, are as follows: As a result of successive selections to higher posts, he became Chief Controller (a Class III service post) in 1950. In March 1951 he was selected by a selection board for the post of Assistant Superintendent, Railway Telegraphs, which was a gazetted post in Class II Officers' cadre. He joined duty in the new post in July 1951. In 1953 his superior officer made certain adverse remarks against him in his confidential report for the year ending March 1953. The views expressed in this report were confirmed by another superior officer soon after. These remarks were placed before the General Manager who wrote:

> I am disappointed to read these report. He should revert as a subordinate till he makes good the shortcomings noticed in this chance of his as an officer. Portions underlined red to be communicated.

The appellant made a representation against the remarks made against him. But this did not produce any favourable result. By August 1953 orders were issued reverting him to Class III. He appealed unsuccessfully first to the General Manager, then to the Railway Board, and finally to the President of India through a representation. In 1955 he filed a writ petition in the Punjab High Court. The judge who heard the petition declared that since Purushotam Lal was not given an opportunity to show cause against the action proposed to be taken in regard to him, provisions of Article 311 were violated and hence the action taken against him was invalid. On a Letters Patent Appeal filed by the Union of India, a Division Bench of the High Court consisting of two judges reversed the above order and dismissed the writ petition. Hence the appeal to the Supreme Court by the petitioner.

The Supreme Court was divided four to one in its decision. Speaking on behalf of the majority, Chief Justice Das made the following important observations:

> Subject to exceptions contemplated by the opening words of Article 310(I), *e.g.* Articles

1. A.N.D'Silva *vs.* The Union of India (1962) II S.C.J 126.
2. 1958, S.C.J. 217.

124, 148,218 and 324, our Constitution has adopted by the said Article 310(I) the English Common Law Rule that public servants held office during the pleasure of the President or the Governor as the case may be and it has by Article 311 imposed two qualifications for the exercise of that pleasure; in other words, the provisions of Article 311 operate as a proviso to Article 310(I). Upon Article 311 two questions arise; namely, (1) who are entitled to protection and (2) the ambit and scope of protection.

To limit the operation of the protective provisions of this Article to persons holding permanent civil posts or who are permanent members of the services will be to add qualifying words to the Article which will be contrary to sound principles of interpretation of the Constitution or a statute. There could also be no rational basis for the distinction. The Article makes no distinction between the two clauses, permanent and temporary (officiating, provisional and on probation included), both of which, therefore, are within its protections.

The two protections under the Article are (1) against being dismissed or removed by an authority subordinate to that by which the appointment had been made and (2) against being dismissed, removed or reduced in rank without being heard. The words "dismissed", "removed" and "reduced in rank" have acquired a special meaning at the time of the Constitution and it is only in those cases where the Government intends to inflict those three forms of punishment that the Government servant must be given reasonable opportunity of showing cause against the action proposed to be taken in regard to him. Therefore, if the termination of service is sought to be brought about otherwise than by way of punishment, then the Government servant whose serivce is so terminated cannot claim the protection of Article 311(2).

The principle is that when a servant has a right to a post or to a rank either under the contract of employment, express, or implied, or under the Rules governing the conditions of service, the termination of service of such a servant or his reduction to a lower post is by itself and *prima facie* a punishment for it operates as a forfeiture of his rights to hold the post or the rank and to get the emoluments and other benefits attached thereto; but if the servant has no such right to the post or the rank as when he is appointed to a post permanent or temporary either on probation or on an officiating basis and whose temporary service has not ripened to a quasi-permanent service under the appropriate Rules, the termination of his employment does not deprive him of any right and cannot therefore by itself be a punishment. In other words if the Government has the right to terminate the employment at any time then such termination in the manner contemplated by the contract or by the Rules is *prima facie* and *per se* not a punishment and does not attract the protection provisions of Article 311.

Even in such cases if the Government chose to proceed against the servant on the basis of misconduct, inefficiency and the like and inflict on him the punishment of dismissal, removal or reduction carrying with it penal consequences, the servant will be entitled to protection under Article 311(2).

The two tests to be applied by Courts are (1) whether the servant had a right to the post or the rank or (2) whether he has been visited with evil consequences. If the case satisfied either of the two tests then it must be held that the servant had been punished and the termination of service must be taken as a dismissal or removal from service or the reversion to his substantive post must be regarded as a reduction in rank, attracting the provision in Article 311(2) and the provision thereof must have been complied with; otherwise the termination of service or reduction in rank must be held to be wrongful.

The appellant was appointed to the higher post on an officiating basis and under the Railway Code and Fundamental Rule he has no right to continue in that post. Such appointment was terminable at any time, on reasonable notice, by Government and so his reversion did not operate as a forfeiture of any right and could not be described as 'reduction in rank' by way of punishment. It would not amount also to 'dismissal or removal' because of Note 1 to Rule 1729 of the Railway Code (applicable to the appellant). Further it did not entail the forfeiture of his future chances of promotion or affect his seniority in his substantive post. He cannot complain that the requirements of Article 311(2) were not complied with.[1]

In his dissent, Justice Bose agreed generally with the interpretation of Article 311 by the majority. But he said that the words 'dismissal, removal and reduction in rank' have special meaning and that Article 311(2) applies when penal consequences ensue, that the article is attracted wherever a right is infringed thereby. He said:

The test must always be whether evil consequences over and above those that would ensue from a 'contractual termination' are likely to follow and Article 311(2) cannot be confined to the penalties prescribed by the various rules or in other words the Article cannot be evaded by saying in a set of rules that a particular consequence is not a punishment or that a particular kind of action is not intended to operate as a penalty.

In the instant case, though the order of reversion is non-committal, the General Manager's remarks or the otherwise irrelevant administrative notings which form the real foundation for the order, *i.e.*, ... till he makes good his shortcomings noticed in this chance of his as an officer' cannot be ignored and Article 311(2) is attracted thereby.

The real hurt does not lie in any of those things—the form of action or the procedure followed or what operated in the minds of a particular officer—but in the consequences that follow and, in my judgment, the protections of Article 311 are not against harsh words but against hard blows. It is the effect of the order alone that matters; and in my judgement Article 311 applies whenever any substantial evil follows over and above a purely 'contractual one'. I do not think that the Article can be evaded by saying in a set of rules that a particular consequence is not a punishment or that a particular kind of action is not intended to operate as a penalty.

What is the precise nature and scope of the expression 'reasonable opportunity of showing cause against the action proposed'? The Court was called upon to go into this question in Khemchand *vs.* Union of India.[2] In this case, the Deputy Commissioner of Delhi had accepted the report of an officer who enquired into the charges of embezzlement, acceptance of illegal gratification *etc.* against the appellant, an officer of the Delhi Administration, found him guilty of all the charges and suggested that dismissal should be the proper form of punishment in the case and confirmed the suggestion as to the punishment proposed. Without giving the appellant the further opportunity to show cause against the dismissal proposed, the order of dismissal was passed. This the Court held was invalid because Section (2) of Article 311 was not fully complied with and the applicant had not had the benefit of all the constitutional protection.

According to Justice Bose:

The reasonable opportunity of showing cause against the action proposed includes:

(a) an opportunity to deny his guilt and establish his innocence which he can do only if he is told what the charges levelled against him are and the allegations on which the charges are based;

(b) an opportunity to defend himself by cross-examining the witnesses produced against him and by examining himself or any other witnesses in support of his defence; and finally,

---

1. The Court reiterated its position in K.H. Phadnis *vs.* State of Maharashtra, A.I.R. 1971, S.C. 998 and State of Punjab *vs.* Krishan Das, A.I.R. 1971, S.C. 766. See also State of Bihar *vs.* S.B. Mishra, A.I.R. 1971, S.C. 1011.
2. 1958 S.C.J. 497. See also Kukumchand Malhotra *vs.* Union of India, 1959, S.C.J. 419 and T.C.M. Pillai *vs.* Technology Institute, Guindy, A.I.R. 1971, S.C. 1811.

(c) an opportunity to make his representation as to why the proposed punishment should not be inflicted on him which he can only do if the competent authority after the enquiry is over and after applying his mind to the gravity or otherwise of the charges proved against the government servant tentatively proposes to inflict one of the three punishments and communicates the same to him.

The principle that has been established as a result of this decision is extremely important. It removes the element of uncertainty that prevailed after the decision in Joseph John's case in which the Court held that "giving opportunity... does not imply giving more than one such opportunity." Khemchand's case fully establishes the principle that the opportunity is to be given after a stage has been reached where the charges have been established and the competent authority has applied its mind to the gravity or otherwise of the proved charges tentatively and proposed a particular punishment. The fact that an opportunity has been given at the enquiry stage is not in itself enough to satisfy the requirements of Article 311(2).

Can the services of a government servant be terminated on the ground of 'subversive activities'? This question arose in Balakotiah *vs.* Union of India[1] in which the appellant challenged the validity of the notice under Rule 3 of Railway Services (Safeguarding of National Security) Rules, 1949, and the order of suspension and dismissal served on him. It was contended on behalf of the appellant that the Security Rules were void as they militated against the Constitutional protections under Article 311 and the Fundamental Rights guaranteed under Article 14 (equality before law and equal protection of laws) and 19(1) (c) (right to form associations). The Court rejected these contentions and unanimously held:

1. It may be that the connotation of the words 'subversive activities' in Rule 3 of the Security Rules is wide but that is not to say it is vague and indefinite. The object of the Rules as recited in the short title is safeguarding the national security which is emphasized in the proviso to Rule 3. The word 'subversive activities' in the context of national security is sufficiently precise to sustain a valid classification. The Security Rules, 1949, are not illegal as being repugnant to Article 14 of the Constitution.

2. The appellants have no doubt a fundamental right to association under Article 19(1) (c) (and to be members of the Community Party and trade unions); but they have no fundamental right to be continued in employment by the State and when their services are terminated by the State they cannot complain of the infringement of any of their constitutional rights when no question of violation of Article 311 arises.

3. The terms of employment (applicable to the appellants) provide for their services being terminated on a proper notice and so no question of premature termination arises. Rule 7 of the Security Rules preserves their right to all the benefits of pension, gratuities and the like they would be entitled to under the rules. The orders terminating their services stand on the same footing as an order of discharge under Rule 148 of the Railway Establishment Code and it is neither one of dismissal nor or removal so as to attract Article 311 of the Constitution.

4. The rules are clearly prospective in that action thereunder is to be taken in respect of subversive activities which either exist now, or are likely to be indulged in, in future. That the materials for taking action in the latter case, as in the notices in the instant cases,

1. 1958, S.C.J. 451.

are drawn from the conduct of the employees prior to the enactment does not render them retrospective.

Under what conditions can the Union or a State Government be justified in dismissing a civil servant from service without holding an enquiry in the interest of the security of the State? In Jayantilal *vs.* F.N. Rana[1] the Supreme Court held that the 'satisfaction of the President' under Article 311(2) (c) has to be of the President personally and not of an authorized officer acting for the President. The specific mention of the President in the clause requires that the President should apply his mind personally to the case. The powers of the President under this clause, therefore, cannot be delegated. This means that in every case when a civil servant is dismissed from service without holding an enquiry in the interest of the security of the State, the matter will have to be brought to the personal notice of the President before the Union Government takes executive action in the name of the President.

The above interpretation was reaffirmed by the Court in B.K. Sardari lal *vs.* Union of India.[2] In this case seventeen members of the Delhi Police were dismissed from service without holding an enquiry. The order was passed under Article 311(2) (c) by the Joint Secretary of the Government in the name of the President of India dispensing with the enquiry in the interest of the security of the State. The High Court of Delhi uphled the validity of the order. On appeal, however, the Supreme Court applying the principle enunciated in the jayantilal case held that it is the President or Governor alone who has to be satisfied that in the interest of the security of the State it is not expedient to hold the enquiry.[3]

Can a government servant join an association of civil servants which has not been recognized by the Government? The Supreme Court answered the question in the positive and declared Rule 4-B of the Central Services (Conduct) Rules, 1955, to be unconstitutional and void. It was unconstitutional because it contravened Article 19(1) (c) of the Constitution which guaranteed the right to form associations by prohibiting a government servant from joining or continuing to be a member of any association of government servants which has not been recognized or whose recognition has been withdrawn by the Government.[4] By the same decision the Court declared that Rule 4-A, which prohibits any form of demonstrations, was also a violation of the government servant's rights. But in so far as the said rule prohibited a strike, it could not be struck down for the reason that there was no fundamental right to resort to strike.

Has the State the power under Article 310 to punish a government servant for acts unconnected with his official duties? This question was answered in the affirmative by the Allahabad High Court in the case of L.N. Pande.[5] Delivering the judgement of the Court Justice Dhawan said that the action taken against the official would be justified if the Government was of the opinion that the act in question amounted to misconduct, unbecoming or unworthy of a Government official or violated the unwritten code of conduct, provided that the Government complied with the provisions of Article 311 and gave a

1. A.I.R. 1964, S.C. 648.
2. A.I.R. 1971, S.C. 1547.
3. See also in this connection B.C. Das *vs.* The State of Assam, A.I.R. 1971, S.C. 2004.
4. E.X. Joseph *vs.* The Accountant-General (1963) S.C.J. Supp. I S.C.R. 789.
5. Indian Institute of Public Administration, *News Letter*, April 1959, p. 7.

reasonable opportunity to the accused official to show cause against the action proposed to be taken against him. He further pointed out that if the contention that a government servant was not answerable to the Government for misconduct committed in his private life was correct, the result would be that however reprehensible or abominable a government servant's conduct in his private life might be, the Government would be powerless to dispense with his services unless and until he committed a criminal offence or committed an act which was specifically prohibited by the government servant's Conduct Rules. This would clothe government servants with an impunity which would place the government in a position worse than that of an ordinary employer. It would be almost destructive of the principle laid down in Article 310 that every government servant held office during the pleasure of the President or Governor, as the case might be. The power of the State to dispense with the services of any government servant, though hedged with safeguards contained in Article 311 and other provisions of the Constitution, was real.

All India Services

Article 312 provides for the creation of All India Services. An All India Service is different form the Central and the State Services. It has been pointed out earlier that under Article 309, the States are entitled to create their own civil services and lay down their own conditions of service just as the Centre is entitled to create its own services, make recruitment and lay down conditions of service. Thus, while Article 309 provides for separate jurisdictions for the Centre and the States, Article 312 takes away to some extent the autonomy of the States in this field by vesting in the Centre the authority to create All India Services. However, the framers were anxious to see that the vesting of such authority in the Centre should be with the consent of a substantial majority of the representatives of the States. This is why Article 312 provides that an All India Service can be created only if the Council of States declares by a resolution supported by not less than a two-thirds majority that it is necessary in the national interest to create one or more such All India Services. Such a resolution should be considered as tantamount to an authority given by the States. When such a resolution is passed, Parliament is competent to constitute such an All India Service and lay down details connected with it.[1]

All India Services, by their very nature, are instruments of national integration and unity. They ensure the maintenance of common standards all over the country in certain vital fields of administration. They facilitate the existence of a hard core of officials in every State who, because of their membership in a service which falls within the jurisdiction of the Centre, feel more free and independent to advise the Government and to act with a national outlook keeping in view the national interests. The framers of the Constitution had originally no intention of creating such All India Services. This was why the Draft Constitution did not make any provision in this regard. But the partition of the country and the creation of Pakistan, and the extremely unsettled conditions that prevailed in the country in the early days of Independence convinced those in authority of the necessity of such services as powerful instruments for the preservation of national unity. The example of the Indian Civil Service provided the necessary experience for the creation of such All India Services.

Until 15 August 1947, when power was transferred, the Indian Civil Service had

1. See in this connection D.S. Grewal *vs.* State of Punjab 1959, S.C.J. 399.

been entrusted with the administration of the country. Recruitment to the I.C.S. came to an end with the termination of the British regime. Most of the European members of that Service retired soon after, and a large number of Muslim members of the Service went away to Pakistan. As a result, the ranks of the I.C.S. were greatly depleted. At the same time, it was found that in the interests of both uniformity and efficient administration, All India Services were necessary. It was, therefore, decided to constitute new All India Services such as the Indian Administrative Service and the Indian Police Service. This was done with the consent of the States. The constitutional basis as embodied in the Council resolution ensures that only with the backing of a substantial majority of the State representatives can such a measure be undertaken.

Originally, besides the old Indian Civil Service, there were only two All India Services, namely, the Indian Administrative Service and the Indian Police Service. Although the Union was keen to establish more such All India Services, most of the States were opposed to the idea as they did not like further extension of the Union's authority in their administrative sphere. Nevertheless, by 1961 they were persuaded to accept the proposal for the creation of three new All India Services and the formal authority to pass the necessary legislation to set them up was vested in Parliament by a Resolution of the Council of States in December 1961. The three new All India Services so approved are: (1) The Indian Service of Engineers, (2) The Indian Forest Service and (3) The Indian Medical and Health Service. Two more all India Services were created in 1965, namely, the Indian Agricultural Service and the Indian Educational Service (Secondary and Technical Education). The States are not willing to create more All India Services.

The Union has, however, created a number of Central Services. The more important of these are:

CENTRAL SERVICE : GROUP 'A' SERVICES

(i) Indian Foreign Service
(ii) Indian P & T Accounts & Finance Service
(iii) Indian Audit and Accounts Service
(iv) Indian Customs and Central Excise Service
(v) Indian Defence Accounts Service
(vi) Indian Revenue Service
(vii) Indian Ordinance Factories Service
(viii) Indian Postal Service
(ix) Indian Civil Accounts Service
(x) Indian Railway Traffic Service
(xi) Indian Railway Accounts Service
(xii) Indian Railway Personnel Service
(xiii) Posts of Assistant Security Officer in Railway Protection Force
(xiv) Indian Defence Estates Service
(xv) Indian Information Service
(xvi) Indian Trade Service
(xvii) Post of Assistant Commandant in Central Industrial Security Force
(xviii) Posts of Deputy Superintendent of Police, in the Central Bureau of Investigation

GROUP 'B' SERVICES

(xix) Central Secretariat Service

(xx) Railway Board Secretariat Service

(xxi) Armed Forces Headquarters Civil Service

(xxii) Customs Appraisers' Service

(xxiii) Delhi and Andaman & Nicobar Islands, Lakshwdeep, Daman & Diu and Dadra & Nagar Haveli Civil Service

(xxiv) Pondicherry Civil Service

2. INDIAN FOREST SERVICE

3. ENGINEERING SERVICES

(i) Indian Railway Service of Engineers

(ii) Indian Railway Stores Service

(iii) Central Engineering Service

(iv) Military Engineer Service

(v) Survey of India Service

(vi) Central Water Engineering Service

(vii) Assistant Executive Engineer (Civil) in P & T Building Works Service

(viii) Central Engineering Service (Roads)

(ix) Assistant Executive Engineer (Civil) in Border Roads Engineering Service

(x) Indian Ordnance Factories Service (Engineering Branch)

Public Services and Welfare State

Viewing the constitutional provisions as a whole, there can be no doubt that they are intended to build up a Public Service that would fit in with the changed character of the State in India. Of course, a civil servant must possess the traditional service virtues of integrity, loyalty, and efficiency. His honesty should be above reproach, his loyalty unquestioned and his efficiency in conformity with recognized standards. The British in India had artificially created a kind of self-styled dignity in the higher services which aimed at a deliberate aloofness from the general public. Such a position ceases when the Government of the Union and the States under the Constitution are dedicated to achieve mass welfare at a fast pace. The Public Services today are expected to have a growing passion for social service and to identify themselves with the people. Efficiency today means something more than an efficient performance of routine duties. It implies the active direction of the economic life of the people with the declared object of ultimately eliminating poverty, disease and ignorance.

In this task, the cooperation of the Public Services—the permanent wing of the Government—with the Ministers, the political wing, is of utmost importance. Control of the administration is no more the responsibility of the Civil Service. It is the responsibility of the representatives of the people. The Services must devote themselves to the service of the people under the direction of the people's representatives. It is the Minister's business to determine the policy. Once a policy is determined, it is the business of the civil servant to carry it out with goodwill and devotion, whether he personally agrees with it or not.

At the same time, it is the traditional duty of the civil servant to make available to his political chief all the information and experience at his disposal in order to help him to arrive at a right decision. The civil servant will not be able to do this, sometimes at the risk of displeasing his chief, unless he has security of tenure. The civil servant can, under the Constitution, give his advice without fear or favour in the interests of efficient administration.

One of the virtues of a parliamentary democracy is the ample opportunity that it affords for the harmonization of two different and even conflicting parts in the same machinery. By nature and training the permanent civil servant is conservative, narrow in outlook, and is often apt to exaggerate the importance of technicalities. He looks at things with the eye of an expert and displays a bureaucratic attitude. A politician on the other hand, by nature and experience, is well versed in human affairs. his vision is broad, his attitude compromising and ideas progressive. He has got the qualities of initiative and judgement. His broad outlook and strong common sense, born out of a long experience of human affairs, bring about a healthy and constructive outlook on all problems. A combination of these two—the administrator and the politician, the civil servant and the Minister—should produce wholesome results.

While the permanent services maintain the continuity of the administrative process, the Minister provides the basis for its popular character. The Minister serves as a link between the Legislature and the administration and ensures the coordination of the two to the best advantage of the country. It is in the interest of efficient administration that these two wings of the Government should maintain their separate identity. The civil servant should maintain his rigid neutrality in politics and the Ministers should scrupulously adhere to this principle and appreciate the attitude of the civil servant. Then only can the permanent services become a real link between successive Ministries and provide stability and continuity of administration.

There are, however, a number of obstacles in India which still hamper the harmonious collaboration of the services and ministerial wings in the Government. These are found more in the States than in the Centre. The Government at the Centre, unlike most of the States, has had the unique advantage of political stability. Not only has the same Party been in power for long periods but also the top leadership has remained almost unchanged. One must add to this also the better calibre of the Ministerial wing in the Central Government. In contrast, most of the States have been suffering from many disadvantages. There have been frequent changes in the top leadership of several States, although the same Party has continued to stay in power in many of them. The reorganization of States brought about many changes, territorial and personnel. As a result, many new Ministers who lacked administrative experience joined the Government in the States. There have been many and frequent changes also in the top ranks of the members of the civil services in the States. A high percentage of the older and more experienced officers left the States for positions of greater importance at the Centre. Those who replaced them had not the same experience as their predecessors.

Analysing the situation that existed in the country soon after the inauguration of the Constitution, A.D. Gorwala made the following observation:

While it is not unusual in many parts of the country to hear in private enthusiastic appreciation of the work of individual government servants by ministers, it would be idle to deny that though working together for a common end there is still generally speaking a feeling of separateness in the minds of both sections of public servants. Not all Ministers have become accustomed to regard the machine as part of themselves. They still look upon it as something outside. They may be responsible for it but they do not feel that it belongs to them.

It must be recognised that it takes a magnanimous mind to forger that while it and its class was suffering deprivation of freedom and intense privation, the servants who now take their orders from its members and call them 'Sir', were living comparatively luxurious lives in the service of those whom it regarded as its oppressors. Magnanimity unfortunately is not a very common quality, although it should be recognised that it is more often among the second rank of politicians that this feeling of difference persists than among the first. To this cause of separateness which lies in past history must be added what may be termed the professional reason. In the Minister this often takes the form of want of experience, in the Government servant of want of adaptability. The best of the Ministers is filled with a burning zeal. He wishes to alter things, to make them different, he wants to build nearer to his heart's desire. The best of civil servants performs his duty zealously. He must point out the snags in the Minister's policy. He must give advice according to his lights. He must suggest consideration and examination. It is scarcely surprising that in the circumstances a certain amount of friction arises, more especially, when either one or the other or both do not belong to the category which may be termed the best. Then it is that want of experience begins to be termed ignorance by the one and the absence of adaptability, woodenness by the other.[1]

The main reasons that contribute to the lack of harmony between the two wings of the Government, in the opinion of the same author, are the following:

Lack of understanding, generally speaking, of their respective roles is perhaps the most fertile cause of friction and misunderstanding. In a Parliamentary system of Government of the British type, there is a place for the Minister, a place for the Secretary, a place for the Head of a Department and a place for the Executive Officer. Everyone of them is essential and everyone has his proper part to play. The Minister's functions, for instance, are the formulation of policy and the superintendence of its implementation. The first he discharge along with his colleagues and with the help of his Secretary. The bulk of the second he delegates to the Secretary and to the Head of the Department, keeping an overseeing eye on the whole position. The Secretary's task is to help in the formulation of policy, to formulate 'subsidiary' policy and to assist the Minister in superintendence and implementation. It will conduce greatly to the efficiency and despatch of public business and the establishment of cordial relations. If all concerned understand their respective spheres and refrain from encroachment on those that legitimately lie within the duty of others.

Another not infrequent reason for discouragement on the part of the Government servant is the dictatorial attitude adopted by some Ministers. Thus, for instance, a minister will sometimes write an order on a carefully worked out proposal in the simple words, 'I don't agree'. He will give no indication of his reasons for disagreement. In fact it would seem as if he regarded the previous noting as a piece of insolence which should not have appeared on the file. Again, occasionally, arbitrary decisions are not unknown. If on similar facts in two or more cases the decisions are different, work becomes difficult for a conscientious government servant. He does not quite know where he stands. Similarly, decisions based on interest rather than on merit are likely to contribute to strained relations. In the present circumstances, the advantage in point of knowledge and experience, generally speaking, is likely to be on the side of the official. This too is apt to create awkardness as it sometimes leads to a feeling that the official is adopting an attitude of superiority.

1. *Report on Public Administration*, pp. 29-30.

As regards government servants, intellectual arrogance has, of course, always been the besetting sin of their highest ranks. In the circumstances of the present time, a very special duty rests upon such of them as are inclined to be occasionally affected by it to avoid it altogether. In this sin perhaps is the origin of the habit formed by some government servants of comment in social conversation upon the abilities and idiosyncrasies of ministers. This seems to have attracted unfarouable comment in ministerial circles in many part of the country. Freedom of private conversation is, of course, always desirable, nor was conversation of such a nature altogether unusual in the past, but since the effect of its transmission has obviously some not altogether desirable repercussions there should be no difficulty in avoiding it, more especially when no purpose is served by such discussion in social circles.

It is also a habit with some government servants to criticise in their social moments in the hearing of outsiders, the policies of government with which they disagree. Now the proper forum for the expression of opinions about policy is at the stage of giving advice to the minister before its formulation. Then an officer has a perfect right to say quite frankly what he feels about it. Once, however, the policy has been accepted after due deliberation and has become the policy of Government, criticism by a government servant outside the range of his official duties is likely to be misunderstood and must be avoided.

Another reason sometimes given for the absence of warmth and cordiality between some Ministers and some government servants is what is termed as the unresponsiveness of some government servants. It is said that they behave with the same sense of formalism as in the past and that they do not seem to feel with a real sense of urgency the need of the great change that must take place in the life of the country. The observance of due formality is by no means a bad thing for persons occupying public positions. What is really essential is that an officer should treat everybody with complete courtesy, be prepared to listen patiently to suggestions, and co-operate whole-heartedly in carrying out such as in his judgement appear to be for the public weal. It is of course obvious that there is no room in modern administration for an attitude of superiority. The first duty of the Government servant is full acceptance of the fact that he is the servant of the public, that the public is in a very real sense his master and that he only exists for the purpose of serving its true interests. The addition of zeal to efficiency is accordingly most desirable, but where responsiveness involves hopeful elation and enthusiasm, the official by his very nature and training, cannot but be somewhat backward. Since this is a point frequently raised, it is interesting to see what Sir Edward Bridges has to say about it:

> A civil servant's life makes him above all, a realist. He is less easily elated, less readily discouraged than most men by everyday happenings. Outwardly, he may appear cynical or disillusioned, and perhaps to be disinclined to put up a fight for things which excite others, but that is because he has learnt by experience that the Walls of Jericho do not nowadays fall flat even after seven circumambulations to the sound of the trumpet, and that many of the results which he wants to see come about in the most unexpected of ways. Once the crust of apparent disillusion is pierced, you will find a man who feels with the fiercest intensity for those things which he has learnt to cherish—those things, that is to say, which a lifetime of experience has impressed upon him as matters which are of vital concern for the continued well-being of the community.

From all that has been said it is clear that the problem of maladjustment is one of misunderstandings rather than of any real difference of opinion as to aims and objectives. There is very considerable need for the best minds on both sides to come closer together. It may well be that if they do, separateness will disappear and in its place will be engendered feelings of the deepest cordiality.

One thing which would aid very largely in this matter would be a clearer understanding of the position of ministerial responsibility. The constitutional responsibility of ministers to

Parliament and the public covers every action of their subordinates, whether done with their specific authority or by delegation expressed or implied. Accordingly, in the legislatures of several other countries, it is the custom never to mention a responsible subordinate official or even a whole department. It is the Minister who is responsible. He takes the praise for that which is well done; and the blame for that which is ill done is his. So far as responsibility goes, the Minister is the department. If there have been mistakes of malafide practices, it is for him to take action against the officers. They are not to be exposed to attacks in the legislature or elsewhere.

The acceptance of this convention would be of great value in the circumstances of this country, where in some legislatures the unedifying spectacle is not uncommon of officers being blackguarded by name by legislators with Ministers listening unmoved or putting up occasionally not too enthusiastic protests. So, too, the attacks on government servants by organs of the political party in power serve no useful purpose. All that they do is to dishearten the government servants and make them lose confidence in their masters. There should be no need in a well-constituted State for the certificate which the Prime Minister or other members of the Cabinet feels compelled to give from time to time to the good work of government servants as a rebuff to the allegations made against them by members of their own party.

All concerned—ministers, legislators and the people—must recognise that there is no way of doing without the government servant. He is essential and has to stay. Without him the work of government cannot be done. Consequently, it is in the interests of all concerned that he should have confidence in, and be encouraged to work for, the benefit of his employer, the State.[1]

As against these causes which contribute to lack of understanding and disharmony, there are some which make for amity and unity. Of these, the most important seems to be the common objective to which both the Ministers and the civil services are committed. The directive principles embodied in the Constitution provide that common objective and it has become a common ideology that animates the economic and social foundations of independent India and which permeates the mind of every educated Indian today. So long as there is unity in this basic objective, those who are charged with the responsibility of translating this objective into reality will have to work together with understanding and such understanding is bound to emerge in the natural course of events. On the political plane, with the emergence of a more and more democratic society resulting from successive general elections based upon adult suffrage, many of the old prejudices will disappear and greater tolerance and understanding will ensue. Finally, those who harboured illwill and even animosity in pre-independence days—politicians as well as civil servants—are fast disappearing. A new generation is taking their place and members of this new generation are free from such illwill or suspicion. With the building up of healthy traditions and conventions, there should be little difficulty for laying the sound foundations of a system where the members of the ministerial and service wings work hand in hand as inseparable limbs of the same organism.

A relative recent phenomenon however, requires close attention for remedial action. It is the collusion between corrupt politicians and their counterparts in the public services. Speaking on this aspect, a top ranking civil servant remarked that in recent years the situation is worse in some States but even in the best it is bad enough ! Who is responsible for this? The health of the State bureaucracy is entirely the responsibility of the State Government and nothing stops the State political leadership from ensuring that the bureaucracy works well on the basis of the accepted principles. If the higher civil services lose their credibility, the confidence of the citizens in their integrity and efficiency will disappear and public administration will no more remain a dependable instrument for the welfare state ideal under a democratic system of government.

***

1. Ibid., pp. 32-5.

43

ADMINISTRATIVE TRIBUNALS

AMONG the many innovative provisions adopted by the Forty-second Amendment of the Constitution (1976) a measure of far-reaching importance was the provision for the setting up of Administrative Tribunals. Part XIV A which consists of two Articles—323A and 323B—deals with these Tribunals.

Section (I) of Article 323-A provides for the adjudication or trial by administrative tribunals of disputes and complaints with respect to recruitment and conditions of service of persons appointed to public services and posts in connection with the affairs of the Union or of any State or of any local or other authority within the territory of India. The power to constitute such Tribunals is vested exclusively in Parliament.

Section (2) of the same Article provides that a law made by Parliament under Section (I) may:

(*i*) provide for the establishment of an Administrative Tribunal for the Union and a separate Administrative Tribunal for each State or for two or more States;

(*ii*) specify the jurisdiction, powers and authority which may be exercised by such tribunals;

(*iii*) provide for the procedure to be followed by these tribunals; and

(*iv*) exclude the jurisdiction of all courts except the special jurisdiction of the Supreme Court under Article 136.

Article 323-B empowers Parliament or State Legislature to set up tribunals for matters other than those covered by clause (2) of Article 323-A. The matters to be covered by such tribunals are as follows:

(*i*) Levy, assessment, collection and enforcement of any tax

(*ii*) Foreign exchange, import and export across customs frontiers;

(*iii*) Industrial and labour disputes;

(*iv*) Matters connected with land reforms covered by Article 31-A;

(*v*) Ceiling on urban property;

(*vi*) Elections to either House of Parliament or Legislature of the States; and

(*vii*) Production, procurement, supply and distribution of food-stuffs or other essential goods.

A law made under the above provisions may provide for the establishment of a hierarchy of tribunals and specify the jurisdiction, powers and authority which may be exercised by each of them. Such law may also provide for the procedure to be followed by these tribunals and exclude the jurisdiction of all except the Supreme Court of India.

The Scheme of Administrative Tribunals envisaged by Part XIV-A of the Constitution as several other provisions of the Forty-second Amendment of the Constitution was looked upon with suspicion and misgivings by certain sections of political and public opinion in the country and that was reflected in the attempt of the Janata Government (1977-79) to abolish these provisions. The Forty-fourth Amendment (1978) among other things sought to abolish Part XIV-A altogether. However, this attempt of the Janata Government was unsuccessful as it could not muster adequate support in Parliament.

The basic objective of Administrative Tribunals is to take out of the purview of the regular courts of law certain matters of dispute between the citizen and government agencies and make the judicial process quick and less expensive. The fact that there has been a phenomenal increase in the number of disputes in which administrative authorities are involved has to be recognised. If all these disputes go to the ordinary judicial system where there is provision for appeals to successive higher courts one after another, there will be no speedy settlement of such disputes and they might linger for years or decades. Inordinate delay and enormous cost are the two distinguishing features of the ordinary judicial system. The number of cases that are pending before the High Courts and the Supreme Court today is legion. No one can normally expect any speedy disposal of most of them. At the same time, there are matters of social concern which require reasonably quick disposal. Administrative tribunals facilitate this and that is the strongest argument in their favour.

Administrative Tribunals are not an original invention of the Indian political system. Such tribunals are now well established in all democratic countries of Europe as well as the United States of America. Britain which until a few decades ago looked upon administrative tribunals with suspicion has, in recent times, recognises their beneficial role and therefore has set up many of them. The experience of India during the past three decades has demonstrated that administrative tribunals have an effective role to play in a country which has embarked upon a programme of rapid socio-economic change.

***

44

ELECTIONS

THE CONSTITUTION of India has provided a separate chapter on elections. In this respect, it has made a departure from the usual practice of constitutions to leave elections as a comparatively unimportant subject to be dealt with by the Legislature. The fact that detailed provisions in this regard have been made in the Constitution shows how anxious the Constitution-makers had been to safeguard this political right as an integral part of the Constitution itself. With a view to ensuring this objective, the Constituent Assembly entrusted its Committee on Fundamental Rights to deal with this problem also. The Committee recommended that the independence of elections and the avoidance of any interference by the Executive in the elections should be regarded as a fundamental right and necessary provisions should be made in this regard. But the Assembly decided that, although it was a matter of fundamental importance, its place was not in the chapter on Fundamental rights but elsewhere. Accordingly, the Drafting Committee made special provisions of a detailed character and embodied them in a separate chapter of the Constitution.

The Committee had two alternatives: either to provide for a permanent Commission consisting of three or more persons, or an ad hoc body appointed by the President every time there was an election. The Committee, however, steered a middle course. According to this it decided in favour of a permanent officer called the Election Commissioner so that a skeleton machinery would always be available. Elections, no doubt, would generally take place at the end of every five years, but by-elections might take place at any time. A State Legislative Assembly or the House of the People might be dissolved before its normal period of five years had expired. Consequently the electoral roll should be kept up to date all the time so that the new election might take place without any difficulty. Hence it was thought that the Chief Election Commissioner's office should be permanent.[1]

The Legal Framework

Under the Constitution the Election Commission is entrusted to deal with the following matters:

(a) election of the President of India;
(b) election of the Vice-President of India;
(c) Parliament and the composition of its two chambers;
(d) qualifications of members of Parliament;

1. C.A.D. VII, pp. 905-7.

(e) composition of State Legislatures;
(f) qualifications of members of State Legislatures;
(g) duration of Parliament and the State Legislatures;
(h) elections to Parliament and State Legislatures;
(i) reservation of seats in the House of the People and the State Assemblies for the Scheduled Castes and Tribes; and
(j) the determination of population for purposes of election

Under Article 327, Parliament is vested with the supreme power to legislate on all matters relating to elections, including elections to State Legislatures. Under Article 328, the States also have been vested with certain limited powers of legislation with respect to elections. But such legislation should not be in conflict with any Parliamentary legislation in this matter. Explaining the reason for vesting the power of conducting even the elections to State Legislatures in the Election Commission Ambedkar said:

> This has become necessary because of the mixture of population in the States. Along with what may be called the original inhabitants, there are other people residing there, who are racially, linguistically or culturally different from the dominant people who are the occupants of the State. It has been brought to the notice of the Drafting Committee and the Central Government that in these States the Executive Government is instructing or managing things in such a manner that those people who do not belong to the category of original inhabitants are not included in the electoral rolls. No person should be excluded merely as a result of the prejudice of a local government or the whim of an officer. That could cut at the very root of democratic government. In order to prevent such injustice being done by the State Governments, it is felt desirable to depart from the original proposal of having a separate Election Commissioner for each State.[1]

Parliament passed two major measures laying down the detailed law under which elections were to be held. The first was the Representation of the People Act, 1950, which provided for qualifications of voters and matters connected with the preparation of electoral rolls. It also laid down the procedure for delimitation of constituencies, and allocated the number of seats in Parliament to the States and fixed the number of seats in the respective State Legislatures. The second, *viz.*, the Representation of the People Act, 1951, provided for the actual conduct of elections and dealt in detail with subjects like administrative machinery for conducting elections, the poll, election disputes, by-elections, etc. Under these two Acts, statutory rules were made by the Central Government and these were respectively called the Representation of the People (Preparation of Electoral Rolls) Rules, 1950, and the Representation of the People (Conduct of Elections and Election Petitions) Rules, 1951. Subsequently the two Acts and Rules were amended as and when changes became necessary. One of the most important of these amendments is with regard to the preparation of electoral rolls. Originally it was provided that separate rolls should be prepared for the Parliamentary and Assembly constituencies. The amendment has prevented a considerable amount of duplication of work by laying down that only one electoral roll need be prepared for all constituencies.

It is within this framework of law that the General Elections have been held. The law seems to have come, as the occasion arose. Now it is high time that this mass of election law scattered over too many legislative enactments is codified into a simple comprehensive legislation on the subject.

---

1. C.A.D. VIII, p. 907.

One General Electoral Roll

At first, it may appear that the constitutional provisions in this regad are superfluous. But there is a history behind it. During the British rule, under the pressure of communal politics, separate electorates were established in India. Accordingly, in every constituency there were as many lists of electoral roll as there were communities recognized for the purpose. Thus, the Muslims all over India had a separate electoral roll and voted only to candidates who stood for election from the constituency reserved for the Muslims. How unnatural was this system of communal electorate needs no special emphasis. Article 325 is a declaration that separate electorates have been abandoned. As a result the people of India irrespective of their religion, race, caste, or sex will belong to one general electoral roll in every territorial constituency for election. In this way, an unnatural system that prevailed in India for a few decades has been removed and a composite political community has been re-established by the Constitution.

Universal Adult Suffrage

One of the outstanding features of the Constitution is adult suffrage. It means that every person—man or woman—who is not less than eighteen years of age* has the right to vote in the election to the House of the People and the State Legislative Assembly. The only grounds for disqualification are (i) non-residence, (ii) unsoundness of mind, (iii) crime, and (iv) corrupt or illegal practice. This provision has been hailed as the "fountainspring of India's democracy". For, it has swept away at one stroke all the antiquated and undemocratic qualifications prescribed to be eligible for voting. Property, income, status, title, educational qualifications and so on.

The cumulative effect of the above two provisions on democracy in India is indeed far-reaching. Under the Government of India Act, 1919, there were only three per cent of India's population who were entitled to exercise their franchise. Under the Act of 1935, with a more broad-based franchise, only ten per cent exercised this elementary right of citizenship. But now, every citizen is entitled to it. The principle of one man, one vote, one value, has become a constitutional right. The removal of the notorious system of communal electorates which had broken up Indian society statutorily into religious and communal compartments is in perfect harmony with the establishment of adult suffrage. As a result, the citizens of India will not vote as individuals and not as Hindus, Muslims, Sikhs or Christians.

Universal adult suffrage was one of the controversial subjects in the Constituent Assembly. Its introduction in India at one stroke looked upon with suspicion and scepticism by many leading constitutionalists and politicians both in and outside the Constituent Assembly. They thought that it was too early for a country like India with mass illiteracy to adopt adult suffrage so suddenly when advanced nations of the West took several centuries to introduce gradually such a system. According to them, the right to vote given to a politically ignorant person was like a loaded gun given to be handled by a child. Instead of furthering the cause of democracy, it might prove suicidal to the very existence of democracy in a comparatively backward country like India. Political demagogues, who

*As originally provided, the minimum age was twenty-one years. The sixty-first Amendment (1989) however lowered the minimum age to eighteen years.

trade on wild utterances and sentimental outburst, might sway the credulous masses and exploit their votes for the establishment of a dictatorship in place of a democracy.[1] Speaking on the subject, P.K. Sen said:

...Before we launch our bark on the uncharted ocean of adult franchise, we have to be careful as to how to proceed. After all, ours is an infant democracy and we have yet to know the shoals and sand banks and all the risks and perils of voyage...[2]

No doubt, there was considerable force in this argument. Yet the Constituent Assembly could not accept it in view of the practical difficulties involved. "What should be the criterion of qualifications for voters? Is literacy or any educational qualification a guarantee for political consciousness for an independent use of the right to vote?" The result was the incorporation of adult suffrage in the Constitution. The thirteen General Elections that have taken place have proved the wisdom of the provision and amply demonstrated that the doubters were in the wrong. Among those who supported adult franchise vigorously was P. Subbaroyan. He said:

I have no fears for adult franchise. The Indian humanity is such that they have enough common sense, enough horse-sense which will make it possible for them to choose their rulers with discrimination and to choose the people whom they think would be able to carry on the administration in a manner which will be for the benefit of the common man of whom we have talked so much in this House.[3]

The Electoral Machinery

In one vitally important respect, the Indian Constitution is almost unique and has followed the example of Canada. The *sine qua non* for a true democracy is the holding of fair and free elections for choosing the people's representatives to the legislative bodies. The elections, in other words, must be conducted in a completely non-partisan spirit and provision was accordingly made in the Constitution to ensure that the party in power, at no time, may be placed in a position to influence the conduct of the elections for its own benefit.

Article 324 enacts that the superintendence, direction and control of all elections in India are vested in an independent body called the Election Commission.

The Election Commission consists of the Chief Election Commissioner and as many Election Commissioners as the President may from time to time fix. They are all appointed by the President. During the General Elections in 1951-52 two Regional Commissioners were temporarily appointed by the President to assist the Election Commission with headquarters at Bombay and Patna respectively. In connection with the second General Elections, 1957, three Deputy Election Commissioners were temporarily appointed with headquarters at Delhi. No Regional Commissioners were appointed for the second elections. The same arrangement continued for later General Elections also until 1994, when two Election Commissioners were appointed.

The Commission is an independent body. Its independence is secured by Article 324(5) which provides that the Chief Election Commissioner shall not be removed from office except in like manner and on like grounds as a judge of the Supreme Court and that

1. C.A.D. X, pp. 622 and 638.
2. C.A.D. X, p. 830.
3. C.A.D. X, p. 693.

any other Election Commissioner shall not be removed except on the recommendations of the Chief Election Commissioner. However, it must be pointed out that the independence of the Election Commissioners is not of the same nature as that of the judges of the Supreme Court. A Judge of the Supreme Court once appointed holds office until he completes the age of 65 years while the Chief Election Commissioner can be appointed for any limited period.[1] The Constitution also provides for the availability of adequate staff facilities for the discharge of the functions of the Election Commission.

At the State level, during the General Elections of 1951-52, the Chief Electoral Officer of a State did not have any statutory status or functions. It was felt later than he should be given a legal status and vested with specific powers and duties. The term 'Chief Electoral Officer' was accordingly defined in the Rules as an officer appointed by a State Government to perform the functions of the Chief Electoral officer under the Rules. In the light of the experience gained so far, the Election Commission is of the opinion that part-time officers seldom find time to make extensive tours of the districts and hence lose touch with the election officers at the district level which is of utmost importance. However, the Commission feels that in case a part-time officer is appointed as the Chief Electoral Officer, a junior wholetime officer should be made available to him as his Deputy.

At the district level, the machinery varies from State to State. In some States there is a wholetime District Election Officer in every district with a nucleus of his own which is strengthened during election time. In some others, an officer belonging to the normal administrative set-up in the district is placed in charge of election work with a nucleus of his own. In yet others, there is no definite scheme at present and the work is done haphazardly during the peak election time by the normal administrative machinery. It is, therefore, necessary that the machinery should be systematized and put on a permanent and more satisfactory basis.

In regard to the preparation and maintenance of the electoral rolls of a constituency, the permanent machinery consists of the Election Commission, the Chief Electoral Officer and the Electoral Registration Officer of the constituency. There is an electoral Registration Officer for each Assembly constituency and it is his responsibility to prepare and revise annually the electoral roll for the constituency as required by law. The law has also made provision for the appointment of one or more Assistant Electoral Registration Officers to assist the Electoral Registration Officers to assist the Electoral Registration Officer in the performance of his functions.

For each Parliamentary or Assembly constituency, a Returning Officer is appointed by the Election Commission. He has to be an officer of the Government. One or more persons who are also officers of the Government are appointed as Assistant Returning Officers to assist him in the performance of his functions.

The actual poll is conducted by a large number of Presiding and Polling Officers. For every polling station, a Presiding Officer and a few polling officers are appointed in respect of each separate election, Parliament and Assembly. In case elections are held

1. Speaking on this aspect of the Commission, K.M. Munshi said that the Election Commission could not become a kingdom within a kingdom nor could it be allowed to sit as a super-government. C.A.D. VIII, p. 925. According to present practice the Chief Election Commissioner is appointed for a period of six years.

simultaneously for Parliament and the Assembly, some of these officers are appointed to take charge of both at a polling station. They are usually assisted by as many policemen and other staff as may be necessary.

First General Elections (1951–52)

The first Genéral Elections in India were a historic event and attracted widespread interest and attention in the country and abroad. The organization and conduct of the elections on such a vast scale naturally presented many difficulties which had to be surmounted. It stands to the credit of the political consciousness and orderliness of the Indian people, a large percentage of whom are illiterate, that the General Elections of such a gigantic magnitude were held in a successful manner. Writing about the success of the Elections, R.R. Diwarkar observed:

> The General Elections were not only a national enterprise but also a great experiment in democracy. This was the biggest ever held in history. Apart from the hugeness, there were misgivings in the minds of some on account of mass illiteracy, want of uniformity, adequate communications and such other facilities. But now it can be said with some pride that the masses of India have acquitted themselves admirably well. More than 50 per cent have actually gone to the polls and in some large tracts about 80 per cent have voted. There have been very few polling-day clashes. A sufficiently intelligent choice has been made by the voters. Therefore, it can be said that more than literacy, it is the general level of understanding and culture and the realization of the soundness of democratic and peaceful methods by the common man that are important. The Congress, in the course of its long history of active mass contact for more than a quarter of a century, have always striven to convey the message of liberty, democracy and social justice to the millions of India. It can now be said that it has done so with some success. Without mass education of that kind, peaceful election on such a big scale by so many million would have been difficult of achievement.[1]

A notable feature of the Election was the wholehearted participation of a number of political parties. It has been admitted by all that the Elections were free and fair and were held in a truly democratic atmosphere. There were in all some 17,500 candidates to fill 3,278 seats in State Assemblies and 1,823 to fill 493 seats in the House of the People. Not less than 75 parties, big and small, national and regional, moderate and extremists, participated. Of these many were new parties. Most of them have now faded away. All this is clear proof of the democratic atmosphere, the emergence of various points of view and the eagerness of a large number of men and women to serve the people through the legislatures.

By conducting Elections in a peaceful, orderly and efficient manner, the Election Commission justified its position as an independent body. Elaborate arrangements had been made and every possible precaution taken by the Commission to see that during the election the independence of the voter and the secrecy of the ballot were fully maintained. Approximately a staff of 560,000 were engaged in handling 600 million ballot papers.

The total number of the electorate in the first Elections was 171,747,300. The results showed that the Congress Party gained 364 of the 489 elected seats and became the first party to organize the first Indian Government after Independence. It had to its credit some 45 per cent of the votes polled. In the States, the Congress tally was on an average good, with overwhelming victories in some and marginal gains in a few. Thus in the Part A

1. *The Pilgrimage and After*, 1952, pp. 2-3.

States of Assam, Bihar, Bombay, Madhya Pradesh, Punjab, Uttar Pradesh and West Bengal, the electorate almost gave a *carte blanche* to the Congress to form the Government. With the Communists running second with 62 seats to their credit in the Madras Assembly and the Ganatantra Parishad with 34 seats in the Orissa Assembly, the Congress found itself in an uncomfortable position in the two States and had to seek the support of Independent members to form stable Ministries.

Among the Part B States, PEPSU proved the problem State for Congress with the Akali Party securing just 7 seats less than the Congress Party and the Congress itself failing to secure an absolute majority. Rajasthan gave the Congress just a marginal lead and in Travancore-Cochin the Congress had to resort to coalition in order that it could form the government. The mid-term election in Travancore-Cochin in 1954 and the events that followed proved that the Congress as a political party was not very popular in that State ever since the advent of India's Independence. The Second General Election of 1957 only completed the story by providing a crushing blow to the Congress as the leading party there.

All the Part C States gave the Congress unstinted support. From an overall point of view, therefore, the Congress party had gained a commendable success in the first General Elections.

The Party which came next to the Congress, although nowhere near in commanding position, was the Socialist Party of India with over 10 per cent of the total votes polled in its favour. But the number of seats won by the Party was disproportionately small in comparison to the percentage of votes secured by it. For, in Parliament it could win only 12 seats. In all the State Assemblies together it won 126 seats. The three all-India Parties which came next to the Socialist Party in order were the Kisan Mazdoor Praja Party, the Communist Party and the Bharatiya Jan Sangh. The KMPP[1] had a total of about 5.5 per cent of the total votes polled, the Communists some 3.8 per cent and the Jan Sangh a little of over 3 per cent. In proportion to the percentage of votes polled the Communists secured the best results in comparison with the other Opposition Parties by winning 16 Parliamentary and 105 State Assembly seats.

Second General Elections 1957

Reporting on the Second General Elections, the Election Commission stated:

> The second general elections were less of an adventure or novelty as compared to the first when even the most optimistic people had felt doubtful as to how far a large country which had only just attained its independence and had yet to settle down to a democratic form of government could successfully carry through a country wide programme of democratic elections based on adult suffrage.[2]

However, the reorganization of the States in 1956 introduced a considerable amount of uncertainty and at one stage it became doubtful as to whether it was possible to see through the legal and administrative formalities to enable the elections to be held according to the schedule. It was in fact felt by some sections of the public that an amendment to the Constitution to extend the life of the first Indian legislature was an imperative necessity.

1. The Socialist Party and the KMPP merged to become the Praja Socialist Party of India soon after the first General Elections.
2. *Report on the Second General Elections in India*, vol. I, p.1.

But it stands to the credit of the Election Commission that it set its face boldly against any such contingency and achieved a seemingly impossible task thereby averting a bad precedent in the annals of constitutional government in free India.

Thus the elections to the House of the People and all the State Assemblies (excepting for the Union territory of Himachal Pradesh and the Kangra district of Punjab) were completed by March 1957. The streamlining of the election machinery in the light of the experience gained during the first Elections enabled the reduction of the period of poll from 17 weeks in the first Election to just over a fortnight in 1957.

The second General Elections created parliamentary history by putting the Community Party at the helm of affairs through the ballot in the southern State of Kerala; this event, more than anything else, has brought into clear relief the truly federalist character of India's democracy. An electorate of over 193 million in the biggest democracy in the world voted for Congress governments at the Centre and in eleven States. Although the Communists failed to gain an absolute majority in Kerala, they could muster enough support from the independent ranks to form their first Government. In the eastern coastal State of Orissa, neither the Congress Party nor its closest rival, the Ganatantra Parishad, could gain an absolute majority. However, the Congress party managed to obtain the support of some minor parties and Independents in the Assembly to enable it to form the Government.

The magnitude of the elections surpassed even that of the first General Elections, which had to that date been acclaimed as the biggest democratic experiment in the world. The electorate increased by over 20 million and the number of votes polled jumped from 103.8 million to 112.3 million. The votes polled constituted 49.2 per cent of the voting capacity of the country as against the corresponding figure of 44.9 per cent for the 1951-52 elections.

From the point of view of the Election Commission, the task involved the preparation of 510 million ballot papers, deployment of a staff of over a million and the procurement of 2,960,000 steel ballot boxes.

To facilitate the smooth conduct of the elections, immediately after the reorganization of States in 1956, the Commission revised the list of recognized State parties in terms of the newly constituted States. The position of the four all-India parties, *viz.* the Indian National Congress, the Praja Socialist Party, the Communist Party of India and the Bharatiya Jan Sangh, however, remained the same. In the case of State parties slight alterations had to be made according to the changed political map of India; but all the same the minimum, level of 3 per cent of the votes polled in an area was observed as the standard for recognition as a State or regional party. In the second Elections the electorate chose its representatives from as many as 26 parties, from the small Mizo Union, restricted in its activities to a part of Assam hills, to the vast Congress organization.

The Congress Party swept the polls in the Parliamentary elections by securing 371 of the 494 elected seats or roughly 75 per cent of the House. Thus it slightly improved on its record of the first General Elections. In the State Assemblies, the Congressmen numbered roughly 65.1 per cent of the successful candidates. The percentage was also almost the same as the corresponding one for the first Elections. The figures for the rest of the parties in the parliamentary elections were comparatively very low. The Communist Party with 9.8 per cent of the votes could secure only 29 seats. The Praja Socialist Party won 19 seats with 10 per cent of the votes and the Jan Singh 4 seats only with 5.7 per cent votes polled to its credit.

In the Assembly elections these three parties registered a slight improvement over their performance in the 1951-52 elections. Among the other parties the Ganatantra Parishad in Orissa almost turned the table against the Congress.

Reviewing the Assembly election results State-wise, it may be seen that the Congress which had scored 90 per cent success in the first Elections in the then Saurashtra State and Uttar Pradesh failed to repeat its performance. But Madhya Pradesh came very near to giving the Party that high percentage of success by choosing 232 Congress nominees in a House of 288. Almost the same level of achievement was recorded by the party in Madras, Mysore, Punjab and Rajasthan, the respective tallies being 151 (out of 205), 150 (208), 118 (154) and 119 (176) seats. The percentage of Congress success varied from 34 in Kerala to 81 in Madhya Pradesh. The second Elections considerably strengthened the Congress position in Rajasthan where in the first Elections it had secured only a marginal absolute majority of 82 in an Assembly of 160. But, perhaps, the two events of far-reaching importance from the point of view of the Congress were its success in Andhra where it cut into some of the Communist strongholds and its defeat in Kerala where it ran a lame second to the Community Party. While the Congress recorded an impressive victory in Rajasthan at the expense of the Jan Sangh, the Ram Rajya Parishad and the Independents most of whom were rulers of the former Princely States, it failed to beat the challenge of the former rulers of Princely States merged in Orissa, where the Ganatantra Parishad led by the princes prevented the Congress from securing an absolute majority. In fact, the Parishad gained some seats in Congress strongholds. As against the outstanding successes of the Congress in Andhra and Rajasthan, the two big States of Uttar Pradesh and Bombay, which in 1952 ad voted solidly for the Congress, registered a marked decline in the number of Congress candidates returned. Another safe Congress area, Bihar, also returned a lesser number of Congress nominees than it did in the first Elections.

In Madhya Pradesh and Mysore, the Communists could make little or no impression. The Jan Sangh had its highest poll in Uttar Pradesh. The Hindu Mahasabha lost much of its importance in the second Elections. Taking the performance of the three all-India Opposition Parties into consideration, the Praja Socialists came first with 10.1 per cent of the votes polled. But they could secure only 196 seats in all against the Communists who won 203 seats with 9.8 per cent of the votes polled. The Jan Sangh could win only 44 seats in all.

Reporting after the conclusion of the second General Elections, the Election Commission said:

If the first general elections served to teach the vast number of uneducated voters what the vote means, the second general elections familiarised them with the exercise thereof with discrimination and understanding. Another welcome and remarkable feature that had already emerged in the implicit and growing confidence which the Election Commission and the election machinery in the States have come to enjoy in the eyes of the political parties and the general public. Within the space of a few years, therefore, doubts which naturally existed as to the preparedness of the people for democratic self-government or the wisdom of extending universal adult franchise in a country with an overwhelmingly illiterate electorate have been completely dispelled. All observers agree now that an election is no longer a merely novel entertainment provided for the electorate in the cities or the countryside but has come to be a serious political struggle between the contending parties and candidates, the outcome of which ultimately depends on the deliberate choice made by the electorate between the contestants. The degree of political maturity displayed by the electorate even in many backward areas has indeed astonished many impartial observers and students of politics.

Third General Elections (1962)

The most outstanding aspect of the results of the third General Elections was the clear mandate which the Congress Party, led by Prime Minister Nehru, received once again from the electorate to continue its uninterrupted rule of the country for another five years. An equally important but depressing aspect was that after fifteen years of parliamentary democracy, the Nation had not yet found an opposition party of national importance to provide an alternative to the Congress in the foreseeable future. On the national front, however, there were two significant developments: first, the decline of the Praja Socialist Party which until then held the position of the leading opposition and secondly, the emergence of the Swatantra Party as one of the two leading parties in the opposition.

The total strength of the electorate for the third General Election was over 216 million as against 193 million in 1957. Polling was held for 489 seats in the Lok Sabha embracing practically the entire country and 3,121 seats in the State Assemblies. The only two State Assemblies for which there was no general elections in 1962 were those of Kerala and Orissa as in these States mid-term elections were held in 1960 and 1961 respectively. A total of over 114 million votes were cast, approximately 53 per cent of the total electorate. This shows the unmistakable trend of the steadily increasing interest of the electorate to participate in the democratic process.

Of the 1,979 candidates contesting 489 seats in the Lok Sabha, 484 belonged to the Congress Party which won a total of 356 seats including three without contest. In contrast to the Congress, none of the parties in the opposition had candidates in all the States. The Communists had no candidate in Gujarat and Himachal Pradesh, the P.S.P. in Punjab, Rajasthan and Himachal Pradesh, the Jan Sangh in Orissa, Manipur, Tripura and Kerala, and the Swatantra in Assam, Manipur, Tripura, Delhi and Kerala. In some of the States the number of candidates belonging to these parties was negligible. For example, in Madras, Mysore and Maharashtra, none of these parties could put up candidates even for half the number of constituencies in these States. Of the total votes polled, the Congress captured a little over 45 per cent. But from the point of view of the percentage of seats their share was 72.80.

The picture in the States, however, was not so impressive. Out of a total of 3,121 seats in the State Assemblies, the Congress won only 1,917 or a little over 60 per cent. The only State where the Party improved its position impressively was Maharashtra where it secured 215 out of 264 seats in the Assembly. In contrast, its performance in Uttar Pradesh, Madhya Pradesh, Rajasthan and Punjab was disappointing, particularly when compared with the results of the second General Elections. In Madhya Pradesh and Rajasthan the Party failed to get an absolute majority, the figures being 142 out of 288 and 88 out of 176 respectively. In Uttar Pradesh the number of seats won was only 249 out of 430 while the corresponding figure in Punjab was 90 out of 154. Even in States like Bihar, Madras and Mysore which were the strongholds of the Congress, the result showed a downward trend. The party had, however, slightly improved its position in West Bengal, Gujarat and Assam.

In the third General Elections the Communist Party secured the second place with

9.96 per cent of the total votes polled. This was indeed an impressive performance in view of the fact that in 1952 the Party had secured only 3.3 per cent of the total votes polled. On a closer examination, however, it would become clear that between 1957 and 1962 the Party had lost its momentum. For, in 1957 it had secured 8.92 per cent of the total votes polled, almost three-fold increase on its figures of the first General Elections. In the Lok Sabha the party won 29 seats, just two more than in 1957. In the State Assemblies its share was 184. The Communist strength was mainly confined to three States, namely, West Bengal, Andhra pradesh and Kerala. The Party had, however, made some gains in Uttar Pradesh and Punjab.

The third General Elections had shown the decisive decline of the Praja Socialist Party which could secure only 6.84 per cent of the total votes, about 4 per cent less than what it secured in 1957. The Party could win only 12 seats in the Lok Sabha as against 19 in the earlier elections. A total of 179 seats were the Party's share in the State Assemblies as against 208 in 1957. It lost practically all its electoral support in Andhra Pradesh, Punjab, Madras and Rajasthan, halved its strength in Bihar, Maharashtra, Orissa and Uttar Pradesh and lost heavily in most of the other States.

As a new all-India Party, contesting General Elections for the first time, the record of the Swatantra party in 1962 was quite impressive. The Party secured 6.85 per cent of the total votes polled and earned for it the second leading position among the opposition parties. In the Lok Sabha it secured 18 seats and in the State Assemblies a total of 166 seats. But more important than the 166 seats was the fact that the Swatantra became the leading opposition party in three State Assemblies, namely Rajasthan, Gujarat and Bihar. With the merger of the Ganatantra Parishad in Swatantra, in Orissa too the party became the leading opposition.

Although the Jan Sangh had increased its percentage of total votes polled from 5.93 in 1957 to 6.44 in 1962, the third General Elections conclusively proved that it was not really an all-India Party. For, its strength was confined only to the Hindi-speaking areas of Northern India. The Party secured 14 seats in the Lok Sabha a against 4 in 1957, an impressive increase when considered on percentage basis. Similarly, its total in State Assemblies advanced from 46 in 1957 to 116 in 1962. But most of these were concentrated in three States only, namely, Uttar Pradesh, 49, Madhya Pradesh, 41, and Rajasthan, 15.

Although the third General Elections witnessed an increase in the number of all-India parties from four to five, the number of regional parties registered a substantial fall. There were only about a dozen such parties which deserve even a mention in this context. Of these, the only party which made a significant, even spectacular, gain was the Dravida Munnetra Kazhagam (D.M.K.) of Tamil Nadu. Out of a total of 206 seats in the State Assembly, the Party captured 50 and out of a total 41 seats for the State in the Lok Sabha it secured 7. Thus the D.M.K. had established itself as the leading opposition party.

Communal parties like the Akali Dal, the Muslim League, the Hindu Mahasabha and the Ram Rajya Parishad have been steadily losing their appeal to the electorate. Each of them had been able to secure only a few seats. Similarly, parties like the Forward Bloc, Revolutionary Socialist Party, Republican Party, Peasant and Workers Party and Jharkhand Party (of Bihar) have also lost considerable ground between 1959 and 1962. The Socialist Party, a breakway group of the P.S.P., had some success in a few of the Northern States but not significant enough to create any new trend. Viewed in general the regional parties were certainly on the decline and their influence was destined to dwindle.

The number of Independents also had registered a significant decline both in the number of seats contested and the seats won. For example, in the Lok Sabha they held 36 seats in 1952 but the corresponding figures in 1957 and 1962 were 25 and 24 respectively.

Fourth General Elections (1967)

In several ways the Fourth General Elections were remarkable. Jawaharlal Nehru was no more and the Congress Party was fighting a general election for the first time without him. The new leader of the Party was Indira Gandhi and this was the first general election under her leadership which itself was yet to be firmly established. The opposition parties were fully aware of the weaknesses of the ruling party and were bent upon exploiting them in their bid to capture power both at the Centre and the States. There were, however, two developments which made the opposition less united and more divided than during the Third General Elections, First, the Communist Party of India was split into two, the C.P.I. and the Communist Party Marxist C.P.I.(M). Secondly, a number of new smaller parties had emerged in the States, mostly splinter groups taking their origin from the existing parties.

The results of the Fourth General Elections showed that the Congress Party was no more an impregnable fortress that it once was and as a consequence it lost heavily both at the Centre and in the States. For the first time since the inauguration of the Constitution the Party lost control of several States including the States of West Bengal and Madras.

As against 361 seats which the Congress Party had won in the Lok Sabha in 1962 with 44.73 per cent votes, it was able to secure only 284 seats with 40.82 per cent of the total votes polled. Among the opposition, the Swatantra Party got the leading position with 42 seats as against 18 in 1962 and 8.54 per cent votes. Swatantra was followed by the Jan Sangh with 35 seats and 9.29 per cent votes. In 1962 Jan Sangh had only 14 seats in the Lok Sabha. The split had far-reaching adverse effect on both Communist parties. While the C.P.I. got 23 seats as against 29 in 1962, the C.P.M. did rather well with 19 seats in their maiden contest. But together the Communist parties polled only 9.36 per cent (C.P.I. 4.90 and C.P.M. 4.46) votes as against 9.94 by the undivided party in 1962. The S.S.P. bagged 23 seats as against 6 in 1962 with 4.89 per cent of votes. The P.S.P. was able to secure only 13 seats and 3.08 per cent votes. The number of independents had gone up by more than a 100 per cent, from 20 in 1962 to 43 in 1967. They had polled a total of 14.39 per cent votes as against 9.63 in 1967.

The opposition parties, viewed as a whole, had done much better than ever before. From 133 seats in 1962 their strength had gone up to 236 in 1967, a remarkable increase indeed. But viewed from another point of view their performance was unsatisfactory. India's Parliament was still without an officially recognized opposition party. For that status a party required a minimum of one-tenth of the total membership of the Lok Sabha. The Swantantra Party which led the opposition had only 42 members which was 10 short of the required minimum.

The Fourth General Elections for the first time gave several opposition parties opportunity to assume power in the States either alone or in combination. Tamil Nadu provided the mot shocking results for the Congress Party which had been ruling the State continuously for over two decades. A regional party, the Dravida Munnetra Kazhagam (D.M.K.), scored a comfortable victory over the Congress, with an absolute majority of seats in the Legislative Assembly, enabling it to form a new Government on its own strength. The most remarkable feature of the elections there was that every leader of standing in the Congress Party was defeated by a D.M.K. candidate. Even the President of the Congress party, K. Kamaraj, a former Chief Minister of the State, was defeated in an Assembly constituency. The Congress had suffered heavy losses in several other States also. The most important among them were West Bengal, Bihar, Madhya Pradesh, Uttar Pradesh, Punjab and Rajasthan. The only State which continued to be as strong a fortress as ever before was Maharashtra with a performance which was even better than that in 1962.

Fifth General Elections (1971)

Since the General Elections are normally held once in every five years, the Fifth General Elections should have taken place only in 1972. But the ruling party decided to go to the electorate and seek a new mandate a year ahead and hence the Fifth General Elections were held in 1971. From the political point of view the 1967-71 period was notable for unprecedented events. Of these, the most significant was the split in the Congress Party following the election of V.V. Giri as President of India consequent on the sudden death in office of President Zakir Husain in 1969. After the split, the ruling wing of the Party was known as Congress (R) and the organization wing was known as Congress (O). Even before the split, the Party's strength in the Lok Sabha, as we have seen earlier, was not as formidable as in the past. But as a consequence of the split the ruling wing was reduced to a minority having only 228 seats out of a total of 522 in the House. The Congress (O) had 65 members.

Although the decision of the Government of India to hold elections in 1971 was related to parliamentary (Lok Sabha) elections only, some of the States also decided to hold elections to their Assemblies at the same time Tamil Nadu (Madras) was a notable example among them. In the case of some States, mid-term elections to the Assemblies had taken place even earlier than 1971. Uttar Pradesh and Kerala are two examples of this category. In the case of the rest of the States, Assembly elections took place only in 1972. Hence a review of the Fifth General Elections should necessarily cover the results of the elections in 1971 and 1972.

The most striking feature of the 1971 Lok Sabha elections was the outstanding performance of the ruling Congress which captured 362 out of a total 520 elected seats in the House. In the dissolved House the Party had only a minority of 228 seats. That means a gain of 134 seats which enabled the Party to command a clear two-thirds majority in the House. The Party was able to achieve this spectacular electoral triumph in spite of the fact that there was an electoral alliance among some of the opposition parties to forge a united front popularly known as `grand alliance' against it. The Congress (O), Swatantra, Jan Sangh, S.S.P. and a few other smaller parties were members of this United Front.

In contrast to 1967 almost all the opposition parties suffered heavily in the elections of 1971. For example, Swatantra could secure only 7 seats, Jan Sangh 21, Congress (O) 13 and Socialist Party 5. Of the two Communist parties, C.P.I. which had electoral alliance with the ruling Congress secured 24 seats while C.P.M. gained 25 seats largely from West Bengal. Among the regional parties, D.M.K. alone which fought the elections in alliance with the ruling Congress was able to achieve signal success by bagging 23 seats from Tamil Nadu. The number of independents also had come down to 14 from a total of 43 in 1967.

The sweeping victory which the ruling Congress gained in the Lok Sabha elections was reflected in the State elections both in 1971 and later in 1972. The result was that the Party staged a spectacular come-back in every State except Tamil Nadu, Meghalaya and Manipur. In Tamil Nadu the victorious D.M.K. was in alliance with the Congress. Similarly in Meghalaya the All Party Hill Leaders' Conference (A.P.H.L.C.) which won a majority of seats in the State Assembly was in alliance with the Congress. It was only in Manipur that the Party was unable to gain a majority of seats; but even there it was the largest single party in the Assembly. On the whole, the Fifth General Elections marked the massive victory of the ruling Congress Party after the many reverses which the Party suffered during the 1967-71 period.

In its report on the Fifth General Elections (1971-72) the Election Commission has pointed out that 354 successful candidates were elected to the Lok Sabha, each polling more than 50 per cent of the votes polled. Of the remaining candidates, six candidates obtained only between 20 and 30 per cent of the votes polled while 23 candidates between 30 and 40 per cent and the rest between 40 and 50 per cent.

The total number of votes polled was about 151.50 million which was approximately 55.22 per cent of the total electorate of 274 million; 3.24 per cent votes were rejected as invalid.

Speaking about the improved procedure adopted during the 1971-72 elections the Report said: "This time, after the elections were over, very few complaints as to intimidation, coercion or victimisation were received from any quarter of the country and the voters belonging to the weaker sections of the community were, by and large, able for the first time to cast their votes in an absolutely free manner according to their own free will and choice."

The report also pointed out that the Joint Committee of Parliament on amendments to election law had not accepted some of its earlier recommendations including those about the filing of return of election expenses by political parties. "No good ground has been adduced by the Committee for not accepting this highly valuable recommendation", the Report said. It rejected "the suggestion made in some quarters" that the present provisions relating to the election expenses should altogether be scrapped from the election law. That, in the opinion of the Election Commission, "would be a dangerous thing and will wide open the flood-gates of corruption and spell disaster for democracy in this country. It will also have an effect of driving out every candidate with meagre or moderate means from the election arena."

In comparison with the previous General Elections, there was substantial improvement in the manner in which the elections were conducted. The polling throughout the country (except a few constituencies in the snowbound Himalayan regions) was completed in five days and the results were declared in the next three days. This in itself was a remarkable organizational feat in view of the elaborate arrangements required for the conduct of a colossal task involving over 200 million people. Apart from substantially reducing the period of polling, the Commission brought into effect another significant improvement by introducing the marking system. This system eliminated many of the corrupt practices which existed under the old system of a separate ballot box for each candidate. There was considerable anxiety that the marking system might prove a failure due to widespread illiteracy among the electorate. But, on the whole, it proved a success. The Election

Commission deserves a tribute for the meticulous manner in which the arrangements connected with the Elections were worked out. And the Indian people have shown how they could conduct themselves in a peaceful and orderly manner in a nation-wide popular exercise like this which forms one of the foundations of democracy in India.

Sixth General Elections (1977)

The Sixth General Elections brought about a revolution through the ballot. It proved to the whole world that India was politically still a democracy where the citizens freely choose their rulers. In a truly dramatic manner, the ruling Congress Party which held the reins of power for over thirty years, was swept off the ground by the newly-formed Janata Party and its allies.

In the normal course the Sixth General Elections should have been held in 1976. But the life of the Lok Sabha was first extended for a year under the emergency and again through the Forty-second Amendment of the Constitution which extended its duration from five to six years. Thus legally the House could continue until April 1978. But to the astonishment of not only her countrymen but even the whole world, Prime Minister Indira Gandhi suddenly announced in January that the postponed elections would be held in mid-March of 1977. Emergency regulations were relaxed and the process of parliamentary democracy was once again in full swing. A sudden political awareness electrified the 318 million voters of the country.

For the first time in the country's history the Congress Party faced a strong opposition; united, determined and under a strong leadership. The newly formed Janata Party was the leader of the opposition. It consisted of the Old Congress, the Jana Sangh, the Bharatiya Lok Dal (B.L.D.) and the Socialist Party. The merger of all these all-India parties to form a new party was an unprecedented event in India's political life. Jayaprakash Narayan was the architect of the new political party and Morarji Desai its Chairman. The Janata Party was supported by another new party the Congress for Democracy (C.F.D.) which was led by Jagjivan Ram who broke off from the ruling Congress immediately after the announcement of the election. The Marxist Party and some regional parties like the Akali Dal also gave their support to the Janata-C.F.D combination.

The opposition parties took full advantage of the unpopular measures of the Emergency period and denounced the dictatorial tendencies which manifested themselves under Indira Gandhi's leadership during the period. They declared that the real issue in the election was `Dictatorship *vs.* Democracy' whether India wanted democracy or dictatorship. The ruling Congress Party countered it by focussing attention on stability and progress and declared that the real issue was `Democracy *vs.* Chaos'.

The Sixth General Election was gigantic in several respects. As many as 318 million voters were eligible to exercise their franchise. There were 2439 candidates for the 542 seats. The Congress Party had put up 493 candidates leaving the rest for its allies. The Janata Party and its allies contested 538 seats. The C.P.I. had 91 and the C.P.M. 53 candidates. Regional or State parties had 77 candidates while unrecognised parties had 80 candidates. There were also 1222 independents. In all 373,684 polling stations were set up.

The election was free, fair and decisive. The electorate was alert and discriminating too. The illiteracy of the Indian masses did not affect the election. They used their franchise effectively. In the northern parts of the country where the excesses of the emergency had their bitter effect, the voters supported the opposition. The result was dramatic. The Janata Party and its allies swept the poll and scored an overwhelming victory. Not only the Congress Party as a whole, but its leader, Indira Gandhi, and most of her cabinet colleagues were decisively defeated.

The only States where the ruling Congress Party was able to show its popularity were all in the south, Andhra Pradesh, Karnataka and Kerala. In Andhra Pradesh the Congress won 41 out of 42, Karnataka 26 out of 28 and Kerala 20 out of 20. In Tamil Nadu the Congress was in alliance with the All India Anna DMK and it had its salutary effect.

Maharashtra, the traditional strong-hold of the Congress Party had been able to return only 20 Congress candidates out of a total of 48 seats. In Gujarat it could manage to win only 10 out of 26 seats. In Assam, again a traditional citadel of the Congress, the Party could capture only 10 out of 14 seats. The single seat in Sikkim went in favour of the Congress. In Kashmir the Party was able to get a majority of seats.

But the most amazing feature of the results was the almost total rout of the Party in the most populous States in the country, namely, Uttar Pradesh and Bihar. The Party was not able to get even a single seat out of a combined total of 139 seats! The Party's position in the other northern states was no better. It won none in Haryana, Punjab, Himachal Pradesh and Delhi. In Rajasthan it managed to win just 1 out of 25 seats.

The only State where the elections to the State Assembly took place along with the Parliamentary election was Kerala. There the Congress-led united front scored a stunning victory over the opposition including the Janata Party by capturing 111 out of a total of 140 seats in the State Assembly.

Viewing the election results as a whole, it is a fact that the Janata Party with its allies could score a decisive victory over the Congress by capturing over two-thirds of the total membership of the Lok Sabha. At the same time it was clear that this victory was confined largely to the northern part of the country. The four southern States with a total population of 155 million had given an equally near unanimous verdict in favour of the Congress and its allies.

Seventh General Elections (1980)

The massive majority with which the newly formed Janata Party was swept into power in 1977 appeared to be so stable that no one could even dream of another general election to the Lok Sabha within a period of less than three years. But that was what happened in January 1980 when the country went to elect a new Lok Sabha.

The Jatana Party Government headed by Morarji Desai had to submit its resignation in July 1979 as a result of its losing majority support in the Lok Sabha which was the consequence of conflict among different groups within the Party. No alternative government backed by majority support was possible although Charan Singh was given the opportunity by the President to form a new government. Charan Singh failed to get the confidence of the House and thereupon on 22 August 1979 the Lok Sabha was dissolved and fresh elections were ordered.

It was a Herculean task for the Election Commission to hold a nationwide election at short notice. Yet it was able to accomplish it in the same manner as it did in the past. The total electorate numbered over 361 million. Of these, nearly 201.27 million exercised their franchise which works out to 56.29 per cent. This compares well with 60.54 per cent in 1977 and 55.29 per cent in 1971.

If the Lok Sabha election of 1977 was characterised as a "silent revolution" sweeping off the Congress Party from power, the 1980 election was described as a "bloodless coup" facilitating a peaceful change of government, unprecedented perhaps in any of the democracies in developing countries. The Congress (I) headed by Indira Gandhi was swept back to power after a relatively short period of less than three years.

Out of over 200 million votes cast, the Congress (I) secured over 83 million which works out to 42.55 per cent. The Janata Party came next with 37.2 million votes or about 19 per cent. Among the other leading parties the following came next in order: Lok Dal: 9.45 per cent, Communist Party of India (Marxist): 6.05, Congress (U) 5.3 per cent and Communist Party of India 2.61. Independents secured 6.55 per cent.

In terms of seats the position was as follows: Congress (I) 351, Lok Dal 41, CPI(M) 35, Janata 31, DMK 16, Congress (U) 13, CPI 11, AIDMK 2, other parties 16 and Independents 8.

Eighth General Elections (1984)

The Eighth General Elections were held under unprecedented circumstances following the assassination of Indira Gandhi. The tragic end of a powerful and charismatic Prime Minister had cast a pall of gloom as well as uncertainty of India's unity, integrity and political stability. Her son, Rajiv Gandhi, was sworn in as Prime Minister on the very same day of her assassination. The new Prime Minister was eager to get a fresh mandate from the people with a view to legitimising his government. That is why the Eighth General Elections were announced to be held within less than two months after his assumption of office.

The eighth General Elections were held between twenty-fourth and twenty-eighth of December 1984. The total number of the electorate was over 389 million. Nearly sixty per cent of the voters exercised their franchise at the elections.

The results of the eighth General Elections showed the triumphal unprecedented march to success of the Congress Party led by Rajiv Gandhi. The Party won 415 seats out of a total 517 seats contested and secured 48.1 per cent of the total votes polled. This was the first time in thirty-seven years that the Party was able to get in its favour such a high percentage of votes. The only State where the Party's performance was poor was Andhra Pradesh where the Telugu Desam Party held its sway almost unchallenged. That Party secured 30 seats out of the 34 it contested, a record for any State Party.

In comparison, most of the other parties fared badly. For instance, Bharatiya Janata Party which contested 229 seats won only 2 seats! Janata Party contested 219 seats and won only ten. The Communist Party of India contested 66 seats and won only six. The only party which performed better was the Communist Party of India (Marxist) which contested 64 seats and winning 22 of them.

Ninth General Elections (1989)

The ninth General Elections demonstrated the vibrant manner in which parliamentary democracy functioned in India. In spite of the massive majority secured by the Congress Party of Rajiv Gandhi at the eighth General Elections in 1984, at the end of a five-year term in Parliament, that Party was unable to secure even a simple majority in 1989. The Party could secure only 193 seats out of a total of 510 seats contested, although it was the largest Party in the House. Another important aspect of the ninth General Elections was that no political party could secure a majority in Parliament. This was the first time that General Elections in India failed to produce a majority for any party which contested the elections. Yet another striking feature was that the Janata Dal, an altogether new Party in 1989 came second with 143 seats. But perhaps the most surprising aspect of the ninth General Elections was the spectacular performance of the Bharatiya Janata Party which improved its position from a mere two seats in the eighth General Elections in 1984 to 85 seats in 1989. Equally surprising was the debacle of the Telugu Desam Party which sank to two seats from 30 which it held in the Eighth General Elections. The Communist Party of India (Marxist) not only maintained its position but improved on it by capturing 33 seats.

The ninth General Elections was memorable in several other ways. It saw the largest number of political parties participating in the elections, their total number being 117. Of these, eight were national parties, twenty State Parties and 89 unrecognised registered parties. There were in all 6,084 candidates. Of these, 3,928 were independent candidates. 1989 also saw for the first time the lowering of the voting age, from the earlier 21 to 18 years. The lowering of the voting age resulted in a steep rise in the number of the electorate. The total number of the electorate was 498.9 million. Of these, over 300 million exercised their franchise at the elections, roughly 62 per cent.

Tenth General Elections (1991)

The interval between the ninth and tenth General Elections was less than two years. This was the first time that the country had two General Elections within such a short period. The country also saw two governments at the Centre in quick succession within that period, the one formed by the Jatana Dal under the leadership of V.P. Singh and its successor formed by the Samajwadi Janata Dal headed by Chandra Sekhar. The latter was a break-away group consisting of members of the Janata Dal who left the party and formed a new Party of their own. They were supported from outside by the Congress Party of Rajiv Gandhi, thus enabling them to secure a vote of confidence in the Lok Sabha. But this rather opportunistic arrangement did not last long. The Congress Party withdraw its support after a few months necessitating the resignation of the Chandra Sekhar Ministry and the consequent dissolution of the Lok Sabha and the tenth General Elections.

The tragic part of the tenth General Elections was the assassination of Rajiv Gandhi half way through the electoral process. The 1984 Elections were held soon after Indira Gandhi's assassination. The 1991 Elections saw Rajiv Gandhi's assassination before the completion of the last stage of the elections. If Indira Gandhi's assassination influenced the results of the elections in 1984, the tragic end of Rajiv Gandhi had also its influence on the results of 1991. The trend of the voting showed that the Congress Party did much better after Rajiv Gandhi's death than when he was alive. As a result, the performance of the Party in 1991 was much better than its performance in 1989. Even so, it was not able to secure an absolute majority in the Lok Sabha. Its tally was 231 and with the support of its allies with 19 seats, it could claim a total strength of 250.

The Janata Dal which was the number two party in the dissolved House lost its position to Bharatiya Janata Party which improved its position to 121. Janata Dal secured only a total of 59 seats. The CPI(M) won 33 seats while the CPI won only 12 seats. The Samajwadi Janata Party could win only 5 seats. The AIADMK, an ally of the Congress (I) won 11 seats. The Telugu Desam Party won 12 seats.

One of the most unwholesome aspects of the tenth General Elections was the widespread violence, rigging, booth-capturing and other forms of electoral offences that tarnished the fair face of Parliamentary democracy in India. The extent of electoral malpractices was such that the Election Commission of India had to countermand elections in many constituencies and order repoll in thousands of booths.

The final party position in the Lok Sabha at the end of the 1991 General Elections was as follows:

Congress (I) 231, Bharatiya Janata Party 121, Janata Dal 59, Communist Party (Marxist) 33, Communist Party of India 21, Telugu Desam Party 12, All India Anna Dravida Munnetra Kazhagam 11, Jharkhand Mukti Morcha 6, Samajwadi Janata Dal 5, Shiva Sena 4, Indian Union Muslim League 2 and others 24.

Eleventh General Elections (1996)

For the second time in the history of Independent India, no Party could win a decisive number of seats in Lok Sabha to form a new government. The three political formations, the Congress, the Bhartiya Janata Party and the National Front, were desperate to create a favourable support base among the electorate by creating a focus on the broad spectrum of issues: corruption, stability, national security, secularism and economic policies.

The voter's mood, however, seemed to sway from confusion to almost total indifference. It was because the Election commission had managed to take the colour out of the campaigning blitzkrieg by imposing a code of conduct on political parties and candidates. Also it appeared that the average voter's hatred for politicians had now mounted to contempt for the political system. There was a general feeling that no single party was going to be able to secure an absolute majority in the Lok Sabha.

The BJP for the first time in India's parliamentary history emerged as the single largest party with 161 seats. It was indeed a sign of the tremendous strides it had made in the preceding few years. The BJP had three poll allies, the Shiva Sena, the Samata Party and the Haryana Vikas Party. Together they won 26 seats. Thus the strength of BJP and allies together was 187. The Congress (I) which was expected to emerge as the single largest party had to be satisfied with the second position. The National Front (Janata Dal and allies) and the Left Front (two Communist Parties and their allies) in all could win only 114 seats, the position of a poor third. The biggest surprise, however, was the emergence of a number of regional parties, the combined strength of which was as much as near any of the national parties. They in all won a total of 101 seats.

The final tally was as follows: BJP and allies 187, Congress (I) 146, Janata Dal 45, CPI (M) 28, CPI 22, Samajwadi Party 17, Forward Block 3, RSP 5, DMK 17, Tamil Manila Kazhagam 20, Telugu Desam 16, BSP 11, Akali Dal 8, Indira Congress 4, AGP 5 and Independents and others 19.

Twelfth General Elections (1998)

Hardly two years had passed since the Eleventh General Elections when the announcement for the Twelfth General Elections was made. The contest was largely among three groups, the Bharatiya Janata Party and its allies, the Congress and its allies and the United Front consisting of the left parties, the Janata Dal and a number of small regional parties. Everyone promised a stable government if elected to power but the electorate did not give a clear verdict in favour of any group.

The BJP secured more seats than it did in 1996 and with its allies were in the lead but was not enough to have a majority in the Lok Sabha. However, BJP with the support of its allies and some other parties supporting it from outside formed the Government but no one could say how long such a government would last. Once again the country appeared to be heading towards political instability at the Centre.

The final tally of seats was as follows: BJP and Allies 262, Congress and Allies: 160, United Front: 96 and others 20.

Thirteenth General Elections (1999)

When elections become too frequent the interest of voters becomes less. This was evident in the General Elections of 1999. Only 58.30 per cent voters cast their votes, the smallest percentage so far.

The fall of the thirteen month old BJP-led National Democratic Alliance (NDA) Government led by A.B. Vajpayee by a solitary vote in the Lok Sabha in the vote of confidence paved the way for the dissolution of the House on 23 April 1999 and ordering of fresh elections by the President. Although the Congress (I) made an effort to form an alternate government, its attempt was not fruitful.

The total number of eligible voters was 620.4 million. There were 773708 polling stations for handling this huge number of voters. The total expenditure for the thirteenth general elections was estimated as Rs. 845 crores. Along with the Lok Sabha elections, simultaneous Assembly elections in the states of Karnataka, Sikkim, Andhra Pradesh, Maharashtra and Arunachal Pradesh also were conducted.

The contest was mainly between the National Democratic Alliance led by the BJP and its allies and the Congress (I) and its allies. A total of over 200 smaller, regional parties also were in the fray. With such a large number of parties in the electoral arena, there was general apprehension that once again there will emerge a hung Parliament. The results, however, produced a different picture, the National Democratic Alliance led by Vajpayee and their allies emerging successful with a majority, just enough to form the Government. Their main rival the Congress party although campaigned for a single party stable government, was far behind. In fact, the thirteenth General Elections saw the Congress emerging with the lowest total ever. From 364 in 1952 the number came down to 146 in 1996 and 126 in 1999.

At the same time, the 1999 elections marks the BJP's coming of age. In the nineteen eighties it was a party of city-dwelling upper castes mainly in the Hindi speaking northern areas of the country. By 1999, however, it has become truly an all-India party with its numbers in almost every State and its influence in every region. But the emergence of the regional parties which began in the early nineties seems to have become a stable feature of India's political life. The Vajpayee Government is one of twenty-four parties which means that coalition governments at the Centre, just as coalition governments in some of the States, have come to stay.

This is the first time that the country faced another general election a year after the previous one. The Vajpayee Government which was in power following the General Elections of 1998 could hardly complete a year when it had to face a confidence motion as a result of the withdrawal of the AIADMK party from the Government. The motion of confidence was defeated in the Lok Sabha by one vote and consequently the Vajpayee Government submitted its resignation. Although there was an attempt on the part of the Congress Party to form an alternate government, it did not succeed. There was thus no other alternative except dissolution of the Lok Sabha and ordering of new elections.

The thirteenth General Elections were fought by the Bharatiya Janata Party in alliance with a number of smaller political parties, most of whom were with it in the Government that lost the confidence vote. They joined together under the banner of the National Democratic Alliance with a common programme. The alliance parties, however, maintained their individual identities. The national Democratic Alliance was able to win 300 seats in the elections and therefore earned the right to form a new government.

The final tally of seats of the major political parties was as follows:

BJP,	182	AIADMK	10
Congress,	116	RJD	7
CPM	33	CPI	4
TDP	29	BSP	14
JD (U)	22	Samajvadi Party	26
Siv Sena	15	NCP	9
DMK	11	National Conference	4
Trinamul Congress	8		

The rest of the seats went to smaller parties and independents.

Fourteenth General Elections

Unlike the Thirteenth General Elections, the fourteenth General Elections saw the National Democratic Alliance entering the electoral arena with full confidence of its victory. They expected Vajpayee to head the Indian Government for one more term. Unfortunately the NDA hopes were dashed to the ground and falsifying all expert election forecasts the Congress Party and its allies were declared victorious. BJP which expected to win 300 seats could get only 138 whereas the Congress Party won 145 seats. In the Thirteenth General Elections the BJP had won 182 seats whereas the Congress had only 116. The Marxist Communist Party secured 43 seats as against 33 in 1999. Among other parties, the DMK (16), RJD (21), NCP (9), CPI (10) were all with the Congress Party.

If in the First General Elections in 1952 the total number of voters was 17.1 million, fifty-two years later in 2004, the total electorate was 670 million. The world has never seen an electorate as large as that. There were over 700,000 polling stations. The total number of candidates was 5435. For the first time Electronic Voting Machines were used throughout the country. Millions of officials were deployed for the conduct of the elections. It was indeed the biggest ballot show ever. It was a relatively peaceful and free and fair elections. The overall percentage was 57.86 in 1999 it was 59.99. There were only 44 women among the 539 elected members.

Election 2004 is acclaimed by many–not the constituents of NDA–as a triumph of secularism, one of the basic principles of the Constitution of India. But if secularism means endorsing a modern view which does not see religious distinctions among the electorate as a hindrance to cooperative state action, their number seems to have given been rather small. On the other hand a large number of voters seem to have given greater importance to their basic needs and economic well being than anything else. It this sence Election 2004 was a triumph of secularism.

Another aspect of the election which was widely canvassed by the NDA and its allies was the foreign origin of Sonia Gandhi, the Congress leader The electorate in general seems to have given no great importance to this issue. This too may be considered as a triumph of secularism. On the whole, Election 2004 has been a watershed in the onward march of democracy in India.

Party Performance and Success Rates

Major parties	*Seats contested*	*Seats won*	*Vote share*	*Success rate*
Congress Party	417	145	26.69	34.77
Bharatiya Janata Party (BJP)	364	138	22.16	37.91
Communist Party of India (Marxist)	69	43	5.69	62.32
Samajwadi Party	237	36	4.21	15.19
Rashtriya Janata Dal	41	21	2.19	51.22
Bahujan Samaj Party	435	19	5.35	4.37
Dravida Munnetra kazhagam	16	16	1.79	100.00
Biju Janata Dal	12	11	1.29	91.67
Communist Party of India	34	10	1.40	29.41
Nationalist Congress Party	32	9	1.78	28.13
Janata Dal (United)	73	8	2.19	10.96
Shiromani Akali Dal	10	8	0.89	80.00
Telugu Desam Party	33	5	3.00	15.15

Fifteenth General Elections (2009)

The Fifteenth General Elections brought the Congress Party and its allies once again to success with increased majority. Even though the Left Parties (the Marxist Communist Party and its allies) withdrew their support to the Manmohan Singh Government, the election saw the Congress Party and its allies triumphant. In West Bengal, after many years, the left parties were defeated decisively and the Congress and the Trinamul Congress alliance were victorious. The Congress Party alone captured 204 seats nationally. In a State like Kerala where the Left Parties had won 18 seats out of 20 seats in 2004 could win only 4 seats. The performance of the BJP was also disappointing with 118 seats. On the other hand the Congress fared much better in most of the States. In Delhi the party won 7 out of 7, in Uttarakhand 5 out of 5, in Haryana 9 out of 10, in Rajasthan 20 out of 26, in Andhra Pradesh 32 out of 41, and in Maharashtra 25 out of 48. In Jammu and Kashmir the alliance between Congress and the National Conference, won 5 out of 6 in Kerala the UDF won 16 out of 20.

The stability of the Government of India was reassured with Dr. Manmohan Singh sworn in as Prime Minister of India for the second time and Sonia Gandhi re-elected as the Chief of the UPA.

Of the total 543 seats in the Lok sabha, 261 seats went to the U.P.A., 158 to the NDA, 23 to the Left Parties and the remaining 101 to the rest.

The final tally of seats was as follows:

Congress Party	204	AIADMK	8
BJP	118	Akali Dal	4
SP	24	RLD	4
BSP	20	RJD	4
Janta Dal (U)	20	CPI	4
Trinamul Congress	19	Janta Dal (S)	3
DMK	18	Muslim League	2
CPM	16	Forward Block	2
BJD	14	RSP	1
Siva Sena	10	PRP	1
NCP	9	Kerala Congresss (M)	1

The Fifteenth General Elections of India was the largest of its kind the world has ever witnessed. The total number of voters was 714 million. Because of its extraordinary size, the Election Commission conducted it in five phases, from April 16 to May 15. The poll schedule was finalised only after a series of meetings with political parties. Chief Secretaries of State Governments, Directors-General of Police and Railway Board officials.

Consequent on the announcement of the schedule of the General Election, the model code of conduct for the guidance of the political parties and candidates came into operation with immediate effect from the day the announcement was made by the Chief Commissioner of Elections.

The total number of the electorate had increased by 43 million, from 671million to 714 million in 2009. To achieve maximum participation, polling stations across the country had been increased by over 1.42 lakhs to 828804 from 687402 in 2004; the date of the Fourteenth General Elections.

Electoral Reforms

Right from the first General Elections the need for electoral reforms has been a subject of intense debate and discussion. Seminars, Workshops and Conferences have from time to time made many recommendations. The reports of the Election Commission of India, after every General Elections, have been making proposals for electoral reforms. A committee with representatives of all leading political parties under the Chairmanship of Dinesh Goswami, a leading member of Parliament, made a thorough study of electoral problems and proposed a number of recommendations. The report of the Committee was unanimously adopted by Parliament. The Lok Sabha has also unanimously passed a resolution on electoral reforms. Successive governments at the Centre have been making promises about electoral reforms. Yet the matter is still hanging fire. No serious steps have been taken by any government all these years.

Free and fair elections have become largely a myth than reality. From booth capturing, snatching of ballot papers and stuffing them in ballot boxes, intimidation of voters, in fact every form of electoral malpractice has been on the increase in election after election. Muscle power and money power have been very much on the increase. It is in this context that the cry for electoral reforms has become persistent and yet nothing tangible has happened so far.

Unless electoral reforms are brought about and strictly enforced, democratic elections will become an ornamental euphemism than a reality worth cherishing.

On criminalisation of polities, the Election Commission of India has urged the Government that there was a need to bar persons who were charge-sheeted for offences punishable with imprisonment for five years and more from contesting elections. The commission hoped that the Government will take electoral reforms as priority number one.

This chapter may be concluded with a brief mention of the commendable manner in which the elections were conducted by the Election Commission. Conduct of an election involving over 600 million voters is unprecedented in history. When we also consider that this gigantic exercise was to be conducted among a voting population which is predominantly illiterate, we get the true magnitude of the achievement. The Commission was able to handle it not only efficiently but in record time. If in 1977 the polling was concluded in four days, in 1980 it was concluded in two days. Most of the results were declared within twenty-four hours after the conclusion of the polling. Experience has made it possible to introduce a measure of sophistication in the conduct of elections in spite of the country's large size and huge population, differing climatic conditions and inadequate facilities for transport and communication. The Election Commission deserves a tribute for the efficient manner in which all the arrangements connected with the elections were handled by it. And the people of India have also shown how they could conduct themselves in a relatively peaceful and orderly manner in a nation wide popular exercise like this which forms one of the foundations of a democratic system of government.

***

45

OFFICIAL LANGUAGE

FEW CONSTITUTIONS have such elaborate provisions dealing with the official language as the Constitution of India. Ordinarily, official language is not a subject which requires any special treatment in a constitutional enactment. This is because, in most countries, a single language is employed as the common medium of expression of the entire population, or at least of an overwhelming majority. There are, of course, exceptions to this general pattern in some parts of the world, and some countries have made even special provisions to solve the problems arising out of bilingualism or multi-lingualism within their borders.

Switzerland provides perhaps the best example of the successful solution of the problem of multi-lingualism created by the existence of the polyglot population comprising of peoples speaking the German, French, Italian and Romonsch languages. The Swiss have designated all these four languages as national languages. The official languages of the country, however, are only the major three-German, French and Italian[1] and all these are used in all official dealings between the Confederation and the Cantons and between the Cantons themselves. All federal laws and publications are issued in all three languages. Canada has a bilingual problem of some 75 per cent English-speaking and twenty-five per cent French-speaking people. [2] Both English and French are recognized as official languages. While the working language of the Federal Government is English, letters written in French are answered in French. In parliamentary debates both languages are used. So also are both allowed in the courts. In Belgium, where there are three languages, German, French and Flemish, French and Flemish are official languages. The former U.S.S.R. had a multi-lingual problem. Official reports show that there are some 200 languages and dialects. But most of these are very little developed. There are however a dozen or more of these languages which are comparatively advanced. Of these, the Russian language has an outstanding position as the mother tongue of some 100 million people. Another advantage of the Russian language was that it was the only official language for purposes of political life, education and administration throughout the Csarist period. This pre-eminent position which Russian enjoyed naturally has made its status different even under the present regime. Nevertheless, the Government of the U.S.S.R. followed a liberal and progressive policy towards the regional languages by encouraging them in every possible way. After the breakup of the Soviet Union the language problem of Russia became comparatively simple.. Russian became the undisputed official language.

---

1. Of the total population, 72 per cent speak German, 20 per cent French, 6 per cent Italian, 1 per cent Romonsch and the rest others.
2. The French-speaking Canadians are mainly in the unilingual Province of Quebec.

In contrast, the language problem in India is complex and is indeed one of the most difficult which any multi-lingual country has ever faced. According to the Linguistic Survey of India, there are 179 languages and 544 dialects, and philologists have classified these into four distinct family groups-Indo-Aryan, Dravidian, Austro-Asiatic and Tibeto-Burman. For the Linguistic evolution of India over recent historic times, the two most important families are the Indo-Aryan and the Dravidian. At present, the Dravidian languages are mainly confined to the southern part of the country and among them are four well-developed languages, Tamil, Telugu, Kannada and Malayalam. Of these, Tamil has the oldest continuous literary tradition going back to pre-Christian times. Kannada literature too is very old while Telugu is believed to be relatively a century or two younger. Malayalam, considered by some as the younger sister of Tamil, is probably the youngest of these literary speeches. Although these languages have thus their own long-established and well-developed literature, nevertheless, the large proportion of Sanskrit words in their vocabularies, each in a varying degree, is a testimony to the historical synthesis in the Dravidian and Aryan culture pattern and forms of speech that came about over centuries of intercourse and communion between the two peoples.

Sanskrit was the first Indo-Aryan-language to develop a great literature and in the early Christian era and for many centuries thereafter it was the language *par excellence* of culture amongst the men of letters in most part of the country. Yet, it was not the spoken language of the masses who used many colloquial and corrupt forms of it in different parts of northern and central India. Gradually, these different local and regional corrupt forms developed into the modern Indian languages of the northern and central parts of the country. The most important of these are Assamese, Bengali, Gujarati, Hindi, Marathi, Oriya, Punjabi and Sindhi.

Between the thirteenth and the seventeenth centuries, as a result of Muslim invasions of India and the establishment of successive Muslim ruling dynasties in the northern parts of the country, a new element, Persian, entered the linguistic complex of the Indian sub-continent. It was, however, not the pure form of Persian that was used as the official language of the Muslim rulers but a mixed form of Persian, Arabic and Turkish. During the Moghul period, it developed into a distinct form of its own and came to be known as Urdu. While this new language employed the Persian script and large element of Persian vocabulary, it adopted a grammar and syntax identical to that of Hindi. As a result, it became alternatively known as Hindustani. This language remained the official language of the major part of northern India almost up to the middle of the nineteenth century.

Although the British had become the major political power in India by the end of the third quarter of the eighteenth century, the English language had not acquired any prominence in the country until the middle of the nineteenth century. Following the famous minute by Macaulay on the necessity of teaching the English language to the 'natives', a resolution was passed by the Governor-General, Lord William Bentinck, in 1835 laying down that "all the funds at the disposal of Government will henceforth be spent in imparting to Indians a knowledge of English literature and science." In the course of the next two decades, English became the official language of the British Indian administration. That was the position in 1947 when power was transferred to Indian hands.

The table on next page will throw light on the linguistic problem of India as it was obtained at the time of the adoption of the Constitution.

According to the report of the Official Language Commission, 1956, the main features and landmarks of the contemporary linguistic scene are the following.

Although the number of languages and dialects enlisted for census purposes runs into several hundreds, the principal languages that have to be reckoned in the language problem of India are about a dozen regional languages which are prevalent in fairly compact areas of the country; all these have amongst them, though in varying degrees, strong elements of identity and affinity; all of them suffer from identical deficiencies as linguistic tools for the requirements of expression in modern societies, arising out of their common supersession in recent decades in certain fields of activity and thought; amongst them the Hindi language had by far the largest proportion of speakers among the Indian population although in the total population this proportion constitutes a minority as compared to the number of speakers in all other languages put together; and in absolute terms, apart from proportions, these regional languages are spoken by large numbers of speakers and many of them would rank high in point of numbers in a world list of languages.

The following table will throw light on the linguistic problem of India :

Table 12

Language	Number of people Speaking (in millions)				Percentage of Total population
	1951	1961	1971	1981	
Assamese	5	6	9	19	2.8
Bangali	25	31	45	54	8.0
Gujarati	16	20	26	34	5.0
Hindi, Urudu, Hindustani, and Punjabi	150	183	209	270	40.0
Kannada	14	17	22	37	5.3
Malayalam	13	16	21	25	3.6
Marathi	27	33	42	63	9.2
Oriya	13	16	22	26	3.7
Tamil	27	33	38	48	7.0
Telugu	33	40	45	53	7.4
Others	30	40	70	54	8.0
Total	356	435	549	683	100

1. These figures are based on the 1951, 1961, 1971 and 1981 Census Data.

After pointing out the main features of the linguistic scene in such terms, the Commission proceeded to state the language problem in the following words:

We have surveyed the Indian linguistic scene and seen how we have current, in different and more or less distinct and compact parts of the country, a dozen great regional languages, several of them spoken by as large a number as or even a larger number of people than the speakers of some of the advanced languages of the West. While there is this multiplicity and variety of forms of speech, there is a large measure of similarity and affinity amongst all these languages. This kinship amongst the Indian languages is only a reflection of the fundamental bedrock of a common cultural inheritance which underlies the apparent variety amongst the linguistic and cultural groups of the Indian community. During the last hundred years or so of British rule, while immense changes were taking place in the country, these great languages happened to be cut away from all significant levels of activity, both governmental and private, and the English language gradually came to supersede the Indian languages in the work, activities and thought-processes of the higher intelligentsia of all the linguistic regions. English, in course of time, became the sole means of inter-communication at the all-India level, or the *lingua franca*, of all persons holding positions of authority or prominence in private and public life. With a rich and well-developed language like English at hand, which was the sole means of communication at all-India levels of intercourse, the official language of governance, the medium of instruction for all advanced education and also the language of all the learned professions, no wonder the indigenous languages languished and failed to develop a sufficiently rich and precise vocabulary for the requirements of modern social life during this period when the progress of scientific knowledge wrought a great revolution in the physical conditions of living in the country. Normally, languages develop in response to the requirements of communication and intercourse felt by societies which speak those languages. Now with the attainment of independence, the problem that presents itself to us is to devise a linguistic medium which obviously needs to subserve the political unity of the country, and, in the words of Article 351 of the Constitution, as a medium of expression for all the elements of the composite culture of India. The problem has also another aspect, *viz.*, that of developing the different regional languages and also Hindi, as the Union Language, so as to made them adequate vehicles of thought and expression in their appropriate spheres on the eventual displacement of the English language. This, in short, is the language problem of India.[1]

How much more difficult and complex is this problem in India than in other countries with bilingual or multi-lingual problems may be seen from the following observations of the Commission:

The difficulty and complexity of the language problem that the country has to tackle are manifest. We seek to find a medium of expression for the strong elements of identity in the cultural life of the country and as a linguistic counterpart of the political unity which the country has rediscovered after many centuries, In doing so, we seek to replace a working system based on the English language which, albeit foreign to the people, is one of the world's richest and most widely spoken languages and has many general merits to recommend it. The languages we can replace English by are at present insufficiently developed for the multifarious occasions of official and non-official intercourse that arise in a modern community. Several of these dozen or so languages are however spoken by numbers in excess of many current European languages claiming to be advanced means of communication and are thus, in point of the number of people who speak them, entitled to a high place in the world's roll of languages. Hindi has been chosen as the Union Language on the principal, and we think sufficient, ground that amongst the regional languages it is spoken by the largest number of people in the country. In the U.S.S.R., the Russian language currently enjoys, and has always had historically, such an outstandingly more important place in the national life than any of the other languages of the different regions that the choice of the national *lingua franca* must have been fairly obvious and incontrovertible. The problem cannot be solved as in Swtzerland

1. *Report of the Official Language Commission*, p.31

or Belgium or Canada by the easy means of recognizing all the competing languages equally for official purposes and carrying on by dint of a wide-spread multi-lingualism, inasmuch as such a solution is obviously impracticable when the number of languages is not two or three but more than a dozen. Some of the different elements in the Indian problem have been severally and individually met and tackled successfully elsewhere in the world; but for the successful tackling of the complex situation wherein all these difficulties are compacted, there is no precedent to our knowledge. We believe, however, that a successful solution can be achieved and we feel confident that, given good sense and an appropriate perspective, it would be done.[1]

During the course of the discussion on the official language, the Constituent Assembly witnessed some of the most agitated scenes, surcharged with emotion riding on the crest of linguistic fanaticism. The problem of the official language had assumed formidable proportions even in the early stages of the deliberations of the Assembly when some of the members insisted upon the business of the House being conducted in Hindi. They also demanded the official text of the Constitution to be adopted by the Assembly in the Hindi language and not in English. The President, however, managed to tide over the situation by assuring these members that the Hindi version of the Constitution would simultaneously be made ready with its text in English. Mainly because of the sharp difference that existed between the pro-Hindi group and those who opposed them, the Assembly postponed the consideration of the question of the official language to almost the very last stages of its deliberations. The deep interest of the members in this problem was evident from the fact that there were more than three hundred amendments to the draft articles on the official language-indeed, a record number of amendments to any provision of the Draft Constitution.

At the very outset of the discussion on this subject, the President cautioned and warned the Assembly which in itself was an unusual thing. For, he never had done it before. He said:

> There is no other item in the whole Constitution which will be required to be implemented from day to day, from hour to hour, I might say, from minute to minute in actual practice... The decision of the House should be acceptable to the country as a whole. Even if we succeed to get a particular proposition passed by majority, if it does not meet with the approval of any considerable section of people in the country either in the north or in the south, the implementation of the Constitution will become a most difficult problem.[2]

He then requested the members that while they spoke on this question they should be particularly careful to appeal to reason and not to feelings or passion.

The person who was entrusted with the task of moving the official amendment to the draft provisions on behalf of the Drafting Committee was Gopalaswami Ayyangar. Moving the motion, Ayyangar made the following points :

1. Although members were sharply divided in their opinion on this questin, there was a "fairly unanimous conclusion that we should select one of the languages in India as the common language of the whole of India, the language that should be used for the official purposes of the Union.

2. It was decided that Hindi should be selected for that purpose.

3. Although the decision in favour of Hindi was taken, it was also decided that "we

1. *Report*, pp. 268-9.
2. C.A.D. IX, p. 1312.

could not afford to give up the English language at once." It was further decided that the period for the transition should last at least fifteen years.

4. The numerals to be used for all official purposes should be the all-India form of Indian numerals.

5. "While we could recognise Hindi as the language for the official purposes of the Union, we must admit also that this language is not today sufficiently developed. It requires a lot of enrichment in several directions... So we have put into this Draft an article which makes it the duty of the State to promote the development of Hindi so that it may achieve all the enrichment and will in due course be sufficiently developed for replacing adequately the English language."

6. "We consider it very fundamental that English shall continue to be used in the Supreme Court and the High Courts until Parliament after full consideration, after Hindi has developed to such an extent that it can be a suitable vehicle for law-making and law-interpretation, comes to the conclusion that it can replace the English language... Law-making and law-interpretation require an amount of precision; they require a number of expressions and words which have acquired a certain definite meaning; and until we reach that stage in regard to the Hindi language, it should not become the language to be used in the highest courts." [1]

Ayyangar concluded his observations in the following terms:

> The draft is the result of a great deal of thought, a great deal of discussion. It is also a compromise between opinions which were not easily reconcilable. It is a compromise in respect of which very greatly cherished views and interests have been sacrificed for the purpose of achieving this draft in a form that will be acceptable to the full House... (Therefore), the scheme of the Chapter should be looked upon as a whole. It is an integrated whole; if you touch one part of it, the other things fall to pieces.

The discussion that followed Ayyangar's speech, contrary to earlier hopes and expectations, was acrimonious, agitated and, at times, undignified. While the advocates of Hindi pleaded in addition to the provisions of the draft also for the acceptance of the Devanagari form of the numerals as is used in Hindi, others threatened that any attempt to press the issue would compel them to withdraw their support to the Ayyangar amendment as a whole. The Muslim members of the Assembly in general advocated the adoption of Hindustani in place of Hindi and both the Devanagari and Urdu scripts. They pointed out that this was the solution of the language problem as envisaged by Mahatma Gandhi and it was also that for which the Indian National Congress had stood for decades.

Speaking of behalf of the Anglo-Indian community, Frank Anthony said:

> I accept the premise that if India is to achieve real unity, a real sense of Indian nationality, then we must have a national language.... That should be Hindi. I cannot understand, however, the almost malicious and vindictive attitude towards English.... Bitterness towards the Britisher should not be imported into our attitude towards the English language. It is one of the few good things that the British, incidentally perhaps unthinkingly, gave to this country and so opened up a treasure-house of literature, thought and culture....[2]

Commenting on the importance of the decision which the Assembly was about to

1. C.A.D.IX, p. 1317
2. C.A.D.IX, p. 1360

take, Shyama Prasad Mukherji said that it was something which had never been attempted in the history of India during the last thousand years.

> Let us, therefore, at the very outset realise that we have been able to achieve something which our ancestors did not achieve... The House is making a real contribution to the national unity of India of which we and those who come after us may be legitimately proud.... National unity must be achieved by allowing those elements in the national life of our country which are today vital to function and function in dignity, in harmony and in self-respect.... Unity in diversity is India's keynote and must be achieved by a process of understanding and consent....[1]

Maulana Abul Kalam Azad drew the attention of the House to the two difficulties that stood in the way of finding a quick and easy solution to the language problem. First, India had no national language as such which could immediately take the place of English.... Secondly, there was no common language in the country. As a result, they were compelled to choose one language for the purpose of developing as a national language while English was still employed for administrative purposes in order to see that efficiency in administration did not suffer.[2]

Supporting the amendment moved by Ayyangar, Prime Minister Nehru said:

> .... Not because it is perfect in every way, but it is the result of continuous effort and endeavour, thought and consultation, and as a result, some integrated thing took shape..... However good and important English may be, we cannot tolerate that there should be an English knowing elite and a large mass of our people not knowing English. Therefore, we must have our language. But English must continue as a most important language in India which large numbers of people learn and learn perhaps compulsorily.

Some members suggested that the whole question should be held in abeyance until a more opportune time for a solution presented itself. At that time, they argued, Parliament could easily pass necessary legislation in this regard. There were a few members who advocated the adoption of Sanskrit as the national language. But these were voices in the wilderness. The Assembly was bent upon arriving at a decision. After two days of heated and animated debate which occasionally became unruly, suddenly a compromise solution[3] was worked out modifying Ayyangar's amendment and this was accepted by the House almost unanimously. The provisions that are embodied in the Constitution are the product of this compromise.

Language of the Union (Arts. 343 and 344)

The main provisions dealing with the official language of the Union as embodied in Articles 343 and 344 are as follows:

1. Hindi written in Devanagari script will be the official language of the Union.

2. For a period of fifteen years from the commencement of the Constitution,[4] however, the English language will continue to be used for all official purposes of the Union. But during this period, the President may authorize the use of Hindi in addition to English.

---

1. C.A.D.IX, p. 1389.
2. C.A.D.IX, 1452.
3. K.M. Munshi played an important role in this compromise.
4. The Constitution was inaugurated on 26 January 1950.

3. Even after fifteen years, Parliament may provide for the continued use of English for any specific purpose.

4. At the end of five years from the commencement of the Constitution, the President shall appoint a Commission to make recommendations for the progressive use of the Hindi language and on the restrictions on the use of English and other allied matters. The President is obligated to appoint such a Commission at the end of ten years after the commencement of the Constitution for the same purpose. While making their recommendations, the Commission should give due regard to the industrial, cultural and scientific advancement of India, and the just claims and the interests of persons belonging to the non-Hindi speaking areas in regard to the Public Services.

5. The Commission's recommendations will be examined by a thirty-man Committee of Parliament (20 members from the Lok Sabha and 10 from the Rajya Sabha) elected in accordance with the system of proportional representation and the Committee will make a report to the President. The President may issue directions on the basis of the report of the Committee.

In accordance with the constitutional provision, in June 1955, at the end of five years after the commencement of the Constitution, the President appointed a Commission consisting of twenty-one members with B.G. Kher as its Chairman. Its terms of reference were as follows:

It shall be the duty of the Commission to make recommendations to the President as to

(a) the progressive use of the Hindi language for the official purposes of the Union;
(b) restrictions on the use of the English language for all or any of the official purposes of the Union;
(c) the language to be used for all or any of the purposes mentioned in Article 348 of the Constitution;
(d) the form of numerals to be used for any one or more specified purposes of the Union;
(e) the preparation of a time schedule according to which and the manner in which Hindi may gradually replace English as the official language of the Union and as a language for communication between the Union and State Governments and between one State Government and another.

The Commission submitted its report to the President by the middle of 1956. The report which runs into some five hundred pages is an impressive document dealing with every one of the questions referred to the Commission in a thorough-going manner. The Report, however, set off one of the bitterest controversies in the country. One of the serious defects of the Report was the strong and utterly uncompromising minutes of dissent by two of its prominent members representing two major languages of the country, namely Bengali and Tamil. Nevertheless, the report is a very valuable document for understanding the immensity and complexity of the language problem of India.

The Commission has dealt with the question of the language of the Union for official purposes at length in the light of the Constitutional provisions detailed above.[1] It gave due consideration to the importance of the English language as a medium of internal as

1. *Report of the Official Language Commission*, 1956, Chapter IV.

well as international communication. According to the Commission, no one can ignore the fact that, today, English is the official language of India and the language of higher education in the country. It is also the sole medium of communication for official purposes. Besides, apart from the English language there is no other common medium of expression in the country. All these factors would seem to be forceful enough to favour the retention of English in the country. Yet, the majority in the Commission was not satisfied that India should perpetuate English as the official language of the Union. The more important of its arguments in favour of discarding English were the following:

1. Consideration of national self-respect are not without relevance in respect of language, which touches the entire national life of a people so intimately and which is, besides, such a sensitive point of honour in the field of international contacts.

2. It is not suggested that English is to be rejected merely because it is a foreign language. But there is a vital distinction between using a foreign language as a second language for specific purposes and for certain categories of persons, and its use as the principal or exclusive medium of education or for the conduct of the day-to-day business of the country. It is perfectly feasible to devise a solution whereby the necessary knowledge of the English language for the appropriate personnel is fully provided for and, at the same time, a change-over is brought about in the general linguistic media in the fields of education, administration and law courts, so as to bring them into a live and continuous communion with the common people of the country.

3. Only through the medium of Indian languages would India be able to bring about that massive resurgence of national life in the service of the ordinary citizen which is implied in the adoption of adult franchise, free and compulsory education, promotion of social justice and equal opportunity and fundamental rights and the directive principles of State policy embodied in the Constitution.

4. The 1951 Census shows that the number of persons with some degree of knowledge of the English language in the whole country is a negligible fraction of the total population, some 3.8 million or a little over one per cent.

5. Even when the ideal of compulsory primary education for all children until the completion of the age of fourteen years as envisaged under the Constitution is realized, the number of English-knowing people will not substantially increase, as instruction at the primary stage is through the medium of the mother tongue. Further, the existence of a high percentage of literates in Indian language will enhance the claim for the change-over in order to make the business of government understandable to the common man. Today when every citizen is a potential beneficiary of Welfare State and has a vote to exercise, it is manifest that the business of the government can be carried on only in a language or languages which admit of the possibility of each citizen taking an intelligent interest in the affairs of the State and exercising his power of franchise with understanding.

6. If the conduct of the official business of the country at the Union as well as at State levels, and the business of law, courts, etc. cannot possibly be carried on indefinitely in the existing medium of the English language in view of the imperative requirements of the situation, the point for consideration is, so far as the Union level is concerned what the linguistic medium should be.

7. The constitutional provisions have laid down that the official language of the Union and the language for inter-state communication shall be the Hindi language.

8. Comparisons are often instituted amongst the Indian languages, as between Hindi and the other regional languages, generally to the disadvantage of the former. The point to remember is that Hindi has been adopted in the Constitution for the official business of the Union and for the purposes of inter-state communication not because it is better developed than the other regional languages are; not because a greater or more varied wealth of literature is available in it; nor because it has presently a larger number of books available in the sciences and in other branches of modern knowledge. It is chosen for performing the job of the official medium on all-India level because it happens that a much larger number of Indian speak it than any other language. Apart from the forty-two per cent of the total population returned in census figures as speaking this language as their mother tongue, it is understood to a considerable extent outside the Hindi-speaking areas, in the market places in cities, at railway stations and in places of pilgrimage where persons hailing from different regions of India and not knowing English have occasion to converse. Besides, owing to the affinity of this language to others like Marathi, Gujarati, Oriya and Bengali, it is for those who speak those languages, a language relatively easy to acquire. Indeed ever since the question of a common language for India began to be discussed in Indian public life, there has never been any serious doubt as to what language should be adopted for the purpose. The status of the official language is not an award for literary merit in a language. A Tagore or a Tulsidas or a Jnanadeva or a Kabir is a literary phenomenon, acting on its own laws inscrutable to us, which raises the status of thought and expression in the linguistic medium of its choice to unprecedented elevations with the flash of its inspired perceptions. For the work-a-day purposes of conducting the administration of the country, enacting statutes and meeting out justice through law courts, the quantum of such grace and benediction bestowed on a language is not the decisive factor, however profoundly important it may otherwise be. Here, we are concerned merely with the prevalence of knowledge of the language in relation to the appropriate sectors of activity and the conclusive guidance relevant is the one to be obtained from the census figures.

9. The constitutional provisions regarding the Union language are framed in the same general spirit of liberalism and catholicity in which the other language provisions of the Indian Constitution are framed. India's cultural heritage is remarkable for its variety of patterns and origins; the harmonizing of these diversities has been the distinguishing feature of the Indian tradition. Language is the loom on which cultural patterns are woven. As we sustain and cherish the various elements entering into India's cultural life, so we must sustain and cherish the different languages adopted as their media by the different cultural groups. The matter of cultural rights is not to be determined merely by brute majorities. The Constitution has, therefore, enacted specific guarantees for the cultural and educational rights of minorities. A positive duty is cast on the State to provide facilities to the minorities for their education in the mother tongue at the primary school stage, apart from the constitutional guarantee to such minorities of the right to establish and administer educational institutions of their own choice.

The main points of the two dissenting members who differed fundamentally from the majority are the following:[1]

According to S.K. Chatterji:

---

1. See, for the full text, the *Report*, pp. 275-314.

.... The provisions in the Constitution regarding the use of Hindi as the official language of the Union in certain contexts have been extended in the Report in a manner which will bring about a total revolution in our Education, in the Administration of Law and Justice, in the Central Legislature, and in the Public Services, a revolution which many do not think to be desirable in the best interest of India in her present situation. If the recommendations are sought to be implemented from the Centre, it will bring about immediate chaos in our public life as a whole. It will mean for non-Hindi peoples the starting of a progressive imposition of Hindi in most spheres of life. The Report has been prepared on the assumption (on the basis of the present Constitution, of course) that Hindi has been already voluntarily accepted by the whole of India, that non-Hindi peoples are as much eager for its use in most spheres of our all-India affairs as speakers of Hindi, and that it will be something anti-national not to try to replace English in the entire administrative, legal and political frame of India, and largely in the educational cadre also. The entire outlook is that of the Hindi speakers in the Indian Union, who alone are to profit immediately, and for a long time to come, if not for ever, I fear that in the entire report there is very little evidence of an attempt to understand the feelings and the intellectual approach of the non-Hindi speaking people for their own language, and also for English (as it is sincerely regarded by them to be the most necessary thing for the development of science and letters in India, for the preservation of the unity of India, and for the maintenance of the pre-eminence of India in the modern world). The attitude is far from democratic — it is just a case of imposition of one kind of mentality over the rest, as the only natural and at the same time politically sound mentality for the whole of India. The fact that India is a polyglot country where people have now become or are becoming aggressively proud of their own language is ignored. A particular language has been sought to be given priority over everything else in our national life. As it strikes us, uniformity through Hindi is sought to be brought about as quickly as possible even at the risk of jeopardising the unity of India gained through the English language.

The Recommendations will, in my opinion, bring about the immediate creation, without intending to do so, of two classes of citizens in India—Class I citizens with Hindi as their language, obtaining an immense amount of special privileges by virtue of their language only, and Class II citizens who will be suffering from permanent disabilities by reason also of their language. This is bound to be the situation so long as non-Hindi speakers like (those from) Assam, Bengal, Orissa, Andhra, Madras, Maharashtra and other peoples do not acquire a command over Hindi which can compare favourable with that of those persons who have Hindi as their only language of education, either along with or to the exclusion of English.

The Recommendations appear to ignore the consequences which may result from them. The Report envinces a subdued but desperate haste to bring in Hindi for the whole of India: 1965 still remains with the Report a target date, although it ruefully admits that 'it has not been possible for us to furnish a regular time table by dates and stages as to how Hindi should be introduced into the business of the Union so as to accomplish the general change-over within the period fixed by the Constitution. I submit the situation now is hardly ripe for bringing in this revolutionary change over in Indian affairs, while Hindi is not yet ready on the one hand, and the non-Hindi peoples too are not ready either on their part.

In his dissent, among other things, P. Subbaroyan said:[1]

The Report in my opinion is trying to prescribe certain programmes, rules and regulations from the Centre, without much reference either to the actual situation in the sphere of language in India or to future reactions and repercussions among large sections of our people. It is also seeking to place as something conclusive before the non-Hindi peoples of India that it will be both an act of patriotic duty and an urgent and necessary reform to replace English by Hindi as quickly as possible, and to take in Hindi to saturation in their judicial and administrative spheres,

1. See for the full text, *Report*, pp. 315-30.

in their educational set-up, and consequently in every aspect of their life. Many of my colleagues are of the opinion that if India is to be completely independent it must give up the use of the English language as early as possible. I regret I cannot agree with this point of view as in my opinion the official language which we are to adopt eventually for the country must be a language which has been fully developed and till such time we must perforce continue to use English. Much more important is the economic and industrial development of the country if it is to maintain its independence and progressively develop, and any steps as we may take to introduce an official language other than English must take into account whether its immediate introduction will hamper economic and industrial progress.

I feel that certain fundamental and vital issues have been totally ignored in the Report. The provisions in the Constitution regarding the use of Hindi as the official language of the Union in certain contexts have been extended in the Report in a manner which will bring about an abrupt and a total revolution in our education, in the administration of law and justice, in the Central Legislature and in the Public Services. In my opinion the recommendations made in the Report go far beyond the terms of reference. If those recommendations are sought to be implemented by the Union Government it will result in the immediate imposition of Hindi on non-Hindi speaking people which will lead to confusion and even chaos in our public life as a whole. The Report has been prepared on the assumption that under the present Constitution Hindi has been already voluntarily accepted by the whole of India, that non-Hindi speaking peoples are as eager for it as speakers of Hindi, and that it will be something anti-national not to try to replace English by Hindi.

The recommendations in the Report appear to ignore the consequences which may result from the implementation of them. The Report evinces a desperate haste to bring in Hindi for the whole of India; 1965 still remains a target date in the Report. After having heard the evidence in both Hindi and non-Hindi speaking States, I am convinced that nine years from now will certainly not be enough for non-Hindi speaking States to get prepared for this eventuality. This is a very vital question which the Report has ignored.

The recent events in many parts of India have brought home to me the imperative necessity to keep intact our most precious treasure of Indian unity. It is, therefore, important to consider seriously about the extent to which we should push Hindi and the speed with which we should try to make it the official language of India. Many honestly feel that there are already signs of the danger of an incipient 'Hindi Imperialism' which will be all the more anti-national as Hindi has not yet acquired any pre-eminence over the other languages of India except its weight of numbers. The Hindi speaking people, like all human beings, are not free from linguism and their expectations have been raised very high. It is also my conviction, after careful observation and thinking, that the relegation of English to a secondary place in our education and public life will certainly not be for the good of the country. Hence I venture to differ from the findings and recommendations of the majority of the Commission and present my specific proposals.

The trend of events in India, particularly during the last few years after independence, has given rise to anxious thoughts about the future among our people who are alive to the realities of the situation, both at home and abroad and who have wide vision which goes beyond the horizon of regionalism and sectarianism. During these eight years, attempts have been made and are being made to prepare Hindi from its position as one of the languages of the country (although used and understood in its numerous ungrammatical forms by a good percentage of the people of North India) to that of 'the first among equals' among the languages of India. It was thought that with the support of the State and the exertions of the people, both within and outside the Hindi areas, Hindi could easily be transformed into a fit and proper vehicle which will adequately express both the composite culture of India and the requirements of modern life in science and technology, and thought and literature. Attempts have also been made to spread the knowledge of Hindi in the non-Hindi areas. To develop or support the growth of Hindi as an expressive modern language and to diffuse its knowledge, considerable sums of money have been spent and are being spent by the Centre, and also by some of the States, but the result has been far from commensurate.

I have already pointed out that the acceptance of Hindi in the Constitution was done in an atmosphere of certain hasty beliefs and impressions and was thought to be a very simple matter by its enthusiastic supporters. Now we are face to face with the stark realities of the situation. After the move at the Centre and in the Hindi-using States to establish Hindi, a move which is becoming more and more insistent, the linguistic problem, which until now was never one of much practical importance or urgency in our country, has been made to assume (at least in certain quarters) a very great importance. It has taken the form of rivalry between Hindi (as a regional language in Hindi speaking States) and the regional languages of the non-Hindi States; between the regional languages and English and between English and Hindi (Hindi both as a regional language and as the proposed official language); and the attitude to the last aspect of the problem is different in non-Hindi States from that in Hindi States. Many matters of prime importance, which we never thought of in our haste through optimistic enthusiasm, are now presenting themselves; and these now appear even to jeopardise both the basic unity of India and her intellectual pre-eminence, and already show signs of lowering administrative efficiency.

As provided for in the Constitution a thirty-member Committee of Parliament with the Home Minister of the Union Government as its Chairman examined the recommendations of the Commission. The Report of the Committee was submitted to Parliament on 8 February 1958. While the Committee had expressed the definite opinion that adherence to the Constitutional settlement which envisaged the replacement of English by Hindi for Union purposes and by the regional languages for the official requirements of the States was the only safe and practicable course to adopt, the approach to the question of final change-over had to be flexible and practical. Thus, the Committee has in general endorsed the recommendations of the Official Language Commission except that it emphasizes the necessity for flexibility in the change-over.[1]

Regional Languages

Each State Legislature is empowered under Article 345 to adopt any one or more of the languages in use in the State for all or any of the official purposes of the State concerned. But so far as communication between a State and the Union or between one State and another is concerned, the official language of the Union will be the authorized language. In order to protect the linguistic interests of minorities in certain States, the Constitution has incorporated a special provision. This is in addition to the cultural rights that are guaranteed as fundamental rights under Article 29 of the Constitution. According to this, the President is empowered under Article 347 to direct a State Government to recognize a particular language for official purposes either for the whole or a part of the State, if he is satisfied, on a representation made to him in this regard, that a substantial proportion of the population of the State desires such recognition. This power in the hands of the Centre will help to curb any tendency towards linguistic fanaticism and the domination of a majority over linguistic minorities in different States.

Language in Courts

Under Article 348, the Constitution makes a special provision for the retention of the English language if Parliament so decides even after the fifteen-year period for the

1. For details see *Report of the Committee of Parliament on Official Language* (1958).

following purposes:

(i) All proceedings in the Supreme Court and the High Courts.

(ii) Authoritative texts of Bills, Acts, Ordinances, orders, rules, regulations and bye-laws issued under the Constitution or under any law.

However, Parliament is empowered to stop the use of English even in the Courts whenever it likes, once the fifteen-year period is over. It is also provided that Hindi or any regional language may be used even earlier for conducting the proceedings in a High Court if the President gives his consent for the measure.

Dealing with the question of the language of legislation, the Language Commission made the following recommendations:[1]

1. A distinction must be made between the language to be adopted for the proceedings and deliberations of legislative bodies and the language of the enactments which they legislate. The former should be done progressively in Hindi and the regional languages while the latter may continue to be made in English.

2. Even after 1965 a Presiding Officer may permit a member to express himself in Parliament or in the State Legislatures through the medium of English if he is unable to express himself in Hindi or the State language concerned.

Apart from the authoritative enactment which, in our opinion, ought to be eventually in Hindi, both in respect of parliamentary legislation and State legislation, there may be need, for the sake of public convenience, to publish translations of the enactments in different regional languages. In respect of State legislation, this would be normally necessary in the regional language(s) prevalent in the State, wherein in respect of parliamentary legislation it may be necessary in all the important regional languages current in the country.

We consider that it is essential, when the time comes for this changeover, that the entire statute book of the country should be in one language which cannot of course be other than Hindi. Therefore the language of legislation of the States as well as of Parliament and also of course consequently the language of all statutory orders, rules, etc. issued under any law should be the Hindi language.

With regard to the language of law courts, the Commission recommended:[2]

It is only natural that justice should be administered in a country in its indigenous languages and provided the change is brought about systematically the prospect should not provoke alarm or cause apprehensions about its basic practicability.

So far as the language of the Supreme Court is concerned, eventually there can be only one language, *i.e.*, Hindi, in respect of the entire court proceedings and records, including of course the judgements and orders. When the time comes for the change-over, the Supreme Court will have to function only in the Hindi language. The authoritative texts of reported judgments of the Supreme Court will also be published in the same language.

Processes issued in Hindi by the Supreme Court, when addressed to non-Hindi regions or against a person whose mother-tongue is not Hindi, should be accompanied by a translation for the convenience of the concerned party.

Provision should also be made for reliable translations of Supreme Court decisions being made available in the State languages in separate regional language series.

1. *Report*, p. 412.
2. Ibid, p. 413.

The pros and cons of the regional and Hindi languages are carefully examined so far as the linguistic medium of the High Courts is concerned. There are several strong and, in our opinion, conclusive reasons in favour of deciding that when the time for the change-over arrives, the language of the judgements, decrees and orders of the High Courts must be in a common linguistic medium for the whole country and therefore these should be in the Hindi language in all regions.

Having regard to the recommendations made by the States Reorganisation Commission regarding transfer of High Court judges and the proposals about a single judicial service, it might be worth considering whether certain minimum language test in appropriate regional languages and Hindi should not be adopted in the case of High Court judges.

Apart from the opinion of delivering judgements in English, there may be an option to High Court judges to deliver judgments in their regional languages provided English or Hindi translations of such judgements are authenticated by them.

Provision may be made for granting leave by presiding judges to Counsel, in suitable cases, to argue in English in the Supreme Court and in English or the regional languages in the several High Courts even after the general change-over in the linguistic medium has taken place.

Special Directives

The Constitution embodies certain special directives with a view to safeguarding the interests of linguistic minorities. Thus, under Article 350 every person is entitled to submit a representation for the redress of any grievance to any officer or authority of the Union or a State in any of the languages used in the Union or in the State as the case may be. In addition, there are two special directives which have been incorporated as a result of the recommendations of the States Reorganization Commission through the Seventh Amendment of the Constitution in 1956. According to these:

1. It shall be the endeavour of every State and of every local authority within the State to provide adequate facilities for instruction in the mother tongue at the primary stage of education to children belonging to linguistic minority groups. The President is empowered to issue such directions to any State as he considers necessary or proper for securing the provision of such facilities.

2. The President will appoint a Special Officer for linguistic minorities. It is the duty of this special officer to investigate all matters relating to the safeguards provided for linguistic minorities under the Constitution and report regularly to the President. The reports of the Special officer are to be laid before each House of Parliament and sent to the Government of the States concerned.[1]

The Constitution also embodies a directive for the development and enrichment of the Hindi language with a view to making it serve as a real medium of expression for all elements of the composite culture of India. Such enrichment may be secured by drawing primarily on Sanskrit and secondarily on other languages. According to the Language Commission, 'other languages' means all other languages and not necessarily the languages of India specified in the Constitution. Hence, in the process of development and enrichment of the Hindi language there is no inhibition as to drawing from any language including the English language.[2]

1. For a comprehensive account on the problems affecting linguistic minorities in the country and how they are being tackled, see the *Second Report of the Commissioner for Linguistic Minorities* (1960), Government of India, Ministry of Home Affairs.
2. *Report of the Official Language Commission*, pp. 52-5.

The Government of India has been extending wholehearted assistance and giving every possible encouragement with a view to enriching Hindi and developing it as the official language of the country. Simultaneously, there has also been steady extension in the use of Hindi for transaction of official business. Necessary rules have been framed for this purpose by the Ministry of Home Affairs of the Government of India and all Central Government offices have been asked to strictly enforce these rules. These rules make it obligatory for officers to use Hindi in reply to communications received in Hindi. They should also use Hindi for correspondence with the Hindi-speaking areas—Delhi, Himachal Pradesh, Haryana, Rajasthan, Uttar Pradesh, Madhya Pradesh and Bihar. Hindi has to be used also for correspondence between Central Government offices located in Hindi-speaking areas. The only exception to this is for writing demi-official letters, communication involving technical and legal matters, and circular letters addressed to all the State Governments.

Government officers have been permitted to use Hindi for noting on files and for preparation of drafts without any obligation for submitting English translations. The Ministry's orders, however, make it compulsory for the officers to use both Hindi and English for general orders, rules, notifications, resolutions, administrative and other reports, contracts, agreements, licences, permits, notices and forms of tenders. Both Hindi and English are to be used for papers to be laid on the table of Parliament, press communiques, invitation cards for Government functions, forms, seals, rubber stamps, letter heads and sign boards. The Government advertisements meant for all-India coverage or for Hindi-speaking areas are also to be written in both English and Hindi.

Eighth Schedule
[Article 344(1) and 351]

The Eighth Schedule of the Constitution lists the following languages:[1]

LANGUAGES

1. Assamese	7. Malayalam	13. Tamil	19. Bodo
2. Bengali	8. Marathi	14. Telugu	20. Dogri
3. Gujarati	9. Oriya	15. Urdu	21. Maithili
4. Hindi	10. Punjabi	16. Konkani	22. Santhal
5. Kannada	11. Sanskrit	17. Manipuri	
6. Kashmiri	12. Sindhi	18. Nepali	

In spite of the controversies and bitterness that still exist in the country on the language problem, it must be admitted that the adoption of the provisions dealing with the official language by the Constituent Assembly marked a triumph of Indian unity. It showed that even in the face of the most acute differences emanating from deep-seated sentiments, men of goodwill who have the good of the nation at heart can find a solution to the most

---

1. Originally the Schedule contained only fourteen languages. The Constitution (Twenty first Amendment) Act, 1967, enlarged the Schedule by adding Sindhi to it. This was in response to the representation of the Sindhi-speaking people in the country.

The Seventy-first Amendment of 1992 amended the Eighth Schedule further to include in it three new languages, namely, Konkani, Manipuri and Nepali.

baffling problem. That realization should augur well for the future of the country and the urge for preserving the unity and integrity of the nation, and should help Indians to find solutions for every problem that threatens to divide them. One might recall what President Rajendra Prasad said in the Constituent Assembly immediately after the adoption of the chapter on the official language, emphasising the momentous nature of the decisions. He said:

> I think we have adopted a chapter for our Constitution which will have very far-reaching consequences in building up the country as a whole. Never before in our history did we have one language recognised as the language of rule and administration in the country as a whole... We have now achieved political unification of the country; we are now going to forge another link which will bind us all together from one end to the other... Our Constitution so far has evoked many controversies, and raised many questions which had very deep differences; but we have somehow or other managed to get over them all. This was one of the biggest gulfs which might have separated us... This language which we will use in the Centre will tend to bring us together, nearer and nearer. The English language brought us together. An Indian language in its place is bound to bring us close together, in particular because our traditions are the same... If we did not accept this formula, the result would have been either a large number of languages to be used for the country as a whole, or separation of provinces which did not like to submit or accept any particular language under pressure. We have done the wisest thing possible.. and I hope posterity will bless us for this.[1]

***

1. C.A.D. IX, p.1489.

46

SPECIAL PROVISIONS RELATING TO CERTAIN CLASSES

A SPECIAL feature of the political life in India under the British was the existence of communal electorates. Nationalist opinion was always opposed to it. Yet it continued, and in course of time established a pattern of communal politics unknown in any other country. According to this, almost every religious minority in India, the Muslims, the Sikhs, the Christians and others, had a certain number of seats reserved for it in the Legislatures. This privilege was extended to the Anglo-Indians and the Europeans also. Under the Constitution Act of 1935, the Scheduled Castes also were to be treated as a separate community and given separate representation. But the historic fast of Gandhi at Poona in 1933 prevented it and the Scheduled Castes were given reservation in constituencies based upon joint electorates with other Hindus. In 1947 when India became independent, this was the prevailing situation.

Although the country was divided between India and Pakistan on a religious basis, the partition of the country did not by itself solve the problem of religious minorities. Pakistan became a 'Muslim' State, but all the Muslims of undivided India did not migrate to that State. Some fifty million Muslims still remained in India. Besides, there were large groups of other religious minorities such as Christians, Sikhs, Anglo-Indians and others. The Scheduled Castes and Tribes were still treated on par with religious minorities deserving special consideration. When the Constituent Assembly took up this question in 1947 there was nothing fundamentally different from the old ideas on the subject. The Assembly formed a committee, the Advisory committee on Fundamental Rights and Minorities with Sardar Patel as its Chairman, to study the different aspects of the problem and make recommendations to the Assembly so that these recommendations could be given due recognition in the provisions of the new Constitution.

Moving the Report of the Committee in the Assembly, Patel gave a detailed picture of the deliberations of the Committee, [1] He said that the original stand of the minorities was, in general, for the continuation of some sort of reservations in the Legislatures. There were, of course, a few who advocated the total abolition of reservations [2]. At the other extreme, there were others who wanted the continuance of the old system of communal electorates. In between these two extremes there were many sections who wanted joint

1. C.A.D.VIII, pp.261-72
2. H.C. Mukherjee and Rajkumari Amrit Kaur were the most prominent among them

electorates but who stood for the reservation of a minimum number of seats for each minority based on the strength of its population.

A sub-committee composed of Patel, Rajendra Prasad, Nehru, Munshi and Ambedkar was appointed by the committee to study in detail the various aspects of the problem and report to it. It took some time for the sub-committee to submit its report. It was of the opinion that some form of reservation was necessary to satisfy the minorities. The Advisory Committee studied these recommendations and decided to recommend them in the form of definite proposals to the Assembly. In the meantime, Independence and the problems created by partition brought about a new outlook and a substantial change in the attitude of many members who belonged to the various minority communities in the Assembly. H.C. Mukherjee took the lead and moved in the committee the motion for dropping the clause on reservation of seats in the Legislatures on a population basis. When this proposal was moved, Muniswami Pillai, representing the Scheduled Castes, moved an amendment to the effect that the provision for reservation, so far as the Scheduled Castes were concerned, might be continued for a period of ten years. The committee also accepted certain special provisions safeguarding the interests of some backward classes belonging to the Sikh community. Patel advised the Assembly to accept the recommendations of the committee with the following appeal:

> ...[I]n the long run, it would be in the interest of all to forget that there is anything like majority or minority in this country and (to realise) that in India there is only one community.

Many members participated in the discussion that followed Patel's statement, highlighting the changed circumstances in the country which necessitated a change of outlook. Almost every one spoke against the retention of communal representation as it existed during the British rule.[1] H.C. Mukherjee advanced perhaps the most powerful argument against reservation. He said that reservations of seats in the legislatures on the basis of religious minorities would strike at the very root of the ideal of a secular State. It also went against the concept of one nation. "To the majority I say: Once for all we are placing the responsibility of looking after us fairly and squarely on your shoulders." He also appealed for goodwill and understanding from the minorities and said that he was of the opinion that the majority had done enough to command confidence and trust.[2] According to Aizaz Rasool:

> Reservation is a self-destructive weapon which separates the minorities from the majority for all time. It gives no chance to the minorities to win the goodwill of the majority. It keeps up the spirit of separatism and communalism alive which shouid be done away with once for all.[3]

Jerome D'Souza said that the fundamental rights safeguarding the rights of the individual and the guarantee of these rights by the Supreme Court should allay the fears of the minority.[4]

The case of the Anglo-Indian community was a special one, both because of its mixed racial character and language. Further, it was a very small community whose members were concentrated mainly in the big cities of the country. They had been enjoying,

1. The only members who spoke in its favour of reservation were M. Ismail and Pocker, Muslim League members from Madras.
2. C.A.D.VIII, pp. 298-300
3. Ibid., pp. 300-2
4. Ibid., pp. 306-7

under the British rule, a number of special privileges. If they did not receive any special consideration, that would have meant serious hardship to them. The Advisory Committee, fully recognizing these factors, had recommended certain special safeguards for the community. Appreciating the spirit behind these measures, Frank Anthony, the Anglo-Indian leader in the Constituent Assembly, paid a handsome tribute to the majority community and particularly the Chairman of the Advisory Committee, Sardar Patel. He said that his (Patel's) attitude was

> ...[N]ot inspired by logic, not by strict reasonableness, not by academic theories but by an attempt to understand the real feelings and psychology of the minority mind.... And this is why we have these provisions granted to us, provisions which we had no right to ask for, on a strictly logical or academic basis.... Sir, may I say this about the decisions of the Advisory Committee? They represent no imposed decisions; they represent decisions which have been arrived at as a result of friendly understanding, compromise and unanimous agreement. I believe, in bringing these decisions to fruition, Sardar Patel has helped-as perhaps none else in the past few years could have done-to bind the minorities with hoops of steel to the cause of national integration and progress.[1]

Apart from the Scheduled Castes and the Anglo-Indians, another community that received special treatment at the hands of the Assembly was the Scheduled Tribes. Speaking about the tribal people, Ambedkar said:

> The tribal people in areas other than Assam are more or less Hinduised, more or less assimilated with the civilisation and culture of the majority of the people in whose midst they live. With regard to the tribals in Assam that is not the case. Their roots are still in their own civilisation and their own culture. They have not adopted mainly or in a large part either the modes or the manners of the Hindus who surround them. Their laws of inheritance, their laws of marriage, customs and so on are quite different from those of the Hindus... The position of the tribals in Assam is somewhat analogous to the position of the Red Indians in the United States as against the white emigrants there.... The political authority that we have given to the tribal people (Assam) through the constitution of the Regional Council or District Councils is all the sphere of influence to which they will be entitled. On the other hand, the tribal people will have representation in the Assam Legislature itself as well as in Parliament so that they will play their part in making laws for Assam and also for the whole of India. Now if these cycles of participation, *viz.*, representation... are not binding forces, what else can ? As a result, the tribals and the non-tribals can politically come together, influence each other, associate themselves with each other and learn something from one another.[2]

The decisions of the Constituent Assembly arising out of the discussions on the recommendations of the Advisory Committee opened a new trend in India politics. The main features of this new trend were (i) abolition of separate electorates, (ii) abolition of reservation of seats in the legislatures, and (iii) abolition of special safeguards to the minorities. The only exceptions made were with regard to the three communities, Scheduled Castes, Scheduled Tribes and Aglo-Indians, each of which had a special case. But even in these cases the special provisions were to exist only for a limited period of ten years from the commencement of Constitution. These provisions are embodied in a separate chapter of the Constitution.

---

1. Ibid., pp. 327-8
2. C.A.D. IX, p. 1024.

Representation of Anglo-Indians in the Legislatures

The Constitution empowers the President under Article 331 to nominate a maximum of two members of the Anglo-Indian community to the House of the People, if he is of the opinion that the community is not adequately represented. From a population point of view, the Anglo-Indian community was not entitled even to one seat in Parliament.[1] The President will act on the basis of this constitutional provision only when no Anglo-Indian has been elected to the House of the People in the General Elections. At present there are two nominated Anglo-Indian members in the House of the People.

Just as the President is empowered to make these nominations, the Governor of a State is empowered under Article 333 to nominate such number of Members of the Anglo-Indian community to the State Legislative Assembly as he considers appropriate, if, in his opinion, the community needs representation in the State Assembly and has not been adequately represented. At present, there is one Anglo-Indian nominated member each in the Legislative Assemblies of Andhra Pradesh, Bihar, Maharashtra, Kerala, Madhya Pradesh, Tamil Nadu, Karnataka, Uttar Pradesh and West Bengal. Thus, the community has now been given representation in the Legislative Assemblies of all the States in which their population is over two thousand.

Reservation in Services (Art. 336)

Under Article 336, the Anglo-Indian community had been given special consideration with regard to appointments in certain services. Accordingly, during the first two years after the commencement of the Constitution, they would be appointed to posts in the railways, customs, postal and telegraph services on the same basis as immediately before 15 August 1947. This reservation would be progressively reduced at the rate of ten per cent after every two years and it would completely cease at the end of ten years. Such reservation, however, did not bar the members of the community from being appointed to any post under the Government if found qualified for appointment on merit as compared with the members of other communities. It may be mentioned that in spite of such reservation the response from the Anglo-Indians for the posts reserved for them was extremely poor.[2] Since the ten-year period was over long ago, Article 336 has little relevance now.

Grants for Educational Benefits

The Anglo-Indian community was entitled to special educational grants under Article 337 of the Constitution for a period of ten years. During the first three years, this grant would be equal to what the community had been receiving in 1947. Thereafter, it would be progressively reduced at the rate of ten per cent at the end of every three years and it would completely cease as a special concession to the community at the end of ten years. It is further provided that at least forty per cent of the annual admissions in the Anglo-Indian educational institutions receiving such grants should be made available to members of other communities.

These provisions, on the whole, show the genuine desire of the framers of the Constitution to accommodate the special interests of a small community like the Anglo-

1. According to 1951 Census, the total population of Anglo-Indians in India was 111,637 spread over thirteen States and three Union Territories.
2. Report of the Commissioner for Scheduled Castes and Tribes (1957-58), p.154.

Indians and infuse confidence in them. When the British left India in 1947, the Anglo-Indians were apprehensive of their future in free India. But soon, the members of the community found that not only were their interests safe but the leaders of independent India were prepared to give them even special consideration so that they could continue as Indian citizens with hope and confidence.

Scheduled Castes and Tribes

According to the 1971 Census, there were some 123.6 million people who are entitled to the benefits provided under the special provisions of the Constitution. Of these, the Scheduled Castes alone numbered some 82.4 millions. They are divided into several groups and are spread all over the country. The Scheduled Tribes number some 41.1 millions. Most of them are in the States of Bihar, Assam and Madhya Pradesh. The Backward Classes, which include the ex-criminal tribes, have not been precisely defined yet, but they are believed to number over 5 million.

Reservation in Legislatures

Under Article 330, a certain number of seats are reserved for the Scheduled Castes and Tribes in the House of the People. The number of these seats is in proportion to their population and is specified in the list of seats allotted to each State. As has been pointed out earlier, there are no separate electorates for these communities. During the first two General Elections they were returned through reservation in plural constituencies where each voter had two votes-one for the general seat and the other for the reserved seat. That system has now given place to one under which separate single member constituencies are specially earmarked for them. At present, there are 119 seats reserved in the House of the People for these communities. Of these 79 are reserved for the Scheduled Castes and the rest for the Scheduled Tribes. (See table No.1).

Not only in Parliament but also in the State Legislatures, the political interests of the Scheduled Castes and Tribes are protected by reservation. Here again, the method adopted is the same, namely, that of special constituencies, and representation proportionate to the population. (See table No.2).

Reservation of a prescribed number of seats in the House of the People and the State Legislative Assemblies does not mean that the maximum number of seats available to the Scheduled Castes and Tribes is limited to such reservation. On the contrary, members of these communities are free to contest as many additional seats as they choose to do. For example, in the Third General Elections, in addition to the reserved seats, six members from the Scheduled Castes and three from the Scheduled Tribes were returned to the Lok Sabha against unreserved seats. Thus in a House of 494 elected seats, members of these two communities had a total of 116 seats. Similarly, in the State Assemblies too, representatives of these communities were elected against fifteen unreserved seats. Of these eight were members of the Scheduled Castes and the rest from Scheduled Tribes. Thus, in a total of 3105 seats [1] in the State Assemblies 706 seats were held by members of these communities. It is also interesting to note in this connection that these figures are proportionately higher than those held by the members of these communities as a result of the earlier General Elections. Under the present provisions of the Constitution, these

1. This figure does not include the 75 seats of the Jammu and Kashmir Assembly.

reservations will last until 2009. Originally, the reservation was only for ten years. But this was extended by another ten years by the Eighth Amendment of the Constitution in 1960 and, again, by another ten years by the Twenty-third Amendment of the Constitution in 1969 and again by the Forty-fifty Amendment in 1980, and again in 1989 by the Sixty-second Amendment and again 1999 by the Seventy-ninth Amendment. This would mean that the reservation would extend to a period of sixty years.

RESERVED SEATS IN LOK SABHA

Name of State/Union Territory	Total No of setas	No. of seats Reserved for	
		Scheduled Castes	Scheduled Tribes
STATES			
1. Andhra Pradesh	42	6	2
2. Arunachal pradesh	1	-	-
3. Assam	14	1	2
4. Bihar	53	8	5
5. Delhi	7	1	-
6. Gujarat	26	2	4
7. Goa, Daman and Diu	2	-	-
8. Haryana	10	2	-
9. Himachal Pradesh	4	1	-
10. Jammu and Kashmir	6	-	-
11. Karnataka	28	4	-
12. Kerala	20	2	-
13. Madhya Pradesh	40	6	9
14. Maharashtra	48	3	4
15. Manipur	2	-	1
16. Meghalaya	2	-	2
17. Mizoram	1	-	-
18. Nagaland	1	-	-
19. Orissa	21	3	5
20. Punjab	13	3	-
21. Rajasthan	25	4	3
22. Sikkim	1	-	-
23. Tamil Nadu	39	7	-
24. Tripura	2	-	1
25. Uttar Pradesh	85	18	-
26. West Bengal	42	8	2

UNION TERRITORIES			
1. Andaman and Nicobar Islands	1	-	-
2. Chandigarh	1	-	-
3. Dadra and Nagar Haveli	1	-	-
4. Lakshadweep (Laccadive)	1	-	-
5. Pondicherry	2	-	-
Special Representation Anglo-Indian	2		
Total	544	79	40

TABLE 2
RESERVED SEATS IN LEGISLATIVE ASSEMBLES

Name of State/Union Territory	*No. of Elected Seats*	*No. of seats Reserved for*	
		Scheduled Castes	*Scheduled Tribes*
STATES			
1. Andhra Pradesh	294	39	15
2. Arunachal Pradesh	30		
3. Assam	126	8	16
4. Bihar	324	48	28
5. Delhi	56	9	
6. Gujarat	182	13	26
7. Goa, Daman and Diu	30	1	
8. Haryana	90	17	-
9. Himachal Pradesh	68	16	3
10. Jammu and Kashmir	76	6	-
11. Karnataka	224	33	2
12. Kerala	140	13	1
13. Madhya Pradesh	320	44	75
14. Maharashtra	288	18	22
15. Manipur	60	1	19
16. Meghalaya	60	-	-
17. Mizoram	30	-	-
18. Nagaland	60	-	-
19. Orissa	147	22	34
20. Punjab	117	29	-
21. Rajasthan	200	33	24
22. Sikkim	32	2	-
23. Tamil Nadu	234	42	3
24. Tripura	60	1	17
25. Uttar Pradesh	425	92	1
26. West Bengal	294	59	17

UNION TERRITORIES			
1. Pondicherry	30	5	-
Total	3997	551	303

Special Consideration in Services

Under Article 335, a general direction to the Union and State Governments is given for giving special consideration to the members of these communities in the services consistent with the maintenance of efficiency in administration. This means that candidates from the Scheduled Castes or Tribes should satisfy at least the minimum educational and other qualifications prescribed for various posts of the different services under the State. It must be noted, however, that there is no fixation of a percentage of jobs in the Constitution for these communities. There is also no fixed period for the continuation of this preferential treatment. Naturally, the State is expected to continue such treatment until these communities make substantial progress educationally and economically and reach a certain level of equality with the rest of the Indian society.

In the light of the constitutional provisions, the Government of India reconsidered the position of the Scheduled Castes and Tribes in 1950. As a result, a new policy was laid down according to which their share of recruitment was fixed at twelve and a half per cent for All India Services on the basis of open competition and sixteen and two-thirds per cent for direct recruitment. The maximum age limit prescribed for them for appointment was also raised by three years. In 1952, this rule was further relaxed raising their age limit to five years above the maximum prescribed for others. All these provisions are also in conformity with the exception provided under Article 16(4) to the Fundamental Right of equality of opportunity in public appointments.

Further, there is a special provision in the Constitution under which, in the States of Bihar, Madhya Pradesh and Orissa, there will be a Minister in charge of Tribal Welfare who may, in addition, be in charge of the welfare of the Scheduled Castes and Backward Classes. At present, there are separate Ministries or Departments for the welfare of these communities in almost all the States. In 1958 there were no less than 17 Ministers and 12 Deputy Ministers in the State Governments belonging to these communities. Besides, there were two Ministers in the Union Government, one of whom was a Cabinet Minister and the other a Deputy Minister. Their position has been steadily improving ever since as every time there was a reconstitution of Ministries, they were better represented.

Special Officer

Under Article 338, the President is empowered to appoint a Special Officer for the Scheduled Castes and Tribes to investigate on all matters relating to the safeguards provided for them under the Constitution, namely (i) representation in legislatures, (ii) claims to representation in services, and (iii) the operation of the Fundamental Rights, and to report to him on these at regular intervals. Under this provision the Special Officer is also entrusted with the interests of the Backward Classes as well as the constitutional safeguards of the Anglo-Indian community.

The first Special Officer, designated as the Scheduled Castes Commissioner, was appointed under this provision in November 1950. He is now assisted by ten Assistant

Regional Commissioners, each in charge of a region. The Commissioner submits every year a report to the President. The report is laid before each House of Parliament.

By virtue of the sixty-fifth Amendment of the Constitution in 1990, the Special Officer's post under Article 338 of the Constitution was substituted by the National Commission for Scheduled Castes and Scheduled Tribes. The Commission consists of a Chairperson and a Vice Chair person and five other members to be appointed by the President. The duties of the Commission include (a) investigation and monitoring of all matters relating to the safeguards provided for the SCs/STs under the Constitution or any other law; (b) Enquiry into specific complaints relating to the deprivation of rights and safeguards of SCs/STs; (c) planning and evaluating the socio-economic development of the SCs and STs; (d) presenting to Parliament annually a report on the working of various safeguards etc.

Parliament is supposed to take suitable action on the reports submitted by the National Commission.

Commissions of Investigation

Under Article 340 of the Constitution, there is provision for the appointment of two Commissions by the President, one to investigate and report on the administration of the Scheduled Areas and the welfare of the Scheduled Tribes and the other to investigate the conditions of socially and educationally backward classes and to make recommendations as to the steps that should be taken by the Union or any State to remove such difficulties. The reports shall be laid before both Houses of Parliament together with statements explaining the government's action on them. The appointment of the first commission within ten years after the commencement of the Constitution was obligatory. Moreover, the Union Executive is empowered to issue directions to the States for implementation of the recommendations of the Commission. The second Commission relating to Backward Classes is optional, and the Union Executive can only advise the States to implement its recommendations. However, it must be emphasized that these are intended to provide the machinery for enquiring into the operation of those Fundamental Rights and Directive Principles which are meant for the advancement of the Backward Classes and the Scheduled Tribes.

Under Article 340 of the constitution, the President appointed the Backward Classes Commission in January 1953. The Commission was charged with the main task of determining the criteria under which any section of the people of India (in addition to the Scheduled Castes and Tribes) should be treated as socially and educationally backward classes; and in accordance with such criteria, prepare a list of such classes setting out their approximate numbers and their territorial distribution. The Commission submitted its Report in March 1955. The Government, after giving careful thought to the Report of the Commission, found it impossible to accept its recommendations. The main drawback of the Report was that the Commission could not find objective tests and criteria for classifying socially and educationally backward classes. The result was a list containing as many as 2,399 communities out of which 913 alone accounted for an estimated population of 115 million. [1]

---

1. *Memorandum on the Report of the Backward Classes Commission,* Ministry of Home Affairs (1956), pp. 1-5.

In its bid to prepare a list of the Backward Classes, the Government of India sought the assistance of the State Governments to make *ad hoc* surveys for determining the precise criteria for the purpose. But the replies received from the State Governments were not satisfactory to the Centre which thereafter entrusted the task to the Office of the Registrar General of India. The Report prepared by that Office forms the basis for determining the list of socially and educationally Backward Classes for the purpose of extending to them governmental help for their progress.

The Constitution vests in the President the power to notify the castes, races and tribes to be included in the Scheduled Castes Lists of a State. But once the notification is issued, his power comes to an end and he cannot revise or modify the list. Any such revision or modification can be made only by Parliament. The same procedure is prescribed for the delimitation of the tribes and tribal communities.[2]

The Union Ministry of Home Affairs is responsible for the formulation and implementation of schemes for the welfare of the Scheduled Castes and Scheduled Tribes and other backward classes and maintains liaison with the States.

A Commission for the Scheduled Castes and Tribes consisting of a Chairman and four members, including the Commission for Scheduled Castes and Scheduled Tribes, was set up in August 1978. The Commission is to investigate all matters relating to constitutional safeguards, reservation in public services, to study the implementation of the Protection of Civil Rights Act, 1955, with particular reference to the objective of removal of untouchability and invidious discrimination arising therefrom, and to ascertain the socio-economic and other relevant circumstances responsible for the commission of offences against persons belonging to Scheduled Castes and Tribes with a view to recommending appropriate remedial measures.

The Government of India had also set up three Parliamentary Committees, the first in 1968, the second in 1971 and third in 1973 to examine the implementation of the constitutional safeguards for the welfare of the Scheduled Castes and Schedule Tribes. The Committee has since been constituted as a Standing Committee of Parliament, the tenure of the members being one year. This Committee consists of thirty members, twenty from the Lok Sabha and ten from the Rajya Sabha.

The State Governments and the Union Territory administrations have separate departments to look after the welfare of the Scheduled Castes and Tribes and other backward classes. The administrative set up in this connection varies from State to State. In Bihar, Madhya Pradesh and Orissa, separate Ministers have been appointed to look after Tribal welfare as prescribed under Article 164 of the Constitution. Some other States have set up committees of members of State Legislature on the pattern of the Parliamentary Committee at the Centre.

States with a large population of Scheduled Castes have set up Scheduled Castes Development Corporations which have branches or subsidiaries at the district level. The Corporation is intended to perform the role of the catalyst. It will organize assistance to scheduled caste families for the provision of income generating assets. The specific problems

1. For details regarding the Scheduled Castes and Tribes including their names and the States and other areas to which they belong, see Parts I to XII of the Schedule to the Constitution (Scheduled Castes) Order, 1950; p. 398 onwards of the Constitution of India (as modified up to 19 May 1972). Government of India Press.

of the Scheduled Castes which have been largely by passed by the general sector programmes are expected to be tackled effectively in this way.

Strategy for Tribal Development

In the Fifth Plan a new strategy for tribal development was evolved. According to the strategy, areas having 50 or more percent of tribal concentration were delineated and tribal sub-plan prepared in 18 States and Union Territories namely, Andhra Pradesh, Assam, Bihar, Gujarat, Himachal Pradesh, Karnataka, Kerala, Madhya Pradesh, Maharashtra, Manipur, Orissa, Rajashtan, Tamil Nadu, Tripura, Uttar Pradesh, West Bengal, Andaman and Nicobar Islands and Goa, Daman and Diu. The states and union territories with predominant tribal population, namely, Aruanachal Pradesh, Meghalaya, Mizoram, Nagaland and Lakshadweep and Dadra and Nagar Haveli were not included in the tribal sub-plan approach as their state plans are, in fact, plans for the development of the tribal people.

The broad objectives of the tribal sub-plan are (i) to narrow the gap between the levels of development of tribal areas and other areas; and (ii) to improve the quality of life of the tribal communities.

In order to achieve these objectives elimination of all forms of exploitation of tribals particularly in land, money-lending, malpractices in the exchange of agricultural and forest produce was given high priority. The tribal sub-plans envisaged total physical and financial efforts for integrated development of the tribal areas. The investments in the sub-plan areas flow from state plans, central outlays from central ministries and departments, institutional finance and special central assistance. During the Fifth Five Year Plan (1974-78) the outlay under special central assistance was Rs. 1200 million. During the Sixth Plan 1980-85, the outlay for special central assistance has been kept at Rs. 6000 million.

The tribal sub-plan areas in the 18 states and union territories are grouped into 180 Integrated Tribal Development Projects as operational units. During the Sixth Plan, Tribal majority pockets which have a total population of 10,000 and 50 per cent or more of tribal population, are also to be taken up under the modified Area Development Approach as a part of the tribal sub-plan strategy. The concept of tribal sub-plan itself has been kept flexible and has been adapted to the local situation. Programmes undertaken include, agriculture and allied sectors, irrigation, ,marketing, co-operation, education, *etc.* The most backward groups among the tribal primitive tribes are given special attention by preparing separate plans for them.

Central Schemes as a Whole

The plan programmes for the welfare of backward classes fall into three main groups: centrally-operated, centrally-sponsored and state sector. Important schemes being implemented under these categories are briefly described below.

With a view to helping the scheduled castes and scheduled tribes to secure employment, two schemes, namely, pre-examination training centres and coaching-cum-guidance centres, have been started. Under the first scheme, there are seven centres located at Allahabad and Shillong which impart coaching to scheduled castes and scheduled tribes for all-India services examination conducted by the Union Public Service Commission. Centres for imparting training to candidates for state service examinations have also been set up in the States of Andhra Pradesh, Bihar, Gujarat, Haryana, Karnataka, Kerala, Madhya Pradesh, Orissa, Uttar Pradesh, West Bangal and the Union Territory of Delhi. Two centres for imparting coaching for engineering service examinations have also been set up at Allahabad and Tiruchirapalli.

Four coaching-cum-guidance centres, one each at the employment exchange in Delhi, Kanpur, Jabalpur and Madras have been set up to conduct courses of 'confidence building and interview techniques' for the scheduled caste and scheduled tribe applicants on the live registers of the concerned employment exchanges for Group "C" posts.

Post-matric scholarships to scheduled castes and tribes are awarded to a limit on their guardian's income. The rates of maintenance allowance for medical and engineering degree student hostellers have been increased substantially from January 1978. Book banks have also been started from the academic year 1978-79 for the same category of students.

Under the scheme, financial assistance is given to state and union territory governments for the construction of new hostels and to expand existing ones at any place where the facilities for girls belonging to these classes are inadequate. A sum of Rs. 19.6 million was spent on the scheme during the Fourth Plan. This sum was substantially increased subsequently.

There are at present 11 Tribal Research Institutes in the country. To co-ordinate their activities, a 30-member Central Research Advisory Council has been set up. The Council provides guidance on policy formulation and services as a clearing house for the Institutes, central and state governments and other research organizations connected with tribal problems.

Scholarships to deserving scheduled castes and scheduled tribes students for studies in foreign countries are being awarded by the union government since 1955. The number of such scholarships every year is 10 for scheduled castes, six for scheduled tribes, one for denotified nomadic and semi-nomadic tribes and three for other backward classes and one for neo-Buddhist. Tourist class air passage is also provided to students who receive foreign scholarships from other sources without travel grants.

Table 3

Percentage Progress in Employment of SCs/STs from 1971 to 1991 in Central Government Services

Category	Group 'A' 1971-91	Group 'B' 1971-91	Group 'C' 1971-91	Group 'D' 1971-91
SC	2.6–9.1	4.1–11.8	9.6–15.7	18.4–21.2
ST	0.4–2.5	0.4–2.4	1.7–4.9	3.7–6.8

Source: Planning Commission, Government of India, Eighth Five-Year Plan: 1992-1997, Vol. II, P.49.

In the course of the last five decades and more, the Scheduled Castes, Scheduled Tribes and Backward Classes have made remarkable progress. Fifty years back, they were some of the most backward peoples anywhere in the world. Most of them were the so-called 'Untouchables' with the lowest social status and living in abject poverty, ignorance and illiteracy. But today, many of them have climbed considerable heights in the social ladder and many more are fast following them. Every successive Report of the

Commissioner registers the all-round increase in the tempo of the work relating to the welfare of these classes. Perhaps, the original provision in the Constitution where it deals with these classes is the provision for the appointment of a Special Officer charged with the responsibility of watching the progress of these communities.

The drive towards the rapid alround progress of these communities is directed mainly through three channels, the social, the economic and the educational. In the social field, the campaign for the removal of untouchability is gathering momentum and has already produced excellent results. The general awareness that the members of the Scheduled Castes and Tribes are fellow citizens with equal rights and privileges and are entitled to the same courtesy and consideration is fast growing among the so-called upper castes. In the economic field, with the enactment of many labour welfare laws, minimum wage laws, co-operative and land distribution laws, they are making substantial progress. Many cottage industries such as weaving and leather industries are providing members of these communities an additional income. The greatest stress has been laid on the provisions for educational facilities and the progress in this field has been indeed remarkable. Thousands of fellowships, scholarships, studentships and freeships are given every year to the members of these communities by the Union and the State Governments. A sum of over Rs. 300 million was spent for the welfare of these communities under the first Five Year Plan with extremely encouraging results. Under the Second Plan the amount so spent was Rs. 794 million. The Third Plan provided for programmes estimated to cost about Rs. 1004 million. The Fourth Plan placed the figure for the same purpose at Rs. 1727 million. The corresponding figures for the Fifth and Sixth Plans are Rs. 2888 and Rs. 2400 respectively. In addition, the Sixth Plan provides also for special Central assistance of Rs. 5500 million for the Scheduled Castes and Rs. 4700 million for the Scheduled Tribes. Every successive Five Year Plan has been increasing the financial assistance to the Scheduled Castes and Tribes substantially. Thus with the active interest of the State in the rapid advancement of these communities there is every reason to hope that they will soon catch up with the rest of the Indian society and play an equally vital role in the all-round progress of the nation.

To Gandhi, the father of the Nation, the Scheduled Castes were *harijans*, the people of God. One of his life-goals was the amelioration of the lot of the *harijan* and to lead him out of the centuries-old social degradation to which he had descended. During his own lifetime a large part of his time and energy was directed towards this task and, to some extent at least, he was successful in his efforts. But the problem was so deeply involved in the socio-economic fabric of India and the task was so stupendous that a single individual's efforts, however great or powerful he might be, could not produce the desired results in a limited time. It is gratifying to note in this context that the Constitution and the different governments established under it at the Centre as well as in the States played a role of signal importance to translate the Gandhian ideal into reality. While the achievements so far have been significant, there is still a long way to go to eradicate completely the deep-seated social prejudices, the economic backwardness and political handicaps of the Scheduled Castes, Tribes and other backward classes.

***

47

AMENDMENT OF THE CONSTITUTION

FEDERAL CONSTITUTIONS as a rule are rigid as most of them have extremely difficult and even complicated procedures of amendment. Amending a federal constitution like that of the United States is perhaps the most difficult. Under the Australian Constitution, too, the amending process is complex. In contrast, the Constitution of India presents a much simpler picture.

A constitution is a fundamental document. It is a document which defines the position and powers of the three organs of the State, the Executive, the Legislature and the Judiciary. It also defines the powers of the Executive and the Legislature as against the citizens. In fact, the purpose of a constitution is not merely to create the organs of the State but also to limit their authority because if no limitation is imposed upon the authority of the organs, there will be tyranny and oppression. Naturally, such a fundamental document as a constitution should not undergo too frequent and easy changes as that would undermine the confidence of the citizens in the abiding nature of the constitution. Further, it would make it impossible to provide a reasonably ascertainable standard against which the conduct of the various organs of government can be measured. The case of a federal constitution is particularly significant in this context because it delimits not only the powers of the different organs of government but also achieves a balance which is often delicate between the Centre and the units of the federation. These considerations are powerful enough to preserve intact the original document which gives expression to the manner in which the governmental system is to be ordered into existence. As such, any amendment of a constitution should be justified by compelling reasons and circumstances.

It should be understood at the same time that a constitution is a dynamic document. It should grow with a growing nation and should suit the changing needs and circumstances of a growing and changing people. Sometimes, under the impact of new, powerful, social and economic forces, the pattern of government will require major changes. If a constitution stands as a stumbling block to such desirable changes, it may, under extreme pressure, be destroyed. A constitution as such cannot have any claim to permanence; nor should it, because it has been adopted and has been working ever since, claim sanctity. As Prime Minister Nehru pointed out in the Constituent Assembly:

> When we want this Constitution to be as solid and permanent as we can make it, there is no permanence in constitutions. There should be a certain flexibility. If you make anything rigid and permanent, you stop the nation's growth of living, vital, organic people. ….. In any event, we could not make this constitution so rigid that it cannot be adapted to changing conditions.

When the world is in turmoil and we are passing through a very swift period of transition, what we may do today may not be wholly applicable tomorrow[1].

So long as the government established under the Constitution continues to be a responsible government, so long as there is parliamentary democracy where, as Ambedkar said, "the government is all the time on the anvil, on trial, responsible to the people, responsible to the judiciary", constitutional changes are nothing but a reflection of the needs of the nation that it serves. The Constitution should facilitate such changes smoothly and easily. These were the basic considerations that guided the framers of the Constitution in formulating the principles governing any amendment of the Constitution.

Speaking on these principles, Ambedkar said that the provisions for amendment, while they embodied a certain measure of rigidity with regard to some parts of the Constitution, were flexible and afforded facilities for a simple process of amendment with regard to others. Pointing out the details of the scheme, he stated:

....We propose to divide the various articles of the Constitution into three categories. In one category we have placed certain articles which would he open to amendment by Parliament by simple majority. (Provisions such as those which deal with the establishment or abolition of Upper Houses in the States are examples of this type.) The second set of articles (for amendment) require a two thirds majority of Parliament. (Parts III and IV of the Constitution which deal with the Fundamental Rights and Directive Principles respectively belong to this category.) The third category requires a two-thirds majority of Parliament plus ratification by the States. The States are given an important voice in the amendment of these matters. These are fundamental matters where States have important powers under the Constitution and any unilateral amendment by Parliament may vitally affect the fundamental basis of the system built up by the Constitution. (Provisions dealing with the division of legislative power between the Union and the States fall in this category.) [1]

Article 368

The procedure of amendment is detailed under Article 368 of the Constitution. According to this, an amendment may be initiated only by the introduction of a Bill for the purpose in either House of Parliament. When the Bill is passed in each House by a majority of the total membership of that House and by a majority of not less than two-thirds of the members of that House present and voting, it shall be presented to the President for his assent. When the President gives his assent, the Constitution stands amended in accordance with the terms of the Bill.

But, as pointed out earlier, in the case of certain amendments, ratification by the Legislatures of not less than one half of the States by resolutions to that effect is required before the amending Bill is presented to the President for assent. The following provisions of the Constitution fall under this category:

1. Articles 54 (Election of President), 55 (Manner of election of the President), 73 (Extent of the executive power of the Union), 162 (Extent of the executive power of States), or 241 (High Courts for Union Terrotories)
2. Chapter IV of Part V (The Union Judiciary), Chapter V of Part VI (The High Courts in the States), Chapter I of Part XI (Legislative relations between the Union and the States);

1. C.A.D. IX, p. 1569.

3. Any of the Lists in the Seventh Schedule;
4. The representation of States in Parliament; and
5. Provisions dealing with amendment of the Constitution.

There is hardly another federal constitution which provides a comparable example, combining rigidity and flexibility in a manner exemplified in the above-mentioned provisions.[1] They show that:

> ...[T]he Assembly has not only refrained from putting a seal of finality and infallibility upon the Constitution by denying the people the right to amend the Constitution as in Canada, or by making the amendment of the Constitution subject to the fulfilment of extraordinary terms and conditions as in America or Australia, but has provided a most facile procedure.[2]

Yet, there were may critics of the amending provisions of the Constitution. Some of them thought that these provisions were inflexible. "Why should a two-thirds majority be imposed on the future Parliament to amend the Constitution while the Constituent Assembly could settle it by a simply majority? The Constitution should be amendable by a simple majority at least for some years." Dealing with this criticism Ambedkar said that the argument was subtle and ingenious:

> It is said that this Constituent Assembly is not elected on adult suffrage while the future Parliament will be elected on adult suffrage and yet the former has been given the right to pass the Constitution by a simple majority while the latter has been denied the same right. It is paraded as one of the absurdities of the Constitution. I must repudiate the charge because it is without foundation.....
>
> What is said to be the absurdity of the amending provisions is founded upon a misconception of the Constituent Assembly and of the future Parliament. The Constituent Assembly in making constitution has no partisan motive. Beyond securing a good and workable constitution it has no eye on getting through a particular measure. The future parliament, if it met as a Constituent Assembly, its members will be acting as partisans seeking to carry amendments to the Constitution to facilitate the passing of party measures which they have failed to get through Parliament by reason of some Article of the Constitution which has acted as an obstacle in their way. Parliament will have an axe to grind while the Constituent Assembly has none. That is the difference between the Constituent Assembly and the future Parliament. That explains why the Constituent Assembly though elected on limited franchise can be trusted to pass the Constitution by simple majority and why the Parliament though elected on adult suffrage cannot be trusted with the same power to amend it.[3]

During the first seven years of the Constitution it was amended seven times. In the next seven years there had been ten more amendments. In the next twelve years, the number of amendments went up by another twenty-five. Such rapid succession of amendments during such a short time in the life of the Constitution has been attacked by many of its critics as a sign of weakness in the Constitution. Some of them thought that the Constitution should not be made so cheap as to admit of amendment so quickly and easily.[4] There is an element of truth in this criticism. Yet, on close examination, it will be seen that there

---

1. Some members in the Constituent Assembly, however, were not happy about the flexible character of the amending provisions. See C.A.D. VII, P.384.
2. Ambedkar, C.A.D.X, p.975.
3. C.A.D.VII, p.43.
4. For example, see the debates in the various State Assemblies and Parliament on the Third Amendment of the Constitution.

were compelling circumstances which led to constitutional amendment during a momentous period of stabilization and consolidation of the political freedom won just a decade earlier. While some of the amendments were a natural product of the eventual evolution of the new political system established under the Constitution in 1950, there were others necessitated by practical difficulties in the working of certain provisions of the Constitution. The reorganization of States and the consequent constitutional amendment is the best example of the former type while the amendments dealing with the right to property provides a good example of the latter type.

For seventeen years since the inauguration of the Constitution there was no doubt about the meaning of Article 368 of the Constitution dealing with Amendment. During that period there were as many as twenty Amendments. Of these, the First, Fourth and the Seventeenth Amendments had dealt with Fundamental Rights and Parliament's right to amend any provision of the constitution in accordance with the procedure laid down in Part XX of the Constitution was never questioned. (The First Amendment Act, 1951, was challenged, among others, on the ground that it was passed by the Provisional Parliament consisting of only one House whereas the amending procedure laid down in the Constitution envisaged two House—the Lok Sabha and the Rajya Sabha.[1] The Supreme Court did not accept this argument and upheld the competence of Parliament as it was then constituted to amend the Constitution including Fundamental Rights. The Court reaffirmed its stand regarding Parliament's competence to amend Fundamental Rights in 1965 in the Sajjan Singh case.[2] Thus until 1967 the law as embodied in the Constitution as well as interpreted by the Supreme Court was that Parliament had the power to amend the Constitution. In 1967, however, the Court by its decision in the Golak Nath Case [3] amended the law and declared by a majority of six against five that Parliament had no 'power' to amend the Fundamental Rights embodied in Part III of the Constitution. This virtually meant that through its interpretational authority the Supreme Court had brought about a fundamental change in the meaning of the Constitution. The main argument of the majority in the meaning of the Constitution. The main argument of the majority in this decision was that Part XX of the Constitution deals with the 'procedure' for passing amending bills. What provisions of the Constitution can be amended depends on the 'power' of Parliament. This power can be seen where the federal power of law-making is given to Parliament under Articles 245, 246 and 248 read with the Seventh Schedule of the Constitution. So read, the 'power' is to be found under the last residuary item 97 of List I. It was in this connection that the majority pointed out that since this was an ordinary topic of legislation it would be caught by the clutches of Article 13(2) if the amendment infringed any Fundamental Rights. Thus, with the decision of the Court in the Golak Nath Case, parliament became incompetent to amend any of the Fundamental Rights, i.e. Articles 12 to 35 of the Constitution.

The Golak Nath decision has undoubtedly been the most controversial of all decisions of the Supreme Court of India. In fact, that decision made even the very role of the Court under the Constitution controversial. It was indeed a case of judges making law and not merely declaring it.

Naturally, this was resented by many members in Parliament as an unwarranted

---

1. Shankari Prasad Case, A.I.R.1951, S.C. 458.
2. A.I.R. 1965, S.C. 845.
3. A.I.R. 1967, S.C. 1643.

invasion on Parliament's authority. To meet this new situation and restore to Parliament what was taken away by the Golak Nath decision (the power to amend Fundamental Rights) a bill to amend Article 268 was introduced by Nath Pai in the Lok Sabha in 1967. A Select Committee was appointed which, after examining witnesses, submitted a report. In the meantime, the Supreme Court gave its verdict in Gujarat vs. Shantilal Mangaldas [1] giving effect to the Fourth amendment which made the adequacy of compensation non-justiciable. It is perhaps this decision or the uncertainty of getting Nath Pai's Bill passed, or both, that contributed to keep the Bill in cold storage. In 1970, however, the Court again reversed its stand through its decision in the Bank Nationalization Case[2] and nullified that effect of the Fourth Amendment which it had restored earlier. A year later, by its decision in the Privy Purse case,[3] the Court reaffirmed its stand in the Nationalization Case. The fifth General Elections were held soon after. The Government came back with an overwhelming majority in the Lok Sabha and the Twenty-Fourth Amendment of the Constitution reestablishing its "power" to amend any part of the Constitution in the following terms.

Be it enacted by Parliament in the Twenty-second year of the Republic of India as follows:

1. This Act may be called the Constitution (Twenty-Fourth Amendment) Act, 1971.

2. In Article 13 of the Constitution, after clause (3), the following clause shall be inserted, namely:

"(4) Nothing in this article shall apply to any amendment of this Constitution made under Article 368"

3. Article 368 of the Constitution shall be re-numbered as clause (2) thereof, and-

(a) for the marginal heading to that article, the following marginal heading shall be substituted, namely:

"Power of parliament to amend the Constitution and procedure therefor".

(b) before clause (92) as so re-numbered, the following clause shall be inserted, namely:

"(1) Notwithstanding anything in this Constitution, Parliament may in exercise of its constituent power amend by way of addition, variation or repeal any provision of this Constitution in accordance with the procedure laid down in this article.",

(c) in clause (2) as so re-numbered, for the words "it shall be presented to the President for his assent and upon such assent being given to the Bill" the words "it shall be presented to the President who shall give this assent to the Bill and thereupon" shall be substituted;

(d) after clause (2) as so re-numbered, the following clause shall be inserted, namely:

(3) Nothing in Article 13 shall apply to any amendment made under this article".

Subsequently, Parliament passed the Twenty-Fifth amendment Act, 1971 amending further Article 31 of the Constitution dealing with the Right to Property. Again, it passed the Twenty-Ninth Amendment Act, 1971, to enable the inclusion of two Kerala Acts dealing with land reforms in the Ninth Schedule of the Constitution.

---

1. (1969) 3 S.C.R. 341.
2. R.C. Cooper vs. Union of India (1980) 3 S.C.R. 530.
3. Madhav Rao vs. Union of India (1970) 3 S.C.R. 9.

The Kerala enactments were challenged as invalid [1] by a group of landlords who contended that their rights to Property safeguarded under Part III of the Constitution were violated by these enactments. On behalf of the Kerala State it was argued that in view of the Twenty-Fourth, Twenty-Fifth and the Twenty-Ninth Amendments of the Constitution, the provisions of the impugned enactments were valid.

Because of the momentous nature of the issues involved, a Special Constitutional Bench consisting of thirteen judges of the Supreme Court was constituted to hear these cases. It was the largest Bench ever constituted to hear any case by the Court. As many as 93 leading lawyers in the country were engaged by the different parties in these cases, including State Governments and the Government of India. Sixty-nine days of arguments made the hearings the longest ever in the history of the Supreme Court. The verdict of the Court was pronounced on 14 April 1973, well over eight months after the cases were admitted on 11 August 1972.

The most significant part of the Court's decision was its unanimous overruling of its earlier decision in Golak Nath Case. Parliament was "given back" its "power" to amend Fundamental Rights. The Court upheld the Twenty-Fourth, the Twenty-Fifth and the Twenty-Ninth Amendments of the Constitution.

In the words of Justice A.N. Ray, "The power to amend is wide and unlimited and this means the power to add, alter or repeal any provision of the Constitution. There can be no distinction between essential and inessential features of the Constitution to raise any impediment to amendment of alleged essential features. Parliament in exercise of constituent power can amend any provision of the Constitution."

According to Justice K.K. Mathew, "The power to amend under Article 368 as it stood before the twenty-Fourth Amendment was plenary in character and extended to all the provisions of the Constitution."

Emphasizing the need for amending the Constitution, including the Fundamental Rights, Justice H.R. Khanna said that "no generation has a monopoly of wisdom nor has it a right to place fetters on future generations to mould the machinery of governments". Provision for amendment of the Constitution, he pointed out, was made with a view to overcoming the difficulties which might be encountered in future in the working of the Constitution. "If no provision were made for amendment of the Constitution, the people would have recourse to extra-constitutional methods like revolution to change the Constitution", he observed. Dealing with the argument that there is possibility for abusing the power of amendment by Parliament, justice Khanna said that it was no ground for denying its existence. "The best safeguard against abuse of power is public opinion and the good sense of the majority of the members of Parliament. It was also not correct to assume that if Parliament was held entitled to amend the Constitution, it would automatically and necessarily result in abrogation of all Fundamental Rights".

"The power of amendment under Article 368", according to Justice Khanna, "does not include the power to alter the basic structure or framework of the Constitution. Subject to the retention of the basic structure or framework of the Constitution, the power of amendment is plenary and includes within itself the power to amend the various Articles of the Constitution, including those relating to Fundamental Rights as well as those which

1. In Kesavanada's case (1973), Supp. S.C.R.1.

may be said to relate to essential features. No part of a Fundamental Right can claim immunity from amendatory process by being described as essence or core of that right. The power of amendment would also include within itself the power to add, alter or repeal the various Articles."

The decisions of different judges in the Kesavananda case, however, showed the conflicting views that still prevailed then. Yet, for the first time, nine of the thirteen judges thought it fit to give the following summary of conclusions which the majority had reached:

1. Golak Nath's case is overruled.

2. Article 368 does not enable Parliament to alter the basic structure or framework of the Constitution.

3. The Constitution (Twenty-fourth Amendment) Act, 1971, is valid.

4. Sections 2(a) and 2(b) of the Constitution (Twenty-fifth Amendment) Act, 1971, are valid.

5. The first part of Section 3 of the Constitution (Twenty-fifth Amendment) Act, 1971, is valid. The second part, namely, "and no law containing a declaration that it is for giving effect to such policy shall be called in question in any court on the ground that it does not give effect to such policy," is invalid.

6. The Constitution (Twenty-ninth Amendment) Act, 1971, is valid. The Constitution Bench will determine the validity of the Constitution (Twenty-sixth Amendment) Act, 1971 (relating to abolition of Privy Purses and privileges of princes) in accordance with law.

By the year 2000 the constitution was amended 82 times.

We have dealt with the various amendments while discussing the relevant parts of the Constitution. Nevertheless, it seems appropriate here to recount them in the chronological order.

The First Amendment (1951) amended Articles 15, 19, 31, 85, 87, 174, 176, 341, 342, 372 and 376. It also added a new Schedule (Ninth Schedule) to the Constitution. The main purpose of the amendment was the removal of certain practical difficulties experienced in the working of some of the fundamental rights, particularly rights under equality before law, freedom of speech, and the right to property.

This Amendment was passed by the Provisional Parliament which existed between the date of commencement of the Constitution (26 January 1950) and the First General Elections (1951). It consisted of only one House as the bicameral system envisaged under the Constitution was to be constituted after the general elections. The passing of the Amendment by Provisional Parliament was challenged as unconstitutional before the Supreme Court mainly on the ground that the power of amending the Constitution was conferred not on "Parliament" but on the "two Houses of Parliament as designated body" and, therefore, the Provisional Parliament was not competent to exercise the power. [1] The matter was disposed of by a unanimous Court, upholding the validity of the Amendment. It held:

> The power of effecting amendments contemplated in Articles 4, 169 and 240 is explicitly conferred on 'Parliament', that is to say the two Houses of Parliament and the President (Article

1. Shankari Prasad Singh Deo v.s. The Union of India 1951 S.C.J. 775.

79). So in the absence of a clear indication to the contrary, the power of effecting amendments under Article 368 must be presumed to have also been conferred on the same body, namely, Parliament, for the requirement of a different majority, which is merely procedural, can be no reason for entrusting the power to a different body. Each of the component units of Parliament is to play its allotted part in bringing about the amendment of the Constitution. There is no force in the suggestion the Parliament would have been referred to specifically if that body was intended to exercise that power. Having mentioned each House of Parliament and the President separately and assigned to each its appropriate part in bringing about constitutional changes, the makers of the Constitution presumably did not think necessary to refer to the collective designation of the three units.

The Second Amendment (1952) amended Article 81 in order to remove the prescribed limit of 750,000 of the population for one member to be elected to the House of the People. According to the original provision, at least one member was to be elected to the House of the People for every 750,000 of the population. It was further provided that the maximum number of elected members to the House should not be adhered to in practice in the light of the actual size of the country's growing population.

The Third Amendment (1954) brought about changes in the Seventh Schedule consisting of the three legislative lists. As a result, the scope of the Union's legislative power was enlarged by substituting entry 33 of the Concurrent List by a new one, including foodstuffs, cattle fodder, raw cotton and jute as additional items whose production and supply can be controlled by the Union, if expedient in the public interest.

The Fourth Amendment (1955) further amended Article 31 and 31A (Right to Property). It also amended Article 305 and the Ninth Schedule.

The Fifth Amendment (1955) amended Article 3 and provided a new procedure for ascertaining the will of a State Legislature with respect to territorial or boundary changes affecting it.

The Sixth Amendment (1956) further amended the Seventh Schedule. It also amended Articles 269 and 286 dealing with interstate sales tax.

The Seventh Amendment (1956) brought about comprehensive changes in the Constitution. The amendment, as was stated earlier, was primarily concerned with the reorganization of States. Along with such reorganization, a large number of consequential changes had to be effected. Thus, the Amendment affected substantially the First and the Fourth Schedules besides many articles of the Constitution.

The Eighth Amendment (1959) amends Article 334 so as to extend the special provision relating to the reservation of seats for the Scheduled Castes and Scheduled Tribes and the representation of the Anglo-Indian community by nomination in the House of the People and the legislative Assemblies of States for a further period of ten years from 26 January 1960.

The Ninth Amendment (1960) amends the First Schedule to the Constitution in order to give effect to the transfer of certain territories to Pakistan in pursuance of the agreements entered into between the Governments of India and Pakistan in September 1958.

Similarly, the **Tenth Amendment (1961)** integrates the areas of free Dadra and Nagar Haveli with the Union of India and provided for their administration under the regulation-making powers of the President (Article 240).

The Eleventh Amendment (1961) obviates the necessity of the joint meeting of the two Houses of Parliament (Article 66) by constituting them into an electoral college for the election of the Vice-President. It also amended Article 71 so as to make it clear that the election of the President or the Vice-President shall not be challenged on the ground of any vacancy for whatever reason in the appropriate electoral college.

The Twelfth Amendment (1962) integrates Goa, Daman and Diu with the Union of India with effect from 20 December 1961 by adding them to the First Schedule as the eighth Union territory and by providing for their administration under Article 240.

The Thirteenth Amendment (1962) provided, along with the creation of Nagaland as the sixteenth State of the Indian Union under the State of Nagaland Act (1962), for certain special protections to the Nagas. According to these, notwithstanding anything in the Constitution, no Act of Parliament in respect of religious or social practices of the Nagas, Naga customary law and procedure, administration of civil and criminal justice involving decisions according to Naga customary law, and ownership and transfer of land and its resources, shall apply to the State of Nagaland unless the legislative Assembly of Nagaland by a resolution so decides. The Amendment provides also for the vesting of certain special responsibilities in the Governor of Nagaland.

The Fourteenth Amendment (1962) provided for the incorporation of the former French Establishment in India, under the name Pondicherry, as an integral part of the territory of the Indian Union. It also amended Article 81 to increase, from a maximum of twenty to twenty-five, the number of seats assigned in the Lok Sabha for the Union Territories. Further, it inserted a new Article 239A providing for the creation of local Legislatures or Council of Ministers or both in the Union Territories of Himachal Pradesh, Manipur, Tripura, Goa, Daman and Diu, and Pondicherry.

The Fifteenth Amendment (1963) seeks to raise the retiring age of High Court judges from 60 to 62 years. It also empowered the various High Courts to hear cases against the Union Government. Another feature of this Amendment was that it restricted the scope of Government servants to appeal against government decisions in disciplinary matters. Accordingly, they will have only one opportunity as against two opportunities they enjoyed until 1963.

The Sixteenth Amendment (1963) empowered Parliament to make laws providing penalty for any person questioning the sovereignty and integrity of India. Under the provisions of this Amendment, a person shall not be qualified to be chosen to fill a seat in Parliament or in the Legislature of a State unless, *inter alia*, he makes or subscribes before a person authorized by the Election Commission an oath or affirmation that he will bear true faith and allegiance to the Constitution and will uphold the sovereignty and integrity of India.

The Seventeenth Amendment (1964) amends the definition of the term "estate" in Article 31A to include lands held under ryotwari settlement and also other lands in respect of which provisions are normally made in land reform enactments. The Amendment has retrospective effect from 26 January 1950, the day on which the Constitution was inaugurated. It also amends the Ninth Schedule of the Constitution to include therein 44 State enactments relating to land reforms in order to remove any uncertainty or doubt that may arise in regard to their validity.

The Eighteenth Amendment (1966) amends Article 3 of the Constitution to confer power on Parliament to form a new State or Union territory by uniting a part of any State or Union territory to any other State or Union territory.

The Nineteenth Amendment (1966) insaerts Article 324 as a consequence of which the existing provisions for the appointment of Election Tribunals has been abolished.

The Twentieth Amendment (1966) inserts a new Article 233A immediately after Article 233 in order to validate the appointments of District Judges which might not have conformed fully to the different constitutional requirements which were in existence prior to 1966.

The Twenty-first Amendment (1967) amends the Eighth Schedule of the Constitution and includes Sindhi as one of the fifteen languages listed in the Schedule.

The Twenty-second Amendment (1969) inserts a new Article 244A immediately after Article 244 to facilitate the formation of a new autonomous State, Meghalaya, within the State of Assam comprising specified tribal areas. The same Amendment amends Article 275 and also inserts a new Article 371B to provide for the consequential changes arising out of the formation of the new State.

The Twenty-third Amendment (1969) deals with the question of reservation of seats in Parliament and State Assemblies for Scheduled Castes, Scheduled Tribes and Anglo-Indians and further extends the period of reservation by another ten years, which means in effect thirty years from the commencement of the Constitution.

The Twenty-fourth Amendment (1971) amends Articles 13 and 368 with a view to removing all possible doubts regarding the power of Parliament to amend the Constitution and procedure therefor. A new clause was inserted and it reads as follows: "Notwithstanding anything in this Constitution, Parliament may in exercise of its constituent power amend by way of addition, variation or repeal any provision of this Constitution in accordance with the procedure laid down in this Article [368]". The Amendment further provides (1) that "it shall be presented to the President who shall give his assent to the Bill", and (2) that "nothing in Article 13 shall apply to any amendment made under this Article".

The Twenty-fifth Amendment (1971) amends Article 31 and inserts a new Article 31C after Article 31B. The Amendment reads as follows:

In Article 31 of the Constitution,

(a) for clause (2), the following clause shall be substituted, namely:

"(2) No property shall be compulsorily acquired or requisitioned save for a public purpose and save by authority of a law which provides for acquisition or requisitioning of the property for an amount which may be fixed by such law or which may be determined in accordance with such principles and given in such manner as may be specified in such law; and no such law shall be called in question in any court on the ground that the amount so fixed or determined is not adequate or that the whole or any part of such amount is to be given otherwise than in cash:

Provided that in making any law providing for the compulsory acquisition of any property of an educational institution established and administered by a minority referred to in clause (1) of Article 30, the State shall ensure that the amount fixed by or determined under such law for the acquisition of such property is such as would not restrict or abrogate the right guaranteed under that clause."

(b)after clause (2A), the following clause shall be inserted, namely:

"(2B) Nothing in sub-clause (f) of clause (1) of Article 19 shall affect any such law as is referred to in clause (2)"

After Article 31B of the Constitution, the following article shall be inserted, namely:

"31C, Notwithstanding anything contained in Article 13, no law giving effect to the policy of the State towards securing the principles specified in clause (b) or clause (c) of Article 39 shall be deemed to be void on the ground that it is inconsistent with, or takes away or abridges any of the rights conferred by Article 14, Article 19 or Article 31; and no law containing a declaration that it is for giving effect to such policy shall be called in question in any court on the ground that it does not give effect to such policy:

Provided that where such law is made by Legislature of a State, the provisions of this article shall not apply thereto unless such law, having been reserved for the consideration of the President, has received his assent."

The Twenty-sixth Amendment (1971) abolishes Articles 291 and 362 of the Constitution and also inserts a new Article 362A after Article 363. The cumulative effect of these changes is the end of the recognition granted to the former Rulers of Indian States and the abolition of privy purses.

The Twenty-seventh Amendment (1971) amends Articles 239A and 240 and inserts a new Article 371C after 371B facilitating the formation of two new Union Territories in the north-eastern part of the country, namely Mizoram and Arunachal Pradesh.

The Twenty-eighth Amendment (1972) deletes Article 314 of the Constitution, which had given protection to the I.C.S. officers' conditions of service and privileges and inserted a new Article 312-A.

The Twenty-ninth Amendment (1972) amends the Ninth Schedule of the Constitution to include in it two Kerala Acts on Land Reforms, Act 35 of 1969 and Act 25 of 1971.

The Thirtieth Amendment of the Constitution (1972) amended Article 133(1) dealing with appeals from the High Courts to the Supreme Court in civil matters.

The Thirty-first Amendment (1973) raised the upper limit of members in the Lok Sabha from 500 to 525. At the same time, it reduced the upper limit for the representation of the Union Territories from 25 to 20 members.

The Thirty-second Amendment (1974) amended Article 371(1) and inserted Articles 371D and 371E. It also amended Entry 63 of List I of the Seventh Schedule.

The Thirty-fourth Amendment (1974) sought to protect land ceiling and land tenure reform laws (seventeen in all) enacted by thirteen States against litigation. These enactments were added to the 66 Acts which were already included in the Ninth Schedule of the Constitution.

The Thirty-fifth Amendment inserted a new Article 2A after Article 2 of the Constitution conferring on Sikkim the Status of associate state of the Indian Union. It also added a new Schedule-Tenth Schedule-to the Constitution embodying the terms and conditions of association of Sikkim with the Union.

The Thirty-sixth Amendment (1975) provided for the creation of a Legislative Assembly for Sikkim. It also gave representation for Sikkim in the Parliament of India.

The Thirty-seventh Amendment (1975) replaced the existing Pradesh Council in the Union Territory of Arunachal Pradesh by a Legislative Assembly.

The Thirty-eighth Amendment of (1975) amended Articles 123, 213, 239B, 352, 356, 359 and 360. Articles 123 and 213 deal with the powers of the President and the Governor respectively to promulgate ordinances. The amended Articles make the satisfaction of the President or the Governor regarding the existence of circumstance necessitating the promulgation of the Ordinance final and conclusive and declares that it shall not be questioned in any court of law on any ground.

Article 352 deals with the Proclamation of Emergency. Two new clauses (4) and (5) have been added to the Article. The power conferred on the President by clause (4) shall include the power to issue different proclamations on different grounds, war or external aggression, internal disturbance or imminent danger of war or external aggression or internal disturbance, whether or not there is a Proclamation already issued by the President under clause (1) and such proclamation is in operation.

Clause (5): Notwithstanding anything in this Constitution (a) the satisfaction of the President mentioned in clause (1) and clause (3) shall be final and conclusive and shall not be questioned in any Court on any ground.

(b) Subject to the Provisions of clause (2), neither the Supreme Court nor any other Court shall have jurisdiction to entertain any question, on any ground, regarding the validity of (i) declaration made by Proclamation by the President to the effect stated in clause (1); or (ii) the continued operation of such Proclamation.

Amendment of Article 356 : In Article 356, after clause (4), the following clause shall be inserted :

"(5) Notwithstanding anything in this Constitution, the satisfaction of the President mentioned in clause (1) shall be final and conclusive and shall not be questioned in any Court on any ground."

Amendment of Article 359 : In Article 359, after clause (1), the following clause shall be inserted :

"(1A) While an order made under clause (1) mentioning any of the rights conferred by Part III is in operation, nothing in that part conferring those rights shall restrict the power of the State as defined in the said part to make any law or to take any executive action which the State would but for the provisions contained in that part be competent to make or to take, but any law so made shall, to the extent of the incompetency, cease to have effect as soon as the order aforesaid ceases to operate, except as respects things done or omitted to be done before the law so ceases to have effect."

Amendment of Article 360: In Article 360, after clause (4), the following clause shall be inserted:

"(5) Notwithstanding anything in this Constitution-(a) the satisfaction of the President mentioned in clause (1) shall be final and conclusive and shall not be questioned in any court on any ground; (b) subject to the provisions of clause (2) neither the Supreme Court nor any other Court shall have jurisdiction to entertain any question, on any ground regarding the validity of (1) a declaration made by Proclamation by the President to the effect stated in clause (1); or (2) the continued operation of such proclamation."

The Thirty-ninth Amendment (1975) amends Article 71 dealing with the election of the President and the Vice President, According to this amendment, Parliament may by law regulate any matter relating to or connected with the election of the President or the Vice President including the grounds on which such election may be questioned provided that the election of a person as President or Vice President shall not be called in question on the ground of the existence of any vacancy for whatever reason among the members of the electoral college electing him.

(2) All doubts and disputes arising out of the election of the President or Vice President shall be inquired into and decided by such authority or body and in such manner as may be provided for by or under any law referred to in clause (1).

(3) The validity of any such law as is referred to in clause (1) and the decision of any authority or body under such law shall not be called in question in any Court.

The Fortieth Amendment (1975) further amends the Ninth Schedule of the Constitution to include 38 more legislative enactments dealing with a variety of subjects including land reforms, industrial development, conservation of foreign exchange, etc.

The Forty-first Amendment (1976) raised the retirement age of the members of the State Public Service Commissions from 60 to 62.

Forty-second Amendment (1976)

Of all the amendments of the Constitution during a period of twenty-six years since its inauguration, the Forty-second Amendment stands out as the most comprehensive. It also became the most controversial. No proposal for amendment of the Constitution had attracted so much attention and criticism in the past as this amendment.

The Union Law Minister, who piloted the Bill claimed on its behalf that "a Constitution to be living must be growing. If the impediments to the growth of the Constitution are not removed, it will suffer a virtual atrophy. The Amendment was necessitated for removing the difficulties which had arisen in achieving the objective of socio-economic revolution which would end poverty and ignorance, disease and inequality of opportunity. The democratic institutions provided in the Constitution are basically sound and the path for progress does not lie in denigrating any of these institutions. However, there could be no denial that these institutions have been subjected to considerable stresses and strains and that vested interests have been trying to promote their selfish end to the great detriment of the public good".

Those who criticized and opposed the amendments alleged that they were intended to destroy the democratic character of the Constitution as it was originally enacted and it was a determined attempt to pave the way for the eventual establishment of a dictatorial regime.

Briefly the Amendment brings about changes in the following provisions of the Constitution; Preamble; Fundamental Rights (Arts. 31 and 32); Directive Principle of State Policy (Arts. 32, 43 and 48); A new Part, Part IV-A entitled "Fundamental Duties"; Union Executive (Arts. 55, 74 and 77); Parliament (Arts. 81, 82, 83, 100, 103, 105 and 118); Union Judiciary (Arts. 131, 139, 144 and 145); Comptroller and Auditor-General of India (Arts 150); State Executive (Art. 166); State Legislature (Arts. 170, 172, 189, 191, 192, 194 and 208); High Courts (Arts. 217, 226, 227 and 228); Relations between the Union and the States (Art. 257); Service (Arts. 311 and 312); A new Part entitled

"Tribunals" (Art 323); Emergency Provisions (Arts. 352, 353, 356, 357, 358, and 366); Amendment of the Constitution (Art. 368); Seventh Schedule (Union List, State List and the Concurrent (List).

Forty-third Amendment (1978)

The Forty-third Amendment deleted Article 31D, which was a part of the Forty-second Amendment and which had empowered Parliament to deal with anti-national activities. The Amendment also restored the power of the Supreme Court to decide on the constitutionality of State laws and that of the High Courts to go into the constitutional validity of Central laws which they had lost under the Forty-second Amendment. The Amendment also specifies that the duration of the House of the People and of the State Assemblies shall be five years and not six years as was made by the 42nd Amendment.

Forty-fourth Amendment (1979)

The Forty-fourth Amendment (1979) aims at correcting some of the distortions which crept into the Constitution as a result of the adoption of the Forty-second amendment. The most important among them are: Article 22(4) is amended to make the conditions of preventive detention more rigorous in the interest of the individual. Article 31 which deals with the right to property has been altogether omitted. Consequently changes have been made in Articles 31A and 31C. Also Article 19 was amended to take away the right to acquire, hold and dispose of property as a fundamental right. The following proviso was added to Article 74; "Provided that the President may require the Council of Ministers to reconsider such advice, either generally or otherwise, and the President shall act in accordance with the advice tendered after such reconsideration." The Forty-second amendment had made the duration of the Lok Sabha and Legislative Assemblies of the States six years. These have been amended to restore the original position, namely, five years. In Article 352 dealing with emergency provisions, the words "internal disturbance" was omitted and "armed rebellion" was substituted. Also Article 356 was amended to reduce the period of President's rule in a State from one year to six months at a time and the total period not to exceed one year.

Forty-fifth Amendment (1980)

The Forty-fifth amendment (1980) seeks to extend the reservation of seats for Scheduled Castes and Scheduled Tribes and the representation of Anglo-Indians in the Lok Sabha and the State Assemblies for ten years. This means that these reservations will now be available until January 25, 1990.

Forty-sixth Amendment (1982)

The forty-sixth amendment (1982) enables the State Governments to plug loop holes and realise sales tax dues on the one hand and on the other aims at bringing about some uniformity in tax rates in case of certain items.

The Constitution (Forty-seventh Amendment) Act, 1984

This amendment is intended to provide for the inclusion of certain land reforms Acts in the Ninth Schedule to the Constitution with a view to obviating the scope of litigation hampering the implementation process of those Acts.

The Constitution (Forty-eighth Amendment) Act, 1984

The proclamation issued by the President under article 356 of the Constitution with respect to the State of Punjab could not be continued in force for more than one year unless the special conditions mentioned in clause (5) of the said article were satisfied. As it was felt that the continued force of the said proclamation was necessary, therefore the present amendment was effected so as to make the conditions mentioned in clause (5) of article 356 inapplicable in the instant case.

The Constitution (Forty-ninth Amendment) Act, 1984

The Government of Tripura recommended that the provisions of the Sixth Schedule of the Constitution may be made applicable to the tribal areas of that State. The amendment involved in this Act is intended to give a constitutional security to the autonomous District Council functioning in the State.

The Constitution (Fiftieth Amendment) Act, 1984

By article 33 of the Constitution, Parliament was empowered to enact laws determining to what extent any of the rights conferred by Part III of the Constitution shall, in their application to the members of the Armed Forces or the Forces charged with the maintenance of public order, be restricted or abrogated so as to ensure the proper discharge of their duties and the maintenance of discipline among them.

Article 33 was amended so as to bring within its ambit –

(i) the members of the Forces charged with the protection of property belonging to, or in the charge or possession, of the State, or

(ii) persons employed in any bureau or other organisation established by the State for purposes of intelligence or counter-intelligence; or

(iii) persons employed in, or in connection with, the telecommunication systems set up for the purpose of any Force, bureau or organisation.

Experience has revealed that the need for ensuring proper discharge of their duties and the maintenance of discipline among them was of paramount importance in the national interest.

The Constitution (Fifty-first Amendment) Act, 1984

Article 330 has been amended by this Act for providing reservation of seat for the Scheduled Tribes in Meghalaya, Nagaland, Arunachal Pradesh and Mizoram in the Parliament and Article 332 has been amended to provide similar reservation in the legislative assemblies of Nagaland and Meghalaya to meet the aspirations of the local tribal population.

The Constitution (Fifty-second Amendment) Act, 1985

It amends the Constitution to provide that a member of Parliament or a State Legislature who defects or is expelled from the Party which set him up as a candidate in the election or if an independent member of the House joins a political party six months from the date on which he takes seat in the House shall be disqualified to remain a member of the House. The Act also makes suitable provisions with respect to splits in, and merger of political parties.

The Constitution (Fifty-third Amendment) Act 1986

This has been enacted to give effect to the Memorandum of Settlement of Mizoram which was signed by the Government of India and the Government of Mizoram with the Mizoram National Front on 30 June, 1986. For this purpose, a new article 371 G has been inserted in the constitution inter alia preventing application of any Act of Parliament in the State of Mizoram in respect of religioum or social practices of the Mizos' Customary law and procedure. Administration of civil and criminal practice involving decisions according to Mizos' Customary law and ownership and transfer of land unless a resolution is passed in the Legislative Assembly to that effect. This, however, will not apply to any Central Act already in force in the State of Mizoram before the commencement of this amendment. The new article also provides that the Legislative Assembly of Mizoram shall consist of not less then forty members.

The Constitution (Fifty-fourth Amendment) Act, 1986

The Act increases the salaries of the Supreme Court and High Court Judges and detailed below :

Chief Justice of India	...Rs. 10,000 per month
Judges of the Supreme Court	...Rs. 9,000 per month
Chief Justice of the High Court	...Rs. 9,000 per month
Judges of a High Court	...Rs. 8,000 per month

This Act amended Part 'D' of the Second Schedule to the Constitution to give effect to the above increases in the salaries of Judges and to make an enabling provision in articles 125 and 221 to provide for changes in the salaries of Judges in future by Parliament by law.

The Constitution (Fifty-fifth Amendment) Act, 1986

This Amendment seeks to give effect to the proposal of the Government of India to confer statehood on the Union Territory of Arunachal Pradesh and for this purpose, a new Article 371H has been inserted which, inter alia, confers, having regard to the sensitive location of Arunachal Pradesh, special responsibility on the Governor of the new State of Arunachal Pradesh with respect to law and order in the State and in the discharge of his functions the Governor shall after consulting the Council of Ministers exercise his individual judgement, as to the action to be taken and this responsibility shall cease when the President so directs. The new article also provides that the new Legislative Assembly of the new State of Arunachal Pradesh shall consist of not less than thirty members.

The Constitution (Fifty-sixth Amendment) Act, 1987

The Government of India had proposed to constitute the territories comprised in the Goa district of the Union Territory of Goa, Daman and Diu as the State of Goa and territories comprised in the Daman and Diu districts of that Union Territory as a new Union Territory of Daman and Diu. In this context, it was proposed that the Legislative Assembly of the new State of Goa shall consist of forty members. The existing legislative Assembly of the Union Territory of Goa, Daman and Diu had thirty elected members and three nominated members. It was intended to make this Assembly with the exclusion of two members representing Daman and Diu Districts the provisional Legislative Assembly for the new State of Goa until elections were held on the expiry of the five year term of the existing Assembly. It was, therefore, decided to provide that the Legislative Assembly of the new State of Goa shall consist of not less than 30 members. The special provision required to be made to give effect to this proposal was carried out by this amendment.

The Constitution (Fifty-seventh Amendment) Act, 1987

The Constitution (Fifty-seventh Amendment) Act, 1987 was enacted to provide for reservation of seats in the House of the People for the Scheduled Tribes in Nagaland, Meghalaya and Arunachal Pradesh and also for reservation of seats for Scheduled Tribes in the Legislative Assemblies of Nagaland and Meghalaya by suitably amending Article 330 and 332.

The Constitution (Fifty-eighth Amendment) Act, 1987

There has been a general demand for the publication of authoritative text of the Constitution in Hindi. It is imperative to have an authoritative text of the Constitution for facilitating its use in the legal process. Any Hindi version of the Constitution should not only conform to the Hindi translation published by the Constituent Assembly, but should be in conformity with the language, style and terminology adopted in the authoritative texts of Central Acts in Hindi. The Constitution has been amended to empower the President of India to publish under his authority the translation of the Constitution in Hindi signed by the Members of the Constituent Assembly with such modifications as may be necessary to bring it in conformity with the language, style and terminology adopted in the authoritative texts of Central Acts in Hindi language. The President was also authorised to publish the translation in Hindi of every amendment of the Constitution made in English.

The Constitution (Fifty-ninth Amendment) Act, 1988

The Act amends Article 356(5) of the Constitution so as to facilitate the extension of Presidential Proclamation issued under clause (1) of Article 356 beyond a period of one year, if necessary, up to a period of three years, as permissible under clause (4) of Article 356 with respect to the State of Punjab because of the continued disturbed situation there. The Act also amended Article 352 of the Constitution pertaining to the Proclamation of Emergency in its application to the state of Punjab and includes "internal disturbance" as one of the grounds for making a proclamation in respect of the State of Punjab only. As a consequence of amendment in Article 351, Articles 358 and 359 in relation to the State of Punjab was to be operative only for a period of two years from 30 March, 1988, which was the date of commencement of the amendment.

The Constitution (Sixtieth Amendment) Act, 1988

The Act amends clause (2) of Article 276 of the Constitution so as to increase the ceiling of taxes on professions, trades, callings and employment from two hundred and fifty rupees per annum to two thousand and five hundred rupees per annum. The upward revision of this tax was to help the State Governments in raising additional resources. The proviso to clause (2) has been omitted.

The Constitution (Sixty-first Amendment) Act, 1988

This amendment amended Article 326 and lowered the voting age form twenty-one to eighteen years.

The Constitution (Sixty-second Amendment) Act, 1989

This amendment further extended the Reservation for Scheduled Castes and Scheduled Tribes in Parliament and State Legislative Assemblies from 1989 to 1999. (In effect, the reservation would extend to a total of fifty years.)

The Constitution (Sixty-third Amendment) Act, 1990

This Amendment abolished the amended provisions of Article 356 and 369A brought about by the Fifty-ninth Amendment of 1989 related to the State of Punjab.

The Constitution (Sixty-fourth Amendment) Act, 1990

This amendment, again dealt with Punjab. It provided for amending the duration of the Presidential Proclamation of 1987 from three years to three years and six months.

The Constitution (Sixty-fifth Amendment) Act, 1990

It amended Article 338 of the Constitution and provided for a National Commission for Schedulde Castes and Scheduled Tribes. The National commission for Scheduled Castes and Tribes shall consist of a Chairperson, a Vice-Chairperson and five other members. They shall be appointed by the President by warrant under his hand and seal. The Commission shall have powers to regulate its own procedure.

The Constitution (Sixty-sixth Amendment) Act, 1990

The Amendment added a further group of land reforms enactments passed by the State legislatures to the Ninth Schedule of the Constitution, thus taking them out of the purview of judicial review.

The Constitution (Sixty-seventh Amendment) Act, 1990

This Amendment, again, dealt with Punjab and extended the Presidential Proclamation of 1987 by another six months.

The Constitution (Sixty-eighth Amendment) Act, 1991

This Amendment too was related to Punjab and provided for extension of the Presidential proclamation by yet another six months.

The Constitution (Sixty-ninth Amendment) Act, 1991

This Amendment provides for a new administrative set up for Delhi as the National Capital by creating a Legislative Assembly and a Council of Ministers.

The Constitution (Seventieth Amendment) Act, 1992

This Amendment amends Articles 54 and 55 to include within the scope of the term "State" the National Capital Territory of Pondicherry.

The Constitution (Seventy-first Amendment) Act, 1992

This Amendment amends the Eighth Schedule of the Constitution with a view to including in it at the appropriate places three new languages namely, Konkani, Manipuri and Nepali.

The Constitution (Seventy-second Amendment) Act, 1992

This Amendment amends Article 332 of the Constitution, after clause (3A) and fixes the number of seats reserved for the Scheduled Tribes in the Legislative Assembly of the State of Tripura, to reflect the tribal population in relation to the total population of the State.

The Constitution (Seventy-third Amendment) Act, 1993

This is a landmark amendment of the Constitution, which provides for an elaborate system of establishing Panchayats, as units of self-government, which for the first time in the Constitutional history of independent India, details of the Constitution of Panchayats, duration for which they would function, membership of Panchayats, constitution of Finance Commission to review financial position of Panchayats and several other related matters. It also adds a new Schedule, namely, Eleventh Schedule to the Constitution, listing 29 subjects which are to be handled by the Panchayats.

The Constitution (Seventy-fourth Amendment) Act, 1993

This again is a very important Amendment and deals with the establishment of Municipalities as a part of the constitutional system. Just as in the case of Panchayati Raj system, this amendment spells out various details connected with the different types of municipalities, including their powers, duration, election, finance and other related matters. It also adds a new Schedule to the Constitution, namely, the Twelfth Schedule, listing 18 subjects which are to be handled by the Municipalities.

The Constitution (Seventy-fifth Amendment) Act, 1994

It amends Article 323-B in Part XIV-A of the Constitution so as to give timely relief to the rent of litigants by providing for setting up of State-level Rent Tribunals in order to reduce the tiers of appeals and to exclude the jurisdiction of all courts, except that of the Supreme Court under Article 136 of the Constitution.

The Constitution (Seventy-sixth Amendment) Act, 1994

This Amendment raises the reservation quota of Government jobs and seats for admission in the educational institutions in favour of socially and educationally backward classes to 69 percent in Tamil Nadu.

Further, the Amendment Act has been included in the Ninth Schedule of Constitution to exempt it from the purview of judicial scrutiny.

The Constitution (Seventy-seventh Amendment) Act, 1995

It inserted clause (4A) in Article 16 dealing with reservation in the matter of promotion.

The Constitution (Seventy-eighth Amendment) Act, 1995

It amends the Ninth Schedule to the Constitution with a view to putting entries 257 and 284 in proper order.

Constitution (Seventy-ninth Amendment) Act, 1999

In Article 334 of the Constitution, for the words "Fifty Years" the words "Sixty Years" shall be substituted. As a result the reservation of seats for the Scheduled Castes and the Scheduled Tribes and the representation of the Anglo-Indian community by nomination to the Lok Sabha and the Legislative Assemblies of the States stand extended by another ten years.

Constitution (Eightieth Amendment) Act, 2000

The Union Government accepted the recommendations of the Tenth Finance Commission for sharing the taxes collected between the Centre and the States. Accordingly Articles 269 and 270 were amended and Article 272 was omitted. As a result the share of the States was enhanced beyond 29 percent.

In order to implement this decision, the Act amended Articles 269, 270 and 272 of the Constitution so as to bring several Central Taxes and duties like Corporation tax and Customs Duties at par with personal income-tax as far as their constitutionally mandated sharing with the States was concerned.

Constitution (Eighty-first Amendment) Act, 2000

Article 16 was amended to insert the following clause after clause (4A) :

(4B) Nothing in this Article shall prevent the State from considering any unfilled vacancies of a year which are reserved for being filled up in that year in accordance with any provision for reservation made under clause (4) or clause (4A) as a separate class of vacancies to be filled up in any succeeding year or years and such class of vacancies shall not be considered together with the vacancies of the year in which they are being filled up for determining the celling of fifty percent reservation on total number of vacancies of that year.

Constitution (Eighty-second Amendment) Act, 2000

Amendment of Article 335. The following proviso was added at the end of the Article :

"Provided that nothing in this Article shall prevent in making of any provision in favour of members of the Scheduled Castes and the Scheduled Tribes for relaxation of qualifying marks in any examination or lowering the standards of evaluation, for reservation in matters of promotion to any class or classes of services or posts in connection with the affairs of the Union or of a State."

Constitution (Eighty-third Amendment) Act, 2000

In Article 243 M of the Constitution, after clause (3), the following clause shall be inserted :

"(3A) Nothing in Article 243 D, relating to reservation of seats for the Scheduled Castes, shall apply to the State of Arunachal Pradesh."

Constitution (Eighty-fourth Amendment) Act, 2001

Amendment of Article 81. In Article 81 of the constitution in the proviso to clause (3)

(1) for the figure "2000" the figure "2026" shall be substituted. Similar amendments were made in Articles 82, Article 170, Article 330 and Article 332. The effect of these Amendments was the freezing of the present number of seats in the Lok Sabha and State Legislative Assemblies until the year 2026.

Constitution (Eighty-fifith Amendment) Act, 2001

This Amendment shall be deemed to have come into force on 17 June 1995.

Amendment of Article 16 : In Article 16 of the Constitution, in clause (4A) for the words "in matters of promotion to any class", the words "in matters of promotion with consequential seniority to any class" shall be substituted.

Constitution (Eighty-sixth Amendment) Act, 2002

Insertion of new Article 21 A : After Article 21 of the Constitution, the following Article shall be inserted, namely :

"21A. *Right to education*–The State shall provide free and compulsory education to all children of the age of six to Fourteen years in such manner as the State may, by law determine."

Substitution of new Article for Article 45 :

"45. Provision for early childhood care and education to children below the age of six-years—The State shall endeavour to provide early childhood care and education for all children until they complete the age of six years."

Amendment of Article 51.A.–In Article 51 A of the Constitution after clause (1) the following clause shall be added, namely; (k) who is a parent or guardian to provide opportunities for education to his child or, as the case may be, ward between the age of six and fourteen years."

Constitution (Eighty-seventh Amendment) Act, 2003

Amendment to Article 81 of the Constitution :

In clause (3) in the proviso, for the figure "1991" figure "2001" shall be substituted. Similar amendments have been brought about in Article 82, in Article 170 and Article 330.

Constitution (Eighty-eighth Amendment) Act, 2003

Insertion of a new Article 268 A after Article 268. "268 A–Service tax levied by Union and allocated and appropriated by the Union and the States—

(1) Taxes on services shall be levied by the Government of India and such tax shall be collected and appropriated by the Government of India, and the States. In the manner provided in clause(2).

(2) The proceeds of any financial year of any such tax levled in accordance with the provisions of clause(1) shall be (a) collected by the Government of India and the States; (b) appropriated by the Government of India and the States in accordance with such principles of collection and appropriation as may be formulated by Parliament by law.

Amendment to Article 270–In Article 270 of the Constitution in clause (1) for the words and figures "Articles 268 and 269", the words, figures and letter "Articles 268, 268A and 269" shall be substituted.

Amendment to Seventeenth Schedule–In the Seventh-Schedule of the Constitution in the Union List, after entry 92 B, the following entry shall be inserted : 92C, "Taxes on Services".

Constitution (Eighty-ninth Amendment) Act, 2003

Amendment of Article 338-established two Commissions, namely, the National Commission for Scheduled Castes and the National Commission for Scheduled Tribes. Each Commission will have a Chairperson, a Vice-Chairperson and three members. The Amendment lists also the functions and powers of each Commission.

Constitution (Ninetieth Amendment) Act, 2003

Amendment of Article 332 of the Constitution–After clause (6) the following proviso shall be inserted :

"Provided that for elections to the Legislative Assembly of the State of Assam, the representation of the Scheduled Tribes in the constituencies included in the Bodoland Territorial Areas District, so notified, and existing prior to the constitution of the Bodoland Territorial Areas District, shall be maintained."

The Constitution (Ninety–first Amendment) Act, 2003

Amendment of Article 75–In Article 75 of the Constitution, after clause (1) the following clauses be inserted :

"(IA) The total number of Ministers, including the Prime Minister, in the Council of Ministers shall not exceed fifteen percent of the total number of members of the House of the People.

(IB) A member of either House of Parliament belonging to any political party who is disqualified for being a member of that House under paragraph 2 of the Tenth Schedule shall also be disqualified to be appointed as a Minister under clause (1) for duration of the period commencing from the date of his disqualification till the date on which the term of his office as such member would expire or where he contests any election to either House of Paliament before the expiry of such period, till the date on which he is declared elected which ever is earlier.

Amendment of Article 164-In Article 164 after clause(1) the following clauses shall be inserted, namely,

"(IA) The total number of Ministers including the Chief Minister in the Council of Ministers in a State shall not exceed fifteen percent of the total number of members of the Legislative Assembly of that State. Provided that the number of Ministers including the Chief Minister, in a State shall not be less than twelve.

Provided further that where the total number of Ministers, including the Chief Minister, in the Council of Ministers in any State at the commencement of the Constitution (Ninety-first Amendment) Act, 2003 exceeds the said fifteen percent, of the number specified in the first proviso, as the case may be, then, the total number of Ministers in that State shall be brought in conformity with the provisions of this clause within six months from such date as the President may by public notification appoint.

(1B) A member of the Legislative Assembly of a State or either House of the Legislature of a State having Legislative Council belonging to any political party who is disqualified for being a member of that House under paragraph 2 of the Tenth Schedule shall also be disqualified to be appointed as a Minister under clause(1) for duration of the period commencing from the date of his disqualification till the date on which the term of his office as such member would expire or where he contests any election to the Legislative Assembly of a State or either House of the Legislature of a State having Legislative Council, as the case may be, before the expiry of such period, till the date on which he is declared elected, whichever is earlier."

4. *Insertion of new Article* 361B—After Article 361A of the Constitution, the following article shall, be inserted, namely :

361B. *Disqualification for appointment on remunerative political post.*-A member of a House belonging to any political party who is disqualified for being a member of the House under paragraph 2 of the Tenth Schedule shall also be disqualified to hold any remunerative political post for duration of the period commencing from the date of his disqualification till the date on which the term of his office as such member would expire or till the date on which he contests an election to a House and is declared elected, whichever is earlier.

The Constitution (Ninety–second Amendment) Act, 2003

Amendment of Eighth Schedule–In the Eighth Schedule to the Constitution (a) existing entry 3 shall be numbered as entry 5 as so renumbered, the following entries shall be inserted, namely,

"3. Bodo 4. Dogri;

(b) Existing entries 4 to 7 shall respectively be renumbered as entries 6 to 9;

(c) Existing entry 8 shall be renumbered as entry 11 and before entry 11 as so renumbered, the following entries shall be inserted, namely, "10 Maithili "

(d) Existing entries 9 and 14 shall respectively be renumbered as entries 12 to 17.

(e) Existing entry 15 shall be renumbered as entry 19 as so renumbered, the following entry shall be inserted namely "18 Santhal".

(f) Existing entries 16 to 18 shall respectively be numbered as entries 20 to 22.

The Constitution (Ninety-Third Amendment) Act, 2005

Amendment of Article 15 of the Constitution:

After clause (4), the following caluse shall be inserted:

(5) Nothing in this Article or in sub-clause (g) of clause (1) Article 19 shall prevent the State from making any special provision, by law, for the advancement of any socially and educationally backward classes of citizens or for the Scheduled Castes or Scheduled Tribes in so far as such special provision relate to their admission to educational institutions including private educational institutions whether aided or unaided by the State other than the minority educational institutions referred to clause (1) of Article 30.

The Constitution (Ninety-Fourth Amendment) Act, 2006

Amendment of Article 164 : In Article 164 of the constitution in clause (1), in the provisio, for the word "Bihar" the word "Chattisgarh", "Jharkhand" shall be substituted.

***

48

CONSTITUTIONAL REVIEW

In February, 2000 the Government of India set up a Constitution Review Commission consisting of eleven members with justice M.N. Venkatachaliah, former Chief Justice of the Supreme Court, as Chairman.

The Terms of Reference

The Government Notification stated, among other things that :

"The Commission shall examine in the light of the experience of the past 50 years, as to how best the Constitution can respond to the changing needs of efficient, smooth and effective system of governance and socio-economic development of modern India. It shall review the working of the Constitution within the framework of Parliamentary form of Government without tampering with the basic features as stipulated by the Supreme Court."

In its first sitting the Commission has specified the following subjects for its consideration: The constitution and the pace of socio-economic change and development; promoting literacy; generating employment; ensuring social security and removal of poverty; Centre-state relations; the working of Article 356; appointment and removal of governors; decentralisation and devolution of powers; strengthening of Panchayatiraj Institutions; enlargement of Fundamental Rights by specific incorporation of freedom of the media; right to compulsory elementary education, right to privacy and right to information; effective enforcement of the Directive Principles of State Policy in order to achieve the goals enshrined in the Preamble and for good governance and Fundamental Duties under Part IV-A of the Constitution. Also Fiscal and Monetary policies; size of Government expenditure and efficacy of public audit mechanisms.

*[Of the various recommendations, **58** recommendations involve amendment to the Constitution, **86** involve legislative measures and the rest involve executive action.]*

CHAPTER 3 : FUNDAMENTAL RIGHTS, DIRECTIVE PRINCIPLES AND FUNDAMENTAL DUTIES

Fundamental Rights

(1) *In article 12 of the Constitution, the following Explanation should be added :*

'Explanation—In this article, the expression "other authorities" shall include any person in relation to such of its functions which are of a public nature.' [Para 3.5]

(2) *In articles 15 and 16, prohibition against discrimination should be extended to "ethnic or social origin; political or other opinion; property or birth".* [Para 3.6]

(3) *Article 19(1) (a) and (2) should be amended to read as follows :*

"Art, 19(1) : All citizens shall have the right :

(a) to freedom of speech and expression which shall include the freedom of the press and other media, the freedom to hold opinions and to seek, receive and impart information and ideas."

19(2) : "Nothing in sub-clause (a) of clause (1) shall affect the operation of any existing law, or prevent the State from making any law, in so far as such law imposes reasonable restrictions on the exercise of the right conferred by the said sub-clause in the interests of the sovereignty and integrity of India, the security of the State, friendly relations with foreign States, public order, decency or morality, or in relation to contempt of court, defamation or incitement to an offence, or preventing the disclosure of information received in confidence except when required in public interest." [Para 3.8.1]

(4) *A Proviso the article 19(2) of the Constitution should be added as under:*

"Provided that, in matters of contempt, it shall be open to the Court to permit a defence of justification by truth on satisfaction as to the bona fides of the plea and it being in public interest". [Paras 3.8.2 and 7.42]

(5) *The existing Article 21 may be re-numbered as clause (1) there of, and a new clause (2) should be inserted thereafter on the following lines :*

"(2) No one shall be subjected to torture or to cruelm inhuman or degrading treatment or punishment". [Para 3.9]

(6) *After clause (2) in article 21 as proposed in para 3.9, a new clause, namely, clause (3) should be added on the following lines :*

"(3) Every person who has been illegally deprived of his right to life or liberty shall have an enforceable right to compensation." [Para 3.10]

(7) *After article 21, a new article, say article 21-A, should be inserted on the following lines :*

"21-A. (1) Every person shall have the right to leave the territory of India and every citizen shall have the right to return to India.

(2) Nothing in clause (1) shall prevent the State from making any law imposing reasonable restrictions in the interests of the sovereignty and integrity of India, friendly relations of India with foreign States and interests of the general public." [Para 3.11]

(8) *A new article, namely, article 21-B, should be inserted on the following lines :*

"21-B. (1) Every person has a right to respect for his private and family life, his home and his correspondence.

(2) Nothing in clause (1) shall prevent the State from making any law imposing reasonable restrictions on the exercise of the right conferred by clause (1), in the interests of security of the State, public safety or for the prevention of disorder or crime, or for the protection of health or morals, or for the protection of the rights and freedoms of others". [Para 3.12]

(9) *A new article, say article 21-C, may be added to make it obligatory on the State to bring suitable legislation for ensuring the right to rural wage employment for a minimum of eighty days in a year.* [Para 3.13.2]

(10) *As regards article 22, the following changes should be made :*

(*i*) The first and second provisos and Explanation to article 22(4) as contained in section 3 of the Constitution (44th Amendment) Act, 1978 should be substituted by the following proviso and the said section 3 of the 1978 Act as amended by the proposed legislation should be brought into force within a period of not exceeding three months :

"Provided that an Advisory Board shall consist of a Chairman and not less than two other members, and the Chairman and the other members of the Board shall be serving judges of any High Court.

Provided further that nothing in this clause shall authorize the detention of any person beyond a maximum period of six months as may be prescribed by any law made by Parliament under sub-clause (a) of clause (7)".

(*ii*) In clause (7) of article 22 of the Constitution, in sub-clause (b), for the words "the maximum period", the words "the maximum period not exceeding six months" shall be substituted. [Para 3.14.2]

(11) *After article 30, the following article should be added as article 30A:*

"30-A : Access to Courts and Tribunals and speedy justice

(1) Everyone has a right to have any dispute that can be resolved by the application of law decided in a fair public hearing before an independent court or, where appropriate, another independent and impartial tribunal or forum.

(2) The right to access to courts shall be deemed to include the right to reasonably speedy and effective justice in all matters before the courts, tribunals or other fora and the State shall take all reasonable steps to achieve the said object". [Para 3.15.1]

(12) *Article 39A in Part IV should be shifted to Part III as a new article 30-B to read as under :*

"30-B. Equal justice and free legal aid : The State shall secure that the operation of the legal system promotes justice, on a basis of equal opportunity, and shall, in particular, provide free legal aid, by suitable legislation or schemes or in any other way, to ensure that opportunities for securing justice are not denied to any citizen by reason of economic or other disabilities." [Para 3.15.2]

(13) *Article 300-A should be recast as follows :*

"300-A. (1) Deprivation or acquisition of property shall be by authority of law and only for a public purpose".

(2) There shall be no arbitrary deprivation or acquisition of property :

Provided that no deprivation or acquisition of agricultural, forest and non-urban homestead land belonging to or customarily used by the Scheduled Castes and the Scheduled Tribes shall take place except by authority of law which provides for suitable rehabilitation scheme before taking possession of such land." [Para 3.16.2]

(14) *In article 31-B, the following proviso should be added at the end, namely :*

"Provided that the protection afforded by this article to Acts and Regulations which may be hereafter specified in the Ninth Schedule or any of the provisions thereof, shall not apply unless such Acts or Regulations relate :

(a) in pith and substance to agrarian reforms or land reforms;

(b) to reasonable quantum of reservation under articles 15 and 16;

(c) to provisions for given effect to the policy of the State towards securing all or any of the principles specified in clause (b) or clause (c) of article 39." [Para 3.17]

(15) *Clauses (1) and (1A) of article 359 should be amended by substituting for "(except articles 20 and 21)", the following :*

"(except articles 17, 20, 21, 23, 24, 25 and 32)" [Para 3.18.2]

(16) *The relevant provision in the Constitution (93rd Amendment) Bill, 2001 making the right to education of children from 6 years till the completion of 14 years as a Fundamental Right should be amended and enlarged to read as under :*

"30-C. Every child shall have the right to free education until he completes the age of fourteen years; and in the case of girls and members of the Scheduled Castes and the Schedule Tribes until they complete the age of eighteen years." [Para 3.20.2]

(17) *After article 24, the following article should be added :*

"Article 24-A. Every child shall have the right to care and assistance in basic needs and protection from all forms of neglect, harm and exploitation." [Para 3.21.2]

(18) *After the proposed article 30-C, the following article may be added as article 30-D :*

"30-D. Right to safe drinking water, prevention of pollution, conservation of ecology and sustainable development.

Every person shall have the right :

(a) to safe drinking water;

(b) to an environment that is not harmful to one's health or well-being; and

(c) to have the environment protected, for the benefit of present and future generations so as to :

(*i*) prevent pollution and ecological degradation;

(*ii*) promote conservation; and

(*iii*) secure ecologically sustainable development and use of natural resources while promoting justifiable economic and social development". [Para 3.22.3]

(19) Explanation II to article 25 should be omitted and sub-clause (b) of clause (2) of that article should be reworded to read as follows :

"(b) providing for social welfare and reform or the throwing open of Hindu, Sikh, Jaina or Buddhist religious institutions of a public character to all classes and sections of these religions." [Para 23.2]

(20) *It shall be desirable that some optimum level of population with a view to take necessary action under this constitutional provision is prescribed. In article 347 of the Constitution, for the words "a substantial proportion of the population", the words "not less than ten per cent of the population" should be substituted.* [Para 3.24]

Directive Principles

(21) *The Commission recommends that the heading of Part IV of the Constitution should be amended to read as* "DIRECTIVE PRINCIPLES OF STATE POLICY AND ACTION". [Para 3.26.3]

(22) A strategic Plan of Action should be initiated to create a large number of employment opportunities in five years to realize and exploit the enormous potential in creating such employment opportunities. The components of this plan may include :

(1) Improvement of productivity in agriculture that will activate a chain of activities towards increased income and employment opportunities.

(2) Integrated horticulture that will include production of fruits, vegetables and flowers, cut-flowers for export and medicinal plants as well as establishment of bio-processing industries aimed primarily at value-addition of agricultural products.

(3) Intensification of animal husbandry programs and production of quality dairy products.

(4) Integrated Programme of Intensive Aquaculture including use of common property resources like village ponds and lakes.

(5) Afforestation and Wasteland Development to bring an additional 12 million hectares under forest plantation and contribute to rural asset building activity.

(6) Soil and Water Conservation to support afforestation and Natural Resource Conservation towards eco-friendly agriculture.

(7) Water Conservation and Tank Rehabilitation.

(8) Production and use of organic manures through vermiculture and other improved techniques and production of organic health foods from them. [Para 3.27.3]

(23) The Commission recommends that an independent National Education Commission should be set up every five years to report to Parliament on the progress of the constitutional directive regarding compulsory education and on other aspects relevant to the knowledge society of the new century. The model of the Finance Commission may be usefully looked into. [Para 3.31.3]

(24) *After article 47, the following article should be added, namely :*

47-A. "Control of population-The State shall endeavour to secure control of population by means of education and implementation of small family norms." [Para 3.32]

(25) An inter-faith mechanism to promote such civil society initiatives should be set up. This may be done under the auspices of the National Human Rights Commission set up under section 3 of the Protection of Human Rights Act, 1993 which, *inter alia*, provides for the participation of "the Chairpersons of the National Commission for Minorities, the National Commission for Scheduled Castes and Scheduled Tribes and the National Commission for Women" who shall be deemed to be the Members of the Commission for the discharge of functions specified in clauses (b) to (j) of the section 12 of the said Act. This body could, in addition to its other statutory functions, also function in collaboration with the National Foundation for Communal Harmony as a mechanism for promotion of inter-religious harmony for *inter alia* overseeing the installation and working of "Mohalla Committees" and other civil society, initiatives in sensitive areas. With an appropriate statutory enablement by way of enlargement of section 12 of the said Act, the purpose could be achieved without additional expenditure for setting up a separate mechanism. Section 12 of the said Act with consequential amendments to section 3(3) could be amended by the addition of clause (k), which shall read as under :

"(k) promoting through civil society initiatives, inter-faith and inter-religious harmony and social solidarity."

The Chairpersons of the National Commission for the Backward Classes and the National Commission for Safai Karamcharis should be co-opted to this body. [Para 3.34.2]

(26) There must be a body of high status which first reviews the state of the level of implementation of the Directive Principles and Economic, Social and Cultural Rights and in particular (*i*) the right to work, (*ii*) the right to health, (*iii*) the right to food, clothing and shelter, (*iv*) Right to Education up to and beyond the 14th year, and (*v*) the Right to Culture. The said body must estimate the extent of resources required in each State under each of these heads and make recommendations for allocation of adequate resources, from time to time. For ensuring that the Directive Principles of State Policy are realized more effectively, the following procedure should be followed :

(*i*) The Planning Commission should ensure that there is special mention–emphasis in all the plans and schemes formulated by it, on the effectuation–realization of the Directive Principles of State Policy.

(*ii*) Every Ministry/Department of the Government of India should make a special annual report indicating the extent of effectuation/realization of the Directive Principles of State Policy, the shortfall in the targets, the reasons for the shortfall, if any, and the remedial measures taken to ensure their full realization, during the year under report.

(*iii*) The report under item (ii) should be considered and discussed by the Department Related Parliamentary Standing Committee, which shall submit its report on the working of the Department indicating the achievements/failures of the Ministry/Department along with its recommendations thereto.

(*iv*) Both the Reports mentioned at items (ii) and (iii) above should be discussed by the Planning Commission in an interactive seminar with the representatives of various NGOs, Civil Society Groups, etc. in which the representatives of the Ministry/Department and the Departmental Related Parliamentary Standing Committee would also participate. The report of this interaction shall be submitted to the Parliament within a time bound manner.

(*v*) The Parliament should discuss the report at item (iv) above within a period of three months and pass a resolution about the action required to be taken by the Ministry/Department concerned.

A similar mechanism as mentioned above may be adopted by the States.

[Paras 3.35.2 and 3.35.3]

(27) The Report of the National Statistical Commission (2001) stresses the importance of availability of adequate, credible and timely socio-economic data generated by the statistical system, both for policy formulation and for monitoring progress of the sectors of economy and pace of socio-economic change. The Commission endorses the recommendations of the National Statistical Commission and stresses the importance of their implementation. [Para 3.36]

Fundamental Duties

(28) For effectuating Fundamental Duties, the following steps should be taken :

(*i*) The first and foremost step required by the Union and State Governments is to sensitise the people and to create a general awareness of the provisions of fundamental duties amongst the citizens on the lines recommended by the Justice Verma Committee on the subject. Consideration should be give to the ways and means by which Fundamental Duties could be popularized and made effective;

(*ii*) Right to freedom of religion and other freedoms must be jealously guarded and rights of minorities and fellow citizens respected;

(*iii*) Reform of the whole process of education is an immediate but immense need, as is the need to free it from government or political control; it is only through education that will power to adhere to our Fundamental Duties as citizens can be inculcated;

(*iv*) *Duty to vote at elections, actively participate in the democratic process of governance and to pay taxes should be included in article 51-A;* and

(*v*) The other recommendations of the Justice Verma Committee on operationalisation of Fundamental Duties of Citizens should be implemented at the earliest.

[Para 3.40.3]

(29) *The following should also be incorporated as fundamental duties in article 51A of the Constitution :*

(*i*) To foster a spirit of family values and responsible parenthood in the matter of education, physical and moral well-being of children.

(*ii*) Duty of industrial organizations to provide education to children of their employees.

[Para 3.40.4]

CHAPTER 4 : ELECTORAL PROCESSES AND POLITICAL PARTIES

Electoral Processes

(30) While some far-reaching reforms in the electoral processes are necessary, no major constitutional amendment is required. The necessary correctives could be achieved by ordinary legislation modifying the existing laws, or in many cases, merely by rules and executive action. A foolproof method of preparing the electoral roll right at the Panchayat level constituency of a voter and supplementing it by a foolproof voter ID card which may in fact also serve as a multipurpose citizenship card for all adults. A single exercise should be enough for preparing common electoral rolls and ID cards. The task could be entrusted to a qualified professional agency under the supervision of the Election Commission of India (EC) and in coordination with the SECs. The rolls should be updated constantly and periodically posted on the web site of the Election Commission and CDROMs should be available to all political parties or anyone interested. Prior to elections, these rolls should be printed and publicly displayed at the post offices in each constituency, as well as at the panchayats or relevant constituency headquarters. These should be allowed to be inspected on payment of a nominal fee by anyone. Facilities should also be provided to the members of the public at the post offices for submitting their applications for modification of the electoral rolls. [Paras 4.7.3 and 4.8.3]

(31) Introduction of Electronic Voting Machines (EVMs) in all constituencies all over

the country for all elections as rapidly as possible. [Para 4.9]

(32) Under section 58-A of the Representation of the People Act, 1951, the Election Commission should be authorised to take a decision regarding booth capturing on the report of the returning officers, observers or citizen groups. Also, the EC should be empowered to countermand the election and order a fresh election or to declare the earlier poll to be void and order a re-poll in the entire constituency. Further, the EC should consider the use of tamper-proof video and other electronic surveillance at sensitive polling stations/ constituencies. [Para 4.10]

(33) Any election campaigning on the basis of caste or religion and any attempt to spread caste and communal hatred during elections should be punishable with mandatory imprisonment. If such acts are done at the instance of the candidate or by his election agents, these would be punishable with disqualification. [Para 4.11]

(34) The Representation of the People Act should be amended to provide that any person charged with any offence punishable with imprisonment for a maximum term of five years or more, should be disqualified for being chosen as or for being a member of Parliament or Legislature of a State on the expiry of a period of one year from the date the charges were framed against him by the court in that offence and unless cleared during that one year period, he shall continue to remain so disqualified till the conclusion of the trial for that offence. In case a person is convicted of any offence by a court of law and sentenced to imprisonment for six months or more the bar should apply during the period under which the convicted person is undergoing the sentence and for a further period of six years after the completion of the period of the sentence. If any candidate violates this provision, he should be disqualified. Also, if a party puts up such a candidate with knowledge of his antecedents, it should be derecognised and deregistered. [Para 4.12.2]

(35) Any person convicted for any heinous crime like murder, rape, smuggling, dacoity, etc. should be permanently debarred from contesting for any political office. [Para 4.12.3]

(36) Criminal cases against politicians pending before courts either for trial or in appeal must be disposed off speedily, if necessary, by appointing Special Courts. [Para 4.12.4]

(37) A potential candidate against whom the police have framed charges may take the matter to the Special Court. This court should be obliged to enquire into and take a decision in a strictly time bound manner. Basically, this court may decide whether there is indeed a *prime facie* case justifying the framing of charges. [Para 4.12.5]

(38) The Special Courts should be constituted at the level of High Courts and their decisions should be appealable to the Supreme Court only (in similar way as the decisions of the National Environment Tribunal). The Special Courts should decide the cases within a period of six months. For deciding the cases, these courts should take evidence through Commissioners. [Para 4.12.6]

(39) The benefit of sub-section (4) of section 8 of the Representation of the People Act, 1951 should be available only for the continuance in office by a sitting Member of Parliament or a State Legislature. The Commission recommends that the aforesaid provision should be suitably amended providing that this benefit shall not be available for the purpose of his contesting fresh elections. [Para 4.12.7]

(40) The proposed provision laying down that a person charged with an offence punishable with imprisonment for a maximum period of five years or more should be disqualified from contesting elections after the expiry of a period of one year from the date the charges were framed in a court of law should equally be applicable to sitting members of Parliament and State Legislatures as to any other such person. [Para 4.12.8]

(41) In matters of disqualification on grounds of corrupt practices, the President should determine the period of disqualification under section 8-A of the Representation of the People Act, 1951 on the direct opinion of the EC and avoid the delay currently experienced. This can be done by resorting to the position prevailing before the 1975 amendment to the said Act. [Para 4.13.1]

(42) The election petitions should also be decided by special courts proposed in Para 4.12.6. In the alternative, special election benches may be constituted in the High Courts and earmarked exclusively for the disposal of election petitions and election disputes. [Para 4.13.2]

(43) The existing ceiling on election expenses for the various legislative bodies be suitably raised to a reasonable level reflecting the increasing costs. However, this ceiling should be fixed by the Election Commission from time to time and should include all the expenses by the candidates as well as by his political party or his friends and his well-wishers and any other expenses incurred in any political activity on behalf of the candidate by an individual or a corporate entity. Such a provision should be the part of a legislation regulating political funding in India. Further, Explanation 1 to section 77(1) of the Representation of the People Act, 1951 should be deleted. [Para 4.14.2]

(44) The political parties as well as individual candidates should be made subject to a proper statutory audit of the amounts they spend. These accounts should be monitored through a system of checking and cross-checking through the income-tax returns filed by the candidates, parties and their well-wishers. At the end of the election each candidate should submit an audited statement of expenses under specific heads. [Para 4.14.2]

(45) Every candidate at the time of election must declare his assets and liabilities along with those of his close relatives. Every holder of a political position must declare his assets and liabilities along with those of his close relations annually. Law should define the term 'close relatives'. [Para 4.14.5]

(46) Any system of State funding of elections bears a close nexus to the regulation of working of political parties by law and to the creation of a foolproof mechanism under law with a view to implementing the financial limits strictly. Therefore, proposals for State funding should be deferred till these regulatory mechanisms are firmly in position. [Para 4.14.5]

(47) All candidates should be required under law to declare their assets and liabilities by an affidavit and the details so given by them should be made public. Further, as a follow up action, the particulars of the assets and liabilities so given should be audited by a special authority created specifically under law for the purpose. Again, the legislators should be required under law for the purpose. Again, the Legislators should be required under law to submit their returns about their liabilitites every year and a final statement in this regard at the end of their term of office. [Para 4.14.6]

(48) Campaign period should be reduced considerably. [Para 4.15.4]

(49) Candidates should not be allowed to contest election simultaneously for the same office from more than one constituency. [Para 4.15.5]

(50) The election code of conduct, which should come into operation as soon as the elections are announced, should be given the sanctity of law and its violation should attract penal action. [Para 4.15.6]

(51) The Commission while recognizing the beneficial potential of the system of run off contest electing the representative winning on the basis of 50% plus one vote polled, as against the first-past-the-post system, for a more representative democracy, recommends that the Government and the Election Commission of India should examine this issue of prescribing a minimum of 50% plus one vote for election in all its aspects, consult various political parties, and other interests that might consider themselves affected by this change and evaluate the acceptability and benefits of this system. The Commission recommends a careful and full examination of this issue by the Government and the Election Commission of India. [Para 4.16.6]

(52) Intra-State delimitation exercise may be undertaken by the Election Commission for Lok Sabha and Assembly constituencies and the Scheduled Castes and Non-Scheduled Area Scheduled Tribe seats should be rotated. The Delimitation Body should, however, reflect the plural composition of society. [Para 4.17]

(53) *The provisions of the Tenth Schedule of the Constitution should be amended specifically to provide that all persons defecting—whether individually or in groups—from the party or the alliance of parties, on whose ticket they had been elected, must resign from their parliamentary or assembly seats and must contest fresh elections.* In other words, they should lose their membership and the protection under the provision of split, etc. should be scrapped. The defectors should also be debarred to hold any public office of a minister or any other remunerative political post for at least the duration of the remaining term of the existing legislature or until, the next fresh elections whichever is earlier. The vote cast by a defector to topple a government should be treated as invalid. Further, the power to decide questions as to disqualification on ground of defection should vest in the Election Commission instead of in the Chairman or Speaker of the House concerned. [Para 4.18.2]

(54) The practice of having oversized Council of Ministers should be prohibited by law. A ceiling on the number of Ministers in any State or the Union government be fixed at the maximum of 10% of the total strength of the popular house of the legislature. [Para 4.19]

(55) The practice of creating a number of political offices with the position, perks and privileges of a minister should be discouraged and at all events, their numbers should be limited to two per cent of the total strength of the lower house. [Para 4.19]

(56) Independent candidates should be discouraged and only those who have a track record of having won any local election or who are nominated by at least twenty elected members of Panchayats, Municipalities or other local bodies spread out in majority of electoral districts in their constituency should be allowed to contest for Assembly or Parliament. [Para 4.20.3]

(57) In order to check the proliferation of the number of independent candidates and the malpractices that enter into the election process because of the influx of the independent

candidates, the existing security deposits in respect of independent candidates may be doubled. Further, it should be doubled progressively every year for those independents who fail to win and still keep contesting elections. If any independent candidate has failed to get at least five per cent of the total number of votes cast in his constituency, he/she should not be allowed to contest as independent candidate for the same office again at least for 6 years. [Para 4.20.4]

(58) An independent candidate who loses election three times consecutively for the same office as such candidate should be permanently debarred from contesting election to that office. [Para 4.20.5]

(59) The minimum number of valid votes polled should be increased to 25% from the current 16.67% as a condition for the deposit not being forfeited. This would further reduce the number of non-serious candidates. [Para 4.20.6]

(60) It should be possible without any constitutional amendment to provide for the election of the Leader of the House (Lok Sabha/State Assembly) along with the election of the Speaker and in like manner under the Rules of Procedure. The person so elected may be appointed the Prime Minister/Chief Minister. [Para 4.20.7]

(61) The issue of eligibility of non-Indian born citizens or those whose parents or grandparents were citizens of India to hold high offices in the realm such as President, Vice-President, Prime Minister and Chief Justice of India should be examined in depth through a political process after a national dialogue. [Para 4.21]

(62) *The Chief Election Commissioner and the other Election Commissioners should be appointed on the recommendation of a body consisting of the Prime Minister, Leader of the Opposition in the Lok Sabha, Leader of the Opposition in the Rajya Sabha, the Speaker of the Lok Sabha and the Deputy Chairman of the Rajya Sabha. Similar procedure should be adopted in the case of appointment of State Election Commissioners.* [Para 4.22]

(63) All candidates should be required to clear government dues before their candidature are accepted. This pertains to payment of taxes and bills and unauthorised occupation of accommodation and availing of telephones and other government facilities to which they are no longer entitled. The fact that matters regarding Government dues in respect of the candidate are pending before a Court of Law should be no excuse. [Para 4.23]

(64) In order to obviate the uncertainty in identifying certain offices as offices of profit or not, *suitable amendments should be made in the Constitution* empowering the Election Commission of India to identify and declare the various offices under the Government of India or of a State to be 'offices of profit' for the purposes of being chosen, and for being, a member of the appropriate legislature. [Para 4.24.3]

Political Parties

(65) A comprehensive law regulating the registration and functioning of political parties or alliances of parties in India [may be named as the political Parties (Registration and Regulation) Act] should be made. The proposed law should:

(a) provide that political party or alliance should, in its Memoranda of Association, Rules and Regulations provide for its doors being open to all citizens irrespective of any distinctions of caste, community or the like. It should swear allegiance to the provisions of the Constitution and to the sovereignty and integrity of the nation, regular elections at an interval of three years at its various levels of the party, reservation/representation of at least 30 per cent, of its organizational positions at various levels and the same percentage of party tickets for parliamentary and State legislature seats to women. Failure to do so should invite the penalty of the party losing recognition.

(b) make it compulsory for the parties to maintain accounts of the receipt of funds and expenditure in a systematic and regular way. The form of accounts of receipt and expenditure and declaration about the sources of funds may be prescribed by an independent body of Accounts & Audit experts, created under the proposed Act. The accounts should also be compulsorily audited by the same independent body, created under the legislation which should also prepare a report on the financial status of the political party which along with the audited accounts should be open and available to public for study and inspection.

(c) make it compulsory for the political parties requiring their candidates to declare their assets and liabilities at the time of filing their nomination before the returning officers for election to any office at any level of government.

(d) provide that no political party should sponsor or provide ticket to a candidate for contesting elections if he was convicted by any court for any criminal offence or if the courts have framed criminal charges against him.

(e) specifically provide that if any party violates the provision mentioned at sub-para (d) above, the candidate involved should be liable to be disqualified and the party deregistered and derecognised forthwith. [Paras 4.30.1, 4.30.3, 4.30.4, 4.30.5 and 4.34]

(66) The Election Commission should progressively increase the threshold criterion for eligibility for recognition so that the proliferation of smaller political parties is discouraged. Only parties or a pre-poll alliance of political parties registered as national parties or alliances with the Election Commission be allotted a common symbol to contest elections for the Lok Sabha. State legislatures and the Council of States (Rajya Sabha).

[Para 4.31.2]

(67) In a situation where no single political party or pre-poll alliance of parties succeeds in securing a clear majority in the Lok Sabha after elections, the Rules of Procedure and Conduct of Business in Lok Sabha may provide for the election of the Leader of the House by the Lok Sabha along with the election of the Speaker and in the like manner. The Leader may then be appointed as the Prime Minister. The same procedure may be followed for the office of the Chief Minister in the State concerned. [Para 4.33.2]

(68) An amendment in the Rules of Procedure of the Legislatures for adoption of a system of constructive vote of no confidence should be made. For a motion of no-confidence to be brought out against a government at least 20% of the total number of members of the House should give notice. Also, the motion should be accompanied by a proposal of alternative Leader to be voted simultaneously. [Para 4.33.3]

(69) A comprehensive legislation providing for regulation of contributions to the political parties and towards election expenses should be enacted by consolidating such laws. This new law should :

(a) aim at bringing transparency into political funding;

(b) permit corporate donations within higher prescribed limits and keep them transparent;

(c) make all legal and transparent donations up to a specified limit tax exempt and treat this tax loss to the state as its contribution to state funding of elections;

(d) contain provisions for making both donors and donees of political funds accountable. The Government should encourage the corporate bodies and agencies to establish an electoral trust which should be able to finance political parties on an equitable basis at the time of elections;

(e) provide that audited political party accounts like the accounts of a public limited company should be published yearly with full disclosures under predetermined account heads; and

(f) provide for immediate derecognition of the party and enforcement of penalties for filing false or incorrect election returns. [Paras 4.35.2, 4.35.3, 4.35.4 and 4.36]

CHAPTER 5 : PARLIAMENT AND STATE LEGISLATURES

(70) The presiding officers, the minister for parliamentary affairs, and the chief whips of parties should periodically meet to review the work of the departmental parliamentary committees and take remedial action. It should be entirely possible for the Parliament to sanction budgets to secure the services of specialist advisors to assist these committees in conducting their inquiries, holding public hearings, collecting data about legislation and administrative details pertaining to countries which have relevance to the Indian conditions. [Para 5.6.3]

(71) Immediate steps be taken to set up a Nodal Standing Committee on National Economy with adequate resources in terms of both in house and advisory expertise, data gathering and computing and research facilities for an ongoing analysis of the national economy for assisting the members of the Committee to report on a periodic basis to the full House. [Para 5.7]

(72) The Parliament should be associated with the initial stage itself in the matter of formulating proposals for constitutional amendment. The actual drafting should be taken up only after the principles underlying the amendment have been thoroughly considered in a parliamentary forum and subjected to *a priori* scrutiny by the constituent power. A Standing Constitution Committee of the two Houses of Parliament for *a priori* scrutiny of amendment proposals should be set up. [Paras 5.8.2. and 5.8.3]

(73) With the proposed establishment of three new Committees, namely, the Constitution Committee, the Committee on National Economy and the Committee on Legislation, the existing Committees on Estimates, Public Undertakings and Subordinate Legislation may not be continued. [Para 5.9.1]

(74) The Petitions Committee of Parliament has tremendous potential as a supplement to the proposed Lok Pal institution. it should be made more widely known and used for ventilation, investigation and redressal of people's grievances against the administration. [Para 5.9.2]

(75) Major reports of all Parliamentary Committees ought to be discussed by the Houses of Parliament especially where there is disagreement between a Parliamentary Committee and the Government. [Para 5.9.3]

(76) For a more systematic approach to the planning of legislation, the following steps should be taken :

(a) Adequate time for consideration of Bills in committees and on the floor of the Houses as also to subject the drafts to thorough and rigorous examination by experts and laymen alike should be provided.

(b) All major social and economic legislation should be circulated for public discussion by professional bodies, business organisations, trade unions, academics and other interested persons.

(c) The functions of the Parliamentary and Legal Affairs Committees of the Cabinet should be streamlined;

(d) More focussed use of the Law Commission should be made;

(e) A new Legislation Committee of Parliament to oversee and coordinate legislative planning should be constituted; and

(f) All Bills should be referred to the Departmental Related Parliamentary Standing Committees for consideration and scrutiny after public opinion has been elicited and all comments, suggestions and memoranda are in. The Committees may schedule public hearings, if necessary, and finalise with the help of experts the second reading stage in the relaxed Committee atmosphere. The time of the House will be saved thereby without impinging on any of its rights. The quality of drafting and the content of legislation will necessarily be improved as a result of following these steps. [Paras 5.10.1 and 5.10.2]

(77) The Parliament may consider enacting suitable legislation to control and regulate the treaty-power of the Union Government whenever appropriate and necessary after consulting the State Governments and Legislatures under article 253 "for giving effect to international agreements". [Para 5.10.3]

(78) The Parliamentarians have to be like Caesar's wife, above suspicion. They must voluntarily place themselves open to public scrutiny through a parliamentary ombudsman. Supplemented by a code of ethics which has been under discussion for a long time, it would place Parliament on the high pedestal of people's affection and regard. [Para 5.11.1]

(79) Mass media should be encouraged to accurately reflect the reality of Parliament's working and the functioning of Parliamentarians in the Houses. Televising all important debates nationwide in addition to the Question Hours, publication of monographs, handouts, radio, TV, press interviews, use of audio visual techniques, especially to arouse curiosity and interest of the younger generation, and regular briefing of the press will go a long way in making people better acquainted with the important national work that is being done inside the historic parliament building. [Para 5.11.2]

(80) It is a legitimate public expectation that membership of Legislatures should not be converted into an office of lucrative gain but remain an office of service. The question of salaries, allowances, perks and pensions of lawmakers should be looked into on a rational basis and healthy conventions built. [Para 5.11.3]

(81) The parliament and the State Legislatures should assemble and transact business for not less than a minimum number of days. The Houses of State Legislatures with less than 70 members should meet for at least 50 days in a year and other Houses for at least 90 days while the minimum number of days for sittings of Rajya Sabha and Lok Sabha should be fixed at 100 and 120 days respectively. [Para 5.11.4]

(82) In order to maintain basic federal character of the Rajya Sabha, the domiciliary requirement for eligibility to contest elections to Rajya Sabha from the concerned State is essential. This should be maintained. [Para 5.11.5]

(83) Better and more institutionalized arrangements are necessary to provide the much-needed professional orientation to newly elected members. The emphasis should be on imparting practical knowledge on how to be an effective member. [Para 5.12]

(84) The findings and recommendations of the Public Accounts Committees (PACs) should be accorded greater weight. A convention should be developed with the cooperation of all major parties represented in the legislature to treat the PACs as the conscience-keepers of the nation in financial matters. [Para 5.13]

(85) Union Government should take necessary steps for the early enactment of the Fiscal Responsibility Bill pending before Parliament. The State Assemblies should enact similar legislation as provided for in article 293 to put their respective fiscal houses in order. [Para 5.14]

(86) The privileges of legislators should be defined and delimited for the free and independent functioning of Parliament and State Legislatures. It should not be necessary to run to the 1950 position in the House of Commons every time a question arises as to what kind of legal protection or immunity a Member has in relation to his or her work in the House. [Para 5.15.3]

(87) *Article 105(2) may be amended to clarify that the immunity enjoyed by Members of Parliament under Parliamentary privileges does not cover corrupt acts committed by them in connection with their duties in the House or otherwise.* Corrupt acts would include accepting money or any other valuable consideration to speak and/or vote in a particular manner. For such acts, they would be liable for action under the ordinary law of the land. It may be further provided that no court will take cognisance of any offence arising out of a Member's action in the House without prior sanction of the Speaker or the Chairman, as the case may be. *Article 194(2) may be similarly amended in relation to the Members of State Legislatures.* [Para 5.15.6]

(88) An Audit Board should be constituted for better discharge of the vital function of public audit, but the number of members to be appointed, the manner of their appointment and removal and other related matters should be dealt with by appropriate legislation, keeping in view the need for ensuring independent functioning of the Board. [Para 5.16.2]

(89) Though no specific change is needed in the existing provisions of the Constitution in so far as appointment of the Comptroller and Auditor General of India (C&AG) and other related matters are concerned, yet a healthy convention be developed to consult the Speaker of the Lok Sabha, before the Government decides on the appointment of the C&AG so that the views of the Public Accounts Committee are also taken into account. [Para 5.16.3]

(90) The considerations that apply at the Union level in regard to the functioning of the office of C&AG should apply with equal force at the State level. The State Accountant Generals (AGs) should be given greater authority by the C&AG, while maintaining its general superintendence, direction and controi to bring about a broad uniformity of approach in the sphere of financial discipline. The C&AG should evolve accounting policies and

standards and norms for all bodies and entities that receive public funds, such as autonomous bodies and the Panchayat Raj institutions. [Para 5.16.4]

(91) The operations of the office of the C&AG itself should be subject to scrutiny by an independent body. To fulfil the canons of accountability, a system of external audit of C&AG's organization should be adopted for both the Union and the State level organizations. [Para 5.17]

(92) The MP LAD Scheme, as being inconsistent with the spirit of the Constitution in many ways, should be discontinued immediately. [Para 5.19.2]

(93) Legislation envisaged in article 98(2) should be undertaken to reorganise the Secretariats as independent and impartial instruments of Parliament, with special emphasis on upgrading professional competence. [Para 5.20.1]

(94) It would be useful to reform the budgetary procedure for streamlining the work of Parliament. [Para 5.21.2]

(95) The number of days on which voting is considered essential should be reduced to the barest minimum and the time for such voting in a given session be fixed in advance with appropriate whips requiring full attendance of members. [Para 5.21.3]

(96) In order to ensure better scrutiny of administration and accountability to Parliament, parliamentary time in the two houses may be suitably divided between the government and the opposition. [Para 5.21.4]

(97) The best way to deal with issues of procedural reforms in a professional (and not political) manner is to have them studied by a Study Group outside Parliament as was done in U.K. The conclusions and suggestions of the Group can be considered by the Rules Committees of the houses of Parliament. Accordingly, a Study Group outside Parliament for study of Parliament should be set up. [Para 5.21.5]

CHAPTER 6 : EXECUTIVE AND PUBLIC ADMINISTRATION

(98) While improving the nature and institutional response of administration to the challenges of democracy is imperative, the system can deliver the goods only through devolution, decentralisation and democratisation thereby narrowing the gap between the base of the polity and the superstructure. [Para 6.2.8]

(99) District should be considered as a basic unit of planning for development. Functions, finances, and functionaries relating to the development programmes would have to be placed under the direct supervision and command of elected bodies at the district levels of operation to give content and substance to such programmes of development and public welfare. This would, to a substantial degree, correct the existing distortions and make officials directly answerable to the people to ensure proper implementation of development programmes under the direct scrutiny of people. [Para 6.4.1]

(100) India should move to a system where the State guarantees the title to land after carrying out extensive land surveys and computerizing the land records. It will take some time but the results would be beneficial for investment in land. This will be a major step forward in revitalizing land administration in the country as it would enable Right to access, Right to use and Right to enforce decisions regarding land. Similar rationalization of records relating to individuals rights in properties other than privately held lands (which are held in common) would improve operational efficiency which left unattended foment unrest. A

coherent public policy addressed to the modern methods of management would contribute to better use of assets and raise dynamic forces of individual creativity. Run away expansion in bureaucratic apparatus of the State would also get curtailed by new management system. [Para 6.4.2]

(101) Energetic efforts should be made to establish a pattern of cooperative relationship between the State and associations, NGOs and other voluntary bodies to launch a concerted effort to regenerate the springs of progressive social change. State and civil society are not to be treated antithetical but complementary. [Para 6.5.4]

(102) The questions of personnel policy including placements, promotions, transfers and fast-track advancements on the basis of forward-looking career management policies and techniques should be managed by autonomous Personnel Boards for assisting the high level political authorities in making key decisions. Such Civil Service Boards should be constituted under statutory provisions. They should be expected to function like the UPSC. The sanctity of parliamentary legislation under article 309 is needed to counteract the publicly known trends of the play of unhealthy and destabilizing influences in the management of public services in general and higher civil services in particular. [Para 6.7.1]

(103) Above a certain level—say the Joint Secretary level—all posts should be open for recruitment from a wide variety of sources including the open market. Government should specialize some of the generalists and generalize some of the specialists through proper career management which has to be freed from day to day political manipulation and influence peddling. [Para 6.7.2]

(104) Social audit of official working should be done for developing accountability and answerability. Officials, before starting their career, in addition to the taking of an oath of loyalty to the Constitution, should swear to abide by the basic principles of good governance. This would give renewed sense of commitment by the executives to the basic tenets of the Constitution. [Para 6.7.3]

(105) The services have remained largely immune from imposition of penalties due to the complicated procedures that have grown out of the constitutional guarantee against arbitrary and vindictive action (article 311). The constitutional safeguards have in practice acted to shield the guilty against swift and certain punishment for abuse of public office for private gain. A major corollary has been erosion of accountability. It has accordingly become necessary to re-visit the issue of constitutional safeguards under article 311 to ensure that the honest and efficient officials are given the requisite protection but the dishonest are not allowed to prosper in office. A comprehensive examination of the entire corpus of administrative jurisprudence has to be undertaken to rationalize and simplify the procedure of administrative and legal action and to bring the theory and practice of security of tenure in line with the experience of the last more than 50 years. [Para 6.7.4]

(106) The civil service regulations need to be changed radically in the light of contemporary administrative theory to introduce modern evaluation methodology. [Para 6.7.5]

(107) The administrative structure and systems have to be consciously redesigned to give appropriate recognition to the professional and technical services so that they may play their due role in modernizing our economy and society. The specialist should not be required to play second fiddle to the generalist at the top. Conceptually we need to develop

a collegiate style of administrative management where the leader is an energizer and a facilitator, and not an oracle delivering verdicts from a high pedestal. [Para 6.7.6]

(108) A parliamentary legislation under article 312(1) should be enacted. It should be debated in professional circles as well as by the general public. [Para 6.7.7]

(109) Right to information should be guaranteed and needs to be given real substance. In this regard, government must assume a major responsibility and mobilize skills to ensure flow of information to citizens. The traditional insistence on secrecy should be discarded. In fact, we should have an oath of transparency in place of an oath of secrecy. Administration should become transparent and participatory. Right to information can usher in many benefits, such as speedy disposal of cases, minimizing manipulative and dilatory tactics of the babudom, and, last but most importantly, putting a considerable check on graft and corruption. [Para 6.10]

(110) The Union Government should take steps to move the Parliament for early enactment of the Freedom of Information Legislation. It will be a major step forward in strengthening the values of a free and democratic society. [Para 6.11]

(111) To remain actively involved in new development programmes the people would also need the support of well organized, well prepared, knowledge-oriented personnel and well thought out policies. Think tanks and organized intellectual groups would have to be promoted through state funding, etc. without abridging their autonomy. [Para 6.12]

(112) The structural problems of foreign policy would be to constantly aim at making the best possible use of the international order and use it to our advantage. In the country's governance, the duality of foreign and domestic policy should end. The two should not be antithetical. A serious effort is required to combine the two to recast relations and launch a creative initiative to achieve strategic partnerships the world over on the principles of inter-dependence without domestic interests being relegated to the background. This calls for a thorough change in the form, working and structuring of Foreign Affairs mechanisms including the External Affairs Ministry. Foreign policy implementation calls for cutting through the mind-set of a generation. [Para 6.14]

(113) One of the measures adopted in several western countries to fight corruption and mal-administration is enactment of Public Interest Disclosure Acts which are popularly called the Whistle-blower Acts. Similar law may be enacted in India also. The Act must ensure that the informants are protected against retribution and any form of discrimination for reporting what they perceived to be wrong-doing, i.e., for *bona fide* disclosures which may ultimately turn out to be not entirely or substantially true. [Para 6.16.3]

(114) The Government should examine the proposal for enacting a comprehensive law to provide that where public servants cause loss to the State by their *mala fide* actions or omissions, they would be made liable to make good the loss caused and, in addition, would be liable for damages. [Para 6.17]

(115) The Union Government should frame rules, without further loss of time, under Section 8 of the Benami Transactions (Prohibition) Act, 1988 for acquiring *benami* property. Further, a law should be enacted to provide for forfeiture of benami property of corrupt public servants as well as non-public servants. [Para 6.19]

(116) The Government should examine enacting a law for confiscation of illegally acquired assets on the lines suggested by the Supreme Court in *Delhi Development Authority* vs. *Skipper Construction Co. (P) Ltd.* (AIR 1996 SC 2005). There is no need to set up an additional independent Authority to determine this issue of confiscation. The Tribunal constituted under the Smugglers and Foreign Exchange Manipulators (Forfeiture of Property) Act, (SAFEMA) 1976, which could deal with similar situation arising out of other statutes may be conferred additional jurisdiction to determine cases of confiscation arising out of the Benami Transactions (Prohibition) Act, 1988 and the Prevention of Corruption Act, 1988, (as may be amended) and other legislations which empower confiscation of illegally acquired assets. Tribunal will exercise distinct and separate jurisdictions under separate statutes. [Para 6.20.2]

(117) The Prevention of Corruption Act, 1988 should be amended to provide for confiscation of the property of a public servant who is found to be in possession of property disproportionate to his/her known sources of income and is convicted for the said offence. In this case, the law should shift the burden of proof to the public servant who was convicted. In other words, the presumption should be that the disproportionate assets found in possession of the convicted public servant were acquired by him by corrupt or illegal means. A proof of preponderance of probability shall be sufficient for confiscation of the property. The law should lay down that the standard of proof in determining whether a person has been benefited from an offence and for determining the amount in which a confiscation order is to be made, is that which is applicable to civil cases, i.e. a mere preponderance of probability only. A useful analogy may be seen in Section 2(8) of the Drug Trafficking Act, 1994 in United Kingdom. [Para 6.20.3]

(118) *The Constitution should provide for appointment of Lok Pal.* The Prime Minister should be kept out of the purview of the Lok Pal. [Para 6.21.1]

(119) The Union Government should take steps for early enactment of the Central Vigilance Commission Bill, already introduced in Parliament. [Para 6.22]

(120) *The Constitution should contain a provision obliging the States to establish the institution of Lokayuktas in their respective jurisdictions in accordance with the legislation of the appropriate legislatures.* [Para 6.23.2]

(121) When once a Commission of Inquiry is constituted under the Commissions of Inquiry Act, 1952 or otherwise, the Government should consult the Chairperson of the Commission in respect of time required for completion/finalisation of the report. Once such a time is specified, the Commission should adhere to it. The Action Taken Report on the report should be announced by the Government within a period of three months from the date of submission of the report. [Para 6.24.2]

CHAPTER 7 : THE JUDICIARY

(122) In the matter of appointment of Judges of the Supreme Court, it would be worthwhile to have a participatory mode with the participation of both the executive and the judiciary in making recommendations. The composition of the Collegium gives due importance to and provides for the effective participation of both the executive and the judicial wings of the State as an integrated scheme for the machinery for appointment of judges. *A National Judicial Commission under the Constitution should be established.*

The National Judicial Commission for appointment of judges of the Supreme Court shall comprise of :

(1) The Chief Justice of India	:	Chairman
(2) Two senior most judges of the Supreme Court	:	Member
(3) The Union Minister for Law and Justice	:	Member
(4) One eminent person nominated by the President after consulting the Chief Justice of India	:	Member

The establishment of a National Judicial Commission and its composition are to be treated as integral in view of the need to preserve the independence of the judiciary.

[Para 7.3.7]

(123) A committee comprising the Chief Justice of India and two senior most Judges of the Supreme Court will comprise the committee of the National Judicial Commission exclusively empowered to examine complaints of deviant behaviour of all kinds and complaints of misbehaviour and incapacity against judges of the Supreme Court and the High Courts. If the committee finds that the matter is serious enough to call for a fuller investigation or inquiry, it shall refer the matter for a full inquiry to the committee [constituted under the Judges' (Inquiry) Act, 1968]. The committee under the Judges Inquiry Act shall be a permanent committee with a fixed tenure with composition indicated in the said Act and not one constituted *ad hoc* for a particular case or from case to case, as is the present position under section 3(2) of the Act. The tenure of the inquiry committee shall be for a period of four years and to be re-constituted every four years. The inquiry committee shall be constituted by the President in consultation with the Chief Justice of India. The inquiry committee shall inquire into and report on the allegation against the Judge in accordance with the procedure prescribed by the said Act, i.e. in accordance with the sub-sections (3) to (8) of Section 3 and sub-section (1) of Section 4 of the said Act and submit their report to the Chief Justice of India, who shall place before a committee of seven senior most Judges of the Supreme Court. The Committee of seven Judges shall take a decision as to— whether (a) findings of the inquiry committee are proper and (b) any charge or charges are established against the judge and if so, whether the charges held proved are so serious as to call for his removal (i.e. proved misbehaviour) or whether it should be sufficient to administer a warning to him and/or make other directions with respect to allotment of work to him by the concerned Chief Justice or to transfer him to some other court (i.e. deviant behaviour not amounting to misbehaviour). If the decision of the said committee of judges recommends the removal of the Judge, it shall be a convention that the judge promptly demits office himself. If he fails to do so, the matter will be processed for being placed before Parliament in accordance with articles 124(4) and 217(1) Proviso (b). This procedure shall equally apply in case of Judges of the Supreme Court and the High Court except that in the case of a Supreme Court Judge the judge against whom complaint is received or inquiry is ordered, shall not participate in any proceeding affecting him.

In appropriate cases the Chief Justice of the High Court or the Chief Justice of India, may withhold judicial work from the judge concerned after the inquiry committee records a finding against the judge.

[Para 7.3.8]

(124) Article 124(3) contemplates appointment of Judges of Supreme Court from three sources. However, in the last fifty years not a single distinguished jurist has been appointed. From the Bar also, less than half a dozen Judges have been appointed. It is time that suitably meritorious persons from these sources are appointed. [Para 7.3.9]

(125) The retirement age of the Judges of the High Court should be increased to 65 years and that of the Judges of the Supreme Court should be increased to 68 years. [Para 7.3.10]

(126) In the matter of transfer of Judges, it should be as a matter of policy and the power under article 222 and its exercise in appropriate cases should remain untouched. The President would transfer a Judge from one High Court to any other High Court after consultation with a committee comprising the Chief Justice of India and the two senior most Judges of the Supreme Court. [Para 7.3.11]

(127) *A proviso should be inserted in article 129 so as to provide that the power of court to punish for contempt of itself inherent only in the Supreme Court and the High Courts and is available as part of the privilege of Parliament and State Legislatures, and no other court, tribunal or authority should have or be conferred with a power to punish for contempt of itself.* [Para 7.4.7]

(128) *A suitable provision may be inserted in the Constitution so as to provide that except the Supreme Court and the High Courts no other court, tribunal or authority shall exercise any jurisdiction to adjudicate on the validity or declare an Act of Parliament or State Legislature as being unconstitutional or beyond legislative competence and so ultra vires. Such a provision may be made as clause (5) of article 226.* [Para 7.5]

(129) A 'Judicial Council' at the apex level and Judicial Councils at each State at the level of the High Court should be set up. There should be an Administrative Office to assist the National Judicial Council and separate Administrative Offices attached to Judicial Councils in States. These bodies must be created under a statute made by Parliament. The Judicial Councils should be in charge of the preparation of plans, both short term and long term, and for preparing the proposals for annual budget. [Para 7.7]

(130) The budget proposals in each State must emanate from the State Judicial Council, in regard to the needs of the subordinate judiciary in that State, and will have to be submitted to the State Executive. Once the budget is so finalized between the State Judicial Council and the State Executive, it should be presented in the State Legislature. [Para 7.8.1]

(131) The entire burden of establishing subordinate courts and maintaining subordinate judiciary should not be on the State Governments. There is a concurrent obligation on the Union Government to meet the expenditure for subordinate courts. Therefore, the Planning Commission and the Finance Commission must allocate sufficient funds from national resources to meet the demands of the State judiciary in each of the States. [Para 7.8.2]

(132) The presiding officers in courts should be adequately trained. To ensure competence, there should be a proper selection, freedom of action, training, motivation and experience. To maintain their competence it is necessary to have continuing education for the judges. Some national judicial institutions have to be properly structured to give such training. There should be a proper monitoring of moving the judges where work demands such movement from places where there are no arrears of work. There has to be systematic assessment of training needs of judicial personnel at different levels. [Para 7.10.2]

(133) The Government should ensure basic infra-structure needed to all courts and arrange to ensure that courts are not handicapped for want of infra-structural facilities. Governments, both at the Centre and in the States, should constitute committee of secretaries to review government litigation with a view to avoid adjudication, wherever possible, give priority in filling of written statements, wherever required, and instruct government advocates to seek early decision on government litigation. [Para 7.10.4]

(134) In the Supreme Court and the High Courts, judgements should ordinarily be delivered not later than ninety days from the conclusion of the case. If a judgement is not rendered within such time – it is possible that the complexities of the case and the effect the decision may have on another similar situation might compel greater and larger judicial consideration and contemplation – the case must be listed before the court immediately on the expiry of ninety days for the court to fix a specific date for the pronouncement of the judgement. [Para 7.10.5]

(135) An award of exemplary costs should be given in appropriate cases of abuse of process of law. [Para 7.11]

(136) The recommendations of the Law Commission of India in regard to the Nagar Nyayalayas, Conciliation Courts, ADR systems of urban litigation, evidence recording by Commissioners, etc. as incorporated in the Code of Civil Procedure (Amendment) Act, 2000 should be brought into force with such modifications as would take care of a few serious objections. [Para 7.13.3]

(137) The provisions relating to conciliation in the Arbitration and Conciliation Act, 1996 should suitably be amended to provide for obligatory recourse to conciliation or mediation in relation to cases pending in courts. Further, the scope and functions of the Legal Services Authorities constituted under the Legal Services Authorities Act, 1987 should be enlarged and extended to enable the Authorities to set up conciliation and mediation fora and to conduct, in collaboration of other institutions wherever necessary, training courses for conciliators and mediators. [Para 7.13.4]

(138) Each High Court should, in consultation with the judicial councils referred to in para 7.7, prepare a strategic plan for time-bound clearance of arrears in courts under its jurisdiction. The plan may prescribe annual targets and district-wise performance targets. High Courts should establish monitoring mechanisms for progress evaluation. The purpose is to achieve the position that no court within the High Court's jurisdiction has any case pending for more than one year. This should be achieved within a period of five years or earlier. [Para 7.13.5]

(139) The criminal investigation system needs higher standards of professionalised action and it should be provided adequate logistic and technological support. Serious offences should be classified for purpose of specialized investigation by specially selected, trained and experienced investigators. They should not be burdened with other duties like security, maintenance of law and order etc., and should be entrusted exclusively with investigation of serious offences. [Para 7.14.2]

(140) The number of Forensic Science Institutions with modern technologies such as DNA fingerprinting technology should be enhanced. [Para 7.14.3]

(141) The system of plea-bargaining (as recommended by the Law Commission of India in its Report) should be introduced as part of the process of decriminalisation.

[Para 7.14.4]

(142) In order that citizen's confidence in the police administration is enhanced, the police administration in the districts should periodically review the statistics of all the arrests made by the police in the district as to how many of the cases in which arrests were made culminated in the filing of charge-sheets in the court and how many of the arrests ultimately turned out to be unnecessary. This review will check the tendency of unnecessary arrests. [Para 7.14.5]

(143) The legal services authorities in the States should set up committees with the participation of civil society for bringing the accused and the victims together to work out compounding of offences. [Para 7.14.6]

(144) Statements of witnesses during investigation of serious cases should be recorded before a magistrate under Section 164 of the Code of Criminal Procedure, 1973. [Para 7.14.7]

(145) The case for a viable, social justice-oriented and effective scheme for compensation victims is now widely felt. The Government at the Union level and in the States are well advised under the directive principles as well as under International Human Rights obligations to legislate on the subject of an effective scheme of compensation for victims of crime without further delay. [Para 7.15.3]

(146) The tremendous support which the criminal justice might derive from the people once the compensation scheme is introduced even in a modest scale, and the possibilities of advancing the crying need for social justice in a very real sense, are attractive enough for the State to find money to float the scheme immediately. [Para 7.15.4]

(147) The National Informatics Centre in collaboration with or with the assistance of the Indian Law Institute and the Government Law Departments should set up a Digital Legal Information System in the country so that all courts, legal departments, law schools would be able to access and retrieve information from the data bank of the important law libraries in the country. [Para 7.17.2]

(148) Progressively the hierarchy of the subordinate courts in the country should be brought down to a two-tier of subordinate judiciary under the High Court. Further, strict selection criteria and adequate training facilities for the presiding officers of such courts should be provided. In order to cope up with the workload of cases at the lower level and also to curtail arrears and delay, the States should appoint honorary judicial magistrates selected from experienced lawyers on the criminal side to try and dispose less serious and petty cases on part-time basis on the pattern of Recorders and Assistant Recorders in UK. They could set for, say, 100 days in a year and hold court later in the evenings after regular court hours. This would relieve the load on the regular magistracy. [Para 7.18]

(149) Since the issues relating to human rights, more particularly relating to unlawful detention, have now occupied a center-stage, both nationally and internationally, it should be desirable that the Protection of Human Rights Act, 1993 may be suitably amended to provide that, in addition to the powers generally vested in that court, such courts shall have the power to issue directions of the nature of a *habeas corpus* as was available to the High Courts under section 491 of the Code of Criminal Procedure, 1898. Vesting of such power will go a long way in providing help to the indigent and vulnerable sections of the society in view of the proximity and easy accessibility of the Court of Session. [Para 7.19.3]

CHAPTER 8 : UNION-STATE RELATIONS

Legislation

(150) Individual and collective consultation with the States should be undertaken through the Inter-State Council established under article 263 of the Constitution. Further, the Inter-State Council Order, 1990, issued by the President may clearly specify in para 4(b) of the order the subjects that should form part of consultation in the Inter-State Council.

[Para 8.2.13]

(151) *"Management of Disasters and Emergencies, Natural or Man-Made" should included in List III of the Seventh Schedule.* [Para 8.2.14]

Finance

(152) It might be worthwhile to provide explicitly for taxing power for the States in respect of certain specified services. For the Union also an explicit entry would be helpful, rather than leaving it to the residuary power of entry 97. However, it may be better to first let a consensus list of services to be taxed by the States come into force to be treated as the exclusive domain of the States, even if the formal taxing power is exercised by the Union. A *de facto* enumeration of services that can be taxed exclusively by the States should get priority from policy makers with a view to augmenting the resource pool of the States. Specific enumeration of services that may become amendable to taxation by the States should be made. *An appropriate amendment to the Constitution in this behalf should be made to include certain taxes, now levied and collected by the Union, to be levied and collected by the States.* [Para 8.5]

Trade, Commerce and Intercourse

(153) For carrying out the objectives of articles 301, 302, 303 and 304, and other purposes relating to the needs and requirements of inter-State trade and commerce and for purposes of eliminating barriers to inter-State trade and commerce Parliament should, by law, establish an authority called the "Inter-State Trade and Commerce Commission" under the Ministry of Industry and Commerce under article 307 read with Entry 42 of List-I.

[Para 8.8.2]

Resolution of Disputes

(154) *Article 139-A, which confers power on the Supreme Court to withdraw cases involving the same or substantially the same question of law, which are pending in Supreme Court and one or more High Courts, should be amended so as to provide that it can withdraw to itself cases even if they are pending in one court where such questions as to the legislative competence of the Parliament or State Legislature are involved.*

[Para 8.9.4]

(155) As river water disputes being important disputes between two or more States and/or the Union, they should be heard and disposed by a bench of not less than three Judges and if necessary, a bench of five Judges of the Supreme Court for the final disposal of the suit. [Para 8.11.7]

(156) Appropriate provisions may be made as envisaged by article 145(1) in consultation with the Supreme Court or if the Supreme Court so opts to provide for the same by the Supreme Court Rules to appoint Commissioners or Masters and to have the evidence

recorded not by the Supreme Court itself but by the Commissioners or Masters so that the precious time of the Supreme Court is saved. [Para 8.11.8]

(157) Appropriate Parliamentary legislation should be made for repealing the River Boards Act, 1956 and replacing it by another comprehensive enactment under Entry 56 of List I. The new enactment should clearly define the constitution of the River Boards and their jurisdiction so as to regulate, develop and control all inter-State rivers keeping intact the adjudicated and the recognized rights of the States through which the inter-State river passes and their inhabitants. While enacting the legislation, national interest should be the paramount consideration as inter-State rivers are 'material resources' of the community and are national assets. Such enactment should be passed by Parliament after having effective and meaningful consultation with all the State Governments. [Para 8.11.9]

(158) In resolving problems and coordinating policy and action, the Union as well as the States should more effectively utilize the forum of inter-State Council as recommended by the Commission on Centre-State Relations (Sarkaria Commission). This will be in tune with the spirit of cooperative federalism requiring proper understanding and mutual confidence and resolution of problems of common interest expeditiously. [Para 8.12.4]

(159) In order to reduce tension or friction between States and the Union and for expeditious decision-making on important issues involving States, the desirability of prior consultation by the Union Government with the inter-State Council may be considered before signing any treaty vitally affecting the interests of the States regarding matters in the State List. [Para 8.13.3]

Executive

(160) The powers of the President in the matter of selection and appointment of Governors should not be diluted. However, the Governor of a State should be appointed by the President only after in consultation with the Chief Minister of that State. Normally the five year term should be adhered to and removal or transfer should by following a similar procedure as for appointment i.e. after in consultation with the Chief Minister of the concerned State. [Para 8.14.2]

(161) In the matter of selection of a Governor, the following matters mentioned in para 4.16.1 of Volume I of the Sarkaria Commission Report should be kept in mind :-

❖ He should be eminent in some walk of life.

❖ He should be a person from outside the State.

❖ He should be a detached figure and not too intimately connected with the local politics of the State.

❖ He should be a person who has not taken too great a part in politics generally, and particularly in the recent past.

In selecting a Governor in accordance with the above criteria, the persons belonging to the minority groups should continue to be given a chance as hitherto. [Para 8.14.3]

(162) There should be a time-limit – say a period of six months – within which the Governor should take a decision whether to grant assent or to reserve a Bill for consideration of the President. If the Bill is reserved for consideration of the President, there should be a

time-limit, say of three months, within which the President should take a decision whether to accord his assent or to direct the Governor to return it to the State Legislature or to seek the opinion of the Supreme Court regarding the constitutionality of the Act under article 143. [Para 8.14.4]

(163) *Suitable amendment should be made in the Constitution so that the assent given by the President should avail for all purposes of relevant articles of the Constitution.* However, it is desirable that when a Bill is sent for the President's assent, it would be appropriate to draw the attention of the President to all the articles of the Constitution, which refer to the need for the assent of the President to avoid any doubts in court proceedings. [Para 8.14.6]

(164) *A suitable article should be inserted in the Constitution to the effect that an assent given by the President to an Act shall not be permitted to be argued as to whether it was given for one purpose or another. When the President gives his assent to the Bill, it shall be deemed to have been given for all purposes of the Constitution.* [Para 8.14.7]

(165) *The following proviso may be added to article 111 of the Constitution:* "Provided that when the President declares that he assents to the Bill, the assent shall be deemed to be a general assent for all purposes of the Constitution."

Suitable amendment may also be made in article 200. [Para 8.14.8]

(166) Article 356 should not be deleted. But it must be used sparingly and only as a remedy of the last resort and after exhausting action under other articles like 256, 257 and 355. [Para 8.18 and 8.19.2]

(167) In case of political breakdown, necessitating invoking of article 356, before issuing a proclamation thereunder, the concerned State should be given an opportunity to explain its position and redress the situation, unless the situation is such, that following the above course would not be in the interest of security of State, or defence of the country, or for other reasons necessitating urgent action. [Para 8.19.5]

(168) The question whether the Ministry in a State has lost the confidence of the Legislative Assembly or not, should be decided only on the floor of the Assembly and nowhere else. If necessary, the Union Government should take the required steps, to enable the Legislative Assembly to meet and freely transact its business. The Governor should not be allowed to dismiss the Ministry, so long as it enjoys the confidence of the House. It is only where a Chief Minister refuses to resign, after his Ministry is defeated on a motion of no-confidence, that the Governor can dismiss the State Government. In a situation of political breakdown, the Governor should explore all possibilities of having a Government enjoying majority support in the Assembly. If it is not possible for such a Government to be installed and if fresh elections can be held without avoidable delay, he should ask the outgoing Ministry, (if there is one), to continue as a caretaker government, provided the Ministry was defeated solely on a issue, unconnected with any allegations of maladministration or corruption and is agreeable to continue. The Governor should then dissolve the Legislative Assembly, leaving the resolution of the constitutional crisis to the electorate.[Para 8.20.3]

(169) The problem of political breakdown would stand largely resolved if the recommendations made in Chapter 4 in regard to the election of the leader of the House (Chief Minister) and the removal of the Government only by a constructive vote of no-confidence are accepted and implemented. [Paras 8.20.3 and 8.20.4]

(170) Normally, President's Rule in a State should be proclaimed on the basis of Governor's Report under article 356(1). The Governor's report should be a "speaking document", containing a precise and clear statement of all material facts and grounds, on the basis of which the President may satisfy himself, as to the existence or otherwise of the situation contemplated in article 356. [Para 8.20.5]

(171) *In clause (5) of article 356 of the Constitution, in clause (a) the word "and" occurring at the end should be substituted by the word "or" so that even without the State being under a proclamation of Emergency, President's rule may be continued if elections cannot be held.* [Para 8.21.3]

(172) Whenever a proclamation under article 356 has been issued and approved by the Parliament it may become necessary to review the continuance in force of the proclamation and to restore the democratic processes earlier than the expiry of the stipulated period. *For this, new clauses (6) & (7) to article 356 may be added on the following lines :*

"(6) Notwithstanding anything contained in the foregoing clauses, the President shall revoke a proclamation issued under clause (1) or a proclamation varying such proclamation if the House of the People passes a resolution disapproving, or, as the case, may be, disapproving the continuance in force of , such proclamation.

(7) Where a notice in writing signed by not less than one-tenth of the total number of members of the House of the People has been given, of their intention to move a resolution for disapproving, or, as the case may be, for disapproving the continuance in force, of, a proclamation issued under clause (1) or a proclamation varying such proclamation :

(a) to the Speaker, if the House is in session; or

(b) to the President, if the House is not in session,

a special sitting of the House shall be held within fourteen days from the date on which such notice is received by the Speaker, or, as the case may be, by the President, for the purpose of considering such resolution." [Para 8.21.4]

(173) *Article 356 should be amended so to ensure that the State Legislative Assembly should not be dissolved either by the Governor or the President before the proclamation issued under article 356(1) has been laid before Parliament and it has had an opportunity to consider it.* [Para 8.22.3]

(174) Government may consider the demands of the Coorgies for a Sainik School, a Development Board and a University for them in Coorg.[Para 8.23.1]

(175) Steps may be taken for better protection of Sindhi language and culture by setting up of a Centre of Sindhi Language and Culture with the State providing necessary facilities for the same. The difficulties faced by the Sindhi migrants may be examined and corrective measures taken to facilitate grant of citizenship as per the existing law. [Para 8.23.2]

CHAPTER 9 : DECENTRALISATION AND DEVOLUTION

Panchayats

176. Article 243-K and 243Z should be amended on the following lines :

1. **Amendment of article 243-K**

In article 243-K,

(a) for clause (1), the following clauses shall be substituted, namely :

"(1) Subject to the provisions of clause (1A), the superintendence, direction and control of the preparation of electoral rolls for, and the conduct of, all elections to the Panchayats shall be vested in a State Election Commission consisting of a State Election Commissioner to be appointed by the Governor.

(1A) The Election Commission shall have the power to issue any directions or instructions to the State Election Commission for the discharge of its functions under clause (1)".

(b) after clause (4), the following clause shall be inserted, namely :

"(5) The State Election Commission shall submit its annual report to the Election Commission and to the Governor, every year and it may, at any time, submit special reports on any matter which in its opinion is of such urgency or importance that it should not be deferred till the submission of its annual report.".

2. Amendment of Article 243ZA.

In article 243ZA, for clause (1), the following clauses shall be substituted, namely :

"(1) Subject to the provisions of clause (1A), the superintendence, direction and control of the preparation of electoral rolls for, and the conduct of, all elections to the Municipalities shall be vested in the State Election Commission referred to in article 243-K

(1A) The Election Commission shall have the power to issue any directions or instructions to the State Election Commission for the discharge of its functions under clause (1)". [Para 9.6.2]

(177) Panchayats should be categorically declared to be 'institutions of self-government' and exclusive functions be assigned to them, *for this purpose, article 243G should be amended to read as follows* :

"Powers, authority and responsibility of Panchayats

243G. Subject to the provisions of this Constitution, the Legislature of a State shall, by law, vest the Panchayats with such powers and authority as are necessary to enable them to function as institutions of self-government and such law shall contain provisions for the devolution of powers and responsibilities upon Panchayats at the appropriate level, subject to such conditions as shall be specified therein, with respect to :

(a) preparation of plans for economic development and social justice;

(b) the implementation of schemes for economic development and social justice as shall be entrusted to them including those in relation to the matters listed in the Eleventh Schedule".

Similar amendments should be made in article 243W relating to the powers, authority and responsibilities of Municipalities, etc. [Paras 9.7.1 and 9.7.2]

(178) *The Eleventh and Twelfth Schedules to the Constitution should be restructured in a manner that creates a separate fiscal domain for Panchayats and Municipalities. Accordingly, articles 243H and 243X should be amended making it mandatory for the legislation of the States to make laws devolving powers to Panchayats and Municipalities.* [Para 9.8.2]

(179) *In order to enable the Finance Commission to take a macro-level view, the provisions sub-clauses (bb) and (c) of clause (3) of article 280 should be amended. The words "on the basis of the recommendation" in these sub-clauses should be replaced by the words "after taking into consideration the recommendations."* [Para 9.8.3]

(180) *In the part of clause (1) of article 243-I which calls for constitution of State Finance Commission (SFC) at the expiration of every fifth year, in line with article 280(1), the words "or at such earlier time as the Governor considers necessary" may be added after the words "fifth year'.* While it is for the State Legislature to ensure that the Government implements fully its assurances, there should be constitutional obligations for placing the Action Taken Report (ATR) before the legislature within 'six months' after the submission of the report. Clause (4) of article 243-I may need to be amended accordingly. [Para 9.8.4]

(181) *The necessary legislative power of fixing upper limit of taxes on professions, trades, callings and employment under article 276 should be vested in Parliament by suitably amending that article.* [Para 9.8.5]

(182) All local authorities may be allowed to borrow from the State Government and financial institutions. [Para 9.8.6]

(183) *An enabling provision should be made in Part IX of the Constitution permitting the State Legislature to make, by law, provisions that would empower the State Government to confer on the Panchayats full power of administrative and functional control over such staff as are transferred following devolution of functions, notwithstanding any right they may have acquired from State Act/Rules.* They should also have the power to recruit certain categories of staff required for service in their jurisdiction. [Para 9.9.1]

(184) *A proviso to clause (1) of article 243E should be inserted to the effect that a reasonable opportunity of being heard shall be given to a Panchayat before it is dissolved.* [Para 9.10]

(185) *A provision for Constitution of a State Panchayat Council under the chairmanship of the Chief Minister [on the pattern of Gujarat State Council for Panchayats as provided in the Gujarat Panchayats Act, 1993] should be made in the Constitution on the analogy of the provision in article 263 of the Constitution relating to the Inter-State Council.* The leader of the opposition may be made *ex officio* vice-chairman of the Council to provide a consensual approach to the development of Panchayats as fully democratic, efficient and responsible institutions. [Para 9.11]

(186) Necessary provision should be made for audit of Panchayat accounts to ensure that all works related to audit (conduct of audit, submission of audit report and compliance with audit objections, if any) are completed within a year of the close of a financial year. To ensure uniformity in the practice relating to audits of accounts, the Comptroller and Auditor-General of India should be empowered to conduct the audit or lay down accounting standards for Panchayats. [Para 9.12]

Municipalities

(187) Whenever a Municipality is superseded, a report stating the grounds for such dissolution should be placed before the State Legislature. [Para 9.13]

(188) All provisions regarding qualifications and disqualifications for elections to local authorities should be consolidated in a single law and until that is done, each State should prepare a manual of existing provisions for public information. [Para 9.14]

(189) The State Election Commission (SEC) should have the authority to prescribe ceiling of expenses and code of conduct in elections. Further, the State laws should clearly specify the powers of the SEC to disqualify candidates or set aside elections in the event of violations of those laws. [Para 9.15]

(190) It should be the duty of a State and the Union (in case of Panchayats and Municipalities located in Union territories) to ensure the completion of elections within the stipulated limits. It should also be duty of the State Election Commissioner to ensure this and in the event of possible delay make a report to the Governor of the State drawing his attention to the problems and suggesting remedial action to fulfill the requirements of the Constitution. Articles 243K and 243ZA should be suitably amended to specify that the responsibility for the conduct of elections shall include all preparatory steps for the same including the electoral rolls and matters connected therewith and the responsibility for the same shall vest with the State Election Commission. [Para 9.16.2]

(191) The functions and responsibilities of delimitation, reservation and rotation of seats and matters connected therewith should be vested in a delimitation Commission constituted by law by the appropriate legislature and not in the SEC. [Para 9.16.2]

(192) The Representation of the People Act and State laws should specify that common polling stations should be used for elections to local bodies, State Legislatures and Parliament. [Para 9.17.2]

(193) The State laws should provide guidelines for the delimitation work such as parity, as far as possible, in the ratio between the population of a territorial constituency and the number of seats within the same class of Panchayats or Municipalities. [Para 9.17.3]

(194) State laws should specify that changes in the administrative boundaries of districts, sub-divisions, taluks, police stations, etc., should not be made with six months prior to a panchayat or a municipal election. [Para 9.17.4]

(195) *To remove ambiguities, articles 243D and 243T should be suitably amended to provide for rotation and changes only at the time of delimitation and not in between.* State laws should provide the guidelines for the process of reservation which should ensure transparency and adequate opportunities for eliciting voter response. [Para 9.18.2]

(196) *To clarify the precise position of reservation under clause (6) of article 243D and clause (6) of article 243T to be provided by the State law, the overall total of reserved seats and reserved offices in Panchayats and Municipalities should be specified.* [Para 9.18.3]

(197) The State Election Commissioner should have a fixed term of 5 years. He/she should be equal to a Judge of the High Court. The broad qualification for a State Election Commissioner may be specified under the State law. [Para 9.19.1]

(198) *The concept of a distinct and separate tax domain for municipalities should be recognised. The concept should be reflected in a list of taxes in the relevant schedule. Carving out items from the existing State lists such as item 49 (taxes on land and buildings) and item 52 (taxes on entry of goods into a local area for consumption) should not be difficult.* [Para 9.21]

Institutions in North East India

(199) The North Eastern part of India with its large number of tribal communities and emerging educated elites has self-governing village councils and organized tribal chiefdoms. Efforts are to be made to give all the States in this region the opportunities provided under the 73rd and 74th Constitution Amendments. However, this should be done with due regard to the unique traditions of the region and the genius of the people without tampering with their essential rights and giving to each State the chance to use its own nomenclature for systems of governance which will have local acceptance. [Para 9.22.3]

(200) Careful steps should be taken to devolve political powers through the intermediate and local-level traditional political organisations, provided their traditional practices carried out in a modern world do not deny legitimate democratic rights to any section in their contemporary society. The details of state-wise steps to devolve such powers will have to be carefully considered in a proper representative meeting of traditional leaders of each community, opinion builders of the respective communities and leaders of State and national stature from these very groups. A hasty decision could have serious repercussions, unforeseen and unfortunate, which could further complicate and worsen the situation. To begin with, the subjects given under the Sixth Schedule and those mentioned in Eleventh Schedule could be entrusted to the Autonomous District Councils (ADCs). The system of in-built safeguards in the Sixth Schedule should be maintained and strengthened for the minority and micro-minority groups while empowering them with greater responsibilities and opportunities, for example, through the process of Central funding for Plan expenditure instead of routing all funds through the State Governments. The North Eastern Council can play a central role here by developing a process of public education on the proposed changes, which would assure communities about protection of their traditions and also bring in gender representation and give voice to other ethnic groups. [Para 9.23(i)]

(201) Traditional forms of governance should be associated with self-governance because of the present dissatisfaction. However, positive democratic elements like gender justice and adult franchise should be built into these institutions to make them broader based and capable of dealing with a changing world. [Para 9.23(ii)]

(202) The implementation of centrally funded projects from various departments of the Union Government should be entrusted to the ADCs and to revived village councils with strict monitoring by the Comptroller and Auditor-General of India. [Para 9.23 (iii)]

(203) The process of protection of identity and the process of development and change are extremely sensitive. These twin processes need to be understood in the framework of a changing world and the role of all communities, small and large, in that world. Therefore, the North Eastern Council should be mandated to conduct an intensive programme of public awareness, sensitization and education through non-government organizations, State Governments, and its own structure to help bring about such an understanding of the proposals. [Para 9.23(iv)]

(204) The provisions of the Anti-Defection Law in the proposed revised form as recommended in para 4.18.2 of the Report should be made applicable to all the Sixth Schedule areas. [Para 9.23(v)]

(205) Given the demographic imbalance which is taking place in the North-East as a result of illegal migration from across the borders, urgent legal steps are necessary for preventing such groups from entering electoral rolls and citizenship rolls of the country.

Reservations for local communities and minorities from other parts of the country should be made in the State Legislatures. Issuance of multi-purpose identity cards to all Indian citizens should be made mandatory for all Indian residents in the North East on a *high-priority basis* and the National Citizenship Law to be reviewed to plug the loopholes which enable illegal settlers to become 'virtual' citizens in a short span of time, using a network of touts, politicians and officials. [Para 9.23(vi)]

(206) A National Immigration Council should be set up under law to examine and report on a range of issues including Work Permits for legal migrants, Identity Cards for all residents, a National Migration Law, a National Refugee Law, review of the Citizenship Act, the Illegal Migrants Determination by Tribunal Act and the Foreigners Act.

[Para 9.23(vii)]

(207) Local communities should be involved in the monitoring of our borders, in association with the local police and the Border Security Force. [Para 9.23(viii)]

(208) As regards Nagaland, the Naga Councils should be replaced by elected representatives of various Naga society groups with an intermediary tier at the district level. Village Development Boards should be less dependent on State and receive more Centrally-sponsored funds. [Para 9.25]

(209) As regards Assam :

(i) *the sixth Schedule should be extended to the Bodoland Autonomous Council with protection for non-tribal, non-Bodo groups,*

(ii) other Autonomous councils be upgraded to Autonomous Development Councils with more Central funds for infrastructure development; within the purview of the 73rd Amendment but also using traditional governing systems at the village level. [Para 9.28]

(210) As regards Meghalaya,

(i) A tier of village governance should be created for a village or a group of villages in the Autonomous District Councils, comprising of elected persons from the traditional systems plus from existing village councils with not more than 15 persons at each village unit.

(ii) The number of seats in each of the Autonomous District Councils in Meghalaya should be increased by 10 seats, *i.e.,* to a total number of 40 seats. Of the 10 additional seats, having regard to the non-representation of women and non-tribals, the Governor may nominate up to five members from these categories to each of the ADCs. The other five may be elected as follows :

(a) By Syiems and Myntris, from among themselves to the Khasi Autonomous Council.

(b) By Dolois from among themselves to the Jaintia Autonomous District Council; and

(c) By Nokmas from among themselves to the Garo Autonomous District Council.

[Para 9.29]

(211) As regards Tripura :

(i) The Changes which may be made in respect of other Autonomous Councils should also apply in respect of the Autonomous District Council (s) in Tripura.

(ii) The number of elected members in the Council should be increased from 28 to 32.

(iii) The number of nominated members should be increased to six from the current two. The existing non-tribal seats (currently, they have three elected seats) be converted to tribal seats. Three non-tribals may be nominated by the Governor and three tribal women may be nominated by the Chief Executive Member. [Para 9.30]

(212) As regards Mizoram :

(i) An intermediary elected 30-member tier should be developed at the district level in areas not covered by the Sixth Schedule, *i.e.,* excluding the Chakma, Lai and Mara District Autonomous Councils. There would thus be two tiers below the State Legislature : the District and the Village.

(ii) Village Councils in non-Scheduled areas should be given more administrative and judicial powers; two or more villages be combined to from one village council, given the small population in the State.

(iii) Consideration should be given to groups seeking Sixth Schedule status, depending on viability of the demand, including size of population, territorial and ethnic contiguity.

(iv) central funding as outlined in general recommendations should be provided to the ADCs.

(v) Nominated seats for women, non-tribals and Sixth Schedule tribes in non-scheduled area (not to exceed six over and above the size of the Councils, making a total of 36 members); current size of ADCs should be increased to 30 with a similar provision for women and non-scheduled tribes. [Para 9.31]

(213) As regards Manipur :

(i) *the provision of the sixth Schedule should be extended to hill districts of the State,*

(ii) the 73rd Amendment should be implemented vigorously in the areas of the plains where, despite elections, the system is virtually non-existent. [Para 9.32]

CHAPTER 10 : PACE OF SOCIO-ECONOMIC CHANGE AND DEVELOPMENT

(214) The Citizens' Charters be prepared by every service providing department/agency to enumerate the entitlements of the citizens. In case a citizen fails to receive the public goods and the services in the manner and to the extent set out in such charters, he/she should have recourse to an easy and effective system of grievance redressal through chartered Ombudsman. These citizen's charters should include specifically the entitlements of citizens belonging to Scheduled Castes (SCs), Scheduled Tribes (STs) and other deprived classes. In the case of these deprived classes the charters can with advantage provide for National and State Commission for SCs, STs, BCs (Backward Classes), Minorities, women, Safai Karamcharis to function effectively as ombudsman-bodies. The charter of these National and State Commissions and the way they are constituted should be such as to facilitate the role, *inter alia,* as ombudsman-bodies for different deprived classes. [Para 10.3.2]

(215) The Civil Services Boards, recommended to be set up under Chapter 6 for considering promotions and placements, should be directed to specifically consider the performance of officers in promoting the welfare of Scheduled Castes, Scheduled Tribes and other deprived categories. When officers are being considered for promotion and placement economic agencies/ministries, weightage should be given to officers who have worked conscientiously and efficiently to implement constitutional values and norms under the law and rules and regulations for the welfare, development and empowerment of the

above disadvantaged categories and those who have failed in this and those who have not worked at least for five years in the areas and sectors pertaining to these categories should be excluded from placements in economic ministries/agencies. For purpose, the provision should be made for Social Justice Clearance before an officer of class I or class II is promoted along the lines detailed in para 3.2 at pages 1390-1392 of Book-3, Vol. II. [Para 10.3.3]

(216) Reservation for members of the SCs and the STs should be brought under the purview of a statute covering all aspects of reservation, as detailed in para 8.10 at pages 1406-1408 of Book-3, Vol. II, including setting up *Arakshan Nyaya Adalats* or Tribunal to adjudicate upon all cases and disputes pertaining to reservation in posts and vacancies in Government, Public Sector, Banks and other financial institutions, Universities and all other institutions and organisations to which reservations are and become applicable. These Tribunals should have the status of High Courts, appeals lying only to the Supreme Court. These Tribunals should have their main Bench at Delhi and other Benches in the States. The Chairperson, Vice-Chairperson and other Members of the Tribunal and its benches should be selected on the basis of their record in the implementation of Reservation in their earlier positions. The statute should, *inter alia,* have a penal provision including imprisonment for those convicted of wilfully or negligently failing to implement reservation. The statute and related provisions should be brought under the Ninth Schedule to the Constitution. [Para 10.3.4]

(217) The three Constitution amendments enacted in the last two years to undo the harm done in 1997 to the long pre-existing rights of SCs and STs in reservations should be put into effect forthwith. The Central and State Governments should amend the executive orders issued in 1997 regarding the roster and restore the pre-1996 roster. This should also be brought under the purview of the statute mentioned above. [Para 10.3.5]

(218) The Reservation for backward classes should also be brought under a statute which, while containing the specificities of reservation for BCs should also contain provisions for *Arakshan Nyaya Adalats* or Tribunal for providing justice in reservation, penal provisions, etc. as recommended in the case of the statute in respect of SCs and STs. [Para 10.3.6]

(219) It should be mandatorily stipulated in the Memoranda of Understanding (MOUs) of privatisation or dis-investment of public sector undertakings that the policy of reservation in favour of SCs, STs and BCs shall be continued even after privatisation or dis-investment in the same from as it exists in the Government and this should also be incorporated in the respective statutes of reservation. As a measure of social integration there should be a half per cent reservation for children of parents one of whom is SC/ST and the other parent is non-SC/non-ST and this reservation should be termed as reservation for the Casteless. [Para10.3.7]

(220) In view of the weighty opinion against the formal introduction of reservation in the higher judiciary, and the fact that over fifty years, the progress of education, however tardy, has certainly produced adequate number of persons of the SC, ST and BC in every State who possess the required qualifications, having necessary integrity, character and acumen required for Judges of Supreme Court and High Courts for appointment as Judge of the superior judiciary, a way could and should, therefore, be found to bring a reasonable number of SCs, STs and BCs on to the Benches of the Supreme Court and High Courts in the same way in which, in practice, it is found is followed in respect of advocates from

different social segments/regions of the country/States or different religious communities so that on the one hand the overwhelming opinion against formal reservation in the Supreme Court and High Courts in respected and on the other hand, the feeling of alienation of the vast majority of Indians comprising SCs, STs and BCs that, in spite of having persons of requisite calibre and character among them, they are being Ignored in the appointment of judges, is resolved. [Para 10.3.9]

(221) There should be reservation for SCs, STs and BCs (including BC minorities and especially More and Most Backward classes), with a due proportion of women from each of these categories in the matter of allotment of shops under the public distribution system, and other allotments like petrol stations, gas agencies, etc. for distribution of commodities by public authority. There is need for support mechanism to help entrepreneurs among these deprived sections to help them to come up in these business ventures. These measures should be taken on the lines as spelt out in para 4.6 at page 1393 of Book-3 Vol. II. [Para 10.3.10]

(222) Massive programmes of employment should be undertaken and expanded to cover all such people and provide them employment at statutory minimum wage fixed for agricultural labourers at least for 80 days in the year over and above the unsteady employment they normally have. The nature of the work to be undertaken, the mode of payment of wages etc. should be as detailed in para 4.5 at pages 1392 to 1393 of Book-3 of Volume-II. Inclusion of Right to Work as a fundamental right has been recommended in para 3.13.2 of this Report and this will provide the necessary constitutional base and support for this programme. [Para 10.3.11]

(223) Residential schools for SCs and STs should be established in every district in the country—one each for SC boys and SC girls, and ST boys and ST girls, as one item of an important package of comprehensive measures required for the development and empowerment of SCs and STs. Similarly, the Commission recommends that residential schools should be set up for the BCs in every district, one each for BC boys and BC girls, including minorities who belong to BCs and with special attention to More Backward and Most Backward classes among BCs. The proportion of the students of the specific category of weaker sections (say 75 per cent) and of other social categories (say 25 per cent), the principles of location, methodology of covering the Minority B.C., phasing and funding, mode of selection of the candidates, management etc. should be as detailed in paras 5.4 and 6.2 at pages 1395 to 1397 of Book 3 of Volume II. This system has got the support of the precedent and experience for the last two decades in Andhra Pradesh state, providing ground for hope in this important and indispensable measure. In addition, the commission recommends that it is also necessary to see that the SCs, STs and BCs especially the More and Most Backward classes of BCs from poor and middle-class families get due benefit of good and prestigious private educational institutions in the country as well as in foreign educational institutions at all levels and in all disciplines, at state cost. Funding for this can be found by measures outlined in subpara (v) of para 5.4 at page 1396 of Book 3 of Volume II. The measures detailed in sub para (ii) and (iv) of para 5.4 at pages 1395 and 1396 of Book 3 of Volume II should be followed in the matter. [Para 10.4.1]

(224) Incentives should be offered to students to prepare for such courses of study in technical, vocational, scientific and professional disciplines. Only a massive transfer of resources to the educational programmes for the Scheduled Castes and Scheduled Tribes will enable us to achieve the kind of quantitative expansion needed to bring these communities on par with others in terms of skills and knowledge base to engage with the modern world. It is only then that they would be in a position to compete on the basis of their own strength and rise to the leadership role in different spheres of public life. This aspect of measures for building up a reservoir of highly educated professional, scientific and technological manpower among these categories in population equivalent proportion should be borne in mind along with its earlier recommendations regarding residential schools of high quality and elementary education, and provisions and outlays should be made accordingly. [Para 10.4.3]

(225) Social policy should aim at enabling the SCs, STs and BCs (including BC minorities and especially the More and Most Backward Classes among BCs) and with particular attention to the girls in each of these categories to compete on equal terms with the general category. This was always necessary but this becomes more important and increasingly urgent in the context of a knowledge society that is emerging. Reservation has helped the above deprived categories to enter state educational institutions from which they had been debarred and/or otherwise excluded in the past. Reservation continues to be necessary since these adverse factors have not ceased to exist. But with the growth of high quality educational institutions built up by the wealthier sections, almost entirely drawn from non-SC, non-ST, non-BC categories, as a high quality stream distinct and separate from the state educational system, it becomes important to ensure that other measures in addition to reservations are introduced. Without these measures, along with the Commissions recommendations on elementary education, the gap between the SC, ST and BC on the one hand and the rest of society will inexorably continue and even be widened. [Para 10.4.4]

(226) The Employment of Manual Scavengers and Construction of Dry Latrines (Prohibition) Act, 1993, should be strictly enforced to bring to an early end to this degrading practice of manual scavenging so offensive to human dignity without abridgement of the employment and income of existing Safai Karamcharis. Automatic applicability of the Act to all States should be brought about by the amendment suggested in para 7.2 at page 1399 of Book 3 of Volume II. Further, the specifics and details of the abolition of the manual scavenging system and the liberation and rehabilitation of Safai Karamcharis and protection of Safai Karamcharis during the transition period should be as detailed in para 7.3 of pages 1399 to 1401 of Book 3 of Volume II, including its incorporation in the System of Social Justice Clearance of officers at the time of their consideration for promotion. Limitations placed on the National Commission for Safai Karamcharis should be removed and it should be given the same powers and functional autonomy as is being enjoyed by the National Human Rights Commission; it should be adequately equipped to achieve its objective of total liberation and full rehabilitation of Safai Karamcharis. This should form an integral part of a National Sanitation Policy-cum-National Social Justice Policy. [Para 10.5]

(227) The bleak situation will continue to bedevil the SCs and STs and the nation unless appropriate new institutions are created to take charge of the full quantum of outlay of SCP and TSP (i.e. outlay not less than the population equivalent proportion of the total plan outlay of the Centre/each State) and manned by competent experts of SCs and STs and others genuinely working for them, to formulate plans in accordance with the developmental needs and priorities of the SCs and STs and ensure that these plans are implemented effectively. This new institutional system should consist of an integrated network of National Development Council for SCs and STs, and National SCs and STs Development Authority, State SCs and STs Development Authorities and District SCs and STs Development authorities. Out of the total plan outlay of the Centre and of each State, before sectorial allocations are made, an outlay equivalent to the population proportion of SCs and STs should be placed at the disposal of the National and respective State Authorities, as the corpus of SCP and TsP for formulation of plans in accordance with the needs and priorities of SC and ST. For this, the system as detailed in para 9.2 at pages 1409 to 1411 of Book-3, Volume-II should be established. The schemes as illustrated in sub-para (9) of para 9.2 at pages 1410-1411 of Book-3 Volume-II should also be taken up on a massive scale. This will at one stroke remove the various limitations and difficulties faced by the SCP and TSP and create a powerful, integrated instrument of social transformation based on the vision of economic liberation, educational equality and social dignity of the SCs and STs.

[Para 10.6.2]

(228) Land reforms involving distribution and allotment of lands from different sources (i.e. Government lands not required for genuine public use, Bhoodan lands, ceiling surplus lands, etc.) to the SCs and STs along with supportive mechanism in the shape of supply of subsidised capital and credit and extension be made, and development of these lands through irrigation and other means be undertaken. In this context, the measures recommended at (b) of subpara (9) of para 9.2 at page 1410 of Book-3, Volume-II and in para 14 (i) to (vi) at pages 1416 to 1417 of Book-3, Volume-II should be implemented. Similarly, with regard to enforcement of the Minimum Wages Act for agricultural labour, the methodology recommended at (c) of sub-para (9) of para 9.2 of page 1410 Book-3, Volume-II should be followed. Strong legal action is needed to prevent alienation of lands belonging to the tribal communities and effective prior rehabilitation of tribals before displacement due to developmental projects. For this purpose, the measures listed in para 13.2 at page 1414 to 1415 of Book-3, Volume-II should be undertaken. Additionally, the tribal communities have to be associated with the management of forest resources, for not only their livelihoods, but also for protecting their way of life and cultural identity which are indissolubly linked to forests. For this purpose, action as recommended in sub-paras (10) and (11) of para 13.2 at page 1416 of Book-3, Volume-II should be taken. [Para 10.7.1]

(229) In the matter of harmonising the preservation of the land ownership of STs, industrial and other development, action should be taken as outlined in sub-paras (6), (8) and (9) of para 13.2 of pages 1415 to 1416 of Book-3, Volume-II. [Para 10.7.2]

(230) Special safeguards should be provided to protect the wholesome traditions of the cultural heritage and of the intellectual property rights of the tribal people. This is no less important for the tribal identity than the effort to prevent alienation of land and land-related institutional rights of tribal people. [Para 10.7.3]

(231) *All areas governed by the Fifth Schedule to the Constitution should be forthwith transferred to the Sixth Schedule extending the applicability of the Sixth Schedule to tribal areas other than the North Eastern States to which alone the Sixth Schedule now applies, and all tribal areas which are neither in the Fifth Schedule nor in the Sixth Schedule should also be brought forthwith under the Sixth Schedule.* Special Programmes of training and orientation for the elected representatives of the Sixth Schedule bodies and related officials should be undertaken and conducted regularly in order to secure the full potential of local developmental and administrative autonomy envisaged under the Sixth Schedule. [Para 10.7.4]

(232) The Government should step in firmly and clearly, if the gap is to be bridged between private prejudices, in the name of "efficiency" on the one hand and the just aspirations of the SC, ST, BC including BC minorities, and women. For this, the Government should take the initiative along the lines suggested in para 11.3 at pages 1412 and 1413 of Book-3, Volume-II. [Para 10.7.5]

(233) Further, the Government should examine other economic and activity sectors at every level of each such sector and see whether the SCs and STs are adequately represented in each of them. If they are not, remedial measures either through reservation of through other means should be undertaken to see that they are adequately represented at every level in every such sector. Similar action should also be taken with regard to backward classes including BC minorities, especially More and Most Backward Classes and women of all categories. This is possible, if non-economic prejudices are excluded, without watering down the genuine requirements of efficiency. [Para 10.7.6]

(234) Agriculturists and other traditional producing classes face certain adverse effects of sudden and unprepared exposure to the regimes of WTO, IPR, etc. In order to protect them from these adverse effects while at the same time to secure the benefits of those regimes, a national convention should be convened involving Ministers in charge of Ministries connected with globalisation and Ministers in charge of Agriculture and other sectors of traditional produce and authentic representatives of the peasant organizations as well as organisations of other traditional producing classes, to identify remedial steps arrive at a consensus about them and these should be implemented quickly. There should be a continuing mechanism involving all these to continuously monitor implementation and correction and modifications required from time to time. [Para 10.7.7]

(235) Agriculturists and many other traditional producing classes suffer from the adverse effects of natural calamities like drought, cyclone, floods, etc. A similar national convention should identify the measures required to protect them from such adverse effects of natural calamities including crop insurance, preparedness etc., arrive at a consensus about these measures and institute a continuing machinery of continuous monitoring and correction and modifications. [Para 10.7.8]

(236) On the one hand, there should be an effective legal structure to protect the SCs and STs against atrocities and discriminatory practices based on untouchability and along with such structure and its efficient functioning and on the other hand, there should also be attitudinal change of a profound nature in the general society. [Para 10.8.1]

(237) With regard to legal structure, the Scheduled Castes and Scheduled Tribes (Prevention of Atrocities) Act, 1989 needs to be strengthened and its effective enforcement ensured. This include the establishment of special courts exclusively to try offences under this Act, inclusion of certain crimes in the list of atrocities, certain penal provisions where they do not exist, appropriate plugging of certain loopholes and comprehensive rehabilitation of victims and so on. For this purpose, the measures suggested in para 8.2.1, 8.2.2, 8.2.3, 8.3 and 8.4 (a) to (p) of Book-3, Vol. II at pages 1401 to 1404 should be taken.

[Para 10.8.2]

(238) Regarding untouchability which continues to be widely prevalent in old classic forms as well as in new forms in line with modern developments, multi-pronged measures covering human rights education, moral education, building up of a strong democratic movement against untouchability and effective punitive action under the Protection of Civil Right Acts, 1955 (PCR Act) are required. In view of this, the entire gamut of measures suggested in paras 8.6 to 8.8 at pages 1404 and 1405, Book-3, Vol. II should be taken.

[Para 10.8.3]

(239) The National Science and Technology Commission referred to in Chapter 6 should also promote measures for extending the umbrella of modern science and technology and higher scientific and technological research to cover SCs, STs and BCs, women and other poor sections of the society, devise means by which they can also be introduced into this field and potential talent among them identified and nurtured so that they also are enabled to contribute to the advancement to higher scientific and technological research in the country and so that there is no feeling that they are shut out from this important area on account of non-scientific prejudices. [Para 10.9]

(240) The Constitution of India contains distinct provision for the protection and promotion of the interests of Scheduled Castes and Scheduled Tribes, Backward classes, women, minorities and other weaker sections. It is necessary to strengthen these provision by amendments, etc. and certain other similar steps. Accordingly, *the amendments to the Constitution listed in para 15 at pages 1417 and 1418 of Book-3, Vol. II, covering articles 46, 335, 16, 15 and List III of the Seventh Schedule should be carried out* [Para 10.10]

(241) As regards the minorities, the following shall be implemented :

(a) Steps should be taken for improvement of educational standards amongst the minority communities. Special programmes should be drawn up after the widest consultation with the leaders of minority communities including leaders of BCs, SCs and STs among Minorities from academic, professional, business, and socio-political spheres and from low-occupational spheres. Such programmes should be generously funded. Only educational and cultural advancement will help the cause of national integration as well as raise the capabilities of the communities. This is the high road to national cohesion.

(b) At present the political representation of minority communities in legislatures, especially Muslims, has fallen well below their proportion of population. The proportion of BCs among them is next to nil. This can lead to a sense of alienation. It is recommended that in situations of this kind, it is incumbent for political parties to build up leadership potential in the minority communities, including BCs, SCs and STs among them, for participation in political life. The role of the state for strengthening the pluralism of Indian polity has to be emphasised.

(c) Backward classes belonging to religious minorities who have been identified and included in the list of backward classes and who, in fact, constitute the bulk of the population of religious minorities should be taken up with special care along with their Hindu counterparts in the developmental efforts for the backward classes. This should be on the pattern of the approach to the development of Backward Classes formulated by the Working Group for the Development and Empowerment of Backward Classes in the Tenth Plan referred to separately under Backward Classes.

(d) An effort needs to be made to carry out special recruitment of persons belonging to the under represent minority communities in the police forces of States, para military forces and armed forces. [Para 10.11.2]

(242) In every State, the linguistic minorities should be provided the facility of having instruction for their children at elementary stage of education in their mother tongue. Numerous recommendations in this behalf and other matters have been made by the Commissioner for Linguistic Minorities in his successive Annual Reports regarding the various problems faced by the linguistic minorities. The Government of India in the Ministry of Social Justice and Empowerment and the Ministry of Human Resources Development should collate all these recommendations and see that substantive action is taken on each of them. [Para 10.11.3]

(243) The denotified tribes/communities have been wrongly stigmatized as crime prone and subjected to highhanded treatment as well as exploitation by the representatives of law and order as well as by the general society. Some of them are included in the list of Scheduled Tribes and others are in the list of Scheduled Castes and list of backward classes. The special approach to their development has been delineated and emphasized in the Reports of the Working Groups for the Development of Scheduled Tribes, Scheduled Castes and Backward Classes in successive Plans and also in the Annual Reports of the Commissioners for Scheduled Castes and Scheduled Tribes, National Commission for Scheduled Castes and Scheduled Tribes and the National Commission for Backward Classes. There are also special reports available on de-notified tribes. Their recommendations have not received attention. The Ministry of Social Justice and Empowerment and the Ministry of Tribal Welfare should collate all these materials and recommendations contained in the reports of the working groups and the reports of the National Commissions and other reports referred to and strengthen the programmes for the economic development, educational development, generation of employment opportunities, social liberation and full rehabilitation of de-notified tribes. Whatever has been said about Vimuktajatis also holds good for nomadic and semi-nomadic tribes/communities. Similar action should be taken in respect of nomadic and semi-nomadic tribes/communities as done in the case of de-notified tribes or Vimuktajatis. The continued plight of these groups of communities distributed in the list of Scheduled Castes, Scheduled Tribes and Backward Classes is an eloquent illustration of the failure of the machinery for planning, financial resources allocation and budgeting and administration in the country to seriously follow the mandate of the Constitution including article 46. The setting up of an integrated network of National Scheduled Castes and

Scheduled Tribes Development Authority, etc. recommended in para 10.5.2 to 10.5.3 will provide a structural mechanism to deal in a practical way with the Vimuktajatis as well as nomadic and semi-nomadic tribes/ communities with the frame work of SCP and TSP. Similarly the approach to the development of backward classes referred to at para 10.14 contains the approach to deal in a practical way with the Vimuktajatis and nomadic and semi-nomadic tribes/communities who are in Backward Class list. [Para 10.12.1]

(244) The Commission also considered the representations made on behalf of the De-notified and Nomadic Tribal Rights Action Group and decided to forward them to the Ministry of Social Justice and Empowerment with the suggestion that they may examine the same preferably through a Commission. [Para 10.12.2]

(245) The Union legislation for agricultural workers, drafted as far back as 1978-80, should be introduced and passed immediately. A realistic scheme of credible implementation of minimum wages Acts with particular attention to agricultural labours, relying to a suitable degree on the district Collectors/Dy. Commissioners and district superintendents of police, should be immediately put into action. For this purpose the measures suggested in para 17.2 at page 1413 of Book 3 Vol. II should be followed. [Para 10.13.2]

(246) Despite prohibition of beggar and other forms of forced labour by the Constitution, the practice of bonded labour has not ended as it is patronised by the most powerful sections in the rural areas. Child labour too is widespread. In order to deal effectively with this problem in keeping with the mandate of the Constitution, the Commission recommends that a fully empowered National Authority for the Liberation and Rehabilitation of bonded labour, as recommended by the Commission for Rural Labour in 1990-91, should be set up immediately along with similar authorities at the State level. In addition, simultaneous rehabilitation of released Bonded Labourers and education for released bonded child labourers and other measures referred to in para 19.2 at page 1414 of Book 3, Vol. II should be taken. [Para 10.14]

(247) The Government should immediately implement every one of the recommendations of the Working Group on Employment of Backward Classes in the Tenth Plan which covers all aspects and fields of their development–Economic, Educational, social, employment, reservation, etc.–taking in with particular care those backward classes who belong to religious minorities along with their Hindu counterparts in a cohesive manner. For example, some of the residential talent schools earmarked for Backward Classes should be located in areas of concentration of Muslim BCs. Further there should be residential talent schools for backward classes as separately recommended for SCs and STs at the rate of one each for boys and girls in each district, 75% being taken from backward classes and 25% from other categories. The Government should without any delay introduce reservation for backward classes in seats in educational institutions since absence of promotion of their education through reservation and other means when there is reservation of employment is anomalous. [Para 10.15]

(248) Action in accordance with the suggestions made in para 16.2 at page 1412 of Book 3 Vol. II. Covering reservation, development, empowerment, health including malnutrition and maternal anaemia and protection against violence should be taken.

[Para 10.16]

(249) The problems relating to prostitution, child prostitutes and children of prostitutes have been the subject of a landmark judgment of the Supreme Court in Gaurav Jain's case of 9th July, 1997 and the Report of Committee of Secretaries on Prostitution, Child Prostitutes and Children of Prostitutes set up in 1997 as explained in para 20.1 and 20.2 at pages 1414 to 1415 of Book 3 Vol. II. In respect of this area of problem, the Government should take action according to the suggestion listed at para 20.3 at page 1415 of Book 3 of Vol. II, covering implementation of the judgement and the Secretaries' report, eliminating the Devadasi system, provision of development and education and prevention of HIV/AIDS

[Para 10.17]

49

CONCLUSION

A CONSTITUTION when written does not breathe. It comes to life and begins to grow only when human elements gather together and work it. As time passes, it changes in form and content, almost imperceptibly, and assumes a new shape and even a new meaning. This comes of the nature and temper of those who work it. Time and circumstances do have their impact on it. Yet, it is men, more than anything else, who shape and mould the destiny of a written constitution.

As Ambedkar observed:

However good a constitution may be, it is sure to turn out bad because those who are called to work it happen to be a bad lot. However bad a constitution may be, it may turn out to be good if those who are called to work it happen to be a good lot. The working of a constitution does not depend wholly upon the nature of the constitution. The constitution can provide only the organs of State such as the Legislature, the Executive and the Judiciary. The factors on which the working of these organs of the State depend are the people and the political parties they will set up as their instruments to carry out their wishes and their policies. Who can say how people of India and their parties will behave? Will they uphold constitutional methods of achieving their purposes or will they prefer revolutionary methods of achieving them? If they adopt the revolutionary methods, however good the constitution may be, it requires no prophet to say that it will fail. It is, therefore, futile to pass any judgement upon the constitution without reference to the part which the people and their parties are likely to play.[1]

No constitution is perfect and the Constitution of India is no exception to this general rule. But it goes to the credit of India that the urge for constitutional government was so deep-seated in her that she devised a constitution of her own within three years after achieving political independence. The Constitution she adopted was intended to be not merely a means of establishing a governmental machinery but also an effective instrument for orderly social change. The strength and stability of a constitution depends largely on its ability to sustain a healthy and peaceful social system and when occasion demands, facilitate the peaceful transformation of its economic and social order. From this point of view the Constitution has set an ideal which not even its severest critic would characterize as outmoded or reactionary. Its basic objective is to establish a democratic, socialist secular republic with a view to securing justice, liberty, equality and fraternity to all its citizens. It aims to translate into practice the noble concept of a cooperative commonwealth, a blending

1. C.A.D. X, p. 975.

of political democracy with economic and social democracy. It embodies the most comprehensive policy directions to the State and its agencies to ensure the establishment of a Welfare State.

On the eve of the adoption of the Republican Constitution of India, many noble sentiments were expressed on the floor of the Constituent Assembly by its members. Some of them recalled the hoary past of India which was not unfamiliar with the concept of democracy and republicanism. It was perhaps true that the ideals of democratic government and republican institutions were first conceived and practised a thousands years before Christ when the people of Mithila established the world's first republic. Such thoughts about a glorious past have indeed a heart-warming effect. What is important, however, is not the consciousness of our ancient glory but the ability to make democracy as envisaged under the Constitution work effectively in the present circumstances. Historical evidence indicates that in the days of the Buddha or even earlier, certain types of democracy did flourish in parts of India. But the republics of those days were confined to small areas, tribes and clans and operated in a highly decentralized fashion. The system, however, could not withstand the pressure of monarchical ideas and soon became a memory of the past. Hence, references to glorious republican institutions in an obscure era can yield but poor comfort in the context of modern challenges. The challenge that faces the country today is whether a constitution embodying democratic principles and establishing republican institutions, can withstand the pressures of a highly complex administration embracing a country of India's vast size and huge population.

Ambedkar focused the attention of not only the Constituent Assembly but the whole nation as early as 1949 on this aspect of the problem when he asked the following significant questions:

"On the 26th of January, 1950, India will be a democratic country and she will have a democratic Constitution. What should we do to preserve our democracy?" [1] These questions are not easy to answer. Yet it is the duty of everyone who is interested in the preservation of constitutional government and democracy in India to try and answer them.

A democratic system can endure only when citizens as a whole hold fast to constitutional methods for achieving their social and economic objectives. Now that constitutional methods are open and available, they must abandon the bloody or coercive methods of revolution, of civil disobedience, and of non-co-operation. For achieving social and economic objectives, these methods should have no place in the country. Democracy cannot survive long among any people with whom the loudest voice counts as the voice of wisdom, or when coercive pressures take the place of reason and persuasion.

Similarly, no country can remain democratic and no people can preserve a constitutional government, if the generality of the people are imbued with an immoderate sense of hero-worship. As John Stuart Mill said, a people should not lay their liberties at the feet of even a great man or trust him with powers which enable him to subvert their institutions. There is nothing wrong in being grateful to a great man, but as Daniel O'Connel said, "No man can be grateful at the cost of his honour, no woman at the cost of her chastity, and no nation at the cost of its liberty."

Dealing with this matter Ambedkar said:

---

1. C.A.D. X, p. 976.

This caution is far more necessary in the case of India than in the case of any other country. For, in India, *Bhakti* or what may be called the path of devotion or hero-worship, plays a part in its politics unequalled in magnitude by the part it plays in the politics of any other country in the world. *Bhakti* in religion may be a road to the salvation of the soul. But in politics, *Bhakti* or hero-worship is a sure road to degradation and eventual dictatorship."[1]

A political democracy without an economic and social democracy is an invitation to trouble and danger. Politics is more a result than a cause. Often this fact is forgotten in the external manifestations of the authority of the State. Political upheavals occur because of unsatisfactory economic and social conditions. The dictum of Aristotle that extreme inequalities cause revolutions in a democracy, although expressed in the context of Greek politics of a remote past, holds good for all ages. Wherever living standards are satisfactory, political stability is normally assured. Where there is economic instability, upheavals are bound to occur. Hence in order to ensure lasting political stability, its base should be firmly planted in an economic and social democracy. While economic democracy emphasizes the absence of extreme inequalities of wealth and adequate means of livelihood for everyone, social democracy stands for a way of life which recognizes liberty, equality and fraternity as the principles of life. In the words of Ambedkar, "these are not to be treated as separate items of a trinity.[2] They form a union of a trinity." In spite of over fifty years of independence, economic equality and social equality are yet to be realised in a substantial measure. Millions of people still live below the poverty line.

One of the perils of constitutional government and democracy in Asian and African countries is that in these countries political changes have preceded social and economic changes. Europe presents a substantially different picture. There, by and large, political changes followed an economic and social revolution. In most of the European countries, particularly of Western Europe, the Industrial Revolution preceded the emergence of political democracy. This is the reason why Europe is in a better position to preserve its political stability than Asia. Unless Asia can bring about rapid economic and social changes among her people, the measure of political democracy that she has introduced is bound to be destroyed sooner or later. India presents perhaps the most challenging test in this context, as she is struggling to realize rapidly an economic and social democracy, through democratic methods employed under a system of political democracy. If she does not achieve quick and wholesome results in this great experiment, she too, like several of her neighbours, is likely to lose the initiative of a democratic political order and succumb to some form of dictatorship. Equality in politics and inequality in economic and social life is a life of contradiction. Such a life cannot last long. It is necessary, therefore, that every effort should be made to remove this contradiction up to a reasonable measure at the earliest possible opportunity.

The importance of planning and planned development looms large in this context. However, if planning is to succeed, there must be general agreement on basic questions. A democracy reflects different interests in the policies of groups and parties. But the conflict among these different interests and pressure groups should not be on matters of basic significance from a developmental point of view. A wide area of agreement on such basic questions as the necessity of rapid development, the strategy of development to be adopted and general type of measures to be used is necessary for the successful functioning of the

1. C.A.D. X, p. 977
2. Ibid.

democratic system. The opposition must therefore refrain from opportunistic criticism of measures involving sacrifices for development purposes. At the same time both the government and the opposition should realize that democratic planning does involve reconciliation of different economic interests and adjustment of rival economic and social pressures, keeping in view the national interest at all times. In short, rapid economic growth is imperative for the survival of democracy in a country like India and democratic planning indeed offers a promising avenue of approach without sacrificing democratic institutions.

The successful working of a democratic constitution requires in those who work it, a willingness to respect the viewpoints of others, a capacity for compromise and accommodation and a real feeling of forbearance. Inflexibility and intolerance on the part of those who happen to be the rulers of the day will sow the seeds of hatred and vengeance. Constitutional government and democracy have no meaning if decisions are always taken on the strength of a numerical majority and the genuine feelings of the minority are bypassed and ignored. It is true that constitutional government would be brought into contempt if the people do not respect and abide by majority decisions. Yet, wisdom demands the finding of a line of demarcation between the fields where majority opinion should of necessity prevail and where minorities, whether of opinion or of interest, ought to be allowed to prevail if the results do not militate against the security of the State. Persistence in courses of conduct alienating minorities, linguistic or religious, simply because of the strength of a 'brute' majority, is no way to strengthen democracy. In this respect, the developing of healthy conventions and strict adherence to them have an important role to play.

Elsewhere, we have dealt at some length on the necessity of developing a sound party system for the successful working of the parliamentary system of government adopted under the Constitution. But the success of a party system largely depends upon the availability of effective and efficient leadership to the parties. Fortunately for India, the national movement threw up in its onward march a set of leaders, able, devoted and trusted. They guided the country in the initial stages of her independence in settling the problem of the Indian States and the framing of a new Constitution. They also gave a good start to the country in her economic and social transformation. But the old leadership has practically disappeared and its place has been taken up by that of a new generation capable of shouldering fully the new responsibilities and inspiring the confidence of the masses. Often one heard, in the past, that vexed question, "who will succeed Nehru?" That question, fortunately for India, has been answered successively in a most satisfying manner. But what the country needs today and even more tomorrow, is not so much just a top leader as a widespread understanding of the facts and considerations which are relevant to the problem of leadership as such in a parliamentary democracy. No nation can expect to get an efficient top leadership without carefully building up a series of levels lower down of properly selected and trained leadership. Many years ago, Walter Bagehot pointed out that nothing changes the face of politics as the change from one generation to another. While change is inevitable, it is essential to ensure that along with the change of leadership, the qualities that must be common to leadership in every age are not destroyed.

Among such qualities are those of courage, character, integrity and social awareness. But among these, character and integrity are even more important under a democratic system. One often hears of a crisis of character and competence in the country. In a country in which leadership becomes corrupt and character gets corroded, democracy cannot endure. When a nation is engaged in mighty efforts of national consolidation and economic rehabilitation, it needs more and more leaders of great integrity and character. Only such leadership can inspire the masses and create in them the enthusiasm for producing better and better results.

One of the most serious weaknesses of democracy in India is the widespread illiteracy and ignorance of the masses. The introduction of adult franchise at one stroke among a predominantly illiterate people has its own inherent dangers. So long as they are unable to exercise the franchise in an intelligent manner, after analysing the political issues in a rational way, democracy is not safe. For, they may be stampeded through empty slogans and irresponsible promises into becoming camp followers of unscrupulous political adventurers. It is therefore of the utmost importance to educate the masses and instill in them a genuine sense of political consciousness and the right constitutional temper. As Edmund Burke said, "let us educate our masters" for the sustenance of our democratic order.

Since a proper system of education is an effective instrument in the development of right attitudes, the system of education should be so reoriented as to inculcate in the youth the virtues of tolerance, discipline and respect for India's composite culture. It is also necessary that a code of conduct is to be evolved for the political parties as well as the press not to indulge in activities which will artificially whip up passions and generate prejudices hampering an objective assessment of problems and issues of political, economic and social significance.

In a country so large in size and with a perplexing diversity in geography, language, race and culture as India, the stability of the democratic system depends largely on its ability to decentralize authority and build up self-governing institutions of an integrated nature at all levels of the administration. However, in view of the great and urgent need for rapid economic development of the country as a whole, the fathers of the Constitution were compelled in assigning a predominantly leading role to the Central Government in the affairs of the nation. They were justified in doing so in the context of economic and social development in India at the time they framed the Constitution. But if centralization was dictated by the economic necessities of the past decentralization becomes imperative for the political stability of the future. The structure of Indian polity has ultimately to be one based on the solid foundation of self-governing local institutions at the lower levels which facilitate the building up of a hierarchy of well-knit and closely bound units of administration at every successive higher level. The progress of democracy in India is inseparably bound with the extent to which these local institutions are established and the manner in which they function in the years to come. In this respect, the measures so far taken for the establishment of Panchayati Raj institutions [1] all over the country, although not a complete success yet, form a move in the right direction.

While the imperative need for the integrated development of the country at an accelerated pace has been widely recognized as an essential pre-condition for the sustenance of India's democracy, the inter-regional jealousies, lack of co-operation and even conflicts have been hampering such development. This is in spite of a comprehensive system of

1. The term *Panchayati Raj* stands for a system of decentralized democracy at the village, block and district levels of the State Administration.

national planning that has been built up over a period of over five decades. While planning demanded an overall national approach to the difficult socio-economic problems the country faced and effective power at the disposal of the Centre, regionalism which is largely based on unilingual States has been expressing itself in many forms and working against a national outlook and national unity. Frictions between different regions, each of which is characterized by a homogeneous language and culture, have been a frequent occurrence in India especially since the reorganization of States in 1957. To a large extent they arise from substantial disparity between the different State units in levels of economic and cultural growth. The relatively less developed states often smart under a deep sense of neglect and resentment. Such feelings from time to time find expression in linguistic agitations and even riots. The objective of these movements appear to be not so much the preservation or promotion of the separate cultures as to drive out people who speak a different language and who have come from other areas of the country. As observed by two thoughtful critics: "It is the middle-class job-hunter and place-hunter and the (mostly) middle-class politicians who are benefited by the establishment of a linguistic State, which creates for them an exclusive preserve of jobs, offices and places by shutting out, in the name of the promotion of culture, all outside competitors."[1]

Inter-regional jealousies and rivalries and the tension that is generated as a consequence, tend to sap the spirit of cooperative federalism that is so badly needed for the smooth development of democracy under constitutional government in India. Coupled with this is the fear of linguistic domination by the Hindi-speaking people over the non-Hindi speaking area. Linguistic chauvinism has always been a disintegrating force wherever it has manifested itself. That is a lesson from history which India cannot and should not ignore. While any attempt at Hindi hegemony is undesirable because of the natural and spontaneous resistance to it that will gather momentum, the anti-Hindi phobia which some regions artificially whip up is equally undesirable from the national integration point of view. For, Hindi is the only language which in the long run can aspire to become the lingua franca of India as a whole. In the ultimate analysis, inter-regional harmony in India can be established only through balanced regional economic and cultural development as quickly as possible. Simultaneously, there must be opportunity for the widest possible sharing of political power through equitable distribution of important offices of the Union Government among the component units of the Union. Constitutional government and democracy have little real meaning so long as such equitable sharing of political power is not ensured and opportunity for economic development both for the individual and the different regions is not made possible.

The frequent changes of government in the States and even at the Centre in recent years (We have had eight different governments at the Centre in eight years of 1990-1998.) point to the general disregard for institutional norms. Collectively, these developments highlight the need to address a gamut of issues concerning the nature and character of our representative institutions. Popular governments whether led by a single party or a coalition of parties get toppled by intra-party factionalism or counter coalitions which radically misrepresent the electoral mandate. This has become a contagious phenomenon in the country during the last one decade showing the immaturity and instability of Indian democracy.

1. Mukherji and Ramaswami, *Reorganisation of Indian States*, p. 31.

Political parties seem to multiply after every general elections. According to the Election Commission of India there were some 128 political parties in India in 1996. The number has gone up substantially in the past few years. The lure of ministership has been the basic urge to break parties, to manipulate majorities and to destabilise or topple governments. Jumbo cabinets seem to be the order of the day in most of the larger states. The smaller States are not far behind. Some of them have more than half of the Members in the Legislative Assembly as ministers. Bihar, U.P., Haryana, Goa, the States in the North-east are the worst examples.

Failure of Single Party Governments

There is however no special virtue in a single-party government. During the first forty-four years since Independence, India was under single-party rule for as many as thirty-nine years. That has not helped the solving of the country's major problems. In fact, the very reason for the present sharp polarisation seems to be the effect of the failure of a single-party government at the Centre for such a long period. Unfortunately, during the last fifty years, India has not been able to develop a strong party system. As a result, the opposition parties have been irresponsible. They oppose anything proposed by the party in power, whether right or wrong, good or bad just for the sake of opposing. It has become an obsession, even a disease with them.

In 1984, at the end of the eighth General Elections, Rajiv Gandhi was returned to power with a massive unprecedented majority of 415 seats in a House of 543. No government could have expected anything better from the electorate. It was the first time that such an overwhelming majority was won by the party. And yet the Rajiv Gandhi Government was a failure on the whole and that was demonstrated by the ninth General Elections with the Congress Party's poor performance. The functioning of the Government, the functioning of the party, the Central Government's attitude towards the State Governments, particularly towards those ruled by parties other than the Congress, the sweeping manner in which decisions were imposed on Congress Governments in the States by the Central leadership, the conflict between the Prime Minister and the President and above all, the dictatorial character of the internal organisation of the Congress party itself, all these show that a single party government has no special virtue to claim for itself. On the contrary, the poor performance of the single party Congress rule amply demonstrates that a country of India's size and complex problems, social, religious, regional and linguistic, needs a national government which represents the will of the people as a whole.

Another alarming development has been the steady growth of Naxalism in the country. It has spread to many parts of India. the States which are most seriously under Naxal threat are West Bengal, Bihar, Orissa, Andhra Pradesh, Chattisgarh. Madhya Pradesh and Jharkhand. Recently in one of his statements Prime Minister Manmohan Singh had voiced his concern and anxiety on the growth of Naxalism. Every citizen who is interested in the unity and integrity of India was worried over the development of Naxalism in India. The time has come to make a serious and comprehensive study about Naxalism with a view to finding remedial measures and to implement them with all seriousness and urgency.

The Case for a National Government

The case for a national government is so compelling today that anything different will not inspire the confidence of the nation. Parliamentary democracy of the Westminster model has failed in India. It is because our people as a whole and our politicians in particular have not cultivated the spirit of 'Constitutional morality' which is an essential *sine qua non* for its success. Constitutional morality presupposes a code of conduct in public affairs, particularly in the attitude of parties both ruling and opposition. On national issues they must have a common outlook. The opposition is not simply to oppose everything that is put forward by the government of the day and bent upon defeating every official move at any cost but to act in a constructive manner. Similarly, the government of the day is not to act in a manner that smacks of steam-rollerism, of intolerance, of narrow mindedness and of partisanship. There should be a spirit of give and take, an appreciation of constructive criticism, willingness to listen to a different point of view and conceding a credit point to the critic who is making a point of view although different from the official one.

Similarly, there must be a system of power sharing at different levels of the government and administration based on competence and character. The reason why single-party governments have failed in India is because of the misuse of power by the government and the abuse of public offices by power-brokers. Today we have come to a critical stage in the country's history when we are compelled to cast off the single party system. A hung parliament for a third time in four years emphasised the fact that the electorate has lost its faith in the single party system. It is in that context that we should look for an alternative system.

A national government of all the leading political parties on a minimum agreed programme is bound to inspire the people's confidence and instill in those who take up ministerial positions a sense of direction and dedication. They are bound to view the problem from the point of view of the country as a whole rather than the narrow considerations of the Party in power. There is bound to emerge as a result a consensus on all the major problems that confront the country.

However, the formation of a national government depends on the willingness of all the major parties especially the party that has the largest membership in the Lok Sabha. To what extent they all will look at the idea favourably is a matter to be seen after the final results of the elections become clear. It is the responsibility of the leading political party to take the initiative for such a government. The reports that President Venkataraman had taken the initiative for such a government twice in the receipt past shows how, as the Head of the Nation, he was applying his mind to the country's grave problems and challenges. While the President's initiative should be welcome to all concerned, more than the President, it is for the leading political parties and particularly the party which has the largest following in the Lok Sabha to take such initiative, The President can, of course, play a catalyst's role at a crucial moment, but too decisive an action cannot be expected of him under our Constitution.

Case for Coalition Governments

If there is no consensus for a national government, what then is the alternative? The only alternative is a coalition government. Like-minded parties should get together to work out a coalition government. The pattern of friendly parties supporting a government from outside has been tried in the recent past, but each time the experiment failed. The downfall of the V.P. Singh Government and that of Chandra Sekhar and also those of Deve Gowda, Gujral and Vajpayee demonstrates that without actively sharing power and responsibility with the supporting party, no government can remain in office for long. That means that that alternative should be ruled out and a coalition with a minimum platform should be given a fair trial to show a new way at the Centre.

For example, if we have a close look at the manifestoes of all the national political parties, it is not difficult to find a good deal of common ground between the Congress and the Janata Dal and the Left Parties. Why not they get together to form a viable strong coalition government? Let the BJP be in the opposition and play the vital role of a constructive opposition. A coalition government need not necessarily be an everlasting alliance. Once the political situation becomes favourable the coalition partners may part company and seek a fresh verdict from the electorate.

After all, we are not altogether strangers to coalition governments. Both West Bengal and Kerala have shown for a fairly long period that in spite of numerous problems and difficulties in the smooth working of such governments, coalitions can still do reasonably well. The record of these two state governments, although not flattering, has been in fact much better than those of single party governments in several other States in India.

Coalition governments have had an impressive record all over the world during the second half of the twentieth century and they seem to have come to stay as an integral part of the parliamentary system. Germany is a shining example of successive successful coalition governments. Holland, Belgium and some of the Scandinavian countries have also demonstrated how coalition governments can function successfully. Switzerland has been a remarkable example of stable coalition governments. Italy is a classic case where several political parties have been getting together and forming coalition governments from time to time, and performing with reasonable success. All these countries are much different from India from the point of view of the complexity of problems such as regional, linguistic and socio-cultural. Yet they have not been striving for single party governments with too frequent elections aiming at the creation of such governments. In fact, coalition governments seem to offer a new solution for countries like India in the days to come both for stability and wider acceptability of governments.

The present is a momentous moment for our political leaders to think seriously and plan carefully in order to hammer out a new viable and stable coalition government if the idea of a national government is still beyond the realm of reality.

Alround Corruption

Feudal culture and colonial rule were blamed for the cancer of corruption in the country. Independence, it was hoped, would usher in an era of honesty and integrity in public affairs. But this has not happened. On the contrary, as time passed, and by the seventies, eighties and nineties, India graduated to the ranks of the most corrupt in the world. A recent global study shows that China, Pakistan, Indonesia and India are the most corrupt countries of the world today.

This is not an exhaustive list of our ills and evils, faults and failures but only a few examples. In the post-golden jubilee era of India's Independence the country is at the cross roads.

Some Achievements

An optimist may argue that a period of five decades is perhaps too short a period in the life of a nation. As such an evaluation of its performance so far may have only a limited significance. Even so, we have to accept the hard reality that most of the objectives set before the nation are yet to be realised. This should not make us blind to the fact that during this period quite a number of achievements are there to the credit of India. While constitutions have been mended or ended frequently, and political upheavals have been the hall-mark of most countries of Asia, Africa and Latin America, India has remained a bulwark of democracy and constitutional government however unsatisfactory that might have been. We still continue to exist as a democracy. Survival itself is a matter of great significance.

The challenge that faces the nation today is how to strengthen the forces of constructive activity all around and ensure communal and religious amity, along with steady economic growth.

Whatever may be its imperfections, a constitution need not and should not stand in the way of a country's progress. Even if it is made only to suit the conditions and circumstances of one age, it need not fail in another. It is difficult to imagine a Constitution like that of the United States, written in the eighteenth century, suiting the altogether different conditions of the twentieth century. Yet it has worked and worked fairly well. In contrast, France has had no less than five constitutions within nearly the same period. Whether the latest one will help France to secure political strength and stability of an enduring nature is yet to be seen. In the post-war Europe, no constitution was hailed as more democratic than that of the Weimar Republic of Germany. Yet it could not prevent Hilter in his sinister march to power and the establishment of a totalitarian regime.

The fact that Indian Constitution has been amended too frequently has been a subject of severe criticism both in India and outside. The critics consider that the Constitution is a 'sacred document' which should not become the subject of too frequent amendments. There is considerable substance in this criticism. Yet there is another side to the matter. A constitution is only a means to an end and not an end in itself. It has no sanctity. It must conform to the needs and challenges of a developing country and of changing times. In an age like the present, when science and technology have made spectacular changes in the needs of human beings, no constitution can claim rigid permanence and at the same time be able to adapt itself to the changing conditions. It is better to have amendments which will provide easy adaptability to altered conditions, rather than an abrupt end under the weight of revolutionary social changes.

Five decades although not a short period is not a long enough period in the life of a nation. As such, an evaluation of the working of the constitution has only a limited significance. Many of the objectives set before the nation are yet to be realized. But still the trend is unmistakably clear. It was during this period that the initial tests of the constitution were conducted. Thirteen General Elections on the basis of adult suffrage, the reorganization of the States, the establishing of a full-fledged cabinet system of Government both at the Centre and in the States, the setting up of an independent judicial system all over the country with the Supreme Court of India at its apex, the testing of the value and effectiveness of the Fundamental Rights, the passing of a long list of social and economic legislation to give effect to the Directive Principles and systematic programme of planned development through the Five Year Plans—all these have been done in accordance with the provisions of the Constitution. Adequate food production, systematic development of science and technology and the magnificent performance of the judiciary as a whole and the higher judiciary in particular, also are worthy to be recorded as independent India's achievements.

While steady progress has been thus maintained under the Constitution, there have been stresses and strains both due to internal difficulties and external factors. As many as a hundred times or more the emergency provisions had to be invoked in fifty years to set aright the breakdown of constitutional machinery in the States. In 1962 a national emergency was proclaimed by the President as a result of the Chinese aggression on the territory of India with far-reaching consequences. There had been three more proclamations of national emergency by the President, in 1965, 1971 and 1975. The Constitution was also amended many times either to remove the difficulties experienced in its working or to facilitate greater mobility in the social change that it originally envisaged. There have been forty-six such amendments by 1983 and ninety-four by the year 2006. These amendments, however, have not in any substantial manner modified the basic ideals for which the Constitution stood, or altered the framework of governmental machinery it sought to establish.

The complete and unqualified triumph of the rule of law as well as the full realization of the objectives of the Constitution, may still be a distant goal. Nevertheless, India can feel reasonably satisfied that she is well on the right path towards that goal. The Constitution, on the whole, has worked fairly well and continues to remain an inspiring document for the citizens of this land.

***

SELECTED BIBLIOGRAPHY

Section 1 : *Acts, Reports and other Documents*

All India Reporter (from 1950 to date)—*Constitutional Law Decisions*
Cabinet Mission Plan (1946)
Census of India, 1951 1961 and 1991
Constitution of India (Draft—1949)
Constitution of India (Text—1950)
Constitution of India as Modified up to 1 *September* 1951
Constitution of India as Modified up to 1 *November* 1956
Constitution of India as Modified up to 1980
Constitutional Proposals of the Sapru Committee (1945)
Debates in the Central Assembly (India) 1921 to 1945
Debates in the Constituent Assembly of India (10 Vols.)
Debates in the House of Commons (relating to India, particularly 1934-35, 1942-43 and 1945-47)
Debates in the House of Lards (relating to India)
Debates in the Lok Sabha and Rajya Sabha of the Parliament of India (1950 to date)
Federal Court (of India) Reports from 1937 to 1950
Fifth Five Year Plan (An Approach to)
First Five Year Plan (1952)
Fourth Five Year Plan
Gazette of India (Extraordinary), March 15, 1950; July 31, 1959 and October 26, 1962
Government of India Act, 1919
Government of India Act, 1935
Government of India's Despatch on Constitutional Reform
India (A Reference Annual) from 1955 to date
India Code, Vol. I to VII
Indian Independence Act, 1947
Montagu-Chelmsford Report, 1918
Nehru Committee Report, 1928
Presidential Addresses of the Indian National Congress (particularly from 1922 to date)
Proceedings of the Round Table Conferences (2 Vols.)
Quit India Resolution (1942)
Report of the Reforms Enquiry Committee (1924)
Report of the All Parties Conference (1928)
Report of the Simon Commission (1930)
Report of the Federal Structure Committee (1932)
Report of the Joint Parliamentary Committee (1934)
Report of the Joint Select Committee (1935)
Report of the Backward Classes Commission (1955)
Reports (Annual) of the Commissioner for Scheduled Castes and Tribes (from 1951 to 1995)
Report of the Election Commission of India–First General Elections, 1951-52

Report of the Election Commission of India–Second General Elections, 1957
Report of the Election Commission of India–Third General Elections, 1962
Report of the Election Commission of India–The Fourth General Elections, 1967
Report of the Election Commission of India–The Fifth General Election, 1972,
Sixth and Seventh General Elections, 1979-1981
Report of the Study Team on Social Welfare and Welfare of the Backward Classes, Committee on Plan Projects, 1959
Report of the Education Commission (1964-66), Government of India, Ministry of Education, New Delhi
Report of the Monopolies Enquiry Commission (1965), Government of India, New Delhi
Report of the Committee on Distribution of Income and Levels of Living, Part I (1964) and Part II (1969), Planning Commission, Government of India
Report of the National Commission on Labour, Ministry of Labour, Employment and Rehabilitation, Government of India, 1969
Report of the Committee on Unemployment (1973), Government of India (Unpublished)
Report of the Committee of Prevention of Corruption, Government of India, Ministry of Home Affairs (1962)
Reports on the Seminar of Indian Law Institute, New Delhi on (1) Law and
Minorities in India (1971) and (2) Constitutional Developments since Independence (1973)
Report of the States Reorganisation Commission (1955)
Report of the First Finance Commission (1952)
Report of the Second Finance Commission (1957)
Report of the Third Finance Commission (1961)
Report of the Seventh Finance Commission (1978)
Report of the Official Language Commission (1956)
Report of the Committee of Parliament on Official Language (1958)
Reports of the Commissioner of Linguistic Minorities (1962)
Reports of the Union Public Service Commission (1951 to date)
Review of Education in India, Ministry of Education (1961)
Review of the First Five Year Plan (1957)
Second Five Year Plan (1956)
States Reorganisation Act, 1956
Statement issued by the Conference on National Integration (1961)
Supreme Court Reports (from 1950 to date)
*Third Five Year Plan (*1961*) and Fifth Five Year Plan* (1974)
Towards Equality, Report of the Committee on the Status of Women in India (1976)
White paper on Indian States (Government of India, Ministry of States, 1950)

Section 2 : Books

AGARWAL, P.P., *The System of Grants-in-aid in India* (1959)
AGGARWALA, OM PRAKASH, *Fundamental Rights and constitutional Remedies* (3 Vols.)
AGGARWALA, OM PRAKASH, *Supreme Court Digest, Vols. I to III*
AIYER, ALLADI KRISHNASWAMI, *The Constitution and Fundamental Rights* (Srinivasa Sastri Memorial Lectures, 1955)
AIYER, ALLADI KRISHNASWAMI and AIYANGAR, N.R., *Government of India Act, 1935 with a Commentary, Critical and Explanatory* 1937)
AIYER, SIVASWAMY, *Indian Constitutional Problems* (1928)

ALEXANDER, H., *India since Cripps* (1944)
ALEXANDROWICZ, CHARLES H., *Constitutional Developments in India* (1957)
ANANT, SANTOKH SINGH, *The Changing Concept of Caste in India* (1972)
ANDREWS, C.F., *India and the Simon Report* (1930)
ALTEKAR, A.S., *State and Government in Ancient India* (2nd revised and enlarged edn.), 1955
AMBEDKAR, B.R., Ranade, *Gandhi and Jinnah* (1943)
AMBEDKAR, B.R., *Thoughts on Linguistic States* (1955)
AMERY, L.S., *India and Freedom* (1942)
APPADORAI, A., *Towards a Just Social Order* (1970)
ARCHIBOLD, W.A.J., *Outline of Indian Constitutional History* (1926)
AUSTIN, GRANVILLE, *The Indian Constitution: Cornerstone of a Nation* (1972)
AZAD, MAULANA ABUL KALAM, India Wins Freedom (1959)
BAILEY, S.D., *Parliamentary Government in Southern Asia* (1953)
BAINS, J.S. (editor), *Studies in Political Science* (1961)
BANDURANT, G.V., *Regionalism versus Provincialism—A Study in Problems of Indian National Unity* (1958)
BANERJEA, P., *Public Administration in Ancient India* (1916)
BANERJEE, BENODE BEHARI, *Outline of the Dominion Constitution for India*
BANERJEE, A.C., *The Making of the Indian Constitution*, 1939-47 (extracts from documents)
BANERJEE, A.C., *Indian Constitutional documents*, 1758-1945, 3 Vols. (1946)
BANERJEE, A.C., *The Constituent Assembly of India* (1947)
BANERJEE, A.C., and BOSE, D.R., *The Cabinet Mission in India* (1946)
BANERJEE, B.N., *Natural Justice and Social Justice before the Supreme Court* 1950-59 (1960)
BANERJEE, D.N., *Early Administrative System of the East India Company in Bengal* (1943)
BANERJEE, D.N., *Partition or Federation, a Study in Indian Constitutional Problems*.
BANERJEE, D.N., *The Draft Constitution of India: A Critique* (1949)
BANERJEE, R.D., *The Age of the Imperial Guptas* (1933)
BANERJEE, SURENDRANATH, *A Nation in Making* (1925)
BARKAT ALI, M., *Indian Constitution together with the Government of India Act*, 1919'
BASU, DURGA DAS, *Commentary on the Constitution of India* (1952)
BASU, DURGA DAS, *Cases on the constitution of India* (2 Vols.)
BEARCE, GEORGE D., *British Attitudes Towards India*, 1784-1858 (1961)
BENI PRASAD, *A Few Suggestions on the Problem of the Indian Constitution* (1928)
BENI PRASAD, *The State in Ancient India* (1942)
BENI PRASAD, *Hindu-Muslim Questions* (1941)
BEOTRA, B.R., *The Two Indias* (1932)
BETEILLE, ANDRE, *Inequality and Social Change* (1972)
BEVERIDGE, LORD, *India Called Them* (1947)
BHAGAT, K.P. *The Kerala Mid-term Elections of 1960* (1962)
BHALLA, R.P., *Elections in India*, 1950-1972 (1973)
BHAMBRI, C.P., *Administrators in a Changing Society* (1972)
BHANJDEO, P.C., *Financial Position of the Government of India* (1935)
BHARGAVA, R.N., *The Theory and Working of Union Finance in India* (1956)
BHARGAVA, R.N., *Indian Public Finance* (1962)
BHARATAN KUMARAPPA and others, *Cultural Foundations of Indian Democracy* (1955)
BLANT, SIR EDWARD, *The Indian Civil Service* (1937)
BOSE, SUBHAS CHANDRA, *The Indian Struggle* (1932)
BOSE, SUBHAS CHANDRA, *Crossroads* (1962)
BOWLES, CHESTER, *Ambassador's Report* (1965)
BOWLES, CHESTER, *The Makings of Just Society* (1963)

BRAILSFORD, H.N., *Rebel India* (1931)
BRIGHT, J.S. (editor), *Selected Writings of Jawaharlal Nehru* (1950)
BROCKWAY, A. FENNER, *The Indian Crisis*
BROWN, D. MACKENZIE, *The Nationalist Movement: Indian Political Thought from Ranade to Bhave* (1961)
Cambridge History of India, Vols. V and VI (1913)
CAMPBELL-JOHNSON, ALLAN, *Mission with Mountbatten* (1951)
CHAUDHRI, A.S., *Constitutional Rights and Limitations* (1956)
CHANDA, A.K., *Indian Administration* (1960)
CHANDA, ASOK, *Under the Indian Sky* (1971)
CHANDRAN, J.R. and THOMAS, M.M (editors), *Religious Freedom* (1956)
CHATURVEDI, R.G., *Natural and Social Justice* (1970)
CHIROL, VALENTINE, *Indian Unrest*
COATMAN, JOHN, *The Indian Riddle* (1932)
COATMAN, JOHN, *India—The Road to Self-Government* (1941)
COUPLAND, R., *Cripps Mission* (1942)
COUPLAND, R., *The Indian Problem*-1833-1935 (1942)
COUPLAND, R., *India, a Re-statement* (1945)
COUPLAND, R., *Constitutional Problems in India* (1949)
COWELL, HERBERT, *History and Constitution of the Courts and Legislative Authorities in India* (1936)
COX, PHILIP, *Beyond the White Paper: A Discussion of the Evidence Presented before the Joint Select Committee on Indian Constitutional Reforms* (1934)
CUMMING, SIR JOHN, *Modern India* (1932)
CURTIS, LIONEL, *Letters to the People of India on Responsible Government*
DA COSTA, ERIC P., *Economic Growth with Social Justice: Challenge and Response* (1972)
DALAL, M.N., *Whither Minorities*?
DAS, BANKA BEHARI, *Indian Economy and Socialism* (1971)
DEAN, V.M., *New patterns of Democracy in India* (1959)
DESAI, A.R., *Social Background of Indian Nationalism* (1954)
DIVETIA, KUMUD, *The Nature of Inter-Relations of Governments in India* (1957)
DODWELL, HENRY, *A Sketch of the History of India from 1858 to 1918* (1925)
DOUGLAS, W.O., *We the judges* (1956)
DUFFETT, W.E., HICKS, A.R. and PARKIN, J.R., *India Today* (1942)
DUNCAN, ARTHUR, *India in Crisis* (1931)
DUNLOP, JOHN T., *The Theory of Wage Determination* (Proceedings of the International Economic Association)
DUTT, ISWARA, *Indian Constitutional Reform*
DUTT, PALME R., *India Today* (1946)
EDDY, J.P. and LAWTON, F.H., *India's New Constitution: As Survey of the Government of India Act,* 1935
FARUQI, ZIYA-UL-HASAN, *The Deoband School and the Demand for Pakistan* (1963)
FISHER, F.B., *India's Silent Revolution* (1920)
FORBES, ROSITA, *India of the Princes* (1939)
FRIEDMANN, W., *Law in a Changing Society* (1959)
GADGIL, D.R., *Federating India* (1945)
GADGIL, D.R., *Some Observations on the Draft Constitution* (1949)
GAJENDRAGADKAR P.B., *Constitution of India*: Its Philosophy and Basic Postulates 91969)
GAJENDRAGADKAR, P.B., Law, *Liberty and justice* (1965)
GAJENDRAGADKAR, P.B., *The Indian Parliament and Fundamental Rights* (1972)
GAJENDRAGADKAR, P.B., *Political Freedom and Social Justice* (1974)
GANDHI, M.K., *India's Struggle for Swaraj* (1921)

GANDHI, M.K., *Communal Unity* (1949)
GANGULEE, N., *The Making of Federal India* (1936)
GANGULEE, N., Constituent Assembly for India (1942)
GARRAT and THOMPSON, *Rise and Fulfillment of British Rule in India* (1935)
GLEDHILL, A., *Fundamental Rights in India* (1956)
GLEDHILL, A., *Republic of India, the Development of its Laws and Constitution*
GOREY, V.K., *United States of India, a Constructive Federal Solution*
GOUR, SIR HARI SINGH, Future Constitution of India (1938)
GREGORY, T., *India on the Eve of the Third Five Year Plan* (1961)
GRIFFITHS, SIR PERCIVAL, *The British Impact on India* (1952)
GWYER, M. and APADORAI, A. (editors), *Speeches and Documents of the Indian Constitution*, Vols. I and II (1957)
HAKSAR and PANIKKAR, *Federal India*
HANGEN, WELLES, *After Nehru, Who?*
HAQQI, S.A.A., *The Colonial Policy of the Labour Government*, 1945-1951 (1961)
HARI CHAND, *The Amending Process in the Indian Constitution* (1972)
HARRISON, SELIG, India—*The Most Dangerous Decades* (1960)
HARTOG, LADY, *India, New Pattern* (1955)
HEGDE, K.S., *Crisis in Judiciary* (1973)
HEGDE, K.S., "*Directive Principles of State Policy in the Constitution of India*", I.C.P.S. (1972)
HORNE, E.A., *Political System of British India with Special Reference to the Recent Constitutional Changes* (1922)
HULL, WILLIAM I., *India's Political Crisis*
ILBERT, COURTNAY, *Government of India: A brief Historical Survey of Parliamentary Legislation Relating to India* (1922)
INDIAN INSTITUTE OF PUBLIC ADMINISTRATION, *Organisation of the Government of India* (1958)
INDIAN NATIONAL CONGRESS-AICC, *Chief Ministers Speak*: being a resume of the activities of the Governments, Central and State, during the 3 years 1947-50
INDIAN NATIONAL CONGRESS-AICC, *Economic Freedom and Economic Planning: a Symposium*
INDIAN NATIONAL CONGRESS-AICC, *Constitution of the Indian National Congress* (1961)
IQBAL NARAIN, *Twilight or Dawn-The Political Change in India*, 1967-71 (1972)
IRWIN, LORD, *Some Aspects of the Indian Problem* (1932)
ISSACS, HAROLD R., *India's Ex-untouchables* (1965)
ISWARI PRASAD, *Medieval India* (1943)
JAIN, H.M., *Right to Property under the Indian Constitution* (1968)
JAYASWAL, K.P., *Hindu Policy* (2nd ed., 1953)
JENNINGS, SIR IVOR, *Some Characteristics of the Indian Constitution* (1953)
KALE, V.G., *Gokhale and Economic Reforms* (1916)
KARUNAKARAN, K.P. (editor), *Modern Indian Political Tradition* (1963)
KEITH, ARTHUR BERRIEDALE, *Constitutional History of India*, 1600-1935 (1937)
KHAN, SIR S. AHMAD, *Indian Federation* (1937)
KHAN, SIR S. AHMAD, *Federal Finance* (1939)
KOCHANEK, S.A., *Business and Politics in India* (1974)
KOTHARI, RAJNI, *Politics in India* (1970)
KRIPALANI, J.B., *Politics of Charkha* (1946)
KRISHNAMACHARI, V.T., *Fundamentals of Planning in India* (1962)
KRISHNAN, K.B., *Problem of Minorities or Communal Representation in India* (1939)
KRISHNAMURTHY, Y.G., *Constituent Assembly and Indian Federation*
KRISHNA SHETTY, K.P., *Fundamental Rights and Socio-economic Justice in the Indian Constitution* (1969)
KUMARAMANGALAM, MOHAN, *Judicial Appointments* (1973)

KUPPUSWAMI, B., *Social Change in India* (1972)
LAJPAT RAI, *The Political Future of India* (1930)
LAL, A.B. (editor), *The Indian Parliament* (1956)
LAL BAHADUR, *The Muslim League* (1954)
LEE-WARNER, *The Native States of India* (1933)
LEVI, WERNER, *Free India in Asia* (1954)
LUMBY, E.W.R., *The Transfer of Power in India* 1944-47 (1954)
LUTHERA, V.P., *The Concept of the Secular State and India* (1964)
MACDONALD, J. RAMSAY, *Government of India*
MACHMAHON, A.W., *Delegation and Autonomy* (1961)
MAHARAJ, HEMINATH, *Is the Republic of India Secular*? (1956)
MAJUMDAR, B.B., (editor), *Public Administration in India* (1953)
MAJUMDAR, R.C., *An Advanced History of India* (1948)
MALENBAUM, WILFRED, *Prospects for Indian Development* (1962)
MALIK, SURENDRA (Ed.), *The Fundamental Rights Cases* (1973)
MALIK, SURENDRA (Ed.), *Supreme Court and Constitutional Law* (1974)
MANSHARDT, CLIFFORD (editor), *The First Decade*: August 15, 1947-August 15, 1957
MARKANDAN, K.C., *Directive Principles in the Indian Constitution* (1966)
MARKANDAN, K.C., *The Amending Process and Constitutional Amendments in the Indian Constitution* (1972)
MARY, COUNTESS OF MINTO, *India, Minto and Morley* (1934)
MASALDAN, P.N., *Evolution of Provincial Autonomy in India*-1858-1950 (1953)
MASANI, M.R., *The Communist Party of India* (1954)
MASHRUWALA, K.G., *Some Particular Suggestions for the Constitution of free India* (1946)
MASHRUWALA, K.G., *Gandhi and Marx* (1951)
MENON, V.K.N., *India Since Independence-From Preamble to the Present* (1970)
MENON, V.P., *The Integration of the Indian States* (1956)
MENON, V.P., *The Transfer of Power in India* (1957)
MEHTA, A., *Politics of Planned Economy* (1953)
MEHTA, ASOKA, *Inside Lok Sabha* (1955)
MERILLAT, H.C.L., *Land and the Constitution in India* (1970)
MISRA, B.R., *Economic Aspects of the Indian Constitution* (1952)
Mitter, b.l., *The Indian Constitution* (1945)
MOON, PENDEREL, *Divide and Quit* (1952)
MONTAGU, E.S., *The Indian Diary* (1930)
MORRIS-JONES, W.H., *Parliament in India* (1957)
MOSLEY, LEONARD, *The Last Days of the British Raj* (1962)
MOTI RAM, *Guide to Constituent Assembly*
MUDALIAR, SIR, A.R., *An Indian Federation* (1933)
MUKHARJI, P.B., "*Three Elemental Problems of the Indian Constitution*", ICPS (1972)
MUKHERJEE, P., *Indian Constitutional Documents Containing Government of India Acts*, 1915 and 1916
MUKERJI, K.P. and MRS. RAMASWAMI, *Reorganisation of Indian States* (1955)
MURTI, A.S.N., *Free State for India with Regional Plan for a New Constitution*
MURTHY, P.N. and PADMANABHAN, K.V., *Constitution of the Dominion of India* (1947)
NAIK, R.B., *Paramountcy in Indian Constitutional Law*: Study of the Legal Aspects of the Relationship between the Indian States and the Government of India from the Days of the East India Company
NANAKCHAND, PANDIT, *Law of Elections and Election Petitions in India* (1951)
NARAYANA, I., *From Dyarchy to Self-government* (1950)
NARAYANA, JAYPRAKASH, *Towards a New Society* (1957)
NARAYAN, SHRIMAN, *Trends on Indian Planning* (1962)

NEHRU, JAWAHARLAL, *An Autobiography*
NEHRU, JAWAHARLAL, *The Unity of India, Collected Writings* 91937-40)
NEHRU, JAWAHARLAL, *Independence and After* (Collection of mportant Speeches from 1946 to 1949)
NEHRU, JAWAHARLAL, *Speeches 1949 to 1953*
NEHRU, JAWAHARLAL, *A Bunch of Old Letters* (1959)
NIHAL SINGH, GURUMUKH, *Landmarks in Indian Constitutional Development*
NORMAN BROWN, *The United States and India and Pakistan* (1962)
O'DWYER, MICHAEL, *India As I Knew It* (1925)
PAL, BEPIN CHUNDER, *The Democratic Swaraj*
PALMER, JULIAN, *Sovereignty and Paramountcy in India* (1930)
PALMER, NORMAN D., *The Indian Political System* (1962)
PANIKKAR, K.M., *The working of Dyarchy in India*, 1919-1928
PANIKKAR, K.M., *A Survey of Indian History* (1954)
PANIKKAR, K.M., *The State and the Citizen* (1956)
PANIKKAR, K.M., *The Foundations of New India* (1963)
PARK, R.L. and TINKER (editors), *Leadership and Political Institutions in India* (1959)
PLANNING COMMISSION-*Research for Planning* 1955-59 (1959)
PARLIAMENT-LOK SABHA SECRETARIAT, SECOND LOK SABHA, *Activities and Achievements* 1957-62 (1959)
PHILLIPS, C.H., *The Evolution of India and Pakistan* 1858-1947 (1962)
PHILLIPS, C.H., *Politics and Society in India* (1963)
PRASAD, BISHESHWAR, *Origins of Provincial Autonomy*-Being a History of the Relations Between the Central Government and the Provincial Governments in British India from 1860 to 1919
PRAVIN, SHAHID, *Role of the Opposition*
PUNNIAH, K.V., *Constitutional History of India* (1925)
RAJKUMAR, N.V., *Indian Political Parties* (1949)
RAMACHANDRAN, V.G., *Law of Preventive Detention* (1954)
RAMASWAMY, M., *Distribution of Legislative Powers in the Future of Indian Federation* (1944)
RARASWAMY, M., *Fundamental Rights* (1946)
RAMASWAMY, M., *Law of the Constitution of India*
RAM GOPAL, *Linguistic Affairs of India* (1966)
RAO, B.N., *India's Constitution in the Making* (1960)
RAO, B. SHIVA and others, *The Challenge to Democracy* (1953)
RAO, SHIVA (Ed.), *The Framing of India's Constitution*, Vol. 4 (1966-68)
RAO, VENKOBA K., *Fundamental Rights* (1953)
RAO, K.V., *Parliamentary Democracy of India* (1961)
RAO, RAMAKRISHNA, *Judicial Review and Elective Franchise* (1956)
RAO, SRINIVASA, *Crisis in India*
RAO, V. VENKATA, *The Prime Minister* (1954)
RAU, B.N. (editor), *Constitutional Precedents* (2 Vols)
RAU, B.N. *India's Constitution in the Making* (1966)
RETZLAFF, R.H., *Village Government in India* (1962)
ROSE, SAUL (editor), *Politics in South Asia* (1963)
ROY, NARESH CHANDRA, Tow*ards Framing the Constitution of I*ndia
ROY, NARESH CHANDRA, *Federalism and Linguistic States* (1962)
RUDRA, A,B., *Problem of India's Constitution-A Solution*
RUTHNASWAMY, M., *Revision of the Constitution* (1928)
SAMPURNANAND, *Memories and Reflections* (1962)
SANDERSON, G.D., *India and British Imperialism* (1951)
SANTHANAM, K., *The Constitution of India* (1951)
SANTHANAM, K., *Union-State Relations in India* (1960)

SAPRE, B.G., *The Growth of the Indian Constitution and Administration* (1928)
SAPRU, TEJ BAHADUR, *Constitutional Proposals of the Sapru Committee* (1946)
SASTRI, NILAKANTA, *The Concept of the Secular State*
SASTRI, V.S. SRINIVASA, *The Congress-League Scheme: An Exposition* (1917)
SASTRY, K.R.R., *Indian States* (1941)
SATHE, S.P., *Fundamental Rights and Amendment of the Indian Constitution* (1968)
SETALVAD, M.C., *The Indian Constitution* 1950-65 (1967)
SCHUSTER, GEORGE AND WINT, GUY, *India and Democracy* (1941)
SEN, D.K., *A Comparative Study of the Indian Constitution* (1960)
SETALVAD, M.C., *War and Civil Liberties* (1946)
SEW, GERTRUDE EMERSON, *Cultural Unity of India* (1956)
SHAH, K.T., *Provincial Autonomy under the Government of India Act,* 1935
SHAH, K.T., and BAHADURJI, GULESTAN J., *Governance of India*: A Commentary on the Government of India Act of 1919 with Additional Chapters on the Indian Local Government, Indian Army, Indian Finance and the Native States.
SHARMA, SRI RAM, *The Supreme Court and Judicial Review in India* (1952)
SHARMA, SRI RAM, *Some Independent-Governmental Agencies in the Indian Constitution* (1953)
SHARMA, SRI RAM, *India's Foreign Policy: The British Interpretations* 1947-57 (1961)
SHARMA, S.R., *How India is Governed* (1954)
SHARMA, S.R., *Democracy in the Saddle* (1940)
SHRIVASTAVA, GUR SHARAN LAL, *Indian Election and Election Petitions*
SHUKLA, V.N., *Constitution: First Amendment Act*, 1951
SIDDIQUI, A.H., *National Integration in India: A Sociological Approach* (1971)
SINGH, BALJIT, *Federal Finance and Underdeveloped Economy* (1952)
SINGH, K.S. (Ed.), *Tribal Situation in India* (1972)
SINGHVI, L.M. (Ed.), "*Bank Nationalization and the Supreme Court Judgement*", ICPS (1971)
SINGHVI, L.M., (Ed.), "*Parliament and Constitutional Amendment*", ICPS (1970)
SINHA, D.C., *Our Legislative Procedure* (1936)
SINHA, MAHINDRA CHANDRA, *The Representation made to Government on the Report on the Constitutional Reforms for India* (1917)
SINHA, V.K. (Ed.), *Secularism in India* (1968)
SIRSIKAR, V.M., *Sovereigns Without Crowns*: A Behavioural Analysis of the Indian Electoral Process (1973)
SITARAMAYYA, PATTABHI, *History of the Indian National Congress*, 2 Vols. (1947)
SMITH, DONALD EUGENE, *India as Secular State* (1963)
SMITH, W.R., *Nationalism and Reforms in India* (1938)
SOCIETY FOR DEMOCRACY (Ed.) *Monopolies and the Public Policy* (1972)
SOVANI, N.V. and DANDEKAR, V.M. (editors), *Changing India* (1961)
SPEAR, PERCIVAL, *India: A Modern History* (1961)
SPRATT, PHILP, *India and Constitution Making* (1948)
SRINIVASAN AND MATHRUBUTHAM, *The Representation of the People Act* (XLIII of 1950) as Amended by Acts LXXXIII of 1950 and XXVII of 1951
SRINIVASAN, N., *Democratic Government in India* (1954)
SRINIVASAN, G.N., *The Language Controversy and the minorities* (1970)
SUBBA RAO, K., *Conflicts in Indian Polity* (1971)
SUBBA RAO, *Social Justice and Law* (1974)
SUNDA, E.S., *Federal Court of India: A Constitutional Study* (1936)
SUNDRAM, LANKA, *A Secular State for India* (1944)
TANDON, B.C. (editor), *The Third Five Year Plan and India's Economic Growth* (1962)
TAYLOR, CARL C., et al, *India's Roots of Democracy* (1965)

TINKER, HUGH, *India and Pakistan: A Short Political Guide* (1962)
THOMPSON, E., *The Other Side of the Medal* (1925)
THOMPSON, E., *Making of Indian Princes*, 1944
TRIPATHY, P.K., *Some Insights into Fundamental Rights* (1972)
TRIPATHY, R.N., *Federal Finance in a Developing Economy* (1960)
TYNE, C.H.V., *India in Ferment* (1923)
VARADARAJAN, M.K. *Indian States and the Federation* (1939)
VENGUSWAMY, N.S., *Congress in Office* (1940)
VENKATARAMA, T.S., *A Treatise on Secular State* (1950)
VENKATARANGAIYA, M., *The Case for a Constitutional Assembly for India*: A Historical and Comparative Study (1946)
VENKATARANGAIYA, M., *Draft Constitution of India* (1949)
VIGHNESWARA, *Our New Rulers* (1961)
WADHWA, K.K., *Minority Safeguards in India: Constitutional Provisions and Their Implementation* (1975)
WATTAL, P.K., *Parliamentary Financial Control in India* (1953)
WEINER, MYRON, *Party Politics in India* (1957)
WEINER, MYRON, *The Politics of Scarcity* (1962)
WEINER, MYRON, *Political Change in South Asia* (1963)
WHITE, SIR FREDERICK, *India: A Federation*? Being a Survey of the Principal Federal Constitutions of the World, with Special Reference to the Relations of the Central to the Local Governments in India
WILSON, PATRICK, *Government and Politics of India and Pakistan*-1855-1955. A biography of works in western languages (1955)
WYLEE, JOHN ALFRED, *India at the Parting of the Ways*: Monarchy or Anarchy?
Y.M.C.A. PUBLISHING HOUSE, CALCUTTA, *The Secular State in India, A Christian Point of View*
Y.M.C.A. PUBLISHING HOUSE, CALCUTTA, *India's Quest for Democracy*
ZACHARIAS, H., *Renascent India* (1933)
ZAFAR IMAM (Ed.), *Muslims in India* (1975)

BOOKS – ADDENDUM

ADISESHAIAH, MALCOLM. *The Why, What and Whither of the Public Sector Enterprises* (New Delhi: Lancer International, 1986)
AGARWAL, M.D. *Studies in Zero Base Budgeting* (Jaipur: Jaipur Research Development Association, 1987)
AGARWAL, R.C. *State Enterprises in India* (Allabhabad: Chaitanya Publishing House, 1961)
AGARWAL, R.C. *Indian Political System*, S. Chand and Company (New Delhi) (2000)
AGGARWAL, N.D. and Mathur, B.I. *Public Enterprises in India* (Jaipur: Ramesh Book Depot., 1983).
AGGARWAL, S.K. *Whither Indian Democracy* (New Delhi: UDH Publishing House, 1991).
AGGARWALA, R.N. *Financial Committees of the India Parliament* – A Study in Parliamentary Control Over State Enterprises in India (Delhi: S Chand & Co. 1966)
AIYAR, S.P. (editor) *Perspectives on the Welfare State* (1966) Manaktala, Bombay
Alexander, P.C., India in the Twenty-first Century (2001)
ALI, CHOWDHURY RAHAMAT, *Pakistan* (Cambridge: Cambridge University Press, 1946).
ALLADI KUPPUSWAMY, *The Constitution*: What it Means to the People Today (2000)
ALTEKAR, A.S. *State and Government in Ancient India* (Delhi: Motilal Banarsidas, 1962)
ANAND RAO, C.P. *Public Enterprises and Parliamentary Committees in India* (Allahabad: Chugh Publications, 1982)
ANTHONY, ROBERT N. *Planning and Control Systems*: A Framework for Analysis (Boston: Hardvard University Press, 1965)

APPLEBY, PAUL H. Reexamination of India's Administrative System with Special Reference to Administration of Government's Industrial and Commercial Enterprise (New Delhi: Cabinet Secretariat, 1956)

- *Report on India's Administrative System*: Comments and Reactions (New Delhi: Lok Sabha Secretariat, 1956)
- *Public Administration in India*: Report of a Survey, 1953 (New Delhi: Cabinet Secretariat, Government of India, 1957)

APTER, DAVID E. *Choice and the Politics of Allocation*: A Developmental Theory (New Haven, CH: Yale University Press, 1971).

ARORA, R.S. *Administration of Government Industries*: Three Essays on Public Corporation (New Delhi: Indian Institute of Public Administration, 1969)

ARORA, RAMESH L. ed., *Administrative Change in India* (Jaipur: Aalekh Publishers, 1974)

- et al. Eds. *The Indian Administrative System* – Essays in honour of Ziauddin Khan (New Delhi: Associated Publishing House, 1978
- ed. *People's Participation in Development Process*: Essays in Honour of B. MEHTA (Jaipur: The HCM State Institute of Public Administration, 1979)
- ed. *Perspectives in Administrative Theory* (New Delhi: Associated Publishing house, 1979)
- and KUKAR, JAGDISH C. *Training and Administrative Development* (Jaipur: HCM State Institute of Public Administration, 1979)
- ed. *Administrative Theory* (New Delhi: Indian Institute of Public Administration, 1984)

AUSTIN, GARNVILLE. *The Indian Constitution*—Cornerstone of a Nation (Oxford: Clarendon Press, 1966).

AVASTHI, *A Central Administration* (New Delhi: Tata, McGraw-Hill Publishing Company Limited, 1980)

- and ARORA, RAMESH K.eds. *Bureaucracy and Development*: Indian Perspectives (New Delhi: Associated Publishing House, 1978)

AYYANAGAR, N. GOPALASWAMY. Report on the Reorganisation of the Machinery of Government (New Delhi: Government of India Printing Press, 1949).

BAGEHOT, WALTER. *The English Constitution* (Cambridge, England: Cambridge University Press, 1963).

BAISVA, K.N. *Financial Administration in India* (Bombay: Himalaya, 1986)

BAKSHI, P.M. *The Constitution of India* (1999) University Publishing Co. New Delhi

Bakshi, P.M., Constitution of India (2000)

BAKSHI, RAJINDER SINGH, *Politicians, Bureaucrats and Development Process* (New Delhi: Radiant Publishers, 1986)

BANARJEE, N.B. *Under Two Masters* (Calcutta: Oxford University Press, 1970)

BANSAL, J.P. *Supreme Court*: Judicial Restraint versus Judicial Activism (Jaipur Unique Publications, 1985)

BARNARD, CHESTER, *The Functions of the Executive* (Cambridge: MA: Hardvard University Press, 1938)

BASHAM, A.L. *The Wonder That Was India* (London: Sedgwick and Jasckson, 1954)

BASU, DURGA DAS. *Commentary on the Constitution of India*, 5th ed. (Calcutta: S.C. Sarkar, 1965)

- *Shorter Constitution of India*, 5th ed., (Calcutta: S.C. Sarkar & Sons, 1967)
- *Limited Government and Judicial Review* (Calcutta: S.C. Sarkar & Sons, 1972)
- *Comparative Constitutional Law* (1984) Prentice Hall

BASU, PRAHLAD KUMAR. *Public Enterprises*: Policy, Performance, and Professionalization (New Delhi: Allied Publishers, 1982)

BAVA, NOORJAHAN. *People's Participation in Development Administration in India* (New Delhi Uppal Publishing Co. 1984)

BAXI, UPENDRA, *Courage, Craft and Contention*: The Indian Superme Court in the Eighties (Bombay: Tripathi, 1985)

BAXTER, CARIG, MALIK, YOGENDRA K. KENNEDY, CHARLES H, and OBSERST, ROBER C. 2nd ed. *Government and Politics in South Asia* (Boulder: Westview Press, 1991)

BELL, DANIEL. *End of Ideology* (Glencoe, IL: The Free Press, 1962)

BENDIX. REINHARD, *Nation-Building and Citizenship*: Studies of our Changing Social Order (New York: John Wiley, 1964)

BETEILLE, ANDRE. *Caste, Class and Power* (The Hague: Mounton Co., 1958)

- *The Backward Classes in Contemporary India* (Delhi: Oxford University Press, 1992)

BHAGAVATHI JAGDISH N. and DESAI, PADMA, *India: Planning for Industrialization and Trade Policies Since 1951* (New Yord: Oxford University Press, 1970)

BHAMBRI, C.P. *Parliamentary Control over State Enterprise in India*: A Study in Public Administration (Delhi: Metropolitan, 1960)

- *Bureaucracy and Politics in India* (Bombay: Vikas Publications, 1971)
- *Administrators in a Changing Society* (Delhi: National Publishing House, 1972)
- *Public Administration in India* (Delhi: Vikas, 1973)
- *Politics in India* 1947-87 (New Delhi: Vikas Publishing House, 1988)

Bhandari, K.C. *Nationalization of Industrial in India* (Calcutta: Academic Publishers, 1962)

BHARGAVA, D.S. *Political Corruption in India* (New Delhi: Services, 1967)

BHASKARA RAO, V. *Employer Relations* A Critical Study of Government of India and Its Employees (Delhi: Concept, 1978)

- and VENKATESWARLU, B. eds. *Parliamentary Democracy in India* (Delhi: Mittal Publications, 1987).

BHATTACHARYA, A. *Recruitment Rules an Civil Services* (New Delhi: Prechi Prakashan, 1984)

BHATTACHARYA, B.B. *Public Expenditure, Inflation and Growth*: A Macro Econometric Analysis (Delhi: Oxford University Press, 1984).

BHATTACHARYA, *Mohit. Bureaucracy and Development Administration* (New Delhi: Uppal, 1979)

BLUNT, EDWARD. *The I.C.S.* (London, Faber and Faber Ltd., 1937)

BANARJEE, N.B. *Under Two Masters* (London: Oxford University Press, 1970)

BOSE, TARUN CHANDRA. Ed. *Indian Federalism*: Problems and Issues (Calcutta: K.P. Bagchi, 1987)

BOUTON, MARSHALL M. *India Briefing*. 1987 (Boulder: West view Press, 1987)

BRAHMA, P.K. *The Decision making Process in Government and Planned Development in India* (New Delhi: Indian Institute of Public Administration, 1981)

BRAIBANTI, RALPH J. ed., *Asian Bureaucratic Systems Emergent from the British Imperial Tradition* (Durham, NC: Duke University Press, 1966)

- ed. *Political and Administrative Development* (Durham) NC: Duke University Press, 1969)
- and Spengler, Joseph. Eds. Tradition, Values and Socio Economic Development (Durham, NC: Duke University Press, 1961)
- and Spendgler, Joseph, eds. Administration Economic Development in India (Dhurham, NC: Duke University Press, 1963)

BRAS. PAUL R. *Caste, Faction and Party in Indian Politics* (Delhi: Chanakya Publications, 1984)

BRECHER, MICHAEL, NEHRU : *A Political Biography* (London : Oxford University Press, 1959)

BURKE, JOHN P. *Bureaucratic Responsibility* (Baltimore: John Hopkins University Press, 1986)

- *Indian Administration*, 2nd ed. (London: Allen & Unwin Ltd., 1967)

CHANDRA, BIPAN. *Communalism in Modern India* (New Delhi: Vikas Publishing House Ltd. 1984)

CHATTERJI, S.K. *Development Administration* (Delhi: Surjeet, 1981)

CHATURVEDI, T.N. ed. *Administrative Accountability* (New Delhi: Indian Institute of Public Administration, 1984)

CHAUDHURI, VALMIKI. *President and the Indian Constitution* (Bombay: Allied Publishers, 1985)

CHETTUR, S.K. *The Steel Frame of India and I* : Life in the Civil Service (Bombay: Asia Publishing House, 1962)

CHINAI, BABUBHAI, India*'s March Towards Democratic Socialism*: A Businessman's Perspective

(Bombay: Brihad Bharatiya Samaj, 1972)

CHOPRA, R.N. *Public Sector in India*: Its Performance, Profitability, and Industrial Relations (New Delhi: Intellectual Publishing House, 1983)

- Green Revolution in India: The Relevance of Administrative Support in its Success (New Delhi: Intellectual Publications, 1985)

CHUGH, RAM I, and UPPAL, J.S. *Black Economy in India* (Delhi: Tata-McGraw Hill Publishing Company Limited, 1986)

CLARKE, M.ed., *Corruption, Causes, Consequences and Controls* (London: Frances Pinter, 1983)

COLLINS, LARRY and LAPIERRE, DOMINIQUE, *Freedom at Midnight* (New Delhi: Vikas Publishing House Pvt. Ltd., 1978)

Congress, Indian National. *Towards a Socialistic order* (New Delhi: All India Congress Committee, 1955)

- *Resolutions on Economic Policy, Programmes and Allied Matters* 1924-1969 (New Delhi: All India Congress Committee, 1969)

- *From Bombay to Delhi* (New Delhi: All India Congress committee, 1970) Constitutional Perspectives (2000) Univ. Law Publishing Co. New Delhi.

CRONIN. A.J. *The Stars Look Down* (Boston: Little, Brown and Company, 1935)

CROSSMAN, R.H.S. *Towards a Philosophy of Socialism* (London: Turnstile Press, 1953)

CROZIER, MICHEL *The Bureaucratic Phenomenon* (Chicago, II: University of Chicago Press, 1964)

DAGLI, VADILAL, ed. *The Public Sector in India*: A Survey (Bombay: Vora & Co. 1969)

DAR, USHA. *Expenditure Control: Problems and Evaluation* (Allahabad: Chaitanya, 1964).

DAS, HARI HARA. and MOHAPTRA, SANJUKTA. *Centre-State Relations in India*: As Study of Sub-national Aspirations (New Delhi: Ashish Publishing, 1986)

DASGUPTA, SUBHAYU, *Hindu Ethos and the Challenge of Change* (Calcutta: The Minerva Associates, 1972)

DATTA, ABHIJIT. *Union-State Relations* (New Delhi: Indian Institute of Public Administration, 1984)

- ed. *Local Government* (New Delhi: Indian Institute of Public Administration, 1984)

DENHARDT, ROBERT B. *Public Administration*: An Action Orientation (Pacific Grove, CA: Books/Cole Publishing Company, 1991)

DESAI, I.P. *Casts, Caste Conflict and Reservations* (Delhi: Ajantha Publications, 1985)

DESAI, MORAJI, *A Minister and His Responsibilities* (Delhi: National Publishing House, 1970)

DEY. S.K. *Community Development*: A Bird's Eye View (New York: Asia Publishing House, 1964)

DHARIA, MOHAN and MALAVIYA, H.D. eds. *Souvenir: Requisitioned Meeting of the AICC Members*, 22-23 November 1969 (New Delhi: AICC, 1969)

DRIEBERG, TREVOR, INDIRA GANDHI: *A Profile in Courage* (Delhi:Vikas Publishing House, 1973)

DUBASHI, P.R. *Essays in Public Administration* (New Delhi: NBO Publishers, 1985)

DUBE, M.P. *Role of the Supreme Court in Indian Constitution* (New Delhi: Deep and Deep Publications, 1987)

DUBE, S.C. *Indian Since Independence* (New Delhi: Vikas Publishing House Pvt. Ltd., 1977)

DUTT R.C. *State Enterprises in a Developing Country*: The Indian Experience (New Delhi: Abhinav, 1990)

DWIVEDI, O.P. and JAIN, R.B. *India's Administrative State* (New Delhi: Gitanjali, 1985)

DYE. THOMAS R. *Understanding Public Policy* 6th ed. (Englewoodd Cliffs, NJ: Prentice Hall, Inc. 1987)

ENSMINGER, DOUGLAS, *Rural India in Transition* (New Delhi: All India Panchayat Parishad, 1972)

ERISSION, ERIK, *Gandhi's Truth*: On the Origins of Militant Non-Violence (New York: W.W. Norton & Company, 1969)

FRANKEL, FRANCINE R, *India's Green Revolution*: Economic Gains and Political Costs (Princeton: Princeton University Press, 1971)

FRIDERICH, CARL J. *The Pathology of Politics, violence, Betrayal*, Corruption, Secrecy and Propaganda (New York: Harper & Row. 1972)

GALANTER, MARC. *Competing Equalities*: Law and Backward Classes in India (Delhi: Oxford University Press, 1984)

GALBRAITH, JOHN KENNETH. *Ambassador's Journal* (Boston: Houghton Mifflin Co., 1963)

GANDHI, MOHANDAS, K. *Socialism of My Conception*, Anand T. Hingorani, ed., (Bombay: Bharatiya Vidhya Bhavan, 1966)

GANGULY, D.S. *Public Corporations in the National Economy* (with Special Reference to India) (Calcutta: Bookland Printers, 1963)

GARDNER, BRIAN. *The East India Company* (New York: Dorset Press, 1971)

GAUS, JOHN M. *Reflections on Public Administration* (Alabama: University of Alabama Press, 1947)

GHOSE, SHANKAR, *Socialism, Democracy and Nationalism in India* (Bombay: Allied Publishers, 1973)

GHOSH, OROON K. *How India Won Freedom* (Delhi: Ajantha Publications, 1989)

GORWALA, A.D. *Report on the Efficient conduct on State Enterprises* (New Delhi: Planning Commission 1951)

Report on Public Administration (New Delhi: Planning Commission, Government of India, 1953)

GOYAL, S.K. ed. *Public Enterprises* (New Delhi: Indian Institute of Public Administration 1984)

GUPTA, ARVIND KUMAR. *Public Enterprises*: Economic Development and Resource Mobilization (New Delhi: Criterion, 1984)

GUPTA, BHARAT BHUSHAN *Problems of Indian Administration* (Allahabad: Chugh Publications, 1975)

GUPTA, B.N. *Government Budgeting*, with Special Reference to India (Bombay: Asia Publishing House, 1967)

GUPTA, K.R. *Economics and Management of Public Enterprises* (New Delhi: Atlantic Publishers and Distributors, 1984)

GUPTA, RAM KISHORE. *Public Enterprises in India* (Agra: Sahitya Bhavan, 1978)

GUPTA, PARANAY. *Mother India*: A Political Biography of Indira Gandhi (Hightstown, NJ: Charles Scrinbner's 1992)

HALAYYA, M. *Emergency: A War on Corruption* (New Delhi: S. Chand & Co. Pvt Ltd.. 1975)

HANDA, K.L. *Programme and Performance Budgeting* (New Delhi: Uppal Publishing House, 1979)

- ed. *Financial Administration* (New Delhi: Indian Institute of Public Administration, 1986)

HARAGRAVE, G. *Administrative Leadership and Rural Development in India* (New Delhi: Light & Life, 1980)

HARDGOPAL. Jr. ROBERT L. *India: Government and Politics in a Developing Nation*, 2nd ed. (New York : Harcourt Brace Jovanovich Inc., 1975)

HARRISON, SELIG. *India : The Most Dangerous Decades* (Princeton, University Press, 1960)

Heginbotham, STANLEY J. Cultures in Conflict : *The Four Faces of Indian Bureaucracy* (New York : Columbia University Press, 1975)

HEIDENHEIMER, ARNOLD J. JOHNSON, MICHAEL and LEVINE, VICTOR T., eds. *Political Corruption*: A Handbook (New Brunswick: Transition Publishers, 1989)

HERRING, PENDLETON, *Public Administration and the Public Interest* (New York: McGraw Hill, 1936)

KAPUR A.C. *Constitution of India* (1985) S. Chand and Company

Administrative Reforms Commission.

Study Team Reports:

1. *Redress of Citizens' Grievances*, August 1966
2. *District Administration*, Vol.I, February 1967. Vol. II, September 1967
3. *Machinery of the Government of India and Its Procedures* of Work, March 1967
4. *On Recruitment, Selection*, U.P.S.C/P.S.Cs. and Training, June 1967
5. *Public Sector Undertakings*, June 1967
6. *Personnel Administration*, August 1967
7. *Centre-State Relationships*, September 1967
8. *State Level Administration*, October 1968

Final Reports

1. *On Public Sector Undertakings*, October 1967
2. *Machinery for Planning*, March 1968
3. *Personnel Administration*, April 1969
4. *Delegation of Financial and Administrative Powers*, June 1969
5. *Center-State Relationships*, June 1969
6. *On State Administration*, November 1969
7. *Administrative Reform and Its Work*: A Brief Summary, June 1970
8. ARC: *Recommendations & conclusions*: A Compendium, July 1970

Report of the Backward Classes Commission, Volumes I & II, 1980 (Shimla: Government of India Press, 1984)

Commission for SC/ST 8th Report, April 1985-March 1986

Report of the Commissioner for Scheduled Castes and Scheduled Tribes (Twenty-Seventh Report), 1982

Ministry of Health & Family Planning, *India's Population:* Demographic Scenarios (New Delhi: Publications Division, 1988)

The Collected Works of Mahatma Gandhi (New Delhi: Publications Division, 1958)

Selected Speeches of Indira Gandhi: January 1966 –April 1969 (New Delhi: Publications Division, 1971)

Nehru Jawaharlal, *Independence and After* (1949) the Publications Division, Government of India.

Department of Personnel and Administrative Reforms. Brochure on Reservations for Scheduled Castes and Scheduled Tribes in Services, 6th ed. (New Delhi: Government of India Press, 1982)

Union Public Service Commission. Civil Services Examination: Report of the Commission on Recruitment Policy and Selection Methods (Kothari Commission, 1976)

Public Service Commissions in India: Golden Jubilee Souvenir, 1926-1976, 1976

Indian National Congress. Resolutions on Economic Policy, Programme and Allied Matters, 1924-1969 (New Delhi: AICC, 1969)

Manifesto of the Congress Party: General Elections, 1989 (Mimeo, no date)

Ismail, M.M. *The President and the Governors in the Indian Constitution* (Madras: Orient Longman, 1972)

Iyer, Krishna V.R. *The Indian Presidency Nascent Challenges and Novel Responses* (New Delhi: Deep & Deep Publications, 1988)

Iyer, Venkat (Editor), Constitution Perspectives (2000)

Jain, R.B. *Contemporary Issues in Indian Public Administration* (Delhi: Vishal, 1976)

- ed. *Panchayati Raj* (New Delhi: Indian Institute of Public Administration, 1980)
- ed. *Panchayati Raj* (New Delhi: Indian Institute of Public Administration, 1981)
- ed. *Public Services in a Democratic Context* (New Delhi: Indian Institute of Public Administration, 1983)

Jain, S.N. Kashyap, Sibash and Srinivasan, N. eds. *The Union and the States* (Delhi: National, 1972)

Jawed, Sohail. *Growth of Socialism in India* (New Delhi: Associated Publishing House, 1980)

Jayakar, Pupul. *Indira Gandhi:* A Biography (New Delhi: Viking, 1992)

Kashyap, Subhash, History of Parliament of India (1994)
- The Ten Lok Sabhas (1952-91)
Kaushik, Susheela ed. *Public Administration*: An alternative Perspective (New Delhi: Ajanta Publications, 1984)
Kaushik. S.L. and Sahni, Pradeep. eds, *Public Administration in India*: Emerging Trends (Allahabad: Kitab Mahal, 1983)
Khan, Rasheeduddin, *Federal India*: A Design for Change (New Delhi: Vikas Publishing House Pvt Ltd. 1992)
Khera, S.S. *District Administration in India* (New Delhi: Indian Institute of Public Administration, 1960)
- *The Central Executive* (New Delhi: Orient Longman Ltd., 1975)
- *Government in Business* 2nd ed. (New Delhi: National Publishing House, 1977)
Kochanek, Stanely A. *Business and Politics in India* (Los Angless: University of California Press, 1974)
- The Congress Party of India: *The Dynamics of One-Party Democracy* (Princeton: Princeton University Press, 1968)
Kohli, Suresh., ed. *Corruption in India* (New Delhi: Chetna Publications, 1975)
Kothari, Rajni, Politics in India (Hyderabad: Orient Longman, 1970)
- *Politics in India* (New Delhi: Orient Longman Ltd., 1972)
- *Democratic Polity and Social Change in India*: Crisis and Opportunities (New Delhi: Allied Publishers, 1976)
- *Politics and the People*: In Search of a Human India, Vols. I & II (Delhi: Ajanta Publications, 1989)
- Ed. *State and Nation Building*: A Third World Perspective (New Delhi: Allied Publishers, 1976)
Kothari, Shanti and Roy, Rameshray, *Relations Between Politicians and Administrators at the District Level* (New Delhi: Indian Institute of Public Administration, 1969)
Kumaramangalam, S. Mohan. *Judicial Appointments* (New Delhi: Oxford and IBH Publishing House, 1973)
Kurian, Mathew and Varghese, P.N. eds. *Centre-State Relations* (Delhi: Macmillan India Limited, 1981)
LALA, R.M.ed *India says no to Nationalization*: An Analysis of Public Reaction to the Current Proposal Affecting Certain Key Industries (Bombay: Rajaji Foundation, 1979)
Lamb, Beatric Pitney, Pitney, India: *A World in Transition*, 4th ed. (New York: Praeger Publishers, 1975)
Laxmi Narain. *Parliament and Public Enterprises in India* (New Delhi: S.Chand, 1979)
- *Principles and Practice of Public Enterprises in India* (New Delhi: S. Cahnd, 1980)
- *Workers' Participation in Public Enterprises* – A Macro & Micro Level Survey and Report of a National Seminar (Bombay: Himalaya, 1984)
- And Murty, B.S. eds. *Public Enterprises and Fundamental Rights*: Basic Papers and Discussions of National Level Seminar (Bombay: N.M. Tripathi, 1984)
Limaye, Madhu, *Indian Politics in Transition* (New Delhi: Radiant Publishers, 1990)
Luthera, V.P. *The Concept of the Secular State and India* (Calcutta: Oxford University Press, 1964)
Macmillan, Margaret. *Woman of the Raj* (New York: Thames and Hudson, 1988)
Madan K.D. et al. Eds. *Policy making in Government*: Selected Readings (New Delhi: Publications Division Government of India, 1982)
Madan, K.D. Deish, K. Pradhan, Ashok and Sekharan, Chandra C. eds. *Policymaking in Government* (New Delhi: Government of India Publications Division, 1982)
Maddick, Henry. Panchayati Raj: *A Study of Rural Local Government in India* (London: Longman Group, Ltd., 1970)
Mahajan, V.D. *Constitutional Development and the National Movement in India* (New Delhi: S. Chand & Company Ltd., 1986)
Maheshwari, Shri Ram. *Local Government in India* (New Delhi: Orient Longman, 1971)

- *The Administrative Reforms Commission* (Agra: Lakshmi Narain Agarwal, 1972)
- *Indian Administration*, 3rd Rev. ed. (New Delhi: Orient Longman, 1979)
- Ed. *Administrative Reforms* (New Delhi: Indian Institute of Public Administration, 1984)

Majumdar, R.C. Roychaudhuri, H.C. and Kalikinkar Dutta, *An Advanced History of India* (New York: St. Martin;s Press, 1965)

Malaviya, H.D. *Socialist Ideology of Congress* (New Delhi: A Socialist Congressman Publication, 1966)

Mallya, N.N. *Public Enterprises in India*: Their Control and Accountability (Delhi: National Publishing House, 1971)

Mansukhani, H.L. *Corruption and Public Servants* (New Delhi: Vikas, 1979)

Marathe, Sharad S. Regulation and Development: India's Policy Experience of Controls Over Industry (New Delhi: Sage Publications, 1986)

Mathur, B.C. etal, eds. *Management in Government* (New Delhi; Publications Division, Government of India, 1979)

Mathur, Hari Mohan. Administrative Development in the Third World: Constraints and Choices (New Delhi: Sage Publications and Choices (New Delhi: Sage Publications, 1986)

- *Training of Civil Servants in India* (New Delhi: Government of India, Department of Personnel and Administrative Reforms, Training Division, 1981)

Mathur, Kuldeep. Sources of *Indian Bureaucratic Behaviour* (Jaipur, HCMIPA, 1972)

- ed. *A Survey of Research in Public Administration*, 1970-1979 (New Delhi: Concept Publishing Company, 1986)

Mechery, F.A. and Tikekar, Maneesha, *Indian Socialism*: Past and Present (Bombay: Himalaya Publishing House, 1985)

Mehta, Asok. *Studies in Asian Socialism* (Bombay: Bharatiya Vidya Bhavan, 1959)

Mehta, Balwantray. *Report of the Team for the Study of Community Projects and National Extension Service* (Delhi: Committee on Plan Projects, *1959)*

Mehta, Haroobhai and Patel, Hasmukh, eds. Dynamics of Reservation Policy (New Delhi: Patriot Publishers, 1985)

Mehta, V.D. and Meheshwari, P.D. *Public Undertakings and Labour in India* (Bhopal: Progress Publishers, 1974)

Mende, Tiber. *Conversations with Nehru* (New York: George Braziller, 1956)

Menge, Paul Erich. *Management for Development*: Executive Budget-making in Indian Government (Durham, NC: Duke University Ph.D. Thesis, 1970)

Menon, P.R.K. *Budgeting for Developing Countries* (with Special Reference to India (Ernakulam: Vidya Prints, 1983)

Mishra, Jagannath *New Dimensions of Federal Finance of India* (New Delhi: Vikas, 1983)

- *Current Perspectives in Public Enterprise Management* (Delhi: Ajanta, 1985)

Misra, B.B. *The Administrative History of India*, 1834-1947 (London: Oxford University Press, 1970)

- *The Bureaucracy in India*: An Historical Analysis of Development up to 1947 (Delhi: Oxford University Press, 1977)
- *Government and Bureaucracy in India*: 1947-1976 (Delhi: Oxford University Press, 1986)

Montiero, J.B. *Corruption* : Control of Maladministration (Bombay : Manaktalas, 1966).

Morris-Jones, W.H. *The Government and Politics in India* (London: Hutchinson University Library, 1967)

Mukarji, Nirmal and Arora, Balveer. *Federalism in India*: Origins and Developments (New Delhi: Vikas Publishing Pvt Ltd. 1992)

Mukerji, Mohan and Arora, Ramesh K. *The Collectors Recollect* (Jaipur: R.B.S.A. Publishers, 1987)

Muttalib, M.A. *Union Public Service Commission* (New Delhi: Indian Institute of Public Administration, 1967)

- *Democracy, Bureaucracy and Technology*: Assumptions of Public Management Theory (New Delhi: Concept Publishing Co. 1980)

Myrdal, Gunnar, Asian Drama: *An Inquiry Into the Poverty of Nations* Vols. I & II (New York: Twentieth Century Fund 1968)

Namboodiripad, E.M.S. *Economics and Politics of India's Socialist Pattern* (New Delhi: People's Publishing House, 1966)

Narain, Iqbal, etal, *Panchayati Raj administration*: Old Controls and New Challenges (New Delhi: Indian Institute of Public Administration, 1970)

Narain, Laxmi, *Worker's Participation in Public Enterprises* (Bombay: Himalaya Publishing House, 1984)

- and Murty, B.S. eds. *Public Enterprises and Fundamental Rights* (Bombay: N.M. Tripathi Private Limited, 1984)

National Front, *National Front*: Lok Sabha Elections, 1989, Manifesto (New Delhi: Windsor Place, 1989)

Nayar, P.K.B. *Leadership, Bureaucracy and Planning in India*: A Sociological Study (New Delhi: Associated Publishing House, 1969)

Nehru, Jawaharlal. *Autobiography* (London: Bodly Head, 1936)

Glimpses of World History (London: Lindsay Drummond Limited, 1949)

- *Towards a Socialistic Order* (New Delhi: Indian National Congress, 1955)
- *Speeches*, Vols. I & II & III (New Delhi: Government of India Publications Division, 1956)
- *A Bunch of Old Letters* (New York: Asia Publications House, 1960)

Padma Ramachandran, *Minorities and Secularism* (1991) Institute of Management Trivandram.

Pai M.R. *Socialism in India*: A Commentary (Bombay: Popular Prakashan, 1967)

- *A Decade of Planning in India* (Bombay: Popular Prakashan 1969)

Pal, Chandra, Center-State Relations and Cooperative Federalism (New Delhi: Deep & Deep Publications, 1983)

Palkhivala, N.A. We the People (Bombay: Strand Bookstall, 1984)

Palmier, Leslie. *The Control of Bureaucratic Corruption*: Case Studies in Asia (New Delhi: Allied Publishers, 1985)

Pandey, Ram Darshan. *Fundamental Rights and Constitutional Amendments* (Delhi: Capital Publishing House, 1985)

Palmer Norman D. *Indian Political System* (1961) Univ. of Penn. Press

Panigrahi, D.D. *Centre-State Financial Relations in India* (Delhi: Vikas, 1985)

Palkiwala, Nani, *We, the People* (1994) Vikas Publishing House

Punjabi, Kewal L. *The Civil Servant in India* (Bombay: Bharatiya Vidya Bhavan 1965)

Patton, Carl V. and Sawicki, David S. Basic *Methods of Policy Analysis and Planning* (Englewood Cliffs, NJ: Prentice Hall, 1986)

Potter, David C. *India's Political Administration*: 1919-1983 (Oxford: Claredon Press, 1986)

Prasad, Anirudh. *Social Engineering & constitutional Protection* of Weaker Sections in India (Delhi: Deep & Deep Publications, 1980)

- *Centre-State Relations in India: Constitutional Provisions*, Judicial Review, Recent Trends (New Delhi: Deep & Deep Publications, 1985)

Prasad, Kamta.ed. *Planning and Its Implementation* (New Delhi: Indian Institute of Public Administration, 1984)

Puri, B,N, *History of Indian Administration* (Bombay: Bharatiya Vidya Bhavan, 1968)

Puri, K.K. *Public Administration*: Indian Spectrum (Allahabad: Kitab Mahal, 1985)

Pylee, M.V. *Constitutional Government in India*, 3rd rev. ed. (London : Asia Publishing House, 1977).

- *India's Constitution*, Rev. ed. (Bombay : Asia Publishing House (P) Ltd., 1979).
- *Constitutional History of India*, 1600-1950, 2nd Rev. ed. (Bombay : Asia Publishing House (P) Ltd., 1980).

Pylee M.V. *India's Constitution at Work*, Patna University Press (1955),

- *The Federal Court of India* (Revised Edn.) Vikas Publishing House (1998).
- *Industrial Policy*, A S C I, Hyderabad (1963).

- *Worker Participation in Management*, Vikas Publishing House (1998).
- *Crisis Conscience and the Constitution*, Asia Publishing House, Bombay (1982).
- *An Introduction to the Constitution of India*, Vikas Publishing House, (1998)
- *Emerging Trends of Indian Polity*, Regency Publications, New Delhi (1998).
- *Our Constitution, Government and Politics*, Universal Law Publishing Company, New Delhi (2000)
- *Constitutions of the World*, Universal Law Publishing Company, New Delhi (2000).

Rabin, Jack and Bowman, James, eds. *Politics and Administration* (New York : Marcel Dekkar, 1984).

Raghvulu, C.V. *Organizational Conflict in Indian government Organizations* (Delhi : Academic, 1984).

Rai, Hardwar and Singh, Sakendra Prasad, *Current Ideas and Issues in Indian Administration* : A Developmental Approach (New Delhi : Uppal, 1979).

Raju, M.P., *Wadhwa Commission Report,* A Critique, Media House, Delhi (1994).

Rai, Mangat E.N. *Commitment My Style* : Career in Indian Civil Service (Delhi : Vikas, 1973).

Ramayyar, M.S. *Indian Audit and Accounts Department* (New Delhi : Indian Institute of Public Administration, 1967).

Rana, M.S. *Writings on Indian Constitution* (Meerut : Orient, 1987).

Rao, C.R. Anand, *Public Enterprises and Parliamentary Committees in India* (Allahabad : Chugh, 1982).

Rao, P.V.R. Red Tape and White Cap (Delhi : Orient Longman, 1970).

Rao, B. Shiva, ed, *The Framing of India's Constitution* : A Study, Vols. I-V (New Delhi : Indian Institute of Public Administration, 1968).

Rath, Sharada, *Federalism Today* : Approaches, Issues and Trends (New Delhi : Sterling Publishers Private Ltd., 1984).

Ray, Amal. *Inter-Governmental Relations in India*: A Study of Indian Federalism (Bombay: Asia Publishing House, 1966)

Reddy, G.Ram ed. *Government and Public Enterprises* – Essays in Honour of Prof. V.V., Ramanahdam (London: Frank Cass, 1983)

Robson, W.A. *Public Enterprises in a Socialist State* (New Delhi: Indian Institute of Public Administration, 1960)

Rothermund, Dietmar. *An Economic History of India*: From Pre-Colonial Times to 1986 (London: Croom Helm, 1988)

Rudolph, Loyd I. and Rudolph, Susan Hoeber. *The Modernity of Tradition*: Political Development in India (Chicago, IL : Chicago University of Chicago Press, 1987)

- *In Pursuit of Lakshmi* : The Political Economy of the Indian State (Chicago : The University Press, 1967).

Sachdeva, D.R. and Dua, B.D. *Studies in Indian Administration* (Allahabad: Kitab Mahal, 1969)

Sadasivan, T.N. *Citizen and Administration* (New Delhi: Indian Institute of Public Administration, 1984)

Saigal, Krishan *Policy making in India*: An Approach to Optimization (New Delhi: Vikas, 1983)

Santhanam, K. *Union-State Relations* (Bombay: Asia Publishing House, 1960)

- Report of the Commission on Prevention of Corruption (New Delhi: Government of India Press, 1964)

Sapru, R.K. *Civil Service Administration in India* (New Delhi: Deep & Deep Publications, 1985)

Sastri, K.V.S. *Federal–State Fiscal Relations in India*: A Study of the Finance Commission and the Techniques of Adjustment (Bombay: Oxford University Press, 1966)

Sathe, Vasant. *Restructuring the Public Sector in India* (New Delhi: Vikas Publishing House, 1989)

Seshadri, S. *Parliamentary Control over Finance*: A Study of the Public Accounts Committee of Parliament (Bombay: Allied Publishers, 1975)

Shakdar, S.L. *The Budget and the Parliament* (New Delhi: National, 1979)

Shama Sastry, R. Kautilya's Arthasastra. 8th ed. (Mysore: Mysore Printing a Publishing House, 1967)

Sharaf, H.K. Sadque, ed. *Public Enterprise in Asia*: Studies on Coordination and Control (Kuala Lumpur: Asian Centre for Development Administration, 1976)

Sharma, B.R. *Administrative Stress* (New Delhi: Indian Institute of Public Administration, 1986)

Sharma, M.P. *Public Administration* in Theory and Practice (Bombay: Kitab Mahal 1958)

Sharma, O.P. *Financial Relations Between Centre, States and Local Self-Government in India* (New Delhi: Altantic Publishers & Distributors, 1988)

Sharma, O.P. Bishnoi, R.N. and Panandikar, Pai V.A. *Development Bureaucracy* (New Delhi: Oxford & IBH, 1983)

Sharma, Sudesh Kumar, eds. *Dynamics of Development: An International Perspective*, 2 Vols. (Delhi: Concept, 1978)

Shukla, J.D. Indianization of All-India Services and its Impact on *Administration*: 1834-1947 (New Delhi: Allied Publishers, 1982)

Shourie, Arun, *Individuals, Institutions, Processes*: How One May Strengthen the Other In India (New Delhi: Viking, 1990)

Singh, Mohinder and Sharma. R.N. *Civil Service and Personnel Administration*. An Annotated Biography (New Delhi: Indian Institute of Public administration, 1981)

Sinha, R.K. *Fiscal Federalism in India* (New Delhi: Sterling 1987)

Sinha, V.M. The Superior Civil Services in India (Jaipur: The Institute for Research and Advanced Studies, 1985)

Sitaramaiah, Pattabhi. *The History of the Indian National Congress*, Vol. I, 1885-1935 (Bombay: Padma Publications, 1946)

\- *The History of the Indian National Cong*ress, vol. II, 1935-1947 (Bombay: Padma Publications, 1947)

Singvi L.M. *Freedom on Trial* (1991) Vikas Publishing House

Smith, D.E. India as a Secular State (Princeton, NJ: Princeton University Press, 1963)

Sondhi, Krishan, *Communication, Growth and Public Policy*: The Indian Experience (New Delhi: Break-through Publications, 1983)

Sorabjee, Soli, Singh, L.P. and Narain, Govind. *The Governor: Sage or Saboteur* (New Delhi: Roli Books International, 1985)

Srinivasan, N. Jain, S.N. and Kashyap, Subash C.eds. *The Union and the States* (Delhi: National, 1972)

Steele, Shelby, *The Content of our Character* (New York: St. Martin's Press, 1990)

Stillman II, Richard J. *Preface to Public Administration*: A search for Themes and Directions (New York: St. Martin's Press, 1991)

Sunder Raman *Constitutional Amendments in India*

Subramaniam, V. *Managerial Class in India* (New Delhi: All India Management Association, 1971)

\- *Social Background of India*'s Administrators: A Socio-Economic Study of the Higher Civil Service of India (New Delhi: Publications Division, Ministry of I & B, 1971)

\- *Transplanted Indo-British Administration* (New Delhi: Ashish Publishing House, 1977)

Sunder Raman, *Constitutional Amendment in India* (1989) Estern Law House

Subhesh Mathur, *Our Constitutional Head Latesh Prakashan*, Jodhpur (1981)

Sylvia, Ronald V. Meier, Kenneth J. and Gunn, Elizabeth. Program Planning and Evaluation for the Public, Manager (Monetary, CA: Brooks/Cole Publishing Company, 1985)

Taube, Richard, *Bureaucrats Under Stress*: Administrators and Administration In India (Berkeley: University of California Press, 1969)

Taylor, Carl C. et al. *India's Roots of Democracy* (Bombay: Orient Longman's, 1965)

Tharoor, Shashi. *The Great Indian Novel* (New York: Arcade Publishing, 1989)

Thavaraj, M.K. Financial Management of Government of India (New Delhi: Sultan Chand & Sons, 1978)

Tummala, Krishna K. *Elements of Public Administration* (Tenali: Kaviraja Publishers, 1962)

- Public *Administration in India* (1994) Times Academic Press
- *Dynamics of the Politics of Confrontation*: The Case of India (Laramie: University of Wyoming, Institute of Policy Research Publication # 226, October 1977)
- *Committed Bureaucracy*: An Attempted Mutation of the Weberian Neutral Construct in India (Laramie: University of Wyoming, Institute of Policy Research Publication 284, April 1979)
- *The Ambiguity of Ideology and Administrative Reform* (New Delhi: Allied Publishers, 1979)
- ed. *Administrative Systems Abroad*, Rev. ed. (Lanham, MD: University Press of America, 1983)
- ed. *Equity in Public Employment Across Nations* (Lanham, MD: University Press of America, 1989)

Thakur, L.D. (editor) *Democracy*, Secularism and Society (1989) Lucknow

UNESCO. *Public Administration and Management*: Problems of Adaptation in Different Socio-Cultural Contexts (Paris: UNESCO, 1985)

Tribe, Lawrence, H. *Constitutional Choices* (2000)

Varadachari, V.K. *President in the Indian Constitution* (New Delhi: Deep and Deep Publishers, 1985)

Varma, R.S. *Bureaucracy in India* (Bhopal: Progress Publishers, 1973)

Vepa, Ram K. *Change and Challenge in Indian Administration* (New Delhi: Manohar, 1978)

Verma, S.P., ed. *Development Administration* (New Delhi: Indian Institute of Public Administration, 1984)

Viet, Lawrence A. *India's Second Revolution*: The Dimensions of Development (New York: McGraw Hill Book Company, 1976)

Wadhwa, C.D. ed. *Some Problems of India's Economic Policy* (Bombay: Tata McGraw Hill, 1973)

Wani, A.A. Exclusion of *Judicial Review*: Administrative Efficiency Confronts Legitimacy of Power (New Delhi: Metropolitan, 1987)

Weiner, Myron. *Politics of Scarcity* (Chicago: Chicago: University Press, 1962)

- India at the Polls: *The Parliamentary Elections* of 1977 (Washington, D.C: American Enterprise Institute, 1978)
- and Katzenstein, Mary with Narayan Rao, K.V. *India: Preferential policies*, Migrants, the Middle Classes and Ethnic Equality (Chicago: The University of Chicago Press, 1981)

Wholey, Joseph S. Newcomer, Kathryn A. and Associates. *Improving Government Performance*: Evaluation Strategies for Strengthening Public Agencies and Programs (San Francisco, CA: Jossey-bass Publishers, 1989)

Woodruff, Philip, *The Men who Ruled India*: The Guaradians (New York: Schocken Books, 1964)

Zaidi. A.M. ed. *Promises to Keep*: A Study of the Election Manifestoes of Indian National Congress 1937-1985 (New Delhi: Indian Institute of Applied Political Research, 1986)

Zakaria, Rafik. ed. *A Study of Nehru* (Bombay: Times of India Publications, 1959)

Section 3 : Articles, Papers, etc.

GENERAL

ABEL, M., '*Problems of* Indian Democracy', *Modern Review*, Vol LXXXII, No. 5, p. 359

AGARWAL, SHRIMAN NARAYAN, 'The Gandhian Constitution', *Modern Review*, Vol. LXXXIII, No. 6, p. 485

APPADORAI, A., 'The Indian Constitution', *Asiatic Review*, Vol. XLV, p. 483

ATULANANDA VATSYAYANA, 'Democracy—*made in India*', Vigil, Vol. 3, No. 52 p. 8.

AYYAR, C.S.S., 'Conventions and the Indian Constitution', *S.C.J.*, I, 1961

BANERJEE, D.N., 'The Sapru Committee and Leading Principles of a New Constitution for India', *Modern Review*, Vol LXXXIX, No. 3, p.173

BANERJEE, D.N. 'Swiss System of Government and its Applicability to India', *Modern Review*, Vol. LXXIX, No. 2, p. 9

BASU, DURGA DAS, 'Stability of the State under the Constitution of India', *F.L.J.*, Vol. 12, p.1

BASU, DURGA DAS, 'The Indian Constitution Through American Eyes', *F.L.J.*, Vol. 12, p. 147

BASU, K.K., 'Constitution of India', *I.L.R.*, Vol. 7, p. 15

BATLIWALA, C.J., 'India and Parliamentary Democracy' (abstract of a thesis), *Journal of the University of Bombay*, Vol. 21. P.84

BLUM, H., 'Constitution in a Modern Democracy', New York state Bar Association Bulletin, *Washington Avenue*, Vol. 25, p.268

BOSE, S.C., 'A Constitution of Myths and Denials', F.L.J., Vol. 13, p. 331

BRADEN, G.D., 'Constitutional Law in India', Conecticut Bar Journal, Vol. 29, p. 299; Vol. 30, p.33

BROWN, MARY ALICE, 'Some Aspects of India's Foreign Policy', *United Asia*, Vol. 12, 1960, p. 493

CHAGLA, M.C., 'Some Aspects of the Constitution of India', *The Modern Review*, Vol. 107, April 1960, p. 269

CHATTERJI, NANDLAL, 'Prospects of Democracy in Free India', *Modern Review*, Vol. LXXXX, No. 4, p. 269.

DEENER, D.R., 'International Law Provisions in Post-World War II Constitutions', *Cornell Law Quarterly*, Vol. 36, 0.505

DOUGLAS ENSMINGER, 'Democratic Decentralisation: A New Administrative Challenge', *The Ind. Jour. Of Pub. Admn.*, Vol. 7, 1961, p.287

D'SOUZA, J., 'The Foundations of Democracy in India', *Social Action*, Vol. 3, 0.232

'Executive vs. Judiciary' (Editorial Comments), *The Modern Review*, Vol. 107, No. 5, Jan.-June 1960, p. 342

FREEMAN, H.A., 'New Constitutions of Europe, Asia and South America', Cornell University, Vol. 34, p.1

GHOSH, ARUN COOMAR, 'The Law of the Indian Constitution', *Modern Review*, Vol. LXXXXVII, No. 2, p. 112.

GOYAL, KAILASH NATH, 'Salient Features of the Draft Constitution', *A.L.J.*, Vol. XLVII, p. 37.

GRIFFITHS, SIR PERCIVAL, 'The Republics of the Indian Sub-Continent', *Asiatic Review*, Vol. 50, p. 105

HAQQI, S.A.H., 'Problems and Prospects of Parliamentary Democracy in India', *I.J.*P. Sc., Vol. 20, No. 3, p. 205

HOYT, EDWIN C., 'Foreign Politics of India and the United States', *India Quarterly*, Vol.17, July-Sept., 1961, p. 277

'India's Constitution (Leading Article), *Eastern Economist*, Vol. 9, No. 7, P. 248

'India's New Constitution' (Article), *Leading Eastern Economist*, Vol. 11, No. 26, p. 1102

IQBAL NARAIN, 'The Idea of Democratic Decentralization', *The Ind. Jour. Of Pol. Sc.*, Vol. 21, No.2, 1960, p. 184

KABADI, SUNDER, 'India: A Commonwealth Republic', *Asiatic Review*, Vol. 46, p. 974

KING, F.C., 'A Republic within the Commonwealth', *Irish Law Times, Dublin*, Vol. 84, p. 41

KOGEKAR, S.V., 'Some Observations on the Constitution of India', *I.J.P.* Sc. Vol. 11, No. 2, p. 61

'The Law of the Constitution' (Leading Article), *Eastern Economist*, Vol. 21, No. 7, p. 257

LAWRENCE, LORD PETHICK, 'Indian Constitutional Government', *Asiatic Review*, Vol. 50, p. 3

'The Liberal Awakening' (Leading Article), Eastern Economist, Vol. 16, No. 22, p. 879

MAVALANKAR, P.G., 'Parliamentary and Social Democracy in India', Asian Review. Vol. 55, No. 201, Jan. 1959, p. 3

MAZUMDAR, ASOK KUMAR, 'The Constitution of India', Hindustan Review, Vol. LXXXVI, February 1950, p. 79; March 1950, p. 148

MEHROTRA, S,R., 'Gandhi and the British Commonwealth', India Quarterly. Vol. 17, Jan-March, 1961, p. 44

MISRA, HAREKRISHNA, 'Democratic Basis of the New Constitution', I.J.P. Sc., Vol. 11, No. 4, p. 77

MORRIS-JONES, W.H., 'Mahatma Gandhi : Political Philosopher', *The Ind. Jour. of Pol. Sc.*, Vol. 21, No. 3, 1960, p. 203.

MORRIS-JONES, W.H., 'Recent Political Developments in India', Parliamentary Affairs, Vol. XI, 1957-58

MUKHERJEE, SILA KUMAR, 'Parliamentary Democracy in India', Modern Review, Vol. LXXXXV, No. 4, p. 273

NAG, D.S., 'Fundamentals of the "Gandhian Constitution', Modern Review, Vol LXXX, No. 6, p. 465

NAMBIAR, M.K., 'American Borrowings in the Indian Constitution', S.C.J., Vol. 17, p. 151

NARAIN, IQBAL, 'The Indian Constitution: On the Anvil', Modern Review, Vol. LXXXXIV, No. 6, p. 445

NARAYAN, JAYAPRAKASH, 'Decentralized Democracy-Theory and Practice', The Indian Jour. Of Pub. Admn., Vol. 7, 1961, p. 271

NAVAR, V.K.S., 'An Analysis of the Major Influences in the Drafting of the Constitution of India', American Political Science Review, September 1956

'The New Constitution' (Leading Article), Eastern Economist, Vol. 10, No. 1, p.17

NICHOLAS, H.S., 'Constitution of India', Australian Law Journal, Vol. 23, p.638

O'NORMAIN, CATHAL, 'The Influence of Irish Political Though on the Indian Constitution', The 2nd Year Book of International Affairs, Vol. 1, p. 156

PANDE, A.C., 'The New Constitution of India', I.J.P. Sc., Vol. 9, No. 4, p. 54

PARTHASARTHI (Mrs.), 'India: A New Democracy', Asiatic Review, Vol. XLVI, p. 1080

PRASAD, RAJENDRA, 'The New Constitution', *Parliamentary Affairs* (London), Vol. 5, p. 420

PYLEE, M.V., 'The Constitution of India', *The German year Book of Public Law* (1955), p. 155

RAJAN, M.S., 'Indian Foreign Policy in Action', *India Quarterly*, Vol. 26, July-Sept., 1960, p. 201

RAMACHANDRAN, V.G., 'Sir Ivor Jennings on the Indian Constitution', *All India Reporter*, September 1957, pp. 76-9

RAMASWAMY, M., 'Constitution of the Indian Republic', *The Canadian Bar Review*, Vol. 28, p.1

RAO RAJESWARA, 'The Outlook of Constitutionalism', *S.C.J.*, Vol. 16, p. 91

RAU, B.N. 'The Indian Constitution', *India Quarterly*, Vol. 5, No. 4, p. 273

ROBSON, WILLIAM A., 'Indian Revisited', *Pol. Quar.* (London), Vol. 31, March 1960, p. 422

SEERVAI, H.M., 'Constitutional Law of India', *Law Quar. Rev.*, Vol. 78, 1962

SHARMA, B., 'Reflections on Parliamentary Government in India', *I.J.P. Sc.*, Vo. 10, No. 3, p. 19

SHARMA, S.R. 'Sir Ivor Jennings and Constitutional Laws of India', *I.J.P. Sec.* Vol. 14, No. 2, p. 145.

SHARMA, S.R., 'Some Aspects of the Indian Constitution', *Modern Review*, Vol. LXXXV, No. 2, p. 115

SILVA, M.A., 'Parliamentary Government in Underdeveloped Democracies', Parliamentary Affairs, (London), Vol. 7, p. 420

SINGH, SUSHIL CHANDRA, 'The New Constitution-An Appraisal', *I.J.P. Sc.*, Vol. 11, No. 4, p. 82

SINHA, L.P., 'Towards a Partyless Democratic State', *The Ind. Jour, of Pol. Sc.*, Vol. 21, No. 4, Oct.-Dec. 1960, p. 347

SIRCAR, RAJ KISHORE, 'The Constitution of India—Its Salient Features', *A.L.J.*, Vol. XLVIII, p. 127

SRIVASTAVA, G.P., 'Second Thoughts on Indian Foreign Policy', *The Ind. Jour. Of Pol. Sci.*, Vol. 21, No. 2, April-June, 1960, p. 143

VENKUDRA, S.D., 'The Concept of the Secular State', *I.J.P. Sc.*, Vol. II, No. 3, pp. 328

VARADACHARIAR, S., 'Indian Constitution—a Brief Study', *India Quarterly*, Vol. 6, No. 3, p. 213

VENKATARAMA SASTRI, T.R., 'Secular State and Legislation', *M.L.J.*, Vol. 1, p. 78

VIJAYALAKSHMI PANDIT, 'The Pattern of India Today', *Asain Review*, Vol. 55, No. 202, April 1959, p. 105

HISTORICAL BACKGROUND

ALEXANDER, P.C., 'The Proposed Constituent Assembly: Can It Solve India's Constitutional Problems? *I.J.P., Sc.*, Vol. 7, No.3, p. 434

ALEXANDER, P.C., 'Cabinet Mission's Scheme and Division of Powers-The Problem of a Weak Centre and Strong Units', *I.J.P. Sc.*, Vol. 8, No. 3, p. 736

'Ambedkar on Draft Constitution' (Editorial Notes), *Modern Review*, Vol. LXXXIV, No. 6, p. 421

AMERY, L.S., 'Indian Constitutional Development: The War Years', *Asiatic Review*, Vol. 49, p. 254

APPADORAI, A., 'The Task Before the Constituent Assembly', *India Quarterly*, Vol. 2, No. 3, p. 231; and Vol. 3, No. 1, p. 10

BANERJEE, D.N., 'Indian States and the Future Constitution of India', *Modern Review*, Vol LXXXV, No. 2, p. 105

BASU, A., 'Education and the Draft Constitution', *Indian Law Review*, Vol. V

'The Constituent Assembly's First Bill' (Leading Article), *Eastern Economist*, Vol. 11 No. 23, p. 959

'Constituent Assemblies: A Retrospect' (Editorial Notes), *C.W.N.*, Vol. L, No. 27

'The Constituent Assembly', (Leading Article), *Eastern Economist*, Vol. 6, No. 21, p. 851

DESHPANDE, N.R., 'The Problem of Constitution-making in India', *I.J.P. Sc.*, Vol. 6, No. 4, p. 189

'The Draft Constitution' (Contributed), *India Quarterly*, Vol. 5, No. 1, p.3

'The Draft Constitution' (Leading Article), *Eastern Economist*, Vol. 10, No. 1, p. 425

'The Draft Constitution of India', Report of Members of the Bar at Calcutta, *I.L.R.*, Vol. 2, p. 9

GHOSAL, A.K., 'Some Aspects of the Draft Constitution of India', *Modern Review*, Vol LXXXIV, No. 1, p. 23; No. 2, p. 110; No. 3, p. 193; No. 4, p. 275; No. 5, p. 360

GUPTA, A. C., 'Notes on Some Articles of the Draft Constitution of India', *I.L.R.*, Vol. 2, p. 26

GWYER, SIR MAURICE, 'Approaches to the Indian Constitutional Problem', *India Quarterly*, Vol. I, p. 5

'Hurdles in Constitution-making' (Editorial Notes), C.W.N., Vol. L, No. 34

'India's Draft Constitution' (Editorial Notes), *Modern Review*, Vol. LXXXIII, No. 4, p.254

KIBE, M.V., 'The Task Before the Constituent Assembly', *Hindustan Review*, Vol. LXXX, p. 232 and Vol. LXXXI, p. 13

MAHAJAN, VIDYADHAR, 'What is Wrong with the Draft Constitution?', *Hindustan Review*, Vol. LXXXII, p. 183 and p. 259

MAZUMDAR, A.K., 'Some Aspects of our Draft Constitution', *Hindustan Review*, Vol. LXXXII, p. 231

MCWHINNEY, E. 'Constitutional History-Democratic Constitutionalism in South-East Asia-Constitution-making in India, Ceylon and Pakistan', *Howard Law Journal*, Vol. I, p. 149

MITRA, S., 'The Draft Constitution of India', *The Indian Law Review*, 1948

MUKHERJI, SUDHANSU SEKHAR, 'Improvement of the Draft Constitution of India', *Modern Review*, Vol. LXXXIV, No. 6, p. 455

MUKHERJI, SUDHANSU SEKHAR, 'Linguistic Provinces and the Draft Constitution', *Modern Review*, Vol. LXXXIV, No. 4, p. 281

NAMBIAR, M.K., 'The Framework of the New Constitution', *F.L.J.*, Vol. 9, p. 52

'Our Constituent Assemblies' (Editorial Notes), C.W.N., Vol. L, No. 19 'Paramountcy and Indian States' (Editorial notes), *C.W.N.*, Vol. LI, No. 31

"Prime Minister" and "Cabinet" in India' (Editorial Notes), *C.W.N.*, Vol. LI, No. 4

PULLAN, A.G.K., 'A Constitution in the Making', *Journal of the Society of Comparative Legislation*, London, Vol. 31, p. 74

RAJAN, M.S., 'India and the Commonwealth 1954-56', *India Quarterly*, Vol. 16, 1960, p. 31

RAM, V.S. and MASALADAN, P.N. "Status and Powers of Provinces in the Future Constitution of

India', *I.J.P. Sc.*, Vol. 7, No. 4, p. 449

RAMAMURTI, PRATAPGIRI, 'The Draft Constitution of India', *I.J.P. Sc.,* Vol. 10, No. 3, p.9

RAMASWAMY, M., 'Constitutional Developments in India, 1600-1955', *Stanford Law Review*, Vol. 8, p. 326

RAO, P. KODANDA, 'Is the Indian Consembly Sovereign?', *Hindustan Review*, Vol. LXXX, October 1949, p. 201

RAO, P. KODANDA, 'The Draft Constitution', *New Review*, Vol. 27, April 1948, p. 311; May 1948, p. 286; June 1948, p. 462

'Reactions to the Cabinet Mission Proposals' (Supplement), *Modern Review*, Vol. LXXIX, No. 6, p. 485

SEN, D.K., 'The Indian Constitution in the Making', *I.L.R.*, Vol. 3, p. 10

SEN GUPTA, N.C., 'Some Outstanding Features of the Draft Constitution of India', *Indian Law Review*, 1948 and F.L.J., Vol. 12, p. 40

SHARMA, R.K., 'Genesis of Indian Democracy', *Modern Review*, Vol. Cx, No. 3, 1961 (Sept.), p. 197

SRIVASTAVA, V.N., 'India-A Union of States Under the Draft Constitution', *I.J.P. Sc.*, Vol. 10, No. 3, p. 45

SRINIVASAN, N., 'A Review of Some Constitutional Schemes', *I.J.P. Sc.,* Vol. 8, No. 1, p. 620

TEMPLEWOOD, VISCOUNT, 'Recent Indian Constitutional History', *Asiatic Review*, Vol. XLVIII, p. 243

'Thoughts on the Cabinet Mission' (Editorial Notes), C.W.N., Vol. L, No. 20

VENKATARANGAIYA, M., 'Some Recent Developments in Asia-constitutional', *India Quarterly*, Vol. 9, No. 3 p. 209

VENKATAKRISHNAN, S., 'A Survey of the Draft Constitution', *F.L.J.*, Vol. II, p. 48

PREAMBLE

DESHPANDE, V.S., 'People and the Constitution', Vol. 16 *J.I.L.I.* (1974), p.1

RAMACHANDRAN, V.G., 'Sovereignty of the Indian Republic', *M.L.J.*, Vol. II (1955), p. 23

RAMACHANDRAN, V.G., 'Sovereignty in the Indian Republic', *A.I.R.* (1956), p. 49

RAO, V. VENKATA, 'The Preamble', *I.J.P.* Sc., Vol. 12, No. 2, p.1

SHARMA R. 'Understanding Indian Constitution and the Preamble', *Political Scientist*, July-December 1971, p. 89

CITIZENSHIP

BINDRA, C.J.S., 'Indian citizenship', *Modern Review*, Vol. 95, No. 5, p. 377

'Citizenship of India' (Editorial Notes), *Modern Review*, Vol. LXXXVI, No. 3, p. 184

'Citizenship in the Indian Union' (Editorial Notes), *C.W.N.,* Vol. LI, No. 28 and Vol. LI, No. 29

"Citizenship of the Indian Union' (Editorial Notes), *C.W.N.*, Vol. LII, April 1948

PANIKKAR, K.M., 'The Citizen and the State', *Eastern Economist*, Vol. 36, No. 14, p. 571 and No. 15, p. 605

TERRITORY

ARORA, S.K., 'The Reorganization of the Indian States', *Far Eastern Survey*, Vol. XXV(2), p. 27

ARORA, V.K., 'The States After Reorganization', *Indian Affairs Record* (1956), p. 4

ARUNACHALAM, N., 'States Barriers', *S.C.J.*, 1960

AURNACHALAM, N., 'States Barriers, Administrative Relations', *S.C.J.*, 1960

Bhargava, G.S., 'India is a Multi-Lingual Nation, not a Multi-National State', *Economic Weekly*, 8(9) : (1956), p. 4

'Bilingual Bombay', *The Eastern Economist*'s Blue Supplement, Vol. II, No.2, August 31, 1956

BOSE, S. M., 'The States and the New Constitution', *Modern Review*, Vol. LXXX, No. 2, p. 107

CHANDA, NAGENDRA NATH, 'States in Indian Constitution', *Modern Review*, Vol. LXXIX, No. 5, p. 375

'Consolidation of Indian States' (Editorial Notes), *Modern Review*, Vol. LXXXIII, No. 2, p. 98

'Constitutional Developments: Constitution of India: Scope of Article 3', (Reference to State Legislatures for their opinion: judgement of the Bombay High Court), *Journal of Parliamentary Information* (1957), p. 381

DANTWALA, M.L., PUNEKAR, S.D., AMIN, R.K., GORWALA, A.D. and HAJI, S.N., 'The New Face of India', A quintet of economic opinion, *United Asia*, 9(5) : p. 379 (1956)

'Delimitation and the Constitution' (The week's notes), *Eastern Economist*, Vol. 18, No. 26, p. 997

'Draft Bill on Reorganization of States, Main Provisions Analysed', *Commerce*, 92(1956), pp. 545 & 595

DUTTA, A.K., 'Some Reflections on the Report of the States Reorganization Commission', *C.W.N.*, LX (17), p. 63

GUNDAPPA, D.V., 'The Indian States and the Linguistic Problem', *The Second Year book of International Affairs*, Vol. III, Part I, p. 35

GUPTA, S., 'Reactions to the SRC Report-A Survey', *Indian Affairs Record*, November 1955, p. 1

GUPTA, S., 'The Task Before the States Reorgnaisation Commission', *Indian Affairs Record*, Vol. I, No. 1, p. 5

GUPTA, S., 'States Reorganisation-The Latest Phase', *Indian Affairs Record* (February 1956), p. 4

'The Indian States' (Leading Article), *Eastern Economist*, Vol. 9, No. 7, p. 250.

'The Integration of States' (Leading Article), *Eastern Economist*, Vol. 11, No. 26, p. 1103

'Kashmir and the Indian Constitution' (Leading Article), *Eastern Economist*, Vol. 19, No. 5, p. 157

MAHARAJA OF BIKANER, 'The Indian Constitution and the States', *Asiatic Review*, Vol. XLII, p. 161

MAHESHWARI, S., 'Evolution of States in India', *I.J.P.A.* (1976), p. 307

MEHRA, M.P., 'Indian States Reorganised', A.I.C.C. *Economic Review*, Issue No. 14, p. 21 (November 1956)

MEHTA, N. JIVARAJ, 'Integration of Indian States', *Asiatic Review*, vol. XLV, p. 719

NARAYAN, JAYAPRAKASH, 'The Question of States Reorganization', *Janata*, XI (3): p. 3 (February 1956)

NARAYAN, SHRIMAN, 'On States Reorganization', A.I.C.C. *Economic Review*, Issue No. 1, p. 18 (May 1956)

'New Political Map of India After States Reorganization', *Economic Weekly*, 8(45): November 1956, p. 1317

PANIKKAR, K.M., 'Indian States Reorganization', *Asian Review*, 52 (192), p. 247 (October 1956)

PARAS, DIWAN, 'Kashmir and the Indian Union-The Legal Position', The International and Comparative Law Quarterly, Vol.2, p.333 (1953) 'Princes and Indian Union' (Editorial Notes), *C.W.N.* Vol. LI, No. 12, February 1947

RAY, CHUNNILAL, 'The States Reorganization Commission's Report', *Modern Review*, 90(1), p. 43

'Reorganization of States', *Commerce*, 92(2352), p. 597

'Reorganization of States', *Commerce*, 93(2383), p. 845

SARAF, OM PRAKASH, 'Kashmir's Constitutional Status in India', *Janata*, XI (36), p. 13

SASTRI, K.N.V., 'A Few Administrative Problems Created by the S.R.C.', *Indian Journal of Political Science*, 17(1), p. 28

'The States Reorganization Commission' (Editorial Notes), *C.W.N.* LX (2 and 3), pp.5 and 6

'The States Reorganization Bill', *Eastern Economist*, XXVI (12), p. 473

VENKATARAMAN, T.S.,'The Integration of Indian States', *F.I.J.*, Vol. 11, p. 1.

VENKATARANGAIYA, M., 'States in Part B-The Paramountcy', *I.J.P. Sc.*, Vol. 11, No. 4, p. 55

VENKATA RAO, V., 'The Political Map of India', *I.J.P. Sc.*, Vol. 17 (2), p. 176

VIDWANS, M.D., 'Zonal Reorganization of India', *S.C.J.*, February 1956, p. 14

WINDMILLER, MARSHALL, 'The Politics of States Reorganization in India: The Case of Bombay', *Far Eastern Survey,* 15(9), p. 129 (September 1956)

FUNDAMENTAL RIGHTS

ACHARYA, B.N., 'A Note on Article 22(1) of the Constitution of India', *A.I.R.,* Vol. 41, p. 37

AGGARVAL, A.P., "Freedom of Association in Public Employment", Vol. 14 *J.I.L.I.* (1972), p. 1

ALEXANDER, P.C., 'Equality as a Fundamental Right in India', *I.J.P. Sc.,* Vol. 9, No. 1, p.54

ALEXANDER, P.C., 'Liberty of the Press – Its Legal Restrictions', *I.J.P. Sc.,* Vol. 8, No.1, p.683

ALEXANDROWICZ, C.H., 'Common Law Prerogative Writs in India', *The Indian year Book of International Affairs,* Vol. 1, Part III, p.199

ARUNACHALAM, N., "The Individual under the Indian Constitution, *S.C.J.,* Vol. 22, p. 68

AYYAR, C.S.S., 'Procedural Due Process or Procedural Safeguards as a Fundamental Right', *S.C.J.,* Vol. 22, p.156

BANERJEE, D.N., 'Some Aspects of the Fundamental Rights, *I.J.P., Sc.,* Vol. II, No.4, p. 26

BANERJEE, D.N., 'Some Aspects of Our Constitution' (Fundamental Rights), *Modern Review,* (i) Vol. 96, No. 4, 1954; (ii) Vol. 96, No. 5, p. 374, 1954; (iii) Vol.97, No.1, 1955; (iv) Vol. 97, No.3, p.361, 1955; (v) Vol. 97, No.5, p. 361, 1955; (vi) Vol.98, No.1, p.25, 1955; (vii) Vol.99, No.1, p.25, 1956; (viii) Vol.99, No.4, p.277, 1956. Also Modern Review, January 1956, p. 32, April 1956, p. 277, July 1956, p.3, January 1957, pp.23-6, March 1957, pp.210-13, July 1957, pp.25-38, October 1957, pp. 277-89, January 1958, pp. 25-39.

BHARGAVA, S.P., 'Fundamental Rights and the Indian Constitution, *I.J.P. Sc.,* Vol. 9, Nos.2 and 3, p.24

BASU, DURGA DAS, 'The Seven Freedoms of the Constitution of India', *F.L.J.,* Vol. 12, p.9

BASU, DURGA DAS, 'Some Aspects of the Habeas Corpus under the Constitution of India'' *F.L.J.,* No. 12, p.73

BANERJEE, D.N., 'A Note on Fundamental Rights and Constitutional Safe-guards', *Modern Review,* Vol. LXXXI, No.3, P.219

BINDRA, C.J.S., 'Freedom of Speech and Expression', *A.I.R.,* Vol. 41, p.62

BISWAS, A.R., "Property in a Changing Society", Vol. 15, *J.I.L.I.* (1973), p.1

BISWAS, N.R., 'Fundamental Rights and the Writs under the Constitution', *A.I.R.,* Vol. 38, pp. 63 and 65-6

CHOWDHURI, C.C., 'Ultra Vires Legislation Abridging Civil Liberty and the Doctrine of Severability', *I.L.R.,* Vol.4, p.158

'Civil Liberty in India Since 1947' (Eleven articles contributed by different authors), *I.J.P. Sc.,* Vol. 13, Nos. 3 and 4, pp.1-108

'The Constitution and the Communal Rule' (The Week's Notes), *Eastern Economist,* Vol. 16, No.17, p.684

'The Constitution and the Right to Freedom of Religion' (Editorial), *C.W.N.,* Vol. LVII, No. 24

DAS, P.R., "The Draft Constitution" and Personal Liberty', *I.L.R.,* Vol.2, p.192

DAS, P.R., 'Civil Liberties in India, *Hindustan Review,* Vol. LXXXVI, P.6

DAS, TARAKNATH, 'Fundamental Rights', *Modern Review,* Vol. LXXXIII, NO.2, P.69

DESHPANDE, V.S., "Rights and Duties under the Constitution, Vol. 15, *J.I.L.I.* (1973), p.94

'Despotism in the First Amendment' (Leading Article), *Eastern Economist,* Vol. 16, No. 2, p. 794

'Detention Without Trial in Free India' (Editorial Notes), *Modern Review,* Vol. LXXXVI, No.4, p.260

'The Devil's Advocate' (Criticises Dr. Ambedkar's defence of the First Amendment of the Constitution) Leading Article, *Eastern Economist,* Vol. 16, No.21, p.839

D'SOUZA, J. 'Using Freedom to Destroy Freedom' (A note on the Preventive Detention Bill), *Social Action,* Vol. 1, p.120

DUTTA, A.K., 'Fundamental Rights Analyzed', *C.W.N.,* LXI (6), p.23

DUTT, P., 'Preventive Detention under the Indian Constitution', *The Modern Review,* Vol. 109, No. 1, Jan.-June 1961, p.21

'Ex-post facto Laws and Article 20(1) of the Constitution' (Editorial Notes), *C.W.N.*, Vol. LVII, No.38

'The Fourth Amendment', *Thought,* March 26, 1955

'The Fourth Estate' (Leading Article), *Eastern Economist,* Vol.16, No.21, p.841

'Fredom and the Constitution' (Leading Article), *Eastern Economist*, Vol. 16, No. 15, p. 597.

'Freedom, the Constitution and the Press' (Editorial Notes), *Modern Review,* Vol. LXXXIX, No. 6, p.425

'Fundamental Rights' (Leading Article), *Eastern Economist*, Vol. 9, No.7, p.248

GADGIL, N.V., 'Amendment of Article 31 of the Constitution', *I.A.R.,* Vol.1, No.3, p.1

GAE, R.S., "Power to Acquire Property", Vol. 13, *J.I.L.I.* (1971), p.189

GARG, RAMESH R., "Phantom of Basic Structure of the Constitution", Vol.16, *J.I.L.I.* (1974), p. 243

GLEDHILL, ALAN, 'India's Fundamental Rights', *The Indian year Books of International Affairs,* Vol. 1, p.9

GUPTA, A.C., 'Reasonable Restrictions', I.L.R., Vol. 5, p.71

GUPTA, SISIR, 'Amendment of the Constitution' Article 31), A.I.C.C. *Economic Review,* Vol. 6, p.73

GUPTESWAR, K., 'The Rule against Double Jeopardy under the Indian Constitution', *S.C.J.,* April 1956, p.53

GYAN PRAKASH, 'Our Constitution and our Right to Equality, Liberty and Property', *A.L.J.*, Vol. LII, p.5

'Hammer on the Anvil: 4yh Amendment Bill' (Leading Article), *Eastern Economist*, Vol.24, No.5, p.613

'Immunity from Self Incrimination. Article 20(3) of the Constitution, Recent Full Bench Decision' (Editorial Notes), *C.W.N.*, Vol. LV, No. 32

JANAKIKUTTY, AMMA K., 'Fundamental Rights in Relation to the Indian Constitution', *I.J.P. Sc.*, Vol.9, Nos.2 and 3, p.19

KRIPALANI, J.B., 'Preventive Detention', *Vigil,* Vol.3, No.2, p.6

KRIPALANI, J.B., 'Civil Liberties', *Vigil,* Vol.4, No.5, p.5

KRIPALANI, J.B., 'Fight for Civil Liberties', *Vigil,* Vol. XI (14), p.215

'The Law and the Press' (Leading Article), *Eastern Economist,* Vol. 17, Nov.10, p.411

'The Liberty of the Individual' (Leading Article), *Eastern Economist*, Vol.20, No.29, p.973, June 1953

MITTER, B.L., 'A Note on Article 15 of the Draft Constitution', *I.L.R.*, Vol. 2, p.209

NAMBIAR, M.K., 'Our Fundamental Rights', *M.L.J.,* Vol. II, p. 41

NAMBIAR, M.K., 'The Role of Double Jeopardy in the Indian Constitution', *M.L.J.*, Vol. II, p.75

NARAYAN, J.P., 'Civil Liberties in India', *Vigil,* Vol. 5, No.10, p.12, No.11, p.7

'On Preventive Detention' (Editorial Notes), *C.W.N.*, Vol. LVI, No. 13

PANDE, D.C., "Offences Against Religion' (A Critical Review of Ramji Lal Modi vs. State of (U.P.), *M.L.J.,* Vol 13 (1958), p.42

PARAS, DIWAN, 'Freedom of Speeach *vs* Defamation of Public Servants', *M.L.J.*, Vol. 11, p. 4.

PARAS, DIWAN 'Nationalization Under the Indian Constitution', *S.C.J.,* Vol.16, p.21

'Pardon by President in Contempt Cases', *Indian Law Quarterly Review*, September 1957, p.415

'Pre-constitution Statute and Equal Protection Clause' (Editorial Notes), *C.W.N.,* Vol. LVII, No.37

'Preventive Detention and the Judiciary (Editorial Notes), *C.W.N.*, Vol. LIV, No.3

PUNTAMBEKAR, S.V., 'The Secular State: A Critique', *I.J.P. Sc.,* Vol.10, Nos.1 and 2, p. 58

RAI, MOHAN 'Fundamental Rights in the Indian Constitution;', *New Age,* 7(5), May, 1958

RAJGOPALAN, S., 'Amending the Constitution' (Article 31), *Vigil,* Vol.5, No.15, p.5, and No.18

RAMACHANDRAN, V.G., 'The Test of Reasonable Restriction in Article 19 of the Indian Constitution', *S.C.J.*, Vol. 16, p.86

RAMACHANDRAN, V.G., 'The Law of Preventive Detention', *S.C.J.*, Vol. 17, p.181

RAMACHANDRAN, V.G., 'Liberty *vs.* Personal Liberty', *M.L.J.*, Vol. 1, p. 40

RAMACHANDRAN, V.G., 'The Constitutional Amendment of Article 31', *S.C.J.*, Vol. 20, p. 35.

RAMACHANDRAN, V.G., 'The Charter of Personal Freedom in England, America and India', *S.C.J.*, Vol. 21, p.9

RAMALINGAM, T., 'Freedom From Law', *S.C.J.*, Vol. 19, p.83

RAMASWAMI, V., 'Law in the Secular state', *Indian Law Review,* Vol. III, 1949

RAO, C. APPA, 'Fundamental Rights vis-à-vis Directive Principles in Indian Constitution', *S.C.J.*, Vol. II, 1961

RAO, APPA, 'Fundamental Rights in the Draft Constitution', *I.J.P. Sc.,* Vol. 10, Nos.1 and 2 p.90

RAO, K. VENKOBA, 'Liberty and Social Control', *S.C.J.*, Vol. 16, p.203

RAO, P. RAJESWARA, 'Fundamental Rights', *Modern Review*, Vol. LXXXVI, No.5, p.361

'Reasonable Restriction Clause in Article 19 of the Constitution' (Editorial Notes), *C.W.N.,* Vol. LX, No.33

'The Restored Freedom (1st Amendment)', Leading Article, *Eastern Economist*, Vol. 17, No.9, p.369

ROY, PRAPHULLA KUMAR, 'Property and Article 19 of the Constitution', *C.W.N.*, Vol. LVI, No.38

SASTRI, C.L.R., "Freedom of Person and Expression', *Modern Review,* Vol. LXXXVI, No.1, p.25

SASTRI, C.L.R., 'When Constitutions Become Flexible and Curvaceous?, *Modern Review*, Vol. LXXXX, No. 4, p. 285

SATHE, S.P., "Standing to Assert Fundamental Rights of Third Parties: An Analysis of Judicial Policy", Vol. 14, *J.I.L.I.* (1972), p. 325

SATYAM, 'Freedom to Propagate Faith', *Swatantra*, Vol. II, No. 31, p. 17

SCHWARTZ, B., 'Comparative View of the Gopalan Case', *F.L.J.*, Vol. 14, p. 276

'Selected Approval (1st Amendment)', Leading Article, *Eastern Economist*, Vol. 16, No.22, p.881

SENGUPTA, N.C., First Amendment of the Constitution', *I.L.R.*, Vol. 5, p. 135

SETALVAD, M.C., 'Equality Before Law', *Journal of Parliamentary Information*, October 1955, p.124

SHAHNAI, T.K., 'Fundamental Rights in Relation to the Indian Constitution', *I.J.P. Sc.*, Vol. 9, Nos.2 and 3, p.12

SHINN, LARRY D., "Indian Communalism and the Secular State", *I.J.P.Sc.*, Vol. XXXII, p.32

SHARMA, B.K., 'A Pragmatic Evaluation of Fundamental Rights', *S.C.J.,* 1960

SHARMA, F.C., 'Fundamental Rights in Draft Constitution of India', *I.J.P., Se.*, Vol. 10, No. 3, p. 32.

SHARMA S.R., 'Fundamental Rights in Our Constitution', *New Review*, Vol. 32, p. 265

SMITH, DONALD E., 'Gandhi and Nehru on the Concept of the Secular State', *Nagpur University Pol. Sc. Assn. Bulletin,* 1954-55

SUBRAHMANYAM, C.S., 'Administrative Discretion and Equality before the Law', *S.C.J.,* Vol. 21, p.255

SUDA, J.P., 'Fundamental Rights and Personal Liberty under Our Constitution', *I.J.P. Sc.*, Vol. II, No.4, p.37

SOUZA, T.P., 'Freedom of Religion under the Indian Constitution', *I.J.P. Sc* Vol. 13 (1952)

'A Supreme Court Judgment on Detention' (Editorial Notes), *C.W.N.*, Vol. LVII, No. 31

'Supreme Court Judgment on Preventive Detention. Articles 22 (5) and (6) of the Constitution', *C.W.N.*, Vol. LV, No.22

THIRUVENKATACHARI, V.K., 'The Unconstitutional Statues', *S.C.J.,* August 1957, p.131

TRIPATHI, P.K., 'India's Experiment in Freedom of Speech: The First Amendment and Thereafter', *S.C.J.*, Vol. 15, p.106

TRIPATHI, P.K., 'Free Speech in the Indian Constitution', *Yale Law Journal,* January 1958, p. 584

'Two Notable Decisions (First Amendment)', The Week's Notes, *Eastern Economist,* Vol. 16, No.22, p. 885

VARADACHARIAR, S., 'Fundamental Rights in the New Constitution', *India Quarterly*, Vol. 5, No.3, p.195

VAZE, S.G., 'Amendment of Article 31 of the Constitution – a Criticism', *Indian Affairs Record,* Vol. I, No.3, p.3

VENKATARAMAN, K., 'Equal Protection of the Laws and Classification', *S.C.J.,* Vol. 16, p.51

VENKATRAMAN, S., 'Judicial Review and Guaranteed Rights', *S.C.J.,* Vol. 17, p.37

VENKATARANGAIYA, M., 'Fundamental Rights in a New Indian Constitution', *I.J.P., Sc.*, Vol. 6, No.2, p. 114

'When Judges Disagree' (On the judgment in the Gopalan Case), Editorial, *Vigil*, Vol. 1, No. 14, p.3

WEINER, MYRON, 'The Struggle for Equality in India', *Foreign Affairs,* Vol. 40, No.4, 1962

WILSON, J.N., 'Foreign Missionaries and the Christian Church and Community in India', *Modern Review*, Vol. LXXXVI, No.4

DIRECTIVE PRINCIPLES

AGARWAL, S.N., 'Village Panchayats in the Indian Constitution', *Modern Review*, Vol. LXXXIX, No.2, p. 146

AIYAR, ALLADI KRISHNASWAMI, 'Separation of Judiciary from the Executive', *M.L.J.,* Vol.2, p.15

BANERJEE, D.N., 'Dr. Katju and the "Separation of the Executive and Judicial Functions" – A Critique', *I.L.R.*, Vol. 3, p.99

BASU, A., 'Education and the Draft Constitution', *I.L.R.*, Vol. 2, p. 141

DESAI, M., 'The Executive vs. the Judiciary', *Harijan*, Vol. 17, No. 36, p.282

KARVE, D.G., 'Public Administration and Directive Principles of the Constitution', *Indian Journal of Public Administration*, January 1955, p.8

KATJU, J.N., 'Separation of the Executive and Judicial Functions', *F.L.J.,* Vol.2, p.200

NARAIN, IQBAL, 'Directives of State Policy', *Modern Review*, Vol. 93, No.2, p. 105

NARAYAN RAO, T.S., 'Directive Principles of State Policy', *I.J.P. Sc.*, Vol.10, No.3, p. 16

PILLAY, K.K., 'The New Constitution of India and "Panchayat Raj", *I.J.P. Sc.,* Vol. 12, p. 13

PURKAYASTHA, K.M., 'Limits of Non-justiciability of Directive Principles', *Vigil,* Vol. 3, No. 36, p.8

RAMACHANDRAN, V.G., 'The Social Welfare State in India in its International Bearings', *C.W.N.*, LX(10), pp.34, 38

RAO, P. KODANDA, 'Prohibition and the Constitution', *Harijan*, Vol. 17, No.8, p.62

RAO, T.S., 'Constitution and Compulsory Education', *Organiser*, Vol. XI(22), p.6

RAMACHANDRAN, V.G., 'Social Structure in Welfare State with Particular Reference to India', *S.C.J.,* Vol. 19, p.37

RAMA RAO, T.S., 'Some Problems of International Law in India', *The Indian Year Book of International Affairs*, Vol. VI, p.3

SASTRY, K.R.R., 'On Article 51 of India's Constitution', *S.C.J.*, Vol. 15, p. 48

'Separation of the Executive and the Judiciary' (Editorial Notes), *C.W.N.,* Vol. LIV, No. 43

SHUKLA, GAYA PRASAD, 'The Hindu Code Bill and the Constitution', *A.L.J.,* Vol. XLVIII, p. 101

TOPE, T.K., 'Provisions of the Indian Constitution Regarding International Relations', *S.C.J.*, Vol. 18, p.305

TRIPATHI, P.K., 'Directive Principles of State Policy: The Lawyer's Approach to them hitherto Parochial, Injurious and Unconstitutional', *S.C.J.,* Vol. 17, p.7

UMESH KUMAR, "Regulation of Concentration of Economic Power", Vol. 17, *J.I.L.I.* (1975), p.539

WIDWANS, M.D., 'Nature of Directive Principles', *All India Reporter*, May 1956, p.37 and June 1956, p.41

THE UNION EXECUTIVE

AGARWAL, P.P., 'The Planning Commission', *Ind. Jour. Of Pub. Admn.*, Vol.3, 1957

AIYAR, S.L.K., 'The President and the Cabinet', *All India Reporter,* October 1957, pp. 81-3

AYYAR, C.S.S., 'Is the President of India a mere Constitutional Head?, *S.C.J.*, I, 1961

BANERJEE, D.N., 'Position of the President of India', *Modern Review*, Vol. LXXVII, No. 6, p. 450, June 1950; Vol. LXXXVII, No.6, p. 454, December 1950; and Vol. LXXXIX, pp. 365 and 451

BANERJEE, D.N., 'The Indian Presidency', *Political Quarterly*, London, March 1955

BANERJEE, D.N., 'The Powers of the President of India', *The Modern Review,* Vol. 109, Jan-June 1961, p.17

BANERJEE, M., 'The President of the Indian Republic', *I.J.P. Sc.,* Vol. 11, No.4, p.101

BASU, DURGA DAS, 'The President of India', *F.L.J.*, Vol. 12, pp.49, 91

BASU, K.K., 'The President of India', *Modern Review*, Vol. LXXXVIII, No.3, p.202, September 1950' Vol. LXXXIX, No.2, p. 141, February 1957, Vol. LXXXX, No. 3, p. 206

'Cabinet Government' (Leading Article), *Eastern Economist*, Vol. 14, No. 22, p. 867, June 1950

CHATTERJEE, M.C., 'Control of the Legislative Powers of Administration'. *S.C.J.*, Vol. 21, p.68

CHOPRA, D.S., 'Doctrine of Pleasure: Its Scope, Implications and limitations', *I.J.P.A.* (1975), p.92

DESHPANDE, V.S., 'The President, His Powers and Their Exercise', Vol. 13, *J.I.L.I* (1971), p.326

GHOSAL, A.K., 'Union Executive in the Indian Constitution', *Modern Review,* Vol. LXXXXI, No. 1, p.31, January 1952: No.2, February 1952 and No.3

GHOSH, RAMESH CHANDRA, 'The Powers of the President of India and the Cabinet System', *I.J.P. Sc.*, Vol. 13, Nos. 3 and 4

HINTON, R.W.K., 'The Prime Minister as an Elected Monarch', *Parliamentary Affairs,* Vol. 13, 1959-60, p. 297

HOLMES, JR., HENRY, W., "Powers of the Indian President" *Myth or Reality*", Vol. 12, J.I.L.I. (1970), p. 367 (also see in the same number of the Journal, "A Plea for the Study of Powers of the President of India", p.400)

JENA, B.B., 'Vice-Presidency under a Parliamentary Democracy', *Modern Review,* October 1954, p.273

MATHUR, R.N., 'The Constitutional Position and Powers of the President of the Indian Union', *S.C.J.*, I, 1962

PARIKH, R.N., 'The Executive, Legislative and Judiciary of the Union of India' (A comparative study), *Modern Review*, Vol. LXXXIII, No.5, p. 357

PURKAYASTHA, K.M., 'Will Cabinet Government Suit Us?', *Vigil,* Vol. 3, No.21, p.6

'The President' (Leading Article), *Eastern Economist*, Vol. 18, p. 691

PYLEE, M.V., "Presidential Power", Quest, April-June 1970, p.9

RAMASWAMY, M., 'The Constitutional Position of the President of the Indian Republic', *Canadian Bar Review*, Vol. 28, January 1950

RAMASWAMY, M., 'The Indian Union Executive', *India Quarterly,* Vol. 3, No.3, p.222

RAO, P. NAGARAJ, 'Internal Executive Power and its Constitutional Validity', *M.L.J.,* Vol. II, p.45

RAO, P. RAJESWARA, 'Union Executive and the Legislature', *Modern Review,* Vol. LXXXVII, No. 1, p. 29.

RAO, K.V., 'President's Resignation in the New Constitution', *Modern Review*', Vol. LXXXIX, No. 3, p.199

RUTHNASWAMY, M., 'The Swiss Executive: Model for India', *New Review,* Vol. 24, p. 386

SATHE, P.S., 'The Ordinance-making Power of President of India', *S.C.J.*, Vol. 22, p. 231

SEN, S.R., 'Planning Machinery in India', *Ind. Jour. Of Pub. Admn.,* Vol. 7, 1961

SHARMA, B.M., 'The President of the Indian Republic', *I.J.P. Sc.*, Vol. II No. 4, p.1

SHARMA, S.R., 'The President of the Indian Republic', *Modern Review,* Vol. LXXXVIII, No.1, p. 39

SRIVASTAVA, G.P., 'The Prime Minister of India', *Modern Review*, Vol. LXXXIX, No.3, p.193

SRIVASTAVA, V.N., 'The Union Executive in the Constitution of India', *I.J.P. Sc.*, Vol. 12, No.2, p.19

TOPE, T.K., 'Power of President of India', *S.C.J., Vol.* 19, p. 118

THE UNION LEGISLATURE

ANDREWS, WILLIAM G., 'Some Thoughts on the Power of Dissolution', *Parliamentary Affairs*, Vol. 13, 1960, p. 286

ALI, SADIQ, 'My Impression of Parliament', *Vigil*, Vol. 1, No. 11, p.8

BANERJEE, D.N., 'The Growth of Parliamentary Government in India', *Parliamentary Affairs*, London, Vol. 9, No.2, p.160

BANERJEE, D.N., 'The Role of Indian Speaker', *Modern Review*, Vol. LXXXXII, No. 2, p. 113

CHOUDHRY, L.P., 'The Council of States in the Indian Republic', *I.P.O., Sc.,* Vol. II, No.4, p.55

CHOWDHURI, C.C., 'Validity of Delegated Legislation', *I.L.R.*, Vol. 4, p.53

'The Council of States' (Leading Article), *Eastern Economist*, Vol. 18, No.11, p. 411

'India's First Elected Parliament' (An Assessment), *Economic Weekly*, Vol. IX, No.3, pp. 139 and 192

DAS, R.K. and DAS, S.R., 'Rise of the Indian Parliament', *Modern Review*, Vol. 93, No.4, p. 273

DE, JATINDRA RANJAN, 'Parliamentary Government in India', *Modern Review*, Vol. 100(3), p.198

DE SOUZA, J.P., 'Parliamentary Government in India', *Journal of the University of Bombay*, Vol. 21, p. 84

GHOSAL, A.K., 'Party, Government and State', *Modern Review*, Vol. 90, p.459

GUPTA, SISIR, 'The First Parliament of India', *A.I.C.C. Economic Review*, Issue No. 17, p. 92

'The House of the People' (Leading Article), *Eastern Economist*, Vol. 18, No. 10, p. 375

JAIN, D.G., "Judicial Review of Parliamentary Privileges: Functional Relationship of Courts and Legislatures in India", Vol.9, *J.I.L.I.* (1967), p.205

KAUL, M.N., 'Position and Functions of the Deputy Speaker', *Journal of Parliamentary Information*, October 1957, p.145

'The Legislative Process' (Leading Article), *Eastern Economist*, Vol. 15, p. 537.

'The Legislative Process' (Leading Article), *Eastern Economist*, Vol. 21, November 7, p.258

MATHUR, R., 'Legislative Control of Delegated Legislation', *The Ind. Jour. of Pol. Sc.*, Vol. 21, Jan-March 1960, p.25

MAVALANKAR, G.V., 'The Office of the Speaker', *Journal of Parliamentary Information* April, 1956

MAVALANKAR, G.V., 'The Development of Parliamentary Procedure in India', *Asiatic Review*, Vol. 49, June 1953

NAG, S.K., 'Parliamentary Privileges in India', *The Modern Reviews*, Vol. cx, 1961, 293

PARAS, DIWAN, 'Parliamentary Democracy and Political Parties', *S.C.J.*, Vol. 16, p. 103

'Parliament and Finance' (Leading Article), *Eastern Economist*, Vol. 22, No.11

'The Private Member' (Leading Article), *Eastern Economist*, Vol. 21, No.18, p.315

'Privileges and Parliament', *Civic Affairs*, Vol. 5(5), p. 18

PYLEE, M.V. and MAZUMDAR, V., (Mrs.), 'The Speaker under Our Constitution', Social Studies, Vol. I, p.32 and Parliamentary Democracy (*Report of the First All India Seminar*), p. 74

RAMSWAMI, V., 'Parliamentary Government and a Planned Society', *M.L.J.*, Vol. II, p.1

RANJAM, JATINDRA, 'Is Second Chamber a Superfluity?, *Modern Review*, Vol. 97, No.5, p.371

SAINI, M.K., 'A Study of No-confidence Motions in the Indian parliament (1952-70)', *I.J.P. Sc.*, Vol. XXXII, p. 297

RAO, K.V., 'The Council of States', *Modern Review*, Vol. LXXXXI, No.4, p.272

RAO, P. KODANDA, 'Parliamentary Democracy and Political Parties', *Swatantra*, Vol. II, No.4, p.13

SASTRI, K.N.V., 'The Struggle for Second Party in India', *I.J.P. Sc.*, Vol. 7, No.4, p.508

SINHA, K.P., 'Delegated and Conditional Legislation', *S.C.J.*, Vol. 13, p. 67

SRIVASTAVA, G.D., 'House of the People: Its Personnel', *Modern Review*, Vol. 95, No.1, p.21

SURYANARAYANASWAMY, D., 'Preparation, Pattern and Passing of Bills', *A.I.R.* (1958), p. 19

VENKATARAMA SASTRI, T.R., 'Powers of 'Provisional Parliament', *M.L.J.*, Vol. I, p.63

THE UNION JUDICIARY

ANANTANARAYANA, M., 'Some Juristic Norms and the Indian Constitution', *The Indian Year Book of International Affairs,* Vol. V, p.104

BASU, DURGA DAS, 'Interpreting the Constitution', *S.C.J.*, Vol. 13, p.2

BEHARI, GOPAL, 'Reform of Judicial System', *A.L.J.*, Vol. XLVIII, p. 92

BETH LOREN, P., 'The Supreme Court and the Future of Judicial Review', *Pol. Sc. Quar.*, Vol. 76, March 1961, p.22

BOSE, VIVIAN, 'The Rule of Law', *A.I.R., Selections III* (1), p.26

'Chagla Commission Report and Article 136 of the Constitution' (Editorial), *C.W.N.*, Vol. LXII (13), p.43

CHOBE, B.N., 'The Work of the Supreme Court for the First Session', *A.L.J.,* Vol. XLVIII, p. 177

'The Constitution and the English Writs' (Editorial Notes), *C.W.N.,* Vol. LV, No.29

DESHPANDE, V.S., "Judicial Review: Expansion and Self-Restraint", Vol. 15, *J.I.L.I.* (1973), p. 531

GAUR, RAM NARAYAN, 'Administration of Justice Under the New Constitution', *A.L.J.*, Vol. XLIV, p. 23

GHOSH, RAMESH CHANDRA, 'Constitutional Decisions of the Supreme Court of India', *I.J.P. Sc.*, Vol. 14, No.2, p. 98

'High Prerogative Writs in India' (Editorial Notes), *C.W.N.*, Vol. LI, No. 30

'Independence of Judiciary' (Editorial Notes), *Vigil,* Vol. 1, No. 39, p.4

'India's Supreme Court' (Editorial Notes), *C.W.N.*, Vol. LI, No. 37, August 1947

'Judiciary Under the Proposed Constitution' (Editorial Notes), *C.W.N.,* Vol. LII, No. 18, March 1948

'Judges Under the Proposed Constitution' (Editorial Notes), *C.W.N.*, Vol. LII, April, 1948

KAUL, A.K., "Article 131 of the Indian Constitution: Some Observations", Vol. 13, *J.I.L.I.*(1971), p. 121

MARKOSE, A.T., 'Judicial Control of Administrative Action in India, *S.C.J.,* Vol. 15, p. 1.

MARKOSE, A. T., 'Judiciary and the Executive in India: Some Suggestions for Reform', *S.C.J.*, Vol. 16, p.111

MATHUR, R.N., 'Rule of Federal Judiciary in Modern Federation', *S.C.J.*, Vol. 21, p. 208.

MATHUR, R.N., 'Interpretation of the Constitution', *S.C.J.*, Vol. 21, p.35

MISRA, R.K., 'The Doctrine of Severability under the Constitution of India', S.C.J., II, 1961

MITTER, S.C., 'Judiciary in Free India', *Modern Review*, Vol. LXXXIII, No.5, p.366

MUKHERJEE, T.B., 'Supreme Court as a Guardian of the constitution of India', *I.J.P. Sc.*, Vol. 12, No.2, p.52

'Our Supreme Court' (Editorial Notes), C.W.N., Vol. LII, No. 15, March 1948

PYLEE, M.V., '*Judicial Review*', S.C.J., Vol. 16, p.67

RAMACHANDRAN, V.G., 'The Role of Judiciary in Independent India', *A.I.R.*, Vol. 43, p.95

RAMACHANDRAN, V.G., 'The Need for Judicial Corrective in Administrative Proceedings', *S.C.J.*, Vol. 21, p. 49

RAMALINGAM, T., 'The Supreme Court of India and the Doctrine of Stare Decisis', *S.C.J.*, Vol. 19, p.9

RAMASWAMY, P.N., 'Judiciary: Its Personnel and Equipment', *M.L.J.*, Vol. I, p.1

RANADE, RAM KESHAV, 'Justice in Democratic India' *A.I.R.*, 1948, p. 41

RUDRA, (KUMARI) SUSHILA 'Concept of Justice in Our Constitution', *Modern Review*, Vol. LXXXXIV, No.3 p. 234

'Rule of Law in India' (Editorial), *C.W.N.*, Vol. LV, No. 22

RUTHNASWAMI, M., 'Concept of Justice', *A.I.R., Selections III* (1), p.49

SASTRY, D. GOPALAKRISHNA, 'Lower Pecuniary Limit in Civil Appeals to the Supreme Court', *S.C.J.*, Vol. 18, p.201

SIRCAR, RAJ KISHORE, 'The Position of the Judiciary under the Constitution of India', *A.I.R.*, Vol. 38, p. 27

SPENS, SIR PATRICK, 'The Judiciary of India and Pakistan', *Asiatic Review*, Vol. XLV, p. 449

SRINIVASACHARYA, R.S., "Recruitment to the Judiciary", *M.I.J.*, Vol. II, p. 45

SUBRAMANIAN, N.A., 'The Judiciary in India', *Indian Year Book of International Affairs*, Vol. IV, Part II, 1955, p. 275

GOVERNMENTAL STRUCTURE IN THE STATES (THE EXECUTIVE)

AGARWALA, S.K., 'The Governor and His Role', *S.C.J.*, Vol. 20, p. 136

BOURNE, FREDERICK, 'Constitutional Governors before and after', *Asiatic Review*, Vol. 46, p. 1111

CHATTERJEE, S., 'The Role of Governor in Indian Politics since 1967', *I.J.P. Sc.*, Vol. XXXII, p. 522

DESHPANDE, N.R., 'The Role of the Governor', *I.J.P. Sc.*, Vol. XX, p. 15

GHOSAL, A.K., 'State Governor in the New Constitution and before', *Modern Review*, Vol. LXXXVIII, No. 6, p. 441

GHOSAL, A.K., 'State Governor in the Constitution', *I.J.P. Sc.* Vol., 12, No. 1, p. 51

Governor's Powers in New India' (Editorial Notes), *C.W.N.*, Vol. L1, No. 38, August 1947

MURTHY, V.L., 'Governors in the Indian Republic', *Triveni*, October 1957, pp. 212-18

SINGH, M.P., "Governor's Power to Dismiss Ministers or Council of Ministers—An Empirical Study", Vol. 13, *J.I.I.I.*, (1971), p. 612

THE STATE LEGISLATURE

ALI, SADIQ, 'Glimpses of a State Legislature', *Vigil*, Vol. 3, No. 24, p. 9

CHERIAN, P.V. and MRS. CHERIAN, 'The Work of an Indian State Legislature', *Asiatic Review*, LIII (196), p. 235

THE HIGH COURTS

'Ambit of Court's Power Under Article 226 of the Constitution' (Editorial Notes), *C.W.N.*, Vol. LV, No. 12

'Article 226 of the Constitution and the Increased Scope of Government Function', *C.W.N*, Vol. LVI, No. 14

'Article 226 of the Constitution—Order of Removal from Service' (Editorial Notes), *C.W.N.*, Vol. LVI, No. 15

GUPTA, ATUL CHANDRA, 'Speaking Order—Article 226', *C.W.N.*, Vol. LVIII, No. 9

KODANDA RAO, P., 'Politician and Judges', *The Eastern Economist*, Vol. 37, 1961, p. 688

KODANDARAMAYYA, P., 'Article 226 and Alternative Remedy', *S.C.J.*, 1960

MARKOSE, A.T., 'The Administrative Jurisdiction of the Indian Judiciary: The Nature and Scope of the Remedies under Article 226 and 32 of the Constitution of India', *S.C.J.*, Vol. 17, p. 155

MENON, P.B., 'Revisional Jurisdiction and Article 226 of the Constitution of India', *A.I.R.*, Vol. 41, p. 37

'Parallel Courts in the States Under the Proposed Constitution' (Editorial), *C.W.N.*, Vol. LII, No. 42

'Scope of Article 226 of the Constitution. Recent Case of the Supreme Court' (Editorial Notes), *C.W.N.*, Vol. LVII, No. 9

SIKRI, S.M., 'Does Article 226 of the Constitution Need any Amendment?', *Madras Law Journal*, February 1958, po. 11

'Trial by Jury to Stay' (Editorial Comments), *The Modern Review*, Vol. 107, Jan.-June 1960, p. 9

'Writs outside the Territory of the State under Article 226 of the Constitution: Should Article 226 be Amended?' (Editorial Notes), *C.W.N.*, Vol. LVII, No. 5

'Expediting Work of High Courts' (Editorial Notes), *C.W.N.*, LXI, No. 33

'High Courts in India' (Editorial), *C.W.N.*, Vol. LI, No. 36

'Non-Judicial Work for High Court Judges' (Editorial Notes), *C.W.N.*, Vol. LVII, No. 10

'Writs Outside the Territories of State for any Other Purpose : Scope of Article 226' (Editorial), *C.W.N.*, Vol. LVII, No. 17

THE FEDERAL SYSTEM

AIYAR, S.P., 'India's Emerging Cooperative Federalism', *The Ind. Journ. of Pol. Sc.*, Vol. 21, 1960, p. 307

ALEXANDROWICZ, C.H., 'Quasi-Federation in India', *Lawyer*, August 1957, p. 9

ALEXANDROWICZ, C.H., 'Is India a Federation?', *Int. and Comp. Law Quarterly*, Vol. 3, 1964

'Award of the Finance Commission I—Review of State Finance', *Economic Weekly*, IX (48), p. 1535

'Award of the Finance Commission II—The Devolutions Recommended', *Economic Weekly*, IX (49), p. 1567

BASU, DURGA DAS, 'Inter-State Trade, Commerce and Intercourse under the Indian Union', *S.C.J.*, Vol. 13, p. 37

BASU, DURGA DAS, 'Repugnancy between Provincial and Federal Legislation', *I.L.R.*, Vol. 36, p. 17

'The Centre and the States' (Editorial Notes), *The Eastern Economist*, XXIX (2), p. 33

'Distributive Justice and the Constitution', *Economic Trends*, Vol. 2, p. 115

DASH, S.C., 'Emergency Provisions and Union-State Relations in India', *Ind. Journ. of Pol. Sc.*, Vol. 22, 1961

DOUGLAS, W.O., 'Bill of Rights, Due Process, and Federalism in India', *Minnesota Law Review*, Vol. 40, p. 1

DUBHASHI, P.R., Unitary Trends in a Federal System', *Ind. Jour. of Pub. Admn.*, Vol. 6, 1960

'A Fair Deal to the States (Editorial Notes), *Eastern Economist*, XXIX (21), p. 760

'Federal Finance' (Leading Article), *Eastern Economist*, Vol. 9, No. 7, p.287

'Federal Grants-in-aid to States: Principles Governing Distribution', *Capital*, Vol. CXXXVIII (1957), p.862

'Finance Commission', *Commerce*, Vol. LXXXIII, P.36

'Financial Clauses of the Constitution' (Leading Article), *Eastern Economist*, Vol.10, No.1, p.539

GANGAL, S.C., 'An Approach to Indian Federalism', *Pol. Sc. Quarterly*, June 1962

GHOSAL, A.K., 'Balance of Powers Under the New Constitution', *I.J.P., Sc.*, Vol. 11, No.4, p.66

GHOSAL, A.K. 'Federalism in the Indian Constitution', *The Calcutta Review* (1956), pp.33 and

GHOSH, S.C., 'Federalism in Indian Constitution', *The Calcutta Review* (1956), pp. 33 and 153

GHOSH, R.C., 'The Impact of Treaty Implementation on the Distribution of Powers', *I.J.P. Sc.*, Vol. 15, p. 89

'Gift to the States, Comments on Finance Commission II-Report' (Editorial Notes), *Economic Weekly*, IX (46), p. 1465

'The Indian Dominion and the States', *The world Today* (London), Vol. 5, No.1

GOYAL, O.P., 'Indian Federation and National Unity', *The Modern Review*, Vol. CX, 1961, p.471

HAQQI, S.A.A., 'Position of the States under the Indian Constitution', *Ind. Jour. of Pol. Sc.*, Vol. 22, 1961

JAGANNADHAM. V., 'Division of Powers in the Indian Constitution', *I.J.P. Sc.*, Vol. 8, p.742

JAIN, C.M., 'Centre-State Relations in India' : A Case Study of Rajasthan', *I.J.P. Sc.* (1970) p. 265.

JAIN, S.N. and JACOB, ALICE, "Centre-State Relations in Water Resources Development", Vol. 12, *J.I.L.I.* (1970), p.1

JAIN, P.C., 'The Union Finance under the Draft Constitution', *New Review*, Vol. 30, pp. 2 and 38.

JAIN, P.C., 'Task Facing the Finance Commission', *Commerce*, Vol. LXXXIII, p.1068

JENA, B.B., 'Contradictions of Equal Sovereignties in India', *Ind. Jour. Of Pol. Sc.*, Vol.23, 1962

MAHAJAN, MEHAR CHAND, 'Amend the Constitution to Make Unitary Government', *Organiser*, February 27, 1956

MUKHERJI, K.P., 'Is India a Federalism?', *I.J.P. Sc.*, Vol.15, p.177

MUNSHI, K.M., 'The New India: Central and the Units', *Hindustan Review*, Vol. LXXXVII, p. 164

MUNSHI, K.M., 'The Distribution of Powers between the Centre and the Units', *I.L.R.*, Vol. 4, p. 5.

MUNSHI, M.C., 'Grants-in-aid in Federal finance', *Eastern Economist*, Vol.10 (Special Number), p.60

MURTHY, D.C.S., 'Case for a Unitary State', *Swatantra*, Vol. II, No.5, p.37

NAMBIAR, M.K., 'Distribution of Legislative Powers in India', *F.L.J.*, Vol. 12, p.51

NARAIN, IQBAL, 'Federalism in the New constitution', *Modern Review*, Vol. 93, No.6, p.442

NAYAK, R.K., "Education: The Centre-State Legislative Relationship", Vol. 14, *J.I.L.I.* (1971), p. 562

PAL, KHAGENDRA CHANDRA, 'The Relations between Indian Union and the State of Jammu and Kashmir', *I.J.P., Sc.*, Vol. 14, No.4, p.333

PARIKH, R.N., 'Some Salient Characteristics of Federal Governments', *Modern Review*, Vol. LXXXV, No. 3, p. 189

'Provincial Finance' (Leading Article), *Eastern Economist*, Vol. 10, No. 13, p. 597

RAMACHANDRAN, V.G., 'Federal Supremacy in the Indian Constitution', *S.C.J.*, Vol. 15, p.39

RAMACHANDRAN, V.G., 'Is the Constitution of India Federal?', *S.C.J.*, Vol. 22, p.97

RAO, K.V., 'Encroachments on Provincial Autonomy in the New Draft Constitution for India', *Modern Review*, Vol. LXXXIV, No.6, p. 455

RAO, K.V., 'Centre-State Relations in Theory and Practice', *I.J.P. Sc.*, Vol. 14, No.4, p.347

RAO, P.K., 'India Should Have Unitary Government', *Organiser*, x (i), p.6 (August, 1956)

RAO, T.S.N., 'Distribution of Legislative Powers', *I.J.P. Sc.*, Vol. Ii, No.4, p.43

SAHAY, VISHNU, et al, "Union-State Relations (Administrative Aspects)", *I.J.P.A.* (1970), July-September issue, special number

SEHGAL, P.L., 'The Relation between the Centre and the States in the Indian Constitution', *Modern Review*, Vol. 95, No. 5, p. 373

SCHOENFELD, B.N., 'Federalism in India', *I.J.P., Sc.*, Vol. 20, pp.52 and 191

SEN, MANKUMAR, 'Centralisation – The Negation of Democracy', *Modern Review*, Vol LXXXIX, No.3, p.236

SHARMA, B.M., 'Relation between the Centre and the Units in the Indian Constitution', *I.J.P. Sc.*, Vol. 11, No.3, p.45

SHARMA, BODH RAJ, 'Position of the Centre in the New Constitution', *I.J.P. Sc.*, Vol. 11, No.4, p.57

SHARMA, S.K., "Inter-State Council – An Aspect of Cooperative Federation", *I.J.P.A.* (1976), p. 539

SHIVKUMAR, J., "Union-State Financial Relations", *I.J.P.A.* (1970), p.203; Also see Vol. XVIII (1972), p.539

SINHA, K.N., 'The Constitution of India-More Unitary than Federal', *Modern Review*, Vol. 98, No.6, p.448

SINGH, D.B., 'The Income-tax as a Balancing Factor in Indian Federal Finance', *Jour, Ind. Eco. Assn.*, Dec. 1953

SINGH, D.K., "Trade, Commerce and Intercourse in India: A reappraisal of Some Constitutional Problems", Vol.14, *J.I.L.I.* (1972), p.39

SINGH, SUSHIL CHANDRA, 'The Centre under the New Constitution', *I.J.P. Sc.,* Vol. 10, Nos.1 an d2, p.84

SRIVASTAVA, G.P., 'Impact of Planning on Union-State Relations in India', *Ind. Jour. of Pol. Sc.*, Vol. 22, 1961

TOPE, TRIMBAK K., 'Freedom of Trade and Commerce under the Indian Constitution', *S.C.J.*, I, 1962

VERMA, V.P., 'Towards Monistic Federalism in India', *Ind. Jour. of Pol. Sc.*, Vol. 22, 1961

VENKATARANGAIYA, M., 'The Centre and the Units in the New Constitution', *I.J.P. Sc.*, Vol. 11, No.1

WATSON, RICHARD A., 'Federalism vs. Individual Rights: The Legal Squeeze on self-incrimination', *The American Political Science Review*, Vol. 54, 1960, p.887

EMERGENCY PROVISIONS

GOPALKRISHNAN, P., 'The Constitutional Implications of President's Rule in Kerala', S.C.J., Vol.22, p.161

SHARMA, I.D., 'Emergency Government Provision in the Indian Constitution', *Ind. Jour. of Pol. Sc.*, Vol.21, No.4, Oct.-Dec. 1960, p.355

SHARMA, SRI RAM, 'Crisis Government in the Indian Constitution, *I.J.P. Sc.,* Vol.10, No.4, p.11

'Failure of the Constitutional Machinery in the States and Issue of Proclamations by the President under Article 356 of the Constitution', *Journal of Parliamentary Information,* April 1957, p.46

PUBLIC SERVICES

AGGARWAL, A.P., 'Strike by Public Employees – Law and Public Policy', Vol.14, *J.I.L.I.* (1972), p.358

'Civil Servants: Right to Form Associations or Unions' (Editorial), *C.W.N.*, LXII (16), p.55

'Constitutional Protection for Civil Servants', *Civic Affairs,* 5(5), p.29

'Constitutional Relations between Minister and Secretary', *Civic Affairs*, 5(8), p.20

CROZIER, M., 'Power Relationships in Modern Bureaucracies', *The Ind. Jour. Of Pub. Admn.* Vol. 7, 1961, p.32

DEY, B.K. , "Professionalism in Civil Service", *I.J.P.A.* (1970), p.234

GHOBE, B.N., 'Services under the Constitution of India', *S.C.J.*, Vol. 16, p.181

JAIN, R.B., "Operation of the Merit System in India", *I.J.P.Sc.*, Vol. XXXIII, p.186

JOSHI, R.C., "Bureaucrats and Politicians: Role and Relationship", *I.J.P.A.* (1976), p.15

KOCHUKOSHY, C.K., 'All India Services—Their Role and Future',*I.J.P.A.*, (1972), p. 67

KRISHNA MENON, V.K., 'Civil Services in Parliamentary Democracy', *Civic Affairs,* 4(10), p.17

MAHESHWARI, S.R., "The Indian Bureaucracy: Its Profile, Malady and Cure", *I.J.P.Sc.* (1970), p.222

MOTIWAL, OM PRAKASH, 'Doctrine of Pleasure in Article 310 of the Constitution of India', *S.C.J.*, II, 1962

MOTIWAL, OM PRAKASH, "Public Services in Parliamentary Form of Government", Vol.16, *J.I.L.I.* (1974), p.461

PANIKKAR, K.M., 'India's Administrative Problem – Services under Democracy', *Eastern Economist,* XXVI (10), P.408

'Parliament's Assessment of Civil Services', Civic Affairs, 5(8), p.24

PATNAIK, K.C., 'Civil Service – What it Means?', *Cuttack Law Times*, Vol. XXIII, p.15

'Public Corporations and Government Servants' (Editorial Notes), *C.W.N.*, LX(41), p.157

'Minister's Constitutional Responsibility for his Subordinates' Actions', *Civic Affairs*, 5(8), p.22

'Report of the Public Services Committee', *Civic Affairs*, 5(2), p.18
SHARMA, BODH RAJ, 'Public Services under the New Constitution', I.J.P. Sc., Vol.11, No.4, p.88
SHARMA, P.D., "Parliamentary Control over Administration in India", I.J.P. Sc., Vol. XXXVII, p.96
SINGH, L.P., "Training of Civil Servants-The Wider Perspective", *I.J.P.A.* (1969), p.5
SNOWISS, LEO M., 'The Education and Role of the Superior Civil Service in India', *The Ind. Jour. of Pub. Admn.* Vol. 7, 1961, p.6
SRINIVASAVARADAN, T.C.A., 'Some Aspects of the Indian Administrative Service', *The Ind. Jour. of Pub. Admn.*, Vol.7, 1961, p.26
SRIVASTAVA, B.P., 'Protection to Civil Servants' (A Review of Dhingra vs. Union of India), *S.C.J.*, Vol. 21, p.137
SRIVASTAVA, G.P., 'The Indian Civil Service', *Modern Review*, Vol. LXXXXVI, No.1, p.21
SUBRAMANIAM, V., 'Role of Civil Service in Indian Political System', *I.J.P.A.* (1971), p.238
TRIVEDI, K.D., "Our Administrative Culture: Some Postulates", *I.J.P.A.*(1975), p.119
VENKATACHAR, C.S., 'Indian Administration-The Inventory', *The Eastern Economist*, Vol. 37, 1961, p.741
VENKATACHAR, C.S., 'Indian Administration-Myths of the Legacy', *The Eastern Economist*, Vol. 37, 1961, p.691
VENKATACHAR, C.S., 'Indian Administration-What is the New Look?', *The Eastern Economist*, Vol. 37, 1961, p.793

PUBLIC SERVICE COMMISSIONS

JAIN, R.B., "The Union Public Service Commission and the State Public Service Commissions in India: The Case for an Institutional Linkage", *I.J.P.A.* (1976), p.363
SRIVASTAVA, G.P., 'Public Service Commission: Some Aspects of the Union', *Modern Review*, Vol. LXXXIX, No.6, p.485
SRIVASTAVA, R.P., 'Role of Public Service Commission in the New Indian Constitution', *I.J.P.Sc.*, Vol.11, No.2, p.13
'Union Public Service Commission', *Commerce*, Vol. LXXXIII, p.662
'Whether Art. 320(3) (c) of the Constitution is Mandatory?', (Editorial Notes), *C.W.N.*, LXI (13), p.45

ELECTIONS

AVASTHI, A., 'Political Parties in India', *I.J.P. Sc.*, Vol.12, No.1, p.6
BANERJEE, D.N., 'Can Democracy Function in a One-party State?', *Modern Review*, Vol. LXXXV, No.5, p.357
BHALLA, R.P., "Electoral Mechanism in India (1951-71)", *I.J.P. Sc.* (1972), p.27
CHANDRA BASU, 'The Returning Officer' (Leading Article), *Eastern Economist*, Vol. 18, No.16, p.179
CHOWDHRY, L.P., 'Indian Political Parties', *I.J.P. Sc.*, Vol.11, No.1
DASTUR, ALOO J., 'Twenty-five Years of Indian Socialism', *India Quarterly*, Vol. 16, April-June 1960, p.103
DESHMUKH, R.N., 'Proportional Representation for Illiterate Electorates', *I.J.P. Sc.*, Vol. 10, Nos.1 and 2, p.73
DHEBAR, U.N., 'General Elections and the Congress', *A.I.C.C. Economic Review*, No.24, p.3
'The Elections and After', *Eastern Economist*, XXVIII (13), p. 469
'Elections and the Law' (Leading Article), *Eastern Economist*, Vol. 25, No.1, p.468
GADGIL, N.V., 'The Government and the Party', *Ind. Jour, of Pub. Admn.*, Vol. 3, 1957

GHOSH, AJOY, 'The Communist Party and the General Election', *New Age,* v (9), September 1956 p.1

HUMAYUN KABIR, 'Congress Ideology', *India Quarterly,* Vol. 16, Jan-March 1960, p.3

JHA, CHETKAR, 'Future of Indian Political Parties', *I.J.P. Sc.*, Vol.12, No.1, p.1

JITENDRA SINGH, 'Communism in Kerala', *Pol. Quar.*, Vol.31, 1960, p.185

L.N.S., 'India and the Party System', *Swatantra,* Vol.11, No.22, p.9

MALIK, S.C., 'India's Second General Elections', *A.I.C.C. Economic Review,* No.21, p.15

MENON, V.K.N., 'Proportional Representation for India', *I.J.P. Sc.*, Vol.7, No.4, p.495

MORE, S.S., 'Reform of the Indian Electoral System', *A.I.C.C. Economic Review,* 9(5), p.16

MORRIS-JONES, W.H., 'Indian Voting Behaviour' (A Review Article), *Pacific Affairs*, xxx (3), p.265.

NAIR, KUSUM, 'The Two General Elections in India', *Asian Review,* LIV (197), January 1958

NARAYAN, SHRIMAN, 'The Elections and After', *A.I.C.C. Economic Review,* No.33, p.6

'Probe into the Elections' (Editorial), *Vigil*, Vol.3, No.2, p.3

RAO, V.V., 'The Reform of the Electoral System', *I.J.P. Sc.* (1075), p.379

RAY, NIRMAL, 'Parties and Democracy in India', *I.J.P. Sc.,* Vol. II, No.2, p.39

ROACH, JAMES R., 'India's 1957 Elections', *Far Eastern Survey*, Vol. XXVI (5), p.65

SCALAPINIO, ROBERT A;, 'Moscow, Peking and the Communist parties of Asia'' *Foreign Affairs*, Vol.41, No.2, Jan.1963

SHARMA. BODH RAJ, 'Some Suggestions for the improvement of our Electoral Laws', *Modern Review*, Vol. LXXXXVI, No.1, p.31

SHELVANKAR, K.S., 'The Indian General Election', *Asian Review*, LIII (195), p.159

TINKER, IRENE and WALKER, MILL, 'The First General Elections in India and Indonesia', *Far Eastern Survey*, 25(7), p.97

UJWAL, H.D., 'Evils of Present Party System in Government', *The Modern Review,* Vol. CX, 1961, p.407

OFFICIAL LANGUAGE

CARIAPPA, K.M., 'A Case for English as our National Language for All Time', *Organiser*, XI 1(7), (6 January 1958), p.8

'Education Through the Medium of English and the Constitution; (Editorial Notes), *C.W.N.*, Vol. LVIII, No.33

'The Language Issue' (Leading Article), *Commerce*, XCIII (2380), P.698

NARAYAN, SHRIMAN, 'The Language Controversy', *A.I.C.C. Economic Review,* 8(10), p.3

PITT, MALCOLM, 'Language Loyalities Challenge India', *Foreign Policy Bulletin,* 35 (12), p.89

RAO, V.V., "Language Politics in India", *I.J.P. Sc.* (1970), p.203

SEN, K.C., 'The Official Language of the Union', *Economic Weekly*, IX (42), p.1359

SUBBARAMAN, K.M., 'A New Official Language for India', *Indian Finance*, 57(25), p.1150

SPECIAL PROVISIONS TO CERTAIN CLASSES

'The Backward Classes' (Leading Article), *Eastern Economist,* Vol. 17, No.21, p.849

CLUMP, C.C., 'Constitutional Position of Backward Classes', *Social Action,* Vol. I, p.383

DESAI, MAGANBHAI, 'Backward Classes and the Constitution', *Harijan,* No.25, p.195

'Safeguards for Minorities' Rights (Editorial Notes), *Modern Review*, Vol. LXXXV, No.6, pp.429 and 431

SHARMA, BODH RAJ, 'The Treatment of Minorities in the Draft Constitution of India', *I.J.P. Sc.*, Vol.10. No.3, p.38

SOUZA, S.D., 'The Problem of Minorities', *Modern Review*, Vol. LXXXXVI, No.3

AMENDMENT

'Amendment of the Constitution' (Editorial Notes), *Modern Review*, Vol. LXXXIX, No.6, p.430

'Amending Our Constitution' (Editorial Notes), *C.W.N.*, Vol. LV, No.23

'Amending the Constitution-the Fourth Amendment', *Commerce*, Vol. XC, No.2296, p.346

'Amending the Constitution (Article 31)-A Dangerous Pastime', *Commerce*, Vol. LXXXVIII, p. 1213

'Amendments to the Constitution' (Leading Article), *Eastern Economist*, Vol. 25, No.241, p.88

'Amendment of the Constitution', *The Modern Review*, Vol. 107, Jan-June 1960, p.2

'Amendment to article 31', *New Age Weekly*, March 1955

'Another somersault by Government' [Article 31 (2)], *Commerce*, Vol XC, No. 2302, p. 657

'Article 19(1) (f), and Article 31 of the Constitution' (Editorial Notes), *C.W.N.*, Vol. LVI, No. 38

'Authority above, Challenge-Fourth Amendment' (Leading Article), *Eastern Economist*, Vol. 24, No.1

CHATTERJI, N.C., 'Constitution amendment Bill', *C.W.N.*, Vol. LV, No.25

'Constitution and Social Progress, *The Modern Review*, Vol. 107, Jan-June 1960, p.92

'Constitutional Amendments' (Editorial Notes), *C.W.N.*, Vol. LVIII, No.35

IYER, SUBRAMANIA, 'Express and Implied Limitations on the Amending Power under Article 368 of the Constitution', *S.C.J.*, Vol. 18, p. 101

MASSEY, I.P., "The Process of Amendment of the Constitution—A Study in Comparatives", Vol.14, *J.I.L.I.* (1972), p.407

NAMBYIR, M.K., 'Seventeenth Amendment of the Constitution', *S.C.J.*, II, 1963

RANGACHAR, H., Constitution and Changes', *Swatantra*, 2 April, 1955

RATH, S.N., "Amendability of Fundamental Rights: Indian Parliament", *Political Scientist*, July-December 1971, p.101

ROY, P.K., 'Proposed Amendment of the Constitution', *C.W.N.*, Vol. LVIII, No. 35

SASTRI, D. GOPALAKRISHNA, 'President's and Supreme Court's Views on Constitution Amending Process', *S.C.J.*, Vol. XXIII, 1960

'The Changing Constitution' (Leading Article), *Eastern Economist*, Vol. 20, No. 22, p. 367

INDEX

INDEX OF CASES

A

B

C

O

P

Q

R

S

T

U

GENERAL INDEX

***